*The preservation of the sacred fire of liberty
and the destiny of the republican model of government
are justly considered as deeply, perhaps as finally,
staked on the experiment entrusted to the hands
of the American people.*

GEORGE WASHINGTON
First Inaugural Address
April 30, 1789

WHAT PEOPLE ARE SAYING

Secular historians ignore George Washington's ward Nelly Custis, who wrote that doubting his Christian faith was as absurd as doubting his patriotism. But they cannot ignore this mountain of evidence suggesting Washington's religion was not Deism, but just the sort of low-church Anglicanism one would expect in an eighteenth century Virginia gentleman. His "sacred fire" lit America's path toward civil and religious liberty.

WALTER A. MCDOUGALL
Pulitzer Prize winning Historian
Professor of History and International Relations, University of Pennsylvania
Author of *"Freedom Just Around the Corner: A New American History, 1585-1828*

George Washington's actions as a soldier and statesman made republican government a reality and shaped the American understanding of liberty as a divine blessing and a sacred trust. Washington's actions were, in no small measure, the products of his character. Washington's character, as Peter Lillback shows in *George Washington's Sacred Fire*, was deeply informed by his Christian faith. Dr. Lillback buries the myth that Washington was an unbeliever—at most a "Deist'—under an avalanche of facts. He demonstrates that our founding father's commitment to kindling and nurturing "the sacred fire of liberty," far from reflecting a rejection of Christian beliefs, flowed directly from them.

ROBERT P. GEORGE
McCormick Professor of Jurisprudence and Director of the
James Madison Program in American Ideals and Institutions, Princeton University

An enlightening, engaging, and long overdue correction of the falsehood that Washington lacked faith.

RODNEY STARK
Baylor University

For several decades, there has been a consensus among academics that George Washington was not really a Christian, but instead was a Deist. Peter Lillback's work demolishes this conventional wisdom. He provides comprehensive evidence and penetrating arguments which demonstrate that Washington was indeed a consistent Christian and in particular that his religious beliefs were those typical of a devout low-church Episcopalian in eighteenth-century Virginia. This volume will enable today's Christians to refute the current falsehoods being propagated about the faith of this greatest of America's founding fathers and to speak a truth that has great meaning in the historical and cultural debates of our own time.

JAMES KURTH
Department of Political Science
Swarthmore College

History is a powerful tool. Used to press an agenda in the guise of recording facts it can yield dangerous results. These results are the more nefarious because the means of handling the facts appear so neutral. Hence the confusion about America's founding fathers. For generations George Washington has been portrayed as an Enlightenment Deist. This view helps reduce the likelihood of a strong Christian influence in early America, which in turn helps promote the cause of secularism today. Peter A. Lillback has given us a nearly exhaustive reckoning with the true Washington, who turns out to be no Deist at all, but a professing Christian, a humble yet zealous follower of Christ. This volume will move the reader as well as persuade him that America's first president was also a premier man of God, whose religion was quite contrary to that of Thomas Paine or Lord Shaftesbury. Neither his life nor his leadership make any sense apart from his commitment to the church and to biblical faith. We praise Dr Lillback for the enormous labor, a labor of love to be sure, but a giant effort dedicated to the truth. We owe it to his thorough research and engaging polemics to give a hearing to *George Washington's Sacred Fire*. When we do, we will discover, in the bargain, that we have here history as it ought to be.

WILLIAM EDGAR
Professor of Apologetics, Westminster Theological Seminary

The reconstruction of the private religious convictions of a public leader is always a most tricky and complicated historical task. In English history, the figure of Oliver Cromwell has proved enigmatic, as historians have sought to co-ordinate his private statements and actions with his public deeds as army general and then Lord Protector. In George Washington, American history has its own Cromwell: a leader of such enormous stature, and who arouses such passionate emotions, that it is difficult to separate the facts from the fiction. For a long time it has been assumed that this founding father was a man of the Enlightenment, a Deist; yet, with this book, Dr Lillback seeks to challenge that, and marshals awesomely detailed evidence that another category, that of a broadly orthodox Anglicanism, provides a more accurate way of setting Washington's religious convictions in context. Whether one agrees or disagrees, it is clear this book is a significant and serious challenge to the typical historiography which can clearly no longer be taken for granted.

CARL TRUEMAN
Professor of Historical Theology
Chairman of the Church History Department, Westminster Theological Seminary
Editor of *Themelios*

George Washington's

SACRED
FIRE

George Washington's
SACRED FIRE

PETER A. LILLBACK
with Jerry Newcombe

 PROVIDENCE FORUM PRESS

DEDICATION OF
George Washington's Sacred Fire

To the children of America—past, present, and future,
especially to those who have ever wondered,
"Was George Washington a Christian?"

Contents

Acknowledgements

George Washington's Sacred Fire was a spark of an idea that first glimmered in my heart over twenty years ago. Somehow, it never was extinguished even though it flickered in the winds of pressing duties and weightier concerns. But over the last ten years, and then especially so in the last two, the spark became a flame and finally *George Washington's Sacred Fire* was ablaze and ready to shed its light on the debate over Washington's religious faith.

The fuel for a fire is the *sine qua non* of its existence. And so the many friends, institutions, and libraries that have assisted in this work have been the very fuel for *George Washington's Sacred Fire*. Although I'm sure I cannot fully remember nor recount each one who has contributed their valued support, I wish to do the best I can to thank those who have made this book a reality.

The kindling for *George Washington's Sacred Fire* is the people who have shared the vision for its creation and have invested their wisdom, skills, time, energy, and resources to make it happen. To each of the following I express my deepest and sincere gratitude:

My family—To my wife, Debbie, for her love, encouragement, and long and gracious patience throughout the almost never ending process of completing this book. To my daughters, Cara and Priscilla, for their interest, thoughtful comments, contributions, typing, and help.

My Team Mates on the Project—To Jerry Newcombe who signed on to make sure that my scholarly smoke didn't eclipse the clarity of the flame by writing, coaching, editing, enabling, and motivating. To the Board of Trustees of The Providence Forum, whose inspiration and support have fueled the vision from its first serious start. To Jack and Pina Templeton whose generosity and encouragement are extraordinary and legendary. To my brother in ministry, the Reverend Paul Karlberg, who recruited Jerry and shouldered the extra burden of ministry created by this project during those many days when all I could do was keep on writing. To the entire Pastoral Staff at Proclamation Presbyterian Church who joined Paul in bearing the extra stresses created by the creation of this book. To all of the support staff at Proclamation Presbyterian Church who have been typing tidbits (and much more) for *George Washington's Sacred Fire* for at least a decade! Especially to these gracious ladies who have helped through the years: B.J. Dunn, Genie Herrell, Felicia Horton, Lisa Moneymaker, Kathy Olson, Marian Rebuck, Bonney Scott, Marion Sacks, April

McKenzie. To Jim Browne who has shared his busy office staff in keeping this project moving forward. To Liz Fabiani who has been doing long, forced marches of service to get everything typed by our deadlines. Especially to Alex Thompson who has read every word at least three times, corrected thousands of mistakes, organized everchanging and growing chapters and titles, and tracked down more stray endnotes than Washington had soldiers in his entire Army. To the support team at The Providence Forum: Carolyn Jewett, Jody Vanmeter, and Carolyn Giosa, each of whom has provided unique contributions to make this book possible, to Silvia Augstroze for final proofreading, and to Aaron Bradford and Matthew McGowen for their excellent service as an interns. To Judy Mitchell for her creative energy in the lovely graphic design of the maps of Washington's Virginia. To our publicists, Larry Ross and Steve Yount and the ALRC team, for their excellent efforts to spread the word about this project. To Peter Roark and Roark Creative for capturing the essence of this work in the cover and interior design. To our printer, Dickinson Press, for their excellent efforts in bringing this book to completion. To our extraordinary marketing and business savvy executive director of The Providence Forum, Ralf Augstroze, who made sure that every picture, every deadline, every budget, and every communication was met according to plan. To all of our friends at Coral Ridge Ministries who gave this project new life, and Nancy Britt for editing assistance. To the entire production team at Coral Ridge who has shared the news of this book with America, and to Dr. D. James Kennedy for his passionate scholarship in regard to the faith of our founding father. To every friend who has asked for updates, prayed, and shared articles and ideas to help with the effort.

My special ministry team—the elders, deacons, members, pastoral staff, and office staff, past and present, of Proclamation Presbyterian Church, to the Board and staff of The Providence Forum, to the faculty, staff, and board of Westminster Theological Seminary, to the Board and staff of *Proclaiming the Word* radio broadcast.

To special scholars who have granted interviews and provided invaluable information, wisdom, and guidance on this project, including Mary Thompson, historian of Mount Vernon; Reverend Donald Binder Ph.D., rector at Pohick Church in Lorton, VA; Dr. James Hutson, Chairman of the Manuscript Division of the Library of Congress; Karen Hedelt of the Visitors' Center of Fredericksburg, VA.

The Historical Organizations—I also wish to express my sincere thanks to the many organizations that provided invaluable access and information to further my research. Without their commitment to the history of our nation, and our founding father, this project could never have been completed. Pohick Church in Lorton, VA.; Christ Church in Alexandria, VA.; Falls Church in Falls Church, VA.; St. Peters

Church, Philadelphia; Christ Church, Philadelphia; Trinity Church, New York City; Visitor Center, Fredericksburg, VA; Mother Bethel AME Church, Philadelphia; George Washington Masonic Memorial, Alexandria, VA.; The Presbyterian Church in Morristown, NJ, and to Swain's of Morristown and Thomas B. Vokes Galleries for their technical support.

Along with the people and the organizations, I must remember to thank the libraries, archives, and those who have granted permission to use their photographs and images in this work. I wish to thank each of the following institutions and their libraries and staffs for their exemplary commitment to scholarship which has provided the foundational materials that have made this research possible: Westminster Theological Seminary, and each of its extraordinary library personnel, Villanova University, University of Pennsylvania, Haverford College, Bryn Mawr College, Swarthmore College, Harvard University, Eastern University, Cabrini College, the Library of Congress, Massachusetts Historical Society, The Boston Athenaeum, Library Company of Philadelphia, The Historical Society of Pennsylvania, George Washington Memorial Chapel in Valley Forge, Connecticut Historical Society, and Mount Vernon's research library.

Finally, I wish to thank Divine Providence for the privilege and blessing of having had the inestimable honor of studying the life and faith of our founding father, George Washington. Indeed, I can do no better than to quote Washington himself, "I feel the most lively sentiments of gratitude to that divine Providence which has graciously interposed for the protection of our Civil and Religious Liberties." (*WGW*, vol. 27, 11-10-1783. To the United Dutch Reformed Churches.) And a hearty thank-you to you, dear reader, for seeking to do your part, as well to protect our civil and religious liberties that were so dear to Washington.

Foreword

In many of America's secondary schools and schools of higher education, history is considered irrelevant to the post-modern and multi-cultural world. Entire curricula on American history have been written with only passing reference to our founding fathers, including George Washington.

But this is not a sudden event. The roots of this historical revisionism go back to the early nineteen hundreds as many elite leaders and educators in America began, intentionally, to move in a direction away from America's Christian heritage.

George Washington, the preeminent figure at the beginning of America as a new, independent nation, has been subjected to the reinterpretation of American history by numerous, secular scholars. Motivated by a world view that rejects the foundational doctrine of George Washington's world view—Divine Providence—these scholars have filtered out and misrepresented the extensive evidence of George Washington's faith. As a result, they have created a secular George Washington as a truncated figure from the heroic figure known by his contemporaries.

One cannot begin to understand the totality of George Washington and the faith which animated him unless one first explores the strong orthodox Christian upbringing which he experienced as a youngster. From his early years, he embraced a lifelong dedication to his Anglican faith. How he lived his faith was very much influenced by his passion for self-discipline, self-control, and rectitude. His personality caused him to avoid laying his heart on his sleeve.

Nevertheless, Washington's contemporaries clearly saw in him his strong Christian faith and his appeal to, and trust in, "Providence," to which "he regularly gave thanks, publicly and privately."[1]

It was only many decades after his death that some historians began to interpret Washington's values and beliefs, more from their own frame of reference, rather than by the extensive writings and utterances of Washington during his lifetime. Because some early American patriots, like Thomas Paine, were Deists, that is those who believed in a distant and remote Deity, many more recent historians have tried to label a number of the luminaries of the founding fathers of America as also being Deists. For example, it is often said today that Thomas Jefferson and Benjamin Franklin were Deists. Yet, each man in a variety of contexts spoke earnestly of their conviction as Theists—that God was both approachable by man and that God played an ever-active

17

role in the affairs of man. Consider Thomas Jefferson's declaration: "God who gave us life gave us liberty. And can the liberties of a nation be thought secure when we have removed our only firm basis, a conviction in the minds of the people that these liberties are the gift of God?" It is not surprising, therefore, that Thomas Jefferson and his fellow founders would have referred four times in the Declaration of Independence to a Creator God of Providence. Likewise, consider the statement of Benjamin Franklin delivered at the Constitutional Convention in Philadelphia in 1787: "I have lived, Sir, a long time, and the longer I live, the more convincing proofs I see of this truth: that God governs in the affairs of man."

In the case of George Washington, this book *George Washington's Sacred Fire* documents with exhaustive detail and analysis that Washington was not only a Theist, as seen in his very frequent references to Providence, but that Washington was also an orthodox Trinitarian Christian. First, in regard to the impact of a Providential God, Washington later in his public life said: "It is the duty of all nations to acknowledge the Providence of Almighty God, to obey his will, to be grateful for his benefits, and humbly implore his protection and favor." (Thanksgiving Proclamation, October 3, 1789)

From his deep Christian faith, Washington also found occasion to advocate Christianity. In a speech to the Delaware chiefs on May 12, 1779, he said: "This is a great mark of your confidence and of your desire to preserve friendship between the Two Nations to the end of time, and to become One People with your Brethren of the United States. My ears hear with pleasure the other matters you mention. Congress will be glad to hear them too. You do well to wish to learn our arts and ways of life, and above all, the religion of Jesus Christ. These will make you a greater and happier people than you are."

Later, during the Revolutionary War, amidst a continuing series of disappointments and setbacks, Washington said: "While we are zealously performing the duties of good citizens and soldiers we certainly ought not to be inattentive to the higher duties of religion. To the distinguished character of patriot, it should be our highest glory to add the more distinguished character of Christian."

But for Washington, the true mark of conviction was how one behaved and what one did. From his lifelong commitment to rectitude and Christian moral principle, Washington stressed in his orders and directives and exhibited in his personal life, that a Christian faith is not just how one speaks but how one acts. As commander in chief, he set high standards for Christian worship and Christian behavior: "We can have little hope of the blessing of Heaven on our arms if we insult it by our impiety and folly.

Let vice and immorality of every kind be discouraged, as much as possible in your brigade; and as a chaplain is allowed to each regiment, see that the men regularly attend divine Worship." This precedent was established earlier in his life as the widely recognized leader of Virginia's Militia. He emphasized that his troops should "pray, fast, attend worship and observe days of thanksgiving."[2]

Finally, it is helpful to reflect on those many, many times in his life when Washington was not sure that he was up to the task of the heavy burden of responsibilities he was called upon to fulfill. When he was selected, unanimously, by the Continental Congress to serve as commander in chief of the Continental Army, he said: "I beg it may be remembered, by every gentleman in the room, that I, this day, declare with my utmost sincerity, I do not think myself equal to the command I am honored with." Many times during the eight long years of the Revolutionary War, Washington experienced more failures than successes. Because the conflict was so protracted, he faced continuing high rates of desertion of various state militias during the War. While Washington maintained great conviction in the merits of the American cause, he nevertheless clearly turned again, and again, to prayer that the Lord God would give him strength and sustain him.

For a man of such probity and such self-restraint, the truest reflection of George Washington's conviction and practice as an orthodox Christian requires exhaustive and thorough scholarship to bring together the totality of George Washington's devotion as a Christian. This book, by the Reverend Dr. Peter Lillback in conjunction with Jerry Newcombe, gives us all a much truer understanding of the man who as "Father of Our Country" was indispensable to the success of securing, not only American independence, but, more importantly, the survival of America's bold experiment in republican representative government. *George Washington's Sacred Fire* is an attempt to let Washington speak for himself, and to address, in a definitive manner, the evidence of his Christian faith and conviction. This book makes a unique and authoritative case for the underlying faith of George Washington which sustained him and guided him throughout his remarkable life.

John M. Templeton, Jr., M.D.

Introduction

In the popular culture of late twentieth and early twenty-first century America, two schools of thought about George Washington are doing battle. As evidenced by sermons and books by conservative religious leaders and numerous websites launched by people with an axe to grind, at least in regard to his religious beliefs, the Washington one finds on the internet appears to be a candidate for diagnosis as a multiple personality. He is either a rabid evangelical Christian or else is described as a Deist, a term which seems to be equivalent in the modern parlance of these polemicists to agnostic—someone who feels that there is no way to know if there is or is not a God, so they refuse to take a stand either way, and, if there is a God, he/she/it is unknowable. Perhaps Washington's seeming personality disorder can be traced to the fact that, depending on which site one reads, he was either raised by pietistic parents or was the son of a man who spurned the Christian faith.

These differing views of Washington in the contemporary United States reflect the historical scholarship of the last two centuries. For over one hundred years following Washington's death, his biographers tended to view their subject as a deeply religious man. Popular writers reflected that same opinion, but often elaborated on the religious theme; stories came into the popular imagination of Washington the perfect man, who broke up fights between children at school as a boy, was always in church each Sunday, had religious visions, and certainly never lied.

All that changed about seventy years ago. At that point, historians began trying to strip away the myths that had grown up around Washington, in order to make him more human and understandable to a twentieth century audience. While this was a laudable goal—and one that contemporary historians and museums are still striving to do in the face of some particularly imbedded beliefs, such as the wooden teeth legend—they began to cast doubt on the view of Washington as a devout Christian. The most influential of those works was historian Paul Boller's *Washington and Religion*, which essentially described Washington as a person who, though raised in the Anglican Church, was at best only nominally Christian, who found that religion useful for keeping the lower classes in order, but did not seriously believe the tenets of the faith. Religion, moreover, was a subject in which he had very little interest. Boller's position has been the standard interpretation of this facet of Washington's life since its publication more than forty years ago. Most recently, scholarly examinations of the subject have suggested that Washington's spiritual life was more greatly influenced by

Stoic philosophy than Judeo-Christian theology.

There is evidence that the historical tide may again be turning. While not directly dealing with Washington, Edward L. Bond and John K. Nelson have written convincing explorations of the Anglican Church in Virginia, which take seriously the depth of faith of the American colonists and challenge the notion that the state church was solely a means by which the upper classes controlled the rest of society. Other scholars—Daniel L. Dreisbach, James H. Hutson, and Garrett Ward Sheldon, to name just a few—have reexamined the place of religion in the lives of Washington's contemporaries and show their readers a group of men and women with a strong belief in God and an intense interest in matters of religion. Quite recently, still others have turned their attention to Washington himself. Vincent Phillip Munoz produced a fine article on Washington's ideas on church and state, while Michael and Jana Novak have just (2006) published a book-length investigation into the identity of the God mentioned in Washington's writings, as well as what the country's most famous founding father meant when he wrote, so very often, about "Providence."

Peter Lillback, with Jerry Newcombe, has written *George Washington's Sacred Fire* as a means of redressing some of the past wrongs in interpreting the place of God and religion in Washington's life. Striving for balance, the man to whom Dr. Lillback introduces his readers is decidedly Christian, but hardly an evangelical in the modern sense. He was an active churchman, whose relationship with the Anglican Church underwent change throughout his life, but never altered his relationship with God. Unlike many of the popular writers who have tried to resurrect belief in a very devout Washington, Dr. Lillback has taken great care to document his sources. His fifteen years of research are clearly evident, with very complete notes and appendices, so that readers wishing to explore further can follow the trail to additional sources. The author also brings an understanding of the eighteenth century church in America, which is invaluable in putting Washington into the context of his time and place.

So, if the historical tide is beginning to turn—a slow process at best—then scholars are in the first stages of reappraising Washington's faith. As part of that reassessment, I would like to invite you to read *George Washington's Sacred Fire*. It is now your turn to weigh the evidence and decide how you would answer the question of whether George Washington, America's founding father, was a Christian or not.

Mary V. Thompson
Research Specialist
George Washington's Mount Vernon Estate

PART I

The
Controversy

ONE

Introduction:
The Controversy

"Broadly speaking, of course, Washington can be classified as a Deist."
Paul F. Boller, Jr. 1963[1]

"On my honor and the faith of a Christian..."
George Washington, 1763[2]

George Washington has been described by recent authors as "a lukewarm Episcopalian,"[3] a "warm Deist,"[4] "not a deeply religious man,"[5] "not particularly ardent in his faith,"[6] "one who avoided as was the Deist custom, the word 'God.'"[7] No wonder Professor Paul Boller wrote, "Broadly speaking, of course, Washington can be classified as a Deist." Yet paradoxically, this was the man who stood trembling before his new nation to give his First Inaugural Address[8] and spoke of "the sacred fire of liberty."[9] This was not a secular fire. It was a flame fueled by the holy.

Surprising perhaps, but as we will see, Washington's description of himself repeatedly used the words "ardent," "fervent," "pious," and "devout." There are over one hundred different prayers composed and written by Washington in his own hand, with his own words, in his writings. His passions flared in a letter, when his church vestry considered not honoring his purchase of a family pew in his local church. He described himself as one of the deepest men of faith of his day when he confessed to a clergyman, "No Man has a more perfect Reliance on the alwise, and powerful dispensations of the Supreme Being than I have nor thinks his aid more necessary."[10]

Rather than avoid the word "God," on the very first national Thanksgiving under the U.S. Constitution, he said, "It is the duty of all Nations to acknowledge the providence of Almighty God, to obey his will, to be grateful for his benefits, and humbly to implore his protection and favor."[11] Although he never once used the word "Deist" in his voluminous writings, he often mentioned religion, Christianity, and the Gospel. He spoke of Christ as "the divine Author of our blessed religion." He encouraged missionaries who were seeking to "Christianize" the "aboriginals." He took an oath in a private letter, "on my honor and the faith of a Christian." He wrote of "the blessed religion revealed in the Word of God." He encouraged seekers to learn "the religion of Jesus Christ." He even said to his soldiers, "To the distinguished Character of Patriot, it should be our highest Glory to add the more distinguished Character of Christian." Not bad for a "lukewarm" Episcopalian!

George Washington is known by Americans as the founding father of our nation. However, there has been great confusion and debate about his faith. The historic view was that he was a Christian. The consensus of scholars that has developed since the bicentennial of Washington's birth in 1932 is that he was a Deist, that is, one who believes in a very remote and impersonal God. (We will define this term more fully in the following chapter.)

Who is correct in their assessment of Washington—the recent historians of Washington or Washington himself? We believe this is a fair question. Our purpose is to address the question of Washington's religion and to answer it in a definitive way, using Washington's own words. Was he a Christian or a Deist?[12] We believe that when all the evidence is considered, it is clear that George Washington was a Christian and not a Deist, as most scholars since the latter half of the twentieth century have claimed.

One of the interesting proofs of the significance of George Washington in American history is that we read into him what we want to see. To a secularist, Washington was a secularist. To a Christian, Washington was a church-going believer. It is natural that people want to make Washington in their own image. This is even true to a humorous degree. For example, George Washington wearing a baseball cap recently graced the front page of the USA Today in reference to Washington, D.C., getting its own baseball team.

Everybody wants to claim Washington for their own. The Christians want to make him a devout evangelical. The skeptics want to make him a skeptic. We believe the truth, however, is that he was an 18th century Anglican. He was an orthodox, Trinity-affirming believer in Jesus Christ, who also affirmed the historic Christian Gospel of a Savior who died for sinners and was raised to life. But then again, we also believe it would not be accurate to call him an "evangelical" (by modern standards of the word).

What are the facts of history? And do they matter? The importance of this study is more than historical. Establishing that George Washington was a Christian helps to substantiate the critical role that Christians and Christian principles played in the founding of our nation. This, in turn, encourages a careful reappraisal of our history and founding documents. A nation that forgets its past does not know where it is or where it is headed. We believe such a study would also empower, enable, and defend the presence of a strong Judeo-Christian worldview in the ongoing development of our state and national governments and courts. We set out to provide the necessary foundation for an honest assessment of the faith and values of our founders and the government they instituted.

NO LONGER A HERO?

Can an historic national hero become irrelevant? This seems to have happened to George Washington and many other "politically incorrect" founding fathers, at least in the minds of some leading educators. In fact, many of our founders—despite all their sacrifices to establish our great country with unparalleled freedoms—have been denigrated to the category of the irrelevant history of "dead white guys." In fact, the *Washington Times* reported: "George Washington, Thomas Jefferson, and Benjamin Franklin are not included in the revised version of the New Jersey Department of Education history standards, a move some critics view as political correctness at its worst."[13]

The impact of this approach to history can perhaps be seen in a recent Washington College Poll. It found that more Americans had a higher respect for Bill Clinton's job performance as the nation's forty second president than they did George Washington's.[14] Thus, George Washington is no longer considered to be the hero he once was.

NO LONGER A CHRISTIAN?

Pick up most books and articles on Washington from 1932 or earlier, and generally, with a few exceptions, you will read about George Washington the Christian. That began to change with the iconoclastic scholarship of the mid-twentieth century that sought to tear down the traditional understanding of our nation and its origins.

In particular, the leading modern study of George Washington the Deist, *George Washington & Religion*, was authored by historian Paul F. Boller, Jr.[15] Boller's conclusion can be summarized in a single sentence: To the "unbiased observer" George Washington appears as a Deist, not a devout Christian.[16]

While there have been studies before Boller's that argued that Washington was a Deist and not a Christian, Boller's book is clearly now considered the definitive standard book on the subject.[17] After his book, very few scholars asserted that George Washington was a Christian. Consequently, it has become the accepted "fact" of history that Washington was a Deist. The interesting thing about Boller's book is that, to our knowledge, it has never been fully rebutted. Using historical scholarship, we want to address and answer Boller's arguments and go beyond them in a way that is accessible to all serious readers.

Even Boller admits that religion was important to Washington as a leader. For instance, Boller writes, "…he saw to it that divine services were performed by the chaplains as regularly as possible on the Sabbath for the soldiers under his command."[18] But shouldn't this lead us to ask why chaplains would be important to a Deist? Boller even admits there are testimonials of Washington's consistency in attending church: "John C. Fitzpatrick's summation of Washington's church-going habits (which he examined carefully) seems fair enough: 'Washington…was a consistent, if not always regular churchgoer.'"[19]

This is an important admission on Boller's part because later writers have gone far beyond Boller's argument and asserted that Washington did not even attend church as a mature adult.[20]

The erosion of accurate historicity is disconcerting: One scholar casts Washington in a Deistic mold. The next goes further and states—without citing evidence—that he didn't even go to church. What will the next generation of scholars claim? This ignorance of the facts is what requires us to pursue our question concerning Washington's religion by constant interaction with his own written words and the unquestionable records of his actions.

As we have said, many recent writers don't see Washington as a Christian. A "tongue-in-cheek" book on him claims to be based on nothing but the facts, but listen to the unsubstantiated extent it goes concerning Washington and religion. Marvin Kitman in his, *The Making of the President* 1789 (Harper & Row, New York, 1989) describes a busy few days where Washington attended various churches. Without the least regard to Washington's vast writings, Kitman inaccurately and falsely states:

And here was a man who didn't even believe in God, some of his political enemies said, paraphrasing his own minister, who had been complaining about the way Washington never mentioned the word God—he did use Providence regularly—didn't come to take sacrament, or do this or that. He was big with the Deist vote, however.[21]

Kitman is incorrect on many fronts, as we will see throughout the book. For starters, Washington believed in God; referred to God (by many names intended to honor Him) hundreds of times; did, indeed, speak of Providence some 270 times; and, in fact, there are written records that Washington partook of Christian communion both before and after the War. Furthermore, the alleged "Deist vote" would have been quite marginal at best. Benjamin Hart notes that at the beginning of the American Revolution, 98.4% of the Americans claimed to be Protestant; 1.4% claimed to be Roman Catholic——thus, 99.8% were professing Christians. This certainly corroborates Benjamin Franklin's telling observation published in 1794 on the faith of his contemporary fellow Americans in the midst of Washington's presidency:

The almost general mediocrity of fortune that prevails in America obliging its people to follow some business for subsistence, those vices that arise usually from idleness are in great measure prevented. Industry and constant employment are great preservatives of the morals and virtue of a nation. Hence bad examples to youth are more rare in America; which must be a comfortable consideration to parents. To this may be truly added, that serious religion, under its various denominations, is not only tolerated, but respected and practiced. Atheism is unknown there, infidelity rare and secret; so that persons may live to a great age in that country without having their piety shocked by meeting with either an atheist or an infidel. And the Divine Being seems to have manifested his approbation of the mutual forbearance and kindness with which the different sects treat each other, by the remarkable prosperity with which He has been pleased to favour the whole country.[22]

A DEVOUT EIGHTEENTH CENTURY ANGLICAN

We believe that an honest look at the facts of history show that George Washington was a devout eighteenth century Anglican. This means he believed the basics of that orthodox Trinitarian faith that proclaimed the substitutionary saving death of Jesus Christ for sinners. Some have declared that Washington stopped attending Communion during the War. Should this be correct—and let's assume so for the sake of argument—does this prove he was not a believing Christian?

Could other reasons better explain the question? Could it have been because he had broken Communion with the head of the Anglican Church (King George III)? Perhaps during the stresses of the War, he got out of the habit of receiving the Lord's Table on a regular basis. And what should we make of the historical testimonies that he did attend Communion after the War from time to time?

As we analyze the written evidence from Washington himself, we will find that he had an exemplary private prayer life. His biblical literacy suggests the he read the Scriptures regularly, and we can also show that he used the 1662 *Book of Common Prayer* from the Church of England, which was a very orthodox guide for Christian worship of the Trinity. In fact, the 1662 *Book of Common Prayer* is more theologically sound than the average book available in a Christian bookstore today.

In this present book, we are taking what Christian philosopher Gary Habermas, in another context, calls "the minimalist facts approach." We are only going to say what can be proven beyond a reasonable doubt. We are not going to present a hagiography of George Washington, i.e., we will not make him into an ecclesiastical saint. But we do believe that his own words and actions show that he was a Christian and not an unbelieving Deist.

George Washington was not a perfect man. He occasionally lost his temper; he drank wine—maybe even too much when he was a young man.[23] He was involved with activities that some would find fault with: he had a revenue producing distillery on his Mount Vernon Estate;[24] he loved to fox hunt; he went to the theatre, and occasionally to the horse races. And, sadly, he owned slaves, something all Americans today would find immoral, but which was not uncommon for a Southern gentleman of his day.

Like other human beings, he struggled with personal challenges such as illness, fatigue, pain, deaths of loved ones, loneliness, financial pressures, and step-parenting challenges, to name but a few. Yet, as we can see from his writings, he attempted to walk according to the duties of the Christian faith. We find this in a letter that he wrote to his life-long friend, Reverend Bryan Fairfax (Lord Fairfax), who had been the pastor of Washington's church in Alexandria, Virginia. Writing from Mount Vernon on January 20, 1799, only months before he died, Washington looked back over his very full life and described his spiritual walk:

> The favourable sentiments which others, you say, have been pleased to express respecting me, cannot but be pleasing to a mind who always walked on a straight line, and endeavoured as far as human frailties, and perhaps strong passions, would enable him, to discharge the relative duties to his Maker and fellowmen, without seeking any indirect or left handed attempts to acquire popularity.[25]

Remember that Washington was a land surveyor by training who specialized in setting long straight boundary lines. He speaks of such "straight lines" in his letters. But here he tells us, as he surveys his remarkable life, that he also had sought to walk a "straight line" in discharging his duties to his "Maker and fellow-men." Accordingly, he openly spoke of his own "fervent prayer" to his soldiers. Consider this concluding line of a December 5, 1775, private letter that Washington wrote to his then faithful officer, Benedict Arnold:

> ...give him all the Assistance in your Power, to finish the glorious Work you have begun. That the Almighty may preserve and prosper you in it, is the sincere and fervent Prayer of, Dear Sir, Your Humble & Obedient Servant, George Washington.[26]

Similarly, he often expresses his own deep faith in God's Providence with such heartfelt language as the following from his May 13, 1776, letter to his close friend in Boston, Reverend William Gordon. Referring to God's "...many other signal Interpositions of Providence," he declares that they "must serve to inspire every reflecting Mind with Confidence." And then he describes himself with these striking worsof spiritual commitment:

> No Man has a more perfect Reliance on the all-wise, and powerful dispensations of the Supreme Being than I have nor thinks his aid more necessary.[27]

DISESTABLISHMENT IN VIRGINIA

It is true that as a young man and for much of Washington's adult life, Virginia had an established church—the Anglican Church. By law one was required to attend services and pay tithes. That was part of the responsibility of a colonist in Virginia. However, that changed in 1786 with the Act for Establishing Religious Liberty. This great step forward in terms of religious liberty was especially the work of Thomas Jefferson and James Madison.

One of the key arguments Jefferson made in this statute was that Almighty God has made the mind free and that any punishments that men mete out against religious opinion deemed to be false are a departure from "the plan of the holy author of our religion, who being lord both of body and mind, yet choose [sic] not to propagate it by coercions on either, as was in his Almighty power to do, but to exalt it by its influence on reason alone…"[28]

In other words, Jefferson argues, because Jesus Christ could have forced men to believe in Him, but did not, and instead gave us the personal responsibility to believe, then who are we as mere men to punish others for their religious opinions, no matter how wrong these opinions may be? Secularists sometimes interpret Jefferson's argument here as a plea for unbelief. Not so. He uses the example of Christ to argue for religious freedom. In fact, religious liberty in America especially stems from two great Christian clergymen who prepared the way for America's religious liberty. They were also two of our nation's settlers—Roger Williams and William Penn.

After Virginia disestablished the Anglican Church, men and women were no longer required by state law to worship there. But Washington did not stop attending church after disestablishment. He kept attending his church long after that—until he died.

GOD IN THE SPEECHES AND WRITINGS OF WASHINGTON

George Washington's mention of God in his private letters as well as his public speeches and writings is frequent, especially when we understand the vast variety of terms he employed for the Almighty including, "the great disposer of events," "the invisible hand," "Jehovah," or his favorite term—"Providence." We cannot escape the alternatives—Washington either truly cared about God or he employed God-talk for mere political or manipulative ends, while he himself didn't believe the words he was speaking. The latter appears difficult to accept from a man who insisted, "Honesty is the best policy."

We are all familiar with politicians talking about God in their public speeches—even if their private behavior belies that God-talk. Was George Washington this type of public figure? We don't think so, nor does the historical evidence support it.

Boller quotes a nineteenth century Anglican minister who laments that Washington allegedly never mentioned Jesus. Anglican minister Bird Wilson said, "I have diligently perused every line that Washington ever gave to the public, and I do not find one expression in which he pledges himself as a professor of Christianity."[29] Here is a sampling of what Bird Wilson could have perused. Washington said that America will only be happy if we imitate "the divine author of our blessed religion."[30]

This is referring to Jesus Christ. This was not an obscure letter; it is the climax of a critical farewell letter the commander in chief wrote to the governors of all the states at the end of the War. Furthermore, it seems that Wilson didn't know about the letter General Washington wrote to the Delaware Indian chiefs. They asked him for advice on teaching their young ones. He responded that they do well to learn our way of life and arts, "but above all, the religion of Jesus Christ."[31]

Furthermore, Washington talks about the need to be a good Christian, using the word "Christian" in several different letters and communiqués. Thus, we find phrases such as the following in Washington's public and private writings: "A Christian Spirit," "A True Christian," "Be more of a man and a Christian," "Christian soldiers," "The little Christian," "To the distinguished character of Patriot, it should be our highest glory to add the more distinguished character of Christian."[32]

What makes these affirmations of Christianity personal for Washington is his deeply held view that strong leadership must be coupled with consistency and integrity. One of Washington's "Rules of Civility" comes into play here.[33] The forty-eighth says, "Wherein you reprove another be unblameable yourself, for example is more prevalent than precepts." Thus he wrote to Lord Stirling, March 5, 1780, "Example, whether it be good or bad, has a powerful influence, and the higher in Rank the officer is, who sets it, the more striking it is." He wrote as follows to James Madison, March 31, 1787, "Laws or ordinances unobserved, or partially attended to, had better never have been made; because the first is a mere nihil [utterly useless], and the second is productive of much jealousy and discontent." He also wrote to Col. William Woodford, November 10, 1775, "Impress upon the mind of every man, from the first to the lowest, the importance of the cause, and what it is they are contending for." And writing to James McHenry on July 4, 1798, he declared,

> A good choice [of General Staff] is of . . . immense consequence. .
> . . [They] ought to be men of the most respectable character, and of
> first-rate abilities; because, from the nature of their respective
> offices, and from their being always about the Commander-in-

Chief, who is obliged to entrust many things to them confidentially, scarcely any movement can take place without their knowledge. . . . Besides possessing the qualifications just mentioned, they ought to have those of Integrity and prudence in an eminent degree, that entire confidence might be reposed in them. Without these, and their being on good terms with the Commanding General, his measures, if not designedly thwarted, may be so embarrassed as to make them move heavily on.[34]

The point of all of this is that Washington believed that a leader's actions and integrity must illustrate his own commitment to his commands to his followers. A successful leader must lead by example. Washington could not have called on his men to be such authentic Christians, if he was not trying to be such a Christian as well. So it would seem that Bird Wilson did not search thoroughly enough for the Christianity of Washington in his writings. Furthermore, if you read the text of the prayers in the 1662 *Book of Common Prayer* that Washington and his fellow worshipers read regularly in the weekly worship services, you would repeatedly see the exaltation of Jesus Christ.

CONCLUSION

We believe that modern skeptics have read into Washington their own unbelief. Just as many Christians have read too much piety into the man, we believe modern skeptics have read too much skepticism into George Washington. The skeptics, however, are on even shakier ground than the pietists that Professor Boller ridicules for their uncritical reliance on unsubstantiated anecdotes and stories that turn Washington into a paragon of devotional piety. The skeptics have remade Washington into their own unbelieving image—even though:

- He was clearly and deeply biblically literate. As we will see from his private and public writings, his pen inks scriptural phrases and concepts from all parts of the Bible.
- He was a committed churchman, attending regularly when it was convenient and inconvenient; he not only attended service, but he diligently served the church, primarily in his youth, as a lay leader; throughout his life, he generously donated money and material goods for the well-being of the church.
- He was generally very quiet about anything pertaining to himself, including his faith, yet he was always concerned to respect the faith of others,

attempting to practice his Christian faith privately, even while he at times openly affirmed his Christian beliefs in public. There are numerous accounts from family and military associates—too numerous to be dismissed—of people coming across Washington in earnest, private prayer.

- He repeatedly encouraged piety, public and private; he insisted on chaplains for the military and legislature; he often promoted "religion and morality" and recognized these as essential for our national happiness, and even called on the nation's leaders to follow Christ's example.

- He turned away from the opportunity to become a king, even though a lesser man would have seized such power; he had not fought the king in order to become a new king, even though men wanted to make him that after he won the War. Indeed, Washington is a striking model of what Christians have called a servant-statesman.

These and many other indicators show that the scholars of recent years have been misreading George Washington and ignoring the spiritual realities of our founding father. By so doing, they have presented a very truncated picture of "his Excellency."

George Washington's Sacred Fire intends to convince you that when all the available evidence is considered, the only viable conclusion is that George Washington was a Christian and not a Deist. What enflamed Washington's passion and stirred his heart was that which was sacred to his soul—his utter dependence on the hand of Divine Providence.

His passion is important for us as well. Where a nation began determines its destiny. Is the Judeo-Christian heritage of America a reality or an interloper aimed at suppressing the secularism of the founders? Or, is it the other way around? Are today's secularists trying to recreate the faith of our founding father into the unbelief of a Deist in order to rid our nation of Washington's holy flame of faith? Was it a secular flame or a "sacred fire" that Washington ignited to light the lamp for America's future? If we look carefully at Washington's words, it is clear that it was a "sacred fire." Throughout the rest of this book, we will continue carefully to consider his words. And as we do, we believe that they will fuel the "sacred fire of liberty" and continue to illumine the path to America's future.

TWO

Deism Defined: Shades of Meaning, Shading the Truth

"The man must be bad indeed who can look upon the events of the American Revolution without feeling the warmest gratitude towards the great Author of the Universe whose divine interposition was so frequently manifested in our behalf."
George Washington 1789[1]

"The hand of Providence has been so conspicuous in all this, that he must be worse than an infidel that lacks faith"
George Washington, 1763[2]

Deism: n. [Fr. *Deisme*; Sp. *Deismo*; It. Id.; from L. *deus*, [God]. The doctrine or creed of a Deist; the belief or system of religious opinions of those who acknowledge the existence of one God, but deny revelation: or deism is the belief in natural religion only, or those truths, in doctrine and practice, which man is to discover by the light of reason, independent and exclusive of any revelation from God. Hence deism implies infidelity or a disbelief in the divine origin of the scriptures.

Deist: n. [Fr. *Deiste*; It. *Deista*.] One who believes in the existence of a God, but denies revealed religion; one who professes no form of religion, but follows the light of nature and reason, as his only guides in doctrine and practice; a freethinker.
Noah Webster, 1828 Dictionary of the American English Language[3]

Before we begin our study, we should define our terms. A Deist is one who believes that there is a God, but He is far removed from the daily affairs of men. God made the world and then left it to run on its own. The Deist's God does not take an active interest in the affairs of men. He is not a prayer-answering God. Praying to Him has no value. Deism is in some ways the natural outworking of exalting reason alone—that is, human reason apart from divine revelation.

The meaning of Deism has changed through the years. What Deism meant in Washington's day and what it meant later is an important point in terms of understanding the religious milieu of George Washington. Because of these shades of meaning, there has been scholarly confusion over the use of the word "Deism." Deism, in general, whether in Washington's day or after, has not believed what the New Testament declares: "In the beginning was the Word, and the Word was with God and the Word was God....And the Word became flesh and dwelt among us..." (John 1:1, 14, NASB). In other words, a Deist, most decidedly, did not accept the Christian claim of the incarnation—that is, that God entered time and space to reveal himself to humanity through his son Jesus Christ.

Scholars identify our founders with secularism or Deism. Does this mean that they did not believe in God's providential actions in American history? Or is it possible that in this period of history there was an earlier form of Deism that still prayed and believed in Providence, but denied that the Bible was the revelation of God? The difference between the two can be described by what we will call "hard Deism" and "soft Deism."

Hard Deists rejected more elements of Christianity than soft Deists. A hard Deist not only denied that God had revealed himself in scripture, but he also denied that God acts in history, which is usually described by the word "Providence." Thomas Paine, the best representative of what we are calling hard Deism, in his *Age of Reason*, rejected the idea of Providence, calling it one of the five deities of Christian mythology.[4] Hard Deists also typically rejected a belief in God's hearing and answering prayer. The movement from the original soft Deism to the fully developed hard Deism is reflected in Crane Brinton's comment in *The Shaping of Modern Thought*: "One of the most remarkable examples of the survival of religious forms is found when professed Deists indulge in prayer, as they occasionally did. After all, the whole point about the Deist's clockmaker God is that he has set the universe in motion, according to natural law and has thereupon left it to its own devices. Prayer to such a god would seem peculiarly inefficacious."[5] This is clearly the conclusion that Thomas Paine reached in the *Age of Reason*.[6] In other words, Deism means an absentee God.

Many consider Washington to have been a soft Deist. Supposedly, this would mean that Washington did not believe that God revealed himself in the Bible. It also means that he did not accept the Christian claims of Christ's divine nature, nor of His atoning death for man's sin and his resurrection from the dead, but that he may well have believed in prayer and Providence, in some sense. Further, while not even the strictest skeptic accuses Washington of being a hard Deist, there is a tendency to inappropriately compare Washington and Paine. Boller, for example, writes that both Washington and Paine used similar deistic names for God. Yet there was a deep divide between the two. The tension between Paine and Washington began over Paine's book the *Rights of Man*.[7] Before this, their friendship had been strong; Washington had loved *Common Sense* and loved Paine's logical arguments that called for the American Revolution that he so ably put forth.[8] But Paine's criticism of Washington in the context of the *Rights of Man* is captured by Washington biographer Thomas Flexner:

> Another complaint is that, in acknowledging copies of the *Rights of Man*, which Paine had sent him, Washington had coldly sidestepped all comment. As a matter of fact, the president, who wished to remain nonpartisan, had used common sense. Paine would undoubtedly have published any compliment Washington sent him. Jefferson was, indeed, to get into hot water by having a letter he wrote to an American printer appear as an introduction and seeming endorsement of Paine's extremely controversial work.[9]

Moreover, Thomas Paine never forgave Washington for his utter silence to his cries for help when he was imprisoned during the violence of the French Revolution. When Paine made it back to America, he used every occasion he could to attack his erstwhile friend, while Washington never responded publicly.[10] The complete severance of their former relationship is underscored by the words of George Washington scholar, John C. Fitzpatrick. This passage begins with Washington's rebuttal to an open letter Paine had written, criticizing our first President: "...absolute falsehoods. As an evidence whereof, and of the plan they are pursuing, I send you a letter from Mr. Paine to me, Printed in this city and disseminated with great industry." The letter, "Printed in the city and disseminated with great industry," was dated July 30, 1796, and published by Benjamin Franklin Bache, a newspaper publisher and a contemporary of George Washington who was severely critical of our founding father—not a popular stance at the time. It was republished in Dublin and London in 1797. It ended thus:

"As to you sir, treacherous in private friendship (for so you have been to me, and that in the day of danger) and a hypocrite in public life, the world will be puzzled to decide, whether you are an apostate or an imposter; whether you have abandoned good principles or whether you ever had any."

So when Boller suggests a parallel between the theological vocabulary of Washington and Paine, in the following statement, in light of the above, it is clear that he entirely neutralizes the intense disagreement that an authentic description of their relationship requires.

> Most of Washington's official communications during the Revolution contained no references to the Christian religion itself. The appeal, as we have seen, was customarily made to "Heaven," "Providence," "Supreme Being,""supreme disposer of all events," and to "the great arbiter of the Universe." All of these were, of course, expressions that a good Deist— like Thomas Paine, for instance—could use in all sincerity without in any way committing himself to the theology and doctrines of the Christian church.[11]

DEISM IN WASHINGTON'S LANGUAGE?

Part of the shading of the truth in this debate is attempting to identify Washington's language with that of the "hard Deist" Thomas Paine by pointing to his use of phrases such as "Heaven," "Providence," "Supreme Being," "Supreme Disposer of all events," and "the great Arbiter of the Universe." But let's take Boller at his own words. Are the names for God used by Washington "expressions that a good Deist— like Thomas Paine—could use in all sincerity, without in any way committing himself to the theology and doctrines of the Christian Church"? First we must ask, if Paine believed that Providence was a Christian mythology, how could he employ each of these terms that argue for God's direct governance in human history? It seems clear to us, however, that Paine himself sensed the incongruity implicit in Boller's claim, since Paine *did not* use these terms in the *Age of Reason*. Instead, Paine's truncated Deistic theological terminology limited itself to the meager list of merely "God," "Creator," and "Almighty." When the variety of names for God that Washington used throughout his writings is considered, however, one discovers around a hundred different titles for God.[12] These titles are remarkably diverse. It's almost as though Washington did not want to use the same title for God a second time. Yet he did use the word "God" over a hundred times and the word "heaven" over a hundred times. The honorific titles for

God such as "the Great Author of the Universe" or the "Great Disposer of Human Events" are only samples of his vast theological vocabulary by which he sought to honor God.

So, while Paine does not use these titles that Washington so frequently employs, we have also found these same titles for God in the writings of other great Christian preachers of Washington's day, whose messages were among the sermons that Washington purchased, collected, and bound, and were found in his library when he died. Reverend Samuel Miller is an example of an orthodox minister of Washington's day using terms for God that our President used. Reverend Miller was a Presbyterian minister and certainly no Deist. His July 4, 1793, message based on 2 Corinthians 3:17 was received by Washington and was bound in Washington's sermon collection.[13] Reverend Miller's sermon, entitled "A Sermon on the Anniversary of the Independence of America," refers to God in the following ways:

- "the supreme Arbiter of nations"
- "the grand Source"
- "the Deity himself"
- "the Sovereign Dispenser of all blessings"
- "the Governor of the universe"
- "thou exalted Source of liberty"[14]

When George Washington used his multitude of respectful titles for God, he was simply employing a Baroque style popular among many of the ministers at the time.[15] He was not showing that he harbored some sort of secret, unspoken code of unbelief that would take two centuries for scholars to decode.[16]

SILENCE FROM WASHINGTON'S DIARIES

One of the arguments we have to assess is the completeness of Washington's diaries—or really, incompleteness. Boller claims that Washington's Christianity is not tenable based on his church attendance recorded in his private diary.[17] If Washington didn't note it, so the argument goes, he didn't attend. But there is a problem here, both with the source and the logic. First, many of Washington's diaries are missing. Second, the silence of the record does not prove it did not happen, or that it was not important to him. The records of his diaries are important. But it is difficult to make a definitive case from the brief and incomplete entries that Washington made in them. For example, when he presided over the Constitutional Convention, he barely wrote a word in his diaries about these epoch-making events.[18] Moreover, he never entered a word about the historic debates that occurred there. Does that mean he barely attended the sessions (not so) or was indifferent to them? By this same logic, one could infer that Washington's breeding and care of his hunting hounds were more important than the Constitutional Convention, since in his diaries he so often mentions his dogs by name! Here we choose not to follow Boller in imposing an uncertain and questionable standard to discern George Washington's spiritual history. Instead of arguments from silence, we choose to accent the written words and substantiated actions of Washington to make our case for his Christian faith.

FAMILY INFLUENCES

We will show from the historical data that Washington was deeply influenced by his godly mother, Mary Ball Washington, and his older half-brother, Lawrence, who provided him with careful instruction in the Christian faith as evidenced by his childhood school papers and his school books, as well as by their active family and personal participation in their church. Along with his family's impact on his faith, we need to also recognize the influence of his religious neighbors—the British noble family of the Fairfaxes that owned vast sections of the Old Dominion. Records show that they went to church together, that Washington was urged by the cousin of Lord Fairfax to have prayers for his troops as a young soldier. His childhood and life-long friend, Bryan Fairfax, actually was the pastor of the Episcopal Church in Alexandria for a time, where Washington worshiped after his return from the Revolutionary War, as well as after his return from the presidency. We will consider the family testimony about Washington's faith—those who were in a position to know his faith the best. We will find that the family witness to his faith is uniform. In their minds there was no doubt that George Washington was a Christian. Perhaps this is why Professor Boller and many recent scholars pass over this extensive evidence in utter silence, treating it as though it were historically irrelevant.

THE CHURCHMAN

George Washington is famous for being a churchman. During the Revolutionary War, he at times actually rode on horseback some twenty miles to get to a church. The Reverend John Stockton Littell, Rector of St. James' Church in Keene N.H., in his 1913 book *George Washington: Christian*[19] records a story that reportedly took place in Litchfield in New England, where Washington saw some of his soldiers throwing stones at an old Anglican church building. He said, "Stop throwing the stones! I am a churchman, and we should not deal with the church in this way." Whether or not one accepts the historicity of this anecdote, Washington's own records show he worshiped in Christian churches not only in his native Virginia, but also from New England to Georgia as he traveled on horseback through the vast and largely unsettled United States. He went to church all of his life, from the time he was a young boy to when he became a soldier. He led in devotions in his camp, when there was no church or chaplain present. As commander in chief and as president, he sought to set an example for his followers by regular worship. When he became a retired president and proprietor of Mount Vernon, he continued to be a consistent worshiper.

In 1755, Washington played the role of Chaplain when he led a funeral service for his commanding officer General William Braddock. Washington read the funeral service by torchlight, as his British soldiers were fleeing from the Indian warriors, whose surprise attack had killed or wounded every officer. Washington was the only officer to escape unharmed. In the service he read from the 1662 *Book of Common Prayer*, giving his fallen General a Christian funeral.[20] The Scriptures and prayers Washington read that sorrowful night by torchlight included:

> I AM the resurrection and the life, saith the Lord: he that believeth in me, though he were dead, yet shall he live: and whosoever liveth and believeth in me shall never die. St. John xi. 25, 26.
>
> I KNOW that my Redeemer liveth, and that he shalt stand at the latter day upon the earth. And though after my skin worms destroy this body, yet in my flesh shall I see God: whom I shall see for myself, and mine eyes shall behold, and not another. Job xix. 25, 26, 27.
>
> WE brought nothing into this world, and it is certain we can carry nothing out. The Lord gave, and the Lord hath taken away; blessed be the Name of the Lord. 1 Tim. vi. 7. Job I. 21.
>
> O MERCIFUL God, the Father of our Lord Jesus Christ, who is the resurrection and the life; in whom whosoever believeth shall live, though he die; and whosoever liveth, and believeth in him, shall not die eternally; who also hath taught us, by his holy Apostle Saint Paul, not to be sorry, as men without hope, for them that sleep in him; We meekly beseech thee, O Father, to raise us from the death of sin unto the life of righteousness; that, when we shall depart this life, we may rest in him, as our hope is this our brother doth; and that, at the general Resurrection in the last day, we may be found acceptable in thy sight; and receive that blessing, which thy

well-beloved Son shall then pronounce to all that love and fear thee, saying, Come, ye blessed children of my Father, receive the kingdom prepared for you from the beginning of the world. Grant this, we beseech thee, O merciful Father, through Jesus Christ, our Mediator and Redeemer. *Amen.*

Thus, we know that the lips of Washington spoke the name of Jesus Christ as he shared the comfort of the Gospel through the historic liturgy of the Anglican Church.

Later in his life, he was very active in worship. The records show that he went to church on Sundays while he served in the office of the presidency. When he retired, he continued to worship in the church. For much of his life, Pohick Church in Lorton, Virginia, was his main church; after the War, Christ Church in Alexandria was his place of worship. Both buildings are still standing today. If you visit them, you can still see the pew boxes he worshiped in and that his records show he purchased for himself and his family. What did Washington pray when he went to these churches? They included Christian prayers from the *Book of Common Prayer* that he prayed aloud with the entire congregation. These prayers are confessions of sin and repentance and calling upon Jesus Christ for mercy and forgiveness. To the retort that the prayer book was not that important to Washington, consider that he not only ordered a family Bible for Mount Vernon, he also ordered prayer books for each member of his family, and specially ordered one for himself that was to be sized to fit in his pocket, so he could carry it with him.[21]

THE COLONIAL CHURCH'S REREDOS

At the Anglican churches Washington worshiped in or visited, the parishioners would read from the "reredos" during the service. This was a large wall plaque behind the altar with words painted on it. These words were from the Bible and Christian teaching and were usually emblazoned on three panels. One consisted of the Apostles' Creed;[22] the next had the Lord's Prayer.[23] And the third panel listed out Exodus 20, i.e., the Ten Commandments,[24] and sometimes included the Golden Rule of Matthew 7:12.[25] There was a very practical motive for these texts to be placed on the main wall of the church—books and printing were very expensive in colonial America. This was a more economical means to provide the essentials of the Children's Catechism and the essentials of the Anglican *Book of Common Prayer* for an entire congregation.

The authors of this present book visited Christ Church in Alexandria, Virginia, and they have a reredos there. That particular reredos is said to be the very one that was used in Washington's day. We also discovered a similar reredos when we visited Pohick Church in Lorton. (The Union Army occupied the abandoned and deteriorating colonial brick church building and inflicted further damage. It was restored to a reasonable facsimile of its colonial interior during the years 1901-1916.) You can also see the Apostles' Creed, the Lord's Prayer, and the Ten Commandments at Bruton Parish Church in Williamsburg, where Washington attended when he was participating in the House of Burgesses. This is true also of Trinity Church in Newport, Rhode Island, where Washington also had his own pew. (Please see the different reredoses in the photos.) As the congregation followed the Anglican liturgy, they would read out loud these holy texts from the reredos.

WASHINGTON'S WORSHIP IN VIEW OF HIS CONSCIENCE AND CHARACTER

Washington was a man with a sensitive conscience and a strong character. We want to take a moment to develop that point, so we can return with a clearer understanding of Washington's religious practices. Why would a man of integrity engage in so many Christian activities, unless he really believed the Christian message?

The force of this question is strengthened by Washington's repeated statements concerning the power of his own conscience and his deep concern for his character.[26] To General Nathanael Greene, he wrote on October 6, 1781, "I bore much for the sake of peace and the public good. My conscience tells me I acted rightly in these transactions, and should they ever come to the knowledge of the world I trust I shall stand acquitted by it." On Dec. 7, 1783, he wrote to the Legislature of New Jersey, "For me, it is enough to have seen the divine Arm visibly outstretched for our deliverance, and to have received the approbation of my Country, and my Conscience...." To Henry Lee he wrote on September 22, 1788, "While doing what my conscience informed me was right, as it respected my God, my Country and myself, I could despise all the party clamor and unjust censure...." If Washington did not believe in something, his conscience would not permit him to participate. If he did not subscribe to the Apostles' Creed, why then would he have said it? If he did not believe in Jesus Christ, why would he not have passed on participating in the service? This is particularly pertinent, since it was his character that caused him to be the unquestioned leader of our youthful nation. Consider what congressional leader and future President John Adams wrote to his wife Abigail on February 21, 1777,

Many persons are extremely dissatisfied with numbers of the

45

general officers of the highest rank. I don't mean the Commander-in-Chief. His character is justly very high, but Schuyler, Putnam, Spencer, Heath, are thought by very few to be capable of the great commands they hold.[27]

In this context, consider Washington's consistently strong words about his deep commitment to candor, honesty, and character. To the Earl of Loudoun, in March 1757, Washington wrote, "My nature is open and honest and free from guile." To Henry Knox he wrote on July 16, 1798, "But my dear Sir, as you always have found, and trust ever will find, candor a prominent trait of my character." To President John Adams, he wrote on September 25, 1798, "…let the purity of my intentions; the candor of my declarations; and a due respect for my own character, be received as an apology." In the same letter he said, "…I would have told you with the frankness and candor which I hope will ever mark my character…." To General Gates he wrote on January 4, 1778, "Thus Sir, with an openness and candor which I hope will ever characterize and mark my conduct have I complied with your request." To James McHenry, he wrote on April 8, 1794, "…with my inauguration, I resolved firmly, that no man should ever charge me *justly* with deception." He wrote from Valley Forge on January 2, 1778 to the President of Congress, "I did not, nor shall I ever [accept a gentleman as a friend that I regard as an enemy], till I am capable of the arts of dissimulation. These I despise…." In other words, Washington sought to act so that he could not be accused of telling lies. To Alexander Hamilton, he wrote on August 28, 1788, "I hope I shall always possess firmness and virtue enough to maintain (what I consider the most enviable of all titles) the character of *an honest man*…." To Edmund Randolph, July 31, 1795, "I am [not] disposed to quit the ground I have taken, unless circumstances more imperious than have yet come to my knowledge should compel it; for there is but one straight course, and that is to seek truth and pursue it steadily." He wrote to Timothy Pickering, February 10, 1799, "Concealment is a species of misinformation." To Timothy Pickering, August 29, 1797, "Candor is not a more conspicuous trait in the character of Governments than it is of individuals." To James Madison, November 30, 1785, "It is an old adage, that honesty is the best policy. This applies to public as well as private life, to States as well as individuals." To Richard Washington, April 15, 1757, "What can be so proper as the truth?"

To say Washington was a Deist—even a "soft Deist"—would imply that he did not have a problem violating his conscience each time he worshiped in his church. It is difficult to imagine how Washington, with his expressed concern for his character and his open commitment to honesty and candor, along with his sensitive conscience, could repeatedly and consistently make a public reaffirmation of a faith that he really did not believe.

The burden of proof is clearly on the side of those who claim that Washington was a Deist. To Washington, integrity and conscience were vitally important. A good conscience and hope of divine approval were essential for Washington's sense of integrity. Thus he wrote August 18, 1786, to Marquis de Chastellux, "Perhaps nothing can excite more perfect harmony in the soul than to have this string [avoidance of vanity and false humility] vibrate in unison with the internal consciousness of rectitude in our intentions and an humble hope of approbation from the supreme disposer of all things."

As a man of honor, he did not determine his actions for outward recognition. To his friend the Marquis De Chastellux, he wrote on August 18, 1786, "I consider it an indubitable mark of mean-spiritedness and pitiful vanity to court applause from the pen or tongue of man." To Dr. James Craik, March 25, 1784 he wrote, "I will frankly declare to you, my dear doctor, that any memoirs of my life, distinct and unconnected with the general history of the war, would rather hurt my feelings than tickle my pride whilst I lived. I had rather glide gently down the stream of life, leaving it to posterity to think and say what they please of me, than by any act of mine to have vanity or ostentation imputed to me . . . I do not think vanity is a trait of my character."

George Washington was either a true churchman or spiritual imposter. He once wrote to Robert Stewart on April 27, 1763. To guarantee the truth of his letter, he used the phrase: "On my honor and the faith of a Christian." Clearly his honor and integrity meant a great deal to him. From this statement, we see that his honor was inseparable from and strengthened by his faith as a Christian.

WASHINGTON AND THE EUCHARIST

One of the main arguments Paul Boller (and other skeptics of Washington's Christianity) makes is that Washington rarely, if ever, received Communion. This is an important matter and must be considered. First of all, there are eye witness written accounts that the General did receive communion regularly as a young man, when his church provided it three or four times a year.[28] Second, there is both oral and written testimony that he received Communion on occasion, both during the Revolutionary War and as President. Third, does one have to receive Communion each time it's offered to be a Christian?

During his presidency in Philadelphia, it was Washington's regular custom to *not* receive the Eucharist. To Boller, this is evidence he was not a Christian. This is, however, not a proof that he was a Deist. Washington was joining many in his parish who left after the completion of the service proper and before the Lord's Supper service was to be held. Bishop William Meade explains,

> If it be asked how we can reconcile this leaving of the church at any time of the celebration of the Lord's Supper with a religious character, we reply by stating a well-known fact,—viz: that in former days there was a most mistaken notion, too prevalent both in England and America, that it was not so necessary in the professors of religion to communicate [receive communion] at all times, but that in this respect persons might be regulated by their feelings, and perhaps by the circumstances in which they were placed. I have had occasion to see much of this in my researches into the habits of the members of the old church of Virginia. Into this error of opinion and practice General Washington may have fallen, especially at a time when he was peculiarly engaged with the cares of government and a multiplicity of engagements, and when his piety may have suffered some loss thereby.[29]

Washington's adopted granddaughter, Nelly Custis, confirms this fact: "On communion Sundays he left the church with me, after the blessing, and returned home, and we sent the carriage back for my grandmother."[30]

Washington biographer Jared Sparks suggests a reason from his military days that may have prompted his non-participation. "It is probable that after he took command of the army, finding his thoughts and attention necessarily engrossed by the business that devolved upon him, in which frequently little distinction could be observed between the Sabbath and other days, he may have believed it improper publicly to partake of an ordinance which, according to the ideas he entertained of it, imposed severe restrictions on outward conduct, and a sacred pledge to perform duties impracticable in his situation."[31]

We believe Sparks was correct when we consult Washington's diaries and letters as to what he did on Sundays after church, these provide a reason why he left after the worship service was complete and before the periodic communion service began. In his letters he relates that this was one of the few times he had in a profoundly busy military, political, and business life to handle his vast private correspondence and to address the massive responsibilities of running his huge Mount Vernon Plantation.[32]

The secret of Washington's ability to accomplish so much was his mastery of time management. Consider his statements on time. "What to me is more valuable, my time, that I most regard," he wrote to James McHenry, September 14, 1799. Similarly, he wrote to James Anderson on December 10, 1799, "...time, which is of more importance than is generally imagined."

One might well disagree with Washington's choice between his personal demands and the participation in the Eucharist. But it is clear that it is a non-sequitur to infer, as Boller and those who argue for Washington's Deism do, that Washington's choice demonstrates a disbelief in Christ. His decision to not commune on many Sundays cannot cancel out his faith demonstrated in countless acts of Christian conduct and publicly expressed in phrases such as "the divine author of our blessed religion,"[33] and privately expressed in affirmations such as "on my honor and the faith of a Christian."[34]

Finally, Boller did not take the time to investigate all the evidence for Washington's communing, or if he did, he chose not even to acknowledge the significant evidence that George Washington did receive Communion as president. This testimony comes from the daughter of his fellow general, Phillip Schuyler. Why should we trust the testimony of Elizabeth Schuyler?—because her married name was Mrs. Alexander Hamilton. She claimed to have communed with President Washington on the day of his inauguration in New York.[35] But there may be an even far better explanation. Two subsequent chapters will explore this question in depth: Did Washington take Communion? Why did Washington not commune as president in Philadelphia?

CONCLUSION

George Washington either was a Christian or he manipulated Christian actions, words, and worship for political ends, merely pretending to be a Christian. Why would he so often refer to God, Providence, Heaven, and the Divine unless he really meant it? Why did he insist on having chaplains? Why did he attend church so consistently, when it was difficult to get there? Was Washington just putting on a show when he spoke about God—even in private correspondence—and for whom? Again, it seems to us that Paul Boller and other modern scholars are remaking George Washington in a secular image, just as much, even more so than the "pietists" that Boller so pointedly criticizes for supposedly remaking Washington in their image. For Washington to use religion for such personal ends may seem consonant with modern and post-modern values. But for Washington to have conducted himself this way, he would have been utterly inconsistent with all of his own claims for his character and the ideals of his era. Moreover, to accomplish this re-creation of Washington, not only is he removed from his historical Anglican and Virginian context, but a great deal of evidence must be either ignored, suppressed, or left unconsidered or undiscovered. Instead, we desire to let the full weight of the evidence be heard.

That evidence includes such humble admissions on his part that he was being saddled with a great responsibility—a responsibility he could only possibly fulfill with the help of the Almighty. We close this chapter with this earnest prayer that he offers for his reputation and with his own promise to seek to perform his daunting duties. This comes from the June 19, 1775, letter he wrote to his brother-in-law, Burwell Bassett:

> I am now embarked on a tempestuous Ocean, from whence perhaps, no friendly harbor is to be found. I have been called upon by the unanimous Voice of the Colonies to the Command of the Continental Army. It is an honor I by no means aspired to. It is an honor I wished to avoid, as well from an unwillingness to quit the peaceful enjoyment of my Family, as from a thorough conviction of my own Incapacity and want of experience in the conduct of so momentous a concern; but the partiality of the Congress, added to some political motives, left me without a choice. May God grant, therefore, that my acceptance of it, may be attended with some good to the common cause, and without Injury (from want of knowledge) to my own reputation. I can answer but for three things, a firm belief of the justice of our Cause, close attention in the prosecution of it, and the strictest Integrity.[36]

THREE

Did Washington Avoid the Name of Jesus Christ?

Addressing a Fundamental Argument

"...there is no direct allusion to Christ, and the word Christ has been found in none of Washington's almost countless autographs"
Rupert Hughes, 1926 [1]

"You do well to wish to learn our arts and ways of life, and above all, the religion of Jesus Christ. These will make you a greater and happier people than you are."
George Washington, 1779 [2]

Let's begin by noting that Washington historian Rupert Hughes is wrong when he writes in 1926, "...there is no direct allusion to Christ, and the word Christ has been found in none of Washington's almost countless autographs."[3] For George Washington wrote in 1779, "You do well to wish to learn our arts and ways of life, and above all, the religion of Jesus Christ. These will make you a greater and happier people than you are."[4] This incident clearly establishes that Washington was openly willing to use the name of Jesus Christ. Washington here was speaking to Delaware Indians, who had come seeking to learn the Christian religion and the ways of the Americans. They had even brought the sons of their chiefs to become students in their educational quest. In this context, Washington freely spoke the name of Jesus Christ to them since he was affirming the religious task of the Christian mission to the Indians. In his mind, the Delawares were doing well to learn the ways of the Americans, but their learning the religion of Jesus Christ was "above all" the other matters of their intended learning. We will later consider Washington's high personal commitment to the evangelization of the Indians or "the Christianization of the aborigines" as he calls it, in the chapter on Washington's Anglican Virginia and the Christian Mission to the Indians.

Author Paul Boller, Jr—again the author of the 1963 landmark book declaring Washington a Deist that has never been fully answered—seeks to dismiss the force of this quote by claiming it was an unthinking acquiescence to his aide's theological viewpoint since he was pressed for time: "Secular freethinkers, reacting against the exuberances of the pietists, have been fond of pointing out that in all of Washington's voluminous writings, there does not appear even a single reference to Jesus Christ. They are in error; there is one such reference. In a speech to the Delaware Chiefs at Washington's Middle Brook headquarters on May 12, 1779 (which the pietists have unaccountably overlooked), appears this passage: 'You will do well to wish to learn our ways of life, and above all, the religion of Jesus Christ. These will make you a greater and happier people than you are.' But his speech, like many of Washington's speeches during the Revolutionary period, was probably written by one of his aides, Robert Hanson Harrison, and Washington, who must have been pressed for time, seems simply to have signed the document without making any revisions." [5] The problems with Boller's feeble argument are patent. First, Boller himself will later quote Fitzpatrick, the editor of the thirty-seven volumes of the *Writings Of George Washington*, "Washington 'dominated his correspondence,' Fitzpatrick went on to say, 'and cannot be denied complete responsibility for it.'[6] Second, Boller does not have a shred of historical evidence for his claim. Note his words: "probably written by one of his aids," "Washington … must have been pressed" and "seems simply to have signed." So much for Boller's insistence that his case for Washington's Deism would be made only by evidence that would "hold up in a court of law." We accept his own verdict of such flimsy explanations, namely, they "must be dismissed as totally lacking in any kind of evidence that would hold up in a court of law."[7]

Finally, the implied irresponsibility in Boller's explanation of Washington's letting something stand under his signature reflecting his faith and values which he did not believe; and further, his having a subordinate who was so unaware of his commanding officer's real beliefs that he would unwittingly impose them on his chief; and on top of this, for it to have been done in such a hurried non-methodical manner, especially when he was acting on behalf of the Congress of the United States, his ultimate superiors, ...all make Boller's argument so unlike all that is known about Washington's character and conduct, that it exposes the utter unhistorical depths to which the skeptics must stoop to make Washington into a Deist!

And since this quote is Washington's, which all the facts indicate it must be, it alone utterly destroys the thesis that Washington was a Deist. No Deist would, or could, say that "above all" learning available to a student, the best is to learn "the religion of Jesus Christ." Boller, who often seeks to compare Washington to Jefferson and Paine, will not find even a hint of such praise for the Christian religion in their writings. The inescapable conclusion is that Washington was a Christian.

JESUS, HUMAN OR DIVINE?

Nevertheless, Washington scholar Rupert Hughes argued, "Jefferson said that Washington was a Deist."[8] But even Washington recognized the possibility that Jefferson may not have understood matters that were important to him.[9] The reliability of Jefferson's assessment of Washington is at least unclear, given that Washington's most gracious appeal could not prevent him from resigning his position as Secretary of State on Washington's cabinet, due to an intractable disagreement with Alexander Hamilton.[10] Nevertheless, let's take Hughes' claim seriously.

If Washington were a Deist, he would have seen Jesus merely as a human, albeit perhaps an extraordinary teacher and a unique religious personality.[11] This is important for our discussion, because when one takes a mere human view of Jesus, as did Thomas Jefferson and Thomas Paine, it actually causes one to be more casual in referring to Jesus. After all, in the view of the Deist, Jesus was only a man, even though a noteworthy person of history.

But for those who hold an historic Christian view of Jesus, He is "fully God and fully man in one person." This was the view of Washington's Anglican tradition that followed the ancient Council of Chalcedon.[12] In fact, the 1662 *Book Of Common Prayer* that Washington worshipped with until the birth of the Episcopal Church in 1789,[13] required the regular use of what has been called the Athanasian Creed.[14] At the conclusion of the Evening Prayer, the heading of Washington's 1662 *Book of Common Prayer* gave this instruction: "Upon these Feasts; Christmas-day, the Epiphany, S.

Matthias, Easter-day, Ascension-day, Whitsunday, S. John Baptist, S. James, S. Bartholomew, S. Matthew, S. Simon and S. Jude, S. Andrew, and upon Trinity-Sunday, shall be sung or said at Morning Prayer, instead of the Apostles Creed, this Confession of our Christian faith, commonly called the Creed of S. Athanasius, by the Minister and People Standing." So on some thirteen Sundays each year, the Anglican Church affirmed these historic words of faith in the Trinity. If we very conservatively assume that Washington only made one of these Sunday services each year of his life until he became President at the age of fifty-seven, and at which time the newly organized American Episcopal *Book of Common Prayer* made this creed optional, that means that he would have already publicly affirmed the following words some fifty times:

> Whoever will be saved: before all things it is necessary that he hold the Catholick Faith. Which faith, except every one do keep whole and undefiled: without doubt he shall perish everlastingly. And the Catholick faith is this: That we worship one God in Trinity, and Trinity in Unity; Neither confounding the Persons; nor dividing the Substance. For there is one Person of the Father, another of the Son: and another of the Holy Ghost. But the Godhead of the Father, of the Son, and of the Holy Ghost, is all one: the Glory equal, the Majesty co-eternal. Such as the Father is, such is the Son and such is the Holy Ghost. The Father uncreate, the Son uncreate, and the Holy Ghost uncreate. The Father incomprehensible, the Son incomprehensible: and the Holy Ghost incomprehensible. The Father eternal, the Son eternal, and the Holy Ghost eternal. And yet they are not three eternals: but one eternal....So the Father is God, the son is God and the Holy Ghost is God. And yet they are not three Gods: but one God . . . And in this Trinity none is afore, or after other: none is greater or less than another; But the whole three Persons are co-eternal together: and co-equal. So that in all things, as is aforesaid: The Unity in Trinity, and the Trinity in Unity is to be worshipped. He therefore that will be saved: must thus think of the Trinity.
>
> Furthermore, it is necessary to everlasting salvation: that he also believe rightly the Incarnation of our Lord Jesus Christ. For the right Faith is, that we believe and confess: that our Lord Jesus Christ the Son of God, is God and man; God of the Substance of the

Father, begotten before the worlds: and man of the Substance of his mother, born in the world. Perfect God and perfect man: of reasonable soul, and human flesh subsisting. Equal to the Father, as touching his Godhead: and inferior to the Father, as touching his Manhood. Who although he be God, and Man: yet he is not two, but one Christ;…Who suffered for our salvation: descended into hell, rose again the third day from the dead. He ascended into heaven; he sitteth on the right hand of the Father, God Almighty: from whence he shall come to judge the quick and the dead. At whose coming all men shall rise again with their bodies: and shall give account for their own works. And they that have done good, shall go into life everlasting: and they that have done evil, into ever lasting fire. This is the Catholick Faith: which except a man believe faithfully he cannot be saved.[15]

The point to see here is that these words, (not to mention those found in the Apostles Creed), which no Deist could honestly recite, were for a devout Anglican a declaration that the name of Jesus was not just a human name, but a divine name too. As we will see over and over in this book, those who hold that Washington was a Deist have ripped him out of his eighteenth century Anglican context.

THE HISTORICAL ANGLICAN CONCERN FOR THE SACRED NAME OF JESUS

It was not merely a commonplace fact of historical discussion when one spoke of Christ. Rather, Jesus was a sacred name that had to be guarded and kept holy. Accordingly, as the rerodos—the wall behind the altar with sacred writings—that Washington read from instructed him: "Thou shalt not use God's name in vain." His childhood "Rules of Civility" reinforced this in rule 108, "When you speak of God or his attributes, let it be seriously and with reverence." Thus in his commonplace activities of farming, military action, business, and politics, the holy name of Jesus Christ would not normally be spoken aloud, if one was outside at a worship setting. In this instance, to "avoid" speaking or writing this holy name should not be construed as an act of unbelief, but of reverence instead.[16] A parallel with the Jewish tradition is observable here. Observant Jews have historically avoided speaking the name of Jehovah (YHWH); similarly, Christians have avoided saying the name of Jesus in common parlance.

The careful personal use of Christ's name by a devout Anglican in the eighteenth century would have been coupled with an equal concern to prevent the profane use of his sacred name. Deists, by contrast, not sharing these scruples, might actually use Jesus' name far more frequently. Such is the case with Jefferson and Paine. Jefferson often speaks of Jesus from his Unitarian perspective[17] that denied both the miracles and the deity of Jesus, but nevertheless honored his teaching.[18] Paine's *Age Of Reason* refers to the human Jesus often since, in his view, Jesus is not divine.[19] But if one holds to the full deity of Christ, as expressed in the Nicene Creed[20] (from the 1789 American edition of the *Book Of Common Prayer*) that Washington regularly recited as President until his death, there is a deep feeling of reverence that is coupled with the name of Jesus Christ that seeks to preserve the sanctity of Christ's name.

We believe that this is exactly what is found in Washington's writings. In his General Orders, for example, he declares that his "feelings" had been "continually wounded" by the profanity and swearing of the soldiers. In his General Orders of July 29, 1779, he declares,

> Many and pointed orders have been issued against that unmeaning and abominable custom of Swearing , not withstanding which, with much regret the General observes that it prevails, if possible, more than ever; His feelings are continually wounded by the Oaths and Imprecations of the soldiers whenever he is in hearing of them.
>
> The Name of That Being, from whose bountiful goodness we are permitted to exist and enjoy the comforts of life is incessantly imprecated and prophaned in a manner as wanton as it is shocking. For the sake therefore of religion, decency and order, the General hopes and trusts that officers of every rank will use their influence and authority to check a vice, which is as unprofitable as it is wicked and shameful. If officers would make it an invariable rule to reprimand, and if that does not do punish soldiers for offences of this kind it could not fail of having the desired effect.[21]

Men throughout Western history, in difficult circumstances such as those encountered regularly by soldiers at war, have resorted to cursing, swearing, and profanity to express distress, anger, disgust, contempt, bravado or pain. The most poignant examples of this are not only when God's name in general is profaned, but also when the name of Jesus Christ is irreverently hurled in a epithet of profane contempt. [22]

HONORIFIC TITLES FOR DEITY

Finally, and consistent with this discussion, we believe that on those occasions when Washington referred to Jesus Christ, he preferred to do so with titles of honor that were customary for his era. A devout Anglican in Washington's day would have been careful to employ honorific titles to preserve the sanctity of this name that is "above every name." (Philippians 2:9) Thus, we find in Washington's writings various titles for Christ intended to bring him honor, and avoid placing his name into common communication. Examples include: "our gracious Redeemer,"[23] "Divine Author of our blessed Religion,"[24] "the great Lord and Ruler of Nations,"[25] "the Judge of the Hearts of Men,"[26] "Divine Author of Life and felicity,"[27] "the Lord, and Giver of all victory, to pardon our manifold sins,"[28] "the Lord, and Giver of Victory,"[29] "Giver of Life."[30]

Moreover, even Washington's use of the names "God" and "Lord" and his many other names for deity are likely to include clear references to the deity of Christ as well.[31] This is because of the Trinitarian context of early Virginia, well reflected by the Anglican commitment to the Nicene Creed and the Athanasian Creed. The Athanasian Creed of Washington's Anglican Church insisted: "So that in all things, as is aforesaid: The Unity in Trinity, and the Trinity in Unity is to be worshipped. He therefore that will be saved: must thus think of the Trinity." In fact, Virginia's Trinitarian faith is evident in the title page of the *Virginia Almanack* that Washington used day after day and year after year to record his brief daily diary entries.[32] The title pages of these almanacks do not simply say, "in the year of our *Lord* 1769" but instead they read, "in the year of our *Lord God* 1769." The significance of this is increased, since in 1766 Washington did not use a *Virginia Almanack*, but instead (for some reason) used *The Universal American Almanack* printed in Philadelphia. Its title page says, "in the year of our *Lord* 1766."[33] In the religiously pluralistic Quaker city of

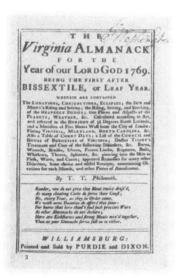

Title page of The Virginia Almanack, signed by Washington, which he used to record his daily diary entries

Philadelphia, the explicitly Trinitarian title "Lord God" was not used by the *Universal Almanack*. This Anglican emphasis upon the Trinity was later evident in the opening words of the peace treaty between America and Great Britain that ended the Revolutionary War. It began with unmistakably Trinitarian words: "In the Name of the Most Holy and Undivided Trinity. Amen."

While Washington was also judicious in his use of the word Christian and Christianity, he employed them much more frequently. We will explore his interaction with Christian teaching in the chapter on Washington's Christianity.

WASHINGTON'S ALLUSIONS TO THE GOSPEL OF CHRIST

Finally, is it really true, as Boller asserts, that Washington never refers to Jesus in his role as a teacher?[34] Perhaps he is technically correct in that Washington never explicitly discusses Jesus' teaching ministry in any of his writings. But this in itself is hardly surprising, given the nature of his daily work and normal professional concerns. But it is, nevertheless, very clear that Washington often alludes to the teachings of Jesus recorded in the Gospels. Thus there are references to Jesus' birth and its celebration.[35] There are references to Jesus' death in his childhood papers and in his adult writing: "the blessed religion revealed in the Word of God will remain an eternal and awful monument to prove that the best Institutions may be abused by human depravity."[36] Washington's lifelong worship with the *Book Of Common Prayer*, as well as his commitment to the Anglican *Thirty-Nine Articles Of Religion*, give insight into his views of the resurrection of Christ.[37]

Although Boller entirely ignores them, there are numerous Gospel phrases in Washington's writings from the teachings of Jesus, the one whom Washington publicly called "the Divine Author of our Blessed Religion." Washington's extensive references and allusions to the teachings of Jesus include: duties to God and man (the two great commandments, Matthew 22:36-40),[38] eternal rules (God's Law, Matthew 5:17-19),[39] doing as one would be done by (the Golden Rule, Matthew 7:12),[40] the will of God (Matthew 6:10),[41] daily bread (Matthew 6:11),[42] deliver us from evil (Matthew 6:13),[43] Benign Parent (Good Father, Matthew 7:11),[44] enlightening sounds of the Gospel (Luke 2:10-15; Mark 1:14-15),[45] propagating the Gospel (Matthew 28:19-20),[46] professors [i.e. believers] of Christianity (John 3:16),[47] narrow path (Matthew 7:13),[48] thorny path (Matthew 13:3-7),[49] paths of life (Matthew 7:14),[50] way of life (John 14:6),[51] road to Heaven (John 14:5-7),[52] pour out His Holy Spirit (John 15:26),[53] ministers of the Gospel (Mark 10:43-45),[54] the jot (Matthew 5:13),[55] house divided, divide and we shall become weak (Matthew 12:25),[56] concern for one's neighbor (Luke 10:29-37),[57] give to the poor (Matthew 5:42),[58] forgive and forget (Matthew 6:14-15; 5:43-44),[59] forgiveness a divine attribute (Mark 2:5-8),[60] repent and be forgiven (Luke 17:3),[61] God's care for His people (Matthew 6:30-33),[62] your good father ... a good Providence which will never fail to take care of his Children (Luke 11:9-13),[63] instruct the ignorant and reclaim the devious (Matthew 18:15-22),[64] the wise man who counts the cost (Luke 14:28),[65] the widow's mite (Mark 12:41-44),[66] appeal to God and man for justice (Luke 18:1-8),[67] the millstone around one's neck (Luke 17:1-2),[68] take up bed and walk (Mark 2:9),[69] good and faithful servant (Matthew 25:21, 23),[70] the wheat and the tares (Matthew 13:24-30),[71] war, pestilence, famine (Matthew 24:6-7),[72] wars and rumors of wars (Matthew 24:6),[73] cast lots (Matthew 27:35),[74] the aggravated vengeance of God (Luke 21:22),[75] the last trumpet (Matthew 24:31),[76] the roar of distant thunder, (Luke 21:25; John 12:28-29),[77] raise the dead to life again (Matthew 10:8; 17:23; Luke 7:22),[78] life eternal (Matthew 25:46),[79] eternal disgrace or reproach (Luke 6:22; 11:45),[80] bitterest curse this side of the grave (Mark 11:21; Matthew 25:41),[81] powers of hell (Matthew 16:18),[82] the demon of party spirit (Luke 11:20-26),[83] Lucifer (Luke 10:18),[84] angels and men (Matthew 2:11-13),[85] eternal glory (Matthew 6:13),[86] eternal happiness (Matt. 25:21, 23, 34, 46),[87] and Heaven (Matthew 6:10; 4:17).[88]

CONCLUSION

As we conclude this introductory summary of Washington's understanding of Jesus' teachings in the Gospels, we should first recognize that his biblical literacy encompasses the entire Bible, not just the Gospel teachings we have presented here. We will consider Washington's Bible literacy in a later chapter on Washington and the Bible. Perhaps in light of the evidence already offered, it is no longer so far-fetched to accept the view of earlier scholars that claimed that Washington was a serious student of the Bible. Be that as it may, it appears that Washington knew his Bible far better than Paul Boller knew Washington's use of the Bible, given that Boller claimed that Washington never referred to the Bible except "for whimsy."[89]

The point of all of this is that Washington's written words about Jesus, his reverential use of his name and titles of honor, as well as careful use of his teaching clearly distance Washington from any legitimate possibility of identifying him as a Deist. Also significant is his life-long worship in an explicitly Trinitarian Christian setting with a Christologically orthodox prayer book. Scholars' assumptions and inferences cannot overturn these explicit statements. We require written proof to show that Washington, the man of honesty and candor, did not really mean what he said when he wrote in 1779, "You do well to wish to learn our arts and ways of life, and above all, the religion of Jesus Christ. These will make you a greater and happier people than you are."

PART II

The Historical Background of George Washington

FOUR

Washington's Virginia and The Anglican Mission to the Indians

"I retire from the Chair of government . . . I leave you with
undefiled hands, an uncorrupted heart, and with ardent vows to heaven
for the welfare and happiness of that country in which I and my forefathers
to the third or fourth progenitor drew our first breath."
George Washington, 1796[1]

George Washington was born in 1732 into a Virginia that was British, Anglican, wary of Indians, dependent upon slaves, and aware that some of her citizens may have come to the New World due to a breach of the common law, or to escape the power of the crown. The concerns that molded the new civilization helped form the character of Washington. To understand Washington, we must have a working knowledge of colonial Virginia.

In the last part of the sixteenth century, while Elizabeth sat on the throne, emissaries of the Virgin Queen began the colonization of the New World and named the territory "Virginia" in her honor. The first two attempts (including the "Lost Colony of 1587") failed, presumably because of violent interactions with the Native Americans. The first English settlement in Virginia to survive began in 1607. The first permanent city of the colony was named Jamestown for the reigning monarch, King James, whose legacy lives on in the popular name for the authorized version of the English Bible, the King James Version (KJV), published in 1611. Thus it is no accident that the King's Church, the Anglican Church, came with the settlers to "The Old Dominion."

One of the first acts of the settlers of Jamestown when they landed in Virginia in 1607 was to erect a wooden cross on the shore at Cape Henry, giving symbolic expression to the Virginia Charter of 1606.[2] It declared that one of the reasons for coming to America was to spread the Christian faith to the Indians—that is, to those who "as yet live in Darkness." Furthermore, words given to the settlers as they departed England for the New World reminded them of the necessity of God's providential care, declaring "every plantation which our heavenly Father hath not planted shall be rooted out."[3]

Virginia's first governing body was called the House of Burgesses, which was under the superior rule of the King and his ministers in London. As a spiritual community, Virginia observed the established Church of the motherland, which meant that church and state were intimately connected.

In 1611, the year of the publishing of the *King James Version* of the Bible, the colonists wrote one of America's first civil documents, the Third Charter of Virginia and in 1619, the first representative assembly in America was held in the church of Jamestown. Thus, to the original settlers of Virginia, there was a visible and unmistakable link between church and state. Reverend Richard Bucke led the House of Burgesses in prayer that God would guide and sanctify their proceedings to his own glory and the good of the plantation. They issued laws requiring church attendance, believing that men's affairs could not prosper where God's service was neglected. In 1619, they also observed the first American Day of Thanksgiving.[4]

THE CHALLENGES FACING VIRGINIA'S FIRST CHURCH AND CLERGYMEN

The Anglican faith, following the ancient tradition of the Roman Catholic Church, was governed by a hierarchy of Bishops. But the Anglican Church in Virginia eventually became relatively independent, in comparison to the English mother church, since there were no Bishops in the new world to oversee the church's growth and development. After years without the oversight and concern of a caring

Episcopate, many pulpits were empty. By the time of George Washington's birth, spiritual care usually fell to the laity[5] of the parish since many churches were cared for by a single traveling curate who had to first travel to England to receive "holy orders" from the hands of the Bishop of London.[6]

Some Virginian Anglican priests had initially been professionals, such as physicians and lawyers, who were serving as vestrymen and churchwardens and were persuaded by the laity to take up the clerical vocation due to the severe ecclesiastical shortfall. In the early years of the colony, the pay was so low for a Virginia clergyman that daughters from upper class English families were rarely allowed to marry an Anglican priest who was planning to minister in the New World.[7] Although some clergymen were wealthy Virginians who entered ministry as a second career, ministers were more likely to be poor, single, and of less than exemplary piety, and often those who could not find a call in England.[8] Eventually the compensation for the clergy improved, but if the colonial clergymen's gifts were perhaps not as strong as their English counterparts, the law of supply and demand and the law of the King that guaranteed and established their religious positions had a tendency to make them largely unaccountable.[9] Since the cash crop for the colony and the means of payment for the clergy was tobacco, tobacco production was destined to be the primary emphasis in Virginia.[10]

TOBACCO—VIRGINIA'S MEANS OF EXCHANGE

As an undeveloped culture, early Virginia lacked many of the foundations of a civilized culture, including roads and currency. The settlers lived close to the land and depended upon the rivers as their only sure roads to the city of Jamestown and to the international markets across the sea. And insomuch as money is a means of exchange, tobacco was, in effect, the money for colonial Virginia for much of its existence. To farmers and planters, tobacco was the cash crop that paid the clergy and the many other bills for goods that had to be imported from the mother country. Indeed, George Washington, like most Virginia planters, paid for his pastor's salary in tobacco.[11]

What the English government and investors expected from their colony in America was a strong return for their past investments, accompanied by an unquestioning obedience. This is amply illustrated by the well-known story of Reverend James Blair's efforts to obtain an endowment for his proposed college in Virginia (a forerunner to William and Mary which never materialized). He obtained the charter and a grant of 2,000 British pounds. Sir Edward Seymour, one of the leading figures of Virginian politics, objected to the grant. Reverend Blair told Commissary Seymour that the college was designed to educate ministers and that people in Virginia had souls to be saved as well as people in England. In one of the more striking historical disagreements between a civil and a religious leader, Seymour intoned: "Souls! Damn your souls! Make tobacco."[12]

INDIANS, CONVICTS, AND SLAVES

By the time George Washington was out surveying the wilderness tracts of land for Lord Fairfax, the proprietor of the Northern Neck's vast expanse, the Indians were no longer an immediate menace, since they had been driven far back into the forests by the previous generations of armed colonists. The Native Americans were still, however, the masters of the vast unsurveyed lands of the upper reaches of the rivers that extended into the Virginian frontier, which at that time included parts of Maryland and Western Pennsylvania. As a young man, George Washington engaged in a surveying expedition into this frontier. He kept a journal of this expedition, and he noted his impressions of some of their customs, such as the Indians' strange way of dancing.[13]

Adding to the woes of the already spiritually impoverished Virginia, King James decided to turn the Colony into a destination for English convicts. One-hundred convicts arrived in America in 1619, the first of many such shipments. (Even a captain that sailed one of George Washington's commercial ships had commanded a convict ship for many years before being employed by Washington.) This commerce did not end until the Revolution closed American ports to the crown's penal exile of English criminals. Australia's Botany Bay would eventually become the next home for these unwanted prisoners of the crown.

In fact, Washington's first teacher had been "bought" by George's father and brought to America to tutor the young George. As a white English convict who had run afoul of the common law, he found a new opportunity in the colony as an indentured servant, serving simultaneously as a sexton for the church, a gravedigger for the cemetery, and a teacher of a small field school. Soon thereafter, also in 1619, a Dutch vessel delivered to Jamestown the first shipload of slaves ever brought to American shores. Indeed, to make tobacco in large enough quantities to satisfy the needs and the quotas from markets in England, the Virginia nobility—the true gentlemen farmers—became accustomed to building and maintaining their vast plantations by the utilization of great numbers of slaves, who cared not only for their masters' fields, but also for their bodies, their horses, their houses, and their children. In fact, one of George Washington's closest friends was William "Billy" Lee, "my Mulatto man William (calling himself William Lee)."[14] In his will, Washington emancipated Billy and provided him with a lifetime annuity.[15]

Virginia's culture and its laws were thus a reflection of its unique origins as the first English settlement in the new world. From 1607 on, the interpenetration of the English state, the Anglican Church, the farm, the Indian, the slave and the convict continued. There needed to be laws for the church, the state, and the soldier.

VIRGINIA'S DIVINE, MARTIAL, AND MORAL LAW

As we have already seen, the beginning of the Episcopal Church of Virginia was inseparably connected with the planting of the colony. The First Charter of Virginia was written in 1606, followed by revisions in 1609 and 1611. Thus, Virginia's code of law developed when "religion was painted upon banners" and law was "divine, martial and moral"—in the words of Bishop William Meade.[16] Bishop Meade's contemporary, B. B. Minor, put it this way, "No one can properly study, write, or appreciate Virginia history who does not largely and heartily enter into those parts relating and devoted to religion and the Church."[17] The roots of religion were planted all the more deeply, given the understanding by the colonists that it must have been God's Providence that had allowed Virginia to survive so many close calls with extinction, due to sheer struggle with the wilderness and fierce warfare with the local aboriginal masters of the New World. This was the culture Washington's ancestors found when they arrived in Virginia around 1657.

THE FIRST CHRISTIAN MISSION TO THE INDIANS

When the first colonists arrived in 1607, Captain John Smith soon became their leader. Reverend John Hunt, the colony's first preacher, provided its spiritual leadership. A 1631 pamphlet described their spiritual life in their rustic original church with a roof made of an old sail, and pews of "unhewed trees and a pulpit of a bar of wood nailed to two neighbouring trees." The pamphlet adds:

> . . . yet we had daily Common Prayer morning and evening, every Sunday two sermons, and every three months the holy communion, till our minister died, (the Reverend Mr. Hunt.) . . . Our order was daily to have prayer with a psalm, at which solemnity the poor savages much wondered.[18]

Concern for the souls of the "savages" was part of the mission into Virginia. When this courageous band had been sent off from England, the Reverend Mr. William

Crashaw reminded the colonists, "that the end of this voyage is the destruction of the devil's kingdom, and the propagation of the Gospel."[19] The King's 1606 patent for Virginia explained that the purpose of their mission to the New World was that:

> So noble a work may, by the Providence of God, hereafter tend to the glorie of his divine majestie, in propagating of Christian religion to such people as sit in darkness and miserable ignorance of the true knowledge and worship of God, and may in time bring the infidels and savages (living in those parts) to human civility and quiet government.[20]

The King's instructions included that "all persons should kindly treat the savages and heathen people in these parts, and use all proper means to draw them to the true service and knowledge of God."[21] As early as 1588, Sir Walter Raleigh had given 100 pounds for the "propagation of Christianity in Virginia."[22]

Two centuries later, when Washington spoke of the "earnestly desired" and "laudable undertaking" of "converting the Indians to Christianity," he reflected the concern of Sir Walter Raleigh. This can be seen in Washington's May 2, 1788, response to a March 28, 1788, letter and pamphlet that he received from Reverend John Ettwein, a Bishop of the Society of the United Brethren.[23] Washington responded: "So far as I am capable of judging, the principles upon which the society is founded and the rules laid down for its government, appear to be well calculated to promote so laudable and arduous an undertaking, and you will permit me to add that if an event so long and so earnestly desired as that of converting the Indians to Christianity and consequently to civilization, can be effected, the Society of Bethlehem bids fair to bear a very considerable part in it. I am, Reverend Sir, with sentiments of esteem, &c."[24]

The principles and rules upon which the society was founded, were deeply Christian.[25] Washington approved their principles and rules, which he deemed "well calculated to promote so laudable and arduous an undertaking."[26] The text of the Brethren's pamphlet read and approved by Washington included, in part,

> Whereas we the subscribers are fully convinced of the Christian zeal and godly concern, wherewith the evangelical Church, known by the name of the Unitas Fratrum or United Brethren, has at all times endeavored to spread the saving knowledge of Jesus Christ, and to carry the same even to the remotest Heathen nations; for which

purpose also in this part of the world a mission among several Indian nations was begun by said Church, and with blessing and good success continued near fifty years: And as we ourselves are members of said Church, which has the salvation of men so near at heart, we cannot but most ardently wish to further this great work of God, conversion of the Heathen, by all just and possible means.

Therefore we have resolved, in the name of God, to form ourselves into a Society by the name of 'A Society of the United Brethren for propagating the Gospel among the Heathen' And do herewith unanimously agree upon the following articles as the stated rules of this Society....

Article XIV.

And as we have hereby no other view or aim but the furtherance and propagation of the knowledge of Jesus Christ among the poor benighted Heathen, ...promise to do all what they do for the benefit of the Society, *gratis.*

Article XV.

...Therefore the missionaries and their assistants shall, in conformity to the rules of the Brethren, set aside all temporal views and interests, and their sole and only care and endeavours shall be, to preach the gospel to the Heathen, to instruct them faithfully in the doctrine of Jesus and his apostles, and so by their word and examples to encourage them to virtue and industry.[27]

George Washington clearly shared the foundational Virginian concern to "Christianize the savages" dwelling in the Virginia Colony. On July 10, 1789, in response to an address from the directors of the Society of The United Brethren for Propagating the Gospel Among the Heathen, Washington stated:

In proportion as the general Government of the United States shall acquire strength by duration, it is probable they may have it in their power to extend a salutary influence to the Aborigines in the extremities of their Territory. In the meantime, it will be a desirable thing for the protection of the Union to co-operate, as far as circumstances may conveniently admit, with the disinterested [unselfish] endeavours of your Society to civilize and Christianize the Savages of the Wilderness.[28]

A Deist, by definition, rejected Christianity and accepted the equivalence of all religions' worship of God. So no Deist could see the plan for the "conversion of the heathen" outlined by Bishop Ettwein and the Brethren as both "laudable" and "earnestly desired." Yet those are Washington's words. Nor could a Deist say, as Washington wrote, "It will be a desirable thing ...to co-operate, as far as circumstances may conveniently admit, with the disinterested endeavours of your Society to civilize and Christianize the Savages of the Wilderness." Washington's assessment of the Brethren's Christian missionary work to the Indians not only reflected his historic Anglican and Virginian roots, but his own Christian faith as well.

THE STARVING TIME

The 1607 colony and its spiritual mission were nearly a total failure, almost meeting extinction as the earlier settlements had. When the next ship arrived in 1610 under the lead of Sir Thomas Gates and Sir George Summers, accompanied by the Reverend Mr. Richard Bucke, the 500 settlers had been reduced to a mere sixty emaciated survivors, who called this period "the starving time." The staggering loss of life was due to both famine and the assaults of the Native Americans. Hunger pains brought on the most desperate inhumanity:

> So great was our famine, that a savage we slew and buried, the poorer sort took him up again and eat him, and so did divers one another, boiled and stewed with roots and herbs. And one of the rest did kill his wife, powdered her, and had eaten part of her before it was known, for which he was executed, as he well deserved.[29]

According to Reverend William Crashaw, the early historian of this period, upon seeing the tragic state of the colony, Gates, Summers, and Bucke went immediately to the ruined and empty church and rang its bell. Crashaw writes: "Such as were able to crawl out of their miserable dwellings repaired thither that they might join in the zealous and sorrowful prayer of their faithful minister, who pleaded in that solemn hour for his afflicted brethren and himself before the Lord their God."[30] Years later, in 1774, when George Washington and his fellow Virginians participated in a colony-wide day of prayer and fasting in the face of the looming crisis with England, it continued a faith tradition of the earliest Virginians who also prayed for divine aid in severe trial.[31]

70

PROVIDENTIAL HELP

The sixty survivors entered the ship that only had a few days' provisions left and prepared to sail to safer harbors in Newfoundland, with "none dropping a tear, because none had enjoyed one day of happiness."[32] They had suffered so much, they were beyond weeping. The last act of the rescued colonists was to bury their weapons and armor. As they began to sail from Jamestown, their farewell to the abandoned colony was given with a woeful "peal of shot," and they began going down the river, leaving behind hundreds of graves, a failed colony, and a ghost town. But at that precise moment, a second ship unexpectedly arrived under the command of Lord De la War (whose name later designated a colony and then a state—Delaware).

Bishop Meade writes: "Behold the hand of Heaven from above, at the very instant, sent in the Right Honorable De la War to meet them at the river's mouth, with provision and comforts of all kind. If he had stayed but two tides longer [in other words, just a day later], he would have come into Virginia and found not one Englishman."[33]

They returned to Jamestown immediately, where, upon landing, Lord De la War fell to his knees and prayed a lengthy silent prayer. This was next followed by a sermon by Reverend Mr. Bucke. And only then, did Lord De la War present to the people his documents authorizing his leadership over the colony. At once he gave orders for the church to be repaired.[34] With the "starving times" behind them, the colony of Virginia was securely established, and began to make the illustrious history for which it is renowned.

RENEWAL OF THE MISSION TO THE INDIANS

Lord De la War's short stay concluded in 1611, but the settlement had been resuscitated and its Gospel mission to the Indian inhabitants of the new land was remembered. A 1612 pamphlet "The New Life of Virginia" expressed the spiritual concerns for the salvation of the Indians:

> And for the poor Indians, what shall I say? But God, that hath many ways showed mercy to you, make you show mercy to them and theirs, and howsoever they may seem unto you so intolerably wicked and rooted in mischief that they cannot be moved, yet consider rightly and be not discouraged. ...This is the work that we first intended, and have published to the world, to be chief in our thoughts, to bring those Infidel people from the worship of Devils to the service of God. . . .

> Take their children and train them up with gentleness, teach
> them our English tongue and the principles of religion. Win the
> elder sort by wisdom and discretion; make them equal to you
> English in case of protection, wealth, and habitation, doing justice
> on such as shall do them wrong. Weapons of war are needful, I
> grant, but for defence only.... [35]

This was the program that George Washington approved many years later. In a speech to the Delaware Chiefs on May 12, 1779, he encouraged "...You do well to wish to learn our arts and ways of life, and above all, the religion of Jesus Christ. These will make you a greater and happier people than you are. Congress will do every thing they can to assist you in this wise intention; and to tie the knot of friendship and union so fast, that nothing shall ever be able to loose it."[36]

The most famous story of reaching a Native American for the Gospel is that of Pocahontas.[37] A painting of her Christian baptism is one of the eight massive murals painted for the rotunda of the U.S. Capitol Building.[38]

REQUIRED DAILY PRAYERS AND PRAYERS FOR THE SALVATION OF THE HEATHEN

As was mentioned above, the colonists "had daily common prayer morning and evening." This practice of daily prayer in the colony of Virginia is worth a further consideration. The daily religious services enjoined by this early colonial Virginia were linked directly with the work parties as they assembled. The day was infused with prayer and worship, including early morning, midday, and evening.[39]

The idea of morning and evening prayer led by a military officer was part of the Virginia in which Washington was raised.[40] Along with the prayers of the *Book of Common Prayer*, a special prayer was composed, particularly for the Morning and Evening Guard. It was to be offered up by "the Captain himself, or some one of his principal men or officers." Some nine substantive paragraphs of prayer in all, the sixth implored the Lord for the salvation of the unbelieving Gentiles that surrounded them.

> And now, O Lord of mercy! O Father of the spirits of all flesh! Look
> in mercy upon the Gentiles who yet know thee not! And seeing
> thou hast honoured us to choose us out to bear they name unto the
> Gentiles, we therefore beseech thee to bless us, and this our

plantation, which we and our nation have begun in thy fear, and for thy glory. We know, O Lord! We have the Devil and all the gates of Hell against us; but if thou, O Lord, be on our side, we care not who be against us! Oh, therefore vouchasafe to be our God, and let us be a part and portion of thy people; confirm thy covenant of grace and mercy with us, which thou hast made to thy Church in Christ Jesus. And seeing, Lord, the highest end of our plantation here is to set up the standard and display the banner of Jesus Christ even here where Satan's throne is, Lord, let our labour be blessed in labouring for the conversion of the heathen. And because thou usest not to work such mighty works by unholy means, Lord, sanctify our spirits, and give us holy hearts, that so we may be thy instruments in this most glorious work.[41]

As the spiritual vitality of Jamestown began to flourish again, a Cambridge graduate, Alexander Whittaker, left his mark. The Reverend Whittaker, a son of an illustrious theologian who helped draft the Lambeth Articles in 1595,[42] wrote a stirring call to England for greater support in the ministry to the colonists and the missionary outreach to the Indians, which by then he himself had pursued for three years. His message to his clerical peers in England was based on the text, "Cast thy bread upon the waters, and thou shalt find it after many days." He called on them to join him in the evangelization of the original inhabitants of Virginia:

Wherefore, my brethren, put on the bowels of compassion, and let the lamentable estate of these miserables enter into your consideration. One God created us. They have reasonable souls and intellectual faculties as well as we. We all have Adam for our common parent; yea, by nature the condition of us both is all one, the servants of sin and slaves of the Devil. Oh, remember, I beseech you, what was the state of England before the Gospel was preached in our country.[43]

Although Virginia had a promising start to evangelize the Indians,[44] it proved to be very slow-going.[45] Few Indians accepted the Gospel, and the Native Americans and the new settlers by-and-large had many conflicts.[46] Subsequently, it was not a promising mission field to would-be ministers (or missionaries).[47] No Bishop would be willing to serve in the wild world of Virginia. In fact, America as a whole never had a bishop until the Revolutionary War had ended.

WASHINGTON'S "CONNEXION" WITH LADY HUNTINGDON'S MISSION

An etching of Lady Huntingdon was placed by Washington in his Mount Vernon Estate following her death.

Washington's involvement and interest in the "Christianization" of the Indians reached its climax in a connection with British royalty and the evangelist George Whitefield, strange connections, indeed, for the leader of the American Revolution and an alleged Deist! The royal figure that made this connection was a "well-connected" woman, Selina, Countess of Huntingdon (1707-91), the daughter of Earl Ferrers. In 1728, she married the Ninth Earl of Huntingdon, Theophilus Hastings. His sister, Mary Hastings, introduced Selina to the Methodist message. In 1739, she became a member of the first Methodist Society in Fetter Lane and was a supporter and friend of John and Charles Wesley, the founders of the Methodist movement in England. Eventually, she founded what became known as "Lady Huntingdon's Connexion."

The Countess of Huntingdon's Connexion was part of the eighteenth century Evangelical Revival closely associated with John Wesley and George Whitefield. Although touching the upper class, it was a religious movement that touched the local population as well. It had a college for the training of ministerial skills and established several interconnected chapels in England. Following the pattern of Wesley, the movement, although originating in the Anglican fold, eventually seceded, and The Connexion became a denomination of its own with its own creed and ordination.[48]

Washington's first connection with "Lady Huntingdon's Connexion" was probably in late 1774, either during or just after his return from the First Continental Congress in Philadelphia. In his diary for 1774, November 5, we read: "Mr. Piercy a Presbeterian [sic] Minister dined here." It is possible that Washington had met Piercy while in Philadelphia. Donald Jackson and Dorothy Thwohig, editors of *Washington's Diaries* write,

> Mr. Piercy was probably William Piercy (Percy), a Calvinistic Methodist and disciple of George Whitefield. Piercy was chaplain

to Selina Hastings, countess of Huntingdon, a devoted follower of the new Methodist movement. In order to give protection to Methodist preachers, she appointed large members of them to the nominal position of chaplain in her household. She had sent Piercy from London to Georgia in 1772 to act as president of Whitefield's Orphan House, or college, at Bethesda, near Savannah, and to preach wherever he could collect an audience in the colonies. Piercy had preached at various locations in Philadelphia during the year. He had given a farewell sermon in late October at the Arch Street Presbyterian meetinghouse, and was probably at this time on his return to his headquarters in Georgia.[49]

The day after Piercy's visit was Sunday, and Washington's diary says, "November 6. Went to Pohick Church." From this point on until the end of the Revolutionary War, there is no mention of Lady Huntingdon's ministry in Washington's writings.

However, at the conclusion of the American Revolution, Washington heard personally from Lady Huntingdon, who wrote to him in 1783, when she was seventy-six years of age. Unfortunately, while her February 20, 1783, letter is not extant we do have Washington's letter in response that allows us to construct what the Countess had in mind. Washington responded to Lady Huntingdon's letter from Headquarters on August 10, 1783:

> My Lady: Within the course of a few days I have received the Letter you was pleased to Honor me with from Bath, of the 20th of febry. and have to express my respectful Thanks to your Goodness, for the marks of Confidence and Esteem contained therein.
>
> Your Ladyships benevolent Designs toward the Indian Nations, claim my particular Attention, and to further so laudable an Undertaking will afford me much pleasure, so far as my Situation in Life, surrounded with many and arduous Cares will admit. To be named as an Executor of your Intentions, may perhaps disappoint your Ladyships Views; but so far as my general Superintendence, or incidental Attention can contribute to the promotion of your Establishment, you may command my Assistance.
>
> My Ancestry being derived from Yorkshire in England, it is more than probable that I am entitled to that honorable

Connection, which you are pleased to mention; ...[50]

The Lady's letter had obviously asked Washington to be an executor of her missionary plan to the Indians, and in the same letter had proposed the possibility that Washington and Lady Huntingdon were related. Historians have established that the common ancestor of the Countess and Washington was Lawrence Washington of Sulgrave Manor (1500-1584).[51] But Washington, true to form, never bothered to establish the connection.[52] Yet Washington was interested in the Countess' mission to the Indians. Although his plans for retirement prevented taking on the task of executor, he pledged himself to her cause "so far as my general Superintendence, or incidental Attention can contribute to the promotion of your Establishment, you may command my Assistance."[53]

This offer of assistance was more than enough for the royal Lady's purposes. She wrote back on March 20, 1784, with striking words. She did not merely call upon Washington to assist her in her American version of her Gospel Connexion, namely, the evangelization of the Indians; instead, she addressed him with Messianic terms as she boldly applied the biblical texts of Isaiah 41:2 and 8 to the triumphant American commander in chief. If Washington were a Deist, this would have been a most awkward misunderstanding. Lady Huntingdon wrote,

> Sir, I should lament the want of expression extremely did I believe it could convey with the exactness of truth the sensibility your most polite kind and friendly letter afforded me. Any degree of your consideration for the most interesting views of my grant which stands so connected with the service of the Indian nations eminently demands my perpetual thanks.
>
> No compliments can be accepted by you, the wise providence of God having called you to, and so honoured you in, a situation far above many of your equals. And as one mark of His favour to His servants of old was given—"the nations to your sword and as the driven stubble to your bow" [Isa. 41:2]—[this] allows me then to follow the comparison till that character shall as eminently belong to you—"He was called the friend of God." [Isa. 41:8]. May therefore the blessings obtained for the poor, so unite the temporal with the eternal good of those miserable neglected and despised nations that they may be enabled to bless you in future ages whose fatherly hand has yielded to their present and everlasting comfort.

I am obliged to say that no early or intemperate zeal, under a religious character, or those various superstitious impositions, too generally taken up for Christian piety, does in any measure prevail with my passions for this end. To raise an altar for the knowledge of the true God and Jesus Christ whom he hath sent "where ignorance alike of him and of themselves so evidently appears" is my only object. And this to convey the united blessings of this life, with the lively evidence of an eternity founded on the sure and only wise testimony of immutable truth is all my wants or wishes in this matter. And my poor unworthy prayers are for those providences of God that may best prepare the way to so rational and great an end.[54]

How would a Deist answer this biblical plea to help an evangelical establish Christian missionaries "to raise an altar for the knowledge of the true God and Jesus Christ"? While various letters between the Countess of Huntingdon and Washington have not survived, we do have several which establish Washington's views of Lady Huntingdon's Gospel mission to the Indians. His responses are those of a Christian. Washington wrote to Lady Huntingdon on February 27, 1785,

My Lady: ...With respect to your humane and benevolent intentions towards the Indians, and the plan which your Ladyship has adopted to carry them into effect, they meet my highest approbation; and I should be very happy to find every possible encouragement given to them. ....I have written fully to the President of Congress, with whom I have a particular intimacy, and transmitted copies of your Ladyships plan, addresses and letter to the several States therein mentioned, with my approving sentiments thereon. ...[55]

Writing on January 25, 1785, to Sir James Jay, friend of the Countess and the brother of American political leader John Jay, Washington says,

I am clearly in sentiment with her Ladyship, that christianity will never make any progress among the Indians, or work any considerable reformation in their principles, until they are brought to a state of greater civilization; and the mode by which she means to attempt this, as far as I have been able to give it consideration, is as likely to succeed as any other that could have been devised...As I am well acquainted with the President of Congress, I will in the course of a few days write him a private letter on this subject giving the substance of Lady Huntington's plan and asking his opinion of the encouragement it might expect to receive from Congress if it should be brought before that honorable body. ...Without reverberating the arguments in support of the humane and benevolent intention of Lady Huntington tochristianize and reduce to a state of civilization the Savage tribes within the limits of the American States, or discanting upon the advantages which the Union may derive from the Emigration which is blended with, and becomes part of the plan, I highly approve of them...[56]

Writing to Richard Henry Lee, the President of the Congress on February 8, 1785, Washington explains:

Towards the latter part of the year 1783 I was honored with a letter from the Countess of Huntington, briefly reciting her benevolent intention of spreading Christianity among the Tribes of Indians inhabiting our Western Territory; and Expressing a desire of my advice and assistance to carry this charitable design into execution....Her Ladyship has spoken so feelingly and sensibly, on the religious and benevolent purposes of the plan, that no language of which I am possessed, can add aught to enforce her observations. ...[57]

Writing finally with the disappointing news of lack of success to the Countess of Huntingdon on June 30, 1785, Washington explained that resistance to the plan had been encountered in Congress for various reasons, including the concern of placing British subjects on America's frontier as a possible future source of political destabilization:

My Lady: In the last letter which I had the honor to write to you, I informed your Ladyship of the communication I had made to the President of Congress of your wishes to obtain Lands in the

Western Territory for a number of Emigrants as a means of civilizing the Savages, and propagating the Gospel among them. ...I will delay no longer to express my concern that your Ladyships humane and benevolent views are not better seconded.[58]

Nevertheless, when General Washington became President Washington, he continued to view "a System corresponding with the mild principles of Religion and Philanthropy towards an unenlightened race of Men" to "be as honorable to the national character as conformable to the dictates of sound policy."[59]

The last we hear of Lady Huntingdon in Washington's writings is on January 8, 1792. Washington wrote a brief note of acknowledgment to Robert Bowyer for an engraved portrait print of the Countess of Huntingdon, made from Bowyer's painting.[60] The Countess had died the year before. Obviously Washington did not want the "connection" with Lady Huntingdon to end. We honestly wonder how many Deists through the years have secured engraved portraits of the world's great Christian missionaries and evangelical philanthropists.

WASHINGTON'S VIRGINIA ROOTS

Washington was an American and a Virginian. He never forgot his rich legacy. In the first draft of his Farewell Address, President Washington accented his roots:

I retire from the Chair of government . . . I leave you with undefiled hands, an uncorrupted heart, and with ardent vows to heaven for the welfare and happiness of that country in which I and my forefathers to the third or fourth progenitor drew our first breath.[61]

In fact, when he was retiring, our first president attempted to trace his roots. He was asked by a high ranking British official for this information. So on November 15, 1796, when he was in Philadelphia, George Washington wrote to his nephew, Captain William Augustine Washington:

Without any application, intimation, or the most remote thought or expectation of the kind, on my part; Sir Isaac Heard, Garter and principal King at Arms, wrote to me some years since enclosing our Armorial [coat of arms]; and requesting a genealogical account of our progenitors since the first arrival of them in this country. ...and

*Tomb stone placed by Washington's family on the crypt
several years after his death with the inscription from John 11:25.*

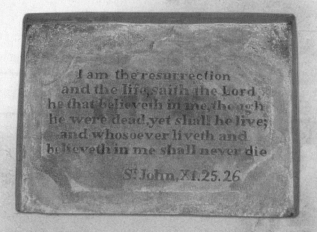

although I have not the least Solicitude to trace our Ancestry, yet as
this Gentleman appears to interest himself in the research, common
civility requires that he should obtain the aids he asks, if it is in our
power to give it to him. Let me request of you, therefore, to give me
what assistance you can to solve the queries propounded in his
letter, if you have only old papers which have a tendency towards it:
if not, or whether or not, by examining the Inscriptions on the
Tombs at the Ancient Vault, and burying ground of our Ancestors,
which is on your Estate at Bridges Creek. And if you are able to do
it, trace the descendents of Lawrence Washington who came over
with John, our Progenitor. [62]

In other words, Washington was asking his nephew for help in tracing his roots
back to England, including reading tombstones, if necessary. Although Washington
had no personal interest in his family's genealogy, he had already been thinking about
his ancestors' tombstones for over a decade. On December 18, 1784, Washington wrote
that he "might soon expect to be entombed in the dreary mansions of my father's."[63]
We don't know what inscriptions Washington's nephew found on the tombs of their
early Virginian ancestors. But we do know what Washington's ancestors ultimately put

on his Mount Vernon tomb. Should you visit Washington's tomb at Mount Vernon, you will read "I am the resurrection and the Life." (John 11:25), the very first words of the funeral service in the *Book of Common Prayer*. Strange indeed that the immediate descendants of a Deist would have a Gospel text quoting Jesus' teaching on the resurrection on the alleged Deist's tomb! Either Washington's heirs were quite confused about the faith of Virginia's greatest son, or they knew George Washington's faith better than most recent historians do.

CONCLUSION

Thus, the tapestry of early Virginia was intricately interwoven with the commerce of tobacco production, a sincere commitment to the church and the Christian mission to the Native Americans, alongside the tragic realities of trading in slaves, the assimilation of convicts and conflict with Native Americans. It was to this faltering yet consciously Christian colony that Washington's family emigrated some fifty years after the establishment of Jamestown. Accordingly, Washington's life was deeply marked by the culture and values of Virginia, "that country in which" he and his "forefathers to the third or fourth progenitor drew" their "first breath."[64] Whether as General, a private citizen, or as president, Washington never swerved from an expressed commitment to the Christian evangelistic mission to the Native Americans that was a legacy bequeathed to him by the very first Anglican settlers of the colony of Virginia. The skeptics who argue for Washington the Deist must explain his lifelong and heartfelt commitment to Christian missionary work. Moreover, nothing less than both written evidence and recorded deeds from Washington himself will be sufficient to explain how he could simultaneously explicitly advocate Christian missionary evangelism, and yet as a Deist deny the teachings of Christianity.

FIVE

George Washington's Virginian Ancestors

"Honour and obey your natural parents altho' they be poor."
Rule of Civility: 108th Copied by George Washington
in his school paper. c.1746[1]

Colonel John Washington (1632-1677) and his brother Lawrence (1635-1677) were the first of the Washington family to come to the New World. John was George's great-grandfather. They came as planters and businessmen in 1657. Their father back in England was the Reverend Lawrence Washington (1602-1652), an Anglican clergyman. One report says Lawrence may have been a heavy drinker.[2] Whether that is true or not, he was loyal to the king, and that meant he was on the wrong side of Oliver Cromwell, the "Lord Protector," in the aftermath of the English Civil War, during the days when England was kingless (1640-1660).

The seeds of Civil War were planted, in part, by the Anglican Church, which actively persecuted those who did not conform to its established worship. This persecution is what prompted the Pilgrims and the Puritans to come to American shores. King James died in 1625, and his son Charles I ascended to the throne, and he got into so many conflicts with Puritan nonconformists in his realm that it eventually

The Genealogy of
George Washington

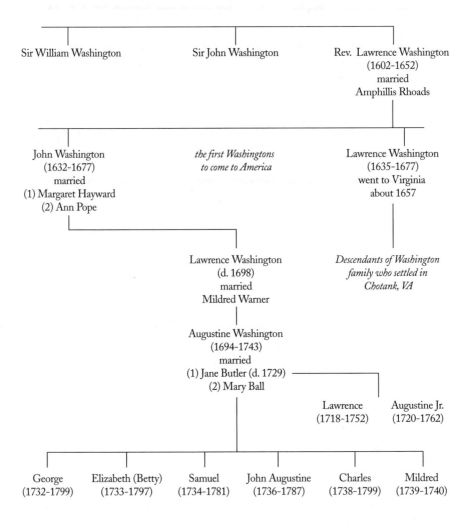

Sir William Washington

Sir John Washington

Rev. Lawrence Washington
(1602-1652)
married
Amphillis Rhoads

John Washington
(1632-1677)
married
(1) Margaret Hayward
(2) Ann Pope

*the first Washingtons
to come to America*

Lawrence Washington
(1635-1677)
went to Virginia
about 1657

Lawrence Washington
(d. 1698)
married
Mildred Warner

*Descendants of Washington
family who settled in
Chotank, VA*

Augustine Washington
(1694-1743)
married
(1) Jane Butler (d. 1729)
(2) Mary Ball

Lawrence
(1718-1752)

Augustine Jr.
(1720-1762)

George
(1732-1799)

Elizabeth (Betty)
(1733-1797)

Samuel
(1734-1781)

John Augustine
(1736-1787)

Charles
(1738-1799)

Mildred
(1739-1740)

led to England's Civil War. Charles lost to a coalition of Puritans, Presbyterians, and Independents, led by independent Oliver Cromwell. Having been condemned by his conquerors as a tyrant, Charles was beheaded in 1649.

The twenty year period from 1640 to 1660 has been termed the Puritan inter-reg-num. There was no King between Charles I and his son Charles II who assumed his hereditary throne in 1660. During this inter-regnum, those still loyal to the throne were out of favor. Thus, the Washington brothers left to attempt a new life in the New World. When George Washington looked back to this era, he referred to the Puritan victory over the King in the British Civil War as the "usurpation" of Oliver Cromwell.[3] Along with their royal sympathies, the Washington brothers brought with them a Christian heritage in the Anglican tradition.

WASHINGTON'S CHRISTIAN ANCESTORS: "BY THE MERITS OF JESUS CHRIST"

Both of the brothers had wills drawn up and recorded in Virginia that underscored their religious beliefs. Both wills were made in 1675, eighteen years after their arrival in the New World. They were probated only four days apart in 1677, suggesting that they had both died in the same year. Lawrence Washington said in his will,

> I give and bequeath my soul unto the hands of Almighty God, hoping and trusting through the mercy of Jesus Christ, my one Saviour and Redeemer, to receive full pardon and forgiveness of all my sins. . . .[4]

John Washington, George Washington's great-grandfather directed that a funeral sermon be preached and that a tablet with the Ten Commandments be ordered from England and given to the church. This would likely have been part of an improvement of the reredos in his local Anglican church.

The impact of John Washington on the history of Virginia, and thus on his great-grandson, was far-reaching. Washington parish was named for John, not, as many today would naturally assume, for his world famous descendant George, who would be born three generations later. John, like the future General Washington, was a military man.[5] His fame in the parish was due to his military prowess as command-er-in-chief of the Northern Neck—the approximately 1,400 square miles of land between the Potomac and Rappahannock Rivers, granted to the Culpepper family by Charles II, which eventually came into the possession of the Fairfax family.[6]

JOHN WASHINGTON—GEORGE'S GRANDFATHER AND HIS FIRST ANCESTOR IN AMERICA

John was elected to the House of Burgesses in 1667, after ten years in the colony. Tradition says he was a surveyor, a seemingly trustworthy claim given the large tracts of land the early Washingtons accumulated in Virginia's unsettled wilderness.[7] Eight years later he was made a Colonel—the same year he made his will, 1675—and was sent with a force of a thousand men to assist the settlers in Maryland to defeat the Susquehannocks. John's life anticipated George's in many respects: a land surveyor, a successful soldier, a man with a keen sense of justice,[8] an elected political leader, a man honored by lands being named in his memory, a Christian man.

John Washington earned a nickname among the Indians that was also applied to George a hundred years later. Great-grandfather John Washington had not only fought the Indians in Maryland, but he had also been the leader of the colonial army that drove the Indians far from the settlements along the lowland rivers in Virginia. The Indians named him, *Conotocarious*. When translated, this name can mean either "Town Taker" or "Devourer of Villages." Joseph D. Sawyer writes, "From the site of the future Mount Vernon twenty-five hundred savages were driven over the hills into the Shenandoah Valley, in that early Indian war, by that first American Washington, who gained the name of "Conotocarius" (Devourer of Villages) through his prowess as an Indian fighter."[9]

Years later, in 1753, in the unsettled wilderness, this name was also, according to author Frank E. Grizzard, Jr. "given to Washington by the Half-King, a prominent Seneca chief allied with the British against the French in the struggle for control of the Ohio Country."[10] In the Biographical Memoranda of 1786, written for his first and only approved biographer David Humphreys, Washington confirms this story. Speaking of himself, he says that he "was named by the Half-King (as he was called) and the tribes of Nations with whom he treated, *Caunotaucarius* or in English, the *Town taker*; which name being registered in their Manner and communicated to other Nations of Indians, has been remembered by them ever since in all their transactions with him during the late War."[11] George Washington, like his ancestor, John Washington, was a successful Indian fighter.

BACON'S "REBELLION" OR RESISTANCE TO TYRANNY?

Returning to the days of the Washington brothers, in the second half of the seventeenth century, the battles with the Indians took on a new significance in the two years between the time the Washington brothers made their wills in 1675 and died in

1677. In what has come to be called Bacon's Rebellion, the Virginians produced one of the earliest civil wars in America as a byproduct of the ongoing conflict between the Native Americans and the settlers.

The nearly autonomous Sir William Berkeley, the longest serving governor of Virginia, ruled from 1641 to 1651 and again from 1660 to his death in 1677. With then capital Jamestown as his base, he governed his colony with a near absolute power. One of his critics was the Reverend William Drummond, who had recently arrived to serve the church. When the two met for the first time, Gov. Berkeley immediately issued a death sentence to his clerical critic: "I am more glad to see you than any man in Virginia. You will hang in half an hour." The governor made good his fatal promise—only an hour and half late.

The settlers living on the frontiers were constantly under the threat of the Indians, while the settlers closer to Jamestown were far more secure. Petitions to Governor Berkeley, however, did not produce the protection they desired, apparently due to a conflict of interest. According to Washington historian Joseph D. Sawyer, Gov. Berkeley "knowingly allowed the Indians to sell him pelts [animal skins] with one hand while they tomahawked Virginians with the other."[12]

Nathaniel Bacon was a member of the Virginia House of Burgesses, who represented a parish that suffered from frequent Indian attacks. (Back then, Virginia was divided into parishes as opposed to counties, much like Louisiana is to this day.) When Bacon failed in securing permission from the governor to raise and lead a militia for the purpose of assaulting the Indians, he determined to take matters into his own hands. He raised a troop on his own to attack the warring Indians and was successful in his mission to drive away the marauding warriors.

Gov. Berkeley, however, declared that Bacon was a rebel. Bacon's grateful constituents, nevertheless, reelected him to office in the House of Burgesses. The Governor decided not to prevent him from taking his seat. But when Bacon repeated his attacks upon the Indians, contrary to the Governor's will, Gov. Berkeley raised his own army to quell the rebellious Indian fighter. However, Bacon's smaller force, with its greater military experience, successfully attacked Jamestown. In 1676, Bacon's force drove out Gov. Berkeley and his army and burned the city and its church to the ground to prevent the Governor from returning to Jamestown and making it his stronghold. The fighting finally ceased when King Charles II, the restored British monarch, finally recalled the beleaguered and much-hated governor.

When King Charles II summarized the governor's reign of terror, he declared that Berkley had hanged more Englishmen (in Virginia) than he himself had executed in avenging the beheading of his father (in England).[13]

What makes this tumultuous history important is that it was part of the Washington family history. For, as Sawyer points out, "John Washington. . . joined Nathaniel Bacon—often called 'the young Cromwell'—in hurling defiance at loot-saturated Governor Berkeley of hated memory."[14] Three generations later, Washington himself would be in a similar position to his forbearer John. He too would feel compelled to take up the just cause of colonists against the tyranny of royal officials in the New World. It is ironic that Washington referred to Oliver Cromwell's leadership in the English Civil War by the use of the term "usurpation."

LAWRENCE WASHINGTON: GEORGE WASHINGTON'S GRANDFATHER

Colonel John Washington died in 1677 in his early forties. He left behind his sixteen-year-old son, Lawrence Washington (1660-1698). Lawrence was George's grandfather.[15] Death came all too early, all too frequently in the colonial era. John buried not only his first wife, but also two of their children. Lawrence was born to John and his second wife. Lawrence was given the name of his Uncle Lawrence, who had come to America at the same time as John. Both had John's clergyman father, Lawrence Washington (the allegedly drunken vicar), as their namesake.

While not much is known about his life, Lawrence (George's grandfather) was also a military man and was known as Captain Washington. When he died in 1698, at his home at Bridges Creek in Westmoreland County Virginia, he was only thirty-eight. He left behind his wife, Mildred Warner Washington, and three children, the second being four-year-old Augustine Washington, future father of George. Lawrence's will divided his estate between his wife and children. He directed that his children were to continue under the care and support of their mother until they were married or came of age.

GEORGE'S FATHER, AUGUSTINE

In the spring of 1700, two years after Lawrence died, Mildred (George's grandmother) married again. She wed a Virginian, George Gayle, who was originally from England. Soon after the marriage, George Gayle moved young Augustine Washington and the family to England to live. But in January 1701, Mildred died in childbirth, when Augustine was only seven. Gayle proved to be a caring stepfather, and he enrolled his young stepson at Appleby School in Westmoreland, England. Again, Augustine Washington (1694-1743) was the father of George, and as we will see in a subsequent chapter, Augustine's studies at Appleby School would directly impact George by bringing "The Rules of Civility" into his childhood education. One of those Rules was the 108th: "Honour and obey your natural parents altho' they be poor," which George copied in his school papers as a young teenager.

Meanwhile, in 1704, John Washington of Chotank, Virginia, (a cousin of Lawrence and the executor of his estate, descending from Lawrence Washington, the younger of the two Washington brothers who first arrived in Virginia) was awarded custody of the three children of their now deceased parents, Lawrence and Mildred Washington. So, while George Washington's father spent a few early years in England, Augustine was soon to return to his native Virginia.

Augustine returned to Virginia at the age of ten, and for the next decade lived in Chotank, not far from his deceased father's farm at Bridges Creek. This plantation became Augustine's in 1715, when he came of age.

Whether Augustine was named in honor of the early Church father (St. Augustine), who was so much appreciated by Protestants (and Catholics alike), is unknown, as there is no record as to the source of the name of this first Augustine Washington. Others of the Washington family, however, would bear his name. Generally, the name of Augustine is derived from the great fourth century Christian theologian and Bishop of Hippo in North Africa.

Apparently, young Augustine thought highly of his education at Appleby and likewise appreciated his stepfather, George Gayle, back in England, for Augustine sent his first two sons (George's older half-brothers Lawrence and Augustine, Jr.) to be educated at Appleby. Furthermore, Augustine, Sr., named his third son George—the first of several Washingtons to be named George, presumably after George Gayle, his stepfather. Thus, George Washington seems to have been named after his father's stepfather, George Gayle.[16]

Shortly after George's father, Augustine, turned twenty-one in 1715, he inherited his late father's Bridges Creek plantation. Grizzard describes what he received:

> Augustine's inheritance included more than 1,000 acres of land (much of it under cultivation by that time); a sizeable amount of tobacco; a half dozen slaves; farm implements and other tools; and livestock consisting of four horses, six sheep, twenty-two cattle, and forty-four hogs. In addition he received a large assortment of house hold goods and eleven books.[17]

About that time, Augustine married his first wife, a Virginia girl from Westmoreland County named Jane Butler (1699-1729), whose holdings increased his lands to over 1700 acres.

Before Jane died at thirty years of age, she and Augustine had four children—George not being among them. One died in infancy, another in early childhood, and two boys—Lawrence (1718-1752) and Augustine, Jr. or "Austin" (1720-1762)—reached adulthood. These two brothers were George's half-brothers. Again, they would attend Augustine's Appleby School in England.

In 1731, Augustine remarried. His second wife was Mary Ball (1708-1789), mother of George, Augustine, Sr., and Mary, who was sixteen years younger than her husband, had six children. They were George (1732-1799), Samuel (1734-81), John or "Jack" (1736-1787), Charles (1738-99), Elizabeth or "Betty" (1733-97), and Mildred (1739-1740).

Augustine was active in the Washington family business of land acquisition and development. He farmed, operated an iron works, and was active in the life of the church. He built a home on Popes Creek at a picturesque point where it entered into the Potomac (an Indian word meaning "river of swans").

What did George's father look like? He was tall and athletic, like his world-famous son. Robert Lewis, George Washington's nephew (son of Betty, his only sister) passed along a description of George's father made by: "Mr. Withers of Stafford, a very aged gentleman." Withers "remembered Augustine as being six feet tall, of noble appearance, and most manly proportions, with the extraordinary development of muscular power for which his son [George] was afterward so remarkable." According to Withers' recollections, when Augustine was the agent for the Principio Iron Works, he had been known to "raise up and place in a wagon a mass of iron that two ordinary men could barely raise from the ground." Despite such physical prowess, Withers also remembered Augustine as a gentle man, "remarkable for the mildness, courtesy, and amiability of his manners."[18]

When the family home was lost in a fire, the couple, with their firstborn child George, moved to a farm near Fredericksburg on the Rappahannock River. This residence became the childhood home of George. Known as Ferry Farm, one can still visit the grounds and a replica of the house to this day.

ACTIVE IN CHURCH DUTIES

Shortly after their move, Augustine Washington assumed the office of vestryman on November 18, 1735, when George, his first-born son by his second marriage, was only three years old. A vestryman was a lay-leader in the church. The oath required for Augustine Washington to become a vestryman was: "I, A B, do declare that I will be conformable to the Doctrine and Discipline of the Church of England, as by law established." What did those Doctrines of the Church of England include? The classic teachings of Christianity: a belief in the Trinity, the deity of Christ, His atoning work on the cross, His resurrection from the dead, His ascension into heaven, His second coming, and the inspiration and authority of the Bible.[19]

Nearly thirty years after his father, George took the same oath on August 19, 1765, having been elected to the vestry of Truro Parish on October 25, 1762. The Vestry book of Pohick Church has the following record: "George Washington Esqr. took the oaths according to Law repeated and subscribed the Test and subscribed to the Doctrine and Discipline of the Church of England in order to qualify him to act as a Vestryman of Truro Parish."[20]

THE DEATH OF GEORGE WASHINGTON'S FATHER

Augustine died in April 1743, after he caught a cold by riding his horse in a severe storm. George was only eleven years old. Writer Benson Lossing describes the details:

> One day early in April, 1743, Mr. Washington rode several hours in a cold rain storm. He became drenched and chilled. Before midnight he was tortured with terrible pains, for his exposure had brought on a fierce attack of hereditary gout. The next day he was burned with fever. His malady ran its course rapidly, and on the 12th he died at the age of forty-nine years. His body was laid in the family vault at Bridges Creek.[21]

Mary Washington was only thirty-seven. Lossing adds, "She submitted to the Divine Will with the strength of a philosopher and the trustfulness of a Christian."[22]

A family tradition recorded by George's adopted stepgrandson gives a glimpse of Augustine's dying scene:

> The father of the Chief made a declaration on his deathbed that does honor to his memory as a Christian and a man. He said, "I thank God that all my life I never struck a man in anger, for if I had I am sure that, from my remarkable muscular powers, I should have killed my antagonist, and then his blood at this awful moment

would have lain heavily on my soul."[23]

Like father, like son. Augustine's son, who would become the "Chief," would also have a reputation for extraordinary strength and would also die of an infection from a cold caught after riding in a storm—and have a deathbed narrative to leave for posterity.

Augustine's business acumen enabled him to divide 10,000 acres of land and nearly fifty slaves in his will. His estate provided for his wife Mary, and the bulk of the rest was given to his three oldest sons—Lawrence, Augustine, and George. Augustine, Jr., received the Pope Creek farm, where he had continued to live after the family had moved. Lawrence received the plantation that he would rename Mount Vernon, in honor of a commanding officer he had served with in military duty. Of course, this would eventually become the property of George, when Lawrence died. (Lawrence's only heir, a daughter, died in childhood.) From his father's estate, George received the farm in Fredericksburg that was known as the Ferry Farm because a ferry crossed the river by their land. This, however, was kept under the guardianship of his mother, until he came of full age.

Furthermore, George's two older half-brothers—Lawrence and Augustine, Jr.— would serve as surrogate fathers for young George, when Augustine died. Both brothers were in their mid-twenties at that time. Because his father died so early, with insufficient funds available, plans to send George to Appleby School in England had to be scrapped. It is intriguing to wonder if George would have become the leader of the American Revolution had he attended Appleby.

CONCLUSION

Thus, our illustrious founding father came of age in a Virginia steeped in a long history of English and Anglican values, where the Indians were no longer a threat, and an agricultural culture was built on vast lands, tobacco, and slave labor. The unhurried life of the gentleman farmer had become a reality. The rural routine and pastoral pleasures of the plantation gentry were periodically interspersed by a journey to lead, serve, and socialize with others of the ruling class in the House of Burgesses, meeting in Williamsburg. Ideally, a Virginia nobleman's son should have been educated in England. But Augustine's untimely death prevented his young son from having the benefit of this experience. However, young Washington still needed to be properly educated, and he was. We will next consider his early childhood and education, which would prepare him for service to the community and impact him throughout his unique and renowned life.

PART III

The Life of
George Washington

SIX

The Childhood of George Washington

"...for you know it has been said, and truly, 'that as the twig is bent so it will grow. This, ... shows the propriety of letting your inexperience be directed by maturer advice."
George Washington, 1796[1]

The early years of Washington's life are known more through tradition,[2] legend[3] and myth,[4] than reliable historical evidence. It is sometimes impossible to sort out which of these questionable historical sources best describes the various stories and anecdotes that have come down to posterity. Historians usually reject definitive statements from this part of his life, often adding a disparaging word about the "moralizing" of Parson Weems, Washington's first popular biographer.

Some of the traditional stories of his early life focus on parental training for moral values. Did youthful Washington really reveal his honest character by telling his father, "I cannot tell a lie, I chopped down the cherry tree"? While virtually all historians today dismiss this as folklore, it is interesting to note that years before Parson Mason Weems immortalized the story in his hagiography of our founding father (written in the early eighteen hundreds) the story must have had some circulation. The evidence for this is

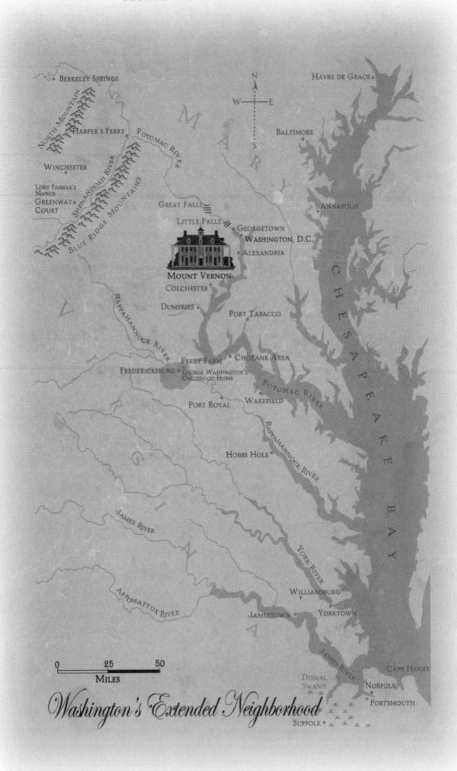

Washington's Extended Neighborhood

a vase made in Germany around the time of
the American Revolution (between the 1770s and the
1790s), honoring its leader, by depicting George as a
young boy with a hatchet and cherry tree and bearing the
initials "G.W."[5]

German made vase from 1790s
depicting the cherry tree incident
several years before Parson Weems
supposedly created the story.

Did George Washington again show his commitment to truth when he immediately told his mother that
her favorite colt died while he was trying to break it in?[6]
In any event, it seems that George, even as a young man,
was beginning to develop a reputation of honesty. We do
know that Washington desired to be known as an honest
man. In a letter to Reverend William Gordon on
December 23, 1788, he wrote: "For the great Searcher of
human hearts knows there is no wish in mine, beyond
that of living and dying an honest man, on my own farm."[7]

There is yet another story that his father, Augustine Washington, planted cabbage
seeds so that when they grew, they would spell out GEORGE WASHINGTON,
allowing George to discover this phenomenon on his own. Then, when the young boy
told his father about it, George was instructed in the truths concerning the Designer
and Creator of the universe.

Whether Washington ever saw his name growing by the design of his father
through planted cabbage seeds, he did delight in the intelligent design[8] he saw in
the work of the "Creator" as he says in his acceptance letter to the American
Philosophical Society:

> In the philosophic retreat to which I am retiring, I shall often
> contemplate with pleasure the extensive utility of your Institution.
> The field of investigation is ample, the benefits which will result to
> Human Society from discoveries yet to be made, are indubitable,
> and the task of studying the works of the great Creator,
> inexpressibly delightful.[9]

While stories such as the cabbage seeds must remain in the region of uncertainty
and apocryphal legend,[10] there is a fair amount of important evidence to help us
learn about George Washington's childhood and teen years that imparted to him a
deeply rooted concept of God.[11] His training was also sufficient for the mastery of

prerequisite knowledge and values required for a young man destined to assume a leadership role in the military, church, and government of his state of Virginia.

A BRIEF SUMMARY OF WASHINGTON'S CHILDHOOD

We do know he was born in 1732 (per the new dating or 1731 by the old dating)[12] in Pope's Creek, which was built by his father Augustine Washington in the mid-1720s. This was a part of Bridges Creek Plantation, the original seat of the Washington family in Virginia. It was located in Westmoreland County. Later the plantation would be called "Wakefield." George Washington lived there for about three years until the house burned down in 1735. A handful of books survived the fire, some with signatures of Augustine and Mary Washington, and dates of 1727, for example.

In 1735, the Augustine Washington family with three-year-old George moved about sixty miles up the Potomac River to live near Little Hunting Creek, which would later be named Mount Vernon. The Pope Creek property they left behind was entrusted to George's half brother Augustine, Jr., who was then about seventeen. Augustine, Jr.'s son, William Augustine, would take over the estate at about age seventeen, nearly thirty years later in 1774.

In 1738, six-year old George Washington and family moved again to Ferry Farm in King George County (later renamed Stafford County after the Declaration of Independence in 1776), located just across the Rappahannock River from Fredericksburg, Virginia. Washington lived in the Fredericksburg area for about fifteen years, until he was twenty-one in 1753, at which time he began his military career. Mary Washington, his mother, lived at Ferry Farm, while Lawrence, his older brother, lived in Mount Vernon until he died. George grew up under the care of his mother and older brother, enjoying periods of time at both of these large farms.

Childhood letters of the youthful George Washington were claimed to have been in existence in the Civil War years. Benson Lossing cites two of these alleged childhood letters that passed between Richard Henry Lee and young George Washington.[13]

George Washington received his education in Fredericksburg, which we will address in the next chapter. He also attended church at St. George's Anglican Church, where he began his life-long habit of church-attendance.[14]

The young George Washington was remarkably strong and athletic. Written accounts claim he was capable of throwing a stone across the Rappahannock River, and all the way from the ground to the top of the natural bridge in Virginia.[15] His diaries are filled with accounts of foxhunting, hunting, gunning, fishing, canoeing, and horseback riding.[16] His power as a wrestler and thrower of the iron bar were legendary.[17]

He was accomplished and graceful in the more gentlemanly activities of dancing and horsemanship.[18] As part of his training for a career in the military, he took fencing lessons from Jacob Van Braam, a Dutch officer in the British military service.[19]

WASHINGTON'S APPROVED DESCRIPTION OF HIS YOUTH

While it is clear that we don't know much about Washington's early life, we do know that the following description about his childhood by David Humphreys was not only read, but also corrected by Washington. As far as we know, Humphrey's draft was the only biography approved by Washington. This work was almost lost to history, and was not printed until the late 1990s.[20]

By a domestic tutor (which was then generally & is now frequently the mode of education practiced in that part of the Continent) he was betimes instructed in the principles of grammar, the theory of reasoning, on speaking, the science of numbers, the elements of geometry, and the highest branches of mathematics, the art of mensuration, composing together with the rudiments of geography, history and the studies which are not improperly termed "the humanities." In the graceful accomplishments of dancing, fencing, riding and performing the military exercises, he likewise made an early and conspicuous proficiency. In short, he was carefully initiated into whatever might be most useful to him, in making his way to preferment in the British army or navy, for which he was designed.

Though he was rather unsure & reserved in his appearance; he was frequently animated and fluent in conversation & always descreed [discreet] in conduct. & In the performance of any business committed to him, he was active, indefatigable, persevering. [He was noted for] His tall stature, for he was clear six feet high without his shoes; his gentiel deportment, for he had something uncommonly noble in his manners; his modest behaviour, which, without being the result of ill-becoming diffidence.

[He was] remarkably robust & athletic. I several times heard him say, he never met any man who could throw a stone to so great a distance as himself; and, that when standing in the valley beneath the natural bridge in Virginia, he has thrown one up to that stupendous arch.

[H]unting & Surveying – the first gave him activity & boldness – the second the means of improving the *Coup d'oeil* in judging of military positions & measuring by the eye the distance between different places. – Patience & perseverance in reconnoitering – how often he spent whole days on horseback, braving the ravages of the most violent heat & cold that ever was experienced in our climate.

As it was the design of his Father that he should be bred for an Officer in the British navy, his mental acquisitions & exterior accomplishments were calculated to give him distinction in that profession. <GW note: it was rather the wish of my eldest brother (on whom the several concerns of the family devolved) that this should take place & the matter was contemplated by him–My father died when I was only 10 years old.> At 15 years old, he was entered a midshipman on board of the [blank] & his baggage prepared for embarkation: but the plan was abandoned in consequence of the earnest solicitations of his Mother.[21]

We get a sense of the childhood home and grounds where George Washington grew up from an advertisement he placed in November 1772 to sell the property:

> A TRACT of 600 acres, including about 200 of cleared land on the north side of Rappahannock river, opposite to the lower end of Fredericksburg. On this tract (a little above the road) is one of the most agreeable situations for a house that is to be found upon the whole river, having a clear and distinct view of almost every house in the said town, and every vessel that passes to and from it. Long credit, if desired, will be given.[22]

The man who bought the farm was Dr. Hugh Mercer of the city of Fredericksburg, who was a close friend of George's. He would later become a general in the Revolutionary War and die at the Battle of Princeton in 1777. He bought the entire farm in 1774 for 2000 pounds Virginia currency, to be paid in five annual installments. In 1743, tragedy struck when George was only ten years old. His father Augustine suddenly died. (The account of his death was related in the prior chapter.) According to

Mason Weems, George was not home when his father turned ill and did not return in time to see him before he died. However, another account says that George was there for his father's final moments. Washington-biographer Edward C. M'Guire writes, "It was in the Easter holydays that Mr. Washington was taken sick. George was absent at the time, on a visit to some of his acquaintances in Chotanct, King George County. He was sent for after his father's sickness became serious, and reached the paternal abode in time to witness the last struggle and receive the parting benediction of his beloved parent."[23]

The Reverend Mason Locke Weems, the first biographer of George Washington.

WASHINGTON'S BROTHER LAWRENCE INSPIRES HIS INTEREST IN THE MILITARY

Following the death of his father, George spent time with his older stepbrothers. Since Lawrence had married the daughter of Colonel William Fairfax of Belvoir, George not only found himself at Lawrence's Mount Vernon, but also at Belvoir, the neighboring Fairfax estate. Here he encountered a British military family of high nobility. Col. William Fairfax was the cousin of and agent for Lord Thomas Fairfax, Sixth Baron of Cameron, and the owner of the entire Northern Neck. As George spent time at Belvoir, he assimilated many of the courtly graces that would characterize his adult life.

Lawrence was also militarily-minded, having served in the British navy during the war between the British and the Spanish, which had broken out in 1740, when Edward Vernon, commander-in-chief of the British Navy in the West Indies, captured the Spanish stronghold of Porto Bello on the Isthmus of Darien (between Columbia and Panama). Consequently, Spain allied with France in retaliation against England. The colonies in turn raised four regiments to assist England in the defense of the West Indies. Lawrence, with his father's blessing, secured a commission as a captain in the regiment from Virginia and left in 1741 as second-in-command. Thus, Lawrence served under Admiral Vernon in the naval assault against Spanish Cartagena on the South American coast of Colombia.

The conflict ended disastrously, as the English were repulsed. Lawrence returned in 1742 with impaired health, having perhaps contracted tuberculosis during this time. But he also came home with a deep admiration for Admiral Vernon. Reverend Jonathan Boucher's critical assessment of the Washington family referred to earlier reports that Lawrence, while at Cartagena, got into a "scrape with a brother officer," and "did not acquit himself quite so well as he ought, and so sold out" (meaning he quit the military with a measure of embarrassment).[24] Whether such was the case, it is clear that he honored the Admiral.

After his father Augustine died, Lawrence inherited the Hunting Creek farm, and changed its name to Mount Vernon. "Mount" was appropriate, given that the house was built on a majestic premonitory overlooking the Potomac River, situated on the nearly 2,500-acre tract of land. Augustine Washington's Last Will and Testament also stipulated that if Lawrence should die without an heir, the estate was to pass to George.

Lawrence had planned to return to England, where he had attended school, and there join the regular army and seek advancement in the ranks. But before he was to leave, his martial plans were exchanged for marital plans, as he was engaged to Ann Fairfax, the daughter of Col. William Fairfax. William Fairfax, "of the King's Council," was "one of Virginia's foremost men, land agent and cousin to Lord Fairfax, and owner of a fine estate called Belvoir."[25] Lawrence and Ann's spring wedding plans were delayed until midsummer, because of the death of Augustine Washington, father to Lawrence and George. Lawrence was elected to the House of Burgesses, where he served for seven years. His better-known brother was to follow in this same path several years later.

In 1746, George spent a week at the Fairfax family's Belvoir plantation mulling over a major life decision in regard to his military plans. In the context of this stay, the closeness between brothers Lawrence and George was recorded for history. In a September 1746 letter, Col. William Fairfax wrote to his son-in-law Lawrence Washington: "George has been with us, and says He will be steady and thankfully follow your Advice as his best friend."[26] Apparently the military discussions that occurred between Lawrence and Col. Fairfax, along with various visiting friends from former military days, helped to instill in George a desire and a decision for military service. Thus, around this time, Lawrence began to make plans for George to pursue a naval career in the legacy of Admiral Vernon.

A DECISION THAT WOULD HAVE CHANGED WORLD HISTORY

In 1746, George Washington reached a significant, potential turning point in his life. He almost joined the British Navy. Had he followed through on this, world history could have changed.

As we have noted, his talks with Lawrence and Lawrence's father-in-law awakened an interest in the fourteen-year-old George Washington to pursue military service. Given the many ships that docked and passed on the river from across the sea, it was natural to think of naval service as a possibility for the young man. Lawrence, along with the help of Dr. Spencer, Mary Washington's family physician, persuaded George's reluctant mother that his military interest would be well met in the Navy. So, late in 1746, Lawrence secured for fourteen-year-old George a midshipman's warrant.

But his mother had apprehension. His mother's reticence to embrace George Washington's longing for the high seas is seen in a letter written by Robert Jackson, one of Lawrence's friends from Fredericksburg. Apparently, she had initially approved ("her first resolution"), but upon greater input, changed her mind:

> I am afraid Mrs. Washington will not keep up to her first resolution. She seems to dislike George's going to sea, and says several persons have told her it was a bad scheme. She offers several trifling objections, such as a fond, unthinking mother habitually suggests, and I find that one word against his going has more weight than ten for it.[27]

The plans finally received a decisive maternal veto, after she received a letter from London from her brother, Joseph Ball, dated May 19, 1747. His arguments proved to be decisive against a naval career for George,

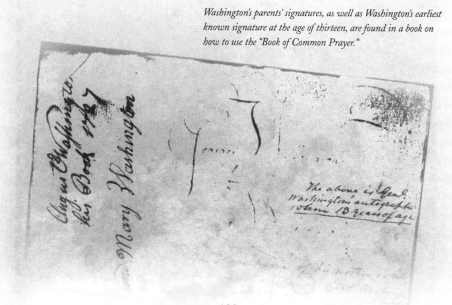

Washington's parents' signatures, as well as Washington's earliest known signature at the age of thirteen, are found in a book on how to use the "Book of Common Prayer."

I understand that you are advised and have some thoughts of putting your son George to sea. I think he had better be put apprentice to a tinker, for a common sailor before the mast has by no means the common liberty of the subject; for they will press him from ship to ship, where he has fifty shillings a month, and make him take twenty-three, and cut and slash and use him like a negro, or rather like a dog. And as to any considerable preferment in the navy, it is not to be expected, as there are always so many gaping for it here who have interest, and he has none.

And if he should get to be a master of a Virginia ship (which it is very difficult to do), a planter who has three or four hundred acres of land and three or four slaves, if he be industrious, may live more comfortably, and leave his family in better stead than such a master of a ship can . . . . He must not be too hasty to be rich, but go on gently and with patience, as things will naturally go. This method, without aiming at being a fine gentleman before his time, will carry a man more comfortably and surely through the world than going to sea, unless it be a great chance indeed. I pray God keep you and yours.

Your loving brother, Joseph Ball[28]

The timing could not have been tighter, since the letter arrived when George's luggage had already been loaded on the ship on which he would have sailed. The historical impact of this decision is profound.

Benson J. Lossing's explanation reflects the significance of this decision from the perspective of an earlier generation of American Washington scholars,

He was destined by Heaven for a far noble career than man had conceived for him. This incident illustrates the truth of the familiar apothegm, "Man proposes but God disposes."[29]

We do not know if the young ex-midshipman George Washington embraced the doctrine of Providence the way that the mature General Washington did as he commanded the army on the land many years later.[30] Here is one sample among several hundred reflecting his belief in Providence. Writing to William Pearce from Philadelphia, near the end of his presidency on May 25, 1794, Washington explains his confidence in Divine Providence:

> I learn with concern from your letter of the 18th. Instant, that your crops were still labouring under a drought, and most of them very much injured. At disappointments and losses which are the effects of Providential acts, I never repine; because I am sure the alwise disposer of events knows better than we do, what is best for us, or what we deserve.[31]

We do not know what George thought about this change in plans, but he obviously submitted to his mother's authority. Respect for higher authority was a principle that Washington maintained throughout his life. Years later, even though entrusted by Congress with the powers of a dictator for a season,[32] and even though given the opportunity to become a new king at the end of the war by his soldiers, Washington never wavered in his immovable commitment to submit to lawful powers over him. This aspect of his character was remarkably highlighted by Alexander Hamilton years later in the midst of the efforts to make Washington King, as seen in a later chapter.[33]

"The maternal hand that bent the twig" never lost the place of honor in the heart of her son. Even to the final years of Mary Washington's life, General Washington called her in his letters "My Revered Mother" or "Honored Madam," but this was also his title for her in his public statements as well. Thus, he wrote to the people in his hometown of Fredericksburg in 1784: "To a beneficent Providence, and to the fortitude of a brave and virtuous Army, supported by the general exertion of our common Country I stand indebted for the plaudits you now bestow; ... my sensibility of them is heightened by their coming from the respectable Inhabitants of the place of my growing Infancy and the honorable mention which is made of my revered Mother; by whose Maternal hand (early deprived of a Father) I was led from Childhood."[34] His consciousness of her impact on his character was implied in his advice given in 1796 to his own young "son," George Washington Parke Custis, "...for you know it has been said, and truly, 'that as the twig is bent so it will grow.' This, ... shows the propriety of letting your inexperience be directed by maturer advice."[35] As Mary had guided young George, so the new young George needed to be guided by a mature adult as well.

Washington had come to trust the wisdom of divine intervention in the events of his life. He also understood the power of a reluctant mother's intervention in a son's decision for military service. In a letter to Landon Carter on April 15, 1777, General

Washington remarked, "I should have been very happy in seeing your Grandson enlisted under the Banners of His country...But a mother's tenderness and Tears too often interpose, and check the ardour of our Youth."[36]

YOUNG GEORGE COMES OF AGE AT MT. VERNON

During the years 1746-48 when George was between fourteen and sixteen years of age, he lived primarily with his brother Lawrence at Mount Vernon. In 1747, at the age of fifteen, George assumed an adult responsibility when he became a godfather to a child in baptism.[37] Throughout his life he became a godfather for some eight children in all. That role required subscribing to the orthodox and Trinitarian doctrines of the Church of England. In conformity with the 1662 *Book of Common Prayer*, the following affirmations were required of the fifteen-year-old Washington, as they were of all godfathers and godmothers:

> *Then shall the Priest speak unto the Godfathers and Godmothers on this wise.*
>
> **DEARLY** beloved, ye have brought *this Child* here to be baptized, ye have prayed that our Lord Jesus Christ would vouchsafe to receive him, to release him of *his* sins, to sanctify him with the Holy Ghost, to give him the kingdom of heaven, and everlasting life. Ye have heard also that our Lord Jesus Christ hath promised in his Gospel to grant all these things that ye have prayed for: which promise he, for his part, will most surely keep and perform. Wherefore, after this promise made by Christ, *this Infant* must also faithfully, for his part, promise by you that are *his* sureties, (until *he* come of age to take it upon *himself,)* that *he* will renounce the devil and all his works, and constantly believe God's holy Word, and obediently keep his commandments.
>
> I demand therefore,
>
> **DOST** thou, in the name of this Child, renounce the devil and all his works, the vain pomp and glory of the world, with all covetous desires of the same, and the carnal desires of the flesh, so that thou wilt not follow, nor be led by them?
>
> [Washington then answered]. I renounce them all.
>
> *Minister.*
>
> **DOST** thou believe in God the Father Almighty, Maker of heaven

and earth? And in Jesus Christ his only-begotten Son our Lord? And that he was conceived by the Holy Ghost; born of the Virgin Mary; that he suffered under Pontius Pilate, was crucified, dead, and buried; that he went down into hell, and also did rise again the third day; that he ascended into heaven, and sitteth at the right hand of God the Father Almighty; and from thence shall come again at the end of the world, to judge the quick and the dead? And dost thou believe in the Holy Ghost; the holy Catholick Church; the Communion of Saints; the Remission of sins; the Resurrection of the flesh; and everlasting life after death?

[Washington then answered] All this I stedfastly believe.

Minister.

WILT thou be baptized in this faith?

[Washington then answered] That is my desire.

Minister.

WILT thou then obediently keep God's holy will and commandments, and walk in the same all the days of thy life?

[Washington then answered] I will.

Then shall the Priest say,

O MERCIFUL God, grant that the old Adam in this Child may be so buried, that the new man may be raised up in him. [Washington then responded] *Amen.*

Grant that all carnal affections may die in him, and that all things belonging to the Spirit may live and grow in him. [Washington then responded] *Amen.*

Grant that he may have power and strength to have victory, and to triumph, against the devil, the world, and the flesh. [Washington then responded] *Amen.*

Grant that whosoever is here dedicated to thee by our office and ministry may also be endued with heavenly virtues, and everlastingly rewarded, through thy mercy, O blessed Lord God, who dost live, and govern all things, world without end. [Washington then responded] *Amen.*

ALMIGHTY, everliving God, whose most dearly beloved Son Jesus Christ, for the forgiveness of our sins, did shed out of his most precious side both water and blood; and gave commandment to his disciples, that they should go teach all nations, and baptize them In the Name of the Father, and of the Son, and of the Holy Ghost: Regard, we beseech thee, the supplications of thy congregation; sanctify this Water to the mystical washing away of sin; and grant that this Child, now to be baptized therein, may receive the fulness of thy grace, and ever remain in the number of thy faithful and elect children; through Jesus Christ our Lord. [Washington then responded] *Amen.*

So, on some eight different occasions, George Washington publicly and explicitly affirmed his Christian faith in these words, a remarkable fact given Washington's powerful conscience. Significantly, Thomas Jefferson, a Unitarian rather than an orthodox Christian, turned down the invitation to be a godfather in 1788, because he could not in good conscience subscribe to the Trinitarian beliefs of the church.[38]

CONCLUSION

In 1748, George took another step as a sixteen-year-old young adult when he joined a surveying trip to Shenandoah Valley with James Genn on behalf of Lord Fairfax. Perhaps we can say that George officially came of age in 1749, when he was appointed a public surveyor. Even here the Christian influences in his life are evident. The very first page of his surveyor notebook has a single sentence inscribed by the youthful Washington's hand. It says, "If you can't find it in the book of Ezekiel, look for it in Israel."

The cryptic message makes sense in light of Washington's Christian training. As Washington was taught the scriptures by his Anglican childhood tutors, he

Cover page of Washington's first surveyor's notebook with reference to Ezekiel and Israel. [39]

learned that Israel was a nation marked out by very clear boundaries (Joshua 13-21), such as would be well understood by surveyors. And the book of Ezekiel concludes with a remarkable survey of the New Jerusalem (Ezekiel 40-48). The young surveyor apparently autographed his official record with this observation. His task in the pristine woods of the New World in some way reminded him of the biblical accounts of marking off expanses of land that had been gifted by God.

Not much is known about George Washington's childhood and early manhood. His father, who was a successful businessman and leader in the church, died young. His mother was a woman of faith. From everything we can tell, he was an obedient son. We do know a little more about his education and, as we shall see next, it was Christian.

SEVEN

The Christian Education of George Washington

"I heartily thank our heavenly Father, that he hath called me to this state of salvation, through Jesus Christ our Saviour."
——*Anglican Catechism taught to George Washington as part of his education*

George Washington's education can be summarized briefly. First, he received a home-based education by tutors who trained him in the topics that were essential for his success as a leader in colonial Virginia. His superlative penmanship and his poor spelling are legendary. Fortunately, his grammar continued to improve throughout his life. His childhood education included extensive instruction in applied mathematics, business law, as well as the teachings of Christianity. His education not only enabled him to become skilled in surveying, real estate law, and land acquisition, but also in local leadership of the Anglican Church. His mother, his church, and his teachers imparted to him a substantial knowledge of the Bible that was manifested in his writings by a high level of Bible literacy.

Second, although he never received a college education, given his disciplined and methodical temperament, he never stopped learning. As author Frank Grizzard, Jr. put it, Washington was "conscious of a defective education."[1] Nonetheless (or perhaps because of this), he strove to overcome it by the continual self-improvement of reading, experimenting, and correspondence. The legacy of his commitment to learning was seen in his extensive library,[2] the many scholarships he gave to young scholars,[3] his generous endowments of schools and universities,[4] as well as a persistent advocacy of the formation of schools of higher education.[5]

In spite of his limited education, he learned enough to make a tremendous mark on the world. The traits of the mature Washington which most impressed his contemporaries were his consistent character and astute and wise judgment. Thomas Jefferson remarked:

> His mind was great and powerful, without being of the very first order; his penetration strong, though not so acute as that of a Newton, Bacon or Locke; and as far as he saw, no judgment was ever sounder. It was slow in operation, being little aided by invention or imagination, but sure in conclusion. Hence, the common remark of his officers of the advantage he derived from councils of war, where, hearing all suggestions, he selected whatever was best; and certainly no general ever planned his battles more judiciously.[6]

Furthermore, the Duke of Wellington, the great British military leader (a generation or so after the American Revolution) described George Washington with these words: "The purest and noblest character of modern time—possibly of all time."[7] We already noted Jefferson's sense of Washington's judgment. He went on to describe his character in terms consistent with the Duke of Wellington:

> His integrity was most pure, his justice the most inflexible I have ever known, no motives of interest of consanguinity, of friendship or hatred, being able to bias his decision. He was, indeed, in every sense of the word, a wise, a good, and a great man. His temper was naturally irritable and high-toned; but reflection and resolution had obtained a firm and habitual ascendancy over it. ...
>
> On the whole, his character was, in its mass, perfect, in nothing bad, in few points indifferent; and it may truly be said that never did

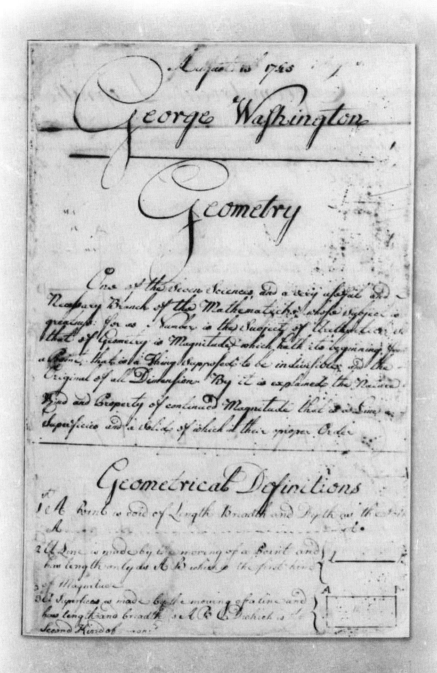

A page of young George's geometry notes from school.
He was remarkably skilled in penmanship and mathematics.

nature and fortune combine more perfectly to make a man great, and to place him in the same constellation with whatever worthies have merited from man an everlasting remembrance.[8]

As we will see, there is evidence that it was a Christian education that formed his great character.

Author Frank Grizzard, Jr. well summarizes the state of the research on George Washington's early education.

> David Humphrey's biography of Washington contains the tantalizing but cryptic statement that "his education was principally conducted by a private tutor." Although many have sought to identify the unnamed tutor, Washington himself edited Humphrey's draft in 1786 without commenting on the passage. It is known that Washington attended school with George Masons' "Neighbour & Your old School-fellow, Mr. [David] Piper," a planter who lived in the vicinity of Washington and Mason's estate but who had been raised in Washington Parish, Westmoreland County, near Washington's birthplace, and a school stood at the nearby Lower Church of the parish.[9]

It is interesting to note that two of George's brothers studied in a way that would have made them less inclined to join the American cause (in the divide between America and Great Britain) had they lived until that time. Indeed, Joseph D. Sawyer writes, "an English college education confirmed the two elder sons of Augustine Washington in Toryism; while plain American schooling, somewhat crudely started by Master Hobby at Falmouth, furthered at the Marye School in Fredericksburg and supplemented by Mr. Williams at Oak Grove, seated George firmly in the colonial saddle. When coupled with sound home training, his modest education turned him into a thoroughgoing American. George Washington never went to college—a fact he is said to have regretted in adult life; his youth was too full of action, perhaps too burdened with responsibility, to allow for a college career. Had his father lived, he would probably have entered Brasenose College, Oxford, the alma mater of his half-brothers and of those earlier Washingtons in England,—including Lawrence, the allegedly drunken Vicar—all of whom enjoyed the advantages of a liberal arts education."[10]

GEORGE WASHINGTON'S CHILDHOOD EDUCATION

The details of George Washington's early education are sketchy. The family moved to Fredericksburg in 1738, when George was six years old. Later, he may have been a student at the Reverend James Marye's school, which had begun in 1740.[11] Reverend James Marye was notable for his evangelical views and sincere piety.[12] Another possibility is that after George's father died, he lived for a time with his older half brother, Augustine, Jr., at his birthplace on Pope Creek farm and went to a school operated by Henry Williams.

We don't have definitive facts on Washington's childhood education. We do know that during the war, someone who wanted to discredit the xommander in chief did so in part by ridiculing his childhood schooling. This critic was Reverend Jonathan Boucher, the tutor Washington himself had hired for his stepson John Parke Custis, affectionately called "Jacky." Reverend Boucher, an Anglican clergyman, wrote with evident disdain, "George, who, like most people thereabouts at that time, had no other education than reading, writing and accounts, which he was taught by a convict servant whom his father bought for a schoolmaster."[13] Boucher wrote these words after he and Washington had parted company over loyalty to the crown. Prior to the politically motivated rupture of their relationship, they had enjoyed an extensive correspondence.[14] As an Anglican clergyman, Boucher's ordination vow included loyalty to the King, a King that Washington viewed as a tyrant and destroyer of American liberty. Boucher's loyalty to the King became so controversial in revolutionary Virginia, that his final sermons preached before leaving for England were delivered from a pulpit graced with two loaded pistols![15]

In Fredericksburg, on the Washington side of the Rappahannock River, there still exists an eighteenth century, small school building adjoining a cemetery. It is a small log cabin structure, with a cemetery and the remains of a church nearby. Tradition holds that Washington received his education in this "field school" from one Master

A Field School similar to the one in which Washington was educated by his tutor Master Hobby.

115

Hobby (sometimes identified as William Groves), who also served as the parish's sexton.

Evidence exists that there was at this time a church sexton who had also held a higher position in the church's life, but had to relinquish it because his legal record in England became known.[16] Boucher's claim that Washington's tutor was a "bought servant" comports with the fact that indentured servitude was a common practice to get a new start on a new life in the New World. Moreover, it is conceivable that an educated person could have run afoul of the common law in the mother country for a non-heinous crime such as debt.[17]

Even author Rupert Hughes (who is generally skeptical of the Christianity of George Washington) supports the notion that young George was taught by a Christian layman, a Mr. Hobby: "This sexton, William Grove, may have been nicknamed 'Hobby' or there may have been another teacher named Hobby. M.D. Conway, in *Washington and Mount Vernon* states that Reverend Dr. Philip Slaughter's researches led him to believe that Hobby was sexton at Fallmouth, two miles above the Washington farm, and that the Washington Children went to school there."[18]

Washington biographer Benson Lossing provides additional information about Hobby. "The sexton of the chapel was Master Hobby, the first school-teacher of George Washington. He reigned over an 'old field' school-house—a log building—as a pedagogue for many years. He had a sort of bullet head and a vast amount of self-esteem. Master Hobby was regarded with great reverence by his pupils as 'wondrous wise,' and as they gazed at him while quaint words of wisdom dropped from his lips, 'Still the wonder grew, How *his* small head could carry all he knew.' When Master Hobby became an old man he often boasted that he was 'the making of General Washington.'"[19]

But whether these accounts of Hobby are factual or not, the foundational claim they make is substantiated by the evidence. Washington was educated in the context of the Anglican Church. Whether it was by a sexton, a clerical tutor, or simply

George Washington son to Augustine & Mary his Wife was Born y[e] 11th Day of February 173½ about 10 in the Morning & was Baptized the 3[d] of April following, Mr. Beverley Whiting & Cap[t]. Christopher Brooks godfathers and Mrs. Mildred Gregory godmother

The handwritten record of Washington's baptism and godparents from the family Bible.

home education, all of the available evidence resoundingly demonstrates this fact.

The religious education of Washington began in the customary Anglican fashion—by baptism with sponsors. In the Washington family Bible is found:

> George William, son to Augustine Washington, and Mary his wife, was born the eleventh day of February, 1731-2, about ten in the morning, and was baptized the 3rd April following, Mr. Bromley Whiting, and Captain Christopher Brooks godfathers, and Mrs. Mildred Gregory godmother.[20]

Whether George himself wrote this record in the Washington family Bible has been debated.[21]

George's training would have included one of the clergy as his religious tutor. Working with his parents—his father the vestryman and his deeply religious mother—the clergyman helped teach George and his siblings the historic Anglican Catechism, which included statements such as "I heartily thank our heavenly Father, that he hath called me to this state of salvation, through Jesus Christ our Saviour. And I pray unto God to give me his grace, that I may continue in the same unto my life's end"[22] as well as the Apostles' Creed, the Ten Commandments, a statement on the doctrine of the Trinity, the Lord's Prayer (the Our Father), and comments on the sacraments of baptism and the Lord's Table. It articulated that we should love God and love our neighbor:

> My duty towards God, is to believe in him, to fear him, and to love him with all my heart, with all my mind, with all my soul, and with all my strength; to worship him, to give him thanks, to put my whole trust in him, to call upon him, to honour his holy Name and his Word, and to serve him truly all the days of my life....
>
> My duty towards my Neighbour, is to love him as myself, and to do to all men, as I would they should do unto me: To love, honour, and succour my father and mother...[23]

The mature Washington clearly remembered these duties to God and man.[24]

WASHINGTON'S CHILDHOOD SCHOOL BOOKS
IN HIS OWN LIBRARY

If you investigate Washington's own library, which we have sought to do, we can see the influence of his Christian education on him. The Boston Athenaeum has done a superlative job keeping Washington's library intact for the most part. Washington's earliest extant signature, portending his famous penmanship and flowing elegant signature, is in a book designed to teach a person to use the *Book Of Common Prayer*.[25] This childhood script is dated by a note of a family member as indicating he was around thirteen years old. A careful examination of this work reveals that portions of its text are stained, perhaps even tear-stained, particularly one of the highly used sections that seeks to bring comfort at the time of death. The book has long been considered one of the textbooks of Washington's early education.

William Coolidge Lane writes, "The volume has been rebacked, otherwise it is in the same binding of old calf as it was when Washington handled and probably studied it in his boyhood."[26] The book certainly seems to have been precious to Washington. It contained a signature of his father, Augustine Washington, dated 1727, along with the signature of his mother, Mary Washington. Washington, the student, also signed his father's name and drew several doodles of the kind that young scholars indulge in when finding their work less than engaging. The above evidences of use corroborate the fact that Washington was carefully instructed in the *Book Of Common Prayer* as part of his education.

Another textbook that survives with George's signature (twice, in fact) is the publication of a series of sermons based on Luke 16:29-31, entitled *The Sufficiency Of A Standing Revelation*. The second sermon, dated February 5, 1700, begins with these words, showing the high view it had of the Scriptures:

> The first thing which I propounded to do in discoursing on these Words, was, the endeavour to show, that the present *Standing Revelation* of God's will, contained in the Books of the Old and New Testament is abundantly sufficient to persuade men to Repentance, if they are not unreasonably blind and obstinate. *They have Moses and the Prophets, (they have also Christ and his Apostles,) let them hear them.*
>
> And if that *Standing Revelation* which God hath made to us of his will in the *Holy Scriptures* can upon any Account be thought insufficient to effect this Design, it must be, I think, either 1.

Because no standing revelation can be sufficient for this Purpose; Or, 2. Because there are some particular defects in that Revelation which we have in the Holy Scriptures which render it not so sufficient for this Purpose, as 'tis possible a Standing Revelation might be.

I have therefore, in a former Discourse upon these words endeavoured to show in general that a Standing Revelation of God's will may be so well contrived, as so well attested as to be sufficient of the Purpose.[27]

This book bears the signatures of other students, who apparently with young George had been exposed to these sermons. Its contents were the Robert Boyle Lectures established to refute the infidelity of deistic thought that had begun to surface in England in the late sixteen hundreds. The force of the sermons that Washington read under his tutor's guidance was designed to refute the Deist claim that there was no divine revelation and so to encourage the historic Protestant view of the sufficiency of Scripture for Christian faith and practice. Robert Boyle, who endowed these lectures, was an Oxford professor, the father of modern chemistry, and a devout Christian.

Another book in his library, dating from this era that had likely been used as a school book, was *The Travels of Cyrus*. This book states that its purpose was, in part, to refute both atheism and Deism.[28] A fictional literary text, *The Travels of Pergrine Pickle*,[29] reveals a sincere belief in divine Providence. Washington even had a copy of Theodore Beza's Latin translation of the New Testament.[30] Beza was a contemporary and compatriot of the Protestant reformer John Calvin in Geneva, Switzerland. Beza is one the four reformers honored on the Reformation Wall in Geneva in the form of gigantic stone statues. He is in the company of Calvin, Knox, and Farel. Washington also had a Latin Concordance of all the words in Homer's *Iliad* dating from this era.[31]

One of the science texts in his library was a work by John Ray (1627-1704/5), an English naturalist, entitled *The Wisdom of God Manifested in the Works of the Creation*. The work addressed all of creation, including the human form, and detailed how each revealed the work of the Creator. Washington saw the study of the works of the "great Creator" as "inexpressibly delightful."[32]

But what is truly amazing, in regard to Washington's early education, is that we know a great deal of the specific assignments he had, because his homework pages still exist.[33] These immediately illustrate his remarkable skill in penmanship and mathematics. But they also reveal the beliefs being transmitted in his childhood education. Two

True Happiness

These are the things, which once possess'd
Will make a life thats truly blest
A Good Estate on healthy Soil,
Not Got by Vice, nor yet by toil:
Round a warm Fire, a pleasant Joke,
With Chimney ever free from Smoke:
A Strength entire, a Sparkling Bowl,
A quiet Wife, a quiet Soul,
A Mind as well as body, whole
Prudent Simplicity, constant Friend,
A Diet which no art Commends;
A Merry Night without much Drinking
A Happy Thought without much Thinking,
Each Night by Quiet Sleep made short
A Will to be but What thou art:
Possess'd of these, all else defy
And neither wish nor fear to Die
        These are things which once Possess'd
        Will make a life thats truly blest

To keep Ink from Freezing or Moulding.
In hard frosty Weather, Ink will be apt to Freeze;
which if once it Doth, it will be Good for Nothing for
it Taketh away all its Blackness & Beauty. To prevent
which (if you have not the Conveniency of keeping
it Warm) Put a few Drops of Brandy or other Spirits into
it, and it will not freeze. And to hinder its Moulding
Put a little Salt therein.

Childhood poem entitled "True Happiness" copied by Washington manuscripts exist that are copies of poems, showing the values of his tutor. One emphasizes moral living, the importance of family, and simplicity for true happiness in life.[34] It appeared in the February 1734 issue of *Gentleman's Magazine* and even earlier in *Universal Spectator*.[35]

A CHRISTMAS POEM

Another youthful school paper of Washington's is his copy of a Christmas poem.[36] It shows that he was exposed to historic Christian teachings concerning Christ's death and resurrection as well as the human and divine nature of Christ. Most scholars only mention this copied poem, or only cite the first two lines.[37] The whole text, however, is valuable, because it illustrates the Christian orthodoxy in which Washington had been trained. Young Washington probably copied this from the February 1743 issue of *Gentleman's Magazine* (London), cited above.

ON CHRISTMAS DAY

Assist me Muse divine to sing the morn,
On which the Saviour of mankind was born;
But oh! what numbers to the theme can rise?
Unless kind angels aid me from the skies?
Methinks I see the tunefull Host descend,
Hark, by their hymns directed on the road,
The gladsome Shepherds find the nascent God!
And view the infant conscious of his birth,
Smiling bespeak salvation to the earth!
For when the important Aera first drew near
In which the great Messiah should appear
And to accomplish His redeeming love
Resign a while his glorious throne above.
Beneath our form every woe sustain
And by triumphant suffering fix His reign
Should for lost man in tortures yield his breath,
Dying to save us from eternal death!
Oh mystick Union! Salutary grace!
Incarnate God our nature should embrace!
That Deity should stoop to our disguise!
That man recovered should regain the skies!

Dejected Adam! From thy Grave ascend
And view the Serpent's Deadly Malice end,
Adorring bless th' Almighty's boundless grace
That gave his son a ransome for thy race!
Oh never let my soul this Day forget,
But pay in grateful praise her annual debt
To Him whom 'tis my trust I shall [adore(?)—illegible.]
When time and sin and death [shall be no more.(?)—illegible.] [38]

Based on this childhood traditional Christian education, Washington's adult writings show that he maintained a deep joy in the Christian celebration of the birth of Christ.[39]

GEORGE WASHINGTON'S "RULES OF CIVILITY"

Virtually all scholars, even those who believe Washington was not a Christian, agree that a set of sayings, originally composed by a Jesuit priest from a century before and often embellished thereafter, was very influential on George Washington.[40] This set of 110 sayings contains many biblical precepts. They are the "Rules of Civility and Decent Behaviour in Company and Conversation"[41] and are viewed as a blueprint that Washington followed his entire life. They are given in their entirety in appendix One.[42]

They were, in fact, very important in the training of students at the Appleby School where George's father and stepbrothers had attended. William Wilbur writes,

> George's father was very familiar with these rules, for they were used at Appleby Grammar School. Among English educators they were generally referred to as Hawkins' rules. They had wide acceptance in English schoolrooms and were so popular that eleven editions were printed between 1640 and 1672. . . the correct title is: "Youth's Behaviour or Decency in Conversation Amongst Men." The title page runs on, "Composed in French by grave persons for the use and benefit of their Youth. Now newly turned into English by Francis Hawkins."[43]

Although we will list only a few of them here, these remarkable and at times humorous rules, as William Wilbur suggests, all fall into the following categories:

RULES Which Taught Character.

On Christmass Day

Assist me Muse divine! to sing the Morn,
On which the Saviour of Mankind was born;
But oh! what Numbers to the Theme can rise?
Unless kind Angels aid me from the Skies!
Methinks I see the tunefull Host descend,
And with officious Joy the Scene attend!
Hark, by their Hymns directed on the Road,
The Gladsome Shepherds find the nascent God!
And view the Infant conscious of his Birth,
Smileing bespeak Salvation to the Earth!

For when the important Æra first drew near
In which the great Messiah should appear;
And to Accomplish his redeeming Love,
Resign awhile his glorious Throne above;
Beneath our Form should every Woe sustain,
And by triumphant Suffering fix his Reign,
Should for lost Man in tortures yield his Breath
Dying to save ... from eternal Death!
Oh mystick Union!—Salutary Grace!
Incarnate God our Nature should embrace!
That Deity should stoop to our Disguise!
That man ... should regain the Skies!
Dejected Adam! from thy grave ascend,
And view the Serpents Deadly Malice end;
Adorning bless th'Almightys boundless Grace
That gave his son a Ransome for thy Race!
Oh never let my Soul this Day forget,
But pay in graitfull praise her Annual Debt
To him, whom 'tis my Trust I shall
When Time, and Sin, and Death ...

*Christmas poem reflecting a rich understanding of the
doctrine of salvation in Christ written in Washington's hand*

RULES Which Counseled Consideration for Others.

RULES That Urged Modesty.

RULES That Advised Compassion.

RULES That Enjoined Respect for Elders and Persons in Positions of Responsibility and Authority.

RULES Which Concern Conduct.

RULES Governing Table Manners and Cleanliness.[44]

Here are a few of the rules. Immediately following, we have supplied a biblical text, of which this maxim is an echo:

RULES OF CIVILITY: 43d Do not express Joy before one sick or in pain for that contrary Passion will aggravate his Misery.

BIBLE: Rejoice with those who rejoice, and weep with those who weep (Romans 12:15, NKJV).

RULES OF CIVILITY: 48th Wherein you reprove Another be unblameable yourself; for example is more prevalent than Precepts.

BIBLE: "Judge not, that you be not judged. For with what judgment you judge, you will be judged" (Jesus in Matthew 7:1-2, NKJV).

RULES OF CIVILITY: 56th Associate yourself with Men of good Quality if you Esteem your own Reputation; for 'tis better to be alone than in bad Company.

BIBLE: "Evil company corrupts good habits" (1 Corinthians 15:33, NKJV).

RULES OF CIVILITY: 82d Undertake not what you cannot Perform but be Carefull to keep your Promise.

BIBLE: When you make a vow to God, do not delay to pay it; for He has no pleasure in fools. Pay what you have vowed—Better not to vow than to vow and not pay (Ecclesiastes 5:4, 5 NKJV).

RULES OF CIVILITY: 108th When you Speak of God or his Atributes, let it be Seriously & [wt.] Reverence. Honour & Obey your Natural Parents altho they be Poor.

BIBLE: Holy, holy holy is the LORD of hosts (Isaiah 6:3).

You shall not take the name of the LORD your God in vain, for the LORD will not hold him guiltless who takes His name in vain....Honor your father and your mother... (Exodus 20:7, 12, NKJV).

RULES OF CIVILITY: 109th Let your Recreations be Manfull not Sinfull.

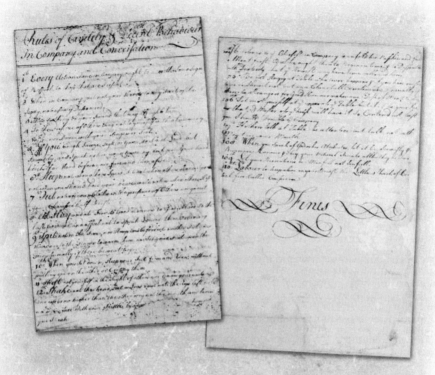

First and last pages of the Rules of Civility, Washington's rules for life.

Note: The 1828 dictionary of Noah Webster defines manful as "noble, honorable."

BIBLE: Flee also youthful lusts… (2 Timothy 2:22, NKJV).

RULES OF CIVILITY: 110th Labour to keep alive in your Breast that Little Spark of Ce[les]tial fire Called Conscience.

BIBLE: Now the purpose of the commandment is love from a pure heart, from a good conscience, and from sincere faith (1 Timothy 1:5, NKJV).

Many of these dignified principles can be summed up in Christ's golden rule: "Whatever you want men to do to you, do also to them." (Matthew 7:12). George Washington not only read the Golden Rule on the rerodos of the church in Alexandria, he quoted it on occasion.[45] These "Rules of Civility" speak volumes about the shaping of the character of George Washington. Marvin Kitman, notes of the "Rules of Civility:" "Those few hundred didactic words say as much about what makes the man tick as multi-volume biographies."[46]

THE YOUNG MAN'S COMPANION BOOK

Along with these most remarkable character values in the Appleby School and "Rules of Civility," there was another text that was a standard for English schoolboys throughout the late sixteen-hundreds to the end of the seventeen hundreds. These are the various editions of *The Young Man's Companion* textbooks. Grizzard refers to the 1727 edition by George Fisher, published in London, from which some of the lessons in Washington's papers were taken.[47] Joseph Sawyer mentions yet another *The Young Man's Companion* written by W. Mather in 1742 and published in England, which "was in its thirteenth edition when owned by Washington. He scrawled his name on the flyleaf of his copy, which is said to have been owned, a century later, by General Ulysses S. Grant. There is probably no copy of the book available in this country today—if anywhere."[48] We here consider passages from the text to appreciate what William Mather was trying to accomplish on behalf of his young masculine readers.

While each edition had its own unique content, there was a common message and spiritual continuity in the various editions. Mather's desire was to bring all sorts of useful knowledge to his young readers in the context of a devout Christian faith. William Mather's 1681 edition, for instance, is entitled *A Very Useful Manual or the Young Man's Companion*, and is 411 pages in length. It contains "plain and easy directions for spelling, reading, and uniting English with easy rules for their attaining to writing, and arithmetick, and the Englishing of the Latin Bible without a Tutor...." Mather writes "To the Reader" giving as his fourth point, "Those that desire to live and walk in the true Religion, must above all heed the outward Teachings, mind the Reproofs of the Spirit of Truth in their own Hearts against all Sin and Evil, otherwise they will turn to the Right Hand, or to the Left into evil. Isa. 30.20, 21, Gen. 6.3, John 3.19." He concludes his introduction by calling for his readers to bring glory to God and by adding this rhyme:

> Remember Man, that the Reproofs of Christ
> For Sin in the Conscience, is the way
> That leads to Life Eternal, if obeyed,
> The everlasting blessed Day.

"The Primer for Children," incorporated into the *Young Man's Companion*, gives about four examples per letter, several of which are important biblical or theological words, including: Chri-sti-a-ni-ty for C, Fel-low-ship for F, "Im-ma-nu-el" for I, and Pro-vi-dence for P. When Washington learned his ABCs, it was with biblical truths. He learned about "The Book of the Ge-ne-ra-ti-on of Je-sus Christ, the Son of Da-vid, the Son of A-bra-ham" as delineated in this textbook. On pages 11-19 there are "Hard Names in the Bible, and some others divided."

With this spiritual message, there are numerous mathematical problems with solutions and hints for solving various types of practical problems. Washington's childhood text also offers hints on measuring things, recommended cures for illnesses, astronomical observations, biblical teachings, insights on the meaning of parts of the *Book Of Common Prayer*, etc. Ultimately, Mathers summarizes his purpose:

> Now Reader, if thy desire is to be truly led to build upon no other Foundation besides the (Rock) Christ Jesus, mark well these Scriptures following, and the Lord give thee an obedient Heart, viz. For the wrath of God is revealed from heaven against all ungodliness and unrighteousness of men. . . .But unto every one of us is given Grace, according to the measure of the gift of Christ; for as many as are led by the Spirit of God, they are the Sons of God...."[49]

To fulfill his spiritual purpose, Mathers' *Young Man's Companion* incorporated:

> The Translation of the Holy Scriptures; The Prophesies of Christ in the Old Testament, fulfilled in the New; The Messiahs Types, Titles, Etc. the Education of Children: The duties of Families; The Mourner comforted for the Death of Friends, together with many other things, to encourage Young Men to the Love of Virtue, with a Table to find the Chiefest Matters herein; Written in a Plain and Easie stile, that a Young man (that lives in the Fear of the LORD) may Attain the same without a Tutor.[50]

Toward the end of his "Loving Epistle to the Young Man, my Reader" in this fifth edition, Mathers declares:

> The Instruction of Words is not so Powerful as the Exhortation of Works, for if they Teach well and neglect to do well, they shall hardly profit their hearers. . . . Let us declare and profess what we will, Men will judge of us after all by our Works. . . .So that it is a

Dishonour to God, a Scandal to Religion, and a cause why many become atheists that men are permitted to Preach and Teach the People, who are unsound in Morals, yea, guilty of some of the Evil above-mentioned.[51]

Mathers' emphasis clearly imparted one of the important principles of Washington's life—that deeds were more important than words.

The point to be seen in the review of Washington's childhood school texts is twofold. First, Washington's schoolbooks were designed to teach practical knowledge to be used in an active Christian life. Second, the theme made here by Mathers of the greater importance of conduct in comparison to words, particularly in leaders, was a theme that marked Washington's own life. His own declaration was "deeds not words."

The Young Man's Companion made it to America and was printed in New York in 1710, and in Philadelphia in 1718, with many other editions in the following years. Some of these versions of the classic text, such as the 1710 New York edition published by William and Andrew Bradford at the publishing house Bible in New York, added a section that contained "a choice collection of acquittances, bills, bonds, wills, indentures, deeds of sale, deeds of gift, letter of attorney, assignments, leases and releases…."

A portion of George's extant collected and existing school papers include the copying of such documents that would be needed by a young man who would often have to do business without the benefit of an attorney at hand.[52] Even these reveal the essentially Christian context of George's early education. One of the documents that George copied was the "Form of a Short Will." In his fine youthful hand, one finds these words written by twelve year old George Washington:

In the Name of God, Amen. The Sixth Day of Oct. In the year of our Lord, 1744, I, A.B. being Sick and Weak of Body but of Sound Judgment and Memory (thanks to God Therefore) Remembering the mortality of my body knowing that it is Determined for all men once to die, Doe make and ordain this my last Will and Testament, That is to say Principally and first of all I recommend my Soul to God Who gave it hoping for salvation in and through the merits and mediation of Jesus Christ, and my body to have buried in a decent manner at the [illegible]
Hoping at [illegible]
Power of God [illegible][53]

A copied will in Washington's hand from one of his manuscript books.
An often overlooked instance of Washington having written the name of Jesus Christ.

ADVICE TO SONS

One of the books that was apparently part of the Washington family training was entitled *Advice to a Son*[54] There is evidence that Martha Washington's first husband, Daniel Parke Custis, used this text. Thus, it is possible that this textbook may have been used by Jack Custis, George Washington's stepson, after Washington married Martha. In fact, there is written an historical note in it of a late-night, secret wedding in the wealthy, Anglican Custis family.[55] That event alone gave reason for the powerful "advice" needed for a young son! Its purpose was to give guidance for "conduct through the various and most important Encounters of this Life." This practical handbook addressed the issues of studies, love and marriage, travel, government and religion.[56] The book is relevant in understanding Washington's religion, in that it reflects the spiritual values and educational tradition that Martha Custis sought to impart to her children during her marriage with young Colonel Washington. The book, *Advice to a Son*, notes this:

> *Of Religion:* Read *the Book of God* with Reverence and in things doubtful take fixation from the *authority* of the *Church*, which cannot be arraigned of a damnable error without questioning that truth, which hath proclaimed her proof against *the gates of Hell.*[57]

The religion advocated by *Advice to a Son* is Protestant, with an emphasis upon a reasonable, biblical faith that respects the established churches and their clergy.

> You will find the Reformation most conformable to the duty we owe to God, and the Magistrate; if not too phlegmatic, in passing by decent Ceremonies, or too choleric and rigid, in obtruding upon weak and tender Consciences. And yet it was no unhappy ran counter in him that said, *A good Religion might be composed out of the Papists* Charity, *the Puritans* words, *and the Protestants* Faith.[58]

It also notes:

> Keep then your *Conscience* tender, but not so raw, as to wince and kick at all you understand not; Nor let it baffle your wit out of the bounds of Discretion, as such do that suffer themselves to be moped by it: to prevent which, keep *Reason* always in your eye; whose light

ought never to be lost in any worldly action, and but eclipsed in what relates to Heaven.[59]

Faith and reason were allies in the father's advice to the young English sons of Britain. In the chapter on "Washington and the Enlightenment," we will see that George Washington agreed.

CONTEMPLATIONS MORAL AND DIVINE

As important as the Bible and the *Book of Common Prayer* may have been for Mary Washington, she also used another historic text in the home education of her children, Sir Matthew Hale's *Contemplations, Moral & Divine*.[60] This

A book used by Washington's mother, Mary as a part of Washington's Christian education

is one of the volumes that George Washington had in his library, in fact bearing his bookplate. According to Joseph D. Sawyer and Benson J. Lossing, it had the signatures of both of Augustine Washington's wives, Jane Washington and Mary Washington. This implies that the book was part of the family training of both Lawrence and Augustine even before George was born.[61]

Author James K. Paulding describes this significant text that Mary Washington used in the education of her family.

> I have now before me a venerable volume, printed in the year 1685, entitled, *Contemplations, Moral and Divine*, by Sir Matthew Hale, late Chief-justice of the Court of King's Bench, in which is written, with her own hand, the name of "Mary Washington." It bears the appearance of frequent use, and particular chapters are designated by marks of reference. It is the volume from which the mother of Washington was accustomed to read daily lessons of piety, morality, and wisdom to her children.[62]

Paulding had received Hale's volume on loan from descendents of Washington who still occupied Mount Vernon in the mid-1850's, along with this correspondence:

> I beg it may be carefully preserved and returned, as one of the family heirlooms which better feelings than pride would retain for future generations to look on, even should they not study it. There

is something in a reverence for religion favourable to a virtuous character; and that reverence is in some measure kept alive by looking on a family Bible, and solid works of divinity, which have descended from past generations. We associate with them recollections of ancestral virtues, and when family tradition assures us they were the counselors of past days, there is a feeling of the heart which turns to them in time of trial, and makes it good, I think, to leave them an honourable station, as friends to those that have gone before, and those who shall come after us, to speak in the cause of truth when we shall sleep in the grave.[63]

Paulding proceeds to quote from Hale for several pages basing his citations in part on the apparent high use of the pages and how they reflect Washington himself.

I shall make some extracts from such portions of this book as appear to have been most used, not only because they contain the finest lessons of piety, morality, and wisdom, but most especially because I think the germ of Washington's character may be traced in the principles and practice they so eloquently inculcate. One of the chapters which appears to have been selected as an ordinary lesson, and marked for the purpose in the table of contents, is denominated "The Great Audit."[64]

One of the passages that Paulding selected from Hale certainly was the practice of Washington throughout his life. Hale writes:

When I undertook any place of power or eminence, first, I looked to my call thereunto to be such as I might discern to be thy call, not my own ambition. Second, that the place was such as might be answered by suitable abilities in some measure to perform. Third, that my end in it might not be the satisfaction of any pride, ambition, or vanity in myself, but to serve Providence and my generation honestly and faithfully.[65]

The reformational understanding of the Gospel as taught by the Chief-Justice[66] and read to the Washington family by Mary Washington is seen in this quote from Hale's chapter, "Of the Knowledge of Christ Crucified:"

> . . . It is easie to see what the Fruits and Effects of all this are. . . .
> Benefits that naturally arise from Christ Crucified, and are enjoyed
> in this life, are these: 1. *Justification* and Acceptation in the sight of
> God; he looks upon us as those that have satisfied his Justice when
> his Son suffered; and as those that performed his Will, when his Son
> performed it: So that as our Lord imputed our sins to our
> Redeemer, so he imputes his Righteousness unto us; and as he was
> well pleased with him, so he was well pleased in him, with as many
> as are received into this Covenant.[67]

Following the tradition of Augustine Washington's first wife, Mary Washington
continued to read great biblical truths to George and his brothers as taught by Sir
Matthew Hale. This tradition of reading sermons to the family continued in George
Washington's family, even when he had become President of the United States.[68]

CONCLUSION

What a man will become is in part due to his education and the books he reads.
George Washington was taught Christian concepts with the use of biblically-oriented
books. These books remained in his library until he died, and there is no evidence that
he threw these beliefs overboard as an older man, as some of his contemporaries did,
in favor of skeptical beliefs. Further, as we will see in the Churchman chapter,
Washington personally assimilated this childhood training and became a leader in the
Anglican Church tradition.
But more significantly, there
is not one written testimony
from Washington that he
ever left or rejected his educational and family training.
Thus, one aspect of the faith
of our founding father can be
clearly seen in his solidly
Christian education.

*Childhood doodles by Washington in his family's book on how to use the
Book of Common Prayer. He wrote his deceased father Augustine's name
and initials.*

EIGHT

The Personality of George Washington

"I consider it ... pitiful vanity to court applause from the pen or tongue of man; ...I believe it to be a proof of false modesty ... to appear altogether insensible to the commendations of the virtuous."[1]
George Washington, 1786

We shall continue to let Washington speak for himself regarding his religion, but we will now address his generally non-disclosing personality in the context of the moral commitments of his character that we have just explored. As we seek to understand Washington, who in many ways was truly a private man, we will next seek to engage the personality of the man himself. His high regard for personal privacy joined with his deep reluctance to speak of himself, have been misinterpreted by many to imply he did not have a Christian faith. We are persuaded by Washington's own self-revealing letters that, to interpret his personality in this way, we will never encounter the real Washington, the human being beneath the aura of glory and the warm-hearted man hidden within a persona of quarried stone.

DESCRIPTIONS OF WASHINGTON BY HIS CONTEMPORARIES

When we consider the momentous character of Washington and the praise he was given by his contemporaries, we can see why it has been difficult to understand him as a humble human being. How can we distinguish between the way his followers saw him and the way he saw himself?

In his book, *Washington on Washington*, Paul M. Zall writes:

> The difference may be inferred from passages that talk about himself in his own writings, both public and private. The public statements fit the Olympian image of Washington in the national memory. The private statements in his journals and letters sometimes reveal a different person—one who will overflow with romantic feelings or wallow in sentimentality or explode with spontaneous wit, even in the privacy of a diary.
>
> A quintessentially private person, Washington had a natural reluctance to express his feelings at all, a reluctance that was rein forced when his words were published to public scorn. He would be known by deeds, not words, but his written words remain to mirror him, often obliquely.
>
> The person and character of Washington did, of course, easily lend themselves to national deification. He was of the stuff of heroes. He even looked the way a hero should look—tall and handsome powerfully built and graceful. Jefferson said of him: "His person was fine, his stature exactly what one would wish, his deportment easy, erect and noble; the best horseman of his age, and the most graceful figure that could be seen on horseback."
>
> His sheer presence impressed everyone. Abigail Adams thought he had more grace and dignity than King George III.[2]

Even one of George Washington's slaves weighed in on the impact of his personality, as Washington biographer Saul Padover writes:

> And his Negro servant, recalling the twenty-seven-year-old
> Washington's marriage to Martha Custis, exclaimed that there was
> nobody, in that glitterin' wedding assemblage, like the young
> Colonel: "So tall, so straight! And . . . with such an air! Ah, sir, he

was like no one else! Many of the grandest gentlemen in their gold lace were at the wedding, but none looked like the man himself."[3]

To some degree, Washington made it difficult for people to know his personality, much less his own private beliefs. Benson Lossing writes, "It was a peculiar trait of his character to avoid everything, either in speech or writing, that had a personal relation to himself."[4]

More than thirty years after his death, Bishop William White wrote on Nov. 28, 1832, "I knew no man who so carefully guarded against the discoursing of himself, or of his acts, or of any thing that pertained to him; and it has occasionally occurred to me when in his company that, if a stranger to his person were present he would never have known from anything said by the President that he was conscious of having distinguished himself in the eye of the world. His ordinary behavior, although exceptionally courteous, was not such as to encourage obtrusion on what he had on his mind."[5]

In confirmation of this observation, Washington himself wrote: "Having been thus unwarily, and I may be permitted to add, almost unavoidably betrayed into a kind of necessity to speak of myself, and not wishing to resume that subject, I choose to close it forever by observing, that as, on the one hand, I consider it an indubitable mark of mean-spiritedness and pitiful vanity to court applause from the pen or tongue of man; so on the other, I believe it to be a proof of false modesty or an unworthy affectation of humility to appear altogether insensible to the commendations of the virtuous and enlightened part of our species."[6]

Thus, the historian has his work cut out for him to try and find the real George Washington. The man himself did not make it easy for us, nor was that his intention.

SHYNESS INTERPRETED AS ALOOFNESS

George Washington certainly carried himself with a reserved dignity. But his shyness was sometimes interpreted as aloofness. In a letter to French Ambassador, Eléonor Francois Élie, Washington apologized for the aloofness of the American people. On March 26, 1788, Washington wrote

> I have even hoped, from the short time of your residence here, and the partial acquaintance you may have had with the characters of the persons, that a natural distance in behavior and reserve in address, may have [not] appeared as intentional coldness and neglect. I am sensible that the apology itself, though it should be well founded,

would be but an indifferent one, yet it will be better than none: while it served to prove that it is our misfortune not to have the same chearfulness in appearance and facility in deportment, which some nations possess. And this I believe, in a certain degree, to be the real fact; and that such a reception is sometimes given by individuals as may affect a foreigner with very disagreeable Sensations, when not the least shadow of an affront is intended.[7]

George Washington was actually commenting in good measure on himself as well. Washington's apparent coldness left people with various reactions. A Mennonite minister from the Netherlands named Francis Adrian Van der Kemp found Mount Vernon, as did many visitors, to be a place "where simplicity, order, unadorned grandeur, and dignity, had taken up their abode," although he detected in his host "somewhat of a repulsive coldness under a courteous demeanour."[8] One visitor described Washington as "morose."[9] U. S. Senator William Maclay from Pennsylvania described the President as "pale, nay almost cadaverous."[10]

Washington's personal sense of decorum and the personal space of office and honor seems to have added to this impression of a cool relational aloofness. Benson Lossing relates a telling anecdote:

> It is related of the Honorable Gouverneur Morris who was remarkable for his freedom of deportment toward his friends, that on one occasion he offered a wager that he could treat General Washington with the same familiarity as he did others. This challenge was accepted, and the performance tried. Mr. Morris slapped Washington familiarly on the shoulder, and said, "How are you, this morning, general?" Washington made no reply, but turned his eyes upon Mr. Morris with a glance that fairly withered him. He afterward acknowledged, that nothing could induce him to attempt the same thing again.[11]

A spiritual variation on the theme of Washington's coolness is seen in the writings of Thomas Coke and Francis Asbury. These two founding Methodist clergymen in America paid a visit to Washington seeking support for their anti-slavery petition.[12] Asbury's record of the May 26, 1785, visit simply said, "We waited on General Washington, who received us very politely, and gave us his opinion against slavery."[13]

But Coke's journal included a more substantial description of their visit,

> The general's seat is very elegant, built upon the great river Potomawk;…He received us very politely, and was very open to access. He is quite the plain country gentleman and he is a friend to mankind. After dinner we desired a private interview, and opened to him the grand business on which we came, presenting to him our petition for the emancipation of the negroes, and intreating his signature, if the eminence of his station did not render it inexpedient for him to sign any petition. He informed us that he was of our sentiments, and had signified his thought on the subject to most of the great men of the State: that he did not see it proper to sign the petition, but if the Assembly took it into consideration, would signify his sentiments to the Assembly by a letter. He asked us to spend the evening and lodge at his house, but our engagement at Annapolis the following day, would not admit of it. I was loth to leave him, for I greatly love and esteem him and if there was no pride in it, would say that we are kindred Spirits, formed in the same mould. O that God would give him the witness of his Spirit!"[14]

Washington's impact on Coke was positive, yet even with Coke's sense of a personal "kindred spirit" with Washington, he left praying for Washington's reception of "the witness of the Spirit." However, by the time of Washington's presidency and later at his death, these founding bishops of the American branch of the Methodist Church viewed Washington as a Christian. Asbury's words at Washington's death were, "Matchless man! At all times he acknowledged the providence of God, and never was he ashamed of his Redeemer. We believe he died not fearing death."[15]

George Washington's leadership style normally maintained a distance that forbade a familiar intimacy or a transparent disclosing of his thoughts or feelings. Yet his reserve in interpersonal relationships did not translate into an arrogant or haughty spirit. Instead, he was also known for his humility

HUMILITY

Washington's humility is reflected in Zall's description of how on one occasion as he was on his way to Mt. Vernon, he was caught in a heavy rainfall. The drenching rain forced him to leave his horse and take a "common stage." Zall writes, "When the coach stopped at a tavern the innkeeper invited the General to the private parlor, but Washington protested: 'No, no. It is customary for the people who travel in this stage always to eat together. I will not desert my companions.'"[16] What is captured in this anecdote is evident in Washington's words as well.

When George Washington was offered the position of commander in chief of the Army of America, he felt unworthy of the task, and he said so. Here is a portion of his speech to the Continental Congress on June 16, 1775:

> Mr. President,
>
> Though I am truly sensible of the high honor done me in this appointment, yet I feel great distress from a consciousness that my abilities and military experience may not be equal to the extensive and important trust. However, as the Congress desire it, I will enter upon the momentous duty and exert every power I possess in the service and for support of the glorious cause. I beg they will accept my most cordial thanks for this distinguished testimony of their approbation. But lest some unlucky event should happen unfavourable to my reputation, I beg it may be remembered by every gentleman in the room, that I this day declare with the utmost sincerity I do not think myself equal to the command I am honored with.
>
> As to pay, Sir, I beg leave to assure the Congress, that as no pecuniary consideration could have tempted me to accept this arduous employment at the expense of my domestic ease and happiness, I do not wish to make any profit from it. I will keep an exact account of my expenses. Those I doubt not they will discharge, and that is all I desire.[17]

He was willing to be reimbursed for his expenses, but he was not willing to receive pay.[18] He expressed his feeling that he was not worthy of the task, but if Congress felt he could lead effectively, he felt honored. He wrote a letter to Martha around that time expressing similar thoughts and also mentioning that he would trust in God to see him through.[19]

About a year and a half later, he explained to Congress: "I have no lust after power but wish with as much fervency as any Man upon this wide extended Continent, for an opportunity of turning the Sword into a plow share."[20] Communicating this same humility, he wrote to his brother Augustine:

> I am now to bid adieu to you, and to every kind of domestic ease, for a while. I am embarked on a wide ocean, boundless in its prospect, and in which, perhaps, no safe harbor is to be found. I have been called upon by the unanimous voice of the Colonies to take the command of the continental army; an honor I have neither sought after, nor desired, as I am thoroughly convinced that it requires greater abilities and much more experience, than I am master of, to conduct a business so extensive in its nature and arduous in its execution. But the partiality of the Congress, joined to a political motive, really left me without a choice; and I am now commissioned a General and Commander-in-Chief of all the forces now raised, or to be raised, for the defense of the United Colonies. That I may discharge the trust to the satisfaction of my employers, is my first wish; that I shall aim to do it, there remains as little doubt of. How far I shall succeed, is another point; but this I am sure of, that, in the worst event, I shall have the consolation of knowing, if I act to the best of my judgment, that the blame ought to lodge upon the appointers, not the appointed, as it was by no means a thing of my seeking, or proceeding from any hint of my friends. I shall hope that my friends will visit and endeavor to keep up the spirits of my wife, as much as they can, as my departure will, I know, be a cutting stroke upon her;[21]

By coupling humility with a sense of official distance, Washington carried himself with what could be called a reserved dignity.

RESERVED DIGNITY

George Washington had a commanding presence that left many with a sense of awe. Zall describes the impact he had on those who knew him or observed him: "Thomas Jefferson said that Washington hated the ceremony of the office but played up to the public's expectations of it. John Adams called Washington 'the best actor of presidency we have ever had.'"[22] In other words, being president called on one to act in a dignified manner—to Adams, George Washington played the part better than anyone. Abigail Adams marveled at the way he could balance the opposite and discordant 'dignity that forbids familiarity' with the 'easy affinity which creates Love and Reverence.' Even British observers wondered at this Socratic art of 'concealing his own sentiments and of discovering those of other men.'"[23]

His impact was felt even on those who did not like him or what he stood for. Zall explains: "Even cynics marveled at his bearing. His natural dignity defied description. Sir James Bland Burges saw him as 'cold, reserved, and even phlegmatic without the least appearance of haughtiness or ill nature,' with an odd compound of pride and 'constitutional diffidence.'"[24]

Washington was even concerned for a balance of humility and honor in his appearance. This is seen as he began to prepare a new American Army to defend the nation in the event of a French invasion in the aftermath of the French Revolution. When the then retired president was asked about his new uniform, he noted, in a letter to James McHenry on January 27, 1799:

> On reconsidering the uniform for the Commander-in-Chief as it respects myself personally, I was against all embroidery."[25] [Similarly, Washington wrote to his nephew and spoke about the dangers of vanity as seen in showing off expensive clothing:] "Do not conceive that fine clothes make fine men any more than fine feathers make fine birds. A plain genteel dress is more admired, and obtains more credit than lace and embroidery, in the Eyes of the judicious and sensible.[26]

A spirit of humility had marked his life from early on. The agent who oversaw his business dealings in London in 1758 once incorrectly called him "ye Honorable." Washington promptly corrected and clarified the potentially flattering bestowal of a prestigious title: "You are pleased to dub me with a title I have no pretensions to—that is, ye Honorable."[27] Washington would not rest in mere words. If he was to be "ye honorable" his deeds, not words alone, would have to prove it so.

DEEDS, NOT WORDS

One of the best ways to interpret George Washington's life is to understand his philosophy of "deeds, not words". Nelly Custis, Washington's adopted granddaughter, said, "His mottoes were, 'Deeds, Not Words'; and 'For God and My Country.'"[28] For example, he wrote Major General John Sullivan on December 15, 1779:

> A slender acquaintance with the world must convince every man, that actions, not words, are the true criterion of the attachment of his friends, and that the most liberal professions of good will are very far from being the surest marks of it.[29]

Washington wrote to Patrick Henry on January 15, 1799: "The views of men can only be known, or guessed at, by their words or actions."[30] Accordingly, he utilized the power of symbolic actions. At the beginning of the Battle of Yorktown, he dug with his own hands into the soil of Yorktown to signify the start of the siege, and once both French and American cannons were in place, he fired the first round. He underscored his written orders by powerful and meaningful visible actions to inspire his men.

Thus, George Washington preferred to be known as a man of "deeds not words." Writing to James Anderson on December 21, 1797, he explained,

> If a person only sees, or directs from day to day what is to be done, business can never go on methodically or well, for in case of sickness, or the absence of the Director, delays must follow. System to all things is the soul of business. To deliberate maturely, and execute promptly is the way to conduct it to advantage. With me, it has always been a maxim, rather to let my designs appear from my works than by my expressions.[31]

Even the words of the motto found on the Washington family's historic British Coat of Arms, *"Exitus Acta Probat"*, when translated from Latin means "The end proves the deed."[32] The Washington heritage emphasized actions rather than words.

We must interpret George Washington on his own terms. To insist that only his written words will give him meaning is to deny the very motivation of his own conduct—actions spoke louder than words. It is important for the debate we pursue in this book to underscore that Washington never declared himself to be a Deist, and he did declare himself to be a Christian. But, as critical as this is,

Washington's book plate bearing the family coat of arms, his motto, "the end proves the deed," and a foreshadowing of the American Flag of stars and stripes

Washington's actions were intended to speak louder than his words. Accordingly,

throughout this book, we will demonstrate his Christian worship, his Christian prayers, his other Christian actions, alongside the words of his writings that also reflect the presence of numerous Christian ideas.

EXPERIENCES THAT TAUGHT WASHINGTON TO GUARD HIS WORDS

It may be that part of Washington's reticence to express his own feelings is that he was "gun shy," so to speak. Apparently, he had recklessly expressed his feelings as a young man, and these expressions came back to haunt him. Two incidents in the 1750s, in particular, come to mind. The first was a hasty signing of a poorly translated agreement of surrender with the French at Fort Necessity, by which Washington unwittingly and incorrectly admitted to having assassinated a French ambassador.[33]

The second incident occurred in this same context. Compounding this misstep (or intentional French deception) during his surrender, Washington sent his brother a letter celebrating the delights of battle: "I heard Bullets whistle and believe me there was something charming in the sound."[34] The French intercepted the letter and subsequently published it throughout the Western world. The remark, when eventually read by British King George II (father of George III), caused him to remark, "He would not say so, if he had been used to hear many."[35] Twenty years later, in 1775, when someone asked if he had actually made that foolish statement, Washington answered, "If I said so, it was when I was young."[36]

Another reason for silence on personal matters was that letters in that day were unreliable and liable to miscarriage, interception, misuse and sometimes, such as in times of war, were even subject to being replaced with spurious letters. Washington was the target of spurious letters and on occasion had to refute them.[37] Along with the obvious reason of preserving their cherished privacy after a very public life, this may have been part of the reason Martha burned their letters after George's death. At any rate, painful personal experiences seem to have helped seal Washington's lips when he was tempted to speak of himself.

WISE ABOUT HISTORY; UNCONCERNED ABOUT LEGACY

Again and again, Washington showed himself to be more of a man of action than words. Yet the lessons of the past mattered to him. He wrote to Major General John Armstrong, March 26, 1781: "We ought not to look back, unless it is to derive useful lessons from past errors, and for the purpose of profiting by dear bought experience. To inveigh against things that are past and irremediable, is unpleasing; but to steer clear of the shelves and rocks we have struck upon, is the part of wisdom."[38] But he did not want to talk about himself. In a letter to his lifelong personal friend and favorite physician, Dr. James Craik, March 25, 1784:

> I will frankly declare to you, my dear doctor, that any memoirs of my life, distinct and unconnected with the general history of the war, would rather hurt my feelings than tickle my pride whilst I lived. I had rather glide gently down the stream of life, leaving it to posterity to think and say what they please of me, than by any act of mine to have vanity or ostentation imputed to me. I do not think vanity is a trait of my character.[39]

In his past as well as in his future conduct, he strove to avoid vanity. In a letter to James Madison, written from Mount Vernon, May 20, 1792, he pointed out that given the existing political divisions, it would be best for the country for him to run for president again, but that he was not seeking reelection for vanity's sake, but for the good of the nation. He hoped no one would misinterpret his motives:

> Nothing short of conviction that my deriliction of the Chair of Government (if it should be the desire of the people to continue me in it) would involve the Country in serious disputes respecting the chief Magestrate, and the disagreeable consequences which might result there from in the floating, and divided opinions which seem to prevail at present, could, in any wise, induce me to relinquish the determination I have formed: and of this I do not see how any evidence can be obtained previous to the Election. My vanity, I am sure, is not of that cast as to allow me to view the subject in this light.
>
> ....In revolving this subject myself, my judgment has always been embarrassed. On the one hand, a previous declaration to retire, not only carries with it the appearance of vanity and self importance, but it may be construed into a manoeuvre to be invited to remain. And on the other hand, to say nothing, implys consent; or, at any rate, would leave the matter in doubt, and to decline afterwards might be deemed as bad, and uncandid.[40]

When he wrestled with the question of becoming the president for the first time at Mount Vernon, one of his favorite military aids had been staying with the Washingtons. David Humphreys became the president's confidant in those interesting days, and in his unfinished biography, he preserved some of the discussions that the two had about Washington's pending history making decision. Out of this trust, Humphreys was given Washington's go ahead to work on his biography, a project he never finished.[41]

HIS OFFICIAL BIOGRAPHY?

He also pointed out that he neither had the time—nor the literary skills—to write up a memoir about his war experience. Below is a comment he made in a letter to David Humphreys, the only man Washington would trust to write a biography of him, dated July 25, 1785:

> If I had the talents for it, I have not leisure to turn my thoughts to Commentaries [on the Revolutionary War]. A consciousness of a defective education, and a certainty of the want of time, unfit me for such an undertaking.[42]

Unfortunately, Humphreys did not finish the task before his death. Yet, of the several chapters he wrote, some of them have been found recently and have been used in our study of Washington.

Meanwhile, Washington perhaps had a little fear about even Humphreys' undertaking such a task, because he did not want to be unduly praised. The retiring president wrote his French friend, Marquis de Chastellux:

> Humphreys (who has been some weeks at Mount Vernon) confirm'd me in the sentiment by giving a most flattering account of the whole performance: he has also put into my hands the translation of that part in which you say such, and so many hand some things of me; that (altho' no sceptic on ordinary occasions) I may perhaps be allowed to doubt whether your friendship and partiality have not, in this one instance, acquired an ascendency over your cooler judgment.[43]

A significant aspect of this letter is Washington's parenthetical aside: "altho' no sceptic on ordinary occasions." His temperament was not normally marked by doubt. Although not a skeptic, and thus not of a temperament that would dispose him to philosophical doubt and unbelief, this does not mean that Washington was a stoic who could not laugh or enjoy the humor of life.

SENSE OF HUMOR

George Washington is often portrayed as if he did not have a sense of humor but that too is inaccurate. As Zall says:

> Just as credible, because evident also in his writings, Washington's stony countenance could dissolve before "an unaffected sally of wit." Congress excused its failure to provide funds because treasurer Robert Morris had his hands full. Washington replied that he wised Morris had his pockets full. When Mrs. Washington chided him for saying grace before dinner with a clergyman at the table, Washington pardoned himself: "The reverend gentleman will at least be assured that at Mount Vernon we are not entirely graceless.[44]

And Zall writes further:

> Natural versus contrived wit bubbles up in writing meant for his eyes only. . . .His diary has such entries as the one recording a Sunday service in York, Pennsylvania. The town lacked an Episcopalian preacher, so Washington attended a Pennsylvania Dutch Reformed church. Since the service was in German and he had understood not a word, he reassured the diary, he had not been converted.[45]

Occasionally Washington even indulged in a bit of sarcasm in the privacy of his diary. He once commented on two sermons he heard while traveling, "I attended Morning & evening Service, and heard very lame discourses from a Mr. Pond."[46] He also critiqued the meager refreshments and decorations of a ball in Alexandria. His diary dubbed it the "bread and butter ball."[47] Zall notes another example of such sarcastic humor, this time aimed at himself:

> Private correspondence also reveals the Washington wit. Former neighbor Eliza Power writes from Philadelphia that the desk he had left behind had a secret drawer containing love letters. He replied

that if she had found warmth in those letters, she must have set them afire.[48]

More than a century before Mark Twain quipped "the reports of my death are greatly exaggerated," Washington noted that the word of his death was premature. After a battle during the French and Indian War, where Washington survived a massacre, he wrote his brother, John Augustine, July 18, 1755:

> Dear Brother, As I have heard, since my arrival at this place, a circumstantial account of my death and dying speech, I take this early opportunity of contradicting the first, and of assuring you, that I have not as yet composed the latter.[49]

Washington's humor could express itself with playful parody of religious themes[50] or in simply giving a description of his daily life.[51]

DEEP PASSIONS UNDER DISCIPLINED CONTROL

Zall writes of an incident after the War where Washington allowed his normally well-concealed emotions to be visible to his brothers-in-arms. At the war's end, he bid farewell to officers in New York. Impulsively, he embraced each one by rank, from rotund Henry Knox on down, while "tears of deep sensibility filled every eye."[52]

> An emotional man at bottom, Washington, the seemingly frosty hero, was capable of the grand, dramatic gesture. His farewell to these officers, on December 4, 1783, at Fraunces' Tavern in New York, was a scene out of a classic play. Standing before the men he had commanded for eight perilous and finally triumphant years, his customary self-control deserted him. Tears filled his eyes as he stood up, filled a glass with a shaking hand, and said in a trembling voice: "I cannot come to each of you to take my leave, but shall be obliged if you will each come and shake me by the hand." Silently they lined up and shook his hand. Then he returned home to Mount Vernon, journeying through communities that moved him deeply with their outpourings of homage, determined to retire from public life. He had started his military career more than thirty years back, and now that he had won independence for his country the

American Cincinnatus, as the newspapers and the orators called him, felt that he merited retirement to the plow. He was only fifty-one and, as he wrote to his friend Lafayette, his sole desire was to be a private citizen, sitting under his "own vine and fig-tree" and "move gently down the stream of life until I sleep with my fathers."[53]

The most open expression of Washington's deep emotions appeared in his General Orders of April 18, 1783, when he publicly declared the ending of hostilities:

> ...Although the proclamation before alluded to, extends only to the prohibition of hostilities and not to the annunciation of a general peace, yet it must afford the most rational and sincere satisfaction to every benevolent mind, as it puts a period to a long and doubtful contest, stops the effusion of human blood, opens the prospect to a more splendid scene, and like another morning star, promises the approach of a brighter day than hath hitherto illuminated the Western Hemisphere; on such a happy day, a day which is the harbinger of Peace, a day which compleats the eighth year of the war, it would be ingratitude not to rejoice! it would be insensibility not to participate in the general felicity.
>
> The Commander in Chief far from endeavouring to stifle the feelings of Joy in his own bosom, offers his most cordial Congratulations on the occasion to all the Officers of every denomination, to all the Troops of the United States in General, and in particular to those gallant and persevering men who had resolved to defend the rights of their invaded country so long as the war should continue. For these are the men who ought to be considered as the pride and boast of the American Army; And, who crowned with well earned laurels, may soon withdraw from the field of Glory, to the more tranquil walks of civil life.
>
> While the General recollects the almost infinite variety of Scenes thro which we have passed, with a mixture of pleasure, astonishment, and gratitude; While he contemplates the prospects before us with rapture; he can not help wishing that all the brave men (of whatever condition they may be) who have shared in the toils and dangers of effecting this glorious revolution, of rescuing

Millions from the hand of oppression, and of laying the foundation of a great Empire, might be impressed with a proper idea of the [dignifyed] part they have been called to act (under the Smiles of providence) on the stage of human affairs: for, happy, thrice happy shall they be pronounced hereafter, who have contributed any thing, who have performed the meanest office in erecting this [steubendous] *fabrick* of *Freedom* and *Empire* on the broad basis of [Indipendency] who have assisted in protecting the rights of humane nature and establishing an Asylum for the poor and oppressed of all nations and religions. The glorius task for which we first fleu to Arms being thus accomplished, the liberties of our Country being fully acknowledged, and firmly secured by the smiles of heaven, on the purity of our cause, and the honest exertions of a feeble people (determined to be free) against a powerful Nation (disposed to oppress them) and the Character of those who have persevered, through every extremity of hardship; suffering and danger being immortalized by the illustrious appellation of the *patriot Army*: Nothing now remains but for the actors of this mighty Scene to preserve a perfect, unvarying, consistency of character through the very last act;[54]

And so the very next day, April 19th, "At noon the proclamation of Congress for a cessation of hostilities was proclaimed at the door of the New Building, followed by three huzzas; after which a prayer was made by the Reverend Mr. Ganno, and an anthem (*Independence*, from Billings,) was performed by vocal and instrumental music."[55]

Because Washington understood the power of human passions he could write: "We must take the passions of men as nature has given them, and those principles as a guide, which are generally the rule of action."[56] He ably answered the passions of his distressed and weary officers as they wrestled with the emotions of a military confrontation with Congress.[57]

HIS EFFORTS TO CONTROL HIS POWERFUL ANGER[58]

To put the word "rapture" and George Washington in the same sentence seems nearly impossible. But still waters run deep, and sometimes they burst forth with tsunami-like force. Washington biographer, John Ferling noted, "Gilbert Stuart, an artist whose livelihood depended in part on his ability to capture the true essence of his subjects, believed Washington's 'features were indicative of the strongest and most ungovernable passions. Had he been born in the forests,' Stuart added, 'he would have been the fiercest man among the savages.'"[59] Zall writes,

> His dignity and self-esteem were such that to a superficial observer he appeared to be cold. Actually he was emotional, tender, and capable of outbursts of violence. An iron discipline, which he imposed upon himself all his life, kept a leash on his passions. "All the muscles of his face," Captain George Mercer, a fellow-soldier, wrote of him "[are] under perfect control, though flexible and expressive of deep feeling when moved by emotion." His infrequent outburst of anger were legendary. On the occasions when his rigid self-control broke under stress, he was, according to a contemporary, "most tremendous in his wrath."[60]

The explosion of joy at the ending of hostilities mentioned above, near the end of the war, reveals Washington's powerful inner passions as well as his ongoing efforts to control them. But so do his infrequent explosions of anger. The fact that George Washington was "tremendous in his wrath" was confirmed by various associates. Lafayette's recollection of Washington's response to General Lee's violation of his orders at the Battle of Monmouth is a case in point.[61] A fellow Virginian, General Lee, disobeyed orders and called for a retreat, for which he was court-martialed. Lee remained a bitter critic of Washington to his death.[62]

Washington's signature evolved through the years.

Other occasions are worthy of note. Zall writes of an incident where President Washington had been criticized in several newspapers hostile to the cause. Thomas Jefferson related, "The presdt . . . got into one of those passions when he cannot command himself, ran on much on the personal abuse which had been bestowed on him, defied any man on earth to produce one single act of his since he had been in the govmt which was not done in the purest motives, that he had never repented but once the having slipped the moment of resigning his office, and that was every moment since, that by god he had rather be on his farm than be made *emperor of the world*, and yet they were charging him with wanting to be a king."[63] Further, the criticism of an old friend, Edmund Randolph, in print, tested Washington's temper: "The president entered the parlor, his face 'dark and lowering.' Someone asked if he had read Randolph's pamphlet, *Vindication* (1795). 'I have,' said Washington, 'and, by the eternal God, he is the damnedest liar on the face of the earth!' he exclaimed as he slammed his fist down upon the table."[64]

A similar passionate outburst of exasperation and anger occurred when Washington was president in 1791, and quietly received word at dinner of St. Clair's defeat by the Indians. According to Tobias Lear, Washington's personal assistant, the emotionally intense episode happened after all the guests, as well as Mrs. Washington, had left the room. He relates,

> The General now walked backward and forward slowly for some minutes without speaking. Then he sat down on a sofa by the fire, telling Mr. Lear to sit down. To this moment there had been no change in his manner since his interruption at table. Mr. Lear now perceived emotion. This rising in him, he broke out suddenly: "It's all over—St. Clair's defeated, routed; the officers nearly all killed, the men by wholesale; the rout complete—too shocking to think of— and a surprise into the bargain!" He uttered all this with great vehemence, then he paused, got up from the sofa and walked about the room several times, agitated, but saying nothing. Near the door he stopped short and stood still for a few seconds, when his wrath became terrible. "Yes," he burst forth, "Here, on this very spot, I took leave of him: I wished him success and honor. 'You have your instruction,' I said, 'from the Secretary of War; I had a strict eye to them, and will add but one word—BEWARE OF A SURPRISE! I repeat it, BEWARE OF A SURPRISE; you know how the Indians fight us.' He went off with that as my last solemn warning thrown into his ears. And yet! To suffer that army to be cut to pieces, hacked, butchered, tomahawked, by a surprise—the very thing I guarded him against! O God, O God, he's worse than a murderer!

How can he answer it to his country? The blood of the slain is upon him—the curse of the widows and orphans—the curse of Heaven!"[65]

A TENDER-HEARTED FRIEND

As a young man, George Washington expressed his joy in friendship and admitted to the power of passion. Both of these occurred in an early letter describing a teenage romance, and his "chaste" struggles to control his "passion." Writing to "dear friend Robin" between 1749-1750 he divulges:

> As it's the greatest mark of friendship and esteem Absent Friends can shew each other in Writing and often communicating their thoughts to his fellow Companions makes me endeavor to signalize myself in acquainting you from time to time and at all times my situation and employments of Life and could wish you would take half the Pains of contriving me a letter by any opportunity as you may be well assured of its meeting with a very welcome reception. My place of Residence is at present at His Lordship's [Fairfax]

This painting by John Ward Dunsmore illustrates good friends
Washington and Lafayette reviewing the encampment at Valley Forge

where I might, was my heart disengaged, pass my time very pleasantly as there's a very agreeable Young Lady Lives in the same house [Mary Cary]. But as that's only adding Fuel to fire, it makes me the more uneasy, for by often, and unavoidably, being in Company with her revives my former Passion for your Low Land Beauty; whereas, was I to live more retired from young Women, I might in some measure alleviate my sorrows, by burying that chaste and troublesome passion in the grave of oblivion or eternal forgetfulness, for as I am very well assured, that's the only antidote or remedy that I shall be relieved by or only recess that can administer any cure or help to me, as I am well convinced, was I ever to attempt anything, I should only get a denial which would be only adding grief to uneasiness.[66]

Friendships mattered to Washington. His inner self was reserved for those who were closest to him. These individuals sometimes received very striking personal revelations in his letters. Moreover, to be his friend was to experience sincere affection, a warm welcome and a hearty embrace. But to become Washington's friend was no easy matter. This seems to reflect his classic "Rules of Civility" number fifty-six that speaks of exercising great care in choosing friends: "Associate yourself with men of good quality, if you esteem your own reputation; for it is better to be alone than in bad company." How to choose a friend was one of the matters of wisdom he sought to impart to his young namesake and adopted grandson, George Washington Parke Custis. Writing from Philadelphia on November 28, 1796, he counseled,

...select the most deserving only for your friendships, and before this becomes intimate, weigh their dispositions and character well. True friendship is a plant of slow growth; to be sincere, there must be a congeniality of temper and pursuits. Virtue and vice can not be allied; nor can idleness and industry....[67]

But when an intimate friendship was established, Washington allowed his closest friends to experience his deep emotions through open and generous expressions of love. Lifelong friendships were made by Washington with neighbors such as Scotch-Irish Presbyterian Dr. James Craik[68] and the Anglican/Episcopalian clergyman, the Reverend Lord Bryan Fairfax.[69] In Washington's adult life, close friendships formed within the circle of his fellow military officers Marquis de Lafayette,[70] Comte Rochambeau,[71] Marquis de Chastellux,[72] Baron Von Steuben,[73] Comte DeGrasse,[74] military aide David Humphreys,[75] Colonel Alexander Hamilton,[76] and General Henry Knox.[77] There was, however, an especially tender place in Washington's heart for the Marquis de Lafayette. Consider these endearing words of affirmation in his letters to his twenty-five-year-younger, surrogate son:

> ...the sincere and heartfelt pleasure that you had not only regained your liberty; but were in the enjoyment of better health than could have been expected from your long and rigorous confinement; and that madame La Fayette and the young ladies were able to Survive ...amongst your numerous friends none can offer his congratulations with more warmth, or who prays more sincerely for the perfect restoration of your ladies health, than I do.[78]

Washington's cool yet gracious countenance was the necessary firewall to contain and to protect his passionate heart.

CONCLUSION: THE LANGUAGE OF WASHINGTON'S HEART

Just as there are largely unknown statements of faith etched on the stairway walls of the Washington Monument as one mounts the stairs to the pinnacle, so inside the marble-like exterior of Washington there was a largely unknown heart of deep feelings, strong emotions, and a reverent personal faith. As he wrote from New York, just at the end of the War to the freeholders and inhabitants of Kings County on December 1, 1783, "...you speak the language of my heart, in acknowledging the magnitude of our obligations to the Supreme Director of all human events."[79] Just as access to the stairs of the monument is restricted, precluding the average American from reading the marvelous testimonials to the faith etched there, so too, many modern historians have cut off access to the real Washington. This book will reopen the stairs, so to speak, to Washington's soul and we will once again read the language of his heart etched throughout his life, which was the language of a deep faith, expressed by a devout Christian in the eighteenth century Anglican tradition. Indeed, the language of Washington's heart was warmed by his passionate soul and the "sacred fire of liberty."

NINE

George Washington the Soldier

"The General hopes and trusts, that every officer and man,
will endeavour so to live, and act, as becomes a Christian Soldier
defending the dearest Rights and Liberties of his country."
George Washington, General Orders, July 9, 1776 [1]

George Washington first secured his place in history as a military leader. From childhood, he had set his sights on a military career. He entered into the Virginia militia as a young adult, and in the midst of struggles over promotion and rank, he affirmed that his "inclinations" were "strongly bent to arms."[2]

His superb leadership, honed from his earliest years in the French and Indian War and perfected when he assumed command in the Revolutionary War, enabled him to ultimately win. But victory was not usually in sight, since he was greatly undersupplied, usually outmanned or outgunned and sometimes outmaneuvered. But Washington had his moments of triumph as well.[3] In this chapter that focuses on George Washington's military career, we discover the early development of his lifelong deep faith in God's powerful Providence, as we find him on duty in the backwoods of Pennsylvania.

WASHINGTON ON DUTY IN THE WILDERNESS OF PENNSYLVANIA

Washington had traveled the Virginian wilderness into the Allegheny Mountains in his work as a sixteen-year-old surveyor for Lord Fairfax. Given his experience, as well as his keen interest in military service, in 1753, Virginia Gov. Dinwiddie gave the then twenty-one-year-old Washington the extraordinary task of trekking across the vast unopened mountainous reaches of what is today the state of Pennsylvania.[4] His mission was to travel to Fort Le Boeuf near modern-day Erie, Pennsylvania, to tell the French military stationed there that they were trespassing on British land, and that they would need to leave. Some have speculated that young George was also willing to go because he was running from a broken heart.[5]

Washington arrived at the Fort on December 11th, having left on October 31st. He soon learned that the French commander St. Pierre had no intention of leaving. He said, "I am here by virtue of the orders of my general, and I entreat you, sir, not to doubt one moment that I am determined to conform myself to them with all the exactness and resolution which can be expected from the best officers."[6] Washington left to carry that news back to Dinwiddie. His return journey however, encountered many dire circumstances, which he narrowly escaped. These included being spared death from an Indian who fired his gun and missed at only fifteen paces away; surviving a near drowning in an ice-swollen river when he was thrown off a makeshift raft; and hiking his way back on foot, since his horse had nearly starved to death on the long, hungry ride, even before facing the cold winter return trip.

A theological book that George Washington owned and signed as a young adult

Washington was sent back to the Fort with troops in 1754, and the first fire under Washington's military command occurred, as well as the first casualties of what was to become the French and Indian War. A surprise attack on a hidden French encampment resulted in ten killed, including the death of Monsieur De Jumonville (the commanding officer), one wounded, and twenty-one prisoners. Ever after this event, the French claimed that Washington was guilty of assassinating an ambassador, while the British claimed that Washington's troops were simply protecting English land against the French intruders and spies. Regardless, Washington's small band retreated, expecting a much larger assault from troops garrisoned at Fort Duquesne, the site of modern day Pittsburgh. The retreat also gave Washington's men time to build Fort Necessity at Great Meadows. Here Washington's soldiers gave a hearty defense until they surrendered before a much larger French force. The surrender was necessitated, in part, due to their rain-soaked weapons and dampened gunpowder. But they negotiated surrender with what Washington believed to be terms of honor. However, when Washington signed the capitulation, due to his limited knowledge of French, he unwittingly signed a paper that declared he had *assassinated* Jumonville.[7] A painful lesson indeed for the young Washington.

WASHINGTON'S LESSON ON PROVIDENCE: SURVIVING A MASSACRE

Today, it is a little known fact that when George Washington was twenty-three, he very easily could have died in a bloody battle that was more of a massacre than a battle. It took place on July 9, 1755, just a year after his surrender at Fort Necessity.

When Jumonville was killed, Washington had, in essence, fired the first shot in what became the French and Indian War. The British continued their defense of their claim on the land north of Florida and south of Canada, from the Atlantic coast to the Mississippi River. From their perspective, the French troops in western Pennsylvania were encroaching on that claim. The Indians were caught in the middle. Some sided with the French, and some with the British. The French and Indian War, pitting England against France, eventually raged over two continents. By the end, Great Britain had won, and France had to withdraw some of its claims in North America. After the War, Great Britain decided to saddle the American colonists with the bill for what they viewed as their defense of America. In 1765, the British Ministry imposed the infamous Stamp Act on America, which Washington criticized as a foolish decision.[8] This and other subsequent new taxes had not been voted on by the colonies. By such taxation without representation,[9] the British put in motion the events that would eventually ignite the American Revolution and result in the loss of their American colonies.[10]

Nineteenth century British author William Thackeray noted Washington's unique role and the irony of all these events:

> It was strange that in a savage forest of Pennsylvania, a young Virginian officer should fire a shot, and waken a war which was to last for 60 years, which was to cover his own country and pass into Europe, to cost France her American colonies, to sever ours from us,

and create the great western republic; to rage over the old world when extinguished in the new; and, of all the myriads engaged in the vast contest, to leave the prize of the greatest fame to him who struck the first blow.[11]

SPARED BY PROVIDENCE

George Washington's life was especially in danger in a couple of instances during the French and Indian War. For example, Washington wrote to his friend and biographer, David Humphreys, of an incident where he was almost killed by "friendly fire":

.... during the time the Army lay at Loyal Hanning, a circumstance occurred which involved the life of George Washington in as much jeopardy as it had ever been before or since. The enemy sent out a large detachment to Reconnoiter our Camp, and to ascertain our strength; in consequence of Intelligence that they were within 2 miles of the Camp a party commanded by a Lieutenant Colonel Mercer of Virginia line (a Gallant & good Officer) was sent to dislodge them between whom a severe conflict & hot firing ensued which lasting some time & appearing to approach the Camp it was conceived that our party was yielding the ground upon which George Washington with permission of the General called (per dispatch) for Volunteers and immediately marched at their head to sustain, as was conjectured the retiring troops. Led on by the firing till he came within less than half a mile, & it ceasing, he detached Scouts to investigate the cause & to communicate his approach to his friend Colonel Mercer advancing slowly in the meantime – But it being near dusk and the intelligence not having been fully disseminated among Colonel Mercers Corps. And they taking us for the enemy who had retreated approaching in another directions commenced a heave fire upon the relieving party which drew fire in return in spite of all the exertions of the Officers one of whom & several privates were killed and many wounded before a stop could be put to it. To accomplish which GeorgeWashington never was in more imminent danger by being between two fires, knocking up with his sword the presented pieces.[12]

In other words, Washington was directly between two lines of soldiers firing at each other. Because they were the same army, Washington tried to stop them from shooting by riding in front of his men on his side of the battlefield and using his sword to push the soldiers' rifles to the sky so no one would be killed. As a result, the person most in danger was Washington himself!

Later, when young Colonel Washington was in the woods of Pennsylvania in 1755, in the midst of the French and Indian War, he faced an extremely close brush with death. British General Edward Braddock was in charge, leading 1300-1400 British soldiers on the way to Fort Duquesne. Only a few miles south of that location, as they crossed the Monongahela River, their path into the forest suddenly came alive with gunfire—all of it one-way—from the Indians and French hidden in the trees and shooting at the unsuspecting British soldiers. The British, who had been trained to march and fight in open field formation were cut to pieces without ever seeing their enemy. In his book, *The Bulletproof George Washington*, David Barton writes: "... not a musket was seen; the enemy was not visible. The blue smoke rising up after every discharge revealed that the firing came from the trees."[13]

Washington had warned Gen. Braddock of the fighting methods of the Indians, but Braddock would hear none of it.[14] His hubris and unwillingness to learn from Washington's wilderness experience of fighting the Indians cost him and his officers their lives, as well as those of many of their men.[15] Tragically, every one of the officers— except Colonel Washington—were wounded or killed.[16]

Someone looking at Colonel Washington at the battle assumed he would die any minute. He reported later, "I expected every moment to see him fall. Nothing but the superintending care of Providence could have saved him."[17] By the end of the "battle" (or really "rout"), Washington alone remained unharmed, with 714 Americans and British either killed or wounded.[18] In contrast, the French and Indians lost three officers and thirty men.

Why was Washington not killed? After this battle, George wrote his brother, John Augustine Washington, and provided his answer to that question—"the miraculous care of Providence":

> Dear Jack: As I have heard since my arrival at this place, a circumstantial acct. of my death and dying speech, I take this early opportunity of contradicting both, and of assuring you that I now exist and appear in the land of the living by the miraculous care of Providence, that protected me beyond all human expectation; I had

4 Bullets through my Coat, and two Horses shot under me, and yet escaped unhurt. We have been most scandalously beaten by a trifling body of men; but fatigue and want of time prevents me from giving any of the details till I have the happiness of seeing you at home; which I now most ardently wish for, since we are drove in thus far. A Weak and Feeble state of Health, obliges me to halt here for 2 or 3 days, to recover a little strength, that I may thereby be enabled to proceed homewards with more ease; You may expect to see me there on Saturday or Sunday...I am Dear Jack, your most Affect. Brother.[19]

His comment is both a demonstration of his wit, as well as a statement of his deep faith in Divine protection.

One of the great Virginian Presbyterian ministers of those days pointed to Washington and expressed his hope that the young Colonel was being prepared by God for great things. Reverend Samuel Davies has been described by Dr. Clarence Edward Macartney as the "most eloquent preacher of Colonial days."[20] What did Reverend Davies say about this remarkable young man who survived all the gunfire despite the incredible odds? "I may point out to the public that heroic youth, Colonel Washington, whom I cannot but hope that Providence has hitherto preserved in so signal a manner for some important service to his country."[21]

This was just one of several close calls with death in the dangers of the French and Indian War in the wilds of the unsettled frontier.[22]

THE INDIAN PROPHECY

Fifteen years later, Washington's diaries show that he and his friend and personal physician, Dr. James Craik, went back to the Fort Dusquesne region and encountered several Indians.[23] As the French had been ousted from America, and the Indians had made peace, they safely made their return trip with the purpose of protecting the lands that Washington and his soldiers had received as payment from the government for their service in the French and Indian War. The remarkable Indian encounter that Washington and Craik had at that time was not recorded by Washington himself, but by Craik, who related it to Washington's adopted grandson, George Washington Parke Custis. Custis records the solemn meeting in his *Recollections of Washington*, preserving what has become known as the "Indian Prophecy."

It was in 1770, that Colonel Washington, accompanied by Doctor

James Craik, and a considerable party of hunters, woodsmen, and others, proceeded to the Kanawha with a view to explore the country, and make surveys of extensive and valuable bodies of lands. At that time of day, the Kanawha was several hundred miles remote from the frontier settlements, and only accessible by Indian path, which wound through the passes of the mountains.

In those wild and unfrequented regions, the party formed a camp on the bank of the river, consisting of rudely-constructed wigwams or shelters, from which they issued to explore and survey those alluvial tracts, now forming the most fertile and best inhabited parts of the west of Virginia.

This romantic camp, though far removed from the homes of civilization, possessed very many advantages. The great abundance of various kinds of game in its vicinity afforded a sumptuous larder, while a few luxuries of foreign growth, which had been brought on the baggage horses, made the adventurers as comfortable as they could reasonably desire.

One day when resting in camp from the fatigues attendant on so arduous an enterprise, a party of Indians led by a trader, were discovered. No recourse was had to arms, for peace in great measure reigned on the frontier; the border warfare which so long had harassed the unhappy settlers, had principally subsided, and the savage driven farther and farther back, as the settlements advanced, had sufficiently felt the power of the whites, to view them with fear, as well as hate. Again, the approach of this party was anything but hostile, and the appearance of the trader, a being half savage, half civilized, made it certain that the mission was rather of peace than war.

They halted at a short distance, and the interpreter advancing, declared that he was conducting a party, which consisted of a grand sachem, and some attendant warriors; that the chief was a very great man among the northwestern tribes, and the same who commanded the Indians on the fall of Braddock, sixteen years before, that hearing of the visit of Colonel Washington to the western country, this chief had set out on a mission, the object of which himself could make known.

The colonel [Washington] received the ambassador with courtesy, and having put matters in camp in the best possible order for the reception of such distinguished visitors, which so short a notice would allow, the strangers were introduced. Among the colonists were some fine, tall, and manly figures, but so soon as the sachem approached, he in a moment pointed out the hero of the Monongahela, from among the group, although sixteen years had elapsed since he had seen him, and then only in the tumult and fury of battle. The Indian was of a lofty stature, and of a dignified and imposing appearance.

The usual salutations were going round, when it was observed, that the grand chief, although perfectly familiar with every other person present, preserved toward Colonel Washington the most reverential deference. It was in vain that the colonel extended his hand, the Indian drew back, with the most impressive marks of awe and respect. A last effort was made to induce an intercourse, by resorting to the delight of the savages — ardent spirit — which the colonel having tasted, offered to his guest; the Indian bowed his head in submission, but wetted not his lips. Tobacco, for the use of which Washington always had the utmost abhorrence, was next tried, the colonel taking a single puff to the great annoyance of his feelings, and then offering the calumet to the chief, who touched not the symbol of savage friendship. The banquet being now ready, the colonel did the honors of the feast, and placing the great man at this side, helped him plentifully, but the Indian fed not at the board. Amazement now possessed the company, and an intense anxiety became apparent, as to the issue of so extraordinary an adventure. The council fire was kindled, when the grand sachem addressed our Washington to the following effect:

"I am a chief and ruler over my tribes. My influence extends to the waters of the great lakes and to the far blue mountains. I have traveled a long and weary path that I might see the young warrior of the great battle. It was on the day when the white man's blood mixed with the streams of our forests that I first beheld this chief: I called to my young men and said, mark yon tall and daring warrior? He is not of the red-coat tribe — he hath an Indian's wisdom, and his warriors fight as we do—himself alone exposed. Quick, let your aim be certain, and he dies. Our rifles were leveled, rifles which, but for you, knew not how to miss—'twas all in vain, a power mightier far than we, shielded him from harm. He can not die in battle. I am old and soon shall be gathered to the great council fire of my fathers in the land of shades, but ere I go, there is something bids me speak in the voice of prophecy: Listen! *The Great Spirit protects that man, and guides his destinies—he will become the chief of nations, and a people yet unborn will hail him as the founder of a mighty empire!*"

The savage ceased, his oracle delivered, his prophetic mission fulfilled, he retired to muse in silence, upon that wonder-working spirit, which his dark "Untutored mind saw oft in clouds, and heard Him in the wind." Night coming on, the children of the forest spread their blankets, and were soon buried in sleep. At early dawn they bid adieu to the camp, and were seen slowly winding their way toward the distant haunts of their tribe. The effects which this mysterious and romantic adventure had upon the provincials, were as various as the variety of character which composed the party. All eyes were turned on him, to whom the oracle had been addressed, but from his ever-serene and thoughtful countenance, nothing could be discovered: still all this was strange, "t'was passive strange." On the mind of Doctor James Craik, a most deep and lasting impression was made, and in the war of the Revolution it became a favorite theme with him particularly after any perilous action, in which his friend and commander had been peculiarly exposed, as the battles of Princeton, Germantown, and Monmouth. On the latter occasion, as we have elsewhere observed, Doctor Craik expressed his great faith in the Indian's prophecy.[24]

It would appear that Providence had preserved George Washington's life for a greater purpose. Multiple witnesses attested to that notion, ranging from a Presbyterian minister, a physician, an Indian sachem to Washington himself. No wonder Washington so often referred to Providence and so willingly expressed his praise and gratitude to the Almighty.

WASHINGTON AND THE REVOLUTIONARY WAR

When the Continental Congress began to prepare for war in 1775, George Washington was the unanimous choice of the colonies as the leader for the Army. He told Congress that he did not feel himself "equal to the command" and he confided in his wife Martha that he didn't feel worthy of this position: "I hope my undertaking this service is designed to answer some good purpose. I rely confidently on that Providence which has heretofore preserved and been bountiful to me."[25]

Historian George Bancroft said that George Washington's decision to accept the post as commander in chief positively changed the colonies' history. "His acceptance changed the aspect of affairs."[26] John Adams, who suggested Washington fulfill this role said: "This appointment will have a great effect in cementing the union of these colonies. The general is one of the most important characters of the world; upon him depend the liberties of America."[27] And so Bancroft observed, "All hearts turned with affection toward Washington. This is he who was raised up to be, not the head of a party, but the father of his country."[28] But even with all of his great abilities, the battles he personally directed and fought resulted in both victories and defeats:

1775	the siege of the British who occupied Boston—Victory
1776	the Battles of Long Island, New York City, Fort Washington—All Defeats
1776	the Retreat through New Jersey—Defeat
1776	the Battle of Trenton—the Christmas Day surprise attack—Victory
1777	the Battle of Princeton—surprise attack—Victory
1777	the Battle of Brandywine—Defeat
1777	the Battle of Germantown—almost victory ending in a Draw or Defeat
1777-1778	the British occupation of Philadelphia and the winter in Valley Forge
1778	the Battle of Monmouth—almost Defeat, ending in Victory
1780	Benedict Arnold's treason at West Point—near Defeat, but plot foiled
1781	the Battle of Yorktown—Victory that forced British surrender

SACRIFICE AND RISK: PROFILES IN COURAGE

Soldiers face great risk each day in war, as they enter harm's way. Part of their training and commitment is to prepare for the "ultimate sacrifice" of laying down their lives for their country. Washington's heroic and martial spirit shone from his earliest military days in his extraordinary survival of enemy fire. But it was also seen in his letters as he grieved over the suffering civilians that he sought to protect with woefully inadequate forces in the aftermath of Braddock's defeat. Writing to Robert Dinwiddie on April 22, 1756, he openly poured out his distressed heart:

George Washington in military regalia

> Your Honor may see to what unhappy straits the distressed inhabitants as well as I, am reduced. I am too little acquainted, Sir, with pathetic language, to attempt a description of the people's distresses, though I have a generous soul, sensible of wrongs, and swelling for redress. But what can I do? If bleeding, dying! would glut their insatiate revenge, I would be a willing offering to savage fury, and die by inches to save a people! I see their situation, know their danger, and participate in their sufferings, without having it in my power to give them further relief, than uncertain promises. In short, I see inevitable destruction in so clear a light, that, unless vigorous measures are taken by the Assembly, and speedy assistance sent from below, the poor inhabitants that are now in forts, must unavoidably fall, while the remainder of the country are flying before the barbarous foe. In fine, the melancholy situation of the people, the little prospect of assistance, the gross and scandalous abuses cast upon the officers in general, which is reflecting upon me in particular, for suffering misconducts of such extraordinary kinds, and the distant prospects, if any, that I can see, of gaining honor and reputation in the service, are motives which cause me to lament the hour, that gave me a commission, and would induce me, at any other time than this of imminent danger, to resign without one hesitating moment, a

command, which I never expect to reap either honor or benefit from; but, on the contrary, have almost an absolute certainty of incurring displeasure below, while the murder of poor innocent babes and helpless families may be laid to my account here!

The supplicating tears of the women, and moving petitions from the men, melt me into such deadly sorrow, that I solemnly declare, if I know my own mind, I could offer myself a willing sacrifice to the butchering enemy, provided that would contribute to the people's ease.[29]

As a young soldier, he had been ready to lay down his life, if necessary. This was true of the commander in chief of the Revolutionary Army as well. Again and again he risked his life, whether in the face of attempted assassination[30] or of deadly fire, as he openly exposed himself to the enemy to rally his men to stand their ground. Referring to the Battle of Germantown, George Washington Parke Custis wrote, "...the exposure of his person became so imminent, that his officers, after affectionately remonstrating with him in vain, seized the bridle of his horse." General Sullivan said, "I saw our brave commander-in-chief...exposing himself to the hottest fire of the enemy in such a manner, that regard for my country obliged me to ride to him and beg him to retire. He, to gratify me and some others, withdrew to a small distance, but his anxiety for the fate of the day soon brought him up again where he remained till our troops had retreated."[31] The same fearlessness was seen at Trenton and Princeton.[32] In the battle for New York, where he was almost captured as his troops were in a panicked retreat, his willingness to expose himself to the enemy may have even had an element of anger or despair.[33] But perhaps the most picturesque example of his seeming immunity to enemy fire occurred at Monmouth,[34] which prompted a reminder from Dr. Craik of the Indian Prophecy. George Washington Parke Custis, writes,

...Heedless of the remonstrances and entreaties of his officers, the commander-in chief exposed his person to every danger throughout the action of the twenty-eighth of June. The night before the battle of Monmouth, a party of the general officers assembled, and resolved upon a memorial to the chief, praying that he would not expose his person in the approaching conflict.

In other words, Washington's men attempted to formally compel their general to not put himself in harm's way. Custis continues,

> His high and chivalric daring and contempt for danger at the battle
> of Princeton, and again at Germantown, where his officers seized
> the bridle of his horse, made his friends the more anxious for the
> preservation of a life so dear to all, and so truly important to the
> success of the common cause. It was determined that the
> memorial should be presented by Doctor Craik, the companion-in-
> arms of Colonel Washington in the war of 1755; but Craik at
> once assured the memorialists that, while their petition would be
> received as a proof of their affectionate regard for their general's
> safety, it would not weigh a feather in preventing the exposure of his
> person, should the day go against them, and the presence of the
> chief become important at the post of danger.
>
> Doctor Craik then related the romantic and imposing incident
> of the old Indian's prophecy, as it occurred on the banks of the Ohio
> in 1770, observing that, bred, as he himself was, in the rigid
> discipline of the Kirk of Scotland, he possessed as little superstition
> as any one, but that really there was a something in the air and
> manner of an old savage chief delivering his oracle amid the depths
> of the forest, that time or circumstance would never erase from his
> memory, and that he believed with the tawny prophet of the
> wilderness, that their beloved Washington was the spirit-protected
> being described by the savage, that the enemy could not kill him,
> and that while he lived the glorious cause of American
> Independence would never die. "Gentlemen," he Craik] said to
> some of the officers, "recollect what I have often told you, of the old
> Indian's prophecy. Yes, I do believe, a Great Spirit protects that
> man—and that one day or other, honored and beloved, he will be
> the chief of our nation, as he is now our general, our father, and our
> friend. Never mind the enemy, they can not kill him, and while he
> lives, our cause will never die." During the engagement on the
> following day,...a cannon ball struck just at his horse's feet,
> throwing the dirt in his face, and over his clothes, the general
> continued giving his orders, without noticing the derangement of
> his toilette. The officers present, several of whom were of the party

the preceding evening, looked at each other with anxiety. The chief of the medical staff [Dr. James Craik], pleased with the proof of his prediction, and in reminiscence of what had passed the night before, pointed toward heaven, which was noticed by the others, with a gratifying smile of acknowledgment.[35]

"THE GAME IS PRETTY NEAR UP"

But even with the seeming personal invincibility of Washington, the ultimate success of the American Army was not a certainty for Washington in the early days of the War. Writing to his nephew Lund Washington on December 10, 1776, he disclosed how close the American Army was to having to say "the game" was "pretty well up."

> In short, your imagination can scarce extend to a situation more distressing than mine. Our only dependence now is upon the speedy enlistment of a new army. If this fails, I think the game will be pretty well up, as, from disaffection and want of spirit and fortitude, the inhabitants, instead of resistance, are offering submission.[36]

Similarly, writing just a week later to his brother John Augustine Washington on December 18, 1776, he said

> In a word my dear Sir, *if every nerve is not strain'd* to recruit the New Army with all possible expedition, *I think the game is pretty near up, owing, in a great measure, to the insidious Arts of the Enemy, and disaffection of the Colonies before mentioned,* but principally to the accursed policy of short Inlistments, and placing too great a dependence on the Militia the Evil consequences of which were foretold [15] Months ago with a spirit almost Prophetick.... You can form no Idea of the perplexity of my Situation. No Man, I believe, ever had a greater choice of difficulties and less means to extricate himself from them. However under a full persuasion of the justice of our Cause I cannot but think the prospect will brighten, although for a wise purpose it is, at present hid under a cloud; [I cannot] entertain an Idea that it will finally sink tho' it may remain for some

time under a Cloud.[37] (emphasis in the original)

But only a few days later at Christmas, Washington pulled off one of the greatest surprise victories in the history of military strategy—The Christmas Day crossing of the Delaware that resulted in the victory at Trenton, and then at Princeton. Military historian, Larkin Spivey explains the events and significance of the Battle of Trenton:

> I think the critical moment in the Revolutionary War came in December 1776. At that time, the revolution was about to be over. Washington and what was left of his army had been defeated on Long Island, and Manhattan and White Plains and had retreated all the way across New Jersey and were more or less huddled on the Pennsylvania side of the Delaware River, waiting to see what was going to happen next. And they were utterly defeated at that point. And the Congress had evacuated Philadelphia and ... the entire cause was on the verge of collapsing.
>
> And at that moment, on Christmas Day 1776, I think Washington took a pure gamble to take what was left of his army back across the Delaware River and strike the garrison at Trenton, which was, manned by Hessian mercenary forces. And it was just a roll of a dice. And for that little attack to have come out as a success took a lot of amazing things to happen, ...the little miracles that enabled Washington to be successful on that day, to defeat this Hessian garrison at Trenton and to totally change the character of that war. That was the spark and it kept the war alive, for another day.
>
> For Washington to be successful, he had to have surprise when he attacked Trenton. He crossed the river at night and his plan was to attack early the next morning. Well, the Hessians at Trenton knew he was coming. They were daily getting reports from across the river from Tory sympathizers and deserters and other people that knew what was coming. And so they knew Washington, this attack, was coming on Christmas Day and they were all ready for it, and, lo and behold, late that afternoon on Christmas Day while Washington was crossing the river, some group of people who

have not really been identified to this day, some small band of colonials attacked the garrison at Trenton, and there was a small battle there and there were some causalities; and then these people disappeared in to the woods and then Colonel Rawl, the Hessian commander, said "Well, that's it. That's the big attack. We were awaiting it, and what a pitiful attack it was." And so they went back to celebrating Christmas and stood down, the troops went in the barracks and everybody had a big hangover the next morning when George Washington appeared with what was left of his army.

The skirmish occurred—this was the night before on Christmas Evening, by this roving band—different historians have different ideas about who these people were—but it's not definitely been determined. But this little attack gave the Hessian garrison at Trenton the false belief that it was over and so they went back to barracks and celebrated Christmas, and history was made the next morning when Washington appeared with his army and attacked the town. And during that attack the Hessians were defeated and surrendered and this was the first real victory of the war.

And after that, everything changed. The Continental Congress came back to Philadelphia; they were able to raise troops, money, the resources to continue the war, based on one little victory. And it was a very small military event. There were only a few casualties, but they had lasting implications for the war.[38]

A few days later, the Americans outwitted the British by secretly moving their forces for a surprise attack on Princeton, as the British moved their troops to attack Washington at Trenton. Washington kept the campfires raging by a small band of soldiers all night, while the rest of the army secretly took a back road to Princeton and executed their attack, yielding another major victory, at least in terms of American morale.[39]

Several months after Trenton, Washington began to reveal some glimmers of hope shining through the "cloud" in regard to "the game." He wrote to Robert Morris on May 25, 1778, at the end of the difficult Valley Forge encampment:

Dear Sir: ...I rejoice most sincerely with you, on the glorious change in our prospects, Calmness and serenity, seems likely to succeed in some measure, those dark and tempestuous clouds which at times appeared ready to overwhelm us, The game, whether well or ill played hitherto, seems now to be verging fast to a favourable issue, and cannot I think be lost, unless we throw it away by too much supineness on the one hand, or impetuosity on the other, God for bid that either of these should happen at a time when we seem to be upon the point of reaping the fruits of our toil and labour, A stroke, and reverse, under such circumstances, would be doubly distressing.[40]

And finally, with Yorktown behind him, Washington wrote to the President of Congress on May 10, 1782: "The British Nation appear to me to be staggered and almost ready to sink beneath the accumulated weight of Debt and Misfortune; if we follow the blow with vigour and energy I think the game is our own."[41]

What kept Washington in the "game" throughout the long years of war was his constant source of hope found in God's divine care. In 1776, he wrote,

> I have often thought how much happier I should have been, if, instead of accepting of a command under such circumstances, I had taken my musket on my shoulder and entered the ranks, or, if I could have justified the measure to posterity and my own conscience, had retired to the back country, and lived in a wigwam. If I shall be able to rise superior to these and many other difficulties, which might be enumerated, I shall most religiously believe, that the finger of Providence is in it, to blind the eyes of our enemies;[42]

In 1778, he affirmed: "Providence has heretofore taken us up when all other means and hope seemed to be departing from us, in this I will confide."[43] In 1780, he declared,

> ...providence, to whom we are infinitely more indebted than we are to our own wisdom, or our own exertions, has always displayed its power and goodness, when clouds and thick darkness seemed ready to overwhelm us. The hour is now come when we stand much in need of another manifestation of its bounty however little we deserve it.[44]

Other "manifestations" of the bounty of Providence seemed to appear for the American Army in various remarkable ways.

GENERAL WASHINGTON'S DEPENDENCE ON THE GOD OF ARMIES AND LORD OF VICTORY

When Washington looked back over the long war that resulted in the American victory and independence, he said the story that historians would tell would be considered fiction. The reason was the sheer advantage the British had over the beleaguered American forces. Washington wrote to Maj. Gen. Nathanael Greene from Newburgh on February 6, 1783:

> If Historiographers should be hardy enough to fill the page of History with the advantages that have been gained with unequal numbers [on the part of America] in the course of this contest, and attempt to relate the distressing circumstances under which they have been obtained, it is more than probable that Posterity will bestow on their labors the epithet and marks of fiction; for it will not be believed that such a force as Great Britain has employed for eight years in this Country could be baffled in their plan of Subjugating it by numbers infinitely less, composed of Men oftentimes half starved; always in Rags, without pay, and experiencing, at times, every species of distress which human nature is capable of undergoing.[45]

There were different times where the hand of God seemed to protect the new nation during the American war for independence. For example, during one of the battles in 1776, Washington and his men were trapped on Brooklyn Heights, Long Island. If the British had wanted to, they could have easily crushed the American army. In fact, they planned to do this the next day. This could have spelled the end of the war and would have been a disastrous end to the conflict. But Washington engaged in a very bold move. Under cover of fog, he risked evacuating all the troops in the night. He used every ship available, from fishing vessels to rowboats. When morning came, it is reported that the fog remained, much longer than normal—just long enough to help the Americans cross the river to safety. It was events like these that caused Washington to point to God's Providence as favoring the American cause.[46]

174

Ironically, in 1783, General Cornwallis tried the same type of escape at Yorktown. Not only was there no fog to help him, but a squall blew up on the Atlantic Ocean, rendering their escape futile and dangerous. The next day he surrendered. He tried to "pull a Washington," if you will. And he failed. Instead, Washington saw God's "astonishing interpositions of providence" at work at Yorktown as well.[47] Other seemingly "miraculous" Providences occurred the same year as the victory at Yorktown, as, for example, the Battle of Cowpens on January 17, 1781,

> ...where American General Daniel Morgan had a line of militia fire into British General Cornwallis' and Colonel Tarleton's dragoons, regulars, Highlanders and loyalists. When the Americans retreated, the British pursued, only to be surprised by American Continentals waiting over the hill. In the confusion, the Americans killed 110 British and captured 830. Cornwallis regrouped and chased the Americans, arriving at the Catawba River just two hours after the Americans had crossed, but a storm made the river impassable. He nearly overtook them again as they were getting out of the Yadkin River, but a torrential rain flooded the river. This happened a third time at the Dan River. British Commander Henry Clinton wrote: "Here the royal army was again stopped by a sudden rise of the waters, which had only just fallen (almost miraculously) to let the enemy over." In March of 1781, General Washington wrote to William Gordon: "We have, as you very justly observe, abundant reason to thank Providence for its many favorable interpositions in our behalf. It has at times been my only dependence, for all other resources seemed to have failed us."[48]

No wonder from the beginning to the end of the War, Washington prayed to the "God of Armies"! In 1777, for example, he prayed:

> Your friendly, and affectionate wishes for my health and success, has a claim to my thankful acknowledgements; and, that the God of Armies may enable me to bring the present contest to a speedy and happy conclusion, thereby gratifying me in a retirement to the calm and sweet enjoyment of domestick happiness, is the fervent prayer, and most ardent wish of my Soul.[49]

As he retired from his command of the Army in 1783, he promised his prayers to the "God of Armies" for his men:

> ...to bid a final adieu to the Armies he has so long had the honor to Command, he can only again offer in their behalf his recommendations to their grateful country, and his prayers to the God of Armies. May ample justice be done them here.[50]

The reason for Washington's prayers to the God of Armies was because he believed, and had come to experience, that God was the source of "victory." In 1776, soon after the start of the War, he repeatedly reminded his men of this fact of his faith:

> We have therefore to resolve to conquer or die: Our own Country's Honor, all call upon us for a vigorous and manly exertion, and if we now shamefully fail, we shall become infamous to the whole world. Let us therefore rely upon the goodness of the Cause, and the aid of the supreme Being, in whose hands Victory is.[51]

And again,

> Thursday the seventh Instant, being set apart by the Honourable the Legislature of this province, as a day of fasting, prayer, and humiliation, "to implore the Lord, and Giver of all victory, to pardon our manifold sins and wickedness's, and that it would please him to bless the Continental Arms, with his divine favour and protection"—All Officers, and Soldiers, are strictly enjoined to pay all due reverance, and attention on that day, to the sacred duties due to the Lord of hosts, for his mercies already received, and for those blessings, which our Holiness and Uprightness of life can alone encourage us to hope through his mercy to obtain.[52]

And again,

> The Continental Congress having ordered, Friday the 17th. Instant to be observed as a day of "fasting, humiliation and prayer, humbly

to supplicate the mercy of Almighty God, that it would please him to pardon all our manifold sins and transgressions, and to prosper the Arms of the United Colonies, and finally, establish the peace and freedom of America, upon a solid and lasting foundation"— The General commands all officers, and soldiers, to pay strict obedience to the Orders of the Continental Congress, and by their unfeigned, and pious observance of their religious duties, incline the Lord, and Giver of Victory, to prosper our arms.[53]

When Washington looked back over the War years, he consistently gave all of the glory to divine Providence for his victory. On June 11, 1783, he wrote to Reverend John Rodgers,

Dear Sir: I accept, with much pleasure your kind Congratulations on the happy Event of Peace, with the Establishment of our Liberties and Independence. Glorious indeed has been our Contest: glorious, if we consider the Prize for which we have contended, and glorious in its Issue; but in the midst of our Joys, I hope we shall not forget that, to divine Providence is to be ascribed the Glory and the Praise.[54]

In the same spirit of worship, Washington wrote to the people of Princeton, New Jersey, on August 25, 1783:

If in the execution of an arduous Office I have been so happy as to discharge my duty to the Public with fidelity and success, and to obtain the good opinion of my fellow Soldiers and fellow Citizens; I attribute all the glory to that Supreme Being, who hath caused the several parts, which have been employed in the production of the wonderful Events we now contemplate, to harmonize in the most perfect manner, and who was able by the humblest instruments as well as by the most powerful means to establish and secure the liberty and happiness of these United States.[55]

All glory was to be ascribed to "that being, who is powerful to save,"[56] for all of Washington's victories.[57] This was instinctive for him, since he could not forget there were moments when he thought that victory was nearly impossible. A great example of this was his immediate response to the victory at Yorktown, the battle that effectively ended the War. The General Orders on October 20, 1781 said,

> Divine Service is to be performed tomorrow in the several Brigades or Divisions. The Commander in Chief earnestly recommends that the troops not on duty should universally attend with that seriousness of Deportment and gratitude of Heart which the recognition of such reiterated and astonishing interpositions of Providence demand of us.[58]

THE CONCATENATION OF CAUSES AND THE FINGER OF PROVIDENCE

From the War to the presidency, Washington believed that the rule of divine Providence meant that order and right would eventually emerge from the dark clouds of confusion. So in 1791 he stated,

> We must, however, place a confidence in that Providence who rules great events, trusting that out of confusion he will produce order, and, notwithstanding the dark clouds, which may threaten at present, that right will ultimately be established.[59]

Thus, America's victory resulted from a providential chain of events, or a "concatenation of causes,"[60] as Washington called them as he wrote on July 8, 1783, to Reverend William Gordon:

> To say nothing of the invisible workings of Providence, which has conducted us through difficulties where no human foresight could point the way; it will appear evident to a close Examiner, that there has been a concatenation of causes to produce this Event; which in all probability at no time, or under any Circumstances, will combine again. We deceive ourselves therefore by this mode of reasoning, and what would be much worse, we may bring ruin upon ourselves by attempting to carry it into practice.[61]

Similarly, just before becoming the first president under the new Constitution,

Washington wrote to Annis Boudinot Stockton on August 31, 1788:

> The felicitations you offer on the present prospect of our public affairs are highly acceptable to me, and I entreat you to receive a reciprocation from my part. I can never trace the concatenation of causes, which led to these events, without acknowledging the mystery and admiring the goodness of Providence. To that superintending Power alone is our retraction from the brink of ruin to be attributed.[62]

The bright future for America under the new Constitution was due to the "remarkably excited" and "invisible hand" of God. Writing to Philip Schuyler on May 9, 1789, Washington explained:

> The good dispositions which seem at present to pervade every class of people afford reason for your observation that the clouds which have long darkened our political hemisphere are now dispersing, and that America will soon feel the effects of her natural advantages. That invisible hand which has so often interposed to save our Country from impending destruction, seems in no instance to have been more remarkably excited than in that of disposing the people of this extensive Continent to adopt, in a peaceable manner, a Constitution, which if well administered, bids fair to make America a happy nation.[63]

A JUST WAR, A RIGHTEOUS CAUSE, AND THE BLESSINGS OF HEAVEN

Washington believed that an army was both appropriate and necessary when it fought for a righteous cause[64] in a just war[65] that was conducted by the laws of war.[66] A strategic policy was to put the enemy in the wrong,[67] so that in the day of battle, heaven's blessings would favor the just army, since God stood with the righteous.[68]

The righteousness of the American cause was an important part of the Washington family's faith. Martha Washington, for example, thus expressed her patriotic support for her husband "to a kinswoman who deprecated what she called 'his folly.'" She wrote in 1774, "Yes, I foresee consequences—dark days, domestic happiness suspended, social enjoyments abandoned, and eternal separations on earth possible. But my mind is made up, my heart is in the cause. George is right; he is always right. God has promised to protect the righteous, and I will trust Him."[69]

The connection between a righteous army and victory meant that worship itself became part of the arsenal of the army. God's blessings needed to rest not just on the men, but even on their "arms." Accordingly, Washington called on his men to "religiously" observe a day of "Fasting, Humiliation and Prayer," so that in the words of the Twenty-Third Psalm, God's "goodness and mercy" would bless the soldiers' weaponry. The purpose of the fasting and prayer was so that the "righteous dispensations of Providence may be acknowledged and His Goodness and Mercy toward us and our Arms supplicated and implored."[70]

We can see then why it was no incongruity for the commander in chief to declare in his General Orders, "The General hopes and trusts, that every officer and man, will endeavour so to live, and act, as becomes a Christian Soldier defending the dearest Rights and Liberties of his country."[71] An army composed of soldiers striving to live and act as Christians should preeminently be a righteous army.

For Washington, righteousness was defined by the eternal rules ordained by heaven or the Ten Commandments. He believed there was "... an indissoluble union between virtue and happiness."[72] Thus, his vocabulary for the divine law includes: "Decalogue,"[73] "duties to God and man,"[74] "infinite obligations,"[75] "goodness and happiness,"[76] "virtue and happiness,"[77] "obligations enjoined by the Creator, and due to his creatures."[78] He made the relationship between obedience to God's "eternal rules" and human "happiness" most clear to the American people in his First Inaugural Address.

> ... the foundations of our National policy will be laid in the pure and immutable principles of private morality; and the pre-eminence of a free Government, be exemplified by all the attributes which can win the affections of its Citizens, and command the respect of the world. I dwell on this prospect with every satisfaction which an ardent love for my Country can inspire: since there is no truth more thoroughly established, than that there exists in the economy and course of nature, an indissoluble union between virtue and happiness, between duty and advantage, between the genuine maxims of an honest and magnanimous policy, and the solid rewards of public prosperity and felicity: Since we ought to be no less persuaded that the propitious smiles of Heaven, can never be expected on a nation that disregards the eternal rules of order and

right, which Heaven itself has ordained: And since the preservation of the sacred fire of liberty, and the destiny of the Republican model of Government, are justly considered as deeply, perhaps as finally staked, on the experiment entrusted to the hands of the American people.[79]

Braddock's defeat brought Washington fame and deepened his lifelong personal faith in Divine Providential care.

As a believer in divine Providence, Washington always wanted the blessings of God on the American side of the battle. This was particularly true as the American army faced the strongest nation on earth. How could a newly organized army succeed in such a contest if they violated God's rules? Throughout his career, from soldier to president, he made a point of emphasizing that happiness or the blessings of heaven could not be expected on America's cause if Americans as a people chose to violate heaven's own rules. Accordingly, Washington used the religiously oriented term "blessing" over 160 times in his writings. Happiness, heaven, and blessing are related concepts for Washington.[80] They come to fullest expression in his phrase, "the blessings of heaven," variations of which he uses some twenty times.[81]

Because of this deep adherence to the interconnection between God's blessings, his soldiers' virtue and victory, he made the role of the military chaplain an important position of leadership in his army.

WASHINGTON'S INSISTENCE ON CHAPLAINS

George Washington insisted on godly conduct and leadership in his army. He did not permit swearing, cursing, or drunkenness, which might impede rather than implore the "blessings of Heaven." Precisely a year before America's Declaration of Independence was dated, Washington's General Orders declared,

> The General most earnestly requires, and expects, a due observance of those articles of war, established for the Government of the army, which forbid profane cursing, swearing and drunkenness; And in like manner requires and expects, of all Officers, and Soldiers, not engaged on actual duty, a punctual attendance on divine Service, to implore the blessings of heaven upon the means used for our safety and defence.[82]

Precisely to help engender such a standard from his Christian soldiers, Washington instituted chaplains in the Revolutionary Army:

> The Hon. Continental Congress having been pleased to allow a Chaplain to each Regiment, with the pay of Thirty-three Dollars and one third pr month—The Colonels or commanding officers of each regiment are directed to procure Chaplains accordingly; persons of good Characters and exemplary lives—To see that all inferior officers and soldiers pay them a suitable respect and attend carefully upon religious exercises. The blessing and protection of Heaven are at all times necessary but especially so in times of public distress and danger—The General hopes and trusts, that every officer and man, will endeavour so to live, and act, as becomes a Christian Soldier defending the dearest Rights and Liberties of his country.[83]

But Washington's understanding of the value of chaplains did not begin with the Revolutionary army. In fact, when he was a young soldier, George Washington found himself in disagreement with his employer, the governor of Virginia, over the issue of chaplains. The young man, only in his twenties, was earnestly seeking chaplains to be a built-in part of the army (at the time, it was the British Army). In theory, chaplains were to be a part of the army. But in practice, it didn't seem to be working out that way. The young Colonel Washington penned a letter to the Royal Governor Robert Dinwiddie on September 23, 1756:

The want of a chaplain, I humbly conceive, reflects dishonor on the regiment, as all other officers are allowed. The gentlemen of the corps are sensible of this, and propose to support one at their private expense. But I think it would have a more graceful appearance were he appointed as others are.[84]

What is Washington saying here? That it reflected badly, in his humble opinion, that chaplains were a low priority to their army and were not there.

The Governor apparently took umbrage at the young man's letter. So Washington wrote him back on November 9, 1756, in an I-was-misunderstood type of apology. He clarified:

As to a chaplain, if the government will grant a subsistence, we can readily get a person of merit to accept the place, without giving the commissary any trouble on the point.[85]

Colonel Washington clarified further in another letter to the Royal Governor, this one dated November 24, 1756:

When I spoke of a chaplain, it was in answer to yours. I had no person in view, though many have offered; and I only said if the country would provide subsistence, we could procure a chaplain, without thinking there was offense in expression.[86]

Washington had persisted in getting a chaplain to their regiment. The Royal Governor Dinwiddie declined his requests and was later recalled in any event. So on April 17, 1758, Colonel Washington wrote to the president of the Virginia Council:

The last Assembly, in their Supply Bill, provided for a chaplain to our regiment. On this subject I had often without any success applied to Governor Dinwiddie. I now flatter myself, that your honor will be pleased to appoint a sober, serious man for this duty. Common decency, Sir, in a camp calls for the services of a divine, which ought not to be dispensed with, although the world should be so uncharitable as to think us void of religion, and incapable of good instructions.[87]

Here was Washington, the young man, long before he became leader of an army that would be opposing the British Army, asserting his belief that the army needed chaplains—a view he never altered.

As leader of the U.S. Army, Washington continued to insist on chaplains for the military. On the ninth of July, 1776, the very day he received the Declaration of Independence, he issued the order we already quoted at the beginning of this section that established Regimental Chaplains in the army. Clearly, Washington operated with the understanding that his army could not win their contest without God's help. Therefore, they had to honor him. Intertwined with the General's goal that the troops hear the Declaration of Independence read aloud were his instructions about how chaplains—men of good character—were to serve in the army.

A CHAPLAIN SPECIALLY HONORED BY GENERAL WASHINGTON

In fact there was one Chaplain, Abiel Leonard from Connecticut, who was so respected by Washington that, as he transitioned in his duty, the General wrote to both honor him and to commend him to Connecticut Governor Jonathan Trumbull.[88] Later, Washington appointed Abiel Leonard to the rank of Regimental Chaplain to Col. Knox, who was one of Washington's closest military friends.[89] Washington heard Leonard preach on at least three occasions.[90]

What makes Chaplain Abiel Leonard particularly noteworthy is that he composed a prayer for the use of Washington's Army. We include it as an appendix to our book, since it was not only a product of Washington's esteemed chaplain, but it was also a published prayer that Washington had bound in his personal collection of pamphlets.[91] Published in Cambridge in 1775, its title is "A prayer, composed for the benefit of the soldiery, in the American Army, to assist them in their private devotions; and recommended to their particular use" by Abiel Leonard, A.M., Chaplain to General Putnam's Regiment in said army.

The Christian character of this prayer, as well as its compatibility with the concerns of General Washington, can be seen by the following selections from the prayer:

> O my God, in obedience to the call of thy providence, I have engaged myself, and plighted my faith, to jeopardy my life in the high places of the field in the defense of my dear country and the liberties of it acknowledging thy people to be my people, their interest my interest, and their God to be my God..... And I desire now to make a solemn dedication of myself to thee in it through

Jesus Christ presenting myself to thy Divine Majesty to be disposed of by thee to thy glory and the good of America. O do thou, I most fervently entreat, wash away mine iniquities, blot them out of thy remembrance, purify and cleanse my soul in the blood of the great Captain of my salvation—accept of—own and bless me!

Teach, I pray thee, my hands to war, and my fingers to fight in the defense of America, and the rights and liberties of it! Impress upon my mind a true sense of my duty, and the obligation I am under to my country!...but may I live to do further service to my country—to the church and the people of God, and interest of Jesus Christ, and see peace and tranquility restored to this land....

Hear me, O my God, and accept of those my petitions through Jesus Christ, to whom with thee, O Father, and the Holy Spirit, one God, be glory, honor and praise, forever and ever. AMEN.[92]

Only a devout Christian could find the ministrations of such a chaplain to be worthy of special commendation to his governor, who also happened to be a clergyman. If Washington was not a devout Christian, then he was not only a remarkable actor, but also a most accommodating Deist, given how well, how often, and how openly he played the role of an interested Christian. Of this much we can be certain, since there is simply no escaping the evidence—Christian chaplains were important to George Washington. Even as president, Washington continued to appoint Christian chaplains to serve in the US Army under the new Constitution.[93]

A SERMON PUBLISHED FOR THE ARMY AND DISTRIBUTED FOR FREE

Chaplains not only pray, but they also preach. One of the remarkable sermons that comes from Washington's collection is by Reverend Israel Evans, Chaplain to Brig. Gen. Maxwell of the Western Army.[94] The title is "A discourse, delivered at Easton, on the 17th of October, 1779, to the Officers and Soldiers of the Western Army, after their return from an expedition against the five nations of hostile Indians. Easton, October 18, 1779." The officers of the Western Army voted to have it printed and "distributed amongst the federal Corps of the Army gratis."[95] Evans' discourse was based on 2 Samuel 22:40, 50, "For thou hast girded me with strength unto the battle: them that rise up against me hast thou subdued under me.—Therefore I will give thanks unto thee, O Lord, among the heathen; and I will sing praises unto thy name."

We cannot consider Evans' extensive sermon at any length, yet there are passages in it worthy of notice, as they reveal the religious beliefs that were held by the chaplains and the commanding officers of the American Army. He provides a Christian perspective on the Revolutionary War (going on at the time he delivered his message), but also the French and Indian War from two decades earlier.

The first text explains their mission and honors the soldiers who confronted the dangers of fighting the Indian tribes in the wilderness, given the universal remembrance of Braddock's disastrous defeat. The second passage explains the Gospel benefits of the soldiers' expedition against the hostile enemies. Evans declared:

> When the tyrant of Britain, not contented to expand his malignant wrath on our sea coasts, sent his emissaries to raise the savages of the wilderness to war, and to provoke them to break their faith with the United States of America; then our defenseless frontiers became the seat of savage fury, and hundreds of our countrymen bled, and hundreds of them suffered more than the tender ear can hear related, or the compassionate heart can endure....But this was a war, from which the boldest and bravest were ready to shrink, and they who had fought an army of regular veterans, dreaded the sudden and hidden attacks of the subtle and bloody savages....Who has resolution enough to expose himself to the secret ambuscade, and risk the unhappy fate of a General Braddock?...Public mercies demand public acknowledgements, and therefore our worthy General has seized this first opportunity for calling us together, to return our most grateful thanks to Almighty God, for the very signal support and success he has been pleased to grant us, during the expedition we have just finished....The pleasure that we shall meet with, when we once more see the illustrious CHIEF of the Armies of the United States, and obtain his approbation, for he knows your worth, will make you forget all your past dangers and toils, and make you pant for an opportunity to distinguish yourselves in his presence.

It is clear that the general and the chief were pleased with the soldiers' successful mission. It is also evident that these same officers, inclusive of Washington, the Chief, had no objection to Chaplain Evans' Christian understanding of the soldiers' mission into the wilderness.

> Before I close this Discourse, suffer me to remind you of other happy consequences of your success. You have opened a passage into the wilderness, where the Gospel has never yet been received....Churches shall rise there, and flourish when perhaps the truths of the Gospel shall be neglected on those eastern shores. For it cannot be supposed, that so large a part of this continent shall for ever continue the haunt of savages, and the dreary abodes of superstition and idolatry. As the Gospel, or Son of Righteousness has only glanced on the shores of this western world, and it is predicted of it, that it shall be universally propagated, it will probably like the Sun, travel to the western extremities of this continent. And when men from other nations, prompted by Liberty and love of the pure Gospel of truth, shall cross the ocean to this extensive empire, they will here find a safe asylum from persecution and tyranny. How honorable then must your employment appear, when considered in all those points of view. How happy to have been the instruments in the hand of God, for accomplishing so great a revolution, and extending the Kingdom of his Son so far. Liberty, and Religion shall have their wide dominion from the Atlantic through the great continent to the western ocean ....promoting the kingdom of our Lord Jesus Christ, ...may you more especially be the partakers of all the benefits and happiness, with which Christ will crown his faithful and dutiful Subjects!

This passage is filled with the American post-millennial theology of the time, that viewed the Christianization of this new nation as a precursor to the second coming of Christ. It also reflects the seeds of America's later idea of "manifest destiny"—the inexorable call of American settlers to occupy the entire North American continent from coast to coast. In another chapter, we will consider how the millennial hope was explicitly part of Washington's personal faith as well.

THE SUFFERING SOLDIER OF CHARACTER AT VALLEY FORGE AND BEYOND

The spiritual strength of the army was necessary not only for confronting the impending assaults of the far stronger British Army, but also for enduring the sheer fatigue, exposure, and near starvation that would be part of the Army's experience before victory was secured. Today, the very name Valley Forge implies heroic sacrifice and perseverance. George Washington described the sufferings of his men at Valley Forge to Virginia Congressman John Banister on April 21, 1778, after the long, brutal winter.

> ...for without arrogance, or the smallest deviation from truth it may be said, that no history, now extant, can furnish an instance of an Army's suffering such uncommon hardships as ours have done, and bearing them with the same patience and Fortitude. To see Men without Cloathes to cover their nakedness, without Blankets to lay on, without Shoes, by which their Marches might be traced by the Blood from their feet, and almost as often without Provisions as with; Marching through frost and Snow, and at Christmas taking up their Winter Quarters within a day's March of the enemy, without a House or Hut to cover them till they could be built and submitting to it without a murmur, is a mark of patience and obedience which in my opinion can scarce be paralleled.[96]

But the sufferings of the American soldiery, that Washington so poignantly described, had already begun before Valley Forge. Writing the summer before to a committee of Congress, composed of Philip Livingston, Elbridge Gerry, and George Clymer on July 19, 1777, Washington explained his men's lack of food, soap, and clothing.

> Gentn.: The little Notice I had of your coming to the Army, and the shortness of your Stay in Camp, will, more than probably, occasion the omission of many matters which of right, ought to be laid before you, and the interruption which my thoughts constantly meet, by a variety of occurrences must apologize for the crude, and indigested manner in which they are offered....
>
> With respect to Food, considering we are in such an extensive and abundant Country, No Army was ever worse supplied than ours with many essential Articles of it. Our Soldiers, the greatest part of the last Campaign, and the whole of this, have scarcely tasted any

kind of Vegitables, had but little Salt, and Vinegar, which would have been a tolerable Substitute for Vegitables, they have been in a great measures strangers to....Soap is another Article in great demand....I have no reason to accuse the Cloathier general of Inattention to his department, and therefore, as his Supplies are incompetent to the wants of the Army, I am to suppose his resources are unequal;... It is a maxim, which needs no illustration, that nothing can be of more importance in an Army than the Cloathing and feeding it well; on these, the health, comfort, and Spirits of Soldiers essentially depend, and it is a melancholy fact, that the American Army are miserably defective in both these respects; the distress the most of them are in, for want of Cloathing, is painful to humanity, dispiriting to themselves, and discouraging to every Officer. It makes every pretension to the preservation of cleanliness impossible, exposes them to a variety of disorders, and abates, or destroys that Military pride, without which nothing can be expected from any Army.[97]

Congress' inability to meet these needs that were already evident in the summer meant that the sufferings of the coming winter at Valley Forge were inevitable.

At any rate, the profoundly patient, sacrificial, and ultimately loyal character that Washington had developed among his soldiers required a national character in return. Nothing less than gratitude and justice by Congress and the American people would be commensurate with such heroic sacrifice. Thus, Washington wrote to Theodorick Bland on April 4, 1783: "We have now a National character to establish; and it is of the utmost importance to stamp favourable impressions upon it; let justice then be one of its characteristics, and gratitude another."[98]

Washington was concerned for many things as a General—food, soap, clothing, shelter, munitions, just payment for his men, and the blessings of heaven. As we contemplate Washington's words and place them in his historical circumstances, it occurs to us that a man so concerned for righteousness in his army, and for military chaplains to lead his men in seeking the blessings of heaven, just might have been a praying man himself. We intend to consider the debate over Washington's prayer at Valley Forge in a subsequent chapter, and when we do, we will further describe the magnitude of the sufferings of the neophyte American Army that shivered and starved in the frigid hills outside of British-occupied Philadelphia in that winter of despair in 1777-1778.

CONCLUSION

We close this chapter with an interesting contrast of Washington with Napoleon. This was made in 1932 on the bicentennial of Washington's birth, by Noel Porter, Arch Deacon of California, when he wrote:

> Finally Washington manifested the spirit of the Cross of Jesus Christ—the spirit of self sacrifice and unselfish service. During the time Washington lived there was another great general in the person of Napoleon. Napoleon was a great military genius, but Washington was a greater man. France can never repay Napoleon for rescuing her from the hands of the despoilers; yet while he waded through the seas of blood he thought only of a crown and a bauble for his son. Washington waded through blood and hunger and privation for his country's sake and when it was done he asked no reward save to be left alone in his Virginia farm. Napoleon asked for a crown and received nothing; Washington asked for nothing and received a crown.[99]

A selfless soldier, committed to his calling, strategically minded, fearless in battle, concerned for the welfare of soldiers and civilians alike, trusting in the hand of Providence, in all of these characteristics, Washington determined the ideal mold for generations of soldiers to come.

TEN

George Washington on Character and Honor

"It gives me real concern to observe ... that you should think it Necessary to distinguish between my Personal and Public Character and confine your Esteem to the former."
George Washington, 1775[1]

"While we are zealously performing the duties of good Citizens and soldiers we certainly ought not to be inattentive to the higher duties of Religion. To the distinguished Character of Patriot, it should be our highest Glory to add the more distinguished Character of Christian."
George Washington, 1778[2]

This book is dedicated to accurately portraying Washington's religion by a thorough examination of his own words. Through our studies of the man, we have come to the conclusion that part of the difficulty in understanding his religious views is due to his generally non-disclosing personality, coupled with the deep moral commitments that formed his character. Washington, both by temperament and by his personal principles, was a private man. How then can we accurately assess his personal religious views more than two centuries later?

In this chapter, we will explore Washington's character and his emphasis on honor. His concern for character and honor contributed to his deep reluctance to speak of himself. Because Washington's principled silence about himself was coupled with his natural shyness, there is a striking connection between Washington the man and the monument that bears his name—tall, majestic, silent, and seemingly impersonal. But did Washington's inwardness and typical silence about the beliefs of his heart mean that he did not have a Christian faith? We believe that Washington's character and personality have been misinterpreted by skeptics and secularists. They claim that his apparent silence on matters of personal religion implies that he did not believe nor live as a Christian. However, we are convinced that to interpret Washington in this way does injustice to the man and is an injustice to his character.

THE WASHINGTON MONUMENT AND ITS SYMBOLIC MESSAGE

It seems to us that the Washington monument is almost as much of a monument to our culture's view of George Washington as it is to Washington himself. The 555-foot-high obelisk is a fitting symbolic declaration of the profound significance of our founding father. After all, Washington was the single dominating figure of our nation's creation. But the statue's towering, faceless height also seems to suggest a transcendent unknowable personality. The highest message of the monument at its very pinnacle declares, "*Laus Deo*" or "Praise to God!" Yet this lofty message at its crowning height is invisible to all who stand below looking on high. Similarly, the many inner messages of the monument that are found chiseled in stone along the ever-rising stairs, such as, "Search the Scriptures," "Holiness to the Lord," "Train up a child in the way he should go, and when he is old he will not depart from it" are left unread, since the mandated way to the top is by speeding elevator, and the daunting and contemplative walk up the stairs is typically closed. All of this adds to the general ignorance Americans have of George Washington's character, personality, faith, and values.

But Washington's seeming unknowability has something to do with his own personality and character as well. Like his monument, he was strikingly attractive and toweringly tall for his day. Yet his quiet, shy, and other-focused demeanor, coupled with his elevated sense of the dignity of rank and office, typically kept his inner thoughts and feelings at a distance from many, if not most of those who occupied his life's activities. But with careful study, we believe we can uncover a great deal of the heart and soul of the man, even though he has been and continues to be draped with the mantle of an almost impenetrable glory from the past and the calloused indifference of the present. In this book we seek to explore the inner staircase of Washington's soul. By careful consideration of the many records of his life that he left for posterity, we plan to show that the highest aspirations of his heart were truly intended to offer *Laus Deo*!

THE PRIMACY OF CHARACTER IN WASHINGTON'S WRITINGS

A careful study of Washington's use of the word "character" shows that it was profoundly important to his view of human conduct. The word itself appears almost fifteen hundred times in his writings. Even his strenuous critic, Loyalist Reverend Jonathan Boucher, tutor of Washington's stepson, had to admit that Washington had a respectable character. "I did know Mr. Washington well, and though occasion may call forth traits of character that never could have been discovered in the more sequestered scenes of life, I cannot conceive how he could, otherwise than through the interested representations of party, have ever been spoken of as a great man. He is shy, silent, stern, slow and cautious; but has no quickness of parts, extraordinary penetration, nor an elevated style of thinking. In his moral character he is regular, temperate, strictly just and honest."[3]

The breadth of Washington's use of the word "character" is remarkable. It encompasses the character of officers[4] and other army officials,[5] militia men,[6] prisoners,[7] deserters,[8] as well as the character of the entire Continental Army.[9] It's clear that to Washington, character mattered.[10] His letters touched on the character of those to whom he was writing[11] and extended to national character,[12] the protection derived from a good character,[13] the character of political divisions,[14] the character of his employees,[15] politicians,[16] judges,[17] governmental positions,[18] and the defense of others from injurious aspersions.[19] He addressed character in terms of business partners and business transactions,[20] foreign affairs,[21] wars,[22] and schools.[23]

His reflections on character also reached to matters of the character of friends,[24] of appropriate suitors of his family members,[25] and of Christian conduct.[26] In this light, one can understand why things that impacted his own character were of deep concern to him as well.[27] This is especially well illustrated in his September 21, 1775, letter to Governor Jonathan Trumbull. Gov. Trumbull was also a clergyman. Washington's response to the Governor shows that he considered one's public and private character to be inseparable, and that they should both reflect the highest standards:

It gives me real concern to observe…that you should think it Necessary to distinguish between my Personal and Public Character and confine your Esteem to the former. [28]

After a careful explanation of the military realities facing the American army, Washington ended his letter to the Governor with this ironic conclusion: "I am, with great Esteem and Regard, for both your *Personal and Public Character*, sir, etc."[29] [emphasis added] As a result of this pointed exchange, Washington and Trumbull became fast friends, with deep, mutual respect for their public *and* private characters. This was evident when the Reverend Gov. died a few years after the War. Washington wrote to his son Jonathan Trumbull on October 1, 1785:

My dear Sir: …You know, too well, the sincere respect and regard I entertained for your venerable father's *public and private character*, to require assurances of the concern I felt for his death; or of that sympathy in your feelings for the loss of him, which is prompted by friendship.[30] (emphasis added)

From his earliest years in the military, Washington had become deeply concerned for the continuity between one's private and public character, because he believed that a man's character ultimately made the difference in a crisis. He recognized this from his earliest military command in 1756. In his first command, he wrote to Gov. Robert Dinwiddie explaining, "I have been obliged to suspend Ensign Dekeyser for Misbehavior till your pleasure is known. See the proceedings of the enquiring Court. His Character in many other respects has been infamous."[31] His concern for character became even more apparent in the midst of the many trials of the American Revolution.

A TIME WHEN CHARACTER MATTERED

If there ever was a time when character mattered, it was in Washington's role in the birth of America. If he had operated with a different set of moral values and a different personal character, America would have had a king or dictator instead of a federal Constitution and representative government.[32] Perhaps even worse, America would never have begun at all.

Consider a pivotal incident where Washington's character changed the direction of America. This occurred at the end of the Revolutionary War, when the American troops were at Newburgh in New York. Although overjoyed with the surrender of Cornwallis at Yorktown, the American troops were restive, since they had rarely been paid. Moreover, Congress' ability to pay in the future was uncertain.

A treacherous solution to this fiscal crisis dawned on some of the officers and insinuated itself into the thinking of others. The army could simply seize power and rule. They had the organized firepower. They could make the great Washington their new King. If Washington were to refuse to accept the crown, the army could stubbornly refuse to disband until they had wrung the guarantees of payment from the impoverished Congress. Either way, the only true barrier to their plan was Washington.

On March 4, 1783, Washington wrote to Alexander Hamilton of the looming dangers. He warned of an American civil war between Congress and the Army because of the financial crisis. Congress was even entertaining the idea of disbanding the unpaid Army to save expenses. Washington's worries and the strength of his own character are both revealed as he reflected on "...the danger that stares us in the face on account of our funds." In ominous language, he evaluated the solution contemplated by Congress:

> Our finances are in so deplorable a state *at this time* . . . The danger, to which the Army has been exposed, to a political dissolution for want of subsistence, ... no observations are necessary to evince the fatal tendency of such a measure....It would...end in blood. Unhappy situation this! God forbid we should be involved in it.[33]

The weight of the possibility of yet another war put tremendous strain on Washington and his hope for America's future.

> The predicament in which I stand as Citizen and Soldier, is as critical and delicate as can well be conceived. It has been the Subject of many contemplative hours. The sufferings of a complaining Army on one hand, and the inability of Congress and tardiness of the States on the other, are the forebodings of evil,...but I am not without hope.[34]

What was Washington's solution? His plan in the short term "as Soldier" was to prevent a civil war by simply continuing to do the right thing. Then, to truly resolve the problem, "as Citizen" he would seek a just solution for his soldiers from the financially strapped Congress. To do this, he began to call for a stronger and a more united Congress. Washington launched an idea that eventually resulted in the Constitutional Convention that finally met in Philadelphia in 1787.

> Be these things as they may, I shall pursue the same steady line of conduct which has governed me hitherto;…the prevailing sentiment in the Army is, that the prospect of compensation for past Services will terminate with the War… for it is clearly my opinion, unless Congress have powers competent to all *general* purposes, that the distresses we have encountered, the expence we have incurred, and the blood we have spilt in the course of an Eight years war, will avail us nothing.[35]

Alexander Hamilton knew Washington's character well. In this context, he had opportunity to express his absolute confidence in Washington's unwavering character to a gathering of political leaders who were concerned with the growing unrest of the army. In James Madison's "Note of Debates in the Continental Congress," February 20th, 1783, Hamilton's remarks are summarized:

> …it was certain that the army had secretly determined not to lay down their arms until due provision and a satisfactory prospect should be afforded on the subject of their pay; …Mr. Hamilton said that he knew Genl. Washington intimately and perfectly, …that his virtue his patriotism and firmness would, it might be depended upon, never yield to any dishonorable or disloyal plans into which he might be called; that he would sooner suffer himself to be cut to pieces; that he, (Mr. Hamilton), knowing this to be his true character, wished him to be the conductor of the army in their plans for redress, in order that they might be moderated and directed to proper objects, and exclude some other leader who might foment and misguide their councils;[36]

WASHINGTON'S EPIC-MAKING SPEECH "TO THE OFFICERS OF THE ARMY"

Washington recognized the possibility of a military coup and of the anonymously called meeting of the officers. But he chose not to attend. Instead, Washington called his own meeting, where he gave one of the most important speeches he ever delivered. As the meeting of his officers began, a few simple words and gestures began to melt their hardened hearts of protest. Col. David Cobb recounted the scene:

> When the General took his station in the desk or pulpit, which you may recollect, was in the Temple, he took out his written address from his coat pocket, and his spectacles, with his other hand, from his waistcoat pocket, and then addressed the officers in the following manner: "Gentlemen, you will permit me to put on my spectacles, for I have not only grown gray, but almost blind, in the service of my country."; This little address, with the mode and manner of delivering it drew tears from [many] of the officers.[37]

Washington's March 15, 1783, speech was simply entitled, "To the Officers of the Army." By his words of moral leadership and example of uncompromising character, Washington simultaneously gave birth to the American tradition of the peaceful transition of power and a civilian-led military. Bespectacled Washington reasoned:

> Gentlemen: By an anonymous summons, an attempt has been made to convene you together; how inconsistent with the rules of propriety! how unmilitary! and how subversive of all order and discipline, let the good sense of the Army decide. In the moment of this summons, another anonymous production was sent into circulation addressed more to the feelings and passions, than to the reason and judgment of the Army....the Address is drawn with great Art,...it is calculated to impress the Mind, with an idea of premeditated injustice in the Sovereign power of the United States, and rouse all those resentments which must unavoidably flow from such a belief....to take advantage of the passions, while they were warmed by the recollection of past distresses,...this dreadful alternative, of either deserting our Country in the extremest hour of her distress, or turning our Arms against it, has something so shocking in it, that humanity revolts at the idea....Can he be a friend to the Army? Can he be a friend to this Country? Rather, is he not an insidious Foe?[38]

Having exposed the treachery of the plan in view, Washington pledged himself to the cause of justice on behalf of the army:

> ... the sincere affection I feel for an Army, I have so long had the honor to Command, will oblige me to declare, in this public and solemn manner, that, in the attainment of compleat justice for all your toils and dangers, ...you may freely command my Services to the utmost of my abilities.[39]

In conclusion, Washington appealed to the lofty nobility of human conduct, when it is marked by the best of human character:

> ...let me entreat you, Gentlemen, on your part, not to take any measures, which, viewed in the calm light of reason, will lessen the dignity, and sully the glory you have hitherto maintained; ...to express your utmost horror and detestation of the Man who wishes, under any specious pretences, to overturn the liberties of our Country, and who wickedly attempts to open the flood Gates of Civil discord, and deluge our rising Empire in Blood. By thus determining, and thus acting, ...You will give one more distinguished proof of unexampled patriotism and patient virtue, rising superior to the pressure of the most complicated sufferings; And you will, by the dignity of your Conduct, afford occasion for Posterity to say, when speaking of the glorious example you have exhibited to Mankind, 'had this day been wanting, the World had never seen the last stage of perfection to which human nature is capable of attaining.'[40]

Had Washington not been the soldier of honor and the citizen of character that he was, "the world would had never seen the last stage" of personal and public leadership "to which human nature is capable of attaining." Given Washington's commitment to a character of moral integrity, we can understand why he strove to be characterized as a man of truth and honesty.

CHARACTER EXPRESSED BY HONESTY AND HONOR

Honesty, truth, and candor were important values to Washington, as we have already emphasized previously. As a young military officer writing to the Earl of Loudoun, in March 1757, he had described himself as without "guile."

> Do not think, my Lord, that I am going to flatter; notwithstanding
> I have exalted sentiments of your Lordship's character and respect
> your rank, it is not my intention to adulate. My nature is open and
> honest and free from guile.[41]

As a man "free from guile," truth was foundational to Washington throughout his life. As President, nearly forty years later in a letter on July 31, 1795, he declared to Secretary of State Edmund Randolph:

> It is not to be inferred from hence that I am, or shall be disposed to
> quit the ground I have taken, unless circumstances more imperious
> than have yet come to my knowledge should compel it; for there
> is but one straight course, and that is to seek truth and pursue it
> steadily.[42]

Similarly, in a letter to fellow Virginian, James Madison, Washington quoted an old proverb that he lived by, "It is an old adage, that *honesty is the best policy*."[43]

Honesty was emphasized by Washington, because it was an inseparable part of honor. The General declared that an ensign had acted "inconsistently with honor and truth" when he violated an oath."[44] When an officer signed "a false return" he did so "to the Injury of his honor and contrary to good order and military discipline."[45] When the commander in chief delivered these verdicts, he was expressing his personal values, not just those of the court-martial of the Revolutionary Army.

As an example, earlier in his career as a young officer in the French and Indian War, Washington had determined to resign from the military. In response, the officers of his Virginia Regiment wrote an address to reveal their deep respect for Washington and his ability to instill "genuine sentiments of true Honor and Passion for Glory":

> Your steady adherance to impartial Justice, your quick Discernment
> and invariable Regard to Merit, wisely intended to inculcate those
> genuine Sentiments of true Honor and Passion for Glory, from
> which the great military Achievements have been deriv'd, first
> heighten'd our natural Emulation, and our Desire to excel…Judge

then, how sensibly we must be Affected with the loss of such an excellent Commander, such a sincere Friend, and so affable a Companion. How rare is it to find those amable Qualifications blended together in one Man?...Adieu to that Superiority, which the Enemy have granted us over other Troops, and which even the Regulars and Provincials have done us the Honor to publicly acknowledge. Adieu to that strict Discipline and order, which you have always maintained. Adieu to that happy Union and Harmony, which has been our principle Cement!...our unhappy Country will receive a loss, no less irreparable, than ourselves. Where will it meet a Man so experienc'd in military Affairs?...Who has so great knowledge of the Enemy we have to deal with?...Who so much respected by the Soldiery?[46]

Washington had won the respect and honor of his inferior officers. But being honored by his superiors truly mattered to Washington. As a young officer, he wrote to Francis Fauquier on December 9, 1758, "If I easily get the better of my present Disorder, I shall hope for the honor of kissing your hand, about the 25th. instant...I shall think myself *honored* with *your* Esteem: Being, with the greatest Respect...."[47]

During these same years, he was faced with a dilemma. Having served in the British military in the war against the French and Indians, he was now confronted with a change of leadership in the British command. The new leader was willing to keep Washington on, but in what technically resulted in a demoted capacity. This was not because of poor performance on the young colonel's part, but because of military politics. In the colonial context, a commission to be a military officer given by the King was automatically viewed by British officers as a higher rank than an equivalent rank given by a colonial Governor. Because honor was so important to him, Colonel Washington felt compelled not to serve under such terms—precisely because he loved the honor of military service. So he wrote to Colonel William Fitzhugh, November 15, 1754:

> You make mention in your letter of my continuing in the service, and retaining my colonel's commission. This idea has filled me with surprise; for, if you think me capable of holding a commission, that has neither rank or emolument [*i.e.* privileges of office] annexed to it, you must entertain a very contemptible opinion of my weakness, and believe me to be more empty than the commission itself.

Besides, Sir, if I had time, I could enumerate many good reasons, that forbid all thoughts of my returning; and which to you, or any other, would, upon the strictest scrutiny, appear to be well founded. I must be reduced to a very low command, and subjected to that of many, who have acted as my inferior officers. In short, every captain, bearing the King's commission. . . would rank before me. . . .

I herewith enclose Governour Sharpe's letter, which I beg you will return to him, with my acknowledgements for the favour he intended me. Assure him, Sir . . . of my reluctance to quit the service . . . Also inform him, that it was to obey the call of honour, and the advice of my friends, I declined it, and not to gratify any desire I had to leave the military line. My inclinations are strongly bent to arms.[48]

Young Colonel Washington had an equally strong commitment to honor as to his calling to serve in the military.

A few months later when General Braddock arrived in America and personally recruited Washington, he immediately reconsidered and signed on to serve with the General. But his motives had changed. Having no hope for a military commission that would allow him a real future in the King's Army, his ambition now was to merit the respect of his countrymen. Washington wrote to William Byrd, a Virginian friend and leader on April 20, 1755:

I am now preparing for, and shall in a few days set off, to serve in the ensuing campaign, with different views, however, from those I had before. For here, if I gain any credit, or if I am entitled to the least countenance or esteem, it must be from serving my country without fee or reward; for I can truly say, I have no expectation of either. To merit its esteem, and the good will of my friends, is the sum of my ambition, having no prospect of attaining a commission.[49]

WASHINGTON'S EMPHASIS ON THE HONOR AND CHARACTER OF LEADERS

The importance that Washington placed on honor is indicated by the sheer magnitude—more than 4,000 instances in all—of his use of the variants of the words containing "honor" or with the older spelling of "honour." General Washington emphasized the far-reaching consequences of officers who were concerned with honor and moral character. This was so important that he claimed that the very existence of the army was at stake. Writing to Gov. Nicholas Cooke on October 12, 1776, he explained,

> The Advantages arising from a judicious appointment of Officers, and the fatal consequences that result from the want of them, are too obvious to require Arguments to prove them; I shall, therefore, beg leave to add only, that as the well doing, nay the very existence of every Army, to any profitable purposes, depend upon it, that too much regard cannot be had to the choosing of Men of Merit and such as are, not only under the influence of a warm attachment to their Country, but who also possess sentiments of principles of the strictest honor. Men of this Character, are fit for Office, and will use their best endeavours to introduce that discipline and subordination, which are essential to good order, and inspire that Confidence in the Men, which alone can give success to the interesting and important contest in which we are engaged. [50]

Washington consistently underscored his view of the "immense consequence" of having "men of the most respectable characters" as the officers surrounding the commanderin chief. He wrote years later to Secretary of War, James McHenry as a new army was being contemplated to address the post-French Revolutionary government:

> To remark to a Military Man how all important the General Staff of an Army is to its well being, and how essential consequently to the Commander in Chief, seems to be unnecessary; and yet a good choice is of such immense consequence, that I must be allowed to explain myself.
>
> The Inspector General, Quartermaster General, Adjutant General, and Officer commanding the Corps of Artillerists and Engineers, ought to be men of the most respectable characters, and of first rate abilities; because, from the nature of their respective

Offices, and from their being always about the Commander in Chief who is obliged to entrust many things to them *confidentially*, scarcely any movement can take place without their knowledge. It follows then, that besides possessing the qualifications just mentioned, they ought to have those of Integrity and prudence in an eminent degree, that *entire* confidence might be reposed in them; without these and their being on good terms with the Commanding General his measures if not designedly thwarted may be so embarrassed as to make them move heavily on.[51]

When character and honor were operative among the officers, daily operations ran smoothly.[52] Character enabled an officer, as Washington himself had learned years earlier, to set aside personal advancement for the well-being of the country.[53] Character and honor were at the heart of military discipline. Unbecoming conduct tarnished the honor and character of the troops.[54] But because an officer's character was sacred, caution had to be exercised in bringing charges.[55] Washington's Army had its share of "unbecoming and unsoldierly conduct."[56] Incidents of soldiers who were "lost to every sense of honor and virtue" included American soldiers plundering civilians,[57] leaving the army in its time of need,[58] misappropriating recruiting funds by diverting them to soldier's salaries[59] and even for gambling.[60] The quality of one's past character made a difference in the process of military discipline. Past bad character took away the leniency of the court.[61] Past good character, however, disposed the court to be lenient.[62]

HONOR, INFAMY, AND THE PURPLE HEART

Character has the power to create a legacy that survives one's death. And the American Revolution left us with the legacy of two of Washington's officers whose names, due to their character or lack thereof, still survive. The first was Maj. Gen. Lord Stirling. In spite of the fact that he carried the British hereditary title of "Lord," he served faithfully as an officer under Washington's command until his death near the end of the Revolutionary War. In a happy play on words, General Lord Stirling was an officer of "sterling character" (a phrase from Middle English meaning a "silver penny" implying something of the highest quality.) This was so much so that at his death, a congressional honor was afforded Major General the Earl of Stirling. Congress reported to Washington:

On motion, Resolved, That the President signify to the Commandr.

in Chief, in a manner the most respectful to the memory of the late Major General the Earl of Stirling, the sense Congress entertain of the early and meritorius, exertions of that general in the common cause; and of the bravery, perseverance and military talents he possessed; which having fixed their esteem for his character, while living, induce a proportionate regret for the loss of an officer who has rendered such constant and important services to his country. [63]

Washington had written near the end of his life about the qualifications of general officers. Stirling had fulfilled Washington's views cited above that ranking officers "ought to have…Integrity and prudence in an eminent degree, that *entire* confidence might be reposed in them; without these and their being on good terms with the Commanding General his measures if not designedly thwarted may be so embarrassed as to make them move heavily on."

Washington also remembered the legacy of another officer with a different character. He had discovered, by a close call with disastrous treason, just how true his words were. The danger of bad character in a military officer echoes through history. Most Americans still recognize the name Benedict Arnold, for it has been a synonym for "traitor" for over two centuries. Washington's General Orders of September 26, 1780, revealed the treachery that could be perpetrated when officers lost their sense of honor:

> Treason of the blackest dye was yesterday discovered! General Arnold who commanded at Westpoint, lost to every sentiment of honor, of public and private obligation, was about to deliver up that important Post into the hands of the enemy. Such an event must have given the American cause a deadly wound if not a fatal stab. Happily the treason has been timely discovered to prevent the fatal misfortune. The providential train of circumstances which led to it affords the most convincing proof that the Liberties of America are the object of divine Protection.
>
> At the same time that the Treason is to be regretted the General cannot help congratulating the Army on the happy discovery. Our Enemies despairing of carrying their point by force are practising every base art to effect by bribery and Corruption what they cannot accomplish in a manly way.
>
> Great honor is due to the American Army that this is the first

instance of Treason of the kind where many were to be expected from the nature of the dispute, and nothing is so bright an ornament in the Character of the American soldiers as their having been proof against all the arts and seduction of an insidious enemy.

Arnold has made his escape to the Enemy but Mr. André the Adjutant General to the British Army who came out as a spy to negotiate the Business is our Prisoner. His Excellency the commander in Chief has arrived at West-point from Harford and is no doubt taking the proper measures to unravel fully, so hellish a plot.[64]

In light of the deadly impact of Arnold's betrayal and its violation of the character of honor required of officers, it is clear why Washington desired to encourage the highest character in his army. He wanted all his soldiers to be men of honor. In that spirit, Washington created the Badge of Merit,[65] originally intended not for officers but for enlisted men. Today, it is known as the Purple Heart.[66] It was granted to "suitable characters" who were worthy of "that honorary distinction."[67] In his General Orders of August 7, 1782, he explained that recipients of this Badge of Merit would be "enrolled in the book of merit which will be kept at the orderly office. Men who have merited this last distinction to be suffered to pass all guards and sentinels which officers are permitted to do." And further, every other soldier should know, "The road to glory in a patriot army and a free country is thus open to all. This order is also to have retrospect to the earliest stages of the war, and to be considered as a permanent one." All of Washington's soldiers were to seek "the road to glory." And just what was the highest glory on this road to glory? Washington had told his soldiers when they were at Valley Forge.

Washington designed the Badge of Merit, now known as the Purple Heart.

OUR HIGHEST GLORY: THE DISTINGUISHED CHARACTER OF CHRISTIAN

Was the "Purple Heart" or "Badge of Military Merit" the highest glory that could be afforded to Washington's soldiers who were being trained to be men of character and honor in pursuit of military glory? Washington didn't think so. At the conclusion of the severe hardships of Valley Forge, Washington declared what he believed was the highest glory for his soldiers. It had to do with character. But it was not just the character of a patriot. That was a high glory to be sure, but not the highest. The highest glory was having the character of a Christian: "While we are zealously performing the duties of good Citizens and soldiers, we certainly ought not to be inattentive to the higher duties of Religion. To the distinguished Character of Patriot, it should be our highest Glory to add the more distinguished Character of Christian."[68] For Washington the "road to glory" led to the "Character of Christian."

CONCLUSION

All Deists, past or present, would deeply disagree with General Washington. But doesn't this tell us something about Washington's views of religion? As a man of candor, honor, character, and strict military discipline and leadership, who was daily pursuing glory on the field of military engagement, it would have been impossible for him to say these words of Christian commitment as a mere rhetorical flourish to rally his men. While perhaps an unscrupulous Deist could have done so, the character required for such deception would have been closer to the character of Benedict Arnold than to Washington's. Let us here emphasize an important point: Washington nowhere, ever even once claimed to be a Deist, in spite of all that skeptics and secularists have written. But on several instances he identified himself as a Christian. His words here from Valley Forge are certainly important, for in his words written for all to read, since they were after all, "General Orders," he declared, "While *we* are zealously performing the duties of good Citizens and soldiers **we** certainly ought not to be inattentive to the *higher duties of Religion*. To the distinguished *Character* of Patriot, it should be **our** *highest glory to add the more* distinguished *Character of Christian*."[69] (emphasis added) A man of honor would never have publicly said the words in bold if he had not meant them.

ELEVEN

"The Sacred Fire of Liberty"

Was George Washington a Godly Leader?

*"The sacred fire of liberty, and the destiny of the Republican
model of Government, are justly considered as deeply, perhaps as finally
staked, on the experiment entrusted to the hands of the American people."*
George Washington, Inaugural Address, April 30, 1789 [1]

*"It is the duty of all nations to acknowledge the Providence
of Almighty God, to obey His will, to be grateful for his benefits,
and humbly to implore His protection and favor."*
George Washington, Thanksgiving Proclamation, October 3, 1789 [2]

Washington's skill as a leader was universally recognized by his contemporaries. His oft-quoted eulogy immortalized him as "first in war, first in peace and first in the hearts of his countrymen." Washington's presidency faced great events that challenged the very core of the new Republic. He was conscious that his every act created a prece-dent for good or ill for all that would follow him.[3] Our purpose here is not to develop the issues and accomplishments of Washington's leadership and administration. Yet we think the following events are important to keep in mind for an understanding of Washington's impact and effectiveness as the formative leader of America.

1781   *Victory at Yorktown* effectively ended the War.

1782   *Commander in chief of victorious army at Newburgh,* New York.

        Urged to become king, and refused because of his republican views.

        Kept army prepared for duty under the provisional treaty of peace.

1783   *Newburgh Conspiracy*—Quelled potential coup instigated by weary and unpaid officers who called for the army to force Congress to meet their demands.

        Cessation of hostilities with Great Britain announced.

        Circular Letter to States calling for justice to the army from the governors.

        Definitive Treaty of Peace signed with Great Britain "In the Name of the Most Holy and Undivided Trinity"

        Wrote his Farewell to the Army, becoming the new "Cincinnatus," the Roman General who retired after victory to return to the plow.

        Last emotional meeting with his officers.

        Resigned his Congressional military commission, and retired to MountVernon, arriving home on Christmas Eve to stay for the first time in eight years.

1784   *Promoted canal projects* to connect the inland rivers with the Virginia coast.

        Advocated union among the states by a stronger central government.

1786   *Annapolis Convention* held. Commissioners from five states sought to change the Articles of Confederation to improve commerce.

        A meeting was called in Philadelphia of state representatives to discuss improvements to the federal government.

1787   *Washington presided over Constitutional Convention* and signed the new Constitution.

1788   *Sought to secure adoption of Constitution* by the states. Nine out of the thirteen states were required for ratification.

1789   *Unanimously declared President* of the United States.
Said farewell to his mother, Mary Ball Washington, who died after his departure for New York.
Inaugurated April 30th in New York City.
Toured northeastern states.
First National Thanksgiving under the Constitution

1790   *Site for the Federal City selected* on the Potomac (Washington, D.C.)
Obligation for Revolutionary War debts accepted by new government.
Debates in Washington's cabinet began to reveal deep differences.

1791   *Toured* southern states.
Gen. Arthur St. Clair defeated by Indian tribes near Wabash River
The Bill of Rights ratified during Washington's first term and became part of the Constitution

1792   *Elected to second term* as president.

1793   *Proclamation of neutrality*—Washington sought to keep America out of European conflicts and wars, thus keeping all as trade partners.
Citizen Edmund Genet sought to gain popular American support for the new government in France. This was contrary to Washington's views of neutrality and Genet was recalled to France.
Thomas Jefferson and Alexander Hamilton, who bitterly disagreed with each other, both resigned from Washington's cabinet as casualties of this debate.
Edmund Randolph assumed Jefferson's position as secretary of state.

1794   *James Monroe sent to France.* Ultimately Washington deeply disagreed with Monroe's views. Along with Jefferson's resignation, this helped to create a new American political party that consciously distanced itself from Washington's (and Adams' and Hamilton's) "federalist" policies, coming to full expression under the presidencies of Jefferson, Madison, Monroe, and Jackson.

Randolph resigned, and Timothy Pickering took his place.

Jay's Treaty: Supreme Court Chief Justice John Jay negotiated with the British with the goal of forcing the British to leave western forts as required by the Treaty of Paris that had ended the Revolutionary War.

Whiskey Rebellion—conflict over the enforcement of excise taxes on distilleries. Washington, in military uniform, personally led the American Army to western Pennsylvania to quell the insurrection.

Gen. Anthony Wayne ("Mad" Anthony Wayne) defeated Indians at Fallen Timbers (Toledo, Ohio).

1795   *Signed Treaty of San Lorenzo with Spain* opening Mississippi River to American shipping and establishing America's southern boundary.

Treaty of Greenville: Indian nations yield lands of what is today Ohio, Indiana, and Michigan.

Jay's Treaty ratified.

1796   *Charles Cotesworth Pinckney* appointed minister to France, but French government refused to receive him, due to French anger over Jay's Treaty with England that partly voided some of America's agreements with France, resulting in American ships being seized by French privateers.

Farewell Address published.

1797   *Washington retired as president* and returned home to Mount Vernon.

XYZ mission to France. President John Adams sent a three-man commission that included Pinckney, which Talleyrand refused to receive. Three parties got involved with the intention of raising loans or bribes of about $250,000 to open the diplomatic doors. Their names were concealed as X,

Y, and Z. Pinckney is supposed to have retorted "millions for defense, sir, but not one cent for tribute."
Preparation for war with France begun by President Adams' contact with Washington.

1798   *Washington appointed commander in chief of the Armies of the United States of America* by President John Adams, in the event of war with post-French Revolutionary government. The army never assembled.

1799   Washington died as he desired—"as an honest man" at Mount Vernon.

WAS WASHINGTON A "GODLY" LEADER?

The purpose of this chapter is to assess how Washington's religion surfaced while he served in public office. Simply put, can we call Washington a "godly" leader? His contemporaries thought so. Consider one of the earliest publications on the life of Washington, by the Reverend Dr. Jedidiah Morse, a clergyman-scholar and correspondent of Washington. At the end of his thirty-three-page long summary of General Washington's life, based upon the anonymously written and approved life of Washington, by David Humphreys, we find the following poem, which probably came from the pen of Humphreys as well.

GENERAL WASHINGTON

GREAT without pomp, without ambition brave—
Proud, not to conquer fellow men, but save—
Friend to the weak—a foe to none but those,
Who plan their greatness on their brethren's woes—
Aw'd by no titles—undefil'd by lust—
Free without faction, obstinately just—
Too wise to learn, form Machiavel's school,
That truth and perfidy by turns should rule.
Warm'd by Religion's sacred, genuine ray,
Which points to future bliss, th' unerring way;
Yet ne'er controul'd by Superstition's laws,
The worst of tyrants in the noblest cause. [4]

Washington would later speak in his Inaugural Address of the "sacred fire of liberty":

Since we ought to be no less persuaded that the propitious smiles of Heaven, can never be expected on a nation that disregards the eternal rules of order and right, which Heaven itself has ordained: And since the preservation of the sacred fire of liberty, and the destiny of the Republican model of Government, are justly considered as *deeply*, perhaps as *finally* staked, on the experiment entrusted to the hands of the American people.[5]

Was Washington's "sacred fire" properly anticipated by Morse's and Humphrey's couplet?:

Warm'd by Religion's sacred, genuine ray,
Which points to future bliss, th' unerring way.

Recent authors will hear none of this and have declared an emphatic no. Willard Randall writes, "Washington was not a deeply religious man."[6] Douglas Southall Freeman says, "He had believed that a God directed his path, but he had not been particularly ardent in his faith."[7] James Thomas Flexner states that "Washington …avoided, as was his deist custom, the word 'God.'"[8] Judging from these writers, Washington could hardly be called a "godly leader." But our conclusion must be drawn from the actual words of Washington and the religious leaders who encountered him. When this is done, we believe that the evidence leads us in a different direction than that of recent historians Randall, Freeman, and Flexner, and what appear to be their unsubstantiated generalizations. By contrast, in addition to being one of Washington's closest military aides in the war, David Humphreys was living with the Washington family at Mount Vernon as he wrote his summation of Washington's daily life, which also had Washington's personal approval.[9]

To begin, let us turn our attention to Washington's remarkable "Circular" that he personally signed and sent to each of the thirteen state governors, who together had just won America's independence.

A LETTER TO THIRTEEN GOVERNORS: WASHINGTON'S CONFESSION OF FAITH

As the war was coming to an end, there were several issues that troubled Washington. We just saw in our last chapter that there was the deep concern for just compensation for the soldiers after their long sacrifice to win independence. But

Washington also had another deep concern. This was the seeming inefficiency and sometimes divisive character of the government established by the Articles of Confederation.

Each state governed itself with such autonomy that, at times, the whole nation suffered. Out of this realization, Washington became one of the earliest proponents for a new kind of government with a more powerful, centralized Congress. His vision ultimately helped to produce the Constitutional Convention. This is the

George Washington's watermark

backdrop for his "Circular to the States." The circular essentially laid out what Washington saw as necessary for an independent America, namely, a union of states under one federal head, a sacred regard for public justice, a proper "peace establishment," and a disposition and temperament among the citizenry that would allow the individual to subjugate their own personal interest in the interest of the larger community. But what is fascinating for our purposes is not just that these concerns of Washington appear in his farewell circular letter to the thirteen governors, but that the entire letter is couched in a theological message. For us, Washington's farewell letter to the governors is his official confession of faith, or what we might call Washington's public theology.

Washington's "Circular to the States" is as close to a statement of religious faith that he ever produced. Given that it was sent to every state, it was clearly intended by him to be his understanding of an American statement of religious faith. There are some thirty references to spiritual realities: heaven's favor; final blessing; gratitude and rejoicing; lot assigned by Providence; moral point of light; a vast Tract of Continent ... all the various soils and climates of the World...peculiarly designated by Providence; heaven crowned all its other blessings; above all the pure and benign light of revelation; not ignorance and superstition; the rights of man; the cup of blessing; stand or fall; confirmation or lapse; a blessing or curse (used twice); aggravated vengeance of heaven; begging daily bread; to implore the divine benediction; earnest prayer; God would have you; holy protection; incline hearts; brotherly affection; love for one another; graciously be pleased; to do justice; love mercy; demean with charity; humility and pacific temper of mind; the Divine Author of our blessed religion; humble imitation of whose example; a happy nation.[10]

The circular, or what we might call, "Washington's Confession of Faith," gives a fair summary of Washington's religion. He had said, "in politics, as in religion my tenets are few and simple."[11] These few and simple religious principles clearly included:

God—"God would have you"

Creation— "a vast Tract of Continent...all the various soils and climates of the World...peculiarly designated by Providence"

Providence—"lot assigned by Providence, designated by Providence"

Deity of Christ—"Divine Author"

Revelation—"pure and benign light of revelation"

Fall—"stand or fall, confirmation or lapse"

Sin—"blessing or curse"

God's Grace—"favor, Heaven crowned all its blessings, incline hearts, graciously be pleased"

Christ—"Our blessed Religion, the Divine Author, whose [Christ's] example, daily bread [the Lord's Prayer], cup of blessing [the Eucharist]"

Worship—"gratitude and rejoicing"

Education—"not ignorance and superstition"

Sanctification—"Holy keeping," "brotherly affection," "love for one another"

Moral Light—"blessing or curse," "justice," "mercy," "demean with love," "humility," "peace"

Prayer—"earnest prayer," "final blessing," "implore the divine benediction"

Civil and Religious Liberty—"rights of mankind," "happy nation"

Heaven—"Heaven's favor," "Heaven crowns"

Judgment—"the aggravated vengeance of Heaven"

The few and simple principles of Washington's religion when summed up are a statement of mere Christianity. Notice too, that while it has been argued that George Washington was unwilling to partake of Christian communion, he even quoted here the biblical phrase that speaks of communion —"the cup of blessing." This was the most public letter in Washington's career to this point, and it was replete with Christian theological references and allusions to scripture. Washington's explicitly Christian and public theological affirmations undercut the entire structure of Deistic thought. How is it possible then to conceive of Washington as a Deist?

NATIONAL WORSHIP: DAYS OF PRAYER, FASTING, AND THANKSGIVING

Throughout his times of leadership, in the military and in the presidency, George Washington participated in proclaiming days of prayer and fasting and thanksgiving. In 1774, the British Parliament, in cahoots with the King, passed the Port Act, which closed the harbor of that most rebellious American city, Boston—home of the Boston Tea Party in December 1773. This was the city Washington was destined to liberate three years later.

Meanwhile, what the British did not count on was that the other colonists would come to the aid of the Bostonians. In fact, they actively tried to discourage other colonies from helping by publishing lies abroad in those colonies. Historian George Bancroft points out, "It was published at the corners of the streets that Pennsylvania would refuse to suspend commerce; that the society of Friends [the Quakers] would arrest every step toward war; that New York would never name deputies to a congress; that the power of Great Britain could not fail to crush resistance."

On June 1, 1774, at midnight, the Port Act went into effect, as scheduled. British ships converged into Boston Harbor to begin an indefinite blockade. George Bancroft describes the somber response from two other American colonies: "At Philadelphia, the bells of the churches were muffled and tolled, the ships in port hoisted their colors at half mast . . . In Virginia, the population thronged the churches; Washington attended the service and strictly kept the fast." As we noted earlier, George Washington's diary entry for June 1, 1774, reads, "Went to church and fasted all day." Even as a lay leader, George Washington was participating in a day of fasting and prayer. Later, he would make proclamations for prayer and fasting.

On March 6, 1776, for example, from his headquarters at Cambridge, General Washington issued the command for a Day of Fasting, Prayer and Humiliation:

> Thursday, the 7th instant, being set apart by the honorable Legislature of this Province as a day of fasting, prayer and humiliation, "to implore the Lord and Giver of all victory to pardon our manifold sins and wickedness, and that it would please Him to bless the Continental army with His divine favor and protection," all officers and soldiers are strictly enjoined to pay all due reverence and attention on that day to the sacred duties at the Lord of hosts for His mercies already received, and for those blessings which our holiness and uprightness of life can alone encourage us to hope

through His mercy obtain.[12]

In recent decades, the First Amendment to the Constitution has been construed to mean that there must be a strict separation of church and state and that there should be no religious expression allowed in the public arena. The first sentence of the amendment simply says, "Congress shall make no law respecting an establishment of religion, nor prohibiting the free exercise thereof." The very men who gave the First Amendment did not intend to impose a radical separation of church and state that is advocated by so many today. In fact, the day after Congress adopted the words of the First Amendment, they sent a message to President Washington, asking him to declare a day of thanksgiving to God to show America's appreciation to God for the opportunity to create America's new national government in peace and tranquility. So on October 3, 1789, President Washington made a Proclamation of a National Day of Thanksgiving. He declared:

> Whereas it is the duty of all nations to acknowledge the Providence of Almighty God, to obey His will, to be grateful for his benefits, and humbly to implore His protection and favor; and
>
> Whereas both Houses of Congress have by their joint Committee requested me "to recommend to the People of the United States a day of public thanksgiving and prayer to be observed by acknowledging with grateful hearts the many signal favors of Almighty God, especially by affording them an opportunity peaceably to establish a form of government for their safety and happiness;"
>
> Now, therefore, I do recommend and assign Thursday, the twenty-sixth day of November next, to be devoted by the People of these United States to the service of that great and glorious Being, who is the beneficent Author of all the good that was, that is, or that will be;
>
> That we may then all unite in rendering unto Him our sincere and humble thanks, for His kind care and protection of the People of this country previous to their becoming a Nation; for the signal and manifold mercies, and the favorable interpositions of His Providence, which we experienced in the course and conclusion of the late war; for the great degree of tranquillity, union, and plenty,

which we have since enjoyed, for the peaceable and rational manner in which we have been enabled to establish constitutions of government for our safety and happiness, and particularly the national one now lately instituted, for the civil and religious liberty with which we are blessed, and the means we have of acquiring and diffusing useful knowledge; and in general for all the great and various favors which He hath been pleased to confer upon us.

And also that we may then unite in most humbly offering our prayers and supplications to the great Lord and Ruler of Nations, and beseech Him to pardon our national and other transgressions, to enable us all, whether in public or private stations, to perform our several and relative duties properly and punctually; to render our national government a blessing to all the People, by constantly being a government of wise, just and constitutional laws, discreetly and faithfully executed and obeyed; to protect and guide all Sovereigns and Nations (especially such as have shown kindness unto us) and to bless them with good government, peace, and concord; to promote the knowledge and practice of true religion and virtue, and the increase of science among them and Us; and generally to grant unto all Mankind such a degree of temporal prosperity as He alone knows to be best.

Given under my hand, at the city of New York, the 3rd of October, in the year of our Lord one thousand seven hundred and eighty-nine.[13]

One cannot read those words without realizing how the founders and father of our nation did *not* intend for God to be separated from our official acts. Rather, the founders just did not want a national denomination, as they had experienced in England. They did not want to have an established church, since an established church took away religious liberty. So, the federal government was carefully designed to assure that there would not be an official state church that could force people to worship against their will, or could coerce people to support it with their tax dollars.

THE CONSTITUTION: HUMAN DEPRAVITY REQUIRES LIMITED POWER

Washington had learned, by brutal experience of the difficulties the Continental

Congress had in getting the necessary work done to care for the army. Toward the end of the war, as we observed in the last chapter, he began to call for plans to strengthen the powers of government for the good of the whole nation. Ultimately, his concerns were shared by many, and the Constitutional Convention was held in Philadelphia in 1789. Washington's religion manifested itself in various ways during that critical summer in Independence Hall.

Washington's years of experience with people in the business context taught him the importance of contracts, in light of human nature, and what he termed "the rascallity of Mankind." Writing to Lund Washington, he said,

> If this should be the case, it will be only adding to the many proofs we dayly see of the folly of leaving bargains unbound by solemn covenants. I see so many instances of the rascallity of Mankind, that I am almost out of conceit of my own species; and am convinced that the only way to make men honest, is to prevent their being otherwise, by tying them firmly to the accomplishmt. of their contracts.[14]

The nation, too, needed a solemn covenant to assure its success. Washington's interest in a constitutional document is seen in the sheer frequency with which he speaks of the idea of the Constitution. The word appears over four hundred times in his writings. Even at the start of the War in 1776, he understood the importance of preparing a sound Constitution for excellent governance. Writing to his brother to encourage him in the Virginian effort to compose a new Constitution, Washington said,

> Dear Brother: Since my arrival at this place, where I came at the request of Congress, to settle some matters relative to the ensuing Campaign I have received your Letter ....
>
> To form a new Government, requires infinite care, and unbounded attention; for if the foundation is badly laid[,] the superstructure must be bad, too. Much time therefore, cannot be bestowed in weighing and digesting matters well. We have, no doubt, some good parts in our present constitution; many bad ones we know we have, wherefore no time can be misspent that is imployed in seperating the Wheat from the Tares. My fear is, that

you will all get tired and homesick, the consequence of which will be, that you will patch up some kind of Constitution as defective as the present; this should be avoided, every Man should consider, that he is lending his aid to frame a Constitution which is to render Million's happy, or Miserable, and that a matter of such moment cannot be the Work of a day.[15]

When the U.S. Constitution was under consideration by the nation, Washington himself became a keen political scientist in his own right. In fact, he claimed to have read every available publication that appeared in the debate!

The mind is so formed in different persons as to contemplate the same object in different points of view. Hence originates the difference on questions of the greatest import, both human and divine. In all Institutions of the former kind, great allowances are doubtless to be made for the fallibility and imperfection of their authors. Although the agency I had informing this system, and the high opinion I entertained of my Colleagues for their ability and integrity may have tended to warp my judgment in its favour; yet I will not pretend to say that it appears absolutely perfect to me, or that there may not be many faults which have escaped my discernment. I will only say, that, during and since the Session of the Convention, I have attentively heard and read every oral and printed information of both sides of the question that could readily be procured. This long and laborious investigation, in which I endeavoured as far as the frailty of nature would permit to act with candour has resulted in a fixed belief that this Constitution, is really in its formation a government of the people; that is to say, a government in which all power is derived from, and at stated periods reverts to them, and that, in its operation, it is purely, a government of Laws made and executed by the fair substitutes of the people alone.[16]

From his unique vantage point of having presided at the Constitutional Convention, and from his expertise in pursuing the entirety of the debate, Washington addressed the question of the merits of the proposed Constitution. Simply put, he

Washington's Inaugural Address was a Presidential sermon. Following his inauguration, his next stop was a worship service.

recognized that it was not perfect. The people who would be governed by it would not be perfect either, given human nature.

Writing to Lafayette on February 7, 1788, he expressed his view that the states' agreement on the Constitution was near miraculous. But he also admitted that there were defects in the Constitution. But, his constitutional "creed" had "two great points": the Constitution gave no more power than necessary to have a good government, and, there were constitutional checks and balances on the government's use of power through popular rule, and by the separation of powers among three branches that kept an eye on one another for the good of the nation.[17] Beyond this, the Constitution also provided for its own amendment, when citizens would find this necessary.[18]

Washington's religion manifested itself precisely at this point in the constitutional debate. The ideas he expressed by terms such as "limited power," "the separation of powers," "the rule of the people," "checks and balances," and the "need for amendment," all existed for one simple reason—people abuse power. The idea of the abuse of power and political depravity were openly admitted at the Constitutional Convention,[19] and also seriously pondered by Washington.[20] Political depravity is a theological concept that flows from the doctrine of human sinfulness—a basic postulate of Christian teaching. In fact, Washington asserted that human depravity could ultimately destroy the Constitution, even with the checks and balances it possessed. In his proposed Address to Congress in April 1789, he described how the Constitution, with all of its wisdom, could ultimately come to naught by the depravity of the people and those who govern them, since the Constitution in the hands of a corrupt people was a mere "wall of words" or a "mound of parchment."[21]

THE CONSTITUTION AND THE "COMPLETION OF OUR HAPPINESS"

But if religion was present theologically in the Constitution, why was it not present explicitly or openly? This question was directly asked of Washington by the Presbyterian ministers and elders from the First Presbytery of the Eastward that included clergy from Massachusetts and New Hampshire. The New Englanders had a

Christian commitment that was expressed through their established religion of the Congregational Church and the closely related Presbyterian tradition.[22] They had wished for a direct reference to the Christian faith in the Constitution, but their disappointment was entirely removed by the public and private Christian and pious leadership of Washington! They wrote:

> Whatever any may have supposed wanting in the original plan, we are happy to find so wisely providing in it amendments; and it is with peculiar satisfaction we behold how easily the entire confidence of the People, in the Man who sits at the helm of Government, has eradicated every remaining objection to its form.
>
> Among these we never considered the want of *a religious test*, that grand engine of persecution in every tyrant's hand: but we should not have been alone in rejoicing to have seen some Explicit acknowledgement of the *only true God and Jesus Christ, whom he hath sent* inserted some where in the *Magna Charta* of our country.
>
> We are happy to find, however, that this defect has been amply remedied, in the face of all the world, by the piety and devotion, in which your first public act of office was performed—by the religious observance of the Sabbath, and of the public worship of *God*, of which you have set so eminent an example—and by the warm strains of Christian and devout affections, which run through your late proclamation, for a general thanksgiving.
>
> The catholic spirit breathed in all your public acts supports us in the pleasing assurance that no religious establishments—no exclusive privileges tending to elevate one denomination of Christians to the depression of the rest shall ever be ratified by the signature of the *President* during your administration
>
> On the contrary we bless God that your whole deportment bids all denominations confidently to expect to find in you the watchful guardian of their equal liberties—the steady patron of genuine Christianity—and the bright Exemplar of those peculiar virtues, in which its distinguishing doctrines have their proper effect.
>
> Under the nurturing hand of a Ruler of such virtues, and one so deservedly revered by all ranks, we joyfully indulge the hope that virtue and religion will revive and flourish—that infidelity and the

vices ever attendant in its train, will be banished [from] every polite circle; and that rational piety will soon become fashionable there; and from thence be diffused among all other ranks in the community.[23]

These Presbyterians had not the least suspicion of any presidential Deism.

Did a deistic President Washington desire to correct their mistaken identification of him as the "bright Exemplar" and "steady patron of genuine Christianity"? Here truly was an occasion for a man of candor, honesty, character, honor, and truth to practice his maxim of "honesty is the best policy." Washington's candid reply did not sidestep the issue of the absence of a direct reference to Christianity in the Constitution. Nor did he miss the fact that his clerical correspondents had identified him as a great defender of Christianity, whose piety and actions had successfully assuaged their fears about the omission of such a reference to Christianity and the negative impact it might have had on the ongoing role of Christian faith under the Constitution. Washington's answer was actually theologically astute, as it is a direct allusion to a foundational Presbyterian doctrine—the perspicuity, clarity, or plainness of the Gospel in the scriptures.[24] The president wrote,

> I am persuaded, you will permit me to observe that the path of true piety is so plain as to require but little political direction. To this consideration we ought to ascribe the absence of any regulation, respecting religion, from the Magna-Charta of our country. To the guidance of the ministers of the gospel[,] this important object is, perhaps, more properly committed. It will be your care to instruct the ignorant, and to reclaim the devious, and, in the progress of morality and science, to which our government will give every furtherance, we may confidently expect the advancement of true religion, and the completion of our happiness.[25]

In sum, Washington believed the Gospel was plain and did not need the Constitution to direct it, and this is why there is no explicit regulation concerning religion in the "Magna-Charta" of America. "Ministers of the gospel," such as the Presbyterian clergy, whom he was addressing, were more appropriately given this evangelistic task. Yet Washington pledged his best efforts to further morality and science, which he was confident would result in the advancement not just of religion in general, but of "true religion."[26] In context, this had direct reference to the Presbyterian clergy's phrase, the "Explicit acknowledgement of the *only true God and Jesus Christ, whom he hath sent.*" [emphasis ours] And as to the clergy's identification of Washington with the Christian faith, we find that he embraced this as well, for the expected advancement of true religion would not only result in the "completion" of the clergy's "happiness," a universally understood synonym for salvation in the era,[27] but in the completion of "our" happiness, inclusive of Washington himself.[28] The historical circumstances, the contextual frame of reference for Washington's letter, and his grammar make only one conclusion possible—Washington wanted the clergy to know that they were correct in identifying him as a Christian.

Here then we can see why Washington insisted that religion and morality were "indispensable pillars" of America's political happiness. We will consider the implications of this statement from his Farewell Address in the final section of this chapter.

A PRESIDENTIAL SERMON: WASHINGTON'S FIRST INAUGURAL ADDRESS

The man who refused to be king at the end of the war was unanimously chosen as president at the start of the new constitutional government—the only man to occupy that office who could make that claim. At his inauguration to the presidency, even as at his retirement from the military, he gave evidence for his Christian faith.

In his first Inaugural Address, Washington frequently referred to the Almighty. His very first act as president was to pray. Washington prayed that God would secure the liberties of the new nation:[29] He went on to say that no one should be more grateful to God than the people of the United States of America in light of what he had done for them throughout the war.[30]

Although the new nation had just gone through the tumultuous time after the Revolution of creating a new civil government, this process, fraught with sectional rivalries and tensions, was accomplished in a peacefully unique way that called for "pious gratitude," since this implied even more divine blessings to come.[31] The implication Washington drew from all of this was that America could not expect the continuing "smiles of Heaven" if "the eternal rules of order and right which Heaven itself has ordained" were disregarded.[32]

We must remember that when Washington attended the Anglican churches of his day, he—along with the congregation—recited the Ten Commandments from the reredos behind the altar. In Washington's historical context, "the eternal rules of order and right which Heaven itself has ordained" could only refer to the Ten

Commandments, given that this was the belief of almost every American in Washington's day who read or heard his Inaugural Address.

Along with his solemn Inaugural Address that graced America's first auspicious pageant of civil religion, Washington's inauguration contributed three other religious precedents. Two have continued, and the third has not. The first is the swearing in of the president with the use of the Bible. This Bible has been sacredly kept by the Masons of New York City. The page where Washington placed his hand for the oath of office was marked by the turning down of the corner of the page. Interestingly, the marked page is Genesis 49, the chapter where Jacob, the father of the sons of Israel, bestows his blessing upon them. By this time Washington had long been called "the father of his country." The parallel of the text and the inauguration was not accidental.

The second religious precedent from Washington's inauguration that continues is the addition of the words "So help me God" to his presidential oath of office, which was spoken as Washington had his hand upon the scriptures opened to Genesis 49. These words were not and are not in the Constitution, but every subsequent president in America's history has said them following Washington's lead. Washington's freely taken oath in the name of God has another important significance beyond mere precedent. It eviscerates James Thomas Flexner's claim concerning Washington's Inaugural Address. He states that "Washington ...avoided, as was his deist custom, the word 'God.'" [33] Strange, indeed, that a man who was following Deist custom would scrupulously avoid the name of God in his speech, but then intentionally add it to his oath of office, where it was not even required! Washington's inaugural sermon does not avoid the name of God, but instead employed the honorific titles of deity that were so often used by the clergy of his era. Washington's inaugural vocabulary for deity cannot legitimately be construed to be that of a Deist. Every inauguration after Washington has reminded America that Washington did not avoid the word "God."

A third Washingtonian religious precedent did not continue. This occurred immediately after being sworn in on the Holy Bible—the new president bent down and kissed the sacred book.[34]

But the religious elements of Washington's inauguration were still not complete. Next, he led the congressmen and everyone else across the street from Federal Hall to St. Paul's Chapel for a two hour service of Christian worship to commit the new nation to God.[35] According to Mrs. Alexander Hamilton, she knelt with President Washington as they received the Eucharist together.[36]

WASHINGTON'S PUBLIC WITNESS TO THE RELIGIOUS BODIES OF AMERICA

At various times during Washington's presidency, he had remarkable opportunities to declare his faith, as he was honored by various religious groups. These religious denominations often wrote an address to express their joy in Washington's actions, presence, words, or election to office. With remarkable consistency, Washington acknowledged these letters. In doing so, he also revealed in various ways his personal religious views. There are approximately thirty some addresses that Washington received from religious bodies and that he answered during his presidential years. They reflect the full spectrum of America's religious communities in his era, from both ecumenical clergy groups[37] and individual denominations, such as Roman Catholic,[38] Episcopal,[39] Lutheran,[40] German Reformed,[41] Dutch Reformed,[42] Presbyterian,[43] Congregational,[44] Moravian,[45] Methodist,[46] Baptist,[47] Quaker,[48] Masonic,[49] Universalist,[50] Jewish,[51] and Swedenborgian.[52] In all of his letters, Washington was always polite and clear.

Interestingly, there is no record of any deistic group or atheist group that wrote to Washington. We cannot fully summarize these letters here. But a careful reading of them will demonstrate that they consistently refer to God or divine Providence. They often quote or appeal to scripture, and consistently reflect a Christian faith and understanding on the part of Washington. They also consistently call for civil obedience and the maintenance of religious liberty. They often conclude with the need to pray for the nation or one another, with a wish of blessing for this life and the life hereafter. These letters are some of the best commentaries on Washington's personal religion as well as his vision for the friendly and cooperative relationship between the distinct spheres of church and state. Most significantly, for our purposes, not one of them provides a hint of a deistic unbelief on the part of Washington.

The characteristic spirit of this correspondence is that both Washington and his religious correspondents agreed that both sides represented godly and religious people. To demonstrate this, let's consider a few of the more salient examples. The Lutherans wrote on April 27, 1789, to the new president: "Pleasingly do we anticipate the blessings of a wise and efficient government—equal freedom—perfect safety—a sweet contentment spreading through the whole land—irreproachable manners with pure religion, and *that* righteousness which exalteth a Nation."

In a most non-deistic manner, Washington responded, "I flatter myself opportunities will not be wanting for me to shew my disposition to encourage the domestic and public virtues of industry, economy, patriotism, philanthropy, and that righteousness which exalteth a nation. . . and amidst all the vicissitudes that may await me in this mutable state of existence, I shall earnestly desire the continuation of an interest in your intercessions at the Throne of Grace."⁵³

The Methodist bishops had written to the president, "...we enjoy a holy expectation that you always will prove a faithful and impartial Patron of genuine, vital religion—the grand end of our creation and present probationary existence. And we promise you our fervent prayers to the Throne of Grace that GOD almighty may endue you with all the graces and gifts of his holy spirit, that may enable you to fill up your important station to his glory, the good of his Church, the happiness and prosperity of the United States, and the welfare of mankind."

Washington's response could not have been that of a Deist, unless it was the kind of Deist that delighted in deceiving others by playing the role of a religious charlatan. Only a godly man could have sincerely written Washington's words to the Bishops: "After mentioning that I trust the people of every denomination, who demean themselves as good citizens, [you?]will have occasion to be convinced that I shall always strive to prove a faithful and impartial Patron of genuine, vital religion; I must assure you in particular that I take in the kindest part the promise you make of presenting your prayers at the Throne of Grace for me, and that I likewise implore the divine benedictions on yourselves and your religious community."⁵⁴

His opening line to the German Reformed Congregations on June 1789 was a simple and clear affirmation of Washington's perspective of his own personal piety, "I am happy in concurring with you in the sentiments of gratitude and piety towards Almighty-God, which are expressed with such fervency of devotion in your address; and in believing, that I shall always find in you, and the German Reformed Congregations in the United States a conduct correspondent to such worthy and pious expressions."⁵⁵ This does not sound like someone who "was not a deeply religious man," or someone who "had not been particularly ardent in his faith," or one who "avoided, as was his Deist custom, the word 'God.'"⁵⁶

PRESBYTERIAN PRAISE FOR PRESIDENTIAL PIETY

But Washington's seeming personal godliness not only touched the Lutherans and the Methodists, but the Presbyterians also saw in the President a deeply pious life of Christian faithfulness. The moderator of the Presbyterian General Assembly, Reverend John Rodgers, who had corresponded with Washington during the War about giving Bibles to the American troops,⁵⁷ was a key signatory of a letter emanating from a committee of the General Assembly. The Presbyterians wrote,

We adore Almighty GOD the author of every perfect gift who hath endued you with such a rare and happy assemblage of Talents as hath rendered you equally necessary to your country in war and in peace . . . .the influence of your personal character moderates the divisions of political parties. . . .your present elevated station by the voice of a great and free people, and with an unanimity of suffrage that has few if any examples in history...their confidence in your virtues; . . . we derive a presage even more flattering from the piety of your character. . . .a steady, uniform, avowed friend of the Christian religion, who has commenced his administration in rational and exalted sentiments of Piety, and who in his private conduct adorns the doctrines of the Gospel of Christ, and on the most public and solemn occasions devoutly acknowledges the government of divine Providence. The examples of distinguished Characters will ever possess a powerful and extensive influence on the public mind, and when we see in such a conspicuous station the amiable example of piety to God, of benevolence to men, and of a pure and virtuous patriotism, we naturally hope that it will diffuse its influence and that eventually the most happy consequences will result from it.[58]

Was the Presbyterian committee utterly mistaken about the godliness they had observed in Washington? Their letter bristled with affirmations of Washington's piety—"personal character," "virtues," "piety of your character," "avowed friend of the Christian religion," "rational and exalted sense of piety," "his private conduct adorns the doctrines of the Gospel of Christ," "devoutly acknowledges the government of divine Providence," "amiable example of piety to God," "a pure and virtuous patriotism."

Washington's response to this litany of Presbyterian praise for his spiritual devotion revealed the temperament of a sincere Christian, not the temporizing of a mere politician. First and last, his concern for humility shone through: "...it will be my endeavor to avoid being elated by the too favorable opinion which your kindness for me may have induced you to express...I desire you to accept my acknowledgements for your...prayers to Almighty God for his blessing on our common country and the humble instrument, which he has been pleased to make use of in the administration of its government."[59] But Washington also understood the essence of the Presbyterian letter. They were declaring their belief that Washington himself was a Christian. What was

Washington's response to this? Was it an evasion that would allow for his actual Deism to stand without causing offense to his religious well-wishers?

Instead, his answer was one that reflected a deep sense of faith and dependence upon God: "I reiterate the possession of my dependence upon Heaven as the source of all public and private blessings." His answer also reflected the importance of the kind of piety the Presbyterians had just extolled in him: "I will observe that the general prevalence of piety, philanthropy, honesty, industry and economy seems, in the ordinary course of human affairs are particularly necessary for advancing and confirming the happiness of our country."

Finally, his answer emphasized that authentic Christianity was a matter to be prized, pursued, and proven. While Washington's classic vocabulary might cloud our understanding, we can sense the passion for the Christian faith that motivated his words. His central thought was this, since all Americans enjoyed full religious liberty, it was only reasonable that something would be expected from them in return for this great blessing.[60] What was this? Washington said, "...that they will be emulous of evincing the sincerity of their profession by the innocence of their lives, and the beneficence of their actions."

We need some help here to understand Washington's intent. A modern equivalent of Washington's staid and archaic eighteenth century rhetoric is: "they [i. e., religious Americans] will be ambitious to surpass others in demonstrating convincingly their heartfelt declaration of faith by the sinlessness of their lives and the kindness of their actions." Why must one's faith be demonstrated by such works? Washington's answer stated: "For no man, who is profligate in his morals, or a bad member of the civil community, can possibly be a true Christian, or a credit to his own religious society." In other words, a true Christian was one who possessed moral restraint that blessed the society through good citizenship and brought credibility to his own religious community as well. Washington was, in essence, applying the biblical teachings of James 2 to the spiritual and civil context: "Faith without works is dead."

If this was not a conversation between a group of Christians and a Christian president, then consider the incongruity that occurred here. A committee of pre-eminent theologians and elders representing their entire denomination were utterly deceived about Washington's faith. And Washington, unwilling to disabuse them of their mistaken notion, played along. Instead of honorably explaining their misunderstanding of his views, he furthered the mistake of the misguided Christian clergymen by deceptively expressing a faith he did not possess. Then to add insult to injury, he went on to expound as a false Christian a fundamental question of the Christian religion, namely, who is a true Christian. In so doing he, in essence, alluded to the teaching of the classic biblical text of James 2, which he, as a Deist, did not believe.

This analysis is not intended to be a *reductio ad absurdum*. The fact is, the options are fairly straightforward. Either Washington was a Christian, or he was a deceptive Deist. If he were the latter, his claim to be a man of honesty and character—the very thing the Presbyterians had celebrated in their letter to Washington—was just as much a sham as his counterfeit Christianity and his pretense of piety.

NON-PARTISANSHIP, PROMOTING THE GENERAL GOOD

When we considered Washington's personality several chapters ago, we discovered that he saw himself as a non-partisan leader.[61] He was not one given to partisan politics and petty conflicts, and thus, if he found parties, he tried to reconcile them. Thus, he wrote on July 6, 1796, to Thomas Jefferson, openly expressing some of the pain partisan politics inflicts on those who govern by principle:

> ...and moreover, that I was no believer in the infallibility of the politics, or measures of *any man living*. In short, that I was no party man myself, and the first wish of my heart was, if parties did exist, to reconcile them. To this I may add, and very truly, that, until with in the last year or two ago, I had no conception that Parties would, or even could go, the length I have been witness to; nor did I believe until lately, that it was within the bonds of probability; hardly with in those of possibility, that, while I was using my utmost exertions to establish a national character of our own, independent, as far as our obligations, and justice would permit, of every nation of the earth; and wished, by steering a steady course, to preserve this Country from the horrors of a desolating war, that I should be accused of being the enemy of one Nation, and subject to the influence of another; and to prove it, that every act of my administration would be tortured, and the grossest, and most insidious mis-representations of them be made (by giving one side *only* of a subject, and that too in such exaggerated and indecent terms as could scarcely be applied to a Nero; a notorious defaulter; or even to a common pick-pocket). But enough of this; I have already gone farther in the expression of my feelings, than I intended.[62]

Similarly, George Washington eschewed any form of prejudice. He once stated, "I am uninfluenced by prejudice, having no hopes or fears but for the general good."[63] On the contrary, Washington once declared that his concern first and foremost was the general good:

> I have no object separated from the general welfare to promote. I have no predilections, no prejudices to gratify, no friends, whose interests or views I wish to advance at the expence of propriety.[64]

One of his final written lines on politics was about his desire to keep America neutral in international politics. Writing to Lafayette, on December 25, 1798, Christmas Day only a year before he died, Washington says,

> On the Politics of Europe I shall express no Opinion, nor make any inquiry who is Right or who is Wrong. I wish well to all nations and to all men. My politics are plain and simple. I think every nation has a Right to establish that form of Government under which It conceives It shall live most happy; provided it infracts no Right or is not dangerous to others. And that no Governments ought to interfere with the internal concerns of Another, except for the security of what is due to themselves.[65]

CONCLUSION: WASHINGTON'S PRINCIPLES OF LEADERSHIP

Nevertheless, a political candidate creates competition and rivalry simply by trying to lead. So, in spite of Washington's desire to be non-political, he was often in the midst of political intrigue. This happened when he tried to step down after his first term, but was urged to run again.[66] Only months before Washington died, political intrigue surfaced again at the end of John Adam's first term, when there were those who attempted to persuade him to leave retirement and pursue a third term, fearing that Adams would not be reelected.[67]

How did Washington seek to lead in the midst of a competitive and divisive political context? The answer is found in his concept of seeking the good of "the great whole." A full study of Washington's principles of leadership would be beneficial to all who seek to learn to lead better. But here, we simply present a few insightful comments from the great leader of early America. These principles are simply given in the chronological order they occur in Washington's writings.

Principle # 1: Smaller Groups When Well Led Will Reflect The Unity Of The "Great Whole."

In short, each Brigade should be an epitome of the great whole, and move by similar Springs upon a smaller scale.[68]

Principle # 2: Governance Requires The Best Men So That "The Great Whole" Is Not Mismanaged.

… that each State would … compel their ablest Men to attend Congress; that they would instruct them to go into a thorough investigation of the causes that have produced so many disagreeable effects in the Army and Country; in a word that public abuses should be corrected, and an entire reformation worked;…These, if the great whole is mismanaged must sink in the general wreck and will carry with it the remorse of thinking that we are lost by our own folly and negligence.[69]

Principle # 3: You Can't Please Everyone, So Seek The Good Of "The Great Whole."

To please every body is impossible; were I to undertake it I should probably please no body. If I know myself I have no partialities. I have from the beginning, and I will to the end pursue to the best of my judgment and abilities one steady line of conduct for the good of the great whole. This will, under all circumstances administer consolation to myself however short I may fall of the expectations of others. …The hour therefore is certainly come when party differences and disputes should subside; when every Man (especially those in Office) should with one hand and one heart pull the same way and with their whole strength. Providence has done, and I am perswaded is disposed to do, a great deal for us.[70]

Principle # 4: Jealous Parties Must Be Urged To Exercise The Wisdom Of Being Part Of "The Great Whole."

My first wish now is, that the States may be wise; that they may improve the advantages which they have obtained; that they may consider themselves individually, as parts of the great whole; and not by unreasonable jealousies, and ill-founded prejudices, destroy the goodly fabrick we have been Eight years labouring to erect. But without more liberallity of Sentiment and action, I expect but little.[71]

Principle # 5: Withering Criticism Can Be Weathered By A Consistent Policy Of Never Seeking Merely Local Or Partial Considerations, But By Always Seeking

"The Great Whole's" Substantial And Permanent Interests.

Gentlemen: In every act of my administration, I have sought the happiness of my fellow-citizens. My system for the attainment of this object has uniformly been to overlook all personal, local and partial considerations: to contemplate the United States, as one great whole: to confide, that sudden impressions, when erroneous, would yield to candid reflection: and to consult only the substantial and permanent interests of our country.[72]

Principle #6: Pursue the true interests of the Country rather than popularity.

I know the delicate nature of the duties incident to the part which I am called to perform; and I feel my incompetence, without the singular assistance of Providence to discharge them in a satisfactory manner. But having undertaken the task, from a sense of duty, no fear of encountering difficulties and no dread of losing popularity, shall ever deter me from pursuing what I conceive to be the true interests of my Country.[73]

As we have reviewed Washington's impact as a leader and his leadership principles, we are in a better place to understand the interconnection between the First Inaugural Address on April 30, 1789 and his first Thanksgiving Proclamation of October 3, 1789. In the first, he appealed to the "sacred fire of liberty" that had been entrusted to the American people in their "experiment" in representative government. In the second, he told the new nation how to fan the "sacred fire of liberty" so that it might burn even more brightly. His proposed method was by acknowledging the Providence of Almighty God and humbly imploring his blessing on the nation. Such words would have been most appropriate coming from the lips of a chaplain or a preacher from his pulpit. Yet it is striking just how naturally they came from George Washington as he assumed his pulpit of the presidency as American's first godly leader. Washington had indeed "turned preacher after all."[74]

TWELVE

George Washington's Family Life

"I have always considered
marriage as the most interesting event of one's life,
the foundation of happiness or misery."
George Washington, May 23, 1785[1]

George Washington was self consciously a family man. His extended family spread throughout Virginia,[2] and he knew that his ancestry went back into the prior centuries of English history.[3] As a soldier, he had a military "family."[4] His presidential staff constituted a "family."[5] His slaves and servants,[6] the tutors for his children,[7] and the helpers in his home were all part of his "family."[8] With other "philanthropists," he was concerned for "the happiness of the great family of mankind."[9] No wonder George and Martha decided at one point that the size of their "family" had gotten large enough.[10]

But most important to Washington was his own family. He took pleasure in family life[11] and in being with his family.[12] In the midst of his busy public life, he sought to keep family responsibilities[13] and matters in mind.[14] When he left to lead the Revolution, he knew his goodbye to his family could have been his last.[15] This prompted him to commit his life and his family to the care of Providence[16] and to the family network that surrounded them.[17]

Because of his lengthy absences from home, he deeply valued mail from his family[18] and the support of his close relations.[19] He was authentically concerned for his brothers, relatives and their children's education.[20] And, like most families, Washington worried about family finances, not only for his own home,[21] but also for his aging widowed mother, who needed his financial support.[22] He personally composed his last will and testament carefully, recognizing individual members of his family, including his adopted grandchildren, "the two whom we have reared from their earliest infancy, namely: Eleanor Parke Custis, and George Washington Parke Custis" as well as his "dearly beloved wife Martha Washington."[23]

In Washington's era, the fragility of life, coupled with the primitive state of medical care, raised the constant concern of the family's health[24] and the constant threat of an unexpected death in the family.[25] The youthful Washington had been confident of his physical strength,[26] but soon the toll of warfare made him not so sure.[27] The aging President thought death was never far away.[28] His letters often commented on the various states of health found in his family[29] or when the tragedy of death struck.[30]

While death was all too frequent, divorce was almost unknown. The word "divorce" never appears in all of Washington's writings. He was certainly aware that an "unhappy marriage"[31] could occur, which prompted him to give sage advice to his younger family members[32] or to explain why he hoped to postpone a marriage of his children, even if the proposed marriage seemed like a good match.[33] He even indulged in an occasional aside, prompted by a surprising match or humorous appearance of newlyweds he knew.[34] He frequently commented on the news of weddings or joyfully extended his congratulations to newlyweds.[35] Washington summarized his premarital counseling wisdom in a letter to his brother-in-law Burwell Bassett, as a wedding in the Washington family was beginning to take shape,

> It has ever been a maxim with me thro' life, neither to promote, nor to prevent a matrimonial connection, unless there should be something indispensably requiring interference in the latter. I have always considered marriage as the most interesting event of one's life, the foundation of happiness or misery. To be instrumental therefore in bringing two people together who are indifferent to each other, and may soon become objects of hatred; or to prevent a union which is prompted by mutual esteem and affection, is what I never could reconcile to my feelings; and therefore, neither directly nor indirectly have I ever said a syllable to

Fanny or George upon the subject of their intended connexion. But as their attachment to each other seems to have been early formed, warm and lasting, it bids fair to be happy: if therefore you have no objection, I think the sooner it is consummated the better.[36]

At any rate, knowing something about the Washington family life helps us to address Washington's religious beliefs. To give us an introductory overview and enable us to keep track of his family life, we present the following chronological summary of some of the key events in George and Martha's family life.

THE FAMILY CHRONOLOGY OF GEORGE AND MARTHA WASHINGTON

1731	June 2 —- Martha Dandridge [Custis, Washington] was born.
1732	February 22 (old style, February 11) - George William Washington was born at Bridges Creek, Westmoreland County, Virginia. Father: Augustine Washington; Mother: Mary Ball.
	April 3 —- George William Washington baptized.
1738	December 1 —- Washington family moved to Ferry Farm on the other side of the Rappahannock River from Fredericksburg.
1743	April 12 —- George's father, Augustine, died. George's older half-brother, Lawrence, inherited his father's Hunting Creek farm, which he renamed Mount Vernon in honor of his military commander. George received Ferry Farm, but it was under his mother's control until he came of age.
	July 19 — Lawrence married Anne Fairfax, and so married into the wealthy family that possessed the vast tract of Virginia called the Northern Neck (which today encompasses a vast section of northern Virginia.).
1746	September —- George was encouraged by Lawrence to join the British Navy. After Mary Washington objected, he did not proceed, although he had his commission.
1747	George, having completed his formal schooling, began to live with his brother Lawrence at Mount Vernon and began to learn surveying.
1748	March-April —- Accompanied George William Fairfax on a month long surveying trip of Lord Fairfax's lands in the

Shenandoah Valley, experiencing the frontier and the Indians for the first time.

December 17 — George William Fairfax married eighteen-year-old Sarah ("Sally") Cary, who became a friend to George.

1749 Martha Dandridge married wealthy Virginian, Daniel Parke Custis. George appointed official surveyor of Culpepper County, Virginia.

1750 October 16 —- George bought a tract of land in the Shenandoah and so began his lifelong business of land acquisition.

1751 September 28 —- Traveled to Barbados with Lawrence, who was seeking relief from tuberculosis.

November 17 —- December 12 —- George's Diary recorded, "Was strongly attacked with the small Pox."[37]

1752 January 26 —- George arrived safely back in Virginia

July 26 —- Lawrence died, leaving Mount Vernon to George, if Anne Fairfax Washington died without children.

September 1 —- George joined the Fredericksburg Masonic Lodge

November 6 —- Washington appointed to the rank of major in the Virginia Militia.

1754-1758 Washington's military service in the French and Indian War

1754 John ("Jacky") Parke Custis born to Martha and Daniel Parke Custis.

Mount Vernon became George's, when Lawrence Washington's only daughter died at the age of four.

1757 Martha ("Patsy") Parke Custis born to Martha and Daniel Parke Custis Daniel Parke Custis died suddenly, and Martha Custis became a wealthy widow.

1758 Colonel George Washington paid two spring visits to Martha Custis, whereupon they became engaged.

July 24 —- Washington elected to the Virginia House of Burgesses, where he continuously served until the American Revolutionary War.

1759 January 6 —- George married the widowed Mrs. Martha Dandridge Custis.

April 6 —- Martha and George Washington, with Martha's two children, John Parke Custis and Martha "Patsy" Custis, took up residence at a remodeled Mount Vernon and began their new family life with Col. George Washington, the consummate Virginian gentleman farmer.

1762   October 25 —- Following in his father's footsteps, Washington became a vestryman in the Truro Parish in Fairfax County, a position he held through the Revolutionary War.

1763   October 3 —- Assumed position as Warden of Pohick Church in Truro Parish.

1765   September 20 —- Disapproved of Stamp Act in letter to Martha's uncle, Francis Dandridge in England.

1770   October 5 — Began journey to the Ohio and Kanawha Rivers in Indian Country to secure claims on lands given in payment to himself and fellow soldiers for service in the French and Indian War.

1773   June 19 —- Patsy Parke Custis, Washington's stepdaughter, died at Mount Vernon of what was likely an epileptic seizure.

July 5 —- John Parke Custis wrote to his mother Martha Washington, "Things My dear Mother were going on in this agreeable Manner, till last Thursday, the day I received Pappa's melancholy Letter, giving an account of my dear & only Sister's Death....she enjoys that Bliss prepared only for the good & virtuous,...comfort yourself with reflecting that she now enjoys in substance what we in this world enjoy in imagination & that there is no real Happiness on this side of the grave. ...remember you are a Christian and that we ought to submit with Patience to the divine Will and that to render you happy shall be the constant care of your affectionate and dutiful son."[38]

1774   February 3 —- John Parke Custis married Eleanor Calvert, who became the parents of Nelly Custis and George Washington Parke Custis, who lived after John's death with the Washingtons at Mount Vernon. Mrs. Washington, still being in mourning over the death of Patsy, did not attend the wedding, but is said to have sent a letter of love to Eleanor through George, who did attend.[39]

1775-1783   Commander in chief of the American Army in the Revolutionary War. George's cousin Lund Washington (1737-1796) took care of Mount Vernon during the war.

1775   June 15 — Congress commissions Washington as commander in chief of the American Army.

June 18 —- General Washington writes to Martha that he reluctantly agreed to lead the American Revolutionary Army. As a result, Washington would be gone from Mount Vernon for eight years.

December 11 —- Martha arrived at Cambridge to winter with General Washington at his headquarters. Tradition claims that she said she arrived at the last fire of the last battle of the year, and departed at the first fire of the first battle of the year, throughout the war. She spent every winter of the war with General Washington at his headquarters.

1777   December —- Anna Maria Bassett, Martha Washington's sister, and mother of Fanny Bassett (1767-1796), died.

1779   Granddaughter Eleanor Parke Custis born (1779-1852).

1781   Stepson John Parke Custis served as a civilian aide to General Washington.

Grandson George Washington Parke Custis born (1781-1857).

November 5 — John Parke Custis died less than three weeks after the British surrender at Yorktown. This occurred at Eltham, near Williamsburg at the home of his aunt and uncle, Anna Maria and Burwell Bassett. He had contracted camp fever or typhoid at the Battle of Yorktown. His wife, Eleanor Calvert, Martha Washington, and General Washington were all present when he died.

1783   At Mount Vernon, Mrs. Washington cared for the younger two of the four children of her deceased son, John Parke Custis.

Eleanor Parke Custis ("Nelly") and George Washington Parke Custis ("Tub") would be "adopted" by General and Mrs. Washington. They lived with them at Mount Vernon and at two presidential residences, until Mrs. Washington's death.

Nelly's and George Washington Parke Custis' older sisters, Elizabeth Parke Custis (1776-1732) and Martha Parke Custis (1777-1854) stayed with their mother, Eleanor Calvert Custis, at her home, Abingdon, only a few miles north of Mount Vernon.

December 24 —- On Christmas Eve, General Washington returned to Mount Vernon to stay for the first time since the beginning of the war.

1784–1788   These were years of rebuilding and repairing Mount Vernon after the inescapable neglect caused by the war.

1784   Niece Fanny Bassett, daughter of Martha's deceased sister, Anna Maria Dandridge Bassett, came to live at Mount Vernon in 1784.

1787   May-September —- George Washington lived in Philadelphia as he presided over the writing of the Constitution.

1789-1796   George and Martha Washington moved to New York and Philadelphia to serve as the First President and First Lady under the new Constitution.

During President Washington's two terms in office, Fanny Bassett (niece, daughter of Martha's sister) took care of the domestic responsibilities at Mount Vernon, and her husband, George Augustine Washington (nephew, son of George's brother Charles Washington), managed the Mount Vernon plantation.

1789   April 20 —- Martha wrote "I am truly sorry to tell you that the General is gone to New York...when, or whether he will ever come home again God only knows, - I think it was much too late for him to go into publick life again, but it was not to be avoided, our family will be deranged as I must follow him."

April 30 —- General Washington inaugurated as president in New York City.

May —- Martha Washington and her grandchildren moved to New York City.

August 25 —- Mary Washington died at 83 years of age.

October 23 —- As the nation's first First Lady, Martha finds her social life a challenge, comparing herself to a "state prisoner."

December 26 —- Yet, she willingly became much more active, visible, and effective in her role in support of the President. Martha wrote, "...it is owing to this kindness of our numerous friends in all quarters that my new and unwished for situation is not indeed a burden to me....I am still determined to be cheerful and to be happy in whatever situation I may be, for I have also learnt from experience that the greater part of our happiness or misery depends upon our dispositions, and not upon our circumstances."

1797   Martha, George, the now retired president, and the children returned to Mount Vernon.

1799   February 22 —- George Washington's final birthday celebration.

On this same day, Eleanor "Nelly" Parke Custis married Lawrence Lewis, a nephew of George Washington at Mount Vernon.

November —- Nelly and Lawrence's first child, Frances Parke Lewis, was born at Mount Vernon. They later built their home on land that George Washington had given to them, near Mount Vernon.

December 14 —- George Washington died at home, with Martha seated beside his bed with an open Bible. His last words were "'Tis well." Her first words spoken when she was told he had died were, "'Tis well. All is now over, I shall soon follow him! I have no more trials to pass through!"

1800   April 5 — Martha wrote to a friend, "… your affliction I have often marked and as often have keenly felt for you but my own experience has taught me that griefs like these cannot be removed by the condolence of friends however sincere—If the mingling tears of numerous friends—if the sympathy of a Nation and every testimony of respect of veneration paid to the memory of the partners of our hearts could afford consolation, you and myself would experience it in the highest degree. But we know that there is but one source from whence comfort can be derived under afflictions like ours. To this we must look with pious resignation and with that pure confidence which our holy religion inspires."

December—Martha made arrangements at the courthouse in accordance with Washington's will to free his slaves at Mount Vernon, which took effect on January 1, 1801.

1802   May 22 — Martha Washington died, and her body was placed beside the president's in the family vault at Mount Vernon.

ARGUMENTS AGAINST WASHINGTON'S CHRISTIANITY THAT EMERGE FROM HIS FAMILY CONTEXT

There are generally four key issues raised in Washington's family context to argue against his Christianity.

- First, Washington allegedly rejected the childhood faith of his mother.[40]
- Second, Washington's marriage to Martha, the Christian, was a

passionless marriage of convenience,[41] and that Washington had a lifelong love for Sally Fairfax, who was married to his older friend, George William Fairfax.[42]

- Third, Washington's letters to his children do not reveal any Christian witness, and thus he could not have been a Christian.[43]
- Fourth, his last will and testament was written without any express witness to faith in Christ (although it does begin, as was often the custom, "In the name of God. Amen"), and when he died, he did not call for a clergyman and thus did not receive the Sacrament.[44]

In this chapter, we will consider the relationship between Washington and his mother, Mary. We will also evaluate the claim that Washington's marriage was only a marriage of convenience. But we will not consider Washington's relationship with Sally Fairfax until a later chapter. In this chapter, we will also engage the question of whether there was a Christian witness by Washington to his children. The last two concerns, namely, the absence of a Christian witness in Washington's will and the absence of a clergyman at Washington's death bed, will be discussed in a subsequent chapter as well.

Here we will address these arguments as we summarize Washington's relationship with his mother, his relationship with his wife Martha, and his relationships with his two sets of adopted children: Martha's children from her first marriage, John (Jack) Parke Custis and Martha (Patsy) Parke Custis, and, John Parke Custis' two children that the Washingtons took into their home when John died, namely Eleanor (Nelly) Parke Custis and George Washington (Tub) Parke Custis.

In addressing these arguments, we will discover that some of the strongest testimony for Washington's Christianity comes directly from his family. This evidence has generally been ignored, overlooked, or suppressed by those who claim that Washington was a Deist.

MARY WASHINGTON: WASHINGTON'S MOTHER

Mary Washington was a commanding figure in her own right. By personal traits and personal circumstances, as a young widowed mother of five children, she, by necessity, became a dominating force in her family.[45] George's older cousin Lawrence Washington, of Chotank (1728-1813), one of his childhood friends, gave a compelling description of his Aunt Mary,

> I was often there with George, his playmate, schoolmate, and young man's companion. Of the mother I was ten times more afraid than

I ever was of my own parents. She awed me in the midst of her kindness, for she was, indeed, truly kind. I have often been present with her sons, proper tall fellows too, and we were all as mute as mice; and even now, when time has whitened my locks, and I am the grand-parent of a second generation, I could not behold that remarkable woman without feelings it is impossible to describe. Whoever has seen that awe-inspiring air and manner so characteristic in the Father of his Country, will remember the matron as she appeared when [she was] the presiding genius of her well-ordered household, commanding and being obeyed.[46]

Mary Washington was a commanding presence, indeed.

Washington scholar Willard Sterne Randall (writing in 1997) apparently does not share Lawrence Washington's reverence for Mary Washington, since he gives her one of the least flattering descriptions we have encountered. Randall writes, "Once he left his Bible-thumping mother's household he may never have taken Anglican communion again."[47]

How Randall can legitimately call her by this disrespectful title is not clear, since he provides no written evidence to substantiate his claim. Moreover, given the fact that the epithet "Bible-thumping" is a pejorative and prejudicial word, it would be difficult to label that description a scholarly one. Even if the criticism might be inferred from the fact that Christian materials were used to train George as a child, then the same criticism would have to be targeted toward George's father and older brother Lawrence as well, since in the chapter on Washington's education, we saw how both his father and his mother provided Christian educational materials for George. We might as well say that George came from a "Bible-thumping" family.

In a later chapter, we will discuss the question of whether Washington communed in the Anglican tradition or in other Christian contexts, which he sometimes did (as we shall see). What concerns us here most, however, is the possible implication from Randall's derogatory description of Mary Washington that Washington rejected his mother's faith. Did Washington reject his mother's faith? If scholarship requires written sources to corroborate a scholar's claim, the answer is a resounding "no." There is not a shred of evidence wherein Washington ever claimed to distance himself from the religious tradition in which he was raised. So, as we pursue a scholarly answer to the question of whether Washington abandoned his childhood faith, let us begin by considering the faith of Mary Washington herself.

Mary Washington's strength of character was spiritually motivated. Her last will and testament, for example, reflected her Christian faith, which was anything but perfunctory, even though the words of her last will and testament reflected a common pattern found also in the short form of a will that young George had copied

> In the name of God, Amen. I, Mary Washington, of Fredericksburg, in the county of Spotsylvania, being in good health, but calling to mind the uncertainty of this life, and being willing to dispose of what remains of my earthy estate, do make and publish this, my last Will, recommending my soul into the hands of my Creator, hoping for remission of all my sins through the merits and mediation of Jesus Christ, the Saviour of mankind.[48]

What was Washington's attitude toward his Christian mother? The written evidence makes it abundantly clear that George was always respectful of his mother and openly expressed his love for his brothers and sisters. Consider this letter written by young Col. Washington, only weeks before the disastrous battle that cost General Braddock his life:

> Honour'd Madam: I came to this place last Saturday, and shall set out tomorrow with the General for Wills Creek; where I fear we shall wait some time for a sufficient number of Waggons to transport us over the Mountains.
>
> I am very happy in the General's Family, and I am treated with a complaisant Freedom which is quite agreeable; so that I have no occasion to doubt the satisfaction I propos'd in making the Campaigne.
>
> As we have met with nothing yet worth relating I shall only beg my Love to my Brother's and Sister's; and Compliments to Friends.
>
> I am, Honour'd Madam,
>
> Yr. most Dutiful and Obedt. Son.[49]

He also openly expressed his affection for her in word and deed. Consider the conclusion he penned to his letter to her dated February 15, 1787. His words are "your most dutiful and affectionate Son." He began with "Honored Madam." The letter dated February 14, 1787, to Charles Washington shows the kind of love that Mary

An example of Washington's warm greetings to his family members, followed by a letter to his mother.

Washington instilled in her family for one another. [50] His concluding words here are, "I am ever yours" words that Washington elsewhere reserves for his dear friend Lafayette. [51] He adds the P. S., "My love in which Mrs. Washington joins to my sister and the family." Mary Washington's family seemed to be quite affectionate, for all of her alleged overbearing spirituality. There is only one known extant letter that Mary Washington wrote to George. It was signed "I am my dear George your loving and affectionate mother." [52]

At news of his brother Charles' wedding plans, he wrote to his mother in 1757. He began with the salutation "Honored Madam" and concluded with the words, "I offer my love to Charles and am honored madam, your most dutiful and affectionate Son." [53] Even when Washington had to address several sensitive, financial issues with his mother in 1787, he used very similar language. [54] When he responded to the congratulations of the leaders of Fredericksburg at the end of the war in 1784, he honored her when he wrote, "...my revered Mother, by whose maternal hand (early deprived of a father) I was led from childhood." [55]

In many ways, George was much like his mother in that both had an intense concern for personal privacy and a deep concern for financial resources. For example, Mary Washington somehow engineered the House of Burgesses to consider providing her a pension from the state of Virginia during the War, while Washington was out of state. An embarrassed Washington wrote to the Burgesses and put a stop to the discussion, declaring, "…all of us, I am certain, would feel much hurt, at having our mother a pensioner, while we had the means of supporting her."[56]

While financial issues and a strong desire for privacy by Mary Washington may have strained their relationship at times,[57] they maintained a close enough relationship that allowed George to have close friend Lafayette visit her and converse with her in her role as the General's mother.[58] George Washington's records show that he not only visited her,[59] but he rode to see her sometimes on the coldest winter days.[60] He stopped at her home when traveling.[61]

History also records his emotional farewell visit to his mother when she was dying from cancer as he was leaving to assume the presidency.[62] His words at Mary's death were reflective of his respect, faith, and love for her:

> Awful, and affecting as the death of a Parent is, there is a consolation in knowing, that Heaven has spared her to an age, beyond which few attain, and favored her with the full enjoyment of her mental faculties, and as much bodily strength as usually falls to the lot of fourscore. Under these considerations and a hope that she is translated to a happier place, it is the duty of her relatives to yield due submission to the decrees of the Creator. When I was last at Fredericksburg, I took a final leave of my Mother never expecting to see her more.[63]

As we conclude this section, let us summarize what we have discovered from the evidence found in their rather limited correspondence and records. Mary Washington was a widow who reared five children as a single mother. George, her firstborn son, called her his "revered mother," throughout his life and addressed her as "honored Madam." He cared for her both from affection and from a sense of duty as a son. She clearly managed her children from a place of authority rather than intimacy, although she openly expressed her love for her children. This was unlike George's and Martha's style of parenting, since the letters of their children, as we will see below, reveal that they were called "pappa" and "dearest mamma."

Washington, although busy and under great responsibilities, willingly sacrificed his time, comfort, and resources to meet her legitimate needs. He respectfully and even pointedly disagreed with her when he felt he must. When she grew elderly, he urged her to move in with one of her children,[64] including into his home, yet he openly pointed out why Mount Vernon would never be a place of refuge for her, given her strong desire for privacy, peace, and quiet.

He wrote to her of Mount Vernon, "For in truth it may be compared to a well resorted tavern, as scarcely any strangers who are going from north to south, or from south to north, do not spend a day or two at it."[65] Yet their disagreements did not keep him from visiting her in his hometown of Fredericksburg and worshiping with her there at St. George's Episcopal Church.[66]

Even when he became renowned, Washington did not hide his mother from his illustrious friends. He made sure that he said his last farewell to her, knowing that her declining health and his serving as president in New York almost surely meant she would die while he was gone. He openly wrote of his grief when he learned the news of her passing. He never left a written hint that he had rejected the Christian faith that she had taught him. Instead, he continued to worship in and at times to lead the church of his childhood in which his mother and father had baptized him, the Anglican Church.

Throughout his single and married life, he openly communicated his love and sincere affection to his siblings and their families—siblings that he, as Mary Washington's first born son, had had a role in caring for after his father died,. He even continued her practice of reading sermons to the family and using the *Book of Common Prayer* in his own family.

The inescapable conclusion is that Washington had a noteworthy and respectable relationship with his mother and the faith of his parents.

MR. AND MRS. GEORGE WASHINGTON

As the French and Indian War came to an end, Washington's interests turned to his farm and to the new family he would create with the widowed Mrs. Martha Custis.[67] The wedding of George and Martha was a glorious affair.[68] The marriage of George and Martha gave George a great deal of additional wealth, but also a great deal of additional responsibility.[69] Washington wrote to Martha's uncle, Francis Dandridge, in England in 1765,

Sir: If you will permit me after six years silence, the time I have been married to your Niece, to pay my respects to you in this Epistolary way I shall think myself happy in beginning a correspondence which cannot but be attended with pleasure on my side....I live upon Potomack River in Fairfax County, about ten Miles below Alexandria and many Miles distant from any of my Wife's Relations; who all reside upon York River, and who we seldom see more than once a year, not always that. My wife who is very well and Master and Miss Custis (Children of her former Marriage) all join in making a tender of their Duty and best respects to yourself and the Aunt.[70]

Was George and Martha's marriage just a "marriage of convenience"?[71] The evidence indicates it was much more than that. Washington's concern for Martha is evident in that he referred to "Mrs. Washington" over eight hundred times in his writings.[72] The extended Washington family enjoyed a fair amount of intimacy.[73] Washington openly expressed his love to his brothers and their families.[74] They expressed their love to those in need through acts of compassion.[75] For several years, Washington wore a painted miniature locket of Martha and apparently had it on when he died.[76]

The Washington family in an 1889 lithograph

247

Daily life for the Washingtons was sometimes a mixture of humor, frustration, and normal activities, as can be seen by consulting a few days in a week from Washington's diary.[77] Washington attempted to get regular exercise, even when in office. This included driving his chariot, riding his horse, or walking.

Washington's amusements in his family life were varied.[78] Consulting his diaries, one finds activities such as: cards,[79] theater,[80] fox-hunting, fishing, hunting deer, dancing and balls, constant hospitality with friends and guests to Mount Vernon and to the president's house. There were celebrations and banquets that included Washington's favorite toast, "All our friends." Washington's view of drinking was one of enjoying the "hilarity" of friends but avoiding drunkenness.[81] The family took trips and vacations to the springs and to the mountains. Reading books and sermons were also part of the family entertainment. After he was married, he never recorded attending another cock-fight.[82]

Only two of George and Martha's letters have survived. The others were destroyed by Martha after George's death. Martha burned them, thereby preserving the Washingtons' privacy from future generations. The two surviving letters communicate a spirit of intimacy, both referring to "Providence." George Washington wrote from Philadelphia on June 18, 1775 (just after receiving the commission from Congress to head up the colonial army), "I shall rely therefore, confidently, on that Providence which has heretofore preserved, and been bountiful to me, not doubting but that I shall return safe to you in the fall…"

George again wrote to Martha from Philadelphia on June 23, 1775, "…I go fully trusting in that Providence, which has been more bountiful to me than I deserve, and in full confidence of happy Meeting with you sometime in the Fall."

Like her husband, Martha's letters also mention divine Providence. Writing to Mercy Otis Warren from Valley Forge on March 7, 1778, she says, "…indeed I think providence was very bountiful in her goodness to your state….would bountiful providence aim a like stroke at Genl Howe, the measure of my happiness would be compleat."[83]

Writing to Mrs. Elizabeth Powel on January 18, 1788, Martha said, "She is blessed however with a charming family of children, and providence has been bountiful in giving her resolution and strength of Body and mind to be able to undertake the care that have developed upon her."[84]

The long absences created by the war required Martha to move to the winter quarters of the army so that they could seek to have a measure of family life in the eight-year-long war.[85] Mrs. Washington's first trip to join her husband was to

Cambridge, Massachusetts. She stopped first in Philadelphia, where she wrote to a friend, "I don't doubt but you have seen the Figure our arrival made in the Philadelphia paper— and I left it in as great pomp as if I had been a very great somebody."[86]

By Washington's own testimony, throughout his life, he was a happily married man. On September 20, 1759, he wrote, "I am now I believe fixed at this Seat [Mount Vernon] with an agreeable Consort [Mrs. Martha Washington] for Life and hope to find more happiness in retirement [from service in the British Army at the end of the French and Indian War] than I ever experienced amidst a wide and bustling World."[87]

On June 18, 1775, he wrote, "My Dearest: …You may believe me, my dear Patsy,… that I should enjoy more real happiness in one month with you at home, than I have the most distant prospect of finding abroad, if my stay were to be seven times seven years."[88] On May 23, 1785, he wrote, "I have always considered marriage as the most interesting event of one's life, the foundation of happiness or misery."[89] George did not think he would marry a second time if Martha died before him.[90]

Martha did not like public life, and had, like her husband, hoped to stay at Mount Vernon after his retirement from the military. Yet, she willingly, if reluctantly, followed.[91] She even compared herself at one point to a "state prisoner."[92] But finally, through the help of friends and her own spiritual growth, she was able to make the transition effectively so that she could become a great help to the president in his many responsibilities.[93] It was Martha's practice to keep constantly employed.[94]

Martha's faith as a Christian manifested itself especially as she faced the death of her husband[95] and of her sister.[96] But the death of Patsy, her daughter, was a particular moment of great sorrow and of faith for the entire family. Martha's son, John Parke Custis, wrote a letter reminding Martha of the Christian faith of the family, and in this way sought to comfort her at the time of the loss of Patsy.[97] Washington had expressed his deep concern for the physical sufferings of his stepdaughter Patsy Custis[98] and prayed fervently for her as she died. George Washington Parke Custis wrote of Washington's prayer for Patsy,

> Her delicate health, or, perhaps her fond affection for the only father
> she had ever known, so endeared her to the "general," that he knelt
> at her dying bed, and with a passionate burst of tears, prayed aloud
> that her life might be spared, unconscious that even then her spirit
> had departed.[99]

In his "Diary," Washington wrote: "June 19. At home all day. About five o'clock poor

Patsy Custis Died Suddenly." Writing to Burwell Bassett the next day, he explained the circumstances of Patsy's death and expressed his belief that, "the Sweet Innocent Girl Entered into a more happy and peaceful abode than any she has met with in the afflicted Path she hitherto has trod."[100]

But the ravages of death had not finished their assaults on Martha's family. She had lost her first husband, her sister, her daughter, and soon it would be her son Jacky as well. Although Jacky's prayers had been offered for the General's success,[101] he stayed home and married and raised a family. In 1774 Jacky, i.e., John Parke Custis, married Eleanor Calvert, who became the parents of Nelly Parke Custis and George Washington Parke Custis. Near the end of the war in 1781, John Parke Custis served as a civilian aide to General Washington. But on November 5, 1781, he died—less than three weeks after the British surrender at Yorktown. He had contracted camp fever or typhoid at the Battle of Yorktown. His wife, Martha Washington and General Washington were all present when he died. Writing about his father, George Washington Parke Custis stated, "In a little while the poor sufferer expired. Washington, tenderly embracing the bereaved wife and mother, observed to the weeping group around the remains of him he so dearly loved, 'From this moment I adopt his two youngest children as my own.'"[102]

Finally on December 24th, Christmas Eve, 1783, General Washington returned to Mount Vernon for the first time to stay since the beginning of the war. Martha would enjoy the life with her husband for sixteen more years, until he passed away in 1799. During all of those years, his adopted children Nelly and young George Washington lived in the presence of George and Martha. The children had a most unique opportunity to observe their faith.

WASHINGTON'S ALLEGED LACK OF CHRISTIAN WITNESS TO CHILDREN

The Washingtons had their share of experiences in rearing children, since they reared not only Martha's children, but her grandchildren as well. Martha had her share of trying to get the kids to places,[103] having them practice their music lessons,[104] and making room for a young, newlywed couple in the house until the first children would be born.[105]

As we have seen, Martha was called a Christian by those who wrote to her. Her son Jacky called her a Christian when he wrote a strong comforting Christian message from his college upon hearing of Patsy's death. In that same letter, he declared his belief that Patsy was in "bliss," and George, having prayed for her, wrote that she had entered "a more happy and peaceful abode." Washington was surrounded by Christians in his family. Was Washington himself a Christian? According to author Rupert Hughes, the answer was no. He based his argument on the writings of nineteenth century historian, Moncure Conway:

Etchings of Alfred the Great (AD 849-899), the English king who established the Christian kingdom of England, graced the dinning room at Mount Vernon

The Reverend Doctor Moncure D. Conway makes a statement that is impressive in view of the emphasis unjustifiably laid on the imaginary doctrine that Washington was brought up in an atmosphere of intense religion: "In his many letters to his adopted nephew and young relatives, he admonishes them about their morals, but in no case have I been able to discover any suggestion that they should read the Bible, keep the Sabbath, go to church, or any warning against Infidelity....If Washington were, indeed, so fervent a Christian as to deserve the name of "a soldier of the cross," often given to him by the clergy, it is puzzling that there should be such difficulty in finding a number of fervent proofs of his ardor."[106]

The only problem with Conway's argument is that, even if the preceding is true, it would not prove that Washington was a Deist. It might well reveal an inconsistent Christian, or that Washington was not an effective Christian parent. But these bare facts do not prove that he was a Deist. To prove that Washington was a Deist, Conway would have to show that Washington rejected the Bible as divine revelation; that he denied the deity of Christ, and that he was perhaps anti-clerical or that he denied Providence. But all of these conclusions cannot be drawn from this argument from silence. For example, Washington apparently did not refer to Providence at his death. Does this mean he no longer believed it? Washington never wrote the great Revolutionary War phrase, "No Taxation Without Representation." Does that mean that he did not believe it, or that it was not an issue for him? The argument from silence alone is always inadequate to prove a point.

As we conclude this chapter, we wish to respond to Conway's objections by considering Washington's Christian witness to his adopted grandchildren and their testimony to his Christian faith. First, it is important to remember that the Washington family always provided prayer books and Bibles for their children.[107] Further, Washington was concerned for their well-being and trusted in Providence to protect them.[108] He was deeply concerned to find the right tutor for young George Washington Parke Custis[109] as there had been for his father, John Parke Custis.[110] Washington often imparted moral advice to his family members.[111] He was also concerned to let others know that his political activities would always be governed by principles of moral virtue.[112]

Washington was deeply concerned about the appropriate school to train his children in.[113] Is there a reason why Washington's children never attended William and Mary? Washington was often in Williamsburg for his work with the House of Burgesses and he was asked to be chancellor of the school. One possible reason why Washington's children were at Annapolis, or Princeton, or the University of Pennsylvania, and why Washington loved Harvard (for its high moral standards), is the same as why they did not attend William and Mary—he saw that the students were not receiving adequate discipline as well as the glimmers of the infidelity of Deism that were beginning to be evident in the classroom.[114]

His teaching and counseling of young George Washington Parke Custis reveal a commitment to both morals and biblical ideas. Washington's letters to young George do emphasize wise choices and moral actions.[115] Some emphasize submitting to the authority of the teachers and tutors. But these tutors, such as Reverend Stanhope Smith of Princeton, were eminently Christian scholars.[116] This admonition to submit to the teaching of such a devout Christian scholar was, in fact, a Christian witness. Washington had assured that his step-grandson was being trained by the finest Christian educator in the country.[117] Further, one of the letters is explicitly theological and biblical.[118] In fact, in this letter dated 1798, Washington gives his young grandson a double scriptural admonition: "Dear Washington:…a fear that your *application to books* is not such as it ought to be, and that the *hours* that might be more profitably employed at your studies are mispent in this manner. Recollect again the *saying of the wise man,* "There is *a time for* all things," and sure I am this is not a time for a *boy of your age* to enter into engagements which might end in sorrow and repentance."[119] Washington's remark brings together words from Ecclesiastes 3:1 and 2 Corinthians 7:10. (emphasis ours)

We believe that Washington's actions and words show that he was pointing his children to the Christian faith. When one remembers that Washington took them to church, read sermons to them at home, along with giving them such counsel, and sending them to study under devout Christian teachers, the objections of Conway evaporate. Moreover, it is important to realize that many of these childhood letters between Washington and his grandson have not survived.

So did George Washington Parke Custis believe that his grandfather was a Christian? Conway says that Washington did not give a Christian witness to him. What witness does the younger George give of Washington's faith?

> General Washington was always a strict and decorous observer of the Sabbath. He invariably attended divine service once a day, when within reach of a place of worship. His respect for the clergy, as a body, was shown by public entertainments to them....On Sunday no visitors were admitted to the president's house, save the immediate relatives of the family, with only one exception: Mr. Speaker Trumbull, since governor of Connecticut, and who had been confidential secretary to the chief in the War of the Revolution, was in the habit of spending an hour with the president, on Sunday evenings. Trumbull practiced the lesson of punctuality, which he learned in the service of the olden time, with such accuracy, that the porter, by consulting his clock, could tell when to stand ready to open to the *Speaker's Bell*, as it was called in the family, from the circumstance of no hand other than the speaker's touching the bell on the evenings of the Sabbath.[120]

Later he adds what happened on the presidential Sabbath days.

> On Sundays, unless the weather was uncommonly severe, the president and Mrs Washington attended divine service at Christ church; and in the evenings, the president read to Mrs. Washington, in her chamber, a sermon, or some portion from the sacred writings. No visitors, with the exception of Mr. Speaker Trumbull, were admitted to the [president's quarters] on Sundays.[121]

Apparently Washington's adage of "deeds not words" was utilized to convey to his grandson the importance of the Sabbath, the significance of regular worship, and the value of the reading of the scriptures. Conway's charges are eviscerated in light of the testimony of the one who was allegedly not evangelized by Washington!

Similarly, Washington and his granddaughter, Nelly Custis, were clearly very close. Nelly Custis was counseled by Washington on the topic of falling in love in a most personal and memorable way in a keenly insightful letter.[122] When he heard that her suitor was moving her toward considering marriage, he wanted her to "relate all your feelings to me on this occasion: or as a Quaker would say, 'all the workings of the spirit within.'"[123] Washington soon gave his approval, and a candlelight wedding occurred at Mount Vernon.[124] Washington also provided land for Nelly and her husband to build their new home upon.[125]

Nellie Custis' testimony to Washington's Christianity, in our opinion, given her personal relationship with her parents George and Martha Washington, is conclusive evidence that Washington was not a Deist.

> He was a silent, thoughtful man. He spoke little generally; never of himself. I never heard him relate a single act of his life during the war. I have often seen him perfectly abstracted, his lips moving, but no sound was perceptible. I have sometimes made him laugh most heartily from sympathy with my joyous and extravagant spirits. I was, probably, one of the last persons on earth to whom he would have addressed serious conversation, particularly when he knew that I had the most perfect model of female excellence ever with me as my monitress, who acted the part of a tender and devoted parent, loving me as only a mother can love, and never extenuating or approving in me what she disapproved in others. She never omitted her private devotions, or her public duties; she and her husband were so perfectly united and happy that he must have been a Christian. She had no doubts, or fears for him. After forty years of devoted affection and uninterrupted happiness, she resigned him without a murmur into the arms of his Saviour and his God, with the assured hope of eternal felicity. Is it necessary that any one should certify, "General Washington avowed himself to *me* a believer in Christianity"? As well may we question his patriotism, his heroic, disinterested devotion to his country. His mottoes were, "Deeds, Not Words"; and "For God and My Country."

With sentiments of esteem,
    I am,
    Nelly Custis[126]

Nellie Custis' testimony to Washington's Christianity, in our opinion, given her personal relationship with her grandparents George and Martha Washington, demonstrates the impossibility of conceiving of Washington as a Deist. Her conclusion has no legitimate retort—"Is it necessary that any one should certify, 'General Washington avowed himself to *me* a believer in Christianity'? As well may we question his patriotism, his heroic, disinterested devotion to his country. His mottoes were, 'Deeds, Not Words'; and 'For God and My Country.'"

PART IV

George Washington the Churchman

THIRTEEN

George Washington The Parishioner

"It is with peculiar satisfaction I can say, that,
prompted by a high sense of duty in my attendance on
public worship, I have been gratified, during my residence
among you, by the liberal and interesting discourses which
have been delivered in your church."
George Washington (1797) [1]

Skeptics today often claim that George Washington was not a real Christian, but in our view, the burden of proof is on them to explain why he was consistently in church throughout his life, why the churches he was part of were entirely orthodox in terms of the Trinity and the doctrine of Christ, and why he attended churches where the Bible was regularly preached on Sunday.

Washington went to churches where the leaders had to affirm the key doctrines of the Christian Church. Furthermore, he was elected a lay-leader in the Church and as a leader, he had to take *oaths* affirming foundational Christian doctrines, which included these points and more:

- Christ was fully God and fully man

- Christ died on the cross to atone for sins.
- He rose bodily from the dead.
- He ascended into heaven and now sits at the right hand of God the Father.
- History is moving toward the climax of the return of Jesus Christ.
- The Bible is the Word of God.
- Sinners need to repent and believe in Jesus Christ for salvation, etc.

Indeed, given the facts, the burden of proof is not to prove that Washington was a Christian; the burden of proof is to prove that he was a skeptic who nevertheless sought to act like a Christian believer!

This chapter and the next will explore George Washington's life as an active churchman. Part 1 is his participation in the church as a parishioner. The next chapter will look at his leadership in the Anglican Church.

DIVIDED LOYALTIES?

It was not easy to be an Anglican and lead a revolution against the King of England. But somehow, Washington accomplished that very thing. The difficulties presented to him by the importance of the Anglican (Episcopal) Church in his life are captured in a letter that Lund Washington (1737-1796), his distant cousin and overseer of his farm, wrote to him concerning George's neighbor and close friend Bryan Fairfax (1736-1802). Washington at this time had been in command of the Continental army in Cambridge, Massachusetts, for only a few months. Lund related to General Washington that Bryan Fairfax had:

> ...become a preacher. He gave Public Notice that on such a Day he should preach at his own House. Accordingly on that Day, Many Assembled to hear him, but to their great Confusion & surprise he Advise'd them to return to the Bosom of that Church in which they had been brought up (The Church of England). For he had been at much pains in Examining the Scriptures, & the different modes of Worshiping the Supreme being, which was now adopted by many, to the disgrace of Christianity, & that he found none so pure & undefiled as that prescribed by the Canons of the Church of England.[2]

To Washington's great credit, his friendship never was broken with Bryan Fairfax, who entered holy orders in 1789, the same year that General Washington became President

Washington. We will return to the special friendship between Fairfax and Washington, but here we need to see how difficult it was to be part of a state church that was loyal to the King, even as one was leading a revolution *against* that King! But just as the friendship between these two men survived, the latter never forsook his allegiance to his childhood church; not even a revolution, nor a new constitution could end his loyalty to his Anglican (Episcopalian) tradition.

An anecdote that comes from Washington's military service in New England sets the stage for the written evidence of his role as a churchman. Author William Johnson observes:

> When Washington was passing through Litchfield, Connecticut, during the war, there was some desecration of the church, recalling the treatment of the cathedral in old Litchfield, England, by the soldiers of Cromwell. Washington himself saw some of his soldiers throw a shower of stones at the church, and at once rebuked them. He did not put forward the merely just argument that such acts were disorderly, but he put his personal feeling into what he said: "I am a churchman, and wish not to see the church dishonored and desolated in this manner."[3]

This church was likely an Anglican Church in a Puritan community.

Whether he actually said such or not, we do know that Washington was, from childhood to adulthood to his death, a "churchman." There are two reasons for stating this. The first is indirect—namely, the extensive ecclesiastical jargon that we find scattered through his writings.[4] The second is direct, thanks to the discovery of the old vestry book of Truro Parish in the early nineteen hundreds. Through this invaluable historical record, we can develop a far more accurate understanding of Washington's role as a vestryman and parishioner. (A vestryman was a lay-leader in the Anglican Church; the name is derived from the types of vests they wore.)

The existence of the vestry book was not known to Bishop William Meade, early bishop and historian of the Episcopal Church in Virginia, or to Paul Leicester Ford. Although published, it was not even consulted by Rupert Hughes or William Johnson. Thus, a very incomplete picture of his leadership in his church has resulted.

Early historian Jared Sparks could not properly interpret some pages recording vestry elections, and this resulted in the erroneous view that is still sometimes encountered, that Washington served in two vestries at the same time. The vestry book helps to explain that matter. Reverend Dr. Philip Slaughter explains:

> The present writer has been so fortunate as to find the old vestry book of Truro Parish; so long lost to the public eye that even Bishop Meade said he could hear no tidings' of it. . . It is now possible for the first time to authenticate its history by its own records, which are continuous from 1732 to 1785, when the civil functions of the Vestries were devolved by law upon the Overseers of the Poor.[5]

We will explore in more depth Washington's experience as a vestryman in the next chapter.

RESERVED SEATING

To raise money for the interior designing of the churches, they sold pews to the highest bidders. The Washington family entered the bidding for the choicest pews and was successful. The minutes reveal,

> [Number] twenty eight, one of the Center pews adjoining the north Isle and next to the Communion Table, to [Colonel] George Washington at the price of sixteen pounds. [Number] Twenty nine, one of the Center pews adjoining the north Isle, to Mr. Lund Washington, at the price of thirteen pounds ten shillings.[6]

Washington was tied with George William Fairfax as the highest bidder, as each paid sixteen pounds for their pew. They both bought the two pews that were closest to the Communion Table and to the altar piece that had the Lord's Prayer, Ten Commandments, and Apostles Creed. The pew of nephew Lund Washington was immediately behind George's pew. But George's pew had another feature that may have made his preferable; it was also on the front row and therefore closer to the pulpit. One may appropriately wonder why a vestryman would have bid for and wanted this most conspicuous pew, if he never intended to worship regularly or to partake of Communion.

GENERAL GEORGE WASHINGTON THE PARISHIONER

As we shall see, George Washington was exemplary in his attendance at the meetings of the vestry. So was his attendance at the Sunday services, according to his pastor, Lee Massey, as quoted by Bishop Meade.

> I never knew so constant an attendant in church as Washington. And his behavior in the house of God was ever so deeply reverential that it produced the happiest effect on my congregation, and greatly assisted me in my pulpit labors. No company ever withheld him from church. I have often been at Mount Vernon on Sabbath morning, when his breakfast table was filled with guests; but to him they furnished no pretext for neglecting his God and losing the satisfaction of setting a good example. For instead of staying at home, out of false complaisance to them, he used constantly to invite them to accompany him.[7]

But skeptical writer Paul L. Ford (1903) dismisses Massey's testimony: "This seems to have been written more with an eye to its influence on others than to its strict accuracy."[8]

Given the fact that Ford did not know of the existence of the vestry book, this dismissal of the pastor's credibility concerning Washington is understandable. But it is unfortunate that Paul Boller, Jr., (1962) would rely so heavily on Ford's unsubstantiated comment, given the fact that when he wrote his study on Washington's religion, the vestry book had been available for over a half century.[9] This is even more startling, since Paul Boller cites the vestry book at other points. With Washington's history as a vestryman and churchman, however, the comment by Reverend Massey concerning his attendance at worship seems more likely.

GEORGE WASHINGTON AND SUNDAY WORSHIP

While Washington's diaries are not a perfect source of his activities, they do give us insight into his Sunday worship practices. He grew up in a church-attending family. He went to church with his mother as a young boy, and years later, he went to church with her in Fredericksburg. His fame brought so many to see him at church that, when the over-full balcony let out a loud crack, according to Washington's diary, the congregation rapidly exited, disrupting the worship service.[10]

Washington was familiar with the special worship of the Anglican Church called "Gunpowder"—the service that commemorates the providential deliverance of the crown from Guy Fawkes November 5th plot to blow up Parliament.[11] He also regularly attended worship when there was a preacher in his Pohick Church. He did not generally attend if there was only a reader. Family tradition says that George Washington or someone else read sermons on many Sundays to the family.[12]

While his average attendance of about one time a month or so seems like a minimal commitment today, the fact is that it was substantial in his day, because the Washington family had to travel about nine miles over wilderness, dirt roads, often through mud or snow. Then, when they arrived at the church, it was unheated. (This was to prevent church fires.) Since the preacher was only there about once per month, if there was a preacher at all, or a healthy one available,[13] the Washington family was rather exemplary in worship. The Washington family also frequently suffered with the health maladies that in that day had little medically sound treatment.

From his diaries, we can see that he was a serious, but not a strict Sabbath keeper. Tradition records Washington being stopped in New England, while president, for traveling on the Sabbath day. He promptly cut his journey short and went to worship in this Puritan town. While his diary does not mention being stopped, Washington does record the events of the day.[14]

In Virginia, Washington never hesitated to travel on Sundays. Sundays were a day to travel, so that an early Monday activity could occur, whether for business or pleasure. But he did not fox hunt or work on Sundays, except for the quiet work of writing letters in the privacy of his room. He would give his servant and staff and soldiers Sundays off , if possible, for the opportunity to worship. To answer Boller's charge that George Washington fox hunted on Sundays, we note that on two Sundays Washington does mention fox hunting, but a careful reading of his diary states that he *traveled to* fox hunt, not that he fox hunted.[15] The Mondays following show that he spent the day in this favorite activity. Throughout his diaries, Sundays are always free from work activity or are passed over largely unnoticed, except for church attendance or hospitality given to guests.

Washington often entertained guests going to or coming from church on Sundays, which frequently included local or traveling clergy. In fact, his letters and diaries reveal that he either wrote to or entertained in his home over one hundred different clergymen![16]

We also know from Tobias Lear's notes that while he was George Washington's personal and family assistant when he was president, that either George or Lear read sermons to the family. George Washington Parke Custis, George Washington's adopted grandson, says that the president's Sunday was marked by a strict Sabbath rest.[17] Only the Sunday evening visit of the Speaker of the House was permitted as an exception. The promptness of the Speaker's visit, says Custis, resulted in the Sunday bell being called "The Speaker's Bell."

The diaries do show a period immediately after George Washington's return from the presidency to Mount Vernon of a non-attendance at church. Several reasons come to mind to explain this absence. Washington was likely overwhelmed with Mount Vernon work after eight years in the military, and then, after only a few years break to try to catch up, he had eight more years away from his plantation while president.

Further, his local church of Pohick had basically been closed for Episcopalian worship, with the disestablishment of the Church, and the physical limitations and clerical retirement of Reverend Massey. Massey had lost his front teeth and could no longer preach clearly and having lost tax support from the Virginia legislature, a new clergyman could not be hired. George Washington actually answered a letter from patriot and Presbyterian clergyman Reverend Dr. John Witherspoon about the status of the Pohick church. He answered, saying it had a preacher at the time.[18]

George Washington's interest in the new church in Alexandria was sincere, since he bought a pew there, but it too was a very long drive from Mount Vernon over the same kinds of roads that had made it difficult for George and his family to attend Pohick. As mentioned above, given the fame Washington had acquired, it had to be tempting for George and Martha just to stay home on some Sundays and simply to read the sermons he had begun to collect, and thus avoid the church-going curiosity seekers.

Finally, as a world-renowned leader, his correspondence continued to grow, but he was now without a presidential staff. Sundays had always been correspondence days for George.

But after about a year, George Washington returned to his regular church attendance pattern. While Alexandria by this time had weekly services, so the aging and weary president, who simply wanted to enjoy his "vine and fig tree" of Mount Vernon, chose not to attend every week. He was, however, preparing to meet his own death "with good grace," whenever he would be summoned by "the Giver of Life."[19] His aspiration was to die at Mount Vernon and be buried and be known as "an honest man."[20] When George Washington breathed his last, his funeral was conducted by the Alexandrian Episcopal Church's pastor, Reverend Thomas Davis. He conducted the service at Mount Vernon, where Washington's remains were interred. Years later, when the family crypt was moved to its new (and current site), his heirs put on the vault a text that played a prominent role in the *Book of Common Prayer's Funeral Liturgy* – "I am the resurrection and the life." These, of course, are words found in John 11:25.

All told, Washington's Sundays corroborate the claim that he was a churchman.

THE SWITCH FROM POHICK TO CHRIST CHURCH, ALEXANDRIA

Why Washington ceased his worship at Pohick is not completely known, but one reason seems obvious. As noted earlier, with the retirement of Lee Massey and the loss of governmental support for the established Anglican Church at the beginning of the Revolution, worship services at Pohick became few and far between. As the result of the disestablishment of the Episcopal Church under Jefferson's and Madison's Bill on religious liberty, on Easter, 1786, by Act of Assembly, all vestries were dissolved and the Protestant Episcopal Church was incorporated.[21] This ended the official family connection with Pohick, since Lund Washington's brief tenure as a vestryman in Truro Parish was terminated by the Act.

From this time on, Washington generally attended services at Christ Church in Alexandria. There is example, however, of his still worshiping on occasion at Pohick. On October 2, 1785, a guest preacher was at Pohick, and the Washingtons traveled to hear him. George's diary says,

> Went with Fanny Bassett, Burwell Bassett, Dr. Stuart, George A. Washington, Mr. Shaw and Nelly Custis to Pohick Church to hear a Mr. Thompson preach who returned home with us to dinner, where I found Reverend Mr. Jones, formerly a Chaplain in a Pa. Regiment. After we were in bed about eleven o'clock at night, Mr. Houdon (sent from Paris by Mr. Jefferson and Dr. Franklin to take my Bust, in behalf of the State of Virginia, with three young men, assistants, introduced by Mr. Perin a French gentleman of Alexandria) arrived here by water from the latter place. 3d. October. The two Reverend gentlemen who dined and lodged here went away after breakfast.[22]

On April 25, 1785, Washington signed a bond that bound him and his family "forever" with an annual pew rent for the very pew that he had purchased over a decade before. The attention to detail and the intricacy of this document, which was so typical of Washington, seem to indicate that Washington himself helped write up the agreement:

> We, the subscribers, do hereby agree that the pews we now hold in

the Episcopal Church at Alexandria shall be forever charged with annual rent of five pounds, Virginia money, each; and we hereby promise to pay (each for himself promising to pay) annually, forever, to the Minster and Vestry of the Protestant Episcopal Church in Fairfax Parish, or, if the Parish should be divided, to the Minister and Vestry of the Protestant Episcopal Church in Alexandria, the said sum of five pounds for each pew for the purpose of supporting the Minster in the said Church. Provided nevertheless that if any law of this Commonwealth should hereafter compel us, our heirs, executors and administrators or assigns, to pay to the support of Religion, the pew-rent hereby granted shall, in that case, be considered as part of what we, by such law, be required to pay. Provided also that each of us pay only in proportion to the part we hold of the said pews. For the performance of which payments, well and truly to be made forever annually, within six months after demanded, we hereby bind ourselves (each for himself separately) our heirs, executors, administrators and assigns, firmly by these presents. In witness whereof, we have hereunto set our hands and seals this 25th day of April in the year of our Lord 1785.[23]

This record is corroborated by Nelly Custis Lewis, George and Martha's adopted granddaughter. "General Washington had a pew in Pohick Church and one in Christ Church, Alexandria. He attended the church at Alexandria when the weather and roads permitted a ride of ten miles."[24] You can visit the original pew itself at Christ Church. (The interior of Pohick Church was destroyed by Union soldiers during the Civil War; it has since been restored, and the restoration includes Washington's box pew.)

Some skeptics have argued that he did not attend Communion for the last several years of his life because he didn't believe in the Christian doctrine of atonement. We disagree with the premise of the argument—that he never received Communion once the war started. We will consider that question in a later chapter.

George Washington's religion was quiet and personal—yet, he went to church, taking his family with him. When one looks at Washington, whose creed was "deeds not words," his deeds, at every point, represent a man committed to the Christian faith. He served his church at great sacrifice. He took his personal wealth and invested in church buildings, pews, and various decorations for the church.

His diaries, and other records show that he knew some sixty pastors that were either personal friends or who were entertained by George and Martha in their home. In addition, he wrote letters to over forty pastors from across the country. The records further show that he had prayers at his table when a clergyman was present, and sometimes he led the thanksgiving prayers at his own table (if a minister was not present). Dr. Ashabel Green, one of the chaplains of the Congress from 1792 to 1800 wrote:

> It was the usage under President Washington's administration that the chaplains of Congress should dine with him once in every month, when Congress was in session...the place of the chaplain was directly opposite to the President. The company stood while the blessing was asked, and on certain occasions, the President's mind was probably occupied with some interesting concern, and on going to the table he began to ask a blessing himself. He uttered but a word or two, when, bowing to me, he requested me to proceed...I mention this, because it shows that President Washington always asked a blessing himself when a chaplain was not present.[25]

George Washington said after absent-mindedly praying with a clergyman present, "At least the Reverend Gentleman will know that we are not entirely graceless at Mount Vernon."[26]

On Sunday mornings he went to church. On Sunday nights, he usually read a sermon or a passage of scripture to Martha and the children.[27] One eyewitness, quoted by nineteenth century Washington biographer E. C. M'Guire, shows how regularly Washington was at church attendance. The eye-witness remarked to a visiting friend, who was curious to see the Father of his Country, "You will certainly see him on Sunday, as he is never absent from church when he can get there...."[28] Where could a visitor go to see George Washington? In church.

Eleanor Parke ("Nelly") Custis, who was George and Martha Washington's granddaughter, made a remark that also reflects the man's commitment to church attendance: "No one in church attended the services with more reverential respect."[29] E. C. M'Guire adds this about George Washington's church attendance:

> The interruptions which sometimes occurred, preventing divine

service being performed in camp, did not interfere with attention to the duty on the part of the Commander-in-chief. For one of his Secretaries, Judge Harrison, has often been heard to say, that "whenever the General could be spared from camp, on the Sabbath, he never failed riding out to some neighbouring church, to join those who were publicly worshipping the Great Creator." This was done by him, we presume, when there was no public worship in camp.[30]

Attending church does not make one a Christian per se, but it is a sign of interest in the things of God. By his own accounts and the accounts of others, Washington was a churchman.

CONCLUSION

Washington lived in a Christian context. This compels us to ask, why was he so persistent in Christian worship, if he was a Deist who had denied the foundational truth of Christianity? Clearly, the Church was an important part of George Washington's life—so much so, that he was active in the service of his church. The man who would lead his country honed his leadership skills in serving as a lay-leader in his church. Ultimately, we will next explore George Washington in his service as a vestryman and church warden in the historic Virginian Truro Parish.

FOURTEEN

George Washington The Vestryman

"The regularity of Washington's attendance at the meetings of the Vestry is deserving of special notice."
Philip Slaughter[1]

For years, Washington was a lay-leader (a vestryman, so named because of the vestments they wore) in the Church of England in the Truro Parish in northern Virginia, outside of the city we now call Washington, D.C. The significance of Truro Parish for our nation's existence is immense. Dr. Philip Slaughter, historian of Truro Parish, explains,

> No Parish in the Colony had a Vestry more distinguished in its personnel, or more fully qualified for their positions, than the Parish of Truro. . . Eleven of them sat at various times in the House of Burgesses. Two of them, the Fairfaxes, were members of "His Majesty's Council for Virginia." Another of her vestrymen was George Mason, one of the first among the founders of the State and the great political thinkers of his age; while still another was

declared to be the "Greatest man of any age," the imperial George Washington.[2]

The role of the vestryman in colonial Virginia was captured by Thomas Jefferson,

> Usually the most discreet farmers, so distributed through their Parish that every part of it may be under the eye of some one of them. They are well acquainted with the details and economy of private life, and they find sufficient inducements to execute their charge well in their philanthropy, in the approbation of their neighbors, and the distinction which that gives them.[3]

The vestry book begins with a citation of the Act of the General Assembly that created the parish along with a record of the election of the members and the proceedings of their first meeting. This Act required that the sheriff of the county call the freeholders and housekeepers, to assemble to elect the "most able and discreet persons in the said Parish as shall make up the number of vestrymen in the said Parish twelve and no more."[4] Thus, the first vestry met in 1732, when George was about one year old. At that meeting, five vestrymen were elected, "having taken the oaths appointed by law, and subscribed to be conformable to the doctrine and disciple of the Church of England." Truro Parish took its name from the parish in Cornwall, England, which became the Diocese of Truro.

There are those who have argued that Washington's service in the vestry of the Anglican Church of Virginia really has little to do with his personal faith. For after all, it was a political position of prestige. And even Thomas Jefferson, hardly a strong role model for devout Christians, was elected as a vestryman.[5] Author Paul Boller, Jr. is one such example. But there is a dramatic difference between vestryman Washington in the Truro Parish and vestryman Jefferson in St. Anne's Parish that "passes through Charlottesville."[6] While Bishop Meade affirms that Jefferson was "elected to the vestry of St. Anne's," he adds, "though it does not appear that he ever acted."[7] To be merely elected a vestryman did not make one a "churchman."

Paul Boller, for instance, writes, "it is not possible to deduce any exceptional religious zeal from the mere fact of membership—even Thomas Jefferson was a vestryman for a while."[8] He also added, "…it is impossible to read any special religious significance into his service."[9]

But Washington's long and faithful service stands in marked distinction from

Jefferson's mere election. Washington actually served with great fidelity. We do not want to read anything into this other than what the facts tell us, and the facts are that George Washington's service as a vestryman is commensurate with the highest commitment to the Christianity proposed by the Anglican Church. George Washington's service as a vestryman is summarized by Philip Slaughter,

> The regularity of Washington's attendance at the meetings of the Vestry is deserving of special notice. During the eleven years of his active service, from February, 1763, to February, 1774, thirty-one "Vestries" were held, at twenty-three of which he is recorded as being present. On the eight occasions when he was absent, as we learn from his Diary or other sources, once he was sick in bed, twice the House of Burgesses, of which he was a member, was in session, and three other times certainly, and on the two remaining occasions probably, he was out of the County.[10]

Washington's commitment to service to the church was exemplary, even by modern standards, when we have faster and more convenient means of transportation.

What did it require to be a vestryman? If public surveyors were required to take oaths to serve,[11] it was even more logical that those entrusted with the church

See middle section of the book for a full color and larger view of this map

sanctioned by the state would take oaths as well. George's father, Augustine, had assumed the office of vestryman on November 18, 1735, when George, his first-born son by his second marriage, was only three years old. The oaths required of a vestryman for both Augustine Washington and his son George were the same: "I, A B, do declare that I will be conformable to the Doctrine and Discipline of the Church of England, as by law established." This meant that they declare their faith in the key Christian doctrines, including the divinity of Christ, Christ's death for sinners, and his resurrection from the dead.

Having been elected to the vestry of Truro Parish on October 25, 1762, some thirty years after his father, George took the same oath on February 15, 1763. The vestry book of Truro Parish has the following record: "Ordered, that George Washington, Esq. be chosen and appointed one of the vestrymen of this parish, in the room of William Peake, Gent. Deceased."[12] The Records of the County Court of Fairfax has under the date of February 15th, 1763, "George Washington Esqr. took the oaths according to Law repeated and subscribed the Test and subscribed to the Doctrine and Discipline of the Church of England in order to qualify him to act as a Vestryman of Truro Parish."[13] Speaking of the oaths taken by vestrymen, Slaughter writes, "they were oaths of allegiance and of abjuration of Popery and of the Pretender, etc., and were required of all Civil and Military officers by the laws of England and of Virginia. . . It seems to have required as many as six oaths and subscriptions properly to qualify a Vestryman in those days."[14]

THE HISTORY OF TRURO PARISH'S VESTRY

The history of the vestry is significant to appreciate Washington's role as a churchman. One of the initial duties the vestry had, when a new parish began, was to organize and build churches. So in 1733, the Reverend Lawrence De Butts was called to preach three times a month in various churches, one of those times being "at Occoquan Church," which was the name for the "old Pohick Church." His salary was to be "the sum of eight thousand pounds of tobacco, clear of the Warehouse charges and abatements."[15]

Along with building churches and filling pulpits, the vestry had the duty to secure and to provide for the clergy of the established church. It was the practice for each Anglican church to have a farm. These were called glebes. Thus, one of the responsibilities of the vestry was to provide for these glebes. The Truro Parish glebe began in 1734.[16] Because there were insufficient clergy for the pulpits, the vestry also hired readers. As their name implies, they were to read published Anglican sermons at services and read prayers from the *Book of Common Prayer*.[17] Some of the sermons that would have been read were the Anglican homilies, these are listed in the *Thirty-Nine Articles*, the official confession of faith of the Anglican Church. The need for a resident clergyman was immediately apparent, and in 1734 the vestry began a search for a pastor.[18]

Seventeen-thirty-five was the first year that a Washington family member served on the Truro Parish. On November 18th, the record states, "Augustine Washington gent. being this day sworn one of the members of this Vestry, took his place therein accordingly."[19] The early history of Augustine Washington's vestry shows that the vestrymen in Virginia were serious in their work, as they sought to honor the Anglican heritage and adapt it to the colonial context.

VARIOUS DUTIES OF THE VESTRY

Along with the many duties of the vestry in regard to church building and caring for the clergy, there were also the responsibilities to care for the poor, to protect the historic boundaries of lands, to collect tithables or church taxes, and to prevent and discipline moral violations.

Caring for the poor was especially the duty of the one who occupied the office of Church Warden. His duties included "binding orphan and other indigent children as Apprentices" and imparting "...the duties and morals of those apprenticed, their being taught to read English and the 'Art and mystery' of shoemaking, or of a Carpenter..."[20]

An ancient vestry duty continued in Virginia was the custom of renewing landmarks. This was termed "processioning." Every four years, landowners in good standing were appointed by the vestry to "perambultate" the parish, going around the plantations and assuring the boundaries were still well marked.[21]

Since tobacco was the primary means of exchange for much of colonial Virginia, church funds were likewise paid by the crop. In order to raise the tobacco to pay for the glebe and its mansion house, as well as its resident rector, not to mention the general care and building of the churches themselves, a great deal of tobacco had to be collected. Records not only had to be kept, but the law complicated the collections by further specifying which persons were "tithables" or countable in a collection of the tithe on tobacco for the church's many needs.

> All male persons of the age of sixteen years or upwards, and also negro, mulatto and Indian women of like age, ("except tributary Indians to this government,") were "tithable" or chargeable for

275

county and parish levies. But the Court or vestry, "for reason of charity," could excuse indigent persons from payment, and this was frequently done. In 1733 there were 676 tithables in Truro. Ten years later there were 1,372. This indicates the growth of the population. The Parish Levy varied widely year by year, the average being about 34 pounds of tobacco per poll.[22]

In view of these extensive financial and legal vestry duties, it is understandable why the records also show payments to a vestry clerk to keep the records, to collectors to secure the tithes, and to a church sexton to maintain the property and to bury the dead.

GEORGE WASHINGTON AS VESTRYMAN

Nearly twenty years would pass after Augustine's death until George, at the age of thirty, would follow in his father's footsteps and become a vestryman himself in 1762. During this time, the life of the parish quietly continued with some important intervening events.

In 1742, a new county was created out of Prince William County and was named Fairfax County. The boundary line of Truro Parish and the new county coincided.[23] In 1748, an Act of Assembly established in the new county a town named Alexandria. This city was named for the three Alexander brothers, John, Robert, and Gerard, who had emigrated from Scotland and had there established tobacco warehouses, which had been known before its new name as Hunting Creek Warehouse or Belle-Haven. As early as June 4, 1753, the Reverend Charles Green had been preaching there every third Sunday.[24]

Given the presence of these Scottish businessmen, Alexandria also became a center for Presbyterian settlers, and a strong Presbyterian church community was established. Coming from these Presbyterian settlers was another of George Washington's closest life-long friends, Dr. James Craik. Dr. Craik was Washington's close friend, travel partner, army surgeon general, and personal physician. He was present when Washington died.

What responsibilities were church wardens charged with? In part, they were the protectors of public morals. As Reverend Slaughter states in the *The History of Truro Parish*,

> Among the duties of the Church Wardens was that of presenting to
> the Court of the county persons guilty of gambling, drunkenness,

profanity, Sabbath breaking, failing to attend church, disturbing public worship, and certain other offences against decency and morality. The fines imposed in these cases went to them for the use of the Parish, and sometimes mentioned in the annual statement, though usually they would be included in the Wardens account which are not given in detail. That the Church Wardens of Truro, Cameron and Fairfax Parishes did not fail in their duty of presenting offenders is abundantly shown in records of the county Court. Presentments were usually made through the Grand Jury, the offender's Parish being designated, but sometimes the Church Wardens themselves are named as prosecutors.[25]

Washington was Church Warden in 1764, a year that saw some large changes in the Parish. One of his duties was to auction tobacco at the court house for the vestry, which is described in the vestry minutes,

> Ordered that 31,549 lb. of tobo. In the hands of the Church Wardens for the year 1764, to wit, George Washington and George Wm. Fairfax Esqrs. be sold to the highest bidder, before the Court House door of this County on the first day of June Court next between the hours of 12 and 4, and that publick notice be given of the sale.[26]

One of the issues that occurred at this time was another division of Truro Parish, creating a new Fairfax Parish and the older continuing Truro Parish. Each Parish was to elect its vestry. But the result of the division was not well received by the continuing Truro Parish. Ultimately, the conflict boiled down to an equitable distribution of "tithables." The issue had to be resolved by the House of Burgesses.

Washington was caught in the middle of the conflict. Again Reverend Slaughter notes:

> It is evident that Washington himself, and his immense estate at Mount Vernon, was the principal bone of contention between the mother and daughter Parishes. The lines proposed ran, the one on the south, the other on the north, of the estate. The one finally

adopted divided it leaving far the larger part, however with the mansion house, in Truro. That he would take an active interest in the settlement of the question was inevitable, and doubtless his direct agency is to be seen in the compromise petition which found favor with the House of Burgesses and was the basis of their legislation. The Act which was passed may well have been drawn by his own pen. In contrast with the previous Act it is unusually specific in its details, and would seem to indicate the hand of the Surveyor in its clearly described lines, and of the Church Warden in its accurate enumeration of the property and assets of the Parish.[27]

Another reference revealing Washington's interest in this matter is a manuscript where he lists the results of both the vestry elections in March and the elections in July. It was confusion over seeing Washington's name listed as elected in both that created the misunderstanding that he had been elected to and served in two vestries. Those historians today that deny Washington was a Christian ignore his deep commitment to serving the church. His keen interest in the church is seen by the fact that he was elected to serve in two separate parishes. When the parish he served in was ended and another started, he was immediately willing to serve in the new and was elected a second time.

Slaughter writes:

This paper shows that at the first election, in March, 1765, Col. Washington was elected a Vestryman of the first Fairfax Parish, he being, for the moment, a resident therein. The life of this Parish was exactly four months, and of this Vestry-elect two months and three days, even if its members never qualified or met for organization, of which there is no evidence. In July, Mount Vernon having, in the meantime, been restored to Truro, Col. Washington was again elected a Vestryman of Truro Parish, and was not eligible in any other.[28]

The result of the division was far more equitable since the result was 1,013 tithable in Fairfax Parish and 962 in Truro. But the good news of a successful division of the Parish was soon dampened when the Reverend Charles Green died.

Charles Green's death had a significant impact on Washington. He lost a physician, since his letters reveal that there were times when his pastor also provided medical care, such as the time he wrote for a house call when he was in such pain he could scarcely write the letter, or when Mrs. Washington had contracted the measles.[29] He also wrote to him from the Warm Springs, describing the location and potential health benefits.[30] He clearly lost a long-standing friend from the days of his father's service on the vestry. But the passing of "Parson Green,"[31] as he called him on one occasion, also meant that he and the other vestrymen would have to search for another clergyman for Truro Parish.

The regular duties of the parish did not cease with the passing of Reverend Green. On February 3-4, 1766, Washington and fellow vestrymen determined to build a new church, and Washington was appointed to the building committee of this church.[32] As the contract was signed for this construction project, an attorney named Lee Massey was present and served as a witness. But he also served the vestry in another important way. The vestry record of the same meeting states,

> Whereas Mr. Lee Massey, an Inhabitant of this parish, having this day offered to supply the place of a Minister therein, and the Vestry being of opinion that he is a person well qualified for the sacred function, have agreed to recommend him to the favour of His grace the Bishop of London and of the Governor of this Colony, for an Introduction to this said parish, and to receive him upon his return properly qualified to discharge the said office.
>
> In consequence of the aforesaid Resolve a Recommendation to his Lordship the Bishop of London, and an address to his Honour the Governor of this Colony in favour of Mr. Lee Massey being made out, are ordered hereafter to be recorded.[33]

Washington was present at this meeting, and, as can be seen from the minutes, he signed the letters that were sent to the Bishop and the Governor. Thus, with the approval of Church Warden George Washington, the well-respected Lee Massey was authorized to travel to London for Anglican ordination and thus take his first step to become the new minister of Truro Parish.

GEORGE WASHINGTON ON THE POHICK CHURCH BUILDING COMMITTEE

In 1767, Washington again served as Church Warden. In this very busy year for the parish, he saw the return and reception of the newly ordained Reverend Lee

Massey as the new Minister of Truro Parish. He also was responsible for the oversight of the building of the Falls Church and its vestry house, the sale of the old glebe, and the accounts of the sale of the church's tobacco and of the payments to the parish's employees. But something even more dramatic happened at the annual meeting on November 20, which met to discuss the amount of Parish "tax." This tax or levy was the assessment to be raised from the church members to build new churches and to operate the existing churches. In a vote that included every member of the vestry, since all were present, there was a split vote concerning the building of another new Church.

> Resolved, that a Church be built at or as near the Cross Road leading from Holis's to Pohic Warehouse as water can be had, which resolution was carried by a majority of seven to five.[34]

A tradition has come down from this meeting that was first given by Washington biographer Jared Sparks in his *Life of Washington* and has been repeated by many others, including Bishop Meade.

> The Old Pohick Church was a frame building, and occupied a site on the south side of Pohick run, and about two miles from the present site which is on the north side of the run. When it was no longer fit for use, it is said the parishioners were called together to determine on the locality of the new Church, when George Mason, the compatriot of Washington, advocated the old site, pleading that it was the house in which their fathers worshipped, and that the graves of many were around it, while Washington and others advocated a more central and convenient one. The question was left unsettled, and another meeting for its decision appointed. Meanwhile Washington surveyed the neighborhood, and marked the houses and distances on a well-drawn map, and, when the day of decision arrived, met all the arguments of his opponent by presenting this paper, and thus carried his point.[35]

Pohick Church still stands today. You can visit it in Lorton, Virginia. As of this writing, the Reverend Donald S. Binder, Ph.D., serves as the rector. He notes:

> Washington surveyed the land. He actually argued to have the

church moved here because it was a more centralized location, had a surveyor's map, drawn up so he could win the point with the rest of the vestry, and so the church was moved up here. It's also on very high ground; you can really oversee the whole of Lorton Valley down below and so, he thought it was an appropriate place, to put a church, you know, closer to heaven, more or less, is the thinking.[36]

The old site was closer to Mason's estate, Gunston Hall, while the new site was closer to Washington's Mount Vernon. The first meeting may have occurred at the September 28, 1767, vestry, where four vestrymen were absent although Mason and Washington had been there. The strong opinions expressed on the location seem to be supported by the full attendance of the vestry at its next meeting, and the close 7-5 vote in favor of Washington's location. It is easy to overlook how important the church's life was in this era. At times the churchyard itself was the venue for important discussions and decisions regarding the future of America.[37] It is certainly fascinating to consider that here we find neighbors, Mason and Washington, two statesmen who would become critical to the foundations of a new nation, debating over the location of their church building. Clearly, church and state were important concerns for our Virginian founding fathers. The building committee for the new Pohick Church included both Washington and Mason, which seems to indicate that their debate and its ultimate outcome did not end their ability to work together.

Washington's commitment in serving the church was time-consuming. He spent many hours at these long meetings serving the vestry. An exceptionally long meeting occurred on March 3, 1769. Washington's diary confirms the vestry record: "Mar. 3d. Went to a Vestry at Pohick church and returned abt. 11 o'clock at night."[38]

GEORGE WASHINGTON'S FINAL VESTRY MEETING

With the arrival of 1774, Washington's national leadership was to become a reality, and with it came the necessity to relinquish actual leadership in his local parish's vestry, even though he was once again appointed Church Warden for the next year, 1775. His final meeting as an active vestryman makes clear that he did not leave his church with a spirit of indifference or unbelief. The last vote that he actually participated in says,

Ordered that the new Church near Pohic be furnished with a Cushion for the Pulpit and Cloths for the Desks & Communion

Table of Crimson Velvett with Gold Fring, and that Colo. George Washington be requested to import the same, as also two Folio Prayer Books covered with blue Turkey Leather with name of the Parish thereon in Gold Letters, the Dimensions for the said Cushion and Cloths being left to Wm. Bernard Sears who is desired to furnish Colo. Washington with proper Patterns at the Expense of the Parish.[39]

The vestry adjourned to meet the next day, February 25th. The record states, "Bonds being taken yesterday from Colo. George Washington for himself, and also as Attorney in Fact for Colo. George William Fairfax, now in Britain, . . ."[40]

George remained a nominal vestryman until he resigned in 1782, at the end of the war. His public duties from this time on made it impossible for him to serve in any active way on the Truro Vestry. For example, on July 10, 1783, he wrote to his old friend and former vestryman, George William Fairfax, then residing in London, "I have not been in the State (Virginia) but once since the 4th of May, 1775. And that was at the siege of York. In going thither I spent one day at my own house, and in returning I took 3 or 4, without attempting to transact a particle of private business."[41] In 1784, two years after General Washington resigned, Lund Washington was elected to the vestry in 1784, thus keeping a Washington on the vestry.[42]

But Washington's absence from the vestry and the church at Pohick did not end his influence or his interest. He provided funds for expensive decorations for the church that were done in gold leaf.[43]

NO MORE STATE FUNDS FOR THE CHURCH

When the eventful year of 1776 arrived, there was a profound impact on the parish. Eventually, there would be no state support for the church, which became a final reality in 1786 with Disestablishment. The clergy would now have to be supported by the voluntary contributions of the church. With George Fairfax in England and General Washington leading the Continental Army, the needs of the Truro Parish became so great, that Reverend Massey ceased to preach and began to practice medicine. (Reverend Massey was first a lawyer, then a pastor, and lastly a physician.) The inherent tension between his vow to the King and his loyalty to his congregation may have played a major role as well, given the fact that he concluded his practice of law because of his disdain for moral tension in many of the cases he had to address as an attorney.

The duties of leading an army away from his financial base of plantation life also made it a challenge for George Washington to honor his substantial commitments. His obligations for the Pohick pews also included that of his friend George William Fairfax, who returned to England before the hostilities of arms broke out. On November 22, 1776, the vestry book states,

> Mr. Peter Wagener and Mr. Thomazen Ellzey appointed Church Wardens, and ordered to receive from former Wardens all balances due the Parish, including General George Washington's Bond and that of Col. George William Fairfax for which the General is liable, and to pay the several sums due the Parish Claimants charged this day, amounting to 119 pounds six shillings and four pence.

While it is clear that Washington did not serve as a vestryman in two parishes, although elected to serve in two, it is also clear that Washington determined to have a family pew in both the new Fairfax Parish and the continuing Truro Parish. This may have been an expression of love for the new Christ Church that was being built in Alexandria at the same time as the new church was being built in Pohick, or it may have been due to a sense of duty, since his Mount Vernon estate had been divided between the two parishes by the final redistricting of the new parish. It is even possible that the earlier tensions that had occurred within the vestry over the placement of the Pohick Church, coupled with the departure of his friend George William Fairfax, and the physical infirmities of Lee Massey, were motives for George to have a pew in Christ Church.

What we do know is that Washington paid the highest individual price for the pews that he purchased in both of the new churches, even more than Robert Alexander, for whom the new city had been named. At Pohick, his bid tied that of George Fairfax, for which George became personally liable when the Fairfaxes quietly fled the country in the face of the looming revolution.[44]

The pew Washington purchased at Christ Church still exists and is in the front on the left, with a close view of the Communion table and altarpiece with the Creed, Commandments, and Lord's Prayer. This pew is doubly historical, since Gen. Robert E. Lee later occupied it.[45]

WASHINGTON'S DEEP INTEREST IN THE CHURCH PEWS

Insight into Washington's deep interest in the pew at Christ Church Alexandria is evident in one of the most passionate letters that he ever wrote. For some reason the vestry in the new Fairfax Parish was considering the setting aside of the sale of the pews—which would have been unfair to those (such as Washington) who had already paid goodly sums for such pews. Since Washington was not a vestryman in Fairfax Parish, he had not had a role in this decision. But when he heard that this was under consideration, he wrote a scathing letter in protest. The letter to the vestry is to the attention of John Dalton and is dated February 15, 1773. It was written from Mount Vernon and it shows that Washington's interest in the pew was not a mere show of religiosity or cultural duty.

> Sir: I am obliged to you for the notice you have given me of an intended meeting of your Vestry on Tuesday next. I am an avowed Enemy to the Scheme I have heard (but never till of late believed) that some Members of your Vestry are Inclined to adopt.
>
> If the Subscription to which among others I put my name was set on foot under Sanction of an Order of Vestry as I always understood it to be, I own myself at a loss to conceive, upon what principle it is, that there should be an attempt to destroy it; repugnant it is to every Idea I entertain of justice to do so; ... As a Subscriber who meant to lay the foundation of a Family Pew in the New Church, I shall think myself Injured; ... as every Subscriber has an undoubted right to a Seat in the Church what matters it whether he Assembles his whole Family into one Pew, or, as the Custom is have them dispers'd into two or three; ...
>
> ...considering myself as a Subscriber, I enter my Protest against the measure in Agitation. As a Parishioner, I am equally averse to a Tax which is intended to replace the Subscription Money. These will be my declared Sentiments if present at the Vestry; if I am not I shall be obliged to you for Communicating them, I am, etc. [46]

In no uncertain terms, Washington was decrying the proposal that the vestry of Fairfax County reallocate the church pews, even if he were repaid his subscription money. He had intended to establish a family pew. This vestry action would have removed the family spiritual legacy that George Washington had planned to create. This powerful missive apparently carried the day, since his family pew was awaiting him after the war, when he began his regular attendance in Alexandria, sometime around April 1785.

Washington's place in the church clearly mattered to him. Scarcely any other letter in all of George Washington's writings carries the passion he displays in the above letter for his place in the church.

CONCLUSION

When we think of George Washington, we think of a great leader. One of the places he learned to lead was in the context of the church. The leadership principles that the father of our country put into practice in the army, in presiding over the Constitution, and in the presidency were learned in part in the service to his church.

It should be abundantly clear that not only did the church play an important part in Washington's life, but Washington played an important role in the church as well. The record reveals a faithful and intense commitment of Washington to his churches, far beyond what one might expect from a Deist.

There were substantial requirements for a serious vestryman. He had to affirm the creed of the Anglican Church, which at that time was orthodox Christianity. Did it cost anything in terms of time, energy, and emotion to be more than a figurehead vestryman like Thomas Jefferson? The answer is that it cost a great deal, especially in an intensely busy life like Washington's. Yet, his commitment to his church was not just the highest price for a pew and gold leaf for the sanctuary, but it was consistent attendance at meetings that sometimes went into the wee hours of the unlit, dark, colonial Virginia nights. Boller's mistake is to assume that Washington's activity in the vestry did not reveal any special religious zeal. That assumption is not only refuted by the bare recital of the facts of Washington's vestry service in comparison with Jefferson's inactivity, but Boller's unsubstantiated claim also fails to hear how George Washington chose to speak most loudly and clearly to his family, friends, and neighbors. It is the same way he still speaks to posterity. Deeds not words!

FIFTEEN

George Washington The Low Churchman

"The expediency of an American Episcopate
was long and warmly debated, and at length rejected."
George Washington, May 4, 1772[1]

The Anglican tradition in Virginia at the beginning of the American constitution-al era had two streams of thought. They have been called the High Church and the Low (or broad) Church. The High Church under the leadership of Bishop Samuel Seabury in New England had certain distinctives that were not shared by the members of the Low Church, which was led by Bishop Samuel Provoost in New York. The Low Church reflected the traditional Anglican Church in Virginia, of which Washington was a part. The High Church emphasized apostolic succession. This view claimed an unbroken chain of ordination all the way from the Anglican bishops to the apostles. Adherents of apostolic succession claimed that the Anglican Church was the only church that could properly administer the sacrament of the Lord's Supper. This creat-ed an air of exclusivity and theological distance from other Protestant churches.

The Low Church, on the other hand, while not discounting the value of apostolic succession, felt it was not the foundational doctrine for the Church's life. Instead of emphasizing the continuity of bishops by an unbroken succession of ordination, the Low Church focused on the importance of lay leadership. Instead of emphasizing an exclusive and uniquely legitimate Communion, the Low Church emphasized a broader Communion with other churches within the historic orthodox tradition of Christianity.

Interestingly, this division between the High Church and the Low Church not only reflected different theological ideas, but it also reflected the natural division of geography. The northern church of New England was High Church and the southern church of Virginia was Low Church. In between the two was Philadelphia, governed by Bishop William White and New York, governed by Bishop Samuel Provoost. Initially, these two Bishops espoused the Low Church tradition of Virginia. As a result of the ecclesiastical debates, and even though he was a great patriot and Low Churchman, Bishop White reached out to High Church Bishop Seabury to establish a union between the High and Low Church. This compromise was uncomfortable for the Virginians and bitterly opposed by Bishop Provoost in New York City. This was the milieu in which George Washington found himself in Philadelphia as he worshipped as president. In fact, colonial America had wrestled with the question of whether there should be a bishop in America at all.

Here and in a later chapter, we will seek to explain why Washington was initially opposed to an American Episcopate that would have lessened lay leadership by elevating the rule of bishops and why he also would have been uncomfortable to personally connect with Bishop White, whose alliance with Bishop Seabury thwarted the Low Church's vision for the new Protestant Episcopal church.

We begin this story before the Revolutionary War, where we find Washington serving in the House of Burgesses, having been elected to the new Committee on Religion. The very fact that Washington was on this committee, as well as being a sincere Low Churchman, not only meant that he would be opposed to Bishop Seabury's views and the claims of the High Church, but it also meant he was not a Deist, because the purpose of the Committee on Religion was to check the growing menace of Deism in Anglican Virginia.

WASHINGTON WAS A CHURCHMAN FROM THE LOW CHURCH TRADITION

To understand Washington's religion, we need to appreciate the Virginian Low Church tradition of which he was a part. The Low Church's dominance in Virginia was a natural result of America having no bishop of its own. It was not just that America had no bishop, but New England as well, as Virginia had strenuously resisted having an American Episcopate. The original Congregationalists had, in large part fled England for New England to escape Episcopal persecution. On the centennial of the end of the Revolutionary War, Reformed Episcopalian clergyman, Reverend Mason Gallagher explained:

> In divine Providence, we owe to the tyranny of [Anglican Archbishop] Laud and the Stuarts [the English royal family], the freedom and the independence which now we so greatly enjoy.
>
> If the noble men whom these tyrants subjected to prison, to fine, to mutilation, and other forms of persecution, even to death, had not been driven from the mother country, and their ecclesiastical home, never would there have been reared in this land, a people willing and able to fight for seven years [in the American Revolution] as the descendants of the Pilgrims did, for the privileges of civil and religious liberty, which, thanks to God and to these patriots, we are privileged now to possess.[2]

Since there was no bishop in America, Washington grew up without being confirmed.[3] As a vestryman, he had helped manage the parish churches and called pastors without the immediate aid of a bishop.[4] He was active in the House of Burgesses that oversaw Virginia's Anglican state church that had no resident bishop.[5] This meant that Washington and his fellow Virginians were not only relatively independent, by historical experience, but Washington was also quite knowledgeable in Anglican life and teaching. Washington, by faith and practice, was a Low Church Anglican.

WASHINGTON'S PERSPECTIVE ON ANGLICANISM THROUGH HIS SERVICE IN THE VIRGINIA HOUSE OF BURGESSES

Washington served for many years as a member of the House of Burgesses. His initial plans to run for office brought him into consultation with his pastor, Reverend Green.[6] With his fame from military service, as well as his close connection with the influential Fairfax family,[7] Washington was elected on his second run for office and began his service in May 1759, just four months after marrying Martha Custis,[8] thereby following the family tradition of serving in government. He occupied his seat as a Burgess in the Virginia Assembly, which held its sessions at Williamsburg.[9]

The Burgesses reflected Virginia's Christian tradition, in part because Virginia had an established church. Washington's knowledge of the Anglican tradition was deepened by serving on the Committee on Religion for several years in the Virginia House of Burgesses. On occasion, they even published sermons. One such sermon has George Washington's signature on the cover page, entitled, "The Nature and Extent of Christ's Redemption."

The sermon was presented before the House of Burgesses by the Reverend Stith, president and professor from the Anglican William and Mary College in Williamsburg in 1753.[10] The theme of the sermon addressed the evangelical doctrine of salvation

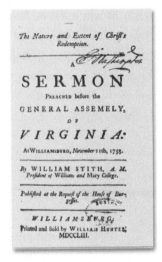

A Christian sermon preached for the Virginia House of Burgesses that Washington had in his library

through faith in "the death of Christ."[11] President Stith argued for what theologians have called the "unlimited atonement" of Christ, or that Christ's death on the cross was intended by God for all humans, not only for his elect. He also wrestled with the perennial Christian missions question of whether the unreached are responsible for not believing in a Gospel they've not yet heard, and how they can gain salvation under such circumstances. In his introduction, Professor Stith suggested that he was at least in part influenced by Christian enlightenment philosopher and theologian John Locke's *The Reasonableness of Christianity*.

The date of Stith's sermon was six years before Washington entered the House of Burgesses. We do not know when Washington signed the sermon, nor the occasion of his securing it. He did, however, include it in his sermon collection that was bound during his life and kept in his library.[12]

From his position in the Virginia House of Burgesses, Washington had opportunity to consider many religious matters that concerned the established Anglican Church of Virginia. These included matters such as: The Two Penny Act and the Parson's Cause,[13] which unveiled Patrick Henry's legal skills,[14] as well as a clergyman's defense against a heresy charge of violating the Anglican confession of faith by a teaching that seemed to deny the deity of Christ.[15] This concern over heretical teaching, by the way, demonstrates that the open denial of Christ's deity was not an acceptable position in English Anglicanism, and would have been even less so in the colonial context. Since Deism by definition denies the deity of Christ, this further supports the incongruity of claiming that Washington was a Deist.

About the time that Washington became a vestryman, he bought *An Exposition of the XXXIX Articles of the Church of England* by Gilbert Burnet Bishop of Sarum,[16] a deeply theological and soundly orthodox statement of Anglican theology, in what was to become known as the broad church or Low Church theology.

Another evidence of Washington's Anglican heritage was that he was offered the position of Chancellor of the Anglican William and Mary College. The school, although not always living up to its purposes in Washington's mind,[17] had very explicit religious duties:

> There are three things which the Founders or this College proposed to themselves, to which all its Statutes should be directed. The First is, That the Youth of Virginia should be well educated to Learning and good Morals. The Second is, That the Churches of America, especially Virginia, should be supplied with good Ministers after the Doctrine and Government of the Church of England; and that the College should be a constant Seminary for this Purpose. The Third is, That the Indians of America should be instructed in the Christian Religion, and that some of the Indian Youth that are well-behaved and well-inclined, being first well prepared in the Divinity School, may be sent out to preach the Gospel to their Countrymen in their own tongue, after they have duly been put in Orders of Deacons and Priests. . . .[18]

The duties of the Master was to "take Care that all the Scholars learn the Church of England Catechism in the vulgar tongue; and that they who are further advanced learn it likewise in Latin. . . .let the president and Masters, before they enter upon these Offices, give their Assent to the Articles of the Christian Faith. . . ."[19] While Washington ultimately decided not to accept the invitation to serve, his decision was reached because of his desire to retire[20] and not because he did not believe these things. The facts of his life show that he did believe them.[21]

WASHINGTON'S SERVICE ON THE COMMITTEE ON RELIGION

Washington's responsibilities in the House of Burgesses included membership on the Committee on Religion. He was elected to the brand new committee in 1769, serving with such illustrious men as Colony Treasurer Robert Carter Nicholas (Chair), Attorney General John Randolph, Richard Bland, Benjamin Harrison, Patrick Henry, Richard Henry Lee, and Edmund Pendleton.[22] Several of these men were the very ones who traveled to the First Continental Congress in 1774 to represent Virginia.[23]

The religious faith of these men is a relevant question to consider. It is clear that they were not Deists, when we consider what Bishop William Meade records of their lives. Speaking of Virginian culture at large, Bishop Meade explains, "There were those, even then, among them [Virginia patriots], who had unhappily imbibed the infidel principles of France; but they were too few to raise their voices against those of Washington, Nicholas, Pendleton, Randolph, Mason, Lee, Nelson, and such like."[24]

Five of the members of the Committee on Religion are here singled out as opponents of the Deist movement in Virginia. Bishop Meade again writes, "If tradition and history and published documents are to be relied on, the patriotic, laborious, self-sacrificing, and eloquent Richard Henry Lee, of the Revolution, must have deeply sympathized with Washington, and Peyton Randolph, and Pendleton, and Nicholas, and Henry, in their religious character and sentiments."[25]

The Christian faith and commitment of these various members of the founding Committee on Religion is written in the pages of Virginia's history and is recorded by Bishop William Meade.[26] Patrick Henry is most known for his fiery, patriotic oratory. But his patriotic fire was strengthened with biblical reflection. In May 1765, the Burgesses passed the Stamp Act Resolves. Years later, on the back of the paper, Henry wrote a note for posterity that highlighted several of the key events that led to the Revolution. His climactic statement declared in bold letters that he was not a Deist.

> This brought on the war which finally separated the two countries and gave independence to ours. Whether this will prove a blessing or a curse, will depend upon the use our people make of the blessings, which a gracious God hath bestowed on us.
>
> If they are wise, they will be great and happy. If they are of a contrary character, they will be miserable.
>
> Righteousness alone can exalt them as a nation. Reader! Whoever thou art, remember this, and in thy sphere practice virtue thyself, and encourage it in others. P. Henry[27]

There was concern over the entrance of Deism into Virginia through the teachers at William and Mary.[28] Was this one of the unspoken reasons why Washington did not want to place his grandson at William and Mary?[29] But there were also concerns about infidelity in the pulpit. Bishop Meade writes,

> I have other reasons for knowing that infidelity, under the specious garb of Universalism, was then finding its way into the pulpit. Governor Page, Colonel Nicholas, and Colonel Bland made complaints against someone preaching in or near Williamsburg about this time for advocating the doctrine with its usual associates, and prevented his preferment... At such a time, when the writings of French philosophers—falsely so called—were corrupting the minds of the Virginia youth, the testimony of such men as Peyton Randolph, Mr. R. C. Nicholas, Colonel Bland, President Nelson, Governor Page, and the recovery of Edmund Randolph from the snare, has peculiar weight.[30]

Again, the names of those openly defending historic Christianity against Deism in Virginia are Washington's fellow members of the Committee on Religion. John Randolph who was on the original committee, left for England when war was beginning to become a possibility.[31] But it was clear that the Randolph family was deeply committed to the defense of the Gospel, having been deeply touched by deistic thought. Bishop Meade relates:

> Mr. Peyton Randolph ever showed himself the warm and steady friend of the Church as well as of his country. He went by the name Speaker Randolph, being for a long time the presiding officer in the House of Burgesses. He was also chosen Speaker of the first, second and third Congress, but suddenly died of apoplexy, during the last. He was buried for a time in Philadelphia, but afterward removed to Williamsburg. In connection with the foregoing notice of Mr. Peyton Randolph, I added something concerning his nephew and adopted son, Edmund Randolph...[the following is an] Extract from a paper written by Edmund Randolph, soon after the death of his wife, and addressed to his children.
>
> Up to the commencement of the Revolution, the Church of England was the established religion, in which your mother had been educated with strictness, if not with bigotry. From strength of

parental example, her attendance on public worship was unremitted, except when insuperable obstacles occurred; the administration of the sacrament was never without a cause passed by; in her closet, prayer was uniformly addressed to the throne of mercy and the questioning of the sacred truths she never permitted to herself or heard from others without abhorrence. When we were united, I was a deist, made so by my confidence in whom I revered, and by the labours of two of my preceptors, who, though of the ministry, poisoned me with books of infidelity. I cannot answer for myself that I should ever have been brought to examine the genuineness of Holy Writ, if I had not observed the consoling influence which it wrought upon the life of my dearest Betsey...for several years since I detected the vanity of sublunary things above; and knew that the good of man consisted in Christianity alone.[32]

The Committee on Religion, in part, saw their concern to impede the advance of Deism in Virginia. In light of this, The Committee on Religion would have been a strange place for a person to serve, if his religious attitudes were actually like those described by Pulitzer-prize winner Joseph J. Ellis in his 2004 bestseller, *His Excellency: George Washington.* If Washington really was "A lukewarm Episcopalian, [who] never took Communion, [and] tended to talk about 'Providence' or 'Destiny' rather than God"[33] he would not have been very effective for the Committee's work.[34] Given the purpose of the Committee,

- Would the Burgesses have begun the committee's work with a founding member who was, according to Ellis, "Never a deeply religious man, at least in the traditional Christian sense of the term."?

- Would a Committee whose purpose was to address Deism select a member who "thought of God as a distant, impersonal force, the presumed wellspring for what he called destiny or Providence."?

- Would the Burgesses have elected a "secular saint" who was not sure "Whether or not there was a hereafter or a heaven where one's soul lived on..."?

- Did the decline of religion in Virginia need someone for whom the question of salvation in heaven "struck him as one of those unfathomable mysteries that Christian theologians wasted much ink and energy trying to resolve"?

- Would it have been a good choice to launch such a committee with one who believed that "The only certain form of persistence was in the memory of succeeding generations, a secular rather than sacred version of immortality...."?[35]

Should Ellis be correct in calling Washington "America's greatest secular saint,"[36] it seems to us that the House of Burgesses might have better elected Washington to the Committee on Deism, since Colonel Washington allegedly had such a deep commitment to the tenets of Deism and such little interest in religion. Just to be clear, however, the Committee on Deism did not exist. Deism was one of the chief issues that the Virginian Committee on Religion sought to address.

THE NEED FOR TEACHERS OF CHRISTIANITY: WASHINGTON ON THE GENERAL ASSESSMENT BILL

According to historian Allan Nevins, the Revolutionary War had brought, "it appears, an increase of crime in Virginia, and this was attributed by many to be a decline of religion. Among those who believed in legislative support of all the churches to check this decline were not only [Patrick] Henry and R. H. Lee, but Washington and John Marshall."[37] Thus, a bill entitled the General Assessment Bill was put under consideration.

The background of the bill was the perceived need to support religion in the post-war era, especially since the Anglican Church in Virginia had been disestablished. Washington had written about the matter to Samuel Chase in January, 1785.[38] The direct effect of the bill would have been state funding of teachers of the Christian religion. Nevins explains

> A plan had found favor with the Presbyterians, and an eloquent advocate in Patrick Henry. Briefly, it proposed that the State should establish all Christian denominations, make them equally state religions, and support them by regular taxation; it was pressed vigorously in the next few years by many outside as well as inside the Episcopal Church.
>
> Henceforth the "general assessment" was the chief religious question before the Legislature. Our available evidence shows that by the end of 1783 the plan of taxing everyone for the support of all

Christian ministers had gained wide favor, and was approved by a majority of Episcopalians, Methodists, and perhaps Presbyterians; but it was opposed by the Baptists and many in all other denominations who agreed with Jefferson that any link whatever between church and state was an evil...[39]

It was this bill that brought forth the famous "Memorial and Remonstrance" of James Madison.[40] Ultimately, the resistance succeeded and the bill failed. The concern was the inherent danger to religious liberty if the government put any funds into religious support, even if the support was broadly conceived and all churches would be beneficiaries.

But Washington did not fully agree with the opponents of this bill that would have provided support for teachers of the Christian religion. Clearly, he was a strong advocate of religious liberty. But he was also a strong advocate of Christian teaching to advance the moral well-being of the community. He believed there was a way both to support the funding of Christian teachers and to protect religious liberty. His political instincts however, told him that the bill could not carry and, if passed, it would probably create ongoing tension, due to an outspoken but substantial minority. In his October 3, 1785, letter to George Mason, Washington explained:

Dr. Sir: I have this moment received yours of yesterday's date, enclosing a memorial and remonstrance against the Assessment Bill, which I will read with attention. At *present* I am unable to do it, on account of company. The bill itself I do not recollect ever to have read: with *attention* I am certain I never did, but will compare them together.

The bill in question was to provide for teachers of the Christian religion in Virginia by means of a specified tax, the money to be paid out on order of the vestries, elders, etc., of each religious society to a teacher or minister of its denomination. It could also be used to provide places of worship.

Altho, no man's sentiments are more opposed to *any kind* of restraint upon religious principles than mine are; yet I must confess, that I am not amongst the number of those who are so much alarmed at the thoughts of making people pay towards the support of that which they profess, if of the denomination of Christians; or declare themselves Jews, Mahomitans or otherwise, and thereby obtain proper relief. As the matter now stands, I wish an assessment had never been agitated, and as it has gone so far, that the Bill could die an easy death; because I think it will be productive of more quiet to the State, than by enacting it into a Law; which, in my opinion, would be impolitic, admitting there is a decided majority for it, to the disquiet of a respectable minority. In the first case the matter will soon subside; in the latter, it will rankle and perhaps convulse, the State.[41]

The point here is that Washington desired to have Christian education supported by state funds if non-Christians could be exempt. Washington's view of the separation of church and state—a phrase that he never used—was a friendly separation that kept the duties of the church and state distinct, but sought to have them cooperate for the good of all.[42]

So Washington was open to the taxation of Christians for Christian causes, as long as non-Christians could find relief from such taxes. If Washington had been a Deist, who rejected all claims of revealed religion, he would have opposed the state sponsorship of Christian programs. He did not view the proposed legislation as a necessary violation of religious liberty if "Jews, Mahomitans or otherwise" could "obtain proper relief." Four years later, serving under the United States Constitution, his idea of the friendly cooperation of the distinct spheres of church and state was still his *modus operandi*. He believed that it was the clergy's duty to "instruct the ignorant, and to reclaim the devious."[43] However, he also felt he could promise under the Constitution or "Magna-Charta" of America, that "in the progress of morality and science, to which our government will give every furtherance, we may confidently expect the advancement of true religion, and the completion of our happiness."[44]

WASHINGTON ON AN AMERICAN EPISCOPATE

As a Low Churchman, a leader of religious matters in his church (as vestryman and church warden) and in his government (as a member of the Committee on Religion), George Washington, was confronted with the question of an American Episcopate. During the Colonial era, the fact that there were no bishops in America caused difficulties for the progress of the Anglican Church. Yet the colonists were wary of the power that bishops would wield in America. Editor of the *Writings of Washington* John C. Fitzpatrick notes,

One of the grievances of the Colonies was this question of the Established Church's rule from London. Young men from America who desired to enter holy orders were obliged to travel to England to be ordained, and few, if any, could stand the expense. The American episcopate was thus, like the American governors, an alien body and not likely to be in sympathy with the people.[45]

So when plans began for the sending of a bishop to America, there was unrest. The fear of the New Englanders was that there was a plot to impose bishops on the colonies against their will. One popular political cartoon depicted an angry mob of New Englanders pushing a ship back toward England, because it was bringing a bishop. The bishop in the cartoon prayed, "Lord, now lettest thou thy Servant depart in Peace."

Other elements of the cartoon included Calvin's writings being thrown at the bishop, and protests of "No Lords Spiritual or Temporal in New England"; "Shall they be obliged to maintain bishops that cannot maintain themselves?" and "Liberty & Freedom of Conscience." To put it mildly, the New England colonies were not ready for an American Episcopate.

Anglican Virginia was not ready for an American Episcopate either. From his vantage point of serving on the Committee of Religion in the House of Burgesses, Washington, the Low Churchman, wrote about an American Episcopate with less than enthusiasm. Writing on May 4, 1772 to Reverend Jonathan Boucher, the tutor of his stepson Jacky Custis, he said: "After a tiresome, and in my opinion, a very unimportant Session, I returned home about the middle of last Month ...."[46] Washington continued:

The expediency of an American Episcopate was long and warmly debated, and at length rejected. As a substitute, the House attempted to frame an Ecclesiastical Jurisdiction, to be composed of a President and four other clergymen, who were to have full power and authority to hear and determine all matters and causes relative to the clergy, and to be vested with the [power] of Suspension, deprivation, and visitation. From this Jurisdiction an Appeal was to be had to a Court of Delegates, to consist of an equal number of Clergymen and Laymen; but this Bill, after much canvassing, was put to Sleep, from an opinion that the subject was of too much Importance to be hastily entered into at the end of a Session.[47]

Having a bishop, even in Washington's Anglican Virginia, was an idea that had not yet achieved support. In fact, when the Committee on Religion had begun in 1769, it had "…drafted plans to block a proposed Anglican episcopate and keep the church under indigenous control."[48]

CHANGES IN THE PRAYER BOOK CAUSED BY THE REVOLUTIONARY WAR

One of the changes to the Anglican faith that Washington personally experienced was the impact of the Revolution on the prayer book he so frequently used. The 1662 *Book of Common Prayer* had the worshipers in morning prayer asking that the Lord would grant the King "long to live," and that he would "strengthen him that he may vanquish and overcome all his enemies…." Obviously, prayers for the King's success could not continue in the church's worship, if the church was convinced that he was assaulting them as a tyrant. After the Declaration of Independence, the vestry of the Bruton Church in Virginia, for example, covered over the prayer for the King. A hand written text replaced the original prayer with a prayer for the President instead:

> O Lord our heavenly Father, the high and mighty Ruler of the universe who dost from thy throne behold all the dwellers upon earth, most heartily we beseech thee, with thy favour to behold and bless thy servant the President of the United States and all others in authority; and so replenish them with the grace of thy Holy Spirit, that they may always incline to thy will and walk in thy way; Endue them plenteously with heavenly gifts; grant them in health; and prosperity long to live and finally after this life to attain everlasting joy and felicity through Jesus Christ our Lord.[49]

After the War, President George Washington would regularly pray this prayer of salvation for himself and his congressional colleagues from his new American version of the *Book of Common Prayer*. As Washington prayed along with all who assembled with him in New York and Philadelphia, he prayed that he as president would "after this life attain everlasting joy and felicity through Jesus Christ our Lord." We know that Washington worshiped regularly on Sundays as president for eight years. If he only worshiped on half of the Sundays, allowing for travel, health issues and other necessary absences, that means that he *publicly* prayed this prayer for himself over two hundred times as president. Nelly remembered his prayers vividly and said, "No one in church attended to the service with more reverential respect."[50] We wonder then, if Washington historian Joseph J. Ellis's description of Washington as a "lukewarm Episcopalian" is the same Washington described by his granddaughter, who sat in the same pew as he did Sunday after Sunday admiring his most "reverential respect"? So then, did Washington ask for the gift of eternal life? We know he did so with deep, reverential respect on at least two hundred occasions.

But before the American *Book of Common Prayer* could become official, the American Episcopal Church had to be structured and its governance had to be addressed.

THE *PROPOSED BOOK OF COMMON PRAYER* OF 1785

With the consecration of Bishop Samuel Seabury[51] in 1784, and Bishop Samuel Provoost[52] and Bishop William White[53] in 1787, an American Episcopacy became a reality in an independent America. The church was no longer under the crown of England or the Bishop of London. Children could be confirmed by American bishops and so be properly admitted to the Eucharist. American clergy could be ordained without traveling to London. And between the times of these two Episcopal consecrations, since White and Provoost were ordained together three years after Seabury, a 1785 American *Proposed Book of Common Prayer* (published in 1786) became available. While there were several changes made in the revised prayer book to the historic 1662 Anglican version, the most important ones for our discussion appear to be:

- It replaced prayers for the King with prayers for the nation;
- Changes were made to the 39 Articles,[54] as well as the Apostles Creed;
- The word "Priest" was replaced on most occasions with the word "minister";
- The Athanasian Creed was removed.[55]

And most interestingly for the new nation, it included an order for the celebration of July Fourth. The Service for July 4th was listed as "A Form of Prayer and Thanksgiving to Almighty God, for the inestimable Blessings of Religious and Civil Liberty; to be used yearly Fourth Day of July" and included the following prayer:

O God, whose Name is excellent in all the earth, and thy glory above the heavens, who as on this day didst inspire and direct the hearts of our delegates in Congress, to lay the perpetual foundations of peace, liberty, and safety; we bless and adore thy glorious Majesty, for this thy loving kindness and providence. And we humbly pray that the devout sense of this signal mercy may renew and increase in us a spirit of love and thankfulness to thee its only author, a spirit of peaceable sub mission to the laws and government of our country, and a spir it of fervent zeal for our holy religion, which thou hast preserved and secured to us and our posterity. May we improve these inestimable blessing for the advancement of religion, liberty, and science throughout this land, till the wilderness and solitary place be glad through us, and the desert rejoice and blossom as the rose. This we beg through the merits of Jesus Christ our Saviour. *Amen*[56]

The *Proposed Book of Common Prayer* of 1785 was especially the work of the patriots of the Revolution, with much of the work having been done by Reverend William White. Reverend Mason Gallagher explained the importance of this book from the perspective of the Low Church tradition:

The same spirit which led the Puritans under Elizabeth and James to struggle and suffer for freedom of conscience, and for the unadulterated truths of Holy Scripture, animated the Congregational, Presbyterian, Dutch and Lutheran pastors of the Revolution, and were it not for their incessant stirring, patriotic appeals from the pulpit and the rostrum, and their presence in the army, where they both fought and prayed, I feel assured that the War of Independence would never have issued in the success of the Colonists. I am aware that there were noble exceptions to the course of the Protestant Episcopal clergy in espousing the cause of the mother country. The names of Bishops White and Provoost, Dr. William Smith of Philadelphia, Peter Muhlenberg, and Dr. Griffith, (Bishop-elect) of Virginia, and Robert Smith of South Carolina, afterwards a bishop, were foremost among those who sympathized with the struggles of the patriot army; while Bishop Seabury of Connecticut, and his disloyal friends were exiled or imprisoned for giving aid and comfort to the oppressors of our grandsires.

... in this city [New York City] of Revolutionary fame, that Bishops White and Provoost, with Dr. Wm. Smith and Dr. Griffiths, were among the framers of the *Prayer Book* of 1785,...on whose principles this country first received its Episcopacy.[57]

What the Low Church clergyman would have us understand is that there were two streams of Episcopalian thought in post-revolutionary America. The movement under Bishop Seabury represented the Loyalist High Church view. The clergy of this tradition had been Tories and opposed Washington and the American Revolution. The second stream was the Low Church, composed of those clergymen who chose to stand with the patriots led by General Washington. Consistent with their patriotic spirit was the inclusion of the special service to celebrate the Fourth of July in the *Proposed Prayer Book*. This did not seem to them to be inappropriate, since it paralleled the Anglican annual celebration of the Gunpowder Plot's providential deliverance of the King and Parliament from Guy Fawkes' destruction on November 5, 1605.[58]

A CHURCH LED BY LAYMEN

As the issue of governance surfaced, the historic concerns over bishops in America again arose, but not just in New England. This occurred in the South as well, as independent minded Americans felt a natural connection with their practice of lay-led churches. The Low Church Reverend Mason Gallagher wrote,

It is well known that the fear of the Establishment of an Episcopal Hierarchy on these shores was one of the causes which led the Colonists to desire separation from the mother country. The inherent nature of this intolerant system was thoroughly appreciated by the descendants of those who had so greatly suffered by it.

The diocese of South Carolina united with the other dioceses on the condition that no bishop should be placed over them. It afterwards elected Robert Smith, who had served as a private in the siege of Charleston. The conventions of Virginia were at first presided over by a layman. It is well known, also, that John Jay and James Duane, with Provoost and others, earnestly endeavored to prevent all ecclesiastical connection with Bishop Seabury after the Revolution.[59]

Bishop White of Philadelphia, before the possibility of ordaining an American bishop developed, conceived a view of Episcopalian governance that was quasi-Presbyterian in form[60] and would have eventually opened the way for an American bishop.

But the Anglican leaders in New England did not wait. They sent Samuel Seabury to Scotland to be ordained by the Anglican bishops who had remained loyal to Charles Edward Stuart, a descendant of James II. These bishops refused to take an oath of loyalty to William and Mary. Because they had not sworn their oath to the crown, they came to be known as the "Non-Jurors."

Thus, the predominance of laymen was a mark of the early Low Church Episcopal movement. The Reverend Gallagher explains:

> It is eminently worthy of remark, that in the four primary Conventions in which Bishop Seabury was neither allowed presence nor influence, the lay element largely predominated. In all the succeeding Conventions the clergy were in the majority. In the First Convention, which settled the *Prayer Book* of 1785, three-fifths of the body were laymen. In the convention of 1789, which decided to admit Bishop Seabury, three-fifths of the number were clergymen.[61]

CONCLUSION

Washington was a churchman through and through. His life in the Anglican Church in the Colony of Virginia, far away from the Bishop of London, created a spirit of independence and self-sufficiency. These qualities led him and his fellow Virginian Anglicans to be Low Church adherents. But his commitment to the Low Church also meant that he was a believing Christian, and not a Deist. In a subsequent chapter we will address how these struggles between the High Church and the Low Church impacted Bishop William White in Philadelphia, and how this had a natural distancing effect between him and Washington. We believe this helps us to explain why Washington did not commune in Philadelphia.

SIXTEEN

George Washington
and the Bible

"The blessed religion revealed in the Word of God."
George Washington, (1789) [1]

Things that people value manifest themselves in their conversations and compositions. Since George Washington loved farming at his lovely and tranquil Mount Vernon plantation, we anticipate his speaking of growing crops, the amount of rain, or improvements to his buildings. Perhaps surprisingly, or maybe unexpectedly, another of the things Washington valued enough to impact his thinking and writings are the scriptures. His writings are sprinkled with phrases and sentences from the Bible. It shows how well he knew the scriptures. We will here discover that it was second nature for him to use its language repeatedly. Not only was he biblically literate, he was communicating to people who were also biblically literate, since he fully expected his vast biblical vocabulary to illuminate rather than darken the understanding of his correspondents.

We have gone through and counted over two hundred different biblical allusions and expressions that come right into his writings from all parts of the scriptures. We find them repeatedly. The purpose of this chapter is to explore the pervasive impact the

Bible made on his life and his beliefs.

But given what we have just claimed, it is important to note that Paul Boller strongly disagrees. He writes, "…there are astonishingly few references to the Bible in his letters and public statements."[2] This means we are completely incorrect in our claim, or that Boller doesn't know the Bible well enough to see Washington's biblical illusions. Perhaps he expected George Washington to list out the references or perhaps he did not read Washington as carefully as he should have.

However, those who are familiar with the scriptures and employ them in their communications generally don't do that. When Abraham Lincoln said, "a house divided against itself cannot stand," his hearers knew he was quoting the Bible. When Reverend John Winthrop said aboard the *Arabella* that the Pilgrim settlers would be as a "city on a hill," his hearers knew he was quoting Jesus in the Sermon on the Mount. Usually, only a clergyman in a sermon spells out a Bible reference.

As we shall see in this chapter, there are hundreds of places in Washington's writings, private and public, where he used biblical phrases and allusions.

POHICK CHURCH: "HEARING THE WORD OF GOD READ AND PREACHED"

As of this writing, the Reverend Dr. Donald Binder is the rector of Pohick Church, one of the key churches where Washington served for years as a lay leader (a vestryman). He points out that in George Washington's day, the Anglican churches in Virginia placed a special emphasis on the Bible. Speaking of Pohick Church, Dr. Binder notes:

> …this was known as an auditory church. The focus was on the Word of God, not on visual imagery. That was seen as too papist. So some of the things that you may see in the church today, the crosses, the candles, any ornamentation here would not have been here in Washington's day. Those are sort of concessions to modern liturgical practices. In Washington's day, the church was fairly plain, and the emphasis again was listening to the liturgy, participating in the liturgy, hearing the Word of God read and preached, and you have to remember this is a period not long after you were even allowed to hear the Bible in your own language. So this was something that they held as being very precious, something we tend to take for granted today. So the very fact that they could hear the

word of God, expounded upon and read in their own language was just a very important thing to them, and so they set up their churches that way. You can see the pulpit looms over top of the boxes. It's given really the focal point of the worship.[3]

THE PROMINENT ROLE OF THE BIBLE IN WASHINGTON'S LIFE

Following a common tradition, a Washington family Bible recorded his birth and baptism.[4] He ordered Bibles for his children with their names printed on them in gold.[5] He ordered a large family Bible.[6] His stepson's training included the Greek New Testament.[7] He had Theodore Beza's (a famous Protestant reformer) Latin Bible in his library that contained his late teenage signature.[8] His children's school textbooks often addressed biblical themes (as did his own childhood textbooks).[9]

Washington took the oath of office on a Bible from the Masonic Hall in New York City. When he did so, he also kissed it and added to the constitutional language, the phrase, "So help me God" as every subsequent president has done.[10] The idea, given to him by Reverend John Rogers, to provide the entire Revolutionary soldiers with the newly printed Aiken's American Bible pleased him.[11]

He told Charles Thomson that he read the first part of his translation of the Septuagint that Thomson had sent to him.[12] His name was at the head of subscribers of an evangelical study Bible named, *Brown's Self-Interpreting Bible*,[13] which we will consider in the next section of this chapter.

He inherited an English bishop's Bible, which he bequeathed to Bryan Fairfax,[14] his childhood and adult friend and fellow fox-hunter, who also became his pastor in later life when he began worshipping in Alexandria. Bryan Fairfax's friendship with Washington survived Fairfax's outspoken Tory sympathies, his assumption of the title of Eighth Lord of Cameron after the War, and the establishment of the Constitution. Fairfax was ordained as an Anglican minister. A printed sermon by Fairfax, at about the time he was Washington's pastor, is thoroughly orthodox and points to the doctrine of salvation by faith in Christ's death on the cross.[15] The sermon in its entirety is in the Appendix.

While he was president, Washington read a chapter from the Bible to his family before the family went to church on Sundays, according to his personal secretary Tobias Lear's records.[16] There are many anecdotes of Washington seen reading his Bible in devotions by those who were with him in his home or in his military quarters.[17] The Bible was open at his bedside as he died, with his wife Martha at his side. Mrs. Washington's grandson, who lived at Mount Vernon, says: 'In that last hour, prayer was not wanting at the throne of grace. Close to the couch of the sufferer, resting her head upon that ancient book, with which she had been wont to hold pious communion a portion of every day for more than half a century, was the venerable consort [Mrs. Washington] absorbed in silent prayer."[18]

WASHINGTON'S ENDORSEMENT OF BROWN'S SELF-INTERPRETING BIBLE

Paul Boller writes, "In 1792, when the 'Self-Interpreting Bible' of John Brown of Haddington, a Scotch Presbyterian, was published in New York, the list of subscribers was headed by 'George Washington, Esq. President of the Untied States of America.' The John Brown Bible had a wide circulation in the United Sates, but we have no way of knowing what use Washington made of his own copy."[19] George Washington was one of more than a hundred investors in the book—making its publishing possible by subscribing to it. While we do not know how extensively Washington used this Bible, we do know some very important things that Boller chose *not* to reveal if he was aware of them. First, we must understand how evangelical and biblically focused Brown's Bible was. To demonstrate this, we must let the book speak for itself. So, consider the title page and the first introductory remarks:

The
Self-Interpreting Bible
Containing
The Sacred Text
Of the
Old and New

TESTAMENTS

Translated from the Original Tongues,
and with the former Translations
Diligently Compared and Revised.

To which are annexed,
MARGINAL REFERENCES AND ILLUSTRATIONS,
AN EXACT SUMMARY OF THE SEVERAL BOOKS,
A PARAPHRASE ON THE MOST OBSCURE OF IMPORTANT PART
AN ANALYSIS OF THE CONTENTS OF EACH CHAPTER
EXPLANATORY NOTES,

AND EVANGELICAL REFLECTIONS
by the late
Reverend John Brown
Minister of the Gospel at Haddington

*Search the Scriptures, for in them ye think ye have eternal life, and
these are they which testify of me, John v. 39 – To him give all the
prophets witness, that, through his name, whosoever believeth
in him shall receive remission of sins, Acts X. 43.
Where a testament is, there must also of necessity be the death
of the testator,
Heb. 9:16.
The Lamb slain from the foundation of the world, Reverend 13:8.*

New York: Printed by Hodge and Campbell
And sold at their respective book stores
[1792]

The Providence of God is particularly manifested in the preservation of the Holy Scriptures. To the Jews were committed the
Oracles of God, and so faithful have they been to this sacred truth,
that when copies of the law of the prophets were transcribed, they
not only diligently compared the one with the other, but even counted the number of the letters in each and compared the numbers.

Like manner, Christians have always manifested the greatest care,
not only when they transcribed, but also when they translated the
Scriptures into their respective languages.

…to…enable every serious reader to judge for himself what
doctrine ought to be believed and what duties practiced by the
Christian; are the avowed aims of this publication.

In the copious INTRODUCTION, the principal proofs of the Divine
authority of the Old and New testaments, and the rules necessary to
promote the profitable perusal of the oracles of God therein con-

tained, are largely exhibited. The connected scheme of the HEBREW LAWS, and their evangelical signification, and of the fate of nations, narrated or predicted in Scripture, as subservient to the glorious work of our redemption,—together with the large CHRONOLOGICAL INDEX,—form a summary of the most celebrated labours of the learned world on these diversified subjects. An accurate attention thereto will, through the blessing of God, greatly assist in searching the Scriptures with success.

The CONTENTS of the Sacred books, and their respective chapters, are an accurate, full, and explicatory interpretation of their subject.—Properly attending to these, the reader must discern of whom, or of what the HOLY GHOST there speaks, and understand that passage accordingly....

In our SAVIOUR'S delightful discourses and the epistles of his inspired messengers, our holy religion is most delineated; and there the explication is peculiarly extensive, and attempts to exhibit the substance of...learned and expensive commentaries, in a manner which, attending to the beautiful connectedness, unfolds the scope and meaning of the SPIRIT OF GOD....

But, as every Protestant must allow the Scripture itself to be its own best interpreter – as God, to oblige men to a diligent search of his word, comparing spiritual things with spiritual, has seldom fully unfolded any of his more important truths in one particular passage – the uncommon collection of parallel scriptures, such as not to be found any where else that I know of, has formed the most laborious, and will ... be found *by far* the most valuable, part of the work....I can truly say, that my labour, in collecting the parallel texts in this work, has afforded me much more PLEASANT INSIGHT into the oracles of God than all the numerous commentaries which I ever perused.

Thus we may listen to and converse with God, and lay our consciences open to the inspired arrows of our...REDEEMER;—we find his words, and eat them, to the joy and health of our soul; we hide them in our heart, that we may not sin against him; we become mighty in the Scriptures, and expert in handling this sword of the SPIRIT, in opposition to every enemy of our soul: in fine, we are made wise unto salvation; are…instructed in righteousness, and perfectly furnished for every good work. May the Lord himself prosper it for these ends!

J. Brown

There is no question, then, that this Bible was an evangelical study Bible. It is impossible to believe that the sitting president of the United States would be identified as the leading subscriber of such a Bible without his support. And as Boller notes, when convenient for his argument, Washington did not choose to support everything he was asked to endorse.[20]

But a second important matter to observe here as well is that many other subscribers are listed to this work. Conspicuous by their absence are the known Deists of the day, such as Thomas Paine, Ethan Allen, Elihu Palmer, and closet atheists such as Joel Barlow, who did not subscribe to its publication. Even the soft Deists like Thomas Jefferson did not affix their names to the subscription pages. The Christian, yet Unitarian-leaning, John Adams also did not subscribe.

But Washington clearly identified himself with the biblically committed evangelicals of his day by subscribing to Brown's Bible at the strategic time of his first term in office. Should it be said Washington did so for political motivations, let us not forget that Washington was unanimously elected to the presidency twice. Appeasing the evangelical vote was not a concern in either of his elections.

Simply put, how can Washington be construed as a Deist, given his open admission of interest in Christianity? Interestingly, for a discussion that we will have in a later chapter, Washington's Bible still exists. It is kept on visible display at the Washington Masonic Memorial in Alexandria, Virginia. The real question, however, is whether Washington ever got around to reading a Bible, since owning a Bible and reading a Bible are two different things? The answer is a resounding yes, as we will now see as we consider Washington's biblical literacy.

WASHINGTON'S DOCTRINE OF SCRIPTURE

George Washington, even though not a theologian, had a theological doctrine of scripture. This is most important since, by definition, a Deist denied the Christian doctrine of written revelation. God was a distant and remote Creator, and had never communicated with his creation. In Deism, there was no doctrine of scripture, because there was no scripture.

Yet Washington referred to the Bible and its teachings in a variety of ways that reflected his own commitment to Christian teaching on the doctrine of scripture. Washington's theology of scripture included such concepts as scripture, the Word of God, revealed religion, benign light of revelation, heaven-ordained rules, the precepts of heaven, Holy Writ, and so on. Each of these titles reflected his doctrine of scripture and his reverence for the scriptures. Here we consider a few examples, wherein we emphasize the key phrases in context.

- He referred to both Christianity and the Bible, as we would expect from a Christian, calling the scriptures the *Word of God*. Note his astute point about how the Bible's teaching on man's sinfulness impacts both church and government: "The blessed *Religion revealed in the word of God* will remain an eternal and awful monument to prove that the best Institutions may be abused by human depravity; and that they may even, in some instances be made subservient to the vilest of purposes."[21] (emphasis ours)

- In his First Inaugural Address (1789), he said this: "We ought to be no less persuaded that the propitious smiles of Heaven, can never be expected on a nation that disregards *the eternal rules of order and right, which Heaven itself has ordained*: (emphasis ours)"

  To his mostly-Christian hearers that meant the rules found in the Bible. The best summary of them can be found in the Ten Commandments. (Don't forget that he attended church regularly, where the copy of the Ten Commandments—from Exodus 20—would be read aloud, as a congregation from the colonial churches' rerodos).

- In a letter to Marquis de Chastellux, April 25[-May 1], 1788, Washington indirectly called the Bible "revealed religion." He wrote: "For certainly it is more consonant to all the principles of reason and *religion (natural and revealed)* to replenish the earth with inhabitants, rather than to depopulate it by killing those already in existence..."[22] (emphasis ours)

God tells man in the beginning of the Bible to be fruitful and fill the earth with inhabitants (Genesis 1:28). This is an allusion to that principle, which comes from revealed religion. During this period in history, the leaders of the deistic side of the Enlightenment were challenging the whole notion of revealed religion, insisting there was only natural religion. Washington, however, following historic Christian teaching, believed in both revealed and natural religion.

• In his *Circular to the States* (June 8, 1783), as commander in chief, the general contrasted superstition with revealed religion. He wrote: "Here [in the United States], [the citizens] are not only surrounded with every thing which can contribute to the completion of private and domestic enjoyment, but Heaven has crowned all its other blessings, by giving a fairer opportunity for political happiness, than any other Nation has ever been favored with. Nothing can illustrate these observations more forcibly, than a recollection of the happy conjuncture of times and circumstances, under which our Republic assumed its rank among the Nations; The foundation of our Empire was not laid in the gloomy age of Ignorance and Superstition, but at an Epocha when the rights of mankind were better understood and more clearly defined, than at any former period, the researches of the human mind, after social happiness, have been carried to a great extent, the Treasures of knowledge, acquired by the labours of Philosophers, Sages and Legislatures, through a long succession of years, are laid open for our use, and their collected wisdom may be happily applied in the Establishment of our forms of Government; the free cultivation of Letters, the unbounded extension of Commerce, the progressive refinement of Manners, the growing liberality of sentiment, *and above all, the pure and benign light of Revelation,* have had ameliorating influence on mankind and increased the blessings of Society. At this auspicious period, the United States came into existence as a Nation, and if their

Citizens should not be completely free and happy, the fault will be entirely their own."[23] (emphasis ours)

This is an outstanding passage. Washington is saying that the United States owes its political happiness to several strands that have come together. But "above all" the greatest of these strands is "the pure and benign light of Revelation"—another way of his describing the scriptures. Therefore, when we have had such an auspicious start as a nation, we have only ourselves to blame if we are not a free and happy people.

- Another phrase he used to describe what is found in the Bible is: *"the precepts of Heaven."*[24] (emphasis ours) Here is what he wrote in another letter to Marquis de Lafayette, July 25, 1785, "I stand before you as a Culprit: but to *repent* and *be forgiven* are the precepts of Heaven: I do the former, do you practice the latter, and it will be participation of a divine attribute."[25] Because he has been remiss in corresponding in a timely manner with his friend, he confesses that he is a "Culprit." In a friendly way, the general reminds Lafayette of one of the key points of the Christian religion: repentance leads to forgiveness, according to "the precepts of Heaven," and so when people forgive the penitent they do what God does.

- We also find these phrases in Washington's writings as well: "as the Scripture expresses it,"[26] "strictly warranted by the scriptures,"[27] "the wonders recorded in Holy Writ,"[28] and "strong as proof of Holy Writ in confirmation of it."[29] Scriptural teaching not only gives promises,[30] but is also plain[31] and makes true religion[32] possible.

To summarize Washington's writings, then, the Bible was the Word of God, the scriptures, or Holy Writ. Since revelation was available, man was not limited to natural religion alone, but he also possessed revealed and true religion. The scriptures expressed the precepts of heaven, offered heaven's eternal and ordained rules of order and right, recorded wonders, warranted conduct, provided strong proof and confirmation as well as promises, all the while being plain in its basic truths.

Although Washington operated only in the English Bible, he read a portion of the English translation of the Septuagint (the Greek translation of the Old Testament). He had a Latin Bible in his library from school days, and had his son trained by an Episcopal clergyman in the reading of the Greek Testament. He approved of the Bible being given to his soldiers.

It is thus clear that he did not approve of the Deist rejection of the Christian claim that the Bible is divine revelation. It is also evident why he felt no personal incongruity as president in subscribing to an explicitly evangelical study Bible. What we will see next is that Washington's doctrine of scripture was matched with Washington's personal knowledge of scripture. He affirmed biblical doctrines and was also very biblically literate.

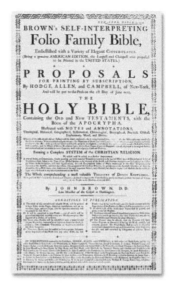

Washington's name appeared prominently on this new evangelical study Bible as its most illustrious sponsor

BELIEF IN ORIGINAL SIN

George Washington believed in the biblical doctrine of original sin. He wrote to his nephew Lund Washington on December 17, 1778: "I see so many instances of the rascallity of Mankind, that I am almost out of conceit of my own species; and am convinced that the only way to make men honest, is to prevent their being otherwise, by tying them firmly to the accomplishmt of their contracts."[33]

Washington believed in a doctrine critical to a proper understanding of man: original sin. "It is vain to exclaim against the depravity of human nature on this account; the fact is so, the experience of every age and nation has proved it and we must in a great measure, change the constitution of man, before we can make it otherwise. No institution, not built on the presumptive truth of these maxims can succeed."[34]

In a letter to Bartholomew Dandridge, dated December 18, 1782, Washington is discussing how to deal with "a most consummate villain"—one Mr. Posey: "The most hardened villain, altho' he Sins without remorse, wishes to cloak his iniquity, if possible, under specious appearances..."[35] As Washington's intended speech to Congress said, "The best institutions may be abused by human depravity."[36]

EXAMPLES OF WASHINGTON'S BELIEF IN THE CREATOR

Here are just a few samples of Washington referring to the Creator or the biblical doctrine of creation:

In a letter to John Parke Custis, January 22, 1777 (7.53), he writes, "...I do not think that any officer since the creation ever had such a variety of difficulties..."[37]

In a letter to Brigadier General Thomas Nelson, August 20, 1778, Washington pens, "...the strangest vicissitudes that perhaps ever attended any one contest since the creation..."[38]

To the American Philosophical Society in Philadelphia, December 13, 1783, the general wrote to extol their work of scientific investigation, which would benefit society at large: "The field of investigation is ample, the benefits which will result to Human Society from discoveries yet to be made, are indubitable, and the task of studying the works of the great Creator, inexpressibly delightful."[39]

On November 28, 1796, the president wrote this to his adopted grandson, George Washington Parke Custis: "The assurances you give me of applying diligently to your studies, and fulfilling those obligations which are enjoined [i.e., through scripture] by your Creator and due to his creatures, are highly pleasing and satisfactory to me."[40]

To Doctor James Anderson, July 25, 1798, President Washington observes, "...a man was not designed by the All wise Creator to live for himself alone..."[41]

In a letter to Elizabeth Parke Custis, German Town, September 14, 1794, our first president wrote, "That as the allwise dispensor of human blessings has favored no Nation of the Earth with more abundant, and substantial means of happiness than United America, that we may not be so ungrateful to our Creator."[42]

From a draft of his Farewell Address, enclosed in Washington's letter to Alexander Hamilton, May 15, 1796, read,

> That as the allwise dispensor of human blessings has favored no Nation of the Earth with more abundant, and substantial means of happiness than United America, that we may not be so ungrateful to our Creator; so wanting to ourselves; and so regardless of Posterity, as to dash the cup of beneficence which is thus bountifully offered to our acceptance.[43]

And we could cite example after example of this.

WASHINGTON'S FAVORITE BIBLE VERSE: THE VINE AND FIG TREE

Probably, George Washington's favorite biblical allusion referred to each man sitting under his own vine and fig tree. Washington used this phrase more than forty times in his writings. It comes from Micah chapter 4, verse 4: "But they shall sit every man under his vine and under his fig tree; and none shall make them afraid: for the mouth of the Lord of hosts hath spoken it." He saw the new nation and especially his own Mount Vernon as places where each citizen, including himself, could enjoy the fruit of his own labor without fear of government intrusion.

Mary Thompson, research specialist at Mount Vernon, said this about Washington, the Bible and the vine and fig tree allusion:

> He clearly, in his writings, uses biblical language, and makes reference to two events in the Bible. He talks about Noah, he talks about Haman, he uses the phrase—the most famous one, of course—is the vine and fig tree, which he uses in terms of coming back to Mt. Vernon and retiring. But there are many others in his writings that he hasn't been given credit for, so he's clearly very familiar with the Bible.[44]

The vine and fig tree example is so common that we could list example after example. Here are just a few:

- *To Marquis de Lafayette,* June 19, 1788: "...every one (under his own vine and fig-tree) shall begin to taste the fruits of freedom..."[45]
- *To the Hebrew congregation of Newport*, August 17, 1790: "...every one shall sit in safety under his own vine and fig-tree, and there shall be none to make him afraid."[46]
- *To William Pearce,* February 21, 1796: "...under my own Vine and fig tree..."[47]
- *To Landon Carter,* October 17, 1796: "...in the shades of Mount Vernon under my Vine and Fig Tree; where at all times I should be glad to see you."[48]
- *To George Clinton,* February 28, 1797: "...I shall be extremely happy to see you under the shade of my vine and fig tree."[49]
- *Doctor James Anderson,* April 7, 1797: "I am once more seated under my own Vine and fig tree, and hope to spend the remainder of my days..."[50]
- *To the Secretary of the Treasury,* May 15, 1797: "...if ever this

happens it must be under my own Vine and Fig tree as I do not think it probable that I shall go beyond the radius of 20 miles from them."[51]

- *To Thomas Pinckney,* May 28, 1797: "...I got seated under my Vine and Fig tree..."[52]
- *To Charles Cotesworth Pinckney,* June 24, 1797: "As for myself I am now seated in the shade of my Vine and Fig tree..."[53]
- *To Louis Philippe,* Comte De Segur, June 24, 1797: "...at no period have I been more engaged than in the last three months, to re-establish myself comfortably, under my Vine and Fig tree."[54]
- *To Rufus King,* June 25, 1797: "...having taken my seat in the shade of my Vine and Fig tree..."[55]
- *To John Quincy Adams,* June 25, 1797: "I am now, as you supposed the case would be when you then wrote, seated under my Vine and Fig-tree; where, while I am permitted to enjoy the shade of it, my vows [i.e. prayers] will be continually offered for the welfare and prosperity of our country..."[56]
- *To David Humphreys,* June 26, 1797: "...after I had left the chair of Government, and was seated in the shade of my own Vine and Fig-tree."[57]
- *To the Earl of Buchan,* July 4, 1797: "...as my glass is nearly run, I shall endeavor in the shade of my Vine and Fig tree..."[58]
- *To the Earl of Radnor,* 1797: "I am now placed in the shade of my Vine and Fig tree..."[59]

This expression is not only a longing of his own heart, it is also his goal for the nation to enjoy the peace and contentment the concept offers of God's anticipated peaceable kingdom on earth. Again, it is the Bible that provides this motif that Washington uses dozens of times in his writings. We will also see in another context Washington's view of the "Millennial" hope of God's peace on earth.[60]

WASHINGTON'S BIBLICAL HUMOR

From what we have seen so far, we can see how misguided Paul Boller is in claiming that Washington's use of scripture was minimal and only for "whimsy."[61] Yet we do not want to suggest that Washington did not enjoy the humorous use of the

Bible that is part of the Christian tradition as well. Two marvelous examples of friendly biblical humor can be found in Washington's letters. The point here is that Washington is not laughing in derision or in opposition to the scriptures, but he is laughing with the scriptures. The first is written to his brother-in-law, Burwell Bassett, celebrating the birth of their new child, and protesting Noah's inclusion of certain creatures on the ark.

> Dear Sir: I was favoured with your Epistle wrote on a certain 25th of July when you ought to have been at Church, praying as becomes every good Christian Man who has as much to answer for as you have; strange it is that you will be so blind to truth that the enlightning sounds of the Gospel cannot reach your Ear, nor no Examples awaken you to a sense of Goodness; could you but behold with what religious zeal I hye me to Church on every Lords day, it would do your heart good, and fill it I hope with equal fervency; but heark'ee; I am told you have lately introduced into your Family, a certain production which you are lost in admiration of, and spend so much time in contemplating the just proportion of its parts, the ease, and conveniences with which it abounds, that it is thought you will have little time to animadvert upon the prospect of your crops &c; pray how will this be reconciled to that anxious care and vigilance, which is so escencially necessary at a time when our grow-ing Property, meaning the Tobacco, is assailed by every villainous worm that has had an existence since the days of Noah (how unkind it was of Noah now I have mentioned his name to suffer such a brood of vermin to get a birth in the Ark) but perhaps you may be as well of as we are; that is, have no Tobacco for them to eat and there I think we nicked the Dogs, as I think to do you if you expect any more; but not without a full assurance of being with a very sin-cere regard etc.[62]

The second letter is written to Annis Boudinot Stockton, sister of Elias Boudinot and wife of Richard Stockton, both of whom had signed the Declaration of Independence. Here his humor includes a keen understanding of the Roman Catholic tradition, as well as of the Bible.

You apply to me, My dear Madam, for absolution as tho' I was your father Confessor; and as tho' you had committed a crime, great in itself, yet of the venial class You have reason good, for I find myself strangely disposed to be a very indulgent ghostly Adviser on this occasion; and, notwithstanding "you are the most offending Soul alive" (that is, if it is a crime to write elegant Poetry) yet if you will come and dine with me on Thursday and go through the proper course of penitence, which shall be prescribed, I will strive hard to assist you in expiating these poetical trespasses on this side of purgatory. Nay more, if it rests with me to direct your future lucubrations, I shall certainly urge you to a repetition of the same conduct, on purpose to shew what an admirable knack you have at confession and reformation; and so, without more hesitation, I shall venture to command the Muse not to be restrained by ill-grounded timidity, but to go on and prosper.

You see Madam, when once the Woman has tempted us and we have tasted the forbidden fruit, there is no such thing as checking our appetites, whatever the consequences may be. You will I dare say, recognize our being the genuine Descendents of those who are reputed to be our great Progenitors.

Before I come to the more serious Conclusion of my Letter, I must beg leave to say a word or two about these Fine things you have been telling in such harmonious and beautiful Numbers. Fiction is to be sure the very life and Soul of Poetry. All Poets and Poetesses have been indulged in the free and indisputable use of it, time out of Mind. And to oblige you to make such an excellent Poem, on such a subject, without any Materials but those of simple reality, would be as cruel as the Edict of Pharaoh which compelled the Children of Israel to Manufacture Bricks without the necessary Ingredients. Thus are you sheltered under the authority of prescription, and I will not dare to charge you with an intentional breach of the Rules of the decalogue in giving so bright a colouring to the services I have been enabled to render my Country; though I am not conscious of deserving any thing more at your hands, than what the purest and most disinterested friendship has a right to claim; actuated by which, you will permit me, to thank you in

320

the most affectionate manner for the kind wishes you have so happily expressed for me and the partner of all my Domestic enjoyments. Be assured we can never forget our friend at Morven; and that I am etc.[63]

To enjoy humor like this, Washington had to have had a deep Christian experience in the scriptures and in Christian theology. His humor toward the scriptures and toward the Roman Catholic tradition in his second letter are simultaneously accurate and in good taste. His humor avoids derision, but still evokes a smile.

SAFETY AND PEACE: NO SANCTION GIVEN TO BIGOTRY

Washington's every-man-under-his-own-vine-and-fig-tree concept discussed earlier was not merely an expression to our first president. This biblical notion was a profound vision of what America was intended to be (and has indeed become for millions). Again, it's the idea of safety and peace, regardless of your religious or political persuasion. In America, there was to be no sanction given to bigotry.

Washington thus received and answered letters from the Hebrew congregation of Newport, Rhode Island, and from the clergy of Newport. In replying to the former he said: "May the children of the Stock of Abraham, who dwell in this land, continue to merit and enjoy the good will of the other inhabitants, while every one shall sit in safety under his own vine and fig-tree, and there shall be none to make him afraid. May the Father of all mercies scatter light and not darkness in our paths, and make us all in our several vocations useful here, and in his own due time and way everlastingly happy."[64]

Here are some of the many biblical allusions found in this one letter:

1) children of the Stock of Abraham (Acts 13:26)
2) who dwell in this land, continue to merit and enjoy the good will of the other inhabitants (Deuteronomy 12:10)
3) while every one shall sit in safety under his own vine and fig-tree ("And Judah and Israel dwelt safely, every man under his vine and under his fig tree...") (1 Kings 4:25)
4) there shall be none to make him afraid ("But they shall sit every man under his vine and under his fig tree; and none shall make

them afraid...") (Micah 4:4)

5) Father of all mercies (2 Corinthians 1:3)

6) scatter light and not darkness in our paths (Psalm 119:105; Proverbs 4:18);

7) make us all in our several vocations useful here (Ephesians 4:1)

8) in his own due time and way (Ecclesiastes 3:11);

9) everlastingly happy (Isaiah 35:10)

Earlier in that same letter, Washington pointed out that our country is a place where religious bigotry is not to be countenanced by the government: "For happily the government of the United States, which gives to bigotry no sanction, to persecution no assistance, requires only that they who live under its protection should demean themselves as good citizens, in giving it on all occasions their effectual support." Rabbi Daniel Lapin, an orthodox rabbi and the head of Toward Tradition, points out.

No country in the last two thousand years has provided the same haven of tranquillity and prosperity for Jews as had the United States of America. And, this is not in spite of Americans being Christian; it is because of it. You might say that America's Bible belt is the Jewish communities' safety belt.[65]

The Bible has played a pivotal role in the founding of America, just as it did in the life and thinking of George Washington.

A PERSONAL LETTER FROM WASHINGTON FILLED WITH SCRIPTURE

Since most of this chapter consists of various snippets of letters, let's look at an example of a short letter in its entirety with an eye to scriptural references. Washington wrote a personal letter to his dear friend Marquis de Lafayette (a small portion of which we cited earlier in this chapter) in which he uses several different biblical allusions in the same correspondence. This is not the result of a speech writer. It is totally private, purely Washington, and remarkably saturated with scripture. To Marquis de Lafayette, July 25, 1785.

As the clouds which overspread your hemisphere are dispersing, and peace with all its concomitants is dawning upon your Land, I will banish the sound of War from my letter: I wish to see the sons and daughters of the world in Peace and busily employed in the more agreeable amusement of fulfilling the first and great commandment, *Increase and Multiply*: as an encouragement to which we have opened the fertile plains of the Ohio to the poor, the needy and the oppressed of the Earth; any one therefore who is heavy laden, or who wants land to cultivate, may repair thither and abound, as in the Land of promise, with milk and honey: the ways are preparing, and the roads will be made easy, thro' the channels of Potomac and James river.[66] (emphasis ours)

Here are some of the biblical allusions:

1) increase and multiply (Genesis 1:28)

2) first and great commandment (Matthew 22:38)

3) poor and needy (Deuteronomy 24:14)

4) heavy laden (Matthew 11:28)

5) land of promise (Exodus 12:25)

6) with milk and honey (Exodus 3:8)

7) ways are preparing (Isaiah 40:3)

EXTENSIVE BIBLICAL ALLUSIONS REFLECTING MASTERY OF THE BIBLE

There are several other examples we could use of several different themes from the Bible. When one looks at all these he can see that here was a man very familiar with the Bible from Genesis to Revelation, who was clearly communicating to men and women that he expected to be likewise familiar with the sacred volume.

Adam & Eve (Genesis 3)

To Mrs. Annis Boudinot Stockton, September 2, 1783:

"....You see Madam, when once the Woman has tempted us and we have tasted the forbidden fruit, there is no such thing as checking our appetites, whatever the consequences may be."[67]

A Time for All Things (Ecclesiastes 3:17)

To George Washington Parke Custis, June 13, 1798, in a reference Washington makes to the wise teacher who wrote Ecclesiastes, sometimes identified as Solomon.

"Recollect again the saying of the wise man, 'There is a time for all things,' and sure I am this is not a time for a *boy of your age* [emphasis in the original] to enter into engagements which might end in sorrow and repentance."[68] ("Sorrow and repentance" is a further biblical allusion to 2 Corinthians 7: 10.)

Blessings of Heaven (Genesis 49:25)
From a proposed address to Congress:
"...the blessings of Heaven showered thick around us..."[69]

Count the Cost (Luke 14:28-33)
Jesus told two parables to the effect that those who were thinking about becoming his disciples should first sit down and count the cost (See Luke 14:28-33). To his largely Christian audience, Washington could refer to this text and instantly they would understand what he meant. It's almost like today's mass media or movies. Someone could say someone had a "Grinch-like" attitude toward the holidays, and we instantly know what he means. So in the same way, when Washington (and the settlers and the founders in general) spoke, it was in a biblically literate milieu.
To The Secretary At War, January 5, 1785:
"In humble imitation of the wise man, I have set me down to count the cost..."[70]

No Peace in Israel (Jeremiah 6:14)
To Gov. Jonathan Trumbull, August 30, 1799:
"I will venture to predict, without the gift of "*second sight*" that there will be "no peace in Israel." Or, in other words, that the restless, ambitious, and Intriguing spirit of that People, will keep the United States in a continual state of Warfare with the numerous tribes of Indians that inhabit our Frontiers."[71]

Righteousness exalts a nation (Proverbs 14:34)

–AND–

The Throne of Grace (Hebrews 4:16)
To the German Lutherans of Philadelphia, April 27, 1789:
"I flatter myself opportunities will not be wanting for me to shew my disposition to encourage the domestic and public virtues of industry, oeconomy, patriotism, philanthropy, and that righteousness which exalteth a nation. . . and amidst all the vicissitudes that may await me in this mutable state of existence, I shall earnestly desire the continuation of an interest in your intercessions at the Throne of Grace."[72]

Recoil on their Own Head (Psalm 7:15-16)
To Colonel Adam Stephen, July 20, 1776:
"Dear Sir: Your Letter of the 4th. came duly to hand. I thank you for yr. kind congratulations on the discovery of the vile Machinations of still viler Ministerial Agents. I hope the untimely fruit of their Intentions will in the end recoil upon their own heads..."[73]

Rise as One Man (Judges 20:8)
To Theodorick Bland, July 8, 1781:
"Would to God they could rise as one Man, and extirpate Lord Cornwallis and his whole Band."[74]

Haman's Gallows (Esther 6:4)
To President Joseph Reed, December 12, 1778:
"...the most attrocious of each State was hung in Gibbets upon a gallows five times as high as the one prepared by Haman."[75]

To Open the Eyes of the Blind (John 10:21)
To The Secretary of State, April 16, 1798:
"....One would think that the measure of infamy was filled, and the profligacy of, and corruption in the system pursued by the French

Directory, required no further disclosure of the principles by which it is actuated than what is contained in the above Dispatches, to open the eyes of the blindest";[76]

Blind the Eyes of the Enemy (2 Kings 6:12-20)
To Joseph Reed, January 14, 1776:
"....If I shall be able to rise superior to these and many other difficulties, which might be enumerated, I shall most religiously believe, that the finger of Providence is in it, to blind the eyes of our enemies; for surely if we get well through this month, it must be for want of their knowing the disadvantages we labour under."[77]

Blessing vs. Curses (Deuteronomy 28)
From a Circular to the States, June 8, 1783:
"...considered as a blessing or a curse: a blessing or a curse..."[78]

Engraved on the heart (Jeremiah 17:1; Jeremiah 31:31)
To the Earl of Buchan, May 26, 1794:
"The sentiments which are expressed in your lordship's letter of the 30th of June, do honor to the goodness of your heart, and ought to be engraved on every man's heart."[79]

In His Good Time (Ecclesiastes 3:11)
To Major General Israel Putnam, October 19, 1777:
"Dear Sir: Your favor of the 16th. I received Yesterday morning, and was much obliged by the interesting contents. The defeat of Genl. Burgoyne is a most important event, and such as must afford the highest satisfaction to every well affected American breast. Should providence be pleased to crown our Arms in the course of the Campaign, with one more fortunate stroke, I think we shall have no great cause for anxiety respecting the future designs of Britain. I trust all will be well in his good time. ..."[80]

Peace of Mind (Isaiah 26:3)
To the President of Congress, September 24, 1776:
"...but experience, which is the best criterion to work by, so fully,

clearly, and decisively reprobates the practice of trusting to Militia, that no Man who regards order, regularity, and oeconomy; or who has any regard for his own honour, Character, or peace of Mind, will risk them upon this Issue."[81]

All Must Die (Hebrews 9:27)
To Major General Israel Putnam, October 19, 1777:
"I am extremely sorry for the death of Mrs. Putnam and Sympathise with you upon the occasion. Remembring that all must die, and that she had lived to an honourable age, I hope you will bear the misfortune with that fortitude and complacency of mind, that become a Man and a Christian."[82]
Washington is commending facing death as a Christian. Found in Washington's writings are several references toward being Christian—all are positive.

The Decalogue (The Ten Commandments) (Exodus 20)
To Annis Boudinot Stockton, September 2, 1783:
"Thus are you sheltered under the authority of prescription, and I will not dare to charge you with an intentional breach of the Rules of the decalogue in giving so bright a colouring to the services I have been enabled to render my Country."[83]

The race not to the swift (Ecclesiastes 9:11)
In his circular to the northern states on January 31, 1782:
"...altho', the race is not always to the swift, or the Battle to the strong, yet without presumptuously waiting for Miracles to be wrought in our favour, it is our *indispensible Duty* , with the deepest gratitude to Heaven for the past, and humble confidence in its smiles on our future operations, to make use of all the Means in our power for our defence and security";[84]

Solemn Covenants (Genesis 26:28)
This is a phrase not directly found in the Bible, but the concept comes from the scriptures. The context of this letter is that George Washington is writing about a man who was allegedly conducting

his business in a shady way.

To Lund Washington, December 17, 1778:

"If this should be the case, it will be only adding to the many proofs we dayly see of the folly of leaving bargains unbound by solemn covenants."[85]

Rising of the Sun to the setting of the same (Psalm 113:3; 50:1)
All is Vanity (Ecclesiastes 1:2)

To William Vans Murray, Mount Vernon, December 3, 1797:

"....what with the plague and trouble proceeding from the number of workmen I have been obliged to employ, and of other matters little interesting to any but myself I have been occupied from the 'rising of the sun to the setting of the same,' and which as the wise man has said 'may be all vanity and vexation of spirit,' but as I did not seek it a source of happiness, but entered upon as a case of necessity, a line may be drawn between his disappointmts. and mine."[86]

To Doctor James Anderson, November 4, 1797:

"...I promise myself more real enjoyment than in all the bustling with which I have been occupied for upwards of 40 years of my life which as the wise man says, is little more than vanity and vexation."[87]

Bricks made of straw (Exodus 5:7)

To Joseph Jones, June 7, 1781:

"....to require Brick without straw was the complaint of old time."[88]

Swords Into Plowshares (Isaiah 2:4)
"The nations learn war no more"[89]

To Marquis de Chastellux, April 25[-May 1], 1788:

"...for the sake of humanity it is devoutly to be wished, that the manly employment of agriculture and the humanizing benefits of commerce, would supersede the waste of war and the rage of conquest; that the swords might be turned into plough-shares, the spears into pruning hooks, and, as the Scripture expresses it, 'the nations learn war no more.'"[90]

To Do Justice, To Love Mercy and Walk Humbly with Your God (Micah 6:8)

Circular letter to the governors of the States, June 8, 1783:

"I now make it my earnest prayer, that God would have you, and the State over which you preside, in his holy protection, that he would incline the hearts of the Citizens to cultivate a spirit of subordination and obedience to Government, to entertain a brotherly affection and love for one another, for their fellow Citizens of the United States at large, and particularly for their brethren who have served in the Field, and finally, that he would most graciously be pleased to dispose us all, *to do Justice, to love mercy, and to demean ourselves with that Charity, humility and pacific temper of mind, which were the Characteristicks of the Divine Author of our blessed Religion, and without an humble imitation of whose example in these things, we can never hope to be a happy Nation.*"[91] (emphasis ours)

An interesting aspect of this letter is that Micah 6:8, to which George Washington is alluding, actually says "do justice, love mercy and walk humbly with you God." But Washington turns Micah's phrase "walk humbly with *your* God" into a direct reference to Jesus Christ. By direct implication, he was equating Jesus with God, a doctrine he subscribed to as an eighteenth century Anglican. Furthermore, Washington is making a profound point that modern Americans would do well to heed: unless we imitate Jesus Christ in his commitment and example with respect to his love (charity), humility, and peace (pacific temper of mind), we cannot hope to be a happy nation.

For George Washington, walking humbly with your God meant: "*and to demean ourselves with that Charity, humility and pacific temper of mind, which were the Characteristicks of the Divine Author of our blessed Religion,* and without an humble imitation of whose example in these things, we can never hope to be a happy Nation."

Broken Reed (Isaiah 36:6)

To John Sullivan, November 20, 1780:

"To depend, under these circumstances, upon the resources of the Country, unassisted by foreign loans will I am confident, be to lean on a broken Reed."[92]

The Filling of the Measure of Iniquity (Genesis 15:16)
To Charles Cotesworth Pinckney, June 28, 1788:
"May this be the case, before that inconsiderate People shall have filled up the measure of iniquity before it shall be too late!"[93]
Here's another example: To James Warren, March 31, 1779:
"Our conflict is not likely to cease so soon as every good Man would wish. The measure of iniquity is not yet filled."[94]

Ascribe Glory (Deuteronomy 32:3, Psalm 115:1)
To Reverend John Rodgers, June 11, 1783:
"Dear Sir: I accept, with much pleasure your kind Congratulations on the happy Event of Peace, with the Establishment of our Liberties and Independence. Glorious indeed has been our Contest: glorious, if we consider the Prize for which we have contended, and glorious in its Issue; but in the midst of our Joys, I hope we shall not forget that, to divine Providence is to be ascribed the Glory and the Praise."[95]

Six…Yea Seven (a pattern set in Proverbs 6:16)
To Benjamin Lincoln, August 28, 1788:
"But I trust in that Providence, which has saved us in six troubles yea in seven, to rescue us again from any imminent, though unseen, dangers. Nothing, however, on our part ought to be left undone."[96]

Led like sheep to the slaughter (Romans 8:36)
To the officers of the Army, March 15, 1783:
"…if Men are to be precluded from offering their Sentiments on a matter, which may involve the most serious and alarming conse-quences, that can invite the consideration of Mankind, reason is of no use to us; the freedom of Speech may be taken away, and, dumb and silent we may be led, like sheep, to the Slaughter."[97]

Yoke of slavery (Galatians 5:1)
To Henry Laurens, April 30, 1778: (written from Valley Forge)

"...should Britain from her love of tyranny, and lawless domination attempt again to bend our Necks to the yoke of slavery, and there is no doubt but she would, for her pride and ambition are unconquerable..."[98]

In His Holy Keeping (Num. 6:24-26; Ps. 121:5; Isa. 6:3.)
To The Provisory Executive Council of France, written May 24, 1793:
"...I pray God to have them and you, very great and good friends and allies, in his holy keeping."[99]
The draft, in the writing of Jefferson, is in the Jefferson Papers in the Library of Congress. Speechwriters are often accused of imposing their views on Washington. This, it has been claimed, is the source of George Washington's use of Providence and spiritual references. We are quite prepared to agree that Washington used speechwriters. But did they impose their beliefs on George Washington or did they know George Washington's beliefs and reflect them in the letter they drafted for him, knowing that he was always careful to review and if necessary change those drafts? We believe this citation alone shows that the latter is true. For here, the draft was written by Thomas Jefferson, who was probably the closest of all the elected founding fathers to being a Deist. Yet, Jefferson's draft is filled with a biblical spirit of prayer and it is based on a classical biblical passage–the Aaronic blessing. If Thomas Jefferson was essentially a Deist, would he not have reflected his own deistic faith, especially since George Washington was allegedly a Deist? But instead of that, we find exactly the reverse. George Washington's Christian witness is known well enough by his then Secretary of State, Thomas Jefferson that he wrote it with a Christian spirit.

Spy Out Land (Numbers 13:2)
To Marquis de Lafayette, October 12, 1783:
"The Dutch Minister, after a passage of near 16 weeks, is just arrived at Philadelphia. Many foreigners are already come over to that and other places, some in the Mercantile line, some to make a tour of the Continent, and some (employed) no doubt to spy out the

Land, and to make observations upon the temper and disposition of its Inhabitants, their Laws, policy &ca."[100]

Land of Promise (Exodus 12:25)
To Gilbert Simpson, February, 23, 1773:
"Lund Washington who is now going up to Alexandria will Inclose you an Acct. of what things he will get there with the prices of each respective Article all of which I hope will not only get safe to your hands but safe to the Land of Promise..."[101]

Lord of Hosts (1 Samuel 1:3)
In his General Orders, vol. 4, March 6, 1776:
"Thursday the seventh Instant, being set apart by the Honourable the Legislature of this province, as a day of fasting, prayer, and humiliation, "to implore the Lord, and Giver of all victory, to pardon our manifold sins and wickedness's, and that it would please him to bless the Continental Arms, with his divine favour and protection"—All Officers, and Soldiers, are strictly enjoined to pay all due reverance, and attention on that day, to the sacred duties due to the Lord of hosts, for his mercies already received, and for those blessings, which our Holiness and Uprightness of life can alone encourage us to hope through his mercy to obtain."[102]
Note the other biblical phrases here as well, such as mercies received, and holiness and uprightness of life.

The God of Armies (1 Samuel 17:45)
The Farewell Orders to the Armies of the United States, November 2, 1783 (speaking of himself in the third person as "The General"):
"He flatters himself...they will do him the justice to believe, that whatever could with propriety be attempted by him has been done, and being now to conclude these his last public Orders, to take his ultimate leave in a short time of the military character, and to bid a final adieu to the Armies he has so long had the honor to Command, he can only again offer in their behalf his recommendations to their grateful country, and his prayers to the God of Armies. May ample justice be done them here, and may the choicest of heav-

en's favours, both here and hereafter, attend those who, under the devine auspices, have secured innumerable blessings for others; with these wishes, and this benediction, the Commander in Chief is about to retire from Service."[103]

And we could go on and on with other examples, but please see the summary chart in appendix 2 for a further demonstration of George Washington's extensive knowledge of the Bible.

CONCLUSION

The point of all this should be obvious. Clearly, George Washington was a man familiar with the Word of God. He must have read the Bible often. What Dr. Donald S. Lutz of the University of Houston said about the founders in general—that "they knew the Bible down to their fingertips"—certainly applies to George Washington.

E. C. M'Guire wrote a biography of George Washington in the early eighteen-hundreds, when some of his sources were still alive. We conclude the chapter with what he said about Washington and the scriptures:

> We before adduced the testimony of one of his aids in the French and Indian War, to his habit of reading the Scriptures and praying with his troops on Sundays, in the absence of the chaplain. This same individual, Col. B. Temple, has often been heard to say in con-nexion [sic] with the above, "that on sudden and unexpected visits into his (Washington's) marquee, he has, more than once, found him on his knees at his devotions."[104]

Based upon the extensive evidence of George Washington's mastery of the Bible, this anecdote appears to not only be believable, but to be necessary.

SEVENTEEN

The Spirituality of George Washington

*"I feel the most lively sentiments of gratitude to that
divine Providence which has graciously interposed for the protection
of our Civil and Religious Liberties."*
George Washington, November 10, 1783 [1]

Did George Washington have an understanding of the human spirit that would enable him to express a personal relationship with God marked by faith, prayers, and a sense of the inner working of the Holy Spirit? For many, the question is impossible to answer two hundred years after Washington's death. Others, having declared that he was a Deist, know that such views are inconsistent with Deism, so it is obvious, that in their minds, the answer has to be "no."

If we are to answer this question, we will have to find our evidence in the self-reflective writings of Washington. Is there enough data to establish this point? Did he even take notice of the human spirit, let alone the spiritual world and man's spiritual relationship with God?

The evidence shows that he did.

In terms of the human spirit, Washington recognized that there is a spiritual energy in the human being. He viewed this spiritual energy as a potential power for either good or evil. To substantiate this, consider the vast use he makes of the concept of the human spirit.

WASHINGTON'S USE OF THE WORD "SPIRIT"

First, let us summarize Washington's use of the human spirit in a negative sense. Phrases such as these are found in his writings: "so fatal a spirit," "a dangerous spirit," "a shocking spirit," and "a spirit not to be encouraged." This would include a spirit of "criticism," "retaliation," "revenge," "plundering," "anarchy," "disaffection," "insurrection," "turbulence," "jealousy," "hostility," "opposition," "complaint," "gambling," "impatience," "wanton cruelty."[2]

Positively, Washington understands the human spirit as a powerful force for good. Thus, he speaks of "spirited men" acting with "the spirit of a soldier." The "spirit which breathes" on such can be described as a spirit of "discipline," "enterprise," and "liberty." "Spirited" men are those who act "with spirit" who possess "the spirit and zeal," "bravery and spirit," "spirit and perseverance," "spirit and order," "fortitude and spirit."

"A man of spirit" or "men of spirit and influence" not only have the "proper spirit," rather than a "discordant spirit," "mercenary spirit," "rebellious spirit," or "refractory spirit," but they "raise the spirit" and "keep up the spirit" of others. As a general, George Washington wished that there would be "the like spirit in others" as can be seen in his terse prayer: "Would to God a like spirit . . . ."

Given the power of the human spirit for good or ill, General Washington concerned himself frequently with the "martial spirit" or "military spirit." If "impetuous spirits" became "the spirit which blazed out," the result might be the "spirit of desertion," "the spirit of mutiny," or the "spirit of disaffection." If "officers of spirit" did not lead, the army would experience a "depression of spirit" or have "damps on their spirits," "drooping spirits," a "want of spirit," or serve "with little spirit." The result was an "insipid and spiritless" army, "as full of spirit as an egg shell is of meat." To win the arduous military conflict, the army needed an "heroic spirit," a "noble spirit," "spirit and rapidity," "good spirits," to act with "great spirit," "diligence and spirit," relying on the "innate spirit of freedom." Indeed, "the requisite spirit for the exigencies of war," included "that spirit which is always derived from a corps being full," as well as a "martial spirit and thirst of glory," "a patriotic spirit," and "the generous spirit of chivalry."[3]

Washington perceived the pervasive role of the human spirit not only in his military life. but also in the realm of civil society, government, and the home. Thus, he wrote "I fear the spirit . . ." and observed the "spirit of the times," "the spirit pervades," "the spirit prevailing," and the "effects of the spirit begin to be visible." Civilian life included not only the "commercial spirit," "spirit and industry," but the evils of "the spirit of "land jobbing," "thieving," "meanness," as well as "mean spiritedness," an "irritable spirit," "factious spirit," "animal spirits," "domineering spirit." In the context of government we find such phrases as "Public spirit," "spirit of our Constitution," "spirit of justice," "spirit of republicanism," "spirit of justice and patriotism," "laws, the spirit and tendency." As a married man, he was concerned to "keep up the spirits of my wife."[4]

When Washington noted his own "vexation of spirit,"[5] he also employed a biblical phrase. Other examples of biblical allusions to man's spiritual experience include: "spirit and letter,"[6] "letter and spirit,"[7] "spirit rather than the letter,"[8] "prophetic(k) spirit,"[9] "spirit of prophecy,"[10] "spirit almost prophetick,"[11] "spirit of divination,"[12] "licenscious spirit,"[13] "licentious spirit,"[14] "spirit of licentiousness,"[15] "May a spirit of wisdom and rectitude,"[16] "spirit of perfect good will and conciliation,"[17] "actuated by one spirit,"[18] "spirit which is at work,"[19] "spirit which was at work."[20]

The religious nature of man's spiritual life is also noted by Washington. Positively, he mentions a "spirit of the religions,"[21] "spiritual concerns,"[22] "spiritual felicity,"[23] "temporal and spiritual felicity,"[24] "genuine spirit,"[25] "warm-spirited,"[26] "spiritual good."[27] The negative realities of the spirit are also noted by Washington by the terms: "evil spirits,"[28] "daemon of party spirit,"[29] "spirit of persecution,"[30] and "spiritual tyranny."[31]

Washington also refers to Christianity's idea of the spiritual life when he uses such terms as "Holy Spirit,"[32] "true Christian spirit,"[33] "pure spirit of Christianity," and[34] "Christian-like spirit."[35] In a letter to a family member, he explicitly and consciously employs a "Quaker" phrase when he asks about "all the workings of the Spirit within."[36] As he contemplates death, he affirms that he is traveling "for the land of spirits"[37] or the "world of spirits."[38] When addressing Native Americans, Washington speaks of the "Great Spirit."[39]

Washington's extensive interest in the human spirit and its impact on human behavior is further corroborated by a prayer he wrote, dated January 27, 1776, and sent to his fellow commanding officer Gen. Philip Schuyler. He prays, "That the supreme Dispenser of every Good may bestow Health, Strength and Spirit to you and your Army, is the fervent wish of Dear Sir, your most affectionate and obedient servant, George Washington."[40] The word "Spirit" since it is capitalized could refer to the divine Spirit, which would make his prayer, already significant enough, a very religiously significant matter indeed. But even if "Spirit" here refers to the human spirit, the point is still religiously significant, since Washington is offering a prayer asking God, the "supreme Dispenser of every Good" to give the positive energy of a good human spirit to an entire army, and thereby recognizing that the best of the human spirit is a gift "Dispensed" by divine grace.

WASHINGTON AND THE DIVINE SPIRIT

As we continue our assessment of Washington's spirituality, we should here note that Washington not only referred to God (about one hundred forty six times)[41] and Providence (some two hundred seventy times),[42] but he often spoke of God by many honorific titles, such as "the invisible hand" (approximately ninety different instances)[43] and frequently referred to Heaven as well (around one hundred thirty three times).[44] Moreover, he insisted that God should be worshiped,[45] acknowledged,[46] adored[47] and praised.[48] But was this personal for him?

First, it is important to note that Washington's writings depict a rich prayer life that includes a substantial vocabulary of prayer. His ledgers show that he bought prayer books for his children, his wife, and himself.[49] His diary shows that he participated in a day of prayer and fasting.[50] When he refers to "my prayers"[51] in his letters, they are described with such words as "devout,"[52] "sincere,"[53] "earnest,"[54] "ardent,"[55] "unfeigned,"[56] and "fervent."[57] Such descriptions reflect a personal spirituality that simply could not be counterfeited for show by a man who prized truth and honor the way that Washington did.

He uses many synonyms for prayer that include such terms as "supplications,"[58] "vows,"[59] "wishes,"[60] "pious entreaties,"[61] "beseech,"[62] "intercession,"[63] "divine benediction,"[64] "implore,"[65] "oath,"[66] "pious exultation,"[67] "blessing,"[68] "devotion,"[69] and "praise."[70] He refers to prayer by such words over one hundred times in his writings.

It is valuable to see the examples of how he personalizes prayer, to address the common retort that these prayers are foisted upon him by speech writers and surrogate composers of letters who had an eye for popular appeal. It is true that we find prayer language that reflects his public role: "prayer time,"[71] "thanksgiving and prayer,"[72] "fasting, humiliation and prayer,"[73] "prayer to be observed,"[74] "prayers to Almighty God,"[75] "pray the Great Spirit,"[76] and the generic "pray heaven."[77]

But we also find personalized phrases such as "I pray God,"[78] "with my prayers for your health," "I pray as a member of it," "a safe return, I pray," "I must pray Heaven," "I pray heaven," "I pray to heaven," "I pray that heaven," "I devoutly pray," "I pray devoutly," "I most devoutly pray," "pray devoutly," "most fervent prayer of my soul," "I unite my prayers most fervently," "I ardently pray," "my ardent prayer ascends," "more ardently prays," "my most ardent prayers," "most ardently pray," "my earnest prayer," "I earnestly pray," "is my sincere prayer," "very great sincerity," "we pray God to keep," "his prayer to the God of Armies," "reciprocate prayers," "your prayer for me is reciprocated," "offering our prayers and supplications," "all good men pray," "praying as becomes every good Christian," "the prayer of your ever faithful," "we pray," "they pray," "your prayers," "our prayers," "our fervent prayers," "the prayer of every good citizen."

Perhaps all of this will allow us to believe Washington, when he writes to a Polish friend on June 18, 1798, "I do not forget to pray,"[79] and when he reflects in his May 28, 1784, letter to the state of South Carolina, the classic biblical prayer text of 1 Thessalonians 5:17, declaring, "my prayers for the welfare of your State, shall never cease."[80]

It is also fascinating to consider to whom Washington was writing when he mentioned these personal prayers. We might call them Washington's prayer list. They included the army,[81] patriots,[82] the governors of each state in the new union,[83] Marquis de Lafayette,[84] John Hancock,[85] Benjamin Franklin,[86] Gov. Navarro,[87] the citizens of Baltimore,[88] his hometown of Fredericksburg,[89] the State of South Carolina,[90] the Reformed Dutch Church in Albany,[91] the Dutch Reformed churches,[92] the Fairfax family,[93] the nation of Ireland,[94] the King of France,[95] the Queen of Portugal,[96] preachers such as Reverend William Gordon,[97] his good friend from Boston, his own wife Martha,[98] and even Thomas Jefferson[99]—not an orthodox believer in Jesus by virtually anybody's reckoning.

While we will not list them here, intending to do so in a subsequent chapter, we discover that Washington's letters contain scores of prayers in various lengths, from a short sentence to even a lengthy paragraph.[100]

Washington also clearly spoke of himself as a man of faith. Referring to himself he wrote, "altho' no sceptic on ordinary occasions,"[101] therefore making it clear he was not an unbeliever or Deist. Frequently, we find the phrases "I believe," "I hope," "I trust" with the Providence of God in view. Some of these strong statements of faith are:

> I go fully trusting in that providence, which has been more
> bountiful to me than I deserve....[102]

> I have always believed, and trusted, that that Providence which
> has carried us through a long and painful War with one of the most
> powerful Nations in Europe, will not suffer the discontented among
> ourselves, to produce more than a temporary interruption to the
> permanent Peace and happiness of this rising Empire.[103]

It is to be hoped, that if our cause is just, as I do most religiously believe it to be, the same Providence which has in many Instances appear'd for us, will still go on to afford its aid.[104]

I have often thought how much happier I should have been, if, instead of accepting of a command under such circumstances, I had taken my musket on my shoulder and entered the ranks, or, if I could have justified the measure to posterity and my own conscience, had retired to the back country, and lived in a wigwam. If I shall be able to rise superior to these and many other difficulties, which might be enumerated, I shall most religiously believe, that the finger of Providence is in it, to blind the eyes of our enemies.[105]

But I have the same reliance on Providence which you express, and trust that matters will *end well*, however unfavourable they may appear at present....[106]

Without expressing any opinion with respect to the Embassy which Sailed from this Country; I will hope for the best: Being among those who believes that *Providence* after its numberless favours toward us, will still continue an outstretched arm to help, and deliver us from the evils with which we have been, and continue to be, assailed.[107]

But that superintending Providence, which needs not the aid of numbers, will lead us I hope to a more fortunate Event.[108]

"We must, however, place a confidence in that Providence who rules great events, trusting that out of confusion he will produce order, and, notwithstanding the dark clouds, which may threaten at present, that right will ultimately be established."[109]

The fortunate discovery, of the Intentions of Ministry, in Lord George Germain's Letter to Govr. Eden is to be Rank'd among many other signal Interpositions of Providence, and must serve to inspire every reflecting Mind with Confidence. No Man has a more perfect Reliance on the alwise, and powerful dispensations of the Supreme Being than I have nor thinks his aid more necessary.[110]

Providence has heretofore taken us up when all other means and hope seemed to be departing from us, in this I will confide.[111]

Tis from dispositions like these that we may hope to avoid an interruption of the numerous blessings which demand our gratitude to Heaven....[112]

Satisfied therefore, that you have sincerely wished and endeavoured to avert war, and exhausted to the last drop, the cup of reconciliation, we can with pure hearts appeal to Heaven for the justice of our cause, and may confidently trust the final result to that kind Providence who has heretofore, and so often, signally favoured the People of these United States.[113]

What may have been the ministerial Views, which have precipitated the present Crisis, Lexington, Concord, and Charles Town can best declare. May that God, to whom you then appealed, judge between America, and you. Under his Providence, those who influence the Councils of America, and all the other Inhabitants of the united Colonies at the Hazard of their Lives are determined to hand down to Posterity those just and invaluable Privileges, which they received from their Ancestors.[114]

As the Cause of our common Country, calls us both to an active and dangerous Duty, I trust that Divine Providence, which wisely orders the Affairs of Men, will enable us to discharge it with Fidelity and Success.[115]

But I trust in that Providence, which has saved us in six troubles yea in seven, to rescue us again from any imminent, though unseen, dangers. Nothing, however, on our part ought to be left undone.[116]

Along with Washington's deep faith in divine Providence, we also find clear statements of a personal commitment to God. On September 22, 1788, to Henry Lee, Washington says, "While doing what my conscience informed me was right, as it respected my God, my Country and myself, I could despise all the party clamor and unjust censure. . . ."[117]

Such a commitment to God is discernable in the young Washington who wrote in 1756, "It gave me infinite concern to hear by several letters, that the Assembly are incensed against the Virginia Regiment; and think they have cause to accuse the officers of all inordinate vices; but more especially of drunkenness and profanity! How far any *one* individual may have subjected himself to such reflections, I will not pretend to determine, but this I am certain of; and can with the highest safety call my conscience, my God! and (what I suppose will still be a more demonstrable proof, at least in the eye of the World) the Orders and Instructions which I have given, to evince the purity of my own intentions and to shew on the one hand, that my incessant endeavours have been directed to discountenance Gaming, drinking, swearing, and other vices, with which all camps too much abound: while on the other, I have used every expedient to inspire a laudable emulation in the officers, and an unerring exercise of Duty in the Soldiers."[118]

Thus, in Washington's writings we find personal affirmations of faith in God such as "I hope in God"[119] and "I trust in God."[120] These statements of a personal relationship with God and trust in God are also coupled by Washington's commitment to fulfilling his duties to God and to his neighbor as taught by scripture. Consider his comments in a letter to his close life-long friend and pastor, Lord Bryan Fairfax, written near the end of his life on January 20, 1799, in which his life walk is paralleled to a surveyor's "straight line" in seeking to fulfill his duties to God and man:

> Lady Huntington as you may have been told *was* a correspondent of mine, and did me the honor to claim me as a relation; but in what degree, or by what connexion it came to pass, she did not inform me, nor did I ever trouble her Ladyship with an enquiry. The favourable sentiments which others, you say, have been pleased to express respecting me, cannot but be pleasing to a mind who always walked on a straight line, and endeavoured as far as human frailties, and perhaps strong passions, would enable him, to discharge the relative duties to his Maker and fellow-men, without seeking any indirect or left handed attempts to acquire popularity.[121]

On December 12, 1796, to his adopted grandson, George Washington Parke Custis, Washington writes, "…know how anxious all your friends are to see you enter upon the grand theatre of life, with the advantages of a finished education, a highly cultivated mind, and a proper sense of your duties to God and man…."[122]

Washington is conscious that humans live their lives in the presence of God. Thus we encounter phrases such as "justified in the sight of God,"[123] "May that God to whom you appealed judge between America and you,"[124] "we might have appealed to God and man for justice,"[125] "answerable to God,"[126] "accountable to God alone."[127] Living in God's presence touches the human heart: "God who knows all hearts,"[128] "God alone is the judge of the hearts of men,"[129] and God "inclines the hearts"[130] of men.

WASHINGTON ON HIS OWN PIETY: PROPAGANDA OR PRIORITY?

In 1936, Franklin Steiner, wrote: "Washington may be closer to a 'warm deist.' Washington was undoubtedly a moral and perhaps religious man—in his own way. But revising history to pull so many of our founding fathers into the Christian tent is merely propaganda." [131]

Can Steiner's claim be proved by Washington's own words? It is unfortunate that so many scholars like Steiner make unsubstantiated claims that they have never bothered to demonstrate with scholarly care. Now that we have seen that Washington was self conscious about the spiritual side of human life, including his own spirit, it is appropriate to ask whether this became a religious spirituality. That is, did his spirit seek to connect with the Divine Spirit? The word that often has been used to describe this type of spirituality is reverence to God or more simply, piety. Did his spirituality express itself in piety? Do Washington's words demonstrate that piety was important for himself and others? If his words count as proof, and they are, in fact, the only sufficient proof, the answer is a resounding "yes."

First of all, Washington was comfortable with people who practiced piety. So he welcomed the "pious wishes" for his happiness from clergymen,[132]—and again, he had contact with roughly one hundred of them. He in turn was comfortable in wishing "all the blessings which flow from piety and religion"[133] upon the leaders of the Reformed Church at Raritan.

In fact, Washington was even comfortable in declaring his views of piety to the Presbyterian clergy. On one occasion he wrote, "I will observe that the general prevalence of piety, philanthropy, honesty, industry, and oeconomy seems, in the ordinary course of human affairs, particularly necessary for advancing and confirming the happiness of our country."[134] On a second occasion, he explained "you will permit me to observe that the path of true piety is so plain as to require but little political direction."[135]

Second, he openly supported and expressed approval for the Protestant and Catholic efforts to bring Christianity to the Native Americans. He described such piety by saying, "the pious and humane purposes"[136] of Lady Huntington's missionary work to the Indians as he wrote to Sir James Jay. In 1785, he wrote to the President of Congress, that he "wou'd give every aid in my power, consistent with the ease and tranquility, to which I meant to devote the remainder of my life, to carry her plan into effect," a plan that he described as "her pious and benevolent designs."[137]

In fact, Washington thought that Lady Huntington's pursuit of evangelism among the Indians was only possible because of her piety. For a less pious person, the complexity of ministering among Native Americans "would discourage any person possessed of less piety, zeal and philanthrophy than are characteristick of Lady Huntington."[138] Similarly, he thanked the Roman Catholic missionary to the Indians, John Carroll, the first Roman Catholic bishop in the United States, for his "pious and benevolent wishes to effect this desirable end, upon the mild principles of Religion and Philanthropy."[139]

Washington even promised his own pious prayers in a private letter. So he affirmed to George Martin, that he would "extend my pious Entreaties, that Heaven may establish them [the citizens of Ireland] in a happy and perpetuated Tranquility."[140]

But Washington's pious prayers were not just for distant countries. He wrote, "there can be no harm in a pious wish for the good of one's Country."[141] Thus, he taught piety to his soldiers at Valley Forge. As we have already noted, Washington not only called on his men to pursue "our highest Glory to add the more distinguished Character of Christian" but he went on to emphasize the importance of the Christian's piety as well. He added, "The signal Instances of providential Goodness which we have experienced and which have now almost crowned our labours with complete Success, demand from us in a peculiar manner the warmest returns of Gratitude and Piety to the Supreme Author of all Good."[142]

General Washington actually commanded the pursuit of piety among "all officers, and soldiers." They were "to pay strict obedience to the Orders of the Continental Congress, and by their unfeigned, and pious observance of their religious duties, incline the Lord, and Giver of Victory, to prosper our arms."[143]

The normally, emotionally staid Washington admitted to Jonathan Trumbull, one of the most devout of the New England Puritans that he knew, that they might properly break out in a thankful and reverent jubilance to Providence in light of the successful adoption of the new Constitution. With palpable emotion he wrote, "we may, with a kind of grateful and pious exultation, trace the finger of Providence through those dark and mysterious events, which first induced the States to appoint a general Convention and then led them one after another (by such steps as were best calculated to effect the object) into an adoption of the system recommended by that general Convention."[144]

America's success in achieving independence and the reality of the peaceful new constitutional government prompted the president to speak of piety in his historic and public inaugural remarks to the nation. He declared that the new office of president could not begin "without some return of pious gratitude."[145]

And even as he left office, after two terms of service, he had not forgotten the importance of religion and morality for the entire nation, including, "The mere Politician, equally with the pious man."[146] It is patent that Washington did not intend to be numbered with the "mere Politician."

But the most explicit proof that Washington intended to be known as a man of piety is in his response to a sermon preached by Chaplain Israel Evans that made direct reference to General Washington.[147] The general thanked Evans for his kind words, but he said that the words were only a "partial mention." What had Evans left out in his description of Washington? The general went on to explain that the "the first wish of my heart" was to assist Evans in his "pious endeavours to inculcate a due sense of the dependance we ought to place in that all wise and powerful Being on whom alone our success depends."[148]

Evans' sermon had not mentioned Washington's pious support for the gospel ministry of the chaplains. It was rare indeed for Washington to correct a clergyman. He did so here on the very matter that secularists deny—his heart commitment to piety and its gospel expression. In essence, he was declaring that he was not indifferent to revealed religion and that he ought not to be construed as

Bronze Statue by Donald DeLue of George Washington praying, displayed at Freedoms Foundation at Valley Forge

what some today might call a "warm Deist."

Strange that the scholars who are so insistent in making Washington a Deist, have not considered what he himself said on this instance to a clergyman who had failed to affirm the heartfelt support of the chaplain's "pious endeavours." It leaves one wondering who is guilty of propaganda instead of serious scholarship—either that or it is a case of sloppy scholarship. If we are permitted, we would like to borrow the words of Steiner, but we will employ them consistently with Washington's words about his personal piety. "Revising history to pull our founding father into the Deist tent is merely propaganda" indeed.

"ACQUAINTED WITH MY HEART:" THE EVIDENCE OF WASHINGTON'S PIETY

To fully understand Washington's piety, we must become acquainted with his heart, as Alexander Hamilton had. He wrote to his close confidant Alexander Hamilton, "you and some others who are acquainted with my heart."[149] To become such intimates of Washington's heart, we need to discover what was first in his heart, what brought ardor and fervency to his soul, what his soul abhorred, what he wished for, what wounded his feelings. As unlikely as it may appear at first blush, it is possible to discover such things because he left a rich collection of personal letters and written documents that give us just such information.

What was in Washington's heart? We've already seen that the "first wish" in Washington's "heart" was to aid the "pious" ministry of the chaplains, like Israel Evans, who was advancing the honor of God.[150] While a wish always comes from the heart, it is not necessarily a prayer. But when the word "devout" is used in context with a wish, it is turning a heartfelt longing into the form of a prayer. The word "devout" implies something that is "deeply religious; pious, displaying reverence or piety, sincere; earnest."[151] It is clear from Washington's use of the word that it is a synonym for a prayer. Writing to Edmund Pendleton,

> Your friendly, and affectionate wishes for my health and success, has a claim to my thankful acknowledgements; and, that the God of Armies may enable me to bring the present contest to a speedy and happy conclusion, thereby gratifying me in a retirement to the calm and sweet enjoyment of domestick happiness, is the fervent prayer, and most ardent wish of my Soul.[152]

Similarly writing to Landon Carter, Washington used the phrase, "the first wish, and most fervent prayer of my Soul."[153]

Somehow secularists have overlooked the fact that Washington used the word "devout" some sixty two times. Some forty six times he used the word "devout" and "wish" in the same context. On nineteen occasions Washington employed "wish" and "prayer" in the same context. And what's truly significant is that Washington openly used the word "devout" of himself. For example, on six instances he wrote, "I devoutly hope," "I devoutly wish," or "I devoutly pray." Secularists who deny that Washington was devout must answer the question of how they can deny Washington's consistent self testimony of being devout.

Washington wanted to have both a pure heart[154] and a sincere heart.[155] He was conscious of the sin of ingratitude: "I am much concern'd, that your Honour should seem to charge me with ingratitude for your generous, and my undeserved favours; for I assure you, Hon'ble Sir, nothing is a greater stranger to my Breast, or a Sin that my Soul abhors, than that black and detestable one Ingratitude."[156]

But what was in Washington's heart? What did he wish for from his soul? What were his deepest feelings? Only on a few occasions did he openly declare them for posterity. For after all, one of his wishes was to be utterly private and unnoticed as he concluded his life: "For I wish most devoutly to glide silently and unnoticed through the remainder of life. This is my heartfelt wish; and these are my undisguised feelings."[157] Nevertheless, Washington's pen revealed the inner thoughts of his heart and soul on a few occasions. And these are the things that were deepest in his heart and soul:

- his children,[158]
- his dearest friends,[159]
- the approval of his fellow citizens,[160]
- his return to Mount Vernon to stay,[161]
- to conclude the war with speed and success,[162]
- retirement and Elysium [the abode of the blessed after death in classical thought],[163]
- the gradual abolition of slavery.[164]

But along with these, there was one unifying, pious desire. His duties to his God constituted the heart language of Washington's soul.

> Gentlemen: While you speak the language of my heart, in acknowledging the magnitude of our obligations to the Supreme Director of all human events; suffer me to join you in celebration of the present glorious and ever memorable Æra, and to return my best thanks for your kind expressions in my favour....
>
> For my own part, Gentlemen, in whatever situation I shall be hereafter, my supplications, will ever ascend to Heaven, for the prosperity of my Country in general; and for the individual happiness of those who are attached to the Freedom, and Independence of America.[165]

It is precisely this well-hidden burning passion of emotions and affections,[166] coupled with the sacred fire of piety in Washington's heart and soul, that caused him to openly confess his hurt feelings by the cursing, swearing, and oaths of his men. The language of his heart bristled when the language of his soldiers defiled the language of his heart:

> Many and pointed orders have been issued against that unmeaning and abominable custom of *Swearing*, not withstanding which, with much regret the General observes that it prevails, *if possible*, more than ever; His feelings are continually wounded by the Oaths and Imprecations of the soldiers whenever he is in hearing of them.
>
> The Name of That Being, from whose bountiful goodness we are permitted to exist and enjoy the comforts of life is incessantly imprecated and profaned in a manner as wanton as it is shocking. For the sake therefore of religion, decency and order the General hopes and trusts that officers of every rank will use their influence and authority to check a vice, which is as unprofitable as it is wicked and shameful.[167]

Washington seems to have given these orders not only "for the sake of religion, decency and order," but also for the sake of his own "pious entreaties," "fervent prayers," and "most ardent wishes of his Soul."

When one becomes acquainted with the heart of Washington, he discovers something much more than a "warm Deist," that is:

- Unless Deists are known for ardent and devout wishes, fervent prayers, and hearts that speak the language of one's infinite obligations to God.
- Unless Deists are those that abhor the "black and detestable sin" of ingratitude, that devoutly hope, that devoutly wish, that devoutly pray and find their feelings wounded by those who do not honor the name of the divine source of every blessing in life.
- Unless Deists are those who long from the first wish of their hearts to help Christian clergymen in their "pious endeavors to inculcate a due sense of the dependence we ought to place in that all wise and powerful Being on whom alone our success depends."

If that is what a "warm Deist" is, then such should come and worship at a Christian church, for they will be most welcome indeed.

EIGHTEEN

George Washington
and Prayer

"...That the God of Armies may Incline the Hearts
of my American Brethren to support, and bestow sufficient abilities
on me to bring the present contest to a speedy and happy conclusion,...
is the first wish, and most fervent prayer of my Soul."
George Washington, April 15, 1777 [1]

One night during the Revolutionary War, a kindly couple who lived near the woods close to the Hudson River took in a stranger. He sought shelter at the home of this farm couple because of a severe thunderstorm. During the night, the man came to check on his guest's room and overheard him in audible prayer. The next day, when the stranger was to leave, he revealed his identity. It was General George Washington himself.[2] This story that Washington was found in prayer was told over and over by different sources and in different places. Are these accounts true, or are they, as Paul Boller and others hold, mere pietistic legends?

Clearly, Washington did not wear his religion on his sleeve in the midst of his life of action and leadership. Was he a man of prayer? We believe the evidence demonstrates that George Washington *was* a man of prayer. It also appears clear to us that he followed the historic Christian practice of secret prayer, as taught in such texts as Matthew 6:5,6. Edward M'Guire, who wrote a biography of George Washington in 1836, attempting to highlight his Christian faith, makes the following pointed remark: "He who prays habitually in secret, furnishes the best possible evidence of his sincerity. Such a one cannot be a dissembler. He has regard to no eye, but that of his Maker."[3]

But this means we have an interesting challenge in our investigation of Washington's religion. How can one establish the reality of a man's prayer life if it was largely done in secret? Alleged secret prayers, since they are unobserved, could be no prayers at all. To start our discussion, it is relevant to note one fairly credible written record that evidences the prayer life of Washington. Bishop William Meade printed a letter from General Lewis, of Augusta County, Virginia, to the Reverend Mr. Dana, of Alexandria, dated December 14, 1855.

> Reverend and Dear Sir: - When (some week ago) I had the pleasure of seeing you in Alexandria, and in our conversation the subject of the religious opinions and character of General Washington was spoken of, I repeated to you the substance of what I had heard from the late General Robert Porterfield, of Augusta, and which at your request I promised to reduce to writing at some leisure moment and send to you. I proceed now to redeem the promise. Some short time before the death of General Porterfield, I made him a visit and spent a night at his house. He related many interesting facts that had occurred within his own observation in the war of the Revolution, particularly in the Jersey campaign and the encampment of the army at Valley Forge. He said that his official duty (being brigade-inspector) frequently brought him in contact with General Washington. Upon one occasion, some emergency (which he mentioned) induced him to dispense with the usual formality, and he went directly to General Washington's apartment, where he found him on his knees, engaged in his morning devotions. He said that he mentioned the circumstance to General Hamilton, who replied that such was his constant habit.[4]

Is there evidence in the writings of Washington to substantiate his alleged prayer life?

THE DAILY SACRIFICE

In the 1890s, a small book of handwritten prayers was found among some of George Washington's effects. Some scholars purported that these were in Washington's own handwriting. Some proposed that he had authored them. Others claimed he merely copied them. Regardless of the confusion over their authorship, they were considered by many to be authentic. This seemed to advance the argument over Washington's faith in the Christian direction, especially since these prayers were marked by a deep Christian piety. But are they authentic? Evangelicals today often quote these prayers with the assertion that they are his. The reality, however, is that we cannot *prove* that at this juncture.

Meanwhile, we *can* prove within reason a host of other points related to the prayer life of Washington, including his use of the 1662 *Book of Common Prayer*. And note well, the alleged Washington prayer book, known as *The Daily Sacrifice*, contains prayers which in tone, theology, and piety are quite similar to the 1662 Church of England's *Book of Common Prayer*.

Again, we take the minimalist facts approach here. Since it can be demonstrated that Washington used that liturgical guide, we prefer to promote that book rather than *The Daily Sacrifice*, which cannot be proven to be authentically his. There is no doubt, however, that this handwritten prayer guide was in his possession, since it was found among his effects. There is doubt as to whether it was in his handwriting. Boller diminishes the significance of these prayers being in Washington's effects by arguing that while such a "book" was found among his papers, writings by Deist Thomas Paine were also found in his library. Moreover, how do we know he even read them?

But we should keep some things in mind as we respond to Boller's claim here. First, George Washington did not have Paine's *Age of Reason* in his library. Further, there is no parallel example of a written manuscript in George Washington's possession that advocated a Deist viewpoint, which at least leads us to ask why Washington even bothered to have such spiritual writings in his possession at all?

The entire text of *The Daily Sacrifice* prayers is found in appendix 4. But there was another prayer book that Washington did in fact use for his daily sacrifice of prayer to his God. This was the 1662 edition of the *Book of Common Prayer*. The evidence clearly shows that this book he bought, he read, he shared with others, and used for his prayers.

THE 1662 *BOOK OF COMMON PRAYER*

From a careful consideration of the evidence, it is clear that Washington was a regular user of the 1662 edition of the *Book of Common Prayer* of the Anglican Church. The next major edition of the *Book of Common Prayer* did not occur until after the Revolutionary War and at the inauguration of the U.S. Constitution in 1789, when the Anglican Church in America became the Episcopal Church.

As we consider the 1662 *Book of Common Prayer* it is important to remember that it was a theologically orthodox book, teaching prayer and worship consistent with historic Christian doctrine. Throughout his lifelong pattern of worship in the Anglican Church, whenever Washington worshiped, the parish priest or lay-reader would use this liturgical guide. Furthermore, Washington's papers show that he even ordered a pocket-sized edition of the prayer book, so he could carry it with him.

> INVOICE OF GOODS TO BE SHIPD BY ROBERT CARY & CO.
> FOR THE USE OF GEO. WASHINGTON, POTOMACK RIVER, VIRGINIA, VIZ.
> July 18, 1771.
> A Prayr. Book with the new Version of Psalms and good plain type, covd. with red Moroco., to be 7 Inchs. long 4 wide, and as thin as possible for the greatr. ease of caryg. in the Pocket. [5]

Here's an example of the morning prayers during a daily service, coming from the 1662 *Book of Common Prayer*, with the scripture verses and prayers that Washington and fellow-worshipers would have recited:

> The Order for Morning Prayer,
> Daily Throughout the Year.
>   At the beginning of Morning Prayer the Minister shall read with a loud voice some one or more of these Sentences of the Scriptures that follow....
>   WHEN the wicked man turneth away from his wickedness that he hath committed, and doeth that which is lawful and right, he shall save his soul alive. Ezek. 18:27.
>   I acknowledge my transgressions, and my sin is ever before me. Psalm 51:3.

Hide thy face from my sins, and blot out all mine iniquities. Psalm 51:9.

The sacrifices of God are a broken spirit: a broken and a contrite heart, O God, thou wilt not despise. Psalm 51:17.

Rend your heart, and not your garments, and turn unto the Lord your God: for he is gracious and merciful, slow to anger, and of great kindness, and repenteth him of the evil. Joel 2:13.

To the Lord our God belong mercies and forgivenesses, though we have rebelled against him; neither have we obeyed the voice of the Lord our God, to walk in his laws which he set before us. Daniel 9:9, 10.

O Lord, correct me, but with judgment; not in thine anger, lest thou bring me to nothing. Jer. 10:24. Psalm 6:1.

Repent ye; for the Kingdom of Heaven is at hand. St. Matt. 3:2.

I will arise and go to my father, and will say unto him, Father, I have sinned against heaven, and before thee, and am no more worthy to be called thy son. St. Luke 15:18, 19.

Enter not into judgment with thy servant, O Lord; for in thy sight shall no man living be justified. Psalm 143:2.

If we say that we have no sin, we deceive ourselves, and the truth is not in us; but if we confess our sins, God is faithful and just to forgive us our sins, and to cleanse us from all unrighteousness. 1 St. John 1:8, 9.[6]

These scriptures provide an outline of the historic Christian Gospel—we are sinners before a just God. We need to repent of our sins and turn to the Lord for forgiveness. After reading these convicting Bible verses, the worshipers would recite the following prayers of repentance and of forgiveness:

A general Confession to be said of the whole Congregation after the Minister, all kneeling.

ALMIGHTY and most merciful Father; We have erred, and strayed from thy ways like lost sheep. We have followed too much the devices and desires of our own hearts. We have offended against thy holy laws. We have left undone those things which we ought to have done; And we have done those things which we ought not to have done; And there is no health in us. But thou, O Lord, have mercy upon us, miserable offenders. Spare thou them, O God, who confess their faults. Restore thou them that are penitent; According to thy promises declared unto mankind in Christ Jesus our Lord. And grant, O most merciful Father, for his sake; That we may hereafter live a godly, righteous, and sober life, To the glory of thy holy Name. Amen.

The Absolution, or Remission of sins, to be pronounced by the Priest alone, standing; the people still kneeling.

ALMIGHTY God, the Father of our Lord Jesus Christ, who desireth not the death of a sinner, but rather that he may turn from his wickedness, and live; and hath given power, and commandment, to his Ministers, to declare and pronounce to his people, being penitent, the Absolution and Remission of their sins : He pardoneth and absolveth all them that truly repent, and unfeignedly believe his holy Gospel. Wherefore let us beseech him to grant us true repentance, and his Holy Spirit, that those things may please him, which we do at this present; and that the rest of our life hereafter may be pure, and holy; so that at the last we may come to his eternal joy; through Jesus Christ our Lord.

The people shall answer here, and at the end of all other prayers, Amen.[7]

Whatever may have been Washington's personal faith, it is clear that the guide for worship used by his church, his family, his soldiers, and himself was unmistakably Christian.

WASHINGTON'S USE OF THE PRAYER BOOK AT BRADDOCK'S FUNERAL

During the French and Indian War, George Washington presided over the funeral of his British commanding officer, General Edward Braddock, shot in the massacre at Monongahela on July 9, 1755. For this funeral service, Washington again used the 1662 *Book of Common Prayer*, and he did so by candlelight. They buried Braddock in the middle of the trail, so that Indians would not find and desecrate his grave.

The service he would have said that fateful night began with these three Bible verses. (Note that the first was put on Washington's own tomb thirty years after he died):

The Order for the Burial of the Dead.

I AM the resurrection and the life, saith the Lord: he that believeth in me, though he were dead, yet shall he live: and whosoever liveth and believeth in me shall never die. *St. John* 11:25, 26.

I KNOW that my Redeemer liveth, and that he shalt stand at the latter day upon the earth. And though after my skin worms destroy this body, yet in my flesh shall I see God: whom I shall see for myself, and mine eyes shall behold, and not another. *Job* 19:25, 26, 27.

WE brought nothing into this world, and it is certain we can carry nothing out. The Lord gave, and the Lord hath taken away; blessed be the Name of the Lord. 1 *Tim.* 6:7. *Job* 1:21.

Then, after reading a Psalm, the priest (on in this case, the lay-leader) was to read from the Resurrection chapter:

1 Cor. 15. 20

NOW is Christ risen from the dead, and become the first-fruits of them that slept. For since by man came death, by man came also the resurrection of the dead. For as in Adam all die, even so in Christ shall all be made alive....Behold, I shew you a mystery: We shall not all sleep, but we shall all be changed, in a moment, in the twinkling of an eye, at the last trump, (for the trumpet shall sound,) and the dead shall be raised incorruptible, and we shall be changed. For this corruptible must put on incorruption, and this mortal must put on immortality. So when this corruptible shall have put on incorruption, and this mortal shall have put on immortality; then shall be brought to pass the saying that is written, Death is swallowed up in victory. O death, where is thy sting? O grave, where is thy victory? The sting of death is sin, and the strength of sin is the law. But thanks be to God, which giveth us the victory through our Lord Jesus Christ. Therefore, my beloved brethren, be ye stedfast, unmoveable, always abounding in the work of the Lord, forasmuch as ye know that your labour is not in vain in the Lord.

After other prayers (such as the Lord's Prayer) are said and other scriptures are read, the leader closes with this prayer and the attached benediction

> O MERCIFUL God, the Father of our Lord Jesus Christ, who is the resurrection and the life; in whom whosoever believeth shall live, though he die; and whosoever liveth, and believeth in him, shall not die eternally; who also hath taught us, by his holy Apostle Saint Paul, not to be sorry, as men without hope, for them that sleep in him: We meekly beseech thee, O Father, to raise us from the death of sin unto the life of righteousness; that, when we shall depart this life, we may rest in him, as our hope is this our brother doth; and that, at the general Resurrection in the last day, we may be found acceptable in thy sight; and receive that blessing, which thy well-beloved Son shall then pronounce to all that love and fear thee, saying, Come, ye blessed children of my Father, receive the kingdom prepared for you from the beginning of the world: Grant this, we beseech thee, O merciful Father, through Jesus Christ, our Mediator and Redeemer. *Amen.*
>
> THE grace of our Lord Jesus Christ, and the love of God and the fellowship of the Holy Ghost, be with us all evermore. *Amen.*[8]

Again, how could a Deist say all these words in good conscience? The point is simply this: George Washington was an eighteenth century Anglican, and we do injustice to his memory by ripping him out of that context, as many modern scholars consistently do.

WASHINGTON'S SUPPORT FOR PUBLIC AND PRIVATE CALLS FOR PRAYER

As a military and political leader, George Washington called for prayer on a multitude of occasions or he received such requests from Congress and church leaders, and then passed them on to others with his blessing and commitment to participate. Excellent examples of the Congressional calls for prayer come from 1777[9] and 1779. On the second date, Washington, acting on Congress' request, not only ordered his men to pray but in the process, mentioned "our gracious redeemer," the "light of the gospel," "the church," "the light of Christian knowledge," and "the Holy Spirit." Washington proceeded to command his chaplains to promulgate this message to the whole army.[10]

After the end of the War, General Washington explained how the surrender of the British would be proclaimed to the troops, making sure that he gave thanks to God first.

> General Orders
>
> Friday, April 18, 1783.
>
> The Commander in Chief orders the Cessation of Hostilities between the United States of America and the King of Great Britain to be publickly proclaimed tomorrow at 12 o'clock at the New building, and that the Proclamation which will be communicated herewith, be read tomorrow evening at the head of every regiment and corps of the army. After which the Chaplains with the several Brigades will render thanks to almighty God for all his mercies, particularly for his over ruling the wrath of man to his own glory, and causing the rage of war to cease amongst the nations.[11]

During the Constitutional Convention in 1787, when a passionate plea to turn to God for help came from none other than Benjamin Franklin, Washington ostensibly was in complete agreement.[12] As the new president, Washington wrote to the ministers, church wardens, and vestry-men of the German Lutheran Congregation in and near Philadelphia on April 27, 1789: "I shall earnestly desire the continuation of an interest in your intercessions at the Throne of Grace."[13] In short, Washington said: keep praying for me.

This biblical allusion reminded his hearers (who were likewise biblically literate) of Hebrews 4:16: "Let us therefore come boldly unto the throne of grace, that we may obtain mercy, and find grace to help in time of need." Washington repeated this allusion to" "the Throne of Grace" in his May 29, 1789, letter to the bishops of the Methodist Episcopal Church in the United States of America.[14]

Since America now had a president and Congress was operating under the new Constitution, Congress sent word to Washington to call for a day of thanksgiving and prayer. Thus, Washington issued a call for prayer to the nation on America's first official Thanksgiving. The purpose was to thank God for the chance to peaceably assemble and operate under the new government. Washington complied and on October 3, 1789, he issued a proclamation (which is found in full in this chapter.) We quote the opening here to show that our first president believed that prayer had a place in society:

> ...it is the duty of all nations to acknowledge the Providence of Almighty God, to obey His will, to be grateful for his benefits, and humbly to implore His protection and favor....[15]

In his Sixth Annual Address to Congress on November 19, 1794 he again called the nation to prayer:

> Let us unite, therefore, in imploring the Supreme Ruler of nations, to spread his holy protection over these United States: to turn the machinations of the wicked to the confirming of our constitution: to enable us at all times to root out internal sedition, and put invasion to flight: to perpetuate to our country that prosperity, which his goodness has already conferred, and to verify the anticipations of this government being a safe guard to human rights.[16]

In his final, Eighth Annual Address to Congress, dated December 7, 1796, Washington again referred to his prayers for the nation:

> The situation in which I now stand, for the last time, in the midst of the Representatives of the People of the United States, naturally recalls the period when the Administration of the present form of Government commenced; and I cannot omit the occasion, to congratulate you and my Country, on the success of the experiment; nor to repeat my fervent supplications to the Supreme Ruler of the Universe, and Sovereign Arbiter of Nations, that his Providential care may still be extended to the United States; that the virtue and happiness of the People, may be preserved.[17]

WASHINGTON'S WRITTEN PRAYERS

At the heart of the Deist perspective is the sense that God is not involved in human history. So if a Deist prays, it is really inconsistent with his worldview, since prayer is not a central tenet of their belief system. So it is consistent for those historians who argue that Washington was a Deist to deny or to diminish any claims of Washington's alleged prayers. This is evident in the rejection of the story of Washington's prayer at Valley Forge. It is what motivates the strident criticisms that have been leveled at the use of what has been called Washington's prayer for America. And it certainly is one of the motivations for the absolute rejection of the significance of the "Daily Sacrifice" prayers that have often appeared in the debate concerning Washington's faith, prompting some to rename them, the "Spurious Prayers."

So it may be unexpected to discover that there are more than, one hundred *written* prayers in Washington's vast correspondence! How many preachers could find that many written prayers in their letters? What makes this significant is not just the sheer quantity. What Washington revealed in these prayers is also quite important for the question of his religious beliefs. There is always the ready argument available to set aside the force of these prayers—Washington didn't write them, they were put in his writings by his secretaries and speech writers.[18] But that argument just won't work as we will now see.

For example, one of the draft letters containing a prayer was prepared by Thomas Jefferson, who was not known as a particularly religious man of prayer. This is significant because it answers this allegation that these written prayers were foisted on Washington by his hyper-religious military staff that hailed from the Puritan New England states. Consider Jefferson's draft that was written during Washington's first term, at the time of the opening of the new government in the wake of the French Revolution:

> *To THE PROVISORY EXECUTIVE COUNCIL OF FRANCE*
> I assure you, with a sincere participation, of the great and constant friendship, which these U.S. bear to the French nation. of the interest they feel in whatever concerns their happiness and prosperity, and of their wishes for a perpetual fraternity with them, and I pray God to have them and you, very great and good friends and allies, in his holy keeping.[19]

Similarly, Washington's staff member Alexander Hamilton also knew to put in prayers in Washington's letters:

> *To GOVERNOR DIEGO JOSEPH NAVARRO [of Havana]*
> Head Quarters, Middle Brook, March 4, 1779.

With my prayers for your health and happiness, and with the greatest respect I have the honor etc.[20]

So Washington's staff, like Thomas Jefferson and Alexander Hamilton, knew that the commander in chief expected prayers to be in his letters. But at least on one occasion, when a prayer had been overlooked in the draft, Washington himself personally added one. This happened in the following letter, also drafted by Alexander Hamilton. Note that the words in brackets are those that Washington himself added to Hamilton's draft.

To COMTE DE ROCHAMBEAU
New Windsor, February 26, 1781.
I have an increase of happiness from the subsequent intelligence you do me the favour to communicate respecting Count D'Estaings suc-cess. This repetition of advices justifies a confidence in their truth [which I pray God may be confirmed in its greatest extent.] (WGW Note: The draft is in the writing of Alexander Hamilton. The words in brackets are in the writing of Washington.)[21]

So what we present here is a sampling of the many written prayers that are encountered throughout the papers of Washington. A much fuller presentation of Washington's written prayers is found in appendix 3. The simple point to be made is this: If someone wrote so many prayers, is it hard to believe that he quietly prayed many unwritten prayers as well? We think that Washington could not have composed such a vast number of prayers had he not been a man committed to the spiritual discipline of prayer. This reality seems to make the story of Washington's prayer at Valley Forge, preserved by the oral history of the Revolutionary era, something more than a mere myth, even if all of the elements of the story cannot at the end of the day be historically verified.

WASHINGTON'S RECIPROCAL PRAYERS

Another expression of Washington's faith revealed in his prayers are in some of his letters where the correspondents say that they are praying for him, and he in return writes back and says he is reciprocating or praying the same thing for them as well. This is a gracious custom that could be construed as a mere civility. But in some instances, this cannot be offered as the explanation. That is because some of the prayers are so explicitly Christian and biblical, that to affirm a reciprocal prayer would be to confess a Christian faith. If Washington intended to be the honest, candid person that he claimed to be, and yet also was the Deist that so many have claimed him to be, he could not have offered a reciprocal prayer in such instances. Yet, that is exactly what Washington did on various occasions.

The first example shows that the reciprocation can be in terms of God's blessings on earthly matters such as "life and public usefulness."

> *From* THE ARTILLERY COMPANY OF THE TOWN
> OF NEWPORT, RHODE ISLAND
> Feb. 27, 1794:
> Humbly beseeching the Supreme Giver of all good gifts to continue your life and public usefulness, and that they with their fellow citizens, may still gratefully reciprocate the satisfaction resulting from a faithful discharge of important duties.[22]
> *To* THE ARTILLERY COMPANY OF THE TOWN
> OF NEWPORT, RHODE ISLAND
> February, 1794:
> Gentlemen: For your kind congratulations on the anniversary of my birthday, and the other obliging expressions of your Address I pray you to accept my grateful thanks.
> To cherish those principles which effected the revolution, and laid the foundation of our free and happy Government, does honor to your patriotism; as do the sentiments of commiseration for the sufferings of the unfortunate, and the good wishes for the happiness of the great family of mankind, to your philanthropy.
> Your prayer for me, is reciprocated by the best vows I can offer for your welfare.[23]

The next example "The Humble Address of the Ministers, Elders and Deacons of the Reformed Protestant Dutch Church in Kingston." As we consider what these church leaders write, we discover that the reciprocation can also be in terms of the deepest spiritual realities pertaining to the Christian doctrine of salvation:

> To the Excellency George Washington Esquire General and Commander in Chief of the American Army etc:

Amidst the general joy which instantly pervaded all ranks of people here on hearing of your Excellency's intended visit to this place, We the Ministers, Elders and Deacons of the Protestant Reformed Dutch Church in Kingston; participated in it; And now beg leave with the greatest respect and esteem to hail your arrival.

The experience of a number of years past has convinced us that your wisdom, integrity and fortitude have been adequate to the arduous task your country has imposed upon you. Never have we in the most perilous of times known your Excellency to despond, nor in the most prosperous to slacken in activity: But with the utmost resolution persevere until by the aid of the Almighty you have brought us thus near to independence, freedom and peace.

Permit us to add: that as the loss of our religious rights was partly involved in that of our civil, and your being instrumental in restoring the one, affords us a happy presage that the Divine Being will prosper your endeavors to promote the other.

When the sword shall be sheathed and peace reestablished, whensoever it is the will of Heaven that your Excellency has lived long enough for the purposes of nature, then may you enter triumphantly thro' the Blood of the Lamb, into the Regions of Bliss there to take possession of that Crown of Glory, the Reward of the Virtuous and which fadeth not away.

By Order of the Consistory Kingston, November 15, 1782.[24]

The Christian view of eternal life in heaven through the work of Christ is unmistakable in the Consistory's words, "then may you enter triumphantly thro' the Blood of the Lamb, into the Regions of Bliss there to take possession of that Crown of Glory, the Reward of the Virtuous and which fadeth not away." Surely Washington, if he were a Deist, could not reciprocate such a prayer. But he did. And this was not a mere oversight. For in so doing, he consciously emphasized the theme of "eternal happiness" and its religious significance in distinction from "temporal happiness." In his November 16, 1782, answer he wrote these striking words,

In return for your kind concern for my temporal and eternal happiness, permit me to assure you that my wishes are reciprocal; and that you may be enabled to hand down your Religion pure and undefiled to a Posterity worthy of their Ancestors. I am Gentlemen, Etc., GW.[25]

Washington responded to the Consistory with an unequivocal Christian letter.

Another example of an explicitly Christian reciprocal prayer by Washington is found in the letters that were exchanged between Reverend William Linn and Washington. The Reverend Linn had written from New York on May 30, 1798, stating:

> Excuse the liberty I take in enclosing to you a discourse delivered on the late fast day. The reasons for the publication in the manner in which it appears you will see in the preface. To confirm some of my sentiments, I have quoted in the notes a few passages from your address on your resignation and I was sorry that more could not be conveniently introduced from a performance immortal as your fame. I beg leave only to express my wishes, that the evening of your busy and eventful life may be peaceful and happy; that you may see your country established in the enjoyment of those blessings you toiled to secure; and that, when removed from this earthly scene you may, through the merits of the Redeemer, receive a crown of glory in heaven. I am with the highest respect, Your Most Obedient Wm. Linn.[26]

Washington's response is as follows:

> Mount Vernon, June 4, 1798. Revd. Sir: I received with thankfulness your favour of the 30th. Ulto., enclosing the discourse delivered by you on the day recommended by the President of the United States to be observed as a general Fast. I have read them both with pleasure; and feel grateful for the favourable sentiments you have been pleased to express in my behalf; but more especially for those good wishes which you offer for my temporal and eternal happiness; which I reciprocate with great cordiality, being with esteem and respect, Revd. Sir Your etc.[27]

What makes Washington's statements here so powerful is that Linn's sermon is a direct attack against Deism and the views of Thomas Paine.[28] How he could have read this sermon "with pleasure" and have been a Deist is incoherence at the highest level. Washington simply could not have said this and have been a Deist. Moreover, the reciprocal prayers for eternal happiness that Washington affirmed here were explicitly made in the context of the saving work of the Redeemer—Jesus Christ, and the concomitant hope of a "crown of glory in heaven." If Washington had not really meant these words in this context, it would not only have been intentionally deceptive, it would have been anything but an expression of "cordiality," "esteem," and "respect."

EXAMPLES OF WASHINGTON'S WRITTEN PRAYERS

As a way of summarizing Washington's many written prayers, we next consider several categories that illustrate the breadth of Washington's interest in prayer.

1. For his family in a time of war.

> *To MRS. MARTHA CUSTIS, July 20, 1758.*
>
> Since that happy hour when we made our pledges to each other, my thoughts have been continually going to you as another Self. That an all-powerful Providence may keep us both in safety is the prayer of your ever faithful and affectionate friend.[29]
>
> *To JOHN AUGUSTINE WASHINGTON, New York, April 29, 1776.*
>
> I am very sorry to hear that my Sister was Indisposed with a sore Breast when you last wrote. I hope she is now recover'd of it, and that all your Family are well; that they may continue so, and that our once happy Country may escape the depredations and Calamities attending on War, is the fervent prayer of, dear Sir, your most affectionate brother. [30]

2. A prayer for himself and his Army.

> *To LANDON CARTER, Morristown in New Jersey, April 15, 1777.*
>
> That the God of Armies may Incline the Hearts of my American Brethren to support, and bestow sufficient abilities on me to bring the present contest to a speedy and happy conclusion, thereby enabling me to sink into sweet retirement, and the full enjoyment of that Peace and happiness which will accompany a domestick Life, is the first wish, and most fervent prayer of my Soul.[31]

3. A Day of Thanksgiving as the New General of the American Army.

GENERAL ORDERS, Head Quarters, Cambridge, November 18, 1775.

The Honorable the Legislature of this Colony having thought fit to set apart Thursday the 23d of November Instant, as a day of public thanksgiving "to offer up our praises, and prayers to Almighty God, the Source and Benevolent Bestower of all good; That he would be pleased graciously to continue, to smile upon our Endeavours, to restore peace, preserve our Rights, and Privileges, to the latest posterity; prosper the American Arms, preserve and strengthen the Harmony of the United Colonies, and avert the Calamities of a civil war." The General therefore commands that day to be observed with all the Solemnity directed by the Legislative Proclamation, and all Officers, Soldiers and others, are hereby directed, with the most unfeigned Devotion, to obey the same.[32]

4. Prayers for God's blessings at the end of the war.

To THE MILITIA OFFICERS OF THE CITY AND LIBERTIES OF PHILADELPHIA,

Philadelphia, December 12, 1783.

While the various Scenes of the War, in which I have experienced the timely aid of the Militia of Philadelphia, recur to my mind, my ardent prayer ascends to Heaven that they may long enjoy the blessings of that Peace which has been obtained by the divine benediction on our common exertions.[33]

FAREWELL ORDERS TO THE ARMIES OF THE UNITED STATES,

Rock Hill, near Princeton, November 2, 1783.

To the various branches of the Army ... he can only again offer in their behalf his recommendations to their grateful country, and his prayers to the God of Armies. May ample justice be done them here, and may the choicest of heaven's favours, both here and hereafter, attend those who, under the devine auspices, have secured innumerable blessings for others; with these wishes, and this benediction, the Commander in Chief is about to retire from Service. The Curtain of seperation will soon be drawn, and the military scene to him will be closed for ever.[34]

5. A Prayer for the legislators of Massachusetts.

To THE MASSACHUSETTS SENATE AND HOUSE OF
REPRESENTATIVES,

Head Quarters, August 10, 1783.

Impressed with sentiments of Gratitude for your benevolent Expressions for my personal Happiness and prosperity, I can make you no better return, than to pray, that Heaven, from the Stores of its Munificence, may shower its choisest blessings on you Gentlemen, and the People of the Commonwealth of Massachusetts, and to entreat that Our Liberties, now so happily established, may be continued in perfect Security, to the latest posterity. With Sentiments of high Veneration etc. (This reply to the Address of the Legislature was transmitted to Samuel Adams, then President of the Massachusetts Senate.)[35]

6. A Prayer for each of the thirteen newly independent states.

CIRCULAR TO THE STATES,

Head Quarters, Newburgh, June 8, 1783

I now make it my earnest prayer, that God would have you, and the State over which you preside, in his holy protection, that he would incline the hearts of the Citizens to cultivate a spirit of subordination and obedience to Government, to entertain a brotherly affection and love for one another, for their fellow Citizens of the United States at large, and particularly for their brethren who have served in the Field, and finally, that he would most graciously be pleased to dispose us all, to do Justice, to love mercy, and to demean ourselves with that Charity, humility and pacific temper of mind, which were the Characteristicks of the Divine Author of our blessed Religion, and without an humble imitation of whose example in these things, we can never hope to be a happy Nation.[36]

7. A Prayer for Princeton, and its historic college.

To THE INHABITANTS OF PRINCETON AND
NEIGHBORHOOD, TOGETHER WITH THE PRESIDENT
AND FACULTY OF THE COLLEGE,

Rocky Hill, August 25, 1783.

I now return you Gentlemen my thanks for your benevolent wishes, and make it my earnest prayer to Heaven, that every temporal and divine blessing may be bestowed on the Inhabitants of Princeton, on the neighbourhood, and on the President and Faculty of the College of New Jersey, and that the usefulness of this Institution in promoting the interests of Religion and Learning may be universally extended.[37]

8. A Prayer for New York City.

COMMONALTY OF THE CITY OF NEW YORK,

[April 10, 1785]

I pray that Heaven may bestow its choicest blessings on your City. That the devastations of War, in which you found it, may soon be without a trace. That a well regulated and benificial Commerce may enrichen your Citizens. And that, your State (at present the Seat of the Empire) may set such examples of wisdom and liberality, as shall have a tendency to strengthen and give permanency to the Union at home, and credit and respectability to it abroad. The accomplishment whereof is a remaining wish, and the primary object of all my desires.[38]

9. A Prayer for God's providential blessings at the start of the new government.

To REVEREND SAMUEL LANGDON,

New York, September 28, 1789.

The man must be bad indeed who can look upon the events of the American Revolution without feeling the warmest gratitude towards the great Author of the Universe whose divine interposition was so frequently manifested in our behalf. And it is my earnest prayer that we may so conduct ourselves as to merit a continuance of those blessings with which we have hitherto been favored. I am etc.[39]

10. The Prayer for the First National Thanksgiving.

THANKSGIVING PROCLAMATION,

City of New York, October 3, 1789.

Whereas it is the duty of all Nations to acknowledge the providence of Almighty God, to obey his will, to be grateful for his benefits, and humbly to implore his protection and favor, and Whereas both Houses of Congress have by their joint Committee—requested me "to recommend to the People of the United States a day of public thanks-giving and prayer to be observed by acknowledging with grateful hearts the many signal favors of Almighty God, especially by affording them an opportunity peaceably to establish a form of government for their safety and happiness."

Now therefore I do recommend and assign Thursday the 26th. day of November next to be devoted by the People of these States to the service of that great and glorious Being, who is the beneficent Author of all the good that was, that is, or that will be. That we may then all unite in rendering unto him our sincere and humble thanks, for his kind care and protection of the People of this country previous to their becoming a Nation, for the signal and manifold mercies, and the favorable interpositions of his providence, which we experienced in the course and conclusion of the late war, for the great degree of tranquillity, union, and plenty, which we have since enjoyed, for the peaceable and rational manner in which we have been enabled to establish constitutions of government for our safety and happiness, and particularly the national One now lately instituted, for the civil and religious liberty with which we are blessed, and the means we have of acquiring and diffusing useful knowledge and in general for all the great and various favors which he hath been pleased to confer upon us.

And also that we may then unite in most humbly offering our prayers and supplications to the great Lord and Ruler of Nations and beseech him to pardon our national and other transgressions, to enable us all, whether in public or private stations, to perform our several and relative duties properly and punctually, to render our national government a blessing to all the People, by constantly being a government of wise, just and constitutional laws, discreetly and faithfully executed and obeyed, to protect and guide all Sovereigns and Nations (especially such as have shown kindness unto us) and to bless them with good government, peace, and concord. To promote the knowledge and practice of true religion and virtue, and the encrease of science among them and Us, and generally to grant unto all Mankind such a degree of temporal prosperity as he alone knows to be best.[40]

11. Washington's prayers for the nation at his farewell from the presidency.

In looking forward to the moment, which is intended to terminate the career of my public life.... your support was the essential prop....I shall carry it with me to my grave, as a strong incitement to unceasing vows that Heaven may continue to you the choicest tokens of its beneficence; that your Union and brotherly affection may be perpetual; that the free constitution, which is the work of your hands, may be sacredly maintained; that its Administration in every department may be stamped with wisdom and Virtue; that, in fine, the happiness of the people of these States, under the auspices of liberty, may be made complete, by so careful a preservation and so prudent a use of this blessing as will acquire to them the glory of recommending it to the applause, the affection, and adoption of every nation which is yet a stranger to it.[41]

12. A Prayer for peace at a time of impending war.

To THE OFFICERS OF THE TENTH AND NINETY-FIRST REGIMENTS OF THE VIRGINIA MILITIA,

Mount Vernon, October 24, 1798.

That there may be no occasion to gird on the Sword, none more ardently prays than I do; and no one, with more truth could add, that, if unfortunately, in defence of our rights we shall be compelled to unsheath I hope, after the object is attained, would return it to its Scabbard with more heart-felt satisfaction. But to avert the evil, or to meet it like men it is necessary under the present aspect of our Affairs to hold it in our hands, and be united in one band.

Your prayers, and kind wishes in my behalf, I reciprocate with great Cordiality [42]

13. Washington's final written prayer in 1799. Preparing for death, Washington referred to God. He used the Christian custom of beginning this official document in God's name.

Last Will And Testament

In the name of God amen.

I *George Washington* of Mount Vernon, a citizen of the United States, and lately President of the same, do make, orda[in] and declare this Instrument; w[hic]h is written with my own hand [an]d every page thereof subscribed [wit]h my name, to be my last Will and [Tes]tament, revoking all others.[43]

FOR WHOM AND FOR WHAT DID WASHINGTON PRAY?

It is fascinating to consider to whom Washington was writing when he composed these personal prayers. Above, we've already considered some of the names on Washington's prayer list. Yet Washington's letters contain many more written prayers in various lengths. A study of Washington's prayers reveal the specifics for which he prayed, manifesting the breadth of his prayer life. The references after the following headings refer to appendix 3, and the specific section where these prayer requests can be found.

Prayer Requests Expressed By Washington for Days of Prayer and Fasting: (Section 2)

    Confession and forgiveness of sin

    Averting war

    Addressing the grievances of Americans against Britain

    Providential mercy

    Protection and success

Prayer Requests Expressed By Washington for Himself and Family: (Section 3)

    To continue to deserve the good sentiments of people.

    Safety for Martha

    For his fears of the ruin of the military

    For health concerns.

    For escaping the calamities of war

    For provisions for the successful conclusion of the war

    For his retirement and return to domestic happiness and peace

    For happiness

Prayer Requests Expressed By Washington for His Army and His Officers: (Section 4)

    To finish the work

    To be preserved and to prosper

    To never again be in a state of the severe lack of needed items for life

    For success and a safe return from a mission

    To avert another campaign

    For justice

    For heaven's favor here and in the hereafter

    For peace

Prayer Requests Expressed By Washington for Peace: (Section 5)

Prayer Requests Expressed By Washington for Citizens and Cities: (Section 6)

    For aid in their efforts for liberty

For the favour of heaven

To recover ease and happiness

For the choicest blessings

For liberties to continue to the latest posterity

For the traces of war to be gone

For enriched commerce

To set examples of wisdom and liberality so that the union would be permanent at home and respected abroad.

Prayer Requests Expressed By Washington for Native American Tribes: (Section 12)

That they would be wise and strong

That they would walk the right path

That they would not be deceived and turn against America

That the Great Spirit would preserve them

Prayer Requests Expressed By Washington For A National Thanksgiving: (Section 13)

Pardon of sins

To perform our duties

That government would be a blessing

For growth in knowledge, religion, virtue, science and temporal prosperity

Prayer Requests Expressed By Washington For Legislative Activity: (Section 14)

That his doubts about the value of a new law would not be realized

For the success of negotiations

Prayer Requests Expressed By Washington For Government Leaders: (Section 7)

To be in God's holy keeping

For health, happiness and prosperity

For their welfare

For health and long life to enjoy blessings

Prayer Requests Expressed By Washington For Royalty: (Section 11)

For God's holy protection

For guidance

For health and happiness

Prayer Requests Expressed By Washington For the American States: (Section 8)

Peace

Possession of their rights

For the prospering of their arms

Harmony of colonies

To avert calamities

Divine mercies

The overruling of wrath and the making of war to cease

Prayer Requests Expressed By Washington For the United States: (Section 10)

Peace to the end of time

Protection

That the citizens would be obedient to government

Brotherly love

Disposed to do justice

To love mercy

Humility

Pacific temper of mind

For a humble imitation of the Divine Author of our blessed religion

Happiness

Long uninterrupted felicity

Such conduct that would merit continuing blessings

Wisdom

A wise and virtuous use of blessings

That all may turn out for the best

That the nation would not become a prey to anarchy or despotism

Prayer Requests Expressed By Washington For Churches: (Section 15)

For present and future happiness

For the blessings a gracious God bestows upon the righteous

For the preservation of civil and religious liberties

For the extension of knowledge, virtue, and true religion

To be conspicuous for religious character

To pass on religion to posterity in a pure and undefiled form

Because this book is about Washington's religion, it is appropriate to distill some of the items that we might call Washington's religious or spiritual prayer requests. The numbers attached to the following list refer to Washington's written prayers found in appendix 3.

Some of the Religious Prayer Requests Expressed by Washington in His Written and Reciprocal Prayers

The extension of True Religion (13.4, 15.2)

Spiritual felicity (15.4)

Forgiveness of sins. (2.2, 2.5, 2.9, 80)

Mercy. (2.5, 60)

Favor in the hereafter. (6.7)

Spiritual and eternal happiness. (15.3, 21.9, 21.10)

Providential or temporal felicity. (57, 77)

God's holy keeping. (7.1)

The blessings of a gracious God. (5.8, 68)

Virtuous conduct flowing from imitating Christ, the Divine Author of Christianity. (10.2)

A conspicuous religious character. (10.7)

Passing on the Reformed Church's religion to posterity in a pure and unde filed form. (15.3)

The reciprocated prayer to "enter triumphantly thro' the Blood of the Lamb, into the Regions of Bliss there to take possession of that Crown of Glory, the Reward of the Virtuous and which fadeth not away." (21.8)

The reciprocated prayer that "When removed from this earthly scene you may, through the merits of the Redeemer, receive a crown of glory in heaven." (21.10)

A benediction for justice and heaven's favor here and hereafter. (6.7)

This summary is an unanswerable critique of the Deist claim that Washington was not a Christian.

CONCLUSION

Normally, Deists rarely pray. But a Deist would never pray in such Christian terms. The prayers summarized in this chapter demonstrate that Washington was a practicing Christian. No Deist whose ethic may have permitted him to misrepresent his faith for political advantage could have simultaneously prayed so Christian-like, so extensively, and yet so falsely. Having established the unassailable evidence of Washington's prayer life, we will next turn our attention to the question, "Did Washington really pray at Valley Forge?"

NINETEEN

Valley Forge:
The Crucible of Washington's "Sacred Cause"

"The General ... persuades himself, that the officers
and soldiers, with one heart, and one mind, will resolve to surmount
every difficulty, with a fortitude and patience, becoming their profession,
and the sacred cause in which they are engaged."
George Washington, December 17, 1777 [1]

Washington led his patriot army to the wintry hills northwest of Philadelphia in late December 1777, after being defeated at Brandywine (September 11, 1777) and Germantown (October 4, 1777). In so doing, he did more than secure an outpost with a strategic advantage for the work of his army. He also forged the legacy and character of his nation.

The proximity and height of the hills of Valley Forge provided surveillance of the British Army enjoying a comfortable winter in captured and civilized Philadelphia. But the sheer barrenness of the woods and fields of Valley Forge, with its raw exposure to the inclement elements, created a daily and deadly enemy for Washington's half-naked and undersupplied army. The frigid struggle for survival by the American Army in its "sacred cause" of liberty gave Valley Forge symbolic meaning, for the winter of 1777-78 would be the lowest "valley" of American hope and morale.

Yet the struggles and doubt endured were to "forge" the character of a nation. The anvil of perseverance struck by the unyielding blows of the hammer of suffering formed not just an army. When the hope of spring was buoyed with the commitment of the aid of the King of France, Washington's army left Valley Forge with a spring in its step and a character formed in the indelible likeness of General Washington. For it was his exemplary leadership and steadfast character that kept the beleaguered patriot army from disbanding in the face of deprivation, death, and despair.

WASHINGTON WAS PRESENT WHEN AMERICA OPENED IN PRAYER

Unaccustomed as most Americans have become to the beliefs of our founders, it may be a surprise to learn that America was begun in prayer. If that's a surprise to us, it was not to Washington, because he was there. Remembering this fact helps to explain why Washington saw his Army as the champions of a "sacred cause."

To set the stage for Valley Forge, we need to go back a little over three years and consider America's first step toward independence begun in Philadelphia at Carpenter's Hall. The First Continental Congress could not meet at the Pennsylvania State House, today called Independence Hall, because their discussions were viewed as too radical for the Pennsylvania legislature, which was loyal to the King. So the local carpenters' guild shared their newly constructed building, Carpenter's Hall.

When the American delegates gathered, they knew why they had come—to address the crisis that had begun in Boston. But how should they go about their work? The Congress decided that its first official act would be to open in prayer.

This was not a simple decision, as can be seen in John Adams' letter to his wife Abigail, written from Philadelphia on September, 16, 1774:

> ...When the Congress first met, Mr. Cushing made a motion that it should be opened with prayer. It was opposed by Mr. Jay, of New York, and Mr. Rutledge of South Carolina, because we were so divided in religious sentiments, some Episcopalians, some Quakers, some Anabaptists, some Presbyterians, and some Congregationalists, that we could not join in the same act of worship. Mr. Samuel Adams arose and said he was no bigot, and could hear a prayer from a gentleman of piety and virtue, who was at the same time a friend to his country. He was a stranger in Philadelphia,

but had heard that Mr. Duche (Dushay they pronounce it) deserved that character, and therefore he moved that Mr. Duche, an Episcopal clergyman, might be desired to read prayers to the Congress, tomorrow morning. The motion was seconded and passed in the affirmative. Mr. Randolph, our president, waited on Mr. Duche, and received for an answer that if his health would permit he certainly would. Accordingly, next morning he appeared with his clerk and in his pontificals, and read several prayers in the established form; and then read the Collect for the seventh day of September, which was the thirty-fifth Psalm. You must remember this was the next morning after we heard the horrible rumor of the cannonade of Boston. I never saw a greater effect upon an audience. It seemed as if Heaven had ordained that Psalm to be read on that morning.

...After this Mr. Duche, unexpected to everybody, struck out into an extemporary prayer, which filled the bosom of every man present. I must confess I never heard a better prayer, or one so well pronounced. Episcopalian as he is, Dr. Cooper himself (Dr. Samuel Cooper, well known as a zealous patriot and pastor of the church in Brattle Square, Boston) never prayed with such fervor, such earnestness and pathos, and in language so elegant and sublime— for America, for the Congress, for the Province of Massachusetts Bay, and especially the town of Boston. It has had an excellent effect upon everybody here...[2]

Dr. Jacob Duché's prayer in Carpenter's Hall, Philadelphia given at the first meeting of the First Continental Congress in September, 1774 says,

Our Lord, our Heavenly Father, high and mighty King of Kings, Lord of Lords, who dost from thy throne behold all the dwellers upon the earth, and reignest with power supreme and uncontrolled over all kingdoms, empires, and governments, look down in mercy, we beseech thee, upon these American States who have fled to Thee from the rod of the Oppressor, and thrown themselves upon Thy gracious protection, desiring to be henceforth dependent only upon Thee.

To Thee have they appealed for the righteousness of their

cause. To Thee do they now look up for that countenance and support which Thou alone canst give. Take them, therefore, Heavenly Father, under Thy nurturing care. Give them wisdom in council and valor in the field. Defeat the malicious design of our cruel adversaries. Convince them of the unrighteousness of their cause, and if they still persist in their sanguinary purpose, O let the voice of Thine own unerring justice, sounding in their hearts, constrain them to drop their weapons of war from their unnerved hands in the day of battle. Be Thou present, O Lord of Wisdom, and direct the Council of the honorable Assembly. Enable them to settle things upon the best and surest foundation, that the scene of blood may speedily be closed; that order, harmony, and peace may effectually be restored, and truth and justice, religion and piety, prevail and flourish amongst Thy people.

Preserve the health of their bodies, the vigor of their minds. Shower down upon them, and the millions they here represent, such temporal blessings as Thou seeist expedient for them in this world and crown them with everlasting glory in the world to come. All this we ask in the name and through the merits of Jesus Christ, Thy Son, our Savior. Amen.[3]

Washington was part of this Congressional prayer meeting. In 1875, the Library of Congress produced a placard that summarized various reports from the founders on the impact that this first prayer had on the Continental Congress. It reads,

Washington was kneeling there, and Henry, Randolph, Rutledge, Lee, and Jay, and by their side there stood, bowed in reverence, the Puritan Patriots of New England, who at that moment had reason to believe that an armed soldiery was wasting their humble households. It was believed that Boston had been bombarded and destroyed.

They prayed fervently 'for America, for Congress, for the Province of Massachusetts Bay, and especially for the town of Boston,' and who can realize the emotion with which they turned imploringly to Heaven for Divine interposition and—'It was enough' says Mr. Adams, 'to melt a heart of stone. I saw the tears

Washington reviewing the encampment at Valley Forge

gush into the eyes of the old, grave, Pacific Quakers of Philadelphia."[4]

The rumor of Boston's destruction turned out to be false. But the next year, 1775, at the Second Continental Congress, Washington was commissioned by Congress as the commander in chief and sent to defend Boston.

VALLEY FORGE: THE CRUCIBLE OF THE "SACRED CAUSE"

And it was in Boston where Washington made his first written and public claim that the American cause was fired by a holy flame. In August 1775, a potent salvo from Washington penned to General Gage criticized the unjust treatment of American prisoners:[5] "I purposely avoided all political Disquisition; nor shall I now avail myself of those Advantages, which the sacred Cause of my Country of Liberty, and human Nature, give me over you."[6] The "sacred Cause" was a theme Washington spoke of to Gov. Jonathan Trumbull[7] and his officers,[8] and to the president of the Congress. As General Washington wrote to the president, he concluded with a brief prayer that focused on the "sacredness of the cause":

I trust through Divine Favor and our own Exertions they will be disappointed in their Views, and at all Events, any advantages they may gain will cost them very dear. If our Troops will behave well, which I hope will be the case, having every thing to contend for that Freemen hold dear, they will have to wade thro' much Blood and Slaughter before they can carry any part of our Works, if they carry them at all; and at best be in possession of a Melancholly and Mournfull Victory. May the Sacredness of our cause inspire our Soldiery with Sentiments of Heroism, and lead them to the performance of the noblest Exploits.[9]

But it was at Valley Forge that the true cost of the sacrifice for such a holy cause would be measured. Washington wrote to John Banister, a Virginia delegate to Congress from Valley Forge on April 21, 1778.

> ... for without arrogance, or the smallest deviation from truth it may be said, that no history, now extant, can furnish an instance of an Army's suffering such uncommon hardships as ours have done, and bearing them with the same patience and Fortitude. To see Men without Cloathes to cover their nakedness, without Blankets to lay on, without Shoes, by which their Marches might be traced by the Blood from their feet, and almost as often without Provisions as with; Marching through frost and Snow, and at Christmas taking up their Winter Quarters within a day's March of the enemy, without a House or Hut to cover them till they could be built and submitting to it without a murmur, is a mark of patience and obedience which in my opinion can scarce be parallel'd.[10]

Only their unity, courage, and the "sacred cause" could enable the men to make the required sacrifice. As a challenge to their faith in the cause, they began their trek to Valley Forge in conformity with the Congressional Proclamation, with "thanksgiving and praise" and "...grateful acknowledgements to God for the manifold blessings he has granted us."[11] Washington's General Orders explained:

> ...the General ... persuades himself, that the officers and soldiers, with one heart, and one mind, will resolve to surmount every difficulty, with a fortitude and patience, becoming their profession, and the *sacred cause* in which they are engaged. He himself will share

in the hardship, and partake of every inconvenience. To morrow being the day set apart by the Honorable Congress for public Thanksgiving and Praise; and duty calling us devoutly to express our grateful acknowledgements to God for the manifold blessings he has granted us. The General directs that the army remain in its present quarters, and that the Chaplains perform divine service with their several Corps and brigades. And earnestly exhorts, all officers and soldiers, whose absence is not indispensably necessary, to attend with reverence the solemnities of the day. (emphasis added.)[12]

One of the sermons preached by the chaplains on that tenuous Thanksgiving Day was by Israel Evans, Chaplain to Gen. Poor's New Hampshire brigade.[13] Printed for the army and distributed free of charge, Evans' sermon called on the soldiers to "look on" "his Excellency General Washington" "and catch the genuine patriot fire of liberty," "and like him, reverence the name of the great Jehovah."[14]

In Chaplain Evans' mind there was an intimate connection created by Washington between the "genuine patriot fire of liberty" and "the great Jehovah," the one who had given his name in sacred fire at the burning bush. Washington did not read Evans' sermon immediately. But he did read it, and when he did, he wrote to Evans on March 13, 1778:

Revd. Sir: Your favor of the 17th. Ulto., inclosing the discourse which you delivered on the 18th. of December; the day set a part for a general thanksgiving; to Genl. Poors Brigade, never came to my hands till yesterday.

I have read this performance with equal attention and pleasure, and at the same time that I admire, and feel the force of the reasoning which you have displayed through the whole, it is more especially incumbent upon me to thank you for the honorable, but partial mention you have made of my character; and to assure you, that it will ever be the first wish of my heart to aid your pious endeavours to inculcate a due sense of the dependance we ought to place in that all wise and powerful Being on whom alone our success depends; and moreover, to assure you, that with respect and regard....

Washington promised to assist Evans in advancing the sacred cause by fanning the divine fire. It was a good thing he did, because there was little else that winter at Valley Forge to keep his men warm, as the uncharming sound of the whistling, winter wind pierced the freezing ears and ragged coats of General Washington's soldiers.

Washington's promise to Chaplain Evans proved to be more than mere pleasantries. After his March 13, 1778, letter promising to aid the chaplain in inculcating his men's dependence on Jehovah, Washington makes one of his clearest calls for his men to be Christians. On July 9, 1776, he had called on his men to be "Christian soldiers."[15] But on May 2, 1778, six weeks after his letter to Evans, near the end of the Valley Forge encampment, he again challenged his men to be Christians. To their "distinguished character of Patriot," which was a high calling, since they were after all the Patriot Army,[16] it was to be their "highest glory to add the more distinguished character of Christian."[17]

With this command, Washington began to assist the chaplains in their "pious endeavours to inculcate a due sense of the dependence" that he thought he and his Army "ought to place in that all wise and powerful Being."

We should note well that when Washington selected the word "inculcate," he chose a strong word. It meant "to teach or impress by urging or frequent repetition; instill." It is derived from the Latin word *inculcare*, meaning "to force upon." The literal meaning of the word is "to trample," or "to stomp in with one's heel" which is evident since it combines the words "*in*" and "*calcare*," which in turn is built on the word "*calx*" meaning "heel." Apparently, Washington's efforts became a matter of discussion that traveled outside the ranks of the camp. According to the notebook of German Lutheran clergyman, Reverend Henry Melchior Muhlenberg, it seems that Washington did more than simply issue an order about becoming a Christian. Reverend Muhlenberg wrote,

> I heard a fine example today, namely that His Excellency General Washington rode around among his army yesterday and admonished each and every one to fear God, to put away wickedness that has set in and become so general, and to practice Christian virtues. From all appearances General Washington does not belong to the so-called world of society, for he respects God's Word, believes in the atonement through Christ, and bears himself in humility and gentleness. Therefore, the Lord God has also singularly, yea, marvelously preserved him from harm in the midst

of countless perils, ambuscades, fatigues, etc., and has hitherto graciously held him in his hand as a chosen vessel.[18]

Reverend Muhlenberg was in a significant position to know of such activity in the camp, not only because he was a pastor in Trappe, near Valley Forge, but also because he was the father of one of Washington's generals, Reverend John Peter Muhlenberg. The Reverend General Peter Muhlenberg had also been a Lutheran pastor in Virginia, where he had known Washington before the war.[19]

WASHINGTON'S UNDERSTANDING OF THE "SACRED"

Since Washington was calling on his army to support the "sacred cause," it is important to understand what he meant by the word "sacred." He used the word fifty two times in his writings. There were two primary senses of the word in Washington's use. The first use implied that something was dedicated or set aside exclusively for a single purpose or person. Second, when something was sacred, it meant that it was holy or set apart as a duty to God, and thus the object was worthy of reverence or the utmost respect.

Examples of the first use, where something was dedicated or set aside exclusively for a single purpose or person, includes the time given by an employee to an employer,[20] money to be saved,[21] boats to be used only for the military.[22] Other examples from the military include the loyalty of a soldier that prohibits desertion,[23] the flag of truce,[24] the honor of a promotion in rank,[25] the administration of justice belonging only to the civil magistrate and not the military,[26] the distribution of food,[27] maintaining the secrecy of passwords,[28] the boundary line with the enemy,[29] and the soldier's arms.[30] Washington's papers that he possessed[31] and those that were in the government archives[32] were also sacred in this sense.

There are also several examples of the second use, where something is holy or set apart as a duty to God, and thus the object or activity is worthy of reverence or the utmost respect. In the diplomatic arena, this included the safety of an ambassador[33] or the King.[34] In military life, this included the discipline and character of an officer,[35] the honor of the officer.[36] The life and protection of the prisoner of war was a "faith held sacred by all civilized nations."[37] The government had sacred compacts and treaties,[38] and citizens had sacred privileges.[39] The president's use of the powers of the Constitution was a sacred duty.[40] The nation and the citizens possessed sacred ties,[41] and sacred engagements.[42] Honor and veracity were sacred enough to "extort" the truth even from a devious person.[43] The nation had a duty to keep a sacred regard for public justice[44] and have a sacred regard to the property of each individual.[45] When war was pending, everything dear and sacred was at risk.[46] In the more spiritual sense, there were books ordered for children that contained sacred classics,[47] the private and sacred duties of the office of the chaplain,[48] and the sacred duties due from everyone to the Lord of Hosts.[49]

It is clear that when Washington spoke of the "sacred cause," he was using the phrase in the second sense, of something that was holy due its relationship with God. In a letter written to John Gabriel Tegelaar, he underscored that heaven's favor and protection were deeply concerned with the survival of liberty.

> May Heaven, whose propitious smiles have hitherto watched over the freedom of your republic still Guard her Liberties with the most sacred protection. And while I thus regard the welfare of your Country at large, permit me to assure you, that I shall feel a very particular desire that Providence may ever smile on your private happiness and domestic pleasures.[50]

And ultimately, Washington even believed that the sphere of the sacred extended to the realm of politics. He claimed that even when freemen disagreed over political issues, this was not a fault, since "they are all actuated by an equally laudable and sacred regard for the liberties of their Country."[51]

If Heaven guarded liberty with "sacred protection" it surely was appropriate for citizen soldiers to pursue the "sacred cause" on earth. Such a precious gift was worthy of the greatest sacrifice, the kind the patriot army made at Valley Forge.

"...WITHOUT A HOUSE OR HUT TO COVER THEM...."[52]

As the army prepared to move out to Valley Forge, the general sought to put on the best face he could to address his soldiers' desperate circumstances. On Dec. 17, 1777, Washington explained the army's success, failures and hopes,

> The Commander in Chief with the highest satisfaction expresses his thanks to the officers and soldiers for the fortitude and patience with which they have sustained the fatigues of the Campaign. Altho' in some instances we unfortunately failed, yet upon the whole Heaven hath smiled on our Arms and crowned them with signal success; and we may upon the best grounds conclude, that by a

spirited continuance of the measures necessary for our defence we shall finally obtain the end of our Warfare, Independence, Liberty and Peace. These are blessings worth contending for at every hazard. But we hazard nothing. The power of America alone, duly exerted, would have nothing to dread from the force of Britain. Yet we stand not wholly upon our ground. France yields us every aid we ask, and there are reasons to believe the period is not very distant, when she will take a more active part, by declaring war against the British Crown. Every motive therefore, irresistably urges us, nay commands us, to a firm and manly perseverance in our opposition to our cruel oppressors, to slight difficulties, endure hardships, and contemn every danger. The General ardently wishes it were now in his power, to conduct the troops into the best winter quarters. But where are these to be found?

There were reasons why the "best winter quarters" could not be found:

Should we retire to the interior parts of the State, we should find them crowded with virtuous citizens, who, sacrificing their all, have left Philadelphia, and fled thither for protection. To their distresses humanity forbids us to add. This is not all, we should leave a vast extent of fertile country to be despoiled and ravaged by the enemy, from which they would draw vast supplies, and where many of our firm friends would be exposed to all the miseries of the most insulting and wanton depredation. A train of evils might be enumerated, but these will suffice. These considerations make it indispensibly necessary for the army to take such a position, as will enable it most effectually to prevent distress and to give the most extensive security; and in that position we must make ourselves the best shelter in our power.

And what would be "the best shelter in our power"?

With activity and diligence Huts may be erected that will be warm and dry. In these the troops will be compact, more secure against surprises than if in a divided state and at hand to protect the country. These cogent reasons have determined the General to take post in the neighbourhood of this camp;

To make it all work, it would indeed be a matter of the "officers and soldiers" working "with one heart, and one mind." They would have to "surmount every difficulty, with a fortitude and patience" and not forget "the sacred cause in which they are engaged." Washington's commitment to "share in the hardship, and partake of every inconvenience" was surely one of the elements of the next day's "public Thanksgiving and Praise."[53]

So on the next day, Thursday Dec. 18, 1777, plans for the huts were disseminated:

A field officer was to supervise a squad of twelve. The dimensions were to be 14' x 16' of logs, roof of split slabs, sides with clay, 18" thick on inside fireplace, door at street, side 6' high.[54]

On Friday Dec. 19, 1777, the cold wind began to blow, piercing the soldiers' threadbare garments as the snow began to fall. At 10 a.m., the American Army began its march to Valley Forge and upon arrival immediately began to lay out the grounds for their respective cantonments.

Saturday Dec. 20, 1777 saw the beginning of felling trees: "Soldiers cutting firewood are to save such parts of each tree as will do for building, reserving sixteen or eighteen feet of the trunk for logs to rear their Huts with."[55] Commands for straw governed a seventy mile region, requiring straw for beds, whereby each farmer had to thresh half his grain by February 1st, and the other half by March 1st for use by the soldiers, otherwise the army would seize all that the owner had.

On Sunday Dec. 21, 1777, a model of a hut was ready to be viewed at headquarters. While no enemy bullets flew at Valley Forge, there were many battles to be fought nevertheless. The immediate battle was over shelter, or the huts. The generals, who longed to head for their own homes for winter quarters, were not permitted to leave until all huts were done (General Orders of Dec. 27.) Washington, of course, never left for Mount Vernon until the war was over.

About the time of the battle of Germantown (October 1777), the northern American Army had won an astounding victory at Saratoga, under General Gates, who had just replaced Gen. Schuyler. But this victory to the north added pain for General Washington, not only in what became known as the Conway Cabal, which we will review later, but it also caused pain for the soldiers at Valley Forge. It was sarcastically observed that "Genl Burgoyne and his defeated Army are to be returned to Britain to sit out the War in the cold discomforts of the London Coffee Shops while we shall remain here in our warm, cozy Hutts living *en prince* off this generous land and enjoying our liberty."[56] Such was the ordeal of crafting the huts that, as human nature is so apt to do to cope with a difficult situation, the men wrote a poem about the pain and progress of the task:

> Of ponderous logs:
> Whose bulk disdains the winds or fogs
> The side and ends are fitly raised
> And by dove-tail each corner's brac'd;
> Athwart the roof, young sapling lie
> Which fire and smoke has now made dry-
> Next, straw wraps o'er the tender pole,
> Next earth, then splints o'erlay the whole;
> Altho' it leaks when show'rs are o'er,
> It did not leak two hours before.
> Two chimneys plac'd at op'site angles
> Keep smoke from causing oaths and wrangles.
> Three windows, placed all in sight
> Through oiled paper give us light;
> One door, on wooden hinges hung,
> Lets in the friends, or sickly throng.[57]

Christmas Day saw the soldiers slowly finishing their huts, still shivering in their tents, with hot smoke in their eyes when they tried to warm themselves by a fire, and with cold, piecing wind to greet them when they tired of the smoke.

By New Years Day, many soldiers were covered with good huts, as the soldiers worked like "a family of beavers."[58] But all huts still were not finally finished until February 7, 1778.

THE SOLDIERS' SUFFERING AT VALLEY FORGE

Alongside the battle for shelter was the battle for clothing. The need for clothing—since uniforms were utterly impossible to find—was dramatized by the order that required the soldiers immediately to return their tents once their hut was completed, lest they cut them into clothing. Clothing was so scarce, that Washington was forced against his will to seize it from the surrounding countryside: "His Excellency regrets the necessity of the measure of seizure of Cloathing. It was unavoidable. The alternative was to dissolve the Army."[59] The capture of a British Brig enabled the arrival of some officers clothes.[60]

The lack of clothing became so severe that "The unfortunate soldiers are in want of everything; they have neither coats, hats, shirts or shoes. Their feet and legs have frozen until they become black, and it is often necessary to amputate them.[61] The Cloathing of those who have died in the Hospitals is to be appraised and delivered to those who have recovered and who stand in need thereof.[62] "We still want for uniformity of Cloathing. We are not, like the Enemy, brilliantly and uniformly attired. Even soldiers of the same Regiment are turned out in various dress; but there is no excuse, as heretofore, for slovenly unsoldierly neglect.[63] The insufficiency of clothing impacted everyone: Our sick are naked, our well naked, our unfortunate men in captivity naked!"[64]

There were not enough shoes. "As reported the 23rd inst., not less than 2898 men are unfit for duty by reason of their being barefoot and naked. We want for shoes, blankets, stockings…[65] Troops are still wanting in shoes. While we have hides, gained from the slaughtering of beef, there are few shoemakers."[66] No soap or vinegar had been had by the troops since the Battle of Brandywine, which was three months past. "Soldiers have no kettles for boiling oil and soap."[67] The lack of salt gave a whole new meaning to the saying "with a grain of salt"—that's the most that anyone had.[68] Leather and wax were almost unavailable. "Writing paper is still in short supply."[69]

Since there were no cattle, there was no meat.[70] One soldier wrote, "Our present situation is the most melancholy that can be conceived. No meat, and our prospect is of absolute want."[71] This scarcity of food created soldiers' chants and imprecations. One soldier wrote, "Provisions are scarce. A general cry thro' the Camp this evening among the soldiers, 'No meat! No meat!' The distant vales echoed back the melancholy sound, 'No meat! No meat!'" One of the soldierly cadences heard at Valley Forge was the antiphonal chorus of hungry soldiers chanting.

'What have we for dinner boys?'

'Nothing but Fire, Cake & Water, Sir!'"[72]

"Our situation for want of Cloathing, while mending, is yet distressing. Supplies are scanty; to give one part of the Army is to take from another. The Soldiers also say, 'No bread, no soldier.'"[73]

The very essentials of the military were in short supply. "This army is short of powder....There is a deficiency of wagons."[74] The horses had starved due to lack of forage.[75] Consequently, artillery was simply left because it could not be moved.[76] "The carcasses of horses about the Camp, and the deplorable leanness of those which still crawl in existence, speak the want of forage equal to that of human food.[77] Forage is wanting. Our horses starve, as do their masters. If help does not arrive, and forage does not appear, we shall not have one horse left."[78] Wood was becoming scarce due to the huts, and the need to heat them. "Now the trees have been burnt and firewood is being carted from a distance."[79]

Medical issues were always a concern. Fortunately, it could be said that "Sanitation has not become a Camp problem.[80] The Commander in chief urges caution with the drinking water, hitherto gathered from the little springs about the Camp."[81] Prevention of small pox was a critical concern. "More than two thousand men in Camp are to be inoculated for the Small Pox."[82] The lack of blankets and the insufficiency of straw contributed greatly to the mortality of the troops. "Unprovided with straw or materials to raise them from the cold earth, sickness and mortality have spread through the quarters of the Soldiers to an astonishing degree."[83] One of the tools to soften the pain and to lighten the burden was through an occasionally generous ration of spirits. "This morning a gallon of spirits was drawn for each Officer's mess, in all Brigades, against these raw and bitter days. Each man is to have a Gill of Rum."[84]

But there were many other nagging problems that Washington's army had to face, which meant they were ever before the commander in chief. "The discontent prevailing in the Army, from various causes, has become all too prevalent. Unless some measures can be adopted to render the situation of the Officers more comfortable than what it has been for some time past, it will increase.[85] The whole Army in general has three months pay in arrears, not counting the months extra pay voted by the Congress.[86] His Excellency expressed his superabundant sentiments of compassion for the miseries of the soldiery which are neither in his power to relieve or prevent. He is said to have written his doubt that unless some great and capital change suddenly take place in the Commissary Department, this Army must inevitably be reduced to one or the other of three things: starvation, dissolution or dispersal in order to obtain subsistence in the best manner it can.[87] The soldiers are scarcely restrained from mutiny by the eloquence and management of our officers.[88] Unless our future efforts to provide clothing are more effectual it will be next to impossible to keep our Army in the field.[89] Even our Officers are tempted to steal fowls,—if they could be discovered, perhaps even a whole hog.[90] Diverse soldiers, some on horseback, have been plundering the inhabitants; this probably arises at least from the rolls not being regularly call'd.[91] To prevent the commission of those crimes, the Genl positively orders: 1st, That no Officer, under the degree of Field Office, or Officer commanding a Regiment, gives passes to non-commissioned Officers, or Soldiers, on any pretence whatever; 2nd, That no non-commissioned Officer, or Soldier, have with him Arms of any kind, unless he is on duty; 3rd, That every non-commissioned Officer or Soldier, caught without limits of the Camp, not having a pass, or with his Arms, shall be confin'd and punish'd. 4th, That the rolls of each Company be called frequently, and that every evening, at different times, between the hours of eight and ten o'clock, all the men's quarters be visited…"[92] Extortion in the name of Washington even began to occur: "…making use of his Excellency's name to extort from the inhabitants by way of sale (or gift) any necessaries they want for themselves."[93]

Problems with officers began to surface. Resignations, often prompted by complaints from home, began to occur. "Patriotism is not enough to carry men through a long war which makes demands on the families and men.[94] Yesterday upwards of fifty Officers of Genl Greene's Division resign'd their Commissions. Six or seven in the Connecticut Regiments did so today. This is occaision'd by Officers families being so much neglected at home…[95] One of the complicated causes of complaints in this Army is the lavish distribution of rank.[96] Major Genl John Sullivan was today refused leave of absence. Strenuous exertions of all the Officers are wanted to keep this Army together. Personal disputes should be settled amicably and they should not be brought to Court Martial or to the Genl as arbiter and referee."[97]

Problems from the non-military people also appeared. "Sutlers have been selling spirituous liquors near the several pickets and out-lines of the Camp, which practice is to be stopp'd.[98] Our money daily grows more worthless, and prices have become so excessive as to cause infinite difficulties. This proceeds more from currency depreciation and from general avarice than from real scarcity of many essential articles."[99] Prostitutes disguised as nurses[100] and incidents of venereal disease[101] prompted various attempts to correct the problem. "Pernicious consequences have arisen from suffering [permitting] Persons (women in particular) to pass and repass from Philada to Camp under pretence of coming out to visit Friends in the Army, but really with an intent of luring the soldiers and enticing them to desert."[102] But the arrival of the women could also mean that needed supplies were available. "Ten teams of oxen, fit for slaughtering, came into Camp, driven by loyal Philadelphian women. They also brought 2000 shirts, smuggled from the City, sewn under the eyes of the enemy."[103]

POLITICAL INTRIGUES AT VALLEY FORGE

And on top of all of the enormity of the human struggle for life itself, there were the political intrigues of those who desired to remove Washington from power. The blame game was in full force at Valley Forge. "The want of Provisions in this Army stems in part from the defect in the system, but more from the indolence, disaffection & arrogance of the Commissaries.[104] Some are disposed to ask why cannot Genl Washington grasp Genl Howe in the same fashion that Genl Gates seized Gentleman Johnny Burgoyne.[105] Rumors circulate that Genl Conway wrote to Genl Gates with these words: 'Heaven has been determined to save your Country, or a weak General and bad counselors would have ruined it.' It is said that the Commander in Chief himself copied these words into a paper and introduced them with "Sir" and concluded with "I am your humble servant" and sent it to Genl Conway.[106] Genl Lee [who had been captured by the Britishin New Jersey the previous year] will be formally exchanged tomorrow...Genl Gates continues his machinations.[107]

"Rumors late today that Congress has appointed the Marquis de la Fayette, Genl Conway and Brigadier Genl Stark to conduct an eruption into Canada. This comes from the Board of War, of which Genl Gates is the President, and was made without the knowledge of his Excellency. Rumors also come that Genl Lee is to placed at the head of this Army. The calm of his Excellency in face of these efforts to detach valiant Officers from this Army or to replace them, move him not. He says that as soon as the public grows dissatisfied with his services in an office he did not solicit he will quit the helm with much satisfaction and retire to a private station with as much content as ever the wearied pilgrim felt upon his safe arrival in the Holy Land."[108]

Even though the enemy armies were in winter quarters, the hostilities never completely ended. "News today that Dr. Franklin was assassinated by a person who had concealed himself in his lodging room. The good Doctor was not wounded so as to be mortal, although this was thought to be so by the perpetrator.[109]...The Senecas and Cayugas can no longer be regarded as friends.[110] They are endeavouring to ensnare the people by specious allurements of peace.[111] The Tory paper...presents a scandalous forgery. Under the guise of a genuine Act of Congress it puts forth a statement that all men drafted to serve in the Continental Army are to be forced to serve for the whole war. The Enemy seeks thereby to encourage desertion."[112]

The pacifist Quakers refused to take an oath or affirmation of allegiance to the American cause.[113] Loyalists or Tories sought to hamper the American cause.[114] Punishments of civilians occurred giving instances of whippings, confiscation of personal property and real estate. Active Loyalists even faced military judges in court martial with severe sentences that could result in "hard labour" or even execution.[115]

Ultimately, the battles at Valley Forge were fought in big and small ways. Sometimes the humor of Washington helped.[116] But the biggest help was in the hope for the assistance of France and her allies due to the loyalty of Lafayette: "…the accounts from France are that the French, Spanish, Prussian and Polish Courts all have declared for the Independency of America by acknowledging them, and that a Treaty of Commerce was concluded by Dr. Franklin and the French Court for thirty years."[117] Eventually British support for the war would have to end given the debt they were accumulating.[118] Oaths of allegiance were signed forcing out Loyalists.[119] Morals were enforced, "But for the virtuous few of the Army, we are persuaded that this Country must long before this have been destroyed. It is saved for our sakes, and its Salvation ought to cause Repentance in us for all our sins, if evil and Misery are the consequences of Iniquity."[120]

Military discipline was dramatically increased through the arrival of Baron Von Steuben. "The impression which our Camp has made upon the Baron is another matter. Our arms are in horrible condition, covered with rust…A great many of the men have boxes instead of pouches,…His description of our dress is not easily repeated…[121] Baron De Steuben…drills them himself twice a day, seeking to remove the English prejudice which some Officers entertain, namely that to drill a recruit is a sergeant's duty and beneath the station of an officer.[122] The old system of manoeuvres is today suspended, as uniformity of disciplinary exercises is being established under the new Inspector Genl.[123] Daily this Army looks more like a military force and less like an armed horde. We parade clean, dressed in proper regimentals, with proper arms and accoutrements."[124]

And through it all, Washington sought to never lose his grace. When one hundred medical books intended for a British physician were captured, the record states "His Excellency magnanimously allows these volumes to be return'd to the Doctor to show that we do not war against the sciences.[125] I have not indulged myself in invective against the present rulers of Great Britain, nor will I even now avail myself of so fruitful a theme."[126] The presence of Mrs. Washington made a difference.[127] The ministry support of the women of Bethlehem also helped.[128] And there even was an occasional dance, or play to provide some entertainment.[129]

And finally the day came when "the Genl addressed his warmest thanks to the virtuous Officers and Soldiery of this Army for that persevering Fidelity and Zeal manifest in all their conduct."[130]

Washington expressed his sense of gratitude at the end of this long winter when he wrote to fellow Virginian Landon Carter from Valley Forge on May 30, 1778,

> My friends therefore may believe me sincere in my professions of attachment to them, whilst Providence has a joint claim to my humble and grateful thanks, for its protection and direction of me, through the many difficult and intricate scenes, which this contest hath produced; and for the constant interposition in our behalf, when the clouds were heaviest and seemed ready to burst upon us.
>
> To paint the distresses and perilous situation of this army in the course of last winter, for want of cloaths, provisions, and almost every other necessary, essential to the well-being, (I may say existence,) of an army, would require more time and an abler pen than mine; nor, since our prospects have so miraculously brightened, shall I attempt it, or even bear it in remembrance, further than as a memento of what is due to the great Author of all the care and good, that have been extended in relieving us in difficulties and distress.[131]

As we conclude this chapter, we turn our attention to the question of whether Washington really prayed at Valley Forge. Given all of the above, it seems to us that a more legitimate question to ask is how he could have survived Valley Forge without prayer!

DID WASHINGTON PRAY AT VALLEY FORGE?

When Washington was at Valley Forge, during the brutal winter of 1777-1778, it was alleged that he was overheard in prayer by a Tory-sympathizer, a Quaker named Isaac Potts. This man supposedly came across General Washington in prayer in the woods and then came home and declared to his wife, "Our cause is lost." He feared that the rebels would win the war, because he heard their leader in earnest audible prayer and had become convinced there was no way that God would not honor that prayer.

Boller discounts this story as part of unreliable oral tradition.[132] Earlier generations of Americans, however, accepted it as historically reliable. Consider, for example, the 1903 Episcopal Washington Memorial Chapel in Valley Forge built to commemorate the story; a 1928 two-cent U.S. postage stamp of Washington in prayer at Valley Forge; a 1955 stained-glass window of the scene in the Prayer Room in the U.S. Capitol building; and a bronze rendition of Washington's "Gethsemane" in the

George Washington praying at Valley Forge.
The eyewitness Isaac Potts can be seen illustrated behind the trees on the left side of this etching.

Sub-Treasury Building in New York City.

Why does Boller think this story is apocryphal? In part, because of differences that exist in the traditional story. One version has the man's name as Isaac Potts. Other versions have a different name for the Quaker as well as his wife. Moreover, the Potts family that owned the house, still known as Washington's Headquarters, have no records that would indicate that Potts made a trip that winter to Valley Forge, where he would have had the occasion to have stumbled on Washington kneeling in the snow in private prayer.

As Boller presents it, there is no hard evidence that the story ever occurred. All we have is the mythic legend preserved in the unsubstantiated story told by the Reverend Mason Weems. Yet, Boller admits that there were others who gave evidence to the account.[133] Rather than engage them, he simply dismisses them with his uncritical remark, "…scores of witnesses attesting to the event (many years later) have been dug up by champions of the story; and many details have been added by later writers to Weems's original account. . . .The Valley Forge story is, of course, utterly without foundation in fact."[134]

What is the extent of Boller's proof? Only the words just cited. That is all he has to say about the subject that built a million dollar church, created one of the best selling postage stamps in history, is reflected on two U.S. government buildings, and prompted President Ronald Reagan to say, "The most sublime picture in American history is of George Washington on his knees in the snow at Valley Forge. That image personifies a people who know that it is not enough to depend on our own courage and goodness; we must also seek help from God, our Father and Preserver."[135] Doubt and criticism are good tools for the historian, but when they allow a historian to fail to do his work and to reach a scientifically justifiable conclusion, they are no longer tools, but expressions of a hostile, prejudicial philosophy.

Our purpose here is not to do the extensive research that would be required to demonstrate what elements of truth are extant in the oral history and accounts that have preserved the tradition of Washington's prayer at Valley Forge. Moreover, our argument for Washington's Christianity is not dependent upon the validity of this anecdote in any way. The evidence we have employed is built directly on Washington's own words. However, we believe that a respectable, historical discussion of this matter at least requires an awareness of the information that Boller simply sweeps under the rug of his skepticism.

All told, there are five different individuals who gave an account of Washington praying at Valley Forge. They are: Reverend Mason L. Weems,[136] Washington historian Benson J. Lossing,[137] Reverend Devault Beaver,[138] Dr. N. R. Snowden, who claimed to have heard it directly from Isaac Potts himself,[139] and General Henry Knox.[140]

Could this story be true? By the strictest, critical standards of historical investigation, we cannot establish its validity. We have no letter from Washington or Isaac Potts declaring that this is what happened. There is no contemporary newspaper account that relates these facts. By the standards of oral history, however, it appears to have a legitimate claim for being considered as a possible historical event. Oral history recognizes that rigorous, critical, historical proof is not the only way history is preserved. It is one thing to say that an oral report of an incident cannot be proven by an eyewitness or a participant's written report; it's another thing to say it did not happen. The multiplicity of testimony and the claim of a remembered interview recorded for posterity suggest that something may well have happened in the snowy woods of Valley Forge.

Our purpose here is not to prove the story, but to show that Boller's cavalier approach to the facts of oral history also reflect his lack of consideration of the written record of Washington and his contemporaries. So even though Boller asserts, "The Valley Forge story is, of course, utterly without foundation in fact," we wish to determine what are the critical and historical facts that we do know about George Washington as a man of prayer? And what we know argues decisively that Washington prayed at Valley Forge, whether Isaac Potts saw him or not.

First, there is indisputable, written evidence from George Washington that he fervently prayed for himself and for the success of his army only months before the painful winter of Valley Forge. In a letter to Landon Carter that Washington wrote from Morristown on April 15, 1777,

> Your friendly and affectionate wishes for my health and success has a claim to my most grateful acknowledgements. That the God of Armies may Incline the Hearts of my American Brethren to support, and bestow sufficient abilities on me to bring the present contest to a speedy and happy conclusion, thereby enabling me to sink into sweet retirement, and the full enjoyment of that Peace and happiness which will accompany a domestick Life, is the first wish, and most fervent prayer of my Soul.[141]

Clearly, Washington wanted the war to end and had already been longing to go home. If Washington fervently prayed for this before the sufferings of Valley Forge, it seems certain that he prayed at Valley Forge, when all he had to count on for victory was the bare hope that God might answer his prayers. To show that this was not a misstatement on Washington's part, it is significant that virtually the same words were used by Washington just three days earlier in a letter to Edmund Pendleton,

> Your friendly, and affectionate wishes for my health and success, has a claim to my thankful acknowledgements; and, that the God of Armies may enable me to bring the present contest to a speedy and happy conclusion, thereby gratifying me in a retirement to the calm and sweet enjoyment of domestick happiness, is the fervent prayer, and most ardent wish of my Soul.[142]

Second, there are dire circumstances of Valley Forge found in Washington's description already quoted of the sufferings of his men that winter of defeat and despair. The capitol city of Philadelphia lay in the conquerors' hands, and Congress had been forced to flee to Lancaster and York. Clearly, this was an occasion for the deepest groanings of prayer for a man of faith. Given that Washington's life and writings show he practiced daily prayer, it is no stretch of historical credibility to affirm that Washington was praying at Valley Forge. The point here is that we don't need the alleged Quaker to prove that General Washington was given to "fervent prayer." His own pen tells us that such was the case.

Also, if we are looking for testimonies of Washington's prayer life by those who observed it, why pursue Isaac Potts, when there are so many other historical examples that are readily at hand? There are other traditional accounts of Washington praying at Valley Forge beyond those that we've mentioned so far, such as his prayer for a dying soldier at Valley Forge.[143] But we will not appeal to this account, even if it may have an element of authenticity. After all, we have already seen that there are over one hundred written prayers in Washington's writings, which we have already addressed in the chapter on Washington and prayer. Beyond this, there are the historical affirmations that Washington was a man of prayer.

> …it was Washington's custom to have prayers in the camp while he was at Fort Necessity.[144]

> He regularly attends divine service in his tent every morning and evening, and seems very fervent in his prayers.[145]

> Throughout the war, as it was understood in his military family, he gave a part of every day to private prayer and devotion.[146]

> … the Reverend William Emerson, who was a minister at Concord at the time of the battle, and now a chaplain in the army, writes to a friend: There is great overturning in the camp as to order and regularity. New lords, new laws. The Generals Washington and Lee are upon the lines every day. New orders from his Excellency are read to the respective regiments every morning after prayers.[147]

> Some short time before the death of General Porterfield, I made him a visit and spent a night at his house. He related many interesting facts that had occurred within his own observation in the war of the Revolution, particularly in the Jersey campaign and the encampment of the army at Valley Forge. He said that his official duty (being brigade-inspector) frequently brought him in contact with

General Washington. Upon one occasion, some emergency (which he mentioned) induced him to dispense with the usual formality, and he went directly to General Washington's apartment, where he found him on his knees, engaged in his morning devotions. He said that he mentioned the circumstance to General Hamilton, who replied that such was his constant habit.[148]

...when ...Elizabeth Schuyler was a young girl, before her marriage to Alexander Hamilton, she was with her father, General Philip Schuyler, one of Washington's aides, at Valley Forge, and saw the terrible sufferings of our men, and heard at that time Washington's fervent prayer that all might be well.[149]

Third, Washington prayed in the winter following Valley Forge. Although Washington's soldiers faced great sacrifice, in this instance provision came to meet the needs of the troops. And this prompted his "ardent" prayer. He wrote to Eldridge Gerry, from Morris Town on January 29, 1780,

With respect to provision; the situation of the army is comfortable at present on this head and I ardently pray that it may never be again as it has been of late. We were reduced to a most painful and delicate extremity; such as rendered the keeping of the Troops together a point of great doubt.[150]

Washington had not forgotten how difficult it was when the army's needs had not been met. He prayed that the painful circumstances would not be repeated, though the need had been met. If he prayed in a time of provision, would it have been likely that he would not have prayed in the midst of great need in the first instance? Would we not expect him to have prayed, especially since the record of his consistency in prayer was written repeatedly in undeniable, historical records?

Finally, we can verify one time when Washington prayed at Valley Forge from his own writings. This is found in his General Orders for April 12, 1778, that called for prayer following the Congressional Proclamation.

The Honorable Congress having thought proper to recommend to The United States of America to set apart Wednesday the 22nd.

instant to be observed as a day of Fasting, Humiliation and Prayer, that at one time and with one voice the righteous dispensations of Providence may be acknowledged and His Goodness and Mercy toward us and our Arms supplicated and implored; The General directs that this day also shall be religiously observed in the Army, that no work be done thereon and that the Chaplains prepare discourses suitable to the Occasion.[151]

CONCLUSION

The last time Washington wrote the phrase "sacred cause" was as his men were heading for Valley Forge. It was as if the sacred cause had been internalized, or become a reality. The next dramatic moment when he would return to this powerful image would be in his First Inaugural Address where his "sacred cause" had become the "sacred fire of liberty." Not only had freedom's holy light not gone out, but it was burning brightly ready to ignite other hearts and other nations.

So could a Quaker have found Washington on his knees in secret prayer, in the snow, at Valley Forge? If we could have asked the opinion of the colonial Lutheran minister Reverend Muhlenberg, he would have not have found the claim unbelievable about the one who was "graciously held" in God's "hand as a chosen vessel."

Thus, the question can no longer really be whether Washington prayed at Valley Forge and was seen by a pacifist Quaker who converted to the American cause. Those events may have happened, but they cannot ultimately be proven. The question instead must be whether Washington prayed at Valley Forge. The only possible answer consistent with all that we know is "yes."

But perhaps the more relevant question is why scholars are insistent on telling the truncated secular version of Washington's encampment at Valley Forge? Why would they tell the story of Washington's great triumph in the battle over doubt and despair without reference to his "sacred cause?" without reference to Washington's faith in Jehovah? without reference to his call for his men to be Christians? Were not these the things that produced "the sacred fire of liberty" that kept his men united in spite of their extreme exposure to the frigid winter winds of Valley Forge? Why then would scholars censure the sermon of Chaplain Israel Evans made at Valley Forge when it had the full approval of Washington? We can no longer tell the story of the Valley Forge encampment without looking on "his excellency General Washington" as Israel Evans admonished,

… Look on him, and catch the genuine patriot fire of liberty and independence. Look on him, and learn to forget your own ease and comfort; like him resign the charms of domestic life, when the genius of America bids you grow great in her service, and liberty calls you to protect her. Look on your worthy general, and claim the happiness and honour of saying, he is ours. Like him love virtue, and like him, reverence the name of the great Jehovah. Be mindful of that public declaration which he has made, "That we cannot reasonably expect the blessing of God upon our arms, if we continue to prophane his holy name. Learn of him to endure watching, cold and hardships, for you have just heard that he assures you, he is ready and willing to endure whatever inconveniencies and hardships may attend this winter. Are any of you startled at the prospect of hard winter quarters? Think of liberty and Washington, and your hardships will be forgotten and banished.[152]

Perhaps the reason the secularists have forgotten the inseparable connection between Washington's "sacred cause," his "patriot fire of liberty," and his "all wise and powerful Being" is because they have been so intent on finding a Deist Washington. As a result of their quest, they clearly have not shared "the first wish of his heart." This wish was "to aid pious endeavours to inculcate a due sense of the dependance we ought to place in that all wise and powerful Being on whom alone our success depends." General Washington was here referring to Jehovah, the God of the burning bush, and the inexhaustible energy of the "sacred fire of liberty."

PART V

The Debate Over George Washington and Communion

TWENTY

George Washington and Communion:

Did Washington Take Communion?

"Such is our situation, and such are our prospects:
but notwithstanding the cup of blessing is thus reached out to us,
notwithstanding happiness is ours, if we have a disposition
to seize the occasion and make it our own."
George Washington September 19, 1796[1]

One of the most often repeated arguments against the thesis of George Washington the Christian is the fact that during a significant period in his later life he apparently did not participate in communion. This issue has been repeated so often and emphasized so much that we devote the next three chapters to consider the matter with care. We believe those who hold George Washington to have been a Deist have ignored some significant facts related to the communion argument. The claims of this argument against Washington's Christianity cried out for a cross-examination.

DID WASHINGTON PARTICIPATE IN THE LORD'S SUPPER?

The claim that Washington allegedly did not participate in the Lord's Supper has carried weight on both sides of the debate.

Some of the chief arguments for the debate of this question are:

1. Washington's clergy said they did not see him partake of the Lord's Supper.

2. For example, Reverend Abercrombie of Christ's Church Philadelphia preached a sermon against not partaking of the Eucharist on a Communion Sunday when Washington was present. Washington never attended there on a Communion Sunday thereafter. Unlike modern Episcopal churches that have weekly Communion, Communion in Washington's Virginia was practiced about three or four times per year, depending on the availability of a clergyman.

3. Washington's granddaughter, Nelly Custis, said that he left with her after the worship service was over, (i.e., before Communion) and the carriage was sent back for Martha Washington.

4. The conclusion reached from this by those who hold that Washington was a Deist is that this proves that he was not a Christian who believed in the atonement of Christ. Since Washington was not a hypocrite, his non-communing fits this consistently held Deistic perspective.

In addition to the above, however, the following must be considered as well:

1. It was universally reported that Washington always communed before the Revolution.

2. Partaking of Communion would be consistent with his highly active and faithful role as a parishioner, vestryman, and church warden.

3. His personally selected most expensive pews in two different Virginia churches were close to the Communion Table in the churches he attended in Virginia (Pohick in Lorton and Christ Church in Alexandria).

4. Even his non-participation during and after the War is open to question:

    a. A strongly held Presbyterian tradition argues that he communed at a Presbyterian Church in Morristown, New Jersey, during the Revolutionary War.

    b. The German Reformed tradition claims that he communed on one occasion in their church in Germantown, outside of Philadelphia, during his presidency.

    c. Reports from officers—Major Popham and General Porterfield—claim that they witnessed his communing in New York City when he was president.

    d. Mrs. Alexander Hamilton told her family that she communed with President Washington on the day of his presidential Inauguration, April 30, 1789, in New York City.

    e. Various testimonies reported by Bishop William Meade and Reverend E. C. M'Guire support Washington's communing.

Nevertheless, all agree on this: There is indisputable evidence that Washington did not commune for a period of time. To put the question as pointedly as possible—does non-communing mean that one is not a Christian? A variation on the question is also important for our concerns here as well. Does cessation of Communion for a lengthy period of time imply that one has rejected Christianity? Are there other explanations that are historically consistent and also consistent with Christian faith and practice that provide an explanation?

As we seek to address this matter in relationship to Washington's religion and to his Christianity, we have come to a point where written documentation directly from the lifetime of Washington is minimal. This means that we cannot appeal to church records, for these sorts of records, if they ever were kept, are no longer in existence (to our knowledge). In some cases, we cannot even prove who all of the pastors were in Washington's home church of Pohick during his lifetime. Similarly, we cannot establish with absolute certainty who the clergyman was who baptized Washington.

If such ecclesiastical records do not exist, it is not startling that we do not have records that indicate when or how often Washington communed. Similarly, we do not possess quotations from Washington declaring his desire to commune at the Lord's Table or his specific rejection thereof, although, as we will see, there is early written testimony that such a written record may have existed.

We thus must keep in mind a basic premise established earlier. Washington may give us written clues about his beliefs, but he never wanted or intended to create an explicit statement of faith. Instead, he claimed that his deeds spoke more loudly than his words. So if and when we discover that Washington communed, and if and when we discover that he chose not to, we must ask what those actions meant.

As we seek to interpret them, we must do so in a manner that reflects what we already know about his life, previous actions, and expressed and written beliefs. We must seek both his deeds, and where possible, we must explain them in conjunction with his words. The words of those closest in time to Washington's life are also important for our debate. So let us start with the summary of this question, as penned by Bishop Meade, who wrote the following more than half a century after Washington's death:

> One question only remains to be settled: Was Washington a communicant of the Church? That he was might be reasonably inferred from the indication of youthful piety, his religious, his ministerial offices at the head of his regiment, the active part taken in the concerns of the parish, his habits of devotion, his regular attendance at church, his conscientious observance of the Sabbath, his strict fasting on appointed days.
>
> It is also believed that he was a communicant, from the testimony of the Reverend Lee Massey, as handed down through his family, and also of others which have come down to us. The testimony which has often been adduced to prove that, during the war, he did commune on a certain Sabbath in a Presbyterian church at Morristown, New Jersey, ought to be enough to satisfy a reasonable man of the fact. Add to these the declaration of so many, in the sermons and orations at the time of his death. But still it has been made a question, and it may be well to consider on what ground. It is certainly a fact, that for a certain period of time during his Presidential term, while the Congress was held in Philadelphia, he did not commune. This fact rests of the authority of Bishop White,

under whose ministry the President sat, and who was on the most intimate terms with himself and Mrs. Washington. I will relate what the Bishop told myself and others in relation to it. During the session or sessions of Congress held in Philadelphia, General Washington was, with his family, a regular attendant at one of the churches under the care of Bishop White and his assistants. On Communion-days, when the congregation was dismissed, (except the portion which communed,) the General left the church, until a certain Sabbath on which Dr. Abercrombie, in his sermon, spoke of the impropriety of turning our backs on the Lord's table,—that is, neglecting to commune,—from which time General Washington came no more on Communion-days. Bishop White supposes that the General understood the "words turning our backs on the Lord's table" in a somewhat different sense than was designed by the preacher; that he supposed it was intended to censure those who left the church at the time of its administration, and, in order not to seem to be disrespectful to that ordinance, thought it better not to be present at all on such occasions. It is needless to attempt to conjecture what may have been the reason of this temporary (as we hope it was) suspension of the act of communicating. A regard for historic truth has led to the mention of this subject. The question as to his ever having been a communicant has been raised on this fact, as stated by Bishop White, and we have thought it best to give the narrative as we heard it from the lips of the Bishop himself.[2]

So a key objection made to the claim that Washington was a Christian is that for a while, perhaps even years, he went without receiving Communion. While it can be asserted that one can be a Christian and not always partake of the Lord's Table, still, this raises a legitimate question concerning Washington's religious beliefs. Was Washington a disbeliever in the atonement, to which the Communion points?

Paul Boller cites sources—namely Reverend Bird Wilson—that he believes demonstrate that Washington in his later years disregarded the sacrament: "Dr. James Abercrombie, assistant rector of Christ Church in Philadelphia, which Washington attended while President had confided to him [Reverend Bird Wilson] that Washington never partook of the sacrament of the Lord's Supper during his presidency. On sacrament days, Wilson quoted Abercrombie as saying, 'Washington's custom was to rise, just before the ceremony commenced, and to walk out of church."'[3]

Abercrombie also wrote the following—although he would not own up to these words when asked about them later: "That Washington was a professing Christian is evident from his regular attendance in our church; but, Sir, I cannot consider any man as a real Christian who uniformly disregards an ordinance so solemnly enjoined by the divine Author of our holy religion, and considered as a channel of divine grace."[4]

Yet, Boller is also honest to cite a source that undercuts this point. Reverend William Jackson of Alexandria, Virginia states, "Universal tradition in the families of those whose parents or friends were acquainted with the General, is, that he was a regular communicant."[5] Others, such as Moncure Conway, argued that George Washington in mature life was a Deist—his earlier practices then being nullified by his practices later in life.[6]

As we proceed with this debate, let us note two things. First, Boller's argument does not appeal to Washington's writings. Boller cannot produce anything written by George Washington himself to substantiate Washington's alleged non-communing, or even more importantly, that he did not believe in Christ's atonement. This means his entire argument is built on silence overlaid with Boller's doubt. Second, to support his claim, he relies entirely on the historical data collected from others' words. So, we will follow his example and answer his claim from the testimony of others who addressed this matter. But, we will do more than this. At the conclusion of this chapter, we will also appeal to Washington's writings, for we do not have to appeal merely to an argument from silence. Washington does refer indirectly to the Eucharist in his writings, and does so in very visible places.

WRITTEN TESTIMONIES OF THOSE WHO SAW WASHINGTON TAKE COMMUNION

Mrs. Washington's granddaughter, who lived for twenty years in the Washington family, wrote: "I have heard my mother say General Washington always received the Sacrament with my grandmother before the Revolution."[7] Some of the testimonies of Washington's partaking of Communion have been preserved by Bishop William Meade and Reverend E. C. M'Guire.

One such affirmation of Washington's partaking of Communion is from the testimony of General Robert Porterfield, preserved in a letter from General S. H. Lewis, of Augusta County, Virginia, to the Reverend Mr. Dana, of Alexandria, dated December 14, 1855.

General Porterfield said ... that he had known General Washington personally for many years... "[Washington] was a pious man, and a member of your Church, [the Episcopal.] I saw him myself on his knees receive the Sacrament of the Lord's Supper ...."[8]

Additional testimony corroborating this tradition was secured through the research of E. C. M'Guire in 1836,

Among the aged persons residing in the neighbourhood of Mount Vernon, and the descendants of such others as have recently gone down to the grave, there is but one opinion in regard to the fact of his having been a communicant in Pohick Church, previous to the revolutionary war. The writer himself had it from a respectable lady, that she once heard her mother unqualifiedly declare, that General Washington was a communicant in that church, in the vicinity of which she had her residence, and on the services of which she attended. A living grand-daughter of the Reverend Lee Massey, rector of Mount Vernon Parish, for some years after Washington's marriage—says, her grandfather on a specified occasion, told her the same thing in answer to a particular inquiry on the subject.[9]

Another account of Washington communing is given by M'Guire. He gives the testimony of one who claimed to witness Washington partake of communion. In this instance it was in New York City. M'Guire writes,

The following extract is from a volume of sermons recently published by Dr. Chapman, of Portland, Maine. It is here added, because of the authenticity and conclusiveness of the testimony furnished by it, on the subject before us. He [George Washington] lived at a period when there were less verbal pretensions on the subject of religion, than have become exceeding fashionable in modern times. And the consequence is, that in his life, we have more of the substance than the parade of piety. Still he was an open and avowed follower of the Lord of glory. From the lips of a lady of undoubted veracity, yet living, and a worthy communicant of the church, I received the interesting fact, that soon after the close of the revolutionary war, she saw him partake of the consecrated symbols of the body and blood of Christ, in Trinity Church, in the city of New –York.[10]

Another testimonial from an eyewitness of seeing George Washington receiving Communion also refers to a later time in his life—the time he served as president. This comes from Major Popham, who served with Washington during the Revolutionary War.[11]

It was my great good fortune to have attended St. Paul's Church in this city with the General during the whole period of his residence in New York as President of the United States. The pew of Chief-Justice Morris was situated next to that of the President, close to whom I constantly sat in Judge Morris's pew, and I am as confident as a memory now labouring under the pressure of fourscore years and seven can make me, that the President had more than once—I believe I say often- attended at the sacramental table, at which I had the privilege and happiness to kneel with him. And I am aided in my associations by my elder daughter, who distinctly recollects her grandmamma—Mrs. Morris—often mention that fact with great pleasure. Indeed, I am further confirmed in my assurance by the perfect recollection of the President's uniform deportment during divine service in church. The steady seriousness of his manner, the solemn, audible, but subdued tone of voice in which he read and repeated the responses, the Christian humility which overspread and adorned the native dignity of the saviour of his country, at once exhibited him a pattern to all who had the honour of access to him. It was my good fortune, my dear madam, to have had frequent intercourse with him. It is my pride and boast to have seen him in various situations,—in the flush of victory, in the field and in the tent,—in the church and at the altar, always himself, ever the same.[12]

WASHINGTON'S COMMUNING AT THE PRESBYTERIAN CHURCH OF MORRISTOWN NEW JERSEY

Another account of Washington communing is from Morristown, New Jersey, during the Revolutionary War. This remarkable account alleges that Washington

H. A. Ogden's rarely acknowledged painting of George Washington
receiving Holy Communion at Morristown in the spring of 1777
This painting appears in color in the middle of this book

partook of Communion in a Presbyterian setting. Given that the English Civil War of the 1640s was fought by Puritan Congregationalists and Presbyterians against Anglican Loyalists, and that tensions had carried over into the colonies of the New World, one would not have expected an Anglican to commune at a Presbyterian table. The unexpected character of such an event is part of what makes this tradition plausible. It is difficult to understand how the story would have been concocted, let alone have gained credence, in the era from which it emanated, had there not been something that prompted the story's development.

Generally speaking, oral history, although imperfectly, does preserve traditions that are rooted in history. Although there is no extant, eyewitness, written account of the event, the testimony supporting the traditional story is worthy of consideration, given the letters already cited from military persons who claimed that they had participated with Washington in Communion services.

Moreover, even though there are no written historical records immediately from that era to establish the event, earlier generations affirmed its authenticity. For example, it was included in the *Presbyterian Encyclopedia* published in the late eighteen hundreds under the article entitled, "General Washington."[13] Similarly, an historical marker was placed in Morristown, New Jersey, by the Daughters of the American Revolution to commemorate the event.[14] Also, a painting of the Washington Communion story hung for many years in the Presbyterian Hospital of Philadelphia.

Today, this painting is in the parish house of the Presbyterian Church in Morristown, New Jersey.

The tradition of Washington's partaking of Communion in this Presbyterian setting can be assembled from several early written sources. Support for the claim that Washington had the freedom of conscience to commune outside of his Anglican tradition is added by J. I. Good, historian of the German Reformed tradition in America. Dr. Good writes:

> When Washington was driven out of Philadelphia by the yellow fever in 1793, he made his home for several months in the family of Reverend Mr. Herman, the pastor at Germantown. There is a tradition that he attended the Reformed church then, and on one occasion took communion with the congregation.[15]

The first printed story of the Morristown event was in 1829. The account was written by Reverend Dr. Samuel H. Coxe, who was then the pastor of Laight Street Presbyterian Church in New York City.[16] According to Coxe, during the week preceding the semiannual celebration of the Lord's Supper in the Presbyterian church, Washington rode to the home of the pastor of the church, Reverend Timothy Johnes, to inquire whether a non-Presbyterian could commune at the service. The answer Washington received affirmed that Christians from other denominations were welcomed. Washington then declared his intent to be present for the service.

Washington's worshiping at the Morristown Church is also affirmed by an article in the 1859 edition of *Harper's Magazine*, "The pulpit of the Morristown Presbyterian Church was occupied by Doctor Timothy Johnes, whose contemporaries describe him as a mild but eminently persuasive preacher, and as a most admirable pastor. Washington was a constant attendant on his preaching, both winters he spent in Morristown."[17]

What transpired on the communion Sunday is described by an article from the *Presbyterian Magazine*,

> It is the Sabbath. The congregation are assembled in an orchard, in a natural basin which Providence had made for them, to pay their homage to the Most High, and to commemorate the love of the Redeemer, even in the winter. Among their number is the commander in chief of the American army. With a willing and

devout spirit he unites with the people of God in the ordinances of religion. After a solemn sermon from a venerable minister, a hymn is sung, and the invitation given to the members of sister churches to unite in the celebration of the Lord's Supper. A well-known military form rises in response to the invitation. With solemn dignity and Christian meekness he takes his seat with Christ's people and partakes of the bread and wine. It is Washington at the communion table.[18]

The fact of Washington attending an outdoor worship service is also affirmed in a history of Morristown, "that Washington and other American officers and soldiers occasionally attended open-air services, held in the orchard in the rear of the Presbyterian parsonage, is now too well authenticated to question."[19]

Some of the authentication of this story was assembled by Reverend E. C. M'Guire in 1836. In response to his inquiries if there was any written documentation still in existence of Washington's request to be included in the Communion service at Morristown, he received letters from two individuals, Asa S. Colton and Dr. James Richards.

Asa Colton wrote, "Mrs. Johnes…gives it as an unquestioned family tradition, that General Washington wrote the note in question, and partook of the sacrament as it has been commonly reported. … the family are still in possession of the orchard, and point out the very tree under which the sacrament was then administered, the church being at that time occupied as a hospital. The fact in question is regarded as certain by the older residents of the place, beyond all room for doubt."[20]

Dr. Richards, the pastor who followed Dr. Johnes in the pulpit of Morristown, wrote,

> I can only say in reply, that I never saw the note to which you allude,—but have no doubt that such a note was addressed by Washington to Dr. Johnes, of Morristown, on the occasion to which you refer. I became a resident in that town in the summer of 1794, while Dr. Johnes was still living—and was afterwards the regular pastor of that congregation for about fourteen years. The report that Washington did actually receive the communion from the hands of Dr. Johnes, was universally current during that period, and so far as I know, never contradicted. I have often heard it from the members

of Dr. Johnes' family, while they added that a note was addressed by Washington to their father, requesting the privilege, and stating that though connected with the Episcopal Church, he felt a freedom and desire to commune with those of another name, if acceptable to them. Very often too have I heard this circumstance spoken of as evidence of that great man's liberality, as well as piety.

There were hundreds at Morristown during the time of which I speak, who might if the fact of Washington's receiving the communion there be true, have witnessed that fact—and who would not be slow to contradict it, on the supposition that it had not been witnessed by them or their friends. It is barely possible, that such a report might be put in circulation through error or mistake, and afterwards gain credit by time; but in my judgment in no degree probable, when all the circumstances of the case are duly considered. The family of Dr. Johnes, sons and daughters, were of mature age, and some of them active members of society, when this note is said to have been written, and the fact to which it related took place. It is scarcely possible that they should have been deceived; and their characters are too well known to suppose them willing to deceive others.[21]

All of this, then, prompts the question of why would they be worshiping outdoors in an apple orchard, particularly if it was winter? The *Presbyterian Magazine* explains,

> There was a vast amount of sickness and suffering in the army; the smallpox prevailed fearfully, the Presbyterian and Baptist churches, and courthouse, were occupied as hospitals...so that there was no place for the meeting of the congregation, except in the open air.[22]

The most extensive source of information for this event comes from an 1851 letter to the editor of the *Presbyterian Magazine* written in response to its article concerning Washington's communing at the Presbyterian Church in Morristown. The correspondent was Reverend O. L. Kirtland, who had lived in Morristown since 1837. He had married into the family of the Reverend Dr. Johnes. Reverend Kirtland was at that time the pastor of the Second Presbyterian Church at Morristown. Writing of his own wife, Reverend Kirtland explained to the editor,

The father of Mrs. Kirtland was the son of the Reverend Doctor Timothy Johnes—lived with him, and took care of him in his old age, and till his death—remained in the homestead of his father, and died there in his 83rd year, November, 1836. Mrs. Kirtland was born in the same house, and never had her home elsewhere till a short time since. She recollects very distinctly that she was accustomed to hear her father speak of the fact that the religious services of the congregation *were conducted in the orchard, in the rear of the house,* whilst Washington was here during the Revolutionary War. This was one of the familiar facts often repeated during her early years. She has no doubt that a part of the familiar subject of the conversation of her father with the family, and with visitors, was, that the communion which General Washington attended was held in the orchard.

In the orchard there is a natural basin several feet deep, and a few rods in diameter. The basin was formerly considerably deeper than at present, having been partly filled in the process of tilling ever since the Revolution. Mrs. Kirtland recollects that her father used to say, that when the people assembled for worship, they occupied the bottom of that basin for their place of meeting. The minister stood on one side of the basin, so as to be elevated above his congregation. The whole field inclines towards the morning and mid-day sun. The rising grounds in the rear would, to a great extent, shield the congregation from the usual winds of winter. Indeed, the basin was formerly so deep, that the wind from any direction would mainly pass over them.

A brother of Mrs. Kirtland, several years older than herself, and other members of the family, tell me that their recollections are distinct, and in harmony with hers, touching the meetings in the orchard, the communion, and the presence of Washington there.[23]

How does Boller disprove all of this historical evidence? The fact is that he doesn't. The best he can muster is to just express his doubt and heap contempt on oral history. Boller writes,

Washington certainly could have attended a service at Morristown church during the Revolution. Theologically, he had, as the story put it, no "exclusive partialities"; and from time to time he did attend churches other than the Anglican church of which he was a member. The request for the sacrament, however, is extremely dubious, for there are strong reasons for doubting that Washington was in the habit of participating in the sacrament, even in his own church. And like the Potts story [the prayer story at Valley Forge], the Morristown episode, even in its simplest form, rests on nothing more than oral tradition. There is no reference to Timothy Johnes in any of Washington's extensive writings. And the indefatigable efforts of nineteenth century authors to locate a written record of some kind substantiating the tale invariably ended in frustration and failure.[24]

But let us for a moment analyze Boller's argument. It is based on two things: doubt and the inadequacy of oral tradition. Doubt is an essential ingredient for all research into the facts of things. Yet, if one so desires, the bar of doubt can be placed so high that nothing can ever move anything to the level of sufficient certainty for acceptance. In fact, even written records can be disputed and claimed to be false or inadequate by a thoroughgoing doubt. This type of scholarly doubt enables one to distinguish between an authentic written document and a spurious or counterfeit text.

But doubt alone is not a sufficient argument. The only honest standard that can be employed in historical research is the same that is used in a legal process, namely, "beyond a reasonable doubt." So how does one establish a fact that is "beyond a reasonable doubt" in historical matters? If something existed for a period of time in oral tradition before it was written down, does that make it necessarily false? When Boller wrote in the 1960s, perhaps a facile rejection of oral history was acceptable. Such a sweeping and uncritical rejection of oral history today is simply unacceptable, given the vast amount of anthropological study done about pre-literary cultures' use of oral history and the extensive historical research that has been done by oral history in the past several decades.[25]

Probably the most startling example of a living oral tradition that is accepted by everyone in regard to Washington is the continuing use of his own words at his inauguration as the first president under the Constitution. The famous phrase, "So help me God," is not found in Washington's vast writings, because it was not written down by Washington. Nor is it in the Constitution, yet, every president following Washington has said these same words when he has taken the oath of office. The reason those words are still used today is due to the fact that this oral tradition was later recorded by others, who claimed to be eyewitnesses of Washington having said those words. Each president following Washington has kept this oral tradition of Washington's words alive.[26]

The oral history in regard to Washington's communing in Morristown is as strong as oral history—the only known historical evidence available in this instance—can be. Boller's simple dismissal of this entire record is inexcusable, since he himself appeals to the non-witnesses of Bishop White and Reverend Abercrombie as decisive. Yet all that their testimony proves is that they themselves did not see Washington commune when they were presiding in a service that he was attending, but not that he never communed or that he did not believe in Communion.

Boller's appeal to doubt coupled with his wholesale denial of oral history means that he makes no effort to answer the massive, consistent and credible witnesses and their testimonies that assert Washington's communing in Morristown and beyond. When a tradition preserved by oral history is able to be traced to the original source by highly credible testimonies, and when multiple witnesses were involved and available to contradict the oral history, but never controverted the claims of that tradition, and when there was no evident reason for such an unexpected event to occur in the first place, there is a strong presumption for the historical character of the tradition.[27] Moreover, if there is a sound historical explanation consistent with Washington's known beliefs as well as the facts of his non-communing in Philadelphia, but his communing in New York, Morristown, and elsewhere, then we have a substantial reason to accept the reliability of the tradition as being beyond reasonable, historical doubt.

Simply put, oral history is susceptible to embellishments and erroneous interpolations. Yet, it still can provide important historical data, particularly when it can be tested by many other sources, such as a large agreement of witnesses who lived during or close to that era. Before we provide the historical explanation that attempts to construct this data, we must complete our summary of other witnesses to Washington's communing.

Yet another credible, written record of Washington's communing exists. This is from Elizabeth Schuyler, the daughter of patriot, statesman, and General Phillip Schuyler. Elizabeth Schuyler is better known as Mrs. Alexander Hamilton.

MRS. ALEXANDER HAMILTON—WITNESS THAT WASHINGTON WAS A COMMUNICANT OF THE CHURCH

The evidence for Washington's communion in this case emerges from the family of Alexander Hamilton. The occasion for the story to first be told was a family reunion held in New York in May of 1854. Mrs. Alexander Hamilton, Sr., was then ninety-seven years old. In spite of her age, she was remarkably well and her recollections were very clear. She had been able to travel to join the family all the way from Washington, D.C. She was even able to get in the coach on her own.

The story of this day was preserved by Reverend Alexander Hamilton, Mrs. Alexander Hamilton's great-grandson. At the time of the 1854 reunion, although he was only seven years old, Mrs. Hamilton took Alexander, her young great-grandson, to visit the former house of the Alexander Hamilton family and to see St. Paul's Church in New York City. The people on the trip were: Mrs. Alexander Hamilton, the young Alexander Hamilton, and Mrs. John Church Hamilton, who was Mrs. Alexander Hamilton's daughter-in-law and the young Alexander Hamilton's grandmother.

The Reverend Hamilton never forgot how Mrs. Alexander Hamilton related the exact details of the story of George Washington's communion at St. Paul's on the day of his presidential inauguration in 1789, when she would have been only thirty one years old. Her desire to tell the story had been prompted by the debate that had begun over whether or not George Washington was a communicant of the church. She told her great-grandson that she wanted him to know that she had been an eyewitness of Washington taking communion, so that he could inform future generations of the truth of Washington's faith. The details of her account included:

- Mrs. Washington was not at the inaugural.
- Washington rode away from Mount Vernon with only two attendants.
- The Inauguration was at Federal Hall.
- The procession walked from Wall St. to Fulton instead of riding.
- The inaugural service was at St. Paul's, instead of Trinity Church, because Trinity had been burned and had not yet been rebuilt.
- St. Paul's was a chapel of Trinity Church.
- Bishop Provoost was Rector of Trinity Parish, although he was bishop of New York as well.

- She had taken Communion with Washington at the service

Her words to her young great-grandson were, "If anyone ever tells you that George Washington was not a communicant of the Church, you say that your great-grandmother told you to say that she 'had knelt at this chancel rail at his side and received with him the Holy Communion.'"[28] She also told her great-grandson of her being at Valley Forge with her father, General Phillip Schuyler. There she said she had heard George Washington praying fervently that all would be well for the soldiers. Mrs. Alexander Hamilton died five months later on November 8, 1854, at the age of ninety-seven.

Elizabeth Schuyler Hamilton

Some seventy years later, around 1924, the Reverend Hamilton, rector and rector emeritus of Christ Church in Westport, Connecticut, from 1918 until his death on June 3, 1928, related this story to Miss Edith Beach, who was an officer of the Woman's Auxiliary to the Board of Missions of the Protestant Episcopal Church. Since the annual meeting of the Woman's Auxiliary was being held in the area, Miss Beech invited Reverend Hamilton to speak. She requested that he tell the story of the family reunion and how Mrs. Alexander Hamilton told him of communing with George Washington. Reverend Hamilton also related how the story had been confirmed to him by his maternal aunt as well. He also explained that his great-uncle Alexander, the son of the illustrious Alexander Hamilton, when visiting him at Mount Vernon, had also told him that Washington had invited many prominent men to attend church with him.

By 1925, Reverend Hamilton had prepared a written account of the events, which was published under the title "George Washington: Leader of Men and Communicant of the Church." But the story did not stop here. *The New York Herald Tribune* printed the Reverend Alexander Hamilton's testimony four years after his death on January 26, 1932. A member of the Church Missions Publishing Company related the story to the paper, as 1932 was "Washington Year" (the two-hundredth anniversary of Washington's birth).

The news story in the *Tribune* was read by Linson H. De Voe of East Orange, New Jersey. De Voe wrote a letter to the "contributor" of the story on the same day it was printed. De Voe had had a childhood connection with the Hamiltons. Many years earlier, he overheard a conversation in which the Rector of Christ Episcopal church was commenting on George Washington's alleged unorthodoxy. Another member of the Hamilton family, General Schuyler Hamilton—Mrs. Alexander Hamilton's grandson and the father of Reverend Alexander Hamilton—proceeded to relate the same narrative that had just been printed in the *Tribune*. Thus, by De Voe's experience, the story was shown to have been preserved and verified through a second line of testimony.

The historicity of Mrs. Alexander Hamilton's testimony of George Washington communing is confirmed by two independently preserved testimonies: Mrs. Alexander Hamilton's grandson and great-grandson.

This leaves us, then, with the final question. Is Mrs. Alexander Hamilton's witness credible? She claimed to have visited Valley Forge with her father as a young adult of around twenty years old. This seems credible, since she met General Washington's young supporting officer, Alexander Hamilton, during the war. Being married to one of Washington's most trusted advisors, and having lived in New York, it would not be surprising that she would be at Washington's inauguration when she was around thirty one years old.

Mrs. Alexander Hamilton is buried next to her husband. She died nearly fifty years after Alexander was killed in the infamous duel with Aaron Burr. Her testimony given to her family declares that she communed with President Washington on the day of his inauguration in New York.

Historical accuracy was consistent with her marked concern for the heritage of the Federalists, the political party originally led by Washington and championed by her husband. Historical accuracy was also consistent with her marked concern for the heritage of the Hamiltons, one of the true patriotic American military dynasties—whose history in the military had been duly recorded. Since her health was clearly excellent and she lived in Washington, she was in a position to know about the debate that had surfaced over Washington's religious practices. There was proof that her long-term memory was excellent, given the accuracy of the other details that her family remembered hearing from her.

Finally, what motive would she have to lie? Given her lifelong character as a woman of integrity, intentional deception seems impossible.[29]

ADDITIONAL TESTIMONIES TO WASHINGTON'S COMMUNING AND FAITH

When Washington died in 1799, the nation was filled with sermons and orations that honored his legacy. These messages both affirmed his status as a communicant and denied that he was a Deist. Mr. Sewell of New Hampshire wrote,

> To crown all these moral virtues, he had the deepest sense of religion impressed on his heart—the true foundation-stone of all the moral virtues. He constantly attended the public worship of God on the Lord's Day, was a communicant at His table, and by his devout and solemn deportment inspired every beholder with some portion of that awe and reverence for the Supreme Being, of which he felt so large a portion.[30]

David Ramsay, a historian from South Carolina wrote around the same time,

> Washington was the friend of morality and religion; steadily attended on public worship; encouraged and strengthened the hands of the clergy. In all his public acts he made the most respectful mention of Providence, and, in a word, carried the spirit of piety with him, both in his private life and public administration. He was far from being one of those *minute philosophers* who think that death is an *eternal sleep*, or of those who, trusting to the sufficiency of human reason, discard the light of divine revelation.[31]

WHY DID WASHINGTON NOT COMMUNE DURING THE WAR?

But even with this testimony of Washington's communing both before, during, and after the war, and also as president, we still must address why the charge of his non-communing exists.

Other suggestions have been offered as well. Perhaps it might be argued that since communion was infrequently celebrated in colonial America, it had not become a foundational spiritual discipline in Washington's mind. The church only provided the Eucharist three or four times a year. "It was the custom in the colonial churches to administer communion only at Christmas, Easter, and Whitsuntide [Pentecost Sunday], and it was not an uncommon practice for communicants to receive only once a year."[32] Perhaps Washington was simply following the practice that was common for Virginians, as Bishop William Meade described,

> … in former days there was a most mistaken notion, too prevalent both in England and America, that it was not so necessary in the professors of religion to communicate [receive communion] at all times, but that in this respect persons might be regulated by their feelings, and perhaps by the circumstances in which they were placed. I have had occasion to see much of this in my researches into the habits of the members of the old church of Virginia. Into this error of opinion and practice General Washington may have fallen, especially at a time when he was peculiarly engaged with the cares of government and a multiplicity of engagements, and when his piety may have suffered some loss thereby.[33]

Perhaps caring for the needs of their young grandchildren also was a concern. Washington's adopted granddaughter, Nelly Custis wrote, "On communion Sundays he left the church with me, after the blessing, and returned home, and we sent the carriage back for my grandmother."[34]

Washington biographer Jared Sparks elaborates on this "Washington was too busy for Communion" explanation. He suggests the inability to conform his daily duties of leadership with the spiritual demands of communing was a likely reason for his non-participation. "It is probable that, after he took command of the army, finding his thoughts and attention necessarily engrossed by the business that devolved upon him, in which frequently little distinction could be observed between the Sabbath and other days, he may have believed it improper publicly to partake of an ordinance which, according to the ideas he entertained of it, imposed severe restrictions on outward conduct, and a sacred pledge to perform duties impracticable in his situation."[35]

This notion may be supported by the sheer demands on Washington's time. Washington's diaries and letters show that Sunday after church was one of the few times he had in a profoundly busy military, political, and business life to handle his vast private correspondence and to address the massive responsibilities of running his huge Mount Vernon plantation. He wrote to James McHenry, September 14, 1799, "…the loss of time, and incidental expences, are not to be compared."[36] Similarly, he wrote to

James Anderson on December 10, 1799, "...time, which is of more importance than is generally imagined."[37]

Mary Thompson, a Washington scholar and research specialist at Mount Vernon, explains that Washington's chief objection to participating in the Eucharist was in the very literal fact that Washington, the leader of the American Revolution, could no longer commune with the head of the Anglican Church. She observes:

> George Washington, according to his family, took communion before the Revolutionary War. He did not take communion after the war. We have evidence from Washington's financial papers that he supplied wine to Pohick Church for communion; we know that he gave money for the crimson hangings and things that would decorate the altar of the communion table. I don't think this is a man who has a problem with communion, at least prior to the war. So, we have to ask ourselves, what would make his practice change? Why would he act differently after the war? And there are a number of reasons that he may have changed the way he was doing things.

What would such changes possibly be? We need to back up for a second and look at the word "Communion." It means that you are in fellowship with others around the table. Washington realized that he could not be in fellowship with a king——the head of the Anglican Church, no less——that he viewed as a tyrant who was killing and stealing from his own people. And so, at the beginning of the Revolutionary War, we know Washington did not continue in the Anglican Communion.

Thus, how could a man like General Washington, a man of principle who was leading the active resistance to the King, the head of the church, at the same time commune in that same church? Hypocrisy was not for George Washington.[38] Here is what Mary Thompson adds on the subject:

> Prior to the Revolution, Washington was made a vestryman at his church; he remained a vestryman until shortly after he returned home from the Revolution. Almost immediately after he gets home he writes to the church, the local church, and says [in effect], "I'm sorry, but I'm going to have to give up being a vestryman." He had to do that, because he had just led a revolution against the king—a

revolt against the King of England, who was the head of the Anglican Church. And as a vestryman, he would've had to swear allegiance to the king and to be subject to the doctrine and discipline of the Anglican Church. He couldn't do that anymore. And I think that problem influenced his taking communion.[39]

In light of all of this, it is virtually a miracle that Washington ever returned to the Church of England (which became the Episcopal Church) after the war. He also continued his membership in his church after the state Church of Virginia was disestablished in 1786, and attendance was no longer a matter of law.

Nevertheless, none of these reasons really seem to warrant Washington's choice not to participate in the Eucharist after the war was over, when he was in Philadelphia serving as the president under the spiritual care of Bishop William White and his assistant Reverend James Abercrombie. While it is a non-sequitur to infer, as Boller and those who argue for Washington's Deism do, that Washington's choice to not participate in Communion necessarily demonstrates a disbelief in Christ; nevertheless, his decision to not commune on many Sundays does not easily comport with his faith expressed in the phrase, "on my honor and the faith of a Christian." Nor does it fit comfortably with his self-description as, "a mind who always walked on a straight line, and endeavoured as far as human frailties, and perhaps strong passions, would enable him, to discharge the relative duties to his Maker and fellow-men...."

Is there a better explanation? We believe there is. And so we will address this question in depth in the chapter entitled, "The Struggle for the Episcopal Church: Washington's Non-Communication and Non-Communion in Philadelphia."

WASHINGTON AND THE RECONCILIATION OF THE CUP OF BLESSING

As the Revolutionary War created the inevitable fault lines between the Tories or Loyalists on the one side and the Patriots on the other, the clergy were compelled to take a stand. Their decision was complicated by the fact that every Anglican curate had taken a vow of loyalty to the King. Communion in the Anglican context was not only with the King of Kings and Lord of Lords, but it was also with the head of the earthly English kingdom, King George III. In fact, the 1662 *Book of Common Prayer's* service for the Communion included two prayers explicitly for King George—one just after the "Collect of the Day"[40]—and then later in the service, a prayer for the church militant included another prayer for the King.[41] But this crisis of conscience for a patriot did not just appear at the communion service, as the daily "Morning Prayer Service" also included "A Prayer for the King's Majesty."[42]

After the British evacuation of Boston in 1775, worship services were held in the city. On January 1, 1776, Christ Church, an Anglican congregation, was made ready for worship at the request of Mrs. Washington, who had come to winter with the General. In the diary of Dorothy Dudley, under that date, we learn of the beginning of American changes to the *Book of Common Prayer*,

> Yesterday service was held in Christ Church. I was invited to be present. Colonel William Palfrey, at request of Mrs. Washington, read the service and made a prayer of a form different from that commonly used for the King . . . . General and Mrs. Washington, Mrs. Gates, Mrs. Morgan, Mrs. Mifflin, Mrs. Curtis, and many others, including officers were present. The General is loyal to his church as to his country, though he had identified himself with our parish [congregational] during his residence among us . . . . The General's majestic figure bent reverently in prayer as with devout earnestness he entered into the service.[43]

As the conflict began to divide the Loyalist clergy and the patriotic people, particularly in the Anglican churches, close friendships began to be strained. This phenomenon impacted Washington and the clergymen that he knew. Washington's struggle with Anglican clergy in the pre-revolution and revolution eras is especially highlighted by three individuals: his lifelong friend, Bryan Fairfax, his son's tutor, Reverend Jonathan Boucher, and Reverend Jacob Duché, the rector of Christ Church, Philadelphia.

Washington's ability to continue to relate to and to forgive these individuals is a testimony to his inner spirituality. To Washington's and Fairfax's credit, their friendship was never broken, even though Fairfax was a Loyalist. After all, he was to become the next "Lord Fairfax, Earl of Cameron." He was given safe passage through American lines by Washington so he could sail to Britain to pursue efforts at reconciliation and perhaps for ordination as well. But he was not given permission to go to England by the British, because he refused to take the severe oaths that were required. Thus, he returned and spent the war years quietly in Virginia. Fairfax wrote a thank you letter to Washington on Dec. 8, 1777, that described the impact of the grace he had been extended by Washington:

> There are Times when Favours conferred make a greater Impression than at others, for, tho' I have received many, and hope I have not been unmindful of them, yet that, at a Time your Popularity was at the highest and mine at the lowest, and when it is so common for Men's Resentments to run high against those that differ from them in Opinion You should act with your wonted Kindness towards me, hath affected me more than any Favour I have received; and could not be believed by some in N: York, it being above the Run of common Minds.

In a most remarkable letter of encouragement, written on March 1, 1778, from a most painful place—Valley Forge—Washington steered his friend to the comfort of God's providential wisdom in the deep disappointment of his life.

> The sentiments you have expressed of me in this Letter are highly flattering, meriting my warmest acknowledgements, as I have too good an Opinion of your sincerity and candour to believe that you are capable of unmeaning professions and speaking a language foreign from your Heart. The friendship I ever professed, and felt for you, met with no diminution from the difference in our political Sentiments. I know the rectitude of my own intentions, and believing in the sincerity of yours, lamented, though I did not condemn, your renunciation of the creed I had adopted. Nor do I think any person, or power, ought to do it, whilst your conduct is not opposed to the general Interest of the people and the measures they are pursuing; the latter, that is our actions, depending upon ourselves, may be controuled, while the powers of thinking originating in higher causes, cannot always be moulded to our wishes....The determinations of Providence are all ways wise; often inscrutable, and though its decrees appear to bear hard upon us at times is nevertheless meant for gracious purposes; in this light I cannot help viewing your late disappointment.[44]

Later, Fairfax would go to England to become ordained as a curate, and for a time be the pastor of Washington's church in Alexandria. Fairfax later returned to England to receive his hereditary title also.

Washington's relationship with Reverend Boucher was far more volatile. William Lane explains,

> Having had friendly and even intimate relations with Washington, Boucher was very angry with the latter for his failure to use his influence in the country to protect him from the insults he endured, and under this feeling of resentment he wrote in August, 1775, a reproachful and bitter letter to Washington…"And yet you have borne to look on, at least as an unconcerned spectator, if not an abettor, whilst, like the poor frogs in the fable, I have in a manner been pelted to death. I do not ask if such conduct in you was friendly: was it either just, manly, or generous? It was not: no, it was acting with all the *base malignity* of a virulent Whig. As such, sir, I resent it: and, oppressed and overborne as I may seem to be by popular obloquy, I will not be so wanting in justice to myself as not to tell you, as I now do with honest boldness, that I despise the man who, for any motives, could be induced to act so mean a part. You are no longer worthy of my friendship: a man of honour can no longer without dishonour be connected with you. With your cause I renounce you."[45]

When the war was over, Boucher sent him a copy of his book on the American Revolution that began with a five-page dedication to Washington. It revealed a great change of sentiment toward his former friend. To Washington's great credit, he responded on August 15, 1798, with a graciousness borne of a forgiving spirit,

> For the honour of its dedication, and for the friendly and favourable sentiments therein expressed, I pray you to accept my acknowledgments and thanks. Not having read the book, it follows of course that I can express no opinion with respect to its political contents; but I can venture to assert beforehand, and with confidence, that there is no man in either country more zealously devoted to peace and a good understanding among the nations than I am; no one more disposed to bury in oblivion all animosities which have subsisted between them and the individuals of each.[46]

The case of Reverend Jacob Duché is also one of a powerful reversal in sentiments. Duché had preached a sermon on Galatians 5:1 in Philadelphia before the war began that called for a bold stand for civil and religious liberty in Christ. This sermon he dedicated to Washington:

> I have made choice of a passage of scripture, which will give me an opportunity of addressing myself to you as FREEMEN, both in the spiritual and temporal sense of the word, and of suggesting to you such a mode of conduct, as will be most likely, under the blessing of Heaven, to ensure to you the enjoyment of these two kinds of Liberty. STAND FAST, THEREFORE, IN THE LIBERTY, WHEREWITH CHRIST HATH MADE US FREE. . . . If spiritual Liberty calls upon its pious Votaries to extend their view far forward to a glorious HEREAFTER, CIVIL LIBERTY must at least be allowed to secure, in a considerable degree, our well-being here. And I believe it will be no difficult matter to prove, that the latter is as much the gift of GOD in CHRIST JESUS as the former, and consequently, that we are bound to stand fast in our CIVIL as well as our SPIRITUAL FREEDOM. . . .let us, nevertheless, 'STAND FAST' as the Guardians of LIBERTY."[47]

But when the British had successfully conquered Philadelphia, and Americans were shivering in the cold of Valley Forge, Reverend Duché realized that his oath to the King could not easily be set aside as he remained behind at Christ Church in Philadelphia. He chose to "stand fast" in the liberty of Christ on the side of the King, rather than to "stand fast" with the patriots' in their Christian cause of religious and civil liberty. Duché wrote an obsequious and treasonous letter to Washington that simultaneously defamed Congress. He explicitly called upon Washington to quit the struggle and to end the war for the nation's good. Duché, turned Tory, wrote on October 8, 1777, calling for Washington to leave the field and negotiate a peace with Britain to end the war and give up the impossible dream of independence. [48]

To this letter Washington responded with a brief note, and then wrote to the President of Congress on October 16, 1777,

> I yesterday thro' the hands of Mrs. Ferguson of Graham Park, received a Letter of a very curious and extraordinary nature from

Mr. Duché which I have thought proper to transmit to Congress. To this ridiculous, illiberal performance, I made a very short reply by desiring the bearer of it, if she should hereafter, by any accident, meet with Mr. Duché, to tell him I should have returned it unopened, If I had had any idea of the contents, observing at the same time, that I highly disapproved the intercourse she seemed to have been carrying on and expected it would be discontinued. Notwithstanding the Author's assertion, I cannot but suspect that this Measure did not originate with him, and that he was induced to it, by the hope of establishing his interest and peace more effectually with the Enemy.

In spite of this letter, calling on Washington to capitulate and to forfeit the cause of independence, years later after the war, Duché wrote to Washington requesting help with returning to his homeland of America. Washington's response again revealed a kind restraint and a gracious spirit.

Headquarters, August 10, 1783

I have received your letter of the 2nd of April and reflecting on its contents, I cannot say but that I am heartily sorry for the occasion that has produced it. Personal enmity, I bear none to any man, so far therefore as to your return to this country depends on my private voice, it would be given in favour of it with chearfulness. But removed as I am from the people and the policy of the state in which you formerly resided and to whose determination your case must be submitted, it is my duty, whatever may be my inclination, to leave its decision to its constitutional judges. Should this be agreeable to your wishes, it cannot fail to meet my entire approbation.

Reverend Duché was buried at St. Peter's Episcopal Church in Philadelphia only a few years after his return.

The point illustrated by these three Anglican clergymen that Washington knew personally was that his role as leader of the patriot army meant that he was almost certainly under the critical eye of the curates of his own church. It was not just with the King that he could not commune. He could hardly commune with a curate at any

Anglican Communion service. This ecclesiastical reality created awkwardness for Washington that led him to worship in other churches. It is thus clear that his initial ceasing of partaking of communion coincides with the start of the Revolution, when Communion with the King and most of the clergy of the Anglican Church was broken. But notice too, that reconciliation and Christian forgiveness seem to have been part of his relational style with these clerical leaders who had opposed him.[49]

Forgiveness of one's enemies is never an easy matter. Nor was it for Washington. But if Washington did not commune, it is at least clear that he lived out the ethics of the Eucharistic "cup of blessing."[50] He was able to reconcile with his clerical brethren who had stood against him: Reverend Fairfax the Tory, Reverend Boucher the bitter critic, and Reverend Duche the turncoat. A man with such magnanimity of Christian grace would normally be a partaker of the Lord's Table.

Whether the evidence here is sufficient to convince the skeptic that Washington was a communicant at the Lord's Table, there is indisputable evidence that Washington directly appealed to the offering of the Communion Chalice. In the skeptics' haste to dismiss the alleged minimal use of scripture by our founding father, they have entirely missed his repeated references to the Christian sacrament of Communion.

The fact is that Washington does use the biblical Eucharistic phrase—"cup of blessing" as well as variations on this theme. The phrase "cup of blessing" is a direct quote of the Eucharistic text of the King James Version's rendering of 1 Corinthians 10:16. This is the very verse that provides the English word "communion" to describe the Lord's Table. The text says, "The cup of blessing which we bless, is it not the communion of the blood of Christ? The bread which we break, is it not the Communion of the body of Christ?" Washington's actual words are,

> At this auspicious period, the United States came into existence as a Nation, and if their Citizens should not be completely free and happy, the fault will be entirely their own.
>
> Such is our situation, and such are our prospects: but notwithstanding *the cup of blessing is thus reached out to us*, notwithstanding happiness is ours, if we have a disposition to seize the occasion and make it our own.[51] (emphasis ours)

Not only does he use the Eucharistic words, but he employs the phrase in a Eucharistic sense of America itself being at the divine Communion table. The cup of blessing is being reached out to America, if America will receive the proffered gift. The significance of this text only increases when it is placed in its immediate and greater context. What Washington wrote just before this was:

> ...the Treasures of knowledge, acquired by the labours of Philosophers, Sages and Legislatures, through a long succession of years, are laid open for our use, and their collected wisdom may be happily applied in the Establishment of our forms of Government; the free cultivation of Letters, the unbounded extension of Commerce, the progressive refinement of Manners, the growing liberality of sentiment, *and above all, the pure and benign light of Revelation,* have had ameliorating influence on mankind and increased the blessings of Society. At this auspicious period, the United States came into existence as a Nation, and if their Citizens should not be completely free and happy, the fault will be entirely their own.
>
> Such is our situation, and such are our prospects: but notwithstanding *the cup of blessing is thus reached out to us,* notwithstanding happiness is ours, if we have a disposition to seize the occasion and make it our own. (emphasis added)

The context of Washington's remark is his declaration that what has most blessed America is the gift of divine revelation. This revelation, of course, is where the image of the Communion cup of blessing is to be found. And most significantly, this passage occurs in one of Washington's most public documents—his circular letter to the thirteen governors at the end of the war on June 8, 1783. These two items—the excellence of divine revelation and the imagery of the communion cup—were not topics a Deist would have chosen to employ.[52]

Although it has been argued that

Washington's pew in St. Paul's chapel, New York City, where he worshipped as President

433

George Washington was unwilling to partake of Christian Communion, the fact that he quotes the very verse that speaks of Communion in his most public letter only further corroborates the written testimonies of his communing.

As we turn to his further use of this biblical Eucharistic language, we will see that this was not an anomaly or something interpolated into his otherwise deistic perspective by speech writers. This is evident because he returns to this same phrase in his self-composed first draft of his presidential Farewell Address, which he enclosed in a letter to Alexander Hamilton on May 15, 1796. Following his custom to avoid using the precise phrase a second time, this time "cup of blessing" is presented with the synonymous "cup of beneficence." He also places the phrase in a deeply spiritual context with phrases such as the "all wise dispensor of blessings," "favor," "happiness," "our Creator," "bountifully offered:"

> That as the allwise dispensor of human blessings has favored no Nation of the Earth with more abundant, and substantial means of happiness than United America, that we may not be so ungrateful to our Creator; so wanting to ourselves; and so regardless of Posterity, as to dash the cup of beneficence which is thus bountifully offered to our acceptance.

Washington uses this biblical idea of the metaphor "the cup of _____" in other contexts as well. Consider, for example:

> *The Cup of Reconciliation:* to The President of the United States, Mount Vernon, July 13, 1798: "Satisfied therefore, that you have sincerely wished and endeavoured to avert war, and exhausted to the last drop, the cup of reconciliation…"

> *Cup of National Felicity:* To Jonathan Trumbull, July 20, 1788: …at least we may, with a kind of grateful and pious exultation, trace the finger of Providence through those dark and mysterious events, which first induced the States to appoint a general Convention and then led them one after another (by such steps as were best calculated to effect the object) into an adoption of the system recommended by that general Convention; thereby, in all human probability, laying a lasting foundation for tranquillity and

happiness; when we had but too much reason to fear that confusion and misery were coming rapidly upon us. That the same good Providence may still continue to protect us and prevent us from dashing the cup of national felicity just as it has been lifted to our lips, is the earnest prayer of My Dear Sir, your faithful friend...

This is perhaps the most striking example of the Eucharistic imagery used by Washington. It reflects the Anglican custom of the common chalice being presented to the communicant's lips. The imagery of "dashing the cup" suggests being deprived of the Communion cup, because it was dropped just as one was about to drink from it. This use of the image is presented in a spiritual context as well: "grateful and pious exultation," "trace the finger of Providence," "dark and mysterious events," "the same good Providence may still continue to protect," "earnest prayer."

But the scriptures also use the imagery of the cup in a negative sense as well. So when Washington speaks of drinking the "bitter cup," he forcefully alludes to Matthew 26:39, a passage that depicts the sufferings of Gethsemane. The point of his remarks is the horrific suffering of the prisoners of war. Written from his own sufferings at Valley Forge, he says to The President of Congress, March 7, 1778:

> ...impeding the progress both of drafting and recruiting, by dejecting the Courage of the Soldiery from an Apprehension of the Horrors of Captivity, and finally by reducing those, whose Lot it is to drink the bitter Cup, to a Despair, which can only find Relief by renouncing their Attachments and engaging with their Captors.

In yet another negative variation on the phrase, Washington uses the image of "the cup of folly" when he writes to Thomas Johnson, October 15, 1784: "I trust that a proper sense of justice and unanimity in those States which have not drunk so deep of the cup of folly may yet retrieve our affairs."

CONCLUSION

Let's recap the main points we've discovered so far in this discussion of Washington's participation in the Lord's Supper:

1) Washington was a regular communicant all his life in the Anglican Church until the Revolutionary War;

2) During the Revolutionary War, when he was leading a rebellion against the King, the earthly head of that church, the general ceased communing in the Anglican context;

3) On occasion, during the war, there are credible reports he received communion in churches of other denominations;

4) After the war, there are credible reports that he did again on occasion receive Communion from his own denomination; and did so in a state of forgiveness and restoration toward the Anglican clergy that had rejected him or his views before or during the war;

5) In none of his extensive writings did he ever deny his belief in the doctrines of his native church (including the atonement of Christ, his passion for the forgiveness of sins, which is the focus of communion). This is significant, since Washington, as a man of honor, had made vows as a vestryman and church warden, therein affirming his belief in the doctrines of the Anglican Church that included a belief in the atonement of Christ and the Communion of the Lord's Table;

6) Instead, he actually uses the biblical Eucharistic imagery of "the cup of blessing" in public and private writings, a phrase he employs in highly biblical and spiritual contexts, even aptly using an allusion to the "bitter cup" of Gethsemane to reflect the sufferings of prisoners of war as he wrote from the crucible of Valley Forge.

7) Washington seemingly never lost communion with his faith, even though communion with the King was broken forever, and communion with his home church and its clergy was broken for awhile. But why then, as president, did he not commune in Philadelphia?

TWENTY ONE

Shadow Or Substance?:

Putting Professor Boller's Evidence for Washington's Deism on Trial

"I contend, that it is by the substance,
not with the shadow of a thing, we are to be benefited."
George Washington February 2, 1787[1]

In this chapter we continue to address the objection that Washington was not a Christian because he did not partake of Christian Communion. As we have already seen in the last chapter, the very way the argument has been presented by Professor Paul Boller, Jr., author of *George Washington & Religion*, is flawed. In this chapter we intend to take Professor Boller at his word, when he claimed that he would use only evidence that would hold up in a court of law.[2] As we cross-examine his argument, we find that it woefully fails, based upon the very standard he erected for himself. Our point will be to show that when credible witnesses from an historical perspective are permitted to speak, which Professor Boller permits when convenient for his argument, Washington's Communion practices fit consistently with all of the known facts and with his Christian character.

THE EPISCOPAL CLERGYMEN AND "MRS." CUSTIS TAKE THE STAND

It is claimed by Professor Boller that Washington never communed at all, because of the statements made by Philadelphia Bishop William White and his assistant, the Episcopal priest Reverend Dr. James Abercrombie. But the facts speak otherwise. The evidence we have already considered in the previous chapter argues that Washington communed in Virginia, in Morristown, New Jersey, and in New York City.[3]

There is significance in the fact that Washington communed under the new government and under the new bishop, Samuel Provoost, as testified by Mrs. Alexander Hamilton. In essence, his return to the Episcopal table was an affirmation of his historic Anglican faith, yet it was still consistent with his belief that the breach with the British crown was a just and righteous act of resistance to monarchical tyranny. The Episcopal Church was no longer the Anglican Church, although its clergy still were ordained in the order and succession of the Anglican prelates or bishops, overseen by the Archbishop of Canterbury and the head of the Episcopal Church in the United States was not the King.

The American version of the *Book of Common Prayer* now had prayers for the president and Congress, but not for King George. The American head of state, however, was not the head of the Episcopal Church, even if he was Episcopalian. Washington's lofty, political position did not translate into a high, ecclesiastical position. This meant that Washington held the anomalous position of being the leader of his country, but only a follower in his church's government. He was an honored member of his church, but his views of ecclesiastical matters, whatever they may have been, or however deeply held, were merely personal. As we shall see, his strongest ecclesiastical view he chose to reveal to history only in the quietness of his diary. Otherwise, we are left to explain his views mainly by his basic motto—deeds not words.

The facts do indicate that he did not commune while he served as president in Philadelphia. This is admitted by all sides of the debate concerning Washington's religion, as we will see in a moment. Just to put this into context, we need to explain a few aspects of the customs of that time. In the Episcopal Church in the late 1780s, it was customary to have Communion only three or four time per year. (Only later did the Episcopal Church change to have the sacrament each Sunday morning). Second, it was customary for the service to contain a break between part one of the service——the liturgy of the word—which included the sermon, and part two, the liturgy of the

Table, which included Communion. Often during that time, according to the record of Reverend James Abercrombie, who will be quoted below, "the greater part of the congregation" would get up and leave—Washington often being one of them. That being said, people on all sides of the debate on George Washington and religion have agreed that it was his custom to not receive Communion while he was in Philadelphia attending services at Christ Church. Reverend John Stockton Littell, advocate of Washington's Christianity writes, "It is a fact that Bishop White could not testify to Washington's making his communions nor even to his religious faith."[4]

Similarly, advocate of Washington's Deism, historian Rupert Hughes wrote,

> His refusal to take communion was admitted by his own clergyman, William White, Bishop of the Episcopal Church in America from 1787 to 1836. Colonel Mercer had written to ask if General Washington "occasionally went to the communion," or "if he ever did at all." Bishop White answered:
>
> "Truth requires me to say that General Washington never received the communion in the church of which I am parochial minister. Mrs. Washington was an habitual communicant... I have been written to by several on the point of your inquiry; and have been obliged to answer them as I now do you." Bishop White had previously written the same to Colonel Mercer, in 1832: "As your letter seems to intend an inquiry on the point of kneeling during service, I owe it to truth to declare that I never saw him in the said attitude."

Thus, we have seen, it is clear that Bishop White said he never heard Washington give a statement of faith in Christianity to him. The bishop also declared that he never saw Washington commune or kneel in the worship services. It is also true that Rector James Abercrombie, another of Washington's clergyman, preached a sermon on the duty of communing that resulted in Washington never attending thereafter on a Communion Sunday at this church in Philadelphia. In fact, Reverend Abercrombie later called Washington a Deist. Allegedly, he said to one who was pursuing the question of Washington's Christianity or Deism, "*Sir, Washington was a deist!*"[5]—although subsequently retracting his statement, saying instead, that he could not conceive of someone being a Christian if he did not commune regularly.[6]

Moreover, Boller cites a letter from Reverend Abercrombie that explains his sermon and gives a report from an unnamed senator to the effect that Washington heard the message and took the rebuke and intended to respond by not attending on a Sunday when the Eucharist was celebrated. Dr. Abercrombie had an even more interesting story to tell about Washington and the sacrament. It appeared in his letter to Origen Bacheler in 1831 and Bacheler, for obvious reasons, chose not to make it public:

> ...observing that on Sacrament Sundays, Gen'l Washington immediately after the Desk and Pulpit services, went out with the greater part of the congregation, always leaving Mrs. Washington with the communicants, she invariably being one, I considered it my duty, in a sermon of Public Worship, to state the unhappy tendency of example, particularly those in elevated stations, who invariably turned their backs upon the celebration of the Lord's Supper. I acknowledge the remark was intended for the President, as such, he received it. A few days later, in conversation with, I believe, a Senator of the U.S., he told me he had dined the day before with the President, who in the course of the conversation at the table, said, that on the preceding Sunday he had received a very just reproof from the pulpit, for always leaving the church before the administration of the Sacrament; that he honored the preacher for his integrity and candour; that he had never considered the influence of his example; that he would never again give cause for the repetition of the reproof; and that, as he had never been a communicant, were he to become one of them, it would be imputed to an ostentatious display of religious zeal arising altogether from his elevated station. Accordingly, he afterwards never came on the morning of Sacrament Sunday, tho' at other times, a constant attendant in the morning.[7]

And it is also the fact that Washington noted earlier that he did not commune, even though Mrs. Washington did, since he and his granddaughter left prior to communion, and then sent the carriage back for Mrs. Washington after the communion service was complete. This is supported by a letter from "Mrs. Nelly Custis," written to Washington historian Jared Sparks.[8]

CROSS-EXAMINATION OF PROFESSOR BOLLER'S EVIDENCE

Nelly Custis' letter is highly significant for our purposes. Washington's adopted granddaughter, Nelly Custis, was a married woman by the time she wrote this letter. Boller writes, "according to Mrs. Custis...."[9] He overlooks her married name, which was Mrs. Nelly Custis Lewis. Nelly was born in 1779, and was only ten in 1789 when the Washingtons took her and her younger brother George Washington Parke Custis to New York to be with them as he served as president. She was only about seventeen when the president's second term was done. She did not marry until February 22, 1799, Washington's birthday, the last one he lived to see. So her name was Mrs. Nelly Lewis, although she signed her letter Nelly Custis, her maiden name. But she did not sign it Mrs. Nelly Custis.

We can forgive Professor Boller's oversight, for it doesn't greatly impact the argument. We are also grateful that the professor is not insistent on full consistency with the logic of his argument. Thankfully, he does not make the faulty inference that Miss Custis must have been a Deist, since she didn't stay for Communion either. And since Reverend Abercrombie noted that Washington left "with the greater part of the congregation," we don't suppose that Professor Boller would have us infer that the majority of Episcopalians in Washington's day at the Reverend Abercrombie's church were Deists too.

A more honest explanation can be offered, since most Deists throughout history have not been in the habit of attending Christian churches. It should be remembered that the 1662 *Book of Common Prayer* Morning Prayer Service was twelve pages long plus a full length sermon, and the Communion service was an additional twenty-six pages long, plus the time required for the administration of the Eucharist.[10] The reason for the "greater part of the congregation leaving" likely had to do with the reason that twelve-year-old Miss Nelly and ten-year-old Master George Washington Parke Custis left with their grandfather, while Mrs. Washington spent the remainder of the morning in worship. We do not intend to suggest that the president didn't take Communion in Philadelphia primarily because of child care. Overlooking such minor considerations, we cannot, however, overlook that grown up Mrs. Nelly Custis Lewis, writing to historian Jared Sparks on February 26, 1833, profoundly disagrees with the inference that Boller draws from her letter. She did not write her letter to show that General Washington was a Deist. Instead, after a full recital of Washington's Christian life, she concluded,

I should have thought it the greatest heresy to doubt his firm belief in Christianity. His life, his writings, prove that he was a Christian....Is it necessary that any one should certify, "General Washington avowed himself to *me* a believer in Christianity"? As well may we question his patriotism, his heroic, disinterested devotion to his country.[11]

This leaves us wondering whether Professor Boller in his research did not carefully read Mrs. Nelly Custis Lewis' well-known letter, or if he simply chose to suppress its real thrust because it made his claims for Washington's alleged Deism so tenuous. Further, why does Professor Boller take Mrs. Nelly Custis Lewis' letter out of context? Her remarks were not intended to argue that Washington had never communed in his life, but that he had never communed in Christ Church and St. Peter's Church in Philadelphia under Reverend Abercrombie and Bishop White.

It is clear that the context of her statement limits his leaving the service during the time of her own childhood while they were in "New York and Philadelphia" where "he never omitted attendance at church in the morning, unless detained by indisposition. . . . No one in church attended to the service with more reverential respect."[12] Nelly, of course, would have had no recollection of Washington's communing on April 30, the day of his Inauguration, as reported by Mrs. Alexander Hamilton, since Miss Nelly, young George Washington, and Mrs. Washington had not yet arrived in New York. And certainly the custom of leaving early and sending the carriage back would not have applied when the family was back at Mount Vernon, where a trip to church required a nine mile bouncing journey over muddy and rutted country roads to either the Pohick church or the church in Alexandria.

HEARSAY EVIDENCE—A CRITICISM OF CONVENIENCE

Next, let us consider Professor Boller's evaluation of the evidence that he offers as proof of his theory that Washington's non-communing in Philadelphia proves that he was a Deist. He states,

> Abercrombie's report that Washington "had never been a communicant" together with the statements of Mrs. Custis and Bishop White, surely must be regarded as conclusive. . .By contrast, the various stories collected by the pietists to prove that Washington received the sacrament at Morristown and elsewhere are based on mere hearsay statements made many years after

Washington's death.[13]

Professor Boller declares that his evidence is vastly superior to that of the "pietists" who argue for Washington's communing on "hearsay" reports. His is based on the report of Reverend Abercrombie, "Mrs. Custis," and Bishop White. But let's take a moment and consider the "report" of Reverend Abercrombie:

> A few days later, in conversation with, I believe, a Senator of the U.S., he told me he had dined the day before with the President, who in the course of the conversation at the table, said, that on the preceding Sunday he had received a very just reproof from the pulpit....

Notice that the Reverend Abercrombie's report is not built on a personal conversation with the president. From whom did the reverend receive it? From an unnamed senator. Or was it a senator, since the Reverend Abercrombie says, "I believe, a Senator of the U.S."? Strange indeed that an Anglican clergyman ministering in the nation's capitol at the time could have had such a confidential conversation about the faith of the president with one of his closest confidants and not even know if he was a senator!

The point here is not to argue that Reverend Abercrombie's "hearsay" evidence cannot be true, but to note that Professor Boller's claim of superior evidence is questionable. The claims for Washington's communing in Morristown are built on exactly the same kind of evidence as here given by Reverend Abercrombie and relied upon by Professor Boller—that is an eye witness account, once or twice removed. During the Revolutionary War, George Washington reportedly received Communion in a Presbyterian service in Morristown, New Jersey. The report of this comes from Reverend Dr. Timothy Johnes' son-in-law, Reverend Dr. James Richards, who was also a minister. Both sources fall into the category of oral history; both can be presumed to be trustworthy, and thus, neither one is necessarily superior.

Further, when a careful consideration is given of the words allegedly said by the unnamed possible senator, it becomes clear that Washington was not making universal pronouncements about his lifetime views of Communion. He was merely stating his practice in the churches in question. The words of the Reverend Abercrombie (referring to Washington) again are clear,

> ...that he had never considered the influence of his example; that he

would never again give cause for the repetition of the reproof; and that, as he had never been a communicant, were he to become one of them, it would be imputed to an ostentatious display of religious zeal arising altogether from his elevated station.

These words are addressing the actions of the president serving in Philadelphia in his busy and "elevated station," not those of the vestryman and church warden from Virginia, or the believer who felt drawn to commune beyond the bounds of his own communion in the midst of war, disease, and exposure to the elements. To interpret these "hearsay" words of "he had never been a communicant" would be to deny his leadership in the Anglican Virginian parish and vestry as church warden, and to select one piece of questionable historical data and give it an unwarranted and undocumentable prominence over the other equally legitimate, oral, historical claims.

At best, these words, which we accept as authentic, argue that Washington did not commune as president in Philadelphia. Since we agree with Professor Boller on this point, it is incumbent upon us to explain why such would be the case. We must answer the question of what made communing in Philadelphia different than communing in New York, Morristown, and Virginia. But, before we address this central question, there is one last reason why Professor Boller's argument will not stand up "in a court of law."

PROFESSOR BOLLER'S LOGICAL FALLACY

Even after exposing all of these weaknesses in Professor Boller's theory, there is still another problem with his claim that Washington was a Deist because he did not commune in Philadelphia under the ministry of Bishop White and the Reverend James Abercrombie. At the heart of the professor's claim that Washington was a Deist, there is a logical inconsistency. The following argument's logical fallacy is immediately apparent:

> Ostriches do not fly.
> George Washington did not fly.
> Therefore George Washington was an ostrich.

Yet compare it with this logic:

> Deists do not commune.

George Washington did not commune.

Therefore George Washington was a Deist.

While less apparent, the same logical fallacy is at work. The fact is that many who have considered themselves to be Christians have not communed for various reasons— the Quakers and the early Schwenkfelders never communed at all on theological and moral principles. Many Protestants have felt they could not commune in good conscience because they were not in communion with the clergy, the church, or the political head of the church where they have worshiped. Sometimes Christians have believed that it would be inappropriate for them to commune because of various personal challenges, difficulties, demands, or moral issues.

To put it logically, for the same reason that shoes are not crows just because both are black, so Washington and Deists are not both non-Christians because neither partook of Communion in Philadelphia at Christ Church.

Finally, let us notice the critique that the Reverend Abercrombie gives against Washington: "I cannot consider any man as a real Christian who uniformly disregards an ordinance so solemnly enjoined by the divine Author of our holy religion." We do not disagree with the words of the Reverend Abercrombie. But, we do disagree with the verdict that he delivered against Washington's whole life. The evidence does not suggest that he never communed. While not communing under Bishop White in Philadelphia, the evidence is that Washington communed under Bishop Provoost in New York City.

CONFLICTING TESTIMONY—OR ARE BOTH TRUE?

To balance the charge brought by the testimony of the Reverend Abercrombie, which has been so heavily relied upon by Professor Boller, we submit the testimony of the Reverend Alexander Hamilton of the historic and illustrious Alexander Hamilton family:

> It was a beautiful morning in May 1854, that the family coach drew up in front of the family home, 17 w. 20th. Street, New York City. There Mrs. General Hamilton (who had come on from Washington, D. C., with her son), her daughter-in-law, Mrs. John Church Hamilton, and A. Hamilton (the writer of this letter and present Reverend Alexander Hamilton) entered and rode to Wall Street, corner of Broad, New York City.

Then Mrs. General Hamilton, her daughter-in-law and great-grandson, Alexander, entered the former house of Alexander Hamilton. Going to the front window, Mrs. Hamilton said, "I, with Mrs. Knox and other ladies, looked from this window over to Federal Hall and saw George Washington inaugurated first President of the United States.

"Then we all walked up Broadway to St. Paul's Chapel, Fulton Street. Washington, Chancellor Livingston, Genera Knox and your great-grandfather (meaning General Hamilton), went into the chapel and occupied the pew on the north side. We ladies sat just back of them, but Mrs. Washington was not present, being yet at Mount Vernon. A festal celebration was held, sermon preached by the rector, and the Holy Communion was also celebrated, at which Washington, members of his party and many others partook."

Mrs. Hamilton then said to me, "My son, I have taken you to Wall Street and there depicted the inauguration; then to St. Paul's Chapel, where Washington attended divine service, and received the Holy Communion. I want you to transmit these facts to future generations, as some have asked, "Was Washington a communicant of the Church, did he ever partake of the Holy Communion?"[14]

So who should we believe in regard to their testimonies about Washington's communing or non-communing? Reverend Abercrombie? Reverend Hamilton? Reverend Johnes? We believe all of them, because there is clear evidence that supports why Washington would have communed in Virginia, Morristown, New Jersey, and New York, but not in Philadelphia.

So as we conclude this section, we believe that the appropriate question to ask is whether a Christian can be a good Christian and not always commune? Reverend John Stockton Littell, author of *George Washington: Christian*, answered this question in regard to General Washington: "During a short period it is probable that while he did not give up assisting in worship, he left the Church before Communion. It would perhaps be too much to expect that at all times he should have maintained an equally strong religious life, or that his perseverance was perfect and without a flaw."[15] However one answers this question, the point is that Washington's non-communing in Philadelphia is not proof that he was a Deist. But why did Washington not commune in Philadelphia?

The reason that George Washington did not commune in Philadelphia, as we shall see in the next chapter, is due to a combination of concerns. First, there was the factor of his massive and accumulating duties as president and his constantly pressing need to keep his Mount Vernon plantation profitable after eight years of neglect and absence during the War. He had served the entire time as commander in chief without salary and so disposable cash was limited. Now after just a few years back at home, he had to leave for another substantial absence to serve as president that turned out to be eight more years away from home. Sunday was his only day for personal matters and for staying abreast of his vast personal correspondence.

But, on top of this pressure to use every moment for his personal concerns, there also was a major struggle occurring between the High Church and the Low Church in the new Episcopal denomination that also impacted Washington. In the next chapter, we will consider Washington's relationship with Bishop Samuel Provoost in New York. Washington, like Bishop Provoost, was an adherent of the Low Church theology. When Washington came to Philadelphia, however, he chose to keep a studied distance from Bishop William White, who had compromised the Low Church position with the High Church bishop Samuel Seabury of New England. This contributed to the lack of connection between Washington and Bishop White. How Bishop White's connection with Bishop Seabury impacted the Low Church and influenced Washington's connection with Bishop White will be the focus of our next chapter.

THE DEIST EXPLANATION DOES NOT FIT THE KNOWN FACTS

The fact is that the explanation that Washington was a Deist, and that is why he did not commune in Philadelphia, does not account for all the known facts. Obviously, we have no direct statement from Washington as to why he did or did not commune. So whatever explanation one offers, it must fit all of the known facts. That is the problem with the Deist explanation. It does not fit.

As we continue to see, there are may reasons why Washington could not have been a Deist. He described himself as a Christian on various occasions,[16] but he never used the word Deist, let alone even once claiming to be a Deist. He criticized the Deist beliefs that rejected divine Providence[17] as well as the Deist rejection of the necessary support of religion and morality for political happiness.[18] He repeatedly and openly affirmed key Christian doctrines, the very ones that, when affirmed, necessarily prohibit one from being a Deist, including: the existence and superior value of revelation, the Bible being the word of God, scripture and Holy Writ,[19] the existence of true religion, the reality of both revealed and natural religion,[20] the excellence of the

Christian religion,[21] the divinity of Christ, the depravity of human nature, his first national Thanksgiving Proclamation calling on the nation to find forgiveness of sins in the "Lord and Ruler of Nations,"[22] a New Testament title for Christ (Revelation 12:5; 19:16), the importance of imitating Christ,[23] the desire to advance Christianity and encourage its missions to non-Christians,[24] and the looking forward to the millennial era of peace on earth.[25]

He even bore Christian witness while president on several occasions, such as in his Inaugural Address that was so openly Christian that the Presbyterians no longer worried that Christianity was not directly mentioned in the new U.S. Constitution.[26] He delighted in Christian prayers and participated in distinctively Christian reciprocal prayers.[27] He approved of biblical and Gospel-based sermons and even commended anti-Deist sermons;[28] all of this coupled with his open and unstinting support of religion and morality, piety, and ministers of the Gospel.[29] Then, as we saw in the previous chapter, using the very same type of evidence that Professor Boller accepts when convenient for his argument, we find that Washington was also a communicant.

CONCLUSION: WASHINGTON'S ALLEGED DEISM — IF IT DOESN'T FIT, YOU MUST ACQUIT

The thesis that Washington was a Deist simply does not fit the facts and must be rejected. Since Washington never wrote a single word saying that he no longer believed in Communion, or that he rejected Christianity, the claim that he rejected Christianity and Communion is built entirely on an argument from silence. The claim that Washington was a Deist is deafeningly refuted by the host of explicit Christian declarations from his pen and actions. Washington wanted to be interpreted by his actions, and so he often left a few words to help us to know what his actions meant. Given his motto was "Deeds not Words,"[30] as Nelly Custis also wrote in the same letter misapplied by Professor Boller to defend a Deist interpretation of Washington, we must now ask what combination of words and deeds explains his communing in some places, but not as president in Philadelphia? Whatever explanation we offer, it must comport with all of the known facts.

TWENTY TWO

The Struggle for the Episcopal Church:

Washington's Non-Communication and Non-Communion in Philadelphia

"Monday October 10th [1785].... A Mr. Jno. Lowe,
on his way to Bishop Seabury for Ordination, called & dined here.
Could not give him more than a general certificate, founded on
information, respecting his character; having no acquaintance
with him, nor any desire to open a Correspondence
with the new ordained Bishop."
George Washington's Diary [1]

In this chapter, we will give possible reasons why Washington did not commune in Philadelphia. While Washington nowhere gave an explicit reason for not communing under the ministry of Bishop William White of Christ Church, Philadelphia, there appears to be pertinent reasons to understand why he might have chosen not to do so. It is clear to us, that the Deist explanation simply does not fit the facts for several reasons.

Washington communed elsewhere and, according to the history of the German Reformed Congregation of Germantown, Washington even communed with them as president while in Philadelphia, when he was sequestered from the city during the yellow fever epidemic. During this time, he spent several weeks at the home of the German Reformed clergyman, Reverend Lebrecht Herman, where he kept his office.[2] Washington never hinted that he had changed his faith in any way, and continued to identify himself as a Christian by his words and actions. So what reasons might there be to explain his non-communion at the Episcopal church in Philadelphia?

First, there was Washington's Low Church (also referred to as "broad church") tradition that impacted his attitude toward the three first American bishops. Further, we believe Washington's relationship with Bishop William White in Philadelphia was significantly influenced by the struggle in the Episcopal Church over the theological views advocated by the High Church. These circumstances, when coupled with the pressures of time, made the temptation to not remain for the lengthy Communion service compelling.

Moreover, Washington's massive and growing duties of the presidency, as well as the continuing demands on his time for the successful management of his vast Mount Vernon plantation, not only resulted in his limited communication with Bishop White, but in his non-communing at the Eucharist where Bishop White presided. The common practice of many of the Episcopal congregants of not remaining for the Communion service became Washington's habit while president in Philadelphia. So Bishop White never saw Washington commune in the churches where he officiated.

Similarly, time demands and the tyranny of the urgent compelled him to protect Sunday afternoons for his personal concerns and voluminous correspondence. Sunday was his only day off, which often was inadequate to address the constant problems that Washington faced from the Mount Vernon front as well as his desire to maintain correspondence with the many who were dear to his heart and important to his life. Time pressures became so severe as president that he nearly forgot his gracious and dignified manner when he bluntly refused to sit for any more portraits unless a reputable group requested him to do so.[3]

WASHINGTON'S CONCERNS WITH BISHOP SEABURY

When the New England Anglicans began the first American Episcopate, it is clear that Washington and other Low Church adherents did not support the first American bishop, Samuel Seabury. In the privacy of his diary, Washington wrote what was probably his strongest written statement on an ecclesiastical matter,

> "Monday 10th [1785]. Thermometer at 68 in the Morng. 70 at Noon and 74 at Night. Thunder about day. Morning threatning but clear & pleasant afterwards. A Mr. Jno. Lowe, on his way to Bishop Seabury for Ordination, called & dined here. Could not give him more than a general certificate, founded on information, respecting his character; having no acquaintance with him, nor any desire to open a Correspondence with the *new* ordained Bishop.[4]

Why would Washington not have wanted to correspond with the newly ordained Bishop Samuel Seabury? In part, it was due to the differences they had over the cause of liberty. As a New England Anglican, Seabury had been a keen Loyalist and stinging critic of the American revolutionary cause.[5] Furthermore, Bishop Seabury was also an adherent to the High Church doctrine of apostolic succession, a view that was de-emphasized by the Anglican Low Church.[6] Washington's diary shows that he carefully chose his words spoken to his guest John Lowe (who was himself a Scottish Anglican and a tutor in the Washington household)[7] before he recorded his personal lack of desire to correspond with the newly ordained Seabury.

Bishop Samuel Seabury was the first American bishop. He was a High Churchman and an opponent of the American Revolution. Washington wrote in his diary that he did not wish to open correspondence with Bishop Seabury following his ordination as Bishop.

This was not a rejection of bishops per se, for Washington was always open to Episcopal bishops, including Bishop Provoost in New York and Bishop White in Philadelphia. As we will see throughout this chapter, he also enjoyed correspondence with an Anglican bishop[8] and was remembered in the will of another, receiving from him a Bible which Washington subsequently bequeathed to his lifelong friend, neighbor, and, pastor, the Loyalist Reverend Lord Bryan Fairfax.[9] His diary note emphasized the "*new* ordained Bishop"

Below the surface of Washington's studied silence and carefully chosen words, there was a major problem that had only begun to be addressed in the Anglican fold.

As noted above, Bishop Seabury from Connecticut had been ordained as the first American Episcopal bishop in 1783.[10] Washington's problem was not with bishops; it was with Bishop Seabury. He had sought ordination independent of the concerns of Anglicans in the Low Church tradition, and he did so from the hands of Scottish bishops, who were more sympathetic to the Catholic side of the royal family, not the normal bishop of London, who had Protestant sympathies. This ecclesiastical maneuvering left the Low Church patriotic laymen in America feeling uncomfortable with Bishop Seabury and with little incentive or enthusiasm to embrace his leadership.

Washington never revealed this attitude outside of his diary, except in his method of deeds, not words. His silence toward Bishop Seabury spoke loudly. Seabury never attempted to open dialogue with Washington; however, Seabury's ally, Reverend John C. Ogden, did contact him. Washington never answered the letter, even though Ogden wrote several plaintive letters appealing to him to help the New England Episcopacy, since they faced stiff opposition from the New England Congregationalists.[11]

As we have seen, Washington's silence was reserved for those with whom he simply did not want to risk having an embarrassing or explosive conversation. Examples of this include: Thomas Paine;[12] irate opponents of the Jay Treaty;[13] and New England High Churchman, the Reverend John C. Ogden.[14] Washington's unwillingness to correspond with Bishop Seabury, who had been ordained by Scottish rather than English bishops, also seems to be consistent with his determination to avoid bringing European conflicts onto American soil.[15]

APOSTOLIC SUCCESSION IN THE ANGLICAN TRADITION[16]

In a popular study on apostolic succession that Washington had in his library, Bishop Seabury wrote an explanation for the Anglican Church that openly criticized the other English Protestant churches.[17] In his view, no other church's ordination or celebration of the Lord's Supper were valid if they could not directly establish an unbroken line of the laying on of hands all the way back to the apostles.[18] In Seabury's mind, the ability to establish this unbroken apostolic succession for the Anglican clergy was what gave the Anglican Church its validity.

These beliefs of Seabury and many High Church Anglicans had a tendency to separate the Episcopal Church from other Protestant bodies descending from English sources, like Presbyterians and Independents. Not only did Seabury oppose Washington politically, he opposed Anglicans and Presbyterians communing together, as Washington had done at Morristown. Washington was comfortable to commune with Christians of other denominations because he was a Low Churchman. Seabury opposed such ecumenical fellowship, since his doctrine of apostolic succession insisted on the exclusiveness of the Anglican Church.

Low Churchman, the Reverend Mason Gallagher, explains how the Low Church tradition, reflected by George Washington and his close friend, fellow-churchman, and Supreme Court Justice, John Jay, distanced itself from the apostolic succession view of Bishop Seabury. We read that "Mr. Jay finding, on his removal to Bedford, no Episcopal Church in the vicinity, constantly attended one belonging to the Presbyterian nor did he scruple to unite with his fellow Christians of that persuasion commemorating the passion of their common Lord."[19] In other words, John Jay did not have a problem worshiping with his Presbyterian brothers in Christ, even though he was an Episcopalian. This mentality exemplifies the Low Church Anglican tradition, to which Washington also belonged.

When Washington was encamped with his army at Morristown, he allegedly wrote a note to Reverend Dr. Johnes, the Presbyterian pastor, inquiring whether he would be welcome to partake of the semi-annual Communion in his church on the following Lord's Day. He stated that he was a member of the Church of England, but was without exclusive partialities as a Christian. "He accepted the invitation, and received with his fellow Christians of other name the memorial of the dying love of their common Lord."[20]

Washington's magnanimous spirit of Low Church Anglicanism was well reflected in his letter to Marquis de Lafayette. "Being no bigot myself to any mode of worship, I am disposed to indulge the professors of Christianity in the church, that road to Heaven, which to them shall seem the most direct plainest easiest and least liable to exception."[21] This view was anathema to High Churchman Seabury. But Washington did not keep his broad church views close to his chest and only communicate them to his close friends, like Marquis de Lafayette. He actually seized a moment in answering a public address from the General Convention of Bishops to make this point. Writing from New York on August 18, 1789, the president answered an address from the General Convention of Bishops, clergy, and laity of the Protestant Episcopal Church in New York, New Jersey, Pennsylvania, Delaware, Maryland, Virginia, and North Carolina:

> On this occasion…it would ill become me to conceal the joy I have
> felt in perceiving the fraternal affection, which appears to increase

every day among the friends of genuine religion. It affords edifying prospects indeed, to see Christians of different denominations, dwell together in more charity and conduct themselves in respect to each other, with a more Christian-like spirit than ever they have done in any former age, or in any other Nation.[22]

What Washington described as a gracious "Christian-like spirit" differed markedly from the impact of the High Church practice. Low Churchman advocate Reverend Gallagher writes referring to President Washington and Chief Justice John Jay:

When one considers the offensiveness of language and action which unfortunately so largely characterizes the Protestant Episcopal Church, with respect to fellowship with the greater bodies of Evangelical Christians around them, it is refreshing to contemplate the spirit and action of these two greatest and grandest of American Episcopal laymen.[23]

So the Low Church's critique of the narrower apostolic succession view of the High Church manifested itself in Washington's lack of desire to correspond with the newly ordained Bishop Seabury. When Washington wrote to the Episcopal Church leaders and celebrated the ecumenicity of the churches in America, this actually was only true of the Episcopal Church in its Low Church expression, such as that seen in Virginia and under Bishop Samuel Provoost of New York City, and initially of Bishop William White of Philadelphia. Thus, Washington's letter of ecumenical diversity marked by a "more Christian-like spirit than ever" was a gracious yet challenging critique of the Episcopal Church, wherein several of its clergy maintained the apostolic succession teaching of Bishop Seabury. Therefore, those who hold up as evidence that Washington was a Deist and that's why he refused to have anything to do with Bishop Seabury are reading too much into the matter.

GEORGE WASHINGTON VERSUS REVEREND JAMES ABERCROMBIE

A similar but less obvious expression of Washington's theme of Christian grace in his Anglican Church appears in his response to a letter from the rector, church wardens, and vestrymen of the United Episcopal Churches of Christ Church and St. Peter's. This was in response to Bishop White and his church leaders as Washington was leaving Philadelphia at the end of his second term in office. Written on March 2,

1797, the president acknowledged the expression of their approval of his work and the promise of their prayers. He was confident that he would enter retirement with a heartfelt satisfaction stemming from his own conscience, the people's approval, coupled with the hope of future happiness. But Washington also commented on an aspect of his experience in the local church context. He said,

> It is with peculiar satisfaction I can say, that, prompted by a high sense of duty in my attendance on public worship, I have been gratified, during my residence among you, by the liberal and interesting discourses which have been delivered in your Churches.[24]

One can understand President Washington's high sense of duty in attending public worship, since the congregation prayed for the president's salvation every public service. But Washington also affirmed his peculiar satisfaction with the "liberal and interesting discourses delivered in your churches." (In this context, the word "liberal" means charitable or gracious.)

Apparently he even embraced the public rebuke given by the Reverend James Abercrombie to the president for leaving before the Communion service.[25] That certainly was an "interesting" sermon. But had it been a "liberal" or a generously charitable sermon? Perhaps with the same gracious and challenging manner as was proffered in his answer to the Episcopalians' address eight years earlier, Washington was giving a gentle critique. Did the churches under Bishop White and Reverend James Abercrombie's leadership allow "room" or "latitude"[26] for varying views and practices that inevitably existed in the church? In other words, Washington was rebuked from the pulpit for leaving before Communion was served. He here not only received the rebuke, but gently made the case for a Low Church, instead of the High Church approach.

While we wish to respect fully Reverend Abercrombie's theological concerns, it has often seemed strange to us that a newly ordained understudy of a bishop would seek to preach a sermon consciously to rebuke the President of the United States that worshiped in the bishop's church. Would it not normally have been the prerogative of the bishop of the church to privately discuss such things and minister to the spiritual needs of the president? Was this due to Abercrombie's theological zeal, his immaturity of ministry, or was it due to an expression of a personal vindication? It seems to us that all three of these causes were involved.

James Abercrombie had been trained under Bishop White and so shared his views. He was a late arrival in ministry due to several adversities that had kept him in various business positions which he had disdained. He had only been ordained a year or so when he unleashed his sermonic assault aimed at the president. So immaturity was clearly a factor, but there seems to have been a principle of personal vindication as well. As it turns out, Washington had passed over Abercrombie for a government position, even though he came with strong advocates and recommendations.

Apparently, in 1793 Abercrombie had sought the office of treasurer, but Washington denied the application in compliance with a resolution forbidding the appointment of two persons from the same state in any one department. Frustrated and disappointed, Abercrombie renewed his efforts to be ordained as an Episcopal priest and rapidly succeeded.[27]

In his new role, Abercrombie was now in a position—consciously or unconsciously—to assuage his frustration toward Washington, who had rejected him as treasurer. So in his historic sermon aimed in large part toward President Washington, Reverend Abercrombie simultaneously pressed a High Church insistence on consistent Communion and seemed to even the score with the president as well.

This interpretation would appear uncharitable if it weren't also sustained by Reverend Abercrombie's judgmental remarks years later where he exclaimed that President "Washington was a Deist!" He then begrudgingly backed away from his verdict, admitting that George Washington was a member of the same church as Abercrombie was and thus was a professing Christian.[28]

THE BATTLE OF THE BISHOPS: BISHOP WHITE CASTS THE VOTE THAT BREAKS THE TIE

As we continue our story of the development of the Episcopal Church's government in the United States after the Revolutionary War and its influence on Washington, we turn next to Washington and Bishop White. William White, the Bishop of Philadelphia was undoubtedly a patriot, holding fast during the war (when other Anglicans were Tories). White was an ecclesiastical diplomat to the differing factions of the church. Bishop White was also an outstanding visionary of the church. All of these things would seem to qualify him for the ear, let alone the heart of his fellow Episcopalian, the president. To understand Washington's studied silence to Bishop White, consider the struggle that existed between America's first three ordained Episcopalian bishops. We believe the simple answer is that Washington did not agree with Bishop White's choices in some complicated church politics. While outwardly a Low Churchman, he sometimes acted as a High Churchman, to

Washington's displeasure.

Samuel Provoost and William White were ordained in 1787 by the Anglican Bishop of London. They had been keen supporters of the American cause. In fact, White had been the successor to Reverend Jacob Duché, after he had left his role as chaplain to Congress and fled to England in the wake of British conquest of Philadelphia. White not only served in Duché's stead at Christ Church Philadelphia, but also as his replacement as the chaplain to the Continental Congress.

Bishop William White

Bishop Provoost served as chaplain to the Senate under the new Constitution. Provoost was such a loyal American and Low Churchman that he did all he could to prevent the union of his Episcopal churches in New York with the leadership of Loyalist and High Church Bishop Seabury.

How then could there be a united Episcopal Church in America, given the Tory and High Church sympathies of Seabury and the patriotism and Low Church perspectives of White and Provoost? These latter two bishops, as Low Churchmen, were sympathetic in some measure with the theological school called "Latitudinarianism." This system was so named by its opponents because of its desire to give greater "Latitude" in theological and ecclesiastical matters.[29] One of the Latitudinarian distinctives was the broader view of Communion we have already mentioned. This meant that the Anglican clergyman could minister in good conscience to those outside the Episcopalian sphere. Thus Latitudinarians, like the early Bishop White and Bishop Provoost, held a theological perspective that did not emphasize the primacy of the apostolic succession of the Anglican or Episcopal tradition which was so critical for Seabury's view of the church.[30]

The process of creating the Protestant Episcopal Church began on September 27, 1785, when the General Convention met in Christ Church in Philadelphia, the church where the then Reverend William White served. Bishop Seabury refused to attend, because no provision had been made for a bishop to preside. Reverend Samuel Provoost was not yet a bishop at this time, and Provoost refused to work with Seabury, since he was a Loyalist and had advocated for the meeting to be conducted without the presiding of a bishop.[31] The newly-ordained Seabury rightly feared the impact that the spirit of independence of the American laity could have on his rule in the church.

The Reverend White, also not yet consecrated as a bishop, was chosen to preside.

The assembly drew up a plan for obtaining the episcopate and began to elect bishops. William White became the bishop-elect for Philadelphia and David Griffith was the bishop-elect for Virginia. In New York, the choice fell to Samuel Provoost.

The second General Convention of the Episcopal Church met in Philadelphia on June 20, 1786. An attempt was made to deny the validity of Seabury's ordination, but bishop-elect White managed to defuse this action. Later, a letter dated July 4th arrived containing the good news that the British Parliament had authorized the consecration of American bishops. Before adjourning, testimonials were signed for the consecration of White, Provoost, and Griffith. Reverend Griffith from Virginia, however, could not raise the money for the trip, so Provoost and White left for England and were consecrated on February 4, 1787, in Lambeth Palace.

In this instance, the Low Church views of Washington's Virginia spoke loudly, when no one stepped forward to provide the funds to send their bishop-elect, the Reverend David Griffith, to London to be consecrated as their new bishop. Virginia's resistance to an American Episcopate continued to be expressed.

When the news of White's and Provoost's departure reached Seabury, he was in a state of anxiety. What was to become of him and the churchmen of New England? His emphasis on Episcopal authority and his exclusion of the laity from church councils had made him unpopular outside of his own sphere in New England. Episcopalians outside of New England, especially in the South, where clergy and laity saw little need for bishops, shared Washington's lack of desire to work with Bishop Seabury. This was especially seen in the opposition of now newly ordained Bishop Samuel Provoost.

Bishop Seabury determined it was time to pursue a diplomatic course and wrote conciliatory letters of congratulations to the two men. He urged them to meet with him to discuss a plan for church union. Bishop Provoost never answered Seabury's letter, but Bishop White responded diplomatically, welcoming the joint meeting.

The members of the Episcopal Constitutional Convention met in Christ Church, Philadelphia, July 28, 1789, but Bishop Provoost pleaded illness and was unable to attend. Bishop White presided over a single body, or chamber. Although many may not have liked Seabury, all factions had become weary of discord. To refuse to recognize Bishop Seabury's consecration would perpetuate the divided state of the church. Finally, it was unanimously resolved, "that the consecration of the Right Reverend Dr. Seabury to the Episcopal Office is valid." The way was then open for the reconciliation of Episcopalians throughout the country.

A further amendment created a House of Bishops. White also wrote to Bishop

Seabury affirming his support. By creating two houses, the General House of Laymen and the Body of Bishops, a bi-cameral system of governance was established that in some ways paralleled the United States bi-cameral House of Representatives and the United States Senate.

The second session opened on September 30th. Bishop Provoost, feeling that harmony in the church had been bought at too high a price, refused to attend. On October 16, 1789, the *Constitution and Canons* and the *Book of Common Prayer* were ratified by "the Bishops, the Clergy, and the Laity of the Protestant Episcopal Church in the United States of America...."[32]

Bishop White's cooperation with Bishop Seabury, however, came at the expense of Low Churchman Bishop Provoost. The bi-cameral government of the church meant that the bishops would ultimately rule in the Protestant Episcopalian Church through the House of Bishops. Consequently, Bishop William White cast the vote that broke the tie in favor of the High Church views of Bishop Seabury. But the Low Church sentiments of Anglicans such as Washington, Supreme Court Chief Justice John Jay, and Bishop Samuel Provoost did not disappear. Low Churchmen remained loyal to their new church, but also as much as possible to their Low Church principles.

WASHINGTON'S RELATIONSHIP WITH THE THREE AMERICAN BISHOPS

Washington was cognizant of the battle of the bishops and he knew of or had met all three newly ordained American bishops.

One of the special duties of a bishop was to ordain the clergy. Washington's diaries twice mention ordination. As we have already seen, the first was the ordination of Bishop Seabury. The second was the service of ordination that Washington saw in June 1787 by Bishop White in Philadelphia. This was history-making for Washington. He had never seen an ordination, since previously the laying on of hands had to be done in England.

Normally,[33] the Bishop of London had ordained the American Anglican clergy. Given this Episcopalian epic-making event of an American ordination, it is no surprise that Washington recorded the event in his diary. Washington's diary mentions that two gentlemen were ordained to be deacons: "June 1787, Sunday. 17th. Went to Church. Heard Bishop White preach, and see him ordain two Gentlemen Deacons."[34]

Because Washington was a Low Churchman and had an interest in the ordination of clergy by the new American bishops, it is important to understand his relationships with these bishops. He would not correspond with High Church Bishop Samuel Seabury. But what was his relationship to Low Church Bishop Samuel Provoost and mediating Bishop William White? True to Washington's and Provoost's Low Church principles, there is evidence of warm interfaith fellowship. This ecumenical fellowship occurred during Washington's presidency in the New York context under Bishop Provoost.

George and Martha Washington entertained Chief Justice John Jay and his wife, the vice president and Mrs. Adams, who were Congregationalists and Low Churchman Bishop Provoost as well as others. His diary records a meal shared on Sunday, April 11, 1790, which included Provoost and others.[35]

Such a fellowship meal occurred again in December. Washington's diary shows that in December 1789, Bishop Provoost, Chaplain of the Senate and Bishop of New York City, Chief Justice John Jay, as well as Reformed Clergyman and Chaplain of the House of Representatives, William Linn were present for dinner also.

Washington's ecumenical spirit[36] enabled him to be close to Reformed clergyman Reverend Linn. During the war, he had forged deep friendships with Reformed and Presbyterian churches and their leaders.[37] Presbyterian clergyman, Reverend Samuel Davies had prophesied of Washington's service for his nation in the aftermath of the Braddock disaster. Also, his warmth toward his Reformed and Presbyterian clerical acquaintances is born out in letters and friendships between Dr. James Craik, Reverend William Linn, Dr. John Witherspoon, and Reverend William Gordon. As noted earlier, Washington chose to stay with the Reformed pastor Limbrecht Herman in Germantown for several weeks in 1793, during the yellow fever epidemic in Philadelphia.

Thus, Washington's Low Church ecumenical spirit also explains why he was comfortable with the image of the Eucharist and used it in strategic places in his public writings. This fact strips Professor Boller's conjecture regarding Washington's alleged non-communing of all its force: "It is quite probable that at no time in his life—though we have no firsthand evidence of any kind for the pre-Revolutionary period—did Washington consider his mind and heart in a proper condition to receive the sacrament. Hypocrisy is surely no Christian virtue; and the pietists might well have applauded Washington's basic honesty and integrity in this matter."[38]

Would not the height of hypocrisy be to quote the very biblical verse that gives us the name of the chalice—"the cup of blessing"—and do so in a context that describes all Americans being offered such a cup to drink as a symbol of national blessing, and yet all the while not believing in the image at all? Rather, Washington's use of the image underscored his own historic practice and willingness to come to the Table and, so symbolically called on the entire nation to come to the national Table of spiritual blessing. In so writing, Washington was not reflecting the exclusivity of the apostolic succession view of the High Church. As a Low Churchman, he called on all Americans to partake of the divine blessings given at the Table of national liberty.

Washington's Low Church sympathies and friend-ship with Low Churchman Bishop Samuel Provoost, John Jay, as well as Reformed Clergyman William Linn[39] and his antipathy to Bishop Seabury, set the stage for Washington's limited relationship with Bishop William White. The ecumenical gatherings assembled by President Washington in New

Bishop Samuel Provoost of New York was a patriot, a Low Churchman and a personal friend of Washington. He served as chaplain to the U.S. Senate while it met in New York City.

York at the family table do not seem to have occurred in Philadelphia, when Washington was under the spiritual jurisdiction of Bishop White.[40] Why did Washington choose to change this? Did Bishop White's compromise with the High Church Bishop Seabury, at the expense of Washington's Low Church Virginian Episcopal views and the Low Church views of his friends Bishop Provoost and Chief Justice John Jay, help to make this a reality? It is an argument from silence, but it seems to conform with the known facts in a much greater way than the superficial charge that Washington was a Deist because he didn't take Communion in Philadelphia.

WASHINGTON'S NON-COMMUNICATION WITH BISHOP WILLIAM WHITE

We concur that all of the evidence indicates that George Washington did not communicate with Bishop White about spiritual matters in Philadelphia, nor commune at his church's Table. We believe that this can be explained in part when we understand the significant results that occurred from Bishop White's relationship with Bishop Seabury. When Bishop White cast the swing vote for Bishop Seabury, he not only set aside the rule of laymen in the Episcopal church, a view that Washington's Virginia Committee on Religion had advocated for years, but he also set aside the 1785 *Proposed Prayer Book* with its July Fourth service. The new Episcopal Church had gone the opposite direction of what Low Churchmen, such as Washington's friend John Jay, had hoped to establish.

Washington's careful silence concerning controversial or difficult matters was habitual, whether in matters of ecclesiastical or government politics.[41] Even though he clearly did not approve of the Bishop Seabury approach, with his reserved dignity, Washington remained silent, yet loyal to his church.

Bishop White had compromised with Bishop Seabury, and in so doing, distanced himself from Bishop Provoost. The results of the compromise were sweeping. A summary of these results can be listed as follows:

1. An elevation of the High Church's emphasis on apostolic succession.

2. A rejection of the Latitudinarian or Broad Church spirit of ecumenical fellowship and communion

3. The elevation of the episcopacy over the governance by laymen.

4. An implicit rebuke of Virginian Episcopalianism, as practiced by Washington for all of his life before the war.

5. A rejection of the views of his friends John Jay and Bishop Samuel Provoost of New York.

6. A negative light was cast on Washington's closeness with Presbyterian and Reformed churches and his acts of communing with them.

7. An honoring of the Tory clergy, such as the Reverends Ogden, Seabury, Duché, Inglis, placing them on par with the pro-Revolutionary clergy, such as Bishop Provoost and Bishop White himself.

8. The loss of Washington's ecumenical fellowship meals under his presidency in Philadelphia, as had been previously held in New York with Reverend Linn, Chief Justice Jay, and Bishop Provoost.

9. The rejection of the American *Proposed Book of Common Prayer.*

10. The loss of the July 4th service, which would have been a natural American commerative service to replace the historic British November 5th celebration of Guy Fawkes Day.

11. The possible creation of tension between Washington's presidential leadership and personal church membership, due to the elevation of the exclusive apostolic succession view.[42] This

naturally created ongoing worries for non-Anglican churches that feared possible religious pressures or persecutions from the new government.[43]

12. The addition of a sacerdotal or priestly element by the inclusion of the word "priest" for "minister" in the new prayer book. George Washington never used the word "priest" for any Protestant clergyman, even though he carefully honored Roman Catholic leaders, while not embracing their theology.[44]

Due to Washington's reserved dignity, he would never have disclosed such critical and personal views to Bishop White for the very same reasons he chose not to correspond with Bishop White's Episcopal partner, Bishop Seabury. We believe this explanation of why Bishop White would not know George Washington's faith views is consistent with all of the known and relevant facts.

WHY DID PRESIDENT WASHINGTON NOT COMMUNE WHILE IN PHILADELPHIA?

So finally, then, why did Washington not commune as president in Philadelphia? We reiterate that we have no explicit writing from Washington's hand as to why he did not commune in Philadelphia. Since he never said so directly, we cannot be dogmatic. But this we can say with confidence, that there is no need, nor evidence, that points to the Deist explanation of professor Boller and others. The explanation offered here is consistent with Washington's Christian faith, his Christian church, and numerous explicit statements in his writings.

Washington, while in Philadelphia, was under the ministry of Bishop White, whose compromise forfeited the Low Church's position in the Church by his reconciliation with the High Church leader, Bishop Seabury—at the expense of Washington's friend, Bishop Samuel Provoost of New York. Thus, his non-communing under Bishop White, who allowed Seabury to subjugate the patriotic Low Church, could have been an expression of his strong conscience.

Perhaps, the absence of any record of personal or inter-denominational and ecumenical fellowship under Bishop White is also a clue. Perhaps, the strong apostolic succession views of Bishop Seabury, openly accommodated by Bishop White, left Washington concerned that as president, he might be too committed to the Episcopal Church, creating fears of an established church in America.

However these matters may be interpreted, it is also clear that Washington's relationship with the Philadelphia Episcopal churches was only complicated by Abercrombie's indirect but intentional criticism of Washington in his sermon.[45]

Finally, given Washington's Low Churchmanship, he was not a frequent communicant by principle and by habit. He had not taken Communion often to begin with. For good or for ill, this was the Virginian Low Church tradition. By personal temperament, Washington would not have discussed this with Bishop White.[46]

Because of Washington's methodical nature, when he would have decided to commune, given that he had no scruple about the frequency of Communion, as a Virginia Low Churchman, it would have been according to his own plan and at what he conceived to be the most appropriate time. As president, he had immense duties, and limited time. As a land owner and citizen he had farm, financial, and family duties.

Given his non-intimacy with Bishop White, his burdens of responsibility that demanded his time, his sense of disappointment that he would be communing under a bishop who took away lay leadership, the Episcopal celebration of of July 4th, and gave a Tory bishop the dominant voice in his childhood church, it is not surprising that Washington chose not to commune in Philadelphia.

Lastly, but not unimportantly, Washington did not commune because of his strict conscience. When the Reverend James Abercrombie issued his sermonic rebuke to the congregation, and specifically to President Washington, he was speaking with the theology of Bishop Seabury. Washington heard it with the spirit of a Low Churchman and respectfully disagreed. Non-communing in this instance comported with his character and personality as well as his conscience.

These same reasons probably governed his Communion practices in New York as well, but clearly to a lesser degree, since the evidence argues he communed on various occasions in New York under Bishop Provoost. His communing on Inauguration Day would be a perfect example of a time when Washington's spiritual and civic duties coincided, and he thus openly communed.

CONCLUSION

The important point to understand here is that George Washington's non-communing did not make him a Deist. Perhaps Washington should have communed more. But then, if we had Washington's strong conscience and extraordinarily busy schedule, and understood his mind, perhaps we would think differently. The point is that the explanation offered here is consistent with Washington himself, honors all the known facts, and in no way requires the incongruent claim that Washington was a Deist.

Again, the facts are that Washington never criticized Christ or Christianity. He did criticize Deism. He also maintained his distance from Bishop Seabury and was uncomfortable with an Episcopacy operated by the High Church principle of apostolic succession. Thus, we conclude that Washington had personal, theological, and ecclesiastical reasons not to commune in Philadelphia. But none of them required him to have been a Deist.

PART VI

George Washington the Deist?

TWENTY THREE

George Washington and the Enlightenment

*"We have abundant reason to rejoice that in this
Land the light of truth and reason has triumphed over the power
of bigotry and superstition, and that every person may here worship
God according to the dictates of his own heart.*

*"In this enlightened Age and in this Land of equal liberty it is
our boast, that a man's religious tenets will not forfeit the protection
of the Laws, nor deprive him of the right of attaining and holding the
highest Offices that are known in the United States."*
George Washington 1793[1]

George Washington came of age during the Age of Reason and thus was influenced by the Enlightenment. But it is a critical point, often missed today, that the Enlightenment was not only an expression of Deistic thought, but it had a Christian expression as well. Scholar and author Michael Novak points out that if the founding fathers were influenced by the Enlightenment, it wasn't the skeptical branch of the same: "The Founders' Enlightenment was not the Enlightenment of Voltaire; it was the Enlightenment of John Locke, a man ever at pains not to tread heavily on Christian sensibilities."[2]

It is disingenuous on the part of some scholars today to present America's founders, including our first president, as men of the Enlightenment, without pointing out the diversity of that umbrella term, "Enlightenment." The views of Enlightenment thinker David Hume, for example, were poles apart from the thinking of Enlightenment thinker Sir William Blackstone, the British jurist who had great influence on America's founders and was a strong advocate of the Holy Bible.

Throughout his long public career, George Washington consciously and consistently spoke and acted as an enlightened leader, advancing reason and eschewing superstition. But that does not mean he did not believe in orthodox Christianity, as some modern writers assert. The purpose of this chapter is to look at George Washington and the Enlightenment.

WASHINGTON AND SUPERSTITION

The confrontation between reason and superstition was part of the Washington family's heritage. The fear of witchcraft that actually prompted a work on the topic by King James himself, was prevalent in Europe, and that fear crossed the ocean with the colonists.

When John Washington, son of Reverend Lawrence Washington, Vicar of Purleigh, came to Virginia in 1657, along with his wife Amphillis and his brother Lawrence, it was feared that a witch had come along on the perilous journey across the high seas to the New World. Captain Prescott immediately determined that he needed no additional risks, and condemned the alleged witch with the fiat: "Hustle this woman into Eternity and save our souls!" So, they tossed the helpless lady into the stormy Atlantic.

Upon their safe arrival in Virginia minus the jettisoned female, John Washington spoke immediately to the authorities, demanding that Captain Prescott be punished for the heartless murder of a helpless woman on the high seas.[3]

Religious persecution had also come to the New World with England's established church, since Anglicanism was enforced by the sword of the crown. James Hutson, chief of the manuscript division for the Library of Congress, describes the painful consequences for those who violated the laws protecting the Church:

> Puritan ministers who refused to conform were fired from their pulpits and threatened with "extirpation from the earth" unless they and their followers toed the line. Exemplary punishments were inflicted on the Puritan stalwarts; one zealot, for example, who

called Anglican bishops "Knobs, wens and bunchy popish flesh," was sentenced in 1630, to life imprisonment, had his property confiscated, his nose split, an ear cut off, and his forehead branded S.S. (sower of sedition).[4]

These were practices that the Washington family neither participated in, nor sanctioned. They had a more humane and just perspective. Lawrence, George's older half-brother and surrogate father, understood the wisdom of religious liberty.

> It has ever been my opinion and I hope it ever will be, that restraints on conscience are cruel in regard to those on whom they are imposed, and injurious to the country imposing them. England, Holland, and Prussia, I may quote as examples, and much more Pennsylvania, which has flourished under that delightful liberty, so as to become the admiration of every man who considers the short time it has been settled. . . .This colony (Virginia) was greatly settled in the latter part of Charles the First's time, and during the usurpation, by the zealous church-men; and that spirit, which was then brought in, has ever since continued; so that, except a few Quakers, we have no dissenters. But what has been the consequence? We have increased by slow degrees, whilst our neighboring colonies, whose natural advantages are greatly inferior to ours, have become populous.[5]

Lawrence mentions Pennsylvania in a positive light (in contrast with Anglican Virginia). You will recall that the northern colony was founded by William Penn (1644-1718), a devout Quaker minister, with the express purpose of providing religious liberty. No one there was to be punished for religious views. Penn called this the "holy experiment," and it succeeded. It attracted many settlers and its capital, Philadelphia, eventually became the capital of the fledgling, new country.[6]

George Washington reflected his forbearers' perspective as he expressed his own views. As General Washington was retiring from his military command, he wrote a circular to each of the thirteen governors of the finally independent states. Writing from "Head Quarters" on June 8, 1783, the enlightened commander of the victorious American army described the "auspicious period" in which "the United States came into existence as a nation."

The foundation of our Empire was not laid in the gloomy age of Ignorance and Superstition, but at an Epocha when the rights of mankind were better understood and more clearly defined, than at any former period, the researches of the human mind, after social happiness, have been carried to a great extent, the Treasures of knowledge, acquired by the labours of Philosophers, Sages and Legislatures, through a long succession of years, are laid open for our use, and their collected wisdom may be happily applied in the Establishment of our forms of Government; the free cultivation of Letters, the unbounded extension of Commerce, the progressive refinement of Manners, the growing liberality of sentiment, and *above all, the pure and benign light of Revelation, have had a meliorating influence on mankind and increased the blessings of Society.* At this auspicious period, the United States came into existence as a Nation, and if their Citizens should not be completely free and happy, the fault will be intirely their own.[7] (emphasis added)

This one passage alone shows that Washington did not view religion in opposition to their enlightened times. The "pure and benign light of Revelation" has a positive impact on society "above all" during their era, an era not marked by "Ignorance and Superstition." "Revelation" here refers to the Bible as the revealed Word of God. Deists and Enlightenment thinkers placed reason above revelation, and they denied that God had revealed himself in the scriptures.[8] Washington, on the other hand, valued revelation as well as reason. Therefore, it is incorrect to call him a Deist. (This is the same letter, by the way, that concludes with the point that America will never be a happy nation unless the citizens imitate Jesus Christ, whom Washington calls "the divine Author of our blessed religion."[9])

CORRESPONDENCE WITH THOMAS PAINE

As the commander of the Continental Army, Washington was a correspondent with none other than Thomas Paine, the author of both the celebrated *Common Sense* (1776) as well as the controversial *Age of Reason* (written in stages some twenty years later—Part 1 in 1794, Part 2 in 1795, and Part 3 in 1807). The former book's potent rhetoric and trenchant reasoning decisively moved colonial public opinion in favor of revolution. With the publication of the latter, Paine's critical mind delivered a poignant critique of revealed religion, and in particular, Christianity. Thereby Paine assumed both the roles of apologist for the American Revolution and later, foremost opponent of Christian orthodoxy and an acknowledged arch-advocate for Deism, the philosophical expression of Enlightenment theology.

Apparently, it was Paine's criticism of the Bible that turned President Washington *against* him. Referring to the *Age of Reason*, the *Funk & Wagnalls New Encyclopedia* notes: "The book alienated George Washington and most of his [Paine's] old friends."[10]

Note what Benjamin Franklin, not known to have been fully orthodox or deeply devout in his faith, wrote to Paine upon receipt of the manuscript of the *Age of Reason*. He did not think it wise for Paine to publish it:

> I have read your manuscript with some attention...the consequence of printing this piece will be a great deal of odium drawn upon yourself, mischief to you, and no benefit to others. He that spits into the wind, spits in his own face. But were you to succeed, do you imagine any good would be done by it?...think about how great a portion of mankind consists of weak and ignorant men and women, and of inexperienced, inconsiderate youth of both sexes, who have need of the motives of religion to restrain them from vice, to support their virtue, and retain them in the practice of it till it becomes habitual, which is the great point for its security. And perhaps you are indebted to her originally, that is, to your religious education, for the habits of virtue upon which you now justly value yourself.[11]

Long before Paine lost whatever faith he may have had,[12] long before he wrote his anti-Christian polemics, he set to writing clever apologies for the American Revolution. General Washington wrote to Thomas Paine on September 18, 1782:

> Sir: I have the pleasure to acknowledge your favor of the 7th. Instant, informing of your proposal to present me with fifty Copies of your last publication, for the Amusement of the Army. [13]

What Washington was referring to was the May 31, 1782, No. XIII edition of Paine's publication, *The Crisis*. One of the earlier editions of *The Crisis* began famously: "These are the times that try men's souls."[14] George Washington was not a superstitious man, yet he did have a sense of humor. The general believed that his army would find amusement, as Paine's wit ridiculed the British. At the end of seven years of war, Paine teased the British mind's superstitious and religious interpretation of the number "seven." This augured well, argued Paine, for an end to the war itself. Paine with obvious relish reasoned,

> I fully believe we have seen our worst days over....I draw this opinion, not only from the difficulties we know they [the British] are in...but from the peculiar effect, which certain periods of time have more or less upon all Men. The British have accustomed themselves to think of the term of seven years in a manner different to other periods of time. They acquire this partly by habit, by religion, by reason and by *superstition*. They serve seven years apprenticeship; They elect their parliament for seven years; They punish by seven years transportation, or the duplicate, or triplicate of that term; Their leases run in the same manner; and they read that Jacob served seven years for one wife and seven years for another; and the same term likewise, extinguishes all obligations (in certain cases) of debt or matrimony; and thus, this particular period, by a variety of concurrences has obtained an influence in their minds superior to that of any other number.
>
> They have now had seven years war, and are not an inch farther on the Continent than when they began. The Superstitious and the populous part will conclude that it is not to be; and the reasonable part will think they have tried an unsuccessful scheme long enough, and that it is in vain to try it any longer."[15] (emphasis added)

Washington highly compliments Paine for this work: "For this Intention you have my sincere thanks, not only on my own Account, but for the pleasure, I doubt not, the Gentlemen of the Army will receive from the perusal of your Pamphlets. Your Observation on the *Period of Seven Years*, as it applies itself to and affects British Minds, are ingenious, and I wish it may not fail of its Effects in the present Instance."[16]

Washington's sense of being part of the more enlightened era, where reason was important, connected him with royalty as well. As Washington enjoyed the retirement interim between his military and presidential careers, he took pleasure in his correspondence with international leaders. His sense of being an enlightened leader on the world stage manifested itself as he corresponded with his close friend, former colleague and French ally, Marquis de Chastellux. The letter received from the royal leader brought along accolades from the King and Queen of France themselves.

Although reluctant to speak of himself, in a letter dated August 18, 1786, Washington assured Chastellux that he was pleased to receive the "*commendations of the virtuous and enlightened part of our species. . . .*" Speaking of himself in the third person of American nobility, he explained to the marquis that "he cannot be indifferent to the applauses of so enlightened a nation, nor to the suffrages of the King and Queen who have been pleased to honor it with their royal approbation."[17]

Washington's description of royal France as an enlightened nation did not imply anti-Christian beliefs. The royal title was "His most Christian King" or "His most Catholic King." In this sense, "enlightened" meant culturally advanced. But the "enlightened" idea of religious liberty that Washington so often celebrated had not yet arrived in France. The Huguenots were still under the crushing weight of royal persecution.

THE DIVERSITY OF ENLIGHTENMENT THINKERS

An important question to consider is this: Was the Enlightenment, by definition, an explosion of unbelief, or were there key elements of the Enlightenment that were Christian in orientation? The answer is the latter. John Locke was a leading figure of the political side of the Enlightenment and has never been considered a Deist. His book, *The Reasonableness of Christianity*, while not completely orthodox in its Christianity, certainly puts Locke in the Christian camp far more than in the Deist camp.

Locke's *2nd Treatise on Government* is held to have been important to the founding fathers, is full of biblical citations to help bolster his points. John Locke wrote many commentaries on the books of the Bible and paraphrases of portions of scripture. About God's Word, he said, "The Bible is one of the greatest blessings bestowed by God on the children of men. It has God for its author; salvation for its end, and truth without any mixture for its matter. It is all pure, all sincere; nothing too much; nothing wanting."[18]

Another example of an "Enlightenment thinker" who was solidly in the Christian camp is Sir William Blackstone (1723-1780), the exceptionally well-known British jurist. Blackstone wrote four volumes of commentaries on the British law considered to be perhaps the most important reflections on laws in the last few centuries. These commentaries were influential to the founders, including Jefferson, as he penned the Declaration of Independence. When Abraham Lincoln taught himself the law, he was able to do so because he had come across the second volume of this four-volume set.

Blackstone's commentaries made a major impact on the United States Supreme Court for several generations of the court.

Blackstone writes, "Thus when the Supreme Being formed the universe, and created matter out of nothing, He impressed certain principles upon that matter, from which it can never depart, and without which it would cease to be."[19]

These principles to which Blackstone refers are "the Law of Nature," which was "coequal with mankind and dictated by God himself."[20] Blackstone sees natural law as the will of God that can be discerned from nature in general. But, because of the sinfulness of man, because man's understanding was "full of ignorance and error," there was a need for revelation. The Bible was that revelation. "The doctrines thus delivered we call the revealed or divine law," Blackstone writes, "and they are to be found only in the holy scriptures."[21]

Thus, there is the law of nature (or natural law) and then there is the law known only by revelation as found in the Bible. Blackstone writes, "Upon these two foundations, the law of nature and the law of revelation, depend all human laws; that is to say, no human laws should be suffered to contradict these."[22] The revealed laws of God are not to be contradicted by man's law. These are the thoughts of a man often categorized as a figure of the Enlightenment. Therefore, we see that the Enlightenment was hardly universally anti-Christian (as is sometimes portrayed today). To the extent that Washington was impacted by "the Enlightenment," it was not by the atheistic, Deistic and anti-Christian side of the movement (as espoused by men like Rousseau and Voltaire).

GENERAL CHARLES LEE AND DEISTIC BELIEFS

Yet, the unbelief, fashionable in some quarters in the last decades of the eighteenth century, impacted even one of Washington's own generals, Charles Lee. General Lee was highly concerned about religious issues and was substantially impacted by Deistic thought. Thus, in his last will and testament we find the following words that take traditional Christianity to task:

The Will of General Charles Lee:

> I desire most earnestly, that I may not be buried in any church, or church-yard, or within a mile of any Presbyterian or Anabaptist meeting-house; for since I have resided in this country, I have kept so much bad company when living, that I do not chuse to continue it when dead.

> I recommend my soul to the Creator of all worlds and of all
> creatures; who must, from his visible attributes, be indifferent to
> their modes of worship or creeds, whether Christians, Mahometans,
> or Jews; whether instilled by education, or taken up by reflection;
> whether more or less absurd; as a weak mortal can no more be
> answerable for his persuasions, notions, or even skepticism in
> religion, than for the colour of his skin.[23]

Charles Lee made another statement, however, where he longed for the practice of what he called "real Christianity."[24]

Washington successfully pursued a court martial of General Lee due to his retreat at Battle of Monmouth. Washington's military leadership as well as his religion stood in stark contrast to that of General Charles Lee.

AN ENLIGHTENED PEOPLE WITH AN ENLIGHTENED PRESIDENT

The Enlightenment emphasis upon reason, with its assault upon superstition and religious bigotry, remained stamped upon George Washington's vocabulary throughout his presidency. Thus, the president was confident that the enlightened Congress would heed his call for funding of the arts and sciences and to secure scholarly and accomplished professors. In his eighth and final address to Congress, dated December 7, 1796, he wrote:

> The Assembly to which I address myself, is too enlightened not to
> be fully sensible how much a flourishing state of the Arts and
> Sciences, contributes to National prosperity and reputation. True it
> is, that our Country, much to its honor, contains many Seminaries
> of learning highly respectable and useful; but the funds upon which
> they rest, are too narrow, to command the ablest Professors, in the
> different departments of liberal knowledge, for the Institution
> contemplated, though they would be excellent auxiliaries.[25]

The word "liberal" here meant well-read or well-studied, and did not have the political or social connotations that the word contains today.

Finally, at the end of his illustrious career, in his Farewell Address he spoke of "the truly enlightened and independent Patriot." Writing to all his fellow citizens, Washington advocated nothing less than a national enlightenment. He wished "that public opinion should be enlightened. . . ." for a great nation needed to be an enlightened people.

> It will be worthy of a free, enlightened, and, at no distant period, a great Nation, to give to mankind the magnanimous and too novel example of a People always guided by an exalted justice and benevolence. . . . [26]

Thus, Washington's letters indicate that he had an appreciation for the more enlightened thinking that was taking hold in America. But this did not distance him from religious leaders, as was seen in the case of the will of General Charles Lee. Instead, Washington, writing to clergyman Reverend John Lathrop on June 22, 1788, spoke of common vision of both "reason and religion":

> How pitiful, in the eye of reason and religion, is that false ambition which desolates the world with fire and sword for the purposes of conquest and fame; when compared to the milder virtues of making our neighbours and our fellow men as happy as their frail conditions and perishable natures will permit *them to be*! I am happy to find that the proposed general government meets with your approbation as indeed it does with *that* of the most disinterested and discerning men. The Convention of this State is now in session, and I cannot but hope from all the accounts I receive that the Constitution will be adopted by it; though not without considerable opposition. I trust, however, that the commendable example exhibited by the minority in your State will not be without its salutary influence in this. In truth it appears to me that (should the proposed government be generally and harmoniously adopted) it will be a new phenomenon in the political and moral world; and an astonishing victory gained by enlightened reason over brutal force. [27]

Washington was delighted that this minister from Massachusetts was pleased with the proposed Constitution. The future president saw the Constitution as a victory of reason over brute force, yet nowhere did Washington imply that "enlightened reason" was an assault against true religion. Instead, "reason and religion" joined together in opposition to selfish ambition's use of war for personal gain.

WASHINGTON ON EDUCATION AS ENLIGHTENMENT

Washington wrote to Mathew Carey on June 25, 1788, discussing Carey's idea of a publication entitled "the American Museum." Washington wanted to see knowledge spread throughout the country, because it safeguarded liberty and improved the morals of an enlightened people:

> For myself, I entertain an high idea of the utility of periodical Publications: insomuch that I could heartily desire, copies of the Museum and Magazines, as well as common Gazettes, might be spread through every city, town and village in America. I consider such easy vehicles of knowledge, more happily calculated than any other, to preserve the liberty, stimulate the industry and meliorate the morals of an enlightened and free People.[28]

In his First Annual Address to Congress, January 8, 1790, the president explained the importance of knowledge to the new republic. Simply, the American experiment would not work if the people were ignorant:

> Knowledge is in every country the surest basis of public happiness… To the security of a free Constitution it contributes in various ways: By convincing those who are intrusted with the public administration, that every valuable end of Government is best answered by the enlightened confidence of the people: and by teaching the people themselves to know and to value their own rights; to discern and provide against invasions of them; to distinguish between oppression and the necessary exercise of lawful authority; between burthens proceeding from a disregard to their convenience and those resulting from the inevitable exigencies of Society; to discriminate the spirit of Liberty from that of licentiousness, cherishing the first, avoiding the last, and uniting a speedy, but temperate vigilance against encroachments, with an inviolable respect to the Laws.[29]

In other words, a well-educated citizenry is essential to maintain both the law and liberty and for having the ability to distinguish between liberty and license. This discernment comes through education. Washington insisted that religion and morality were integral to a sound education.

Washington, along with the other founders, gave us the Northwest Ordinance in 1787, which was then readopted in 1789. The Northwest Ordinance is one of our nation's four founding documents—along with the Declaration of Independence, the Constitution, and the Articles of Confederation. The goal of the Northwest Ordinance was to retain a certain degree of uniformity as new states were being added to the new nation. Article III of the Northwest Ordinance states: "Religion, morality, and knowledge being necessary to good government and the happiness of mankind, schools and the means of education shall be forever encouraged."[30] Clearly, religion and morality, according to our founders, were to be driving forces in America's schools. An enlightened education valued liberty, but rejected licentiousness (doing whatever one's nature might desire, regardless of flaws).

ENLIGHTENMENT VERSUS RELIGIOUS BIGOTRY

Because of Washington's enlightened anti-superstition views, he particularly regretted the religious bigotry he found among some professing Christians. He had hoped that in an era that had learned to celebrate religious freedom, men could have grown beyond that. He wrote to Sir Edward Newenham on June 22, 1792:

> I regret exceedingly that the disputes between the Protestants and Roman Catholics should be carried to the serious alarming height mentioned in your letters. Religious controversies are always productive of more acrimony and irreconcilable hatreds than those which spring from any other cause; and I was not without hopes that the enlightened and liberal policy of the present age would have put an effectual stop to contentions of this kind.[31]

Four months later, he wrote another letter to Newenham, dated October 20, 1792, in which he explained:

> Of all the animosities which have existed among mankind, those which are caused by a difference of sentiments in religion appear to be the most inveterate and distressing, and ought most to be deprecated. I was in hopes, that the enlightened and liberal policy, which has marked the present age, would at least have reconciled Christians of every denomination so far, that we should never again see their religious disputes carried to such a pitch as to endanger

the peace of Society.[32]

Washington's wish has largely been fulfilled in America. While there have been some ugly exceptions:

- Anti-Catholic mobs fighting on the streets of nineteenth century New York City or Philadelphia
- The anti-Mormon persecution, including the slaying of the founder Joseph Smith in 1844
- African-American Pentecostal ministers lynched for preaching the Gospel

Yet, by-and-large, America has *not* seen the kinds of wars of religion that devastated Europe in the wake of the Reformation and Counter-Reformation. For the most part, America has seen religious conflicts fought by argument and reason.

As the first president under the well-reasoned American Constitution, Washington was given an enlightened pulpit from which to speak concerning his views of religious liberty, even to the clergy. Accordingly, President Washington wrote on January 27, 1793, to ecclesiastical leaders of The New Church in Baltimore. The New Church was a new denomination based on the creative ideas of the novel religious thinker Emanuel Swendenborg. Therein, Washington boasted of America's triumph over superstition,

> We have abundant reason to rejoice that in this Land the light of truth and reason has triumphed over the power of bigotry and superstition, and that every person may here worship God according to the dictates of his own heart. In this enlightened Age and in this Land of equal liberty it is our boast, that a man's religious tenets will not forfeit the protection of the Laws, nor deprive him of the right of attaining and holding the highest Offices that are known in the United States.[33]

This conviction came after two or three centuries of wars of religion within outwardly Christian denominations–Catholics vs. Protestants–Protestants vs. other Protestants.

In all the letters that Washington wrote to the many religious groups that contacted him, one of the main points he stressed was America's religious liberty for all. European history was filled with religious intolerance, perpetrated all too often in the name of Christianity. But Washington saw the United States as an asylum where such bigotry would not gain a foothold. However, in taking such a stance, Washington did not become a Deist.

Writing to Benedict Arnold on September 14, 1775, and speaking of Roman Catholics in Canada, he affirmed: "Prudence, policy, and a true Christian spirit will lead us to look with compassion upon their errors without insulting them."[34] He wrote to his soldiers on July 9, 1776, immediately after receiving a copy of the Declaration of Independence: "The General hopes and trusts, that every officer and man, will endeavour so to live, and act, as becomes a Christian Soldier, defending the dearest Rights and Liberties of his country."[35] In short, a belief in religious liberty did not mean a belief in Deism. In fact, the great original advocates of religious liberty in America were Christian clergymen—Reformed and Baptist thinker Roger Williams in Rhode Island, and Quaker William Penn in Pennsylvania.[36]

REASON VS. FAITH?

In Washington's Enlightenment, reason had conquered bigotry and superstition. But had it conquered revealed religion too? The view of common scholars that the Enlightenment was monolithic, and its faith was that of a Deist, is unsound. A careful reading of the original writings of our founders yields their profound insistence on the importance of religion, and even religion of the *revealed* variety found in the Holy Bible.

It is historically untenable that Washington's understanding of an enlightened faith meant a rejection of a biblical Christianity. As a point in fact, consider Washington's biblical allusions in his concluding prayer of his May 1790 letter to the Hebrew congregation in Savannah, Georgia.

> I rejoice that a spirit of liberality and philanthropy is much more prevalent than it formerly was among the enlightened nations of the earth, and that your brethren will benefit thereby in proportion as it shall become still more extensive; happily the people of the United States have in many instances exhibited examples worthy of imitation, the salutary influence of which will doubtless extend much farther if gratefully enjoying those blessings of peace which (under the favor of heaven) have been attained by fortitude in war, they shall conduct themselves with reverence to the Deity and

charity toward their fellow-creatures.

May the same wonder-working Deity, who long since delivered the Hebrews from their Egyptian oppressors, planted them in a promised land, whose providential agency has lately been conspicuous in establishing these United States as an independent nation, still continue to water them with the dews of heaven and make the inhabitants of every denomination participate in the temporal and spiritual blessings of that people whose God is Jehovah.

Consider the many phrases used by Washington in this letter that have their root in the Bible. To highlight the scriptural allusions, we have emphasized them by listing them individually and by placing them in italics:

- *blessings of peace which (under favor of Heaven)* (Numbers 6:23-26) have been obtained by fortitude in war, they shall conduct themselves with;
- *reverence to the Deity,* (Deuteronomy 6:6) and;
- *charity toward their fellow creatures* (Leviticus 19:18)."
- May the *same wonder-working Deity* (Daniel 4:3), who long since;
- *delivering the Hebrews from the Egyptian oppressors* (Exodus 15:11); and
- *planted them in the promised land* (Joshua 22:4)—whose;
- *providential agency has lately been conspicuous in establishing these United States as an independent nation* (1 Samuel 2:7; Psalm 75:7; Isaiah 55:5; Daniel 2:21, 37)—still;
- *continue to water them with the dews of Heaven* (Genesis 27:28) and to make the inhabitants of every denomination participate in the;
- *temporal and spiritual blessings* of that (Genesis 49:25; Ephesians 1:3);
- *people whose God is* (Psalm 33:12);
- *Jehovah* (Exodus 6:3; Psalm 83:18; Isaiah 12:2; 26:4)."[37]

These biblical references are linked together by Washington in a most remarkably integrated manner. They clearly demonstrate that Washington was not opposed to the Bible nor to its extensive use for forming and expounding upon his enlightened views of opposition to religious bigotry. They also underscore his biblical literacy. This is not the writing of a Deist. This kind of biblical synthesis reveals a lifetime of reflection on the scriptures, which is the result of a Christian faith.

CONCLUSION

George Washington saw the United States as an enlightened nation—enlightened by reason and by revelation (the Judeo-Christian revelation of the Holy Scriptures). Thus, Washington wrote in, April 1789:

> The blessed Religion revealed in the word of God will remain an eternal and awful monument to prove that the best Institutions may be abused by human depravity;"[38] "The blessed religion revealed in the word of God" is Christianity.

Perhaps the greatest theologian in American history was Jonathan Edwards. Although he died just years before the great events that triggered the American Revolution, he would have understood Washington's language of the "Word of God" to be consistent with Christianity but not Deism. Jonathan Edwards wrote,

> From what has been said, plainly appears the *necessity* of divine *revelation.* The Deists deny the Scripture to be the word of God, and hold that there is no *revealed religion;* that God has given mankind no other rule but his own reason; which is sufficient, without any word or revelation from heaven, to give man a right understanding of divine things, and of his duty.

What Deists denied, Washington affirmed. Washington accepted the scriptures, rejected superstition, and was comfortable with the reasonableness of faith advocated by the Christian enlightenment that celebrated religious liberty.

TWENTY FOUR

George Washington and Religious Liberty:

A Christian or Deist Idea?

"...I was in hopes, that the enlightened and liberal policy, which has marked the present age, would at least have reconciled Christians of every denomination so far..."
George Washington, 1792 [1]

Religious liberty was born in America, and George Washington made a major contribution toward the establishment of religious freedom under our government. Through the influence of the United States, he made a major impact on the existence of religious freedom in the world as well. In May 1789 he answered a letter from the General Assembly of Presbyterian Churches in the United States:

> While I reiterate the professions of my dependence upon Heaven as
> the source of all public and private blessings; I will observe that the
> general prevalence of piety, philanthropy, honesty, industry,
> and economy seems, in the ordinary course of human affairs,

particularly necessary for advancing and conforming the happiness of our country.

    While all men within our territories are protected in worshipping the Deity according to the dictates of their consciences; it is rationally to be expected from them in return, that they will be emulous of evincing [striving to prove] the sanctity of their professions by the innocence of their lives and the beneficence of their actions; for no man who is profligate in his morals, or a bad member of the civil community, can possibly be a true Christian, or a credit to his own religious society.[2]

How one can be a true Christian, asked President Washington, if one acts like a profligate and is a bad citizen? He did not want any professing Christian to abuse his freedom here in this free land and thereby cross the line from liberty into license.

    Washington maintained that there was a difference between liberty and license, or immoral behavior. Washington simultaneously held the principles of high moral conduct and freedom of religion from any government coercion.

WASHINGTON AS A DELEGATE TO THE CONTINENTAL CONGRESS

    Washington was a member of the first two Continental Congresses. Thus, he and a handful of other Virginians journeyed to Philadelphia to meet together with other delegates representing the other colonies. Out of these congresses, the United States of America was born.

    As surprising as it sounds in a secular America, the first act of the first Congress was to pray, despite a myriad of Christian denominations represented. John Adams wrote to his wife Abigail, explaining what happened on September 6, 1774, and September 7—the first two meetings of the newly formed Congress.[3] This prayer not only began America, but it began the continuing congressional tradition of prayer and the work of chaplains among our government officials. A famous painting from the mid-nineteenth century depicts the classic scene of Reverend Duché praying. George Washington was one of those at prayer as well. In this portrait, he is kneeling.

    As the work of the Congress proceeded, they

John Adams

decided to appeal to England and to reason with the mother country to show the errors of its misguided efforts to force the colonies to pay taxes that were inconsistent with the British constitution and legacy of liberty. The Congress began with a recitation of history:

> WHEREAS the power but not the justice, the vengeance but not the wisdom of Great-Britain, which of old persecuted, scourged, and excited our fugitive parents from their native shores, now pursues us their guiltless children with unrelenting severity...[4]

These words raise a critical point: many wish to separate the settling of America (by the Puritans, the Pilgrims, the Quakers, etc.), which was Christian from the founding of America (by the founding fathers, who allegedly were mostly Deists). Thus, in this view, the settlers were Christian, but the founders were secular-minded.

But the early Congresses did not adhere to Deism—including the very first Congress, which recognized that "our fugitive parents" came to these shores to flee persecution. Congress went on to resolve that it would be wrong not to stand up to their current persecution at the hands of Great Britain, in light of the sacrifice of the settlers of America:

> THAT it is *an indispensable duty which we owe to God*, our country, ourselves and posterity, by all lawful ways and means in our power to maintain, defend and preserve these *civil and religious rights* and liberties for which many of our fathers fought, bled and died, and to hand them down entire to future generations. (emphasis ours)[5]

How, they ask, could they let down their fathers (the settlers of America) or their posterity if they allowed England to run roughshod over their religious liberties? Washington and his congressional patriots believed they owed it to their God and their country to stand boldly for their heritage of liberty.

THE QUEBEC ACT

One act of Parliament in particular worsened the situation. It was the Quebec Act, which especially concerned the Continental Congress, because it seemed to open the door for the Roman Catholic persecution of Protestants. This was an era when severe persecution of Protestants by some leaders in the Roman Catholic Church still occurred.

Some of the men in Congress had ancestors who had been persecuted by Catholics, and had fled such persecution. For example, some of the founders, such as Paul Revere, Alexander Hamilton, John Jay, and Elias Boudinot had ancestors of Huguenot extraction. The Huguenots were French Calvinists persecuted severely for their belief by the French King and the Catholic Church. France under King Louis XIV killed or banished most Calvinists from his kingdom.

As we'll see below, Protestant England had had its own run-in with anti-Protestant terrorists and consequently persecuted Catholics in England. (This was partially the reason for Lord Baltimore founding Maryland as a colony for Catholic refugees from persecution by the Church of England.) But true to the military and political adage, the enemy of my enemy is my friend, England punished Americans for their resistance to the British King by passing the Quebec Act. This law established French-speaking Canada as an official Roman Catholic nation.

In the days before the gift of religious liberty was bequeathed to the world by American Christianity, those in the state were required to follow the official religion of the state. So Roman Catholic Quebec was viewed as a threat to New England. The colonies had been formed, for the most part, by Protestants seeking religious freedom. Their sense of religious freedom was threatened when England allowed Roman Catholic Quebec to exist just north of New England. In this light, one can understand the Congress strong fears aroused by the Quebec Act:

> THAT the late act of Parliament for *establishing the Roman Catholic religion* and the French laws in that extensive country now called Quebec, is dangerous in an extreme degree to the *Protestant religion* and to the civil rights and liberties of all America; and therefore as men and *protestant Christians*, we are indispensably obliged to take all proper measures for our security. (emphasis ours)[6]

A note in the *Writings of George Washington* edited by John Fitzpatrick says:

> By the Quebec Act of 1774 Great Britain, with a view of holding the Colonies in check, established the Roman Catholic religion in Canada, and enlarged its bounds so as to comprise all the territory northwest of the Ohio to the head of Lake Superior and the Mississippi. This attempt to extend the jurisdiction of Canada to the

The first act of the first Congress was to pray. George Washington is the third person from the left who is kneeling

Ohio was especially offensive to Virginia. Richard Henry Lee, in Congress, denounced it as the worst of all the acts complained of.[7]

The American colonists viewed the Quebec Act essentially as an act of war. Thus, Washington voted openly as a Protestant to protect the religious liberty that he and his fellow colonists had enjoyed as "Protestant Christians."

CONGRESS ORDERS THE INVASION OF CANADA

As a response to the Quebec Act, Congress attempted to neutralize the threat of the treaty of Quebec for the colonies. On February 15, 1775, Congress appointed three commissioners—Benjamin Franklin, Samuel Chase, and Charles Carroll (a Roman Catholic)—to meet with the leaders of Canada.[8] They were accompanied by the Reverend John Carroll, a Catholic clergyman, who later became the archbishop of Baltimore. Congress hoped that Carroll's influence with the people of Quebec, on account of his religious principles and character would be useful.

The commissioners arrived at Montreal on April 29, 1775, without Franklin, who returned en route, because his health was unable to sustain the demands of the long and arduous journey. The negotiations were unsuccessful. The American Congress put military might behind their concerns and sent an army under the command of Generals Philip John Schuyler and Richard Montgomery and Col. Benedict Arnold to the city of Montreal. At that time, General Washington wrote a letter to the northern nation, on September 14, 1775:

TO THE INHABITANTS OF CANADA

Friends and Brethren: The unnatural Contest between the English Colonies, and Great Britain has now risen to such a Height, that Arms alone must decide it.

The Colonies, confiding in the Justice of their Cause and the purity of their intentions, have reluctantly appealed to that Being, in whose hands are all Human Events: He has hitherto smiled upon their virtuous Efforts: The Hand of Tyranny has been arrested in its Ravages, and the British Arms, which have shone with so much Splendor in every part of the Globe, are now tarnished with disgrace and disappointment. Generals of approved experience, who boasted of subduing this great Continent, find themselves circumscribed within the limits of a single City and its Suburbs, suffering all the shame and distress of a Siege. While the Freeborn Sons of America, animated by the genuine principles of Liberty and Love of their Country, with increasing Union, Firmness and discipline, repel every attack and despise every Danger.

Above all we rejoice that our Enemies have been deceived with Regard to you: They have persuaded themselves, they have even dared to say, that the Canadians were not capable of distinguishing between the Blessings of Liberty and the Wretchedness of Slavery; that gratifying the Vanity of a little Circle of Nobility would blind the Eyes of the people of Canada. By such Artifices they hoped to bend you to their Views; but they have been deceived: Instead of finding in you that poverty of Soul, and baseness of Spirit, they see with a Chagrin equal to our Joy, that you are enlightened, generous, and Virtuous; that you will not renounce your own Rights, or serve as Instruments to deprive your Fellow subjects of theirs. Come then, my Brethren, Unite with us in an indissoluble Union. Let us run together to the same Goal. We have taken up Arms in Defence of our Liberty, our Property; our Wives and our Children: We are determined to preserve them or die. We look forward with pleasure to that day not far remote (we hope) when the Inhabitants of America shall have one Sentiment and the full Enjoyment of the blessings of a Free Government.

Incited by these Motives and encouraged by the advice of many Friends of Liberty among you, the Great American Congress have sent an Army into your Province, under the command of General Schuyler; not to plunder but to protect you; to animate and bring forth into Action those sentiments of Freedom you have declared, and which the Tools of dispositism would extinguish through the whole Creation. To co-operate with this design and to frustrate those cruel and perfidious Schemes, which would deluge our Frontier with the Blood of Women and Children, I have detached Colonel Arnold into your Country, with a part of the Army under my Command. I have enjoined upon him, and I am certain that he will consider himself, and act as in the Country of his Patrons and best Friends. Necessaries and Accommodations of every kind which you may furnish, he will thankfully receive, and render the full Value. I invite you therefore as Friends and Brethren, to provide him with such supplies as your Country affords; and I pledge myself not only for your safety and security, but for ample Compensation. Let no Man desert his habitation. Let no Man flee as before an Enemy.[8]

Washington appealed to liberty and justice, but the Canadians saw it as an invasion. Eventually, the Americans were defeated at the Battle of Montreal. General Montgomery was killed. Nonetheless, for his great bravery, he was viewed as a hero. Later, the capital city of Alabama was named in his honor. Col Benedict Arnold was wounded. The army retreated. Canada remained loyal to England, and Quebec continued its Roman Catholic religion.

But Washington's orders to Arnold when he began his march to Canada were the true victory of the campaign. They clearly established the principle of religious liberty in his command. America's concern was not to assault Roman Catholicism, but to prevent a state with the establishment of the Roman Catholic religion that could persecute Protestants or attack the colonies due to religious motivations.

WASHINGTON'S PROMOTION OF RELIGIOUS LIBERTY

Before General Washington dispatched Benedict Arnold for this invasion, he wrote a letter to Arnold (before his treachery) essentially saying that while the Canadians may be in error theologically, it is not the army's place to disparage or belittle in any way their Roman Catholic beliefs. That was both wrong and counter-productive:

> As the *Contempt of the Religion* of a Country by ridiculing any of its Ceremonies or affronting its Ministers or Votaries has ever been deeply resented, you are to be particularly careful to restrain every Officer and Soldier from such Imprudence and Folly and to punish every Instance of it. On the other Hand, as far as lays in your power, you are to protect and support the free Exercise of the Religion of the Country and the undisturbed Enjoyment of the rights of Conscience in religious Matters, with your utmost Influence and Authority. Given under my Hand, at Head Quarters, Cambridge, this 14th Day of September one Thousand seven Hundred and seventy-five.
>
> I also give it in Charge to you to avoid all *Disrespect to or Contempt of the Religion* of the Country and its Ceremonies. Prudence, Policy, and a true Christian Spirit, will lead us to look with Compassion upon their Errors without insulting them. While we are contending for our own Liberty, we should be very cautious of violating the Rights of Conscience in others, ever considering that God alone is the Judge of the Hearts of Men, and to him only in this Case, they are answerable. Upon the whole, Sir, I beg you to inculcate upon the Officers and Soldiers, the Necessity of preserving the strictest Order during their March through Canada; to represent to them the Shame, Disgrace and Ruin to themselves and Country, if they should by their Conduct, turn the Hearts of our Brethren in Canada against us. And on the other Hand, the Honours and Rewards which await them, if by their Prudence and good Behaviour, they conciliate the Affections of the Canadians and Indians, to the great Interests of America, and convert those favorable Dispositions they have shewn into a lasting Union and Affection.[9] (emphasis ours)

General Washington understood the importance of religious liberty and religious toleration for the success of his army. Mutual respect in the midst of religious diversity was evident in his General Orders from Head Quarters in Cambridge on November 5, 1775. As we will see in a moment, the date November 5th was quite significant:

> As the Commander in Chief has been apprized of a design form'd for the observance of that ridiculous and childish custom of burning the Effigy of the pope—He cannot help expressing his surprise that there should be Officers and Soldiers in this army so void of common sense, as not to see the impropriety of such a step at this Juncture; at a Time when we are solliciting, and have really obtain'd, the friendship and alliance of the people of Canada, whom we ought to consider as Brethren embarked in the same Cause. The defence of the general Liberty of America: At such a juncture, and in such Circumstances, to be insulting their Religion, is so monstrous, as not to be suffered or excused; indeed instead of offering the most remote insult, it is our duty to address public thanks to these our Brethren, as to them we are so much indebted for every late happy Success over the common Enemy in Canada.[10]

Washington was aghast at the thought his troops would make fun of Catholic customs. Why was the date of this communique—November 5th—so significant? Because it was Guy Fawkes Day.

GUY FAWKES DAY

To understand the bigger picture, including Washington's reference to the burning of effigies of the pope, we will back up for a few moments and explain the significance of Guy Fawkes Day to the American colonists, who were for the most part Protestant Britishers transplanted to a new continent.

America's celebration of her birth on July Fourth has no equivalent celebration in Great Britain. The closest British parallel historically, perhaps, is Guy Fawkes Day. This commemorates the November 5th, 1605 foiling of an attempt to assassinate not only King James the First, but the entire House of Lords along with him. Guy Fawkes was arrested and hung for his plot to ignite several barrels of gunpowder that had been stored under the Parliament Building.

The perpetual dubious honor afforded to Guido Fawkes, the pro-Catholic and anti-Royal leader of the plan, was to be annually burned in effigy. The custom began exactly one year later on November 5, 1606, when his effigy was burned all over the country, since November Fifth already happened to have been a traditional English night for building bonfires. Guy Fawkes had chosen that same day to have a royal bonfire. Guy Fawkes has been part of the British psyche from childhood poems, to a Beatles' song, to a form of worship in the 1662 *Book of Common Prayer*.

A traditional English poem preserves the story of the failed plot and God's providential intervention.

> Remember, remember, the fifth of November,
> Gunpowder, Treason and Plot;
> I see no reason why Gunpowder Treason
> Should ever be forgot.
> Guy Fawkes, Guy Fawkes
> 'Twas his intent
> To blow up the King and the Parliament
> Three score barrels of powder below
> Poor old England to overthrow
> By God's providence he was catched
> With a dark lantern and burning match.
> Penny for the Guy, Hit him in the eye,
> Stick him up a lamp-post [or chimney] and there let him die.

The connection between George Washington and religious liberty appears in that Washington played a pivotal role in his November 5, 1775, orders in helping to end anti-Catholic bigotry in the new nation.

The Guy Fawkes custom had come to America with the historic English anti-Catholic sentiment. As we saw in an earlier chapter, anti-Catholic oaths were required of an Anglican vestryman (or public surveyor) like Washington in colonial Virginia—whereby one swore allegiance to the Protestant King and against the Roman Catholic heir to the throne, as well as the doctrine of transubstantiation. The effigy burned on Guy Fawkes Day in the colonies was not always Guy, sometimes it was the pope himself.

But this historic custom did not continue once America began her pursuit of liberty and ultimately independence. The reason for this can be traced directly to the leadership of George Washington. In the context of the invasion of Roman Catholic Quebec, General Washington prohibited all mockery of the enemy's religion. It is not surprising, however, that at the beginning of the Revolutionary War, King George III or his political advisors began to be burned in effigy. But under Washington's leadership, the pope was no longer symbolically burned at the stake.

FREEDOM FOR CATHOLICS REITERATED BY PRESIDENT WASHINGTON

As president, George Washington affirmed religious freedom for all in America, including Catholics. (Keep in mind that America was a largely Protestant country— 98.4% Protestant Christian and 1.4% Catholic at the beginning of the war.)[11]

On March 15, 1790, according to the *Maryland Journal and Baltimore Advertiser,* a committee of Roman Catholics waited upon the president with a congratulatory address, to which the president replied. Washington said, in part:

> I feel, that my conduct in war and in peace has met with more general approbation than could reasonably have been expected: and I find myself disposed to consider that fortunate circumstance, in a great degree, resulting from the able support and extraordinary candor of my fellow-citizens of all denominations....
>
> ...As mankind become more liberal [charitable], they will be more apt to allow, that all those, who conduct themselves as worthy members of the community are equally entitled to the protection of civil government. I ever [long] to see America among the foremost nations in examples of justice and liberality. And I presume, that your fellow-citizens will not forget the patriotic part, which you took in the accomplishment of their revolution and the establishment of their government; or the important assistance, which they received from a nation in which the roman catholic religion is professed...may the members of your Society in America, animated alone by the pure spirit of christianity, and still conducting themselves as the faithful subjects of our free government, enjoy every temporal and spiritual felicity.[12]

RELIGIOUS FREEDOM FOR ALL

Washington believed there should be religious freedom for all. This was a point he especially emphasized in his letter to the Hebrew congregation in America. He wrote to the Hebrew Congregation in Newport, Rhode Island, a now-famous letter (dated August 17, 1790), declaring:

> It is now no more that toleration is spoken of as if it were the indulgence of one class of people that another enjoyed the exercise of their inherent natural rights, for, happily, the Government of the United States, which gives to bigotry no sanction, to persecution no assistance, requires only that they who live under its protection should demean themselves as good citizens in giving it on all occasions their effectual support....[13]

Washington's respect for religious liberty and freedom of conscience comes into focus in a letter that he wrote to his surrogate son, Marquis de Lafayette, from Philadelphia on August 15, 1787, while the Constitutional Convention was in session:

> ...I am not less ardent in my wish that you may succeed in your plan of *toleration in religious matters. Being no bigot myself to any mode of worship, I am disposed to indulge the professors of Christianity in the church, that road to Heaven, which to them shall seem the most direct plainest easiest and least liable to exception.....*We have abundant reason to rejoice that in this Land the light of truth and reason has triumphed over the power of bigotry and superstition, and that every person may here worship God according to the dictates of his own heart. In this enlightened Age and in this Land of equal liberty it is our boast, that a man's *religious* tenets will not forfeit the protection of the Laws, nor deprive him of the right of attaining and holding the highest Offices that are known in the United States. (emphasis added)[14]

After centuries of persecution within Christendom against dissenting Christians of other denominations, the United States, under the leadership of George Washington, chose a path of liberty of conscience for dissident believers. Religious freedom did not grow out of secularism. It grew out of the unique experience of America, where a nation was settled by Christians seeking to worship Christ in the purity of the Gospel according to their consciences—but in different ways than the state churches they left behind, and in different ways from each other.[15] George Washington respected these differences and charted a path of Christian forbearing for religious disagreements. This can be seen in his letters to Quakers and the Baptists, both of which had experienced significant religious persecution in England and in the American colonies.

In March, 1790, the Society of Free Quakers meeting in Philadelphia delivered a complimentary address to Washington. Washington responded:

> *Having always considered the conscientious scruples of religious belief as resting entirely with the sects that profess,* or the individuals who entertain them, I cannot, consistent with this uniform sentiment, otherwise notice the circumstances referred to in your address, than by adding the tribute of my acknowledgment to that of our country, for those services which the members of your particular community rendered to the common cause in the course of our revolution. And by assuring you that, as our present government was instituted with an express view to general happiness, it will be my earnest endeavor, in discharging the duties confided to me with faithful impartiality, to raise the hope of common protection which you expect from the measures of that government." (emphasis ours)[16]

On May 10, 1789, in addressing the general committee representing the United Baptist Churches of Virginia, President Washington stated:

> If I could have entertained the slightest apprehension that the Constitution framed by the Convention, where I had the honor to preside, might possibly endanger the religious rights of any ecclesiastical Society, certainly I would never have placed my signature to it...[17]

Thus, Washington is on record in opposition to all religious persecution, whether it comes from religious sources or secular sources. In his Farewell Address he declared that religion and morality are indispensable to our political prosperity.

A SACRED FIRE CREATES ASYLUM FOR THE OPPRESSED OF ALL RELIGIONS

The "sacred fire"[18] of Washington's "true religion"[19] blazed with a passion for divine

Providence and religious liberty. The "sacred fire of liberty," lit at his First Inaugural Address, has burned throughout America's history and still beacons from New York Harbor. Although "Lady Liberty's" torch has pointed to the heavens for several generations, her elevation of Washington's "sacred fire of liberty" continues to ignite hope for all who have come to America's shores to find "asylum." Washington was sure America would become the "asylum" of the world for those who had been persecuted for their religious beliefs. In passionate and prescient words of encouragement to his victorious troops in 1783, the general explained to his men:

> While the General recollects the almost infinite variety of Scenes thro which we have passed, with a mixture of pleasure, astonishment, and gratitude; While he contemplates the prospects before us with rapture; he can not help wishing that all the brave men (of whatever condition they may be) who have shared in the toils and dangers of effecting this glorious revolution, of rescuing Millions from the hand of oppression, and of laying the foundation of a great Empire, might be impressed with a proper idea of the dignified part they have been called to act (under the Smiles of providence) on the stage of human affairs: for, happy, thrice happy shall they be pronounced hereafter, who have contributed any thing, who have performed the meanest office in erecting this stupendous *fabrick* of *Freedom* and *Empire* on the broad basis of Independency; who have assisted in protecting the rights of humane nature and establishing an Asylum for the poor and oppressed of all nations and religions. The glorious task for which we first flew to Arms being thus accomplished, the liberties of our Country being fully acknowledged, and firmly secured by the smiles of heaven, on the purity of our cause, and the honest exertions of a feeble people (determined to be free) against a powerful Nation (disposed to oppress them) and the Character of those who have persevered, through every extremity of hardship; suffering and danger being immortalized by the illustrious appellation of the *patriot Army*: Nothing now remains but for the actors of this mighty Scene to preserve a perfect, unvarying, consistency of character through the very last act; to close the Drama with applause; and to retire from the Military Theatre with the same approbation of Angells and men

which have crowned all their former virtuous Actions.[20]

The Fourth of July, for Washington as for all Americans, became synonymous with liberty.[21] In fact, "July IV, 1776" are the solitary words on the tablet held by Lady Liberty"[22] as she welcomes the world to America, the world's greatest asylum for religious liberty.[23] Proposed and designed by Frederic Auguste Bertholdi, a descendant of a persecuted Huguenot, the Statue of Liberty, appropriately bears the poetry of Emma Lazarus, a descendant of a persecuted Jewish immigrant family. Her poem speaks as if with the flaming tongues of Washington's "sacred fire of liberty":

> "Keep, ancient lands, your storied Pomp!" cries she
> With Silent lips. "Give me your tired, your poor,
> Your huddled masses yearning to breath free,
> The wretched refuse of your teeming shore.
> Send these, the homeless, tempest-tossed to me,
> I lift my lamp beside the golden door."

Set afire by Washington's character, "Liberty" holds her lamp aloft to shine the eternal flame of America's sacred fire into the night of the world's despair. Having received the "approbation of Angells and men," Washington's Constitution with its Bill of Rights keeps the lamp ablaze as she awaits the midnight cry. Thankfully, Washington, "Warm'd by Religion's sacred, genuine ray,"[24] has bequeathed his "sacred fire" to the world.[25]

CONCLUSION

Secularists claim that it was secularism (of which Deism was a nascent eighteenth century form) that gave us religious freedom, but this is not so. It was what Washington called "the pure spirit of christianity." Author Bill Federer, compiler of *America's God and Country*, spoke of Christianity and religious liberty in the American experience, of which Washington was the father:

> Tolerance was an American Christian contribution to the world.
> Just as you drop a pebble in the pond, the ripples go out, there was
> tolerance first for Puritans and then Protestants, then Catholics,
> then liberal Christians, and then it went out completely to Jews.
> Then in the early 1900s, tolerance went out to anybody of any faith,

monotheist or polytheist. Finally, within the last generation, tolerance went out to the atheist, the secular humanist and the anti-religious. And the last ones in the boat decided it was too crowded and decided to push the first ones out. So now we have a unique situation in America, where everybody's tolerated except the ones that came up with the idea.[26]

George Washington—the champion of religious freedom—insisted that his "asylum for mankind"[27] is a "capacious asylum"[28] that is an asylum large enough for all of us to be warmed under the "sacred fire of liberty."

TWENTY FIVE

George Washington, Member of the Masonic Order

"Being persuaded, that a just application of the principles,
on which the Masonic fraternity is founded, must be promotive of
private virtue and public prosperity.

"I shall always be happy to advance the interests of the society,
and be considered by them a deserving brother."
George Washington, 1790[1]

One of the objections some people make to Washington's Christianity is that he was a Mason. For example, John Warwick Montgomery, in his *The Shaping of America*, dismisses virtually all the founding fathers as Deists, including our first president:

> Washington's own convictions are revealed by his enthusiastic
> connection with the Freemasons—a connection to which the

architecturally monstrous, but appropriately Babel-like George Washington Masonic National Memorial in Alexandria, Virginia, bears witness…Freemasonry, originating not in the mysteries of Solomon's Temple but in the rationalism of early modern times, is at root Deistic; indeed, the movement may be regarded as a liturgical Deism. It holds to a unitary Supreme Being, the so-called Great Architect of the Universe, denies Christ's unique saviorship and atonement, and reduces religion to a moralistic observance of allegedly common ethical principles.[2]

Thus, Washington was not a Christian, argues Montgomery, because he was an active Mason.

GEORGE WASHINGTON WAS A MASON

It's very clear that Washington was a Mason, as attested by letters in Washington's correspondence to Masonic groups.[3] He participated in the laying of the cornerstone in the United States Capitol Building in the federal city, now Washington, D.C., and he did that as a Mason. Historian Paul Johnson well summarizes Washington's Masonic life:

Washington became familiar with the externals of Masonry as a boy, and in 1752, when he reached the age of twenty, he was inducted as an Entered Apprentice Mason in the Fredericksburg Lodge. Thereafter, Masonry plays an important, if discreet part in his life, as it did among many of the Founding Fathers. Indeed, it is true to say that Masonry was one of the intellectual building blocks of the Revolution. Washington allowed lodges to flourish in several of his war camps. It was a link with advanced thinking in France: when Lafayette visited him in 1784, he gave him a Masonic apron of white satin, which the marquise had embroidered. Washington swore the oath of office as president on the Masonic Bible and when he laid the cornerstone of the capitol in 1793 he invoked the lodges of Maryland and Virginia. Indeed at his funeral all six pallbearers were Masons and the service followed the Masonic rite.[4]

Allyn Cox's painting of Washington laying the cornerstone of the Capitol, September 18, 1793

THE GOD OF WASHINGTON'S MASONIC ORDER: DEIST OR CHRISTIAN?

But just what influence did Washington's participation in the Masonic Order have on his view of the God of Christianity? In Washington historian Willard Sterne Randall's mind, it meant a decisive departure from Washington's Christian faith. Randall writes,

> It may have been at least in part to further this military ambition that on September 1, 1752, he applied to join a new Masonic lodge being organized in Fredericksburg. Washington was one of the first of the initiates on November 4, paying an initiation fee of £2, 3 shillings to become registered as an Entered Apprentice. But Washington was not performing a self-interested connection with the Masons. He would take the Mason's apron and trowel seriously. Eventually he became the highest ranking Mason in the United States and brought to the order a durable political prestige. While he dutifully attended the church services of the established Church of England, he was bored with its priest craft and from that time forward rarely was seen going to Anglican Communion. He put his own interpretation on Civility Rule No. 108: "When you

speak of God or his attributes let it be seriously and with reverence."
He began in his letters to use the word *God* very seldom,
substituting Masonic formulae: The Almighty, the Ruler of the
Universe, Providence, the Supreme Being. He used these forms not
only in private correspondence but as commander in chief during
the Revolution in his General Orders.[5]

But, before we can accept Montgomery's and Randall's claims, we need to notice
just how confused scholars are these days on Washington's religion. Professor Boller
claimed that Washington's names for God were those of the Deists. But author Willard
Sterne Randall here claims that they are the names for the God of the Masons. The
easy retort suggested by Montgomery that the Deists and the Masons were one and
the same does not work. As we will see in a subsequent chapter, Professor Boller argues
that Washington was unsure about the reality of immortality or life after death.[6] Yet a
foundational claim of the Masonic order is eternal life, symbolized in their ritual of
burial by a sprig of the acacia tree, a symbol to them of eternal life.[7]

And what do we do with the Masonic sermons that Washington collected and had
bound in his library,[8] that were written by the orthodox and evangelical clergymen of
the day,[9] who preached the Gospel and evangelical sermons to them at the invitation
of the Masons themselves?[10] And what do we do with the fact that these alleged
Masonic titles for Deity have already been shown to be the very names for God used
by the orthodox clergy of Washington's day?[11] The fact is, these honorific titles for
Deity were neither deistic nor Masonic; they were the vocabulary of the eighteenth
century Christian pulpit.

Moreover, we must disagree with Randall, because Washington's writings show
that he never stopped using the word *God*, and did, in fact, use it throughout his writings. The evidence shows that he used the word *God* some 140 times. We wonder how
Randall established his claim that Washington avoided using of the word *God* after
joining the Masons in 1752. As far as we can tell from our analysis, every known
example of his written use of *God* outside of his school papers occurred *after* he joined
the Masonic Order in 1752, the earliest written example being almost two years after
joining the Masonic Order in a letter on June 12, 1754.[12] Washington clearly did not
avoid the word *God* nor hide his faith in God when, at his Inauguration, he established
the precedent of adding to the constitutional presidential oath the words "So help
me *God*."

We believe the linkage between the Masonic Order and Deism in Washington's day is historically false. The evidence for this is clear. The Masons of Washington's day explicitly rejected Deism. The Masonic Constitution, as presented by the Episcopalian clergyman Reverend Dr. William Smith of the Grand Lodge of Pennsylvania, declared in chapter I, section I, "Concerning God and Religion:"

> ...A *Mason* is also obliged to observe the moral law, as a true *Noachida* (Sons of Noah: the first name for Free Masons); and if he rightly understands the Royal Art, he cannot tread in the irreligious paths of the unhappy *Libertine*, the *Deist*, nor stupid *Atheist*; nor in any case, act against the inward light of his own conscience. He will likewise shun the gross errors of *Bigotry* and *Superstition*; making a due use of his own reason according to that liberty wherewith a *Mason is made free.*[13]

But it's not just that the Masons were not to "tread in the irreligious paths of the... Deist nor stupid Atheist." Before the early eighteen hundreds, Masons in America were by-and-large orthodox, Trinitarian Christians.

CHRISTIAN MASONS

While it may seem strange to many today, the Masons of Washington's day called themselves "Christian Masons."[14] In an explanatory note added to his sermon for its publication, Presbyterian clergyman Reverend Samuel Miller wrote about the relationship between the Masons of his day and the Christian faith,

> The Author [Reverend Miller referring to himself] has said, that the "principles of Masonry so far as they go, coincide with the Christian religion." He would here explain himself. Masonry, as such, and according to its original plan, appears to be founded on natural religion. Hence the institution is found among all nations, who believe in one God, and the accountableness of man to him, as a moral Agent, and an immortal being. But none need to be informed that all the genuine principles of *natural religion*, are adopted in the Christian system, and are inculcated throughout every page of the sacred volume. – But farther; it is to be remembered that this discourse [Miller's sermon] was addressed to *Christian Masons*, or in other words, to Masons professing a belief in

Christianity. It was addressed to a fraternity, who introduce the sacred scriptures into all their lodges; who frequently inculcate even the peculiar doctrines contained therein; and who profess, as a society, to make revelation their constant guide. [15]

When the Reverend Dr. William Smith preached his Masonic sermon on December 28, 1779, a sermon that Washington also had in his collection, he declared that, in effect, Masonry was a form of non-denominational Christianity. He wrote,

Looking far beyond the little distinctions of sect or party (by which too many seek to know, and be known by, each other) we should labor to imitate the great Creator, in regarding those of every Nation Religion, and tongue, who "fear Him, and work righteousness."

Such conduct becomes those who profess to believe that when our Master Christ shall come again to reward his faithful workmen and servants; he will not ask whether we were of Luther or of Calvin? Where we prayed to him in white, black, or grey; in purple, or in rags; in fine linen, or in sackcloth; in a woolen frock, or peradventure in a *Leather-Apron*? Whatever is considered as most convenient, most in character most for edification, and infringes least on Spiritual liberty, will be admitted as good in this case.

But although we may believe that none of these things will be asked in that great day; let us remember that it will be assuredly asked—were we of CHRIST JESUS? "Did we pray to him with the Spirit and with the understanding?" Had we the true Marks of his Gospel in our lives? Were we "meek and lowly of heart?" did we nail our rebellious affections to his Cross, and strive to subdue our spirits to the Rule of his Spirit? But above all, it will be asked us— Were we clothed with the *Wedding-garment* of love? Did we recognize our HEAVENLY MASTER in the Sufferings of those whom he died to save? Did we, for his sake, open our souls wide, to the cries of HIS DISTRESSED POOR? "When they were hungry, did we give them meat? When thirsty, did we give them drink? When strangers, did we take them in? When naked, did we clothe them? When sick, did we visit them? When in prison, did we come unto them," with Comfort and Relief?[16]

And perhaps most tellingly, what do we do with the fact that one of Washington's Masonic brothers was none other than the itinerant Parson Mason Weems?[17] Certainly his entry into the Masons did not destroy his Anglican faith. Clearly, his participation in the craft did not end his Christianity, nor his participation in Communion.

We are not suggesting that all Masons were or are Christians. In fact, the history of the Masonic Order shows that it is Christianity's inherent power that Christianizes the Masonic Order.[18] Nor are we encouraging Christians to become Masons.[19] What we are saying is that the evidence from Washington's day shows that the Masonic Order was anti-Deist and openly Christian and committed to scripture. Therefore, Washington's membership in the Masonic Order of his day is much more a proof of his Christianity than of his alleged Deism.[20] Further, his membership in the Masonic Order also supports the evidence that shows that Washington believed in immortality.

HOW ACTIVE A MASON WAS WASHINGTON IN LATER LIFE?

The evidence from Washington's own pen seems to point to the idea that Washington in later life was less active in Masonry than one would expect. If we are to take Washington literally, he went only once or twice to the Masonic lodge in thirty years of his adult life. The Reverend G.W. Snyder wrote to Washington on September 25, 1798, sending a book he had read entitled, *Proofs of a Conspiracy*, by John Robison. The book argued that the Illuminati, a subversive organization that was anti-religion and anti-government, had penetrated America and had taken refuge in the Masonic fraternities of America.

Washington responded that he had been so busy that he was not aware of this book until Reverend Snyder sent it to him. In fact, his "busy-ness" had kept him away from most Masonic meetings. Furthermore, Washington notes that, to his knowledge, the Illuminati had not made great inroads into American Masonry:

> I have heard much of the nefarious, and dangerous plan, and doctrines of the Illuminati, but never saw the Book until you were pleased to send it to me. The same causes which have prevented my acknowledging the receipt of your letter have prevented my reading the Book, hitherto; namely, the multiplicity of matters which pressed upon me before, and the debilitated state in which I was left after, a severe fever had been removed. And which allows me to add little more now, than thanks for your kind wishes and favourable

sentiments, except to correct an error you have run into, of my Presiding over the English lodges in this Country. The fact is, I preside over none, nor have I been in one more than once or twice, within the last thirty years. I believe notwithstanding, that none of the Lodges in *this* Country are contaminated with the principles ascribed to the Society of the Illuminati.[22]

Apparently, Washington's active years in the Masonic Order, by his own admission, were from 1752 (the year he joined the Masonic Order at twenty years old) to 1768, the date thirty years back from when Washington wrote to Reverend Snyder in 1798. So at about the age of thirty-six or so, he stopped regular attendance at the Masonic Lodge. His active Masonic years were from the start of his military career to about the start of his disagreement with the British government's efforts to raise money in the colonies through means such as the Stamp Act. These were also years in which he was highly active as a vestryman and church warden.

Washington's letter reveals that in the later years of his life, while he continued to be a member of the Masons, he had not been a regular attendee. Thus, his activities thereafter were essentially symbolic and ceremonial. But Washington's letter also shows us that the Masons, of which he was a part during his active years, were not anti-religious, like the Deists. Washington knew of the "nefarious and dangerous plan and doctrines of the Illuminati." But as a member of the Masonic Fraternity, he did not believe the lodges in America had been "contaminated" by them.

So if we take Washington at his word, as he would expect us to, since he insisted that he was a man of candor and honesty, he obviously was far more active in the Christian church during the last three decades of his life than he was in the Masonic Order.

The American Masonic Order, to Washington's knowledge, was not corrupted by the irreligion of the Illuminati—the most radical expression of French Deism. Thus, Washington's involvement with the Masonic Order, based on his own comments, was consistent with our understanding of Washington as a Christian. The Masons were not Washington's regular religion, nor were they against Washington's Anglican faith.

This is why the Reverend Dr. William Smith, Episcopalian clergyman from Philadelphia, was able to have been a member and to have written the Constitution of the Order. (Again, the Constitution of the Masons declared that no Deist or "stupid Atheist" was to participate with the Masons.) This is also why the Reverend Parson Weems, Episcopalian clergyman from Washington's neighborhood, was able to have been a member and also be an outspoken advocate of Washington's Christian faith, even if he wrote an historically unacceptable biography of Washington.

CONCERNS FOR THE LOSS OF CHRISTIANITY IN THE MASONIC ORDER

To corroborate the Christian character of the Masonic Order in Washington's day, we must consider two further testimonies. The first occurs in the story of Reverend Timothy Dwight, the president of Yale College. Dwight had been an officer in the American Revolution, and became one of the leaders of America's Second Great Awakening. President Dwight, in his 1798 sermon, "The Duty of Americans at the Present Crisis," wrote that one of the realities of America's decline in religion was that the Masonic Order was losing its original purpose of friendship and fellowship and was becoming hostile to religion.

> In the meantime, the Masonic societies, which had been originally instituted for convivial and friendly purposes only, were . . . made the professed scenes of debate concerning religion, morality, and government. . . The secrecy, solemnity, mysticism, and correspondence of Masonry were in this new order preserved and enhanced; while the ardor of innovation, the impatience of civil and moral restraints, and the aims against government, morals, and religion were elevated, expanded and rendered more systematical, malignant, and daring.[23]

Dwight's sermon, preached on July 4, 1798, confirms the concerns of Reverend G. W. Snyder's letter of September 25, 1798. Apparently, Washington, however, had not been aware of the relatively recent change in tone in some of the Masonic lodges, given his general non-involvement during the last years of his life.

Further substantiation that the earlier "Christian Masons" of Washington's young adulthood were becoming less Christian during the time that Washington was no longer regularly attending the Masonic lodge is seen in the experience of Charles Thomson. Thomson was the first and only clerk of the Continental Congress. Thomson, from Bryn Mawr, Pennsylvania, was a remarkable classicist and biblical scholar.[24] He has the distinction of being the first to translate the Septuagint (the Greek translation of the Old Testament) into English. Washington, who knew Thomson, actually read a portion of Thomson's translation.[25] Thomson was invited to join the

Masonic Order to help keep its Christian witness alive—an invitation, however, that he did not accept:

> ...the Master of the Masonic Order in Baltimore ... was "determined... to unbosom [his] heart." This man urged Thomson to become a Mason to help him bring the order (which had "deviated from the truth") back to the "first principles" of Christianity. "I am in, you are out," wrote the Masonic Master. "Will you—can you—deem yourself called upon to lend your aid to do much good?" Thomson stayed out. [26]

CONCLUSION

In the early nineteenth century, American Masonry began to experience a decided shift away from traditional Christianity. But the American Masonry of George Washington's day considered itself to be quite compatible with Christianity.

In short, a man could be both a good Christian and a good Mason in the minds of the founders. The evidence is clear that being both a Mason and a Christian was not considered to be antithetical in the American Christian mind until the close of the eighteenth century.[28] While it is a legitimate question to ask just how Christian the Masonic Order is today, for Washington in his day and in his understanding, Christianity and membership in the Masonic Order were compatible. Washington believed that both taught the Christian faith, the moral duties of loving God and neighbor, and human immortality. It is a historical misunderstanding to drive a wedge between Washington and Christianity, because Washington was a Mason as has been done by John Warwick Montgomery,[29] Willard Sterne Randall[30] and Paul Johnson.[31]

TWENTY SIX

More Objections to Washington the Christian:

Slaves, Slander, Passion, and Tripoli

*"I wish from my soul that the Legislature of this
State could see the policy of a gradual Abolition of Slavery;
It would prevent much future mischief."*
George Washington, 1797[1]

George Washington's Sacred Fire was written to answer the objections of scholars who claim that George Washington was not a Christian. We have already considered several arguments utilized to support the claim of Washington's Deism. In this chapter, we will consider four other important objections to Washington's Christianity. These are:

- Washington's ownership of slaves;
- the question of Washington's morality, or what we might

call the question of Washington "slanders," versus the Washington "scandals";

- Washington's passionate temper; and
- Washington's alleged role in the Treaty of Tripoli.

Before we begin to consider these, let's engage the classic objector to Washington's Christianity—Washington historian Rupert Hughes,[2] a skeptical historian who wrote a generation before Professor Boller.

RUPERT HUGHES: THE PARSON WEEMS IN REVERSE OF THE TWENTIETH CENTURY

In 1926, only six years before the bicentennial of Washington's birth in 1932, Rupert Hughes wrote a substantive biography of Washington. His work, in many ways, began the reassessment of Washington's religion that led to the wholesale acceptance of the thesis that Washington was a Deist. The vast majority of the scholars who had written on Washington up to that time had accepted the view that Washington was a Christian. To put it mildly, Rupert Hughes, and others in his perspective, have successfully persuaded subsequent scholars, including Paul Boller, Jr. and Joseph Ellis.

The arguments that Hughes put forward are worthy of a brief response at this point in our study, because we discover that each of his claims were made with dogmatic self-assurance and are clearly incorrect, based upon our analysis of Washington's words and actions. We are reminded of an historian's adage—"The living can make the dead do any tricks they find necessary." The only way to guard against the scholarly slight of hand of historical revisionism is for serious historians to do the painstaking work of going to the original sources to verify their claims.

As we have sought to do that here, our conclusion is that Rupert Hughes can be considered the "Parson Weems in reverse" of the twentieth century Washington scholars. His unsubstantiated assertions, his uncritical acceptance of others' unsubstantiated remarks (such as Dr. Moncure Conway's) have simply been uncritically accepted and then quoted so often that everyone "knows" they are true. But Hughes' claims have about as much support as Parson Weems had for his cherry tree story. However, Weems even had an advantage over Hughes; he knew Washington and at least claimed to have actually investigated the matter from living witnesses.

We don't fault Hughes for not investigating his topic from living sources. That's more than any historian can do 150 years after the fact. But we do fault Hughes for his dogmatic claims that were not based on serious investigation. Hughes' assertions of

Washington's Deism were based solely on a biased, unsubstantiated perception. And sadly, an untested acquiescence to Rupert Hughes' errant claims set the scholarly tone which allowed Boller to write what became a "definitive" argument for Washington the Deist.

To corroborate our criticisms of Hughes, we will cite several of his claims and respond to them briefly with the evidence we have uncovered in our investigation of Washington's religion.

- Rupert Hughes claimed: "Aside from such an instance [the childhood Christmas poem] and one reference to "the Divine author of our blessed religion" in 1783, there is no direct allusion to Christ, and the word Christ has been found in none of Washington's almost countless autographs." We have already seen that Hughes is incorrect about this, since Washington did write the name of Jesus Christ literally and indirectly through honorific titles on several occasions. We discussed this at length in earlier chapters.

   Washington also used various titles for Deity that are biblical titles for Christ. Further, his Trinitarian heritage included the Deity of Christ whenever he spoke of God. Washington was an avowed Trinitarian in his Anglican context. Jefferson, as a Unitarian, could not serve in a Christian context, as he himself said, because of his anti-Trinitarian views. Washington, whose conscience was of the strictest sort, had no scruple to serve in church and in worship in distinctive and open Christian roles.

- Rupert Hughes claimed: "His refusal to take communion was admitted by his own clergyman, William White, Bishop of the Episcopal Church in America from 1787 to 1836. Colonel Mercer had written to ask if General Washington 'occasionally went to the communion,' or 'if he ever did at all.' Bishop White answered: 'Truth requires me to say that General Washington never received the communion in the church of which I am parochial minister....'" We have seen in the three chapters on Washington and Communion how his experience in Philadelphia does not imply a Deist Washington, nor did it depict his whole life. The inference drawn from it is built not only on faulty logic, but incomplete facts. Evidence as strong as Washington's non-communing in Philadelphia is available to show that he communed in Virginia, New York, and New Jersey. The only acceptable explanation is one that addresses all the facts. We have put Washington's communing practices into the historical milieu in which they occurred.

• Rupert Hughes claimed: "Jefferson said that Washington was a Deist." We have also seen that Jefferson was not an intimate of Washington, and those who were closest to Washington simply disagree with Jefferson, whom Washington described as an opponent of his government after he resigned in protest from Washington's cabinet.

• Rupert Hughes claimed: "This [Jefferson's assertion that Washington was a Deist] would seem to be the truth. In his time the deist was a term of fierce reproach, almost worse than atheist, though a deist believed in an all-wise deity who cared for the world and provided a future reward for the good. This deity was not, however, the Israelitic Jehovah and was not the father of Christ, who was considered a wise and virtuous man, but not of divine origin." Strange, that if Washington was a Deist, that he refused to correspond with Thomas Paine after Paine wrote the *Age of Reason*, and even though Washington had a large and well representative library, the *Age of Reason* was not found on his shelf, although several volumes in criticism of Deism and of Paine were. And if Washington's Deity was not the "Israelitic Jehovah," then why did he write to the Hebrew congregation in Savannah, and describe the God he trusted in that had delivered America in the revolution as the "same wonder-working deity" that the Jewish scriptures presented, and which Washington named, "Jehovah"? Is it possible that Rupert Hughes was wrong about Washington's use of the name Jehovah, just as he was about Washington's use of the name "Jesus Christ"? It appears so. But even though Hughes obviously had not done his scholarly due diligence on this topic, like many other scholars, that did not stop him from making definitive—albeit spurious—pronouncements on the subject. And if the term "Deist" brought fierce reproach, why did Paine get the brunt of all of that fierce reproach——so much so that a graveyard could scarcely be found where he could be buried when he died——but Washington was beloved beyond words? Was it that Washington simply pretended to be a Christian, as he called himself on several occasions, simply to hide the fact that he was really a Deist? Then what are we to make of all of his constant claims of candor, honesty, character, and truthfulness?

- Rupert Hughes claimed: "Such was probably Washington's opinion on the subject, though there is little evidence either way. In spite of his incessant allusions to providence, Washington was persistently silent as to his dogmatic beliefs." While Rupert Hughes here hedges his bets by saying "probably" and supports it with the claim that there is little evidence either way, the fact is that there is a vast amount of evidence, and Hughes, believing that there was none, never bothered to look for it. The religious themes and issues in Washington's writings are full enough so that in this work we have been able to establish his Christian worldview, his perspective on the Gospel, his vast biblical literacy, his approval of many evangelical and anti-Deist sermons and writings, and his support for Christian missionary activities, as well as clear critical comments against Deism, to name but a few of our discoveries.

- Rupert Hughes claimed: "The fanatically abused 'atheist,' Jefferson, was far more religious than Washington, and intensely interested in Jesus, whom he revered this side of divinity. … The greatly reviled Thomas Paine believed in God as a loving father, though he denounced the Bible as not His word." While Jefferson could not call Jesus God, Washington did call Jesus Christ "The Divine Author of our Blessed Religion," "The Divine Author of Life and Felicity"; "The Great Lord and Ruler of Nations." If Jefferson was far more religious than Washington, why did Jefferson refuse to be a sponsor in baptism and fail to actively serve as a vestryman, although elected? Washington, on the other hand, on eight occasions accepted the responsibility to sponsor a child in Christian baptism, and his service on the vestry and as warden for several years was exemplary and costly in terms of time, stress, and resources. Why did Washington repeatedly use the words "ardent," "fervent," "devout," and "pious," to describe his prayers, of which there are over one hundred in his own hand? If Paine did not believe the Bible to be God's Word, Washington did, calling it in his own written words, "The blessed religion revealed in the word of God." In so doing, Washington not only disagreed with Paine, he definitively distanced himself from Deism.

- Rupert Hughes claimed: "The Reverend Doctor Moncure D. Conway makes a statement that is impressive in view of the emphasis unjustifiably laid on the imaginary doctrine that Washington was brought up in an atmosphere of intense religion: 'In his many letters to his adopted nephew and young relatives, he admonishes them about their morals, but in no case have I been able to discover any suggestion that they should read the Bible, keep the Sabbath, go to church, or any warning against Infidelity.'" Actually, the facts are quite different than this, if we listen to the records given by these very same children who write of his Christianity, his sabbath keeping, his reading of the Bible to the family, his passionate prayer for the healing for his dying step-daughter, and his concern for religion and reverence in public and private life. Reverend Conway's scholarship apparently never got around to a careful reading of Washington's letters to his adopted grandson, where scripture is quoted and spiritual duties are addressed—duties to "God and man," as he wrote to young George Washington Parke Custis—nor to the testimonies of Washington's stepchildren.
- Rupert Hughes claimed: "Washington had in his library the writings of Paine, Priestly, Voltaire, Frederick the Great, and other heretical works." True enough, but Washington had books that critiqued Deism in his library as well. As can be seen

in the chapter on "Washington's Clergy and Sermons," he wrote letters to clergymen who had written sermons against Deism, and commended them. He said that their teachings were both pleasing to him and sound in doctrine. Thomas Paine's the *Age of Reason* was not in Washington's library, nor was Paine, after writing *The Age of Reason*, any longer on Washington's correspondence list.

- Rupert Hughes claimed: "Dr. Conway, speaking of Washington's Diaries, notes 'his pretty regular attendance at church but never any remark on the sermons.'" While it is true that remarks on sermons were scarce in Washington's diaries, Dr. Conway is incorrect that Washington "never" makes any remark on sermons. But then, what he said about sermons in his diaries is more than what he wrote in his diaries about the discussions of the Constitutional Convention. However, Dr. Conway failed to observe, as has every writer on the Deist perspective of Washington since, that Washington's vast correspondence included extensive writings with clergymen. In fact, Washington commented on several published sermons from these authors in his letters. If Dr. Conway or Rupert Hughes (or Professor Boller for that matter) had read these letters and these sermons, they would have found that Washington's comments show again and again that he was a Christian and not a Deist. We thought this matter so important, we have devoted an entire chapter to it. (Please, see chapter 33 entitled "George Washington's Clergy and Their Sermons").

- Rupert Hughes claimed: "If Washington were, indeed, so fervent a Christian as to deserve the name of 'a soldier of the cross,' often given to him by the clergy, it is puzzling that there should be such difficulty in finding a number of fervent proofs of his ardor." We wish to reply to Rupert Hughes that we have had no difficulty in finding a "number of fervent proofs of his ardor." The problem for us is to relate all the data that pertains to Washington's "sacred fire" to our readers in the limited pages we have been allotted. Washington's words about his own religion and spirituality are a vast and remarkably overlooked field of study. We do not intend to call Washington a "soldier of the Cross," even though it would not be inappropriate to call him a "Christian Soldier," since that was his own phrase for his army, and he did call on his men to attain the "highest glory of the character of a Christian." But perhaps it would not be inappropriate for us to say here that the "fervent prayers," the "ardent prayers," and the "pious entreaties" that Washington described in his writings may well have fanned the "sacred fire" that ignited his love for liberty and put a spiritual dynamic into his motto—"My God and My Country."

Since the objections by Rupert Hughes are without substance, we will proceed to address other arguments that skeptics have brought against the truth of Washington's own claim that he was a Christian, as seen, for example, in his words from a private letter "on my honor and the faith of a Christian."

HOW COULD A TRUE CHRISTIAN OWN SLAVES?

Indeed, another objection to the thesis of George Washington the Christian is that he owned slaves. Yes, that is the sad truth. If there is any good news in this sad fact, Washington freed his slaves upon his death, something Thomas Jefferson never did. Of the nine slave-owning presidents, Washington was the only one who freed them all, albeit at his death.

Meanwhile, the transformation of Washington, as he moved from being an indifferent slave owner to being a principled slave owner, one who would purchase no more slaves and one who would not break up slave families, to finally becoming an emancipator of slaves in his last will and testament, is a fascinating story. Early on, for example, in the Fairfax Resolves of 1774, George Washington and George Mason solemnly judged the slave trade: "After the first day of November next we will neither ourselves import nor purchase any slave or slaves imported by any other person, either from Africa, the West Indies, or any other place." The Fairfax Resolves were early and strong declarations against slavery. But the British authorities kept these resolves from being implemented. (This was long before William Wilberforce and his evangelical comrades led their long, successful crusade to end the slave trade and slavery in the British Empire.)

This objection to Washington as a Christian——that he owned slaves— obvious-

Slave quarters at Mount Vernon

ly cannot be applied uniquely to Washington. The judgment here is against the entire practice of all slave owners, whether in the North or the South. (Indeed, in the colonial era, slavery was tolerated by all of the colonies from New York south.) To understand Washington's complicity in this evil trading in human lives, we must recognize his historical context, and then see how Washington's life began to change as he grew to understand the incongruity of his own quest for freedom, all the while that he owned slaves. Clearly, slavery was a moral wrong. It was, to put it in Christian terms, a sin against God and a sin against one's neighbor. Nevertheless, Washington's process of repentance from the wrong of slave-holding to the right of emancipating his slaves was also a remarkable sign of what Christian theology has termed repentance.

George Washington grew up in a Virginia where, tragically, slaves had been part of the culture for generations. Dr. Martin Luther King, Jr. used to point out that slaves came to the New World a year before the Pilgrim fathers and mothers did. As we saw earlier, a European ship selling slaves came into Jamestown, Virginia in 1619, one year before the voyage of the *Mayflower.*

But the very change in attitude toward slavery in Washington's life actually argues for his Christian identity. This is because he was willing to face a wrong in his life and in his culture and to begin the long hard struggle to make things right. Note the following progression in the attitude of the father of our country toward this terrible injustice that was there 150 years before he ever held a high position of leadership:

- When Washington grew up, he already owned slaves as a child of a Virginia family with a large plantation. We find that early in his life, he actually sold some slaves to buy things like lemons and various products from the Caribbean. They were, for a time in his life, chattel property.[3]

- As he became a young adult and began to be a person who cared about what was true and right, he began to write, "I will never again separate a family by selling my slaves." In other words, he realized that they had a right to a family home, and he would not break up families.[4]

- Later on in his life, he began to say, "Slavery is wrong, and we must do something to end it."[5] But the system was so deeply imbedded in his Virginian plantation culture that he could not entirely break free from the sad practices of slavery[6]—that is, until his death and his liberating will took force.

- By the end of his life, Washington, determined in his will that he would free all the slaves that belonged to him and actually provided for them financially. He also freed one of his closest friends, Billy Lee, a slave that was his body servant. Remembering him by name, Washington gave him a bequest that enabled him to live the rest of his life very comfortably.

So what we see in Washington is what Christianity calls forth from all who follow Christ: a growth in what is right, the beginning to change until, finally, right actions become normative. It took Washington a lifetime. It took America a different generation and a bloody war to get it right, but Washington was one of the leaders that called for the ending of slavery in America.

If we remember that future generations often can see the flaws of the past far more clearly than those who were living in the midst of the struggles, we can understand that Washington's conduct, although slow and over a lifetime, was significant progress for a slave-holding Southern plantation owner. He understood the evils of slavery without the need of a war to point it out to him. Slavery was one of Washington's sins, or moral failures, but the standard for being a Christian is not perfection, it is honestly dealing with one's sin and failures in light of God's life-changing grace. It appears that is exactly what Washington did, and so, even Washington's sin of slavery and how he dealt with it, argues for his Christian identity.

WASHINGTON SLANDERS OR WASHINGTON SCANDALS?

A great deal of discussion has occurred on Washington's possible scandals. It appears, however, that when all of the evidence is in, the alleged moral failures turn out to be slanders rather than scandals. The most thorough debunking of the allegations of Washington's promiscuity was by John Fitzpatrick in his article, "The George Washington Slanders."[7] The essence of his research is that not only is there no evidence to support the claim of promiscuity or of an illegitimate Washington child, there is direct, hard evidence that these accusations were part of the spurious letters that were circulating in Washington's lifetime to discredit him as a leader in order to make it easier to undermine his leadership in the revolution. In other words, the slanders were part of a British propaganda smear campaign that failed. These accusations can be dismissed with confidence as being unfounded and thereby disproved.

Not so easily answered, however, is the question of Washington's alleged lifelong love for Sally Fairfax, who was married to his older friend, George William Fairfax.[8] So next, we will consider Washington's relationship with Sally Fairfax.

WASHINGTON'S RELATIONSHIP WITH SALLY FAIRFAX

The evidence with regard to Washington's relationship with Sally Cary Fairfax and his letters to her are more compelling and must be considered with some care.[9] On September 12, 1758, unmarried, but engaged Col. Washington wrote to Mrs. George William Fairfax from his lonely post in the wilderness of Pennsylvania in the midst of the French and Indian War,

> 'Tis true, I profess myself a votary of love. I acknowledge that a lady is in the case, and further I confess that this lady is known to you... I feel the force of her amiable beauties in the recollection of a thousand tender passages that I could wish to obliterate, till I am bid to revive them. But experience, alas! Sadly reminds me how impossible this is, and evinces an opinion which I have long entertained, that there is a Destiny which has the control of our actions, not to be resisted by the strongest efforts of Human Nature.
>
> You have drawn me, dear Madame, or rather I have drawn myself, into an honest confession of a simple Fact. Misconstrue not

my meaning; doubt it not, nor expose it. The world has no business
to know the object of my love, declared in this manner to you, when
I want to conceal it . . . Adieu to this till happier times, if I ever shall
see them. The hours at present are melancholy dull . . . I dare believe
you are as happy as you say. I wish I was happy also.[10]

Some have tried to explain this letter away by claiming this and similar letters are counterfeit, but scholars have satisfactorily shown them to be genuine.[11]

Mrs. George William Fairfax was eighteen and a newlywed when she met George as a sixteen-year-old at Belvoir, the Fairfax estate. From letters that have survived, it is clear that they became lifelong friends.

Sally's letters to George have not survived, but George's intriguing letters to Sally in 1758 have aroused great interest and have been interpreted in several ways. What makes the letters alluring is that they were written to Sally Cary Fairfax, George William Fairfax's wife, by the lonely, unmarried Col. Washington, who was now engaged to Martha Custis, soon to be Mrs. Martha Washington. (While it is startling to realize that Washington was engaged and writing such letters, the facts are that Washington had met his fiancée Martha only twice, while his friendship with Sally Fairfax had developed over many years). The range of interpretations include: (1) a cryptic expression of a past love affair,[12] (2) a deeply emotional attachment that was morally contained due to their (or Sally's) commitment to honor, (3) a warm, personal relationship that continued as a lifelong friendship between the Washingtons and the Fairfaxes,[13] to (4) a role-playing exercise based upon George's and Sally's love of the theater and courtly romance.[14] As we begin our assessment, we wish to make clear that we accept the authenticity of the letter and its timing of an engaged Washington writing to a married friend's wife, who was also Washington's friend.

ADULTERY?

First of all, passion was not foreign to Washington's experience, even though he was always known as a man under the greatest personal control. His passing comments in various letters give us a hint of his understanding of human nature and its passions.

- To John Banister, April 21, 1778, "We must take the passions of men as nature has given them, and those principles as a guide, which are generally the rule of action."[16]
- To John Jay, August 1, 1786, "We must take human nature as

we find it. Perfection falls not to the share of mortals."[17]

- In a humorous letter referring to poetry, Washington wrote to Mrs. Richard Stockton, September 2, 1783, "When once the woman has tempted us, and we have tasted the forbidden fruit, there is no such thing as checking our appetites, whatever the consequences may be."[18]

Did George Washington commit adultery? We know that Martha Washington burned their letters after George's death. Critical authors have read much into such a burning. Could it be, they speculate, that she was covering up an alleged affair between the father of our country and some wife of the Revolution? Tongue-in-cheek author, Marvin Kitman, makes fun of this bonfire incident:

> No one has ever explained the motive behind this wild letter-burning episode. Martha Washington knew at the time—indeed, the whole world knew—that George Washington was a superstar in the field of history, and that every scrap of his writing would be treasured and printed. Did she feel, as Woodward [W. E. Woodward, *George Washington: The Image and the Man,* 1926] suggests, that his letters to her were so sacred in their intimacy that posterity had no right to read them?
>
> ....Perhaps Lady Washington did not want to cast her husband's pearls before us swine.
>
> "Privacy," explains historian Richard B. Bernstein. "There. You have your explanation."
>
> ....Martha was not as dumb as historians make her seem. She knew something was going on between those two [George Washington and Kit Greene, wife of Nathanael].[19]

With all of his teasing, Kitman never declares Washington committed adultery. Instead, he notes: "I have read a thousand history books, and there is not a single case of an unnatural act—that is, [Washington] sleeping with somebody, not even Molly Pitcher."[20]

Washington-biographer James Thomas Flexner describes George Washington and Sally Fairfax this way:

Washington's existence at Mount Vernon was being troubled and made fascinating by the woman to whom he wrote, when he was old and celebrated, that none of the subsequent events of his career 'nor all of them together have been able to eradicate from my mind those happy moments, the happiest of my life, which I have enjoyed in your company.' What surely was the most passionate love of Washington's life had dark overtones: Sally was married, married to his neighbor and close friend George William Fairfax. Washington's love was no flash fire that burns away quickly. He had first met Sally when she was eighteen and he was sixteen, and she had come to Belvoir as a bride. Her two years' seniority must then have created a significant gap, but the sixteen-year-old grew into the impressive giant whose physical and military adventures electrified all Virginia. The exact nature of their relationship cannot be defined. Washington was to write Sally that he recollected "a thousand tender passages"; and a mutual female friend admonished Washington, just before his defeat at Fort Necessity, to seek "some unknown she that may recompense you for all your trials" and make him abandon "pleasing reflections on the hours past." Whatever transpired did not break Washington's friendship with Sally's husband; the suitor remained welcome at Belvoir.[21]

We believe there is no evidence of an adulterous affair between George Washington and Sally Fairfax. The charge is baseless. But, may we suggest that Washington may well have wrestled with romantic feelings for Sally in his youthful years? In his teen years, Washington admitted his struggle with his romantic feelings— what he called his "chaste and troublesome passion."[21] He did his best to keep his passions under control.

Speaking of yet another young lady he had known as a teenager whose name has been lost to history, he wrote the following.

...but as that's only adding Fuel to fire, it makes me the more uneasy. For by often and unavoidably being in Company with her revives my former Passion for your Low Land Beauty. Whereas was I to live more retired from young Women I might in some measure eliviate my sorrows by burying that chast and troublesome Passion in the grave of oblivion or etarnall forgetfulness. For as I am very well assured that's the only antidote or remedy that I ever shall be releivd by, or only recess than can administer any cure or help to me. As I am well convinced was I ever to attempt any thing I should only get a denial, which would be only adding grief to uneasiness.[23]

The same kind of "chaste and troublesome Passion" seems to have been the case here with Sally as well, since careful research points to no evidence of an incident of unfaithfulness on their part. Perhaps the best way to describe the situation is that in a moment of weakness, facing loneliness and possible death, Washington allowed himself to write words of romantic force to a close friend for whom he had felt romantic emotions.

His fiancée, Martha Custis, was the perfect wife, but he had only met her twice. On the second meeting he proposed and she accepted. But then Washington had to return to war. In that distant place, a young adult and unmarried Washington apparently let his "troublesome Passion" become less than emotionally "chaste." But the true point of the story is that they both conquered the passion. It must have been at least, in part, mutual, for Sally kept the letter all her life, and it was only found years later after her death in England, and then brought to America. But Sally, George, and their spouses became close friends as couples after the French and Indian War. They lived joyfully as neighbors until the Revolutionary War became imminent and the Fairfaxes left for England, never to return again to America. Who then was Sally Fairfax to George Washington? She was a youthful flame that Washington contained. Washington certainly must have been intentionally, although clandestinely autobiographical, as he wrote to his adopted granddaughter, Nelly Custis,

Love is said to be an involuntary passion, and it is, therefore, contended that it cannot be resisted. This is true in part only, for like all things else, when nourished and supplied plentifully with ailment [i.e., that which troubles, or, Washington's "troublesome Passion"], it is rapid in its progress; but let these be withdrawn and it may be stifled in its birth or much stinted in its growth. For example, a woman (the same may be said of the other sex) all beautiful and accomplished, will, while her hand and heart are undisposed of, turn the heads and set the circle in which she moves on fire. Let her marry, and what is the consequence? The madness *ceases* and all is quiet again. Why? not because there is any diminution in the charms of the lady, but because there is an end of hope. Hence it follows, that love may and therefore ought to be under the guidance of reason, for although we cannot avoid first impressions, we may assuredly place them under guard.[24]

Did not Washington say as much in his letter to Sally?

I feel the force of her amiable beauties in the recollection of a thousand tender passages that I could wish to obliterate, till I am bid to revive them. But experience, alas! sadly reminds me how impossible this is, and evinces an opinion which I have long entertained, that there is a Destiny which has the control of our actions, not to be resisted by the strongest efforts of Human Nature.[25]

Francis Rufus Bellamy has put it this way,

Added to these social and religious considerations was the friendship already existing between George Washington and George William, Sally's husband and Lawrence's brother-in-law. Under no circumstances could a man of honor coldly contemplate stealing the wife of his friend and next-door neighbor. Nor if he could, would an intelligent woman permit him. What then was left for two people in such a situation? Surely only inner denial and outward friendship. That something like this was what happened to Washington in his youth seems clear; and that it was not easy goes without saying. For he was in his tumultuous twenties at the time, and he was not born with control over his feelings; he achieved mastery by conscious effort.[26]

As we assess this youthful episode in Washington's life, we see what is again, the authentic struggle of a Christian life. A Christian is not perfect. A Christian will struggle with temptations and desires that are wrong. But in the midst of the duty to do what is right, the temptation can be conquered, and the sin can be forgiven. And as a result, relationships can be maintained. The lifelong friendship and relationship that was marked by honor between the Fairfaxes and the Washingtons is a testimony to the Christian faith that both families practiced.

As we've already seen, even secular Washington historian James Thomas Flexner had to admit: "Whatever transpired did not break Washington's friendship with Sally's husband; [Washington]… remained welcome at Belvoir."[27]

WASHINGTON AND ANGER–A MAN OF PASSION UNDER CONTROL

Just as Washington learned to control his romantic passions, so Washington also learned to control his temper. He was known for occasional flashes of great anger. For example, he was so angry at General Charles Lee's retreat at the Battle of Monmouth that Washington determined to have him court martialed.

Washington was a man who knew the power of passion and had learned to exercise a spiritual control over his powerful emotions. Washington's comments on human passion are not only instructive, but they are reflective of his own spiritual struggles:

- To Gouverneur Morris, May 29, 1778, "We may lament that things are not consonant with our wishes, but cannot change the nature of Men, and yet those who are distressed by the folly and perverseness of it, cannot help complaining."[28]

- To Lafayette, September 1, 1778, "It is the nature of man to be displeased with everything that disappoints a favorite hope or flattering project; and it is the folly of too many of them to condemn without investigating circumstances."[29]

- To a Committee of Congress, January 28, 1778, "A small knowledge of human nature will convince us, that, with far the greatest part of mankind, interest is the governing principle; and that, almost, every man, is more or less under its influence."[30]

- To John Banister, April 21, 1778, "We must take the passions of men as nature has given them, and those principles as a guide, which are generally the rule of action."[31]

- To John Laurens, July 10, 1782, "It is not the public, but the private interest, which influences the generality of mankind, nor can the Americans any longer boast an exception."[32]

- To John Jay, August 1, 1786, "We must take human nature as we find it. Perfection falls not to the share of mortals."[33]

- To John Marshall, December 4, 1797, "Unfortunately the

nature of man is such, that the experience of others is not attended to as it ought to be. We must *feel*, ourselves, before we can think or perceive the danger that threatens."[34]

- To John Jay, May 18, 1786, "Ignorance and design are difficult to combat. Out of these proceed illiberal sentiments, improper jealousies, and a train of evils which oftentimes in republican governments must be sorely felt before they can be renewed."[35]

As we have already seen in the chapter on George Washington's personality, he had a powerful, passionate temper that he faithfully sought to keep under control. Francis Rufus Bellamy shares a fascinating anecdote from the Washington family in this regard:

> Incidentally, the painter's [Gilbert Stuart's] daughter, Jane Stuart, also supplies a sidelight on Washington's reputation as the possessor of a fiery disposition even then. Talking one day to General Harry Lee, her father happened to remark that Washington had a tremendous temper but held it under wonderful control. Light Horse Harry reported the remark to George and Martha at breakfast a few days later. "I saw your portrait the other day, a capital likeness," said Lee, "but Stuart says you have a tremendous temper." "Upon my word," said Mrs. Washington, coloring, "Mr. Stuart takes a great deal on himself, to make such a remark" "But stay, my dear lady," said General Lee, 'He added that the President had it under wonderful control.' With something like a smile, General Washington remarked, "He's right."[36]

Such growth in self-control is a mark of spiritual maturity, a goal of the Christian life.[37]

THE TREATY OF TRIPOLI

The last matter that we will consider here is Washington's alleged involvement in the treaty that the United States established with Tripoli. The Treaty of Tripoli came about because Muslim ships dispatched from the Barbary coast of Africa were attacking American vessels and turning the captors into slaves. This treaty put on paper an agreement to stop this terrible practice.

The relevance of the wording of the Treaty of Tripoli for our discussion is how its text related to Washington's religion, as well as how it reflects our founders' view of the relationship of Christianity and the American Constitution. For example, does it matter for our interpretation of the religion clauses of the First Amendment, whether or not Washington said to the Muslims in Tripoli, "These United States are not in any sense founded on the Christian religion."[38]

We believe that it does matter if Washington said this. If we are to understand the original intent of the Constitution that the founders wrote, we must understand Washington, who presided over the Constitutional Convention.

Did Washington write, "America is in no way founded upon the Christian religion" in the Treaty with Tripoli? Scholars on both sides of the debate regarding Washington's Deism—even Boller, who rejects Washington's Christianity—have concurred that this is a myth,[39] although not everyone has gotten the word.[40] Thus, frequently and unfortunately, it is still stated as though it were a fact.

In fact, there is ambiguity surrounding the authenticity of this phrase in the treaty itself that was signed by President John Adams. Charles I. Bevans states in *Treaties and Other International Agreements of the United Sates of America,*

> This translation from the Arabic by Joel Barlow, Consul General at Algiers, has been printed in all official and unofficial treaty collections since it first appeared in 1797 in the Session Laws of the Fifth Congress, first session. In a "Note Regarding the Barlow Translation" Hunter Miller stated: ". . .Most extraordinary (and wholly unexplained) is the fact that Article 11 of the Barlow translation, with its famous phrase, 'the government of the United States of America is not in any sense founded on the Christian Religion.' does not exist at all. There is no Article 11. The Arabic text which is between Articles 10 and 12 is in form a letter, crude and flamboyant and withal quite unimportant, from the Dey [Governor] of Algiers to the Pasha [ruler] of Tripoli. How that script came to be written and to be regarded as in the Barlow translation, as Article 11 of the treaty as there written, is a mystery and seemingly must remain so. Nothing in the diplomatic correspondence of the time throws any light whatever on the point."[41]

Is it possible that Joel Barlow's explorations of atheism may have induced him to interpolate this phrase into the treaty?[42] At any rate, Washington never wrote nor signed the disputed words of the Treaty of Tripoli. In stark contrast to this dubious statement from the Treaty of Tripoli, Washington wrote on September 19, 1796, "Of all the dispositions and habits which lead to political prosperity, Religion and morality are indispensable supports. In vain would that man claim the tribute of Patriotism, who should labour to subvert these great Pillars of human happiness, these firmest props of the duties of Men and citizens. The mere Politician, equally with the pious man ought to respect and to cherish them. A volume could not trace all their connections with private and public felicity."

CONCLUSION

What the objections of this chapter demonstrate is that Washington was not a perfect man. In Christian terms, he was a man who sinned. But the definition of a Christian is not perfection, and being a sinner does not make a man a Deist. If that were the case, then every Christian would be a Deist, since Christianity affirms the universality of sin.

Perhaps a more appropriate definition of a Christian is a person who practices faithful and faith-filled repentance. Washington's repentance of slavery at the end of his life, his repentant control over the misplaced passions of temptation, and his self-control over his explosive anger are each indicative of a spiritual life. While Washington never wrote, "America is in no way founded upon the Christian religion" in the Treaty with Tripoli, it is clear to us that the Christian religion is what Washington's spiritual growth was founded upon.

TWENTY SEVEN

"Minds of Peculiar Structure":

George Washington vs. Deism

"Whatever may be conceded to the influence of refined education on minds of peculiar structure, reason and experience both forbid us to expect that National morality can prevail in exclusion of religious principle."
George Washington, 1796[1]

As we have already seen, reason was in the air during the seventeen hundreds. By reason, man now knew he was no longer the center of the universe, but also by reason he was sure he would be its master. German philosopher Immanuel Kant declared, "*Sapere aude!*—Dare to reason! Have the courage to use your own minds!—is the motto of enlightenment."[2] Alexander Pope's "Essay On Man" reflected the intoxicating optimism that was the enticement of enlightenment thought: "O happiness! Our being's end and aim! Good, pleasure, ease, content! Whate'er thy name."[3]

This enlightenment spirit sometimes expressed itself as Deism, which Noah Webster's 1828 *American Dictionary* defined as, "The doctrine or creed of a deist; the belief or system of religious opinions of those who acknowledge the existence of one God, but deny revelation: or deist is the belief in natural religion only, or those truths, in doctrine and practice, which man is to discover by the light of reason, independent and exclusive of any revelation from God. Hence deism implies infidelity or a disbelief in the divine origin of the scriptures."[4]

DEISM AND THE FOUNDING FATHERS

But this emphasis upon the power of human reason did not mean that our founding fathers agreed on everything, or that all of them became Deists. Norman Cousins has well written, "To say that the Founding Fathers were the products of the Age of Enlightenment does not mean that they had a uniform view of religion or politics or anything else. All the Enlightenment did, and this was enough, was to give men greater confidence than before in the reach of the human intelligence."[5]

In fact, some of them, like John Adams, were explicitly opposed to Deism. John Adams wrote to fellow founder Dr. Benjamin Rush on January 21, 1810:

> Learned, ingenious, benevolent, beneficent old friend of 1774! Thanks for "the light and truth," as I used to call the Aurora, which you sent me. You may descend in a calm, but I have lived in a storm, and shall certainly die in one....
>
> I have not seen, but am impatient to see, Mr. Cheetham's life of Mr. Paine. His political writings, I am singular enough to believe, have done more harm than his irreligious ones. He understood neither government nor religion. From a malignant heart, he wrote virulent declamation, which the enthusiastic fury of the times intimated all men, even Mr. Burke, from answering, as he ought. His deism, as it appears to me, has promoted rather than retarded the cause of revolution in America, and indeed in Europe. His billingsgate, stolen from Blounts' Oracles of Reason, from Bolingbroke, Voltaire, Be¢renger, &c., will never discredit Christianity, which will hold its ground in some degree as long as human nature shall have any thing moral or intellectual left in it. The Christian religion, as I understand it, is the brightness of the glory and the express portrait of the character of the eternal, self-existent, independent, benevolent, all powerful and all merciful creator, preserver, and father of the universe, the first good, first

perfect, and first fair. It will last as long as the world. Neither savage nor civilized man, without a revelation, could ever have discovered or invented it. Ask me not, then, whether I am a Catholic or Protestant, Calvinist or Arminian. As far as they are Christians, I wish to be a fellow-disciple with them all. [6]

Benjamin Franklin, like John Adams, was clearly not an advocate of the perspective of Thomas Paine. Writing to Paine on July 3, 1786, Franklin declared, after reviewing a draft of the *Age of Reason*:

> I would advise you, therefore, not to attempt unchaining the tiger, but to burn this piece before it is seen by any other person; whereby you will save yourself a great deal of mortification by the enemies it may raise against you, and perhaps a good deal of regret and repentance. If men are so wicked *with religion*, what would they be *if without it*. I intend this letter itself as a *proof* of my friendship, and therefore add no *professions* to it; but subscribe simply yours, B. Franklin. [7]

In the same letter to Paine, he likened defying God (which the book did) to spitting in the wind wherein it lands right back on one's own face.

But it is clear that some of our founding fathers did embrace elements of the Deistic perspective. For example John Marshall was a church attender but not a communicant. However, he was converted to the Christian faith at the end of his life. [8] Similarly, Virginia Burgessman Edmund Randolph recanted his youthful Deism as he got older. [9] Deism's rejection of revelation in favor of an exclusive dependence upon human reason brought with it in many instances an overt hostility to the clergy as well. [10] In mid-eighteenth century Virginia, there was already a growing concern over the emergence of Deism. We can see by a summary in the 1761 *Virginia Almanack* of a book entitled, *An Impartial Enquiry into the True Nature of the Faith, which is required in the Gospel as necessary to salvation, In which is briefly shown, upon how righteous terms Unbelievers may become true Christians: And the Case of Deists is reduced to a short Issue.* This was the *Almanack* that George Washington used for the period of May 24 through October 22, 1761, to write his diary notes. There is a high likelihood that Washington read it in its entirety, since he handled it nearly everyday for six months and because the value of the short 54-page long *Almanack* was enhanced by the

THE
VIRGINIA
ALMANACK
FOR THE
Year of our LORD GOD 1761.

BEING THE FIRST AFTER

BISSEXTILE, or LEAP-YEAR.

WHEREIN ARE CONTAINED

The LUNATIONS, CONJUNCTIONS, ECLIPSES; the Sun and Moon's Rising and Setting; the Rising, Setting and Southing, of the HEAVENLY BODIES; WEATHER; &c. CALCULATED ACCORDING TO ART; and referred to the HORIZON of 38 Degrees North Latitude, and a Meridian of Five Hours West from the City of London; fitting *Virginia*, *Maryland*, *North-Carolina*, &c.—Also, A Table of COURT-DAYS; Description of the ROADS through the CONTINENT; a List of the COUNCIL and HOUSE of BURGESSES of *Virginia*; Directions for making a *Travelling-Umbrella*, which may be carried without the least Inconvenience, with Remarks on the Propriety of Dress; Directions for making common Small-Beer, as pleasant as fine Ale, without any additional Expence: A certain Method of preserving Buildings from the fatal Effects of Lightning, with a few Queries to the Superstitious; a Method for preserving Virtues of Lemons and Oranges for Years; Limes in Cookery; a wholsome Liquor made from Ind'ian Corn; Directions how to prepare the Body for Inoculation, in the Small-Pox; by observing of which not one in 300 will lose their Lives, whereas, in the common Way of Infection, one den out of five.

To WHICH IS ADDED AN APPENDIX,

Containing a Collection of approv'd MAXIMS, entertaining EPIGRAMS, curious ANECDOTES, diverting STORIES, &c. &c. Calculated for INSTRUCTION and AMUSEMENT.

By THEOPHILUS WREG. Philom.

I will behold the Heavens, even the Works of thy Fingers, the Moon and Stars which thou hast ordained. Psal. viii. 3.

WILLIAMSBURG:
Printed and Sold by WILLIAM HUNTER.

Contained in the Virginia Almanack that Washington used in 1761 for his diary was the above summation of a book presenting the importance of Christian teaching versus that of Deism.

Sexes, Plantations, Riches, Prophecies, Ambition, Masks and Triumphs, Nature, and Natural Disposition in Men, Custom and Education, Fortune, Usury, Youth and Age, Beauty, Deformity, Building, Gardens, Negociating, Followers and Friends, Suitors, Studies, and the Reading of Books, Factions, Ceremonies, Praise, Vain-Glory, Honour and Reputation, Office of a Judge, Anger, Vicissitude of Things, Fragment of an Essay of Fame, Essay touching Helps for the Intellectual Powers, a Civil Character of Julius Cæsar, a Civil Character of Augustus Cæsar, a Civil Character of Henry VII. Felicities of Queen Elizabeth, Parables, Discredits of Learning, and the Answer, Discredits of Learning from the Objections of Politicians, &c. Discredits of Learning from Learned Mens Fortunes, Discredits of Learning from Learned Mens Studies, &c. Peccant Humours in Learning, Dignity of Learning, Human Proofs and Arguments, Influence of Learning in Military Affairs, Influence of Learning in Moral Virtue, Power and Sovereignty and Pleasures of Learning, Acts of Merit towards Learning, Defects in these Acts, History of Learning, Dignity and Difficulty of Civil History, Partition of Civil History, Ecclesiastical History, Appendages of History, Poetry, Triumphs of Man, Knowledge of Man's Body, Memory, Rhetorick, Critical and Pedantical Knowledge, Moral Knowledge, Civil Conversation, Architect of his Fortune, Inspired Divinity. Price 15s.

An Impartial Enquiry into the TRUE NATURE of that FAITH, which is required in the Gospel, as necessary to SALVATION. In which is briefly shown, upon how righteous Terms Unbelievers may become true Christians: And the Case of the DEISTS is reduced to a short Issue. Containing Section 1. Nature of Faith, or Belief, in the general. 2. Showing how much, and how readily, all Men act, in the most important Affairs of this World, upon Faith, or upon Grounds less certain. 3. True Nature of the Christian Faith. 4. In which the Nature of Christian Faith is more fully explained, by examining the Properties of Abraham's Faith, which Christians are bound to imitate. The first Property attributed to Abraham's Faith is considered; viz. That it was grounded on Reason. 5. In which the second Property of Abraham's Faith is considered; viz. The Righteousness of his Faith. 6. In which the third Property of Abraham's Faith is considered; viz. That it was a full Persuasion of his Mind. 7. In which the fourth Property of Abraham's Faith is considered; viz. That he gave Glory to God. 8. Shows in what Sense the Practice of Virtue is necessary to the Producing of Faith, in Christ Jesus. 9. Showing that no Man can attain to true Christian Faith, without the Assistance of the Divine Spirit influencing his Soul. 10. Concerning the due Submission of Reason, with regard to the Mysteries of Religion: In which the Nature of a Christian Mystery is explained. 11. In which the Influence and Efficacy of Divine Faith is considered. 12. Containing a summary Account of the

24

inclusion of informative charts and tables as well as humorous excerpts.[11]

THE MOST INFLUENTIAL DEISTS

Meanwhile, Deists in England felt the need to evaluate everything, including religion, in light of the new emphasis on reason. One of the intellectual leaders of the Deists was Lord Herbert of Cherbury (1581-1648), often called the father of English Deism. He wrote *Religion of the Gentiles With the Causes of their Errors*. His essential articles of faith were: (1) the existence of God; (2) His Worship; (3) the practice of virtue; (4) repentance of sin; and (5) a faith in immortality. These truths he believed to be self-evident and accessible by all men everywhere since these beliefs were rationally based. Undergirding his perspective was the notion that all claims of revealed religion must be tested by reason.[12] Lord Herbert found the Christian Gospel by salvation through faith in Jesus Christ untenable under the scrutiny of reason.[13]

The early English-language Deists writers included the English: Lord Herbert of Cherbury, John Toland, Robert Collins, Matthew Tindal (not to be confused with Bible translator of the Reformation age William Tyndale), William Wollaston, Charles Blount, Henry St. John Bolingbroke, Thomas Chubb, Samuel Clarke, and John Leland. The earliest French Deist writers were Voltaire and Diderot. But the Deist that most Americans became aware of was Thomas Paine, author of the anti-Christian Deistic work the *Age of Reason* in which he declared, "The Christian theory is little less than the idolatry of the ancient mythologists, accommodated to the purposes of power and revenue; and it yet remains to reason and philosophy to abolish the amphibious fraud."[14]

DEISM VS. CHRISTIAN PHILOSOPHY ON CAMPUS

It was inevitable that Deistic thought would cross the ocean and enter the thinking of America's young scholars. Examples of Deistic thought appeared in colonial Virginia in the context of William and Mary College.[15]

Ezra Stiles and Timothy Dwight, the presidents of Yale College during the years of George Washington's presidency, were keenly aware of the threat of Deism to orthodox Christianity. As early as 1759, Stiles wrote to Thomas Clap, then president of Yale, "Deism has got such Head in this Age of Licentious Liberty that it would be in vain to try to stop it by hiding the Deistical Writings: and the only Way left to conquer & demolish it, is to come forth into the open Field & Dispute this matter on even Footing—the evidences of Revelation in my opinion are nearly as demonstrative as Newton's Principia, & these are the Weapons he used."[16]

Stiles' successor to the presidency of Yale was Timothy Dwight. His approach to the problem of Deism can be seen in his address to the graduating class of Yale. In September 1797, he gave lectures (published the next year at the request of his students) entitled, "Two Discourses On The Nature and Danger of Infidel Philosophy."[17] This publication by Dwight was sent to George Washington by Reverend Zachariah Lewis, a young tutor at Yale that had been Washington's adopted grandson George Washington Parke Custis' tutor at the University of Pennsylvania in Philadelphia.

President Washington responded to Lewis on September 28, 1798, telling him: "I thank you for sending me Doctor Dwights Sermons to whom I pray you to present the complimts. of Yr. etc." The word "compliments" is an expression of "praise, admiration or congratulation." Ultimately, we do not know how extensively Washington agreed with the discourses, but they are valuable, because they represent an acknowledged study of what "infidel philosophy" looked like in Washington's day in the context of a respected college. Given this fact, our purpose here is to capture the essence of what the deistic thinkers of Washington's day were actually saying about their beliefs and about deistic ethical conduct and practice. And then, we want to compare these deistic ideas with Washington and see if his beliefs and ethical practices conformed to the deistic writers summarized by Dr. Dwight, the president of Yale College. The "infidel" philosophers specifically critiqued by President Dwight included the Deists: Blount, Lord Shaftesbury, Collins, Woolston, Tindal, Chubb, Lord Bolingbroke, Lord Herbert, Voltaire; and the philosophers Thomas Hobbes and David Hume.

Dwight's treatise is significant for it gives expression to the Christian enlightenment, or the cooperation of faith and reason, thereby providing an alternative to the secular wing of the enlightenment that expressed itself in Deism. Dwight explains, "That philosophy only, which is opposed to Christianity, is the subject of the following observations."[18]

Further, Dwight excludes the philosopher John Locke from the ranks of the Deists. Dwight is clear that Locke is a Christian:[19]

> Infidels have been ingenious men; that some of them have been learned men; and that a few of them have been great men. Hume, Tindal, and a few others, have been distinguished for superior strength of mind, Bolingbroke for eloquence of the pen, Voltaire for brilliancy of imagination, and various others for respectable talents

of different kinds. But I am wholly unable to form a list of Infidels, which can, without extreme disadvangage, be compared with the two Bacons, Erasmus, Cumberland, Stillingfleet, Grotius, Locke, Butler, Newton, Boyle, Berkeley, Milton, Johnson, etc. In no walk of genius, in no path of knowledge can Infidels support and claim to superiority, or equality with Christians.[20]

Thus, argues Timothy Dwight: Isaac Newton, John Locke, Hugo Grotius, John Milton, Robert Boyle were first-rate geniuses and believers in Jesus—whereas, Deists were lesser rate geniuses.

THE THEOLOGY OF THE DEISTS VS. WASHINGTON'S THEOLOGY

Dwight next highlights the theological doctrines of the Deists to show in what ways they departed from historic Christian thought. Here we will summarize the thinking and representative doctrines of some of the leading philosophers considered by Dwight, followed by a summary of a theological statement from Washington's writings to show that he disagreed with the Deists at every point.

Lord Herbert believed that all "Revealed Religion" (viz. Christianity) was "absolutely uncertain, and of little or no use." Washington believed that the pursuit of the Christian character should be our "highest glory."[21]

Thomas Hobbes' concept was that man was a "mere machine," and that the soul was "material and mortal." In contrast, Washington looked forward to a "glorious immortality."[22]

Charles Blount declared that divine revelation was unsupported because men could not agree on the truth of it. Washington declared that heaven had given the "treasures of knowledge" to the citizens of America.[23]

Lord Shaftesbury believed that the scriptures were an invention and miracles "ridiculous" and inconsequential. Washington spoke of the "word of God"[24] and found the scriptures to be so trustworthy that he referred to "the proof of holy writ" to confirm the truth of his words.[25]

Robert Collins saw the prophets as "fortunetellers" and thus, Christianity was based on a false foundation. Washington wrote of the veracity of Christianity in terms of "true religion," "true piety," and "a true Christian."[26]

William Tindal asserted that the scriptures were contradictory, confusing, and incomprehensible. *Washington* found the scriptures to contain the eternal rules of order and right, which heaven itself has ordained,[27] and the path of faith "so plain."[28]

Thomas Chubb declared that God was indifferent, prayer improper, Christ's life and teachings ridiculous and useless, the apostles imposters, and their teaching unworthy. Washington wrote of "good Providence,"[29] and he prayed faithfully as he "earnestly emplored" the "divine Being, in whose hands are all human events."[30] He called on America to imitate "the Divine Author of our Blessed Religion."[31]

David Hume, in a notably perverse logic, conceived that what is seen as God's "perfection," may in reality be defects, and his truly excellent nature is one of malice, folly, and injustice. Washington wrote consistently about the goodness of Providence, that "all wise and merciful disposer of events."[32]

Lord Bolingbroke acknowledged providences, yet argued there was no foundation for belief in them. God was ultimately unconcerned with man, and there would be no final judgment."[33] Washington attested to the goodness of Providence, "which will never fail to take care of his Children," and recognized the wrath of God, "the aggravated vengeance of Heaven."[34]

The clear conclusion from this survey is that Washington's doctrines stood in utter contrast from each of these representative Deists at every point. He cannot be classified as a Deist.

THE ETHICS OF THE DEISTS VS. WASHINGTON'S ETHICS

The sermon sent to George Washington by young Zechariah Lewis that was written by President Timothy Dwight not only criticized the theology of Deism, but also the ethics of Deism as well. A simple perusal of the Deist philosophers' ethics summarized by Dwight, the president of Yale, will show that they were as alien to Washington's personal values as rape, plunder, and atrocity were to the values of his army. As far as we can find, the issue of the ethics of Deism in the debate over Washington's religion has not been raised until now.

As we consider the vast chasm that emerges when Washington's ethics and the ethics of the Deists are compared, even the most strenuous advocate of Washington's Deism would have to admit that it is ludicrous to think that any of these beliefs reflect Washington's ethics. Washington's ethical values were distinctively Christian. So let us again compare Washington with the Deist writers identified by President Dwight.

Lord Herbert claimed that men were not accountable for their sinful actions. Washington, however, repeatedly warned his men to avoid vice and immorality,[35] and called them to "unfeignedly confess their Sins before God, and supplicate the all wise and merciful disposer of events."[36]

Hobbes espoused that civil law was the only true law by which men could be judged, and where civil law lapsed, men were to judge for themselves right from wrong. Washington appealed to the eternal rules of order ordained by heaven as the truest standard of morality.[37]

Lord Shaftesbury held that there was no true virtue, only virtue motivated by the mercenary concerns of final judgment.[38] Washington looked forward to "the benediction of Heaven,"[39] and "the future reward of good and faithful Servants."[40] He believed that the response to the goodness of Providence was true gratitude and virtue, and that he must be "worse than an infidel,"[41] that lacks faith, and "the man must be bad indeed who can look upon the events of the American Revolution without feeling the warmest gratitude towards the great Author of the Universe."[42]

Tindal asserted that judgment is conditional upon circumstances, and men are to consider the circumstances for each offence in order to pass judgment. Washington recognized the need to seek God's forgiveness for man's "manifold sins and wickedness."[43]

Chubb taught that there would be no ultimate judgment for impiety, ingratitude to God, or sinful behavior, but only for "injuries to the public." Washington warned of the consequences of impiety[44] and considered ingratitude to God a "black and detestable" sin.[45]

Hume's reverse logic claimed that self-aggrandizing, living only for self, and even suicide, were virtuous acts worthy of pursuit. Washington wrote often of self-denial,[46] the value of humility,[47] and sought to avoid anything which might lead one to suicide.

Lord Bolingbroke also affirmed that gratifying the flesh was the chief end of man, and thus adultry and polygamy were worthy pursuits."[48] Washington insisted his men avoid lewdness,[49] sexual immorality, and pursue moral purity.[51]

The ethical tenets of Deism, as here summarized by President Dwight, were viewed with horror in the American culture of Washington's day. Beyond the Deist's writings, such ethical teaching began to be openly advocated only at the arrival of the sexual revolution in the mid-twentieth century, and only became culturally normative with the expressive individualism of post-modernity. Yet the precursors for these views were the Deists of Washington's day. Washington was not one of the forerunners of the sexual revolution, precisely because he was not a Deist.

LIAR, LORD, OR LUNATIC? WASHINGTON'S ENDORSEMENT OF TWO SERMONS

It is clear that Deism was making a major impact on early America. Preachers gave sermons with challenges like the following:

If we regard as we ought, our Master's interest; if we feel that benevolence to our fellow-men, which the Gospel dictates, and that compassion to immortal Souls, perishing in their sins which it inspires, we shall be led to pursue every possible method, in order to make a determined opposition to the flood of infidelity, which is increasing with such rapidity.

But of all methods of opposing infidelity, none we believe is so efficacious as a holy life. To live the life of the Righteous, to exhibit in our daily deportment, a specimen of the christian virtues, is a constant practical defence of the Gospel. It shows the power of divine grace on the heart, and is a convincing proof, of the superlative excellency of Christianity. While we neglect no proper mean of defending our cause, let us be careful to set before unbelievers, this striking evidence in favour of our divine Master. Let our lives convince every beholder, that Religion is an undoubted reality. Let them see in our practice, that is inconceivably the most benevolent, and humane system, ever revealed to man; and that our belief of it is cordial and unshaken. This argument will certainly carry conviction home to their consciences; and without it no other defence will be productive of lasting benefit.[52]

One could be sure that a Deist like Thomas Paine would have to smile at the success of his beliefs and also disagree very deeply with a clergyman who sought to stop the advance of his views. Clearly, it would be wonderful if we had known what George Washington thought about a sermon like this. If he disagreed, clearly he would have been in the Deist camp. And if he found the doctrine sound, he would have to have been a Christian. The only other alternative is that Washington said something that he didn't believe, which runs contrary to all that we know about his commitment to character and personal integrity. Well, we now can answer the question of what Washington thought of this sermon, because he wrote a letter about it and declared his view.

At first blush, it may seem strange to raise the issue of sermons that Washington had read and endorsed at this point in our study. An argument for Washington's Christianity based on the mere fact that he possessed Christian sermons would not be conclusive by any standard of historical evaluation. Moreover, Professor Boller claims that what we can determine about Washington's attitudes toward the doctrinal content of any of the sermons that he possessed leaves us in a state of uncertainty anyway:

> In only two instances did Washington express his opinion on the
> content of sermons which had been forwarded to him. In August
> 1797, when he received a collection of sermons from Reverend
> Zechariah Lewis, twenty-four-year-old tutor at Yale College, he
> wrote to say: The doctrine in them is sound, and does credit to the
> author." Unfortunately, we do not know whose sermons they were
> (they were not Lewis', for the young tutor had published nothing at
> this time), and consequently we have no way of knowing what the
> doctrine was that Washington considered "sound."[53]

Our research shows that Boller is wrong. The letter from Washington to Zechariah
Lewis was from Mount Vernon on August 14, 1797. Washington wrote, "For the
Sermons you had the goodness to send me I pray you to accept my thanks. The doc-
trine in them is sound, and does credit to the Author."

Professor Boller has seemingly done the necessary scholarly work to establish his
point. This is seen, for example, when he assures us that young Lewis had not written
anything at the time this letter was written. From this, it is easy to assume that he has
also established that we really "do not know whose sermons they were ... and consequently we have no way of knowing what the doctrine was that Washington considered "sound." Should we trust Boller here? We do not think so.

Instead, we should find the letter that Zechariah Lewis wrote to Washington to
see if it gives us any clues. Fortunately, for our purposes, his letter is extant. We do not
know why Professor Boller did not consult this letter. If he had, he would have
discovered that we can clearly establish "whose sermons they were." Zechariah Lewis',
July 17, 1797, letter from Yale College in New Haven says:

> Permit me, Sir, to beg your acceptance of the two Sermons, lately
> preached by my Father, which accompany this letter. The political
> sentiments contained in the one, which was preached before the
> Gove[r]nor & Legislature of Connecticut, accorded with the
> feelings of a very crowded assembly; & appears to be the prevailing
> sentiments of this State. This is the only apology I offer for
> troubling you with the Sermon. I am Sir, with the highest
> affectation & respect for yourself & family Your much Obliged &

very Obedt Servt. Zechariah Lewis.

As we note the details of the letter, we discover several facts. There were "two sermons." They were "lately preached." They were preached by Reverend Zechariah Lewis' "Father." One clearly was a "political" sermon, preached "before the Governor."

The name of Zechariah Lewis' father was Isaac Lewis. When we consult the Evans Collection of Early American Imprints, we discover that there were three published sermons by Reverend Isaac Lewis. Two were preached relatively close together, satisfying the clue in the phrase "lately preached." The political sermon is easy to identify: "The Political Advantages of Godliness. A Sermon, preached before His Excellency the Governor, and the honorable Legislature of the State of Connecticut, convened at Hartford on the Anniversary Election" preached May 11, 1797.[54]

Isaac Lewis' second sermon was entitled, "The Divine Mission of Jesus Christ Evident from his Life, and From the Nature and Tendency of His Doctrines." The sermon is based on the text John 8:46, "Which of you convinceth me of sin? And if I say the truth, why do ye not believe me?" (King James Version)

Washington's letter in answer to Lewis for the gift of the sermons is significant. Again, he wrote, "For the Sermons you had the goodness to send me I pray you to accept my thanks. The doctrine in them is sound and does credit to the author."[55] Washington spoke of both sermons, since he used the word "Sermons" in the plural. Similarly, he referred to the sermons in the plural, since he used the plural pronoun "them" rather than "it." Washington had only one "author" in mind for these sermons. Thus, the letter comports exactly with Lewis' letter. Therefore, Washington's evaluation of the sermons referred to both the political and the more spiritual sermon. What was the sound doctrine in both of these sermons by Isaac Lewis?

We need to take a careful look at each, because both sermons that Washington declared to have been sound doctrine affirm the Christian faith and reject Deism. The first sermon sent by Lewis to Washington, "The Political Advantages of Godliness," was based on I Timothy 4:8, "*Godliness is profitable unto all things, having promise of the life that now is, and of that which is to come.*" In this sermon, Reverend Lewis not only affirms the necessity of Christianity for sound civil government, but he also lifts up Washington as the exemplar of Christian leadership. He writes,

> In all situations and conditions of life, true religion is of the first importance...Godliness is a term used in two senses; the one limited, and the other more general. In its limited sense, it includes

only the duties of piety toward God…that they may be divided into four classes, the duties we owe to God, to Christ, to our fellow-men, and to ourselves.

In the first of these, are comprised supreme love to God, a fixed dependance on, and a humble trust in him, a cordial submission to his providential dispensations, together with conformity to his revealed will.

In the second, are included faith in the mediator, accompanied with a daily and sincere attention to him, considered as our teacher, our example and lawgiver, our advocate and intercessor with the father.

In the third, are contained universal love to mankind, mercy, justice, beneficence, truth and the forgiveness of injuries.

The fourth, comprehends the graces of humility, meekness, prudence, fortitude and self-government.

…[Washington] whose distinguished talents and eminent abilities, faithfully consecrated to his country's service, have not only in an unexampled manner endeared him to his fellow-citizens, but rendered him the object of the veneration of the world. From that valuable legacy of political experience and sentiment, which he bequeathed to his country, in his address accompanying his resignation, I gladly introduce the following passages.

"Of all the dispositions and habits, says he, which lead to political prosperity, religion and morality are indispensable supports. In vain would that man claim the tribute of patriotism who should labor to subvert these great pillars of human happiness, these firmest props of the duties of men and citizens. The mere politician equally with the pious man ought to respect and to cherish them. A volume could not trace all their connections with private and public felicity. Let it simply be asked, where is the security for property, for reputation, for life, if the sense of religious obligation desert the oaths, which are the instruments of investigation in the courts of justice? And let us with caution indulge the supposition, that morality can be maintained without religion. Whatever may be conceded to the influence of refined education on minds of a peculiar structure; reason and experience both forbid us to expect, that national morality can prevail in exclusion of religious principle.

"It is substantially true, that virtue or morality is a necessary spring of popular government. The rule indeed extends with more or less force to every species of free government. Who that is a sincere friend to it, can look with indifferency on attempts to shake the foundation of the fabric?..."

The importance of supporting Christianity is undeniable. All the political benefits, which can be rationally expected from any religion ever taught in this world, may certainly be expected from the Christian, and in a much higher degree than from any other, in proportion to the superior excellency of its moral precepts. The candid enemies of our faith confess, that the morality taught in the gospel is the most pure, and the best adapted to the purposes of social happiness, of any moral system ever published to men. If then some religion be necessary to answer the purposes of civil government, Christianity even on political views ought to be preferred to all others, as it possesses far the greatest tendency to promote the important designs already mentioned. If its morals are the purest, its tendency to promote social happiness is the greatest, and therefore good policy requires its support.

It is not however our wish that any thing similar to the religious establishments of Europe, should be introduced into our country. We hope never to see our magistrates employed, in prescribing articles of faith; nor in the exercise of the least coercive power to compel men to adopt this, or that creed, or submit to any one mode of worship in preference to another. May liberty of conscience, in this land, be never violated. But if there be important political advantages to be derived from Christianity, which cannot be so effectually secured by any other means, as appears evident from the preceding observations, then is it as much the duty of government to endeavor its preservation, as in any other way to seek the public good. ...

No Deist could ever have said that this sermon was sound in its doctrine, unless Deists affirmed, "...the importance of supporting Christianity is undeniable;" and that in "the duties we owe ... to Christ, ...are included faith in the mediator, accompanied with a daily and sincere attention to him, considered as our teacher, our example and lawgiver, our advocate and intercessor with the father;" or, that it is "…as much the duty of government to endeavor its [Christianity's] preservation, as in any other way to seek the public good." This sermon draws on George Washington himself to make its point. If Washington disagreed or did not wish his name to be used in such a manner, he would have stated as such. Instead, he approves the sermon.

But even more explicitly Christian was the second sermon sent by Zechariah Lewis to Washington. It was entitled, "The Divine Mission of Jesus Christ Evident from his Life, and From the Nature and Tendency of His Doctrines." In many ways, this article by Isaac Lewis anticipates the same logic that another Lewis—C. S. Lewis—would make 150 years later in his book, *Mere Christianity*. Isaac Lewis said,

> Either Jesus Christ was what he professed to be, the *Sent of God*, and the Saviour of the world; or he was a deluded enthusiast, who thought himself the subject of a divine mission, and of divine revelation, when in fact he was not; or he was the grossest and most designing, impostor, who ever lived. One, or the other of these, must have been the truth; for a supposition distinct from all of them, cannot be named. If then his life, and doctrines were such, as it is impossible to suppose they should have been, had he have acted the part, either of an enthusiast, or a deceiver, it must follow, that he was the person, he claimed to be, and that the Religion he taught, is of God. …
>
> I proceed to consider the supposition, of his having been an intentional deceiver. If he was no enthusiast, either he was what he asserted of himself, or the grossest deceiver the world has ever produced. His pretensions, on the supposition of his having been a deceiver, were the most blasphemous, and his conduct the most studiedly deceitful, and the most extravagantly bold, and daring. If then his life, and doctrines were such, as are altogether inconsistent with his having been such a monster of wickedness, the only consequence which can be fairly drawn is, that he was in truth the *Sent of the Father*, and ought to be received as such, by all to whom the Gospel comes….
>
> The life, then, and the nature and tendency of the doctrines, of our Saviour, are clear proofs of his divine mission. And if Christ

received his mission from God, Christianity is established on an immoveable basis. The nations may rage, and the people imagine a vain thing, but the counsel of God shall stand, and he will do all his pleasure. The Church rests on an unshaken foundation, and the gates of hell shall never finally prevail against it. I will further add, that only on the supposition that the life, and doctrines of our Saviour, do clearly evince his divine mission, can we understand the true import of our text. "Which of you convinceth me of sin? And if I say the truth, why do ye not believe me?"....

The most successful engine which they have ever made use of against revealed Religion, is ridicule. An argument in order to carry conviction, must contain reason, or at least the appearance of reason. But by the power of ridicule, a laugh may easily be excited, and the most sacred truths represented in a ludicrous point of light. Though this mode of treating the subject of Religion, has been sufficiently exposed, and clearly proved to carry in it meanness and injustice, yet infidels persist in it, because they find by experience, that men of little information, and still less stability, may easily be laughed out of all regard to Religion. But such conduct as this betrays a weak cause, and evidently manifests, that their opposition to Christianity is not founded in principle, but in enmity and disaffection.

...If Christ be undoubtedly the Sent of God, and the Saviour of the world, then is Christianity not only true, but all-important. Whatever men of prostituted talents may say, or write; or men of vicious inclinations may believe, it infinitely concerns all the friends of morality and religion, to unite in its defense. The gift of Christ, is infinitely the most important gift, which Heaven has bestowed on the children of men.

To have the Gospel supported, and maintained in the world is of far greater importance, than everything else, which can possibly interest the human race. It is of the highest importance in this life, as it respects the civil, and political happiness of society. It is of inconceivable and eternal importance to the future felicity of mankind, as it provides the only possible way of escaping God's eternal wrath, and of obtaining his divine favor. If then the enemies of our holy religion are improving every opportunity and making use of every art, to disseminate error, falsehood and blasphemy, certainly her friends ought to be equally industrious in spreading the favour of this divine knowledge, as extensively as possible. If they are indefatigable in their work, we ought to be much more so in ours. If they unite all their strength in order to give weight, and influence to the cause of vice, and infidelity, both ministers and private Christians ought to pursue the same measures, in the support of the all important interests of religion.

President Washington was not a Deist, if he found "the doctrine" in this sermon by Reverend Isaac Lewis to have been "sound." It clearly affirms the Deity of Christ, something no Deist would subscribe to.

MORAL VALUES UPHELD AND VICES OPPOSED BY WASHINGTON

The ethics of George Washington and the morality of his religion demonstrate resoundingly that he was not a Deist in faith or in practice. He desired his army and his nation to be free from the vices that afflicted humanity: "Our Men are brave and good; Men who with pleasure it is observed, are addicted to fewer Vices than are commonly found in Armies."[56] But his men and family had to face the dangers of vice of all kinds.[57] In his Farewell Address he asked the American people to,

> Observe good faith and justice towds. all Nations. Cultivate peace and harmony with all. Religion and morality enjoin this conduct;...Can it be, that Providence has not connected the permanent felicity of a Nation with its virtue? The experiment, at least, is recommended by every sentiment which ennobles human Nature. Alas! is it rendered impossible by its vices?[58]

Washington's concern was for men who were self-sacrificing, who cared for character.[59]

> It is with inexpressible concern, the General sees Soldiers fighting in the Cause of Liberty, and their Country, committing Crimes most destructive to the army, and which in all other Armies are punished with Death—What a shame and reproach will it be if Soldiers fighting to enslave us, for two pence, or three pence a day, should be

more regular, watchful and sober, than Men who are contending for every thing that is dear and valuable in life.[60]

One of the ways that the very life of the new nation and the army that was called to defend its liberty was able to survive and succeed, given the many who resisted the effort for independence from within the country and from without, was through the use of the oath. The oath was a promise that one made to man calling on God to be the witness of the promise, and thus admitting that the one taking the oath would someday be held accountable for that promise by God and, possibly, in the court of law on earth. In the historic Judeo-Christian setting of revolutionary America, the oath was extremely important and powerful.[61] It was because of the importance of the oath for the work of justice in the courts, that Washington warned America of the dangers of the Deist "mind of peculiar structure."[62]

A Deist was far more easily tempted to lie under oath, since he claimed that God had no interest in human activities. In some cases the Deists denied the Final Judgment, so men who had, in fact, lied under oath would never have to give an account of their intentional deception. The oath that Americans were required to take at Valley Forge declared:

> I _____ do acknowledge The United States of America to be Free, Independent and Sovereign States and declare that the People thereof owe no Allegiance or Obedience to George the Third, King of Great Britain and I renounce refuse and abjure any Allegiance or Obedience to him, and I do swear (or affirm) that I will to the utmost of my Power support, maintain and defend the said United States against the said King George the third, his heirs and Successors and his and their Abettors, Assistants and Adherents and will serve the said United States in the office of _____ which I now hold with Fidelity according to the best of my skill and understanding.
>
> Sworn before me at _____ this day of _____ A.D.[63]

As we have noted in earlier chapters, there were various vices that Washington vigorously opposed.

He opposed Drunkenness. Washington was not opposed to drinking alcoholic beverages per se for himself or for his men. Nevertheless, he was keenly aware of the destructive power of alcoholism and drunkenness on his army and on his workmen and their families. Numerous times we find Washington commanding his men to avoid drunkenness, or writing letters to counsel people who were struggling with alcohol abuse.[64]

Washington opposed gambling. Even as a young man, he could see gambling's corrosive influence. He wrote this letter as Colonel Washington to Governor Richard Dinwiddie when he was in his twenties, February 2, 1756:

> I have always, so far as was in my power, endeavored to discourage gambling in camp, and always shall while I have the honor to preside there...[65]

Later, as head of the U.S. Army, George Washington issued this directive against gambling on October 2, 1775:

> Any officer, non-commissioned officer, or soldier who shall hereafter be detected playing at toss-up, pitch, and hustle, or any other games of chance, in or near the camp or village bordering on the encampments, shall without delay be confined and punished for disobedience of orders. The General does not mean by the above to discourage sports of exercise or recreation, he only means to discountenance and punish gaming.[66]

In a similar vein, Washington recognized the great danger of gambling in civilian life. As he gave counsel to his nephew, heir, and future Supreme Court Chief Justice Bushrod Washington, he wrote:

> The last thing I shall mention, is first of importance and that is, to avoid Gaming. This is a vice which is productive of every possible evil. equally injurious to the morals and health of its rotaries. It is the child of Avarice, the brother of inequity, and father of Mischief. It has been the ruin of many worthy familys; the loss of many a man's honor; and the cause of Suicide. To all those who enter the list, it is equally fascinating; the Successful gamester pushes his good fortune till it is over taken by a reverse; the loosing gamester, in hopes of retrieving past misfortunes, goes on from bad to worse; till grown

desperate, he pushes at every thing; and looses [loses] his all. In a word, few gain by this abominable practice (the profit, if any, being diffused) while thousands are injured.[67]

This concern runs throughout his writings.[68]

Washington opposed cursing and swearing. George Washington's first order was against blasphemy, gambling, and abuse of alcohol. This command came on July 4, 1775. He ordered that his men follow strict discipline and that they participate in "divine services" (in other words, Christian worship services) if they were not otherwise-occupied. Here is what the commander-in-chief ordered on July 4, 1775:

> The General most earnestly requires and expects a due observance of those articles of war established for the government of the army, which forbid profane cursing, swearing, and drunkenness. And in like manner he requires and expects of all officers and soldiers, not engaged in actual duty, a punctual attendance on Divine service, to implore the blessing of Heaven upon the means used for our safety and defence.[69]

This drives home the point of Washington the Christian. He was deeply concerned with American soldiers not offending God by taking His name in vain or by missing worship services.[69] The values of the Deists—"minds of peculiar structure"—were advocates of values-free culture, and that was diametrically opposed to the moral order that Washington advocated for his army and his family.

CONCLUSION

Washington's concern for ethical behavior, and his equal concern for doctrine that sustained such moral conduct, reflected his Christianity. For these same reasons, he cannot be considered a Deist.

While a thoroughgoing Deist either doubted or denied Providence, Washington connected Providence and virtue and called on America to make a vast moral experiment, as he said his farewell to the nation. The experiment is still worth considering. The president wrote, "Can it be, that Providence has not connected the permanent felicity of a Nation with its virtue? The experiment, at least, is recommended by every sentiment which ennobles human Nature."[71] The experiment was the heartfelt proposal of George Washington, a Christian political scientist who feared the chaos that would eventuate from a thoroughgoing deistic ethic, the very thing that occurred in the deistic French Revolution.

PART VII

George Washington the Christian

TWENTY EIGHT

George Washington's God:

Religion, Reason, and Philosophy

"The blessed Religion revealed in the word of God..."
George Washington, 1789 [1]

It is claimed that George Washington did not have an orthodox belief in God and that he even avoided speaking of God. In his book, *The Indispensable Man*, James Thomas Flexner writes, "Washington...avoided, as was his deist custom, the word 'God.'"[2]

It has also been alleged that Washington did not use the word "God" at all, but instead spoke of an impersonal "Providence." Similarly, Paul Boller claims that Washington used names for God that were the kind that a Deist would use.[3]

The fact that such claims have been made of Washington is actually an indication of how little, careful research has been done in regard to this question. Instead of Washington avoiding the use of "God" or not having an historic Christian view of God, the empirical data in relationship to this question proves the exact opposite. What we shall do here is list the many titles and phrases that are found in Washington's writings that manifest his understanding of God. There is much material to summarize, since he uses the words God (at least 146 times), Divine (at least 95 times), Heaven (at least 133 times), as well as many honorific titles for God (at least 90 times), the term Providence (at least 270 times) for a total of over 700 instances. When one thinks about it, that's a lot for a military man, who was neither a theologian nor intending to address religious themes on a daily basis.

Because of this vast data, it is possible to construct a "systematic theology" of George Washington's idea of God. By carefully collecting and organizing his terminology for deity, we can assemble a Washingtonian theology.

THE ACTIVITIES OF GOD

All of the following references come right out of his writings.[4] As to the attributes or titles that he uses to modify or describe "God," we find: Almighty, My God, Gracious, Benevolent, Great goodness, the mercy of Almighty God, God of Armies, Glory, Holy, Omnipotence of that God, Great Spirit above, In the name of God.

The *works* of God in Washington's writings encompass such phrases as: Incline the hearts of my Americans,[5] Providence of Almighty God, Powers which God has given, Favors of Almighty God, Make wise and strong, Blessings a gracious God bestows, Overruling Wrath of man to his own glory, Under God, Under His providence, Crown you, Deserve His future blessing, The source and benevolent bestower of all good, When God is ready, God will direct, Please him to pardon all our sins, Whose divine aid, Causing the rage of war to cease amongst the nation.

God's *works* are also identified with such terms as: Creates, Orders, Providence, Governs, Rules, Guides, Dispenses, Directs, Disposes, Searches, Arbiter, Forgives, Saves, Gives (life, felicity, care, good, victory, blessing.)

Among God's *works*, we find Washington's affirmation of God's *revelation*. Revelation is affirmed with such terms as revelation, revealed, Bible, Scripture, Holy Writ, Word of God, Greek Testament, ordains, promises, sanctions.

He refers to God's *knowledge* with phrases such as: God only knows, God knows (when), God who knows all hearts, God knows, as an expression of one's own human uncertainty.

He addresses God's *saving and preserving work* with statements such as: God save the friendly powers of Europe, God save the American States, God prosper you with it, God Almighty restore you, and Keeping and protection of Almighty God, Should please God to spare life, Should please God to advance a life.

Washington recognizes that man lives in *the sight of God*. Thus, he writes: Justified in the sight of God, God who knows all hearts, May that God to whom you appealed judge between America and you, We might have appealed to God and men for justice, God alone is the judge of the hearts of men, and Answerable to God, What, Gracious God is man!, Accountable to God alone.

Since faith in God is a personal matter, he uses the following phrases to describe *God and the heart*: Knows all hearts, Grateful hearts, Incline the hearts, and God alone is the judge of hearts.

He expresses his *dependence upon God* with such phrases as: My God, I hope in God, I trust in God.

Mankind's *worship of or duties to God* are described in such words as: Acknowledge providence of Almighty God, Worship God according to dictates, Unfeignedly confess sins before God, In the service of their God, To adore the supreme Providence of Almighty God, Worship Almighty God agreeably to conscience, along with Proper sense of duties to God and man, and Deserve His future blessing. He also uses the ecclesiastical term, godson.

He affirms man's duty to express *thanksgiving* to God with phrases such as: To express my humble thanks to God, Solemn thanksgiving to almighty God, Grateful hearts [to God], Thank God, Thankfulness to God, To express our grateful acknowledgement to God, You might thank God. (And, of course, like many of our presidents, he declared national days of thanksgiving.)

In regard to *prayer*, we find the following: Prayers to the Almighty God, Would to God, May that God, Pray God, I pray God, The Throne of Almighty God, the Throne of grace, That God would have you, God grant, Which God send, Supplicates (the mercy of almighty God).[6]

He also understands that there is a relationship between *God and country*. This is seen in the terms: My God, my country, and myself; In the service of their God and their country; Answerable to God and their country.

But Washington not only speaks of Deity with the word "God," he also employs several additional names for God. Some of these names are *traditional,* like God, Deity and Divinity. He also utilizes *biblical* names for God. These include: Creator, Maker, Lord, Lord of Hosts, Lord of Nations, Lord of Armies, Jehovah, Wonder Working Deity, Father of all mercies, Gracious Father of lights, Benign Parent [i.e. Good Father], Author, Searcher, Almighty, Guide, Giver of Life, Ruler.

Occasionally he uses *philosophical* names for God, such as Supreme Being, Greater and efficient Cause, the greatest and best of Beings.[7]

On occasion, when writing to Masons, he uses the Masonic name for God: Great

Architect of the Universe.[8]

Living in the eighteenth century, he also often used many of the *honorific* titles that were often used by the great clergy of his day. These include: Governor, Disposer, Dispenser, Power, the great Power above, Providence, Heaven, Providence, Arbiter, the supreme Arbiter of human events, Director, Infinite Wisdom, and Eye of Omnipotence.

On a few occasions, when writing to Indian tribes, he made use of the phrase "Great Spirit." Like a good politician, and a competent statesman, Washington reflected the traditional biblical injunction to be "all things to all men" (1 Corinthians 9:22).

Since George Washington believed in God's existence, he expressed his views of God's nature. Some of the *attributes of God* identified by Washington's titles for Deity include, Omnipotence, All wise, Majesty (Great, Grand, Glory), Omnipresence (God's presence in the universe, nations, hearts, all events), Rule, Sovereign, Gracious, mercy, Good, forgiving, Kind, Holy, Eternal Existence (was, is, to come).

The idea of the Trinity[9] is implied by his theological vocabulary. 1) Jehovah: "there is a good Providence which will never fail to take care of his children;" Benign parent, the Father of all mercies, Gracious Father of lights. 2) Jesus Christ: his use of the phrase, "Divine Author of our blessed religion" in reference to Christ, and 3) his use of the divine name, "Holy Spirit."

Given the above, it seems impossible to read George Washington in his own words and conclude that he never spoke about God or that his views of God were unorthodox.

A WASHINGTONIAN CREED: "ON MY HONOR AND THE FAITH OF A CHRISTIAN"

Since there is so much theological material to work with, we have created a creed from Washington's theology, using his words found throughout his writings. Since we are using Washington's very words, we have chosen to entitle it "On My Honor and the Faith of a Christian."[10]

> I believe in God,[11] the Lord,[12] the Deity,[13] The Divinity,[14] The Great Spirit,[15] in heaven.[16] He is Jehovah,[17] the Wonder working Deity,[18] who can be called the Supreme Being,[19] Infinite Wisdom,[20] and the Eye of Omnipotence,[21] because He is the Almighty,[22] the great,[23] glorious,[24] almighty,[25] omnipotent,[26] and all wise,[27] the Supreme Disposer of all things,[28] the great power above.[29]

No Man has a more perfect Reliance on the all wise, and powerful dispensations of the Supreme Being than I have nor thinks his aid more necessary.[30] As an inexhaustible subject of consolation, remember that there is a good Providence which will never fail to take care of his Children.[31] I shall always strive to prove a faithful and impartial Patron of genuine, vital religion.[32]

He is the Great Creator,[33] a Greater and more Efficient Cause,[34] the greatest and best of Beings,[35] supreme[36] and grand architect of the universe.[37]

He is the good[18] and gracious,[39] supreme,[40] benevolent,[41] author of all good,[42] life,[43] felicity,[44] and victory,[45]

He is the Lord of Hosts,[46] the God of Armies,[47] The Great Director,[48] and Great All wise disposer of all human events,[49]

From his divine nature there is blessing,[50] goodness,[51] government, grace,[52] and mercy,[53]

He is the all-powerful guide,[54] great governor[55] and ruler of the universe[56] through his all-kind,[57] powerful,[58] gracious, good, overruling,[59] and superintending Providence.[60] In His Divine Providence,[61] He is the Lord[62] and supreme ruler of the nations,[63] the sovereign arbiter[64] of both nations[65] and the universe itself,[66] as well as being the supreme dispenser of every good.[67]

This Great Searcher of hearts[68] has provided both natural and revealed religion,[69] but above all divine revelation,[70] and the blessed religion revealed in the Word of God,[71] the religion of Jesus Christ,[72] as well as the eternal rules ordained by Heaven.[73] Because He is powerful to save[74] and forgiveness is a Divine attribute,[75] you do well

Washington spoke of the "Eye of Omnipotence," also called the "Eye of Providence," or the all-seeing eye of God, encased in the Trinitarian triangle and placed on the back of the Great Seal of the United States. Providence Forum Press, publisher of this book, incorporated this distinct symbol of divine Providence in its publisher's mark.

PROVIDENCE
FORUM PRESS

to learn the religion of Jesus Christ,[76] as I was led in my growing infancy by my revered mother.[77]

So I now make it my earnest prayer that you do justice, love mercy, and imitate the divine author of our blessed religion.[78]

Washington, of course, never assembled this creed. But all of the words used above are directly cited from his writings. We will see in the chapters on "Washington and Christianity," "George Washington and Prayer," and Washington's interaction with clergy and sermons, that he gave his direct approval to the core message of the Gospel—the divine Son of God, dying for sinners in order to forgive them before a holy God. We also see in the chapter on "George Washington and Communion," the outline of the one public confession of faith George Washington wrote, which occurred when he retired as general of the army.

HIS NAMES FOR GOD

Consider the following list of Washington's terms for God.

[Divine] Providence – 270x

All Powerful Guide – 1x

All powerful guide – 1x

All wise & powerful being – 1x

All wise – 2x

All wise disposer of events – 1x

Almighty – 8x

Almighty Being – 1x

Almighty God – 11x

Almighty Ruler of Universe – 1x

Architect of the universe – 1x

Author of all good – 2x [Lord] & giver of all victory – 1x

Author of Life – 1x

Beneficent author – 1x

Deity – 2x

Divine – 1x

Divine [author] of life and felicity – 1x

Divine [author] of our blessed religion – 1x

Divine author of life and felicity – 1x

Divine author of our blessed religion – 1x

Divine Blessing – 1x

Divine Goodness – 1x

Divine Government – 1x

Divinity – 3x

Eye of Omnipotence – 1x

Giver of Life – 1x

God – 146x

God of Armies – 2x

Grand architect – 1x

Great & Glorious Being – 1x

Great & Good Being – 1x

Great author of all care and good – 1x

Great Director of events – 1x

Great disposer of all human events – 1x

Great Disposer of Human Events – 1x

Great Governor of universe – 2x

Great Power – 1x

Great ruler of events – 5x

Greater and more Efficient Cause – 1x

Greater and More Efficient Cause – 1x

Greatest & Best of Beings – 1x

Heaven – 133x

Infinite Wisdom – 1x

Lord and giver of all victory – 1x

Lord and ruler of Nations – 1x

Lord of Hosts – 1x

Omnipotent Being – 1x

Overruling Providence – 1x

Ruler of Nations – 2x

Ruler of the Universe – 5x

Sovereign arbiter of nations – 1x

Superintending Providence – 4x

Supreme architect – 1x

Supreme author of all good – 1x

Supreme Being – 7x

Supreme dispense of every good – 1x

Supreme ruler of nations – 1x

Supreme ruler of the universe – 2x

That being who – 3x

So what shall we say about Washington's alleged use of Deist titles for God? The problem with this objection is that there is no list of what are "Deist" titles for God.[79]

GEORGE WASHINGTON'S USE OF THE TERM "DIVINE"

To this remarkable list of titles for "deity," we must also summarize Washington's use of the word "Divine." Washington's understanding of this word is fairly broad. It refers to God's help as seen in such phrases as: divine providence (19x), Knights of Divine Providence (3x), divine protection (5x), divine interposition (4x), divine aid (2x), divine government (1x), the divine arm (1x).

It refers directly to God in the phrases: Divine Author (2x), Divine Being (1x), Divine Benefactor (1x), and Divinity (1x).

Washington uses it to refer to God's nature in phrases, such as: divine will (2x), divine purposes (1x), divine goodness (1x), divine grace (1x), divine attribute [forgiveness] (1x), and divine favor (5x).

God's work is in view when he uses the word as follows: divine benediction (3x), divine blessing (2x), divine wisdom (1x), divine source of light (1x), and in the sight of the divinity (1x).

He uses the word divine in the sense of "theology" when he employs phrases such as: questions human and divine (1x), obligations divine and human (1x), sanction of divinity (1x), and a point of divinity (1x).

He also uses the word in terms of supernatural knowledge: spirit of divination (3x), no divining (1x), and to divine (3x).

Finally, he uses the word in the sense of the worship of the church or its clergy: divine service (21x), divine worship (2x), services of a divine (1x), and that venerable divine (1x).

The point to be understood here is that Washington did not avoid the use of God, but instead, had a profoundly rich, theological vocabulary that suggested a vast range of the Christian faith's beliefs and practices in regard to God. When one remembers he was a military officer, a farmer, and a politician, and not a clergyman or theologian, this is truly astonishing. Washington's vocabulary for Deity is not that of a Deist, but of a devout eighteenth century Anglican Christian.

THE COMPATIBILITY AND CONSOLATION OF RELIGION AND REASON

Washington's view of God and religion was definitely impacted by the eighteenth century's renewed emphasis on human reason and philosophy. But in his mind, they were viewed as entirely complementary. Thus, we find in Washington the phrases "reason and religion,"[80] "reason, religion, and philosophy," or "religion and philosophy,"[81] Washington speaks of his philosophy as that "mild philosophy"[82] that is concerned with "human happiness."[83] He believed his faith had a rational basis.[84] He evaluated human conduct and decisions in terms of moral certainty.[85]

Religion was closely connected to reason and philosophy, as can be seen from an excerpt of his letter to Martha Washington's nephew, Burwell Bassett, April 25, 1773. After the death of Bassett's daughter, Washington wrote to console him:

> ...the ways of Providence being inscrutable, and the justice of it not to be scanned by the shallow eye of humanity, nor to be counteract-ed by the utmost efforts of human power or wisdom, resignation, and as far as the strength of our reason and religion can carry us, a cheerful acquiescence to the Divine Will, is what we are to aim...[86]

Having offered comforting words, he added the assurances of a reasonable religion, namely that God knows what he is doing and that it is our job to submit cheerfully to his will.

Similarly, he wrote his friend David Humphreys, after the loss of the latter's parents:

> I condole with you on the loss of your Parents; but as they lived to a good old age you could not be unprepared for the shock, tho' it is painful to bid an everlasting adieu to those we love, or revere. Reason, Religion and Philosophy may soften the anguish of it, but time alone can eradicate it.[87]

For Washington, reason and religion were not mortal enemies. In a time of grief, he counseled his great general, Henry Knox, on March 2, 1789:

> But [it]is not for man to scan the wisdom of Providence. The best he can do, is to submit to its decrees. Reason, religion and Philosophy, teaches us to do this, but 'tis time alone that can ameliorate the pangs of humanity, and soften its woes.[88]

Again, to Washington, reason, religion, and philosophy were allies.

DISTINCTION BETWEEN NATURAL AND REVEALED RELIGION

Washington distinguished between "natural and revealed religion," and could thus speak of the "blessed religion revealed in the Word of God." The first phrase comes from his letter to Marquis de Chastellux:

> For certainly it is more consonant to all the principles of reason and religion (natural and revealed) to replenish the earth with inhabitants, rather than to depopulate it by killing those already in existence.[89]

In a 1789 unpublished letter he had written and considered sending to Congress, Washington said:

> The blessed Religion revealed in the word of God will remain an eternal and awful monument to prove that the best Institutions may be abused by human depravity; and that they may even, in some instances be made subservient to the vilest of purposes.[90]

It is important, then, to see that Washington's philosophy was not that of a skeptic. It was a "mild philosophy" that was not only consistent with his desire to be under his Mount Vernon "vine and fig tree," but this philosophy was also consistent with the source of this most favorite of all quotations by Washington—the Holy Scriptures. His mild philosophy was the pursuit of happiness in God's peace. Thus, his religion was consistent with his philosophy.

And this helps us to understand why, when Washington wants to describe something as absolutely sure or certain, he speaks of it as a "moral certainty." Morals were from God. Whatever commandments came from God were absolutely certain. So by inference, anything that was certain was the equivalent of what was morally certain. Washington will use the phrase "moral certainty" some fifty-five times. A striking example of this is from his letter to the president of Congress, November 11, 1778:

> It seems to me impolitic to enter into engagements with the Court of France for carrying on a combined operation of any kind, without a moral certainty of being able to fulfil our part, particularly if the first proposal came from us.
>
> ....So far from their being a moral certainty of our complying with our engagements, it may, in my opinion, be very safely pronounced, that if the Enemy keep possession of their present posts at New York and Rhode Island, it will be impracticable either to furnish the men, or the other necessary supplies for prosecuting the plan.[91]

Also indicative of Washington's sense of the compatibility of faith and reason is his use of the phrases "rational hope" or "a rational ground of belief." Here's an example:

> ...I agree in Sentiment with the Honorable Body over whom you preside that we may entertain a rational ground of belief, that under the favor of divine providence the Freedom, Independence and happiness of America will shortly be established upon the surest foundation...[92]

WASHINGTON CONSIDERED RELIGIOUS BY HIS ENEMIES

George Washington was considered religious not just by his friends and colleagues, but even by his enemies. Remarkably, in the midst of the War, *The London Chronicle* in the September 21 to 23, 1779, issue carried an article that affirmed Washington's religious nature. It was entitled, "Character of General Washington, by an American Gentleman now in London, who is well acquainted with him." It states,

> General Washington, altho' advanced in years is remarkably healthy, takes a great deal of exercise, and is very fond of riding on a favourite white horse; he is very reserved and loves retirement. . . . He regularly attends divine service in his tent every morning and evening, and seems very fervent in his prayers.[93]

If this is an insult, it is a back-handed one.

As mentioned earlier, Reverend Jonathan Boucher was the tutor to Washington's adopted son, Jack Custis. As a result of this educational connection, Boucher became a regular writer to Washington. But when the Revolution came, he chose the Loyalist side, and their relationship ended. Reverend Boucher was so hated for his opposition to the colonial resistance to the British, he even had to have armed protection when he was in the pulpit.[94]

His views naturally led him to strenuous disagreement and criticism of Washington. But in spite of all of this, he still begrudgingly admitted Washington's religious character. Such a testimony has to carry great weight, since it comes from an Anglican clergyman who had every reason to criticize Washington and certainly nothing to gain by making the affirmation of Washington's religious commitment. Thus, his remarks are striking both for what they critique, and for what they affirm. This text comes from his autobiography:

> I did know Mr. Washington well.... He is shy, silent, stern, slow and cautious; but has no quickness of parts, extraordinary penetration, nor an elevated style of thinking. In his moral character he is regular, temperate, strictly just and honest (excepting that as a Virginian, he has lately found out that there is no moral turpitude in not paying what he confesses he owes to a British creditor), and, as I always thought, religious; having heretofore been pretty constant, and even exemplary, in his attendance on public worship in the Church of England.[95]

Their final meeting occurred on the Potomac River, as McGoldrick explains,

> Washington and Boucher had a dramatic meeting as their boats were passing on the Potomac River. Boucher was returning home, and Washington was on his way to Philadelphia. The rector there pleaded with his friend not to support the movement for war. Washington assured Boucher that he had no desire to see an armed conflict, and the two friends parted, never to meet again.[96]

These un-coerced testimonies by opponents of George Washington have to carry far greater weight than recent historians, who blithely assert that he was "not a religious man."[97]

WASHINGTON'S PERSONAL SENSE OF RELIGION

Washington's use of the word "religiously" shows us that it is a word of great seriousness. He can use it in a very literal way, where it means having a serious religious way of life. But Washington also uses it in a way that implies a strict and exact obedience, the complete truthfulness of a claim, or a deep moral commitment either to do or to believe something. In all instances of his utilization of the word "religiously," it is deemed a very honorable quality.

Examples of having a serious religious life:

He wrote to Gov. Wm. Livingston from Head Quarters in Morristown, on February 22, 1777:

> No person, I hope, can be so lost to Virtue, as to except against Colo. Newcombe on Account of his being *religiously* disposed. The relaxed Discipline and want of Order in the Regiment, I believe were among the principle objections to him; these added to his Inactivity and that want of Confidence mentioned in a former Letter, obliged me to displace him.[98]

Apparently, Col. Newcombe (no known relation to the coauthor of this book) was lax in his military duties, but defended himself by claiming that he was being criticized because of his religion.

Examples of a strict and exact obedience:

We can see this use in his commitment to free his slaves. Washington begins his last will and testament with the classic words, "In the name of God, amen." He later declares:

> And I do moreover most pointedly, and most solemnly enjoin it upon my Executors hereafter named, or the Survivors of them, to see that *this* [cl]ause respecting Slaves, and every part thereof be *religiously* fulfilled at the Epoch at which it is directed to take place; without evasion, neglect or delay.[99]

He absolutely wanted to make sure this was carried out.

General Orders from Head Quarters in Newburgh on Thursday, November

14th, 1782 declare:

> Congress having been pleased to set a part Thursday the 28th. instant as a day of Solemn thanksgiving to [G]od for all his Mercies, The General desires it may be most *religiously* observed by the army; and that the Chaplains will prepare discourses suitable to the occasion.[100]

Several other examples of this can be observed.[101]

Examples of the complete truthfulness of a claim:
To Patrick Henry he writes from Mount Vernon on October 9, 1795:

> I persuade myself, Sir, it has not escaped your observation, that a crisis is approaching that must if it cannot be arrested soon decide whether order and good government shall be preserved or anarchy and confusion ensue. I can most *religiously* aver I have no wish, that is incompatible with the dignity, happiness and true interest of the people of this country.[102]

To Edmund Pendleton he writes from Philadelphia on January 22, 1795:

> A month from this day, if I live to see the completion of it, will place me on the wrong (perhaps it would be better to say, on the advanced) side of my grand climacteric; and altho' I have no cause to complain of the want of health, I can *religiously* aver that no man was ever more tired of public life, or more devoutly wished. for retirement, than I do.[103]

Examples of a deep faith in something include:
In a Circular Letter from Head Quarters, near Passaic Falls on October 18, 1780, he writes,

> I am *religiously* persuaded that the duration of the War and the greatest part of the misfortunes and perplexities we have hitherto experienced, are chiefly to be attributed to the System of

temporary enlistments.[104]

And we could go on and on. We still use the same word in the same way today. For instance, when we say that someone works out religiously.

But there's a deeper meaning to this. George Washington thought of religion as a positive force in society. He was not like the French skeptic, Diderot, who looked for the dawning of the new age when the last king on earth would be strangled with the entrails of the last priest on earth. It was views like those of Diderot and fellow traveler Voltaire that inspired the bloody French Revolution. While Thomas Jefferson may have applauded that revolution to some degree, George Washington certainly did not. This parallels what we saw earlier in regard to Washington's statement on his piety and pious and devout wishes and prayers.

WASHINGTON'S COMMITMENT TO RELIGION

There are several examples from Washington's writings where his own personal commitment to religion is evident. As a young officer in the French and Indian War, he declared his interest in religion, as he pleaded for a chaplain for his troops.

> The last Assembly, in their Supply Bill, provided for a chaplain to our regiment, for whom I had often very unsuccessfully applied to Governor Dinwiddie. I now flatter myself, that your Honor will be pleased to appoint a sober, serious man for this duty. Common decency, Sir, in a camp calls for *the services of a divine, and which ought not to be dispensed with, altho' the world should be so uncharitable as to think us void of religion*, and incapable of good instructions. [105]

While polite society is often reminded never to discuss religion and politics, Washington compares the two in terms of his view of their each being composed only a few simple tenets:

> I have no inclination to touch, much less to dilate on politics. For *in politics, as in religion my tenets are few and simple*: the leading one of which, and indeed that which embraces most others, is to be honest and just ourselves, and to exact it from others; medling as little as possible in their affairs where our own are not involved.[106]

The purpose of our book is to establish with precision from Washington's writings what his "few and simple" religious tenets were. From what we have learned so far, and what he wrote to the Methodist bishops, it is clear these tenets enabled him to promise, "*I shall always strive to prove a faithful and impartial Patron of genuine, vital religion.*"[107] Such a view of religion, in Washington's mind at least, was consistent with the inherent faith in God that he believed was evident from the very beginning of America.

Washington's vital religion evoked strong words about gratitude to God and its opposite. Here's what he wrote to Reverend Samuel Langdon on September 28, 1789:

> The man must be bad indeed who can look upon the events of the American Revolution without feeling the warmest gratitude towards the great Author of the Universe whose divine interposition was so frequently manifested in our behalf. And it is my earnest prayer that we may so conduct ourselves as to merit a continuance of those blessings with which we have hitherto been favored.[108]

RELIGIOUS DISPUTES

Washington addresses the reality of differing religious sentiments as he considers various plans for chaplains in the army. He promoted chaplains to the army, and he addressed a key argument against chaplains that they may introduce debates over religion:

> Among many other weighty objections to the Measure, It has been suggested, that it has a tendency to introduce religious disputes into the Army, which above all things should be avoided, and in many instances would compel men to a mode of Worship which they do not profess. The old Establishment gives every Regiment an Opportunity of having a Chaplain of their own religious Sentiments, it is founded on a plan of a more generous toleration, and the choice of the Chaplains to officiate, has been generally in the Regiments.[109]

His recognition of this issue appears in another letter written to a friend in Europe years later.

> I was sorry to see the gloomy picture which you drew of the affairs

of your Country in your letter of December; but I hope events have not turned out so badly as you then apprehended. Of all the animosities which have existed among mankind, those which are caused by a difference of sentiments in religion appear to be the most inveterate and distressing, and ought most to be deprecated. I was in hopes, that the enlightened and liberal policy, which has marked the present age, would at least have reconciled *Christians* of every denomination so far, that we should never again see their religious disputes carried to such a pitch as to endanger the peace of Society.[110]

He saw that America could help lead the way in showing the world how Christians of all stripes could get along with each other. When he left the White House, he received a thank you letter from several leading clergymen of Philadelphia in gratitude for his half-century of service to America. He wrote back on March 3, 1797. Note how he envisions religion playing a key role to American life:

Believing, as I do, that Religion and Morality are the essential pillars of civil society, I view, with unspeakable pleasure, that harmony and brotherly love which characterizes the Clergy of different denominations, as well in this, as in other parts of the United States; exhibiting to the world a new and interesting spectacle, at once the pride of our country and the surest basis of Universal Harmony.[111]

He not only believed in Christianity undergirding the morals of the American people, he looked forward to the idea of American Christians showing how believers could work together in love. For the most part, his vision has been fulfilled.

He included Jews in that vision. And America has not persecuted Jews. In fact, she has proven to be a haven for this persecuted people. Washington wrote to the Hebrew congregations of Philadelphia, New York, Charleston and Richmond (December 1790):

Gentlemen: The liberal sentiment towards each other which marks every political and religious denomination of men in this country stands unrivalled in the history of nations. The affection of such people is a treasure beyond the reach of calculation; and the repeated proofs which my fellow citizens have given of their attachment to me, and approbation of my doings form the purest source of my temporal felicity. The affectionate expressions of your address again excite my gratitude, and receive my warmest acknowledgements.[112]

As Washington saw it, America was to be an asylum for those suffering religious persecution. And that is precisely what she became.

CONCLUSION

George Washington was no skeptic. He was no religion-hater. He had a vision for religious tolerance and respect for all, despite creed. He had no desire to violate anyone's conscience. Furthermore, he saw religion as playing a key role in society. Note what he said to the Synod of the Dutch Reformed Churches in North America (October 9, 1789): "While just government protects all in their religious rights, true religion affords to government its surest support."[113] That's quite an affirmation for an alleged Deist to make.

TWENTY NINE

Washington and the Doctrine of Providence

*"While I sincerely condole with you on the loss
of your good father; you will permit me to remind you, as an inexhaustible
subject of consolation, that there is a good Providence which will
never fail to take care of his Children: and be assured, Sir, it will always
give me real satisfaction to find that prosperity and felicity
have been attendant on all your steps."*
George Washington, 1788[1]

Modern skeptics argue that George Washington was a Deist and not a Christian. We believe they are wrong, but no one on any side of the debate can argue that George Washington did not believe in Providence. As a repeated theme in his collected works, he refers constantly and consistently to Providence in his personal letters and public addresses.

Historian James Flexner admitted this fact when he summarized his claim that Washington and our other founding fathers were Deists:

Washington subscribed to the religious faith of the Enlightenment:

like Franklin and Jefferson, he was a deist. Although not believing in the doctrines of the churches, he was convinced that a divine force, impossible to define, ruled the universe, and that this "Providence" was good. With what passion he now turned for reassurance and guidance to this force is revealed by the inaugural address he delivered with trembling voice and trembling hands on April 30, 1789, to a joint meeting of the houses of Congress. The religious passages took up almost a third of the address. Speaking not for conventional effect but from his own heart, he avoided, as was his deist custom, the word "God."[2]

But what exactly did Washington mean by the term? Did Providence mean essentially the God of the Bible or was it rather some impersonal force? In this chapter, we explore what Washington said about Providence. As we do, we shall see that he was consciously referring to God in a biblical and Christian way.

WASHINGTON'S PERSONAL EXPERIENCE OF DIVINE PROVIDENCE

We have already related the remarkable survival of young Colonel Washington in the deadly fire of Braddock's defeat. Of this event, he wrote to his brother that by a "miracle of Providence" he was still alive. Washington had learned of Providence years earlier in his childhood training in the Anglican Church. Given his fame from the French and Indian War, years later, when the army was established in 1775, George Washington was the unanimous choice of the colonies as the leader for the effort. He proved to be a great military leader, doing much with few resources and little backing.

There were different times during the war when the hand of God seemed, in Washington's mind, to protect the new nation during the struggle for independence. For example, during one of the battles in 1776, Washington and his men were trapped on Brooklyn Heights, Long Island. If the British had chosen to, they could have easily crushed the American army which, in fact, they planned to do the next day. This could have spelled the end of the war and would have been a disastrous end to the conflict.

However, Washington engaged in a bold move born of desperation. Under the cover of a black foggy night, he evacuated all of his troops. He used every ship available, from fishing vessels to rowboats. When morning came, it is reported that the fog remained longer than normal and lifted just in time for the British army to see the last American boat crossing the Delaware River to safety, just beyond reach of their guns.

Events such as this were the evidence for Washington that God's Providence favored the American cause.

Ironically, at the battle of Yorktown, British General Charles Cornwallis tried to repeat Washington's nighttime escape strategy. But instead of fog to hide their attempts to escape by boats, the British experienced a terrible storm and churning seas that thwarted their plans. No wonder George Washington marveled at God's help during the war.[3]

HUMANLY SPEAKING, AMERICA SHOULD HAVE LOST THE WAR

The Reverend Dr. Donald Binder currently serves as the rector for Pohick Church, one of George Washington's most frequented churches. Here's what Dr. Binder says about Washington and Providence when we asked him if our first president was a Deist.

> It's quite evident from Jefferson's writings that he [Jefferson] was a Deist, and that's sometimes laid at Washington's feet because he was fairly quiet and introverted about his faith, but he had this great belief in Divine Providence and really saw, especially, the coming together—-he called it a "concatenation of events"—-with the Revolutionary War. There was no way we should have won that war. The odds were so highly stacked against us that the very fact that they were able to sustain themselves for the longest war in American history, and then achieve a victory over the greatest force on the planet at that time, was for him a miracle. And he always attributed that to God's Divine Providence. Now that clashes with one of the tenets of Deism, which [is that] God is sort of behind [the scenes and] sort of sets the world off and spins it into motion and doesn't have any type of interactivity with it. But the whole notion of Divine Providence, which Washington espoused, clashes totally with that. He saw God's hand in bringing him the victories and in sustaining him and his troops throughout the war.[4]

Washington would have agreed. While in 1776 he wrote to his brother John Augustine,

> *I think the game is pretty near up...* You can form no Idea of the perplexity of my Situation. No Man, I believe, ever had a greater

choice of difficulties and less means to extricate himself from them. However under a full persuasion of the justice of our Cause I cannot but think the prospect will brighten, although for a wise purpose it is, at present hid under a cloud...[5]

Amazingly, five years later, he recognized that God's Providence came through again and again, bringing hope of victory,

We have, as you very justly observe, abundant reason to thank providence for its many favourable interpositions in our behalf. It has, at times been my only dependence for all other resources seemed to have fail'd us.[6]

DID WASHINGTON BELIEVE IN AN IMPERSONAL PROVIDENCE?

As already noted, Washington spoke of Providence some 270 times in both his public utterances and private writings. Some modern writers imply that to Washington, Providence was not the God of the Bible per se, but rather some impersonal force. However, it is clear that Providence was not impersonal for Washington. In writing to Pierre Charles L'Enfant in 1788 Washington noted: "While I sincerely condole with you on the loss of your good father; you will permit me to remind you, as an inexhaustible subject of consolation, that there is a good Providence which will never fail to take care of his Children: and be assured, Sir, it will always give me real satisfaction to find that prosperity and felicity have been attendant on all your steps."[7] Clearly, if Providence can be "good" and "never fail to take care of his children," it cannot be an impersonal force.

Was Providence an impersonal "it," a force, but not the God of the churches? It can be argued that at times, Washington uses "Providence" as the impersonal power of God at work in history that can properly be described as an "it."[8] Similarly, Washington uses impersonal relative pronouns to describe this providential agency, such as "which"[9] or "that."[10] This impersonality is suggested again by simply referring to it as an "agency of a Providence."[11]

This however is only part of the story. Although sometimes impersonal, he frequently desires to personify this Providential power as seen in his frequent use of "smiles,"[12] "hand,"[13] finger,"[14] and "arm,"[15] with respect to this force. In his desire to reflect his delight in this divine Providential reality, he sometimes refers to Providence as "she,"[16] and "her."[17]

A further response to the question of the alleged impersonal force for Providence in Washington's mind is seen in the fact that he frequently used his words for Deity in tandem with the word Providence. When Washington did this, he consistently spoke of God in *personal* terms, and then distinguished Providence as the actions that God took. This then explains why he spoke of Providence at times in an impersonal way. God the person acts through his decrees or interpositions. Actions are not personal, but they reflect the personality of the person who does, in fact, act.

This then not only explains the impersonal references to Providence, but it also accounts for the personal references that Washington used with respect to Providence. These personal occurrences of Providence, however, cannot be accounted for if Washington viewed Providence as an impersonal force that was intended to take the place of the God of the church.

Thus, we find in Washington's writings and speeches that Providence is also used in a personal way with the masculine personal pronoun "he"[18] as well as with the personal relative pronoun "who" and "whose."[19] Providence is not just an impersonal force, but a "Being."[20] Providence is constantly associated with Deity by being defined as "Divine Providence" and as "Divine Government."[21] Moreover, Washington never refers directly to God as an "it," as he does occasionally with Providence. God is personal, while Providence in itself is not, unless the term is being used figuratively for Deity.

Parallel to this, Washington's use of "Heaven" follows a similar pattern. Heaven is a place and thus is impersonal. But since it is the place of God's dwelling, by figurative language and association, heaven takes on the personality of God.[22] Because of Washington's identification of the impersonal actions of Providence with the Divine Agent behind Providence, in Washington's mind, Providence becomes a legitimate object of divine adoration.[23]

THE BIBLICAL SOURCE OF GEORGE WASHINGTON'S UNDERSTANDING OF PROVIDENCE

Is there a Rosetta Stone or a translation in Washington's own words, where he defines what he means by Providence? We believe the answer is, yes. It is found in a letter he wrote in response to the Hebrew congregation of Savannah, Georgia. He said this:

> May the same wonder-working Deity, who long since delivering the
> Hebrews from their Egyptian Oppressors planted them in the

promised land—whose Providential Agency has lately been conspicuous in establishing these United States as an independent Nation—still continue to water them with the dews of Heaven and to make the inhabitants of every denomination participate in the temporal and spiritual blessings of that people whose God is Jehovah.[24]

The significance of this letter is that it confirms that when George Washington referred to Providence, he was thinking in terms of the God of the Bible. By saying that the same God who delivered the ancient Hebrews in the exodus from Egypt was the same God who delivered America, and by calling him the "Providential Agency," Washington is giving us his translation of the term Providence. For Washington, Providence is the work of Jehovah, the God of the Bible.

Likewise, when we met with Mary Thompson, research specialist at Mount Vernon, we asked her opinion about Washington and his faith. She explained that Washington's beliefs were not those of a Deist. Here's what she said:

For about the last 40 years the standard interpretation has been that George Washington was a Deist. I started research about seven years ago on his religious beliefs in order to answer an inquiry from a visitor. And what I found very early on was that this was a man who believed that God took an active role in the founding of the United States, a man who believed that God took an active interest in people's lives, and that the way a person behaved in reference to God would influence how God related to him. And that's not the belief of a Deist.

She adds this comment in reference to George Washington and Providence:

I would think that God and Providence are synonymous in Washington's mind. When you look at a number of the letters, it becomes obvious that he feels that Providence is all-knowing, all-wise, that Providence is involved in what happens in the world.[25]

WASHINGTON CONSIDERED HIMSELF "A PREACHER OF PROVIDENCE"

General Washington once said of himself that he could become, should time and circumstances permit, "a preacher" of Providence. He made this pronouncement based on the fact that he had so often witnessed what he believed to be the Almighty intervening on behalf of the American cause. After several years of battle, the most powerful army in the world could not subdue a rag-tag assembly of farmers. So awestruck was Washington by God's intervention that he said that an American who would not acknowledge God's help to the American cause was "worse than an infidel." An infidel, by the way, was a synonym for a Deist in Washington's day.[26] These points, and more, Washington made in a private letter to Brigadier General Thomas Nelson, August 20, 1778:

> It is not a little pleasing, nor less wonderful to contemplate, that after two years Manoeuvring and undergoing the strangest vicissitudes that perhaps ever attended any one contest since the creation both Armies are brought back to the very point they set out from and, that that, which was the offending party in the beginning is now reduced to the use of the spade and pick axe for defence. The hand of Providence has been so conspicuous in all this, that he must be worse than an infidel that lacks faith, and more than wicked, that has not gratitude enough to acknowledge his obligations, but, it will be time enough for me to turn preacher, when my present appointment ceases; and therefore, I shall add no more on the Doctrine of Providence....[27]

Thus, in many ways, Washington did indeed become a "preacher of Providence."

"THE DOCTRINE OF PROVIDENCE" ACCORDING TO GEORGE WASHINGTON

Washington's writings show that not only was he a "preacher" of Providence, but in fact, he had a clearly developed "Doctrine of Providence," which can be seen when his more than 270 usages of the words "Providence" and "Providential" are summarized. What follows is a complete summary of Washington's "Doctrine of Providence." Washington's basic idea of "the Doctrine of Providence"[28] is captured by several key concepts:

1. Providence is divine,[29] that is, a property of God himself.
2. Since Providence reflects God's nature, it shares in the properties of Deity also:
   a. Providence is all-powerful.[30]
   b. Providence is mysterious[31] or inscrutable.[32]
   c. Providence is immutable[33] or unchangeable.
   d. Providence is all-wise and all-knowing.[34]
3. Providence is God's superintending[35] or overruling[36] of human events.
   a. Providence is God's invisible workings[37] and interpositions[38] in human history.
   b. Thus Providence is the fulfillment of his purposes.[39] It is his ordering,[40] design,[41] and good pleasure.[42]
   c. God's Providential agency includes his determinations,[43] his presiding,[44] his ruling of great events,[45] his governing of all events, (including storms)[46] whereby through his divine will,[47] he not only permits things to happen,[48] but also brings about the final results.[49]
   d. God's Providence is actualized through his just acts and decrees[50] that are accomplished through his smile of Providence,[51] his arm of Providence,[52] his hand of Providence,[53] or his finger of Providence.[54]
      1. When these events are signal,[55] singular,[56] or favorable interpositions,[57] they are gracious,[58] good,[59] benign,[60] wondrous,[61] merciful,[62] bountiful,[63] beneficent,[64] kind,[65] and even indulgent,[66] including every blessing,[67] favor,[68] and even miraculous care.[69]
      2. When they are signal or severe[70] strokes one must submit[71] without lament,[72] murmur,[73] or repine,[74] knowing that God can bring good from evil,[75] even if He scourges[76] mankind or causes him to walk through a labyrinth, or live in darkness,[77] or to struggle,[78] as he tests man's patience, fortitude, and virtue,[79] so that ultimately a man can declare, "whatever is, is

right,[80] because his Providence is righteous."

4. When man understands that he lives "under Providence,"[81] then he must learn to respond correctly to God's providential government of his world.

    a. Thus, he is to acknowledge[82] God's Providence, showing gratitude[83] and thanksgiving.[84] He is in humility[85] to adore,[86] and give glory[87] and praise[88] for God's Providence, looking up for light and direction,[89] with appropriate piety,[90] and sometimes even astonishment.[91]

    b. God's Providence gives man a rational ground for believing[92] and hope,[93] confidence,[94] trust,[95] dependence,[96] reliance.[97]

    c. Since God's Providence makes man sure,[98] he is to pray[99] and invoke[100] God's Providence, committing himself and others to Providential care,[101] thereby finding consolation[102] and assistance.[103]

    d. God's Providence, however, does not excuse a man from his duty,[104] his own human efforts at "providential" foresight,[105] nor his own endeavor to reach ahead by not neglecting or slighting his own gifts.[106] Rather than tempting Providence by half-hearted effort,[107] he is to consider Providence without doubting,[108] and be persuaded by it,[109] so that he can deserve better of Providence,[110] aiming at felicity and virtue.[111]

5. Washington's faith in Providence was not simply connected with a theological or philosophical perspective. His faith indeed taught him to believe that Providence "never fails to take care of His children,"[112] and that Providence "has appeared in many instances"[113] with its "peculiar mark"[114] or "token of Providential agency." But Washington's perspective on Providence was not only a matter of faith, which he sometimes struggled to maintain.[115] He also saw illustrations of divine Providential activity in daily life, as well as in the War of Independence and in the life of the new nation. A summary of Washington's

extensive experiences of Providence include the following:

a. In daily life, Washington's vast belief in Providence is connected with: one's lot and station in life,[116] blessings,[117] preservation,[118] protection,[119] guiding and direction,[120] aid and assistance,[121] bountiful prosperity,[122] happiness,[123] provision,[124] being upheld and cared for,[125] being used as an instrument of God's will,[126] and finding assistance in one's own inadequacy in facing the future.[127] Providential matters even impacted Washington's approach to business. Thus, the crops he grew were under God's care,[128] and consideration of difficult Providential actions determined how his landlords should collect rents from his tenants.[129]

b. In terms of war, God's Providence was involved in unjust war[130] and with the passions of men.[131] Divine Providence extended to matters of safety,[132] success,[133] victory,[134] prisoners,[135] including a vast array of struggles in regard to the enemy (battles,[136] blinding their eyes,[137] discovering their intentions,[138] disabling them,[139] losses,[140] evacuations,[141] opportunities to defeat,[142] forming a regiment in retreat,[143] preventing their plans,[144] disappointing their plans,[145] having advantages over them,[146] defeating them,[147] preventing them from taking vigorous measures).[148] Divine Providence also rendered assistance with direction,[149] rescue,[150] deliverance,[151] and intervention at strategic moments[152] and peace.[153] No wonder soldiers considered participation in the Knights of Divine Providence.[154]

c. In terms of the new nation, Providence was seen by Washington in the directing of public officials,[155] in divine favor on the nation[156] which included preventing the dashing the cup of national happiness,[157] inducing the people to adopt the new Constitution,[158] bringing order out of confusion,[159] ordaining the very disagreements of people over issues,[160] the prevention of disease,[161] preserving peace,[162] increasing prosperity,[163] tranquility, liberty, and independence.[164]

In light of all of the above, we can truly understand the sincerity of Washington in his opening remarks upon his assumption of the presidency as well as his final prayer for the nation. In each, the theme is the same—America is a nation under divine Providential care.[165]

WASHINGTON'S TRUST IN PROVIDENCE

There is no better way to capture Washington's heart of faith than to read his words of reliance, trust, and dependence and faith in God's Providential care. For the sake of clarity, we will highlight in italics, Washington's words of faith. So here is a sampling of the many references in George Washington's writings to Providence.

He wrote Martha a letter on June 18, 1775:

> I shall *rely*, therefore, *confidently* on that Providence which has heretofore preserved and been bountiful to me, not doubting but that I shall return safely to you in the fall.[166]

He wrote his wife again on June 22, 1775, wherein he stated:

> I go *fully trusting* in that Providence, which has been more bountiful to me than I deserve and in full confidence of a happy meeting with you sometime in the Fall.[167]

Long after the war and during the year between the writing of the Constitution (1787) and its adoption (1789), George Washington wrote of his own "pious exultation" to Connecticut governor, Jonathan Trumbull, on July 20, 1788:

> Or at least we may, with a kind of *grateful and pious exultation*, trace the finger of Providence through those dark and mysterious events, which first induced the States to appoint a general Convention and then led them one after another (by such steps as were best calculated to effect the object) into an adoption of the system recommended by that general Convention....
>
> That the same good Providence may still continue to *protect* us

and prevent us from dashing the cup of national felicity ...[168]

George Washington wrote a letter to his brother, John Augustine Washington on March 31, 1776. This was after a major strategic victory for the American cause. For more than a year, the Americans surrounded British-occupied Boston, trying to strangle the bottled up red backs into submission. In early March 1776, Washington and his men managed to secretly assemble major artillery aimed at the then indefensible British garrisons and ships. Through the ingenuity of Henry Knox, whom Washington assigned the task, the Americans managed to sled more than two hundred gigantic cannons and weaponry from the captured Ft. Ticonderoga through countless miles of wilderness tract of ice and snow. In the middle of the night, without the British noticing or stopping them, the Americans placed this artillery upon the heights at Dorchester, looking down at the British. By the time the British discovered this, it was too late. Thus, the British, under General William Howe, suffered a humiliating setback. All they could do was flee the city and the big guns as quickly as possible. To whom did Washington give the praise for this remarkable turn of events? To God. He wrote these words to his brother:

> Upon their discovery of the works next morning, great preparations were made for attacking them; but not being ready before the afternoon, and the weather getting very tempestuous, much blood was saved, and a very important blow, to one side or the other, was prevented. That this most remarkable Interposition of Providence is for some wise purpose, *I have not a doubt.*[169]

Indeed, the remaining Loyalists chose to risk the elements rather than the fury of the returning citizens. Washington continues:

> When the Order Issued therefore for Imbarking the Troops in Boston, no Electric Shock, no sudden Clap of thunder, in a word the *last Trump,* could not have struck them with greater Consternation. They were at their Wits' end, and conscious of their black ingratitude chose to commit themselves in the manner I have above describ'd to the Mercy of the Waves at a tempestuous Season rather than meet their offended Countrymen.[170]

George Washington wrote a letter to Major General John Armstrong on the 4th of July, 1777. He noted that the evacuation of the British troops from New Jersey occurred just before the harvest—too early to burn the nearly-ripe crops, but not too early or late for the Americans to harvest the grain:

> The evacuation of Jersey at this time, seems to be a peculiar mark of providence, as the Inhabitants have an Opportunity of Securing their Harvests of Hay and Grain.[171]

He wrote to Major-General Israel Putnam on October 19, 1777, and said, "Should Providence be pleased to crown our arms in the course of the campaign with one more fortunate stroke...*I trust all will be well in His good time...*"[172] The Providence of God worked in God's sovereign time in Washington's thoughts, based in part on the biblical text of Ecclesiastes 3:11.

General Washington wrote a letter to Landon Carter on October 27, 1777, in which he discussed prisoners rounded up by the American patriots in the North. He notes:

> This singular instance of Providence, and of our fortune under it, exhibits a striking proof of the advantages which result from unanimity and a spirited conduct in the militia...
>
> I flatter myself that a superintending Providence is ordering everything for the best, and that, in due time, all will end well.[173]

From his Farewell Address, 1796, we read these words:

> Observe good faith and justice towards all Nations. Cultivate peace and harmony with all. Religion and morality enjoin this conduct; and can it be that good policy does not equally enjoin it? It will be worthy of a free, enlightened, and, at no distant period, a great Nation, to give to mankind the magnanimous and too novel example of a People always guided by an exalted justice and benevolence. Who can doubt that in the course of time and things the fruits of such a plan would richly repay any temporary advantages wch. might be lost by a steady adherence to it? *Can it be, that Providence has not connected the permanent felicity of a Nation*

with its virtue? The experiment, at least, is recommended by every sentiment which ennobles human Nature. Alas! is it rendered impossible by its vices?[174]

In short, Washington is saying that a nation is happy according to its level of virtue. Here are remarks he made in his Circular Letter to the States, June 8, 1783:

> The Citizens of America, placed in the most enviable condition, as the sole Lords and Proprietors of a vast Tract of Continent, comprehending all the various soils and climates of the World, and abounding with all the necessaries and conveniencies of life, are now by the late satisfactory pacification, acknowledged to be possessed of absolute freedom and Independency; They are, from this period, to be considered as the Actors on a most conspicuous Theatre, *which seems to be peculiarly designated by Providence* for the display of human greatness and felicity...[175]

To Reverend John Rodgers, Head Quarters, June 11, 1783:

> Glorious indeed has been our Contest: glorious, if we consider the Prize for which we have contended, and glorious in its Issue; but in the midst of our Joys, I hope we shall not forget that, *to divine Providence is to be ascribed the Glory and the Praise.*[176]

To Marquis de Lafayette, June 19, 1788:

> I do not believe, that *Providence* has done so much for nothing.[177]

And we could go on and on and on and on.

To George Washington, Providence is omniscient (knows all things), omnipotent (can do all things), and omnipresent (everywhere at the same time). These are the very same attributes of God outlined by the historic Christian faith.

CONCLUSION

To squeeze Washington into a secular image requires that substantial evidence be ignored, distorted or suppressed. When one realizes that the use of the term

"Providence" was Washington's favorite and most frequent way of referring to God, then it is clear that he consciously and constantly referred to God throughout his entire life. To hold that Washington was a Deist is to make the self-professed preacher of Providence into the very opposite of what he claimed to be.

THIRTY

George Washington's Christian Worldview

> *"It is vain to exclaim against the depravity*
> *of human nature...the experience of every age and nation*
> *has proved it...No institution, not built on the presumptive*
> *truth of these maxims can succeed."*
> *George Washington, 1778*[1]

While a Christian worldview may be defined differently by various scholars, it seems clear to us that a thoroughgoing Christian worldview will include an affirmation of the following:

1. God's existence
2. An affirmation of the three persons of the Trinity
3. The deity of Christ (a subset of #2)
4. God's decree, plan or will
5. God's self-revelation in the scriptures and in nature
6. The doctrine of Creation
7. Mankind's sinfulness

8. God's saving work in Christ
    a. His birth
    b. His exemplary life
    c. His teaching
        1) The two great commandments
        2) The Golden Rule
        3) Acquaintance with other teachings of Jesus
    d. His Crucifixion
    e. A recognition of his Resurrection
9. An understanding of the Gospel
    a. The reality of and the way to heaven
    b. God's judgment upon sin and the pains of hell
    c. Man's spiritual nature
    d. The difference between true and false religion
    e. The importance of faith and unbelief
    f. The need for justification before God
    g. The forgiveness of sins by God, and man's repentance
10. God's providential care of his people
11. The life of the Christian and the work of the church
    a. The work of ministers of the Gospel
    b. The importance of missionary work to non-Christians
    c. The Christian practice of forgiveness
    d. The importance of the church, the clergy, and worship
    e. A call for Christian conduct that is pleasing to
       God's nature
12. An ultimate hope
    a. The Second Advent
    b. The blessings of heaven
    c. The millennial state
    d. Eternal life

Would a person who affirmed all of these things be called a Deist or a Christian? The answer is obvious. What is listed above is a simple, but fairly full, outline of the basics of the Christian faith. Apparently it has not been so obvious in recent years that Washington affirmed all of these things! His simple beliefs, written throughout his papers, and his consistent pattern of worship in the Christian tradition preserved by the

Anglican Church, reflected all of these Christian teachings. There is simply no honest way that a man who believed such things can be called a Deist. We will now demonstrate our claim that these beliefs composed the faith and practice—a Christian worldview—of our Christian founding father.

WASHINGTON'S STATEMENTS THAT SUPPORT A CHRISTIAN WORLDVIEW

1. GOD'S EXISTENCE

In our chapter on Washington's view of God, we found that he clearly believed in God and used the word "God" some 140 times in his writings. Furthermore, Washington used approximately 90 different respectful titles of God (some from the Bible, some not—Almighty, Great Governor of the Universe, Lord of Armies). On top of this, he used the word "Providence" approximately 270 times. Like the preachers of his day, Providence was either another name for God, or referred to the work of God in human history.

2. AN AFFIRMATION OF THE THREE PERSONS OF THE TRINITY

This too was touched on briefly in the chapter on Washington's view of God. We will now consider further evidence.

In his diary on April 3, 1768, we read, "Went to Pohick Church."[2] April 3rd that year was Easter Sunday. This is significant in this context, since we also know that he attended church eight weeks later on May 29th of the same year. His diary entry for May 29th says, "Went to St. Paul's Church and Dined at my Brother's."[3] When Washington attended church on May 29th, eight weeks after Easter, it was Trinity Sunday. What did Washington pray when he was present for the Trinity Sunday liturgy? The 1662 *Book of Common Prayer* provided these words of praise for the Trinity:

> Trinity-Sunday.
> *The Collect.*
> Almighty and everlasting God, who hast given unto us thy servants grace, by the confession of a true faith to acknowledge the glory of the eternal Trinity, and in the power of thy Divine Majesty to worship the Unity; We beseech thee, that thou wouldst keep us steadfast in this faith, and evermore defend us from all adversities,

who livest and reignest, one God, world without end. *Amen.*[4]

The scripture readings for Trinity Sunday included Revelation 4, where John receives a vision of the triune God being worshiped in heaven. It also includes John 3, the famous evangelistic verses of Jesus where he speaks of the necessity of being "born again," and where Jesus promises "eternal life" for "whosoever believeth in him."

3. GOD'S DECREE OR PLAN

We have devoted an entire chapter on George Washington and Providence, in which we demonstrate from his own writings that Providence for Washington is the God of the Bible, or God's powerful plan being worked out in human history. Washington believed in God and counseled others to trust in him and to submit to his will, even when circumstances were difficult. Providence was the personal Divine Father, as we see in his words of consolation to Pierre L'Enfant: "While I sincerely condole with you on the loss of your good father; you will permit me to remind you, as an inexhaustible subject of consolation, that there is a good Providence which will never fail to take care of his Children."[5] Providence is also, in Washington's mind, the sovereign plan of God that accomplishes his decrees. In this case, Washington speaks of Providence with the impersonal "it." He used the same type of language commonly employed by eighteenth century American Christians, as seen in these examples:

- On March 1,1778, he wrote his childhood friend (turned Tory), Bryan Fairfax: "The determinations of Providence are all ways wise; often inscrutable, and though its decrees appear to bear hard upon us at times is nevertheless meant for gracious purposes..."[6]
- He wrote Elizabeth Parke Custis Law (on March 30, 1796): "Mrs. Lear was good and amiable, and your Society will feel the loss of her. But the Dispensations of Providence are as inscrutable, as they are wise and uncontroulable. It is the duty therefore of Religion and Philosophy, to submit to its decrees, with as little repining as the sensibility of our natures, will permit."[7]
- He wrote to his nephew William Augustine Washington (February 27, 1798): "...these are the decrees of an Allwise Providence, against whose dictates the skill, or foresight of man

can be of no avail; it is incumbent upon him therefore, to submit with as little repining as the sensibility of his nature will admit."[8]

• He wrote to Reverend Jonathan Boucher (his stepson's old tutor in happier days) (August 15, 1798): "What will be the consequences of our Arming for self defence [against a potential invasion by France], that Providence, who permits these doings in the Disturbers of Mankind; and who rules and Governs all things, alone can tell. To its all powerful decrees we must submit, whilst we hope that the justice of our Cause if War, must ensue, will entitle us to its Protection."[9]

And examples like these, as is true of virtually all these points, abound. While the language may sound a bit impersonal, this was a common way that orthodox Christian teachers and leaders referred to God in America at the time. For example, no one doubts the orthodoxy of the devout Presbyterian clergyman, Reverend Dr. John Witherspoon, the president of the College of New Jersey (later known as Princeton University). Congress declared that May 17, 1776, should be a National Day of Fasting, Humiliation, and Prayer. Reverend Witherspoon preached a sermon at the College entitled "The Dominion of Providence over the Passions of Men." He said, "...we give praise to God, the Supreme Disposer of all events, for His interposition on our behalf..."[10] This is just a sample of the way eighteenth century American Christians spoke. To interpret Washington's language as that of a Deist, means that Reverend Dr. Witherspoon would also have to be classified as a Deist. That, of course, would be absurd. Thus, this argument is both erroneous and illogical.

4. THE DEITY OF CHRIST

The climax of George Washington's great Circular Letter to the state governments on June 8, 1783, at the conclusion of the war, when he was hanging up his sword, notes that without a humble imitation of "the Divine Author of our blessed religion," we could never hope to be a "happy nation."[11] Here Washington is speaking about Jesus Christ.

Washington, of course, had subscribed to the doctrines of the church when he assumed the role of a vestryman. In so doing, he affirmed his belief in the second article of the *Thirty-Nine Articles of Religion of the Anglican Church*. That article reads as follows:

II. *Of the Word, or Son of God, which was made very man.*

The Son, which is the Word of the Father, begotten from everlasting of the Father, the very and eternal God, and of one substance with the Father, took man's nature in the womb of the blessed Virgin, of her substance: so that two whole and perfect natures, that is to say, the Godhead and manhood, were joined together in one person, never to be divided, whereof is one Christ, very God and very man, who truly suffered, was crucified, dead, and buried, to reconcile His Father to us, and to be a sacrifice, not only for original guilt, but also for all actual sins of men.[12]

Furthermore, Washington used the title (referring to Jesus) of "the great Lord and Ruler of Nations." To Washington's largely Christian audience, this had reference to Jesus Christ, whom the Bible calls "KING OF KINGS AND LORD OF LORDS" (Revelation 19:16) [Emphasis in the original]. The Bible says of Mary, "she brought forth a man child who was to rule all nations" (Revelation 12:5, KJV). In that light, note what Washington declared in his Thanksgiving Proclamation of October 3, 1789: "And also that we may then unite in most humbly offering our prayers and supplications to the great Lord and Ruler of Nations and beseech him to pardon our national and other transgressions, to enable us all, whether in public or private stations, to perform our several and relative duties properly..."[13] Similarly, Washington said in his Sixth Annual Address to Congress (November 19, 1794): "Let us unite, therefore, in imploring the Supreme Ruler of nations, to spread his holy protection over these United States..."[14] Washington also refers to Christ when he speaks of "the Divine Author of light and felicity."[15]

5. GOD'S SELF-REVELATION IN THE SCRIPTURES AND IN NATURE

Consider these statements from George Washington about the Word of God. (Keep in mind, much of this has been covered in Chapter 13 on "Washington and the Bible.")

- In a message he prepared for Congress in April 1789, the new President wrote, "The blessed Religion revealed in the word of God will remain an eternal and awful monument to prove that the best Institutions may be abused by human depravity; and that they may even, in some instances be made subservient to the vilest of purposes." [16]

- In a letter to Marquis de Chastellux, April 25[-May 1], 1788, Washington indirectly called the Bible "revealed religion." He wrote: "For certainly it is more consonant to all the principles of reason and religion (natural and revealed) to replenish the earth with inhabitants, rather than to depopulate it by killing those already in existence..."[17] God tells man in the beginning of the Bible to be fruitful and fill the earth with inhabitants (Gen. 1:28). This is an allusion to that principle, which comes from revealed religion. (Note that at that point in history, the leaders of the deistic side of the Enlightenment were challenging the whole notion of revealed religion.)

- In the famous Circular Letter that he wrote to the States, resigning as commander in chief, the General contrasted superstition with revealed religion. He wrote: "...The foundation of our Empire was not laid in the gloomy age of Ignorance and Superstition, but at an Epocha when the rights of mankind were better understood and more clearly defined, than at any former period...the free cultivation of Letters, the unbounded extension of Commerce, the progressive refinement of Manners, the growing liberality of sentiment, and above all, the pure and benign light of Revelation, have had ameliorating influence on mankind and increased the blessings of Society."[18]

This last quote is an outstanding passage. Washington is saying that the United States owes its political happiness to several strands that have come together. But "above all" the greatest of these strands is "the pure and benign light of Revelation"—another way of describing the scriptures. Therefore, he goes on to say, when we have had such an auspicious start as a nation, we have only ourselves to blame if we are not a free and happy people.

6. THE DOCTRINE OF CREATION

Washington affirmed his belief in what the Bible says about the Creator and his creation. Here are just a few samples:

- In a letter to John Parke Custis, January 22, 1777, he writes, "...I do not think that any officer since the creation ever had such a variety of difficulties..."[19]
- In a letter to Brigadier General Thomas Nelson, August 20, 1778, Washington pens, "...the strangest vicissitudes that perhaps ever attended any one contest since the creation..."[20]
- On November 28, 1796, the president wrote this to his adopted grandson, George Washington Parke Custis: "The assurances you give me of applying diligently to your studies, and fulfilling those obligations which are enjoined [i.e., through scripture] by your Creator and due to his creatures, are highly pleasing and satisfactory to me."[21]
- To Doctor James Anderson, July 25, 1798, President Washington observes, "...a man was not designed by the All wise Creator to live for himself alone..."[22]
- From a draft of his farewell address, enclosed in Washington's letter to Alexander Hamilton, May 15, 1796, read, "That as the allwise dispensor of human blessings has favored no Nation of the Earth with more abundant, and substantial means of happiness than United America, that we may not be so ungrateful to our Creator; so wanting to ourselves; and so regardless of Posterity, as to dash the cup of beneficence which is thus bountifully offered to our acceptance."[23]

And, as in virtually all these points, we could cite example after example of this.

7. MANKIND'S SINFULNESS

Like almost every founding father, George Washington believed in the doctrine of original sin. He believed that man was sinful; he believed in human depravity. We do not pursue this here, since we addressed it in a previous chapter. Let this single instance then illustrate our point:

It is vain to exclaim against the depravity of human nature on this account; the fact is so, the experience of every age and nation has proved it and we must in a great measure, change the constitution of man, before we can make it otherwise. No institution, not built on the presumptive truth of these maxims can succeed.[24]

8. GOD'S SAVING WORK IN CHRIST

As we summarize this aspect of Washington's experience, we wish to point especially to the teachings of the *Book of Common Prayer* that Washington used throughout his life for worship.

HIS BIRTH

In the Christian understanding, men are incapable of saving themselves, so God provided his son for mankind's redemption. As an Anglican, Washington celebrated Christmas, which on some occasions included attending church that day, where he would have read prayers acknowledging the historic Christian faith in Christ and the Gospel.[25] The service continued with readings from Hebrews 1 and John 1 (included in this endnote), Bible passages which affirm that Jesus Christ, whose birth is celebrated at Christmas, was divine.[26]

Another example of Washington's worship at Christmas is on December 25, 1770. This year Christmas fell on a Tuesday. His entry for this date says, "Went to Pohick Church and returnd to Dinner."[27] Christmas Sundays in the Anglican tradition were also Sundays when the Lord's Supper was celebrated.

When he wasn't fighting battles on Christmas,[28] he was celebrating Christmas like other Christians.

CHRIST'S EXEMPLARY LIFE

In his classic Circular Letter to the States (June 8, 1783), Washington prayed that God "would most graciously be pleased to dispose us all, to do Justice, to love mercy, and to demean ourselves with that Charity, humility and pacific temper of mind, which were the Characteristicks of the Divine Author of our blessed Religion, and without an humble imitation of whose example in these things, we can never hope to be a happy Nation."[29] Thus, Washington affirmed that Jesus was loving, humble, and peace loving (pacific) and worthy of imitation.

CHRIST'S TEACHING

The Two Great Commandments

Jesus gave two great commandments to his people: to love God and to love one's neighbor as themselves (Mark 12:30-31). Our first president affirmed this when he wrote to his adopted grandson, George Washington Parke Custis on December 19,

A Description of the Leap year, Dominical
Letter, Golden Number, Cycle of the Sun
Roman Induction Epact &c
With Memorial Verses on the Ecclesiastical
and civil Kalender

The Golden Number or Prime is a circular Revolution of 19
years in which term of years it hath been anciently supposed that the Sun
& Moon do make all the Variety of Aspects one to another

The Cycle of the Sun maketh its Revolution in 28 Years be
cause in that time all the Variety of y Dominical Letters & Leap Years
are Expired & the 29 Year the Cycle doth begin again which Number
is is to find out the Dominical Letter for any Year Past Present or to
come

The Roman Induction consisteth of 15 Years & is set Down in
the Charters & Writings of the Pronotaries of the Pope of Rome for once
in 15 Years the Nations were to Pay tribute to the Romans

The Epact is a Number never exceeding 30 Days it is the 11 Days
& 5 Hours which added to the Lunar Year being 354 Days do make it
equal to the Solar Year which is 365 Days

The Leap Year is every fourth Year which hath one Day More
in it than Common Year this Day is made up in 4 Years by the Addi
of Six Hours that are ever y above y 365 Days which Day is added after
the 28th of Febry So that in y Leap Year Febry has 29 Days. And here
note that y Prime y Dominical Letters & the Cycle of the Sun Change
the first of January, and the Epact the first of March, & the Roman In
diction the first of September

To Know if it be Leap Year
Divide the Year by 4 what is left shall
be for Leap Year o for Past 1 2 or 3
Example Anno 1707
4/1707/426
40
Ansr 3 Year after Leap Year

*In these two illustrations, Washington's childhood school papers show that he was taught
the mathematical method of how to find the date of Easter in any given year, past or future.*

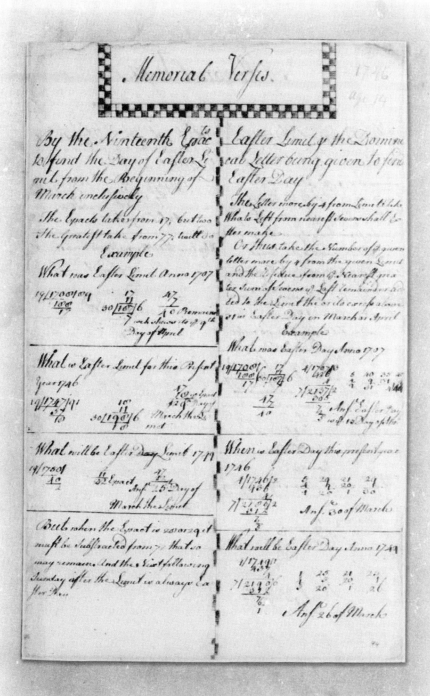

Even his math training reflected his ecclesiastical and christian education

1796: "...you are well acquainted with my sentiments on this subject, and know how anxious all your friends are to see you enter upon the grand theatre of life, with the advantages of a finished education, a highly cultivated mind, and a proper sense of your duties to God and man..."[30]

Also, he wrote to Reverend Bryan, Lord Fairfax (January 20, 1799): "The favourable sentiments which others, you say, have been pleased to express respecting me, cannot but be pleasing to a mind who [sic] always walked on a straight line, and endeavoured as far as human frailties, and perhaps strong passions, would enable him, to discharge the relative duties to his Maker and fellow-men, without seeking any indirect or left handed attempts to acquire popularity."[31]

The Golden Rule

At Christ Church in Alexandria, Virginia, where Washington worshiped and maintained a pew, you can see on the reredos the Golden Rule. The Golden Rule as taught by Jesus Christ states: "All things whatsoever ye would that men should do to you, do ye even so to them" (Matthew 7:12). Washington not only said those words at church, he tried to live by them. He wrote, for example, to Mr. Chichesters (April 25, 1799): "I should have hoped, that upon the principle of doing as one would be done by, they would not have been injured by my Neighbours."[32]

Acquaintance with other teachings of Jesus

In George Washington's writings, he used phrases that come from various aspects of the teachings of Christ, which we have already seen in earlier chapters.[33] Some examples of these are: The wise man counting the cost, the "jot or tiddle," widow's mite, millstone hung to the neck, repent and be forgiven, take up my bed and walk, heavy laden, wheat and tares, stumbling block, lead into temptation, good and faithful servant, war and rumors of war.

CHRIST'S CRUCIFIXION.

As a devout Anglican, Washington affirmed Jesus' death for sinners every time he attended church. As Washington used his prayer book for daily prayers during the Passion Week, he would have prayed as follows:

Good Friday.[34]
The Collects.
Almighty God, we beseech thee graciously to behold this thy family, for whom our Lord Jesus Christ was contented to be betrayed, and given up into the hands of wicked men, and to suffer death

upon the cross, who now liveth and reigneth with thee and the Holy Ghost, ever one God, world without end. *Amen.* ...

The Collect from the <u>First Day of Lent</u> is to be read every day in Lent after the Collect appointed for the Day.

The First day of Lent, Commonly called Ash-Wednesday.

The Collect.

Almighty and everlasting God, who hatest nothing that thou hast made and dost forgive the sins of all them that are penitent; Create and make in us new and contrite hearts, that we, worthily lamenting our sins, and acknowledging our wretchedness, may obtain of thee, the God of all mercy, perfect remission and forgiveness; through Jesus Christ our Lord. *Amen.*

A RECOGNITION OF HIS RESURRECTION

In 1768, Easter fell on April 3rd. Washington's diary for that date says, "Went to Pohick church and returnd to Dinner."[35] The prayers that Washington said that day from *The Book of Common Prayer* affirm a hearty belief in the resurrection of Christ.

Easter-Day.

At Morning Prayer, instead of the Psalm, O come, let us sing, *&c. these Anthems shall be sung or said.*

Christ our Passover is sacrificed for us : therefore let us keep the feast; Not with the old leaven, nor with the leaven of malice and wickedness : but with the unleavened bread of sincerity and truth. 1 *Cor.* 5:7 Christ being raised from the dead dieth no more : death hath no more dominion over him. For in that he died, he died unto sin once : but in that he liveth, he liveth unto God. Likewise reckon ye also yourselves to be dead indeed unto sin : but alive unto God through Jesus Christ our Lord. *Rom.* 6:9...

The Collect.

Almighty God, who through thine only-begotten Son Jesus Christ hast overcome death, and opened unto us the gate of everlasting life; We humbly beseech thee, that, as by thy special grace preventing us thou dost put into our minds good desires, so by thy continual help we may bring the same to good effect; through Jesus Christ our Lord, who liveth and reigneth with thee and the Holy Ghost, ever one God, world without end. *Amen.*

The Gospel reading was John 20, which declares how Jesus rose from the dead and appeared to His disciples. It includes the passage where Thomas earns the moniker "Doubting Thomas" because he declared he wouldn't believe the Resurrection until he actually touched the risen Jesus.

Easter was an important part of Washington's early education. In his mathematical school papers, after dealing with surveying, measuring, and gauging, he writes of the cycle of the sun and how to determine the exact date of Easter in any given year.[36]

9. AN UNDERSTANDING OF THE GOSPEL

We will not develop the Gospel section here, since this will be the focus of the next chapter. But there we will see that Washington's writings refer to:

    a.   The reality of and the way to heaven

    b.   God's judgment upon sin and the pains of hell

    c.   Man's spiritual nature and the work of the Holy Spirit.

Man's spiritual nature and need of the Holy Spirit is especially seen in Washington's General Orders for November 27, 1779, that declared Congress's day of thanksgiving:

> RESOLVED, That it be recommended to the several states, to appoint Thursday, the 9th of December next, to be a day of public and solemn thanksgiving to Almighty God for his mercies, and of prayer for the continuance of his favor...that he would grant to his church the plentiful effusions of divine grace, and pour out his *Holy Spirit* on all ministers of the gospel; that he would bless and prosper the means of education, and spread the light of Christian knowledge through the remotest corners of the earth...."[37]

This theology of "the plentiful effusions of divine grace" and of pouring "out his Holy Spirit" reflected the Christian understanding of Pentecost. Washington's experience with the book of prayer in the military resulted in his participation in a Pentecost Sunday service.

We know from Washington's diary entry for June 2, 1754, that there was a prayer service that he attended as a soldier. He wrote, "Two or three families of the Shawanese and Loups arrived: We had prayers at the Fort."[38] There were several reasons for this prayer service. First, they just had finished the fort the day before, according to the entry. Second, he saw the arrival of the Indians, and may have remembered his friend George Fairfax's instruction to not to forget prayers, especially when Indians were present. And finally, June 2nd in 1754 was a Sunday and fell precisely seven Sundays after Easter, which we know was on April 14th in that year. This meant this Sunday was Whitsunday, or Pentecost Sunday. The prayer that Washington and his fellow soldiers prayed that day said,

> God, who as at this time didst teach the hearts of thy faithful peo-
> ple, by the sending to them the light of thy Holy Spirit; Grant us by
> the same Spirit to have a right judgment in all things, and evermore
> to rejoice in his holy comfort, through the merits of Christ Jesus our
> Saviour, who liveth and reigneth with thee in the unity of the same
> Spirit, one God, world without end. Amen.[39]

Since no chaplain had been provided for these soldiers, as seen in Washington's frequent appeals for the provision of one, Washington, as the commanding officer, likely followed the ancient Virginia custom of the officer in charge leading the prayers for the men. Thus, Washington would have on this day led the Pentecost Sunday prayer service with its cry for the work of the Holy Spirit. He would have also read the great biblical texts from *The Book of Common Prayer* that teach the coming of the Holy Spirit: the Epistle reading being Acts 2 and the Gospel reading being John 14.

    d.   The difference between true and false religion

As we saw in the last chapter on Washington and the doctrine of Providence, Washington spoke sometimes of "true religion" or the "true spirit of Christianity." Implied in that is the notion that there are the false practices of so-called Christians. Here is one of those quotes: "While just government protects all in their religious rights, true religion affords to government its surest support."[40]

    e.   The importance of faith versus unbelief

On August 20, 1778, George Washington wrote to Thomas Nelson, Jr., wherein he noted how God was helping the American cause in the war. He said that God's hand was so obvious that Americans would be ingrates if we didn't recognize it. He wrote: "The Hand of Providence has been so conspicuous in all this that he must be worse than an infidel that lacks faith, and more wicked that has not gratitude to acknowledge his obligations…"[41]

    f.   The need for justification before God

Washington used phrases like "answerable to God," "so much to answer for," "justifiable in the eyes of God and men."[42] Washington had affirmed the *Thirty-Nine Articles* when he became a vestryman. This included the classic reformational doctrine of justification by faith alone in Christ alone. [43]

    g.   *The forgiveness of sins by God, and man's repentance*

In a letter to his surrogate son, Marquis de Lafayette (July 25, 1785), Washington begins in a joyful mood, drawing on their shared understanding of Christian teaching on sin and forgiveness: "I stand before you as a Culprit: but to *repent & be forgiven* are the precepts of Heaven: I do the former, do you practice the latter, and it will be participation of a divine attribute."[44]

The Gospel message is clearly seen as Washington gave his General Orders on November 27, 1779:

> The Honorable Congress has been pleased to pass the following proclamation.
>
> Whereas it becomes us humbly to approach the throne of Almighty God, with gratitude and praise for the wonders which his goodness has wrought in conducting our fore-fathers to this western world; for his protection to them and to their posterity amid difficulties and dangers; for raising us, their children, from deep distress to be numbered among the nations of the earth; and for arming the hands of just and mighty princes in our deliverance...and above all, that *he hath diffused the glorious light of the gospel, whereby, through the merits of our gracious Redeemer, we may become the heirs of his eternal glory:* therefore,
>
> RESOLVED, That it be recommended to the several states, to appoint Thursday, the 9th of December next, to be a day of public and solemn thanksgiving to Almighty God for his mercies, and of prayer for the continuance of his favor and protection to these United States;...that he would in mercy look down upon us, pardon our sins and receive us into his favor....[45] (emphasis ours)

Washington did not hesitate to communicate to his army this congressional message concerning the Redeemer, Jesus Christ.

10. GOD'S PROVIDENTIAL CARE OF HIS PEOPLE

In our chapter on Washington's views of Providence, we saw that he refers to this doctrine some 270 times. But there is a fascinating experience of God's Providence in Washington's life that occurred in November of 1751, when he was in Barbados with his brother Lawrence. On November 11th, we read in his diary, "Dressed in order for Church but got to town two Late. Dined at Majr. Clarkes with ye S: G: went to Evening Service and return'd to our Lodgings."[46]

It is difficult to pin down the exact day of the week this was. It appears to have been a Sunday. The problem is, that in the Gregorian calendar of 1751, November 11th is a Thursday, and in the

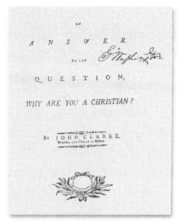

Washington's signature on a book in his collection

Julian calendar it is a Monday. Given these uncertainties, we cannot place the date for sure. It is possible that this trip to church was to celebrate St. Martin's day that is on November 11th. But it seems fairly unlikely that they would have made a special trip for morning prayer for a non-Sunday celebration of a saint's day. The one thing we do know, however, is that they attended evening prayer.

The two collects for evening prayer focus on God's providential care. The significance of this is found in Washington's diary entry for November 17th, "Was strongly attacked with the small Pox: sent for Dr. Lanahan whose attendance was very constant till my recovery, and going out which was not 'till Thursday the 12th of December."[47] That Washington contracted small pox when he was young and in a very warm climate was a providential blessing for the future American cause.[48] During the American War for Independence, more American soldiers were killed by disease than in battle.

Consider what Washington himself will say of his own army's sufferings with this profoundly life-threatening disease, on December 20, 1776, 25 years later, "Brigadier Read of New Hampshire [does] not I presume mean to continue in Service, he ought not, as I am told by the Severity of the small Pox he is become both blind and deaf."[49] Washington's life could have been taken, since small pox did not spare generals. Washington writes to Brig. Gen. John Sullivan on June 13, 1776, "Having received Intelligence of the unfortunate Death of General Thomas, occasioned by the small Pox he had taken, the Command of the Army in Canada devolves on you."[50]

In light of this, the prayers offered by young Washington in his evening prayers just before his own onset of small pox have a certain poignancy, "O God, from whom all holy desires, all good counsels, and all just works do proceed; Give unto thy servants that peace which the world cannot give, that both our hearts may be set to obey thy commandments, and also that by thee we being defended from the fear of our enemies, may pass our time in rest and quietness, through the merits of Jesus Christ our Saviour. *Amen.*" The next prayer said, "Lighten our darkness, we beseech thee, O Lord, and by they great mercy defend us from all perils and dangers of this night, for the love of thy only Son our Saviour Jesus Christ. Amen."[51]

11. THE LIFE OF THE CHRISTIAN AND THE WORK OF THE CHURCH

We have seen throughout our study that Washington actively supported the work of the church and practiced Christian principles in his work and relationships.

a. The work of ministers of the Gospel

George Washington believed in the validity of the work of ministers. In his letter to the First Presbytery of the Eastward, Newburyport, October 28, 1789, he made it clear that religion should not be mandated, convinced, instead, that "the path of true piety is so plain as to require but little political direction." Indeed, instead, he charged the clergy to "instruct the ignorant, and to reclaim the devious, and, in the progress of morality and science, to which our government will give every furtherance, we may confidently expect the advancement of true religion, and the completion of our happiness."[52]

b. The importance of missionary work to non-Christians

We saw in our earlier chapter in "The Anglican Mission to the Indians" that George Washington believed strongly in the need for Indians to be civilized. He saw the Gospel of Jesus Christ as playing a critical role. He corresponded with those engaged in or financially supporting such missionary endeavors. This is akin to what he said in a speech to the Delaware Indian chiefs (May 12, 1779) that they do well to learn our way of life——but "above all, the religion of Jesus Christ."[53]

c. The Christian practice of forgiveness

Washington believed what Christianity affirms—that those who repent should be forgiven. He wrote to his adopted grandson, George Washington Parke Custis (June 4, 1797): "your resolution to abandon the ideas which were therein express, are sincere, I shall not only heartily forgive, but will forget also, and bury in oblivion all that has passed."[54]

We also saw, in a previous chapter, how George Washington was magnanimous in showing forgiveness to those who had hurt him during the war. His childhood friend, Bryan Fairfax, turned Tory during the war. Afterwards, George forgave him. So also did George forgive Reverend Jacob Duché, who led the first Congress in the moving prayer (September 7, 1774), and Reverend Jonathan Boucher, who was the tutor of Washington's stepchildren. All of these made peace with Washington and he with them after the war.[55]

    d.   The importance of the Church, the clergy and worship

Not only was George Washington a committed churchman, early in life he was a committed lay leader. Furthermore, throughout his life he had several friendships with clergymen. A review of the index in his diaries will reveal that some sixty pastors actually visited Washington and stayed in his home at Mount Vernon. Some of these visited many times and were clearly among his personal friends. He corresponded with over forty pastors from all over the country. He was clearly comfortable with the clergy. The record shows that he usually had prayers at his table, and sometimes he led the prayer, even when a minister was present, although he usually asked the clergyman present to lead in the prayers for the meal.[56]

    e.   A call for Christian conduct that is pleasing to God's nature

In his First Inaugural Address (1789), George Washington said this: "We ought to be no less persuaded that the propitious smiles of Heaven, can never be expected on a nation that disregards the eternal rules of order and right, which Heaven itself has ordained."[57] To his mostly-Christian hearers that meant the rules found in the Bible.

12. AN ULTIMATE HOPE

Washington believed that religion provided hope. He wrote to Benjamin Lincoln (February 11, 1788): "Time *alone* can blunt the keen edge of afflictions; Philosophy and our Religion holds out to us such hopes as will, upon proper reflection, enable us to bear with fortitude the most calamitous incidents of life and these are all that can be expected from the feelings of humanity; is all which they will yield."[58] (emphasis in the original)

    a.   The millennial state

As most American's have come to know, the word millennium means one thousand years. It is based on the biblical text in Revelation 20, which speaks of a one thousand-year kingdom on earth. Washington's use of this word in the below examples points to the historic Puritan understanding which saw the one thousand-year kingdom as one of global peace, before Christ would make his second return. This peaceful kingdom is brought about through the leadership and ministry of Christians worldwide. Technically, this is known as the "postmillennial" view, or Christ will come again only *after* the one thousand year reign of peace on earth.

Note that Washington's view of the sinfulness of man, caused him to doubt that the millennial state was to come any time soon! He wrote to the Earl of Buchan (May 26, 1794) that "the restless and malignant passions of man,…place the prospects of peace too far off, and the promised millenium at an awful distance from our day."[59] Similarly, he wrote to Doctor James Anderson (December 24, 1795): "But alas! the millenium will not I fear appear in our days."[60]

He noted to Sir Edward Newenham on August 29, 1788:

> But what shall we say of Wars and the appearances of Wars in the rest of the World? Mankind are not yet ripe for the Millenial State. The affairs of some of the greatest Potentates appear to be very much embroiled in the North of Europe. The question is, whether the Turks will be driven out of Europe or not?[61]

Thus, the Christian understanding of a millennium provided the framework of Washington's understanding of history (that it was progressing to an end, predetermined by God).

    b.   The Second Coming of Christ

Washington implied an understanding of the Second Coming of Christ, or the Second Advent, when he referred to the biblical texts of "separating the wheat and tares," "the last trump," "the sound of distant thunder," "wars and rumors of wars," "a second morning star," "the reward of a good and faithful servant."[62]

    c.   The blessings of heaven

We believe that Washington believed in eternal life or immortality. Since we will discuss this in a subsequent chapter, we simply offer this single quotation that shows his belief in life after death. He wrote this letter to a family member when his stepdaughter died in an epileptic seizure,

> Dear Sir: It is an easier matter to conceive, than to describe the distress of this Family; especially that of the unhappy Parent of our Dear Patsy Custis, when I inform you that yesterday removed [sic] the Sweet Innocent Girl Entered into a more happy and peaceful abode than any she has met with in the afflicted Path she hither to has trod.[63]

The phrase "a more happy and peaceful abode" cannot refer to the tomb. When

Washington speaks of the tomb he calls it "the dreary mansions of my fathers." The more happy and peaceful abode was heaven. Washington referred to heaven over one hundred times in his writings.

d. Eternal life

Washington's use of eternal includes, "eternal life," "eternal glory," "eternal happiness," "eternal rules ordained by Heaven," and the "eternal and awful monument" that the Christian religion gives to the abuse of power by the best of institutions. All of these ideas are consistent with Christianity and inconsistent with Deism.

CONCLUSION

A fully developed Christian worldview emerges from Washington's words and his lifelong worship with the prayer book that he regularly used and shared with his family. In light of this evidence, it cannot any longer be legitimately argued that George Washington believed in the remote absentee God of the Deists. A Christian worldview and a Deist perspective are unable to be harmonized. Washington's expressed beliefs and his worldview are Christian, and thus, undercut the claim that Washington held to a Deist perspective.

THIRTY ONE

The Gospel According to George Washington

"And above all ... he hath diffused the glorious light of the gospel, whereby, through the merits of our gracious Redeemer, we may become the heirs of his eternal glory."
General Orders of Washington,
November 27, 1779, quoting a Congressional Proclamation [1]

The question of George Washington's Christianity is at the heart of the controversy over his religion. As we assemble the evidence of Washington's belief in the Christian Gospel, we wish to highlight a few important considerations.

First, for the sake of argument, we will set aside the authority of the classic anecdotes and oral histories that have traditionally been used to substantiate Washington's Christianity. These are simply rejected as untrue or unproven by those who doubt his Christianity. For example, modern author, Joseph J. Ellis, in his book *His Excellency: George Washington,* says that the cherry tree incident (first popularized by Parson Mason Weems) is "a complete fabrication."[2]

Second, since we have consciously adopted a "minimalist facts" approach, we will not base our arguments on disputed evidence, such as the explicitly Christian *Daily*

Sacrifice prayers that were in the manuscript book found in Washington's effects about a hundred years after his death. Since it cannot be proved beyond a shadow of a doubt that he wrote them or that he read them or used them, but only that he possessed them, we will not appeal to them to establish our claim of Washington's Christianity.[3]

Third, we will engage the opponents of Washington's Christianity, who refuse to accept his own personal approach of "works not words." As we do, we reiterate that if this canon of Washington's self-interpretation were followed, the overwhelming evidence already cited would end the debate. But since the skeptics require *written* proof of his Christian faith, we will proceed to provide it.

Fourth, given Washington's personality and principles, we must recognize that he never intended to provide a personal creed. His daily priorities and profoundly busy life did not give him the leisure or the impetus to compose a personal creed. So we will seek to demonstrate his Christianity through his occasional self-revealing statements, wherein he identifies himself as a Christian or gives us insights into his faith in the Gospel. In the previous chapter, we saw his commitment to the essential elements of a Christian worldview.

A REVIEW OF THE EVIDENCE OF WASHINGTON'S CHRISTIANITY SO FAR

What we have learned about Washington's Christianity thus far can be summarized as follows:

- He was from a British Christian culture, from a colony that had an established Christian church and from a family that had for several generations been explicitly Christian and active in the Anglican tradition.
- His home training was clearly Christian in orientation, in terms of the tutors and texts, as evidenced by extant schoolbooks and school papers. His childhood education was conducted under a Christian father, until Augustine Washington died when George was eleven, and then under his devout Christian mother.
- He pursued a career in the military that brought him into a highly structured environment that regularly had morning and evening prayers in accordance with the liturgical Christian "divine service" of the *Book of Common Prayer*. The military

vocabulary of his era was marked by a direct use of Christian theological terms: pardon, redemption, the atonement, grace, mercy, forgiveness, salvation, justification, imputation of guilt, appeal to heaven.

- He married a devout Christian woman and raised his adopted children under the tutorship of Anglican clergy, buying for his children not only explicitly Christian text books, but also prayer books and Bibles, with their names personally gilded upon them.

- He served in the leadership of the Anglican Church, taking vows not only to the worship and doctrines of the Christianity expressed by the Anglican Church, but his attendance, contributions, and involvement in issues concerning the church in terms of church government and the House of Burgesses were exemplary. His ecclesiastical vocabulary is extensive.

- He served in the role of sponsor of eight children in the sacrament of Christian baptism, something that Thomas Jefferson would not do, because his Unitarianism prevented him from taking the required public vows to the historic Christian faith. Washington had no scruples in this regard and performed this duty willingly, which is particularly significant, given Washington's consistent emphasis upon his personal candor and constant concern for strict personal integrity.

- He openly encouraged the work of the clergy and chaplains in his roles as military, ecclesiastical, and civil leader. When such were not available to do their work, he performed their functions, both leading in prayers, and, even conducting a Christian funeral in the case of General Braddock in 1755.

- His vocabulary is replete with theological concerns. He speaks of God some 140 times, the divine 95 times, heaven 133 times, Providence 270 times, and uses various honorific titles for God some 95 times. He alludes to approximately 200 different biblical texts, some of them scores of times, and does so in a way that shows that he was remarkably biblically literate.

- He was explicitly a praying man, as evidenced by a

custom-sized prayer book that he ordered to fit comfortably in his pocket. More than 100 different prayers (or references to prayer) in his own hand were found throughout his private and public letters.

• His views of religion are discoverable in some measure, even though as a military and government official, as well as a manager of a vast plantation, his extensive duties and writings would normally not be expected to turn in a direction of theology. These views include an overt affirmation of revelation, the reality of both natural and revealed religion, a concern that his Protestant soldiers not ridicule Roman Catholics for their beliefs, and an equal concern that Protestant and Jewish minorities not be fearful of persecution or bigotry from the new federal government he helped to fashion and to initiate.

• Indeed, Washington was keenly aware of the spiritual component of human life, referring again and again to the human spirit, as well as acknowledging the Holy Spirit and the Spirit's work. He frequently reveals his own spiritual concern for prayer, dependence on Providence, and faith and trust in God.

• He was also consciously influenced by the emphasis upon reason emanating from the Enlightenment. But this expressed itself not in hostility to faith, but hostility to superstition. Thus, Washington's writings explicitly criticize the deistic thought of his day. This is seen in phrases like, "worse than an infidel," "that man must be bad who does not believe," and his strong warning in his Farewell Address to those of the deistic mindset who would discountenance the necessary supports of "religion and morality" for political prosperity. His broken relationship with Thomas Paine is illustrative of this as well. Thomas Paine, the highly esteemed best-selling patriotic writer of *Common Sense*, was Washington's friend. But Thomas Paine, the critic of revealed religion, as manifested in the *Age of Reason*, was carefully addressed by Washington's distance and silence. Instead of pursuing reason over revealed religion, Washington's letters manifest a commitment to revelation coupled with a "rational ground for belief," "moral certainty," and a self-description of "no sceptic on normal occasions." In a previous chapter entitled "Washington vs. Deism," we offered a comparison of his views with those of the Deists, and found Washington's beliefs inherently and consistently incompatible with the teachings and ethics advocated by the Deists.

• In fact, it is remarkable that so much of Washington's faith can be discovered at all, given that by habit and principle he was a man who did not talk about himself. This is universally confirmed by the testimonies of those who personally knew him. His personal faith was thus, not easily or often put into words, but rather was expressed in actions according to his motto: "deeds not words"[4] which was also consistent with the motto on the Washington family's Coat of Arms: *Exitus Acta Probat*, meaning, "the end proves the deed." As his granddaughter said, "His mottoes were, "Deeds, Not Words"; and "For God and My Country."

Thus, George Washington's own rule for interpreting himself or anyone else was the necessity of looking at a person's conduct, not primarily reading or hearing one's words. On this basis, the evidence is unimpeachably clear—Washington was a Christian. But given the fact that those who have denied his Christianity have erected a standard of evidence that Washington explicitly did not intend—that is, a verbal, written, self-disclosing personal declaration of his heartfelt beliefs—before they will accept the claim that he was self-consciously a Christian, we will seek to address their concerns.

WASHINGTON'S STATEMENTS THAT IDENTIFY HIM AS A CHRISTIAN

Consider these declarations of George Washington as a Christian. (Many of these have been previously mentioned, but now we here assemble them together for the reader to experience the full impact.):

1. Washington called himself a Christian as part of a faith declaration he made to acknowledge the truth of a personal claim he made in a letter. He freely wrote of his own accord, "On my honor and the faith of a Christian...."[5]

2.   As a military commander he said to the Delaware Indian chiefs that they do well to learn about the Christian religion. He said in May 1779:

> ...Brothers: I am glad you have brought three of the Children of your principal Chiefs to be educated with us. I am sure Congress will open the Arms of love to them, and will look upon them as their own Children, and will have them educated accordingly. This is a great mark of your confidence and of your desire to preserve the friendship between the Two Nations to the end of time, and to become One people with your Brethren of the United States. My ears hear with pleasure the other matters you mention. Congress will be glad to hear them too. You do well to wish to learn our arts and ways of life, and above all, the religion of Jesus Christ. These will make you a greater and happier people than you are.[6]

Similarly, he wrote to Reverend John Ettwein from the Society for the Propagation of the Gospel to the Heathen from Mount Vernon on May 2, 1788:

> ...So far as I am capable of judging, the principles upon which the society is founded and the rules laid down for its government, appear to be well calculated to promote so laudable and arduous an undertaking, and you will permit me to add that if an event so long and so earnestly desired as that of converting the Indians to Christianity and consequently to civilization, can be effected, the Society of Bethlehem bids fair to bear a very considerable part in it....[7]

3.   The records of the Country Court of Fairfax has under the date of February 15, 1763, "George Washington, Esqr., took the oaths according to Law repeated and subscribed the Test and subscribed to the Doctrine and Discipline of the Church of England in order to qualify him to act as a Vestryman of Truro Parish."[8] This doctrine included the following teaching from the eleventh article of the *Thirty-Nine Articles of Religion*:

> We are accounted righteous before God only for the merit of our Lord and Saviour Jesus Christ, by faith, and not for our own works

or deservings; Wherefore, that we be justified by faith only is a most wholesome doctrine and very full of comfort....[9]

As a committed Anglican, Washington regularly prayed the General Confession of the Morning Prayer as he worshiped with the *Book of Common Prayer* throughout his military career and in his lifelong worship in the Anglican/Episcopal tradition:

> ALMIGHTY and most merciful Father; We have erred, and strayed from thy ways like lost sheep. We have followed too much the devices and desires of our own hearts. We have offended against thy holy laws. We have left undone those things which we ought to have done; And we have done those things which we ought not to have done; And there is no health in us. But thou, O Lord, have mercy upon us, miserable offenders. Spare thou them, O God, who confess their faults. Restore thou them that are penitent; According to thy promises declared unto mankind in Christ Jesus our Lord. And grant, O most merciful Father, for his sake; That we may hereafter live a godly, righteous, and sober life, To the glory of thy holy Name. Amen.[10]

4.   On perhaps as many as eight different occasions, Washington said the following in a public worship setting as he stood as a sponsor for a child who was being baptized and answered this question:

> *DOST* thou believe in God the Father Almighty, Maker of heaven and earth? And in Jesus Christ his only-begotten Son our Lord? And that he was conceived by the Holy Ghost; born of the Virgin Mary; that he suffered under Pontius Pilate, was crucified, dead, and buried; that he went down into hell, and also did rise again the third day; that he ascended into heaven, and sitteth at the right hand of God the Father Almighty; and from thence shall come again at the end of the world, to judge the quick and the dead?
>
> And dost thou believe in the Holy Ghost; the holy Catholick Church; the Communion of Saints; the Remission of sins; the Resurrection of the flesh; and everlasting life after death?"

These are all affirmations of the Apostles' Creed. To this question at each of these eight baptisms he publicly declared, "All this I steadfastly believe."[11] Again, Thomas Jefferson could not bring himself to say these words publicly because he did not believe them.[12]

5.   Washington in private settings identified himself as a Christian:
He wrote to comfort Major General Israel Putman on October 19, 1777, saying,

> ...I hope you will bear the misfortune with that fortitude and complacency of mind, that become a Man and a Christian....[13]

Washington wrote to John Christian Ehler on December 23, 1793, calling on him to be more of a Christian,

> ...Don't let this be your case. Show yourself more of a man, and a Christian, than to yield to so intolerable a vice...[14]

In September 1775 he spoke as a Christian to Col. Benedict Arnold:

> ...I also give it in Charge to you to avoid all Disrespect to or Contempt of the Religion [Roman Catholicism] of the Country [Canada] and its Ceremonies. Prudence, Policy, and a true Christian Spirit, will lead us to look with Compassion upon their Errors without insulting them....God alone is the Judge of the Hearts of Men....[15]

6.   Washington in public settings openly identified himself as a Christian:
In his General Orders from Head Quarters in New York on July 9, 1776, he called on his entire army to be Christian soldiers:

> ...The blessing and protection of Heaven are at all times necessary but especially so in times of public distress and danger—The General hopes and trusts, that every officer and man, will endeavor so to live, and act, as becomes a Christian Soldier defending the dearest Rights and Liberties of his country.[16]

Consistent with this are his General Orders from Middle Brook on Monday, April 12, 1779, where he "enjoins" a "strict" keeping of a day of prayer and fasting for the forgiveness of sins:

> The Honorable the Congress having recommended it to the United
> States to set apart Thursday the 6th day of May next to be observed
> as a day of fasting, humiliation and prayer, to acknowledge the
> gracious interpositions of *Providence*; to deprecate deserved
> punishment for our Sins and Ingratitude, to unitedly implore the
> Protection of Heaven; Success to our Arms and the Arms of
> our Ally: The Commander in Chief enjoins a religious observance
> of said day and directs the Chaplains to prepare discourses
> proper for the occasion; strictly forbiding all recreations and
> unnecessary labor.[17]

In his General Orders from Head Quarters in Valley Forge on Saturday, May 2, 1778,
he told his men that it was even more glorious to be a Christian than to be a patriot:

> While we are zealously performing the duties of good Citizens and
> soldiers we certainly ought not to be inattentive to the higher duties
> of Religion. To the distinguished Character of Patriot, it should be
> our highest Glory to add the more distinguished Character of
> Christian.[18]

He wrote to Governor Jonathan Trumbull, also a clergyman, on September 6, 1778.
His words show that he believed, along with the minister, in the sovereignty of God
over life for "his people":

> ...The violent gale which dissipated the two fleets when on the point
> of engaging, and the withdrawing of the Count D'Estaing to
> Boston may appear to us as real misfortunes; but with you I
> consider storms and victory under the direction of a wise providence
> who no doubt directs them for the best of purposes, and to bring
> round the greatest degree of happiness to the greatest number of
> his people.[19]

On June 8, 1783, Washington wrote to every Governor of all thirteen of the new
American states, and in so doing, consciously and explicitly prayed as a Christian:

...the Legacy of One, who has ardently wished, on all occasions, to be useful to his Country, and who, even in the shade of Retirement, will not fail to implore the divine benediction upon it. I now make it my earnest prayer, that God would have you and the State over which you preside, in his holy protection, that he would incline the hearts of the Citizens to cultivate a spirit of subordination and obedience to Government, to entertain a brotherly affection and love for one another, for their fellow Citizens of the United States at large, and particularly for their brethren who have served in the Field, and finally, that he would most graciously be pleased to dispose us all, to do Justice, to love mercy, and to demean ourselves with that Charity, humility and pacific temper of mind, which were the Characteristicks of the Divine Author of our blessed Religion, and without an humble imitation of whose example in these things, we can never hope to be a happy Nation.[20]

On October 28, 1789, Washington wrote to the First Presbytery of the Eastward indicating his sympathy for Christianity in its simplicity with respect to "the path of true piety." He proceeds to declare his intent as leader of the new "government" under its new Constitution or "Magna Charta" to assist these "ministers of the gospel" in the "furtherance" of "true religion":

> I am persuaded, you will permit me to observe that the path of true piety is so plain as to require but little political direction. To this consideration we ought to ascribe the absence of any regulation, respecting religion, from the Magna Charta of our country. To the guidance of the ministers of the gospel this important object is, perhaps, more properly committed. It will be your care to instruct the ignorant, and to reclaim the devious, and, in the progress of morality and science, to which our government will give every furtherance, we may confidently expect the advancement of true religion, and the completion of our happiness.[21]

THE GOSPEL ACCORDING TO GEORGE WASHINGTON

We know that George Washington was not a theologian or an evangelist. So the topics of his daily duties did not directly engage spiritual or biblical themes. Given his inward and shy personality on matters concerning himself, we should not expect a treatise from him that would summarize his "few and simple"[22] points of religion.

But given the reality we have already seen repeatedly, namely, that spiritual truths and Christian ideas surface in his writings, perhaps it is a useful exercise to assemble the elements of the Christian Gospel that have been preserved for us by his own pen. This method has both a strength and a weakness. The strength is that all of the words are Washington's. The limitation is that the distilling of all of this relevant material is ours—the result of careful study and assembly. We believe this presentation of the Gospel according to George Washington is faithful to Washington's writings and to the theology he subscribed to and professed as an eighteenth century Anglican. This exercise will also show Washington's extensive exposure and commitment to the Christian Gospel. It may be compared to the task of systematic theology—carefully discovering theological ideas and then constructing them in the logical order that the material itself suggests.

While the principles of Washington's religion were "few and simple,"[23] they were cognizant of the "gospel."[24] Thus he spoke of "our blessed Religion,"[25] "the Religion of Jesus Christ,"[26] and "the blessed religion revealed in the Word of God."[27] Washington spoke of "true religion"[28] yet coupled it with his gracious spirit declaring that "a true *Christian* Spirit, will lead us to look with Compassion upon their Errors [the inhabitants of Quebec] without insulting them."[29] This true religion was both "natural and revealed."[30] Yet it was especially as revealed religion that it was "above all," since it was available to Americans through "the benign light of revelation,"[31] and was found in "Holy Writ."[32]

Washington was aware of his own inner life, referring often to "my soul."[33] The "Divine Author" of the religion that Washington received when he wrote of "our blessed religion" was none other than the religion of Christ. It was Christ in his "charity, humility and pacific temper of mind" that Washington called all Americans to "imitate."[34] Consoling a friend he wrote, "...our *Religion* holds out to us such *hopes* as will, upon proper reflection, enable us to bear with fortitude the most calamitous incidents of life."[35] Since the "Lord and Ruler of Nations"[36] and the "Divine Author of life and felicity"[37] has come to the earth allowing people to celebrate the "Christmas Hollidays,"[38] George Washington as a child could copy such a Christmas poem:

> Assist me Muse divine to sing the morn,
> On which the Saviour of mankind was born;
> But oh! what numbers to the theme can rise?

Unless kind angels aid me from the skies?

Methinks I see the tunefull Host descend,

Hark, by their hymns directed on the road,

The gladsome Shepherds find the nascent God!

And view the infant conscious of his birth,

Smiling bespeak salvation to the earth!

For when the important Aera first drew near

In which the great Messiah should appear

And to accomplish His redeeming love

Resign a while his glorious throne above.[39]

And as an adult, he could likewise speak openly of Christmas: "I hope the next *Christmas* will prove happier than the present...."[40] "...I may on these accounts venture to hope that you will spend a happy and merry Christmas...."[41] And pray as Washington did on Christmas Day, on December 25, 1770. This year Christmas fell on a Tuesday. His entry for this date says, "Went to Pohick Church and returnd to Dinner." Christmas Sundays in the Anglican tradition were also Sundays when the Lord's Supper was celebrated.

> *The Nativity of our Lord, or the Birthday of Christ, Commonly called Christmas-Day. The Collect:* Almighty God, who hast given us thy only-begotten Son to take our nature upon him, and as at this time to be born of a pure Virgin; Grant that we being regenerate, and made thy children by adoption and grace, may daily be renewed by thy Holy Spirit; through the same our Lord Jesus Christ, who liveth and reigneth with thee and the same Spirit, ever one God, world without end. *Amen.*

And soldiers and congressman together can affirm "the enlightening sounds of the Gospel"[42] that declare that "above all ... he hath diffused the glorious light of the *gospel*, whereby, through the merits of our gracious Redeemer, we may become the heirs of his eternal glory."[43] And so people can prepare for death by writing, as George Washington did in his youth, as he copied a "Form of a Short Will."

> In the Name of God, Amen. The Sixth Day of Oct. In the year of our Lord, 1744, I, A.B. being Sick and Weak of Body but of Sound

Judgment and Memory (thanks to God Therefore) Remembering the mortality of my body knowing that it is Determined for all men once to die, Doe make and ordain this my last Will and Testament, That is to say Principally and first of all I recommend my Soul to God Who gave it hoping for salvation in and through the merits and mediation of Jesus Christ, and my body to have buried in a decent manner ....[44]

Thus "Ministers of the Gospel"[45] have the duty to "prepare [men] for the other world."[46] They do this by "instructing the ignorant and reclaiming the devious,"[47] "propagating the gospel"[48] and seeking "to Christianize"[49] non-believers. "Sin"[50] and "evil men" exist.[51] "Sinners"[52] express their "nature"[53] through "iniquity,"[54] "depravity,"[55] "rascality"[56] and failure to heed "conscience."[57] Thus, men fail to keep their "duties to God and man."[58]

But, because God is "powerful to save,"[59] "we must place a confidence in that *Providence* who *rules* great events, trusting that out of confusion he will produce order, and, notwithstanding the dark clouds, which may threaten at present, that right will ultimately be established."[60] He is the "the *Sovereign* Dispenser of life and health"[61] and the "Supreme Ruler of the Universe, and *Sovereign* Arbiter of Nations."[62] He rules from a "throne of grace,"[63] extending grace,[64] and mercy,[65] from a propitious[66] heaven for the "professors of Christianity" who seek the "most direct plainest and easiest" "road to heaven."[67]

Washington's copied childhood poem described the work of the cross with these words:

Beneath our form every woe sustain
And by triumphant suffering fix His reign
Should for lost man in tortures yield his breath,
Dying to save us from eternal death!
Oh mystick Union! Salutary grace!
Incarnate God our nature should embrace!
That Deity should stoop to our disguise!
That man recovered should regain the skies!
Dejected Adam! From thy Grave ascend
And view the Serpent's Deadly Malice end,
Adorring bless th'Almighty's boundless grace

That gave his son a ransome for thy race![68]

As an adult, Washington described the work of the cross with these words: "The blessed religion revealed in the Word of God will remain an eternal and awful monument to prove that the best Institutions may be abused by human *depravity*; and that they may even, in some instances be made subservient to the vilest of purposes."[69] (emphasis ours)

But "the seventh, now *called the first day*"[70] of the week" has come. And so, Washington was trained as a fourteen-year-old to determine the annual celebration of Easter each year.[71] In 1768, Easter fell on April 3rd. Washington's diary for that date says, "Went to Pohick church and returnd to Dinner." The prayer that Washington said that Easter Sunday from the *Book of Common Prayer* affirmed a hearty belief in the resurrection of Christ:

> Almighty God, who through thine only-begotten Son Jesus Christ
> hast overcome death, and opened unto us the gate of everlasting life;
> We humbly beseech thee, that, as by thy special grace preventing us
> thou dost put into our minds good desires, so by thy continual help
> we may bring the same to good effect; through Jesus Christ our
> Lord, who liveth and reigneth with thee and the Holy Ghost, ever
> one God, world without end. *Amen.*[72]

The need for justification before God was implied by Washington when he used phrases like "answerable to God,"[73] "so much to answer for,"[74] and "justifiable in the eyes of God and men."[75] He declared, "God alone is the Judge of the Hearts of Men, and to him only in this Case, they are answerable."[76] And men have "much to answer for," since their judge is "the supreme Arbiter of human events."[77] Washington warned of "the aggravated vengeance of heaven,"[78] and referenced the "torment of a mental hell,"[79] "the powers of hell,"[80] as well as the reality of "blessing and curse."[81] Washington's view of the curse seems to include a curse after death, as suggested by Washington's phrase "the bitterest curse this side of the grave"[82] and his statement that "*Conscience* again seldom comes to a Mans aid while he is in the zenith of health, and revelling in pomp and luxury upon ill gotten spoils; it is generally the *last* act of his life and comes too late to be of much service to others here, or to himself hereafter."[83]

Thus, Washington and the leaders of the new nation believed that men needed "with united Hearts and Voice *unfeignedly* [to] confess their Sins before God, and

BERKELEY SPRINGS   HAVRE DE GRACE

                              N
                          W ─┼─ E   BALTIMORE
HARPER'S FERRY   S
                  POTOMAC RIVER
WINCHESTER

LORD FAIRFAX'S
MANOR
GREENWAY   ANNAPOLIS
COURT   GREAT FALLS

                   LITTLE FALLS   GEORGETOWN
                                   WASHINGTON, D.C.

                                   ALEXANDRIA

                   MOUNT VERNON
                   COLCHESTER

                   DUMFRIES
                              PORT TABACCO

RAPPAHANNOCK RIVER

                   FERRY FARM   CHOTANK AREA
FREDERICKSBURG   GEORGE WASHINGTON'S
                   CHILDHOOD HOME

                   PORT ROYAL   WAKEFIELD

                              HOBBS HOLE

JAMES RIVER

APPOMATTOX RIVER   YORK RIVER

                              WILLIAMSBURG
                   JAMESTOWN   YORKTOWN

                                             CAPE HENRY
                              DISMAL
                              SWAMP   NORFOLK
0   25   50
|————————————————| PORTSMOUTH
     MILES   SUFFOLK

Washington's Extended Neighborhood

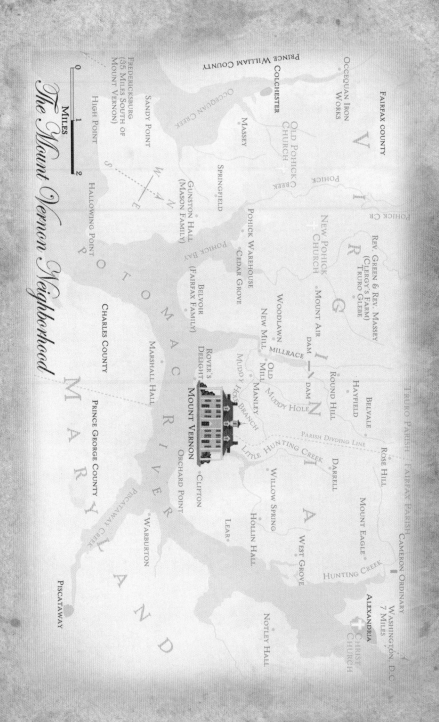

The Mount Vernon Neighborhood

MILES
0 1 2

FAIRFAX COUNTY

PRINCE WILLIAM COUNTY

OCCEQUAN IRON WORKS

COLCHESTER

OLD POHICK CHURCH

MASSEY

OCCOQUAN CREEK

POHICK CREEK

POHICK CR

HIGH POINT

SANDY POINT

SPRINGFIELD

FREDERICKSBURG
(35 MILES SOUTH OF
MOUNT VERNON)

HALLOWING POINT

GUNSTON HALL
(MASON FAMILY)

POHICK WAREHOUSE

CEDAR GROVE

POHICK BAY

BELVOIR
(FAIRFAX FAMILY)

NEW POHICK CHURCH

WOODLAWN

NEW MILL

MOUNT AIR

DAM

MILLRACE

DAM

ROUND HILL

REV. GREEN & REV. MASSEY
(CLERGY'S FARM)
TRURO GLEBE

V I R G I N I A

BELVALE

HAYFIELD

TRURO PARISH   FAIRFAX PARISH   CAMERON ORDINARY

WASHINGTON, D.C.
7 MILES

ROSE HILL

PARISH DIVIDING LINE

LITTLE HUNTING CREEK

MOUNT EAGLE

CHRIST CHURCH

ALEXANDRIA

DARRELL

WILLOW SPRING

HUNTING CREEK

WEST GROVE

HOLLIN HALL

NOTLEY HALL

LEAR

ROVER'S DELIGHT

MOUNT VERNON

CLIFTON

ORCHARD POINT

OLD MILL

MANLEY

MUDDY HOLE

MUDDY HOLE BRANCH

MARSHALL HALL

CHARLES COUNTY

PRINCE GEORGE COUNTY

PISCATAWAY CREEK

WARBURTON

PISCATAWAY

M A R Y L A N D

P O T O M A C   R I V E R

N

S

E

W

This stained glass window is in Mother Bethel AME Church in Philadelphia.
It shows that some in the Masonic order consider themselves compatible with the Christian faith.

The WASHINGTON
COMMUNION
Spring 1777

*George Washington's communing in Morristown is depicted in this stained glass window
in the sanctuary of the Presbyterian Church in Morristown, NJ, the church where the event occurred.*

The mural by painter Allyn Cox of George Washington in Masonic regalia, laying the cornerstone of the US Capitol in 1793.

H.A. Ogden's rarely acknowledged painting of George Washington receiving Holy Communion at Morristown, NJ in the spring of 1777.

E. Percy Moran's painting of the Washingtons at home

Arnold Friberg's
Prayer at Valley Forge

On May 6, 1982,
President Ronald Reagan
said "The most sublime
picture in American history
is of George Washington
on his knees in the snow at
Valley Forge. That image
personifies a people who
know that it is not enough
to depend on our own
courage and goodness;
we must also seek help
from God, our Father
and Preserver."

supplicate the all wise and merciful disposer of events,"[84] and "to *implore* the Lord, and Giver of all victory, to pardon our manifold sins and wickedness's."[85] And "that he would in mercy look down upon us, pardon our sins and receive us into his favor...."[86]

In view of God's great Providential care for the nation, Washington asserted that faith and gratitude were necessary, "The Hand of Providence has been so conspicuous in all this that he must be worse than an infidel that lacks faith, and more than wicked that has not gratitude enough to acknowledge his obligations..."[87] Washington joyfully wrote to his friend Marquis de Lafayette, drawing on their shared understanding of Christian teaching on sin and forgiveness: "I stand before you as a Culprit: but to repent & be forgiven are the precepts of Heaven: I do the former, do you practice the latter, and it will be participation of a divine attribute."[88]

The Gospel message was so well understood that even soldiers utilized words such as "atonement,"[89] "forgiveness,"[90] and "pardon"[91] to describe their work. So these truths called for men to become "Christian soldiers,"[92] to be "more of a man and of a Christian,"[93] and to seek one's highest glory by adding to their character "the more distinguished character of Christian."[94] The work of the "Holy Spirit"[95] was recognized and so Washington could speak of "all the workings of the spirit within,"[96] "a Christian-like spirit,"[97] "a true Christian Spirit,"[98] and the "pure spirit of Christianity,"[99] as well as praying that God would grant "spirit" to his army.[100] Thus, there was the duty to be a "true Christian,"[101] whose life was manifested not in "profligate morals, etc.,"[102] but in "true piety."[103] Christians and Christianity were the friends of government in Washington's mind: "While just government protects all in their religious rights, true religion affords to government its surest support."[104]

Christians were to be active in the support of the government since "true religion affords to government its surest support,"[105] and "religion and morality are indispensable supports for political happiness."[106] But because "the path of true piety is so plain,"[107] no direction for religion per se was provided in the "Magna-Charta" or Constitution of America.[108] So as the Christian seeks to live with the desire to be "justifiable in the eyes of God and man,"[109] he seeks a "glorious immortality,"[110] a "future happiness,"[111] and "happiness hereafter"[112] in "the world of spirits,"[113] "the other world."[114] He knows there is a promised millennium,[115] a last trump,[116] and that when men die, they are facing a "life eternal."[117] He can sooth his conscience by awaiting the approbation of the Supreme Being.[118]

CONCLUSION

This summation of Washington's theology is the Christian Gospel pure and simple. Washington's expressed beliefs presented here are utterly inconsistent with Deism. Even if the arrangement of Washington's theological themes assembled here is deficient, the sheer weight of the volume of the Gospel concepts affirmed by Washington and expressed in his own words militate against any claim of Washington's Deism. The evidence is clear; Washington spoke with consistency and conviction in terms of the Christian Gospel. He could not have been a Deist. There is not a word of unbelief in the Christian faith in the entire body of Washington's writings. The claim for Washington's Deism is a myth without a single word of substantiation.

❋

THIRTY TWO

George Washington and Forgiveness:

A Consideration of the Historicity of Two Classic Washington Anecdotes on Forgiveness

"Your resolution to abandon the ideas which
were therein expressed, are sincere.
I shall not only heartily forgive, but will forget also,
and bury in oblivion all that has passed."
George Washington, 1797 [1]

Washington practiced what Christianity affirms—that those who repent should be forgiven. He wrote to his adopted grandson, George Washington Parke Custis: "Your resolution to abandon the ideas which were therein expressed, are sincere, I shall not only heartily forgive, but will forget also, and bury in oblivion all that has passed." [2] One of Washington's criticisms of King George was that he could neither forget nor forgive.[3]

Washington was magnanimous in showing forgiveness to those who had hurt him during the war. His childhood friend, Bryan Fairfax, turned Tory. Afterwards, George forgave him. Reverend Jacob Duché also rejected the patriot cause, even though he had led the first Congress in a moving prayer (September 7, 1774). Later, Washington forgave him. Reverend Jonathan Boucher, who was the tutor of Washington's stepchildren, verbally attacked Washington, yet Washington forgave him. All of these made peace with Washington and he with them after the War.[4]

WASHINGTON SEEKS FORGIVENESS

An experience in his own life perhaps helped him learn to forgive. There seems to have been a moment in time when Washington needed to seek forgiveness and reconcile with a man with whom he had had a fight. Although the account has often been disputed, Washington scholar John Corbin has argued that it is authentic.[5] Washington biographer Parson Mason Weems' account puts it as follows:

> In 1754, and the 22d year of his age…[Washington] was stationed at Alexandria with his regiment, the only one in the colony, and of which he was colonel. There happened at this time to be an election in Alexandria for members of assembly, and the contest ran high between colonel George Fairfax, and Mr. Elzey. Washington was the warm friend of Fairfax, and a Mr. Payne headed the friends of Elzey. A dispute happening to take place in the courthouse-yard, Washington, a thing very uncommon, said something that offended Payne; whereupon the little gentleman who, though but a cub in size, was the old lion in heart, raised his sturdy hickory, and, at a single blow, brought our hero to the ground. Several of Washington's officers being present, whipped out their cold irons in an instant, and it was believed that there would have been murder off-hand. To make bad worse, his regiment, hearing how he had been treated, bolted out from their barracks, with every man his weapon in his hand, threatening dreadful vengeance on those who had dared to knock down their beloved colonel. Happily for Mr. Payne and his party, Washington recovered, time enough to go out and meet his enraged soldiers; and, after thanking them for this expression of their love, and assuring them that he was not hurt in

the least, he begged them, as they loved him or their duty, to return peaceably to their barracks. As for himself, he went to his room, generously chastising his imprudence, which had this struck up a spark, that had like to have thrown the whole town into a flame. Finding on mature reflection, that he had been the aggressor, he resolved to make Mr. Payne honourable reparation, by asking his pardon on the morrow! No sooner had he made this noble resolution, than recovering that delicious gaiety which accompanies good purposes in a virtuous mind, he went to a ball that night, and behaved as pleasantly as though nothing had happened! Glorious proof that great souls, like great ships, are not affected by those little puffs which would overset feeble minds with passion, or sink them with spleen!

The next day he went to a tavern, and wrote a polite note to Mr. Payne, whom he requested to meet him. Mr. Payne took it for a challenge, and repaired to the tavern not without expecting to see a pair of pistols produced. But what was his surprise on entering the chamber, to see a decanter of wine and glasses on the table! Washington arose, and in a very friendly manner met him, and gave him his hand. "Mr. Payne," said he "to err is nature; to rectify error is glory; I find I was wrong yesterday, but wish to be right to-day. You have had some satisfaction; and if you think that sufficient here's my hand, let us be friends."[6]

Perhaps this episode, wherein Washington needed forgiveness, was a factor in his development as a leader known for clemency.[7] Even the records from Martha Washington's correspondence attest to Washington's forgiving spirit as a military officer.[8]

FORGIVENESS OF AN ENEMY AT VALLEY FORGE: REVEREND PETER MILLER'S APPEAL FOR THE LIFE OF MICHAEL WIDMAN BEFORE GENERAL WASHINGTON

A classic story from Valley Forge tells of a moment when the Christian grace of forgiving one's enemy became a reality under the command of General Washington. Washington, as we have seen, was given to mercy, pardon, and forgiveness of his army, when deemed appropriate.

James Baldwin in *An American Book of Golden Deeds*, tells the story:

> While encamped at Valley Forge one day, a Tory who was well known in the neighborhood was captured and brought into camp. His name was Michael Widman, and he was accused of having carried aid and information to the British in Philadelphia. He was taken to West Chester and there tried by court-martial. It was proved that he was a very dangerous man and that he had more than once attempted to do great harm to the American army. He was pronounced guilty of being a spy and sentenced to be hanged. On the evening of the day before that set for the execution, a strange old man appeared at Valley Forge. He was a small man with long, snow-white hair falling over his shoulders. His face, although full of kindliness, was sad-looking and thoughtful; his eyes, which were bright and sharp, were upon the ground and lifted only when he was speaking. . . .
>
> His name was announced.
>
> "Peter Miller?" said Washington. "Certainly. Show him in at once."
>
> "General Washington, I have come to ask a great favor of you," he said, in his usual kindly tones.
>
> "I shall be glad to grant you almost anything," said Washington, "for we surely are indebted to you for many favors. Tell me what it is."
>
> "I hear," said Peter, "that Michael Widman has been found guilty of treason and that he is to be hanged at Turk's Head to-morrow. I have come to ask you to pardon him."
>
> Washington started back, and a cloud came over his face.
>
> "That is impossible," he said. "Widman is a bad man. He has done all in his power to betray us. He has even offered to join the British and aid in destroying us. In these times we can not be lenient with traitors; and for that reason I cannot pardon your friend."
>
> "Friend!" cried Peter. "Why, he is no friend of mine. He is my bitterest enemy. He has persecuted me for years. He has even beaten me and spit in my face, knowing full well that I would not strike back. Michael Widman is no friend of mine."

Washington was puzzled. "And still you wish me to pardon him?" he asked.

"I do," answered Peter. "I ask it of you as a great personal favor."

"Tell me," said Washington, with hesitating voice," why is it that you thus ask the pardon of your worst enemy?"

"I ask it because Jesus did as much for me," was the old man's brief answer.

Washington turned away and went into another room. Soon he returned with a paper on which was written the pardon of Michael Widman.

"My dear friend," he said, as he placed it in the old man's hand, "I thank you for this example of Christian charity."[9]

E. Gordon Alderfer relates the story this way:

That Peter Miller was a forgiving man is demonstrated by the story of one of his appeals for clemency. Michael Widman, then tavern keeper at what later became the famous Eagle Hotel in Ephrata village, had on several occasions bedeviled the nonresistant prior, hitting him soundly on one occasion and spitting in his face on another. Michael was alleged to be one of the richest Tories in Lancaster County. He got caught expressing his political opinions, was arrested for treason, escaped through a window of his tavern, and fled to Bethania in Ephrata, where he hid. He was soon captured again and was sentenced to be hanged. Miller at once started off on foot to see his friend General Washington at Valley Forge, a grueling journey. The General at first refused to intercede, but when he discovered that his friend had walked sixty miles through snow on behalf of his worst enemy, he relented and granted a pardon. Miller than walked another fifteen miles with the pardon note to West Chester, arriving, it is said, just in time to see Widman being led to the scaffold. The Tory allegedly saw the prior arrive and insensible to the ways of the nonresistant Christian, assumed he had come from Ephrata to gloat. The pardon was pronounced in the nick of time, and Widman was released. It is said that the two men walked back to Ephrata together, Widman no doubt a chastened man. All of the Tory's property was confiscated and sold at auction by orders of the new government. Widman's political views did not change; he was jailed again, won a release, and thereafter disappeared in the west.[10]

A STORY FULL OF HOLES?

But not everyone, of course, is prepared to accept this story as historically valid. Author and Washington biographer Douglas Harper writes, "The story as it stands is full of holes, Why would Washington in Valley Forge send an Ephrata man to be hanged in West Chester, which was then a backwater crossroads with just a school and a tavern? There certainly never was any block house there, and except in the week after the Battle of the Brandywine there was no significant presence of American troops in the region. And why would the many detailed observers of the early West Chester scene (Joseph Townsend, Joseph J. Lewis, William Darlington, Philip Sharpless, etc.), make no mention of such a dramatic event as a near-hanging? Further, why would Washington, as commander in chief attempt to execute a private citizen for a crime that was handled by the civil authorities of the state, and why would those authorities make no complaint, or even mention of the event? The narrative makes it clear that Widman was a private citizen, not a British spy, at the time. And why, if Washington was touched enough to reverse himself and grant a pardon, was he not also touched enough to lend Miller a horse to get him to Turk's Head before the execution? So what are the facts? There may not be enough of them to consign the story to fiction, but there are enough to put it in serious doubt...."[11]

The background of Peter Miller is important to understand in order to appreciate the story of his intercession on behalf of Michael Widman. Miller had come from Germany, having been trained in the Reformed tradition. When he arrived in America, he was ordained in the Presbyterian Church. He went to the Cocalico-Tuplehocken area (Berks County, Pennsylvania) to serve. While there he encountered the German Seventh Day Baptists, who had started the Ephrata Cloister—what amounted to a Protestant monastery.

The leader, Conrad Beisel, ultimately persuaded Miller to join the "Dunkers," which included not only leaving his Reformed pastorate, but becoming a monk, taking a vow of celibacy, receiving believer's baptism, and adopting the pacifist life of the cloister.

To further appreciate the elements of the historicity of the Miller-Widman story, we must go back earlier into the context of the French and Indian War.[12] Braddock's defeat resulted in the unopposed French and Indian raids on the English settlements. Col. Washington had to defend 350 miles of wilderness with little success against the Indians, resulting in constant reports of carnage and slaughter. The need for a safe haven became critical, which impacted the Ephrata community.

Reverend Peter Miller saw the French and Indian War as a possible end time scenario, or at least a season of imminent persecution. To prepare his people for such, he translated into German the massive Dutch work, *Martyr's Mirror*, an Anabaptist equivalent of *Foxe's Book of Martyrs*. When he published it, it became the largest and lengthiest publishing project in colonial America—all accomplished on the frontier at Bethlehem-Ephrata. The entire project, from making paper, translating, printing, etc., was done by Miller and his fellow religionists. Tradition records that Miller only slept hours per night for months until the project was complete. The sheer magnitude of the project, as well as the quality of its finished product, prompted a high admiration for Miller by Philadelphia printer, Benjamin Franklin.

As the French and Indian War raged in Pennsylvania, the cloister, that is, the Ephrata community, became a hospital to meet the needs of the wounded and those dying from camp fever. The pacifists quietly bore the burdens of the war they had not started or believed in by caring for the dying and burying the dead. Washington likely was aware of the Ephrata community during the French and Indian War because of the medical care they provided for wounded and sick soldiers.

At any rate, the end of the world did not come, but the end of the war finally did. Miller's printing achievement, as well as his insights into agricultural matters, such as the best way to grow peas, brought him an invitation to join the American Philosophical Society. In this context, Reverend Miller also became known to Philadelphia patriot and poet, Francis Hopkinson. The point here is that there is strong undeniable historical evidence of the life and ministry of Reverend Miller.

Years earlier, when Reverend Miller left the Reformed Church and joined the Dunkers, he unavoidably offended some of his former parishioners. One of those was a successful innkeeper named Michael Widman, who was an officer in the Reformed church that Miller had pastored. Thereafter, Widman seized opportunities to torment and ridicule his former pastor, the Seventh Day Baptist or "Dunker" pacifist clergyman, Reverend Miller.

The pattern of the Widman-Miller relationship had long been set when Washington came into contact with Reverend Miller, due to the movement of troops, and because of the need for the pacifistic Ephrata community to assist in alleviating the sufferings of Washington's soldiers during the Revolutionary War.

There were other natural connections as well. The Reverend General John Peter Muhlenberg, of Washington's army, was born in Tuplehocken, near Ephrata, and his Lutheran clergyman father still lived there. Records indicate that Gen. Muhlenberg visited his father during the Valley Forge encampment, so there was direct travel occurring on some occasions between Valley Forge and the region of the Ephrata Cloisters minister by Reverend Miller.

The need for hospital care became acute in the aftermath of the Battle of Brandywine in 1777, which brought many wounded soldiers there, including Marquis de Lafayette. This, in turn, brought several officers to Ephrata to visit the wounded in the military hospital there, including General Washington. As they had in the French and Indian War, so now again in the Revolutionary War, the Ephrata Cloister met the needs of the wounded and the soldiers who were dying from camp fever. The pacifists once again bore the burdens created by the War they had not started or believed in, caring for the dying to burying of the dead.

The pacifistic community also helped meet other needs of the patriotic cause. When Philadelphia was captured, Peter Miller's publishing efforts provided a printing press. The paper industry provided the "wads" necessary for loading for the primitive rifles. Tradition says that Miller translated the Declaration of Independence into seven different languages, although there is no proof that he did. Apparently he could have, given his scholarly and European language mastery.

Letters show that Washington's contacts in the area created friendships with other religious groups doing mission work in the area, such as the Brethren, Bishop Ettwein.[13]

THE EVIDENCE FOR THE HISTORICITY OF WASHINGTON'S PARDON OF MICHAEL WIDMAN

As we consider the Michael Widman and Peter Miller story, it is clear that the account fits many of the known facts. There are historical records of both men from the places mentioned. Widman was a tavern owner. Turk's Head existed and was the early name for West Chester, being so named by a sign at the tavern in the town. Widman had human reasons to be an enemy to Miller, given the facts of his conversion to a strange new sect, a fact that is affirmed by Church records on both sides of the ecclesiastical debate.

Washington would have had several reasons to have known Miller, as well as other church leaders from that area. Miller's commitment to pursue clemency and leniency of prisoners was also recorded by contemporaries of Reverend Miller in other instances.

We have also seen that, according to Washington's military records, he was known to issue pardons and offer clemency. Thus, Washington's change of mind toward Widman would not be inconsistent in itself with what is known about Washington's personality and approach to prisoners.

Government records of the confiscation of Widman's property have been found. Not only has a deed been found of Widman as owner of the tavern that preceded the Eagle Tavern in Ephrata, but historical records also reveal another tavern keeper named Widman in the Reading, Pennsylvania, area some years later. Given all of these facts, the story may not be summarily dismissed as lacking historical credibility.

So, in the context of Valley Forge, let us consider Douglas Harper's objections to the historical credibility of the Miller-Widman story. His first and major problem is that the civilian Widman was tried in a military rather than a civilian court. But this, too, comports with circumstances at Valley Forge. On several instances, court martial dealt with civilians, inclusive of meting out the death penalty, as was looming for Widman. Valley Forge historian John Stoudt quotes sources stating:

- "Congress has resolved to try by Courts Martial any Civilian found carrying supplies to the Enemy."[14]
- "William Maddock found guilty of trying to drive Cattle to the Enemy. Confin'd to a Gaol in Pennsylvania, and to have all his real and personal estate taken for the use of the United States of America."[15]
- "The sentence of whippings for the citizens of this State convicted of intercourse with the Enemy was carried out today. A surgeon stopped several whippings because the culprit could stand no more."[16]
- "The besetting of Mr Knox's house is a matter of civil cognizance, but it appears that the prisoner has held correspondence with the enemy and supplied them with provisions, and he will probably suffer death for those offences by sentence of Court Martial."[17]

Civilians were being tried by military courts, even facing capital punishment. So this objection by Harper is clearly specious.

A second objection by Harper is Reverend Peter Miller's walking to rescue Widman, and Washington's clemency being so little moved that he did not provide

Reverend Miller with a horse. Why would Miller have walked and why would Washington not have offered a horse? The simple answer is that at Valley Forge there were no horses available to spare, scarcely being enough even for the troops or for the artillery. The horses were starving, dying, and in fact even being confiscated from Quakers traveling by.

Sources that address the objection of Harper state:

- "We have lost a good many men, and horses, and have had hard fare in our present quarters."[18]
- "Next Sunday the Quakers will be seeking to go to their General Meetings in Philada. This is an intercourse we should by all means endeavor to interrupt, as the plans settled at these Meetings are of a most pernicious kind. If any are riding Horses, these are to be seized and draughted for the Service and they are to be sent to the Quarter Master General."[19]
- "Our horses, being constantly exposed to showers of rain and falls of snow, day and night, are in miserable condition. Many die. The rest are so emaciated as to be unfit for labor. If we be attacked now we shall have to leave our artillery behind for want of horses."[20]
- "The carcasses of horses about the Camp, and the deplorable leanness of those which still crawl in existence, speak the want of forage equal to that of human food."[21]
- "Forage is wanting. Our horses starve, as do their masters. If help does not arrive, and forage does not appear, we shall not have one horse left."[22]

Washington simply could not make a horse available to Reverend Miller's errand of mercy. It perhaps also may explain why Miller himself had not ridden to Valley Forge on a horse—all of the region's available horses had already been seized, or would have been seized. Miller either did not have a horse, since it had already been taken, or, he chose not to risk riding in with a horse for fear of the seizure of one of the cloister's horses. Whether the monastic community put a premium on pilgrimage by foot for mercy ministry is also a question worthy of investigation as well. So, contrary to Harper, the horses were starving to death like the soldiers, and there were none to spare. Harper's second objection is specious as well.

Another problem with the historicity of this story raised by Harper is that there was no "blockhouse" in Turk's Head or West Chester at that time, and why would a prisoner be sent to West Chester anyway? We have already seen that there was a civilian who was "Confin'd to a Gaol in Pennsylvania, and [had] all his real and personal estate taken for the use of the United States of America."[23] The general location of West Chester would have worked for keeping a prisoner, since it was away from British, and yet within traveling distance of Valley Forge. Further, American soldiers had been in the area for a fair amount of time only months before, preparing for the engagement with the British at Brandywine, and the residents there were not hostile to their fellow Americans.

Moreover, there was no way to keep a prisoner at Valley Forge, since there were no buildings, except the meager huts the soldiers had hastily built to survive the winter exposure. There was no food available for prisoners—the soldiers were starving. Given Washington's commitment to humane treatment of prisoners, the closest safe place for a prisoner may well have been in a minor holding location, such as a house or barn used as a temporary "blockhouse" that has basically been lost to history. Washington, in his writings elsewhere, affirms that many records from the War were lost.[24]

So, as we conclude our response to Harper's claim that the Widman-Miller-Washington story is "full of holes," as we see it, the only uncertainties left are those that do not overturn the story.

It is true that the words that Washington spoke that refer to Jesus in the first of the accounts cited are not in the earliest written account. Since it is usually very difficult to establish the actual spoken words in an historical account if they were not immediately recorded, it is not surprising that storytellers have yielded to the temptation to embellish the facts. But we disagree with Harper's claim that Peter Miller could not have made the parallel between Jesus seeking forgiveness for the sins of his enemies from God and his own seeking to have Widman pardoned by Washington.

While Harper calls this a "false parallel," did not Jesus teach his followers to pray for their enemies? Moreover, the Lord's Prayer that Washington, Miller, and Widman all prayed, presents the petition of "forgive us our trespasses as we forgive those who trespass against us." And did not their Bibles teach, "And be ye kind one to another, tenderhearted, forgiving one another, even as God for Christ's sake has forgiven you." (Eph. 4:32.)?

Reverend Miller was not claiming to be the Messiah; he was attempting to intercede on behalf of his enemy. And interestingly, Washington used the term "intercede" in various pardon passages of his military letters as well.[25] So, the words the later account attributed to Miller could have been spoken, and Washington would have understood, even though obviously there is no way to demonstrate that they were or were not spoken.

Finally, it is true that there is no known account of the Widman-Miller-Washington story of pardon coming from the West Chester area. We concur with Harper that a last minute rescue from the hangman's gallows would have been newsworthy—had it been witnessed. We cannot prove or disprove the claim of the dramatic timing of the story. But for our purposes, the timing of the rescue is not the point. The point is that the pardon was given, and Widman lived to disappear in the west. The essential feature of the story is its claim that the pardon was issued by Washington to a clergyman for the clergyman's worst enemy. This feature of the story comports with all the known facts.

CONCLUSION

All that we know about the history of the time and the character of the men supports that this event could have happened along the lines as reported. Miller's involvement in the pardon of Widman reflected Washington's great motto—deeds not words. Peter Miller's deed of gracious intercession spoke to Washington, and Washington's deed of clemency spoke to his sympathy for the Christian value of forgiving one's enemies. Indeed, this is what Washington himself did with his own Anglican clergyman Reverend Fairfax, Reverend Boucher, and Reverend Duché, who as Loyalists had opposed him. Sometimes actions do speak louder than words.

So finally, we must disagree with Harper's conclusion: "There may not be enough [holes] to consign the story to fiction, but there are enough to put it in serious doubt." Rather, the facts show that the story has the hallmarks of an historical event, and, for our purposes here, the act reflects the character of a Christian and further undercuts the claim that Washington was a Deist, unless Deists accept the Gospel teaching of Jesus to forgive one's enemies.

THIRTY THREE

George Washington's Clergy and Their Sermons

"The Commander in chief thinks it a duty to declare the regularity and decorum with which divine service is now performed every Sunday, will reflect great credit on the army in general, tend to improve the morals, and at the same time, to increase the happiness of the soldiery, and must afford the most pure and rational entertainment for every serious and well disposed mind."
George Washington, March 22, 1783 [1]

A common claim of the deistic writers is that George Washington was largely indifferent to the printed Christian sermons that were so important to the early American culture throughout the period of Washington's life. Thus, Washington biographer Franklin Steiner says that in Washington's vast writings, he commented on sermons only twice. [2]

Similarly, Rupert Hughes writes, "Dr. [Moncure D.] Conway, speaking of Washington's diaries, notes 'his pretty regular attendance at church but never any remark on the sermons.'"[3] Our purpose in this chapter is to evaluate these claims and see if Washington was at all interested, as a means of education, spiritual nurture, communication and entertainment, in the many sermons that were being published throughout the eighteenth century. We believe the clear evidence is that Washington did indeed show an interest in these sermons, all of which are orthodox and many of which condemn Deism, the very view that Washington supposedly embraced. This is yet more evidence that Washington was a Christian, not a Deist.

One of the ways to approach this question is to ask if Washington was actively engaged with the clergy of his day. If Washington was not anti-clergy, one of the more typical and visible signs of Deism, then it increases the likelihood that he was a reader of the many sermons he collected throughout his life and which he had bound and kept on his library shelves.

GEORGE WASHINGTON'S CLERGY

Consistent with the evidence that documents the Christianity of Washington is that he was a man who did not reflect, in the least, the anti-clerical spirit so typical of Deists. Instead, Washington's attitude was consistently one of honor for the clergy and for the church. There are approximately sixty-two clergymen identified in Washington's diaries. There are over seventy clergymen to whom Washington wrote letters, exclusive of the many letters he wrote to religious bodies, that we considered above in the chapter entitled, "Washington the Godly Leader."

His writings indicate that the clergyman he knew were his family pastors,[4] his family's tutors,[5] and his lifelong neighbor and childhood friend, Reverend Bryan Lord Fairfax.[6] The clergy in Washington's life assisted him in practical ways,[7] such as with introductions of people visiting in a new city.[8] He also gave assistance to clergymen in various ways.[9] Washington wrote to a group of women that included a pastor's wife,[10] took note of a widowed pastor's wife in a letter,[11] and provided care for the widow of his childhood pastor, Reverend Charles Green, and her estate.[12] He corresponded with several pastors as he gave support to the various compassion-ministries that they supervised.[13]

The clergy were the college educators of his children,[14] the chaplains in his army,[15] and the chaplains in his government,[16] as well as active officers in the army.[17] They were missionaries,[18] counselors,[19] medical care providers,[20] sources of military intelligence,[21] good citizens,[22] scholars,[23] authors,[24] politicians,[25] and historians.[26] Given the struggles of the Revolution, some of the clergy—especially those from his Anglican church—became his opponents and enemies,[27] yet even these Washington was able to forgive.[28]

Given these extensive, positive, and strong pastoral relationships with the clergy from his own life, we find that he also had a positive interest in the sermons the clergymen preached and published.

GEORGE WASHINGTON AND SERMONS

With George Washington's remarkable career, it is no surprise that his life was not only recorded by historians, but also noticed by the clergy, both during and after his life. As the news of his unexpected death spread, literally hundreds of memorial sermons were preached and published across America in the months following his funeral.[29] But what may come as a surprise, given the skeptics' claims we have just cited, is Washington's keen personal interest in both preached and published sermons. The fact is, George Washington called the divine service—the Christian worship service—inclusive of the sermon: "the most pure and rational entertainment" available to his soldiers.[30]

The tradition of the time was to have sermons read to the family.[31] Washington's family and personal assistants both record that he read sermons to his family or had sermons read to them.[32] His cash records show that he purchased sermons.[33] His church often had no preacher, or bad weather or ill health prevented the family from attending services, so it is clear why he as a churchman would have purchased sermons for family worship at home.

Sermons show up in Washington's life for other reasons as well.[34] They were among his family's early books and his schoolbooks.[35] They were widely available, due to the high honor afforded clergy in the early years of America, and thus, widely distributed by booksellers of the time.[36] They conveyed important news, such as funerals or celebrations.[37] They were expressions of honor, as they often were given to or dedicated to important people like Washington himself.[38]

One of the earliest sermons to make note of George Washington was by Reverend Samuel Davies, who commented upon the extraordinary providential escape from the Indians at Braddock's defeat.[39] Davies was a scholarly Presbyterian preacher and theologian, who later left Virginia to become the president of Princeton.

Furthermore, sermons were sent by preachers as a mark of esteem or out of a desire for endorsement by George Washington for their work.[40] They were even printed by the House of Burgesses of Virginia. As saw earlier in the chapter on "Washington the Low Churchman," one of these sermons has George Washington's signature on the cover page. Its title is unmistakably Christian—"The Nature and Extent of Christ's Redemption." It was presented before the House of Burgesses by the Reverend

William Stith, a professor from a prominent Virginia family, who taught at the Anglican William and Mary College in Williamsburg.[41] Since George Washington served on the committee on religion, he would have had opportunity to consider closely the various sermons preached to the burgesses.[42]

Some have dismissed these facts with the retort that Washington had neither time, interest, nor motivation to read sermons, and even if he did, there would be no way to prove it at this late date in history. After all, Washington clearly stated that he had no time to read books.[43] He also expressed humor about preachers—"the lame discourses" of a Reverend Pond[44]—and recorded his disinterest in connecting with another clergyman, the new Anglican Bishop Seabury.[45] He also noted that a sermon he had heard preached in Dutch, since he had not understood a word, had not converted him to the Dutch Reformed denomination.[46]

We also know that he did not read every sermon that was sent to him. Thus, he wrote to Tobias Lear, "I send with my best remembrance a Sermon for Mrs. Washington— n. I presume it is good, coming all the way from New Hampshire; but do not vouch for it not having read a word of it. It was one of your enclosures."[47]

But it would clearly be incorrect to claim that Washington was not a reader at all. The evidence points otherwise. Careful study of Washington's writings reveals a clearer picture. Washington had a deep interest in books and articles and placed a high value on reading: "I conceive a knowledge of books is the basis upon which other knowledge is to be built."[48]

Washington, aware of his "defective education,"[49] sought to overcome its limitations through the power of self-learning through reading. The proof of his reading is evident in the copious notes extant in his papers from historical and agricultural books.[50] Given his profoundly systematic method[51] and his highly disciplined life of time in his study, he certainly had frequent opportunity to read.[52] One of the most astonishing facts of Washington's reading is his written assertion that he had read everything printed on the constitutional debate.[53]

But how do we know what sermons, in particular, were important to him and in fact were read by him? First, we know that he valued sermons, because he signed them,[54] and in several instances thanked the authors for sending them. He then bound them into his own personal hardcover collection of sermons, numbering several volumes in length.[55]

Along with his own collected sermons, Washington had various printed sermons or collections of sermons by clergy such as Reverend James Beattie,[56] Reverend Hugh Blair (published by and purchased from Reverend Mason Weems),[57] Reverend

George Washington and family emerging from Easter services at Christ Church, Alexandria, in 1795.

Laurence Sterne,[58] "Shipley's Sermons" by Reverend Jonathan Shipley,[59] Reverend Gilbert Burnet on the *Thirty Nine Articles of Religion*,[60] Reverend John Wesley, etc.[61] What did Washington write in his letters about these sermons? As we shall see, he commented on many of the sermons sent to him.

SERMONS ALREADY CONSIDERED AND COMMENTED ON BY WASHINGTON

As we turn our attention to the sermons in his collection on which Washington chose to make comment (and that we have shared in our study), we must take careful note of what Washington said concerning them. When we look at his remarks with care, we discover his personal, and therefore significant, testimony about the doctrines he agreed with and wished to see advanced.

We must also note which of these critiqued Deist beliefs. Washington's views of such sermons further corroborate that he was not a Deist, or merely an indifferent, lukewarm, disinterested Christian. Washington's "sacred fire" manifests itself in his open and sincere pleasure in and commitment to the theological and biblical concerns of these sermons that he approved.

But before we consider these additional sermons, we will summarize some of the sermons we have already encountered in our study of Washington's religion.

In the chapter on "Deism: Shades of Meaning and Shading the Truth," we used a sermon written by Samuel Miller and possessed by Washington to evaluate the claim that Washington's terms for deity were deistic. Washington expressed his "thanks" to Miller for this sermon.[62]

In the chapter on "George Washington Versus Deism," we considered two sermons by Reverend Dr. Timothy Dwight and possessed by Washington to summarize the key doctrines and ethical ideas of Deism. Washington expressed his "compliments" to Dwight for these sermons.[63]

In the chapter on "George Washington Versus Deism," we used two sermons by Isaac Lewis that Washington had received and read to establish his views of Christianity and of Deism. It is most significant that Washington declared that the "Doctrine" in these two sermons was "sound," because the sermons are clearly pro-Christian and anti-Deist.[64]

In the chapters on "Spirituality" and "Valley Forge," we used a sermon by Israel Evans to show Washington's self-understanding of his own piety. Washington wrote to Chaplain Evans and told him that he had read the sermon with "equal attention and pleasure" and that he intended to support the "pious endeavors" of Evans in his ministry. It is evident that Washington's use of the phrase "read with pleasure" indicates approval.. This is also evident when we see how he used the phrase "read with pleasure" in his other letters, when he described other works he had read.[65] We discover that he used it in three areas: agriculture, politics, and sermons. The nature of the political and agricultural works shows that this is undeniably an approving pleasure. Washington uses this same language with respect to both pro-Christian and anti-Deist sermons.[66]

In the chapter on "Prayer," we cited a sermon by William Linn to evidence Washington's opposition to Deism. Linn's sermon critiquing America's sins emphasized that one of these main sins was the continuing influence of French Deism in America.[67]

Washington wrote to Linn and told him he had read "the sermon with pleasure." Again, this is an expression of approval. Washington did not find pleasure in what he disagreed with. For that matter, how could any logically consistent American Deist have expressed pleasure in a sermon whose very purpose was to attack the evils of Deism in America? To summarize, then, Washington's comments on the sermons we have considered so far reflect a Christian perspective and reveal both an explicit and implicit opposition to Deism.

ADDITIONAL OVERLOOKED SERMONS FAVORED BY WASHINGTON

At the beginning of this chapter, Franklin Steiner and Moncure Conway were quoted to the effect that Washington did not comment on sermons, or if he did, it was only in two instances. Professor Paul Boller, Jr, generally agrees: "In only two instances did Washington express his opinion on the content of sermons which had been forwarded to him."[68] He argues that these two instances are the sermons sent by Zachariah Lewis and the funeral sermon of Sir William Pepperell.

According to Boller, the sermons sent by Zachariah Lewis to Washington were called "sound" by Washington, but since their identity is unknown, they are essentially irrelevant to the debate. The funeral sermon of Sir William Pepperell, to which Washington wrote his "approbation of the doctrine," was a sermon that no Deist would ever find objectionable. The doctrine presented in the sermon was that great human beings, although god-like, must die like other mere men, as part of God's moral governance of the universe—clearly a doctrine a Deist could readily affirm.[69]

We have already shown that Professor Boller was incorrect about the "unknown" sermons sent by Zachariah Lewis. We have readily found them, accurately identified them, and have shown them to be "sound" Christian teaching and anti-Deist in force. We will consider Professor Boller's assessment of the Sir William Pepperell funeral sermon by Reverend Benjamin Stevens below.

This discussion exposes a fatal inaccuracy that has been part and parcel of the Washington-as-a-Deist case from the beginning. The fact is that Washington did not limit his favorable comments to only these two sermons. As we have just summarized above, in earlier chapters of our study, we have found that Washington also gave his approving pleasure to the sermons of military Chaplain Israel Evans and House of Representatives Chaplain, William Linn. Thus, we have already encountered four sermons approved by Washington that are explicitly Christian and either explicitly or implicitly anti-Deist. And there are still more.

The authors were tempted to include these sermons in their entirety, allowing the reader to experience the text that Washington so enjoyed. However, knowing the difficulty of the language and the depth of the theology they contain, we have opted to summarize the sermons by brief citations from key passages and give a fuller sampling of the text in the endnotes. We encourage the reader to delve into these sermons and thereby recognize just how biblically literate and theologically minded our first president was.

However, before we consider them, how are we to assess the errant scholarship of so many who have argued for Washington's Deism? The stark reality is that there are only two options, neither of which is complimentary to the accomplished scholars who have uncritically followed the unsubstantiated statements of Moncure Conway, Franklin Steiner, and Paul Boller. Either these scholars have failed to do the research they should have done before making their unsubstantiated pronouncements, or even worse, they have intentionally suppressed the incontrovertible evidence that eviscerates their case for Washington's alleged Deism.

At any rate, in spite of the pro-Deist scholars' claims that we should have found only two sermons that Washington commented upon, we must add several others to the list. The sermons we must yet consider here are by Uzal Ogden, Jedidiah Morse, Benjamin Stephens, and Laurence Sterne. Other sermons we will consider in subsequent chapters are by Reverend Dr. John Lathrop and yes, the ever provocative Parson Weems.

We begin our consideration of these next sermons with one by the Reverend Uzal Ogden.[70] Washington received this sermon and wrote back to Reverend Ogden, from West Point on August 5, 1779. Washington wrote,

> Reverend Sir: I have received, and with pleasure read, the Sermon you were so obliging as to send me. I thank you for this proof of your attention. I thank you also for the favourable sentiments you have been pleased to express of me. But in a more especial mannr. I thank you for the good wishes and prayers you offer in my behalf. These have a just claim to the gratitude of Reverend Sir, Yr., etc.

Thus, Washington read the following sermon with pleasure. After reading the first portion of Ogden's sermon, one must ask if a Deist would have or could have read this Christian Gospel presentation with "pleasure" and then have thanked the author who had sent it to him for his prayers. The sermon is addressed "To Christians of Every Denomination." The Christian message of Ogden's sermon is absolutely unmistakable:[71]

A SERMON ON PRACTICAL RELIGION
By the Reverend Uzal Ogden, of Sussex County,
New Jersey
O that they were wise, that they understood this,
that they would consider their latter end! Deuteronomy 32: 29
Behold! Now is the accepted time.

Behold now is the day of salvation. 2 CORINTHIANS 6: 2

...The divine Jesus was appointed by the Father of Mercies to interpose in our favor. He most graciously undertook to restore to man all that he had left, and to deliver him from all the evils to which he is exposed. The Son of God is, therefore, emphatically stiled our Redeemer [Isaiah 59:20], our Deliverer [Romans 11:26], our Saviour [Luke 2:11].

...Thus did the merciful Saviour endeavour to dispose men to be reconciled with their offended Maker. Thus, "was God in Christ reconciling the world unto himself [2 Corinthians 5:19]; restoring us to his favour and friendship."

The medium of reconciliation, is the blood of Jesus [Ephesians 2:16], apprehended by faith [John 3:15], with a disposition of penitence and sincere obedience.

With what fervor of affection are we entreated by the apostle to accept of this favour? "We are ambassadors for Christ," says he "as though God did beseech you by us: We pray you, in Christ's stead, be ye reconciled to God; for he hath made him to be sin for us, who knew no sin, that we might be made the righteousness of God in him [2 Corinthians 5:20-21]."

A more clear statement of the Christian Gospel has scarcely ever been penned. There can scarcely be found a more clear indication that Washington was not a Deist than his personal letter to the author of this sermon, stating that he had "read it with pleasure." Professor Boller does not even acknowledge the existence of this sermon by Ogden, let alone the fact that Washington read Ogden's sermon "with pleasure."

To recap, Boller wrote that Washington did not think much about sermons, and that while he approved a sermon sent by Zachariah Lewis, it is impossible to know what it said. However, we have located that very sermon and discovered that it was written by Lewis' father, Reverend Isaac Lewis, and that it too had a strong Christian message. Furthermore, a sermon preached by Benjamin Stevens, Boller mistakenly identifies as one compatible with a Deist world view. This, too, Washington commended, and it was also distinctively a Christian sermon.

To his credit, Boller acknowledges two other sermons that Washington mentioned, one by Reverend Dr. Jedidiah Morse and one by Chaplain Israel Evans. To Boller's discredit, he does not come to grips with the anti-Deist messages in these sermons that George Washington commended. We have already mentioned Evans' sermon; now we turn to that of Morse.

Listen to even the title and subtitle of Reverend Dr. Jedidiah Morse: "A Sermon Preached at Charlestown November 29, 1798 On the Anniversary [of] Thanksgiving In Massachusetts—With An Appendix Designed to illustrate some parts of the discourse; exhibiting proof of the early existence, progress, and deleterious effects of French intrigue and influence in the United States."[72] Its lengthy title and subtitle show that it is a clear statement against French Deism. But with respect to Morse, Boller briefly considers Washington's letter to Reverend Dr. Morse. Washington wrote from Mount Vernon on February 28, 1799.

> Reverend Sir: The letter with which you were pleased to favour me, dated the first instant, accompanying your thanksgiving Sermon came duly to hand.
>
> For the latter I pray you to accept my thanks. I have read it, and the Appendix with pleasure; and wish the latter at least, could meet a more general circulation than it probably will have, for it contains important information; as little known out of a small circle as the dissimination of it would be useful, if spread through the Community. With great respect etc.

Professor Boller's comments in this context appear to be a fine example of scholarly deflection—noting that something exists, making a depreciating admission about it, and then not bothering to investigate the evidence, as one hastily moves on to another matter.[73] Professor Boller's comments do not address the fact that Washington's pleasure extended to reading both the sermon and the appendix. That a fair reading of his words included his desire that the sermon and the appendix both have a "more general circulation," and if that was not possible, "at least" it would be so for the appendix.

So although Washington's letter does not require us to, let's limit our consideration only to the appendix, since Professor Boller's remarks imply that that was what Washington truly desired to have disseminated and "spread through the community." But Professor Boller did not allow his readers to read what Washington had read. If he had, the reader would have found Dr. Morse arguing against the dangers of Deism in America. This was a continuation and deeper explanation of the theme of his sermon. A sympathetic reading of Washington at this point demands that we at least quote a portion of the text he wanted "to meet a more general circulation." Dr. Morse's appendix declares:

> ...Our political divisions and embarrassments, and much of that Atheistical infidelity and irreligion, which, during the last twenty years, have made such alarming progress among us, are probably but the poisonous fruits of our alliance and intimate intercourse with the French nation. ...
>
> At a time when our holy religion and our government are formidably assailed, by the secret and subtle artifices of foreign enemies, it is incumbent on every friend to Christianity, and to his country, to unite in opposing their insidious and wicked designs. He is unworthy the name of a Christian or a patriot, who, in such a crisis as the present, is silent or inactive. Surely the ministers of religion ought not to be considered as deviating from the duties of their profession, while they unveil those political intrigues, which, in their progress and operation, are undermining the foundations, and blasting the fair fruits of that holy religion, which they preach, and which they are under the oath of God to vindicate against every species of attack.
>
> ....infidelity and licentiousness are too numerous, they are yet the minority of the nation, as we will hope and are now on the decline, both in numbers and influence. The lamentable issue of the great experiment, made in France, of governing a civilized people without the aids of religion, has procured for Christianity many able advocates, and furnished many strong motives to the Christian to cherish his faith. ....How much soever we detest the principles and the conduct of the French, we shall most sincerely wish them well; that they may speedily enjoy the fruits of true repentance and reformation; the blessings of good government, peace, and pure Christianity. Then we will embrace them as FRIENDS; till then, we ought to hold them as ENEMIES.[74]

The words "infidelity" and "irreligion" in his appendix are Dr. Morse's synonyms for Deism, the driving ideology of the French Revolution. The cure for the "atheistical conspirators against religion" in America, according to Reverend Dr. Morse, was for people to be worthy of the names of "Christian" and "Patriot" by a renewed commitment to the "holy religion" of "pure Christianity." Professor Boller chose not to quote his message from Dr. Morse's appendix that Washington wished to have "disseminated" and "spread through the community." Perhaps Professor Boller failed to have read the appendix. Perhaps he did and chose not to disseminate the message of the appendix, because it negates his entire thesis that Washington was a Deist.

ATTEMPTS TO CUT AND PASTE TO SAVE A THESIS WITHOUT FOUNDATION

We have noted that Professor Boller acknowledged that Reverend Benjamin Stevens' sermon was read by Washington and that Washington had approved the doctrine in it. He mentioned Stevens' sermon in a letter written from New York on December 23, 1789 to Reverend Joseph Buckminster of New Hampshire. The president said:

> Sir: Your letter of the 27th of November and the discourse which it enclosed have been duly received.
>
> I consider the sermon on the death of Sir William Pepperell which you were so good as to send me by desire of Lady Pepperell his Relict, as a mark of attention from her which required my particular acknowledgments; and I am sorry that the death of that Lady which I see is announced in the public papers prevents my thanks being returned to her for her respect and good wishes. You, Sir, will please to accept them for your goodness in forwarding the discourse, and my request, that they may be added to the Revd. Author [Reverend Benjamin Stevens, of Kittery or now, Maine] with my approbation of the Doctrine therein inculcated. I am etc.

What was the "doctrine inculcated" in Steven's sermon to which Washington gave his approbation? According to the presentation of it by Moncure Conway and Paul Boller, the message of this sermon is something that a deistic George Washington could readily have accepted.[75] But is this the case? Let us permit Reverend Stevens to speak for himself, without blindly accepting the carefully edited summary that Conway and Boller provide, since they have carefully cut and pasted this sermon so that its presentation might be compatible with a Deist's approval. The sermon is entitled, "A Sermon occasioned by the death of the Honorable Sir William Pepperell, Bart.

Lieutenant-General in his Majesty's Service."[76] First, let us note the introduction of the sermon that was ignored in the presentation by both Moncure Conway and Paul Boller. Stevens introduces his sermon:

> To Lady Pepperrell. ...
>
> Although you have less one of the best friends, yet overlook not your many remaining mercies, nor forget the many arguments of consolation, which our excellent religion affords. You have reason for thankfulness, ... you do not sorrow as others who have no hope. The certainty of a future existence, and of the resurrection of the just to immortal glory and felicity, which the Gospel gives, affords strong consolation to those who are mourning for the death of pious friends: and the comfortable hope you have, that he who is not taken from you is present with the Lord, and that he is now freed as well from the temptations as the pains and sorrows of this state of trial, and is with the spirits of just men made perfect, and that you shall 'ere long meet again in the regions of perfect friendship never be separated more; may justly sooth your grief. Therefore, instead of giving way to dejection of spirit, let it be your concern to maintain the eminency of your character, by giving proof that your religion is your support in a time of affliction, as well as the rule of your conduct in life...I am Madam, your Ladyship's affectionate, and obliged humble servant. Benjamin Stevens.

It is thus clear that Stevens was not intending to give a sermon that was to be compatible with deistic beliefs. When Washington read this sermon, it was obvious that Reverend Stevens intended it to be a Christian sermon. Washington's approval of the doctrine of this sermon extends to the sermon in its entirety. Washington's approval of this sermon's "doctrine" was given without any limitation. So there is no authentic way that Reverend Stevens' Christian sermon can be cut and pasted into a statement that a Deist could make, i.e., Washington approved all of the sermon, not just certain parts of it.

In fact, this sort of dissimulation—affirming the doctrine of a sermon, but only really affirming a part of the doctrine of the sermon—would be inconsistent with Washington's repeated affirmations of honesty, candor, integrity; not to mention his affirmations of Christianity. There was no reason even to address the doctrine of the sermon in his letter, unless Washington had truly wanted to. He could have, as he did on several occasions, simply have given a sincere thank you, or not corresponded at all.

Since it is a lengthy sermon, we will do what Conway and Boller have done, namely, give selections of the sermon. But we do this not to hide the Christian doctrine of this sermon, but to show what was hidden by the cutting and pasting of Conway and Boller.

> A Funeral Sermon. Psalm 82: 7. But ye shall die like men.
>
> ...If such Persons behave well in Life, and view Death in the Light the Gospel represents it to the Righteous; not as the End of our Being, but the Commencement of a happy Immorality: such being conformed to *Him who is the Resurrection and the Life,* have Reason with Thankfulness to adore that gracious Plan of Things which removes them from this World to a better; although the dark Valley of Death be the Passage thereto.—For then, instead of being abased, they shall be exalted to true Dignity. Then they shall be crowned with everlasting honors. Tho' their Bodies lie down in the Dust and see Corruption; tho' they mingle with the common Earth, and with the Dust of the lowest of Men; yet shall they be raised again in the Resurrection of the Just. And at the Judgment of the great Day, those who in this Life faithfully acted the Parts assigned them, shall meet with the Approbation of the universal Judge;— The unerring Discerner of true Worth—and whose Approbation is an Honor infinitely superior to the united Applause and Homage of all Mankind. And those, *who have been faithful over a few Things, shall be made Ruler over many, and enter into the Joy of their Lord.*
>
> ...But before I finish, it deserves Notice, that in these degenerate Days in which too many are asham'd of Christ and his Cross, especially among those who are in high Life, he [Pepperell] consider'd the Christian Character as truly honourable. And as he was favor'd with a Christian Education; so he made a public and open Profession of the Religion of Christ: and his regular Attendance on his holy Institutions, both in his Family, and in the House of God;–his becoming Seriousness and Gravity when engaged in solemn Acts of Worship;–and his Disposition to maintain peace and Order, and to support the Gospel, shew, that he

was not insensible of the sacred Obligations of Christianity....

...*My Little Children*, Be concerned to remember your Creator in the Days of your Youth; let it be your first Concern to be good: In order to which acquaint yourselves with God, with his Son Christ Jesus, and with his Gospel; and live as the Word of God directs you....and you will be Blessings in this World, and happy to all Eternity.... find Consolation in him who so tenderly sympathized with his afflicted Friends in the Days of his Flesh! – In him who is the Resurrection and the Life! – And believing in him may they have Life eternal!

...May we be taught hereby to cease from Man, and to put our Trust in and expect our Happiness from him who is the ever-living God! – the Voice of this Providence speaks aloud to all to prepare for Death; – to prepare to follow him who is gone before us.—Every instance of Mortality enforces with peculiar Energy that important Admonition of our great Instructor Jesus Christ, *Be ye also ready for in such on Hour as you think not, the Son of Man cometh.* None we see are exempted from Death; – its Approach is intirely uncertain, it can be but at a little Distance at farthest, and is besides such an important and interesting Event, that it demands our most serious Consideration and our greatest Solicitude to prepare for it, that so it may be joyful and happy.[77] (emphasis in the original)

Washington's approbation of the doctrine of this sermon was tantamount to an affirmation of the doctrine that stands at the core of the Christian Gospel. And in so giving his approbation, President Washington clearly distinguished himself from the Deists of his day. No wonder the pro-Deists Moncure Conway and Paul Boller made sure that the readers of their works did not even have the chance to read Reverend Stevens' sermon for themselves.

A BRIEF SYNOPSIS OF FOUR ADDITIONAL SERMONS COMMENTED ON BY WASHINGTON

As is becoming apparent, the study of the role of sermons in Washington's theology and Christian thinking has never been adequately pursued by either the "Washington the Christian" thesis, or the "Washington the Deist" thesis supporters. As we have seen, the pro-Deist perspective has generally dismissed the whole topic by erroneously claiming that Washington only commented on two sermons and never did so in his diary entries. Instead, we have found several sermons that Washington interacted with in various ways.

Here we wish to highlight four additional sermons or discourses that are important for the discussion of Washington's faith. These are selected because they further highlight the inherent inconsistency of viewing Washington as a Deist. The first is an important sermon that Washington affirmed and commented on in his diary. Pro-Deist Washington historian, Dr. Moncure Conway, asserted that Washington did not comment on any sermon in his diary, but here we find this to be false. This sermon is by Reverend Dr. Robert Davidson.

A second sermon that Washington considered and commented on was an oration given on the day of prayer and fasting connected with the struggles over the insurrection in western Pennsylvania called the "Whiskey Rebellion," as it was prompted by a reaction to the excise tax that the government had placed on distilled beverages. Written by Alexander Addison, it is significant not only because it, too is Christian and anti-Deist, but it is also a sermon that Washington wrote about to the author, declaring that he had read it with equal attention and satisfaction.

A third sermon is one written by Reverend Mason Weems. Since most historians have assaulted Weems' failures as a historian, it has often been asserted that Weems never met Washington. This is an error, as we will see in a later chapter. But it is important to consider this sermon written by Weems, because Washington not only said he read it, but he wished to see the "doctrine" in it more prevalent in America.

The fourth sermon is actually a collection of sermons that Washington received from the Bishop of Asaph in England, comprised of a series of sermons by the Bishop's father entitled the "Shipley's Sermons." What we will find here is that Washington's letter back to the bishop shows not only his appreciation for the sermons, but his profound respect for the bishop. These comments are utterly inconsistent with what a Deist would have said. When one remembers that this bishop was at the center of a theological movement very close to Washington's theology, namely the "Latitudinarian movement," it again becomes evident how closely Washington himself identified with the Low Church movement in the Anglican tradition. (To pursue these questions more fully, see the chapter on "Washington the Low Churchman" and the appendix entitled "George Washington and Latitudinarianism").

Reverend Dr. Robert Davidson's published sermon was entitled, "A Sermon on the Freedom and Happiness of the United Sates of America, preached in Carlisle, on the 5th Oct. 1794. And published at the request of the Officers of the Philadelphia and

Lancaster Troops of Light Horse. By Robert Davidson, D.D. Pastor of the Presbyterian Church in Carlisle, and One of the Professors in Dickinson College."[78]

Washington wrote in his diary on Oct. 5th, 1794 (Sunday): "Went to the Presbiterian meeting and heard Doctr. Davidson Preach a political Sermon, recommendatory of order & good government, and excellence of that of the United States."[79] While Washington's comments are brief, they express the value he placed on the sermon, since only what Washington wanted to remember and record for future consideration ever made it in his diaries. Certainly he found the emphasis on order and good government and the excellence of the United States' government, supported by Christian biblical exposition an encouragement as he, as president, was leading an army to put down an insurrection of American citizens. There is no hint of a deistic concern for keeping religion out of the discourse of government in Washington's remarks. A brief consideration of Reverend Dr. Davidson's sermon illustrates that it was directly based upon scriptural concerns, and was commendatory of the president and his policy in this situation. Reverend Davidson declared in his sermon:

> ...the management of public concerns, and the duties of citizens are not to be considered as topics foreign to the gospel, but the contrary; because the gospel views man in every condition in which man can be placed,–and especially as a member of society. I shall not, therefore, need to apologize for the sentiments contained in the following discourse; since, in delivering them, especially in present circumstances, I consider myself only doing conscientiously the duties of my office.[80]

He continues to discuss the role of divine Providence in the American cause and how thankful we should be for it.[81] Next, Dr. Davidson traces America's providential history from Columbus to God's providential care of the early settlements. The struggles of the American Revolution occurred since Americans were "confident of the justice of our cause, we committed ourselves into His hand, who disposeth of states and kingdoms at his pleasure..."All of this brought Dr. Davidson to declare,

> These things are mentioned, to shew, that when we compare our condition with that of other nations, we may with great propriety borrow and apply the words of the text, and say,—*What one nation in the earth is like the American people*....Here is liberty and equality,

according to the just acceptation of those favourite terms; liberty, civil and religious, to the utmost extent that they can be, where there is any government at all....[82] (emphasis in the original)

He then addressed the soldiers and the president, saying,

To you, my friends, who are present with us at this time, in the character of *Citizen-Soldiers*, allow me the liberty of a short address....You are in the presence of *Him* who knoweth all hearts; and I trust you are conscious to yourselves, that you have assumed your present character, not from the desire of war, but the love of peace....You have the example of our beloved PRESIDENT, and other exalted characters, to animate you to your duty....You are called to act under the direction and authority of HIM, who never exposed to danger a single life without necessity; and who graced his victories with that clemency which is the greatest ornament of true courage and one of the surest tests of magnanimity. And is not the cause, in which you are engaged, such, that you may safely pray to the omnipotent and just Ruler of the world, for his aid and protection? We are persuaded it is, and would both follow you with our prayers, and beseech you to pray for yourselves, and trust in him who is able to preserve you....And now may God dispose the hearts of our fellow-citizens, every where, to the love of order, justice, and peace! May he establish good government among us! May he long preserve a life which appears so necessary for our public tranquility; and preserve to this country her rights and privileges—WHILE SUN AND MOON ENDURE![83] (emphasis in original)

The second discourse that we consider here is by Alexander Addison. Addison was not a clergyman, but a jurist who lived from 1759 to 1807. This text was mentioned in Addison's letter to Washington on May 17, 1798. Addison wrote, "I take the liberty of sending a pamphlet—and in a separate inclosure a Newspaper." Washington wrote back on June 3, 1798, "I pray you Sir, to accept my thanks for the Pamphlet ...and for the Gazette containing an Oration .... Both of these productions I have read with equal attention & satisfaction...."[84] Unfortunately, the newspaper article from this time and city cannot be found in any archive. However, a newspaper account has surfaced from the *Albany Centinel* of the date 1798. This newspaper article gives the following details:

> At Washington, Pennsylvania, the late Fast day, the people being destitute of a regularly settle clergyman, assembled together and attended to an excellent oration, delivered at the Academy in that town. The oration furnishes a striking display of the crimes and enormities practiced by France towards all the states whom she has *republicanized*; demonstrates the necessity of union and firmness in Americans, to thwart the views of that nation upon our property and independence; paints, with the pencil of truth, the infamous and vile arts of the faction which exists in the bosom of our country; and impresses the necessity of a conduct which is indispensable on the part of the friends of government, (in order to check the currents, thro' which the purelizing streams of deception flow) in the following just and energetic remarks....[85]

Fortunately, Alexander Addison's "Oration" that was printed in the gazette from Washington Pennsylvania that cannot be located was also printed in Philadelphia by publisher John Ormrod in 1798 and is thus available to us. Its title was "An Oration on the Rise and progress of the United States of America, to the Present Crisis; and on the Duties of the Citizens." Some of the important sections of this "Oration" that prompted Washington's "equal attention & satisfaction" when read included the following:

> ...the French government have abandoned all regard to God, to government, to justice, or to decency....Pamphlets and newspapers have been continually issuing from the press, for the avowed purpose of destroying all trust in God, and all confidence in our government. No public character, not even the virtue of a Washington, nor religion itself, has escaped abuse and defamation....Can we expect justice from men who deny it to each other? Will those respect the rights of man, who contemn the rights of God? Can we expect any decency or right from men with power in their hands, who deny a God and a future state?....An house divided against itself cannot stand....When an independent and

free nation has its sovereign rights attacked, and violated by another nation; it is a call of Providence to all the citizens to stand forth, and defend the cause of truth and national liberty....And in the discharge of this duty, to which Providence calls them, they ought to look up with holy confidence to the protection of that Providence which calls them out to trial, and to the strength of the Lord of Hosts, who calls them to battle. His providence and strength America hath heretofore experienced: And the Lord, which delivered us out of the paw of the lion, will deliver us out of the hand of the Philistine. To a trust in God we ought to unite confidence in those men whom Providence hath called to rule over us.

....Let us unite in one band of unity among ourselves, and confidence in our administration; and, to testify this union and confidence to the world, let us unanimously sign an instrument, expressing to our government our confidence in the rectitude of its measures, our firm reliance on the protection of divine Providence, for the support of our independence from a foreign yoke, on this as on a former occasion; and, for this support, now as then, pledging to each other our lives, our fortunes, and our sacred honour.[86]

The third sermon we consider here is the Reverend Mason L. Weems' "The Philanthropist; or, A Good Twelve Cents Worth of Political Love Power, for the Fair Daughters and Patriotic Sons of America," Dedicated to that great *Lover* and *Love* of his Country, George Washington, Esq.[87] The reason that this sermon is significant is twofold. First, it is a sermon by Washington's first biographer, the "infamous" Parson Weems. Second, Washington wrote back to Weems in regard to this sermon and expressed his appreciation for its "doctrine." Thus, it is clear that Washington knew of Weems and actually appreciated his theological concerns. Washington's letter to Weems says,

Revd Sir: I have been duly favored with your letter of the 20th. instant, accompanying "The Philanthropist." For your politeness in sending the latter, I pray you to receive my best thanks. Much indeed is it to be wished that the sentiments contained in the Pamphlet, and the doctrine it endeavors to inculcate, were more prevalent. Happy would it be for *this country at least*, if they were so. But while the passions of Mankind are under so little restraint as they are among us, and while there are so many motives, and views, to bring them into action we may wish for, but will never see the accomplishment of it. With respect, etc.[88]

Weems' sermon demonstrates that Washington's affirmation of its doctrine was again an affirmation of the Christian faith, for in it Weems talks about the importance of the "body" as made up of essential parts. He says,

> Thus has God, the common Parent, removed far from us all ground of pride on the part of the rich, and of dejection on the part of the poor, "the rich and the poor, says Solomon, meet together, the Lord is the maker of them all."....Thus, secure in each others protection, thus abundant and happy in the sweet rewards of their mutual labours, they can eat, drink, and rejoice together like brothers, under the shade of their own vine and fig-tree, none daring to make them afraid. O how goodly a thing it is to see a whole nation living thus together in unity![89]

Weems sermon on unity is based on several biblical texts that again reveal Washington's comfort with and commitment to basic Christian teachings. By openly giving his support to a Christian minister and author, Washington was again distancing himself from a Deist perspective.

Finally, let us note that Washington was comfortable with identifying with Anglican Bishop Shipley when his son, Dr. William Davies Shipley, sent his father's sermons to him. Washington wrote:

> Sir: I have been honored with your polite Letter of the 23d. of May, together with the works of your late Right Revd. father Lord bishop of St. Asaph, which accompanied it. For the character and sentiments of that venerable Divine while living, I entertained the most perfect esteem, and have a sincere respect for his memory now he is no more. My best thanks are due to you for his works, and the mark of your attention in sending them to me; and especially for the flattering expressions respecting myself, which are contained in

your letter.[90]

Washington declared not only his thanks for the works of the Lord Bishop of Asaph, but he also affirmed his "most perfect esteem" for the "venerable Divine's "character and sentiments." Thus, Washington's "sincere respect for his memory" was coupled with appreciation for his ministry.[91]

To sum up this section, we can simply say that whenever Washington's view of sermons come to light, he consistently supports sermons that are pro-Christian in character, many of which were also explicitly anti-Deist in focus. This continues to underscore the erroneous nature of the assertion that Washington was a Deist.

A SUMMARY OF WASHINGTON'S MOST IMPORTANT SERMONS

While the pro-Deist authors have arbitrarily limited Washington's interest in his sermon collection to only two, the fact is that there are so many, we cannot possibly do justice to all of them in this study. The best we can do for now is to summarize the most salient sermons and attempt to show how they relate to Washington's life and faith. Given the vast number and the complexity of the topic, we cannot include the information in the text of this chapter. But in appendix 5, "A Summary of Washington's Most Important Sermons," we have catalogued these sermons in terms of their relevance to Washington's life and, where appropriate, included his comments on the sermon.

CONCLUSION

As we conclude, we believe the combination of the extensive friendship of Washington with the clergy and his consistent appreciation and approval of their sermons, as manifest in this representative sample, establish two points. First, it is patent that Washington's response to these sermons is consistently in agreement with the Christian perspective and logically incompatible with the Deist perspective. Second, the Deistic argument, beginning with Conway and Steiner and continuing up until now under the influence of Professor Boller's study of Washington's religion, that George Washington ignored the sermons he possessed in his library, clearly has been based on flawed scholarship and flimsy evidence. Instead, as we can see in his letter to Reverend H. H. Brackenridge, Washington was even willing to quote Christian sermons to his fellow correspondents. In this case, Washington appealed to a sermon by the Reverend Laurence Sterne,

West Point, September 8, 1779.

Sir: I have to thank you for your favor of the 10th of August, and your Eulogium [i.e. eulogy].

You add motives to patriotism, and have made the army your debtor in the handsome tribute which is paid to the memory of those who have fallen in fighting for their country. I am sensible that none of these observations can have escaped you, and that I can offer nothing which your own reason has not already suggested on this occasion; and being of [Reverend Laurence] Sterne's opinion, that "Before an affliction is digested, consolation comes too soon; and after it is digested, it comes too late: there is but a mark between these two, as fine almost as a hair, for a comforter to take aim at." I rarely attempt it, nor shall I add more on this subject to you, as it would only be a renewal of sorrow, by recalling a fresh to your remembrance things which had better be forgotten.[92]

Later, Washington again appealed to the sermons of Reverend Laurence Sterne. This was when he wrote to Jonathan Trumbull, Jr., at the time of the death of his stepson, Jack Custis, only weeks after the victory at Yorktown in 1781. Washington wrote,

My dear Sir: I came here in time to see Mr. Custis breathe his last. About Eight o'clock yesterday Evening he expired. The deep and solemn distress of the Mother, and affliction of the Wife of this amiable young Man, requires every comfort in my power to afford them; the last rights of the deceased I must also see performed; these will take me three or four days; when I shall proceed with Mrs. Washington and Mrs. Custis to Mount Vernon.

As the dirty tavern you are now at cannot be very comfortable; and in spite of Mr. [Reverend Laurence] Sterne observation the House of Mourning not very agreeable; it is my wish, that all of the Gentn of my family, except yourself, who I beg may come here and remain with me; may proceed on at their leizure to Mount Vernon, and wait for me there. Colo. Cobb will join you on the road at the Tavern we breakfasted at (this side Ruffens). My best wishes attend the Gentn. and with much sincerity and affectn.[93]

Thus, there is clear evidence that Washington not only read the Laurence Sterne sermons that were in his library, but that he even had digested them to the point that he could refer to them and even quote them, whether from memory, or by reading them. Since the quotation of Reverend Sterne comes from Headquarters at West Point in 1779, it is possible that this quotation was from memory, since Washington's library did not travel with him during the war.

As we conclude then, the question in Washington studies can no longer be *if* Washington read the sermons he collected. It is clear that he at least read many of them (if not all). The question, instead, must be whether the scholars who have written on Washington have sufficiently read much of *his own writings*. If they haven't, that is sloppy and substandard scholarship. If they have, and they claim that they have found only two sermons that Washington commented upon, then it is no longer merely a matter of sloppy scholarship. It's worse—it's a case of dishonesty. Our founding father is certainly worthy of better research than that.

THIRTY FOUR

George Washington on Heaven and Eternal Life

*"The Sweet Innocent Girl [his step-daughter Patsy]
Entered into a more happy and peaceful abode than she has met with
in the afflicted Path she hitherto has trod."*
George Washington, March 22, 1783 [1]

"Tis well."
Last words of George Washington, December 14, 1799[2]

Those who believe George Washington was a Deist argue that he essentially did not believe in heaven either, or that he believed that heaven was irrelevant. Joseph J. Ellis in his recent book, *His Excellency,* argues that the only type of "immortality" that Washington believed in was not the Christian kind. He claims that Washington believed that immortality was simply being remembered by future generations. Ellis writes:

Never a deeply religious man, at least in the traditional Christian sense of the term, Washington thought of God as a distant, impersonal force, the presumed wellspring for what he called destiny or providence. *Whether or not there was a hereafter, or a heaven where one's soul lived on, struck him as one of those unfathomable mysteries* that Christian theologians wasted much ink and energy trying to resolve. *The only certain form of persistence was in the memory of succeeding generations, a secular rather than sacred version of immortality....*[3] (emphasis ours)

Meanwhile, as noted repeatedly, the classic work on George Washington's religion is Paul Boller Jr.'s, *George Washington and Religion.*[4] As we have seen, Boller's perspective is well summarized in his phrase, "Washington and his fellow deists."[5] As we turn our attention to the question of George Washington's beliefs about heaven and eternal life, or immortality, we must consider Professor Boller's views in regard to this question. Boller writes, "There is some evidence, though it is far from conclusive, that Washington believed in immortality."[6] But is this very tentative statement regarding immortality even consistent with his thesis of Washington the Deist?

DEIST BELIEF IN IMMORTALITY

It appears to us that this hesitating "far from conclusive" interpretation of the evidence is strange, since if Washington were a Deist, he ought to have believed in immortality, since it was a foundational belief of the Deists. To have doubted or denied immortality would have placed a thinker in Washington's day in the category of an atheist, even beyond a most hardened Deist. Even Thomas Paine, the most vehement Deist of his day, believed in immortality.[7] Thus, in the secularists' quest to make Washington into a Deist, he has been made into even more of an unbeliever than the Deists were!

Consider Lord Herbert of Cherbury (1581-1648), often called the father of English Deism. He evaluated everything, including religion, in light of the new emphasis on reason. As seen in his work, *Religion of the Gentiles With the Causes of their Errors*, published in 1645, his essential articles of faith were: (1) the existence of God; (2) the worship of God; (3) the practice of virtue; (4) repentance of sin; and (5) a faith in immortality. He believed these truths, including immortality, to be self-evident and accessible by all men everywhere, since these beliefs were (supposedly) rationally based.[8]

Thus, if Washington were a Deist, he ought to have believed in immortality, since it was not only a tenet of Deism, but it was also a claim of the other Deist-leaning founders such as Thomas Jefferson and Benjamin Franklin.[9] To the best of our knowledge, there was not a single founding father that denied the immortality of the soul. Not one.

MASONIC BELIEF IN IMMORTALITY

But there is even further reason why we insist that Washington believed in immortality. He was a Mason.[10] As we saw in the chapter on Washington's Masonic beliefs, a foundational claim of the Masonic Order was a belief in immortality. In this context, consider Washington's correspondence with the Grand Lodge of Pennsylvania in 1792. The Lodge wrote,

> To these our grateful acknowledgements (leaving to the impartial pen of history to record the important events in which you have borne so illustrious a part), Permit us to add our most fervent prayers that after enjoying the utmost span of human life, every felicity which the Terrestrial Lodge can afford, you may be received by the great Master Builder of this World and of worlds unnumbered, into the ample felicity of that *celestial lodge* in which alone distinguished virtues and distinguished labors can be eternally rewarded.[11] (emphasis ours)

This is a clear statement of belief in immortality. Washington wrote the following to his Masonic brothers, which reflected a belief in eternal life,

> Fellow Citizens and Brothers of the Grand Lodge of Pennsylvania. I have received your address with all feelings of brotherly affection mingled with those sentiments for the society, which it was calculated to excite.
>
> To have been in any degree an instrument in the hands of Providence, to promote order and union, and erect upon a solid foundation the true principles of government, is only to have shared with many others in a labor, the result of which, let us hope, will prove through all ages a sanctuary for brothers and a lodge for the virtuous.

> Permit me to reciprocate your prayers for my temporal happiness and to supplicate that we may all meet thereafter in that eternal temple, whose builder is the great architect of the universe.[12]

Immortality would have been a strongly held belief of Washington, not just because he was a Mason, but also because Washington's Masonic Order was a fraternity of "Christian Masons."

ANGLICAN BELIEF IN IMMORTALITY

A foundational tenet of Christianity is the certainty of immortality through faith in the saving work of Christ. *The Thirty Nine Articles* of the Anglican Church that Washington had adopted as his confession of faith when he became a vestryman said in the eighteenth Article:

> *Of Obtaining eternal Salvation only by the Name of Christ.*
> They also are to be had accursed that presume to say, That every man shall be saved by the Law or Sect which he professeth, so that he be diligent to frame his life according to that Law, and the light of Nature. For Holy Scripture doth set out unto us only the Name of Jesus Christ, whereby men must be saved.[13]

One of Christianity's foundational claims is eternal life through faith in Christ. So, regardless of how one views Washington in his historical context, whether as Deist, Mason, or Christian, each of these potential identifications of Washington anticipates his belief in immortality.

The scholarly confusion must be set straight concerning Washington's view of immortality. To help us appreciate his views on the reality of heaven, the attainment of eternal life or immortality, we must begin with a discussion of his views of death and dying.

GEORGE WASHINGTON ON DEATH AND DYING

Death came early to the Washington household, since George's father died when he was a child of eleven. George's mother was the second wife of his father Augustine. His first wife had died, and so George had two half-brothers. As we have seen earlier, Mary Ball Washington was a very serious student of the scriptures and raised her family as a single mother. Her key textbook was Sir Matthew Hale's *Contemplations*

Moral and Divine, a copy of which was in Washington's library when he died. This was his mother's copy, with her signature and well-marked and used pages. We have a copy of the 1685 edition—the same one that the Washingtons had. The very first article is, "Of the Consideration of our Latter End and the Benefits of it," a study based on Deuteronomy 32:29, "Oh that they were wise, that they understood this, that they would consider their Latter End!"[14]

Young George's home training and early experiences taught him the reality of death and to prepare to face the "grim king." He wrote to Richard Washington on October 20, 1761, as only a twenty nine-year-old man,

> Dear Sir: Since my last of the 14th July I have in appearance been very near my last gasp; the Indisposition then spoken of Increased upon me and I fell into a very low and dangerous State. I once thought the grim King would certainly master my utmost efforts and that I must sink—in spite of a noble struggle but thank God I have now got the better of the disorder and shall soon be restord I hope to perfect health again.[15]

The primary text in Washington's worship life, of course, was the 1662 *Book of Common Prayer*. The Washington family used a book written by Thomas Comber that taught them how to use the classic book of Anglican worship.[16] When we examined this text in the Boston Athenaeum, we found that it was owned by George's father and signed by both of his wives as well. The book had been well used by the family. In fact, the pages that address coping with the sorrow of death appear to be tear stained. This book bears George's earliest extant signature.

Indeed, George saw many deaths throughout his life. The word "death" appears approximately 555 times in his collected writings. He saw the death of his two stepchildren. His adopted grandson, G. W. P. Custis wrote of the death of Washington's stepdaughter Patsy, "Her delicate health, or, perhaps her fond affection for the only father she had ever known, so endeared her to the 'General,' that he knelt at her dying bed, and with a passionate burst of tears, prayed aloud that her life might be spared, unconscious that even then her spirit had departed."[17] His stepson Jacky Custis died of camp fever in the wake of the victory at Yorktown.[18]

Washington often counseled family and friends at deaths calling on them not to "murmur" but to "submit" to the "will of God" and his sovereign "decrees."[19] He arranged for the funeral of his nephew.[20] He saw his mother for the last time just weeks before she died as he left to assume the presidency.[21] He wrote at the death of his brother Charles, "I was the *first*, and am now the last, of my father's Children by the second marriage who remain."[22] (emphasis in the original) And, of course, he was in charge of the American army in the nation's longest-lasting war, a war which saw terrible death and destruction. No wonder he spoke of death as the "grim King."

Washington had learned as a child to turn to the *Book of Common Prayer* for solace in the face of death, and clearly continued to do so throughout his life. In the chapter entitled "Washington the Soldier," we saw Colonel Washington performing by torchlight "The Order for the Burial of the Dead" for his fallen commander, General Braddock.

Four decades later, on April 9, 1793, he wrote to his friend the Reverend Bryan Fairfax: "Dear Sir: At One o'clock in the afternoon on Thursday next, I mean to pay the last respect to my deceased Nephew, by having the funeral obsequies performed. If you will do me the favor to officiate on the occasion, it will be grateful to myself, and pleasing to other friends of the deceased. No sermon is intended, and but few friends will be present...."[23]

The omnipresence of death in the lives of everyone in the eighteenth century, and particularly so for an active military man, meant that reflection on death was not just a philosophical pursuit. Numerous times throughout Washington's life, he had participated in the "funeral obsequies" of the *Book of Common Prayer*.[24]

At the end of the war, Washington dreamt of "the private walks of life; for hence forward my Mind shall be unbent; and I will endeavor to glide down the stream of life 'till I come to that abyss, from whence no traveler is permitted to return."[25] The traveling image was Washington's euphemism for death: "The want of regular exercise, with the cares of office, will, I have no doubt hasten my departure for that country from whence no Traveller returns;" "He is, I believe not far from that place, from whence no traveler returns."[26]

WASHINGTON AND THE PREVENTION OF PREMATURE DEATH

Understandably, Washington developed an interest in the prevention of premature death. (In Washington's day, premature death often occurred because of an incomplete understanding of human breathing.) His interest in preventing an early death can be seen in his correspondence with Reverend Dr. John Lathrop,[27] who had recently delivered a medical religious discourse to the Humane Society. Lathrop explained how certain medical procedures were applied to people who were considered to be dead—due to a sudden death incident—that sometimes restored them to life.

Washington wrote to Lathrop on June 22, 1788,

> Reverend and respected Sir: Your very acceptable favour of the 16th
> of May, covering a recent publication of the proceedings of the
> Humane Society, have, within a few days past, been put into my
> hands. I observe, with singular satisfaction, the cases in which your
> benevolent Institution has been instrumental in recalling some of
> our Fellow creatures (as it were) from beyond the gates of Eternity,
> and has given occasion for the hearts of parents and friends to leap
> for joy.[28]

This new method was championed by the Humane Society that had started in
Amsterdam. Humane Societies had spread over Europe and now had arrived in
Boston. Their work had had remarkable success in rescuing those "apparently dead."
This included cases of drowning, choking, and those who had been struck by lightning.
In one instance in Europe, a person had been dead for three days. When a physician
looked in the coffin, he decided the body was worthy of an attempt at resuscitation,
which proved to be successful. Lathrop at that point wrote, "This instance should
caution us against hastening the body of our friends to the grave. In cases of sudden
death, the last solemn rite should not be performed until there be evident marks of
putrefaction."[29] As we shall see, Washington readily embraced this advice.

When Washington wrote of his "singular satisfaction" in reading of the work of
the Humane Society, he expressed a level of praise that he offered only on five other
occasions in his vast writings.[30] (Some of those other occasions were in his praise to
Christ-centered sermons.)

The subject of Lathrop's discourse had an evident impact on Washington.
He wrote:

> Sir: I have received your letter of the 28th. Ulto. accompanied by the
> three pamphlets which you did me the honor to send me. You will
> do me the favor, Sir, to accept of my best thanks for the mark of
> polite attention in forwarding your discourses to me.
>
> The one delivered before the Humane Society is upon a subject
> highly interesting to the feelings of every benevolent mind. The
> laudable view of Institutions of this nature do honor to humanity.
> The beneficence resulting from them is not confined to any

particular class or nation; it extends its influence to the whole race of mankind and cannot be too much applauded.[31]

DID "HIS EXCELLENCY" FACE DEATH AS A CHRISTIAN OR A STOIC?

When Washington faced his own "sudden death" experience twelve years later as he lay on his death bed, almost unable to breathe, he made it very clear to his assistant Tobias Lear that he was not to be put in the tomb until three days had passed. But did this in some way suggest an expression of unbelief in Christianity? One might be led to believe so if Joseph J. Ellis' 2004 bestseller, *His Excellency: George Washington*, is considered in this context. Ellis wrote,

> Washington believed that several apparently dead people, including perhaps Jesus, had really been buried alive, a fate he wished to avoid. His statement [to be placed in the vault in less than three days after he died] also calls attention to a missing presence at the deathbed scene: there were no ministers in the room, no prayers uttered, no Christian rituals offering the solace of everlasting life....The historic evidence suggests that Washington did not think much about heaven or angels; the only place he knew his body was going was into the ground, and as for his soul, its ultimate location was unknowable. He died as a Roman stoic rather than a Christian saint.[32]

In this brief paragraph, Ellis piles up several assertions that impact on the topic of Washington's Christian faith—without any attempt to provide evidence. We will here briefly consider the unsubstantiated statements that Ellis offers to discount Washington's Christian faith:

1. "Perhaps, Jesus, had really been buried alive." Ellis here suggests that Washington may have entertained the notion that Jesus hadn't died, but instead swooned on the cross. Let it simply be said that there is not a shred of evidence to substantiate this assertion. It is inconsistent with history, in that the Romans were masters at execution. When they declared one of their victims dead, he was dead. This theory is also inconsistent with the Anglican faith that Washington knew and practiced. And,

as we will see below, the Reverend Dr. Lathrop's message and the work of the Humane Society were deeply committed to historic Christianity. Moreover, modern unbelief did not arise until long after Washington's death. Not until the twentieth century did liberal unbelieving Christianity begin to substitute the swoon of Jesus on the cross for his physical death on the cross to account for his appearance on Easter Sunday morning and to dismiss the biblical claim of bodily resurrection. Ellis' suggestion is entirely out of historical context. The "swoon theory" of Jesus' crucifixion, burial, and resurrection would have been utterly unknown to Washington.

2. "His statement [to be placed in the vault in less than three days after he died] also calls attention to a missing presence at the deathbed scene: there were no ministers in the room,..." It is true that there were no clergy present. But one of Washington's closest lifelong friends was present, namely, Dr. James Craik. Dr. Craik was a devout Scotch-Irish Presbyterian who was later buried in the Presbyterian church yard in Alexandria. Dr. Craik's assessment of Washington's last day of life is significant. Dr. Craik's simple description of Washington's death says, "During the short period of his illness, he oeconomised his time, in the arrangement of such few concerns as required his attention, with the utmost serenity; and anticipated his approaching dissolution with every demonstration of that equanimity for which his whole life has been so uniformly and singularly conspicuous."[33] Dr. Craik, who had known Washington throughout his adult life, saw no change in his dying moments from his whole life. What was the secret of Washington's "utmost serenity" or profound tranquility that was joined with his "conspicuous equanimity," or remarkable calmness? Craik knew Washington's unwavering trust in the care, protection, and provision of divine Providence, as we saw in the chapters on "Washington and Providence" and "Washington the Soldier."

3. "No prayers uttered,..." While it is true that Tobias Lear's account of Washington's death records no uttered prayers, it

should be remembered that Martha Washington was praying with her Bible open at the foot of the bed. Bishop Meade addresses the question this way,

> It has been asked why he did not, in the dying hour, send for some minster and receive the emblems of a Savior's death. The same might be asked of thousands of pious communicants who do not regard the sacrament as indispensable to a happy death and glorious eternity, as some Romanists do. Moreover, the short and painful illness of Washington would have forbidden it. But his death was not without proofs of a gracious state. He told to surrounding friends that it had no terrors for him—that all was well. The Bible was on his bed: he closed his own eyes, and folding his arms over his breast, expired in peace.[34]

4. "No Christian rituals offering the solace of everlasting life...." Along with the comment just cited from Bishop Meade, it should be remembered that Washington's fatal sickness only lasted a mere twenty-four hours. Washington's illness was a swollen throat that was so severe that he could not swallow, and eventually could not even breathe. Even if Washington could have swallowed, as a Low Churchman in the Virginian tradition, he would not have sought the Eucharist on his sickbed.

5. "The historic evidence suggests that Washington did not think much about heaven or angels." This statement is fascinating for three reasons. First, it suggests that Ellis knows what Washington may have been thinking on his deathbed. One may rightly wonder how he has access to such knowledge. If he claims that it is based on Washington's writings, then we simply must disagree. Second, the historic evidence shows, as we will summarize below, that Washington referred to "heaven" over 130 times! Ellis is utterly incorrect. Washington clearly did think much about heaven. And third, as to Washington's alleged non-reflection on angels, Ellis apparently was unaware of the letter that Martha Washington wrote relating her

husband's dream that he had had only weeks before his death that included an angel. We will consider Washington's dream below. It was that very dream that prompted Washington to write his last will and testament, the very document he asked to review as he slipped away in his brief battle for life on his death bed.

6. "The only place he knew his body was going was into the ground,..." It is true that Washington knew he would be buried. His will called for the eventual construction of a new crypt.[35] But when that was done, his family's actions suggested that the Washington family's faith was not just that the body would go in the ground, for they placed on the tomb, the first verse used in the funeral service of the *Book of Common Prayer*, that Washington had prayed and used throughout his life. That verse, John 11:25, gives the words of Jesus, where he declares, "I am the resurrection and the life."

7. "And as for his soul, its ultimate location was unknowable." If this were true, why did he write the prayer to his fellow Masonic brethren, as we just saw above, that declared that after living this earthly life, "that we may all meet thereafter in that eternal temple, whose builder is the great architect of the universe"? We will challenge Ellis' unsubstantiated claims more fully below by a careful consideration of Washington's idea of "heaven," the "hereafter," the "next world," and his use of phrases such as "the road to heaven," "the hope of an approving heaven," "the hope our religion gives," etc.

8. "He died as a Roman stoic rather than a Christian saint." Washington's "serenity" and "equanimity" or tranquility and calm in the face of death may well have resembled a stoic-like resignation. But it was perfectly matched by the same attributes in Mrs. Washington as well. Washington's last words were, "'Tis well." Martha's first words in response to the news of her husband's death were "'Tis well." Her equanimity was the same as her husband's. No one denies that Martha was a Christian. Could it be that Washington's peace and calmness at death were indistinguishable from Martha's because they reflected the

same faith in the sovereign Providence of God? Compare here Washington's words of spiritual consolation with those of Martha. Washington wrote to Frances Bassett Washington, the widow of George Augustine Washington, on February 24, 1793,

> My dear Fanny: To you, who so well know the affectionate regard I had for our departed friend, it is unnecessary to describe the sorrow with which I was afflicted at the news of his death, although it was an event I had expected many weeks before it happened. To express this sorrow with the force I feel it, would answer no other purpose than to revive, in your breast, that poignancy of anguish, which, by this time, I hope is abated. Reason and resignation to the divine will, which is just, and wise in all its dispensations, cannot, in such a mind as yours, fail to produce this effect.[36]

But compare the following from Martha Washington to Mercy Otis Warren, written from New York, June 12, 1790:

> ...But for the ties of affection which attract me so strongly to my near connections and worthy friends, I should feel myself indeed much weaned from all enjoyments of this transitory life. ...
>
> In passing down the vale of time, and in journeying through such a mutable world as that in which we are placed, we must expect to meet with a great and continual mixture of afflictions and blessings. This a mingled cup which an overruling providence undoubtedly dispenses to us for the wisest and best purposes...and as you justly observe, shall we shortsighted mortals dare to arraign the decrees of eternal wisdom—that you and your may always be under the kind of protection and guardianship of the providence is the sincere wish of....

Consider also these words from Martha Washington which she wrote to Janet Livingston Montgomery on April 5, 1800:

...your affliction I have often marked and as often have keenly felt for you but my own experience has taught me that griefs like these can not be removed by the condolence of friends however sincere – If the mingling tears of numerous friends—if the sympathy of a Nation and every testimony of respect of veneration paid to the memory of the partners of our hearts could afford consolation you and myself would experience it in the highest degree but we know that there is but one source from whence comfort can be derived under afflictions like ours. To this we must look with pious resignation and with that pure confidence which our holy religion inspires.[37]

George and Martha's granddaughter, Nelly Custis, saw a spiritual union between her grandparents in this context as well. She wrote, "She [Martha] and her husband were so perfectly united and happy that he must have been a Christian. She had no doubts, or fears for him. After forty years of devoted affection and uninterrupted happiness, she resigned him without a murmur into the arms of his Saviour and his God, with the assured hope of eternal felicity."[38]

WASHINGTON'S AIM TO PREVENT PREMATURE DEATH

Returning then to Washington's positive response to Reverend Dr. Lathrop's advice regarding the delay of burial in the face of sudden death, we then must ask, was there a religious motivation as well as a scientific motivation for Washington's request to delay his entombment for three days? By a quick review of Reverend Lathrop's sermon, we can discover that the answer is yes, and the motive was not Ellis' implication of Washington's disbelief in Christianity. The evidence shows the exact opposite. This is clear in the heading of Reverend Dr. Lathrop's *Discourse*, which quotes Luke 9:56, "The Son of Man is not come to destroy men's lives, but to save them." [39]

DID WASHINGTON BELIEVE IN HEAVEN?

Did Washington even believe in heaven? If we were to listen to Joseph Ellis, it would seem that he did not, but Washington did in fact believe in heaven. This helps us to understand that his idea of immortality was not merely figurative, but was, instead, a reality that informed his daily religious life. First, we must emphasize that Washington used the word "heaven" more than 130 times. Remarkably, heaven as a concept in Washington's theology has been entirely overlooked by the scholars who have addressed his concept of immortality. Since this is the case, it warrants a brief summation of this important concept for Washington. For once his understanding of heaven is established, his remarks about the after-life and immortality make much more sense. (The following phrases are all easily found by using the search feature of the *Writings of Washington* at the Library of Congress.)

1. Washington addressed heaven with phrases such as "prayers" or "vows" to heaven" (16x), "I wish to heaven" (2x), "invoked heaven" (1x), "heaven grant it" (1x) and emotionally laden phrases expressing dread ("Heaven avert"—7x; "Heaven forbid"—2x), longing ("would to heaven"—4x), relief ("Thank heaven"—4x), frustration ("In the name of Heaven"—2x; "By Heaven"—1x; "For Heaven's sake"—3x), confidence ("Heaven knows"—8x; "Heaven alone can foretell"—1x), earnestness ("Heaven is witness"—3x).

2. Accordingly, Washington believed that heaven was active in the affairs of his life, and so in this sense it was a synonym for Providence: "interposing hands of heaven," "events produced by heaven," "events left to heaven"; "Heaven saves" or "rescues," "helps" (3x), "Heaven assist me" (1x), "protects" (5x). And "an appeal to heaven" (3x), was a synonym for a prayer that was offered at the time of battle.

3. The graciousness of heaven was captured by Washington with phrases such as "blessings of heaven" (10x), "smiles of heaven" (11x), "under the smiles of heaven" (2x), "favor of heaven" (5x), "fostering influence of heaven" (1x), "as heaven could flourish" (1x), "heaven crowns blessings" (3x), "bountiful heaven" (1x), "benediction of heaven" (1x), "indulgent care of heaven" (1x), "gracious indulgence of heaven" (1x), "not forsaken by heaven" (1x), "that heaven may continue to you..." (1x). By way of contrast, the nation was reminded that it must consider "the vengeance of heaven." (1x). Washington also used a figure of speech comparing romantic love to heaven: "heaven taken its abode on earth."

4. Washington understood that the work of heaven was sovereign. This is reflected by these phrases, each of which was used once:

"Heaven determined," "heaven ordains," "heaven has spared us," "the will of heaven whose decrees are always just and wise," "heaven inspires," "approved by heaven," "heaven points out," "precepts of heaven," "under heaven" (2x), "moving heaven and earth."

5. Washington wrote of the "road to heaven," "to *repent* and *be forgiven* are the precepts of heaven," [emphasis in the original] and "in the hope of an approving heaven" giving expression to the basic ideas of Christian teaching on salvation.

6. Man's response to heaven is "gratitude" (4x), "sincere acknowledgement" (1x), and "dependence upon heaven" (1x).

Based upon Washington's extensive use of the idea of heaven, it is clear that he held to the concept of the efficacy of prayer and the Providential care of God, according to God's own purposes in history. Because of this vital interconnection between heaven and earth, Washington called on men to have a grateful dependence upon God. Further, Washington affirmed that there was a "road to heaven"[40] for man, and stated that "to *repent* and *be forgiven* are the precepts of Heaven,"[41] and that there was a "hope of an approving heaven."[42] Given this Christian doctrinal matrix that is woven throughout his writings, we must thus take Washington's affirmations of eternal life and eternal destiny in the historic Christian sense. To refuse to do so is to uproot Washington from the historic milieu in which he lived as an Anglican Christian and as a Christian Mason—each of which were deeply committed to immortality.

Not only did Washington have an understanding of heaven, but as we saw in the chapter on Washington's Christian world view, he also had an extensive recognition of the Christian doctrines of the last things. Washington's phrases that reflect the Christian understanding of the last things, or what is called eschatology by theologians, include the following:

- Raise the dead[43]
- Send to life eternal[44]
- Throne of grace[45]
- Reward of good and faithful servant[46]
- Separation of wheat and tares[47]
- Blessings of a gracious God upon the righteous[48]
- Wise man counts the cost[49]

- The millennial state[50]
- Last trump[51]
- Until the globe itself is dissolved[52]

Given all of this, did Washington have a belief in an afterlife in heaven? It seems to us he did. Consider, for example, Washington's remark about the usefulness of conscience:

> Conscience again seldom comes to a Mans aid while he is in the zenith of health, and revelling in pomp and luxury upon ill gotten spoils; it is generally the *last* act of his life and comes too late to be of much service to others here, or to himself hereafter.[53]

In light of Washington's extensive commitment to Christian eschatology, it does not seem inconsistent to understand him to be committed to immortality and eternal life when he speaks of this concept.

WASHINGTON ON IMMORTALITY

Given the Christian understanding of heaven that is at the heart of Washington's perspective, we must take his claims for belief in immortality seriously. He speaks of immortality from a philosophical standpoint: "You see how selfish I am, and that I am too much delighted with the result to perplex my head much in seeking for the cause. But, with Cicero in speaking respecting his belief of the immortality of the Soul, I will say, if I am in a grateful delusion, it is an innocent one, and I am willing to remain under its influence."[54] But he also speaks of immortality with a Christian vocabulary as well: "May the felicity of the Magistracy and Inhabitants of this Corporation, be only limited by the duration of time, and exceeded by the fruition of a glorious immortality."[55] Consistent with this, Washington also uses phrases such as "the other world,"[56] "eternal happiness,"[57] "the Sweet Innocent Girl [his step-daughter Patsy] Entered into a more happy and peaceful abode than she has met with in the afflicted Path she hitherto has trod,"[58] "happier clime,"[59] "happier place,"[60] "happiness here and hereafter,"[61] "heaven's favours here and hereafter,"[62] and "must be happy."[63] Also, in Washington's reciprocal prayers, he affirms the ideas of a heavenly rest,[64] the salvation through the Lamb of God.[65] We have also encountered his use of the concepts of the hope of religion,[66] the hope of the approbation of heaven,[67] the reward of good and faithful servants,[68] the throne of grace,[69] "the gates of eternity,"[70] and "life eternal," and "eternal happiness."[71] To these can be added his phrases "land of spirits,"[72] "world of

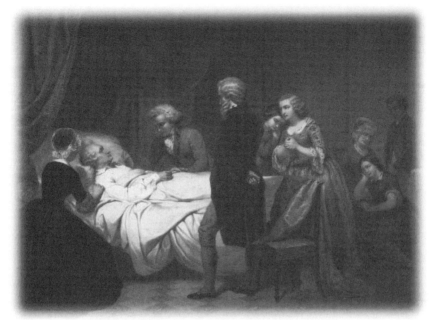

"When the summons comes I shall endeavor to obey it with good grace."

spirits,"[73] and the classical name "Elysium,"[74] the abode of the honored dead.

Given Washington's extensive use of the term "heaven," and the doctrinal ideas that he coupled with it, these multiple phrases are clearly intended to be taken in the sense that a Christian would have normally used them. Simply put, when Washington's writings are taken in his own context, not in the context of secular doubt, then it is completely evident that he was an advocate of immortality. As we have already seen, even the Deists of Washington's day believed as much. Certainly the Christian Masons did as well. It is simply time to dismiss the evasions that have been put forward on this topic by many contemporary historians of Washington.

WASHINGTON'S PREPARATION FOR DEATH

Washington's preparation for death was not only somber, there was even a bit of good-natured humor that was shared by Washington and founding father Robert Morris. (Morris was a signer of the Declaration of Independence. He was known as the financier of the American Revolution. Furthermore, Washington stayed with him during the summer of 1787, when the Constitution was written). Apparently the two made a pact not to die before 1800. Washington only missed his lighthearted promise by a few weeks, since he died on December 14, 1799. (Morris died in 1806.)

On September 22, 1799, just eleven weeks before he died, we find Washington preparing for death as he writes to nephew Burgess Ball from Mount Vernon who had informed him of the death of George's brother:

> Your letter of the 16th inst. has been received, informing me of the death of my brother [Charles Washington]. The death of near relations always produces awful and affecting emotions, under whatsoever circumstances it may happen. That of my brother has been so long expected, and his latter days so uncomfortable to himself [that they] must have prepared all around him for the stroke though painful in the effect.
>
> I was the *first*, and am, now, the *last* of my father's children by the second marriage who remain. When I shall be called upon to follow them, is known only to the Giver of Life. When the summons comes I shall endeavor to obey it with good grace.[75] (emphasis in the original)

These words quietly reflect several Christian ideas. Death for Washington is not just a natural or unavoidable occurrence that is borne with a stoic or Deistic indifference of unyielding resolve. Rather, Washington believed that his death would occur when he was "called upon" by the "Giver of Life," who issues a "summons" that he intended to "obey with good grace." Each of these phrases reflects an element of Christian biblical teaching:

- "called" upon (Romans 8:28)
- "by the "Giver of Life" (Job 1:21)
- who issues a "summons" (Luke 12:20)
- that he intended to "obey with good grace" (Matthew 26:39)

Washington's language is consistent with the lifelong education that he had from his religious tradition and the books he held in his library that addressed this topic. As mentioned before, the childhood family spiritual text read by Mary Washington to her family was Sir Matthew Hale's *Contemplations Moral and Divine* addressed this topic. "Of Our Consideration Of Our Latter End," the first study in Hale's work, finishes with these words:

...we are to be thankful for our life, and not be desirous to leave our Post, our Station, our Business, our Life, till our Lord call us to himself in the ordinary way of his Providence; for he is the only Lord of our lives, and we are not the Lords of our own lives.[76]

Washington's words also seem to echo another book he had in his library entitled, *The Sick Man Visited*. It was published in London in 1745 by the Reverend Nathanael Spinkes, the Prebendary (that is, one who received a stipend from the Church) of Sarum. His prayer "For One of Middle Age" says,

Suffer me not to set my affections upon any thing here below, but upon the eternal enjoyment of thee, and thine inestimable rewards in Heaven; nor to reckon upon the wonted vigour of my age, but upon my present inability, and the nearness I am possibly in to death, and a future state. Teach me a perfect submission to thy holy Will, that I may account of life, only as an opportunity of doing thee farther services; and may use it whilst continued to me, to be in a great readiness for death, that whensover that comes, I may receive its summons without surprise, and may willingly quit all that I have here, to depart, and be with Christ, which is far better. My time at best is short; but if thou art pleased to make it shorter than might have been expected, by taking me away in the midst of my days, I commit myself into thy hands, to do with me as seemeth thee good. Only, I beseech thee, remove me not hence, til thou shalt have fitted me for a better and more lasting state, through Jesus Christ my only Saviour and Redeemer. *Amen.*[77]

And Washington's words above (about his readiness to die) also reflect the classic prayer of "The Order For The Visitation Of The Sick" in 1662 *The Book of Common Prayer* that says, "...give *him* grace so to take thy visitation, that, after this painful life ended, *he* may dwell with thee in life everlasting; through Jesus Christ our Lord. *Amen.*"[78]

WASHINGTON'S LAST WILL AND TESTAMENT: A WILL WITHOUT WITNESS?

We must now address the question of Washington's last will and testament. Why did Washington write his will without any express witness to faith in Christ? It did begin with the traditional words of taking an oath: "In the name of God. Amen." Yet we cannot answer the question of why Washington did not explicitly declare his faith in his will by any statement in Washington's writings. It is possible that Washington felt that a witness in a will, such as the one he had copied as a youth as a writing exercise, was not the best way to express one's faith.

Washington's creed was deeds not words. So while we cannot give an explicit reason in Washington's writings for why he chose not to mention his faith in his will, we would point out that such an act is not required by the Christian faith. Further, if the absence of such a witness is a proof of Deism, then, on the basis of this argument, Martha Washington was a Deist too, since her will makes no mention of her faith in Christ. But this would be clearly false. No one doubts Martha Washington's Christian faith. Thus, the argument is a non sequitur. In fact, Washington uses the name of Jesus more often than Martha, since there seems to be no instance where Martha wrote the name of Jesus Christ.

As we saw in the chapter entitled, "Did Washington Avoid the Name of Jesus Christ?" there was a common practice to refrain from using the name of Jesus Christ to honor Christ's name. This was not intended to be an expression of unbelief. Martha's not writing the name of Jesus Christ could not be used as a testimony against her faith. It seems that the historic Trinitarian use of "God" as captured by the Anglican tradition of using the Athanasian Creed, along with the sincere Virginian Anglican desire not to profane the name of Christ, kept her, like her husband, from writing the name of Jesus Christ in common or ordinary correspondence.

The point here is clear. If this reticence to mention Jesus in writing proves Deism, then it proves that both George and Martha were Deists. But this is clearly absurd. Thus, the argument is specious and can carry no persuasive force. We believe that George was no more a Deist than Martha. Moreover, Washington's will was not explicitly Christian, yet it was implicitly Christian, as one considers what he says he wanted done with regard to his slaves, a specially bequeathed Bible, his views of war, and his love expressed to his family.

THE DREAM BEFORE HIS DEATH

As we consider this important question, let us return to Joseph Ellis' claims that we have already briefly considered. Above, we mentioned that Washington's writing of his will seems to have been motivated by a premonition. This came in the form of a remarkable dream, which was preserved for history through a letter by Martha

Washington. This clearly stands in tension with what Ellis wrote, "The historic evidence suggests that Washington did not think much about heaven or angels." Ellis apparently was unaware of the letter that Martha Washington wrote relating her husband's dream about his death that included an angel.

This incident occurred just a few months before Washington's death. It was this dream that prompted Washington to write his last will and testament, the very document he asked to review on his deathbed as he slipped away in his brief battle for life. Martha wrote:

> At midsummer the General had a dream so deeply impressed on his mind that he could not shake it off for several days. He dreamed that he and I were sitting in the summer-house, conversing upon the happy life we had spent, and looking forward to many more years on the earth, when suddenly there was a great light all around us, and then an almost invisible figure of a sweet angel stood by my side and whispered in my ear. I suddenly turned pale and then began to vanish from his sight and he was left alone. I had just risen from the bed when he awoke and told me his dream saying, "You know a contrary result indicated by dreams may be expected. I may soon leave *you*." I tried to drive from his mind the sadness that had taken possession of it, by laughing at the absurdity of being disturbed by an idle dream, which, at the worst, indicated that I would not be taken from him; but I could not, and it was *not* until after dinner that he recovered any cheerfulness. I found in the library, a few days afterwards, some scraps of paper which showed that he had been writing a Will, and had copied it.[79] When I was so very sick, lately, I thought of this dream, and concluded my time had come, and that I should be taken first.[80] (emphasis in the original)

Clearly this dream had a direct impact on Washington, since it caused him to write his last will and testament.

Washington enjoyed good health for the remaining months before his death—so much so that at the middle of November, Martha and he were invited to attend the dancing assemblies in that town, as they had frequently done. Washington replied:

Mount Vernon, 12th November, 1799.

Gentlemen: Mrs. Washington and myself have been honored by you polite invitation to the Assemblies at Alexandria this winter, and thank you for this mark of attention. But, alas! Our dancing days are no more. We wish, however, all those who have relish for so agreeable and innocent amusement all the pleasure the season will afford them.[81]

WAS THERE NO CHRISTIAN WITNESS AT WASHINGTON'S DEATH?

The two arguments raised against Washington's Christian faith that emerge from his family context are that his last will and testament was written without any express witness to faith in Christ, and that when he died, he did not call for a clergyman, and thus did not receive the Sacrament.[82] While we have already considered these objections, we now address the second in more detail.

On December 13th, just a month from the date of his note declining the opportunity to attend the dance, Washington rode over his farm on horseback for several hours in a storm of sleet. He sat down to dinner without removing his damp clothing, and during the succeeding night he experienced a severe throat infection that nearly prevented both his swallowing and his breathing. Physicians came, and soon so reduced his strength from blood-letting that he did not have enough strength left to fight the disease. He died near midnight on December 14, 1799. His death was marked by an extraordinary peace and confidence in the face of an unexpected illness and sudden death. This was in itself an expression of an ideal of the Christian faith. (See John 14:27.)

CONFIDENCE IN THE FACE OF DEATH

Throughout his life, Washington was constantly reminded that he needed to be ready for death.[83] He was often afflicted with life-threatening illnesses;[84] he had been in danger continually as an officer in combat.[85] From childhood on, he saw several members of his family and several of his own friends die. Whether in spite of these struggles or because of them, his last spoken words were filled with confidence, gratitude, and peace. Tobias Lear, Washington's personal secretary recorded the events as they unfolded, and kept track of many of his statements.[86] They include: (as the now-rejected medical procedure of blood letting commenced), he said, "Don't be afraid. The orifice is not large enough. More, more." Concerning his swollen throat, he said, "Tis very sore." He then called for Mrs. Washington and selected one of two existing wills and had one burned. He remarked, "I find I am going, my breath can not last long. I believed from the first that the disorder would prove fatal."

To Tobias Lear, his secretary, the dying Washington said, "Do you arrange and record all my late military letters and papers. Arrange my accounts and settle my books, as you know more about them than any one else, and let Mr. Rawlins finish recording my other letters which he has begun." He then asked if Lear recollected anything which was essential for him to do, as he had but a very short time to continue among them. Lear said he recollected nothing, but that he hoped he was not so near his end; Washington observed smiling, that he certainly was, and that it [death] was a debt, the debt that all must pay. He looked to the event with perfect resignation.

As Lear assisted him, he said to him, "I am afraid I shall fatigue you too much." When Lear said that it was his wish to give him ease, Washington responded, "Well it is a debt we must pay to each other, and I hope when you want aid of this kind, you will find it." He asked when Mr. Lewis, his nephew, and Washington Custis, his grandson, would return, since they were in New Kent, Virginia. Lear said on the twentieth. At five o'clock Dr. James Craik came again to check on his lifelong friend. Washington said to him, "Doctor, I die hard; but I am not afraid to go; I believed from my first attack that I should not survive; my breath can not last long."

When the doctors had him sit up, he said, "I feel myself going, I thank you for your attentions; but I pray you to take no more trouble about me, let me go off quietly, I can not last long." Lear then heard his last words, "I am just going. Have me decently buried; and do not let my body be put into the Vault in less than three days after I am dead. Do you understand me?" When Lear said he did, Washington spoke his last words, "'Tis well." Martha Washington had been seated by his bed the whole time with her Bible.[87] Lear's narrative concludes, "He expired without a struggle or a sigh! While we were fixed in silent grief, Mrs. Washington (who was sitting at the foot of the bed) asked with a firm & collected voice, 'Is he gone?' I could not speak, but held up my hand as a signal that he was not more. 'Tis well,' said she in the same voice, 'All is now over I shall soon follow him! I have no more trials to pass through!'"[88]

Lear's account concluded on Christmas Day, 1799: "I this day sent to Alexa. for the Plumber to come down & close the leaden Coffin containing the General's Body, as Judge Washington [Bushrod Washington, Washington's nephew and future U.S. Supreme Court Justice, and heir of Mount Vernon] had arrived, and did not incline to see the remains. The Plumbers [those who soldered the coffin shut] came. I went with them to the Tomb—I took a last look—a last farewell of that face, which still appeared unaltered. I attended the Closing of the Coffin—and beheld for the last time that face which shall be seen no more here; but *which I hope to meet in Heaven*."[89] (emphasis in the original)

Washington's death was faced with a confident acceptance of the decrees of God, as a debt that all must pay, to be looked upon with perfect resignation.[90] Thus he could say to his dear friend, Dr. Craik, "I die hard; but I am not afraid to go" and "I pray you to take no more trouble about me, let me go off quietly, I can not last long." So he could address his burial and conclude his life with the last words of "'Tis well." These were expressions of a confident faith.

THE LETTERS OF CONSOLATION TO MRS. WASHINGTON

As we conclude our discussion of Washington's view of immortality, it is significant to note that he not only wrote of his belief in immortality, but those who wrote to Martha and to whom Martha then answered all affirmed their belief in Washington's salvation and entrance into eternal life.

Martha, grieving at the passing of her illustrious husband, was ministered to with words of encouragement such as the following from Theodore Foster, a Rhode Island political figure,

> ...For he was so universally belovd that his Eulogy is now and will continue to be a delightful Theme, for the good, the Sentimental and the ingenious in all future Time. That Almighty God may preserve you, in Health, console you by the Supporting Influence of his Spirit, and bestow on you all possible Happiness is the sincere Prayer...[91]

On behalf of Martha, family secretary Tobias Lear wrote him back:

> While these evidences of respect and veneration paid to the memory of our illustrious Chief, make the most grateful impression on the heart of Mrs. Washington, she finds that the only source of Consolation is from that Divine Being who sends Comfort to the Afflicted, and has promised to be the Widow's God. Your prayers for her health and happiness are received with gratitude, and reciprocates with sincerity.[92]

Meanwhile, Martha herself replied to acquaintance Catherine Garreston with the following,

The kind sympathy which you expressed for my afflictive loss – and your fervent prayers for my present comfort and future happiness, impress my mind with gratitude. The precepts of our holy Religion have long since taught me, that in the severe and trying scenes of life, our only sure Rock of comfort and consolation is the Divine Being who orders and directs all things for our good.

Bowing with humble submission, to the dispensations of his Providence, and relying upon that support which he has promised to those who put their trust in him, I hope I have borne my late irreparable loss with Christian fortitude. To a feeling heart, the sympathy of friends, and the evidences of universal respect paid to the memory of the deceased,—are truly grateful.—But while these aleviate our grief, we find that the only sense of comfort is from above.

It gives me great pleasure to hear that your good Mother yet retains her health and faculties unimpaired,—and that you experience those comforts which the Scriptures promise to those who obey the Laws of God.—That you may continue to enjoy the blessings of this life—and receive hereafter the portion of the Just is the prayer of your sincere friend & obt Serv.[93]

CONCLUSION

Washington lived his life with a hope for the approval of heaven.[94] Those who corresponded with him became convinced that he wrote as a Christian.[95] In the minds of Washington's family and friends, George Washington died as he had lived—as a Christian with the hope of eternal life. It only stands to reason that those who knew him personally are better qualified to testify as to his faith and attitude toward life and death than modern scholars two hundred years later, some of whom seem to have a point to make: that Washington was a Deist.

So, note what Washington's own contemporaries said about him after his death. The Earl of Buchan wrote,

I have this day received from my brother, at London, the afflicting tidings of the death of your admirable husband, my revered kinsman and friend.....He was one of those whom the Almighty, in successive ages, has chosen and raised up to promote the ultimate designs of his goodness and mercy, in the gradual melioration of his creatures and the coming of his kingdom, which is in heaven.... His course is finished...in the hopes afforded by the Gospel of pardon and peace! He therefore, Madam, to continue my parallel, may be accounted singularly happy, since by dying according to his own Christian and humble wish expressed on many occasions, while his credit was nowise impaired, his fame in all it splendor, his relations and friends not only in a state of comfort and security, but of honor, he was probably to escape many evils incident to declining years. Moreover, he saw the government of his country in hands conformable to our joint wishes and to the safety of the nation, and a contingent succession opening, not less favorable to the liberties and happiness of the people.[96]

Washington's close confidant, David Humphreys (Washington's only chosen biographer), wrote,

I know you were ever exposed to listen to the voice of friendship, reason, and religion....he has gone before us from these mutable scenes of trouble to the mansions of eternal rest. We too, are hastening to follow him "to that undiscovered country from whose Bourne no traveller returns."

...and may you not derive some rational comfort from the recollection that the great and good man whom we now mourn as having been subject to the lot of mortality, has faithfully discharged every duty in life; from a belief that he has now entered upon a glorious immortality; and from a conviction that, after having rendered to his country more important services than any other human character ever performed, his example will continue to be a blessing to mankind so long as the globe shall exist as a theater for human action?[97]

Humphreys again wrote,

...It seems not unreasonable to suppose (from the wonderful change of sentiments which has since taken place in France) that his death was ordained by Providence to happen exactly at the point of time, when the salutary influence of his example would be more extensively felt than it would have been at any other period....

In either extremity of life so immediately does the lot of Genl Washington appear to have been the charge of Heaven. Since the mortal as well as the natal hour if unchangeably fixed, it becomes our duty to acquiesce in the wise dispensation of the Deity. The illustrious father of his Country was long since prepared for that event. You will remember, when his life was despaired of at New York, he addressed these words to me: "I know it is very doubtful whether ever I shall arise from this bed and God knows it is perfectly indifferent to me whether I do or not."—Amidst all the successes & all the honours of the world he knew "that no man is to be accounted happy until after death. Happy is it that the seal of immortality is set on the character of his, whose counsels, as well as his actions were calculated to increase the sum of human happiness.[98]

Jonathan Trumbull, the son of one of Washington's closest political allies, Connecticut Gov. Jonathan Trumbull, wrote to Martha:

A second Father, as he has been, in many respects to me, -his Death has opened afresh the deeply impressed Wound, which the Loss of my first venerable parent had formerly occasioned. But he is gone and our Duty, however hard it may be at the first instance, is to Bow submissive to the Divine Will—His own words, written to me on a similar occasion (the Death of my Father) are so peculiarly consolatory at the moment, and are also so particularly applicable to my subject as well as to himself that I am impelled to give them to you without apology, etc[99]

This is the letter where Washington wrote of Governor Trumbull, "All these combining have secured to this memory universal respect and love here, and no doubt immeasurable happiness hereafter."[100] The point is that young Jonathan Trumbull is declaring that Washington's words of his father's immortality applied equally well to Washington. Martha Washington agreed. She wrote in return,

...the good Christian will submit without repining to the Dispensations on Divine Providence and look for consolation to that Being who alone can pour balm into the bleeding Heart and who has promised to be the widows God...your kind letter of condolence of the 30th of December was greatfull to my feeling. ...the loss is ours, the gain is his.

For myself I have only to bow with humble submission to the will of that God who giveth and who taketh away looking forward with faith and hope to the moment when I shall be again united with the Partner of my life. But while I continue on Earth my prayers will be offered up for the welfare and Happiness of my Friends among who you will always be numbered being.

Dear Sir, your sincere and afflicted friend, Martha Washington...[101]

It is clear that Martha believed her husband was a Christian and had entered into the immortality of heaven. Her faith was "I shall be again united with the partner of my life." Martha and her friends believed that Washington had lived and died as a Christian.

Scholars today may not accept that Washington believed in immortality, but it is clear that those who knew him were sure he was a true Christian.[102]

Washington clearly expressed a belief in everlasting life by the mercies of God's grace. When scholars reject Washington's belief in immortality, they do so in spite of the ample record of Washington's faith in eternal life. A scholar's unbelief in immortality, should that be the case, does not permit this conclusive evidence to be dismissed. There is indisputable evidence that Washington, as well as the Washington family as a whole, had a sincere belief in the hope of eternal life.

THIRTY FIVE

The Revenge
of Parson Weems:

Washington's Unparalleled Praise
for an Unexpected Person

"For your kind compliment—'The Immortal Mentor,'
I beg you to accept my best thanks. I have perused it with singular
satisfaction; and hesitate not to say that it is in my opinion
at least, an invaluable compilation. I cannot but hope that a
book whose contents do such credit to its title, will meet
a very generous patronage."
George Washington to Parson Weems [1]

The story of the Reverend Mason Locke Weems (1759 - 1825), or Parson Weems as he is usually titled, is a fascinating topic for Washington studies. The reason is evident: Weems' biography of Washington was the first bestseller on Washington's life. We have intentionally developed our study of the religious ideas of George Washington without dependence on Weems' biography. Nevertheless, neither Weems' life nor his writings can be entirely ignored. And once again, as in other aspects of Washington and religion, a deeper look at the existing evidence argues for the authenticity of our first president's Christianity.

Born in Maryland, Mason Weems was the youngest of nineteen children. He first studied medicine. Later he pursued theology, and in 1784 he was one of the first two Americans to be ordained in the Church of England after the Revolutionary War. He preached for several years in Maryland churches and eventually added to his ministry the publishing and sales of religious books. He wrote several books, including such fascinating titles as: *Hymen's Recruiting Sargeant,* or *The New Matrimonial Tat-too for Old Bachelors; The Philanthropist,* or a *Good Twenty-Five Cents Worth of Political Love-Powder; God's Revenge Against Dueling; God's Revenge Against Gambling; God's Revenge Against Adultery.* He wrote a biography of Francis Marion—the famous "swamp fox," (who was the chief inspiration for Mel Gibson's *The Patriot*) as well as publishing other books aimed at producing good morals or answering the deistic views of Thomas Paine.

WEEMS' *LIFE OF WASHINGTON*

But far beyond these titles, we must recognize the sheer impact Parson Weems' *The Life of Washington* has had on the American historical consciousness of Washington. His biography became wildly successful and went through many printings. First published in 1800, it was so popular that some fifty-nine editions had appeared before 1850. Weems' bestseller even made a significant impact on the youthful Abraham Lincoln. Weems' masterwork is still in print as an important historical work.[2]

The first edition was being written while Washington was alive and began with Weems' inscription:

> Go thy way old George. Die when thou wilt,
> We shall not look upon thy like again.

But Washington died on December 14, 1799, and accordingly, these opening lines were deleted. The most famous of all of his stories is the "cherry tree" incident. Weems' version of the alleged historic anecdote follows:

> When George was about 6 years old, he was made the wealthy
> owner of a hatchet, of which, like most little boys, he was

immoderately fond; and was constantly going about chopping every thing which came in his way. One day, in the garden, where he often amused himself by hacking his mother's pea-sticks, he unluckily tried the edge of his hatchet on the body of a beautiful young English cherry tree, which he barked so terribly, that I don't believe the tree ever got the better of it. The next morning, the old gentleman, finding out what had befallen his tree, which, by the by, was a great favourite, came into the house; and with much warmth asked for the mischievous author, declaring at the same time, that he would not have taken 5 guineas for his tree. Nobody would tell him anything about it. Presently George and his hatchet made their appearance. "George," said his father, "do you know who killed that beautiful little cherry tree yonder in the garden?"

This was a tough question; and George staggered under it for a moment; but quickly recovered himself; and looking at his father, with the sweet face of youth brightened with the inexpressible charm of all-conquering truth, he bravely cried out, "I can't tell a lie, Pa; you know I can't tell a lie. I did cut it with my hatchet." "Run to my arms, you dearest boy," cried his father in transports, "run to my arms; glad am I, George, that you killed my tree, for you have paid me for it a thousand fold. Such an act of heroism in my son is worth more than a thousand trees, though blossomed with silver and their fruits of purest gold."[3]

Because of these sorts of unverifiable stories, as well as Parson Weems' interest in presenting Washington as a model for virtue, he is believed—at least in the minds of most scholars—to have exaggerated elements of Washington's life and to have added unhistorical details whenever it seemed appropriate to him to make his point. Thus, Weems is viewed with great suspicion by serious historians. There is good reason for this suspicion.

With all "honesty," Weems does not score high marks as a careful historian, since he made many factual errors. In the first two chapters alone, he makes several misstatements: the maiden name of the first wife of George's father, Augustine, was not Dandridge, but Butler; the age of Augustine at his marriage was not "at least 40," but only thirty-six; the destination of the sea trip by George and Lawrence (his older step-brother) was not Bermuda, but Barbados. Lawrence did not survive his struggle with tuberculosis long enough to see George's successful military exploits at Fort Necessity in 1752, for he died in 1751; rather, his other stepbrother, Augustine Jr., lived to see it, since he did not die until 1762. Moreover, Weems created the wonderful dialogues of George and his family apparently from his own imagination, since there were no historical records kept of these early family dialogues.

Yet, we should also consider the assessment of Weems by Marcus Cunliffe, the historian who reissued Weems' work on behalf of the Harvard Press in 1962. Cunliffe notes, "He gets his facts wrong, but not entirely wrong."[4] Weems also does something that creates the possibility that he was generally accurate. Namely, he quotes individuals by name, some of whom were still alive at the time of his writing. Thus we find John Fitzhugh, Esq. of Stafford, "who was, all his life, a neighbour and intimate of the Washington family."[5] There are also "Col. Lewis Willis, his play-mate and kinsman," and "Mr. Harry Fitzhugh of Chotank."[6] These people actually existed. Col. Lewis (1734-1813, a cousin of George Washington) was still alive at the time of this book. John Fitzhugh of "Marmion in Stafford" appears in George's diary.[7] If Harry is a nickname for Henry, there also is a Henry Fitzhugh that appears in George's diary.[8] We are not aware of any of these men uttering any protest about what Weems had to say.

Weems explains that the anecdote he was about to present was "related to me twenty years ago by an aged lady, who was a distant relative, and when a girl spent much of her time in the family."[9] Since this ninth edition of Weems' life of Washington was published in 1809, and it is the first version that offered the Washington childhood anecdotes, we would understand Weems to be relating stories he had heard around 1788, or just about when Washington was heading to be the first American president under the Constitution. This was a prime time for the appearance of the question, "Do you remember when?" which so often occurs when a local boy becomes famous.

Many of his claims could be checked by those in the region of Virginia, where Washington's family and friends lived—the very ones to whom Weems sought to sell his books. Thus, it is plausible to assume that his claims based on such local, oral histories had some reliability, simply because of contemporaneous verifiability. Add to this the cover endorsement by Lighthorse Harry Lee (1756-1818), Major General in the U. S. Army as well as associate, neighbor, and friend of Washington. He was also the father of Robert E. Lee. Here is what he said about Weems' book:

> The author has treated this great subject with admirable success in
> a new way. He turns all the actions of Washington to the

encouragement of virtue, by a careful application of numerous exemplifications drawn from the conduct of the founder of our republic from his earliest life. No biographer deserves more applause than he whose chief purpose is to entice the young mind to the affectionate love of virtue, by personifying it in the character most dear to these states.[10]

The point is that Lee understood that Weems' biography was intended to be a call to virtue. It is Lee who says that these anecdotes were "drawn. . .from his earliest life." Would such an illustrious Virginian and closely related friend of Washington fall for entirely unhistorical anecdotes of his hero, whom he himself knew and immortalized with the timeless words, "First in war, first in peace and first in the hearts of his countrymen"?

But these modest arguments for Weems' reliability cannot withstand the subsequent scathing critique of scholars. Writing about the turn of the twentieth century, Henry Cabot Lodge wrote a withering criticism, which set the tone for the standard wholesale scholarly dismissal of virtually everything that Weems ever wrote about Washington:

> Many are the myths, and probably few the facts that have come down to us in regard to Washington's boyhood. For the former we are indebted to the illustrious Weems, and to that personage a few more words must be devoted. Weems has been held up to the present age in various ways, unusually, it must be confessed, of an unflattering nature, and "mendacious" [untruthful] is the adjective most commonly applied to him....Let us therefore consign the Weems stories and their offspring to the limbo of historical rubbish, and try to learn what the plain facts tell us of the boy Washington.[11]

So, as we attempt to look at the Reverend Mason Weems and to evaluate if there is anything of historical value in his bestselling story of Washington, we must begin by looking at the hard data. What exactly do we know about this person who wrote of George Washington?

BACKGROUND OF PARSON WEEMS

Mason Locke Weems (1759–1825) was born in Anne Arundel County, Maryland, spent part of his youth in England, where in 1784 he was ordained a priest of the Anglican Church, returning to Maryland to be rector (1784–89) of All Hallows Parish at South River in Anne Arundel County. Weems supported his wife and their ten children by traveling the east coast promoting and selling popular books, preaching in various sanctuaries (including Pohick Church), and writing moral essays and biographies of American heroes, including his book on Washington.[12]

Thus, we know that he was an itinerant bookseller and preacher in the Anglican Episcopalian tradition and that he had the opportunity to travel through the Mount Vernon region where Washington lived, about fifteen miles south of Washington, D.C. As he traveled to the different churches to fill vacant pulpits, he would preach and share his ministry of books. The book salesman in that day was called a "colporteur," and his efforts were a well understood way of advancing the Christian faith in rural areas during the colonial era and long after.

His claim made on the title page of his bestseller, namely, that he was "Rector of Mount Vernon Parish," has led many to scoff and to declare his utter historical unreliability, since there never was a Mount Vernon Parish in Virginia. However, as we saw in the chapter on George Washington the vestryman, Mount Vernon actually fell between two parishes. So while Weems' title was inaccurate technically, it was not inaccurate ecclesiastically. Mount Vernon had been the central concern in the division of the old Truro parish into the new parishes of Truro and Fairfax. Therefore, while it is true that there was no literal Mount Vernon Parish, there are records that show that Reverend Weems was an Episcopalian minister who preached in the Pohick church where Washington worshiped. Washington biographer Phillip Slaughter writes,

> Towards the close of the century, some say in 1798, the eccentric Mason L. Weems appears upon the scene. There is no proof of his precise relations to the Parish. In his popular *Life of Washington* he calls himself "Late Rector of Mount Vernon Parish," as if he did not know its name. It is certain however that he was officiating there about the beginning of this century. Mr. Davis, a teacher in that section, published a work dedicated to Jefferson, and entitled, *Four and a Half Years in America*. In it he says: "About eight miles from Occoquan Mills is a place of worship called Poheek [sic] Church. Thither I rode on Sunday and joined the congregation of Parson

> Weems, a Minister of the Episcopal persuasion, who was cheerful in his mein that he might win men to religion.... the discourse of Parson Weems calmed every perturbation, for he preached the great doctrines of Salvation as one who had experienced their power.[13]

Apparently, Weems was an evangelical and eccentric preacher who had the ability to make people laugh. Bishop Meade mentions that whenever Parson Weems preached, he unleashed "the risible qualities" in people's souls.[14]

THE RELATIONSHIP BETWEEN WASHINGTON AND WEEMS

The general misunderstanding of the relationship between Weems and Washington is reflected by the following comment excerpted from the 1975 *People's Almanac*, *"Footnote People in U.S. History,"* "Although Weems boasted that he had preached for Washington at Mount Vernon, in truth they had never met."[15]

Not so. In spite of such scholarly assaults on Weems' integrity, not just on his reliability as a historian, we know that Weems had direct encounters with George Washington himself. It is clear that Washington and Weems *had* met, and that this likely occurred in the years between the War's conclusion in 1783 and before his election to the presidency in 1789. The source for this fact is a 1792 letter from Weems to Washington. Weems explains to Washington that he had been "introduced to your Excellency by Doctor [James] Craik [Jr.] . . . some Years ago at M. Vernon."[16]

The encounter between them is also substantiated by Washington's diary entry for Saturday, March 3, 1787, which is most likely the encounter mentioned in his letter:

> The Revd. Mr. Weems, and yg. Doctr. Craik who came here yesterday in the afternoon left this about Noon for Port Tobo.[17]

The younger Dr. James Craik that Washington mentions was the son of Washington's closest friend, Dr. James Craik, who served as surgeon general in the Revolutionary War, and had also been with him in the French and Indian War. Dr. Craik was also with George Washington when he died. Thus, Washington's diary tells us that he entertained the two men and that Weems and Craik spent the night. But why did Reverend Mason Weems, together with the younger Dr. Craik, visit Washington at Mount Vernon in the first place?

The answer is that Weems was married to the cousin of James Craik's wife. The editors of Washington's diaries, Donald Jackson and Dorothy Twohig "In 1785 Weems married Frances Ewell (1775-1843), a cousin of Dr. Craik and daughter of Col. Jesse Ewell of Bel Air, Prince William County, where the Weems family later made their home."[18] Thus, the Weems' family connection to one of Washington's closest friends brought him into contact with Washington himself. That explains why the younger James Craik as well as Weems visited Washington's house together.

So we know that Weems and Washington knew each other; were connected not only by region, but also by friends; and that Weems even had spent the night with Washington at Mount Vernon.

But we also find that Weems had further correspondence with Washington. Weems actually had the opportunity to sell one of the books he had published to Washington. In one of Washington's cash accounts we discover that he purchased a book called *Blair's Sermons*.[19] In 1795, Weems wrote to Washington:

> Highly honored Sir: Herewith I send your Copy of the American Edition of Blair's Sermons, which you were so good as to patronize; and for which you paid. I have taken upon me to circulate moral and religious books among the people, with which I know that your Excellency as the Father of the People, is not displeased. Bishop Maddison, Mr. John Dickinson and Doctor Wharton have set me on a good work, i. e. to reprint, if possible a large and cheap American edition of the good old Bishop Wilson's works. I am not ignorant of the services which your Excellency has had the happiness to render to my county, and hope you will not be angry with me for saying that I have gratitude enough earnestly to wish to make your Excellency a present of an Elegant Copy of the above very valuable Work. Your Excellency's name will greatly help our undertaking, and so render a real blessing to our country as well as a lasting obligation on your Excellency's Well Wishing, Mason L. Weems.[20]

While very little is known about the Bishop Thomas Wilson referred to in Weems' letter, so far as we can tell, Washington did not write back to Weems concerning Bishop Wilson's works, but we do know from his library that he possessed them and that they came to him in 1794 as part of the estate of Bishop Wilson's family. This occurred a year before Weems' letter. Also accompanying the Bishop's works was the three-volume study Bible that had been written by Bishop Wilson as well.[21] Clearly, scholarly clergy on both sides of the Atlantic understood that Washington had a true interest in the Bible.

The topics of the book indicate that the book purchased by Washington from Weems was thoroughly orthodox in perspective. It begins with "View of the Internal Evidence of the Christian Religion," by Soame Jenyns of the British Parliament.[22] Next, Weems' book presents twenty-one of Blair's sermons, with titles such as "On the Union of Piety and Morality," "On the Death of Christ," "On the Government of the Heart," and "On the Compassion of Christ."

Thus, the selling and buying of religious books brought Washington and Weems in contact. Historians today so often dismiss Weems as an eccentric, clerical book peddler and a deficient historian. We have yet to find one who acknowledges the evidence that George Washington himself was an occasional beneficiary or even customer of Christian book-seller Parson Weems! There are at least three other letters in the Washington correspondence that further illuminate the relationship between Weems and Washington. On March 26, 1799, Weems needed a character reference on a potential customer. The parson wrote on behalf of a wealthy friend, concerning a man (James Welch) to whom Washington had sold a piece of property. Weems wanted to know whether Welch had fulfilled his financial obligations, since Welch was now attempting to make a large order on credit from his friend.[23]

Washington's answer was swift, being dated March 31, 1799. He explained his real estate contract with James Welch, concluding with words that likely caused a denial of the extension of credit: "PS. It may not be amiss to add that the first years Rent (due in Jan. last) is not yet paid."[24]

Thus, the need to verify a friend's customer's credit brought them together. Six months later, on August 29, 1799, Washington wrote another letter to Reverend Weems. It was in response to Reverend Weems' printed sermon that called for an end to the divisive, political spirit that had appeared in the political process surrounding the presidential election.

Reverend Sir: I have been duly favored with your letter of the 20th. instant, accompanying "The Philanthropist"

For your politeness in sending the latter, I pray you to receive my best thanks. Much indeed is it to be wished that the sentiments contained in the Pamphlet, and the doctrine it endeavors to inculcate, were more prevalent. Happy would it be for *this country at least*, if they were so. But while the passions of Mankind are under so little restraint as they are among us. And while there are so many motives, and views, to bring them into action we may wish for, but will never see the accomplishment of it. With respect etc.[25]

Washington's view was that even though Weems' "philanthropist" (charitable) proposal was really wishful thinking, he could also wish that "the doctrine it endeavors to inculcate, were more prevalent."

Thus, not only Virginian family and friends, the purchasing of religious materials, and the assisting of business relationships brought Washington and Weems together, but so did a common concern for the divisive, political spirit that was beginning to take root in the young republic's elections. On top of all of this, there apparently was an even deeper reason that Washington and Weems had a common bond.

WASHINGTON'S PRAISE FOR *THE IMMORTAL MENTOR*

To attempt to understand the bond of the Washington and Weems relationship, we might ask, what prompted Weems to send *The Philanthropist* to Washington in the first place? The answer appears to be the response the retired president had sent just weeks before to Weems on July 3, 1799, concerning a publication he had sent. This book was a compilation of writings entitled *The Immortal Mentor*. The full title is sometimes given as *The Immortal Mentor; or Man's Unerring Guide to a Healthy, Wealthy and Happy Life.*[26]

The third letter, then, which highlights the relationship between Washington and Weems' concerns Washington's views of *The Immortal Mentor*. Washington's letter to Weems is most important for our purposes. Washington, expressing his thanks for the gift of *The Immortal Mentor*, says to "The Reverend Mr. Weems":

> For your kind compliment—"The Immortal Mentor," I beg you to accept my best thanks. I have perused it with singular satisfaction; and hesitate not to say that it is *in my opinion at least*, an *invaluable* compilation. I cannot but hope that a book whose contents do such *credit* to its *title*, will meet a very generous patronage.
>
> Should that patronage equal my wishes, you will have no reason to regret that you ever printed the Immortal mentor.
>
> With respect I am Reverend Sir,
> Your most obedient
> Humble Servant,
> George Washington.[27] (emphasis in the original.)

In all of the many letters of Washington, there is no commendation that compares with Washington's affirmation of this work. He not only declares that he "perused" the book, but he showers upon it his "best thanks," his "singular satisfaction," his declaration of his *"opinion"* that it is *"an invaluable compilation"* and a wish for a "generous patronage." In other words, Washington hoped that the book

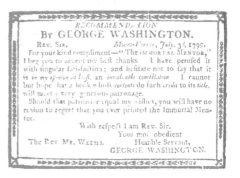

Washington's endorsement appeared as a recommendation in subsequent editions of the Immortal Mentor.

would sell well. Given that he regularly, for consistency's sake, turned down dedications and endorsements from many authors for things that he truly favored, the mere fact that he made such a statement is remarkable.[28]

It should be noted that while in today's conversation, the verb "to peruse" tends to mean to give something a brief look-through, in Washington's day, the word had a very different, in fact, its accurate meaning. Even a current *Webster's Dictionary* defines to "peruse" as "to examine with great care; to read intensively." Thus, when Washington claims to have perused Weems' book, he did so with great care, and most likely read it cover to cover.[29]

Washington's lavish endorsement of Weems' compilation requires us to take a close look at this book "whose *contents* do such *credit* to its *title*."

THE MESSAGE OF *THE IMMORTAL MENTOR: HOW TO BE HEALTHY, WEALTHY, AND WISE*

The *Immortal Mentor* is a compilation of three different authors. The first section is by an Italian author named Luigi Cornaro, entitled, "Man's Unerring Guide to a Long and Healthy Life." Cornaro explains how, by replacing luxury and gluttony with frugality and temperance, even an ill person, as he himself once was, can attain a long and healthy life.

The second section is by Dr. Benjamin Franklin. His two short pieces are "The Way to Wealth" and "Advice to a Young Tradesman." These are intended to instruct a young person on how hard work and thrift will result in the accumulation of wealth.

And the third and final section is by Dr. Thomas Scott.[30] His is the longest selection, comprising more than half the book, and is entitled, "A Sure Guide To Happiness." It is composed of two sections. The first is intended to teach love for God, and the second is to teach "social love," or love for one's neighbor. These two items, often considered the first and second great commandments in the Judeo-Christian tradition, are in Dr. Scott's mind, the sure guide to happiness.

TEMPERANCE AND HEALTH

The Immortal Mentor is designed to explain how a person could be healthy, wealthy, and happy. What makes this book significant for our discussion of Washington's religion is that it demonstrates that Washington truly enjoyed and appreciated a Christian perspective on these foundational questions of health, wealth, and happiness, for *The Immortal Mentor* underscores Christian principles. The first piece by Cornaro explains how temperance helps one to have a long life on earth and to seek forgiveness of sins and eternal life in heaven.

> Cornaro writes,
> ...I must confess, it was not without great reluctance that I abandoned my luxurious way of living. I began with praying to God, that he would grant me the gift of Temperance, well knowing that he always hears our prayers with delight.
> ...that when he shakes hands with his vices, he is no longer a slave to the devil, and finds himself in a better condition of providing for the salvation of his soul: that God, whose goodness is infinite, has ordained that the man who comes to the end of his race, should end his life without any distemper, and so pass by a sweet and easy death, to a life of immortality and glory, which I expect. I hope (said I to him) to die singing the praises of my Creator. The sad reflection, that we must one day cease to live, is no disturbance to me, though I easily perceive, that at my age, that day cannot be far off; nor am I afraid of the terrors of hell, because, blessed be God, I have long ago shaken hands with my sins, and put my trust in the mercy and merits of the blood of *Jesus Christ*.[31]

ATTAINING WEALTH

The second section by Benjamin Franklin shows that when one works hard and exercises thrift and industry, he is able to accumulate wealth. In this regard he offers many practical hints from Franklin's well-known *Poor Richard's Almanack* such as:

Away, then with your expensive follies, and you will not then have so much cause to complain of hard times, heavy taxes, and chargeable families; for

Women and wine, game and deceit,
Makes the wealth small, and the want great.
And farther, "What maintains one vice, would bring up two children."... Beware of little expences; "A small leak will sink a great ship," as Poor Richard says."[32]

The practical advice given to the "Young Tradesman" also helps make a man wealthy:

Remember that time is money....Remember that credit is money. If a man lets his money lie in my hands after it is due, he gives me the interest, or so much as I can make of it during that time....Remember that money is of a prolific generating nature. Money can beget money, and its offspring can beget more, and so on...[33]

Finally, in Franklin's mind, this accumulated wealth has a spiritual context. Under the Providence of God, wealth enables the diligent worker to become a useful neighbor to others.

This doctrine, my friends, is reason and wisdom: but, after all, do not depend too much upon your own industry and frugality, and prudence, though excellent things; for they may all be blasted, without the blessing of Heaven; and therefore, ask that blessing humbly, and be not uncharitable to those that at present seem to want it, but comfort and help them. Remember, Job suffered, and was afterwards prosperous....[34]

In short, the way to wealth, if you desire it, is as plain as the way to market. It depends chiefly on two words, industry and frugality; that is, waste neither time nor money, but make the best use of both. Without industry and frugality nothing will do, and with them every thing. He that gets all he can honestly, and saves all he gets, (necessary expenses excepted) will certainly become *rich*; if that

Being who governs the world, to whom all should look for a blessing on their honest endeavors, doth not, in his wise providence, otherwise determine.[35]

TRUE WISDOM

The third section of the *Immortal Mentor* explains how a person can be truly happy. Dr. Thomas Scott an Anglican clergyman and biblical commentator begins this selection from his vast writings with an affirmation of revelation:

If there be any truth fully ascertained by reason and revelation, it is this, That "*Man is not but to be happy.*" ...Wherein consists the happiness of man?[36]

Dr. Scott teaches that happiness cannot be found in the body. To make this point he offers a graphic depiction of an old man dying:

Nature now sinks apace; his heart labours; his breast heaves; his breathing becomes short and quick; his eyes are hollow and sunk; his voice grows hoarse; he rattles in the throat; his limbs wax cold; his teeth turn black; he foams at the mouth; a feeble convulsion shakes his frame and, with a deep groan, his unwilling spirit takes her leave. Immediately putrefaction and worms begin their loathsome office; and in a little time, this pampered, idolized flesh, returns to the dust of which it was formed.[37]

From this painful image of death, Dr. Scott draws this spiritual lesson:

Who can contemplate this picture, and not bewail with tears of blood, the madness of those who expect their only happiness from such a vile body! O how infinitely superior to these miserable delusions is the Heaven descended philosophy of Jesus Christ! In that divine religion, the body, instead of being exalted as the seat of our happiness, is depreciated as the principal cause of our misery, being, as the poet expresses it, not only a nest of pain and bag of corruption, but the most fruitful source of our sins and sorrows. Christ seldom mentions the body....[38]

Just as happiness cannot be found in the body, nor can it be found in the wealth of this world. Dr. Scott writes,

But the vanity of seeking happiness from riches, honors and pleasures, is yet more convincingly felt when death comes to put a final close to this mortal scene. Ah! my friends, this is the awful hour that strips off the tinsel coverings of folly, stamps vanity on all beneath the sun, and shews that "too low they build, who build beneath the stars."

In that day of terror and despair, what can a vain world offer its poor deluded followers... The remembrance of a life misspent in vain or in guilty pleasures, will fill the soul with pangs of remorse, with agonies of horror, of which none but the wretched sufferers can form any idea. . . . "I have neglected God, and sold my birth-right to heaven! Me, miserable! Whether am I going? My golden sands are all run out! The sun of my life is about to set, and, utterly unprepared, I am going to appear before God." . . . then, when earth, and only earth, hath been the pursuit, what wretchedness to be torn from all that was counted happiness; to leave this dear world behind them forever, to go—Ah! Whither? Not to treasures laid up for them in heaven; not to the place where they have made themselves friends of the mammon of unrighteousness; but where that rich man went who lift up his eyes in torment, because, though rich in this world, he was not rich towards God.[39]

Instead of finding happiness in the pleasures of the body or in the pursuit of wealth, Dr. Scott argues that happiness can only be found in love, a love that is aimed toward God and toward one's neighbor.

"Lay not up for yourselves treasures on earth," says the divine Teacher. ... "but lay up for yourselves treasures in heaven; for where the treasure is, there will the heart be also."—What treasures? Why love,—Love to God and to our neighbour.[40]

The man who loves God, says Dr. Scott, is the only truly wise man. He is the one following the words of "the divine Teacher"—Jesus Christ.

He who loves God is the alone wise, dignified and happy man. For he loves the only good that is worthy the affections of an immortal mind. He loves a friend who alone possesses almighty power to protect him, unerring wisdom to counsel him, and infinite love to bless him. He loves an immortal friend who can never die and forsake him, and an unchangeable friend who will never requite his love with neglect.[41]

And finally, Dr. Scott's teaching of love is much closer to the religion of Paul than that of Mr. Thomas Paine,

But love not only thus marshals an army with banners around us for our safety; it also pours a sweet sunshine of peace and harmony over our days. St. Paul, who was a much safer guide in matters of religion, than Mr. Paine, advises us to walk in love with our neighbours, if we would lead a quiet and peaceable life. For as men naturally perceive a fragrance in the rose, and a sweetness in the honey-comb; so naturally do they discern a heavenly charm and beauty in love.[42]

How does the explicitly Christian content of the Reverend Weems' *Immortal Mentor* impact the question of Washington's views of Christianity?

We believe that it directly impacts the question of Washington's Christianity. Consider again Washington's assessment of Weems' work. Washington wrote to Reverend Weems declaring that he had "perused" (read carefully) his book with "singular satisfaction." In short, he found the book to have been deeply satisfying to his soul. The significance of this statement is that only on one other occasion did Washington ever write such a declaration of approval to a published work. This second instance of Washington's "singular satisfaction" was expressed to the Reverend John Lathrop in regard to the Humane Society's dramatic and successful efforts to save lives from near death situations. He wrote to Reverend Lathrop,

Reverend and respected Sir: Your very acceptable favour of the 16th. of May, covering a recent publication of the proceedings of the Humane Society [of Massachusetts] have, within a few days past, been put into my hands. I observe, with singular satisfaction, the cases in which your benevolent Institution has been instrumental in recalling some of our Fellow creatures (as it were) from beyond the gates of Eternity, and has given occasion for the hearts of parents and friends to leap for joy. The provision made for the preservation of ship-wrecked Mariners is also highly estimable in the view of every philanthropic mind and greatly consolatory to that suffering part of the Community. These things will draw upon you the blessings of those, who were nigh to perish. These works of charity and good-will towards men reflect, in my estimation, great lustre upon the authors and presage an æra of still father improvements. How pitiful, in the eye of reason and religion, is that false ambition which desolates the world with fire and sword for the purposes of conquest and fame; when compared to the milder virtues of making our neighbours and our fellow men as happy as their frail conditions and perishable natures will permit *them to be* ![43]

Thus, Washington greeted Weems' book with the same "singular satisfaction" that he afforded to the Reverend Dr. Lathrop's gift of the report of the Humane Society. The point to be seen here is that the Christian ethic of saving mankind's physical life and the Christian message of saving mankind's spiritual life both brought "singular satisfaction" to Washington's soul.

Washington further declared that he hoped that Weems' book would receive an "extensive patronage," or a broad audience. In his opinion, it was an extremely well-named book, given the selections that were offered. Thus, Washington could delight in and encourage Christian ideas, even though these Christian concepts were circulated by the much maligned Parson Weems.

CONCLUSION: THE REVENGE OF PARSON WEEMS

Whether one agrees or not with Weems' historical writings, it is clear that Washington embraced Weems' theological perspective and had had substantial historical encounters with Weems and his Christian beliefs. This may come as a surprise to many, since no historian who has written on Washington in the last century has even commented on it, let alone considered this evidence of Washington's advocacy of the theology of the consistently ridiculed Reverend Mason Weems. Ironically, Washington here stands as an advocate of Reverend Weems and his theology.

What is the conclusion here? Only a Christian could have taken the views expressed by Washington to a preacher publishing a book with such explicit Christian themes. Washington could not have done so as a Deist.

Scholars know they can't rely on Parson Weems' biography of Washington. Nevertheless, they must trust Washington's own words concerning the Christian book compiled by Parson Weems. With "singular satisfaction," or distinct pleasure, we declare that the only legitimate conclusion that can be drawn from this evidence is that Washington was an advocate of and a believer in the Christian faith.

Conclusion

THIRTY SIX

George Washington's Sacred Fire

*"We ought to be no less persuaded that the propitious smiles
of Heaven can never be expected on a nation that disregards the eternal rules
of order and right, which Heaven itself has ordained: And since the
preservation of the sacred fire of liberty, and the destiny of the Republican
model of Government, are justly considered as deeply, perhaps as
finally staked, on the experiment entrusted to the hands
of the American people."*
George Washington, First Inaugural Address, 1789 [1]

In his First Inaugural Address, Washington explained that an experiment had been entrusted to the American people. What was at stake in America's experiment in self-government was the "preservation of the sacred fire of liberty." This "sacred fire" had been entrusted to Americans by heaven. Liberty's flame was sacred or holy because it was sustained by heaven's "eternal rules of order and right." Washington believed that the great American experiment with the "republican model of government" had no hope of success without regard for these rules and without the aid of the "propitious" or gracious "smiles of Heaven."

711

America's responsibility to keep the divinely given "sacred fire" burning brightly was understood from the birth of our nation. The Continental Congress, of which George Washington was a member, acknowledged this trust in 1774 when they gave their explanation of their understanding of the magnitude of the task on which they were embarking for generations to come,

> ...it is an indispensable duty which we owe to God, our country, ourselves and posterity, by all lawful ways and means in our power to maintain, defend and preserve these civil and religious rights and liberties for which many of our fathers fought, bled and died, and to hand them down entire to future generations.[2]

Is it possible to preserve America's "sacred fire of liberty" if we strip the *divine* from our history and suppress our heroic founders' the concern for the *sacred*?"

THE REPACKAGING OF HISTORY

Reverend Mason Weems, George Washington's first biographer, opened his biography of George Washington with these words: "Go thy way old George. Die when thou wilt, we shall not look upon thy like again."[3] Reverend Weems could never have imagined that his words of praise would be ironically fulfilled by the erasure of Washington's legacy from the minds of America's schoolchildren and the denial of his Christian faith by many of our nation's historians.

But this is happening reflecting the adage that "the living can make the dead do any tricks they find necessary!" The re-creation of George Washington into a Deist has been considered necessary by secular historians in order to create a secular America. This is not to say that everyone who treats Washington as a Deist necessarily subscribes to the theory that the founding fathers were secularists by-and-large. In his book, *A History of the American People,* the esteemed British historian Paul Johnson viewed Washington as a moderate Deist, while Johnson, nevertheless, clearly recognizes the critical role the Christian faith played in the founding of this country.[4] But some scholars have essentially become used to quoting other scholars and have pursued their own original research.[5]

This enterprise of remaking George Washington, in particular, into a Deist has been one of the most successful repackagings of an historical figure ever. But in the process, a great disservice has been done to our founding father. For no longer can it be said that Washington is "first in war, first in peace, and first in the heart of his countrymen." This loss of our historical consciousness of Washington's centrality in our nation's history was preceded by the denial of his Christian faith. Yet the evidence overwhelmingly establishes that Washington was a devout eighteenth century Anglican Christian.

George Washington's Sacred Fire, based on Washington's own words, demonstrates that no other conclusion can honestly and accurately be reached. For if we intend to truly do justice to history, rather than to the hubris of historical revisionism, we must let the words, actions, and primary sources of Washington be determinative in our interpretation of him.

WASHINGTON NEVER CLAIMED TO BE A DEIST

Washington never claimed to be a Deist. In fact, he criticized Deism on various occasions, as we have demonstrated throughout *Sacred Fire* and as summarized below. And further, he openly and repeatedly claimed to be a Christian. His entire life and words opposed the leading themes that Deism sought to establish. Not only did Washington celebrate Christian character, he attacked both publicly and privately the ethics that flowed from Deism. By way of review, Washington's rejection of the foundational tenets of Deism can be seen by the following:

- Deism claimed an absentee God. Washington proclaimed an active God of Providence in history some 270 times;
- Deism rejected divine revelation. Washington declared America's greatest benefit was "the benign light of revelation;" He alluded and referred to the Bible over 200 times;
- Deism held to the non-divinity of Christ. Washington declared Christ to be the "Divine Author of our Blessed religion." Throughout his life, Washington supported Christian missionary efforts, declaring "and above all learn the religion of Jesus Christ."
- Deists considered prayer to be useless. Washington composed over 100 written prayers, openly writing of his "pious," "earnest," and "fervent" prayers. Washington marveled at God's providential care for the American colonies.
- Deism affirmed the equality of all religions. Washington called on America "to imitate" Christ, "the Divine Author of our Blessed Religion," in his "humility, charity, and pacific temper of

mind." He called on Americans to pursue "true religion;" since only in this way could we be "a happy nation."

- Deism sought the exclusion of religion from government. Washington claimed that "true religion is the surest support for government," and that "religion and morality are indispensable supports for political happiness."

- It has been claimed that Washington agreed with Thomas Paine on titles for Deity. But when compared carefully, Washington's robust and extensive theological vocabulary reflects the Christian clergy of his day, and not that of the Deists who had a meager and truncated vocabulary for Deity. Further, he and Paine had a fatal falling-out when Paine committed himself to the Deistic tenets of the French Revolution.

- Deism reflected an anti-clergy spirit that also reflected itself in non-participation in the churches. Washington was a faithful church attendee and superlative vestryman, with literally scores of friends and correspondents who were Christian ministers.

- Washington, in fact, never even used the words "Deist" or "Deism." His closest synonym was "infidel." And when he used that word, he said that a man was "worse than an infidel" who could deny God's Providence in a specific instance during the War. Referring to the same sort of unbelief, he said, "that man is bad indeed." In his Farewell Address, he publicly warned Americans of those whose "peculiar Structure of mind" would lead them to remove the "indispensable supports of religion and morality" from government.

In summation, there is not a hint anywhere in Washington's writings that he ever wanted to be considered anything other than a Christian. His own words show that he desired to be known as an honest man from Virginia who was loyal to his roots, his family, his church, his country, and his God. Those who would transform him into a Deist must produce the requisite written, historical evidence to show that he intended to be viewed as a Deist. Scholars have no authority simply to revise history in an effort to accommodate an increasingly secular America. The facts remain the facts, even when they are manipulated and shaded to hide the truth. And the facts explicitly demonstrate that Washington was a Christian.

We ask every scholar in America this simple request—provide us with only *one* historically verifiable statement from Washington's pen where he declares himself to be a Deist. We only ask for *one*. But the truth is, it cannot be found. There is no evidence for Washington's Deism. It is a scholarly myth. The Deist Washington is an exemplar of the very worst of scholarly, historical revisionism. Meanwhile, as we will reiterate below, there are numerous instances of his professed Christianity.

A SUMMATION OF THE EVIDENCE OF WASHINGTON'S CHRISTIANITY

Throughout *George Washington's Sacred Fire*, we have presented the evidence that proves that George Washington was, without doubt, a Christian. In brief, we have shown that:

1. He was from a British Christian culture and from a Christian family in the Anglican tradition.
2. His childhood home and education were clearly Christian.
3. His military career was layered with liturgical services, prayer, Christian theological terms, and use of the *Book of Common Prayer*.
4. His wife, Martha, was a devout Christian, and her children and George's stepchildren were raised and educated in a Christian environment.
5. He actively served in the leadership of the Anglican Church and sponsored eight children in the Christian sacrament of baptism, something that Thomas Jefferson would not do, because his Unitarianism prevented him from taking the required public vows to the historic Christian faith.
6. He openly encouraged the work of the clergy and chaplains.
7. His theological vocabulary was vast. He spoke of God some one hundred forty times, the divine ninety-five times, heaven one hundred thirty-three times, Providence over two hundred seventy times, and used various honorific titles for God some ninety-five times, and alluded to over two hundred different biblical texts, some

of them scores of times, making the instances of his allusion to scripture to be well over three hundred times. *Thus the total of the theological clues to Washington's faith is over a thousand instances!*

8.   He wrote more than one hundred different prayers in his own hand.

9.   His views of religion are discoverable and include an affirmation of revelation, an understanding of both natural and revealed religion, and a strong belief in religious liberty.

10.   He understood well the spiritual life of man and the work of the Holy Spirit. He frequently revealed his own spiritual concern for prayer, dependence on Providence, and faith and trust in God.

11.   His understanding of the impact of the Enlightenment was revealed in his hostility to *superstition*, but not to the Christian faith. Thus, Washington's writings criticized the deistic thought of his day as we saw above.

12.   Washington's faith can be discovered in spite of his habit and principle of humility and his belief that "deeds not words" should be the measure of the man. As his granddaughter said, "His mottoes were, "Deeds, Not Words;" and "For God and My Country."

13.   Martha, as well as Martha's and George's adopted grandchildren all affirmed that Washington was a Christian.

In addition to the above historical evidence, we have presented Washington's own statements about himself that identify him as a Christian.

WASHINGTON'S STATEMENTS THAT IDENTIFY HIM AS A CHRISTIAN

Here we list only some of the instances where Washington calls himself a Christian.

1.   Washington openly called himself a Christian. He freely wrote

of his own accord, "On my honor and the faith of a Christian...."

2. He encouraged Delaware Indian chiefs that they do well to learn about "the religion of Jesus Christ."

3. He took oaths as a vestryman, which required him to acknowledge his belief in the historic Christian faith as written in *Thirty-Nine Articles of Religion*: As a committed Anglican, Washington regularly prayed the General Confession of the Morning Prayer and worshiped with the *Book of Common Prayer*

4. Washington in various private settings identified himself as a Christian; for example, urging one of his correspondents to be more of "a Man and a Christian."[6]

5. Washington, in public settings, openly identified himself as a Christian, calling on his entire army to be "Christian Soldiers,"[7] and that "to the distinguished Character of Patriot, it should be *our* highest Glory to add the more distinguished Character of Christian."[8] (emphasis added)

6. Writing to every governor of all thirteen of the new American states, he consciously and explicitly prayed as a Christian, saying:

> ...I now make it my earnest prayer, that God would have you and the State over which you preside, in his holy protection, that he would incline the hearts of the Citizens to cultivate a spirit of subordination and obedience to Government, to entertain a brotherly affection and love for one another, for their fellow Citizens of the United States at large, and particularly for their brethren who have served in the Field, and finally, that he would most graciously be pleased to dispose us all, to do Justice, to love mercy, and to demean ourselves with that Charity, humility and pacific temper of mind, which were the Characteristicks of the Divine Author of our blessed Religion, and without an humble imitation of whose example in these

things, we can never hope to be a happy Nation.[9]

Washington never once calls himself a Deist or an unbeliever. Instead, he repeatedly identifies himself as a Christian. Who should we believe—the scholars or Washington?

AN INHERITANCE TO OUR CHILDREN

The impact of the secularist revision of Washington's legacy is profound. To remove Christianity from Washington's life is to take away his "sacred fire." It is to strip him of the core of his essence and to leave him a mere hollow shell of an action hero. Indeed, to uproot Washington from his historical context is to distort Washington's history. Sadly, the living indeed can make the dead do any tricks they find necessary.

In contrast to this secularist revisionism, Washington was viewed very differently both by himself and his contemporaries. Consider, for example, Major General Richard Henry Lee who wrote in 1799,

> Possessing a clear and penetrating mind, a strong and sound judgment, calmness and temper for deliberation, with invincible firmness and perseverance in resolution maturely formed, drawing information from all, acting for himself, with incorruptible integrity and unvarying patriotism: his own superiority and the public confidence alike marked him as the man designed by heaven to lead in the great political as well as military events which have distinguished the era of his life...First in war, first in peace, and first in the hearts of his countrymen, he was second to none in the humble and endearing scenes of private life. Pious, just, humane, temperate, and sincere; uniform, dignified, and commanding, his example was edifying to all around him, as were the effects of that example lasting.[10]

By anyone's standards, this is the description of a man of great character, as well as a man of piety, who should serve as a role model for our children, our citizens, and our statesmen. The list of the moral tributes of his character are striking: Just, humane, incorruptible integrity, drawing information from all, pious, strong, and sound judgment. Indeed President John Adams agreed:

His example is now complete, and it will teach wisdom and virtue to magistrates, citizens, and men, not only in the present age, but in future generations, as long as our history shall be read.[11]

Perhaps Adams should have said, as long as our history is not revised.

THE TESTIMONY OF HIS CONTEMPORARIES

But all of these traits were also formed and informed by Washington's Christian faith. Jonathan Mitchell Sewall, in an oration delivered at Portsmouth, New Hampshire, at the request of the inhabitants wrote:

> To crown all these moral virtues, he had the deepest sense of religion impressed on his heart – the true foundation-stone of all the moral virtues. This he constantly manifested on all proper occasions. He was a firm believer in the Christian religion;…Let the deist reflect on this, and remember that Washington, the saviour of his country, did not disdain to acknowledge and adore a great Saviour, whom deists and infidels affect to slight and despise.[12]

We concur with Sewall, the true foundation stone of all the moral virtues and religion were pressed upon Washington's heart. But this is not hyperbole, for Washington agreed with this assessment as well. He wrote when you "speak of the magnitude of our obligations to the Supreme Director of all human events," "you speak the language of my heart."[13]

And those who knew him best, and experienced him firsthand, agreed. To Timothy Dwight, President of Yale College, the evidence was clear,

> For my own part, I have considered his numerous and uniform public and most solemn declarations of his high veneration for religion, his exemplary and edifying attention to public worship, and his constancy in secret devotion, as proofs, sufficient to satisfy every person, willing to be satisfied. I shall only add that if he was not a Christian, he was more like one than any man of the same description whose life has been hitherto recorded.[14]

Note Timothy Dwight's astute observation; there is sufficient evidence to satisfy every person *willing to be satisfied.* Those who demand and require a Deist Washington will never be satisfied with Washington's own words. They can make the dead do any tricks they find necessary. They will simply refuse to allow their historically unfounded faith to be enlightened by the very words of Washington. To such closed-minded secularists, even though Washington spoke from a soul committed to "honor and the faith of a Christian" his heartfelt words do not matter. The dead Washington must do the tricks the secular historians require. Their view of Washington will not be altered even by the primary sources—the very words of Washington himself.

Yet these high tributes to Washington were not only from individuals alone. We are struck by the declaration of the United States Senate in 1799 at his death:

> Let his countrymen consecrate the memory of the heroic General, the patriotic Statesman, and the virtuous Sage; let them teach their children never to forget that the fruit of his labours and his example are their inheritance.

We believe, as did the Senate in 1799, that Washington was a man whose immense sacrifices and extensive labors for his country deserve better of us who have been entrusted with his legacy. A Christian Washington matters because the Christianity of Washington was the very spirit that put the sacred in Washington's "sacred fire of liberty." Washington knew well that it had been the struggle of the great diversity of Christians seeking to live together in peace that ultimately gave our nation its spirit of religious liberty, and hence our uniqueness as a nation.

AN EYE-WITNESS TESTIMONY OF WASHINGTON'S CHRISTIAN FAITH

When Nelly Custis' father, Jack Custis (George's stepson), died in 1781, George and Martha Washington took her and her younger brother George Washington Parke Custis into their home. Under their care she grew. Her witness of her adopted parents' faith is compelling and yet consistently ignored or diminished by those who claim Washington was a Deist and secularist. We have referred to her testimony repeatedly throughout our study. We cite it here in its entirety so that its full force may be felt. Nelly Custis' testimony is a telling critique of the view that advocates that Washington was a Deist.

...General Washington had a pew in Pohick Church, and one in

Christ Church at Alexandria. He was very instrumental in establishing Pohick Church, and I believe subscribed largely. His pew was near the pulpit...He attended the church at Alexandria when the weather and roads permitted a ride of ten miles. In New York and Philadelphia he never omitted attendance at church in the morning, unless detained by indisposition...No one in church attended to the service with more reverential respect. My grandmother, who was eminently pious, never deviated from her early habits. She always knelt. The General, as was then the custom, stood during the devotional parts of the service. On communion Sundays he left the church with me, after the blessing, and returned home, and we sent the carriage back for my grandmother.

It was his custom to retire to his library at nine or ten o'clock, where he remained an hour before he went to his chamber. He always rose before the sun, and remained in his library until called for breakfast. I never witnessed his private devotions. I never inquired about them. I should have thought it the greatest heresy to doubt his firm belief in Christianity. His life, his writings, prove that he was a Christian. He was not one of those who act or pray, "that they may be seen of men." He communed with his God in secret.

My mother resided two years at Mount Vernon, after her marriage with John Parke Custis, the only son of Mrs. Washington. I have heard her say that General Washington always received the sacrament with my grandmother before the Revolution. When my aunt, Miss Custis, died suddenly at Mount Vernon, before they could realize the event, he knelt by her and prayed most fervently, most affectingly, for her recovery. Of this I was assured by Judge Washington's mother, and other witnesses.

He was a silent, thoughtful man. He spoke little generally; never of himself. I never heard him relate a single act of his life during the war. I have often seen him perfectly abstracted, his lips moving, but no sound was perceptible. I have sometimes made him laugh most heartily from sympathy with my joyous and extravagant spirits. I was, probably, one of the last persons on earth to whom he would have addressed serious conversation, particularly when he knew that I had the most perfect model of female excellence ever with me as my monitress, who acted the part of a tender and devoted parent, loving me as only a mother can love, and never extenuating or approving in me what she disapproved in others. She never omitted her private devotions, or her public duties; she and her husband were so perfectly united and happy that he must have been a Christian. She had no doubts, or fears for him. After forty years of devoted affection and uninterrupted happiness, she resigned him without a murmur into the arms of his Saviour and his God, with the assured hope of eternal felicity. Is it necessary that any one should certify, "General Washington avowed himself to *me* a believer in Christianity"? As well may we question his patriotism, his heroic, disinterested devotion to his country. His mottoes were, "Deeds, Not Words"; and "For God and My Country."

With sentiments of esteem,

I am,

Nelly Custis[15]

Our challenge to the secularist interpreters of Washington is not just to refute Nelly Custis' testimony, but to find merely one statement where Washington claimed to be a Deist. To question Washington's patriotism is absurd. Nelly Custis declares it is just as absurd to question his Christianity.

SACRED FIRE VS. WILDFIRE

The "sacred fire of liberty" that Washington knew and shared with his nation is not in danger of burning out. Instead the danger is that the "sacred fire" is rapidly becoming a secular fire. The eternal flame of the torch of liberty is not burning low; instead, it is in danger of burning out of control. It is like what Washington experienced as a youth when he wrote in his diary on April 2, 1747, "Saterday 2d Last Night was a blowing and Rainy night Our Straw catch'd a Fire that we were laying upon and was luckily Preserved by one of our Mens awaking when it was in a [blaze]."[16]

There is a crucial difference between the sacred and the secular, between a sacred fire and a secular fire, between a fire in the hearth and a fire on the roof, between a Christian Washington and a secular Washington. It is the difference between ordered liberty and moral anarchy, between liberty and licentiousness. Licentiousness is an abuse of liberty. It is a spirit of anything goes. In contrast, Washington believed in ordered liberty, liberty under God's law. Washington was keenly conscious of the

722

distinction between liberty and licentiousness. He addressed this point on various occasions. To the states he wrote:

> We shall be left nearly in a state of Nature, or we may find by our own unhappy experience, that there is a natural and necessary progression, from the extreme of anarchy to the extreme of Tyranny; and that arbitrary power is most easily established on the ruins of Liberty abused to licentiousness.[17]

To John Augustine Washington, he explained,

> Liberty, when it degenerates into licenciousness, begets confusion, and frequently ends in Tyranny or some woeful catastrophe....[18]

In his First Inaugural Address, he declared,

> ...every valuable end of Government is best answered by the enlightened confidence of the people: and by teaching the people themselves ... to discriminate the spirit of Liberty from that of licentiousness, cherishing the first, avoiding the last, and uniting a speedy, but temperate vigilance against encroachments, with an inviolable respect to the Laws.[19]

The difference between "the spirit of liberty" and "licentiousness" is the difference between Washington's "sacred fire of liberty" and the licentious secular fire of Deists like Thomas Paine. This is profoundly illustrated by the differences between the revolutionary "sacred fire" ignited by the American Revolution and the revolutionary wild fire unleashed by the French Revolution which resulted in widespread bloodshed. As we have seen, the differences between religion and morality vs. secularism were a theme often addressed in the sermons that Washington approved. Washington believed that the fires of reason and the fiery passions of a society without the presence of the sacred, refining fire of faith would always burn out of control. A fire lit by human passions alone would be a blaze without limits, without direction, and leave devastation and carnage behind.

George Washington's "sacred fire of liberty" was sacred, precisely because of his ardent Christian faith. He understood that the American nation, under God, possessed a sacred fire to energize, guide, and sustain its "experiment in the republican model of government" that was "finally staked" on the experience and experiment of the American people.

"THE SPIRIT OF LIBERTY"

America's experiment in liberty continues. The question is whether we will light our future with Washington's "sacred fire of liberty" or the wildfire of a culture marked by a rootless, historical amnesia. Washington did not, Prometheus-like, steal the "fire of liberty" from heaven. He received it as a "sacred fire," a divine gift informed by "the eternal rules of order and right, which *Heaven itself has ordained*." (emphasis ours)

Washington knew that the divine flame of freedom would not light the path of a happy nation unless that nation pursued "justice and loved mercy." And further, Washington called upon his nation to follow the "humility, charity and pacific temper of mind" of Jesus Christ as their great example. For this "Divine Author" of Washington's "blessed religion" was the ultimate source of America's "sacred fire of liberty." That which made them a "happy nation."

And finally, the phrase "sacred fire of liberty" manifests Washington's common practice of biblical allusion. "The sacred fire of liberty" is clearly suggested by the sacred book that Washington knew so well. In the Bible, 2 Corinthians 3:17 says, "Now the Lord is that Spirit, and where the Spirit of the Lord is, there is liberty"(KJV). Here is the source of Washington's spirituality and the fuel for his "sacred fire of liberty."

"The preservation of the sacred fire of liberty" Washington said was "entrusted to the hands of the American people." As keepers of this sacred fire, let us never forget that the "destiny of the republican model of government" is "deeply" and "finally" staked" on us, and what we do with the divine gift of liberty. What can we do to assure that the sacred fire will burn as an eternal flame? Clearly, we must pass it on by educating the next generation. Washington understood the power of his legacy for the future generations. Referring to his Congressional Commission to command the Revolutionary Army, he wrote, "If my commission is not necessary for the files of Congress, I should be glad to have it deposited amongst my own papers. It may serve *my grand children* some fifty or a hundred years hence for a theme to ruminate upon, *if they should be* contemplatively disposed."[20] (emphasis in original)

So once and for all, let us refuse to allow the secular revision of our history to extinguish the sacred in the life of Washington. The task is daunting to be sure. But our founding father's words inspire us to press on to success:

As the cause of our common Country, calls us both to an active and dangerous duty, I trust that Divine Providence, which wisely orders the affairs of men, will enable us to discharge it with fidelity and success.[21]

Washington's "sacred fire" can and must burn brightly again.

Appendices

APPENDIX ONE

The Rules of Civility and Decent Behaviour in Company and Conversation

George Washington, sometime before the age of sixteen, transcribed these *Rules of Civility & Decent Behaviour In Company and Conversation*. Most historians of Washington see a great deal of consistency between his life and these rules for "civility and decent behaviour." The evidence is also clear that Washington's father, Augustine, and his two older half brothers were exposed to these rules as well, since they were part of the basic education of the Appleby School in England, where both boys had been educated. Rules 108 to 110 lay the groundwork for a life of exemplary piety. (Original errors in numbering have been corrected; original spelling is unchanged.)[1]

1ST: Every Action done in Company, ought to be with Some Sign of Respect, to those that are Present.

2ND: When in Company, put not your Hands to any Part of the Body, not usually Discovered.

3RD: Shew Nothing to your Freind that may affright him.

4TH: In the Presence of Others Sing not to yourself with a humming Noise, nor Drum with your Fingers or Feet.

5TH: If You Cough, Sneeze, Sigh, or Yawn, do it not Loud but Privately; and Speak not in your Yawning, but put Your handkercheif or Hand before your face and turn aside.

6TH: Sleep not when others Speak, Sit not when others stand, Speak not when you Should hold your Peace, walk not on when others Stop.

7TH: Put not off your Cloths in the presence of Others, nor go out your Chamber half Drest.

8TH: At Play and at Fire its Good manners to Give Place to the last Commer, and affect not to Speak Louder than Ordinary.

9TH: Spit not in the Fire, nor Stoop low before it neither Put your Hands into the Flames to warm them, nor Set your Feet upon the Fire especially if there be meat before it.

10TH: When you Sit down, Keep your Feet firm and Even, without putting one on the other or Crossing them.

11TH: Shift not yourself in the Sight of others nor Gnaw your nails.

12TH: Shake not the head, Feet, or Legs rowl not the Eys lift not one eyebrow higher than the other wry not the mouth, and bedew no mans face with your Spittle, by approaching too near him when you Speak.

13TH: Kill no Vermin as Fleas, lice ticks &c in the Sight of Others, if you See any filth or thick Spittle put your foot Dexteriously upon it if it be upon the Cloths of your Companions, Put it off privately, and if it be upon your own Cloths return Thanks to him who puts it off.

14TH: Turn not your Back to others especially in Speaking, Jog not the Table or Desk on which Another reads or writes, lean not upon any one.

15TH: Keep your Nails clean and Short, also your Hands and Teeth Clean yet without Shewing any great Concern for them.

16TH: Do not Puff up the Cheeks, Loll not out the tongue rub the Hands, or beard, thrust out the lips, or bite them or keep the Lips too open or too Close.

17TH: Be no Flatterer, neither Play with any that delights not to be Play'd Withal.

18TH: Read no Letters, Books, or Papers in Company but when there is a Necessity for the doing of it you must ask leave: come not near the Books or Writings of Another so as to read them unless desired or give your opinion of them unask'd also look not nigh when another is writing a Letter.

19TH: let your Countenance be pleasant but in Serious Matters Somewhat grave.

20TH: The Gestures of the Body must be Suited to the discourse you are upon.

21ST: Reproach none for the Infirmaties of Nature, nor Delight to Put them that have in mind thereof.

22ND: Shew not yourself glad at the Misfortune of another though he were your enemy.

23RD: When you see a Crime punished, you may be inwardly Pleased; but always shew Pity to the Suffering Offender.

24TH: Do not laugh too loud or too much at any Publick Spectacle.

25TH: Superfluous Complements and all Affectation of Ceremonie are to be avoided, yet where due they are not to be Neglected.

26TH: In Pulling off your Hat to Persons of Distinction, as Noblemen, Justices, Churchmen &c make a Reverence, bowing more or less according to the Custom of the Better Bred, and Quality of the Person. Amongst your equals expect not always that they Should begin with you first, but to Pull off the Hat when there is no need is Affectation, in the Manner of Saluting and resaluting in words keep to the most usual Custom.

27TH: Tis ill manners to bid one more eminent than yourself be covered as well as not to do it to whom it's due Likewise he that makes too much haste to Put on his hat does not well, yet he ought to Put it on at the first, or at most the Second time of being ask'd; now what is herein Spoken, of Qualification in behaviour in Saluting, ought also to be observed in taking of Place, and Sitting down for ceremonies without Bounds is troublesome.

28TH: If any one come to Speak to you while you are are Sitting Stand up tho he be your Inferiour, and when you Present Seats let it be to every one according to his Degree.

29TH: When you meet with one of Greater Quality than yourself, Stop, and retire especially if it be at a Door or any Straight place to give way for him to Pass.

30TH: In walking the highest Place in most Countrys Seems to be on the right hand therefore Place yourself on the left of him whom you desire to Honour: but if three walk together the middest Place is the most Honourable the wall is usually given to the most worthy if two walk together.

31ST: If any one far Surpassess others, either in age, Estate, or Merit yet would give Place to a meaner than himself in his own lodging or elsewhere the one ought not to except it, So he on the other part should not use much earnestness nor offer it above once or twice.

32ND: To one that is your equal, or not much inferior you are to give the cheif Place in your Lodging and he to who 'tis offered ought at the first to refuse it but at the Second to accept though not without acknowledging his own unworthiness.

33RD: They that are in Dignity or in office have in all places Preceedency but whilst they are Young they ought to respect those that are their equals in Birth or other Qualitys, though they have no Publick charge.

34TH: It is good Manners to prefer them to whom we Speak before ourselves especially if they be above us with whom in no Sort we ought to begin.

35TH: Let your Discourse with Men of Business be Short and Comprehensive.

36TH: Artificers & Persons of low Degree ought not to use many ceremonies to Lords, or Others of high Degree but Respect and highly Honour them, and those of high Degree ought to treat them with affibility & Courtesie, without Arrogancy.

37TH: In Speaking to men of Quality do not lean nor Look them full in the Face, nor approach too near them at lest Keep a full Pace from them.

38TH: In visiting the Sick, do not Presently play the Physicion if you be not Knowing therein.

39TH: In writing or Speaking, give to every Person his due Title According to his Degree & the Custom of the Place.

40TH: Strive not with your Superiers in argument, but always Submit your Judgment to others with Modesty.

41ST: Undertake not to Teach your equal in the art himself Proffesses; it Savours of arrogancy.

42ND: Let thy ceremonies in Courtesie be proper to the Dignity of his place with whom thou conversest for it is absurd to act the same with a Clown and a Prince.

43RD: Do not express Joy before one sick or in pain for that contrary Passion will aggravate his Misery.

44TH: When a man does all he can though it Succeeds not well blame not him that did it.

45TH: Being to advise or reprehend any one, consider whether it ought to be in publick or in Private; presently, or at Some other time in what terms to do it & in reproving Shew no Sign of Cholar but do it with all Sweetness and Mildness.

46TH: Take all Admonitions thankfully in what Time or Place Soever given but afterwards not being culpable take a Time & Place convenient to let him him know it that gave them.

47TH: Mock not nor Jest at any thing of Importance break no Jest that are Sharp Biting and if you Deliver any thing witty and Pleasent abstain from Laughing there at yourself.

48TH: Wherein you reprove Another be unblameable yourself; for example is more prevalent than Precepts.

49TH: Use no Reproachfull Language against any one neither Curse nor Revile.

50TH: Be not hasty to beleive flying Reports to the Disparagement of any.

51ST: Wear not your Cloths, foul, unript or Dusty but See they be Brush'd once every day at least and take heed that you approach not to any Uncleaness.

52ND: In your Apparel be Modest and endeavour to accomodate Nature, rather than to procure Admiration keep to the Fashion of your equals Such as are Civil and orderly with respect to Times and Places.

53RD: Run not in the Streets, neither go too slowly nor with Mouth open go not Shaking yr Arms kick not the earth with yr feet, go not upon the Toes, nor in a Dancing fashion.

54TH: Play not the Peacock, looking every where about you, to See if you be well Deck't, if your Shoes fit well if your Stokings sit neatly, and Cloths handsomely.

55TH: Eat not in the Streets, nor in the House, out of Season.

56TH: Associate yourself with Men of good Quality if you Esteem your own Reputation; for 'tis better to be alone than in bad Company.

57TH: In walking up and Down in a House, only with One in Company if he be Greater than yourself, at the first give him the Right hand and Stop not till he does and be not the first that turns, and when you do turn let it be with your face towards him, if he be a Man of Great Quality, walk not with him Cheek by Joul but Somewhat behind him; but yet in Such a Manner that he may easily Speak to you.

58TH: Let your Conversation be without Malice or Envy, for 'tis a Sign of a Tractable and Commendable Nature: And in all Causes of Passion admit Reason to Govern.

59TH: Never express anything unbecoming, nor Act agst the Rules Moral before your inferiours.

60TH: Be not immodest in urging your Freinds to Discover a Secret.

61ST: Utter not base and frivilous things amongst grave and Learn'd Men nor very Difficult Questians or Subjects, among the Ignorant or things hard to be believed, Stuff not your Discourse with Sentences amongst your Betters nor Equals.

62ND: Speak not of doleful Things in a Time of Mirth or at the Table; Speak not of Melancholy Things as Death and Wounds, and if others Mention them Change if you can the Discourse tell not your Dreams, but to your intimate Friend.

63RD: A Man ought not to value himself of his Atchievements, or rare Qualities of wit; much less of his riches Virtue or Kindred.

64TH: Break not a Jest where none take pleasure in mirth Laugh not aloud, nor at all without Occasion, deride no mans Misfortune, tho' there Seem to be Some cause.

65TH: Speak not injurious Words neither in Jest nor Earnest Scoff at none although they give Occasion.

66TH: Be not forward but friendly and Courteous; the first to Salute hear and answer & be not Pensive when it's a time to Converse.

67TH: Detract not from others neither be excessive in Commanding.

68TH: Go not thither, where you know not, whether you Shall be Welcome or not. Give not Advice without being Ask'd & when desired do it briefly.

69TH: If two contend together take not the part of either unconstrained; and be not obstinate in your own Opinion, in Things indiferent be of the Major Side.

70TH: Reprehend not the imperfections of others for that belongs to Parents Masters and Superiours.

71ST: Gaze not on the marks or blemishes of Others and ask not how they came. What you may Speak in Secret to your Friend deliver not before others.

72ND: Speak not in an unknown Tongue in Company but in your own Language and that as those of Quality do and not as the Vulgar; Sublime matters treat Seriously.

73RD: Think before you Speak pronounce not imperfectly nor bring out your Words too hastily but orderly & distinctly.

74TH: When Another Speaks be attentive your Self and disturb not the Audience if any hesitate in his Words help him not nor Prompt him without desired, Interrupt him not, nor Answer him till his Speech be ended.

75TH: In the midst of Discourse ask not of what one treateth but if you Perceive any Stop because of your coming you may well intreat him gently to Proceed: If a Person of Quality comes in while your Conversing it's handsome to Repeat what was said before.

76TH: While you are talking, Point not with your Finger at him of Whom you Discourse nor Approach too near him to whom you talk especially to his face.

77TH: Treat with men at fit Times about Business & Whisper not in the Company of Others.

78TH: Make no Comparisons and if any of the Company be Commended for any brave act of Vertue, commend not another for the Same.

79TH: Be not apt to relate News if you know not the truth thereof. In Discoursing of things you Have heard Name not your Author always A Secret Discover not.

80TH: Be not Tedious in Discourse or in reading unless you find the Company pleased therewith.

81ST: Be not Curious to Know the Affairs of Others neither approach those that Speak in Private.

82ND: Undertake not what you cannot perform but be carefull to keep your promise.

83RD: When you deliver a matter do it without passion & with discretion, however mean the person be you do it too.

84TH: When your Superiours talk to any Body hearken not neither Speak nor Laugh.

85TH: In Company of these of Higher Quality than yourself Speak not til you are ask'd a Question then Stand upright put of your Hat & Answer in few words.

86TH: In Disputes, be not So Desireous to Overcome as not to give Liberty to each one to deliver his Opinion and Submit to the Judgment of the Major Part especially if they are Judges of the Dispute.

87TH: Let thy carriage be such as becomes a Man Grave Settled and attentive to that which is spoken. Contradict not at every turn what others Say.

88TH: Be not tedious in Discourse, make not many Digressigns, nor repeat often the Same manner of Discourse.

89TH: Speak not Evil of the absent for it is unjust.

90TH: Being Set at meat Scratch not neither Spit Cough or blow your Nose except there's a Necessity for it.

91ST: Make no Shew of taking great Delight in your Victuals, Feed not with Greediness; cut your Bread with a Knife, lean not on the Table neither find fault with what you Eat.

92ND: Take no Salt or cut Bread with your Knife Greasy.

93RD: Entertaining any one at table it is decent to present him wt. meat, Undertake not to help others undesired by the Master.

94TH: If you Soak bread in the Sauce let it be no more than what you put in your Mouth at a time and blow not your broth at Table but Stay till Cools of it Self.

95TH: Put not your meat to your Mouth with your Knife in your hand neither Spit forth the Stones of any fruit Pye upon a Dish nor Cast anything under the table.

96TH: It's unbecoming to Stoop much to ones Meat Keep your Fingers clean & when foul wipe them on a Corner of your Table Napkin.

97TH: Put not another bit into your Mouth til the former be Swallowed let not your Morsels be too big for the Gowls.

98TH: Drink not nor talk with your mouth full neither Gaze about you while you are a Drinking.

99TH: Drink not too leisurely nor yet too hastily. Before and after Drinking wipe your Lips breath not then or Ever with too Great a Noise, for its uncivil.

100TH: Cleanse not your teeth with the Table Cloth Napkin Fork or Knife but if Others do it let it be done wt. a Pick Tooth.

101ST: Rince not your Mouth in the Presence of Others.

102ND: It is out of use to call upon the Company often to Eat nor need you Drink to others every Time you Drink.

103RD: In Company of your Betters be not longer in eating than they are lay not your Arm but only your hand upon the table.

104TH: It belongs to the Chiefest in Company to unfold his Napkin and fall to Meat first, But he ought then to Begin in time & to Dispatch with Dexterity that the Slowest may have time allowed him.

105TH: Be not Angry at Table whatever happens & if you have reason to be so, Shew it not but on a Chearfull Countenance especially if there be Strangers for Good

Humour makes one Dish of Meat a Feast.

106TH: Set not yourself at the upper of the Table but if it Be your Due or that the Master of the house will have it So, Contend not, least you Should Trouble the Company.

107TH: If others talk at Table be attentive but talk not with Meat in your Mouth.

108TH: When you Speak of God or his Atributes, let it be Seriously & wt. Reverence. Honour & Obey your Natural Parents altho they be Poor.

109TH: Let your Recreations be Manfull not Sinfull.

110TH: Labour to keep alive in your Breast that Little Spark of Celestial fire Called Conscience.

Representative Biblical Quotations and Allusions used by George Washington

All quotations are from the *Writings of Washington*, unless otherwise noted.
PGW refers to the *Papers of George Washington* at the Library of Congress

Biblical Text Used By Washington; Never Cited By Chapter & Verse	Closest Scriptural References In King James Version	Nature of Use of Scripture by Washington	Examples Found in the Writings of Washington	Comments
Replenish the earth	Genesis 1:28; 9:7	Allusion	Vol. 29, 4-25-1788	US West to be inhabited
Sin with their Eyes open	Genesis 3:5-7	Allusion	Vol. 31, 6-19-1791	
Once the Woman has tempted us and we have tasted the forbidden fruit,	Genesis 3:6-7	Allusion	Vol. 27, 9-2-1783	Used in humor of poetry
Sweat of the brow	Genesis 3:19	Quotation	Vol. 35, 7-12-1797	
Return to dust	Genesis 3:19	Allusion	Vol. 28, 10-16-1785	
By description and descent almost from Adam	Genesis 5:1ff	Allusion	Vol. 24, 4-20-1782	
Swept from the face of the earth	Genesis 6:7	Allusion	Vol. 29, 11-5-1786	Expression of judgment
Noah	Genesis 6—9	Allusion	Vol. 37, 8-28-1762	In humor
Bird with olive branch	Genesis 8:11	Allusion	Vol. 29, 7-20-1787	Weather vane at Mount Vernon
Measure of iniquity	Genesis 15:16	Allusion	Vol. 14, 3-31-1779	
Doctrine of Providence	Genesis 22:14	Theological summary	Vol. 12, 8-20-1778	Washington's favorite theological doctrine. Used some 270x.
Solemn covenants	Genesis 26:28	Theological summary	Vol. 13, 12-17-1778	Reflects the Scottish Presbyterian Tradition of the "Solemn League and Covenant"
Water with dews from heaven	Genesis 27:28	Allusion	PGW, Letterbook 38, Image 147	
Poor, needy, oppressed	Genesis 35:10	Theological summary	Vol. 27, 9-2-1783	

Biblical Text Used By Washington; Never Cited By Chapter & Verse	Closest Scriptural References In King James Version	Nature of Use of Scripture by Washington	Examples Found in the Writings of Washington	Comments
The fat of the land	Genesis 45:18	Allusion	Vol. 1, 4-22-1756	
Until I arrive at the end of my pilgrimage.	Genesis 47:9	Allusion	Vol. 32, 9-26-1792	
Temporal and spiritual blessings	Genesis 49:25; Ephesians 1:3	Popular saying	Vol. 25, 11-16-1782; Vol. 27, 11-10-1783	
Staff in your hand	Exodus 4:2	Allusion	Vol. 25, 9-4-1782	Used 3x
Edict of Pharaoh—bricks without straw	Exodus 5:6-7	Allusion	Vol. 21, 3-21-1781	
Jehovah	Exodus 6:3	Quotation	*PGW*, Letterbook 38, Image 147	To synagogue in Savannah
Powerful to save	Exodus 14:30-31	Allusion	Vol. 4, Answer to an Address	
Delivering Hebrews from oppressors	Exodus 15:11	Allusion	*PGW*, Letterbook 38, Image 147	To synagogue in Savannah
Rules of Decalogue	Exodus 20:1-17	Christian saying	Vol. 27, 9-2-1783	In humor
Religious obligation deserts the oaths	Exodus 20:7	Theological summary	Vol. 35, 9-19-1796	Farewell Address
Day of rest	Exodus 20:8-11	Christian saying	Vol. 31, 6-26-1791	
Six days do I labor	Exodus 20:9	Quotation	Vol. 37, 4-23-1799	
I shall not covet	Exodus 20:17	Quotation	Vol. 33, 3-31-1794	
Charity toward fellow creature	Leviticus 19:18	Allusion	Vol. 8, 6-10-1777	General Orders

Biblical Text Used By Washington; Never Cited By Chapter & Verse	Closest Scriptural References In King James Version	Nature of Use of Scripture by Washington	Examples Found in the Writings of Washington	Comments
Seven times seven years	Leviticus 25:8	Allusion	Vol. 3, 6-18-1775	
Blessings of peace	Numbers 6:23-26	Allusion	Vol. 21, 4-15-1781	
Holy keeping	Numbers 6:24-26; Psalm 121:5; Isaiah 6:3.	Christian saying	Vol. 27, 12-23-1783	benediction used often in letters to royalty
Spy out the land	Numbers 13:17, 13:2	Quote	Vol. 27, 10-12-1783	Used 2x
Land of promise flowing with milk and honey	Numbers 13:27	Allusion	Vol. 28, 7-25-1785	
I shall not depart from it by turning either to the right or to the left,	Deuteronomy 2:27	Quotation	Vol. 32, 9-26-1792	
Promised land	Deuteronomy 9:28	Allusion	Vol. 28, 7-25-1785	The US Western frontier
Dwell in the land	Deuteronomy 12:10	Allusion	Vol. 31, 8-14-1790	
Classed among the false prophets, and suffer for evil prediction	Deuteronomy 13:1-5; 18:19-22	Allusion	Vol. 28, 2-8-1785	
Justifiable in the eyes of God and man	Deuteronomy 16:18-20; Acts 4:19	Allusion	Vol. 24, 4-21-1782	Divine law is important for human law
Care of the widow and the fatherless	Deuteronomy 24:19-20	Allusion	Vol. 30, 12-8-1788	
First fruit	Deuteronomy 26:2	Allusion	Vol. 10, 2-8-1778; Vol. 33, 4-11-1794	Used 6x
An outstretched arm to help	Deuteronomy 26:8	Allusion	Vol. 37, 11-22-1799	A symbol used by an early American war flag

Biblical Text Used By Washington; Never Cited By Chapter & Verse	Closest Scriptural References In King James Version	Nature of Use of Scripture by Washington	Examples Found in the Writings of Washington	Comments
Blessing or curse	Deuteronomy 28	Allusion	Vol. 26, 6-8-1783	
Byword in all the earth	Deuteronomy 28:37	Popular saying	Vol. 29, 12-26-1786	A phrase also used by Franklin at the Constitutional Convention
Planted in promised land	Joshua 22:14	Allusion	*PGW*, Letterbook 38, Image 147	
Scourge to mankind	Joshua 23:13	Allusion	Vol. 28, 5-10-1786	
Thorn in side	Joshua 23:13	Allusion	Vol. 29, 3-31-1787	
Providence which needs not the aid of numbers	Judges 7:14	Allusion	Vol. 5, 8-13-1776	
A willing sacrifice	Judges 11:30-36	Allusion	Vol. 1, 4-22-1756	Referring to himself in battle with Indians
Rise as one man	Judges 20:8	Allusion	Vol. 10, 11-20-1777	
Lord of Hosts	1 Samuel 1:3	Quotation	Vol. 4, 3-6-1776	
Providential agency conspicuous	1 Samuel 2:7; Psalm 75:7; Isaiah. 55:5; Daniel. 2:21, 37	Theological affirmation	Vol. 12, 8-20-1778	Used 4x
Second sight	1 Samuel 9:9	Allusion	Vol. 26, 3-31-1783	Used 3x
Powers of hell	1 Samuel 16:15-16; Matthew 16:18	Allusion	Vol. 30, 2-5-1789	Power of music over such
Strength of a giant	1 Samuel 17:4-11; Job 16:14	Allusion	Vol. 35, 5-15-1796	

Biblical Text Used By Washington; Never Cited By Chapter & Verse	Closest Scriptural References In King James Version	Nature of Use of Scripture by Washington	Examples Found in the Writings of Washington	Comments
God of Armies	1 Samuel 17:45	Quotation	Vol. 7, 4-15-1777	In farewell to Army
Vine and fig tree	1 Kings 4:25	Allusion	Vol. 29, 6-19-1788	Washington's favorite biblical image
Double portion	2 Kings 2:9	Allusion	Vol. 15, 5-7-1779	
To blind the eyes of our enemies	2 Kings 6:12-20	Allusion	Vol. 4, 1-14-1776	Note parallel of war contexts
At such a time as this	Esther 4:14	Quotation	Vol. 5, 8-8-1776	
Hung in Gibbets upon a gallows five times as high as the one prepared by Haman	Esther 6:4	Allusion	Vol. 13, 12-12-1778	
Becomes the creatures to submit with patience and resignation to the will of the Creator	Job 1:21; 2:10	Theological summary	Vol. 32, 1-27-1793	
The Lord gives and takes	Job 1:21	Allusion	Fields, *Worthy Partner* p. 339	Letter from Martha at George's death
Recoil on their own heads	Psalm 7:15-16	Allusion	Vol. 5, 7-20-1776	
Goodness and mercy	Psalm 23:6	Quotation	Vol. 11, 4-12-1778	
All the days of your life	Psalm 23:6	Allusion	Vol. 33, 11-3-1793	
Ascribe glory	Psalm 29:1; 68:34	Allusion	Vol. 27, 12-13-1783	
Silent as the grave	Psalm 31:17	Allusion	Vol. 12, 7-3-1778	

Biblical Text Used By Washington; Never Cited By Chapter & Verse	Closest Scriptural References In King James Version	Nature of Use of Scripture by Washington	Examples Found in the Writings of Washington	Comments
People whose God is Jehovah	Psalm 33:12	Quotation	PGW, Letterbook 38, Image 147	To Jewish synagogue
Causing the rage of war to cease amongst the nations	Psalm 46:6-9	Quotation	Vol. 26, 4-18-1783	
Over ruling the wrath of man to his own glory	Psalm 76:10	Theological summary	Vol. 26, 4-18-1783	
Holy-land	Psalm 78:54	Popular saying	Vol. 10, 1-23-1778	To Rev. William Gordon
Verging towards three score and ten	Psalm 90:10	Allusion	Vol. 37, 7-21-1799	
Rising of the sun to the setting of the same	Psalm 113:3; 50:1	Quotation	Vol. 36, 12-3-1797	
Scatter light and not darkness	Psalm 119:105; Proverbs 4:18	Allusion	PGW, Letterbook 38, Image 147	To Jewish synagogue
Slumber nor sleep	Psalm 121:4	Allusion	Vol. 13, 12-18-1778	
Dwell together in more charity	Psalm 133:1	Allusion	Vol. 30, 8-18-1789	To the General Convention of Protestant Episcopal Church
Above all, the benign light of revelation	Psalm 138:2	Theological summary	Vol. 26, 6-8-1783	Phrase aimed at Deism
Searcher of human hearts	Psalm 139:23	Allusion	Vol. 30, 12-23-1788	
The wise man...his whole book	Proverbs 1:5; Ecclesiastes. 12:9	Direct reference to author of Proverbs	Vol. 30, 1-18-1790	Washington's favorite biblical book was Proverbs

Biblical Text Used By Washington; Never Cited By Chapter & Verse	Closest Scriptural References In King James Version	Nature of Use of Scripture by Washington	Examples Found in the Writings of Washington	Comments
Six troubles yea seven	Proverbs 6:16	Allusion	Vol. 30, 8-28-1788	
Whether to prolong or to shorten the number of our days.	Proverbs 10:27; Psalm 90:12	Allusion	Vol. 32, 1-27-1793	
Beware of surety-ship	Proverbs 11:15; 17:18	Quotation	Vol. 30, 1-18-1790	Washington's "favorite" verse
Righteousness that exalteth a nation	Proverbs 14:34	Quotation	PGW, 2:179-181	
For political prosperity, religion, and morality are indispensable	Proverbs 14:34	Theological summary	Vol. 35, 9-19-1796	Farewell Address
Charity may throw her mantle	Proverbs 17:9	Paraphrase	Vol. 35, 5-15-1796	
Turn preacher	Ecclesiastes 1:1-2	Allusion	Vol. 12, 8-20-1778	Washington is speaking of himself
any people (nation) under the Sun	Ecclesiastes 1:3	Allusions	Vol. 32, 8-26-1792	Used 8x
As the wise man has said "may be all vanity and vexation of spirit,"	Ecclesiastes 1:4	Quotation	Vol. 36, 12-3-1797	
"There is a time for all things," and sure I am this is not a time for a *boy of your age* to enter into engagements which might end in sorrow and repentance.	Ecclesiastes 3:1	Quotation	Vol. 36, 6-13-1798	To grandson
In His good time	Ecclesiastes 3:11	Quotation	Vol. 9, 10-19-1777	
Vows to heaven	Ecclesiastes 5:4	Theological summary	Vol. 35, 5-6-1796	One of Washington's synonyms for prayer

Biblical Text Used By Washington; Never Cited By Chapter & Verse	Closest Scriptural References In King James Version	Nature of Use of Scripture by Washington	Examples Found in the Writings of Washington	Comments
The race to the swift, the battle to the strong	Ecclesiastes 9:11	Quotation	Vol. 23, 1-31-82	
Creator	Ecclesiastes 12	Title for deity	Vol. 27, 12-13-1783; Vol. 30, 9-13-1789	
Obligations which are enjoined by your Creator and due to his creatures,	Ecclesiastes 12:1	Allusion	Vol. 35, 11-28-1796	To grandson
Vale of years	Ecclesiastes 12:27	Allusion	Vol. 30, 7-21-1788	
If this maxim was generally adopted Wars would soon cease, and our swords would soon be converted into reap-hooks, and our harvests be more abundant, peaceful, and happy.	Isaiah 2	Allusion	Vol. 34, 12-24-1795	
After our swords and spears have given place to the plough share	Isaiah 2:4	Quotation	Vol. 16, 9-30-1779	To Marquis de Lafayette
And as the Scripture expresses it, "The nations learn war no more"	Isaiah 2:4	Quotation	Vol. 25, 4-29-1788	To Marquis de Chastellux
Swords might be turned into pruning hooks…learn war no more	Isaiah 2:4	Quotation	Vol. 25, 4-29-1788	
Peace of mind	Isaiah 26:3	Allusion	Vol. 6, 9-24-1776	
Everlastingly happy	Isaiah 35:10	Allusion	*PGW*, Letterbook 38, Image 147	To the Hebrew congregation
Broken reed	Isaiah 36:6	Allusion	Vol. 14, 3-20-1779	
Ways preparing, roads will be made easy	Isaiah 40:3	Allusion	Vol. 28, 7-25-1785	To Marquis de Lafayette

Biblical Text Used By Washington; Never Cited By Chapter & Verse	Closest Scriptural References In King James Version	Nature of Use of Scripture by Washington	Examples Found in the Writings of Washington	Comments
Dust in the balance	Isaiah 40:15	Popular saying	Vol. 37, 7-21-1799	
Crying peace, peace	Jeremiah 6:14	Quotation	Vol. 37, 12-25-1798	
No peace in Israel	Jeremiah 6:14	Allusion	Vol. 37, 8-30-1799	To Gov. Trumbull
Engraved on the heart	Jeremiah 31:33	Allusion	Vol. 33, 5-26-1794	
If you can't find it in Israel, look for it in the Book of Ezekiel	Ezekiel	Allusion	PGW, April 13, 1748, Image 2 of 70	Earliest reference to Scripture in Washington—in surveyor's book
Eye of tender pity	Ezekiel 16:5-6; Psalm 103:13	Allusion	Vol. 4, no date	Answer to an address from the Massachusetts Legislature
Reclaim the wicked	Ezekiel 33:11	Allusion	Vol. 33, 9-25-1794	
Same wonder-working deity	Daniel 4:3	Theological summary	PGW, Letterbook 38, Image 147	Jehovah has blessed America even as Israel
Storms for wise purposes	Jonah 1:4	Allusion	Vol. 12, 9-6-1778	
None to make afraid	Micah 4:4	Quotation	Vol. 31, 8-14-1790	In letter Jewish synagogue
Do justice, love mercy	Micah 6:8	Quotation	Vol., 26, 6-8-1783	
Those who run may read	Habakkuk 2:2	Quotation	Vol. 37, 5-29-1797	
Please God to spare your life	Malachi 3:17	Allusion	Vol., 35, 11-28-1796	To grandson
Angels and men	Matthew 2:11-13	Christian saying	Vol. 26, 4-18-1783.	Seeking approval of both

Biblical Text Used By Washington; Never Cited By Chapter & Verse	Closest Scriptural References In King James Version	Nature of Use of Scripture by Washington	Examples Found in the Writings of Washington	Comments
Heaven	Matthew 4:17; 6:10	Popular saying	Vol. 5, 7-21-1776 Washington uses the word heaven 133 times.	A favorite phase is "Blessings of Heaven."
Is strong as "proof of holy writ" in confirmation of it.	Matthew 4:4	Theological statement	Vol. 32, 6-21-1792	As an emphasis of serious fact to Gouverneur Morris
The jot	Matthew 5:13	Popular saying	Vol. 3, 1-31-1770; 8, 7-28-1777; 12, 7-4-1778.	
Eternal rules	Matthew 5:17-19	Theological summary	Vol. 30, 4-30-1789	God's Law
I have never seen, nor heard a tittle from him.	Matthew 5:18	Popular saying	Vol. 37, 1-10-1799	
Give to the poor	Matthew 5:42	Popular saying	Vol. 1, 4-20-1756; 7, 1-21-1777; 21, 3-2-1781, note	Washington called himself a Philanthropist
The will of heaven	Matthew 6:10	Christian saying	Vol. 32, 1-27-1793	Lord's Prayer
The will of God	Matthew 6:10	Christian saying	Vol. 32, 1-27-1793; 3-6-1793	Lord's Prayer
Daily bread	Matthew 6:11	Christian saying	Vol. 26, 6-8-1783	Lord's Prayer
Eternal glory	Matthew 6:13	Military saying	Vol. 17, 11-27-1779	Destiny of courageous soldiers
Who may lead you into temptation	Matthew 6:13	Allusion	Vol. 30, 3-31-1789	Lord's Prayer

Biblical Text Used By Washington; Never Cited By Chapter & Verse	Closest Scriptural References In King James Version	Nature of Use of Scripture by Washington	Examples Found in the Writings of Washington	Comments
Deliver us from (an evil)	Matthew 6:13	Quotation	Vol. 6, 12-6-1776; 37, 11-22-1799	The Lord's Prayer
Forgive and forget	Matthew 6:14-15; 5:43-44	Theological summary	Vol. 35, 6-4-1797	To his grandson
Lucifer	Matthew 6:24; Luke 10:18	Popular saying	Vol. 7, 2-22-1777	Washington's word is "Lucre."
The task of pleasing a Master and Mistress' equal to that of two masters	Matthew 6:24		Vol. 3, 2-15-1774	
God's care for His people	Matthew 6:30-33	Allusion	Vol. 12, 9-6-1778; 17, 11-27-1779	To clergyman Governor Trumbull
Benign Parent	Matthew 7:11	Paraphrase	Vol. 30, 4-30-1789.	The Good Father
Doing as one would be done by	Matthew 7:12	Paraphrase	Vol. 28, 6-30-1786; 37, 4-25-1799	The Golden Rule
Narrow path	Matthew 7:13	Christian saying	Vol. 35, 5-15-97	
Paths of life	Matthew 7:14	Allusion	Vol. 21, 3-26-1781; 27, 2-1-1784	
Raise the dead to life again	Matthew. 10:8; 17:23; Luke 7:22	Christian saying	Vol. 1, 5-28-1755	
Heavy laden	Matthew 11:28	Quotation	Vol. 28, 7-25-1785	
House divided, divide and we shall become weak	Matthew 12:25	Quotation and paraphrase	Vol. 4, 4-23-1776	Lincoln also used in a speech

Biblical Text Used By Washington; Never Cited By Chapter & Verse	Closest Scriptural References In King James Version	Nature of Use of Scripture by Washington	Examples Found in the Writings of Washington	Comments
Thorny path	Matthew 13:3-7	Christian saying	Vol. 36, 7-4-1798	
The cares of this world	Matthew 13:22	Allusion	Vol. 29, 2-15-1787	
The wheat and the tares	Matthew 13:24-30	Allusion	Vol. 5, 5-31-1776	
Instruct the ignorant, and to reclaim the devious	Matthew 18:15-22	Theological summary	Vol. 30, 10-23-1789	Discussing the Constitution
Duties to God and man	Matthew 22:36-40	Theological summary	Vol. 4, 12-8-1775	The two great commandments
Wars and rumors of wars	Matthew 24:6		Vol. 28, 12-1-1785	
War. . .pestilence, famine	Matthew 24:6-7	Allusion	Vol. 28, 8-22-1785	
Good and faithful servant	Matthew 25:21, 23	Allusion	Vol. 1, "To the Speaker and Gentlemen of the House of Burgesses"; 31, 6-15-91; 35, 3-5-97	Uses with respect to clergy, political leaders, servants
Eternal happiness	Matthew 25:21, 23, 34, 46	Christian saying	Vol. 25, 11-16-1782; 36, 6-4-1798	Synonym for heaven
Life eternal	Matthew 25:46	Christian saying	Vol. 1, 9-6-1756	Euphemism for death penalty
Bitter cup	Matthew 26:39	Allusion	Vol. 11, 3-7-1778	Written from Valley forge of prisoners of war

Biblical Text Used By Washington; Never Cited By Chapter & Verse	Closest Scriptural References In King James Version	Nature of Use of Scripture by Washington	Examples Found in the Writings of Washington	Comments
Cast lots	Matthew 27:35	Allusion	Vol. 16, 8-10-79	Actually used to divide a supply of coats to soldiers
Propagating the Gospel (also "Christianize")	Matthew 28:19-20	Theological summary	Vol. 28, 6-30-1785; 29, 5-2-88; 30, 7-6-89, note.	With reference to the Indians
The religion of Jesus Christ	Mark 1:1	Theological allusion	Vol. 15, 5-12-1779	In address to Indian chiefs
Forgiveness a divine attribute	Mark 2:5-8	Theological summary	Vol. 10, 11-21-1777; 28, 7-25-1785	Personal letter to Lafayette
Take up (my) bed and walk	Mark 2:9	Paraphrase	Vol. 15, 7-4-1779; 37, 3-25-1799	Uses of himself once
Ministers of the Gospel	Mark 10:43-45	Christian saying	Vol. 17, 11-27-1779; 30, 10-23-1789	Discussing the Constitution
Bitterest curse this side of the grave	Mark 11:21; Matthew 25:41	Allusion	Vol. 6, 9-30-1776	Euphemism for hell on earth
The widow's mite	Mark 12:41-44	Allusion and Quotation	Vol. 3, 7-20-1770; 26, 1-15-1783; 26, 3-31-1783; 35, 11-15-1796	Nineteen times in all. A favorite phrase to describe his many charitable contributions
Enlightening sounds of the Gospel	Luke 2:10-15; Mark 1:14-15	Allusion	Vol. 37, 8-28-1762	In humor
Eternal disgrace or reproach	Luke 6:22; 11:45	Christian saying	Vol. 3, 8-10-1775; 4, 12-28-1775; 9, 9-4-1777	Cowardly soldiers' destiny
My justification	Luke 7:35	Christian saying	Vol. 24, 5-22-1782	Used 5x

Biblical Text Used By Washington; Never Cited By Chapter & Verse	Closest Scriptural References In King James Version	Nature of Use of Scripture by Washington	Examples Found in the Writings of Washington	Comments
Concern for one's neighbor	Luke 10:29-37	Theological summary	Vol. 8, 6-17-1777; 15, 5-12-1779; 27, 7-10-1783; 37	
Your good father … a good Providence which will never fail to take care of his Children	Luke 11:9-13	Paraphrase	Vol. 29, 4-28-1788	Personal letter to console Charles L'Enfant at loss of his father
The demon of party spirit	Luke 11:20-26	Allusion	Vol. 31, 6-4-1790	
The wise man who counts the cost	Luke 14:28	Quotation	Vol. 25, 1-5-1785	Personal letter
The children of this world	Luke 16:8	Allusion	Vol. 32, 1-27-1793	
Torment of mental hell	Luke 16:24	Figure of speech	Vol. 20, 10-13-1780	Of Benedict Arnold
The millstone around one's neck	Luke 17:1-2	Paraphrase	Vol. 35, 11-28-1796	To grandson
Repent and be forgiven	Luke 17:3	Paraphrase	Vol. 28, 7-25-1785	To Lafayette
Appeal to God and man for justice	Luke 18:1-8	Theological summary	Vol. 28, 7-26-1786	Battle in just war is an "appeal to God" for justice
The aggravated vengeance of God	Luke 21:22	Allusion	Vol. 26, 6-8-1783	In General's Circular Letter to 13 Governors
The roar of distant thunder	Luke 21:25; John 12:28-29	Possible allusion	Vol. 29, 4-25 to 5-1-1788	
Professors [i.e. believers] of Christianity	John 3:16	Allusion	Vol. 29, 8-15-1787	In context of religious liberty
A man to throw the first stone for fear of having it returned to him.	John 8:7	Allusion	Vol. 33, 12-18-1793	

Biblical Text Used By Washington; Never Cited By Chapter & Verse	Closest Scriptural References In King James Version	Nature of Use of Scripture by Washington	Examples Found in the Writings of Washington	Comments
Mansions of my fathers	John 14:2	Saying	Vol. 27, 4-4-1784	For the family crypt
Road to Heaven	John 14:5-7	Allusion	Vol. 29, 8-15-1787	Personal letter
Way(s) of life	John 14:6	Allusion	Vol. 2, 7-1-1757; 15, 5-12-1779.	In the second, "Ways of life" is paralleled with "the religion of Jesus Christ."
Cloak his iniquity	John 15:22	Allusion	Vol. 25, 12-18-1782	
Pour out His Holy Spirit	John 15:26	Quotation	Vol. 17, 11-27-1779	Quotes Congress–Call for prayer
The blessed Religion revealed in the word of God will remain an eternal and awful monument to prove that the best Institutions may be abused by human depravity; and that they may even, in some instances be made subservient to the vilest of purposes	Acts 2:23; 1 Corinthians 2:8	Theological summary	Vol. 30, 4-1789	Washington refers to the crucifixion and how its injustice was justified or permitted by both religious and civil courts
Scales from eyes	Acts 9:18	Allusion	Vol. 30, 6-8-1788	
Children of the stock of Abraham	Acts 13:26	Allusion	Vol. 31, 8-14-1790	
Common parent	Acts 17:26-28	Allusion	Vol. 28, 9-5-1785	
Heaven is my witness	Romans 1:9	Christian saying	Vol. 30, 8-28-1788	
Ungrateful to the Creator	Romans 1:21	Allusion	Vol. 35, 9-19-1796	Farewell Address, uses ingratitude 26x

Biblical Text Used By Washington; Never Cited By Chapter & Verse	Closest Scriptural References In King James Version	Nature of Use of Scripture by Washington	Examples Found in the Writings of Washington	Comments
Sin of ingratitude	Romans 1:21	Allusion	Vol. 1, 5-29-1754	
Abused by human depravity	Romans 1:21-32	Theological summary	Vol. 30, April, 1789	
Breaking faith	Romans 1:31	Allusion	Vol. 17, 11-20-1779	
Depravity of the minds of so many	Romans 1:28	Allusion	Vol. 29, 11-15-1786	Refers to depravity 9x
Genuine Descendents of those who are reputed to be our great Progenitors.	Romans 5:12	Allusion	Vol. 27, 9-2-1783	
Pursuing the right walk of life	Romans 6:4	Allusion	Vol. 26, 1-15-1783	
Providence works in the mysterious course of events "from seeming evil still educing good."	Romans 8:28	Allusion	Vol. 30, 8-18-1788	
Like sheep to the slaughter	Romans 8:36	Allusion	Vol. 26, 3-15-1783	To the officers of the army
Peace and Harmony with all	Romans 12:18	Allusion	Vol. 35, 9-19-1796	Used in public and private letters
To render unto every one their due	Romans 13:7	Quotation	Vol. 30, 1-18-1790	
Worshipping the deity according to one's conscience	Romans 14:1ff	Allusion	Vol. 30, 5-26-1789	Used 2x
Tho' not strictly warranted by Scripture, is nevertheless highly admissible	Romans 14:1; 1 Corinthians 4:6	Theological summary	Vol. 3, 5-21-1772	In humor to his son's clergyman tutor

Biblical Text Used By Washington; Never Cited By Chapter & Verse	Closest Scriptural References In King James Version	Nature of Use of Scripture by Washington	Examples Found in the Writings of Washington	Comments
No eye, no tongue, no thought	1 Corinthians 2:9; Isaiah 64:4	Allusion	Vol. 37, 8-30-1799	
Workings of the Spirit within	1 Corinthians 2:11	Allusion	Vol. 34, 2-10-1796	To his granddaughter
It would be a stumbling block in your way	1 Corinthians 8:9	Christian saying	Vol. 35, 11-28-1796	To nephew; used 9x
Cup of blessing	1 Corinthians 10:16	Quotation	Vol. 26, 6-8-1783	The Communion chalice
Last trump	1 Corinthians 15:52; Matthew 24:31	Allusion	Vol. 4, 3-31-1776	Flight of British from Boston
God of all Mercies	2 Corinthians 1:3	Quotation	Vol. 17, 11-27-1779	
Letter and spirit	2 Corinthians 3:6	Allusion	Vol. 8, 7-16-1777	
Enlightened spirit of liberty	2 Corinthians 3:17	Allusion	Vol. 30, 1-15-1790	
Sacred fire of liberty	2 Corinthians 3:17	Allusion	Vol. 30, 4-30-1789	Used in First Inaugural Address
Eternal glory	2 Corinthians 4:17	Allusion	Vol. 17, 11-27-1779	
True repentance	2 Corinthians 7:9-10	Allusion	Vol. 21, 1-27-1781	
Sorrow and Repentance	2 Corinthians 7:9-10	Allusion	Vol. 32, 6-4-1797	To his grandson
Blessings a gracious God bestows upon the righteous	2 Corinthians 8:1	Allusion	Vol. 24, 6-30-1782	

756

Biblical Text Used By Washington; Never Cited By Chapter & Verse	Closest Scriptural References In King James Version	Nature of Use of Scripture by Washington	Examples Found in the Writings of Washington	Comments
To bless with health or afflict with pain	2 Corinthians 12:7-9; Job 2:1-7	Theological summary	Vol. 32, 1-27-1793	
Yoke of slavery	Galatians 5:1	Allusion	Vol. 11, 4-30-1778	A sermon was dedicated to Washington on this text by Rev. Jacob Duché
Reap the fruit of his labor	Galatians 6:7	Allusion	Vol. 26, 6-8-1783	
Spirit of wisdom/rectitude	Ephesians 1:17	Allusion	Vol. 27, 8-21-1783	
Which Heaven itself has ordained	Ephesians 2:10	Allusion	Vol. 30, 4-30-1789	First Inaugural Address
Several vocations useful	Ephesians 4:1	Allusion	PGW, Letterbook 39, 22 of 222	
Christian Soldier	Ephesians 6:13-18	Allusion	Vol. 5, 7-9-1776	At Valley Forge
The blessed Religion revealed in the word of God	Ephesians 6:17; 1 Thessalonians 2:13	Theological statement	Vol. 30, 4-1789	In an unsent letter prepared for Congress
Happiness depends more upon the internal frame of a person's own mind, than on the externals in the world.	Philippians 4:6-12	Theological summary	Vol. 29, 2-15-1787	To mother
Word of God	1 Thessalonians 2:13; Hebrews 4:12	Theological statement	Vol. 30, 4-1789	
Like a thief	1 Thessalonians 5:2	Allusion	Vol. 35, 11-28-1796	To grandson
Shall not cease to supplicate (pray)	1 Thessalonians 5:17	Allusion	Vol. 35, 3-3-1797	
Worse than an infidel	1 Timothy 5:18	Quotation	Vol. 12, 8-20-1788	Criticism of Deism

Biblical Text Used By Washington; Never Cited By Chapter & Verse	Closest Scriptural References In King James Version	Nature of Use of Scripture by Washington	Examples Found in the Writings of Washington	Comments
Root of Evil	1 Timothy 6:10	Allusion	Vol. 1, 1-14-1756	
Scripture	2 Timothy 3:16	Popular saying	Vol. 37, 5-30-1799	see also Isaiah 2:4
Hope of future happiness	Titus 2:13	Theological summary	Vol. 35, 3-2-1797	
All the wonders recorded in holy writ	Hebrews 2:4	Allusion	Vol. 16, 9-30-1779	In humor to Lafayette
Throne of grace	Hebrews 4:16	Quotation	PGW, 2:179-181	
Divine Author of life and felicity	Hebrews 5:9	Paraphrase	Vol. 35, 3-3-1797	
Distinguish between good and evil	Hebrews 5:14	Quotation	Vol. 1, 12-1756	
Remembering that all must die, and that she had lived to an honourable age, I hope you will bear the misfortune with that fortitude and complacency of mind, that become a Man and a Christian.	Hebrews 9:27	Allusion	Vol. 9, 10-19-1777	Personal letter to console a fellow general, Israel Putnam
Divine Author	Hebrews 12:2	Allusion	Vol. 26, 6-8-1783	Refers to Christ
Gracious Father of lights	James 1:17	Quotation	PGW, Letterbook 38, Image 147	
Supreme Author of all good	James 1:17	Allusion	Vol. 11, 5-2-1778	
True religion	James 1:27	Theological saying	Vol. 30, 10-3-1789	Used 3x

Biblical Text Used By Washington; Never Cited By Chapter & Verse	Closest Scriptural References In King James Version	Nature of Use of Scripture by Washington	Examples Found in the Writings of Washington	Comments
The cries of the distressed, of the fatherless and the widows	James 1:27	Allusion	Vol. 15, 5-18-1779	
Holy writ	1 Peter 1:16	Christian saying	Vol. 32, 6-21-1792; Vol. 16, 9-30-1779	Synonym for scripture
Pilgrim/sojourner	1 Peter 2:11	Allusion	Vol. 35, 5-20-1797; Vol. 10, 1-23-1778	Also used "pilgrimage"
Brotherly love	1 Peter 2:17	Allusion	Vol. 1, 6-18-1754; Vol. 9, 10-27-1777	
Heirs of his eternal glory	1 Peter 3:7	Quotation	Vol. 17, 11-27-1779	In Congressional Call for Prayer
Until the Globe itself is dissolved	2 Peter 3:11	Allusion	Vol. 28, 9-5-1785	
Paradise	Revelation 2:7	Allusion	Vol. 37, 2-20-1774	
Untimely fruit	Revelation 6:13	Allusion	Vol. 5, 7-20-1776	
Lord and Ruler of Nations	Revelation 12:5; 19:16	Theological affirmation	Vol. 30, 10-3-1789	Title for Christ; used in First Thanksgiving Proclamation
'Tis wonderful it should be otherwise and the earth should be moistened with human gore, instead of the refreshing streams, wch. the shedders of it might become, instruments to lead over its plains, to delight and render profitable our labours. But alas! the millenium will not I fear appear in our days.	Revelation 20:6	Allusion	Vol. 34,12-24-1795	Washington had been influenced by post-millennial Puritan thought

Biblical Text Used By Washington; Never Cited By Chapter & Verse	Closest Scriptural References In King James Version	Nature of Use of Scripture by Washington	Examples Found in the Writings of Washington	Comments
Promised millennium	Revelation 20:6	Allusion	Vol. 33, 5-26-1794	Refers to millennium 3x
Morning star	Revelation 22:16	Allusion	Vol. 26, 4-18-1783	

George Washington's Written Prayers

One of the elements of the Christian faith that was suspect, and eventually abandoned by Deism, was the practice of prayer. This was logical since there was little purpose in speaking to a Deity who on principle had abandoned all contact and communication with his creation.

Given this understanding, Washington's lifelong practice of prayer, illustrated by these more than one hundred written prayers, is an undeniable refutation of his alleged Deism. While not all of these prayers were composed by Washington (though most were), that he used them is indisputable, as they are taken directly from his public and private writings. We have organized them by topic for convenience. The sheer magnitude of the number of prayers, coupled with the expansive topics included in his prayers, give substantial credence to the universal testimony of Washington's contemporaries of his practice of corporate and private prayer

This underscores how misplaced contemporary scholars have been in claiming that Washington was a man of lukewarm religious faith.

All the cited prayers can are from the *Writings of George Washington* edited by John C. Fitzpatrick and found online at http://etext.lib.virginia.edu/washington/fitzpatrick/

1.   **His Order for a Custom Made Prayer Book**

1.1   INVOICE OF GOODS TO BE SHIPD BY ROBERT CARY & CO. FOR THE USE OF GEO. WASHINGTON, POTOMACK RIVER, VIRGINIA, VIZ.

July 18, 1771. A Prayr. Book with the new Version of Psalms and good plain type, covd. with red Moroco., to be 7 Inchs. long 4? wide, and as thin as possible for the greatr. ease of caryg. in the Pocket.

2. His Culture – Prayer and Fasting

2.1 DIARY: June 1, 1774. Went to Church and fasted all day." [This was in keeping with the burgesses' vote to fast in support of Massachusetts when the Boston Port bill began.] [Thomas Jefferson wrote:] The day of fasting was observed throughout the colony. The people met generally with anxiety and alarm in their countenances, and the effect of the day, through the whole colony, was like a shock of electricity, arousing every man, and placing him erect and solidly on his center. (See *Jefferson's Works*, vol. I, p. 7.) [Moncure D. Conway noted] The fast was obeyed throughout Virginia with such rigor and scruples, as to interdict the tasting of food between the rising and setting sun. With the remembrance of the King [Minis try?], horror was associated; in churches, as well as in the circles of social conversation, he seemed to stalk like the arch-enemy of mankind. [See Moncure D. Conway's *Biography of Edmund Randolph*. Note in *WGW*.]

2.2 GENERAL ORDERS Head Quarters, Cambridge, July 16, 1775. The Continental Congress having earnestly recommended, that "Thursday next the 20th. Instant, be observed by the Inhabitants of all the english Colonies upon this Continent, as a Day of public Humiliation, Fasting and Prayer; that they may with united Hearts and Voice unfeignedly confess their Sins before God, and supplicate the all wise and merciful disposer of events, to avert the Desolation and Calamities of an unnatural war." The General orders, that Day to be religiously observed by the Forces under his Command, exactly in manner directed by the proclamation of the Continental Congress: It is therefore strictly enjoin'd on all Officers and Soldiers, (not upon duty) to attend Divine Service, at the accustomed places of worship, as well in the Lines, as the Encampments and Quarters; and it is expected, that all those who go to worship, do take their Arms, Ammunitions and Accoutrements and are prepared for immediate Action if called upon. If in the judgment of the Officers, the Works should appear to be in such forwardness as the utmost security of the Camp requires, they will command their men to abstain from all Labour upon that solemn day.

2.3 "His Excellency General Washington was with the troops who passed us here to the Perkiomen. The procession lasted the whole night, and we had all kinds of visits from officers wet to the breast, who had to march in that condition the cold, damp night through, and to bear hunger and thirst at the same time. This robs them of courage and health, and instead of prayers we hear from most, the national evil, curses."—*Muhlenberg's Diary*, Sept. 19, 1777.

2.4 And certainly not all prayers that were offered to God, were not always for the best of motives: From *WGW*: Ford quotes from a letter from Col. John Chester to Col. Samuel B. Webb (January 17): "The inhuman treatment our prisoners met with while in New York is beyond all description. Humanity cannot but drop a tear at sight of the poor, miserable, starved objects. They are mere skeletons, unable to creep or speak in many instances. One vessel lost 27 in her passage from New York to Medford, and 7 died the night they were put ashore; and they are dying all along the roads. Most who have got home in the neighboring towns, are taken with the small pox, which undoubtedly was given them by design—all this does not seem to discourage the few surviving ones. They pray that God would only give them health and strength again, and they are determined to have sweet revenge."

2.5 GENERAL ORDERS Head Quarters, New York, May 15, 1776. The Continental Congress having ordered, Friday the 17th. Instant to be observed as a day of "fasting, humiliation and prayer, humbly to supplicate the mercy of Almighty God, that it would please him to pardon all our manifold sins and transgressions, and to prosper the Arms of the United Colonies, and finally, establish the peace and freedom of America, upon a solid and lasting foundation" — The General commands all officers, and soldiers, to pay strict obedience to the Orders of the Continental Congress, and by their unfeigned, and pious observance of their religious duties, incline the Lord, and Giver of Victory, to prosper our arms. The regiment of Artillery to be mustered, Sunday morning, at eight o'clock, upon the Common, where the Commissary General of Musters will attend.

2.6 GENERAL ORDERS Head Quarters, Morristown, February 4, 1777. The Hon'ble The Governor and Assembly of New Jersey, having directed Thursday the 6th. day of this Month, to be observed as a Day of Fasting, Humiliation and Prayer, by the Inhabitants of the State — The General desires the same may be observed by the army.

2.7 GENERAL ORDERS Head Quarters, V. Forge, Sunday, April 12, 1778. The Honorable Congress having thought proper to recommend to The United States of America to set apart Wednesday the 22nd. instant to be observed as a day of Fasting, Humiliation and Prayer, that at one time and with one voice the righteous dispensations of Providence may be acknowledged and His Goodness and Mercy toward us and our Arms supplicated and implored; The General directs that this day also shall be religiously observed in the Army, that no work be done thereon and that the Chaplains prepare discourses suitable to the Occasion.

2.8   To THE PRESIDENT OF CONGRESS Head Quarters, Middle Brook, April 2, 1779. The Act recommending a day of fasting, humiliation and prayer shall be duly attended to.

2.9   GENERAL ORDERS Head Quarters, Middle Brook, Monday, April 12, 1779. The Honorable the Congress having recommended it to the United States to set apart Thursday the 6th. day of May next to be observed as a day of fasting, humiliation and prayer, to acknowledge the gracious interpositions of Providence; to deprecate deserved punishment for our Sins and Ingratitude, to unitedly implore the Protection of Heaven; Success to our Arms and the Arms of our Ally: The Commander in Chief enjoins a religious observance of said day and directs the Chaplains to prepare discourses proper for the occasion; strictly forbiding all recreations and unnecessary labor.

2.10   To THE PRESIDENT OF CONGRESS Head Quarters, March 23, 1780. The day appointed for Fasting, humiliation and prayer will be observed by the Army, agreeable to the proclamation.

2.11   GENERAL ORDERS Head Quarters, Morristown, Thursday, April 6, 1780. The Honorable the Congress having been pleased by their proclamation of the 11th. of last month to appoint Wednesday the 22nd. instant to be set apart and observed as a day of Fasting Humiliation and Prayer for certain special purposes therein mentioned, and recommended that there should be no labor or recreations on that day; The same is to be observed accordingly thro'out the Army and the different Chaplins will prepare discourses suited to the several objects enjoined by the said Proclamation.

2.12   GENERAL ORDERS Head Quarters, New Windsor, Friday, April 27,1781. Congress having been pleased to set apart and appoint Thursday the 3d. of May next for fasting humiliation and prayer, the General enjoins a strict obedience to it in the Army and calls upon the Chaplains thereof to prepare discourses suitable to the occasion. All duties of Fatigue are to cease on that day.

3.   Prayers for Self and Family

3.1   To JOSEPH REED Cambridge, December 15, 1775. Dear Sir: The accounts which you have given of the sentiments of the people respecting my conduct, is extremely flattering. Pray God, I may continue to deserve them, in the perplexed and intricate situation I stand in.

3.2   To MRS. MARTHA CUSTIS July 20, 1758. We have begun our march for the Ohio. A courier is starting for Williamsburg, and I embrace the opportunity to send a few words to one whose life is now inseparable from mine. Since that happy hour when we made our pledges to each other, my thoughts have been continually going to you as another Self. That an all-powerful Providence may keep us both in safety is the prayer of your ever faithful and affectionate friend.

3.3   To FRANCIS FAUQUIER Fort Cumberland Camp, August 5, 1758. In fine, I said, and did every thing to avert a mischief that seem'd to forebode our manifest Ruin; this is the light it appears to me. I pray Heaven my Fears may prove imaginary only.

3.4   To JOHN AUGUSTINE WASHINGTON New York, April 29, 1776. Mrs. Washington is still here, and talks of taking the Small Pox, but I doubt her resolution. to be inoculated. Mr. and Mrs. Custis will set out in a few days for Maryland. I did not write to you by the 'Squire, because his departure in the first place, was sudden; in the next, I had but little to say. I am very sorry to hear that my Sister was Indisposed with a sore Breast when you last wrote. I hope she is now recover'd of it, and that all your Family are well; that they may continue so, and that our once happy Country may escape the depredations and Calamities attending on War, is the fervent prayer of, dear Sir, your most affectionate brother. Mrs. Washington, Mr. and Mrs. Custis join in love to my Sister and the rest of the Family.

3.5   To EDMUND PENDLETON Morris Town, April 12, 1777. Your friendly, and affectionate wishes for my health and success, has a claim to my thankful acknowledgements; and, that the God of Armies may enable me to bring the present contest to a speedy and happy conclusion, thereby gratifying me in a retirement to the calm and sweet enjoyment of domestick happiness, is the fervent prayer, and most ardent wish of my Soul.

3.6   To LANDON CARTER Morristown in New Jersey, April 15, 1777. Your friendly and affectionate wishes for my health and success has a claim to my most grateful acknowledgements. That the God of Armies may Incline the Hearts of my American Brethren to support, and bestow sufficient abilities on me to bring the present contest to a speedy and happy conclusion, thereby enabling me to sink into sweet retirement, and the full enjoyment of that Peace and happiness which will accompany a domestick Life, is the first wish, and most fervent prayer of my Soul.

3.7   To HANNAH FAIRFAX WASHINGTON Mount Vernon, May 20, 1792. Dear Madam: Mrs. Washington received with much pleasure your kind remembrance and affectionate regards, and would, were she here, where I am come for a few days only, return the same with much sincerity to which permit me to add the best wishes and ardent prayers for your happiness. I am etc.

4.   Prayers For the Army

4.1   To ELBRIDGE GERRY Head Quarters, Morris Town, January 29, 1780 With respect to provision; the situation of the Army is comfortable at present on this head and I ardently pray that it may never be again as it has been of late.

4.2   To JOHN ROBINSON Fort Loudoun, June 10, 1757. Major Lewis is returned with part of the Indians, that went out with him, in consequence of their having taken only eight days' provisions with them. He was unable to prevail with those savages to take more. One party of twenty, with ten soldiers, is gone towards Fort Duquesne, under Captain Spotswood; and another party of fifteen, with five soldiers, under Lieutenant Baker, but they course towards Logstown. God send them success and a safe return, I pray.

4.3   To COLONEL HENRY BOUQUET Camp at Fort Cumberland, August 2, 1758. …we can do nothing more this Fall than to fortify some Post on the other side of the Mountains and prepare against another Campaigne I must pray Heaven, most fervently, to avert! till we find it impracticable at least to prosecute with prudence the Enterprise in hand.

5   Prayers For Peace

5.1   To MARQUIS DE LAFAYETTE Hd. Qrs., Newburgh, March 23, 1783. I hope it is unnecessary to repeat to you, that whether during the continuance of the War, or after the olive branch shall have extended itself over this Land (for which I most devoutly pray) I shall be happy to see you on Columbias shore.

5.2   To THE OFFICERS OF THE TENTH AND NINETY-FIRST

REGIMENTS OF THE VIRGINIA MILITIA Mount Vernon, October 24, 1798. That there may be no occasion to gird on the Sword, none more ardently prays than I do; Your prayers, and kind wishes in my behalf, I reciprocate with great Cordiality

5.3   To GEORGE WASHINGTON MOTIER DE LAFAYETTE Mount Vernon, December 25, 1798. Young gentlemen of the first families, fortunes and expectations in the United States, are offering their Services; but I hope, and most ardently pray, that the Directory in your Country will not, by a perseverance in the insults and injuries which they have heaped on this, make it necessary to resort to Arms to repel an Invasion, or to do ourselves justice.

5.4   To THE INHABITANTS OF RICHMOND [August 28, 1793.] True to our duties and interests as Americans, firm to our purpose as lovers of peace, let us unite our fervent prayers to the great ruler of the Universe, that the justice and moderation of all concerned may permit us to continue in the uninterrupted enjoyment of a blessing, which we so greatly prize, and of which we ardently wish them a speedy and permanent participation.

5.5   To THE MILITIA OFFICERS OF THE CITY AND LIBERTIES OF PHILADELPHIA Philadelphia, December 12, 1783. While the various Scenes of the War, in which I have experienced the timely aid of the Militia of Philadelphia, recur to my mind, my ardent prayer ascends to Heaven that they may long enjoy the blessings of that Peace which has been obtained by the divine benediction on our common exertions.

5.6   To THE EARL OF RADNOR Mount Vernon, July 8, 1797. I reciprocate with great cordiality the good wishes you have been pleased to bestow on me; and pray devoutly, that we may both witness, and that shortly, the return of Peace; for a more bloody, expensive, and eventful War, is not recorded in modern, if it be found in ancient history.

5.7   To CHARLES COTESWORTH PINCKNEY Mount Vernon, December 4, 1797. That the Government of France views us as a divided people, I have little doubt; and that they have been led to entertain that opinion from representations, and the conduct of many of our own citizens, is still less doubtful; but I shall be very much mistaken, indeed, in the mass of the People of the United States, if an occasion should call for an unequivocal expression of the public voice, if the first would not find themselves very much deceived; and the latter (their leaders excepted) to change their notes. I pray devoutly that the Directory may not bring the matter to trial.

5.8 To THE INHABITANTS OF THE CITY OF NEW LONDON [September 2, 1793.] Experienced as we have lately been in the calamities of war, it must be the prayer of every good Citizen that it may long be averted from our land, and that the blessings which a kind providence has bestowed upon us, may continue uninterrupted.

6 **Prayers For Citizens and Cities**

6.1 To COMTE DE ROCHAMBEAU New Windsor, February 26, 1781. I have an increase of happiness from the subsequent intelligence you do me the favour to communicate respecting Count D'Estaings success. This repetition of advices justifies a confidence in their truth [which I pray God may be confirmed in its greatest extent.] Note: The draft is in the writing of Alexander Hamilton. The words in brackets are in the writing of Washington.

6.2 To MAJOR GENERAL HORATIO GATES New York, June 24, 1776. The Distance of the Scene, and the frequent Changes which have happened in the State of our Affairs in Canada, do not allow me to be more particular in my Instructions. The Command is important, the Service difficult, but honourable; and I most devoutly pray that Providence may crown your Arms with abundant Success. Given under my Hand, etc.

6.3 ORDERS AND INSTRUCTIONS TO MAJOR GENERAL ISRAEL PUTNAM Head Quarters, Cambridge, March 29, 1776. Devoutly praying that the Power which has hitherto sustained the American Arms, may continue to bless them, with his divine Protection, I bid you Farewell.

6.4 To THE CITIZENS AND INHABITANTS OF THE TOWN OF BALTIMORE Baltimore, September 8, 1781. I most sincerely thank you for your Prayers and good Wishes. May the Author of all Blessing aid our united Exertions in the Cause of Liberty. And may the particular Favor of Heaven rest on you Gentlemen, and the worthy Citizens of this flourishing Town of Baltimore.

6.5 To COLONEL HENRY BOUQUET Camp Fort Cumberland, August 13, 1758. If you have any Intelligence from Ticonderago, I shou'd be extreme thankful for the acct. We have expected hourly, to hear that Louisburg is in Our hands, pray Heaven we may not be disappointed at last.

6.6 FAREWELL ORDERS TO THE ARMIES OF THE UNITED STATES Rock Hill, near Princeton, November 2, 1783. To the various branches of the Army the General takes this last and solemn opportunity of professing his inviolable attachment and friendship. … and being now to conclude these his last public Orders, to take his ultimate leave in a short time of the military character, and to bid a final adieu to the Armies he has so long had the honor to Command, he can only again offer in their behalf his recommendations to their grateful country, and his prayers to the God of Armies. May ample justice be done them here, and may the choicest of heaven's favours, both here and hereafter, attend those who, under the devine auspices, have secured innumerable blessings for others; with these wishes, and this benediction, the Commander in Chief is about to retire from Service. The Curtain of seperation will soon be drawn, and the military scene to him will be closed for ever.

6.7 To COLONEL BENEDICT ARNOLD Cambridge, December 5, 1775. I have no Doubt but a Junction of your Detachment with the Army under General Montgomery, is effected before this. If so, you will put yourself under his Command and will, I am persuaded, give him all the Assistance in your Power, to finish the glorious Work you have begun. That the Almighty may preserve and prosper you in it, is the sincere and fervent Prayer of, Dr. Sir, &c.

6.8 To THE CITIZENS AND INHABITANTS OF THE TOWN OF BALTIMORE Baltimore, September 8, 1781. I most sincerely thank you for your Prayers and good Wishes. May the Author of all Blessing aid our united Exertions in the Cause of Liberty. And may the particular Favor of Heaven rest on you Gentlemen, and the worthy Citizens of this flourishing Town of Baltimore.

6.9 To THE MAGISTRATES AND SUPERVISORS OF TRYON COUNTY [August 1, 1783.] Accept Gentlemen my thanks for your kind wishes for my welfare be assured it will be my earnest prayer that by the blessing of Providence on the fine Country you possess you may soon be enabled to recover your former ease, and to enjoy that happiness you have so well deserved. I am etc.

6.10 To THE MASSACHUSETTS SENATE AND HOUSE OF REPRESENTATIVES Head Quarters, August 10, 1783. Be assured Gentlemen, that, through the many and complicated vicissitudes of an arduous Conflict, I have ever turned my Eye, with a fixed Confidence on that superintendg. Providence which governs all Events: and the lively Gratitude I now feel, at the happy termination of our Contest, is beyond my Expression.

If, dependg on the Guidance of the same Allwise Providence, I have performed my part in this great Revolution, to the acceptance of my fellow Citizens, It is a source of high satisfaction to me; and forms an additional Motive of Praise to that Infinite Wisdom, which directs the Minds of Men. This Consideration will attend me in the Shades of retirement, and furnish one of the most pleasing Themes of my Meditation. So great a revolution as this Country now experiences, doubtless ranks high in the Scale of human Events, and in the Eye of Omnipotence is introductive to some noble Scenes of future Grandeur to this happy fated Continent. May the States have Wisdom to discern their true Interests at this important period! Impressed with sentiments of Gratitude for your benevolent Expressions for my personal Happiness and prosperity, I can make you no better return, than to pray, that Heaven, from the Stores of its Munificence, may shower its choisest blessings on you Gentlemen, and the People of the Commonwealth of Massachusetts, and to entreat that Our Liberties, now so happily established, may be continued in perfect Security, to the latest posterity. With Sentiments of high Veneration etc.

6.11   To THE MAYOR AND COMMONALTY OF FREDERICKSBURG
February 14, 1784 Gentlemen: With the greatest pleasure, I receive, in the character of a private Citizen, the honor of your Address. To a beneficent Providence, and to the fortitude of a brave and virtuous Army, supported by the general exertion of our common Country I stand indebted for the plaudits you now bestow; The reflection however, of having met the congratulating smiles and approbation of my fellow-Citizens for the part I have acted in the cause of liberty and Independence cannot fail of adding pleasure to the sweets of domestic life; and my sensibility of them is heightened by their coming from the respectable Inhabitants of the place of my growing Infancy and the honorable mention wch. is made of my revered Mother; by whose Maternal hand (early deprived of a Father) I was led from Childhood. For the expressions of personal Affection and attachment, and for your kind wishes for my future welfare, I offer grateful thanks and my sincere prayers for the happiness and prosperity of the Corporate Town of Fredericksburgh.

7   **Prayers For Government Leaders**
7.1   To THE PROVISORY EXECUTIVE COUNCIL OF FRANCE I assure

you, with a sincere participation, of the great and constant friendship, which these U.S. bear to the French nation. of the interest they feel in whatever concerns their happiness and prosperity, and of their wishes for a perpetual fraternity with them, and I pray god [God] to have them and you, very great and good friends and allies, in his holy keeping.

7.2   To GOVERNOR JOHN HANCOCK West Point, November 15, 1783. Be persuaded, my dear Sir, that my wishes and prayers will ever be most ardent for the health and happiness of your Excellency, and for the prosperity of the Commonwealth over which you preside. With sentiments of unalterable respect etc

7.3   To GOVERNOR DIEGO JOSEPH NAVARRO Of [Havana] Head Quarters, Middle Brook, March 4, 1779. With my prayers for your health and happiness, and with the greatest respect I have the honor etc.

7.4   To THE MAYOR, RECORDER, ALDERMEN, AND COMMONALTY OF THE CITY OF NEW YORK [April 10, 1785] I pray that Heaven may bestow its choicest blessings on your City. That the devastations of War, in which you found it, may soon be without a trace. That a well regulated and benificial Commerce may enrichen your Citizens. And that, your State (at present the Seat of the Empire) may set such examples of wisdom and liberality, as shall have a tendency to strengthen and give permanency to the Union at home, and credit and respectability to it abroad. The accomplishment whereof is a remaining wish, and the primary object of all my desires.

8   Prayers For States

8.1   To THE SOUTH CAROLINA SENATE AND HOUSE OF REPRESENTATIVES May 28, 1784. For the favorable wishes you have kindly bestowed on me you have all my gratitude; and my prayers for the welfare of your State, shall never cease.

8.2   To GOVERNOR JOHN HAWKINS STONE Philadelphia, December 23, 1796. With the same entire devotion to my country, every act of my civil Administration has been aimed to secure to it those advantages which result from a stable and free government; and with gratitude to Heaven, I unite with the Legislature of Maryland in the pleasing reflections, that our country has continued to feel the blessings of peace, liberty and prosperity, whilst Europe and the Indies have been convulsed with the horrors of a dreadful and desolating war. My ardent prayers are offered that those afflicted regions may now speedily see their calamities terminated, and also feel the blessings of returning peace. Their kind wishes for my domestic happiness, in my contemplated retirement, are entitled to my cordial thanks. If it shall please God to prolong a life already far advanced into the vale of years, no attending felicity can equal that which I shall feel in seeing the administration of our government operating to preserve the Independence, prosperity and welfare of the American People. With great respect etc.

9   **Prayers For a President**

9.1   To THE PRESIDENT OF THE UNITED STATES Mount Vernon, March 3, 1799. I sincerely pray, that in the discharge of these arduous and important duties committed to you, your health may be unimpaired, and that you may long live to enjoy those blessings which must flow to our Country, if we should be so happy as to pass this critical period in an honourable and dignified manner, without being involved in the horrors and calamities of War.

10   **Prayers For America**

10.1   FAREWELL ADDRESS [First Draft May 15, 1796.] That we may be always prepared for War, but never unsheath the sword except in self defence so long as Justice and our essential rights, and national respectability can be preserved without it; for without the gift of prophecy, it may safely be pronounced, that if this country can remain in peace 20 years longer: and I devoutly pray that it may do so to the end of time; such in all probability will be its population, riches, and resources, when combined with its peculiarly happy and remote Situation from the other quarters of the globe, as to bid defiance, in a just cause, to any earthly power whatsoever.

10.2   CIRCULAR TO THE STATES Head Quarters, Newburgh, June 8, 1783. I now make it my earnest prayer, that God would have you, and the State over which you preside, in his holy protection, that he would incline the hearts of the Citizens to cultivate a spirit of subordination and obedience to Government, to entertain a brotherly affection and love for one another, for their fellow Citizens of the United States at large, and particularly for their brethren who have served in the Field, and finally, that he would most graciously be pleased to dispose us all, to do Justice, to love mercy, and to demean ourselves with that Charity, humility and pacific temper of mind, which were the Characteristicks of the Divine Author of our blessed Religion, and without an humble imitation of whose example in these things, we can never hope to be a happy Nation.

10.3   To JONATHAN TRUMBULL Mount Vernon, July 20, 1788. My dear Trumbull: Humphreys...from the wonderful revolution of sentiment in favour of federal measures, and the marvellous change for the better in the elections of your State, that he shall begin to suspect that miracles have not ceased; indeed, for myself, since so much liberality has been displayed in the construction and adoption of the proposed General Government, I am almost disposed to be of the same opinion. Or at least we may, with a kind of grateful and pious exultation, trace the finger of Providence through those dark and mysterious events, which first induced the States to appoint a general Convention and then led them one after another (by such steps as were best calculated to effect the object) into an adoption of the system recommended by that general Convention; thereby, in all human probability, laying a lasting foundation for tranquillity and happiness; when we had but too much reason to fear that confusion and misery were coming rapidly upon us. That the same good Providence may still continue to protect us and prevent us from dashing the cup of national felicity just as it has been lifted to our lips, is the earnest prayer of My Dear Sir, your faithful friend, &c.

10.4   To NATHANIEL GORHAM Mount Vernon, July 21, 1788.With earnest prayers that you and all the worthy Patriots of America may long enjoy uninterrupted felicity under the New Government.

10.5   To REVEREND SAMUEL LANGDON New York, September 28, 1789. The man must be bad indeed who can look upon the events of the American Revolution without feeling the warmest gratitude towards the great Author of the Universe whose divine interposition was so frequently manifested in our behalf. And it is my earnest prayer that we may so conduct ourselves as to merit a continuance of those blessings with which we have hitherto been favored. I am etc.

10.6   To GEORGE WILLIAM FAIRFAX State of New York, July 10, 1783. I unite my prayers most fervently with yours, for Wisdom to these U States and have no doubt, after a little while all errors in the present form of their Government will be corrected and a happy temper be diffused through the whole; but like young heirs come a little prematurely perhaps to a large

Inheritance it is more than probable they will riot for a while.

10.7   To THE MINISTERS, ELDERS, DEACONS, AND MEMBERS OF THE REFORMED GERMAN CONGREGATION OF NEW YORK New York, November 27, 1783. The establishment of Civil and Religious Liberty was the Motive which induced me to the Field; the object is attained, and it now remains to be my earnest wish and prayer, that the Citizens of the United States would make a wise and virtuous use of the blessings, placed before them; and that the reformed German Congregation in New York; may not only be conspicuous for their religious character, but as exemplary, in support of our inestimable acquisitions, as their reverend Minister has been in the attainment of them.

10.8   To JONATHAN TRUMBULL Mount Vernon, June 8, 1788. Mr. Henry and Colo. Mason are at the head of the opposition; May all things turn out for the best; in respect to this highly favored Continent, is the constant and unfeigned prayer of Yours....

10.9   To JAMES McHENRY Mount Vernon, July 31, 1788. I earnestly pray that the Omnipotent Being who has not deserted the cause of America in the hour of its extremest hazard, will never yield so fair a heritage of freedom a prey to Anarchy or Despotism.

11   Prayers For Royalty

11.1   To THE KING OF FRANCE City of New York, April 6, 1790. We pray God to keep your Majesty under his holy protection.

11.2   To THE QUEEN OF PORTUGAL Philadelphia, February 21, 1791. I pray God to keep you, Great and good Friend, under his holy Protection.

11.3   To THE KING OF FRANCE New York, October 9, 1789. Permit me to assure your Majesty of the unceasing gratitude and attachment of the United States and of our prayers, that the Almighty will be pleased to keep you, our great and beloved Friend and Ally under his constant guidance and protection.

11.4   To THE EARL OF BUCHAN Philadelphia, June 20, 1792. With sincere prayers for the health and happiness of your Lordship; and gratefully impressed with the many marks of attention which I have received from you. I have the honor etc.

11.5   To THE COUNTESS OF HUNTINGDON Mount Vernon, February 27, 1785. My Lady: It will appear evident, from the date of my publication, that

I could not at the time it was promulgated, have had an eye to your Ladyship's plan of emigration; and I earnestly pray that my communication of the matter at this time, may receive no other interpretation than what is really meant....

11.6 To THE KING OF FRANCE New York, October 9, 1789. To our great and beloved Friend and Ally, his Most Christian Majesty. By the change which has taken place in the national government of the United States, the honor of receiving and answering your Majesty's letter of the 7th. of June, to "the President and Members of Congress" has devolved upon me. Permit me to assure your Majesty of the unceasing gratitude and attachment of the United States and of our prayers, that the Almighty will be pleased to keep you, our great and beloved Friend and Ally under his constant guidance and protection.

11.7 To THE KING OF FRANCE City of New York, April 6, 1790. Very great and good Friend and Ally: We pray God to keep your Majesty under his holy protection.

12 Prayers For Indians

12.1 SPEECH TO THE DELAWARE CHIEFS Head Quarters, Middle Brook, May 12, 1779. Brothers: When you have seen all you want to see, I will then wish you a good Journey to Philadelphia. I hope you may find there every thing your hearts can wish, that when you return home you may be able to tell your Nation good things of us. And I pray God he may make your Nation wise and Strong, that they may always see their own] true interest and have courage to walk in the right path; and that they never may be deceived by lies to do any thing against the people of these States, who are their Brothers and ought always to be one people with them.

12.2 TALK TO THE CHEROKEE NATION City of Philadelphia, August 29, 1796. I now send my best wishes to the Cherokees, and pray the Great Spirit to preserve them.

13 Thanksgiving Prayers

13.1 GENERAL ORDERS Head Quarters, Cambridge, November 18, 1775. The Honorable the Legislature of this Colony having thought fit to set apart Thursday the 23d of November Instant, as a day of public thanksgiving "to offer up our praises, and prayers to Almighty God, the Source and Benevolent

Bestower of all good; That he would be pleased graciously to continue, to smile upon our Endeavours, to restore peace, preserve our Rights, and Privileges, to the latest posterity; prosper the American Arms, preserve and strengthen the Harmony of the United Colonies, and avert the Calamities of a civil war." The General therefore commands that day to be observed with all the Solemnity directed by the Legislative Proclamation, and all Officers, Soldiers and others, are hereby directed, with the most unfeigned Devotion, to obey the same.

13.2   To THOMAS McKEAN Mount Vernon, November 15, 1781. Sir: I have the Honor to acknowledge the Receipt of your Favor. of the 31st. ulto. covering the Resolutions of Congress of 29th. and a Proclamation for a Day of public Prayer and Thanksgiving; The Success of the Combined Arms against our Enemies at York and Gloucester, as it affects the Welfare and Independence of the United States, I viewed as a most fortunate Event. In performing my Part towards its Accomplishment, I consider myself to have done only my Duty and in the Execution of that I ever feel myself happy. And at the same Time, as it agurs [sic] well to our Cause, I take a particular Pleasure in acknowledging, that the interposing Hand of Heaven in the various Instances of our extensive Preparations for this Operation, has been most conspicuous and remarkable.

13.3   GENERAL ORDERS Friday, April 18, 1783. The Jersey regiment gives the Guards and the Jersey battalion the fatigues tomorrow. The Commander in Chief orders the Cessation of Hostilities between the United States of America and the King of Great Britain to be publickly proclaimed tomorrow at 12 o'clock...After which the Chaplains with the several Brigades will render thanks to almighty God for all his mercies, particularly for his over ruling the wrath of man to his own glory, and causing the rage of war to cease amongst the nations....on such a happy day, a day which is the harbinger of Peace, a day which compleats the eighth year of the war, it would be ingratitude not to rejoice!...The glorius task for which we first fleu to Arms being thus accomplished, the liberties of our Country being fully acknowledged, and firmly secured by the smiles of heaven, on the purity of our cause, and the honest exertions of a feeble people (determined to be free) against a powerful Nation (disposed to oppress them) and the Character of those who have persevered, through every extremity of hardship; suffering and danger being immortalized by the illustrious appellation of the patriot Army…

13.4 THANKSGIVING PROCLAMATION [*WGW* Note: A copy of this proclamation was sent to the executives of the States by the President in a brief form letter (October 3). This form is recorded in the "Letter Book" in the Washington Papers.] City of New York, October 3, 1789. Whereas it is the duty of all Nations to acknowledge the providence of Almighty God, to obey his will, to be grateful for his benefits, and humbly to implore his protection and favor, and Whereas both Houses of Congress have by their joint Committee requested me "to recommend to the People of the United States a day of public thanks-giving and prayer to be observed by acknowl edging with grateful hearts the many signal favors of Almighty God, especially by affording them an opportunity peaceably to establish a form of government for their safety and happiness." Now therefore I do recommend and assign Thursday the 26th. day of November next to be devoted by the People of these States to the service of that great and glorious Being, who is the beneficent Author of all the good that was, that is, or that will be. That we may then all unite in rendering unto him our sincere and humble thanks, for his kind care and protection of the People of this country previous to their becoming a Nation, for the signal and manifold mercies, and the favorable interpositions of his providence, which we experienced in the course and conclusion of the late war, for the great degree of tranquillity, union, and plenty, which we have since enjoyed, for the peaceable and rational manner in which we have been enabled to establish constitutions of government for our safety and happiness, and particularly the national One now lately instituted, for the civil and religious liberty with which we are blessed, and the means we have of acquiring and diffusing useful knowledge and in general for all the great and various favors which he hath been pleased to confer upon us. And also that we may then unite in most humbly offering our prayers and supplications to the great Lord and Ruler of Nations and beseech him to pardon our national and other transgressions, to enable us all, whether in public or private stations, to perform our several and relative duties properly and punctually, to render our national government a blessing to all the People, by constantly being a government of wise, just and constitutional laws, discreetly and faithfully executed and obeyed, to protect and guide all Sovereigns and Nations (especially such as have shown kindness unto us) and to bless them with good government, peace, and concord. To promote the knowledge and practice of true religion and virtue, and the encrease of science among them and Us, and generally to grant unto all Mankind such a degree of temporal prosperity as he alone knows to be best. [This was the first national Thanksgiving Day proclamation under the Constitution.]

14   **Prayers For Legislation and Negotiation**

14.1   To WILLIAM GRAYSON Mount Vernon, July 26, 1786. I wish very sincerely that the Land Ordinance may answer the expectations of Congress. I had, and still have my doubts of the utility of the plan, but pray devoutly, that they may never be realized, as I am desirous of seeing it a productive branch of the Revenue.

14.2   To WILLIAM VANS MURRAY Mount Vernon, October 26, 1799. You are going to be employed in an important, and delicate Negotiation; for the success of which, in all its relations, no one more ardently, and sincerely prays than I do.

15   **Prayers For Churches**

15.1   To THE MEMBERS OF THE NEW CHURCH IN BALTIMORE [Philadelphia, January 27, 1793.] Your prayers for my present and future felicity are received with gratitude; and I sincerely wish, Gentlemen, that you may in your social and individual capacities taste those blessings, which a gracious God bestows upon the Righteous.

15.2   To THE MINISTERS, ELDERS, AND DEACONS OF THE REFORMED DUTCH CHURCH AT ALBANY Albany, June 28, 1782. Your benevolent wishes and fervent prayers for my personal wellfare and felicity, demand all my gratitude. May the preservation of your civil and religious Liberties still be the care of an indulgent Providence; and may the rapid increase and universal extension of knowledge virtue and true Religion be the consequence of a speedy and honorable Peace. I am etc.

15.3   To THE MINISTER, ELDERS, AND DEACONS OF THE REFORMED PROTESTANT DUTCH CHURCH IN KINGSTON Kingston, November 16, 1782. In return for your kind concern for my temporal and eternal happiness, permit me to assure you that my wishes are reciprocal; and that you may be enabled to hand down your Religion pure and undefiled to a Posterity worthy of their Ancestors.

15.4   To THE MINISTER, ELDERS, AND DEACONS OF THE TWO

UNITED DUTCH REFORMED CHURCHES OF HACKENSACK AND SCHALENBURGH AND THE INHABITANTS OF HACKENSACK November 10, 1783. In retiring from the field of Contest to the sweets of private life, I claim no merit, but if in that retirement my most earnest wishes and prayers can be of any avail, nothing will exceed the prosperity of our common Country, and the temporal and spiritual felicity of those who are represented in your Address.

16   **Prayers For Nations**

16.1   To GEORGE MARTIN Head Quarters, August 10, 1783. I cannot but join with you in my most earnest prayers, that these States may be blessed with Wisdom equal to the arduous Task of rightly formg the Establishment of their New Empire. And while I thus express my Wishes in favor of my Native Country, I would felicitate the Kingdom of Ireland on their Emancipation from British Controul, and extend my pious Entreaties, that Heaven may establish them in a happy and perpetuated Tranquility, enjoying a freedom of Legislation, and an unconfined Extension of Trade, that connecting Link, which binds together the remotest Countries.

16.2   To COMTE DE ROCHAMBEAU New York, October 13, 1789. The Revolution, announced by the intelligence from France, must be interesting to the nations of the world in general, and is certainly of the greatest importance to the country in which it has happened. I am persuaded I express the sentiments of my fellow-citizens, when I offer an earnest prayer, that it may terminate in the permanent honor and happiness of your government and people. With sentiments of respectful affection &c.

16.3   To BARON VAN DER CAPELLEN DE POL Head Quarters, State of New York, August 2, 1783. Your Nation, Sir, and your Character in particular, have indeed merited the confidence and regard of the confederated States of America, and they will long I trust be considered with grateful veneration. The Union so happily commenced, will I hope be cultivated by both with the utmost care and Attention, and I pray to Heaven, that it may be as durable as mutual Interests and reciprocal benefits can render it....May Heaven long Bless your Country with the enjoyment of her liberty, the choicest Earthly layout; and may personal happiness and domestic pleasures, ever attend your footsteps through all your future Walks of Life.

16.4   To MARQUIS DE LAFAYETTE Philadelphia, November 22, 1791. I
cannot conclude this letter without congratulating you most sincerely on the
King's acceptance of the Constitution presented to him by National
Assembly, and upon the happy consequences which promise to flow upon
your Country, as well as to mankind in general, from that event. The prayers
and wishes of the friends to the human race have attended the exertions of
your Nation, and when your affairs are completely settled under an energetic
and equal government the hearts of good men will be gratified, and no one
will rejoice in your felicity, and for the noble and disinterested part you
have acted more than your sincere friend and truly Affectionate &c.

16.5   To MARQUIS DE LA LUZERNE Philadelphia, September 10, 1791. The
complete restoration of our public credit holds us up in a high light abroad.
Thus it appears that the United States are making great progress towards
national happiness, and if it is not attained here in as high a degree as human
nature will admit of its going, I think we may then conclude that political
happiness is unattainable. But at the same time we wish it not to be confined
to this Country alone; and, as it expands through the world, our enjoyments
will expand with it; and that you may find it in your nation, and realize it
yourself, is the sincere prayer of, Sir, &c.

16.6   To MARQUIS DE LAFAYETTE New York, October 14, 1789. The
revolution, which has taken place with you, is of such magnitude and of so
momentous a nature that we hardly yet dare to form a conjecture about it. We
however trust, and fervently pray that its consequences may prove happy to a
nation, in whose fate we have so much cause to be interested and that its
influence may be felt with pleasure by future generations.

17   Prayers For Government in Health Crisis

17.1   To THE TRUSTEES OF THE PUBLIC SCHOOL OF
GERMANTOWN [November 6, 1793.] Where it will be best for Congress
to remain will depend on circumstances which are daily unfolding themselves,
and for the issue of which, we can but offer up our prayers to the Sovereign
Dispenser of life and health. His favor too on our oft, the good sense and
firmness of our fellow Citizens, and fidelity in those they employ, will secure
to us a permanence of good government.

18   Prayers For a University

18.1   To THE INHABITANTS OF PRINCETON AND NEIGHBOR-
HOOD, TOGETHER WITH THE PRESIDENT AND FACULTY OF
THE COLLEGE Rocky Hill, August 25, 1783. I now return you
Gentlemen my thanks for your benevolent wishes, and make it my earnest
prayer to Heaven, that every temporal and divine blessing may be bestowed
on the Inhabitants of Princeton, on the neighbourhood, and on the President
and Faculty of the College of New Jersey, and that the usefulness of this
Institution in promoting the interests of Religion and Learning may be
universally extended.

19   Prayers For Individuals and Friends

19.1   To WILLIAM HEATH Mount Vernon, May 20, 1797. It gives me great
pleasure to hear from yourself, that you are writing Memoirs first published
in Boston in 1798…That you may enjoy health to complete the work to
your entire satisfaction, I devoutly pray, and that you may live afterwards to
hear it applauded (as I doubt not it will be) I as sincerely wish.

19.2   To REVEREND BRYAN, LORD FAIRFAX Mount Vernon, January 20,
1799. For the details contained in these several letters, I pray you to accept my
thanks; and congratulations on your safe arrival in England, although the
Passage, on the whole, was not altogether as expeditious and agreeable as you
expected. To this prayer, let me add my best wishes for the perfect restoration
of your health, and the accomplishment of such other objects as might have
induced you to undertake the Voyage. After which it would give your friends
in this Country much pleasure to hail your return.

19.3   To MARQUIS DE LAFAYETTE Mount Vernon, December 8, 1784. My
fervent prayers are offered for your safe and pleasant passage, happy meeting
with Madame la Fayette and family, and the completion of every wish of your
heart, in all which Mrs. Washington joins me, as she does in compliments to
Capt. Grandchean and the Chevalier [Caraman] of whom little Washington
often speaks.

19.4   To BENJAMIN FRANKLIN New York, September 23, 1789. Dear Sir:
The affectionate congratulations on the recovery of my health, and the warm
expressions of personal friendship which were contained in your favor of the
16th instant, claim my gratitude. And the consideration that it was written
when you were afflicted with a painful malady, greatly increases my obligation

for it.

Would to God, my dear Sir, that I could congratulate you upon the removal of that excruciating pain under which you labour! and that your existence might close with as much ease to yourself, as its continuance has been beneficial to our Country and useful to mankind! Or, if the United wishes of a free people, joined with the earnest prayers of every friend to Science and humanity could relieve the body from pains or Infirmities, you could claim an exemption on this score. ...so long as I retain my memory, you will be thought on with respect, veneration and Affection by Your sincere friend etc.

19.5   To THOMAS JEFFERSON Philadelphia, January 1, 1794. Let a conviction of my most earnest prayers for your happiness accompany you in your retirement; and while I accept with the warmest thanks your solicitude for my welfare, I beg you to believe that I always am &c.

19.6   To THE MARQUISE DE LAFAYETTE Philadelphia, June 13, 1793. While I acknowledge the receipt of your letter of the 13 of March,...I enclose you duplicates of two letters which I had the honor of writing to you on the 31st. of January and 16. of March. To these I can only add my most ardent prayers, that you may be again united to M. de la Fayette, under circumstances that may be joyful to you both; and that the evening of that life, whose morning has been devoted to the cause of liberty and humanity, may be crowned with the best of heaven's blessings.

19.7   To MARQUIS DE LAFAYETTE Philadelphia, June 10, 1792. Hamilton Knox Jay and Jefferson are well and remember you with affection. Mrs. Washington desires to be presented to you in terms of friendship and warm regard, to which I add my most affectionate wishes and sincere prayers for your health and happiness, and request you to make the same acceptable to Madm. le Fayette and your children.

19.8   To JULIAN URSYN NIEMCEWICZ Mount Vernon, June 18, 1798. That your country is not as happy as your struggle to make it so, was Patriotic and Noble, is a matter which all lovers of national Liberty and the Rights of Man, have sorely lamented: and if my Vows, during the arduous contest could have availed, you would now, have been as happy in the enjoyment of these desirable blessings under your own Vine and Fig Tree, as the People of these United States may be under theirs. The flattering expressions of your letter, excites all my Sensibility, and in making a tender of the best wishes of Mrs. Washington and Miss Custis for your polite remembrance of them, I do not forget to pray, although I am persuaded, nothing can eradicate from a mind susceptible as yours is, the recollection of those misfortunes which have befallen your Country, that you may experience in this, such attentions, as may have a tendency to alleviate the poignancy of them.

19.9 To MARQUIS DE LAFAYETTE Mount Vernon, December 25, 1798. Convinced as you must be of the fact, it wd. be a mere waste of time to assure you of the sincere and heartfelt pleasure I derived from finding by the above letters, that you had not only regained your liberty; but were in the enjoyment of better health than could have been expected from your long and rigorous confinement; and that madame La Fayette and the young ladies were able to Survive it attall. On these desirable events I can add with truth, that amongst your numerous friends none can offer his congratulations with more warmth, or who prays more sincerely for the perfect restoration of your ladies health, than I do.

19.10 To DANIEL MORGAN Mount Vernon, April 10, 1799. I assure you my dear sir it gave me not a little pleasure, to find the account of your death in the news papers was not founded in fact and I sincerely pray that many years may elapse before that event takes place, and that in the mean time you may be restored to the full enjoyment of your health and to your usefulness in Society being With very great regard etc.

20 Thanks for Prayers

20.1 To THE RECTOR, CHURCH WARDENS, AND VESTRYMEN OF THE UNITED EPISCOPAL CHURCHES OF CHRIST CHURCH AND ST. PETER'S [in Philadelphia, Pa.] [March 2, 1797.] Gentlemen: To this public testimony of your approbation of my conduct and affection for my person I am not insensible, and your prayers for my present and future happiness merit my warmest acknowledgments. It is with peculiar satisfaction I can say, that, prompted by a high sense of duty in my attendance on public worship, I have been gratified, during my residence among you, by the liberal and interesting discourses which have been delivered in your Churches. Believing that that Government alone can be approved by Heaven, which promotes peace and secures protection to its Citizens in every thing that is dear and interesting to them, it has been the great object of my administration to insure those invaluable ends; and when, to a consciousness of the purity of intentions, is added the approbation of my fellow Citizens, I shall experience in my retirement that heartfelt satisfaction which can only be exceeded by the hope of future happiness.

20.2 To THE GRAND LODGE OF ANCIENT, FREE AND ACCEPTED MASONS OF THE COMMONWEALTH OF MASSACHUSETTS Mount Vernon, April 24, 1797. Brothers: In that retirement which declining years induced me to seek, and which repose, to a mind long employed in public concerns, rendered necessary, my wishes that bounteous Providence will continue to bless and preserve our country in Peace, and in the prosperity it has enjoyed, will be warm and sincere; And my attachment to the Society of which we are members will dispose me, always, to contribute my best endeavours to promote the honor and interest of the Craft. For the Prayer you offer in my behalf I entreat you to accept the thanks of a grateful heart; with the assurance of fraternal regard and best wishes for the honor, happiness and prosperity of all the Members of the Grand-lodge of Massachusetts.

20.3 To JOSEPH REED Fredericksburg in the State of N. York, November 27, 1778. It is eleven O'clock at Night and I am to set out early in the Morning, for which reason I shall only add my thanks for the favourable Sentiments you are pleased to entertain for, and have expressed of me but in a more especial manner for your good wishes and prayers. With sincere esteem and affection, and with Compts. to Mrs. Reed.

20.4 To THE REVEREND UZAL OGDEN "A sermon on practical religion. Inscribed to Christians of every denomination. No. I. (Chatham: Printed by Shepard Kollock)." Revd. Sir: I have received, and with pleasure read, the Sermon you were so obliging as to send me. I thank you for this proof of your attention. I thank you also for the favourable sentiments you have been pleased to express of me. But in a more especial mannr. I thank you for the good wishes and prayers you offer in my behalf. These have a just claim to the gratitude of, Revd. Sir, Your most obedient, obliged, humble servant, G. Washington.

20.5 To ROBERT CARTER NICHOLAS Camp at Cambridge, October 5, 1775. My Respectful compliments to Mrs. Nicholas and the rest of your Fireside, and to any inquiring friends, conclude me, with grateful thanks for the Prayers and good wishes you have been pleased to offer on my account, Dear Sir, etc.

20.6 To REVEREND WILLIAM GORDON New York, May 13, 1776. The

fortunate discovery, of the Intentions of Ministry, in Lord George Germain's Letter to Govr. Eden is to be Ranked among many other signal Interpositions of Providence, and must serve to inspire every reflecting Mind with Confidence. No Man has a more perfect Reliance on the all wise and powerful dispensations of the Supreme Being than I have nor thinks his aid more necessary. The favourable Sentiments you say the Gentlemen of Providence are pleased to entertain of me are exceedingly flattering, and when by an attentive observance, and discharge of my duty I can acquire the good wishes and prayers of our American Friends I shall think myself double happy; happy in their good opinion, happy; in a conscious Integrity...

21   Reciprocal Prayers

21.1   From THE ARTILLERY COMPANY OF THE TOWN OF NEWPORT, RHODE ISLAND Feb. 27, 1794. Humbly beseeching the Supreme Giver of all good gifts to continue your life and public usefulness, and that they with their fellow citizens, may still gratefully reciprocate the satisfaction resulting from a faithful discharge of important duties.

21.2   To THE ARTILLERY COMPANY OF THE TOWN OF NEWPORT, RHODE ISLAND [February, 1794.] Gentlemen: For your kind congratulations on the anniversary of my birthday, and the other obliging expressions of your Address I pray you to accept my grateful thanks.To cherish those principles which effected the revolution, and laid the foundation of our free and happy Government, does honor to your patriotism; as do the sentiments of commiseration for the sufferings of the unfortunate, and the good wishes for the happiness of the great family of mankind, to your philanthropy. Your prayer for me, is reciprocated by the best vows I can offer for your welfare.

21.3   From THE OFFICERS OF THE TENTH AND NINETY-FIRST REGIMENTS OF THE VIRGINIA MILITIA October 6, 1798. To this permit us to add our fervent supplications to Heaven, that you may long live to enjoy these blessings which you have been so instrumental in procuring to your country, and in that repose which you have always sacrificed in obedience to the will of the nation.

21.4   To THE OFFICERS OF THE TENTH AND NINETY-FIRST REGIMENTS OF THE VIRGINIA MILITIA Mount Vernon, October 24, 1798. Your prayers, and kind wishes in my behalf, I reciprocate with great

Cordiality.

21.5   To REVEREND WILLIAM GORDON Philadelphia, July 19, 1791. I ...shall only add my thanks for the prayers and good wishes which you offer for my happiness, and assure you that I reciprocate them with very great sincerity.

21.6   To GEORGE MARTIN Head Quarters, August 10, 1783. I cannot but join with you in my most earnest prayers, that these States may be blessed with Wisdom equal to the arduous Task of rightly forming the Establishment of their New Empire. And while I thus express my Wishes in favor of my Native Country, I would felicitate the Kingdom of Ireland on their Emancipation from British Control, and extend my pious Entreaties, that Heaven may establish them in a happy and perpetuated Tranquility, enjoying a freedom of Legislation, and an unconfined Extension of Trade, that connecting Link, which binds together the remotest Countries.

21.7   To REVEREND WILLIAM GORDON Philadelphia, February 25, 1791. I presume, therefore, it will hardly be necessary to offer an apology to you for the want of punctuality in acknowledging the receipt of your letters. I should, however, be deficient in civility and gratitude was I not to return my best thanks for the elegantly bound volumes of your history, which you have been so polite as to send to me, and for the ardent prayers for my health and happiness which are expressed in your letters. I beg you to be assured that my good wishes attend you, and that I shall always be glad to hear of your prosperity.

21.8   THE HUMBLE ADDRESS OF THE MINISTERS, ELDERS AND DEACONS OF THE REFORMED PROTESTANT DUTCH CHURCH IN KINGSTON November 15, 1782. To the Excellency George Washington Esquire General and Commander in Chief of the American Army etc: Amidst the general joy which instantly pervaded all ranks of people here on hearing of your Excellency's intended visit to this place, We the Ministers, Elders and Deacons of the Protestant Reformed Dutch Church in Kingston; participated in it; And now beg leave with the greatest respect and esteem to hail your arrival. The experience of a number of years past has convinced us that your wisdom, integrity and fortitude have been adequate to the arduous task your country has imposed upon you. Never have we in the most perilous of times known your Excellency to despond, nor in the most prosperous to slacken in activity: But with the utmost resolution persevere until by the aid of the Almighty you have brought us thus near to independence, freedom and peace Permit us to add: that as the loss of our religious rights was partly involved in that of our civil, and your being instrumental in restoring the one, affords us a happy presage that the Divine Being will prosper your endeavors to promote the other. When the sword shall be sheathed and peace reestablished, whensoever it is the will of Heaven that your Excellency has lived long enough for the purposes of nature, then may you enter triumphantly thro' the Blood of the Lamb, into the Regions of Bliss there to take possession of that Crown of Glory, the Reward of the Virtuous and which fadeth not away. By Order of the Consistory Kingston, November 15, 1782. George J: L: Doll. V. D. M.

21.9   To THE MINISTER, ELDERS, AND DEACONS OF THE REFORMED PROTESTANT DUTCH CHURCH IN KINGSTON Kingston, November 16, 1782. Gentlemen: I am happy in receiving this public mark of the esteem of the Minister, Elders and Deacons of the Reformed Protestant Dutch Church in Kingston. Convinced that our Religious Liberties were as essential as our Civil, my endeavours have never been wanting to encourage and promote the one, while I have been contending for the other; and I am highly flattered by finding that my efforts have met the approbation of so respectable a body. In return for your kind concern for my temporal and eternal happiness, permit me to assure you that my wishes are reciprocal; and that you may be enabled to hand down your Religion pure and undefiled to a Posterity worthy of their Ancestors. I am Gentlemen, Etc., GW.

21.10   To REVEREND WILLIAM LINN Mount Vernon, June 4, 1798. Revd. Sir: I received with thankfulness your favour of the 30th. Ulto., enclosing the discourse delivered by you on the day recommended by the President of the United States to be observed as a general Fast. I have read them both with pleasure; and feel grateful for the favourable sentiments you have been pleased to express in my behalf; but more especially for those good wishes which you offer for my temporal and eternal happiness; which I reciprocate with great cordiality, being with esteem and respect, Revd. Sir Your etc. [What makes Washington's statements here so powerful is that the sermon is a direct attack against Deism and the views of Thomas Paine. Moreover, the reciprocal prayers for eternal happiness that Washington affirms here are explicitly made in the context of the saving work of the Redeemer—Jesus Christ and the concomitant hope of a "crown of glory in heaven". If Washington did not really mean these words in this context, it was not only intentionally deceptive, it was anything but an expression of "cordiality," "esteem" and "respect."]

Washington's Synonyms for Prayer

Washington's prayer vocabulary went beyond the simple use of the word prayer. Washington's synonyms for prayer include the phrases vows, wishes and prayers, supplications, imploring, oaths, , entreaties, benediction, invoke, etc.

22.   An example of "wishes and prayers"

22.1   To HANNAH FAIRFAX WASHINGTON Mount Vernon, May 20, 1792. Dear Madam: Mrs. Washington received with much pleasure your kind remembrance and affectionate regards, and would, were she here, where I am come for a few days only, return the same with much sincerity to which permit me to add the best wishes and ardent prayers for your happiness. I am etc.

23.   An example of "wishes and vows"

23.1   To THE INHABITANTS OF SHEPHERDS TOWN AND ITS VICINITY United States, October 12, 1796. Gentlemen: That Beneficent Providence, which, hitherto, has preserved us in Peace, and increased our prosperity, will not, I trust, withdraw its protecting hand; while we, on our part, endeavour to merit a continuance of its favors. For the favorable sentiments you have expressed for me, and for your kind wishes, I sincerely thank you, and reciprocate with great cordiality my vows for your welfare.

24.   Washington frequently uses the word "vow" as a synonym for prayer. Consider these many examples:

24.1   IN WASHINGTON'S FIRST DRAFT OF HIS FAREWELL ADDRESS, [dated May 15, 1796, he outlines his vows or prayers that he promises to carry with him from government to the day he would die. Writing to his "Friends and Fellow Citizens" he declares:] ...the curtain is to drop forever on the public scenes of my life ... All the returns I have now to make will be in those vows which I shall carry with me to my retirement and to my grave, that Heaven may continue to favor the people of the United

States with the choicest tokens of its beneficence; that their union and brotherly affection may be perpetual; that the free Constitution which is the work of their own hands, may be sacredly maintained; that its administration in every department, may be stamped with wisdom and with virtue; and that this character may be ensured to it, by that watchfulness over public servants and public measures, which on the one hand will be necessary, to prevent or correct a degeneracy; and that forbearance, on the other, from unfounded or indiscriminate jealousies which would deprive the public of the best services, by depriving a conscious integrity of one of the noblest incitements to perform them; that in fine the happiness of the people of America, under the auspices of liberty, may be made complete, by so careful a preservation, and so prudent a use of this blessing, as will acquire them the glorious satisfaction of recommending it to the affection; the praise; and the adoption of every Nation which is yet a stranger to it. That as the allwise dispensor of human blessings has favored no Nation of the Earth with more abundant, and substantial means of happiness than United America, that we may not be so ungrateful to our Creator; so wanting to ourselves; and so regardless of Posterity, as to dash the cup of beneficence which is thus bountifully offered to our acceptance....I retire from the Chair of government...I leave you with undefiled hands, an uncorrupted heart, and with ardent vows to heaven for the welfare and happiness of that country in which I and my forefathers to the third or fourth progenitor drew our first breath.

24.2   FAREWELL ADDRESS In looking forward to the moment, which is intended to terminate the career of my public life....your support was the essential prop....I shall carry it with me to my grave, as a strong incitement to unceasing vows that Heaven may continue to you the choicest tokens of its beneficence; that your Union and brotherly affection may be perpetual; that the free constitution, which is the work of your hands, may be sacredly maintained.

24.3   To MARQUIS DE LAFAYETTE Mount Vernon, October 8, 1797. M. Frestal has been a true Mentor to George....Both your son and him carry with them the vows, and regrets of this family, and of all who know them. ...With what concerns myself, personally, I shall not take up your time; further than to add, that I have once more retreated to the shades of my own Vine and Fig tree, where I shall remain with best vows for the prosperity of that country for whose happiness I have toiled many years, to establish its

Independence, Constitution, and Laws, and for the good of mankind in general, until the days of my sojournment, whh. cannot be many, are accomplished.

24.4   To COMTE DE GRASSE Head Quarters Before York, October 19, 1781. I entreat Yr. Excellcy. to accept the sincere and ardent vows which I make for your recovery, and the preservation of a Health so dear to our two Nations.

24.5   To COMTE DE GRASSE October 28, 1781. I am much afflicted at hearing the continuance of Yr indisposition; my ardent vows are repeated for your speedy reestablishment.

24.6   To COMTE DE GRASSE November 5, 1781. I entreat your Excellency to accept my ardent vows for the speedy and perfect reestablishment of your health, and the sentiments of sincere friendship with which I shall ever remain.

24.7   To MARQUIS DE LAFAYETTE Mount Vernon in Virginia, November 15, 1781. If I should be deprived of the pleasure of a personal interview with you before your departure, permit me my dear Marquis to adopt this method of making you a tender of my ardent Vows for a propitious voyage, a gracious reception from your Prince, an honorable reward for your Services, a happy meeting with your lady and friends, and a safe return in the Spring.

24.8   To WATSON & CASSOUL State of New York, August 10, 1782. For your affectionate Vows, permit me to be grateful; and offer mine for true Brothers in all parts of the World; and to assure you of the sincerity with which I am etc.

24.9   To MARCHIONESS DE LAFAYETTE Mount Vernon, April 4, 1784. The charms of your person, and the beauties of your mind, have a more powerful operation. These Madam, have endeared you to me, and every thing which partakes of your nature will have a claim to my affections. George and Virginia (the offspring of your love), whose names do honor to my Country, and to myself, have a double claim and will be the objects of my vows.

24.10   To MARCHIONESS DE LAFAYETTE Mount Vernon, November 25, 1784. The Marquis returns to you with all the warmth and ardour of a newly inspired lover. We restore him to you in good health, crowned with wreaths of love and respect from every part of the Union. That his meeting with you, his family and friends, may be propitious, and as happy as your wishes can make it: that you may long live together revered and beloved, and that you may transmit to a numerous progeny the virtue which you both possess, is consonate with the vow and fervent wish of your devoted and most respectful Humble Servant.

24.11 To CHEVALIER DE LA LUZERNE Mount Vernon, December 5, 1784. If any thing could overcome the present difficulties which impede my desires to pay my respectful homage at your Court, it would be the wish …but I fear my vows and earnest wishes are the only tribute of respect I shall ever have it in my power to offer them in return.

24.12 To MARCHIONESSE DE LAFAYETTE Mount Vernon, May 10, 1786. My Mother will receive the compliments you honor her with, as a flattering mark of your attention; and I shall have great pleasure in delivering them myself. My best wishes and vows are offered for you, and for the fruits of your love, and with every sentiment of respect and attachment. I have the honor, etc.

24.13 To MARQUIS DE LAFAYETTE Mount Vernon, March 25, 1787. I have lately lost a Brother (Colo. John Augt. Washington which I mention to account for the black Seal of this letter) the rest of my friends, and every individual in the Family are tolerably well and join most cordially in every vow that can contribute to the health and happiness of Madam La Fayette yourself and family.

24.14 To THE INHABITANTS OF SHEPHERDS TOWN AND ITS VICINITY United States, October 12, 1796. Gentlemen: That Beneficent Providence, which, hitherto, has preserved us in Peace, and increased our prosperity, will not, I trust, withdraw its protecting hand; while we, on our part, endeavour to merit a continuance of its favors. For the favorable sentiments you have expressed for me, and for your kind wishes, I sincerely thank you, and reciprocate with great cordiality my vows for your welfare.

24.15 To THE CITIZENS OF ALEXANDRIA AND ITS NEIGHBORHOOD [March 23, 1797.] For the prosperity of the Town and neighbourhood, and for your individual happiness, I offer my best vows.

24.16 To THE CLERGY OF DIFFERENT DENOMINATIONS RESIDING IN AND NEAR THE CITY OF PHILADELPHIA [March 3, 1797.] That your labours for the good of Mankind may be crowned with success; that your temporal enjoyments may be commensurate with your merits; and that the future reward of good and faithful Servants may be your's, I shall not cease to supplicate the Divine Author of life and felicity.

24.17 To JOHN QUINCY ADAMS Mount Vernon, June 25, 1797. I am now, as you supposed the case would be when you then wrote, seated under my Vine and Fig-tree; where, while I am permitted to enjoy the shade of it, my vows will be continually offered for the welfare and prosperity of our country; and for the support, ease and honor of the Gentleman to whom the Administration of its concerns are entrusted.

24.18   To SIR EDWARD NEWENHAM Mount Vernon, August 6, 1797. I am now seated in the shade of my own Vine and Fig tree, and shall devote the remainder of a life, nearly worn out to such Agricultural and rural amusements as will afford employment for myself, and cannot, or ought not, to give offence to any one; offering while I am on this Theatre, my sincere vows that the ravages of war, and the turbulence of passions; may yield their scepters to Peace and tranquility that the world may enjoy repose.

24.19   To REVEREND WILLIAM GORDON Mount Vernon, October 15, 1797. Rural employments while I am spared (which in the natural course of things cannot be long) will now take place of toil, responsibility, and the sollicitudes attending the walks of public life; and with vows for the peace, the happiness, and prosperity of a country in whose service the prime of my life hath been spent, and with best wishes for the tranquility of all Nations, and all men, the scene will close; grateful to that Providence which has directed my steps, and shielded me in the various changes and chances, through which I have passed, from my youth to the present moment.

24.20   To GEORGE WASHINGTON MOTIER LAFAYETTE Mount Vernon, December 5, 1797. If my best vows would have contributed to a prosperous Voyage, and a happy meeting with your Parents and Sisters in France, both must have happened to the utmost extent of your wishes 'ere this, for they were offered on the Altar of Sincerity; and are now followed with assurances that, if you should ever return to America again, that you will find the same cordial reception within the Walls of this Mansion, as you have heretofore experienced.

24.21   To THE TRUSTEES OF WASHINGTON ACADEMY Mount Vernon, June 17, 1798. Sentiments like those which flowed from your Pen, excite my gratitude, whilst I offer my best vows for the prosperity of the Academy, and for the honor and happiness of those under whose auspices it is conducted.

24.22   To JULIAN URSYN NIEMCEWICZ Mount Vernon, June 18, 1798. That your country is not as happy as your struggle to make it so, was Patriotic and Noble, is a matter which all lovers of national Liberty and the Rights of Man, have sorely lamented: and if my Vows, during the arduous contest could have availed, you would now, have been as happy in the enjoyment of these desirable blessings under your own Vine and Fig Tree, as the People of these United States may be under theirs.

25.   **Washington also uses the word "supplication" as a synonym for prayer.**

25.1   To THE CLERGY OF DIFFERENT DENOMINATIONS RESIDING IN AND NEAR THE CITY OF PHILADELPHIA [March 3, 1797.] That your labours for the good of Mankind may be crowned with success; that your temporal enjoyments may be commensurate with your merits; and that the future reward of good and faithful Servants may be your's, I shall not cease to supplicate the Divine Author of life and felicity.

25.2   THE FIRST INAUGURAL ADDRESS [April 30, 1789.] Fellow Citizens of the Senate and the House of Representatives. Such being the impressions under which I have, in obedience to the public summons, repaired to the present station; it would be peculiarly improper to omit in this first official Act, my fervent supplications to that Almighty Being who rules over the Universe, who presides in the Councils of Nations, and whose providential aids can supply every human defect, that his benediction may consecrate to the liberties and happiness of the People of the United States, a Government instituted by themselves for these essential purposes: and may enable every instrument employed in its administration to execute with success, the functions allotted to his charge....Having thus imparted to you my sentiments, as they have been awakened by the occasion which brings us together, I shall take my present leave; but not without resorting once more to the benign parent of the human race, in humble supplication that since he has been pleased to favour the American people, with opportunities for deliberating in perfect tranquility, and dispositions for deciding with unparalleled unanimity on a form of Government, for the security of their Union, and the advancement of their happiness; so his divine blessing may be equally conspicuous in the enlarged views, the temperate consultations, and the wise measures on which the success of this Government must depend.

25.3   To THE FREEHOLDERS AND INHABITANTS OF KINGS COUNTY New York, December 1, 1783. For my own part, Gentlemen, in whatever situation I shall be hereafter, my supplications, will ever ascend to Heaven, for the prosperity of my Country in general; and for the individual happiness of those who are attached to the Freedom, and Independence of America.

25.4 THANKSGIVING PROCLAMATION City of New York, October 3, 1789. And also that we may then unite in most humbly offering our prayers and supplications to the great Lord and Ruler of Nations and beseech him to pardon our national and other transgressions, to enable us all, whether in public or private stations, to perform our several and relative duties properly and punctually, to render our national government a blessing to all the People, by constantly being a government of wise, just and constitutional laws, discreetly and faithfully executed and obeyed, to protect and guide all Sovereigns and Nations (especially such as have shown kindness unto us) and to bless them with good government, peace, and concord. To promote the knowledge and practice of true religion and virtue, and the increase of science among them and Us, and generally to grant unto all Mankind such a degree of temporal prosperity as he alone knows to be best.

25.5 EIGHTH ANNUAL ADDRESS TO CONGRESS December 7, 1796. Fellow Citizens of the Senate and House of Representatives: In recurring to the internal situation of our Country, since I had last the pleasure to Address you, I find ample reason for a renewed expression of that gratitude to the ruler of the Universe, which a continued series of prosperity has so often and so justly called forth. The situation in which I now stand, for the last time, in the midst of the Representatives of the People of the United States, naturally recalls the period when the Administration of the present form of Government commenced; and I cannot omit the occasion, to congratulate you and my Country, on the success of the experiment; nor to repeat my fervent supplications to the Supreme Ruler of the Universe, and Sovereign Arbiter of Nations, that his Providential care may still be extended to the United States; that the virtue and happiness of the People, may be preserved; and that the Government, which they have instituted, for the protection of their liberties, maybe perpetual.

25.6 GENERAL ORDERS Head Quarters, Cambridge, July 16, 1775. The Continental Congress having earnestly recommended, that "Thursday next the 20th. Instant, be observed by the Inhabitants of all the english Colonies upon this Continent, as a Day of public Humiliation, Fasting and Prayer; that they may with united Hearts and Voice unfeignedly confess their Sins before God, and supplicate the all wise and merciful disposer of events, to avert the

Desolation and Calamities of an unnatural war." The General orders, that Day to be religiously observed by the Forces under his Command, exactly in manner directed by the proclamation of the Continental Congress.

25.7   GENERAL ORDERS Head Quarters, New York, May 15, 1776. The Continental Congress having ordered, Friday the 17th. Instant to be observed as a day of "fasting, humiliation and prayer, humbly to supplicate the mercy of Almighty God, that it would please him to pardon all our manifold sins and transgressions, and to prosper the Arms of the United Colonies, and finally, establish the peace and freedom of America, upon a solid and lasting foundation"—The General commands all officers, and soldiers, to pay strict obedience to the Orders of the Continental Congress, and by their unfeigned, and pious observance of their religious duties, incline the Lord, and Giver of Victory, to prosper our arms.

25.8   GENERAL ORDERS Head Quarters, New York, June 30, 1776. Upon the Signal for the enemies approach, or upon any alarm, all fatigue parties are immediately to repair to their respective Corps, with their arms, ammunition and accoutrements ready for instant action,...to see that every Soldier is completed to Twenty-four Rounds, and has a good Flint, well fixed into the lock; in short to be well prepared for an engagement is, under God, (whose divine Aid it behooves us to supplicate) more than one half the battle.

25.9   GENERAL ORDERS Head Quarters, near Germantown, September 13, 1777. The General, with peculiar satisfaction, thanks those gallant officers and soldiers, who, on the 11th. instant, bravely fought in their country and its cause. ...Altho' the event of that day, from some unfortunate circumstances, was not so favorable as could be wished, the General has the satisfaction of assuring the troops, that from every account he has been able to obtain, the enemy's loss greatly exceeded ours; and he has full confidence that in another Appeal to Heaven (with the blessing of providence, which it becomes every officer and soldier humbly to supplicate), we shall prove successful.

26.   Examples of "implore" as a synonym for prayer include:

26.1   ANSWER TO AN ADDRESS OF THE MASSACHUSETTS LEGISLATURE July 4, 1775. In return for your affectionate wishes to myself, permit me to say, that I earnestly implore the divine Being, in whose hands are all human events, to make you and your constituents as distinguished in private and public happiness, as you have been by ministerial oppression, and private and public distress.

26.2   GENERAL ORDERS Head Quarters, Cambridge, July 4, 1775. The General most earnestly requires, and expects, a due observance of those articles of war, established for the Government of the army, which forbid profane cursing, swearing and drunkeness; And in like manner requires and expects, of all Officers, and Soldiers, not engaged on actual duty, a punctual attendance on divine Service, to implore the blessings of heaven upon the means used for our safety and defence.

26.3   GENERAL ORDERS Head Quarters, Cambridge, March 6, 1776. Thursday the seventh Instant, being set apart by the Honourable the Legislature of this province, as a day of fasting, prayer, and humiliation, "to implore the Lord, and Giver of all victory, to pardon our manifold sins and wickedness's, and that it would please him to bless the Continental Arms, with his divine favour and protection"—All Officers, and Soldiers, are strictly enjoined to pay all due reverence, and attention on that day, to the sacred duties due to the Lord of hosts, for his mercies already received, and for those blessings, which our Holiness and Uprightness of life can alone encourage us to hope through his mercy to obtain.

26.4   GENERAL ORDERS Head Quarters, White Marsh, November 30, 1777. Forasmuch as it is the indispensible duty of all men, to adore the superintending providence of Almighty God; to acknowledge with gratitude their obligations to him for benefits received, and to implore such further blessings as they stand in need of; and it having pleased him in his abundant mercy, not only to continue to us the innumerable bounties of his common providence, but also, to smile upon us in the prosecution of a just and necessary war, for the defence of our unalienable rights and liberties.It is therefore recommended by Congress, that Thursday the 18th. day of December next be set apart for Solemn Thanksgiving and Praise; that at one time, and with one voice, the good people may express the grateful feelings of their hearts, and consecrate themselves to the service of their divine benefactor; and that, together with their sincere acknowledgements and offerings they may join the penitent confession of their sins; and supplications for such further blessings as they stand in need of. The Chaplains will properly notice this recommendation, that the day of thanksgiving may be duly observed in the army, agreeably to the intentions of Congress.

26.5   GENERAL ORDERS Head Quarters, V. Forge, Sunday, April 12, 1778.

The Honorable Congress having thought proper to recommend to The United States of America to set apart Wednesday the 22nd. instant to be observed as a day of Fasting, Humiliation and Prayer, that at one time and with one voice the righteous dispensations of Providence may be acknowledged and His Goodness and Mercy toward us and our Arms supplicated and implored; The General directs that this day also shall be religiously observed in the Army, that no work be done thereon and that the Chaplains prepare discourses suitable to the Occasion. The Funeral Honors at the Interment of Officers are for the future to be confined to a solemn Procession of Officers and soldiers in number suitable to the rank of the deceased with Revers'd Arms; Firing on those occasions in Camp is to be abolished.

26.6   GENERAL ORDERS Head Quarters, Middle Brook, Monday, April 12, 1779. The Honorable the Congress having recommended it to the United States to set apart Thursday the 6th. day of May next to be observed as a day of fasting, humiliation and prayer, to acknowledge the gracious interpositions of Providence; to deprecate deserved punishment for our Sins and Ingratitude, to unitedly implore the Protection of Heaven; Success to our Arms and the Arms of our Ally: The Commander in Chief enjoins a religious observance of said day and directs the Chaplains to prepare discourses proper for the occasion; strictly forbidding all recreations and unnecessary labor.

26.7   To THE STATE SOCIETIES OF THE CINCINNATI Mount Vernon, in Virginia, October 31, 1786....it only remains for me to express the sense I entertain of the honor conferred by the last General Meeting in electing me their President, and to implore in future the benediction of Heaven on the virtuous Associates in this illustrious Institution.

26.8   FIFTH ANNUAL ADDRESS TO CONGRESS Philadelphia, December 3, 1793. I humbly implore that Being, on whose Will the fate of Nations depends, to crown with success our mutual endeavours for the general happiness.

27.   Examples of "invoke" as a synonym for prayer include:

27.1   To CHEVALIER DE CHASTELLUX New Windsor, May 7, 1781. May you participate in those blessings you have invoked heaven for me, and may you live to see a happy termn. of a struggle which was begun and has been continued for the purpose of rescuing America from impending Slavery, and securing to its Inhabitants their indubitable rights in which you bear a conspicuous part, is the ardent wish of Dr. Sir etc.

27.2   To THE GENERAL ASSEMBLY OF VIRGINIA Virginia, July 15, 1784. For those rewards and blessings which you have invoked for me in this world, and for the fruition of that happiness which you pray for in the one which is to come, you have all my thanks, and all my gratitude. I wish I could insure them to you, and the State you represent, an hundred fold.

27.3   To JAMES MADISON Mount Vernon, May 20, 1792. I take the liberty at my departure from civil, as I formerly did at my military exit, to invoke a continuation of the blessings of Providence upon it; and upon all those who are the supporters of its interests, and the promoters of harmony, order and good government.

28.   Examples of the use of the word "benediction" include:

28.1   To THE MINISTERS, ELDERS, DEACONS, AND MEMBERS OF THE REFORMED GERMAN CONGREGATION OF NEW YORK New York, November 27, 1783. Disposed, at every suitable opportunity to acknowledge publicly our infinite obligations to the Supreme Ruler of the Universe for rescuing our Country from the brink of destruction; I cannot fail at this time to ascribe all the honor of our late successes to the same glorious Being. And if my humble exertions have been made in any degree subservient to the execution of the divine purposes, a contemplation of the benediction of Heaven on our righteous Cause, the approbation of my virtuous Countrymen, and the testimony of my own Conscience, will be a sufficient reward and augment my felicity beyond anything which the world can bestow.

28.2   To THE MILITIA OFFICERS OF THE CITY AND LIBERTIES OF PHILADELPHIA Philadelphia, December 12, 1783. While the various Scenes of the War, in which I have experienced the timely aid of the Militia of Philadelphia, recur to my mind, my ardent prayer ascends to Heaven that they may long enjoy the blessings of that Peace which has been obtained by the divine benediction on our common exertions.

28.3   To THE STATE SOCIETIES OF THE CINCINNATI Mount Vernon, in Virginia, October 31, 1786. Highly approving as I do, the principles on which the Society is now constituted; and pleased to find, so far as I have been able to learn from reiterated enquiries, that it is acceptable to the good people of the United States in general; it only remains for me to express the sense I entertain of the honor conferred by the last General Meeting in electing me their President, and too implore in future the benediction of Heaven on the virtuous Associates in this illustrious Institution.

28.4 To ANNIS BOUDINOT STOCKTON Mount Vernon, August 31, 1788. I hope that you and yours may have the enjoyment of your health, as well as Mrs. Washington and myself: that enjoyment, by the divine benediction, adds much to our temporal felicity.

29. Examples of Washington's use of the word "beseech" as a synonym for prayer:

29.1 GENERAL ORDERS Head Quarters, Moore's House, Saturday, November 27, 1779. The Honorable the Congress has been pleased to pass the following proclamation. RESOLVED, That it be recommended to the several states, to appoint Thursday, the 9th of December next, to be a day of public and solemn thanksgiving to Almighty God for his mercies, and of prayer for the continuance of his favor and protection to these United States; to beseech him that he would be graciously pleased to influence our public councils, and bless them with wisdom from on high, with unanimity, firmness, and success; that he would go forth with our hosts and crown our arms with victory; that he would grant to his church the plentiful effusions of divine grace, and pour out his holy spirit on all ministers of the gospel; that he would bless and prosper the means of education, and spread the light of christian knowledge through the remotest corners of the earth; that he would smile upon the labours of his people and cause the earth to bring forth her fruits in abundance; that we may with gratitude and gladness enjoy them; that he would take into his holy protection our illustrious ally, give him victory over his enemies, and render him signally great, as the father of his people and the protector of the rights of mankind; that he would graciously be pleased to turn the hearts of our enemies, and to dispense the blessings of peace to contending nations; that he would in mercy look down upon us, pardon our sins and receive us into his favor, and finally, that he would establish the independence of these United States upon the basis of religion and virtue, and support and protect them in the enjoyment of peace, liberty and safety.

29.2 FAREWELL ADDRESS, September 19, 1796, ...Though in reviewing the incidents of my Administration, I am unconscious of intentional error, I am nevertheless too sensible of my defects not to think it probable that I may have committed many errors. Whatever they may be I *fervently* beseech the Almighty to avert or mitigate the evils to which they may tend. I shall also carry with me the hope that my Country will never cease to view them with indulgence; and that after forty five years of my life dedicated to its Service, with an upright zeal, the faults of incompetent abilities will be consigned to oblivion, as myself must soon be to the Mansions of rest.

APPENDIX FOUR

George Washington's "Daily Sacrifice Prayers" or "The Spurious Prayers"

Long after George Washington's death, a series of hand-written prayers were found in his personal effects. When these came to public attention in 1891, a debate ensued over their authenticity. Questions debated in this context included:

(1) Did Washington write them?
(2) Did Washington copy them?
(3) Did Washington use them if they had been written by another and given to him?

Because these questions cannot be answered with finality, we have chosen not to use the "Daily Sacrifice" prayers as part of our argument. Instead, we have employed what we have termed "a minimalist facts approach." We have relied only on evidence that is indisputable. But we have included them here since they have been used so frequently in the debate over Washington's Christianity.

For the background to this discussion, we begin by citing the historical summation from Washington historian, Rupert Hughes. Hughes refused to call these prayers "The Daily Sacrifice Prayers" of Washington. Instead he called them "the Spurious Prayers." His summation of the background of these controversial "Daily Sacrifice" prayers of Washington seems accurate enough so we begin by quoting it. Rupert Hughes writes,

> In 1891, there appeared at an auction in Philadelphia, among a
> mass of relics offered for sale by Washington's descendents, a little
> manuscript book found at Mount Vernon and promptly assumed to

be in his autograph. It was also decided that he wrote it when he was about twenty.

Save for one newspaper at the time, nobody seems to have questioned its authenticity and no protest has been made against enshrining it as "without exception the most hallowed of all his writings." Yet there is really every reason to cast this document out as not only the work of some other hand than Washington's, but as a writing that could hardly have been written by anybody during his lifetime. The Reverend W. Herbert Burk, in a privately printed edition of the manuscript, describes it as a confirmation of the story of Washington's prayers at Valley Forge...

Their first publisher, Stan V. Henkels, said of the little memorandum book, "This gem is all in the handwriting of George Washington, when about twenty years old, and is without exception, the most hallowed of all the writings. It is neatly written on twenty-four pages of a little book about the size of the ordinary pocket memorandum."

Mr. Burk describes their discovery:

"By the merest accident Mr. Henkels discovered this document. While making arrangements for the sale, he came across a dilapidated trunk, which Mr. Washington assured him contained only papers of no value, papers which had been rejected by authorities of the Smithsonian Institute when offered for exhibition. In looking them over he came across this document and recognized at once what he considered the penmanship of Washington. His judgment was substantiated by other experts, to whom the manuscript was submitted.

"Mr. W.E. Benjamin, the well-known New York dealer, purchased the manuscript for twelve hundred and fifty dollars, and by him it was sold to the late Reverend Charles Frederick Hoffman, D.D. Naturally the discovery and sale of such an important manuscript of Washington attracted considerable attention and in the columns of the *New York Evening Post* the authenticity of the manuscript was challenged. It is not my purpose to revive the controversy. Where experts disagree a layman's opinion counts for little. Able experts declare the prayers were written by Washington.

One says they were written by a Washington. Another, they are 'written in the unformed hand of the great patriot. It is well-known fact that Washington between the years 1755 and 1763 changed his hand from the angular to the round formation.'

"The ultimate judgment must be based on the chirography, for there are no *a priori* arguments to prove that Washington did not write them.

"What disposition Dr. Hoffman made of the manuscript I have been unable to discover. In Dr. Potter's *Washington a Model in his Library and Life* is the following statement: 'The Reverend Dr. Chas. F. Hoffman has lately purchased "Washington's Prayers," The MSS. [manuscripts] containing morning and evening prayers for various days of the week. He has under consideration, for the benefit of young men and others, a division of this very valuable manuscript, forming a sermon every page, for deposit in the fire-proof libraries of St. Stephen's College, Hobart College, Trinity College, and the University of the South, each institution to have also a complete free circulation of the whole work."

"An analysis of this first prayer shows that it is made up almost entirely of sentences from the *Prayer Book*, and the other prayers are drawn largely from the same source. Almost every part of the Prayer Book has been laid under contribution, showing that the author was very familiar with its entire contents.

"While the Prayer Book is undoubtedly the source of the prayers, the question of this authorship is not determined. Dr. Lyman Abbott and Prof. Upham attributed them to Washington.

"No proof can be given that these prayers were composed by Washington, but, on the other hand, no proof had been produced to show that they were not his work. Professor Lucien M. Robinson is of the opinion that they are taken from some collection of prayers, but has not yet been able to confirm his opinion. I think this is very probable, and have endeavored to discover their source, but so far the search has been in vain. At present, the question is an open one, and its settlement will depend on the discovery of the originals, or upon the demonstration that they are the work of Washington."

These being the arguments in favor of the prayers, the arguments against them may be considered, without dwelling over much on their discovery in a neglected old trunk whose contents, as Mr. Henkels confesses, "had been rejected by the authorities of the Smithsonian Institute when offered for exhibition."[1]

Below are these disputed prayers that some scholars claim were in Washington's own handwriting, while other scholars disagree.

THE DEBATED "DAILY SACRIFICE" PRAYERS OF GEORGE WASHINGTON

Sunday Morning...

Almighty God, and most merciful father, who didst command the children of Israel to offer a daily sacrifice to thee, that thereby they might glorify and praise thee for thy protection both night and day; receive, O Lord, my morning sacrifice which I now offer up to thee; I yield thee humble and hearty thanks that thou hast preserved me from the dangers of the night past, and brought me to the light of this day, and the comforts thereof, a day which is consecrated to thine own service and for thine own honor.

Let my heart, therefore, Gracious God, be so affected with the glory and majesty of it, that I may not do mine own works, but wait on thee, and discharge those weighty duties thou requirest of me; and since thou art a God of pure eyes, and wilt be sanctified in all who draw near unto thee, who doest to regard the sacrifice of fools, or hear sinners who tread in the courts, pardon, I beseech thee, my sins, remove them from thy presence, as far as the east is from the west, and accept of me for the merits of thy son Jesus Christ, that when I come into thy temple, and compass thine altar, my prayers may come before thee as incense; and as thou wouldst hear me calling upon thee in my prayers, so give me grace to hear thee calling on me in thy word, that it may be wisdom, righteousness, reconciliation and peace to the saving of my soul in the day of the Lord Jesus. Grant that I may hear it with reverence, receive it with meekness, mingle it with faith, and that it may accomplish in me, Gracious God, the good work for which thou has sent it. Bless my family, kindred, friends and country, be our God & guide this day and for ever for his sake, who lay down in the Grave and arose again for us, Jesus Christ our Lord. Amen.

*Sunday Evening...*O Most Glorious God, in Jesus Christ my merciful & loving father, I acknowledge and confess my guilt, in the weak and imperfect performance of the duties of this day. I have called on these for pardon and forgiveness of sins, but so

804

coldly & carelessly, that my prayers are become my sin and stand in need of pardon. I have heard thy holy word, but with such deadness of spirit that I have been an unprofitable and forgetful hearer, so that, O Lord, tho' I have done thy work, yet it hath been so negligently that I may rather expect a curse than a blessing from thee. But, O God, who are rich in mercy and plenteous in redemption, mark not, I beseech thee, what I have done amiss; remember I am but dust, and remit my transgressions, negligences & ignorances, and cover them all with the absolute obedience of thy dear Son, that those sacrifices which I have offered may be accepted by thee, in and for the sacrifice Jesus Christ offered upon the cross for me; for his sake, ease me of the burden of my sins, and give me grace that by the call of the Gospel I may rise from the slumber of sin unto newness of life. Let me live according to those holy rules which thou hast this day prescribed in thy holy word; make me to know what is acceptable in thy sight, and therein to delight. Open the eyes of my understanding, and help me thoroughly to examine myself concerning my knowledge, faith and repentance. increase my faith, and direct me to the true object Jesus Christ the way, the truth and the life, bless, O Lord, all the people of this land, from the highest to the lowest, particularly those whom thou hast appointed to rule over us in church & state. continue thy goodness to me this night. These weak petitions I humbly implore thee to hear accept and ans. for thy Dear Son Jesus Christ our Lord. Amen.

Monday Morning...O eternal and everlasting God, I presume to present myself this morning before Thy Divine majesty, beseeching thee to accept of my humble and hearty thanks, that it hath pleased thy great goodness to keep and preserve me the night past from all the dangers poor mortals are subject to, and hast given me sweet and pleasant sleep, whereby I find my body refreshed and comforted for performing the duties of this day, in which I beseech thee to defend me from all perils of body & soul. Direct my thoughts, words, and work, wash away my sins in the immaculate Blood of the Lamb, and purge my heart by thy holy spirit from the dross of my natural corruption, that I may with more freedom of mind and liberty of will serve thee, the ever living God, in righteousness and holiness this day, and all the days of my life. Increase my faith in the sweet promises of the gospel; give me repentance from dead works; pardon my wanderings, & direct my thoughts unto thyself, the God of my salvation; teach me how to live in thy fear, labour in thy service, and ever to run in the ways of thy commandments; make me always watchful over my heart, that neither the terrors of conscience, the loathing of holy duties, the love of sin, nor an unwillingness to depart this life, may cast me into a spiritual slumber, but daily frame me more and more into the likeness of thy Son, Jesus Christ, that living in thy fear, and dying in thy favor, I

The authenticity of these written prayers continues to be strongly debated may in thy appointed time attain the resurrection of the just unto eternal life. Bless my family, friends and kindred, and unite us all in praising and glorifying Thee in all our works begun continued, and ended when we shall come to make our last account before thee blessed saviour, who hath taught us to pray our Father, &c.

Monday Evening...Most Gracious Lord God, from whom proceedeth every good and perfect gift, I offer to Thy Divine Majesty my unfeigned praise and thanksgiving for all Thy mercies towards me. Thou mad'st me at first and hast ever since sustained the work of thy own hand; thou gav'st thy Son to die for me; and hast given me assurance of salvation, upon my repentance and sincerely endeavouring to conform my life to his holy precepts and example. Thou art pleased to lengthen out to me the time of repentance, and to move me to it by thy spirit and by thy word, by thy mercies; and by thy judgments: out of a deepness of thy mercies, and my own unworthiness, I do appear before at this time; I have sinned and done very wickedly, be merciful to me, O God, and pardon me for Jesus Christ sake: instruct me in the particulars of my duty, and suffer me not to be tempted in the particulars of my duty, and suffer me not to be tempted above what thou givest me strength to bear. Take care, I pray thee of my affairs and more and more direct me in the truth, defend me from my enemies, especially my spiritual ones. Suffer me not to be drawn from thee, by the blandishments of the world, carnal desires, the cunning of the devil, or deceitfulness of sin. Worm in me thy good will and pleasure, and discharge my mind from all things that are displeasing to thee, of all ill will and discontent, wrath and bitterness, pride & vain conceit of myself, and render me charitable, pure, holy, patient and heavenly minded. Be with me at the hour of death dispose me for it, and deliver me from the slavish fear of it, and make me willing and fit to die whenever thou shalt call me hence. Bless our rulers in church and state. Bless O Lord the whole race of mankind, and let the world be filled with the knowledge of Thee and Thy Son, Jesus Christ. Pity the sick, the poor, the weak, the needy, the widows and fatherless, and all that mourn or are broken in heart, and be merciful to them according to their several necessities. Bless my friends and grant me grace to forgive my enemies as heartily as I desire forgiveness of Thee my heavenly Father. I beseech Thee to defend me this night from all evil, and do more for me than I can think or ask, for Jesus Christ sake, in whose most holy name and Words, I continue to pray, Our Father, who art in heaven, hallowed be Thy Name....

Tuesday Morning...O Lord our God, most mighty and merciful father, I, thine unworthy creature and servant, do once more approach Thy presence. Though not worthy to appear before Thee, because of my natural corruptions, and the many sins and transgressions which I have committed against Thy Divine Majesty; yet I beseech

Thee, for the sake of Him in whom Thou are well pleased, the Lord Jesus Christ, to admit me to render Thee deserved thanks and praises for Thy manifold mercies extended toward me, for the quiet rest & repose of the past night, for food, raiment, health, peace, liberty and the hopes of a better life through the merit of thy dear son's bitter passion. and O kind father continue thy mercy and favour to me this day, and ever hereafter; prosper all my lawful undertakings; let me have all my direction from thy holy spirit, and success from thy bountiful hand. Let the bright beams of thy light so shine into my heart, and enlighten my mind in understanding thy blessed word, that I may be enabled to perform thy will in all things, and effectually resist all temptations of the world, the flesh, and the devil. preserve and defend our rulers in church & state. bless the people of this land, be a Father to the fatherless, a Comforter to the comfortless, a Deliverer to the captives, and a Physician to the sick. Let Thy blessing be upon our friends, kindred and families. Be our Guide this day and forever through Jesus Christ in whose blessed form of prayer I conclude my weak petitions—Our Father, who art in Heaven, hallowed be Thy Name....

*Tuesday Evening...*Most gracious God and heavenly Father, we cannot cease, but must cry unto Thee for mercy, because my sins cry against me for justice. How shall I address myself unto thee, I must with the publican stand and admire at they great goodness, tender mercy, and long suffering towards me, in that thou hast kept me the past day from being consumed and brought to nought. O Lord, what is man, or the son of man, that thou regardest him; the more days pass over my head, the more sins and iniquities I heap up against thee. If I should cast up the account of my good deeds done this day, how few and small would they be; but if I should reckon my miscarriages, surely they would be many and great. O, blessed Father, let thy son's blood wash me from all impurities, and cleanse me from the stains of sin that are upon me. Give me grace to lay hold upon his merits; that they may be my reconciliation and atonement unto thee,—That I may know my sins are forgiven by His death and passion. Embrace me in the arms of thy mercy; vouchsafe to receive me unto the bosom of Thy love, shadow me with Thy wings, that I may safely rest under Thy protection this night; And so into Thy hands I commend myself, both soul and body, in the name of Thy son, Jesus Christ, beseeching Thee, when this life shall end, I may take my everlasting rest with Thee in Thy heavenly kingdom. Bless all in authority over us, be merciful to all those afflicted with Thy cross or calamity, bless all my friends, forgive my enemies and accept my thanksgiving this evening for all the mercies and favors afforded me;

Hear and graciously answer these my requests, and whatever else Thou see'st needful grant us, for the sake of Jesus Christ in whose blessed Name and Words I continue to pray, Our Father, who art in heaven, hallowed be Thy Name....

*Wednesday Morning...*Almighty and eternal Lord God, the great Creator of heaven and earth, and the God and Father of our Lord Jesus Christ; look down from heaven, in pity and compassion upon me Thy servant, who humbly prostrate myself before Thee, sensible of Thy mercy and my own misery; there is an infinite distance between thy glorious majesty and me, thy poor creature, the work of thy hand, between thy infinite power, and my weakness, thy wisdom, and my folly, thy eternal Being, and my mortal frame, but, O Lord, I have set myself at a greater distance from thee by my sin and wickedness, and humbly acknowledge the corruption of my nature and the many rebellions of my life. I have sinned against heaven and before thee, in thought, word & deed; I have contemned thy majesty and holy laws. I have likewise sinned by omitting what I ought to have done, and committing what I ought not. I have rebelled against light, despised thy mercies and judgments, and broken my vows and promises; I have neglected the means of Grace, and opportunities of becoming better; my iniquities are multiplied, and my sins are very great. I confess them, O Lord, with shame and sorrow, detestation and loathing, and desires to be vile in my own eyes, as I have rendered myself vile in thine. I humbly beseech thee to be merciful to me in the free pardon of my sins, for the sake of thy dear Son, my only Saviour, J.C., who came not to call the righteous, but sinners to repentance; be pleased to renew my nature, and write thy laws upon my heart, and help me to live, righteously, soberly and godly in this evil world; make me humble, meek, patient and contented, and work in me the grace of thy holy spirit. prepare me for death and judgment, and let the thoughts thereof awaken me to a greater care and study to approve myself unto thee in well doing. Bless our rulers in church & state. Help all in affliction or adversity—give them patience and a sanctified use of their affliction, and in Thy good time, deliverance from them; forgive my enemies, take me unto Thy protection this day, keep me in perfect peace, which I ask in the name and for the sake of Jesus. Amen.

*Wednesday Evening...*Holy and eternal Lord God who art the King of heaven, and the watchman of Israel, that never slumberest or sleepst, what shall we render unto thee for all thy benefits: because thou hast inclined thine ear unto me, therefore will I call on there as long as I live, from the rising of the sun to the going down of the same let thy name be praised. among the infinite riches of the mercy towards me, I desire to render thanks & praise for thy merciful preservation of me this day, as well as all the days of my life; and for the many other blessings & mercies spiritual & temporal which thou hast bestowed on me, contrary to my deserving. All these thy mercies call on me to be thankful and my infirmities & wants call for a continuance of thy tender mercies: cleanse my soul, O Lord, I beseech thee, from whatever is offensive to thee, and hurtful to me, and give me what is convenient for me. Watch over me this night, and give me comfortable and sweet sleep to fit me for the service of the day following. Let my soul watch for the coming of the Lord Jesus; let my bed put me in mind of my grave, and my rising from there of my last resurrection; O heavenly Father, so frame this heart of mine, that I may ever delight to live according to thy will and command, in holiness and righteousness before thee all the days of my life. Let me remember, O Lord, the time will come when the trumpet shall sound, and the dead shall arise and stand before the judgment seat, and give an account of whatever they have done in the body, and let me so prepare my soul, that I may do it with joy and not with grief. Bless the rulers and people of this and forget not those who are under any affliction or oppression. Let thy favour be extended to all my relations friends and all others who I ought to remember in my prayer and hear me I beseech thee for the sake of my dear redeemer in whose most holy words, I farther pray, Our Father, &c.

*Thursday Morning...*Most Gracious Lord God, whose dwelling is in the highest heavens, and yet beholdest the lowly and humble upon earth, I blush and am ashamed to lift up my eyes to thy dwelling place, because I have sinned against thee; look down, I beseech thee upon me thy unworthy servant who prostrate myself at the footstool of thy mercy, confessing my own guiltiness, and begging pardon for my sins; what couldst thou have done Lord more for me, or what could I have done more against thee? Thou didst send thy Son to take our nature upon

Note: The manuscript ended at this place, the close of a page. Whether the other pages were lost, or the prayers were never completed, has not been determined.[2]

RUPERT HUGHES' FIVE ARGUMENTS AGAINST THEIR AUTHENTICITY

As we have seen, Rupert Hughes calls Washington's "Daily Sacrifice Prayers" the "Spurious Prayers" of Washington. There are five basic arguments used by Rupert Hughes against the authenticity of these prayers.

(1) George Washington was not a Christian
According to Hughes, Washington was not a Christian, so he wouldn't have written or copied such prayers. (But we have

thoroughly answered and disproved that claim throughout this book. Further, Washington's life long use of and exposure to the Anglican *Book of Common Prayer* would also be an argument for the potential authorship of copying of these prayers that in many ways come from the *Book of Common Prayer*.)

(2) The Differences of Tone and Style

Hughes writes,

To one who has read at all widely in what Washington has written, the tone is as foreign as if they were written in Greek. There is not a misspelled word, not a touch of incorrect grammar, not a capitalized noun or other emphatic word except the titles of the deity. In the final two entries of his Diary for December 12 and 13, 1799, Washington spells the following words with a capital: "Cloudy, Mercury, Moon, Night, Hail, Rain, Snowing, O'clock." The punctuation is precise and faultless.[3]

(3) The Question of Historical Context

Hughes writes,

This is not the place for a theological or bibliological treatise, but one who will read such a work as Reverend Dr. John Wright on *Early Prayer Books of America* will find it hard to believe that either Washington or anybody else could have written this manuscript until the early part of the Nineteenth Century. Washington died in 1799.[4]

(4) Possibility of Another Author

Hughes writes,

Mount Vernon was occupied variously after his death, and some member of the household – probably a woman- may easily have begun a transcript of phrases from the Prayer Book and given it up before the work was done.[5]

(5) Question of Handwriting Styles

Again Hughes notes,

> The rejection of the manuscript neither implies nor excuses any suggestion of fraud in their connection. Sincerity is granted to the believers in it. Forgery is not to be considered since a forger would have given at least an imitation of Washington's penmanship. And of this there is no trace. The little memorandum-book contains twenty-four pages of handwriting consisting of a series of daily prayers headed "The Daily Sacrifice." There is a prayer for each morning and evening, beginning Sunday morning and ending abruptly in the middle of a sentence under Thursday morning.[6]
>
> The impossibility of the work being in Washington's hand should be apparent to the most casual comparison. The writer of the Prayers, for instance always crosses his final "t's" and all his "t's" are squatty and flat. Washington always wrote a tall thin "t," and usually ended it with a mere sidewise uplift. Little words like "and," "the," "this," and "most" are utterly unlike his, nor the familiar "G," nor the "L," nor the "D," nor any of the capitals. The same is true of the small letters, their joining and angles. The dates and days of the week are not in the least like his. Never in his life could Washington have written the sentence as they run. The "round hand" he practiced for a time has no resemblance to this specimen. The tracings herewith may be compared with the facsimiles from Washington's Note Books of 1757 which were written in the so-called "round hand" he used for ten years.[7]

CONCLUSION

Ultimately, the argument for or against the authenticity of these prayers cannot be solved by this current study. Perhaps an extensive forensic science analysis of the handwriting along with a radio carbon-dating assessment of the pages might help clarify the question of whether Washington could have written these prayers largely drawn from the *Book of Common Prayer*. Again, since we have taken the "minimalist facts" approach in this study, our argument is not dependent in any way upon the authenticity of these prayers. We include them here because of their extensive use in the debate over George Washington's Christianity.

Furthermore, simply peruse the prayers found in the *Book of Common Prayer*, and one will find prayers similar to those of the "Daily Sacrifice." Prayers from both sources invoke the mercy of Jesus Christ as well as seeking and accepting his forgiveness. Since Washington was a regular user of the *Book of Common Prayer*, it is easily conceivable that he could have used the prayers of the "Daily Sacrifice" as well.

At the very least, we can ask the question of why a Deist would even bother to have such Christian manuscript prayers in his possession in the first place. If they were given to him, why did he accept them? Why did he keep them? These are the sorts of prayers a Christian would likely have had in his personal possession. This fact coheres with the evidence of Washington's Christian faith.

The bottom line is that the authenticity or non-authenticity of these "Daily Sacrifice Prayers" make no difference to the evidence of Washington's Christianity. Authentic or not, Washington's own one hundred plus written prayers from his own public and private letters are more than sufficient to demonstrate his Christian faith.

A Summary of Washington's Most Important Sermons

The importance of Christian sermons in George Washington's life has been entirely overlooked by recent scholars. Moreover, the full extent of Washington's interest and reading of Christian sermons has never been sufficiently explored. This oversight is unfortunate since it leaves an incomplete understanding of Washington's spirituality. The evidence presented throughout this book makes it clear that Washington read, purchased, received, and commented on sermons.

The authors advocating that Washington was a Deist have arbitrarily limited Washington's theological comments and interaction with his sermon collection to only two such messages. But the fact is that there were so many, we cannot possibly do justice to all of them in this study. The best we can do, for now, is to outline the most salient sermons and attempt to show how they relate to Washington's life and faith. We here provide a "Summary of Washington's Most Important Sermons." We have catalogued them in terms of their relevance to Washington's life, and, where possible, we have included his comments on the sermons.

It should be noted that during the colonial era, printed sermons of leading Christian clergymen were a major means of communication. In a sense, they were like the mass media of the day. John Locke was quoted by many during the founding era. Why? Because he was quoted in sermons. Dr. Donald S. Lutz, co-author (along with Dr. Charles Hyneman) of a ground-breaking study on how the Bible was the most quoted and cited source during the founding era, made this observation about the printed sermon of George Washington's day. Says Dr. Lutz:

> During the founding era, the late 1700's, there were no magazines, newspapers had a very small circulation, there was no television, there was no internet, what did people do for entertainment? They would read pamphlets. Now, of all the pamphlets published during

the last part of the 1700's, more than 80% of them were reprinted sermons.[1]

Washington certainly was not alone in his hobby of collecting and reading printed sermons.

CATEGORIZING THE SERMONS WASHINGTON COLLECTED

There are several ways to organize and summarize the major sermons in Washington's life. For the sake of convenience, these sermons will be presented here in outline form. In a few instances some of the sermons will appear more than once in the following list, because there are various significant features that need to be highlighted. This summary is merely representative and is therefore not complete.

1. **Sermons Washington received and thanked the author for**
   a. Samuel Miller: "A Sermon, preached in New-York, July 4th, 1793. Being the Anniversary of the Independence of America: at the Request of the Tammany Society, or Columbian Order. By Samuel Miller, A.M. One of the Ministers of the United Presbyterian Churches, in the city of New-York." Washington wrote on 8-29-1793, "Sir: It is but a few days since that I had the pleasure to receive your polite letter of the 4 instant, which accompanied the Sermon delivered by you on the 4 of July, and I beg you will accept my best thanks for the attention shewn in forwarding the same to me."[2]
   a. Ezra Stiles: "The United States elevated to Glory and Honor. A Sermon, preached before His Excellency Jonathan Trumbull, Esq. L.L.D. Governor and Commander in Chief, and the Honorable the General Assembly of the state of Connecticut, convened at Hartford, at the Annual Election, May 8th, 1783. By Ezra Stiles, D.D. President of Yale-College. New-Haven: printed by Thomas & Samuel Green." Washington wrote on 2-23-1787, "Sir: I have the pleasure to acknowledge the receipt of your letter of the 7th. Instant and likewise one of the 9th. of November handed to me by the Revd. Mr. Morse together with your election Sermon for which I beg you will accept of my best thanks."[3]
   c. Uzal Ogden: The identification of these sermons or theological articles are unclear. Washington wrote on 7-6-1789, "Your letter of the 12th of June, which was duly received, should have had an earlier acknowledgment and best thanks have been rendered to you for your politeness in sending me the

first number of a new periodical publication which accompanied it, had not my late indisposition prevented. I must now beg your acceptance of my thanks for this mark of attention, and assure you that it always gives me peculiar pleasure to afford every proper encouragement to useful publications, but as I have not been able (from the multiplicity of business which has crowded upon me since my recovery) to peruse the work which you sent me, I cannot, with propriety give it that testimony of my approbation which you desire, and which I dare say it deserves."[4]

d. Isaac Story: "A Discourse, delivered February 15, 1795, at the Request of the Proprietors' Committee; as preparatory to the Collection, on the national Thanksgiving, the Thursday following, for the Benefit of our American Brethren in Captivity at Algiers. By Isaac Story, A.M. Pastor of the Second Congregational Society in Marblehead. Printed by Thomas C. Cushing, Salem." "A Sermon, preached February 19, 1795, (from Ecclesiastes 9:18.) being the Federal Thanksgiving, appointed by our beloved President, the Illustrious George Washington, Esq. By Isaac Story, A.M. Pastor of the Second Congregational Society in Marblehead. Printed by Thomas C. Cushing, Salem." Reverend Story had written, "Deign most respected Sire, to accept of the enclosed, as one of the sermons was composed in obedience to your requisition.—please to accept them as a pledge of my veneration for your person and public administrations. I acknowledge myself a federalist and that I rejoice in the privileges of our excellent constitution. May the blessings of it be preserved, notwithstanding the machination of foreigners and foes within, be increased and handed down in their utmost extent to the latest posterity. While the old officers of government are dropping off around you, may you be like Mount Zion, which cannot be moved. Long may you sway the scepter of our government, long reign in the hearts of every sincere Patriot, and at some far distant period leave this earthly dominion for a crown of glory which fadeth not away. And when you take your ascension may the reins of government like Elijah's mantle drop into the hands of a worthy successor. I am your most obedient and devoted servant, Isaac Story." Washington wrote on 4-14-1795 a brief note of thanks to Reverend Isaac Story, of Marblehead, Mass., for the sermons that he sent.[5]

e. Jeremy Belknap: "A Sermon, delivered on the 9th of May, 1798, the Day of the national Fast, recommended by the President of the United States. By Jeremy Belknap, D.D. Minister of the Church in Federal-Street, Boston.

Printed by Samuel Hall, Boston. 1798." Washington wrote on 6-15-1798, "Your favour of the 29th Ulto. accompanying the Discourse delivered on the day recommended by the President of the U States to be observed for a Fast, was received in the usual course of the Mail, from Boston...For the Discourse, which you were so obliging as to send me, and for the favourable sentiments with which it was accompanied, I pray you to accept the best thanks ."[6]

f. "*Shipley's Works* by Reverend Jonathan Shipley, Anglican Bishop of St. Asaph. Shipley. 2 vols. London, 1792."[7] When his son, Dr. William Davies Shipley, sent his father's sermons to him. Washington wrote:

"Sir: I have been honored with your polite Letter of the 23d. of May, together with the works of your late Right Revd. father Lord bishop of St. Asaph, which accompanied it. For the character and sentiments of that venerable Divine while living, I entertained the most perfect esteem, and have a sincere respect for his memory now he is no more. My best thanks are due to you for his works, and the mark of your attention in sending them to me; and especially for the flattering expressions respecting myself, which are contained in your letter."[8]

2. **Sermons dedicated to Washington to which he made no comment**

   a. Jacob Duché: "The Duty of Standing fast in our spiritual and temporal Liberties, a Sermon preached in Christ-Church, July 7th, 1775."[9]

   b. William White: "A sermon on the reciprocal Influence of Civil Policy and Religious Duty. Delivered in Christ Church, in the City of Philadelphia on Thursday, the 19th of February, 1795, being a Day of General Thanksgiving."[10]

3. **Sermons he received that he said he hadn't read yet**

   a. Unknown sermon. Mentioned to Tobias Lear on 3-28-1791.[11]

   b. Samuel Langdon: "The Republic of the Israelites an Example to the American States. A Sermon, preached at Concord, in the state of New-Hampshire; before the Honorable General Court at the annual Election. June 5, 1788. by Samuel Landon, D.D. Pastor of the Church in Hampton-Falls. Exeter: printed by Lamson and Ranlet." In this letter of 9-28-1789, Washington says, "Sir: You will readily believe me when I assure you that the necessary attention to the business in which I have been lately engaged is the sole cause of my not having sooner acknowledged the receipt of your letter of the 8th. of July, and made a proper return for your politeness in sending me the Sermon which accompanied it. You will now, Sir, please to accept my best thanks for this mark of attention, as well as for the friendly expressions contained in your letter. The man must be bad indeed who can look upon the events of the American Revolution without feeling the warmest gratitude towards the great Author of the Universe whose divine interposition was so frequently manifested in our behalf. And it is my earnest prayer that we may so conduct ourselves as to merit a continuance of those blessings with which we have hitherto been favored."[12]

c. Jedidiah Morse: 5-26-1799. "Revd. Sir: I thank you for your Sermon 'Exhibiting the present dangers, and consequent duties of the Citizens of the United States of America' which came to hand by the last Post: and which I am persuaded I shall read with approbating pleasure, as soon as some matters on which I am engaged at present, are dispatch'd."[13]

d. William White: 5-30-1799. Washington wrote, "The Sermon on the duty of Civil obedience as required in Scripture, which you had the goodness to send me, came safe a Post or two ago; and for which I pray you to accept my grateful acknowledgments. The hurry in which it found me engaged, in a matter that pressed, has not allowed me time to give it a perusal yet: but I anticipate the pleasure and edification I shall find when it is in my power to do it."[14]

4. **Sermons he possessed that were illustrative of his education and faith**

a. Offspring Blackhall: 1717. "The Sufficiency of a Standing Revelation in General, and of the Scripture Revelation in particular. Both as to the Matter of it, and as to the Proof of it; and that new Revelations cannot reasonably be desired, and would probably be unsuccessful. In eight Sermons, preach'd in the Cathedral-Church of St. Paul, London; at the Lecture founded by the Honourable Robert Boyle Esq; in the Year 1700." Childhood textbook signed by Washington and in his library.[15]

b. William Stith: 1753. "The Nature and Extent of Christ's Redemption. A Sermon preached before the General Assembly of Virginia: at Williamsburg, November 11th, 1753. by William Stith, A.M. President of William and Mary College. Published at the request of the House of Burgesses." Signed by Washington.[16]

c. William Gordon: "The Separation of the Jewish Tribes, after the Death of Solomon, accounted for, and applied to the present Day, in a Sermon preached before the General Court, on Friday, July the 4th, 1777. Being the Anniversary of the Declaration of Independency. By William Gordon. Pastor of the Third Church in Roxbury. Boston: Printed by J. Gill, Printer to the General Assembly." 7-4-1777. A sermon dedicated to Washington by a Revolutionary War historian, and one of Washington's closest correspondents throughout the War to the end of his life.[17]

d. Samuel Stanhope Smith: "A Discourse on the Nature and Reasonableness of Fasting, and on the existing Causes that call us to that Duty. Delivered at Princeton, on Tuesday the 6th January, 1795. Being the Day appointed by the Synod of New York and New-Jersey, to be observed as a General Fast, by all the Churches of their Communion in those States; and now published in Compliance with the Request of the Students of Theology and Law in Princeton. By Samuel Stanhope Smith, D.D. Vice-President and Professor of Moral Philosophy and Divinity, in the College of New-Jersey. Philadelphia: printed by William Young, 1795." Smith was the tutor of G. W. P. Custis at Princeton. This sermon reveals the Christian faith of the man under whom Washington insisted that his young grandson, George Washington Parke Custis study.[18]

e. Abiel Leonard: "A Prayer Composed for the Spiritual Benefit of the soldiery in the American army to assist them in their private devotions, and recommended to their particular use. Cambridge, 1775." Leonard's prayer is found here as appendix 6. Leonard was one of Washington's favorite chaplains. See the chapter on "George Washington the Soldier."

f. Samuel Miller: "A Sermon, preached in New York, July 4th, 1793. Being the Anniversary of the Independence of America: at the Request of the Tammany Society, or Columbian Order. By Samuel Miller, A.M. One of the Minister of the United Presbyterian Church, in the city of New York."[19] This Masonic sermon shows the Christian character of the Masonic Order in Washington's day.

g. Uzal Ogden: "A sermon delivered at Morris-Town, on Monday December 27, 1784, it being the Festival of St. John the Evangelist, before the Fraternity of Free and Accepted masons, of Lodge No. 10, in the State of New-Jersey."[20] Masonic sermon. Shows the Christian and anti-Deist spirit of the Masonic Order in Washington's day.

h.   Joel Barlow: "An Oration, delivered at the North Church in Hartford, at the Meeting of the Connecticut Society of the Cincinnati, July 4th, 1787. In Commemoration of the Independence of the United States."[21] It shows the spiritual nature of the Order of the Cincinnati, Washington's military order of honor for the officers of the Revolutionary War. It also shows either a pre-Deist, or pre-Atheist, or secret Deist or Atheist.

5.   **Sermons he did not have but were significant to his life**

a.   Samuel Davies: "Religion and patriotism the constituents of a good soldier. A sermon preached to Captain Overton's Independent Company of Volunteers, raised in Hanover County, Virginia, August 17, 1755. By Samuel Davies, A.M. Minister of the Gospel there."[22] This was the first sermon to take notice of Washington in the aftermath of Braddock's defeat. Davies suggested that Washington's providential deliverance was perhaps a harbinger of significance service for the nation.

b.   Bryan Fairfax: "He that Believeth On Me Hath Everlasting Life." No Date. This was reproduced with permission from a printed version by the Virginia Historical Society. This sermon was written by one of Washington's closest lifelong friends. He was also the pastor of his church in Alexandria for a time. It shows a clear belief in the biblical doctrine of eternal life through faith in Christ's redeeming work on the cross for sinners, that in turn results in good works. It is included here as appendix 7.

6.   **Sermons for which Washington paid "compliments" to the author**

a.   The unique distinction of having this honor goes to Dr. Timothy Dwight, President of Yale for his two sermons entitled, "Nature and Tendency of Infidel Philosophy."

7.   **Sermons which Washington said he read with pleasure**

a.   Israel Evans: A discourse delivered on the 18th day of December, 1777, the day of public thanksgiving, appointed by the Honourable Continental Congress, by the Reverend Israel Evans, A.M. Chaplain to General Poor's brigade. And now published at the request of the general and officers of the said brigade, to be distributed among the soldiers, gratis."[23] Washington responded on 3-13-1778. "I have read this performance with equal attention and pleasure, and at the same time that I admire, and feel the force of the reasoning which you have displayed through the whole, it is more especially incumbent upon me to thank you for the honorable, but partial mention you have made of my character; and to assure you, that it will ever be the first wish of my heart to aid your pious endeavours to inculcate a due sense of the dependance we ought to place in that all wise and powerful Being on whom alone our success depends; and moreover, to assure you, that with respect and regard, I am, etc. "[24]

b.   Uzal Ogden: "A sermon on practical religion. By the Reverend Uzal Ogden, of Sussex County, New-Jersey. [Four lines of Scripture texts] Number I." [Chatham, N.J.][25] Washington responded on 8-5-1779 "Revd. Sir: I have received, and with pleasure read, the Sermon you were so obliging as to send me. I thank you for this proof of your attention. I thank you also for the favourable sentiments you have been pleased to express of me. But in a more especial mannr. I thank you for the good wishes and prayers you offer in my behalf. These have a just claim to the gratitude of Revd. Sir, Yr., etc."[26]

c.   Alexander Addison: "Observations on the Speech of Albert Gallatin, in the House of Representatives of the United States, on the Foreign Intercourse Bill. (Washington [Penn.]."[27] Washington replied, "I pray you, Sir, to accept my thanks for the Pamphlet you had the goodness to send me...and for the Gazette containing an Oration delivered at the Town of W. on the day recommended by the President to be observed as a General Fast. Both of these productions I have read with equal attention & satisfaction:"[28]

d.   William Linn: "A Discourse on national Sins: delivered May 9, 1798." Washington responded on July 4th 1798, "I recd. With thankfulness your favor of the 30th ult. inclosing the discourse delivered by you on the day recommended by the president of the U. States, to be observed as a general Fast. – I have read them both with pleasure—and feel grateful for the favorable Sentiments you have been pleased to express in my behalf."[29]

e.   Jedidiah Morse: "A Sermon preached at Charlestown, November 29, 1798, on the Anniversary Thanksgiving in Massachusetts. With an Appendix, designed to illustrate some Parts of the Disourse; exhibiting proofs of the early existence, progress, and deleterious effects of French intrigue and influence in the United States."[30] Washington replied on 2-28-1799, "Reverend Sir: The letter with which you were pleased to favour me, dated the first instant, accompanying your thanksgiving Sermon came duly to hand. For the latter I pray you to accept my thanks. I have read it, and the Appendix with pleasure; and wish the latter at least, could meet a more general circulation than it probably will have, for it contains important information; as little known out of a small circle as the dissimination of it would be useful, if spread through the Community. With great respect etc."[31]

8. **Sermons upon which Washington offered his prayers or wished for their success**

a. Nathaniel Whitaker: 1777. "An Antidote Against Toryism. Or the Curse of Meroz, in a Discourse on Judges 5th 23."[32] Washington wrote, "...For the honour of the dedication, I return you my sincere thanks, and wish most devoutly that your labour may be crowned with the success it deserves."[33]

b. Masons L. Weems: "The Philanthropist." Reverend M. L. Weems, *The Philanthropist; or A Good Twelve Cents Worth of Political Love Power, for the Fair Daughters and Patriotic Sons of America.* Dedicated to that great *Lover* and *Love* of his Country, George Washington, Esq (Alexandria: John & James D. Westcott, 1799). Washington responded on 8-29-1799 "Revd Sir: I have been duly favored with your letter of the 20th. instant, accompanying "The Philanthropist." For your politeness in sending the latter, I pray you to receive my best thanks. Much indeed is it to be wished that the sentiments contained in the Pamphlet, and the doctrine it endeavors to inculcate, were more prevalent. Happy would it be for *this country at least*, if they were so. But while the passions of Mankind are under so little restraint as they are among us. and while there are so many motives, and views, to bring them into action we may wish for, but will never see the accomplishment of it. With respect etc"[34]

c. Mason L. Weems: *The Immortal Mentor.* Mason L. Weems, *The Immortal Mentor; or Man's Unerring Guide to a Healthy, Wealthy and Happy Life.* In Three Parts. By Lewis Cornaro, Dr. Franklin, and Dr. Scott. Philadelphia: Printed for the Reverend Mason L. Weems, by Francis and Robert Bailey, no. 116 High-Street, 1796. Washington wrote to Weems on 7-3-1799, "For your kind compliment—"The Immortal Mentor," I beg you to accept my best thanks. I have perused it with singular satisfaction; and hesitate not to say that it is *in my opinion at least*, an *invaluable* compilation. I cannot but hope that a book whose contents do such *credit* to its *title*, will meet a very generous patronage.

Should that patronage equal my wishes, you will have no reason to regret that you ever printed the Immortal mentor. With respect I am Reverend Sir,

Your most obedient Humble Servant, George Washington."[35] (emphasis in the original.)

    d.   Jedidiah Morse. 2-28-1799. (see Washington's remarks above in 7.e.)

9.   Sermons upon which Washington directly commented on the doctrine that they contained

    a.   Benjamin Stevens: Funeral Sermon for Lord William Pepperell. Washington replied, "I consider the sermon on the death of Sir William Pepperell which you were so good as to send me by desire of Lady Pepperell his Relict, as a mark of attention from her which required my particular acknowledgments; and I am sorry that the death of that Lady which I see is announced in the public papers prevents my thanks being returned to her for her respect and good wishes. You, Sir, will please to accept them for your goodness in forwarding the discourse, and my request, that they may be added to the Revd. Author with my approbation of the Doctrine therein inculcated. I am etc.[36]

    b.   Isaac Lewis: "The Political Advantages of Godliness. A Sermon, preached before His Excellency the Governor, and the honorable Legislature of the State of Connecticut, convened at Hartford on the Anniversary Election" preached May 11, 1797.[37] Isaac Lewis' second Sermon was entitled, "The divine mission of Jesus Christ evident from his life, and from the nature and tendency of his doctrines. A sermon preached at Stamford, October 11, 1796. before the Consocation of the Western District in Fairfield County. By Isaac Lewis, D.D. Pastor of a consociated church in Greenwich." (New Haven: Printed by T. and S. Green—New-Haven., [1796]). These sermons were discussed in the chapter entitled, "George Washington Versus Deism." On 8-30-1799, Washington wrote in regard to these sermons, "Your favor of the 17th. Ulto came safe, but a good while after date. For the Sermons you had the goodness to send me I pray you to accept my thanks. The doctrine in them is sound, and does credit to the Author."[38]

    c.   Mason L. Weems. "The Philanthropist." 8-29-1799. (see above under 8. b.)

10. Sermons that Washington read with "singular satisfaction"

    a.   Mason L. Weems: *The Immortal Mentor.* 7-3-1799. See above under 8. c.

    b.   John Lathrop: "A Discourse Before the Human Society in Boston." Given 6-2-1787.[39] Washington's letters were 2-22-1788; 6-22-1778. "You will do me the favor, Sir, to accept of my best thanks for the mark of polite attention in forwarding your discourses to me. The one delivered before the Humane Society is upon a subject highly interesting to the feelings of every benevolent mind. The laudable view of Institutions of this nature do honor to humanity. The beneficence resulting from them is not confined to any particular class or nation; it extends its influence to the whole race of mankind and cannot be too much applauded. I am etc."[40] And again, "I observe, with singular satisfaction, the cases in which your benevolent Institution has been instrumental in recalling some of our Fellow creatures (as it were) from beyond the gates of Eternity, and has given occasion for the hearts of parents and friends to leap for joy. The provision made for the preservation of shipwrecked Mariners is also highly estimable in the view of every philanthropic mind and greatly consolatory to that suffering part of the Community. These things will draw upon you the blessings of those, who were nigh to perish. These works of charity and good-will towards men reflect, in my estimation, great lustre upon the authors and presage an æra of still father improvements. How pitiful, in the eye of reason and religion, is that false ambition which desolates the world with fire and sword for the purposes of conquest and fame; when compared to the milder virtues of making our neighbours and our fellow men as happy as their frail conditions and perishable natures will permit *them to be!*"[41]

11. Sermons that Washington quoted in his letters

a. Laurence Sterne: "The Sermons of Mr. Yorick." In his letter to Reverend Hugh Henry Brackenbridge, 9-8-1779, Washington says, "Sir: I have to thank you for your favor of the 10th of August, and your Eulogium. You add motives to patriotism, and have made the army your debtor in the handsome tribute which is paid to the memory of those who have fallen in fighting for their country. I am sensible that none of these observations can have escaped you, and that I can offer nothing which your own reason has not already suggested on this occasion; and being of [Reverend Laurence] Sterne's opinion, that 'Before an affliction is digested, consolation comes too soon; and after it is digested, it comes too late: there is but a mark between these two, as fine almost as a hair, for a comforter to take aim at.' I rarely attempt it, nor shall I add more on this subject to you, as it would only be a renewal of sorrow, by recalling a fresh to your remembrance things which had better be forgotten."[42]

b. Laurence Sterne: In Washington's letter to Jonathan Trumbull, Jr. Washington writes, "My dear Sir: I came here in time to see Mr. Custis breathe his last. About Eight o'clock yesterday Evening he expired. The deep and solemn distress of the Mother, and affliction of the Wife of this amiable young Man, requires every comfort in my power to afford them; the last rights of the deceased I must also see performed; these will take me three or four days; when I shall proceed with Mrs. Washington and Mrs. Custis to Mount Vernon.

"As the dirty tavern you are now at cannot be very comfortable; and in spite of Mr. [Reverend Laurence] Sterne observation the House of Mourning not very agreeable; it is my wish, that all of the Gentn of my family, except yourself, who I beg may come here and remain with me; may proceed on at their leizure to Mount Vernon, and wait for me there. Colo. Cobb will join you on the road at the Tavern we breakfasted at (this side Ruffens). My best wishes attend the Gentn. and with much sincerity and affectn."[43]

12. **Sermons that he possessed and/or commented upon that addressed the topic of Deism**

a. Samuel Langdon: "The Co-incidence of natural with revealed religion." A sermon at the annual lecture instituted in Harvard College by the last will and testament of the Honorable Paul Dudley, Esq; delivered November 1, 1775. By Samuel Langdon, D.D. president of Harvard College. [Three lines from Acts].[44] This was in Washington's library, but there is no letter commenting on it.

b. William Linn: "A Discourse on National Sins" [May 9, 1798] (see Washington's comments in 7.d.).

c. Isaac Lewis. "The Political Advantages of Godliness. A Sermon, preached before His Excellency the Governor, and the honorable Legislature of the State of Connecticut, convened at Hartford on the Anniversary Election" preached May 11, 1797.[45] Isaac Lewis' second Sermon was entitled, "The divine mission of Jesus Christ evident from his life, and from the nature and tendency of his doctrines. A sermon preached at Stamford, October 11, 1796, before the Consocation of the Western District in Fairfield County. By Isaac Lewis, D.D. Pastor of a consociated church in Greenwich." (New Haven: Printed by T. and S. Green—New-Haven., [1796]). These sermons were discussed in the chapter entitled, "George Washington Versus Deism." On 8-30-1799, Washington wrote in regard to these sermons, "Your favor of the 17th. Ulto came safe, but a good while after date. For the Sermons you had the goodness to send me I pray you to accept my thanks. The doctrine in them is sound, and does credit to the Author."[46]

d. Jedidiah Morse: "Sermon preached at Charlestown—Exhibiting proofs of the early existence, progress and deleterious effects of French intrigue" (see Washington's comments in 7.e)

e. Timothy Dwight: "Two Discourses on the Nature and Danger of Infidel Philosophy."[47] Washington's letter of 9/28/1798 to Reverend Zechariah Lewis says, "I thank you for sending me Doctr. Dwights Sermons to whom I pray you to present the complimts."

13. Spiritual writings he possessed and directly or indirectly commented upon that were designed to support his soldiers

a. Abiel Leonard: "A prayer, composed for the benefit of the soldiery, in the American Army, to assist them in their private devotions; and recommended to their particular use: By Abiel Leonard, A.M., Chaplain to General Putnam's Regiment in said Army."[48]

b. Israel Evans: "Discourse to Officers and Soldiers of the Western Army; 10/17/1779"[49]

c. Nathaniel Whitaker: "An Antidote Against Toryism; 1777." (see Washington's comments in 8.a.)
William Gordon: "Sermon on the Anniversary of Declaration of Independence; 7/4/1777" (see Washington's comments in 4.c.)

14. Sermons that brought him recognition and honor, or that were dedicated to him

a. Samuel Davies: "Religion and patriotism the constituents of a good soldier. A sermon preached to Captain Overton's Independent Company of Volunteers, raised in Hanover County, Virginia, August 17, 1755. By Samuel Davies, A.M. Minister of the Gospel there."[50]

b. Jacob Duché: "The duty of standing fast in our spiritual and temporal liberties, a sermon, preached in Christ-Church, July 7th, 1775, before the First Battalion of the city and liberties of Philadelphia; and now published at their request. By the Reverend Jacob Duché, M.A."[51]

c. William White: "A sermon on the reciprocal influence of civil policy and religious duty. Delivered in Christ Church, in the city of Philadelphia, on Thursday, the 19th of February, 1795, being a day of general thanksgiving. By William White, D.D. Bishop of the Protestant Episcopal Church, in the Commonwealth of Pennsylvania."[52]

15. **Sermons that he received, that address the relationship between government and religion**

   a. Isaac Lewis: See above, 12. c. See letter to Zechariah Lewis; Letter, 7/17/1797

   b. William White: "A sermon on the duty of civil obedience, as required in Scripture. Delivered in Christ Church and St. Peter's, April 25, 1799, being a day of general humiliation, appointed by the president of the United States. By Wm. White, D.D. Bishop of the Protestant Episcopal Church, in the Commonwealth of Pennsylvania."[53]

16. **Sermons that he commented upon that present the Gospel**

   a. Uzal Ogden: "A sermon on practical religion. By the Reverend Uzal Ogden, of Sussex County, New-Jersey. [Four lines of Scripture texts] Number I. 1779."[54]

   b. Benjamin Stevens: "A sermon occasioned by the death of the Honorable Sir William Pepperrell, Bart. Lieutenant-General in his Majesty's Service. Who died at his seat in Kittery, July 6th, 1759, aged 63. Preached the next Lord's-Day after his funeral by Benjamin Stevens, A.M. Pastor of the First Church in Kittery."[55] (see Washington's comments in 9.a.).

   c. Isaac Lewis: "The divine mission of Jesus Christ evident from his life, and from the nature and tendency of his doctrines. A sermon preached at Stamford, October 11, 1796, before the Consociation of the Western District in Fairfield County. By Isaac Lewis, D.D. Pastor of a consociated church in Greenwich." (New Haven: Printed by T. and S. Green—New-Haven., [1796]).

17. **Sermons that he possessed, that show the spiritual nature of the education that he desired for his family**

   a. Samuel Stanhope Smith: "A discourse on the nature and reasonableness of fasting, and on the existing causes that call us to that duty. Delivered at

Princeton, on Tuesday the 6th January, 1795. Being the day appointed by the Synod of New-York and New-Jersey, to be observed as a general fast, by all the churches of their communion in those states; and now published in compliance with the request of the students of theology and law in Princeton." By Samuel Stanhope Smith, D.D. vice-president and professor of moral philosophy and divinity, in the College of New-Jersey.[56]

18. Sermons that reveal the nature of the masonic order

    a. Samuel Miller: "A sermon, preached in New-York, July 4th, 1793. Being the anniversary of the independence of America: at the request of the Tammany Society, or Columbian Order." By Samuel Miller, A.M. One of the Ministers of the United Presbyterian Churches, in the city of New-York.[57]

    b. Uzal Ogden: "A Sermon delivered at Morris-Town, on Monday December 27, 1784, it being the Festival of St. John the Evangelist, before the Fraternity of Free and Accepted Masons, of Lodge No. 10, in the State of New-Jersey." By the Reverend Uzal Ogden. Published at the Request of the Lodge. New-York: printed by J. M'Lean, and Co. 1785.[58]

19. Sermons noted in Washington's diaries.

    a. Reverend Dr. Robert Davidson: "A sermon, on the Freedom and Happiness of the United Sates of America, preached in Carlisle, on the 5th Oct. 1794. And published at the request of the Officers of the Philadelphia and Lancaster Troops of Light Horse. By Robert Davidson, D.D. Pastor of the Presbyterian Church in Carlisle, and One of the Professors in Dickinson College."[59] Washington wrote in his diary on Oct. 5th—Sunday, 1794, "Went to the Presbiterian meeting and heard Doctr. Davidson Preach a political sermon, recommendatory of order & good government, and excellence of that of the United States."[60]

    b. "The lame discourses" of a Reverend Pond.[61]

    c. A sermon he had heard preached in Dutch.[62]

    d. November 1789, Sunday 22d. Went to St. Pauls Chappel in the forenoon— heard a charity sermon for the benefit of the Orphans School of this City.[63]

    e. January 8, 1797, Clear & Cold—wind at No. Wt. Went to a charity sermon in Christ Church. Alarmed by a cry of fire while there.[64]

20. Sermons or theological works that Washington purchased.

a. Reverend James Beattie: *Evidences of the Christian religion briefly and plainly stated.* 2 vols., London, 1786.[65]

b. Reverend Hugh Blair: *Sermons. To which is prefixed that admired tract, On the internal evidence of the Christian religion.* 2 vols. Baltimore, reprinted for the Reverend M. L. Weems. 1792-1793. (Published by and purchased from Reverend Mason Weems).[66]

c. Reverend Gilbert Burnet, Bishop of Sarum: *An Exposition of the Thirty Nine Articles of the Church of England.* Written by Gilbert Bishop of Sarum. The sixth Edition corrected. London: printed for J. Knapton, C. Hitch, 1759.[67]

Modern scholars that ignore the sources that George Washington himself drew from have presented a truncated picture of the man. They have remade him into their own secular image, while ignoring his Christian context.

Abiel Leonard's Prayer[1]

We pointed out earlier in the book that the vast majority of the colonists during the American Revolution claimed to be Christian. The statistics are staggering. At the time the American Revolution began in 1775, 99.8% of the citizens claimed to be Christians. Not 90%, not 98%, not even 99%, but 99.8%. Furthermore, 98.4% were Protestant Christians, 1.4% were Roman Catholics.[2]

The following is a prayer designed and printed to enable the soldiers to pray in a uniform manner. It was in Washington's bound collection of pamphlets and sermons. It is important for our study because Abiel Leonard was highly praised by Washington as one of the most exemplary chaplains in his army.

> His General Conduct has been exemplary and praiseworthy: In discharging the duties of his Office, active and industrious; he has discovered himself warm and steady friend to his Country, and taken great pains to animate the Soldiery and Impress them with a knowledge of the important rights we are contending for. Upon the late desertion of the Troops, he gave a Sensible and judicious discourse, holding forth the Necessity of courage and bravery and at the same time of Obedience and Subordination to those in Command.[3]

Leonard's prayer is deeply patriotic and overtly Christian. It is certain, based upon this evidence, that Washington himself read and prayed this prayer.

A prayer, composed for the benefit of the soldiery, in the American Army, to assist them in their private devotions; and recommended to their particular use: By Abiel Leonard, A.M., Chaplain to General Putnam's Regiment in said Army

A Prayer. Most great and glorious God, thy name alone is Jehovah! Thou existest independent of all beings, and art possessed of eternal and absolute perfection! I adore thee as the supreme Governor and Judge among the nations of the earth; who hast in thy wise and good providence divided them, and settled the bounds of their habitations! Thou hast placed the inhabitants of Great-Britain, and of America; not only under the common laws of justice and equity; but also under the most endearing bonds and obligations of brotherly love and kindness towards each other. Those sacred bonds have been violated; and that mutual confidence, harmony and affection, that once subsisted to mutual advantage, in a great measure lost. The enemies of America have sent over a great multitude to cast thy people in this land which thou hast given them to inherit; and to deprive them of their liberties and properties: whereby, O Lord, they have been reduced to the dreadful alternative of submitting to arbitrary laws and despotic government; or of taking up arms in defense of those rights and privileges, which thou, in thy goodness, hast conferred upon them as men and as Christians.

I would adore and bless thy name, that thou hast given thy people a just sense of the value of their important privileges, civil and sacred; and that, that love of liberty and willingness to encounter every temporary difficulty and danger to enjoy it, which glowed in the breasts of their ancestors, and brought them over to settle this land, is enkindled in their breasts; and that they are united in their counsels, and in their measures for their protection, defense and security.O my God, wilt thou be graciously pleased to strengthen and establish the union of their colonies; and favour the Congress with thy blessing and presence! Prosper the means of defense—be the God of the American army, — bless all in general, and in particular command, and grant unto thy servant the commander in chief, wisdom and fortitude suited to his important military station, and crown him with prosperity, success and honor.

O my God, in obedience to the call of thy providence, I have engaged myself, and plighted my faith, to jeopardy my life in the high places of the field in the defense of my dear country and the liberties of acknowledging thy people to be my people, their interest my interest, and their God to be my God. Thou knowest, O Lord, that it is not from a spirit of licentiousness,—lust of independence or delight in the effusion of human blood: but from a sense of that duty; owe to my country and posterity I have voluntarily engaged in this service.—And I desire now to make a solemn dedication of myself to thee in it through Jesus Christ presenting myself to thy Divine Majesty to be disposed of by thee to thy glory and the good of America. O do thou, I most fervently entreat, wash away mine iniquities, blot them out of thy remembrance, purify and cleanse my soul in the blood of the great Captain of my salvation—accept of—own and bless me!

Teach, I pray thee, my hands to war, and my fingers to fight in the defense of America, and the rights and liberties of it! Impress upon my mind a true sense of my duty, and the obligation I am under to my country! And enable me to pay a due and ready respect and obedience to all my officers. Grant unto me courage, zeal and resolution in the day of battle, that I may play the man for my people, and the cities of my God; choosing rather to lay down my life, than either through cowardice or desertion betray the glorious cause I am engaged in. And, O Lord, if it seem good in thy sight, shield and protect me; cover my head in the day of battle; and suffer not the arrows of death that may fly around me, to wound or destroy me: but may I live to do further service to my country—to the church and the people of God, and interest of Jesus Christ, and see peace and tranquility restored to this land.

Give me grace, that I may spend my time in my proper employment as a soldier, furnishing myself with such military skill as may quality me to stand in a day of war, and to speak with the enemy in the gate; wisely filling up my spare hours in acts of religion. May I detest and abhor all sinful oaths, execrations and blasphemies; never using thy name, but on solemn occasions, and then with the most profound reverence! May I never so far lose my liberty, as to become a servant of meats and drinks; but teach me to use thy good creatures soberly and temperately: not enslaving myself to, not losing my reason by indulging a brutal appetite! Enable me to flee all those vices of gaming, rioting, chambering and wantonness which have a destructive and fatal tendency; but as a stranger and pilgrim may I abstain from fleshly lusts which war against the soul! Enable me to put off all anger, wrath, malice and strife; and live in love with and in the exercise of kindness to my fellow soldiers! Bring content with my wages, may I never do violence to any man, nor seize upon his property through covetousness or greediness of spoil! And may I prove myself a faithful follower of Jesus Christ, whom all the armies of heaven follow; fight the good fight of faith; and have my present conflicts against the world, the flesh and the devil crowned with victory and triumph!

Now, O my God, a mind deeply affected with a sense of thy wisdom, power, goodness and faithfulness, I desire to commit all my concerns to thee,—to depend upon thy help and protection, in all the difficulties and dangers; and upon thy care and provision, in all the wants and necessities that can befall me!

And my family and kindred, whom I have left behind, I recommend to thy care; to receive the blessings of God, the comforts and supports of thy providence and the sanctification of thy Spirit.

And, O Thou, who didst preserve the children of Israel from the hand of

Pharaoh and his host,—didst protect and deliver them from all dangers,—didst redeem them out of all their troubles,—and broughtest them out of the land of bondage into the state of liberty,—deliver, I pray thee, thy distressed, afflicted and oppressed people in this land out of all their troubles! Preserve them in truth and peace. In unity and safety, in all storms, and against all temptations and enemies! And by means of the present conflict may the liberties of America be established upon a firmer foundation than ever; and she become the excellency of the whole earth, and the joy of many generations!

And grant, O Lord, that the inhabitants of Great-Britain may arise and vindicate their liberties; and a glorious reunion take place between them and thy people in this land, founded upon the principles of liberty and righteousness; that the Britons and the Americans may rejoice in the King as the minister of God to both for good.

Hear me, O my God, and accept of those my petitions through Jesus Christ, to whom with thee, O Father, and the Holy Spirit, one God, be glory, honor and praise, forever and ever. AMEN

Sermon by the
Reverend Bryan Lord Fairfax

This "lost sermon" was recently rediscovered, thanks to the help of the Virginia Historical Society, and is published here with their kind permission. We include it because it shows the biblical nature of the Gospel preaching of the Reverend Bryan Lord Fairfax. The Fairfax family had the deepest influence of all families, other than Washington's own, on his life and values. Bryan Fairfax not only served as the pastor at Washington's church in Alexandria, but he was a life-long friend, neighbor, confidant, and fellow fox-hunter. The evidence shows that Washington sought Reverend Fairfax's pastoral ministry at times of spiritual need, as when Washington asked Reverend Fairfax to officiate at his nephew's funeral.

The sermon reflects the Gospel preaching that George Washington would have experienced from his personal and pastoral friend. This sermon focuses on the New Testament doctrine of eternal life by faith in Christ's redeeming work on the cross that results in the obedience of good works. It reflects a modified Calvinist theology of the atonement of Christ.

Sermon by the Reverend Bryan Lord Fairfax
Minister of Christ Church,
Alexandria, Virginia

"Verily, verily, I say unto you, he that believeth on Me hath
everlasting life."
St. John 6: 47.

Our blessed Lord, who knew all things, in uttering these words seems to have guarded against their perversion. He knew that their meaning would be perverted, and that they would be strained to bear another, from what they plainly have. Therefore he not only says, He that believeth on Me hath everlasting life, but he introduces it by saying, *Verily, verily* he that believeth on Me hath everlasting life; as if it were to give a greater sanction to the words.

Notwithstanding this, these words and others of the like import, have been often construed to mean something more than the express. For it is very common with interpreters, when they cannot reconcile one part of Scripture with their ideas, or with another, to strain the meaning of one of them, so as to coincide with the other.

It is for this reason, we may suppose, that though it is declared, that a believer in Christ hath everlasting life, yet because good works are elsewhere mentioned as necessary to salvation, it is concluded that believing, means believing and obeying. As this opinion may be an hinderance to salvation, it may be useful to take notice of it.

I shall therefore in the first place show how this opinion may become an hinderance in the way of salvation.

The great point of the Gospel is to trust in the mercy of God, or to have a faith in the meritorious sacrifice of Christ. If, in consequence of this, I repeat to a man the plain words of Christ, that he that believeth on him hath everlasting life, it is well; but if I also add, you must obey him before you can expect life, I then put a clog on him—a hinderance to his faith. For as long as obedience is such an indefinite thing, he can never tell whether his obedience is perfect enough to entitle him so to trust. Many a one is perhaps kept from trusting through a diffidence in his own goodness. The presumptuous, and they who have the best opinion of themselves, will be most apt to do it upon such a ground; whereas the better any man grows, the clearer will he see his imperfections.

The true ground, therefore, is the promises and declaration of God. A right understanding of the Gospel is the best foundation. The Apostle tells the Colossians of the hope that is laid up for them in Heaven, whereof, says he, ye heard before in the word of the truth of the Gospel. It was from the Gospel they derived their hope—not from their obedience, which, being imperfect, can never give a solid hope in the sight of God.

It is remarkable that wherever faith is mentioned as having annexed to it everlasting life, obedience is never joined to it, because that would destroy what the other was intended to produce.

Many things are best illustrated by examples. Suppose a man is shut up in a close room and ready to faint—one calls to him from without, and tells him to open the door and he will revive. Another tells him he must do many other things also, that it is in vain to open the door unless he can and will do so and so. The poor man is discouraged and dies. Now faith is the door of the heart, when a man opens it life enters, and he is then alert and active and ready to do what is required. So Christ says, "Behold I stand at the door and knock, if any man hear my voice and open the door, I will come in to him and sup with him, and he with me." This is the great point, to hear the voice of Christ in the Gospel, and to open the heart and receive him, which is life eternal. For to believe in him is to believe his words; and when you believe them, you receive them, his words of eternal life.

What has obedience or good works to do here? Christ tells us to open our hearts and receive him; and if we do we immediately have life. Spiritual death is the fear of [sic] of God. Believe that he is reconciled, or believe that Christ will save you from wrath, and you revive. If you wait for a more complete obedience before you believe this, you will always be subject to doubts and fears, and perhaps never this way attain to a true and lasting peace. We must keep in mind that the words of Christ as spirit and life; this he said upon the subject of believing in him, when he said he would give his flesh for the life of the world. This is the way we are to obtain life. Whatever inducement God may have to give us life, that is another matter. If our repentance should dispose him to give us life, yet still it is through the name of Jesus Christ, through faith in his blood. And although faith is the gift of God, and it is he which enables us to believe, yet whatever hinders our faith should be removed.

There is the same reason for it in this case as it was in respect to the Apostle Paul, and the people of Galatia. He had planted the Gospel among them; but afterwards there came some and told them, except they were circumcised and kept the law of Moses, they could not be saved. This made the Apostle afraid that he had bestowed upon them labor in vain. Yet he tried to bring them back to seek for justification in Christ, and told them that the new persuasion they were in came not from Him that called them. Hence we see that though it was God who gave them faith, and justified them thereby, yet the Apostle's ministry was made use of to recover them from their error. So it is the duty of ministers to further the faith of others; as it is possible for some, according to the Scripture, to shut up the Kingdom of Heaven against men, which is open to all believers.

When Paul and Silas were asked by a man what he should do to be saved, the answer was, "Believe on the Lord Jesus Christ, and thou shalt be saved and thy house." Here is no mention of works or obedience; neither was there when our Saviour uttered another remarkable saying: "Verily, verily, I say unto you, he that heareth my word and believeth on him that sent me, hath everlasting life, and shall not come into condemnation, but is passed from death unto life." And why did our Lord make this declaration? We may conclude it was for the same reason that his Apostle wrote to the same purport: "These things have I written on you that believe on the name of the Son of God, that ye may believe on the name of the Son of God." His words were spoken, and these were written, that believers might know that they had eternal life.

For however reviving such a faith is, considering the difficulty there is in maintaining it, a positive declaration that such a faith is life, helps them to preserve it, as the last words quoted from St. John do declare. And faith is criterion by which a man may judge of his own state in a more sure and better manner than he can by any obedience, which falls greatly short of perfection. For the comfort of Christians, then, was all Holy Scripture written, as well as to bring them to the knowledge of Jesus Christ; and when they believe in him hereafter they will not be ashamed nor confounded.

One of the Prophets says, They shall not make haste – they will not run to hide themselves in the rocks and mountains, and in the tops of the ragged rocks; all which declarations and the like, indicate great fear, and show that under spiritual death they have a dread of

God; *and this must be removed by a belief in His reconciliation, and in no other manner.* For damnation means condemnation, and this is opposed to life; for some will be raised to life, and some to damnation, or everlasting shame and contempt. The condemnation will be in the sinner's own breast. This he can be delivered from, only by a belief in that satisfaction which the Son of God hath made for his numerous offences.

Our blessed Lord came not to condemn the world, but that the world through him might be saved. And he has told us again and again how that is to be—by believing in him, that is, by believing in him we have life; and as we trust in him he will save us.

Yet however strange it might seem, there are multitudes who do not receive the offered salvation. Some will not, and some cannot. The Scriptures are not easily understood. A man must labor like one who diggeth for hid treasure, to understand the fear of the Lord and to find the knowledge of God. Various constructions are put upon them; some consider salvation in this view, some in that.

Some reckon the great atonement was made for a few only; some consider it as made for all men. The former say it was absolute; the later say it was conditional. These differences become a hinderance to salvation; a hinderance to the great work of God: "For this is the work of God, that you believe on him who he hath sent."

But since I have mentioned the Atonement, it may be proper to observe further: They who think Christ died only for a few, believe he died for them absolutely. They are convinced from Scripture that he made an absolute atonement, and that God was reconciled to all for whom he did die; but as the greater part perish, he must have died only for a few.

The others lay down another principle, and yet make their conclusion for the very same reason. They say, *it is certain that* he died for all; but it could only be conditionally, because the greater part perish.

Now the truth seems to lie right between these opinions, and we must reject the same reason which they both give. The truth seems to be that he made an absolute atonement, and that for all men, without any condition on their part, so as to effect the virtue of this atonement. Many passages in Scripture prove that he died for all men; and none that mention his death look anything like a conditional atonement. This opinion is taken up because of the question, Why then do any perish? it not being discerned how any can be miserable if an absolute unconditional atonement has been made. But if this can be made plain, the difficulty will vanish.

Although we should suppose that God was reconciled to the whole race, on the death of his Son, it does not follow that none will be miserable. Because the atonement of itself makes no alteration in the heart of man, no, not in one of the elect. Christ's dying for sin produces no change; does not qualify any man for heaven, nor even escape wrath. But a faith in that atonement may and does deliver us from the fear of God, and make us fit for heaven.

Now if we only suppose that under spiritual death there may be a great sense of sin and a fear of God's wrath, like that of Adam who fled and hid himself; a man who does not believe that God is reconciled, may be in as great torment as if he was an enemy not be appeased.

When we consider the greatness of the Supreme Being, his power, holiness, and all his glorious perfections, we may easily conceive an offending creature to be extremely miserable when the purity of the Divine Law which he hath broken, and these perfections come to be unveiled. Besides his exclusion from that bliss which others enjoy, and which he thinks he might have shared in will become an additional torment. There shall be weeping and gnashing of teeth, said our Saviour, when ye shall see Abraham, and Isaac, and Jacob, and all the prophets, in the kingdom of God, and you yourselves thrust out. A shame also will arise from having his sins laid open and exposed to the view of all. Hence we see that our Lord Jesus Christ may have made an absolute atonement, and that for all mankind; and yet that the greater part may perish and be miserable. And that he has done it, the resurrection is at once a proof. They are raised from the dead. Because the penalty of the law hath been paid; and they will be raised, and by virtue of that atonement and that alone.

Christ hath atoned for all, but all are not heirs. He has

purchased all. They are all bought with a price, even them that bring upon themselves swift destruction, denying the Lord that bought them. But all are not heirs of glory. Therefore here is the place to introduce conditions. If ye believe, if ye persevere, if through obedience ye continue in the faith, ye will be happy; not that Christ hath atoned for you if you do so and so, for that he hath already done, whether you believe or no: as it is written. "If we be dead with him, we shall also live with him; if we deny him, he also will deny us. If we believe not, yet he abideth faithful, he cannot deny himself."

I come now in the 2d. Place to show how good Works or Obedience are necessary to Salvation, and that consistently with what hath been already said upon this subject. It hath been said, that, according to this doctrine, if a man only believes, he shall be saved, let him live as he will. But this is a wrong conclusion. No man can trust in the Lord and at the same time be living in sin; and no man can continue in faith without a certain degree of obedience; because sin hardens the heart, and introduces unbelief. Every imperfection will not destroy our faith, but deliberate sins will; and till we are humbled by repentance, it will not return. If we cannot continue in the faith without suitable good works or a certain degree of obedience, then this obedience is quite necessary to our final salvation.

But that I may not be supposed to have advanced this at random, and as it is very material, I will point out some Scriptures which confirm it.

St. Paul in writing to Timothy, says: "This charge I commit unto thee, son Timothy, according to the Prophecies which went before on thee, that though by them mightest war a good warfare, holding faith and a good conscience; which some having put away, concerning faith have made shipwreck." Here we see that faith is shipwrecked, or destroyed, by putting away a good conscience, which is done only by sin.

The Apostle also to the Hebrews writes: "Take heed, brethren, lest there be in any of you an evil heart of unbelief, in departing from the living God. But exhort one another daily, while it is called, to-day; lest any of you be hardened through the deceitfulness of sin. For we are made partakers of Christ, if we hold the beginning of our confidence steadfast unto the end." Now, confidence means a confiding—a confiding trust. And this they are told they must hold steadfast to the end. And for this purpose they are exhorted to beware of an evil heart of unbelief, and to take care that they are not hardened through the deceitfulness of sin.

But not only does obedience continue us in the faith, but repentance prepared our heart for it. Yet faith is still the great means of life—as it is written in 3d St. John's Gospel. Not only our Lord himself said it, but John the Baptist also declared: "He that believeth on the Son hath everlasting life; and he that believeth not the Son shall not see life, but the wrath of God abideth on him." The wrath of God abideth on a man till he believeth on the Son, and then he has life, and not before.

To conclude. We find it expressly said, that he that believeth on him, our *Lord Jesus Christ,* hath everlasting life; and that a similar declaration was made, that such as believed on him might know that they had life, and that they might believe on his name.

And when we have this truth laid before us, we should not hinder its effects by blending any other matter with it that does not belong to it. And as we are weak creatures, we should pray to God to help us to this faith; for it is he which enables us to believe.

We read of a man that prayed to Christ to help his unbelief. And the Apostle Paul prayed to God for the Ephesians, that they might be strengthened with might by his Spirit in the inner man, that Christ might dwell in their hearts by faith. So also we have a fragment of one of the holy Fathers, wherein he desires the prayers of other Christians that he might be justified by this faith. All which may be an inducement to us also to pray for this gift where we have it not, and for an increase and continuance of it when we have it. Yet we should also read the Scriptures as the way wherein it comes, or else by hearing them read and expounded. I have not entered into a definition of a saving faith; for if I should fail in that, I might do harm. The only express definition of it in Scripture, we have in Hebrews.

There it is called – the substance of things hoped for; or as some expound it – the substantial expectation of things not seen: and this I think cannot amount to less than a firm persuasion of being saved, and partaking of the heavenly inheritance. And the account there given of several that had died in the faith shows, that they having seen the promises afar off, were persuaded of them and embraced them, and confessed that they were strangers and pilgrims on the earth. And as they desired a better country, God was not ashamed to be called their God; and had prepared for them a city.

May we be enabled to imitate their faith, and enjoy all those good things which God hath laid up for them that love him.

Now to God, the Father, God the Son, and God the Holy Ghost, be ascribed all the glory, power, might, majesty, and dominion, both now and for evermore. Amen.

THE END.[1]

APPENDIX EIGHT

The Wisdom
of George Washington

The following quotations from Washington are arranged in outline form. They represent the many facets of his life, and illustrate the principles by which he lived his life, and the wisdom by which he reached his unwavering decisions. Also, note that an important quotation is found at the head of each chapter throughout this book.

I. Character and Education
II. Virtue and Vice, Personality and Emotions
III. Family
IV. Government and Leadership
V. Military and Patriotism
VI. Business and Finances
VII. Politics and Media
VIII. Slavery

Unless otherwise noted all the quotations are from the *Writings of George Washington* edited by John C. Fitzpatrick and found online at http://etext.lib.virginia.edu/ washington/fitzpatrick/

I. CHARACTER AND EDUCATION
A. Character
1. Character
a) To THE SECRETARY OF STATE, Philadelphia, March 3, 1797.
"I have thought it expedient to notice the publication of certain forged letters which first appeared in the year 1777,...Another crisis in the affairs of America having occurred, the same weapon has been resorted to, to wound my character and deceive the people."

b) To REVEREND ISRAEL EVANS, Head Qrs. Valley-forge, March 13, 1778.

"It is more especially incumbent upon me to thank you for the honorable, but partial mention you have made of my character; and to assure you, that it will ever be the first wish of my heart to aid your pious endeavours to inculcate a due sense of the dependance we ought to place in that all wise and powerful Being on whom alone our success depends."

c) To GOVERNOR JONATHAN TRUMBULL, September 21, 1775.

"It gives me real concern to observe yours of the 15th Inst. that you should think it Necessary to distinguish between my Personal and Public Character and confine your Esteem to the former."

d) To BROWN & FRANCIS, Philadelphia, January 7, 1792.

"In my public capacity you will readily see that such a thing could not be done; and abroad, it would be almost impossible to separate my private from my official character, in a case of this kind."

2. **Deeds**

a) To MAJOR GENERAL JOHN SULLIVAN, December 15, 1779.

"A slender acquaintance with the world must convince every man, that actions, not words, are the true criterion of the attachment of his friends, and that the most liberal professions of good will are very far from being the surest marks of it."

b) To PATRICK HENRY, January 15, 1799.

"The views of men can only be known, or guessed at, by their words or actions."

B. **Education**

1. **Education**

a) To GOVERNOR ROBERT BROOKE, Philadelphia, March 16, 1795.

"It is with indescribable regret, that I have seen the youth of the United States migrating to foreign countries, in order to acquire the higher branches of erudition, and to obtain a knowledge of the Sciences. Altho' it would be injustice to many to pronounce the certainty of their imbibing maxims, not congenial with republicanism; it must nevertheless be admitted, that a serious danger is encountered, by sending abroad among other political systems those, who have not well learned the value of their own. The time is therefore come, when a plan of Universal education ought to be adopted in the United States."

b) To DAVID HUMPHREYS, July 25, 1785.

"If I had the talents for it, I have not leisure to turn my thoughts to Commentaries [on the Revolutionary War]. A consciousness of a defective education, and a certainty of the want of time, unfit me for such an undertaking."

c) To NICHOLAS PIKE, June 20, 1786.

"In my opinion, every effort of genius, and all attempts towards improving useful knowledge ought to meet with encouragement in this country."

d) To ALEXANDER HAMILTON, September 1, 1796

"Education generally [is] one of the surest means of enlightening and giving just ways of thinking to our citizens."

2. **Ignorance**

a) To JOHN JAY, May 18, 1786. "Ignorance and design are difficult to combat. Out of these proceed illiberal sentiments, improper jealousies, and a train of evils which oftentimes in republican governments must be sorely felt before they can be renewed."

3. **Knowledge**

a) CIRCULAR TO THE STATES Head Quarters, Newburgh, June 8, 1783.

"The foundation of our Empire was not laid in the gloomy age of Ignorance and Superstition, but at an Epocha when the rights of mankind were better understood and more clearly defined, than at any former period, the researches of the human mind, after social happiness, have been carried to a great extent, the Treasures of knowledge, acquired by the labours of Philosophers, Sages and Legislatures, through a long succession of years, are laid open for our use, and their collected wisdom may be happily applied in the Establishment of our forms of Government; the free cultivation of Letters, the unbounded extension of Commerce, the progressive refinement of Manners, the growing liberality of sentiment, and above all, the pure and benign light of Revelation, have had ameliorating influence on mankind and increased the blessings of Society. At this auspicious period, the United States came into existence as a Nation, and if their Citizens should not be completely free and happy, the fault will be entirely their own."

4. **Reading**

a) To JAMES MCHENRY, May 29, 1797.

"… in this detail no mention is made of any portion of time allotted for reading; the remark would be just, for I have not looked into a book since I came home, nor shall I be able to do it until I have discharged my Workmen; probably not before the nights grow longer; when possibly, I may be looking in doomsday book."

b) To REVEREND BOUCHER, July 9, 1771.

"I conceive a knowledge of books is the basis upon which other knowledge is to be built."

c) To GEORGE WASHINGTON PARKE CUSTIS, November 13, 1796.

"Light reading (by this, I mean books of little importance) may amuse for the moment, but leaves nothing solid behind."

5. **Students**

a) To TOBIAS LEAR, Mount Vernon, November 7, 1790.

"I lay it down as a maxim, that if the number of the pupils is too great for the tutors, justice cannot be done, be the abilities of the latter what they will. What the *due* proportion, beyond which it ought not to go, is in some measure matter of opinion, but an extreme must be obvious to all."

6. **Scholarships**

a) To WILLIAM MINOR, Mount Vernon, June 16, 1785.

"Moral obligations, or the obligations of humanity therefore induced me to bestow a years schooling on Lawce. Posey, and to effect it I was willing to incur the expence of a years board also;"

II. VIRTUE AND VICE, PERSONALITY AND EMOTIONS

A. Virtues & Vices

1. **Compassion**

a) To BUSHROD WASHINGTON, Newburgh, January 15, 1783.

"Let your *heart* feel for the affliction, and distresses of every one, and let your *hand* give in proportion to your purse; remembering always, the estimation of the Widows mite. But, that it is not every one who asketh, that deserveth charity; all however are worthy of the enquiry, or the deserving may suffer."

b) To the PRESIDENT OF CONGRESS, January 26, 1777.

"I hope your new appointment . . . will make the necessary reform in the hospital and that I shall not, the next campaign, have my ears and eyes too, shocked with the complaints and looks of poor creatures perishing for want of proper care."

c) To JAMES MCHENRY, July 4, 1798.

"Humanity and feeling for the sick and wounded of an army call loudly for skill, attention, and economy in the director of the hospitals."

d) To JAMES ANDERSON, July 25, 1798.

"I, believing that man was not designed by the all-wise Creator to live for himself alone, prepare for the worst that can happen."

e) To GEORGE WASHINGTON PARKE CUSTIS, November 13, 1796.

"Never let an indigent person ask, without receiving *something*, if you have the means." (emphasis in the original)

f) To LUND WASHINGTON, November 26, 1775.

"Let the hospitality of the house [Mount Vernon], with respect to the poor, be kept up. Let no one go hungry away. If any of this kind of people should be in want of corn, supply their necessities, provided it does not encourage them in idleness; and I have no objection to your giving my money in charity, to the amount of forty or fifty pounds a year, when you thing it well bestowed. What I mean by having no objection is, that it is my desire that it should be done. You are to consider, that neither myself nor wife is now in the way to do these good offices. In all other respect, I recommend it to you, and have no doubt of your observing the greatest economy and frugality; as I suppose you know, that I do not get a farthing for my services here, more than my expenses. It becomes necessary, therefore, for me to be saving at home."

2. **Drunkenness**

a) To THOMAS GREEN, Mount Vernon, March 31, 1789.

"… refrain from drink which is the source of all evil, and the ruin of half the workmen in this Country; and next to avoid bad Company which is the bane of good morals, economy and industry. You have every inducement to do this. Reputation the care and support of a growing family and society which this family affords within your own doors which may not be the case with some of the idle (to say nothing worse of them) characters who may lead you into temptation. Were you to look back, and had the means, either from recollection, or accounts, to ascertain the cost of the liquor you have expended it would astonish you. In the manner this expence is generally incurred that is by getting a little now, a little then, the impropriety of it is not seen, in as much as it passes away without much thought. But view it in the aggregate you will be convinced at once, whether any man who depends upon the labour of his hands not only for his own support, but that of an encreasing family can afford such a proportion of his wages to that article. But the expence is not the worst consequence that attends it for it naturally leads a man into the company of those who encourage dissipation and idleness by which he is led by degrees to the perpetration of acts which may terminate in his Ruin; but supposing this not to happen a disordered frame, and a body debilitated, renders him unfit (even if his mind was disposed to discharge the duties of his station with honor to himself or fidelity to his employer) from the execution of it. An aching head and trembling limbs which are the inevitable effects of drinking disincline the hands from work; hence begins sloth and that Listlessness which end in idleness; but which are no reasons for withholding that labour for which money is paid."

3. **Excuses**

a) To HARRIOT WASHINGTON, his niece, October 30, 1791.
"It is better to offer no excuse than a bad one."

4. **Friendship**

a) To GEORGE WASHINGTON PARKE CUSTIS, Philadelphia, November 28, 1796.

"'Tis well to be on good terms with all your fellow-students, and I am pleased to hear you are so, but while a courteous behavior is due to all, select the most deserving only for your friendships, and before this becomes intimate, weigh their dispositions and character *well*. True friendship is a plant of slow growth; to be sincere, there must be a congeniality of temper and pursuits. Virtue and vice can not be allied; nor can idleness and industry; of course, if you resolve to adhere to the two former of these extremes, an intimacy with those who incline to the latter of them, would be extremely embarrassing to you; it would be a stumbling block in your way; and act like a millstone hung to your neck, for it is the nature of idleness and vice to obtain as many votaries as they can.

"I would guard you, too, against imbibing hasty and unfavorable impressions of any one. Let your judgment always balance well before you decide; and even then, where there is no occasion for expressing an opinion, it is best to be silent, for there is nothing more certain than that it is at all times more easy to make enemies than friends. And besides, to speak evil of any one, unless there is unequivocal proofs of their deserving it, is an injury for which there is no adequate reparation. For, as Shakespeare says "He that robs me of my good name enriches not himself, but renders me poor indeed," or words to that effect. Keep in mind that scarcely any change would be agreeable to you at *first* from the sudden transition, and from never having been accustomed to shift or rough it. And, moreover, that if you meet with collegiate fare, it will be unmanly to complain. My paper reminds me it is time to conclude. Affectionately, &c."

b) To BUSHROD WASHINGTON, Newburgh, January 15, 1783.

"That the Company in which you will improve most, will be least expensive to you; and yet I am not such a Stoic as to suppose you will, or to think it right that you ought, always to be in Company with Senators and Philosophers; but, of the young and juvenile kind let me advise you to be choice. It is easy to make acquaintances, but very difficult to shake them off, however irksome and unprofitable they are found after we have once committed ourselves to them; the indiscretions, and scrapes which very often they involuntarily lead one into, proves equally distressing and disgraceful.

"Be courteous to all, but intimate with few, and let those few be well tried before you give them your confidence; true friendship is a plant of slow growth, and must undergo and withstand the shocks of adversity before it is entitled to the appellation."

c) To LAFAYETTE, November, 1784.

"In the moment of our separation upon the road as I travelled, and every hour since, I felt all that love, respect and attachment for you, with which length of years, close connexion and your merits have inspired me. I often asked myself, as our carriages distended, whether that was the last sight, I ever should have of you? And tho' I wished to say no, my fears answered yes. I called to mind the days of my youth, and found they had long since fled to return no more; that I was now descending the hill, I had been 52 years climbing, and that tho' I was blessed with a good constitution, I was of a short lived family, and might soon expect to be entombed in the dreary mansions of my father's. These things darkened the shades and gave a gloom to the picture, consequently to my prospects of seeing you again: but I will not repine, I have had my day..."

d) To LAFAYETTE, West Point, September 30, 1779.

"...your strict and uniform friendship for *me*, has ripened the first impressions of esteem and attachment, which I imbibed for you into such perfect love and gratitude, that neither time nor absence can impair. Which will warrant my assuring you, that, whether in the character of an officer at the head of a corps of gallant French (if circumstances should require this), whether as a major-genl. Commanding a division of the American army, or whether, after our Swords and spears have given place to the ploughshare and pruning-Hook, I see you as a private gentleman, a friend and companion, I shall welcome you in all the warmth of friendship to Columbia's shores; and, in the latter case, to my rural cottage where homely fare and a cordial reception shall be substituted for delicacies of costly living. This, from past experience, I know *you* can submit to; and if the lovely partner of your happiness will consent to participate with *us* in such rural entertainment and amusements, I can undertake, in behalf of Mrs. Washington, that she will do every thing in her power to make Virginia agreeable to the Marchioness .... I assure you, that I love every body that is dear to you. ..."

5. **Finishing**

a) To THOMAS LAW, Mount Vernon, May 7, 1798.

"It has been a maxim with me from early life, never to undertake anything without perceiving a door to the accomplishment, in a reasonable time and with my own resources."

6. **Golden Rule**

a) To THE EMPEROR OF GERMANY, Philadelphia, May 15, 1796.

"As it is a maxim with me not to ask what under similar circumstances, I would not grant, your Majesty will do me the justice to believe, that this request appears to me to correspond with those great principles of magnanimity and wisdom, which form the Basis of sound Policy and durable Glory. May the almighty and merciful Sovereign of the universe keep your Majesty under his protection and guidance."

7. **Gratitude**

a) To LANDON CARTER, Valley Forge, May 30, 1778.

"Were I not warm in my acknowledgments for your distinguished regard, I should feel that sense of ingratitude, which I hope will never constitute a part of my character, nor find a place in my bosom. My friends therefore may believe me sincere in my professions of attachment to them, whilst Providence has a joint claim to my humble and grateful thanks, for its protection and direction of me, through the many difficult and intricate scenes, which this contest hath produced; and for the constant interposition in our behalf, when the clouds were heaviest and seemed ready to burst upon us."

b) To COLONEL JAMES WOOD, July 1758.

"If thanks flowing from a heart replete with joy and Gratitude can in any Measure compensate for the fatigue, anxiety and Pain you had at my Election, be assured you have them . . .

"How I shall thank Mrs. Wood for her favorable Wishes, and how acknowledge my sense of obligation to the People in general for their choice of me, I am at a loss to resolve on. But why? Can I do it more effectually than by making their Interest (as it really is) my own, and doing everything that lyes in my little Power for the Honor and welfare of the Country? I think not; and my best endeavors they may always command. . .

"I am extremely thankful to you and my other friends for entertaining the Freeholders in my name. I hope no Exception was taken to any that voted against me, but that all were alike treated, and all had enough. It is what I much desired."

c) To SELECTMEN OF BOSTON, July 28, 1795.

"While I feel the most lively gratitude for the many instances of the approbation from my country, I can not otherwise deserve it, than by obeying the dictates of my conscience."

d) To MAJOR GENERAL ISRAEL PUTNAM, June 2, 1783.

"Ingratitude has been experienced in all ages, and republics in particular have ever been famed for the exercise of that unnatural and sordid vice."

8. Gambling

a) To BUSHROD WASHINGTON, Newburgh, January 15, 1783.

"The last thing I shall mention, is first of importance. and that is, to avoid Gaming. This is a vice which is productive of every possible evil. equally injurious to the morals and health of its votaries. It is the child of Avarice, the brother of inequity, and father of Mischief. It has been the ruin of many worthy familys; the loss of many a man's honor; and the cause of Suicide. To all those who enter the list, it is equally fascinating; the Successful gamester pushes his good fortune till it is over taken by a reverse; the loosing gamester, in hopes of retrieving past misfortunes, goes on from bad to worse; till grown desperate, he pushes at every thing; and looses his all. In a word, few gain by this abominable practice (the profit, if any, being diffused) while thousands are injured."

9. Honesty

a) FAREWELL ADDRESS

"I hold the maxim no less applicable to public than to private affairs, that honesty is always the best policy."

b) FAREWELL ADDRESS [First Draft, May 15, 1796.]

"In public, as in private life, I am persuaded that honesty will forever be found to be the best policy."

c) To ALEXANDER HAMILTON, Mount Vernon, August 28, 1788.

"Still I hope I shall always possess firmness and virtue enough to maintain (what I consider the most enviable of all titles) the character of *an honest man.*" (emphasis in the orginal)

d) To EARL OF LOUDOUN, March 1757.

"My nature is open and honest and free from guile."

e) To EDMUND RANDOLPH, July 31, 1795.

"There is but one straight course, and that is to seek truth and pursue it steadily."

f) To TIMOTHY PICKERING, February 10, 1799.

"Concealment is a species of misinformation."

10. **Honor**

a) To JACOB GERHARD DIRIKS, Mount Vernon, March 15, 1785.

"It is a maxim with me Sir, to take no liberties with exalted characters to whom I am not personally known, or with whom I have had no occasion to correspond by letter."

b) To COLONEL WILLIAM FITZHUGH, November 15, 1754.

"I herewith enclose Governour Sharpe's letter, which I beg you will return to him, with my acknowledgements for the favour he intended me. Assure him, Sir . . . of my reluctance to quit the service . . . Also inform him, that it was to obey the call of honour, and the advice of my friends, I declined it, and not to gratify any desire I had to leave the military line. My inclinations are strongly bent to arms."

c) To WILLIAM BYRD, Mount Vernon, May 25, 1755.

"If I gain any credit, or if I am entitled to the least countenance or esteem, it must be from serving my country without fee or reward; for I can truly say, I have no expectation of either. To merit its esteem, and the good will of my friends, is the sum of my ambition, having no prospect of attaining a commission..."

d) To PATRICK HENRY, March 28, 1778.

"The approbation of my country is what I wish; and, as far as my abilities and opportunities will permit, I hope I shall endeavor to deserve it. It is the highest reward to a feeling mind; and happy are they, who so conduct themselves as to merit it."

11. Humility

a) REMARKS ON MONROE'S "VIEW OF THE CONDUCT OF THE EXECUTIVE OF THE UNITED STATES"

"Acts of candor when performed, if acknowledged by the party to whom they are said to be rendered, ought not to be boasted of by those who perform them."

b) SPEECH TO CONGRESS, June 16, 1775.

"Mr. President: Though I am truly sensible of the high honor done me in this appointment, yet I feel great distress from a consciousness that my abilities and military experience may not be equal to the extensive and important trust. However, as the Congress desire it, I will enter upon the momentous duty and exert every power I possess in the service and for support of the glorious cause. I beg they will accept my most cordial thanks for this distinguished testimony of their approbation. But lest some unlucky event should happen unfavourable to my reputation, I beg it may be remembered by every gentleman in the room, that I this day declare with the utmost sincerity I do not think myself equal to the command I am honored with.

"As to pay, Sir, I beg leave to assure the Congress, that as no pecuniary consideration could have tempted me to accept this arduous employment at the expense of my domestic ease and happiness, I do not wish to make any profit from it. I will keep an exact account of my expenses. Those I doubt not they will discharge, and that is all I desire."

12. Happiness

a) THE FIRST INAUGURAL ADDRESS [April 30, 1789.]

"The foundations of our National policy will be laid in the pure and immutable principles of private morality; and the pre-eminence of a free Government, be exemplified by all the attributes which can win the affections of its Citizens, and command the respect of the world.... there is no truth more thoroughly established, than that there exists in the oeconomy and course of nature, an indissoluble union between virtue and happiness, between duty and advantage, between the genuine maxims of an honest and magnanimous policy, and the solid rewards of public prosperity and felicity: Since we ought to be no less persuaded that the propitious smiles of Heaven, can never be expected on a nation that disregards the eternal rules of order and right, which Heaven itself has ordained: And since the preservation of the sacred fire of liberty, and the destiny of the Republican model of Government, are justly considered as *deeply*, perhaps as *finally* staked, on the experiment entrusted to the hands of the American people." (emphasis in the orginal)

b) To ANNIS BOUDINOT STOCKTON, Mount Vernon, August 31, 1788.

"A good general government, without good morals and good habits, will not make us a happy People; and we shall deceive ourselves if we think it will."

c) GENERAL ORDERS, Saturday, March 22, 1783.

"In justice to the zeal and ability of the Chaplains, as well as to his own feelings, the Commander in chief thinks it a duty to declare the regularity and decorum with which divine service is now performed every sunday, will reflect great credit on the army in general, tend to improve the morals, and at the same time, to increase the happiness of the soldiery, and must afford the most pure and rational entertainment for every serious and well disposed mind."

d) To THE GENERAL CONVENTION OF BISHOPS, CLERGY, AND LAITY OF THE PROTESTANT EPISCOPAL CHURCH in New York, New Jersey, Pennsylvania, Delaware, Maryland, Virginia, and North Carolina delivered an address to the President, August 18, 1789. Washington stated that "human happiness and moral duty are inseparably connected" and that "It affords edifying prospects indeed to see Christians of different denominations dwell together in more charity, and conduct themselves in respect to each other with a more christian-like spirit than ever they have done in any former age, or in any other Nation."

e) To MARQUIS DE CHASTELLUX, Mount Vernon, August 18, 1786.

"Nor does that mild species of philosophy which aims at promoting human happiness, ever belye itself by deviating from the generous and godlike pursuit."

f) To HENRY LAURENS, March 20, 1779.

"Most of the good and evil things in this life are judged of by comparison."

g.) To MRS. MARY WASHINGTON, February 15, 1787.

"Happiness depends more upon the internal frame of a person's own mind, than on the externals in the world."

h.) To ELEANOR PARKE CUSTIS, January 16, 1795.

"A sensible woman can never be happy with a fool."

i.) To THOMAS PAINE, May 6, 1792.

"As no one can feel a greater interest in the happiness of mankind than I do, . . . it is the first wish of my heart, that the enlightened policy of the present age may diffuse to all men those blessings, to which they are entitled, and lay the foundation of happiness for future generations."

j.) To de la LUZERNE, September 10, 1791.

"The United States are making great progress towards national happiness; and, if it is not attained here in as high a degree as human nature will admit . . . , I think we may then conclude, that political happiness in unattainable."

k.) To JOHN AUGUSTINE WASHINGTON, January 16, 1783.

"*Imaginary* wants are indefinite; and oftentimes insatiable; because they sometimes are boundless, and always changing." (emphasis in the orginal)

l.) To DAVID HUMPHREYS, July 20, 1791.

"In this age of free inquiry and enlightened reason, it is to be hoped, that the condition of the people in every country will be bettered, and the happiness of mankind promoted."

m.) To THOMAS PAINE, May 6, 1792.

"As no one can feel a greater interest in the happiness of mankind than I do, . . . it is the first wish of my heart, that the enlightened policy of the present age may diffuse to all men those blessings, to which they are entitled, and lay the foundation of happiness for future generations."

13. **Habits**

a) To FRANCIS HOPKINSON, Mount Vernon, May 16, 1785.

"In for a penny, in for a pound is an old adage. I am so hackneyed to the touches of the Painters pencil, that I am now altogether at their beck, and sit like patience on a Monument whilst they are delineating the lines of my face. It is a proof among many others of what habit and custom can effect. At first I was as impatient at the request, and as restive under the operation, as a Colt is of the Saddle. The next time, I submitted very reluctantly, but with less flouncing. Now, no dray moves more readily to the Thill, than I do to the Painters Chair."

14. **Idleness**

a) To WILLIAM MINOR, Mount Vernon, June 16, 1785.

"Moral obligations, or the obligations of humanity therefore induced me to bestow a years schooling on Lawce. Posey, and to effect it I was willing to incur the expence of a years board also; ... Was not his Fathers house, if time was to be misspent, the best place for him to waste it in? Can it be supposed I ever had it in contemplation to board him out for the purpose of idleness?"

15. Justice

a) To REVEREND WILLIAM GORDON, Mount Vernon, October 15, 1797. "The spurious letters.... the Agent or tool of those who are endeavouring to destroy the confidence of the people in the officers of Government (chosen by themselves) to dissiminate these counterfeit letters, I conceived it a piece of justice due to my own character, and to Posterity to disavow them in explicit terms; and this I did in a letter directed to the Secretary of State to be filed in his Office the day on which I closed my Administration. This letter has since been published in the Gazettes by the head of that Department."

b) To ROBERT STEWART, August 10, 1783.

"Justice requires and a grateful government certainly will bestow those places of honor and profit, which necessity must create, upon those who have risked life, fortune and Home to support its cause."

16. Luxury

a) To CATHERINE MACAULAY GRAHAM, New York, January 9, 1790. "Mrs. Washington is well and desires her compliments may be presented to you. We wish the happiness of your fireside, as we also long to enjoy that of our own at Mount Vernon. Our wishes, you know, were limited; and I think that our plans of living will now be deemed reasonable by the considerate part of our species. Her wishes coincide with my own as to simplicity of dress, and everything which can tend to support propriety of character without partaking of the follies of luxury and ostentation."

17. Morality

a) To GEORGE STEPTOE WASHINGTON, Philadelphia, December 5, 1790.

"It may be proper to observe that a good moral character is the first essential in a man, and that the habits contracted at your age are generally indelible, and your conduct here may stamp your character through life. It is therefore highly important that you should endeavor not only to be learned but virtuous."

b) To ANNIS BOUDINOT STOCKTON, Mount Vernon, August 31, 1788.

"A good general government, without good morals and good habits, will not

make us a happy People; and we shall deceive ourselves if we think it will."
c) GENERAL ORDERS, Saturday, March 22, 1783.

"In justice to the zeal and ability of the Chaplains, as well as to his own feelings, the Commander in chief thinks it a duty to declare the regularity and decorum with which divine service is now performed every sunday, will reflect great credit on the army in general, tend to improve the morals, and at the same time, to increase the happiness of the soldiery, and must afford the most pure and rational entertainment for every serious and well disposed mind."
d) To CYRUS GRIFFIN, New York, August 18, 1789.

The general convention of bishops, clergy, and laity of the Protestant Episcopal Church in New York, New Jersey, Pennsylvania, Delaware, Maryland, Virginia, and North Carolina delivered an address to the President at this approximate time which, together with Washington's reply, is entered in the "Letter Book" in the *Washington Papers*. In that reply, Washington stated that "human happiness and moral duty are inseparably connected" and that "It affords edifying prospects indeed to see Christians of different denominations dwell together in more charity, and conduct themselves in respect to each other with a more christian-like spirit than ever they have done in any former age, or in any other Nation."
e) To HENRY LEE, Mount Vernon, September 22, 1788.

"Though I prize, as I ought, the good opinion of my fellow citizens; yet, if I know myself, I would not seek Or retain popularity at the expense of one social duty or moral virtue."
f) To THE MINISTERS AND ELDERS REPRESENTING THE MASSACHUSETTS AND NEW HAMPSHIRE CHURCHES which compose the First Presbytery of the Eastward, Newburyport, October 28, 1789.

"I am persuaded, you will permit me to observe that the path of true piety is so plain as to require but little political direction. To this consideration we ought to ascribe the absence of any regulation, respecting religion, from the Magna- Charta of our country. To the guidance of the ministers of the gospel this important object is, perhaps, more properly committed. It will be your care to instruct the ignorant, and to reclaim the devious, and, in the progress of morality and science, to which our government will give every furtherance, we may confidently expect the advancement of true religion, and the completion of our happiness."

18. Philanthropy

a) To MARQUIS DE LAFAYETTE, Mount Vernon, August 15, 1786.

"As a Philanthropist by character, and (if I may be allowed the expression) as a Citizen of the great republic of humanity at large; I cannot help turning my attention sometimes to this subject. I would be understood to mean, I cannot avoid reflecting with pleasure on the probable influence that commerce may hereafter have on human manners and society in general. On these occasions I consider how mankind may be connected like one great family in fraternal ties. I indulge a fond, perhaps an enthusiastic idea, that as the world is evidently much less barbarous than it has been, its melioration must still be progressive; that nations are becoming more humanized in their policy, that the subjects of ambition and causes for hostility are daily diminishing, and, in fine, that the period is not very remote, when the benefits of a liberal and free commerce will, pretty generally, succeed to the devastations and horrors of war."

b) To MARQUIS DE LAFAYETTE Mount Vernon, August 15, 1786.

"Altho' I pretend to no peculiar information respecting commercial affairs, nor any foresight into the scenes of futurity; yet as the member of an infant empire, as a Philanthropist by character, and (if I may be allowed the expression) as a Citizen of the great republic of humanity at large; I cannot help turning my attention sometimes to this subject. I would be understood to mean, I cannot avoid reflecting with pleasure on the probable influence that commerce may hereafter have on human manners and society in general. On these occasions I consider how mankind may be connected like one great family in fraternal ties. I indulge a fond, perhaps an enthusiastic idea, that as the world is evidently much less barbarous than it has been, its melioration must still be progressive; that nations are becoming more humanized in their policy, that the subjects of ambition and causes for hostility are daily diminishing, and, in fine, that the period is not very remote, when the benefits of a liberal and free commerce will, pretty generally, succeed to the devastations and horrors of war."

c) To LAFAYETTE, August 15, 1786.

"[I am] a philanthropist by character, and . . . a citizen of the great republic of humanity at large."

d) To GOUVERNEUR MORRIS, July 28, 1791.

"I believe it is among nations as with individuals, that the party taking advantage of the distresses of another will lose infinitely more in the opinion of mankind, and in subsequent events, than he will gain by the stroke of the moment."

19. Passion

a) To JOHN BANISTER, April 21, 1778.

"We must take the passions of men as nature has given them, and those principles as a guide, which are generally the rule of action."

20. Reconciliation

a) To DAVID STUART, March 28, 1790.

"To constitute a dispute there must be two parties. To understand it well, both parties, and all the circumstances, must be fully heard; and, to accommodate differences, temper and mutual forbearance are requisite."

21. Reputation

a) To BURWELL BASSETT, Philadelphia, June 19, 1775.

"I can answer but for three things, a firm belief of the justice of our Cause, close attention in the prosecution of it, and the strictest Integrity. If these cannot supply the place of Ability and Experience, the cause will suffer, and more than probable my character along with it, as reputation derives its principal support from success; but it will be remembered, I hope, that no desire or insinuation of mine, placed me in this situation. I shall not be deprived therefore of a comfort in the worst event if I retain a consciousness of having acted to the best of my judgment."

b) To LUND WASHINGTON, Col. Morris's, on the Heights of Harlem, September 30, 1776.

"To lose all comfort and happiness on the one hand, whilst I am fully persuaded that under such a system of management as has been adopted, I cannot have the least chance for reputation, nor those allowances made which the nature of the case requires; and to be told, on the other, that if I leave the service all will be lost, is, at the same time that I am bereft of every peaceful moment, distressing to a degree. But I will be done with the subject, with the precaution to you that it is not a fit one to be publicly known or discussed. If I fall, it may not be amiss that these circumstances be known, and declaration made in credit to the justice of my character....I am wearied to death all day with a variety of perplexing circum stances — disturbed at the conduct of the militia, whose behavior and want of discipline has done great injury to the other troops, who never had officers, except in a few instances, worth the bread they eat."

22. Truth

a) To THE SECRETARY OF STATE, [Philadelphia, March 3, 1797.]

"I have thought it a duty that I owed to Myself, to my Country and to Truth, now to detail the circumstances above recited; and to add my solemn declaration, that the letters herein described are a base forgery, and that I never saw or heard of them until they appeared in print."

23. Thrift

a) To PRESIDENT OF CONGRESS, April 23, 1776.

"No person wishes more to save money to the public, than I do; and no person has aimed more at it. But there are some cases in which parsimony may be ill-laced."

24. Virtue

a) THE FIRST INAUGURAL ADDRESS [April 30, 1789.]

"There is no truth more thoroughly established, than that there exists in the oeconomy and course of nature, an indissoluble union between virtue and happiness, between duty and advantage, between the genuine maxims of an honest and magnanimous policy, and the solid rewards of public prosperity and felicity: Since we ought to be no less persuaded that the propitious smiles of Heaven, can never be expected on a nation that disregards the eternal rules of order and right, which Heaven itself has ordained: And since the preservation of the sacred fire of liberty, and the destiny of the Republican model of Government, are justly considered as *deeply*, perhaps as *finally* staked, on the experiment entrusted to the hands of the American people." (emphasis in the orginal)

b) To HENRY KNOX, Mount Vernon, July 16, 1798.

"But my dear Sir, as you always have found, and trust ever will find, candour a prominent trait of my character."

c) THE FIRST INAUGURAL ADDRESS [April 30, 1789.]

"The foundations of our National policy will be laid in the pure and immutable principles of private morality; and the pre-eminence of a free Government, be exemplified by all the attributes which can win the affections of its Citizens, and command the respect of the world. ... there is no truth more thoroughly established, than that there exists in the oeconomy and course of nature, an indissoluble union between virtue and happiness, between duty and advantage, between the genuine maxims of an honest and magnanimous policy, and the solid rewards of public prosperity and felicity: Since we ought to be no less persuaded that the propitious smiles of Heaven, can never be expected on a nation that disregards the eternal rules of order and right, which Heaven itself has ordained: And since the preservation of the sacred fire of liberty, and the destiny of the Republican model of Government, are justly considered as *deeply*, perhaps as *finally* staked, on the experiment entrusted to the hands of the American people." (emphasis in the orginal)

25. **Wisdom**

a) To BUSHROD WASHINGTON, Mount Vernon, November 10, 1787. "If we cannot learn wisdom from experience, it is hard to say where it is to be found."

b) To JAMES ANDERSON, July 25, 1798.

"I, believing that man was not designed by the all-wise Creator to live for himself alone, prepare for the worst that can happen."

26. **Vanity**

a) To JAMES MADISON, Mount Vernon, May 20, 1792.

"...a previous declaration to retire, not only carries with it the appearance of vanity and self importance, but it may be construed into a maneuver to be invited to remain. And on the other hand, to say nothing, implies consent; or, at any rate, would leave the matter in doubt, and to decline afterwards might be deemed as bad, and uncandid....I take the liberty at my departure from civil, as I formerly did at my military exit, to invoke a continuation of the blessings of Providence upon it; and upon all those who are the supporters of its interests, and the promoters of harmony, order and good government."

b) To DR. JAMES CRAIK, March 25, 1784.

"I do not think vanity is a trait of my character."

B. PERSONALITY & EMOTIONS

1. Busy / Overwhelmed

a) To JOHN WEST, Mount Vernon, January 13, 1775.

"I can solemnly declare to you, that, for a year or two past, there has been scarce a moment, that I could properly call my own. What with my own business, my present ward's, my mother's, which is wholly in my hands, Colonel Colvill's, Mrs. Savage's, Colonel Fairfax's, Colonel Mercer's , and the little assistance I have undertaken to give in the management of my brother

Augustine's concerns (for I have absolutely refused to qualify as an executor), together with the share I take in public affairs, I have been kept constantly engaged in writing letters, settling accounts, and negotiating one piece of business or another; by which means I have really been deprived of every kind of enjoyment, and had almost fully resolved to engage in no fresh matter, till I had entirely wound up the old."

2. **Candor**

a) To HENRY KNOX, Mount Vernon, July 16, 1798.

"But my dear Sir, as you always have found, and trust ever will find, candour a prominent trait of my character."

b) To THE PRESIDENT OF THE UNITED STATES, Mount Vernon, September 25, 1798.

"Let the purity of my intentions; the candour of my declarations; and a due respect for my own character, be received as an apology....But if you had been pleased, previously to the nomination, to have enquired into the train of my thoughts upon the occasion, I would have told you with the frankness and candour which I hope will ever mark my character, on what terms I would have consented to the nomination; you would then have been enabled to decide, whether they were admissible or not."

c) To MAJOR GENERAL HORATIO GATES, Valley Forge, January 4, 1778. vol. 10.

"Thus Sir, with an openess and candour which I hope will ever characterize and mark my conduct have I complied with your request."

d) To TIMOTHY PICKERING, August, 29, 1797.

"Candor is not a more conspicuous trait in the character of Governments than it is of individuals."

e) To JAMES MADISON, November 30, 1785.

"It is an old adage, that honesty is the best policy. This applies to public as well as private life, to States as well as individuals."

f) To RICHARD WASHINGTON, April 15, 1757.

"What can be so proper as the truth?"

3. **Clothing**

a) To BUSHROD WASHINGTON, Newburgh, January 15, 1783.

"Do not conceive that fine Clothes make fine Men, any more than fine feathers make fine Birds. A plain genteel dress is more admired and obtains more credit than lace and embroidery in the Eyes of the judicious and sensible."

b) To JAMES MCHENRY, Mount Vernon, January 27, 1799.

"On reconsidering the uniform for the Commander-in-Chief . . . as it respects myself *personally*, I was against *all* embroidery." (emphasis in the orginal)

4. **Color**

a) To ROBERT CARY, & CO., June 6, 1768.

"Green being a color little apt . . . to fade, and grateful to the eye, I would give it the preference."

5. **Despising**

a) To THE PRESIDENT OF CONGRESS, Valley Forge, January 2, 1778.

"If General Conway means, by cool receptions mentioned in the last paragraph of his Letter of the 31st Ulto., that I did not receive him in the language of a warm and cordial Friend, I readily confess the charge. I did not, nor shall I ever, till I am capable of the arts of dissimulation. These I despise, and my feelings will not permit me to make professions of friendship to the man I deem my Enemy, and whose system of conduct forbids it."

6. **Difficulties**

a) To JOHN AUGUSTINE WASHINGTON, White Plains, November 6, 1776. "I am wearied almost to death with the retrograde Motions of things, and I solemnly protest that a pecuniary reward of 20,000£ a year would not induce me to undergo what I do; and after all, perhaps, to loose my Character as it is impossible under such a variety of distressing Circumstances to conduct matters agreeably to public expectation, or even of those who employ me, as they will not make proper allowances for the difficulties their own errors have occasioned."

7. **Emotions**

a) THE FIRST INAUGURAL ADDRESS [April 30, 1789.]

"In this conflict of emotions, all I dare aver, is, that it has been my faithful study to collect my duty from a just appreciation of every circumstance, by which it might be affected....it would be peculiarly improper to omit in this first official Act, my fervent supplications to that Almighty Being who rules over the Universe, who presides in the Councils of Nations, and whose providential aids can supply every human defect, that his benediction may consecrate to the liberties and happiness of the People of the United States, a Government instituted by themselves for these essential purposes: and may enable every instrument employed in its administration to execute with success, the functions allotted to his charge. In tendering this homage to the Great Author of every public and private good, I assure myself that it expresses your sentiments not less than my own; nor those of my fellow-citizens at large, less than either. No People can be bound to acknowledge and adore the invisible hand, which conducts the Affairs of men more than the People of the United States. Every step, by which they have advanced to the character of an independent nation, seems to have been distinguished by some token of providential agency. And in the important revolution just accomplished in the system of their United Government, the tranquil delib-erations and voluntary consent of so many distinct communities, from which the event has resulted, cannot be compared with the means by which most Governments have been established, without some return of pious gratitude along with an humble anticipation of the future blessings which the past seem to presage. These reflections, arising out of the present crisis, have forced themselves too strongly on my mind to be suppressed. You will join with me I trust in thinking, that there are none under the influence of which, the pro-ceedings of a new and free Government can more auspiciously commence....

"I dwell on this prospect with every satisfaction which an ardent love for my Country can inspire: since there is no truth more thoroughly established, than that there exists in the oeconomy and course of nature, an indissoluble union between virtue and happiness, between duty and advantage, between the genuine maxims of an honest and magnanimous policy, and the solid rewards of public prosperity and felicity: Since we ought to be no less per-suaded that the propitious smiles of Heaven, can never be expected on a nation that disregards the eternal rules of order and right, which Heaven itself has ordained: And since the preservation of the sacred fire of liberty, and the destiny of the Republican model of Government, are justly considered as *deeply*, perhaps as *finally* staked, on the experiment entrusted to the hands of the American people." (emphasis in the orginal)

8. **Enmity**

a) To JOHN JAY, Head Quarters, Middle brook, April 14, 1779.

"Conscious that it is the aim of my actions to promote the public good, and that no part of my conduct is influenced by personal enmity to individuals, I cannot be insensible to the artifices employed by some men to prejudice me in the public esteem."

9. **Excellence**

a) To WILLIAM PEARCE, Philadelphia, March 22, 1795.

"I had rather hear it was delayed than that it should be sown before every thing was in perfect order for it; for it is a *fixed* principle with me, that whatever *is done* should be *well done*. Unless this maxim is attended to, our labor is but in vain, and our expectation of a return, is always deceptious; whilst we are ascribing our disappointments to any thing rather than the true cause, namely not laying (by proper preparations) a good foundation, on which to build our hopes." (emphasis in the orginal)

10. **Mixed Emotions**

a) To THE CITIZENS OF NEW BRUNSWICK, New Brunswick, December 6, 1783.

"I cannot bid adieu to the Acquaintances and Connections I have formed while acting in a public character without experiencing a certain pleasing, melancholly sensation, pleasing because I leave my Country in the full possession of Liberty and Independence; Melancholly because I bid my friends a long, perhaps a last farewell."

11. **Moods**

a) To REVEREND BOUCHER, May 21, 1772.

"Inclination having yielded to Importunity, I am now contrary to all expectation under the hands of Mr. [Charles Willson] Peale; but in so grave—so sullen a mood—and now and then under the influence of Morpheus, when some critical strokes are making, that I fancy the skill of this Gentleman's pencil, will be put to it, in describing to the World what manner of man I am."

12. **Mount Vernon**

a) To ARCHIBALD CARY, H.W., Newburgh, June 15, 1782.

"I pant for retirement, and am persuaded that an end of our warfare is not to be obtained but by vigorous exertions. . . I can truly say, that the first wish of my Soul is to return speedily into the bosom of that country, which gave me birth, and, in the sweet enjoyment of domestic happiness and the company of a few friends, to end my days in quiet, when I shall be called from this stage."

b) To LAFAYETTE, February 1, 1784

"At length, my dear marquis, I am become a private citizen on the banks of the Potomac, and under the shadow of my own vine and my own fig-tree, free from the bustle of a camp and the busy scenes of public life, I am solacing myself with those tranquil enjoyments of which the soldier who is ever in pursuit of fame, the statesman whose watchful days and sleepless nights are spent in devising schemes to promote the welfare of his own, perhaps the ruin of other countries, as if the globe was insufficient for us all, and the Courtier who is always watching the countenance of his Prince, in hopes of catching a gracious smile, can have very little conception. I have not only retired from all public employments, but I am retiring within myself, and shall be able to view the solitary walk of private life with heartfelt satisfaction. Envious of none, I am determined to be pleased with all; and this, my dear friend, being the order of my march, I will move gently down the stream of life until I sleep with my fathers."

13. Pain

a) To GOVERNOR HENRY LEE, Philadelphia, May 6, 1793.

"It gives me inexpressible pain to receive such frequent, and distressing accounts from the Western frontiers of this Union (occasioned by Indian hostilities); more especially as our hands are tied to defensive measures...."

14. Quality

a) To P. MARSTELLER, December 15, 1786.

"It is not the lowest priced goods that are always the cheapest—the quality is, or ought to be as much an object with the purchaser, as the price"

15. Retirement

a) To ARCHIBALD CARY, H.W., Newburgh, June 15, 1782.

"I pant for retirement, and am persuaded that an end of our warfare is not to be obtained but by vigorous exertions. . . I can truly say, that the first wish of my Soul is to return speedily into the bosom of that country, which gave me birth, and, in the sweet enjoyment of domestic happiness and the company of a few friends, to end my days in quiet, when I shall be called from this stage."

b) To ROBERT STEWART, New York August 10, 1783.

"I only wait (and with anxious impatience) the arrival of the definitive treaty, that I may take leave of my Military Employments and by bidding adieu to Public life, forever enjoy in the shades of retirement that ease and tranquility to which, for more than eight years, I have been an entire stranger, and for which, a mind which has been constantly on the stretch during that period, and perplexed with a thousand embarrassing circumstances, often times without a ray of light to guide it, stands much in need."

c) To HENRY KNOX, Philadelphia, March 2, 1797.

"To the wearied traveller who sees a resting place, and is bending his body to lean thereon, I now compare myself; but to be suffered to do *this* in peace, is I perceive too much, to be endured by *some* . To misrepresent my motives; to reprobate my politics; and to weaken the confidence which has been reposed in my administration, are objects which cannot be relinquished by those who, will be satisfied with nothing short of a change in our political System. The consolation however, which results from conscious rectitude, and the approving voice of my Country, unequivocally expressed by its Representatives, deprives their sting of its poison, and places in the same point of view both the weakness, and malignity of their efforts.

"Although the prospect of retirement is most grateful to my soul, and I have not a wish to mix again in the great world, or to partake in its politics, yet, I am not without my regrets at parting with (perhaps never more to meet) the few intimates whom I love, among these, be assured you are one." (emphasis in the orginal)

16. Righteousness

a) Martha Washington's comment to a friend. –"George is always right and God is on the side of the righteous."[1]

17. Skeptic

a) To MARQUIS DE CHASTELLUX, Mount Vernon, August 18, 1786.

"...(altho' no sceptic on ordinary occasions) I may perhaps be allowed to doubt whether your friendship and partiality have not, in this oneinstance, acquired an ascendency over your cooler judgment."

18. Sorrow

a) To BURWELL BASSETT, Mount Vernon, June 20, 1773.

"Dear Sir: It is an easier matter to conceive, than to describe the distress of this Family; especially that of the unhappy Parent of our Dear Patsy Custis, when I inform you that yesterday removed[*sic*]the Sweet Innocent Girl Entered into a more happy and peaceful abode than any she has met with in the afflicted Path she hitherto has trod."

III. FAMILY

A. Love

1. To ELEANOR PARKE CUSTIS, Philadelphia, January 16, 1795.

"In the composition of the human frame there is a good deal of inflammable matter, however dormant it may lie for a time, and like an intimate acquaintance of yours, when the torch is put to it, *that* which is *within you* may burst into a blaze; for which reason and especially too, as I have entered upon the chapter of advices, I will read you a lecture drawn from this text.

"Love is said to be an involuntary passion, and it is, therefore, contended that it cannot be resisted. This is true in part only, for like all things else, when nourishes and supplied plentifully with ailment, it is rapid in its progress; but let these be withdrawn and it may be stifled in its birth or much stinted in its growth. For example, a woman (the same may be said of the other sex) all beautiful and accomplished, will, while her hand and heart are undisposed of, turn the heads and set the circle in which she moves on fire. Let her marry, and what is the consequence? The madness *ceases* and all is quiet again. Why? not because there is any diminution in the charms of the lady, but because there is an end of hope. Hence it follows, that love may and therefore ought to be under the guidance of reason, for although we cannot avoid first impressions, we may assuredly place them under guard; and my motives for treating on this subject are to show you, while you remain Eleanor Parke Custis, spinster, and retain the resolution to love with moderation, the propriety of adhering to the latter resolution, at least until you have secured your game, and the way by which it may be accomplished.

"When the fire is beginning to kindle, and your heart growing warm, propound these questions to it. Who is this invader? Have I a competent knowledge of him? Is he a man of good character; a man of sense? For, be assured, a sensible woman can never be happy with a fool. What has been his walk in life? Is he a gambler, a spendthrift, or drunkard? Is his fortune sufficient to maintain me in the manner I have been accustomed to live, and my sisters do live, and is he one to whom my friends can have no reasonable objection? If these interrogatories can be satisfactorily answered, there will remain but one more to be asked, that, however, is an important one. Have I sufficient ground to conclude that his affections are engaged by me? Without this the heart of sensibility will struggle against a passion that is not reciprocated; delicacy, custom, or call it by what epithet you will, having precluded all advances on your part. The declaration, without the *most indirect* invitation of yours, must proceed from the man, to render it permanent and valuable, and nothing short of good sense and an easy unaffected conduct can draw the line between prudery and coquetry. It would be no great departure from truth to say, that it rarely happens otherwise than that a thorough-paced coquette dies in celibacy, as a punishment for her attempts to mislead others, by encouraging looks, words, or actions, given for no other purpose than to draw men on to make overtures that they may be rejected." (emphasis in the orginal)

B. Marriage

1. To BURWELL BASSETT, Mount Vernon, May 23, 1785.

"It has ever been a maxim with me thro' life, neither to promote, nor to prevent a matrimonial connection, unless there should be something indispensably requiring interference in the latter: I have always considered marriage as the most interesting event of one's life, the foundation of happiness or misery; to be instrumental therefore in bringing two people together who are indifferent to each other, and may soon become objects of hatred; or to prevent a union which is prompted by mutual esteem and affection, is what I never could reconcile to my feelings."

2. To GEORGE AUGUSTINE WASHINGTON, Mount Vernon, October 25, 1786. "If Mrs. Washington should survive me there is a moral certainty of my dying without issue, and should I be the longest liver, the matter in my opinion is almost as certain; for whilst I retain the reasoning faculties I shall never marry a girl; and it is not probable that I should have children by a woman of an age suitable to my own, should I be disposed to enter into a second marriage."

3. To BUSHROD WASHINGTON, January, 15, 1783.

"Be courteous to all, but intimate with few; and let those few be well tried before you give them your confidence. True friendship is a plant of slow growth, and must undergo and withstand the shocks of adversity before it is entitled to the appellation."

4. To LUND WASHINGTON, September 20, 1783.

"I never did, nor do I believe I ever shall, give advice to a woman, who is setting out on a matrimonial voyage; first, because I never could advise one to marry without her own consent; and, secondly, because I know it is to no purpose to advise her to refrain, when she has obtained it. A woman very rarely asks an opinion or requires advice on such an occasion, till her resolution is formed; and then it is with the hope and expectation of obtaining a sanction . . . that she applies."

5. To MRS. RICHARD STOCKTON, September 2, 1783.

"When once the woman has tempted us, and we have tasted the forbidden fruit, there is no such thing as checking our appetites, whatever the consequences may be."

6.) To ELEANOR PARKE CUSTIS, January 16, 1795.

"A sensible woman can never be happy with a fool."

C. Mother

1. To BENJAMIN HARRISON, New Windsor, March 21, 1781.

"I do not delay a moment to thank you for [your letter] . . . and to express surprise at that part which respects a pension for my mother. True it is, I am but little acquainted with her *present* situation or distresses, if she is under any. ...confident I am that she has not a child that would not divide the last sixpence to relive her from *real* distress. This she has been repeatedly assured of by me; and all of us I am certain would feel much hurt, at having our mother a pensioner, while we had the means of supporting her; but in fact she has an ample income of her own. I lament accordingly that your letter, which conveyed the first hint of this matter, did not come to my hands sooner; but I request, in pointed terms, if the matter is now in agitation in your Assembly, that all proceedings on it may be stopped, or in case of a decision in her favor, that it may be done away and repealed at my request."

2. To MRS. MARY WASHINGTON, Mount Vernon, February 15, 1787.

"Hond. Madam: In consequence of your communication to George [Augustine]Washington, of your want of money, I take the (first safe) conveyance by Mr. John Dandridge to send you 15 Guineas, which believe me is all I have,...My house is at your service, and [I] would press you most sincerely and most devoutly to accept it, but I am sure, and candor requires me to say, it will never answer your purposes in any shape whatsoever. For in truth it may be compared to a well resorted tavern, as scarcely any strangers who are going from north to south, or from south to north, do not spend a day or two at it.

"... [by] the mode I have pointed out, you may reduce your income to a certainty, be eased of all trouble, and if you are so disposed, may be perfectly happy; for happiness depends more upon the internal frame of a person's own mind, than on the externals in the world. Of the last, if you will pursue the plan here recommended, I am sure you can want nothing that is essential. The other depends wholly upon yourself, for the riches of the Indies cannot purchase it. "Mrs. Washington, George and Fanny join me in every good wish for you, and I am, honored madame, your most dutiful and aff. son."

D. Brother

1. To JOHN AUGUSTINE WASHINGTON, Newburgh, January 16, 1783.

"... how did my brother Samuel contrive to get himself so enormously in debt? Was it by making purchases? By misfortunes? Or sheer indolence and inattention to business? From whatever cause it proceeded, the matter is now the same, and curiosity only prompts me to the enquiry, as it does to know what will be saved, and how it is disposed of. . . . I have lately received a letter from my mother, in which she complains much of the knavery of the overseer at the Little Falls quarter."

E. Wife

1. To MRS. MARTHA CUSTIS, July 20, 1758.

"We have begun our march for the Ohio. A courier is starting for Williamsburg, and I embrace the opportunity to send a few words to one whose life is now inseparable from mine. Since that happy hour when we made our pledges to each other, my thoughts have been continually going to you as another Self. That an all-powerful Providence may keep us both in safety is the prayer of your ever faithful and affectionate friend."

2. To RICHARD WASHINGTON, September 20, 1759.

"I am now I believe fixd at this seat [Mount Vernon] with an agreeable Consort for Life. And hope to find more happiness in retirement than I ever experienced amidst a wide and bustling World."

3. To MARTHA WASHINGTON, Philadelphia, June 23, 1775.

"My Dearest: As I am within a few minutes of leaving this city, I would not think of departing from it with out dropping you a line, especially as I do not know whether it may be in my power to write again till I get to the camp at Boston. I go fully trusting in that providence, which has been more bountiful to me than I deserve and in full confidence of a happy meeting with you some time in the fall. I have no time to add more as I am surrounded with company to take leave of me. I return an unalterable affection for you which neither time or distance can change my best love to Jack and Nelly and regard for the rest of the family; conclude me with the utmost truth and Sincerity, Yr. entire, G. Washington."

F. Martha Washington on her husband George

1. To JANET LIVINGSTON MONTGOMERY, Mount Vernon, April 5th 1800.

"...your affliction I have often marked and as often have keenly felt for you

873

but my own experience has taught me that griefs like these can not be removed by the condolence of friends however sincere—If the mingling tears of numerus friends—if the sympathy of a Nation and every testimony of respect of veneration paid to the memory of the partners of our hearts could afford consolation you and myself would experience it in the highest degree but we know that there is but one source from whence comfort can be derived under afflictions life ours To this we must look with pious resignation and with that pure confidence which our holy religion inspires.

"…but as you justly observe it is certainly a consolation and flattering to poor mortality to believe that we shall meet here after in a better place."[2]

2. To JONATHAN TRUMBALL, Mount Vernon January 15, 1800.

"…the good Christian will submit without repining to the Dispensations on Divine Providence and look for consolation to that Being who alone can pour balm into the bleeding Heart and who has promised to be the widows god - … your kind letter of condolence of the 30th of December was greatfull to my feeling.

"…the loss is ours the gain is his.

"For myself I have only to bow with humble submission to the will of that God who giveth and who taketh away looking forward with faith and hope to the moment when I shall be again united with the Partner of my life But while I continue on Earth my prayers will be offered up for the welfare and Happiness of my Friends among who you will always be numbered being."[3]

IV. GOVERNMENT AND LEADERSHIP

A. Government

1. The Constitution

a) *Spoken as he signed it*, September 17, 1787.

"Should the States reject this excellent Constitution, the probability is that an opportunity will never again offer to cancel another in peace—the next will be drawn in blood."

b) To SELECTMEN OF BOSTON, July 28, 1795.

"The constitution is the guide, which I can never abandon."

c) To ALEXANDER HAMILTON, July 2, 1794.

"The powers of the executive of this country are more definite, and better understood, perhaps, than those of any other country; and my aim has been, and will continue to be, neither to stretch nor relax from them in any instance whatever, unless compelled to it by imperious circumstances."

d) To EDMUND PENDLETON, September 23, 1793.

"I have no object in view incompatible with the constitution, and the obvious interests of this country. . . . I only wish, whilst I am a servant of the public, to know the will of my masters, that I may govern myself accordingly."

2. **Amendment to the Constitution**

a) To BUSHROD WASHINGTON, Mount Vernon, November 10, 1787.

"The warmest friends and the best supporters the Constitution has, do not contend that it is free from imperfections; but they found them unavoidable and are sensible, if evil is likely to arise there from, the remedy must come hereafter; for in the present moment, it is not to be obtained; and, as there is a Constitutional door open for it, I think the People (for it is with them to Judge) can as they will have the advantage of experience on their Side, decide with as much propriety on the alterations and amendments which are necessary [as] ourselves. I do not think we are more inspired, have more wisdom, or possess more virtue, than those who will come after us."

b) To PATRICK HENRY, September 24, 1787.

"I wish the constitution, which is offered, had been made more perfect; but I sincerely believe it is the best that could be obtained at this time. And, as a constitutional door is opened for amendment hereafter, the adoption of it, under the present circumstances of the Union, is in my opinion desirable."

3. **Power of the Constitution**

a) To BUSHROD WASHINGTON, Mount Vernon, November 10, 1787.

"The power under the Constitution will always be in the People. It is entrusted for certain defined purposes, and for a certain limited period, to representatives of their own chusing; and whenever it is executed contrary to their Interest, or not agreeable to their wishes, their Servants can, and undoubtedly will be, recalled."

4. **Time Required to Create a Constitution**

a) To JOHN AUGUSTINE WASHINGTON, May 31, 1776.

"To form a new Government, requires infinite care, and unbounded attention; for if the foundation is badly laid the superstructure must be bad, too much time therefore, cannot be bestowed in weighing and digesting matters well. We have, no doubt, some good parts in our present constitution; many bad ones we know we have, wherefore no time can be misspent that is imployed in seperating the Wheat from the Tares. My fear is, that you will all get tired and homesick, the consequence of which will be, that you will patch up some kind of Constitution as defective as the present; this should be avoided, every Man should consider, that he is lending his aid to frame a Constitution which is to render Million's happy, or Miserable, and that a matter of such moment cannot be the Work of a day."

5. **A Citizen**

a) To GOVERNOR GEORGE CLINTON, Mount Vernon, December 28, 1783.

"I arrived at my Seat the day before Christmas, having previously divested myself of my official character. I am now a private Citizen on the banks of the Powtowmack, where I should be happy to see you if your public business would ever permit, and where in the meantime I shall fondly cherish the remembrance of all your former friendship."

b) To GOVERNOR HENRY LEE, Philadelphia, May 6, 1793.

"As a public character, I can say nothing on the subject of it. As a private man, I am unwilling to say much."

c) To COMTE DE ROCHAMBEAU, Mount Vernon, February 1, 1784.

"My Dear Count: Having resigned my public trust, and with it all my public cares into the hands of Congress, I now address you in the character of an American Citizen from the Banks of the Potomac to which I have been retired, fast locked up by frost and snow ever since Christmas."

6. **The French**

a) REMARKS ON MONROE'S "VIEW OF THE CONDUCT OF THE EXECUTIVE OF THE UNITED STATES"

"Why not,...allow the American government to adopt *some* of the *all* perfect maxims of the French. It will not be denied that, to boast of what they do, and even of what they do not do is one of them."

7. **Impartiality**

a) To ROBERT DINWIDDIE, Fort Loudoun, October 5, 1757.

"If an open, disinterested behavior carries offence, I may have offended; because I have all along laid it down as a maxim, to represent facts freely and impartially."

8. **Immigrants**

a) To JOHN JAY, Philadelphia, November 1 [-5], 1794.

"I have established it as a maxim, neither to invite, nor to discourage emigrants. My opinion is, that they will come hither as fast as the true interest and policy of the United States will be benefited by foreign population."

9. **Indians**

a) To TIMOTHY PICKERING, January 20, 1791.

"Humanity and good policy must make it the wish of every good citizen of the United States, that husbandry, and consequently civilization, should be introduced among the Indians. So strongly am I impressed with the beneficial effects, which our country would receive from such a thing, that I shall always take a singular pleasure in promoting, as far as may be in my power, every measure which may tend to ensure it."

b) To DAVID HUMPHREYS, July 20, 1791.

"I must confess I cannot see much prospect of living in tranquility with them [Indians], so long as a spirit of land-jobbing prevails, and our frontier settlers entertain the opinion, that there is not the same crime (or indeed no crime at all) in killing an Indian as in killing a white man."

10. **International Relations**

a) To JAMES MONROE, August 25, 1796.

"I have always given it as my decided opinion, that no nation had a right to intermeddle in the internal concerns of another; that every one had a right to form and adopt whatever government they liked best to live under themselves."

b) To PATRICK HENRY, October 9, 1795.

"My ardent desire is, and my aim has been . . . to comply strictly with all our engagements, foreign and domestic; but to keep the United States free from political connexions with every other country, to see them independent of all and under the influence of none. In a word, I want an American character, that the powers of Europe may be convinced we act for ourselves, and not for others. This, in my judgment, is the only way to be respected abroad and happy at home; and not, by becoming the partisans of Great Britain or France, create dissensions, disturb the public tranquility, and destroy perhaps for ever, the cement which binds the union."

c) To WILLIAM HEATH, May 20, 1797.

"No policy, in my opinion, can be more clearly demonstrated, than that we should do justice to all, and have no political connexion with any of the European powers beyond those, which result from and serve to regulate our commerce with them."

d) To EARL OF BUCHAN, April, 22, 1793.

"I believe it is the sincere wish of United America to have nothing to do with the political intrigues, or the squabbles, of European nations; but, on the contrary, to exchange commodities and live in peace and amity with all the inhabitants of the earth."

11. National Debt

a) FAREWELL ADDRESS, September 19, 1796

"As a very important source of strength and security, cherish public credit. One method of preserving it is to use it as sparingly as possible: avoiding occasions of expence by cultivating peace, but remembering also that timely disbursements to prepare for danger frequently prevent much greater disbursements to repel it; avoiding likewise the accumulation of debt, not only by shunning occasions of expence, but by vigorous exertions in time of Peace to discharge the Debts which unavoidable wars may have occasioned, not ungenerously throwing upon posterity the burthen which we ourselves ought to bear. The execution of these maxims belongs to your Representatives, but it is necessary that public opinion should cooperate."

12. National Interest

a) To HENRY LAURENS, Fredericksburgh, November 14, 1778.

"I am heartily disposed to entertain the most favourable sentiments of our new ally and to cherish them in others to a reasonable degree; but it is a maxim founded on the universal experience of mankind, that no nation is to be trusted farther than it is bound by its interest; and no prudent statesman or politician will venture to depart from it. In our circumstances we ought to be particularly cautious; for we have not yet attained sufficient vigor and maturity to recover from the shock of any false step into which we may unwarily fall."

b) To PRESIDENT JOSEPH REED, Head Quarters, Bergen County, July 4, 1780. "In general I esteem it a good maxim, that the best way to preserve the confidence of the people durably is to promote their true interest."

13. Nominations

a) To JAMES McHENRY, Philadelphia, April 8, 1794.

"I have experienced the necessity in a variety of instances, of hardening my heart against indulgences of my warmest inclination and friendship; and from a combination of causes, as well as more fitness of character, to depart from first impressions and first intentions with regard to nominations; which has proved most unequivocally, the propriety of the maxim I had adopted, of never committing myself, until the moment the appointment is to be made; when from the best information I can obtain, and a full view of circumstances, my judgment is formed."

14. **Peace**

a) To FIELDING LEWIS, Morris-Town, May 5[-July 6], 1780.

"We shall never have Peace till the enemy are convinced that we are in a condition to carry on the War. It is no new maxim in politics that for a nation to obtain Peace, or insure it, It must be prepared for War."

b) To THE PRESIDENT OF CONGRESS, Head Qurs., Orange Town, August 20, 1780. "Many circumstances will contribute to a negotiation. An Army on foot not only for another Campaign but for several Campaigns, would determine the enemy to pacific measures, and enable us to insist upon favourable terms in forcible language. An Army insignificent in numbers, dissatisfied, crumbling into pieces, would be the strongest temptation they could have to try the experiment a little longer. It is an old maxim, that the surest way to make a good peace is to be well prepared for War."

c) To JAMES McHENRY, Philadelphia, December 11, 1781.

"You know it is an old and true Maxim that to make a good peace, you ought to be well prepared to carry on the War."

d) To JONATHAN BOUCHER, August 15, 1798.

"Peace with all the world is my sincere wish."

e) To GOUVERNEUR MORRIS, June 25, 1794.

"My primary objects, to which I have steadily adhered, have been to preserve the country in peace if I can, and to be prepared for war if I cannot; to effect the first, upon terms consistent with the respect which is due to ourselves, and with honor, justice, and good faith to all the world."

15. **Public Good**

a) To JOHN JAY, Head Quarters, Middle brook, April 14, 1779.

"Conscious that it is the aim of my actions to promote the public good, and that no part of my conduct is influenced by personal enmity to individuals, I cannot be insensible to the artifices employed by some men to prejudice me in the public esteem."

16. **Respect**

a) To BENEDICT ARNOLD, September 14, 1775.

"As the contempt of the religion of a country by ridiculing any of its cere-monies, or affronting its ministers or votaries, has ever been deeply resented, you are to be particularly careful to restrain every officer and soldier from such imprudence and folly, and to punish every instance of it. On the other hand, as far as lies in your power, you are to protect and support the free exercise of the religion of the country, and the undisturbed enjoyment of the rights of conscience in religious matters, with your utmost influence and authority."
b) To LAFAYETTE, August 15, 1787.
"Being no bigot myself, I am disposed to indulge the professors of Christianity in the church with that road to Heaven, which to them shall seem most direct, plainest, easiest and least liable to exception."
c) To the HEBREW CONGREGATION OF NEWPORT,
August, 1790.
"It is now no more that toleration is spoken of, as if it was by the indulgence of one class of people that another enjoyed the exercise of their inherent nat-ural rights. For happily the Government of the United States, which gives to bigotry no sanction, to persecution no assistance, requires only that those who live under its protection should demean themselves as good citizens, in giv-ing it, on all occasions their effectual support. . . .May the Father of Mercies scatter light and not darkness on our paths, and makes us all, in our several vocations useful here, and in his own due time and way everlastingly happy."
d) To THOMAS JEFFERSON, August 23, 1792.
"Without more charity for the opinions and acts of one another in govern-mental matters, or some more infallible criterion by which the truth of spec-ulative opinions, before they have undergone the test of experience, are to be fore-judged, . . . I believe it will be difficult, if not impracticable, to manage the reins of government."

17. **Republic**
a) To LAFAYETTE, September 1, 1778.
"In a free and republican government, you cannot restrain the voice of the multitude. Every man will speak as he thinks."
b) To EDMUND PENDLETON, January 22, 1795.
"Republicanism is not the phantom of a deluded imagination. On the contrary, . . . under no form of government, will laws be better supported, liberty and property better secured, or happiness be more effectually dispensed to mankind."

18. War

a) To BENEDICT ARNOLD, September 14, 1775.

"Prisoners . . . you will treat with as much humanity and kindness, as may be consistent with your own safety and the public interest. Be very particular in restraining . . .your . . . troops . . . from all acts of cruelty and insult, which will disgrace the American arms."

b) To BOARD OF WAR, November 30, 1776.

"You ask my advice as to the propriety of enlisting prisoners of war. I would just observe, that, in my opinion, it is neither consistent with the rules of war, nor politic; nor can I think, that, because our enemies have committed an unjustifiable action, by enticing, and in some instance intimidating, our men into their service, we ought to follow their example."

c) To JOHN BANISTER, April 21, 1778.

"I will venture to assert, that a great and lasting war can never be supported on this principle [patriotism] alone. It must be aided by a prospect of interest or some reward."

d) To DAVID HUMPHREYS, July 25, 1785.

"My first wish is to see this plague to mankind banished from off the earth, and the sons and daughters of this world employed in more pleasing and innocent amusements, than in preparing implements and exercising them for the destruction of mankind."

e) To JOHN BANISTER, April 21, 1778.

"I will venture to assert, that a great and lasting war can never be supported on this principle [patriotism] alone. It must be aided by a prospect of interest or some reward."

19. Washington D.C.

a) To MRS. SARAH FAIRFAX, May 16, 1798.

"A century hence, if this country keeps united, . . . will produce a city, though not as large as London, yet of a magnitude inferior to few others in Europe, on the banks of the Potomac, where one is now establishing for the permanent seat of the government of the United States, . . . a situation not excelled, for commanding prospect, good water, salubrious air, and safe harbour, by any in the world; and where elegant buildings are erecting and in forwardness for the reception of Congress in the year 1800."

B. Leadership

    1. Gifts

        a) To DAVID HUMPHREYS, June 26, 1797.

        "Presents . . . , to me, are of all things the most painful; but I am so well satisfied of the motives which dictated yours my scruples are removed; and I receive the buckles (which are indeed very elegant) as a token of your regard and attachment."

        b) To MRS. MATTHEW ANDERSON, Philadelphia, July 20, 1794.

        "It is to an established maxim of mine, not to accept a Present from any one."

    2. Leadership Principles

        a)   Principles:

            (1) To GOV. JONATHAN TRUMBULL, August 30, 1799.

            "If principles, instead of men, are not the steady pursuit of the Federalists, their cause will soon be at an end."

        b)   Making Decisions:

            (1) To HENRY KNOX, September 20, 1795.

            "If any power on earth could . . . erect the standard of infallibility in political opinions, there is no being . . . that would resort to it with more eagerness than myself, so long as I remain a servant of the public. But as I have found no better guide hitherto, than upright intentions and close investigation, I shall adhere to those maxims, while I keep the watch; leaving it to those who will come after me, to explore new ways, if they like or think them better."

        c)   Precedents:

            (1) To HENRY LEE, October 31, 1786.

            "Precedents are dangerous things."

        d)   Discipline and Reward:

            (1) To COL. WILLIAM WOODFORD, November 10, 1775.

            "Be strict in your discipline; that is . . . require nothing unreasonable of your officers and men, but see that whatever is required be punctually complied with. Reward and punish every man according to his merit, without partiality or prejudice; hear his complaints; if well founded, redress them; if otherwise, discourage them, in order to prevent frivolous ones. Discourage vice in every shape."

        e)   Accountability:

            (1) To DUKE DE LIANCOURT, August 8, 1796.

"Men in responsible positions cannot, like those in private life, be governed solely by the dictates of their own inclinations, or by such motives as can only affect themselves. . . . A man in public office . . . is accountable for the consequences of his measures to others, and one in private life . . . has no other check than the rectitude of his own action."

f) Execution of Plans:

(1) To JAMES MCHENRY, Secretary of War, July 13, 1796.

"Let me in a friendly way impress the following maxims upon the Executive Officers. In all important matters, to deliberate maturely, but to execute promptly and vigorously; and not to put things off until the morrow, which can be done and require to be done today. Without an adherence to these rules, business never will be well done, or done in any easy manner, but will always be in arrear, with one thing treading upon the heels of another."

g.) Enforcement of Rules:

(1) To JOHN JAY, August 1, 1786.

"Experience has taught us, that men will not adopt and carry into execution measures the best calculated for their own good, without the intervention of a coercive power."

(2) To JAMES MADISON, March 31, 1787.

"Laws or ordinances unobserved, or partially attended to, had better never have been made; because the first is a mere nihil, and the second is productive of much jealousy and discontent."

h.) Problem Solving:

(1) To MALMEDY, May 16, 1777.

"We ought not to convert trifling difficulties into insuperable obstacles."

(2) To THE PRESIDENT OF CONGRESS, December 20, 1776.

"Desperate diseases require desperate remedies."

i.) Power of Example

(1) To LORD STIRLING, March 5, 1780.

"Example, whether it be good or bad, has a powerful influence, and the higher in Rank the officer is, who sets it, the more striking it is."

j.) Communicative Mission and Vision:

(1) To COL. WILLIAM WOODFORD, November 10, 1775.

"Impress upon the mind of every man, from the first to the lowest, the importance of the cause, and what it is they are contending for."

k.) Offense is Defense:

(1) To JOHN TRUMBULL, June 25, 1799.

"Offensive operations oftentimes are the *surest*, if not . . . the *only* means of defense." (emphasis in the original)

l.) Use of Power:

(1) To JOSEPH REED, July 4, 1780.

"Extensive powers not exercised as far as was necessary have, I believe, scarcely ever failed to ruin the possessor."

(2) To HENRY LEE, October 31, 1786.

"Influence is no government."

3. **Creating Trust in Leaders:**

a) To THE PRESIDENT OF CONGRESS, Valley Forge, March 7, 1778.

"It may not be a little dangerous, to beget in the minds of our own Countrymen, a Suspicion that we do not pay the strictest Observance to the Maxims of Honor and good Faith. It is prudent to use the greatest Caution, not to shock the Notions of general Justice and Humanity, universal among Mankind, as well in a public as a private View: in a Business, on the side of which the Passions are so much concerned as in the Present, Men would be readily disposed to believe the worst and cherish the most unfavourable Conclusions."

4. **Good Leaders**

a) To THE MASSACHUSETTS SENATORS, [February 24, 1797.]

"I entertain the pleasing hope, that the intelligence and superior information of my fellow citizens, enabling them to discern their true interests, will lead them to the successive choice of wise and virtuous men to watch over, protect and promote them, who while they pursue those maxims of moderation, equity and prudence, which will entitle our country to perpetual peace, will cultivate that fortitude and dignity of sentiment which are essential to the maintenance of our Liberty and independence."

b) To JAMES MCHENRY, July 4, 1798.

"A good choice [of General Staff] is of . . . immense consequence. . . . [They] ought to be men of the most respectable character, and of first-rate abilities; because, from the nature of their respective offices, and from their being always about the Commander-in-Chief, who is obliged to entrust many things to them *confidentially*, scarcely any movement can take place without their knowledge. . . . Besides possessing the qualifications just mentioned, they ought to have those of Integrity and prudence in an eminent degree, that *entire* confidence might be reposed in them. Without these, and their being on good terms with the Commanding General, his measures, if not designedly thwarted, may be so embarrassed as to make them move heavily on."

c) To JAMES MCHENRY, August 10, 1798.

"It is infinitely better to have a *few* good men than *many* indifferent ones." (emphasis in the original)

5. **Public Good**

a) To JOHN JAY, Head Quarters, Middle brook, April 14, 1779.

"Conscious that it is the aim of my actions to promote the public good, and that no part of my conduct is influenced by personal enmity to individuals, I cannot be insensible to the artifices employed by some men to prejudice me in the public esteem."

b) To MAJOR FRANCIS HALKET, August 2, 1758.

"I am uninfluenced by prejudice, having no hopes or fears but for the general good."

c) To THE SELECTMEN OF BOSTON, July28, 1795.

"In every act of my administration, I have sought the happiness of my fellow citizens. My system for the attainment of this object has uniformly been to overlook all personal, local, and partial considerations; to contemplate the United States as one great whole; to confide that sudden impressions, when erroneous, would yield to candid reflection; and to consult only the substantial and permanent interests of our country."

6. **Good of the Great Whole**

a) To JOHN ARMSTRONG, May 18, 1779.

"To please everybody is impossible; were I to undertake it, I should probably please nobody. If I know myself I have no partialities. I have from the beginning, and I hope I shall to the end, pursued to the utmost of my judgment and abilities, one steady line of conduct for the good of the great whole."

7. **Promises**

a) To CHARLES CARROLL, OF CARROLLTON, Mount Vernon, August 2, 1798.

"It is an invariable maxim with me, never, before hand, and until the moment requires it, to pledge myself by promises which I might find embarrassing to comply with."

8. **Prudence**

a) To RICHARD HENRY LEE, December 14, 1784.

"It is easier to prevent than to remedy an evil."

b) To JAMES MCHENRY, August 10, 1798.

"It is much easier at all times to prevent an evil than to rectify mistakes."

9. **Supervisors**

a) AGREEMENT WITH WILLIAM PEARCE, Mount Vernon, September 23, 1793. "But it may not be amiss to repeat that one of the most effectual steps to accomplish all these ends, is to see that the Overseers of the Farms and the Superintendants of other business, are constantly at their posts; for it may be received as a maxim that if they are away or entertaining company at home, that the concerns entrusted to them will be neglected, and certainly go wrong: and it is not less certain that relaxation on his part will serve only to beget liberties on their's; therefore strictness with justice is the sure means of having the business well conducted."

b) To BURGES BALL, Philadelphia, July 27, 1794.

"If you can keep him *always* with your people he will make you a good Overseer; and without it, neither *he* or *any other man* will. With me, it is an established maxim, that an Overseer shall never be absent from his people but at night, and at his meals." [emphasis in the original]

V. MILITARY AND PATRIOTISM

A. Military

1. **The Army's Need of Food and Clothing**

a) To PHILIP LIVINGSTON, ELBRIDGE GERRY AND GEORGE CLYMER, Camp at the Clove, July 19, 1777.

"It is a maxim, which needs no illustration, that nothing can be of more importance in an Army than the Cloathing and feeding it well; on these, the health, comfort, and Spirits of Soldiers essentially depend, and it is a melancholy fact, that the American Army are miserably defective in both these respects; the distress the most of them are in, for want of Cloathing, is painful to humanity, dispiriting to themselves, and discouraging to every Officer. It makes every pretension to the preservation of cleanliness impossible, exposes them to a variety of disorders, and abates, or destroys that Military pride, without which nothing can be expected from any Army."

2. **Military Strength**

   a) To THE PRESIDENT OF CONGRESS, Head Quarters, Camp near German Town, August 10, 1777.

   "It is generally a well-founded Maxim, that we ought to endeavour to reduce our defence, as much as possible, to a certainty, by collecting our Strength and making all our preparations at one point, rather than to risk its being weak and ineffectual every where, by dividing our attention and force to different objects."

3. **Military Academy**

   a) EIGHTH ANNUAL ADDRESS TO CONGRESS, December 7, 1796.

   "The Institution of a Military Academy, is also recommended by cogent reasons. However pacific the general policy of a Nation may be, it ought never to be without an adequate stock of Military knowledge for emergencies. The first would impair the energy of its character, and both would hazard its safety, or expose it to greater evils when War could not be avoided. Besides that War, might often, not depend upon its own choice. In proportion, as the observance of pacific maxims, might exempt a Nation from the necessity of practising the rules of the Military Art, ought to be its care in preserving, and transmitting by proper establishments, the knowledge of that Art. Whatever argument may be drawn from particular examples, superficially viewed, a thorough examination of the subject will evince, that the Art of War, is at once comprehensive and complicated; that it demands much previous study; and that the possession of it, in its most improved and perfect state, is always of great moment to the security of a Nation. This, therefore, ought to be a serious care of every Government: and for this purpose, an Academy, where a regular course of Instruction is given, is an obvious expedient, which different Nations have successfully employed."

4. **Militia**

   a) To LUND WASHINGTON, Col. Morris's, on the Heights of Harlem, September 30, 1776.

   "This time last year I pointed out the evil consequences of short enlistments, the expenses of militia, and the little dependence that was to be placed in them. I assured [Congress] that the longer they delayed raising a standing army, the more difficult and chargeable would they find it to get on and that, at the same time that the militia would answer no valuable purpose, the frequent calling them in would be attended with an expense, that they could have no conception of. Whether, as I have said before, the unfortunate hope of reconciliation was the cause, or the fear of a standing army prevailed, I will not undertake to say; but the policy was to engage men for twelve months only. The consequence of which, you have had great bodies of militia in pay that never were in camp; you have had immense quantities of provisions drawn by men that never rendered you one hour's service (at least usefully), and this in the most profuse and wasteful way.... I am wearied to death all day with a variety of perplexing circumstances—disturbed at the conduct of the militia, whose behavior and want of discipline has done great injury to the other troops, who never had officers, except in a few instances, worth the bread they eat."

b) To JOHN AUGUSTINE WASHINGTON, February 24, 1777.

"Militia, . . . here today and gone tomorrow—whose way, like the ways of Providence are almost inscrutable."

5. **Bunker Hill**

a) To LUND WASHINGTON, Camp at Cambridge, August 20, 1775.

"The People of this government have obtained a Character which they by no means deserved; their officers generally speaking are the most indifferent kind of People I ever saw. I have already broke one Colo. and five Captains for Cowardice and for drawing more Pay and Provisions than they had Men in their Companies; there is two more Colos. now under arrest, and to be tried for the same offences; in short they are by no means such Troops, in any respect, as you are led to believe of them from the accts. which are published, but I need not make myself Enemies among them, by this declaration, although it is consistent with truth. I dare say the Men would fight very well (if properly Officered) although they are an exceeding dirty and nasty people; had they been properly conducted at Bunkers Hill (on the 17th of June) or those that were there properly supported, the Regulars would have met with a shameful defeat, and a much more considerable loss than they did, which is now known to be exactly 1057 killed and wounded; it was for their behaviour on that occasion that the above Officers were broke, for I never spared one that was accused of Cowardice but brot 'em to immediate Tryal."

6. **Hospital**

a) To THE PRESIDENT OF CONGRESS, January 26, 1777.

"I hope your new appointment . . . will make the necessary reform in the hospital and that I shall not, the next campaign, have my ears and eyes too, shocked with the complaints and looks of poor creatures perishing for want of proper care."

7. **Military Family/Band of Brothers**

a) To HENRY KNOX, October 21, 1798.

"My first wish would be, that my military family and the whole army should consider themselves as a band of brothers, willing and ready to die for each other."

8. **Promotions**

a) To THE COMMITTEE OF CONGRESS WITH THE ARMY, [Head Quarters, January 29, 1778.]

"Irregular promotions have also been a pregnant source of uneasiness, discord and perplexity in this army....This, however, shows how indespensably necessary it is, to have some settled rule of promotion, universally known and understood and not to be deviated from, but for obvious and incontestible reasons."

9. **Tensions with General Gates**

a) To JOHN JAY, [Head Quarters, Middle brook, April 14, 1779.]

"I discovered very early in the war symptoms of coldness and constraint in General Gates behavior to me. These increased as he rose into greater consequence; but we did not come to a direct breach, 'till the beginning of last year. This was occasioned, by a correspondence, which I thought rather made free with me between General Gates and Conway, which accidentally came to my knowledge. The particulars of this affair you will find delineated in the packet herewith indorsed "papers respecting General Conway." Besides the evidence contained in them of the genuineness of the offensive correspondence, I have other proofs still more convincing, which, having been given me in a confidential way, I am not at liberty to impart.

"After this affair subsided, I made a point of treating Genl. Gates with all the attention and cordiality in my power, as well from a sincere desire of harmony, as from an unwillingness to give any cause of triumph to our enemies from an appearance of dissension among ourselves. I can appeal to the world and to the whole Army whether I have not cautiously avoided every word or hint that could tend to disparage General Gates in any way. I am sorry his conduct to me has not been equally generous and that he is continually giving me fresh proofs of malevolence and opposition. It will not be doing him injustice to say, that, besides the little underhand intrigues, which he is frequently practising, there has hardly been any great military question, in which his advice has been asked, that it has not been given in an equivocal and designing manner, apparently calculated to afford him an opportunity of censuring me on the failure of whatever measure might be adopted.

"When I find that this Gentleman does not scruple to take the most unfair advantages of me; I am under a necessity of explaining his conduct to justify my own. This and the perfect confidence I have in you have occasioned me to trouble you with so free a communication of the state of things between us. I shall still be as passive as a regard to my own character will permit. I am however uneasy as General — has endeavoured to impress Congress with an unfavourable idea of me, and as I only know this in a private confidential way, that I cannot take any step to remove the impression, if it should be made."

10. **General Conway's Secret Enemy**

a) To MAJOR GENERAL HORATIO GATES, Valley Forge, January 4, 1778. vol. 10. "...given with a friendly view to forewarn, and consequently forearm me, against a secret enemy; or, in other words, a dangerous incendiary; in which character, sooner or later, this Country will know Genl. Conway."

B. **Patriotism**

1. **Patriot**

a) To THE SECRETARY OF WAR, Mount Vernon, February 25, 1799. "It is a maxim with me, that in times of imminent danger to a Country, every true Patriot should occupy the Post in which he can render [his services to his country] the most effectually."

b) To BENEDICT ARNOLD, September 14, 1775. "Every post is honorable, in which a man can serve his country."

c) To COL. JOSIAS C. HALL, April 3, 1778. "From the crisis at which our affairs have arrived, . . . I think every man, who does not merely make profession of patriotism is bound by indissoluble ties to remain in the army."

d) FIRST INAUGURAL, April 30, 1789. ". . . my country, whose voice I can never hear but with veneration and love."

e) To HENRY LEE, July 21, 1793. "I have no wish superior to that of promoting the happiness and welfare of this country."

f) To DAVID HUMPHREYS, June 26, 1797.

"I am clearly in sentiment with you that every man who is in the vigor of life, ought to serve his country, in whatever line it requires and he is fit for."

2. American West

a) To RICHARD HENDERSON, June 19, 1788.

"If I was a young man, just preparing to begin the world, or if advanced in life, and had a family to make a provision for, I know of no country where I should rather fix my habitation than in some part of that region [the West]."

b) To DAVID HUMPHREYS, July 25, 1785.

"Rather than quarrel about territory, let the poor, the needy, and oppressed of the earth, and those who want land, resort to the fertile plains of our western country, the second land of promise, and there dwell in peace, fulfilling the first and great commandment."

VI. BUSINESS AND FINANCES

A. Business

1. Doing Business Well

a) To THE SECRETARY OF WAR, Mount Vernon, July 13, 1796.

"Let me, in a friendly way, impress the following maxims upon the Executive Officers. In all important matters, to deliberate maturely, but to execute promptly and vigorously. And not to put things off until the Morrow which can be done, and require to be done, to day. Without an adherence to these rules, business never will be *well* done, or done in an easy manner; but will always be in arrear, with one thing treading upon the heels of another."

2. System

a) To JAMES ANDERSON, Mount Vernon, December 21, 1797.

"If a person only sees, or directs from day to day what is to be done, business can never go on methodically or well, for in case of sickness, or the absence of the Director, delays must follow. System to all things is the soul of business. To deliberate maturely, and execute promptly is the way to conduct it to advantage. With me, it has always been a maxim, rather to let my designs appear from my works than by my expressions. To talk long before hand, of things to be done, is unpleasant, if those things can as well be done at one time or another; but I do not mean by this to discourage you from proposing any plans to me which you may conceive to be beneficial, after having weighed them well in your own mind; on the contrary, I request you to do it with the utmost freedom, for the more combined, and distant things are seen, the more likely they are to be turned to advantage."

3. **Fair Business Practices**

a) To JAMES ANDERSON, Mount Vernon, September 10, 1799.

"For at the same time that I should expect a reasonable compensation for the use of the property it would be equally my wish that you should find your account in the profit, arising there from. Live, and let live, is, in my opinion, a maxim founded in true policy; and is one I am disposed to pursue."

4. **Commerce**

a) To MARQUIS DE LAFAYETTE, Mount Vernon, August 15, 1786 (vol. 28).

"As a Philanthropist by character, and (if I may be allowed the expression) as a Citizen of the great republic of humanity at large; I cannot help turning my attention sometimes to this subject. I would be understood to mean, I cannot avoid reflecting with pleasure on the probable influence that commerce may hereafter have on human manners and society in general. On these occasions I consider how mankind may be connected like one great family in fraternal ties. I indulge a fond, perhaps an enthusiastic idea, that as the world is evidently much less barbarous than it has been, its melioration must still be progressive; that nations are becoming more humanized in their policy, that the subjects of ambition and causes for hostility are daily diminishing, and, in fine, that the period is not very remote, when the benefits of a liberal and free commerce will, pretty generally, succeed to the devastations and horrors of war."

5. **Self Interest**

a) To ROBERT CARY & COMPANY, Mount Vernon, May 28, 1762.

"As I have ever laid it down as an established Maxim to believe, that every person is, (most certainly ought to be) the best judges of what relates to their own Interest and concerns I very rarely undertake to propose Schemes to others which may be attended with uncertainty and miscarriage."

b) To DOLPHIN DREW, Mount Vernon, February 25, 1784.

"From the first I laid it down as a maxim, that no person who possessed Lands adjoining, should hold any of mine as a Lease, and for this obvious reason, that the weight of their labour, and burden of the crops, whilst it was in a condition to bear them, would fall upon my Land, and the improvement upon

his own, in spite of all the covenants which could be inserted to prevent it."
c) To JOHN AUGUSTINE WASHINGTON, Mount Vernon,
March 27, 1786.
"I had established it as a maxim to accept no Tenants that did not mean to reside on the Land; or who had land of their own adjoining to it, not expecting, in either case, much improvement on, or much justice to mine under these circumstances."
d) To JOHN LAURENS, July 10, 1782.
"It is not the public, but the private interest, which influences the generality of mankind, nor can the Americans any longer boast an exception."

6. **Time**

a) To DOCTOR JAMES ANDERSON, Philadelphia,
December 24, 1795.
"The truth, is so little time is at my disposal for private gratifications, that it is but rarely I put pen to paper for purposes of my own."
b) To JAMES MCHENRY, September 14, 1799.
"What to me is more valuable, my time, that I most regard."
c) To JAMES ANDERSON, December 10, 1799.
"Time is of more importance than is generally imagined."

7. **Time and Money**

a) To JAMES ANDERSON, Mount Vernon, December 21, 1797.
"The man who does not estimate *time* as *money* will forever miscalculate; for altho' the latter is not paid for the former, it is nevertheless a sure item in the cost of any undertaking."

8. **Workmen**

a) To JAMES ANDERSON, Federal City, May 22, 1798.
"I had no intention then, nor have I any desire now, to part with you as a manager; but having made this declaration I shall add (what I believe I then did) that I have no wish to retain any person in my Service who is discontented with my conduct . . . Strange, and singular indeed would it be, if the Proprietor of an Estate . . . should have nothing to say in, or controul over, his own expenditures; Should not be at liberty to square his oeconomy thereto; Nor should, without hurting the feelings of a Manager, point to such alterations . . .

"Where have I been deficient? or in what have you just cause to complain? If I cannot remark upon my own business, passing every day under my eyes, without hurting your feelings, I must discontinue my rides, or become a cypher on my own Estate... If your feelings have been hurt by my remarks on the bad clover Seed that was purchased, I cannot help that; my views and plan have been much more hurt by it ... it is not my wish to hurt the feelings of any one, where it can be avoided, or to do injustice in any respect whatsover;"

b) To WILLIAM GORDON, October 14, 1797.

"Workmen in most Countries I believe are necessary plagues—in this [country] where entreaties as well as money must be used to obtain their work and keep them to their duty they baffle all calculation in the accomplishment of any plan or repairs they are engaged in;—and require more attention to and looking after than can be well conceived."

c) To HENRY KNOX, September 24, 1792.

"My observation on every employment in life is, that, wherever and whenever one person is found adequate to the discharge of a duty by close application thereto, it is worse executed by two persons, and scarcely done at all if three or more are employed therein."

d) To TENCH TILGHMAN, March 24, 1784.

"If they are good workmen, they may be from Asia, Africa or Europe; they may be Mahometans, Jews or Christians of any sect, or they may be Atheists. I would, however, prefer middle aged to young men, and those who have good countenances, and good characters ... to others who have neither."

C. Finances

1. Borrowing

a) To SAMUEL WASHINGTON, July 12, 1797.

"You may be assured that there is no practice more dangerous than that of borrowing money.... For when money can be had in this way, repayment is seldom thought of in time; the Interest becomes a moth; exertions to raise it by dint of Industry ceases—it comes easy and is spent freely; and many things indulged in that would never be thought of, if to be purchased by the sweat of the brow.—In the meantime the debt is accumulating like a snowball in rolling."

2. Debt

a) To JOHN AUGUSTINE WASHINGTON, Newburgh, January 16, 1783.

"...how did my brother Samuel contrive to get himself so enormously in debt? Was it by making purchases? By misfortunes? Or sheer indolence and inattention to business? From whatever cause it proceeded, the matter is now the same, and curiosity only prompts me to the enquiry, as it does to know what will be saved, and how it is disposed of. . . . I have lately received a letter from my mother, in which she complains much of the knavery of the overseer at the Little Falls quarter."

b) To JAMES WELCH, April 7, 1799.

"To contract new Debts is not the way to pay old ones."

c) To ROBERT STEWART, April 27, 1763.

"I wish, my dear Stewart, that the circumstances of my affairs would have permitted me to have given you an order . . . for £400 . . . or even twice that sum . . . But, alas! To show my inability in this respect, I enclose you a copy of Mr. Cary's last account current against me, which upon my honor and the faith of a Christian, is a true one. . .

"This, upon my soul, is a genuine account of my affairs in England."

d) To LUND WASHINGTON, Newburgh, February 12, 1783.

"I have often told you, and I repeat it with much truth, that the entire confidence which I placed in your integrity made me easy, and I was always happy at thinking that my affairs were in your hands—which I could not have been if they had been under the care of a common manager. . . . I want to know before I come home (as I shall come home with empty pockets, whenever Peace shall take place) how affairs stand with me, and what my dependence is."

3. **Security for Loans**

a) To DANIEL McCARTY, Mount Vernon, November 13, 1797.

"It is a maxim with me, to take landed security which from its nature is unchangeable, to personal security which is subject to numberless vissitudes."

b) To BURGES BALL, New York, January 18, 1790.

"I hope you have got through your difficulties on account of your surety-ship for Major Willis, and without loss. When you engaged in this business you neglected the advice of the Wise man, than which no better I believe is to be found in his whole book, or among all his sayings, 'Beware of surety-ship.' Offer my love and good wishes to Fanny and the family, accept the same yourself and those of Mrs. Washington. I am etc."

4. Money Limited

a) To FIELDING LEWIS, Mount Vernon, February 27, 1784.

"You very much mistake my circumstances when you suppose me in a condition to advance money. I made no money from my Estate during the nine years I was absent from it, and brought none home with me. those who owed me, for the most part, took advantage of the depreciation and paid me off with six pence in the pound. those to whom I was indebted, I have yet to pay, without other means, if they will not wait, than selling part of my Estate; or distressing those who were too honest to take advantage of the tender Laws to quit scores with me."

b) To CHARLES CARTER, Philadelphia, March 10, 1795.

"My friends entertain a very erroneous idea of my pecuniary resources, when they set me down for a money lender, or one who (now) has a command of it. You may believe me, when I assert that the Bonds which were due to me before the Revolution, were discharged during the progress of it, with a few exceptions in depreciated paper (in some instances as low as a shilling in the pound). That such has been the management of my estate, for many years past, especially since my absence from home, now six years, as scarcely to support itself. That my public allowance (whatever the world may think of it) is inadequate to the expence of living in this city; to such an extravagant height has the necessaries as well as the conveniences of life, arisen. And, moreover, that to keep myself out of debt; I have found it expedient, now and then, to sell lands, or something else to effect this purpose.

"These are facts I have no inclination to publish to the world, nor should I have disclosed them on this occasion, had it not been due to friendship, to give you some explanation of my inability to comply with your request. If, however, by joining with nine others, the sum required can be obtained, notwithstanding my being under these circumstances, and notwithstanding the money will be to be withdrawn from another purpose, I will contribute one hundred pounds towards the accommodation of your sons wants, without any view to the receipt of interest there from."

c) To SAMUEL WASHINGTON, Mount Vernon, July 12, 1797.

"I perceive by your letter of the 7th Instant that you are under the same mistake that many others are, in supposing that I have money always at Command.

"The case is so much the reverse of it, that I found it expedient before I retired from public life to sell all my Lands (near 5000 Acres) in Pennsylvania in the Counties of Washington and Fayette, and my lands in the Great Dismal Swamp in Virginia, in order to enable me to defray the expences of my station, and to raise money for other purposes."

5. **Rents**

a) To ROBERT LEWIS, Mount Vernon, October 15, 1791.

"From long experience I have laid it down as an unerring maxim that to exact rents with punctuality is not only the *right* t of the Landlord, but that it is also for the benefit of the Tenant, that it should be so; unless by uncontroulable events, and providential strokes the latter is rendered unable to pay them; in such cases he should not only meet with indulgence, but, in some instances with a remittal of the rent. But, in the ordinary course of these transactions, the rents ought to be collected with the most rigid exactness."

VII. POLITICS AND MEDIA

A. Politics

1. **Censure/Criticism**

a) To THE EARL OF LOUDOUN, [January], 1757.

"Therefore, it is not to be wondered at, if, under such peculiar circumstances, I should be sicken'd in a service, which promises so little of a soldier's reward. I have long been satisfied of the impossibility of continuing in this service, without loss of honor. Indeed, I was fully convinced of it before I accepted the command the second time, (seeing the cloudy prospect that stood before me;) and did for this reason reject the offer, (until I was ashamed any longer to refuse,) not caring to expose my character to public censure. But the solicitations of the country overcame my objections, and induced me to accept it."

b) To PRESIDENT JOSEPH REED, West-point, July 29, 1779.

"If I had ever assumed the Character of a Military genius and the Officer of experience. If undr. these false colors I had solicited the command I was honoured with, or if after my appointment, I had presumptuously driven on under the sole guidance of my own judgment and self will, and misfortunes the result of obstinacy and misconduct, not of necessity, had followed, I should have thought myself a proper subject for the lash, not only of his, but the pen of every other writer, and a fit object for public resentment."

c) To MRS. MARTHA WASHINGTON, Philadelphia, June 18, 1775.

"It was utterly out of my power to refuse this appointment, without exposing my character to such censures, as would have reflected dishonor upon myself, and given pain to my friends."

d) To JOHN AUGUSTINE WASHINGTON, Cambridge, March 31, 1776.

"Many of my difficulties and distresses were of so peculiar a cast that in order to conceal them from the Enemy, I was obliged to conceal them from my friends, indeed from my own Army, thereby subjecting my Conduct to interpretations unfavourable to my Character, especially by those at a distance, who could not, in the smallest degree be acquainted with the Springs that govern'd it."

e) To ROBERT DINWIDDIE, Fort Loudoun, September 17, 1757.

"It is hard to have my character arraigned, and my actions condemned, without a hearing."

f) To DAVID HUMPHREYS, June 12, 1796.

"I am attacked for a steady opposition to every measure which has a tendency to disturb the peace and tranquility of it. But these attacks, unjust and unpleasant as they are, will occasion no change in my conduct; nor will they work any other effect in my mind, than to increase the anxious desire which has long possessed my breast, to enjoy in the shades of retirement the consolation of having rendered my Country every service my abilities were competent to, uninfluenced by pecuniary or ambitious considerations as they respected myself, and without any attempt to provide for my friends farther than their merits, abstractedly, entitle them to; nor an attempt in *any* instance to bring a relation of mine into Office. Malignity therefore may dart her shafts; but no earthly power can deprive me of the consolation of knowing that I have not in the course of my administration been guilty of a *wilful* error, however numerous they may have been from other causes." (emphasis in the original)

2. **Politics**

a) To LAFAYETTE, December 25, 1798.

"I wish well to all nations and to all men. My politics are plain and simple. I think every nation has a right to establish that form of government under which it conceives it shall live most happy; provided it infracts no right, or is not dangerous to others; and that no governments ought to interfere with the internal concerns of another, except for the security of what is due to themselves."

3. **Opinions**

   a) To HENRY KNOX, Mount Vernon, September 20, 1795.

   "If any power on earth could, or the great power above would, erect the standard of infallibility in political opinions, there is no being that inhabits this terrestrial globe that would resort to it with more eagerness than myself, so long as I remain a servant of the public. But as I have found no better guide hitherto than upright intentions, and close investigation, I shall adhere to these maxims while I keep the watch; leaving it to those who will come after me to explore new ways, if they like; or think them better."

   b) To JOHN PARKE CUSTIS, February 28, 1781.

   "To be disgusted at the decision of questions, because they are not consonant to our own ideas, and to withdraw ourselves from public assemblies, or to neglect our attendance at them . . . is wrong, because these things may originate in a difference of opinion; but, supposing the fact is otherwise . . . .it is the indispensable duty of every patriot to counteract them by the most steady and uniform opposition."

   c) To THOMAS JEFFERSON, August 23, 1792.

   "Without more charity for the opinions and acts of one another in governmental matters, or some more infallible criterion by which the truth of speculative opinions, before they have undergone the test of experience, are to be fore-judged. . . I believe it will be difficult, if not impracticable, to manage the reins of government."

   d) To ALEXANDER HAMILTON, August 26, 1792.

   "Differences in political opinions are as unavoidable, as, to a certain point, they may perhaps be necessary. But it is exceedingly to be regretted, that subjects cannot be discussed without temper on the one hand, or decisions submitted to without having the motives . . . improperly implicated on the other; and his regret borders on chagrin, when we find that men of abilities, zealous patriots, . . . will not exercise more charity in deciding on the opinions and actions of one another."

4. **Honesty**

   a) To DOCTOR JAMES ANDERSON, Philadelphia,
   December 24, 1795.

   "I have no inclination to touch, much less to dilate on politics. For in politics, as in religion my tenets are few and simple: the leading one of which, and indeed that which embraces most others, is to be honest and just ourselves, and to exact it from others; medling as little as possible in their affairs where our own are not involved. If this maxim was generally adopted Wars would cease, and our swords would soon be converted into reap-hooks, and our harvests be more abundant, peaceful, and happy. 'Tis wonderful it should be otherwise and the earth should be moistened with human gore, instead of the refreshing streams, wch. the shedders of it might become, instruments to lead over its plains, to delight and render profitable our labours. But alas! the millenium will not I fear appear in our days. The restless mind of man can not be at peace; and when there is disorder within, it will appear without, and soon or late will shew itself in acts. So it is with Nations, whose mind is only the aggregate of those of the individuals, where the Government is Representative, and the voice of a Despot, where it is not."

5. **Disputes**

a) FAREWELL ADDRESS, [First Draft, May 15, 1796.]

"That party disputes, among all the friends and lovers of their country may subside, or, as the wisdom of Providence has ordained that men, on the same subjects, shall not always think alike, that charity and benevolence when they happen to differ may so far shed their benign influence as to banish those invectives which proceed from illiberal prejudices and jealousy."

b) To ALEXANDER HAMILTON, October 18, 1787.

"When the situation of this country calls loudly for vigor and unanimity, it is to be lamented that gentlemen of talents and character should disagree in their sentiments for promoting the public weal; but unfortunately this ever has been, and most probably ever will be, the case in the affairs of mankind."

6. **Non-Partnerships**

a) To THOMAS JEFFERSON, Mount Vernon, July 6, 1796.

"I was no party man myself, and the first wish of my heart was, if parties did exist, to reconcile them.

"To this I may add, and very truly, that, until within the last year or two ago, I had no conception that Parties would, or even could go, the length I have been witness to; nor did I believe until lately, that it was within the bonds of probability; hardly within those of possibility, that, while I was using my utmost exertions to establish a national character of our own, independent, as far as our obligations, and justice would permit, of every nation of the earth; and wished, by steering a steady course, to preserve this Country from the horrors of a desolating war, that I should be accused of being the enemy of one Nation, and subject to the influence of another; and to prove it, that every act of my administration would be tortured, and the grossest, and most insidious mis-representations of them be made (by giving one side *only* of a subject, and that too in such exaggerated and indecent terms as could scarcely be applied to a Nero; a notorious defaulter; or even to a common pick-pocket). But enough of this; I have already gone farther in the expression of my feelings, than I intended."

b) To JOHN ARMSTRONG, May 18, 1779.

"To please everybody is impossible; were I to undertake it, I should probably please nobody. If I know myself I have no partialities. I have from the beginning, and I hope I shall to the end, pursued to the utmost of my judgment and abilities, one steady line of conduct for the good of the great whole."

7. Public Sentiment

a) To LAFAYETTE, July 25, 1785.

"It is to be regretted I confess, that democratical states must always *feel* before they can *see*; it is this that makes their governments slow, but the people will be right at last." (emphasis in the original)

b) To EDWARD CARRINGTON, May 1, 1796.

"Whatever my own opinion may be on this or any other subject interesting to the community at large, it always has been and will continue to be my earnest desire to learn, and, as far as is consistent, to comply with, the public sentiment; but it is on great occasions only, and after time has been given for cool and deliberate reflection, that the real voice of the people can be known."

8. Democrat

a) To JAMES MCHENRY, September 30, 1798.

"My opinion is . . . . that you could as soon scrub the blackamore white as to change the principle of a profest Democrat, and that he will leave nothing unattempted to overturn the Government of this country."

9. Franklin

a) To HENRY HILL New York, June 3, 1790.

Benjamin Franklin, bequeathing to him his gold-headed Crabtree walking stick, said: "If it were a scepter, he has merited it and would become it."

10. Lust for Power

a) To PRESIDENT OF CONGRESS, December 20, 1776.

"I have no lust for power."

11. **Minority and Majority**

a) To CHARLES M. THUSTON, August 10, 1794.

"If the laws are to be so trampled upon with impunity, and a minority (a small one too) is to dictate to the majority, there is an end put . . . to republican government; and nothing but anarchy and confusion is to be expected hereafter. Some other man or society may dislike another law, and oppose it with equal propriety, until all laws are prostrate, and every one (the strongest I presume) will carve for himself."

12. **Popularity**

a) To HENRY LEE, Mount Vernon, September 22, 1788.

"Though I prize, as I ought, the good opinion of my fellow citizens; yet, if I know myself, I would not seek Or retain popularity at the expense of one social duty or moral virtue."

b) To THE CITIZENS OF BALTIMORE, [April 17, 1789.]

"I know the delicate nature of the duties incident to the part which I am called to perform; and I feel my incompetence, without the singular assistance of Providence to discharge them in a satisfactory manner. But having undertaken the task, from a sense of duty, no fear of encountering difficulties and no dread of losing popularity, shall ever deter me from pursuing what I conceive to be the true interests of my Country."

13. **Prejudice**

a) To CALEB GIBBS, New York, May 26, 1789.

"Whatever may be my private inclinations and feelings, it will then be my endeavour to find out and nominate such men as shall seem to be best calculated and best entitled in every respect to fill those offices, according to the clearest information I can obtain, and the most unbiassed judgment I can exercise on the subject."

b) To MAJOR FRANCIS HALKET, August 2, 1758

"I am uninfluenced by prejudice, having no hopes or fears but for the general good."

14. **Passions of Men**

a) To JOHN BANISTER, April 21, 1778.

"We must take the passions of men as nature has given them, and those principles as a guide, which are generally the rule of action."

B. Media

    1. Newspapers

        a) To JAMES MCHENRY, April 3, 1797.

        "We get so many details in the gazettes, and of such different complexions, that it is impossible to know what credence to give to any of them."

        b) To OLIVER WOLCOTT, May 15, 1797.

        "There is so little dependence on newspaper publications, which take whatever complexion to the editors please to give them, that persons at a distance, who have no other means of information, are oftentimes at a loss to form an opinion on the most important occurrences."

        c) To EDMUND RANDOLPH, August 26, 1792.

        "If the government and the officers of it are to be the constant theme for newspaper abuse, and this too without condescending to investigate the motives or the facts, it will be impossible, I conceive, for any man living to manage the helm or to keep the machine together."

    2. The Influence of the Media

        a) To JAMES MADISON, May 20, 1792.

        "However necessary it may be to keep a watchful eye over public servants, and public measures, yet there ought to be limits to it; for suspicions unfounded, and jealousies too lively, are irritating to honest feeling; and oftentimes are productive of more evil than good."

        b) To EDMUND PENDLETON, January 22, 1795.

        "It is well known, that, when one side only of a story is heard and often repeated, the human mind becomes impressed with it insensibly."

VIII. SLAVERY

    A. Washington's Early View on Slavery

        1. To CAPTAIN JOSIAH THOMPSON, Mount Vernon, July 2, 1766.

        "With this letter comes a negro (Tom), which I beg the favor of you to sell in any of the Islands you may go to, for whatever he will fetch, and bring me in return from him

            One hhd (Hogshead—a cask containing from 63 to 140 gallons)

            One ditto of best rum

            One barrel of lymes, if good and cheap

            One pot of tamarinds, containing about 10 lbs.

            Two small ditto of mixed sweetmeats, about 5 lbs each.

"And the residue, much or little, in good old spirits. That this fellow is both a rogue and a runaway (tho' he was by no means remarkable for the former, and never practiced the latter till of late) I shall not pretend to deny. But that he is exceeding healthy, strong, and good at the hoe, the whole neiborhood can testify, and particularly Mr. Johnson and his son, who have both had him under them as foreman of the gang; which gives me reason to hope he may with your good management sell well, if kept clean and trim'd up a little when offered for sale.

"I shall very cheerfully allow you the customary commissions on this affair, and must beg the favor of you (lest he should attempt his escape) to keep him handcuffed till you get to sea, or in the bay, after which I doubt not but you make him very useful to you."

B. Washington's Mature View on Slavery

1. To ROBERT MORRIS, April 12, 1786.

"There is not a man living, who wishes more sincerely than I do, to see a plan adopted, for the abolition of slavery. But there is only one proper way and effectual mode by which it can be accomplished, and this by legislative authority."

2. To LAFAYETTE, May 10, 1786.

"To set the slaves afloat, at once would I believe be productive of much inconvenience and mischief; but, by degrees, it certainly might and assuredly ought to be effected, and that, too, by legislative authority."

3. To JOHN FRANCIS MERCER, September 9, 1786.

"I never mean, unless some particular circumstance should compel me to it, to possess another slave by purchase, it being among my first wishes to see some plan adopted by which Slavery, in this country may be abolished by law."

4. To ALEXANDER SPOTSWOOD, November 23, 1794.

"With respect to the other species of property, concerning which you ask my opinion, I shall frankly declare to you that I do not like even to think, much less talk of it. However, as you have put the question, I shall, in a few words, give you *my ideas* of it. Were it not then, that I am principled against selling negroes, as you would do cattle at a market, I would not in twelve moths from this date, be possessed of one, as a slave. I shall be happily mistaken, if they are not found to be very troublesome species of property ere many years pass over our heads."

5. To GEORGE LEWIS, November 13, 1797.

"The running off of my Cook, has been a most inconvenient thing to this family; and what renders it more disagreeable, is, that I had resolved never to become the Master of another Slave by *purchase* ; but this resolution I fear I must break. I have endeavoured to hire, black or white, but am not yet supplied."

George Washington and the Anglican Theology of Latitudinarianism

Our study of George Washington has sought to be accurate and scholarly, but also accessible. So we decided that our discussion of Washington's place in the detailed theological movements of the Anglican tradition did not fit into the main story that we have sought to tell. Nevertheless, an accurate understanding of the theological current in which Washington found himself is a critical link in the argument to establish his Christianity and his non-deistic approach to religion. Accordingly, we've included this discussion as an appendix. The following comparison between the theological school of thought called Latitudinarianism and Washington's writings will establish this point. This discussion, however, necessarily encompasses some theological jargon, and therefore, we must offer some historical and theological background.

A DEFINITION OF LATITUDINARIANISM

As we saw in an earlier chapter discussing Washington's partaking of Christian Communion, Washington was willing to participate in the Eucharist outside of his own Anglican Communion. Washington's personal willingness to commune with those of the Presbyterian tradition reflected his Low Church attitude. This was part of a stream of Anglican theology and practice that had come to be known as the "Latitudinarian" perspective.[1] This movement received its name because it sought to give more theological room—latitude—to those who disagreed with the established church, such as the non-conformists who were often Presbyterians, Congregationalists or Independents. It sought to give more latitude in doctrinal controversy within the church as well. It attempted to soften the hostility against Roman Catholicism, without yielding on historic Christian Orthodoxy or basic Protestant theology. So as a result of this effort at a more gracious spirit of Christian community and theology, "a more Christian-like spirit," to use one of Washington's phrases,[2] the Latitudinarians had the dishonor of being seen as heretics by the stalwarts of nearly every tradition.

As a result, the word "Latitudinarian," at first, became a word of contempt, or theological name-calling.

Martin I. J. Griffin Jr., church historian, explains:

> From the beginning, the term "Latitudinarian," or its occasional early variant "Latitude-Man," denoted heterodoxy or religious laxity. One of the most common charges, often expressed, was that a "Latitude-Man . . . being of no religion himself, is indifferent what religion others should be of." The Latitudinarians, it was said, took no trouble to profess any particular religion, because they considered all religions almost equally saving. Did they not outstrip "a very heathen" in preaching that "a good life will carry men to heaven, though they be Jews, Turks, Antichristians, or never such damnable heretics in point of faith"?[3]

This movement was accused of being Presbyterian,[4] Calvinist,[5] Socinian,[6] Arminian,[7] Pelagian,[8] and Erastian.[9] Some of these beliefs are mutually exclusive. This kind of misunderstanding is what happens when criticism is based only on impressions and not careful study. Griffin, continues,

> Such were the common acceptations of the word "Latitudinarian" in the seventeenth century. Stripped of the confusing inessentials always attendant upon name-calling, the charges against the Latitudinarians can be reduced to three which reflect the main sources of contemporary alarm about their teachings. One was that they tried to make religions too "reasonable." A second was that their doctrine of grace and their scheme of salvation were Pelagian. A third was that they were too permissive and lax in their opinions on Church government and liturgy. The basic theme of the accusations from the side of doctrinaire Calvinism was that the Latitudinarians gave too much to reason, not enough to revelation; too much to nature, not enough to grace. From High Church Anglicans and Roman Catholics came *the charge that they were but Presbyterians in Anglican surplices*, and that they gave insufficient importance to the doctrinal teaching authority of the Church.[10] (emphasis ours)

Later, however, "Latitudinarian" was replaced by the word "Broad church"[11] that has for many come to be synonymous with the "Low Church."[12] The theologian who identified most with this movement was Bishop Gilbert Burnet, the author of the study of the *Thirty-Nine Articles* that Washington had purchased in March 1766. It is important to remember that Washington had taken a vow to uphold the *Thirty-Nine Articles*, there is no evidence that he ever changed his mind. This is a strong argument in favor of his Christian Orthodoxy. Probably the best summary of the *Thirty-Nine Articles'* distinctives, especially as it made itself known as a theological expression in Washington's Virginia, comes again from Griffin:

> The religious strife of seventeenth-century England elicited…their characteristic teachings, which included a rational theology, a minimalism in theology, a tendency to exalt moral theology over speculative theology, and an insistence upon moderation and mutual tolerance in matters of religion and worship that were inessential.[13]

But what makes this movement most interesting for our concerns here is that it was conscious of the Christian doctrines of salvation and was also intentionally anti-Deist. In terms of the doctrines of salvation, we find the following that almost sounds as if it were from Washington himself. Quoting Griffin again:

> "…true philosophy can never hurt sound divinity…." As Glanvill said, the Latitudinarians held as "one of their main doctrines" that "the principles which are necessary for salvation are very few, and very plain, and generally acknowledged among Christians." The Bible alone was a sufficient rule of faith, for in it the few fundamentals of religion were set forth, Fowler said, even to the meanest intelligence, "with such perspicuity and clearness, that nothing but men's shutting their eyes against the light can keep them from discerning their true meaning."[14]

And, important for our purposes, Latitudinarians were not Deists. They affirmed that salvation was revealed in the scriptures, the very thing that Deists denied: "it is sufficient for any man's salvation, that he assent to the truth of the Holy Scriptures, that he carefully endeavor to understand their true meaning, so far as concerns his own duty, and to order his life accordingly."[15]

For our concerns here, did such sympathy for religious tolerance, a historic commitment to Christian Orthodoxy, and a strong emphasis on morality coupled with a belief in salvation and in revelation fit Washington's character? This, in fact, is Washington's theology.

Martin I. J. Griffin, Jr. and Lila Freedman, the scholar who completed Griffin's study for publication after his death, have summarized and characterized Latitudinarianism with the following traits:

(1) Orthodoxy in the historical sense of acceptance of the contents of the traditional Christian creeds;

(2) Conformity to the Church of England as by law established, with its Episcopal government, its *Thirty-Nine Articles*, and the *Book of Common Prayer*;

(3) An advocacy of 'reason' in religion;

(4) Theological minimalism;

(5) An Arminian scheme of justification;

(6) An emphasis on practical morality above creedal speculation and precision;

(7) A distinctive sermon style;

(8) Certain connections with seventeenth-century science and the Royal Society."[16]

While (7) and (8) are only tangentially connected to non-clergyman, and a non-resident of England, the first six items are close approximations of what one finds in Washington's thought. The implications of points (1) and (2) should not be ignored. Like other Latitudinarians, Washington affirmed the doctrines of the Trinity, the Deity of Jesus Christ, the atoning death and bodily resurrection of Jesus, and the authority of the Bible. No Deist could affirm such doctrines.

WASHINGTON'S THEOLOGY FITS THE LATITUDINARIAN PARADIGM

Washington in many ways parallels the distinctives of Latitudinarianism. But with these strong similarities, there are some unique distinctives that Washington himself brings to the discussion. So although Latitudinarianism is usually Arminian in emphasis, Washington seems to have Calvinistic emphases in his thinking as well. For example, Washington places a strong emphasis on God's decree in his statements on Providence. He also shows a deep affinity with the Calvinistic doctrine of sin since he openly and repeatedly emphasizes human depravity. On other occasions, he referred to the hoped for "millennial" era, thereby revealing a Puritan post-millennial vision, which also was a Calvinist view. Given Washington's "few and simple" points of religion, he did not develop any evident Reformed distinctives of salvation and seems to have left these matters much more in the area of human choice, which is closer to the Arminian perspective. He also seems to have wanted to emphasize the moral principles of authentic Christianity as an expression of one's salvation. Thus, human obedience and activity are emphasized rather than the free grace of God. But we must be quick to note that Washington's writings do refer to divine grace. For such reasons it seems appropriate to see a "modified Arminian," or "inconsistent Calvinist" label resting comfortably, if not precisely, on Washington's theological expressions.

If we review the items we've summarized above about Latitudinarianism, we can assemble a list to which we can compare the distinctives of the Latitudinarians with representative statements by Washington. In so doing, we discover Washington's affinity with the Latitudinarian, or Low Church perspective.

A COMPARISION OF WASHINGTON AND LATITUDINARIANISM

(1) *Orthodoxy* in the historical sense of acceptance of the contents of the traditional Christian creeds. Washington was an active worshiper in the Anglican tradition, and thus regularly said all of the creeds. As a sponsor of a child in baptism some *nine* different times, he affirmed the articles of the Apostles Creed, article by article, on *nine* occasions in a worship setting. No Deist could affirm all those key, historic Christian doctrines.

(2) *Conformity* to the Church of England as by law established, with its Episcopal government, its *Thirty-Nine Articles*, and the *Book of Common Prayer*. Washington took all of the required oaths to become a public surveyor and to become a vestryman in the Church of England. He remained an active member and parishioner of the Episcopal Church until he died. There is no record of his ever renouncing any element of the Anglican tradition except for loyalty to the King which was set aside in the Revolution.

(3) Advocacy of '*reason*' in religion. To Burwell Bassett, Washington wrote, "as far as the strength of our reason and religion can carry us…"[17] And to Benjamin Lincoln, "Time *alone* can blunt the keen edge of afflictions; Philosophy and our Religion holds out to us such hopes as will, upon proper reflection, enable us to bear with fortitude the most calamitous incidents of life and these are all that can be expected from the

feelings of humanity; is all which they will yield."[18]

(4) *Theological minimalism*;

To Dr. James Anderson, "I have no inclination to touch, much less to dilate on politics. For in politics, as in religion my tenets are few and simple."[19]

(5) An *Arminian* scheme of justification;

He wrote to Tobias Lear, "It is the nature of humanity to mourn for the loss of our friends...To say how much we loved, and esteemed our departed friend, is unnecessary. She is now no more! but she must be happy, because her virtue has a claim to it."[20]

And his stepson, John Parke Custis, wrote to Martha Washington from Kings College on July 5, 1773,

> I receiv'd Pappa's melancholy Letter, giveing an account of my dear & only Sister's Death... Her case is more to be envied than pitied, for if we mortals can distinguish between those who are deserveing of grace & who are not, I am confident she enjoys that Bliss prepar'd only for the good & virtuous, let these consideration, My dear Mother have their due weight with you and comfort yourself with reflecting that she now enjoys in substance what we in this world enjoy in imagination & that there is no real Happiness on this side of the grave. I must allow that to sustain a shock of this kind requires more Philosophy than we in general are (possest) off, ...I will no longer detain you on a subject which is painful to us both but conclude with beging you to remember you are a Christian and that we ought to submit with Patience to the divine Will and that to render you happy shall be the constant care of your effectionate and dutiful son.
> John Parke Custis[21]

George and Martha Washington instilled a strong Christian worldview upon their son/stepson, so that when death took his sister, he saw the big picture and was not without hope. Washington himself said in a letter to Burnwell Basset informing him of Patsy Custis' sudden passing, "the Sweet Innocent Girl Entered into a more happy and peaceful abode than any she has met with in the afflicted Path she hitherto has trod."[22]

Yet in terms of the sovereignty of Providence, Washington does not fit simply into the "Arminian" category. This is seen when the comment to Tobias Lear (quoted above) (see p. 912(5)) is put in context.

> It is the nature of humanity to mourn for the loss of our friends; and the more we loved them, the more poignant is our grief. It is part of the precepts of Religion and Philosophy, to consider the Dispensations of Providence as wise, immutable, uncontroulable; of course, that it is our duty to submit with as little repining, as the sensibility of our natures is capable of to all its decrees. But nature will, notwithstanding, indulge, for a while, its sorrow's. To say how much we loved, and esteemed our departed friend, is unnecessary. She is now no more! but she must be happy, because her virtue has a claim to it.

And to Burwell Bassett who lost a child just months before the Washingtons, he wrote,

> we sympathize in the misfortune, and lament the decree which has deprived you of so dutiful a child, and the world of so promising a young lady, stands in no need, I hope, of argument to prove; but the ways of Providence being inscrutable, and the justice of it not to be scanned by the shallow eye of humanity, nor to be counteracted by the utmost efforts of human power or wisdom, resignation, and as far as the strength of our reason and religion can carry us, a cheerful acquiescence to the Divine Will, is what we are to aim;[23]

(6) *Practical morality* above creedal speculation and precision;

He wrote to Capt. John Posey, "you must give me leave to say that it is Works and not Words that People will judge from…"[24]

And to John Sullivan, he penned, "A slender acquaintance with the world must convince every man that actions, not words are the true criterion…."[25] As we have seen, this was a theme in Washington's life he was a man of actions, not words. And those actions reflected his active Christian faith.

(7) A distinctive *sermon* style.

Obviously Washington did not preach sermons in the technical sense. But he collected sermons, read sermons to his family, claimed on a couple of occasions he was "turning preacher" and emphasized the great value of the sermon, not only by commending several clergymen in writing for their sermons, but saying the following to his soldiers,

General Orders: "In justice to the zeal and ability of the Chaplains, as well as to his own feelings, the Commander in chief thinks it a duty to declare the regularity and decorum with which divine service is now performed every Sunday, will reflect great credit on the army in general, tend to improve the morals, and at the same time, to increase the happiness of the soldiery, and must afford the most pure and rational entertainment for every serious and well disposed mind. No fatigue except on extra occasions, nor General review or inspections to be permitted on the Sabbath day."[26]

Furthermore, he paid money for pews that were well-situated by the pulpit, and the Communion table so he could hear the sermons. To this day, you can go to see the George Washington box-pews at Christ Church, Alexandria, Virginia; Pohick Church, Lorton, Virginia (where the entire interior has been recreated, including Washington's pew); Trinity Episcopal Church, Newport, Rhode Island; Christ Church, Philadelphia; and St. Paul's Chapel, New York City. Hearing sermons was apparently very important to Washington throughout his life. And, we should add, these were Christian sermons, not deistic ones.

(8) Certain connections with seventeenth-century science and the Royal Society of London.

Washington was a member of scientific societies such as the American Philosophical Society, and he corresponded with members of agricultural societies in England. His science and ideas of creation were complementary. To the American Philosophical Society, "In the philosophic retreat to which I am retiring, I shall often contemplate with pleasure the extensive utility of your Institution. The field of investigation is ample, the benefits which will result to Human Society from discoveries yet to be made, are indubitable, and the task of studying the works of the great Creator, inexpressibly delightful."[27]

(9) Washington's comfort level with the Reformed and Presbyterian churches both in terms of Communion, church life, piety and prayer are remarkable. He communed with Presbyterians in Morristown.[28] He may have communed with German Reformed in Germantown. He sent many collegial letters to Reformed churches with which he had a special bond because of their intimate support of the work of the army in the Revolution. He corresponded openly with their clergy expressing his views of "true religion."

- To the minister of the Reformed Dutch Church, "Your

benevolent wishes and fervent prayers for my personal wellfare and felicity, demand all my gratitude. May the preservation of your civil and religious Liberties still be the care of an indulgent Providence; and may the rapid increase and universal extension of knowledge virtue and true Religion be the consequence of a speedy and honorable Peace."[29]

- To the Synod of the Dutch Reformed Church, Washington asseverated, "I readily join with you that 'while just government protects all in their religious rights, true religion affords to government its surest support.[30]

- To the First Presbytery of the Eastward, Newburyport, October 28. "I am persuaded, you will permit me to observe that the path of true piety is so plain as to require but little political direction."[31]

- To Col. Benedict Arnold (pre-treason). "I also give it in Charge to you to avoid all Disrespect to or Contempt of the Religion of the Country and its Ceremonies. Prudence, Policy, and a true Christian Spirit, will lead us to look with Compassion upon their Errors without insulting them."[32]

- To the General Assembly of the Presbyterian Churches in the United States, "…no man, who is profligate in his morals, or a bad member of the civil community, can possibly be a true Christian, or a credit to his own religious society."[33]

(10) *Rational theology*,

To Tobias Lear: "It is the nature of humanity to mourn for the loss of our friends; and the more we loved them, the more poignant is our grief. It is part of the precepts of Religion and Philosophy, to consider the Dispensations of Providence as wise, immutable, uncontroulable."[34]

To Nicholas Pike: "The science of figures, to a certain degree, is not only indispensably requisite in every walk of civilised life; but the investigation of mathematical truths accustoms the mind to method and correctness in reasoning, and is an employment peculiarly worthy of rational beings. In a clouded state of existence, where so many things appear precarious to the bewildered research, it is here that the rational faculties find a firm foundation to rest upon. From the high ground of mathematical and philosophical demonstration, we are insensibly led to far nobler speculations and sublimer meditations."[35]

(11) An insistence upon moderation

"It is unhappy that a matter of such high importance cannot be discussed with that candour and moderation which would throw light on the subject and place its merits in a proper point of view; but in an assembly so large as your Convention must be and composed of such various and opposite characters, it is almost impossible but that some things will occur which would rouse the passions of the most moderate man on earth."[36]

(12) A mutual tolerance in matters of religion and worship

To Marquis de Lafayette: "I am not less ardent in my wish that you may succeed in your plan of toleration in religious matters. Being no bigot myself to any mode of worship, I am disposed to indulge the professors of Christianity in the church, that road to Heaven, which to them shall seem the most direct plainest easiest and least liable to exception."[37]

To the Hebrew Congregation of Newport, Rhode Island: "For happily the government of the United States, which gives to bigotry no sanction, to persecution no assistance, requires only that they who live under its protection should demean themselves as good citizens, in giving it on all occasions their effectual support....May the children of the Stock of Abraham, who dwell in this land, continue to merit and enjoy the good will of the other inhabitants, while every one shall sit in safety under his own vine and fig-tree, and there shall be none to make him afraid."[38]

(13) Doctrines of salvation affirmed

Answer to an Address from the Massachusetts Legislature: "May that being, who is powerful to save, and in whose hands is the fate of nations, look down with an eye of tender pity and compassion upon the whole of the United Colonies; may He continue to smile upon their counsels and arms, and crown them with success, whilst employed in the cause of virtue and mankind. May this distressed colony and its capital, and every part of this wide extended continent, through His divine favor, be restored to more than their former lustre and once happy state, and have peace, liberty, and safety secured upon a solid, permanent, and lasting foundation."[39]

"Circular to the States," 1783: "I now make it my earnest prayer, that God would have you, and the State over which you preside, in his holy protection, that he would incline the hearts of the Citizens to cultivate a spirit of subordination and obedience to Government, to entertain a brotherly affection and love for one another, for their fellow Citizens of the United States at large, and particularly for their brethren who have served in the Field, and finally, that he would most graciously be pleased to dispose us all, to do Justice, to love mercy, and to demean ourselves with that Charity, humility and pacific temper of mind, which were the Characteristicks of the Divine Author of our blessed Religion, and without an humble imitation of whose example in these things, we can never hope to be a happy Nation."

Proposed Address to Congress, 1789: "The blessed Religion revealed in the word of God will remain an eternal and awful monument to prove that the best Institutions may be abused by human depravity; and that they may even, in some instances be made subservient to the vilest of purposes."[40]

Thanksgiving Proclamation, October 3, 1789: "Whereas it is the duty of all Nations to acknowledge the providence of Almighty God, to obey his will, to be grateful for his benefits, and humbly to implore his protection and favor...And also that we may then unite in most humbly offering our prayers and supplications to the great Lord and Ruler of Nations and beseech him to pardon our national and other transgressions..."[41]

(14) Biblical revelation

"Circular to the States:" "The foundation of our Empire was not laid in the gloomy age of Ignorance and Superstition, but at an Epocha when the rights of mankind were better understood and more clearly defined, than at any former period, the researches of the human mind, after social happiness, have been carried to a great extent, the Treasures of knowledge, acquired by the labours of Philosophers, Sages and Legislatures, ... and above all, the pure and benign light of Revelation..."[42]

(15) Non-deistic

To Reverend William Gordon: "No Man has a more perfect Reliance on the alwise, and powerful dispensations of the Supreme Being than I have nor thinks his aid more necessary."[43]

To Brig. Gen. Thomas Nelson: "...The hand of Providence has been so conspicuous in all this [the success of the American Revoluiton], that he must be worse than an infidel that lacks faith, and more than wicked, that has not gratitude enough to acknowledge his obligations."[44]

To Reverend Samuel Langdon: "The man must be bad indeed who can look upon the events of the American Revolution without feeling the warmest gratitude towards the great Author of the Universe whose divine interposition was so frequently manifested in our behalf. And it is my earnest prayer that we may so conduct ourselves as to merit a continuance of those blessings with which we have hitherto been favored."[45]

Farewell Address, 1796: "Of all the dispositions and habits which lead to political prosperity, Religion and morality are indispensable supports. In vain would that man claim the tribute of Patriotism, who should labour to subvert these great Pillars of human happiness, these firmest props of the duties of Men and citizens. The mere Politician, equally with the pious man ought to respect and to cherish them. A volume could not trace all their connections with private and public felicity. Let it simply be asked where is the security for property, for reputation, for life, if the sense of religious obligation *desert* the oaths, which are the instruments of investigation in Courts of Justice? And let us with caution indulge the supposition, that morality can be maintained without religion. Whatever may be conceded to the influence of refined education on minds of peculiar structure, reason and experience both forbid us to expect that National morality can prevail in exclusion of religious principle. 'Tis substantially true, that virtue or morality is a necessary spring of popular government."[46]

CONCLUSION

Based upon this summation of the Latitudinarian theology of the Low Church, in comparison with Washington's beliefs, it is simply impossible to claim that Washington was a Deist. It is evident that he was an adherent of the Anglican traditional Low Church theology, which was thoroughly rejected by all Deists, and which, in turn, denied the claims of Deism.

Tributes to Washington
By His Contemporaries:
His Christian Faith, Striking
Appearance, and Moral Character

In this appendix, we will assemble several citations from Washington's contemporaries. They are grouped in three sections: his Christianity, descriptions of his appearance, and summations of his character.

I. TESTIMONIES TO WASHINGTON'S CHRISTIAN FAITH BY HIS CONTEMPORARIES

William Johnson writes in *George Washington The Christian*:

> Sermons and orations by divines and statesmen were delivered all over the land at the death of Washington. A large volume of such was published. I have seen and read them, and the religious character of Washington was a most prominent feature in them; and for this there must have been some good cause. 'That Washington was regarded throughout America, both among our military and political men, as a sincere believer in Christianity, as then received among us, and a devout man, is as clear as any fact in our history.'[1]

A. Declarations of His Contemporaries

(1) Major-General Henry Lee

Major-General Henry Lee, member of Congress from Virginia, who served under him during the war, and afterward in the civil department, and who was chosen by Congress to deliver his funeral oration, Thursday, December

26, 1799, at Philadelphia, in the German Lutheran Church. He says in that oration: "First in war, first in peace, and first in the hearts of his countrymen, he was second to none in the humble and endearing scenes of private life. Pious, just, humane, temperate, and sincere; uniform, dignified, and commanding, his example was edifying to all around him, as were the effects of that example lasting."[2]

(2) Joathan Mitchell Sewall

On Tuesday, December 31, 1799, Jonathan Mitchell Sewall delivered an oration at Portsmouth, New Hampshire, at the request of the inhabitants, in which he says: "To crown all these moral virtues, he had the deepest sense of religion impresses on his heart—the true foundation—stone of all the moral virtues.

"This he constantly manifested on all proper occasions. He was a firm believer in the Christian religion; and, at his first entrance on his civil administration he made it known, and adhered to his purpose, that no secular business could be transacted with him on the day set apart by Christians for the worship of Deity.

"Though he was, from principle, a member of the Episcopal Church, he was candid and liberal in the highest degree, not only to all sects and denominations of Christians but to all religions, where the possessors were sincere, throughout the world.

"He constantly attended the public worship of God on the Lord's Day, was communicant at His table, and, by his devout and solemn deportment, inspired every beholder with some portion of that awe and reverence for the Supreme Being of which he felt so large a portion.

"For my own part, I trust I shall never lose the impression made on my own mind in beholding in this house of prayer the venerable hero, the victorious leader of our hosts, bending in humble adoration to the God of armies, and great Captain of our Salvation. Hard and unfeeling indeed must that heart be that could sustain the sight unmoved, or its owner depart unsoftened and unedified.

"Let the deist reflect on this, and remember that Washington, the saviour of his country, did not disdain to acknowledge and adore a great Saviour, whom deists and infidels affect to slight and despise."[3]

(3) Reverend John Thornton Kirkland

In a discourse on the death of Washington, delivered by the Reverend John Thornton Kirkland, minister of the New South Church, Boston, Massachusetts, December 29, 1799, he says: "The virtues of our departed friend were crowned with piety. He is known to have been habitually devout. To Christian institutions he gave the countenance of his example; and no one could express more fully his sense of the Providence of God, and the dependence of man."[4]

(4) Captain Josiah Dunham

Josiah Dunham, Captain of the 16th U.S. Regiment of the Revolution, in his funeral oration pronounced at Oxford, Massachusetts, at the request of the field officers of the brigade, stationed at that place, on the 15th of January, 1800, says of him: "A friend to our holy religion, he was ever guided by its pious doctrines. He had embraced the tenants of the Episcopal Church; yet his charity, unbounded as his immortal mind, led him equally to respect every denomination of the followers of Jesus."[5]

(5) The Hon. David Ramsay

The Hon. David Ramsay, M.D., of South Carolina, the historian, in his oration on the death of Washington, delivered at Charleston, South Carolina, on January 15, 1800, at the request of the inhabitants, says; "He was the friend of morality and religion; steadily attended on public worship; encouraged and strengthened the hands of the clergy. In all his public acts he made the most respectful mention of Providence, and, in a word, carried the spirit of piety with him, both in his private life and public administration. He was far from being one of those minute philosophers who believe that 'death is an eternal sleep'; or, of those, who, trusting to the sufficiency of human reason, discard the light of divine revelation."[6]

(6) The Reverend John M. Mason, D.D.

The Reverend John M. Mason, pastor of the Associate Reformed Church in the city of New York, in the funeral eulogy delivered by appointment of a number of the clergy of New York City, February 22, 1800, uses this language: "That invisible hand which guarded him at first continued to guard and to guide him through the successive stages of the Revolution. Nor did he account it a weakness to bend the knee in homage to its supremacy, and prayer for its direction. This was the armor of Washington, this the salvation of his country."[7]

(7) Jeremiah Smith

In an oration delivered by Jeremiah Smith at Exeter, New Hampshire, February 22, 1800, he says: "He had all the genuine mildness of Christianity with all its force. He was neither ostentatious, nor ashamed of his Christian profession. He pursued in this, as in everything else the happy mean between the extremes of levity and gloominess, indifference and austerity. His religion became him. He brought it with him into office, and he did not lose it there. His first and his last office acts (as he did all the intermediate ones) contained an explicit acknowledgement of the overruling providence of the Supreme Being; and the most fervent supplication for His benediction on our government and nation."

"Without being charged with exaggeration, I may be permitted to say, that an accurate knowledge of his life, while it would confer on him the highest title to praise, would be productive of the most solid advantage to the cause of Christianity."[8]

(8) President Timothy Dwight

Timothy Dwight, D.D., president of Yale College, in a discourse on "The Character of Washington," February 22, 1800, says: "For my own part, I have considered his numerous and uniform public and most solemn declarations of his high veneration for religion, his exemplary and edifying attention to public worship, and his constancy in secret devotion, as proofs, sufficient to satisfy every person, willing to be satisfied. I shall only add that if he was not a Christian, he was more like one than any man of the same description whose life has been hitherto recorded."[9]

(9) Reverend Devereux Jarratt

In an address delivered by the Reverend Devereux Jarratt, in Dinwiddie County, Virginia, he says: "Washington was a professor of Christianity and a member of the Protestant Episcopal Church. He always acknowledged the superintendence of Divine Providence; and from his inimitable writings we find him a warm advocate for a sound morality founded on the principles of religion, the only basis on which it can stand. Nor did I ever meet with the most distant insinuation that his private life was not a comment on his own admired page."[10]

(10) Reverend Jonathan Boucher

The testimony of the Reverend Jonathan Boucher, who, to say the least, was not prejudiced in favor of Washington, is very interesting. He was a minister in the Episcopal Church at Annapolis, Maryland. During the first six months

922

of 1775 he always preached with a pair of loaded pistols lying on the cushion in front of him; and indeed, with no aid from firearms, he was well known to be more than a match for any single member of his congregation. He opposed the independence of the colonies, and returned to England in 1775. He was for a time private tutor to John Parke Custis, the son of Mrs. Washington. His acquaintance with Washington was prior to the Revolution, and, in his own words, he "did know Washington well." In 1776 he writes concerning him; "In his moral character he is regular, temperate, strictly just and honest (except that as a Virginian he has lately found out that there is no moral turpitude in not paying what he confesses he owes to a British creditor), and, I always thought, religious; having heretofore been pretty constant and even exemplary in his attendance on public worship in the Church of England."[11]

(11) President Madison

President Madison says, "Washington was constant in the observance of worship, according to the received forms of the Episcopal Church."[12]

(12) Bushrod Washington

Washington bequeathed Mount Vernon, four thousand acres, including the Mansion House to his nephew, Bushrod Washington, who afterwards became a judge of the Supreme Court of the United States. In 1862 the latter was elected a vice-president of the American Sunday School Union. In replying to an address he said, "Upon the well-intended efforts I have made to secure the due observance of the Sabbath day, upon a spot, where, I am persuaded, it was never violated during the life and with the permission of its venerable owner."[13]

(13) Tradition of the New York Indians

The New York Indians hold this tradition of Washington: "Alone, of all white men, he has been admitted to the Indian Heaven, because of his justice to the Red Men. He lives in a great palace, built like a fort. All the Indians, as they go to Heaven, pass by, and he himself is in his uniform, a sword at his side, walking to and fro. They bow reverently with great humility. He returns the salute, but says nothing." Such is the reward of his justice to the Red Men."[14]

(14) Reverend Israel Evans

The Reverend Israel Evans was a chaplain in the United States army through nearly the entire Revolutionary service. He was a native of New Jersey, a man of education, and capable of appreciating such a character as that of

Washington. The opportunities he enjoyed for social intercourse with him, as well as with other patriots of the Revolution, were very frequent and favorable, and his reverence for Washington was very great. "It is related of Mr. Evans that during his last sickness, thirty years or more after the Revolution, his successor in the ministry, in the New England village where he had been settled, was called in by the family to pray with him, in the evident near approach of the dying hour. Mr. Evans had lain some considerable time in a stupor, apparently unconscious of anything around him, and his brother clergyman was proceeding in fervent prayer to God, that, as his servant was evidently about departing this mortal life, his spirit might be conveyed by angels to Abraham's bosom. Just at his point, the dying man for the first time and for the moment revived, so far as to utter, in an interval of his delirium, '*and Washington's, too*'—and then sunk again into apparent unconsciousness. As if it was not enough to 'have Abraham to his father,' and on whose bosom to repose, but he must have Washington, too, on whom to lean. A signal manifestation of 'the ruling passion strong in death'—and of the lasting hold which that great man had on this mind and heart of one of his early and devoted friends."[15]

B. The Judgment of Washington's Earliest Historians Concerning His Christian Faith

(1) Mason L. Weems

"The noblest, the most efficient element of his character was that he was an humble, earnest Christian."[16]

(2) Aaron Bancroft

"In principle and practice he was a Christian."[17]

(3) Cyrus R. Edmunds

"The elements of his greatness are chiefly to be discovered in the moral features of his character."[18]

(4) John Marshall

Supreme Court Chief Justice John Marshall, who had been the personal friend and frequent associate of Washington, says in his biography, "Without making ostentatious professions of religion, he was a sincere believer in the Christian faith, and a truly devout man."[19]

(5) George Bancroft

"Belief in God and trust in His overruling power, formed the essence of his

924

character…His whole being was one continued act of faith in the eternal, intelligent and moral order of the universe."[20]

(6) Jared Sparks

"A Christian in faith and practice, he was habitually devout. His reverence for religion is seen in his example, his public communications, and his private writings. He uniformly ascribed his successes to the beneficent agency of the Supreme Being. Charitable and humane, he was liberal to the poor and kind to those in distress. As a husband, son, and brother, he was tender and affectionate.

"If a man spoke, wrote, and acted as a Christian through a long life, who gave numerous proofs of his believing himself to be such, and who was never known to say, write or do a thing contrary to his professions, if such a man is not a to be ranked among the believers of Christianity, it would be impossible to establish the point by any train of reasoning…

"After a long and minute examination of the writings of Washington, public and private, in print and in manuscript, I can affirm that I have never seen a single hint or expression from which it could be inferred that he had any doubt of the Christian revelation, or that he thought with indifference or unconcern of that subject. On the contrary, whenever he approaches it, and, indeed, whenever he alludes in any manner to religion, it is done with seriousness and reverence."[21]

(7) David Ramsay

Doctor David Ramsay was a celebrated physician of Charleston, South Carolina. He was a delegate to the Continental Congress in 1782-86. In his biography of Washington, he says: "There are few men of any kind, and still fewer of those the world calls great, who have not some of their virtues eclipsed by corresponding vices. But this was not the case with General Washington. He had religion without austerity, dignity without pride, modesty without diffidence, courage without rashness, politeness without affectation, affability without familiarity. His private character, as well as his public one, will bear the strictest scrutiny. He was punctual in all his engagements; upright and honest in his dealings; temperate in his enjoyments; liberal and hospitable to an eminent degree; a lover of order; systematical and methodical in his arrangements. He was a friend of morality and religion; steadily attended on public worship; encouraged and strengthened the hands of the clergy. In all his public acts he made the most respectful mention of Providence; and in a word, carried the spirit of piety with him both in his private life and public administration."[22]

(8) James K. Paulding

"It is impossible to read the speeches and letters of Washington and follow his whole course of life, without receiving the conviction of his steady, rational, and exalted piety. Everywhere he places his chief reliance, in the difficult, almost hopeless circumstances in which he was so often involved, on the justice of that great Being who holds the fate of men and of nations in the hollow of His hand. His hopes for his country are always founded on the righteousness of its cause, and the blessing of Heaven. His was the belief of reason and revelation; and that belief was illustrated and exemplified in all his actions. No parade accompanied its exercises, no declamation its exhibition; for it was his opinion that a man who is always boasting of his religion, is like one who continually proclaims his honesty—he would trust neither one nor the other. He was not accustomed to argue points of faith, but on one occasion, in reply to a gentleman who expressed doubts on the subject, thus gave his sentiments:

It is impossible to account for the creation of the universe without the agency of a Supreme Being.
It is impossible to govern the universe without the aid of a Supreme being.
It is impossible to reason without arriving at a Supreme Being. Religion is as necessary to reason as reason is to religion. The one cannot exist without the other. A reasoning being would lose his reason in attempting to account for the great phenomena of nature, had he not a Supreme Being to refer to; and well has it been said, that if there had been no God, mankind would have been obliged to imagine one.

"On this basis of piety was erected the superstructure of his virtues. He perceived the harmonious affinity subsisting between the duties we owe to Heaven and those we are called upon to sustain on earth, and made his faith the foundation of his moral obligations. He cherished the homely but invaluable maxim that 'honesty is the best policy,' and held that the temporal as well as the eternal happiness of mankind could never be separated from the performance of their duties to Heaven and their fellow creatures. He believed it to be an inflexible law that, sooner or later, a departure from the strict obligations of truth and justice would bring with it the loss of confidence of mankind, and this deprives us of our best support for prosperity in this world, as well as our best hope of happiness in that to come. In short, he believed and practiced on the high principle, that the invariable consequence of the performance of a duty was an increase of happiness. What others call good fortune, he ascribed to a great and universal law, establishing an indissoluble connection between actions and their consequences, and making every man responsible to himself for his good or ill success in this world. Under that superintending Providence which shapes the ends of men, his sentiments and actions show that he believed, that, as a general rule, every rational being was the architect of his own happiness."[23]

(9) Sir George Otto Trevelyan

"A better churchman—of, at all events, a better man who ranked himself as a churchman—than George Washington it would have been hard indeed to discover. When at home on the bank of the Potomac, he had always gone of a Sunday morning to what would have been called a distant church by any one except a Virginia equestrian; and he spent Sunday afternoons, alone and inapproachable, in his library. In war he found time for daily prayer and meditation (as, by no wish of his, the absence of privacy, which is a feature in camp life, revealed to those who were immediately about him); he attended public worship himself; and by every available means he encouraged the practice of religion in his soldiers, to whom he habitually stood in a kind of fatherly relation. There are many pages in his Orderly Books which indicate a determination that the multitude of young fellows who were intrusted to his charge should have all possible facilities for being as well-behaved as in their native villages.

"The troops were excused fatigue duty in order that they might not miss church. If public worship was interrupted on a Sunday by the call to arms, a service was held on a convenient day in the ensuing week. The chaplains were exhorted to urge the soldiers that they ought to live and act like Christian men in times of distress and danger; and after every great victory, and more particularly at the final proclamation of Peace, the Commander-in-chief earnestly recommended that the army should universally attend the rendering of thanks to Almighty God 'with seriousness of deportment and gratitude of heart.'

"Washington loved his own church the best, and had no mind to leave it; but he was not hostile to any faith which was sincerely held, and which exerted a restraining and correctly influence upon human conduct. 'I am disposed,' he once told Lafayette, 'to indulge the professors of Christianity with that road to Heaven which to them shall seem the most direct, plainest, easiest, and least liable to exception.' His feeling on this matter was accurately expressed in the instruction which he wrote out for Benedict Arnold, when that officer led an armed force of fierce and stern New England Protestants against the Roman Catholic settlements in Canada. The whole paper was a lesson in the statesmanship which is founded on respect and consideration for others, and still remains well worth reading. In after years, as President of the United States, Washington enjoyed frequent opportunities for impressing his own sentiments and policy, in all that related to religion, upon the attention of his compatriots. The churches of America were never tired of framing and presenting addresses which assured him of their confidence, veneration, and sympathy; and he as invariably replied by congratulating them that in their country worship was free, and that men of every creed were eligible to every post of honor and authority."[24]

(10) Henry Cabot Lodge

"He had the same confidence in the judgment of posterity that he had in the future beyond the grave. He regarded death with entire calmness, and even indifference, not only when it came to him, but when in previous years it had threatened him. He loved life and tastes of it deeply, but the courage which never forsook him made him ready to face the inevitable at any moment with an unruffled spirit. In this he has helped by his religious faith, which was as simple as it was profound. He had been brought up in the Protestant Episcopal Church, and to that church he always adhered, for its splendid liturgy and stately forms appealed to him and satisfied him. He loved it too [and it] was the church of his home and his childhood. Yet he was as far as possible from being sectarian, and there is not a word of his which shows anything but the most entire liberality and toleration. He made no parade of his religion, for in this as in other things, he was perfectly simple and sincere. He was tortured by no doubts or questionings, but believed always in an overruling Providence and in a merciful God, to whom he knelt and prayed in the day of darkness or in the hour of triumph with a supreme and childlike confidence.'"[25]

(11) Mason L. Weems

"When the children of the years to come, hearing his great name re-echoed from every lip, shall say to their fathers, 'What was it that raised Washington to such height of glory?' let them by told that it was HIS GREAT TALENTS, CONSTANTLY GUIDED AND GUARDED BY RELIGION."[26]

(12) Duke of Wellington

"The purest and noblest character of modern time — possible of all time."[27]

II. DESCRIPTIONS OF WASHINGTON'S STRIKING APPEARANCE BY HIS CONTEMPORARIES

Unless otherwise noted, all of these citations are found in *Tributes to Washington, Pamphlet No. 3* edited by Albert Bushnell Hart (Washington, D.C.: George Washington Bicentennial Commission, 1931, pages 30 to 39.) They are listed in chronological order.

(1) Captain George Mercer (1759)

"Though distrusting my ability to give an adequate account of the personal appearance of Col. George Washington, late commander of the Virginia Provincial troops, I shall, as you request attempt the portraiture. He may be described as being as straight as an Indian, measuring six feet two inches in his stockings, and weighing 175 pounds, when he took his seat in the House of Burgesses in 1759. His frame is padded with well-developed muscles, indicating great strength. His bones and joints are large, as are his hands and feet. He is wide shouldered, but not a deep or round chest, but is broad across the hips, and has rather long legs and arms. His head is well shaped though not large, but is gracefully poised on a superb neck. A large and straight rather than a prominent nose; blue-gray penetrating eyes, which are widely separated, and overhung by a heavy brow. His face is long rather than broad, with high, round, cheek-bones, and terminates in a good firm chine. He has a clear though rather colorless pale skin, which burns with the sun. A pleasing, benevolent, though commanding countenance, dark brown hair, which he wears in a cue.

"His mouth is large and generally firmly closed, but which from time to time disclosed some defective teeth. His features are regular and placid, with all the muscles of his face under perfect control, though flexible and expressive of deep feeling when moved by emotions. In conversation, deferential and engaging. His voice is agreeable rather than strong. His movements and gestures are graceful, his walk majestic, and he is a splendid horseman."[28]

(2) Dr. James Thacher (1778)

"The personal appearance of the Commander in Chief, is that of the perfect gentleman and accomplished warrior. He is remarkably tall, full six feet, erect and well proportioned. The strength and proportion of his joint and muscles, appear to be commensurate with the preeminent powers of his mind. The serenity of his countenance, and majestic gracefulness of his deportment, impart a strong impression of that dignity and grandeur, which are his peculiar characteristics, and no one can stand in his presence without feeling the ascendancy of his mind, and associating with his countenance the idea of wisdom, philanthropy, magnanimity, and patriotism. There is a fine symmetry in the features of his face indicative of a benign and dignified spirit. His nose is strait, and his eyes inclined to blue. He wears his hair in a becoming cue, and from his forehead it is turned back and powdered in a manner which adds to the military air of his appearance. He displays a native gravity, but devoid of all appearance of ostentation. His uniform dress is a blue coat, with two brilliant epaulettes, buff colored under clothes, and a three cornered hat with a black cockade. He is constantly equipped with an elegant small sword, boot and spurs, in readiness to mount his noble charger."[29]

(3) Dr. James Thacher (1779)

"Yesterday I accompanied Major Cavil to headquarters, and had the honor of being numbered among the guests at the table of his Excellency, with his lady,… It is natural to view with keen attention the countenance of an illustrious man, with a secret hope of discovering in his features some peculiar traces of excellence, which distinguishes him from and elevates him above his fellow mortals. These expectations are realized in a peculiar manner, in viewing the person of General Washington. His tall and noble and just proportions, cheerful open countenance, simple and modest deportment, are all calculated to interest every beholder in his favor, and to command veneration and respect. He is feared even when silent, and beloved even while we are unconscious of the motive.…In conversation, his Excellency's expressive countenance is peculiarly interesting and pleasing; a placid smile is frequently observed on his lips, but a loud laugh, it is said, seldom if ever escapes him. He is polite and attentive to each individual at table, and retires after the compliment of a few glasses."[30]

(4) John Bell (1779)

"General Washington is now in the forty-seventh year of his age; he is a tall well-made man, rather large boned, and has a tolerably genteel address: his features are manly and bold, his eyes of a bluish cast and very lively; his hair a deep brown, his face rather long and marked with the small pox; his complexion sun burnt and without much colour, and his countenance sensible, composed and thoughtful; there is a remarkable air of dignity about him, with a striking degree of gracefulness."[31]

(5) Baron Cromot Du Bourg (1781)

"General Washington came to see M. de Rochambeau. Notified of his approach, we mounted our horses and went out to meet him. He received us with that affability which is natural to him and depicted on his countenance. He is a very fine looking man, but did not surprise me as much as I expected from the descriptions I had heard of him. His physiognomy is noble in the highest degree, and his manners are those of one perfectly accustomed to society, quite a rare thing certainly in America."[32]

(6) Marquis De Chatellux (1781)

"In speaking of this perfect whole of which General Washington furnishes the idea, I have not excluded exterior form. His stature is noble and lofty, he is well made, and exactly proportionate; his physiognomy mild and agreeable, but such as to render it impossible to speak particularly of any of his features, so that in quitting him you have only the recollection of a fine face. He was neither a grave nor a familiar face, his brow is sometimes marked with thought, but he inspires confidence, and his smile is always the smile of benevolence."[33]

(7) Abbe Claude C. Robin (1781)

"Tall and noble stature, well proportioned a fine, cheerful, open countenance, a simple and modest carriage; and his whole mien has something in it that interests the French, the Americans, and even themselves in his favor."[34]

(8) Prince De Broglie 1782

"General Washing is now forty-nine years of age. He is tall, nobly built and very well proportioned. His face is much more agreeable than represented in his portrait. He must gave been much handsomer three years ago, and although the gentleman who have remained with him during all that time say that he seems to have grown much older, it is not to be denied that the general is still as fresh and active as a young man."[35]

(9) John Hunter (1785)

"The General is about six feet high, perfectly straight and well made; rather inclined to be lusty. His eyes are full and blue and seem to express an air of gravity. His nose incline to the aquiline; his mouth is small; his teeth are yet good and his cheeks indicate perfect health. His forehead is a noble one and he wears his hair turned back, without curls and quite in the officer's style, and typed in a long queue behind. Altogether he makes a most noble, respectable appearance, and I really think him the first man in the world.

"... When I was first introduced to him he was neatly dressed in a plain blue coat, white cassimir waistcoat, and black breeches and boots, as he came from his farm... The General came in again, with his hair neatly powdered, a clean shirt on, a new plain drab coat, white waistcoat and white silk stockings."[36]

(10) Jedidiah Morse (1789)

"General Washington in his person was tall, upright, and well made; in his manner easy and unaffected. His eyes were of a bluish cast no prominent, indicative of deep thoughtfulness, and when in action, on great occasions remarkably lively. His features strong, manly, commanding; his temper reserved and serious; his countenance grave, composed, and sensible. There was in his whole appearance an unusual dignity and gracefulness which at once secured him profound respect, and cordial esteem. He seemed born to command his fellow men."[37]

(11) Anonymous Briton (1790)

"It was not necessary to announce his name, for his peculiar appearance, his firm forehead, Roman nose, and a projection of the lower jaw, his height and figure, could not be mistaken by any one who had seen a full-length picture of him, and yet no picture accurately resembled him in the minute traits of his person. His features, however, were so marked by prominent characteristics, which appear in all likeness of him, that a stranger could not be mistaken in the man; he was remarkably dignified in his manners, and had an air of benignity over his features which his visitant did not expect, being rather prepared for sternness of countenance...his smile was extraordinarily attractive. It was observed to me that there was an expression in Washington's face that no painting had succeeded in taking. It struck me no man could be better formed for command. A stature of six feet, a robust, but well-proportioned frame, calculated to sustain fatigue, without that heaviness which generally attends great muscular strength, and abates active exertion, displayed bodily power of no mean standard. A light eye and full–the very eye of genius and reflection rather than of blind passionate impulse. His nose appeared thick, and though it befitted his other features, was too coarsely and strongly formed to be the handsomest of its class. His mouth was like no other that I ever saw; the lips firm and the under jaw seeming to grasp the upper with force, as if its muscles were in full action when he sat still."[38]

(12) Senator William Maclay (1791)

"In stature about six feet, with an unexceptionable make, but lax appearance. His frame would seem to want filling up. His motions rather slow than lively, though he showed no signs of having suffered by gout or rheumatism. His complexion pale, nay, almost cadaverous. His voice hollow and indistinct, owing, as I believe, to artificial teeth before his upper jaw, which occasions a flatness."[39]

(13) Jean Pierre Brissot De Warville (1791)

"You have often heard me blame M. Chastellux for putting too much sprightliness in the character he has drawn of his general. To give pretensions to the portrait of a man who has none is truly absurd. The General's goodness appears in his looks. They have nothing of that brilliancy which his officers found in them when he was at the head of his army; but in conversation they become animated. He has no characteristic traits in his figure, and this has rendered it always so difficult to describe it; there are few portraits which resemble him. All his answers are pertinent; he shows the utmost reserve, and it very diffident; but, at the same time, he is firm and unchanged in whatever he undertakes. His modesty must be astonishing, especially to a Frenchman."[40]

(14) Edward Thornton, of English Legation (1792)

"His person is tall and sufficiently graceful; his face well formed, his complexion rather pale, with a mild philosophic gravity in the expression of it. In his air and manner he displays much natural dignity; in his address he is cold, reserved, and even phlegmatic, though without the least appearance of haughtiness or ill-nature; it is the effect, I imagine, of constitutional diffidence. That cause and circumspection which form so striking and well known a feature in his military, and indeed, in his political character, is very strongly marked in his countenance, for his eyes retire inward (do you understand me?) and have nothing of fire animation or openness in their expression."[41]

(15) Henry Wansey (1795)

"The President in his person is tall and thin, but exact; rather of an engaging than a dignified presence. He appears very thoughtful, is slow in delivering himself, which occasions some to conclude him reserved, but it is rather, I apprehend, the effect of much thinking and reflection, for there is great appearance to me of affability and accommodation He was at this time in his sixty-third year... but he had very little the appearance of age, having been all his life long so exceeding temperate."[42]

(16) Isaac Weld (1797)

"His chest is full; and his limbs, though rather slender, well shaped and muscular. His head is small, in which respect he resembles the made of a great number of his countrymen. His eyes are of a light grey colour; and in proportion to the length of his face, his nose is long. Mr. Stewart, the eminent portrait painter, told me, that there were features in his face totally different from what he ever observed in that of any other human being; the sockets for the eyes, for instance, are larger than what he ever met with before, and the upper part of the nose broader. All his features, he observed, were indicative of the strongest and most ungovernable passions, and had he been born in the forests, it was his opinion the he would have been the fiercest man among the savage tribes."[43]

(17) Anonymous (1798)

"It was in the month of November, 1798, I first beheld the Father of his Country. It was very cold, the northwest wind blowing hard down the Potomac, at Georgetown, D. C. A troop of light-horse from Alexandria escorted him to the western bank of the river. The waves ran high and the boat which brought him over seemed to labor considerably. Several thousand people greeted his arrival with swelling hearts and joyful countenances; the military were drawn up in the long line to receive him; the officers, dressed in regimentals, did him homage. I was so fortunate as to walk by his side, and had a full view of him. Although only about ten years of age, the impression his person and manner then made on me is now perfectly revived. He was six feet one inch high, broad and athletic, with very large limbs, entirely erect and without the slightest tendency to stooping; his hair was white, and tied with a silk string, his countenance loft, masculine, and contemplative; his eye light gray. He was dressed in the clothes of a citizen, and over these blue surtout of the finest cloth. His weight must have been two hundred and thirty pounds, with no superfluous flesh, all was bone and sinew, and he walked like a soldier. Whoever has seen in the Patent Office at Washington, the dress he wore when resigning his commission as commander-in-chief, in December, 1783, at once perceives how large and magnificent was his frame. During the parade, something at a distance suddenly attracted his attention; his eye was instantaneously lighted up as with the lightning's flash. At this moment I see it marvelous animation, its glowing fire, exhibiting strong passion, controlled by deliberate reason.

"In the summer of 1799 I again saw the chief. He rode a purely white horse, seventeen hands high, well proportioned, of high spirit; he almost seemed conscious that he bore on his back the Father of his Country. He reminded me of the war-horse whose neck is clothed with thunder. I have seen some highly-accomplished rider, but not one of them approached Washington; he was perfect in this respect. Behind him, at the distance of perhaps forty yards, came Billy Lee, his body-servant, who had periled his life in many a field, beginning on the heights of Boston, in 1775, and ending in 1781, when Cornwallis surrendered, and the captive army, with unexpressible chagrin, laid down their arms at Yorktown. Billy rode a cream colored horse, of the finest-form, and his old Revolutionary cocked hat indicated that its owner had often heard the roar of cannon trying scenes. Billy was a dark mulatto. His master speaks highly of him in his will, and provides for his support."[44]

(18) Marquis de Lafayette (1824)

"The person of Washington, always graceful, dignified and commanding, showed to peculiar advantage when mounted; it inhibited, indeed, the very *beau ideal* of a perfect cavalier. The good Lafayette, during his last visit to America, delighted to discourse of the 'times that tried men's souls.' From the venerated friend of our country we derived a most graphic description of Washington and the field of battle. Lafayette said, 'At Monmouth I commanded a division, and, it may be supposed I was pretty well occupied; still I took time, to admire our beloved chief, who, mounted on a splendid charger, rode along the ranks amid the shouts of the soldiers cheering them by his voice and example, and restoring to our standard the fortunes of the fight. I thought then, as now,' continued Lafayette, 'that never had I beheld so *superb* a man.'"[45]

(19) George Washington Parke Custis (1826)

"General Washington, in the prime of life, stood six feet two inches and measured precisely six feet when attired for the grave. From the period of the Revolution, there was an evident bending in that frame so passing straight before, but the stoop is attributable rather to the care and toils of that arduous contest than to age; for his step was firm, and his carriage noble and commanding, long after the time when the physical properties of man are supposed to be in the wane.

"To a majestic height, was added correspondent breath and firmness, and his whole person was so cast in nature's finest mould as to resemble the classic remains of ancient statuary, where all the parts contribute to the purity and perfection of the whole.

"The power of Washington's arm was displayed in several memorable instances: in his throwing a stone from the bed of the stream to the top of the Natural Bridge; another over the Palisades in the Hudson, and yet another across the Rappahannock, at Fredericksburg. Of the article with which he spanned this bold and navigable stream, there are various accounts. We are assured that it was a piece of slate, fashioned to about the size and shape of a dollar, and which, sent by an arm so strong, not only spanned the river, but took the ground at least thirty yards on the other side. Numbers have since tried this feat, but none have cleared the water."[46]

(20) Judge Gibson

Judge Gibson in his reminiscences of the Whiskey Rebellion relates: "The rendezvous of the northern division, by far the strongest, was at Carlisle, where the President joined it as Commander-in-chief. Passing through the town without dismounting at the quarters proposed for him, he proceeded at once, under an escort of New Jersey dragoons, to the plain at the south of it, where ten thousand volunteers, the flower of the Delaware, New Jersey and Pennsylvania youth, were drawn up to be reviewed by him. Finer looking fellows were perhaps never brought into line; and their uniforms, arms and accoutrements were splendid. But the observed of all observers was Gen. Washington. Taking off his small revolutionary cocked hat, and letting it fall at his side with inimitable grace, he rode slowly along the front, receiving, with a puff of military pride, the salute of the regiments with drums and colors; of the officers with swords and spontoons; and of the private soldiers with presented arms. His eye appeared to fall on every man in the line; and every man in the line appeared to feel that it did so. No man ever sat so nobly in a saddle, and no man's presence was ever so dignified. To a boy, as the writer then was, it was an impressive spectacle, that review."[47]

III. DESCRIPTIONS OF WASHINGTON'S CHARACTER AND SERVICE BY HIS CONTEMPORARIES

Unless otherwise noted, all of these citations are also taken from Albert Bushnell Hart's, *Tributes to Washington, Pamphlet No. 3* (Washington, D.C.: George Washington Bicentennial Commission, 1931.) They are presented in chronological order.

A. As stated by Americans

(1) Delegate Patrick Henry (1774)

"When Patrick Henry was asked 'whom he thought the greatest man in Congress,' he replied: 'If you speak of eloquence, Mr. Rutledge of South Carolina is by far the greatest orator, but if you speak of solid information and sound judgment, Colonial Washington is unquestionably the greatest man on that floor.'"[48]

(2) Delegate Silas Deane (1775)

"General Washington will be with You soon, possibly by the Time You receive This. His Election was unanimous, his acceptance of the high Trust, modest and polite, his Character I need not enlarge on but will only say to his honor, that he is said to be as fixed and resolute in having his Orders on all Occasion executed, as he is cool and deliberate, in giving them."[49]

(3) President John Hancock (1775)

"The Congress have appointed George Washington, Esqr., General and Commander in Chief of the Continental Army. His Commission is made out and I shall Sign it to morrow. He is a Gentleman you will all like. I submit to you the propriety of providing a suitable place for his Residence and the mode of his Reception. Pray tell Genl. Ward of this with my Respects, and that we all Expect to head that the Military Movements of the Day of his Arrival will be such as to do him and the Commander in Chief great honour....General

Washington will set out in a few Days. ...Pray do him every honour. By all means have his Commission read at the head of the whole Forces."[50]

(4) Delegate John Adams (1775, 1776)

"I can now inform you that the Congress has made choice of the modest and virtuous, the amiable, generous and brave George Washington, Esquire to be General of the American army, and that he is to repair, as soon as possible, to the camp before Boston. This appointment will have a great effect in cementing and securing the union of these colonies.

"There is something charming to me in the conduct of Washington. A gentleman of one of the first fortunes upon the continent, leaving his delicious retirement, his family and friends, sacrificing his ease, and hazarding all in the cause of his country! His views are noble and disinterested. He declared, when he accepted the mighty trust, that he would lay before us an exact account of his expenses, and not accept a shilling for pay.

"I congratulate you, Sir, as well as all the Friends of Mankind on the Reduction of Boston, an event which appeared to me of so great and decisive importance, that the next Morning after the Arrival of the News, I did myself the honour to move, for the Thanks of Congress to your Excellency and that a Medal of God Should be Struck in commemoration of it. Congress have been pleased to appoint me, with two other Gentlemen to prepare a Device."[51]

(5) General Nathanael Greene (1775, 1776)

"His Excellency, General, has arrived amongst us, universally admired. Joy was visible on every countenance, and it seemed as if the spirit of conquest breathed through the whole army. I hope we shall be taught, to copy his example, and to prefer the love of liberty, in this time of public danger to all the soft pleasures of domestic life, and support ourselves with manly fortitude amidst all the dangers and hardships that attend a state of war. And I doubt not, under the General's wise direction, we shall establish such excellent order and strictness of discipline as to invite victory to attend him wherever he goes.

"Greater powers must be lodged in the hands of the General than he has ever yet exercised....I can assure you that the General will not exceed his powers, though he may sacrifice the cause. There never was a man that might be more safely trusted, nor a time when there was a louder call."[52]

(6) Delegate Robert Morris (1777)

"Remember, my good Sir, that few men can keep their feelings to themselves, and that it is necessary for example's sake that all leaders should feel and think boldly in order to inspirit others, who look up to them. Heaven, no doubt for the noblest purposes, has blessed you with a firmness of mind, steadiness of countenance, and patience in sufferings, that give you infinite advantages over other men. This being the case, you are not to depend on other people's exertions being equal to your own. One mind feeds and thrives on misfortunes by finding resources to get the better of them; another sinks under their weight, thinking, it impossible to resist; and, as the latter description probably includes the majority of mankind, we must be cautious of alarming them."[53]

(7) Delegate Abraham Clark (1777)

"I believe the General is honest, but I think him fallible."[54]

(8) An Officer (1777)

"Our army love their General very much, but they have one things against him, which is the little care he take so himself in any action. His personal bravery, and the desire he has of animating his troops by example, make him fearless of danger. This occasions us much uneasiness. But Heaven, which has hitherto been his shield, I hope will still continue to guard so valuable a life."[55]

(9) Colonel Alexander Hamilton (1778)

"The general I always revered and loved ever since I knew him, but in this instance he rose superior to himself. Every lip dwells on his praise, for even his pretended friends (for none dare to acknowledge themselves his enemies) are obliged to croak it forth."[56]

(10) Ex-Minister Governeur Morris (1779)

"Born to high destinies, he was fashioned for them by the hand of nature. His form was noble—his port majestic. On his front were enthroned the virtues which exalt, and those which adorn the human character. So dignified his deportment, no man could approach him but with respect—none was great in his presence. You have all seen him, and you all have felt the reverence he inspired....His judgment was always clear, because his mind was pure. And seldom, if ever, will a sound understanding be met in the company of a corrupt heart.... In him were the courage of a soldier, the intrepidity of a chief, the fortitude of a hero. He had given to the impulsions of bravery all the calmness of his character, and, if in the moment of danger, his manner was distinguishable from that of common life, it was by superior ease and grace.... Knowing how to appreciate the world, its gifts and glories, he was truly wise. Wise also in selecting the objects of his pursuit. And wise in adopting just means to compass honorable ends."[57]

(11) John Bell (1779)

"He has an excellent understanding without much quickness; is strictly just vigilant, and generous; an affectionate husband, a faithful friend, a father to the deserving soldier; gentle in his manners, in temper rather reserved; a total stranger to religious prejudice, which have so often excited Christians of one denomination to cut the throats of those of another; in his morals irreproachable; he was never known to exceed the bounds of the most rigid temperance; in a word, all his friends and acquaintances universally allow, that no man ever united in his own person a more perfect alliance of the virtues of a philosopher with the talents of a general. Candour, sincerity, affability, and simplicity, seem to be the striking features of his character, till an occasion offers of displaying the more determined bravery and independence of spirit. General Washington having never been to Europe, could not possibly have seen much military service when the armies of Britain were sent to subdue us; yet still, for a variety of reasons, he was by much the most proper man on this continent, and probably any where else, to be placed at the head of an American army. The very high estimation he stood in for integrity and honour, his engaging in the cause of his country from sentiment and a conviction of her wrongs, his moderation in politics, his extensive property, and his approved abilities as a commander, were motives which necessarily obliged the choice of America to fall upon him."[58]

(12) Delegate Alexander Hamilton (1783)

"The Commander was already become extremely unpopular, among almost all ranks from his known dislike to every unlawful proceeding; that this unpopularity was daily increasing and industriously promoted by many leading characters; that his choice of unfit and indiscreet persons into his family was the pretext, and with some the real motive; but the substantial one, a desire to displace him from the respect and confidence of the army, in order to substitute General [not listed in source], as the conductor of their efforts to obtain justice. Mr. Hamilton said that he knew General Washing[ton] intimately and perfectly; that his extreme reserve, mixed sometimes with a degree of asperity of temper, both of which were said to have increased of late, had contributed to the decline of his popularity; but that his virtue, his patriotism and firmness, would, it might be depended upon, never yield to any dishonorable or disloyal plans into which he might be called; that he would suffer himself to be cut to pieces."[59]

(13) William Paulett Cary (1789)

"A stranger to profusion, yet generous in every instance where liberality was a virtue; during the late troubles, his fortune was employed in succoring merit, rewarding bravery, promoting discipline in the soldiery, and subordination to the new established government, in the citizens. At a time when the calamities incident to a state of civil warfare, fell heavy on all ranks, but principally on the middle class of his countrymen, his beneficence, which seemed to shun the public eye, would in all probability be lost in oblivion, but for the voice of those whom he freed from the accumulated miseries of famine, sickness, and imprisonment.

"In whatever light we view the character of this truly great man we are struck with fresh cause for esteem and admiration: we every moment discover new and shining traits of humanity, of wisdom, and disinterested heroism: we see united to him the distinguished virtues of a good citizen, an experienced general, an upright senator, and a wise politician; we behold him rising superior to every mean consideration of self-love, hazarding his fortunes in the cause of freedom, cheerfully submitting to bear the name of rebel, and braving an ignominious death, to which he would inevitably have fallen a sacrifice, had Britain triumphed in the contest: we behold him furnishing an example the most interesting to humanity, and capable of nerving the palsied arm of age, or even of cowardice itself…"[60]

(14) Jedidiah Morse (1789)

"It is hoped posterity will be taught, in what manner he transformed an undisciplined body of peasantry into a regular army of soldiers. Commentaries on his campaigns would undoubtedly be highly interesting and instructive to future generation. The conduct of the first campaign, in compelling the British troops to abandon Boston by a bloodless victory, will merit minute narration. But a volume would scarcely contain the mortifications he experienced and the hazards to which he was exposed in 1776 and 1777, in contending against the prowess of Britain, with an inadequate force. His good destiny and consummate prudence prevented want of success from producing want of confidence on the part of the public; for want of success is apt to lead to the adoption of pernicious counsels through the levity of the people or the ambition of their demagogues."[61]

(15) Governor and Council of North Carolina (1790)

"We congratulate ourselves with equal sincerity in beholding you, Sir, in the high department which your virtues merited, and to which your country unanimously and gratefully appointed you. The importance of your situation receives additional dignity by the veneration your Country possesses for your character, and from a confidence that every power vested in you by the Constitution will be exerted for the happiness and prosperity of our country.... We have just received the happy information of your recovery from a disorder which threatened your life; a life we may truly say as necessary as dear to us:—With grateful hearts we return thanks to the great Disposer of event for this beneficent mark of his attention in preserving you. May it long be shewn in continuing you among us, and when the awful day comes which is to separate you from us, may you receive the reward of those virtues, which he only can give."[62]

(16) William Sullivan (1797)

"The following are recollections of Washington, derived from repeated opportunities of seeing him during the last three years of his public life. He was over six feet in stature; of strong, bony, muscular frame, without fulness of covering, well formed and straight. He was a man of most extraordinary physical strength. In his own house his action was calm, deliberate, and dignified, without pretension to gracefulness, or peculiar manner, but merely natural, and such as one would think it should be in such a man. When walking in the street, his movement had not the soldierly air which might be expected. His habitual motion had been formed before he took command of the American armies, in the wars of the interior, and in the surveying of wilderness lands, employments in which grace and elegance were not likely to be acquired. At the age of sixty-five, time had done nothing toward bending him out of his natural erectness. His deportment was invariably grave; it was sobriety that stopped short of sadness. His presence inspired a veneration, and a feeling of awe, rarely experienced in the presence of any man. His mode of speaking was slow and deliberate, not as though he was in search of fine words, but that he might utter those only adapted to his purpose. It was the usage of all persons in good society to attend Mrs. Washington's levee every Friday evening. He was always present. The young ladies used to throng around him, and engaged him in conversations. There were some of the well-remembered belles of that day who imagined themselves to be favorites with him. As these were the only opportunities which they had of conversing with him, they were disposed to use them. One would think that a gentleman and a gallant soldier, if he could ever laugh or dress his countenance in smiles, would do so when surrounded by young and admiring beauties. But this was never so; the countenance of Washington was never softened; nor changed in habitual gravity. One who had lived always in his family said, that his manner in public life was always the same. Being asking whether Washington could laugh: this person said, that this was a rare occurrence, but one instance was remembered when he laughed most heartily at her narration of an incident in which she was a party concerned; and in which he applauded her agency. The late General Cobb, who was long a member of his family during the war, (and who enjoyed a laugh as much as any man could,) said, that he never saw Washington laugh, expecting when Colonel Scammel (if this was the person) came to dine at headquarters. Scammel had a fund of ludicrous anecdotes, and a manner of telling them, which relaxed even the gravity of the commander-in-chief."[63]

(17) President John Adams (1799)

"I have seen him in the days of adversity, in some of the scenes of his deepest distress and most trying perplexities; I have also attended him in his highest elevation and most prosperous felicity; with uniform admiration of his wisdom, moderation, and constancy.

"...Malice could never blast his honour, and envy made her a singular exception to her universal rule. For himself he had lived enough, to life and to glory. For his fellow-citizens, if their prayers could have been answered, he would have been immortal. For me, his departure is at a most unfortunate moment....His example is now complete, and it will teach wisdom and virtue to magistrates, citizens, and men, not only in the present age, but in future generations, as long as our history shall be read."[64]

(18) Representative Henry Lee (1799)

"Will you go with me to the banks of the Monongahela, to see your youthful Washington, supporting, in the dismal hour of Indian victory, the ill fated Braddock; and saving by his judgment and his valour; the remains of a defeated army, pressed by the conquering savage foe? or, when—oppressed America nobly resolving to risk her all in defense of her violated rights—he was elevated by the unanimous voice of Congress to the command of her armies?...

"Who is there that has forgotten the vales of Brandywine—the fields of Germantown—or the plains of Monmouth? Every where present, wants of every kind obstructing, numerous and valiant armies encountering, himself a host, he assuaged our sufferings, limited our privations, and upheld our tottering Republic...

"Possessing a clear and penetrating mind, a strong and sound judgment, calmness and temper for deliberation, with invincible firmness and perseverance in resolution maturely formed, drawing information from all, acting for himself, with incorruptible integrity and unvarying patriotism: his own superiority and the public confidence alike marked him as the man designed by heaven to lead in the great political as well as military events which have distinguished the era of his life...

"First in war, first in peace, and first in the hearts of his countrymen, he was second to none in the humble and endearing scenes of private life: Pious, just, humane, temperate, and sincere; uniform, dignified, and commanding; his example was as edifying to all around him as were the effects of that example lasting.

"To his equals he was condescending; to his inferiors kind, and to the dear object of his effection exemplarily tender: Correct throughout, vice shuddered in his presence, and virtue always felt his fostering hand; the purity of his private character gave effulgence to his public virtues.... Such was the man for whom our nation mourns."[65]

(19) Representative John Marshall (1799)

"Our Washington is no more! The Hero, the Sage and Patriot of America— the man on whom in times of danger, every eye was turned, and all hopes were placed – lives now, only in his own great actions, and in the hearts of an affectionate and afflicted people....

"More than any other individual, and as much as to one individual was possible, has he contributed to found this our wide spreading empire, and to give the western world its independence and it freedom...

"Having effected the great object for which he was placed at the head of our armies, we have seen him convert the sword into the plowshare, and voluntarily sinking the soldier in the citizen....

"We have seen him once more quit the retirement he loved, and in a season more stormy and tempestuous than war itself, with calm and wise determination, pursue the true interests of the nation and contribute, more than any other could contribute, to the establishment of that system of policy which will, I trust, yet preserve our peace, our honour and our independence."[66]

(20) Senate of the United States (1799)

"With patriotic pride, we review the life of our Washington, and compare him with those of other countries who have been pre-eminent in fame. Ancient and modern names are diminished before him. Greatness and guilt have too often been allied; but his fame is whiter than it is brilliant. The destroyers of nations stood abashed at the majesty of his virtue. It reproved the intemperance of their ambition, and darkened the splendor of victory....Let his countrymen consecrate the memory of the heroic General, the patriotic Statesman, and the virtuous Sage; let them teach their children never to forget that the fruit of his labours and his example are their inheritance."[67]

(21) President Smith and New Jersey College (1800)

"Washington was always equal to himself. There was a dignity in the manner in which he performed the smallest things. A majesty surrounded him that seemed to humble those who approached him, at the same time that here was a benignity in his manner that invited their confidence and esteem. His virtues, always elevated and splendid, shone only with a milder light by being placed in the vale of retirement. He was sincere, modest, upright, humane; a friend of religion; the idol of his neighbors as well as of his country; magnificent in his hospitality, but plain in his manners, and simple in his equipage...."[68]

(22) Representative Fisher Ames (1800)

"However his military fame may excite the wonder of mankind, it is chiefly by his civil magistracy that his example will instruct them. Great generals have arisen in all ages of the world, and perhaps most in those of despotism and darkness. In times of violence and convulsion, they rise by the force of the whirlwind, high enough to ride in it, and direct the storm....But such a Chief Magistrate as Washington appears like the pole star in a clear sky, to direct the skilful statesman. His presidency will form an epoch, and be distinguished as the age of Washington. Already it assumes its high place in the political region. Like the milky way, it whitens along its allotted portion of the hemisphere. The latest generations of men will survey through the telescope of history."[69]

(23) Tutor Ebenezer Grant Marsh of Yale (1800)

"Resolute and undejected in misfortunes, he rose superior to distresses, and surmounted difficulties, which no courage, no constancy, but his own, would have resisted. His letters during his most gloomy prospects, announce a hero, conscious of his danger, but still deriving a well grounded hope from the resources of his own mind. His valor was never unequal to his duty or the occasion. He attempted things with means that appeared totally inadequate, and successfully prosecuted what he had boldly resolved. He was never disheartened by difficulties, but had that vigor of mind, which, instead of bending to opposition, rises above it, and seems to have a power of controlling even fortune itself. His character combined a cool and penetrating judgment and prompt decision, caution and intrepidity, patience and enterprise, generous tenderness and compassion, with undaunted heroism....

"In no situation did Washington appear more truly great than at the helm of our federal government. Here he displayed an astonishing extent and precision of political integrity, an incorruptible heart, a constant attention to the grand principles of rational liberty, and an invariable attachment to his country. His genius was equal to the most enlarged views, and minute details, of civil policy. A vigorous mind, improved by the experience and study of mankind, dexterity and application in business, a judicious mixture of liberality and economy. Steadiness to pursue his ends, and flexibility to vary his means, marked his administration. He guided the passions of others, because he was master of his own."[70]

(24) Chief Justice John Marshall (1804)

"The day finally came when his work was finished, and he could be, as he phrased it, 'translated into a private citizen.' Marshall describes the scene as follows: 'At noon, the principal offices of the army assembled at France's [sic] tavern; soon after which, their beloved commander entered the room. His emotions were too strong to be concealed. Filling a glass, he turned to them and said, 'With a heart full of love and gratitude, I now take leave of you: I most devoutly wish that your latter days may be as prosperous and happy, as your former ones have been glorious and honorable.'

"Having drunk, he added: 'I cannot come to each of you to take my leave; but shall be obliged to you, if each of you will come and take me by the hand.' General Knox, being nearest, turned to him. Incapable of utterance, Washington grasped his hand and embraced him. In the same affectionate manner he took leave of each succeeding officer. In every eye was the tear of dignified sensibility, and not a word was articulated to interrupt the majestic silence, and the tenderness of the scene."[71]

(25) Timothy Pickering (1811)

"To the excellency of his virtues I am not disposed to set any limits. All his views were upright, all his actions just."[72]

(26) Ex-President Thomas Jefferson (1814)

"His mind was great and powerful, with out being of the very first order; his penetration strong, though not so acute as that of Newtown, Bacon, or Locke; and as far as he saw, no judgment was ever sounder. It was slow in operation, being little aided by invention or imagination, but sure in conclusion. Hence the common remark of his officers, or the advantage he derived from councils of war, where, hearing all suggestions, he selected whatever was best; and certainly no general ever planned his battles more judiciously. But if deranged during the course of the action, if any member of his plan was dislocated by sudden circumstances, he was slow in a readjustment. The consequence was, that he often failed in the field, and rarely against an enemy in station, as at Boston and York. He was incapable of fear, meeting personal dangers with the calmest unconcern. Perhaps the strongest feature in his character was prudence, never acting until every circumstance, every consideration, was maturely weighed; refraining if he saw a doubt, but, when once decided, going through with his purpose, whatever obstacles opposed. His integrity was most pure, his justice the most inflexible I have ever known, no motives of interest or consanguinity, of friendship or hatred, being able to bias his decision. He was a good, and a great man. His temper was naturally irritable and high-toned; but reflection and resolution had obtained a firm and habitual ascendancy over it. If ever, however, it broke its bonds, he was most tremendous in his wrath...

"On the whole his character was in its mass, perfect, in nothing bad, in few points indifferent; and it may truly be said that never did nature and fortune combine more perfectly to make a man great, and to place him in the same constellation with whatever worthies have merited from man an everlasting remembrance. For his was the singular destiny and merit of leading the armies of his country successfully thought as arduous war, for the establishment of its independence; of conducting its councils through the birth of a government, new in its forms and principles, until it had settled down into a quiet and orderly train; and of scrupulously obeying the laws through the whole of his career, civil and military, of which the history of the world furnishes no other example."[73]

B. Washington's Character as Described by Internationals

(1) Phillips Callbeck (1775)

[American armed vessels took prisoners on the island and St. John's and pillaged defenseless inhabitants. Such conduct, however, could not fail to excite the indignation of the Commander-in-chief, and he released the captives immediately, and orders were given for restoring the goods. The following note was written by Mr. Callbeck, one of the captured officials.]

"I should ill deserve the generous treatment, which your excellency have been pleased to show me, had I not gratitude to acknowledge so great a favor. I cannot ascribe any part of it to my own merit, but must impute the whole to the philanthropy and humane disposition, that so truly characterize General Washington. Be so obliging, therefore, as to accept the only return in my power, that of my grateful thanks."[74]

(2) Peter S. Du Poncheau (1778)

"General Washington received the Baron [Steuben] with great cordiality, and to me he showed much condescending attention. I cannot describe the impression that the first sight of that great man made upon me. I could not keep my eyes from that imposing countenance – grave, yet not severe; affable, without familiarity. Its predominant expression was calm dignity, through which you could trace the strong feelings of the patriot, and discern the father as well as the commander of his soldiers. I have never seen a picture that represents him to me as I saw him at Valley Forge, and during the campaigns in which I had the honor to follow him. Perhaps that expression was beyond the skill of the painter; but while I live it will remain impressed on my memory. I had frequent opportunities of seeing him, as it was my duty to accompany the Baron when he dined with him, which was sometimes twice or thrice in the same week."[75]

(3) "American Gentleman Now In London" (1779)

"General Washington, altho' advanced in years, is remarkably healthy, takes a great deal of exercise, and is very fond of riding on a favorite white horse; he is very reserved, and loves retirement. When out of camp he is only a single servant attending him, and when he returns within the lines a few of the light horse escort him to his tent. When he has any great object in view he sends for a few of the officers of whose abilities he has a high opinion, and states his present plan among half a dozen others, to all which they give their separate judgments: by these means he gets all their opinions, without divulging his intentions. He has no tincture of pride, and will often converse with a centinel with more freedom than he would with a general officer. He is very shy and reserved to foreigners, altho' they have letters of recommendation, from the Congress. He punishes neglect of duty with great severity, but is very tender and indulgent to recruits until they learn the articles of war and their exercise perfectly. He has a great antipathy to spies, although he employs them himself, and has an utter aversion to all Indians. He regularly attends divine service in his tent every morning and evening, and seems very fervent in his prayers. He is so tender-hearted, that no soldiers must be flogged nigh his tent, or if he is walking in the camp, and sees a man tied to the halberds, he will either order him to be taken down, or walk another way to avoid his sight. He has made the art of war his particular study; his plans are in general good and well digested; he is particularly careful always securing a retreat, but his chief qualifications are steadiness, perseverance, and secrecy; any act of bravery he is sure to reward, and make a short eulogium on the occasion to the person and his fellow soldiers (if it be a soldier) in the ranks. He is humane to the prisoners who fall into his hands, and orders everything necessary for their relief. He is very temperate in his diet, and the only luxury he indulges himself in, is a few glasses of punch after supper."[76]

(4) Minster Conrad A. Gerard (1779)

"I have had many conversations with General Washington....I have formed as high an opinion of the powers of his mind, his moderation, his patriotism, and his virtues, as I had before from common report conceived of his military talents and of the incalculable services he has rendered to his country."[77]

(5) Count Axel De Fersen (1780)

"I was at Hartford,...with M. de Rochambeau.... M. de sent me in advance, to announce his arrival, and I had time to see the man, illustrious, if not unique in our century. His handsome and majestic, while at the same time mild and open countenance perfectly reflects his moral qualities; he looks the hero; he is very cold; speaks little, but is courteous and frank. A shade of sadness overshadows his countenance, which is not unbecoming, and gives him an interesting air."[78]

(6) Claude Blanchard (1781)

"This day General Washington, who was expected, arrived [at Newport] about two o'clock. He first went to the *Duc de Burgoyne*, where all our generals were. He then landed; all the troops were under arms; I was presented to him. His face is handsome, noble and mild. He is tall (at the least, five feet, eight inches). In the evening, I was at supper with him. I mark as a fortunate day, that in which I have been able to behold a man so truly great."[79]

(7) Marquis De Chastellux (1781)

"I wish only to express the impression General Washington has left on my mind; the idea of a perfect whole, that cannot be the produce of enthusiasm, which rather would reject it since the effect of proportion is to diminish the idea of greatness. Brave without temerity, laborious without ambition, generous without prodigality, noble without pride, virtuous without severity; he seems always to have confined himself within those limits, where the virtues by clothing themselves in more lively, but more changeable and doubtful colours, may be mistake for faults. This is the seventh year that he has commanded the army, and that he has obeyed the Congress; more need not be said, especially in America, where know how to appreciate all the merit contained in this simple fact. ...

"It will be said of him, AT THE END OF A LONG CIVIL WAR. HE HAD NOTHING WITH WHICH HE COULD REPROACH HIMSELF. If anything can be more marvelous than such a character, it is unanimity of the public suffrages in his favour. Soldiers, magistrates, people, all love and admire him; all speak of him in terms of tenderness and veneration. Does there then exist a virtue capable of restraining the injustice of mankind; or are glory and happiness too recently established in America, for Envy to have deigned to pass the seas?"[80] (emphasis in original. "Civil War" here refers to the American Revolution)

(8) Abbe Claude C. Robin (1781)

"He has ever shown himself superior to fortune, and in the most trying adversity has discovered resource till then unknown; and, as if his abilities only increased and dilated at the prospect of difficulty, he is never better supplied than when he seems destitute of everything, nor have his arms ever been so fatal to his enemies, as at the very instant when they thought they had crushed him for ever...

"Old men, women, and children, press about him when he accidentally passes along, and think themselves happy, once in their lives, to have seen him – they follow him through the towns with torches, and celebrate his arrival by public illuminations. The Americans, that cool and sedate people, who in the midst of their most trying difficulties, have attended only to the directions and impulses of plain method and common sense, are roused, animated, and inflamed at the very mention of his name: and the first songs that sentiment or gratitude has dictated, have been to celebrate General Washington."[81]

(9) Chevalier de Silly (1781)

"Man is born with a tendency to pride and the further he progresses in his career in an elevated rank the more his self love nourishes this vice in him but so far this Washington although born with every superior quality adds to them an imposing modesty which will always cause him to be admired by those who have the good fortune to see him; as for esteem he has already drawn to himself that of all Europe even the heart of his enemies and ours— 'tandemoculi nostril, videuntur honorem et virtutem.'"[82] [at last, all our eyes will see honor and virtue]

(10) Prince De Broglie (1782)

"His physiognomy is mild and open. His accost cold although polite. His pensive eyes seem more attentive than sparkling; but their expression is benevolent, noble and self-possessed. In his private conduct, he preserves that polite and attentive good breeding which satisfies everybody, and that dignified reserve which offends no one. He is a foe to ostentation and to vain-glory. His temple is always even. He has never testified the least humor. Modest even to humility, he does not seem to estimate himself at his true worth. He receives with perfect grace all the homages which are paid him, but he evades rather than seeks them...

"Mr. Washington's first military services were against the French in the War for Canada. He has no opportunity for distinguishing himself, and after the defeat of Braddock, the war having crossed the river St. Lawrence, and the Virginia militia of which he was a Colonel having been sent home, he was not kept in active service; whereupon he retired to his plantation where he lived like a philosopher.

"His estate was quite distant from the seat of the English government, the real hotbed of the insurrection; and his wise character withheld him still further from mixing in its movements, so that he had but little share in the first troubles.

"On the breaking out of hostilities with the mother-country, every body wished a chief who joined a profound sagacity to the advantage of having had military experience. All eyes turned toward Washington, and he was unanimously called to the command of the army. The course of events justified the choice. Never was there a man better fitted to command the Americans, and his conduct throughout developed the greatest foresight, steadiness and wisdom."[83]

(11) Joseph Mandrillon (1782)

"Imposing in size, noble and well proportioned, a countenance open, calm and sedate, but without any one striking feature, and when you depart from him, the remembrance only of a fine man will remain, a fine figure, an exterior plain and modest, a pleasing address, firm without severity, a manly courage, an uncommon capacity for grasping the whole scope of a subject, and a complete experience in war and politics; equally useful in the cabinet and in the field of Mars, the idol of his country, the admiration of the enemy he has fought and vanquished; modest in victory, great in the reverse; why do I say the reverse! Very far from being subdued he has made every misfortune contribute to his success. He knows how to obey as well as command, he never made use of his power or the submission of his army to derogate from the authority of his country or to disobey its commands."[84]

(12) Comte de Segur (1782)

"One of my most earnest wishes was to see Washington, the hero of America. He was then encamped at a short distance from us, and the Count de Rochambeau was kind enough to introduce me to him. Too often reality disappoints the expectations our imagination had raised, and admiration diminishes by a too near view upon which it has been bestowed; but, on seeing General Washington, I found a perfect similarity between the impression produced upon me by his aspect, and the idea I had formed of him. His exterior disclosed, as it were, the history of his life: simplicity, grandeur, dignity, calmness, goodness, firmness, the attributes of his character, where also stamped upon his features, and in all his person. His stature was noble and elevated; the expression of his features mild and benevolent; his smile graceful and pleasing; his manners simple, without familiarity....Washington, when I him, was forty-nine years of age. He endeavored modestly to avoid the marks of admiration and respect which were so anxiously offered to him, and yet no man ever knew better how to receive and to acknowledge them. He listened, with an obliging attention, to all those who addressed him, and the expression of his countenance had conveyed his answer before he spoke."[85]

(13) Chevalier Anne C. de la Luzerne (1784)

"The estate of General Washington not being more than fifteen leagues from Annapolis I accepted an invitation that he gave me to go and pass several days there, and it is from his house that I have the honor to write to you. After having seen him on my arrival on this continent, in the midst of his camp and in the tumult of arms, I have the pleasure to see him a simple citizen, enjoying in the repose of his retreat the glory which he so justly acquired....He dresses in a gray coat like a Virginia farmer, and nothing about him recalls the recollections of the important part which he has played except the great number of foreigners who come to see him."[86]

(14) Charles Varlo (1784)

"I crossed the river from Maryland into Virginia, near the renowned General Washington's, where I had the honour to spend some time, and was kindly entertained with that worthy family. As to the General, if we may judge by the countenance, he is what the world says of him, a shrewd, good-natured, plain, humane man, about fifty-five years of age, and seems to wear well, being healthful and active, straight, well made, and about six feet high. He keeps a good table, which is always open to those of a genteel appearance. He does not use many Frenchified *congees* [formal bows as part of a ceremonial departure] or flattering useless words without meaning, which savours more of deceit than an honest heart; but on the contrary, his words seem to point at truth and reason, and to spring from the fountain of a heart, which being have every one's good word, and those are—the Queen of England and General Washington, which I never heard friend or foe speak slightly of."[87]

(15) Jean Pierre Brissot De Warville (1791)

"He shows the utmost reserve, and is very diffident; but at the same time, he is firm and unchangeable in whatever he undertakes. His modesty must be very astonishing, especially to a Frenchman. He speaks of the American war as if he had not directed it; and of his victories with an indifference which strangers even would not affect. I never saw him divest himself of that coolness by which he is characterized, and become warm but when speaking of the present stat of America ... He spoke to me of M. La Fayette with tenderness. He regarded him as his son; and foresaw with a joy mixed with anxiety, the part he was about to play in the revolution preparing in France."[88]

(16) Member of Parliament Charles James Fox (1794)

"And here, Sir, I cannot help alluding to the President of the United States, General Washington, a character whose conduct has been so different from that, which has been pursued by the ministers of this country. How infinitely wiser must appear the spirit and principles manifested in his late address to Congress, than the policy of modern European courts! Illustrious man, deriving honor less from the splendor of his situation than from the dignity of his mind; before whom all borrowed greatness sinks into significance, and all the potentates of Europe (excepting the members of our own royal family) become little and contemptible! He has had no occasion to have recourse to any tricks of policy or arts of alarm; his authority has been sufficiently supported by the same means by which it was acquired, and his conduct has uniformly been characterized by wisdom, moderation and firmness."[89]

(17) Henry Wansey (1794)

"I confess, I was struck with awe and veneration, when I recollected that I was now in the presence of one of the greatest men upon earth—the GREAT WASHINGTON- the noble and wise benefactor of the world!...Whether we view him as a general in the field vested with unlimited authority and power, at the head of the victorious army; or in the cabinet, as the President of the United States; or as a private gentleman, cultivating his own farm; he is still the same great man, anxious only to discharge with propriety the duties of his relative situation. His conduct has always been so uniformly manly, honorable, just, patriotic, and disinterested, that his greatest enemies cannot fix on any one trait of his character that can deserve the least censure."[90]

(18) Louis, Count de Fontanes (1800)

"The people who so lately stigmatized Washington as a rebel, regard even the enfranchisement of America, as one of the events consecrated by history and past ages. Such is the veneration excited by great characters. He seems so little to belong to modern times, that he imparts to us the same vivid impressions as the most august examples of antiquity with all that they accomplished. His work is scarcely finished when it at once attracts the veneration which we freely accord to those achievements only that are consecrated by time. The American Revolution, the contemporary of our own, is fixed forever. Washington began it with energy, and finished it with moderation. He knew how to maintain it, pursuing always the prosperity of his country; and this aim alone can justify at the tribunal of the Most High, enterprises so extraordinary."[91]

"His administration was as mild and firm in internal affairs as it was noble and prudent toward foreign nations. He uniformly respected the usages of other countries, as he would desire the rights of Americans to be respected by them. Thus in all his negotiations, the heroic simplicity of the President of the United States, without elevation or debasement, was brought into communication with the majesty of the Kings. He sought not in his administration those conceptions which the age calls great, but which he regarded as vain. His ideas were more sage than bold; he sought not admiration, but he always enjoyed esteem, alike in the field and in the Senate, in the midst of business as in the quiet of retirement."

(19) Francis Adrian van der Kemp (1800)

"Washington's character was from his first entrance in public life through its whole course not only unimpeached but highly revered by all, who were admitted to his acquaintance. His active prudence was guided by his intrepid courage:—his vigilant mind, never appalled in the most distressing emergence, was always enliven'd by a manly devotion, and all these virtues, with a vivid sense of his own intrinsic value, were only equaled by his modesty. Remembering that he was a man, Washington made every reasonable allowance for the frailties of human nature, pardon'd its weaknesses, and pity'd her follies, as often they were not blackened by vices, or the Public welfare did not require the infliction of a severer punishment….

"We wrong this eminent man M. H.! [my hearers] in considering him along as a General. Washington's claims, as a statesman, on our on Posterity's respectful regard, are equally solid. We Americans, assent with all heart to this self-evident truth. Let Foreigners –to appreciate the solidity of our judgment, consider maturely Washington's admonitions – when he divested himself of the supreme command—dijudicate our Constitution, as a part of his egregious workmanship, and scrutinize his letter to the Individual states, as President of the Convention, and none of them will longer hesitate to go over in the steps of Columbia's sons. A constitution is adopted, and Washington unanimously chosen President of the United States. Here once more this great and good man sacrifices the delights of his retirement to the toils of a laborious life, for the benefit of his Country—with the same inimitable disinterestedness. What a large—what an immense field of glory for him, or stupefying amazement for us see I here opening!

"The sight of General in his brightest glory is lost in the radiance of this new Politic Luminary. Mine eyes are weakening—dedimmed—bedewed, but my heart in the same moment joyfully expanded by its benign all vivifying influence."[92]

(20) Peter Ivanovitch Poletica (1812)

"All the life of this man, worthy of eternal praise, can be compared to the cleanest of looking glasses. If one can not say that he was always above the situation he occupied, one can however assert that in any case he was always adequate to it. In his private life, Gen. Washington was always a loving husband, ardent and steadfast friend, a just master and a pious Christian."[93]

(21) Lord Byron (1818-1821)

"Can tyrants but by tyrants conquer'd be, And freedom fin not champion and no child

Such as Columbia saw arise when she Sprung forth a Pallas, arm'd and undefiled?

"Or must such minds be nourish'd in the wild,

Deep in the unpruned forest 'midst the roar

Of cataracts, where nursing Nature smiled On infant Washington? Has Earth no more

Such seeds within her breat, or Europe no such shore?

"Not so Leonidas and Washington, Whose every battle-field is holy ground,

Which breathes of nations saved, not worlds undone.

How sweetly on the ear such echoes sound!

While the mere victor's may appal or stun

The servile and the vain, such names will be a watchword till the future shall be free.

"Great men have always scorn'd great recompenses; ...

George Washing had thanks and nought beside,

Except the all-cloudless glory (which few men's is)

To free his country."

"While Franklin's quiet memory climbs to Heaven,

956

"Calming the lightning which he thence had riven,
Or drawing from the no less kindled earth
Freedom and peace to that which boast his birth;
While Washington's a watchword, such as ne'er
Shall sink while there's an echo left to air."[94]

Endnotes

FOREWORD

1   George Washington's quotes are found in the original sources of Washington's writings and also in the very helpful article by Michael Novak and Jana Novak, *Washington's Faith and the Birth of America*, found in *The American Enterprise*, May 2006 issue, pages 20-27.

2   Ibid.

CHAPTER 1

1   Paul F. Boller, Jr., *George Washington & Religion* (Dallas: Southern Methodist University Press, 1963) p. 93.

2   John Clement Fitzpatrick, ed., *The Writings of George Washington, from the Original Manuscript Sources 1749-1799*, 39 vols.(Washington, D.C.: United States Government Printing Office, 1931-1944). The writings of George Washington are now readily and easily available online at http://etext.lib. virginia.edu/washington/. Readers may find quotations by searching by word, date, or recipient. Further references to Washington's writings will be referenced simply by *WGW* followed by the Volume number and date. *WGW* vol. 2, 4-27-63.

3   Joseph J. Ellis, *His Excellency* (New York: Alfred K. Knopf, 2004).

4   Franklin Steiner, *The Religious Beliefs Of Our Presidents From Washington to FDR* (New York: Prometheus Books, 1995).

5   Willard Sterne Randall, *George Washington: A Life* (New York: Henry Holt and Co., 1997).

6   Douglas Southall Freeman, *George Washington A Biography*. 7 Vols (New York:, Charles Scribner's Sons, 1948).

7   James T. Flexner, *Washington: The Indispensable Man* (New York: Signet, 1984).

8   William Maclay, *The Journal of William Maclay, United States Senator from Pennsylvania 1789-1791*, (New York: Albert & Charles Boni, 1927) p. 9.

9   *WGW*, Inaugural Address.

10 Ibid., vol. 37, 5-13-1776.

11 Ibid., vol. 30, 10-3-1789.

12 The eighteenth century in America was a remarkable time. This is not simply because of the political and international events surrounding the birth of our nation. It was remarkable, too, because of many aspects of the modern world that emerged from this period. One of the most important ingredients of the modern world is the elevation of human reason above scriptural revelation. In the 1700s this was beginning to take place among many of the educated. The movement during that time was called "The Enlightenment." One of the central components of the Enlightenment era was a shift from biblical Christianity to a theological viewpoint called "Deism." James Flexner, *Washington: The Indispensable Man*, p. 216, declares, "Washington subscribed to the religious faith of the Enlightenment: like Franklin and Jefferson he was a Deist. Although not believing in the doctrines of the churches, he was convinced that a divine force, impossible to define, ruled the universe, and that this 'Providence' was good." If there is not a Providential God in Deism and Washington is claimed to have been a Deist, how then could he have believed in Providence? Let's consider a historical definition of Deism given by America's first lexicographer, Noah Webster. His personal experience argues that he understood the issues involved, given his own history of intellectualism and unbelief in the Gospel:

> About a year ago an unusual revival of religion took place in New Haven, and frequent conferences of private meetings for religious purposes were held by pious and well disposed persons in the Congregational societies. . . .I closed my books, yielded to the influence which could not be resisted or mistaken, and was led by a spontaneous impulse of repentance, prayer, and entire submission and surrender of myself to my Maker and Redeemer. My submission appeared to be cheerful, and was soon followed by the peace of mind which the world can neither give nor take away. . . .You will readily suppose that such evidence of the direct operation of the divine spirit upon the human heart, I could no longer question or have a doubt respecting the Calvinistic and Christian doctrines of regeneration, of free grace, and of the sovereignty of God. I now began to understand and relish many parts of the scriptures, which before appeared mysterious and unintelligible or repugnant to my natural pride. . . .Permit me here to remark, in allusion to a passage in your letter, that I had for almost fifty years exercised my talents such as they are, to obtain knowledge and to abide by its dictates, but without arriving at the truth, or what now appears to me to be the truth, of the gospel. I am taught now the utter insufficiency of our own powers to effect a change of the heart, and am persuaded that a reliance on our own talents or powers is a fatal error, springing from natural pride and opposition to God, by which multitudes of men, especially of the more intelligent and moral part of society are deluded into ruin. I now look, my dear friend, with regret on the largest portion of the ordinary life of man, spent 'without hope and without God in the world.' I am particularly affected by a sense of my ingratitude to that Being who made me and without whose constant agency I cannot draw a breath, who has showered upon me a profusion of temporal blessings and provided a Savior for my immortal soul . . .In the month of April last I made a profession of faith." ("Noah Webster: Founding Father of American Scholarship and Education" in Facsimile First Edition of *American Dictionary of the English Language* (1828) by Noah Webster (1989), p. 20-21).

His 1828 *American Dictionary of the English Language* provides the following definitions:

> Deism: n. [Fr. *Deisme*; Sp. *Deismo*; It. *Id*.; from L. *deus*, [God]. The doctrine or creed of a Deist; the belief or system of religious opinions of those who acknowledge the existence of one God, but deny revelation: or Deism is the belief in natural religion only, or those truths, in doctrine and practice, which man is to discover by the light of reason, independent and exclusive of any revelation from God. Hence Deism implies infidelity or a disbelief in the divine origin of the scriptures.

> Deist: n. [Fr. *Deiste*; It. *Deista*.]   One who believes in the existence of a God, but denies revealed religion; one who professes no form

of religion, but follows the light of nature and reason, as his only guides in doctrine and practice; a freethinker.

Deism in Washington's day rejected divine revelation, affirmed the preeminence of human reason, but had not yet necessarily denied the validity of Providence. Clearly, Webster's definition of Deism does not prohibit a belief in Providence. As we shall see, Washington did believe in the Providence of God in the affairs of human history. Later Deism may well have rejected this idea, but such was not the case in colonial America. On the basis of this, in the next chapter we will make a distinction between "hard" and "soft" Deism.

13 Ellen Sorokin, "No Founding Fathers? That's Our New History," *Washington Times,* January 28, 2002.

14 Brit Hume, "The Political Grapevine," February 22, 2005, *Fox News.*

15 Boller, *George Washington & Religion.*

16 Ibid., p.86.

17 See for example Frank E. Grizzard, Jr., *George Washington: A Biographical Companion* (Denver: ABC-CLIO, 2002) pp. 268-273. The only scholarly source that Grizzard cites is Boller's book on Washington's religion.

18 Boller, *George Washington & Religion,* p.30.

19 Ibid.

20 See James Flexner quote in note 1 above.

21 Marvin Kitman, *The Making of the President 1789: the Unauthorized Campaign Biography* (New York: Harper & Row, 1989), p. 73.

22 Benjamin Franklin, *Information to Those Who Would Remove to America.* (London: M. Gurney, 1794,) pp. 22, 23.

23 John Corbin, *The Unknown Washington,* (Charles Scribner's sons, 1930), p. 36 writes, "…a tradition handed down in the countryside where he first surveyed land for Lord Fairfax and then, . . . endeavored to protect the settlers from savage butchery. Though not recorded until 1926, it is thoroughly in accord with what we know of the unlicked cub. Having ordered a drink at the bar of a tavern in what is now Martinsburg, West Virginia, he found that he had no money and tendered a coonskin. The change came in rabbitskins, said to have numbered one hundred and fifty-eight. Confronted by this unwieldy heap, and possibly warmed by his liquor, Washington stood treat to all comers until the last rabbit-scut disappeared behind the bar. An eighteenth-century diarist quotes Alexander Hamilton to the effect that Washington had a strong head for liquor—and exercised it daily. One visitor at Mount Vernon found him loquacious after champagne." (*WGW*, vol. 33, note, 10-9-1794.) In preparation for president Washington's riding to western Pennsylvania to address the "Whiskey Rebellion," Bartholomew Dandridge wrote, "As the President will be going, if he proceeds, into the Country of Whiskey he proposes to make use of that liquor for his drink, and presuming that beef and bread will be furnished by the contractors he requires no supply of these Articles from you."

24 *WGW*, vol. 36, 1-10-1798. To Burwell Bassett. "As you kindly offered to become the purchaser of Corn for me, in case I should need any for my Distillery, I now request the favour of you to procure, and send me (not of the gourd seed kind) a Vessel load, say from five to twelve hundred bushels, so soon as all danger of the River freezing, is over."

25 Ibid., vol. 37, 1-20-1799.

26 Ibid., vol. 4, 12-5-1775.

27 Ibid., vol. 37, 5-13-1776.

28 Thomas Jefferson, "A Bill for Establishing Religious Freedom," 1786, Bruce Frohnen, ed., *The American Republic: Primary Sources* (Indianapolis: Liberty Fund, 2002), p. 330.

29 Boller, *George Washington & Religion,* p.16.

30 John Rhodehamel, ed., *George Washington: Writings* (New York: The Library of America, 1997), 526.

31 Ibid., 351.

32 All of these quotes can be found in *WGW*, vol. XI, p. 343.

33 "The Rules of Civility" was a collection of 110 maxims for behavior for a young man. We will consider these rules more fully in the chapter on Washington's childhood education. They are listed in their entirety in appendix 1.

34 *WGW*, vol. 36, 7-4-1798.

CHAPTER 2

1 Noah Webster, 1828 *American Dictionary of the English Language.*

2 *WGW*, vol. 30, 9-28-1789.

3 Ibid., vol. 12, 8-20-1778.

4 "It seems as if parents of the Christian profession were ashamed to tell their children anything about the principles of their religion. They sometimes instruct them in morals, and talk to them of the goodness of what they call Providence, for the Christian mythology has five deities- there is God the Father, God the Son, God the Holy Ghost, the God Providence, and the Goddess Nature." Thomas Paine, *Age of Reason*, Luxembourg, 8th Pluviose, Second Year of the French Republic, one and indivisible. January 27, O. S. 1794. Part I.

5 Crane Brinton in *The Shaping of Modern Thought* (Englewood Cliffs, N.J.: Prentice-Hall, Inc., 1963), p. 137.

6 Thomas Paine's criticism of prayer can be found in *Age of Reason*, Luxembourg, 8th Pluviose, Second Year of the French Republic, one and indivisible. January 27, O. S. 1794. Part I. "Yet, with all this strange appearance of humility and this contempt for human reason, he ventures into the boldest presumptions; he finds fault with everything; his selfishness is never satisfied; his ingratitude is never at an end. He takes on himself to direct the Almighty what to do, even in the government of the universe; he prays dictatorially; when it is sunshine, he prays for rain, and when it is rain, he prays for sunshine; he follows the same idea in everything that he prays for; for what is the amount of all his prayers but an attempt to make the Almighty change his mind, and act otherwise than he does? It is as if he were to say: Thou knowest not so well as I."

7 *WGW*, vol. 31, 6-19-1791. On June 19, 1791, Washington wrote to Tobias Lear showing his still high regard for Paine's writings: "I should

like to see Mr. Payne's answer to Mr. Burke's Pamphlet [*WGW* note: This was Paine's reply to Edmund Burke's *Reflections on the French Revolution*, which constituted what was afterwards the first part of *The Rights of Man*.]; if it is to be had...."

8   For the friendship that Washington originally had toward Paine, see his letter to Richard Henry Lee on June 12, 1784:

Dear Sir: Unsollicited by, and unknown to Mr. Paine, I take the liberty of hinting the services, and distressed (for so I think it may be called) situation of that Gentleman. That his *Commonsense*, and many of his Crisis', were well timed, and had a happy affect upon the public mind, none I believe who will recur to the epochas at which they were published, will deny: that his services hither to have passed off unnoticed, is obvious to all; and that he is chagrined and necessitous, I will undertake to aver. Does not common justice then point to some compensation? He is not in circumstances to refuse the public bounty. New York, not the least distressed, or most able State in the Union have set the example. He prefers the benevolence of the States individually, to an allowance from Congress, for reasons which are conclusive in his own mind, and such as I think may be approved by others; his views are moderate; a decent independency is, I believe, the height of his ambition; and if you view his services in the American cause in the same important light that I do, I am sure you will have pleasure in obtaining it for him. I am, etc. *WGW*, vol. 27, 6-12-1784.

For his appreciation for *Common Sense*, see Washington's letter to Joseph Reed, January 31, 1776, "A few more of such flaming arguments, as were exhibited at Falmouth and Norfolk, added to the sound doctrine and unanswerable reasoning contained in the pamphlet *Common Sense*, will not leave numbers at a loss to decide upon the propriety of a separation." *WGW*, vol. 4, 1-31-1776.

9   James Thomas Flexner, *George Washington Anguish and Farewell (1793-1799)* (Boston: Little, Brown & Co. 1969), p. 323.

10   Washington's policy was not to answer a letter or charge that he believed to have the wrong "tenor." See his July 28, 1795, letter to the Boston Selectmen. *WGW*, vol. 34, 7-28-1795.

"Gentlemen: In every act of my administration, I have sought the happiness of my fellow-citizens. My system for the attainment of this object has uniformly been to overlook all personal, local and partial considerations: to contemplate the United States, as one great whole: to confide, that sudden impressions, when erroneous, would yield to candid reflection: and to consult only the substantial and permanent interests of our country.

Nor have I departed from this line of conduct, on the occasion, which has produced the resolutions, contained in your letter of the 13 [instt.]

Without a predilection for my own judgment, I have weighed with attention every argument, which has at any time been brought into view. But the constitution is the guide, which I never will abandon. It has assigned to the President the power of making treaties, with the advice and consent of the senate. It was doubtless supposed that these two branches of government would combine, without passion, [and with the best means of information], those facts and principles upon which the success of our foreign relations will always depend: that they ought not to substitute for their own conviction the opinions of others; or to scorn expect truth thro' any channel but that of a temperate and well-informed investigation.

Under this persuasion, I have resolved on the manner of executing the duty now before me. To the high responsibility, attached to it, I freely submit; and you, gentlemen, are at liberty to make these sentiments known, as the grounds of my procedure. While I feel the most lively gratitude for the many instances of approbation from my country; I can no otherwise deserve it, than by obeying the dictates of my conscience. With due respect, &c."

The note of *WGW* on this date explains: Addresses of disapprobation of Jay's Treaty, urging that it be not ratified, poured in upon the President from cities, towns, and counties in nearly every State. The earliest being that from the Selectmen of Boston, dated July 13, and the last coming from the citizens of Lexington, Ky., in their meeting of September 8 (forwarded September 10). To most of these addresses the same answer was returned as that to the Boston Selectman, July 28. The text of the addresses, with the president's answers, are entered in the "Letter Book" in the *Washington Papers* . On the "Letter Book" copy of the resolutions of the citizens of Petersburg, Va., August 1, Washington has noted: "Tenor indecent. No answer returned." On the "Letter Book" copy of the resolutions of the inhabitants of Bordentown, Crosswicks, Black Horse, and Reckless Town, N. J., Washington has noted: "No answer given. The Address too rude to merit one." The copyist's note to resolutions of the citizens of Laurens County, S. C., is "The foregoing Resolutions & ca.? were sent under a blank cover, by (it is supposed) Jno. Matthews Esqr. No notice has been taken of them." On the "Letter Book" copy of the remonstrance and petition of the citizens of Scott County, Ky., August 25, Washington has noted: "The Ignorance and indecency of these proceedings forbad an answr." On the "Letter Book" copy of the address from the citizens of Lexington, Ky., Washington has noted: "It would now [be] out of time to answr this address when reed Novr. Indecent besides."

11   Boller, *George Washington & Religion*, p. 60.

12   We will address Washington's many titles for "Deity" in a subsequent chapter, "Washington's God: Religion, Reason and Philosophy."

13   Washington wrote to Reverend Samuel Miller from Philadelphia on August 29, 1793, "Sir: It is but a few days since that I had the pleasure to receive your polite letter of the 4 instant, which accompanied the Sermon delivered by you on the 4 of July, and I beg you will accept my best thanks for the attention shewn in forwarding the same to me." The Title page declares:

A SERMON PREACHED IN NEW YORK, JULY 4TH, 1793
BEING THE ANNIVERSARY OF THE
INDEPENDENCE OF AMERICA:
At the Request of the Tammany Society, or Columbian Order
by SAMUEL MILLER, A.M.
One of the Ministers of the United Presbyterian Churches, in the City of New York

To The Tammany Society, Or Columbian Order

Whose Principles of Association
Merit the Highest Applause –
And Whose Patriotic Exertions
Demand the Warmest Gratitude
of Every American –

THIS SERMON

Delivered published at their Request,
Is respectfully dedicated,
By their Fellow-Citizen,
The Author
In Society, July 4, 1793.

RESOLVED, That the Thanks of this Society by returned to the Reverend Mr. SAMUEL MILLER, for his elegant and patriotic Discourse, delivered by him, before the Society, this Day.

ORDERED, That Brothers Rodgers, Mitchell, and Ker, Be a Committee to wait on Mr. Miller, for this Purpose, and to request a Copy for the Press.

A true Copy from the Minutes, BENJAMIN STRONG, Secretary

ADVERTISEMENT

THE following Discourse is published, almost verbatim, as it was delivered, excepting the addition of the Notes. It was compiled on very short Notice – amidst many pressing Avocations – and, consequently, in great Haste. These Circumstances, together with the want of Abilities and Experience in the Author, must apologize for its indigested and defective Appearance.

CHRISTIANITY
the GRAND SOURCE, AND THE SUREST BASIS
of POLITICAL LIBERTY:
A SERMON.
II. CORINTHIANS, iii. 17.
AND WHERE THE SPIRIT OF THE LORD IS, THERE IS LIBERTY.

14   Ellis Sandoz, ed., *Political Sermons of the American Founding Era, 1730-1805* (Indianapolis: Liberty Fund, 1998), vol. 2, pp. 1154, 1159, 1165, 1166, 1167.

15   See chapter 3, note 47 where a letter from Methodist Bishops Thomas Coke and Francis Asbury on behalf of the Methodist-Episcopal church is cited. This clearly shows that Washington's language for Deity was that of the evangelical preachers of his day. Coke and Asbury write: "We have received the most grateful satisfaction, from the humble and entire dependence on the Great Governor of the universe which you have repeatedly expressed, acknowledging him the source of every blessing,…." Washington responded on the same day "It always affords me satisfaction when I find a concurrence of sentiment and practice between all conscientious men, in acknowledgments of homage to the great Governor of the universe,…."

16   In a subsequent chapter on Washington's sermons, we will consider the collection of sermons that Washington stated in writing that he had read, enjoyed, or approved. An example presented there is "A Sermon Occasioned by the Death of the Honourable Sir William Pepperell etc.," Boston, 1759, to which Washington gave his "approbation" (see *WGW*, letter to Reverend Joseph Buckminster, December 23, 1789). The terms for "God" that Stephens used in this sermon include: "Supreme Ruler of the Universe" "great Governor of the World," "His Providence," "Divinity," "universal Sovereign," "Definition of Infinite Wisdom," "supreme Universal Monarch," "universal Judge," "Discerner of true Worth." Such titles for deity used by Christian preachers of Washington's era, which Washington also employed, are utterly absent from Thomas Paine's deistic *Age of Reason.*

17   Boller, *George Washington And Religion*, p. 28-29, writes, "Parson Weems quoted him [Lee Massey] as saying: I never knew so constant an attendant at Church as Washington. His behavior in the House of God was ever so deeply reverential, and greatly assisted me in my pulpit labors. No company ever withheld him from church. I have often been at Mount Vernon, on Sabbath morning, when his breakfast table was filled with guests; but to him they furnished no pretext for neglecting his God, and losing the satisfaction of setting a good example For instead of staying home out of false complaisance to them, he used constantly to invite them to accompany him. But Massey's statement was made many years after the period to which he referred and, as Paul Leicester Ford suggested, it was probably made "more with an eye to its influence on others than to its strict accuracy." The same comment may be made of George Washington Parke Custis' statement, some years after Washington's death, that his step-grandfather "was always a strict and decorous observer of the Sabbath. He invariably attended divine service once a day, when within reach of a place of worship. If we examine Washington's own record of what he did on Sunday before the Revolution, we find that he was considerably less conscientious about attending church than either Lee Massey or GWP Custis seems to have recollected. According to his diary, Washington went to church four times during the first five months of 1760, and in 1768 he went fifteen times; and these years seem to be fairly typical of the period from 1760 to 1773. It is true, as the pietists have noted, that bad weather sometimes made it impossible to make the trip to church, that illness occasionally kept Washington at home, and that Pohick Church did not hold services every Sunday because the rector had to preach elsewhere in Truro parish. But Washington, we know, also transacted business on Sundays, visited friends and relatives, traveled, and sometimes went fox-hunting, instead of going to church. . . . But at the most it does not seem to have exceeded an average of once a month."

962

Boller's use of Washington's diaries here is methodologically unsound. His conclusions are non-sequiturs. Washington, for example, almost ignores political events. On this count, they were irrelevant too. (Historians have been frustrated by Washington's seeming indifference in his own diary to the world-changing events that he often participated in.) Or by this same logic, church attendance could be construed as even more important than his attendance at the Constitutional Convention—for he never even said a word beyond bare attendance! Or as a *reductio ad absurdum*, by the same logic, consider then the profound significance of the fact that on a Saturday and Sunday at the end of July 1769, Washington chose to give so much detail concerning his hounds. With barnyard clarity, Washington records: "Chaunter again lind with Rockwood" and "The black bitch countess appeard to be going proud" and "was shut up in order to go to the same Dog." And that the next day "Chaunter Lined again by rockwood." By Boller's logic, if importance is established by record and commentary, we are compelled to assume that the breeding of his dogs was the most important thing in his life, since Washington by far presents more on his dog's historical actions than he does of his own actions on Sunday worship or at the Creation of a New American Government! Let it be noted, that a thorough search of Washington's diaries shows that he never fox-hunted on a Sunday. Not being of the Puritan tradition, he had no scruple about traveling on Sunday. The few Sundays in his diaries that mention fox hunting show that he traveled to someone's home to fox hunt. The next day's entry then shows the typical recounting of the foxes that were chased and sometimes killed. While Boller's logic diminishes the faithfulness of Washington's attendance at church, a few other factors should be kept in mind. First, to make his point, he must, in essence, call Reverend Massey and Washington's grandson, who grew up in Washington's house, exaggerators or outright liars. Next, he has to disregard the fact that the trip to church took nearly all day, since it required an approximately nine mile carriage ride through unpaved country roads, and in the winter, it was to a church building that by law could not have a fireplace for heat, lest it be susceptible to catching fire. Further, Boller's portrayal of the minimal attendance of Washington at church overlooks the written record and the physical evidence of Washington's custom of reading a sermon to his family on Sundays. Finally, we will, in a subsequent chapter, consider the training the Washington family gave to their children through Episcopal tutors and that Washington himself received in childhood in regard to the regular use of *The Book Of Common Prayer* which provided a weekly spiritual experience, even when weather, health, distance, or lack of clergy prevented the family from attending worship. As strange as it may sound, in the rural countryside of Virginia, an average of once a month attendance at church gave one high marks for consistency. Consistent with this, when Washington lived in New York and Philadelphia as president, his attendance was far more convenient and far more frequent.

18   Rupert Hughes writes in *George Washington the Human Being and the Hero 1732-1762* (New York: William Morow & Co., 1926), p. 555, "Dr. Conway, speaking of Washington's Diaries, notes 'his pretty regular attendance at church but never any remark on the sermons.'" The same flawed logic as Boller is reflected here by Hughes. Washington did, in fact, comment on the sermons, only rarely in his diaries, but in letters to the preacher/writers of the sermons, he did on some twenty different occasions. We will consider these in a later chapter.

19   Reverend John Stockton Littell, D.D. *Washington: Christian – Stories of Cross and Flag No. 1* (Keene, N.H.: The Hampshire Art Press).

20   William Fairfax, Washington's paternal advisor, had recently counseled him by letter to have public prayers in his camp, especially when there were Indian families there; this was accordingly done at the encampment in the Great Meadows, and it certainly was not one of the least striking pictures presented in this wild campaign — the youthful commander presiding with calm seriousness over a motley assemblage of half-equipped soldiery, leathern-clad hunters and woodsmen, and painted savages with their wives and children, and uniting them all in solemn devotion by his own example and demeanor. Jared Sparks, *The Writings of George Washington: Being His Correspondence Addresses, Messages, and other Papers, Official and Private* (New York: Harper & Brothers, 1847), p. 138.

20   Washington Irving, *Life of George Washington* Part I, p. 203ff. Washington Irving writes, "Dr. Craik dressing his wounds, and Washington attending him with faithful assiduity….Captain Orme, who gave these particulars to Dr. Franklin, says that Braddock "died a few minutes after." This, according to his account, was on the second day; whereas the general survived upward of four days. Orme, being conveyed on a litter at some distance from the general, could only speak of his mood from hearsay…..He died on the night of the 13th at the Great Meadows, the place of Washington's discomfiture in the previous year. His obsequies were performed before break of day. The chaplain having been wounded, Washington read the funeral service. All was done in sadness, and without parade, so as not to attract the attention of lurking savages, who might discover and outrage his grave. It is doubtful even whether a volley was fired over it, that last military honor which he had recently paid to the remains of an Indian warrior. The place of his sepulture, however, is still known, and pointed out."

It is undisputed tradition, according to the recounting of Washington's soldiers, that he became chaplain at such times when there was no other to perform the service. The record that David Humphreys gives in his biography of George Washington is significant, because it is the only biography of his life that Washington read and approved: "General Braddock breathed his last. — He was interred with the honors of War, and as it was left to George Washington to see this performed, & to mark out the spot for the reception of his remains to guard against a savage triumph, if the place should be discovered." In David Humphreys, *Life of George Washington* (University of Georgia Press, 1991), pp. 15-20. Thus, Washington's presiding over the burial service for General Braddock is not mere tradition. Braddock was buried with "the honors of war" and this ceremony would have included the use of the prayers from the *Book of Common Prayer*.

21   See *WGW*, vol. 2, Oct 12, 1761; vol. 3, July 18, 1771, July 15, 1772. Under the date of July 18, 1771 is found: "INVOICE OF GOODS TO BE SHIPD BY ROBERT CARY & CO. FOR THE USE OF GEO. WASHINGTON, POTOMACK RIVER, VIRGINIA, A Prayr. Book with the new Version of Psalms and good plain type, covd. with red Moroco., to be 7 Inchs. long 4? wide, and as thin as possible for the greatr. ease of caryg. in the Pocket."

22   The Apostles' Creed was to be said in both the morning and evening prayer as outlined by the 1662 *Book Of Common Prayer*, as well as the 1789 revision. This historic Christian creed declares: "I BELIEVE in God the Father Almighty, Maker of heaven and earth: And in Jesus Christ his only Son our Lord; Who was conceived by the Holy Ghost, Born of the Virgin Mary; Suffered under Pontius Pilate, Was crucified, dead, and buried; He descended into hell, The third day he rose from the dead; He ascended into heaven, And sitteth on the right hand of God the Father Almighty; From thence he shall come to judge the quick and the dead. I believe in the Holy Ghost; The holy Catholic Church; The Communion of Saints; The Forgiveness of sins; The Resurrection of the body; And the Life

everlasting. Amen."

23   The Lord's Prayer, as given in the 1662 *Book Of Common Prayer* says, " Our Father, which art in heaven, Hallowed be thy Name. Thy kingdom come. Thy will be done in earth, As it is in heaven. Give us this day our daily bread. And forgive us our trespasses, As we forgive them that trespass against us. And lead us not into temptation, But deliver us from evil. Amen." It was to be used daily both in the morning and evening prayer.

24   The Ten Commandments were an essential part of the catechism in the1662 *Book Of Common Prayer.* The public corporate reading of the Ten Commandments provided for in the Communion Service of the 1662 *Book Of Common Prayer* was as follows:

"Then shall the Priest, turning to the people, rehearse distinctly all the TEN COMMANDMENTS; and the people still kneeling shall, after every Commandment, ask God mercy for their transgression thereof for the time past, and grace to keep the same for the time to come, as followeth. Minister.

God spake these words, and said; I am the Lord thy God: Thou shalt have none other gods but me.

People. Lord, have mercy upon us, and incline our hearts to keep this law.

Minister. Thou shalt not make to thyself any graven image, nor the likeness of any thing that is in heaven above, or in the earth beneath, or in the water under the earth. Thou shalt not bow down to them, nor worship them: for I the Lord thy God am a jealous God, and visit the sins of the fathers upon the children unto the third and fourth generation of them that hate me, and shew mercy unto thousands in them that love me, and keep my commandments.

People. Lord, have mercy upon us, and incline our hearts to keep this law.

Minister. Thou shalt not take the Name of the Lord thy God in vain: for the Lord will not hold him guiltless, that taketh his Name in vain.

People. Lord, have mercy upon us, and incline our hearts to keep this law.

Minister. Remember that thou keep holy the Sabbath-day. Six days shalt thou labour, and do all that thou hast to do; but the seventh day is the Sabbath of the Lord thy God. In it thou shalt do no manner of work, thou, and thy son, and thy daughter, thy man-servant, and thy maid-servant, thy cattle, and the stranger that is within thy gates. For in six days the Lord made heaven and earth, the sea, and ail that in them is, and rested the seventh day: wherefore the Lord blessed the seventh day, and hallowed it.

People. Lord, have mercy upon us, and incline our hearts to keep this law.

Minister. Honour thy father and thy mother; that thy days may be long in the land which the Lord thy God giveth thee.

People. Lord, have mercy upon us, and incline our hearts to keep this law.

Minister. Thou shalt do no murder.

People. Lord, have mercy upon us, and incline our hearts to keep this law.

Minister. Thou shalt not commit adultery.

People. Lord, have mercy upon us, and incline our hearts to keep this law.

Minister. Thou shalt not steal.

People. Lord, have mercy upon us, and incline our hearts to keep this law.

Minister. Thou shalt not bear false witness against thy neighbour.

People. Lord, have mercy upon us, and incline our hearts to keep this law.

Minister. Thou shalt not covet thy neighbour's house, thou shalt not covet thy neighbour's wife, nor his servant, nor his maid, nor his ox, nor his ass, nor any thing that is his.

People. Lord, have mercy upon us, and write all these thy laws in our hearts, we beseech thee."

25   The Golden Rule of Matthew 7:12 provides the answer to the catechism in the 1662 *Book Of Common Prayer.* "*Question.* What is thy duty towards thy Neighbour? *Answer.* My duty towards my Neighbour, is to love him as myself, and to do to all men, as I would they should do unto me...."

26   Washington's code of conduct learned as a child, entitled "Rules of Civility," was relevant in regard to his conscience. As a child, Washington had written down rule 110th that said, "Labor to keep alive in your breast that little celestial fire called conscience." Washington's concern for his character will be considered at some length in chapter three.

27   *WGW* vol. 7, 2-4-1777, see Fitzgerald's note.

28   This was long before the Oxford movement of the 1830s impacted the Anglican Church and placed the sacramental and Eucharistic life at the front of the churches' life. Sir Matthew Hale, for example, an exemplar of Anglican piety whose books were used by Mary Washington in the spiritual nurture of her children, wrote that a serious minded believer should commune three times per year. The early Virginia colony only held Communion three times per year, "It was the custom in the colonial churches to administer communion only at Christmas, Easter, and Whitsuntide [Pentecost Sunday], and it was not an uncommon practice for communicants to receive only once a year." (William Johnson, *George Washington the Christian* (Arlington Heights: Christian Liberty Press, 1919), (p.58) A 1631 pamphlet describes early Virginian Anglican worship, "...yet we had daily Common Prayer morning and evening, every Sunday two sermons, and every three months the holy communion, till our minister died.") When one remembers the lack of clergy in the colonial Anglican churches, even this ideal may have been difficult to achieve.

29   Bishop Meade, *Old Churches, Ministers and Families of Virginia vol. 2* (Philadelphia: J.B.Lippencott & Co., 1857) p. 495.

30   Jared Sparks, *The Writings of George Washington;* XII, pp. 405ff.

31   Ibid., p. 409.

32   John C. Fitzpatrick, ed., *The Diaries of George Washington* (Boston: Houghton Mifflin Company, 1925) "Sunday October 11, 1789 'At home all day – writing private letters.' (p. 19); For another example consider November 1, 1789 "Attended by the president of the State (Genl. Sullivan), Mr. Landon, and the marshal, I went in the forenoon to the Episcopal church, under the incumbency of a Mr. Ogden; and in

the afternoon to one of the Presbyterian of Congregational Church, in which a Mr. Buckminster Preached. Dines at home with the marshal, and spent the afternoon in my own room writing letters." (p. 43)

33 Ibid., vol. 26, 6-8-1783.
34 Ibid., vol. 2, 4-27-63.
35 We will detail this story in a later chapter.
36 *WGW,* vol. 3, 6-19-1775.

CHAPTER 3

1 Hughes, *George Washington the Human Being and the Hero,* p. 554.
2 *WGW,* vol. 15, 5-13-1779.
3 Hughes, *George Washington the Human Being and the Hero,* p. 554.
4 *WGW,* vol. 15, 5-13-1779.
5 Boller, *George Washington And Religion,* p. 69.
6 Ibid., p. 74.
7 Ibid., p. 74. C
8 Rupert Hughes, p. 554. (Unfortunately, Rupert Hughes' only source for this claim is Dr. M. D. Conway's monograph, "The Religion of George Washington." *The Open Court,* Oct. 24, p. 1889, p. 1895. For other relevant texts, see Boller, *George Washington And Religion* p. 85,
9 As an illustration of this, a private letter to Gov. Henry Lee, dated August 26, 1794, is pertinent. According to the *WGW* Note on that date: "Lee had written (August 27): '...very respectable gentleman told me the other day that he was at Mr. Jefferson's, and among enquirys which he made of that gentleman, he asked if it were possible that you had attached yourself to G Britain and if it could be true that you were governed, by British influence as was reported by many. He was answered in the following words: 'that there was no danger of your being biassed ? by considerations of that sort so long as you were influenced by the wise advisers, or advice, which you at present had. ' I requested him to reflect and reconsider and to repeat again the answer. He did so, and adhered to every word. Now as the conversation astonished me and is inexplicable to my mind as well as derogatory to your character, I consider it would be unworthy in me to withhold the communication from you. To no other person will it ever be made.'" President Washington addressed "what Mr. Jefferson is reported to have said of" him as follows: "With respect to the words said to have been uttered by Mr. Jefferson, they would be enigmatical to those who are acquainted with the characters about me, unless supposed to be spoken ironically; and in that case they are too injurious to me, and have too little foundation in truth, to be ascribed to him. There could not be the trace of doubt on his mind of predilection in mine, towards G. Britain or her politics, unless (which I do not believe) he has set me down as one of the most deceitful, and uncandid men living; because, not only in private conversations between ourselves, on this subject; but in my meetings with the confidential servants of the public, he has heard me often, when occasions presented themselves, express very different sentiments with an energy that could not be mistaken by *any one* present."
10 In the context of the preparation of his farewell address, Washington wrote to Alexander Hamilton on May 15, 1796, calling Jefferson and Madison " *two* of those characters who are now strongest, and foremost in the opposition to the Government; and consequently to the person Administering of it contrary to their views." See *WGW,* vol.35, 5-15-1796. Washington originally had considered retirement from the presidency at the end of his first term. Madison and Jefferson were aware of his plan as well as his first draft of a farewell address from their assistance to the president when they were closer to him. Ultimately Jefferson resigned his post as Secretary of State. The relationship between Washington and Jefferson continued to deteriorate as their political differences began to be increasingly evident. Washington had attempted in vain to keep Jefferson on his cabinet. This is seen in the following letter that he wrote on October 18, 1792 to Jefferson just before Jefferson resigned. The four years of Washington's second term had elapsed between Washington's heartfelt effort to keep Jefferson on the Cabinet and his painful letter to Hamilton referring to Madison and Jefferson as those "foremost in the opposition to the Government." Washington unsuccessfully sought to mediate between Hamilton and Jefferson with these gracious words: "I did not require the evidence of the extracts which you enclosed me, to convince me of your attachment to the Constitution of the United States, or of your disposition to promote the general Welfare of this Country. But I regret, deeply regret, the difference in opinions which have arisen, and divided you and another principal Officer of the Government; and wish, devoutly, there could be an accommodation of them by mutual yieldings. A Measure of this sort would produce harmony, and consequent good in our public Councils; the contrary will, inevitably, introduce confusion, and serious mischiefs; and for what? because mankind cannot think alike, but would adopt different means to attain the same end. For I will frankly, and solemnly declare that, I believe the views of both of you [Hamilton and Jefferson] are pure, and well meant; and that experience alone will decide with respect to the salubrity of the measures wch. are the subjects of dispute. Why then, when some of the best Citizens in the United States, Men of discernment, Uniform and tried Patriots, who have no sinister views to promote, but are chaste in their ways of thinking and acting are to be found, some on one side, and some on the other of the questions which have caused these agitations, shd. either of you be so tenacious of your opinions as to make no allowances for those of the other? I could, and indeed was about to add more on this interesting subject; but will forbear, at least for the present; after expressing a wish that the cup wch. has been presented, may not be snatched from our lips by a discordance of action when I am persuaded there is no discordance in your *views.* I have a great, a sincere esteem and regard for you both, and ardently wish that some line could be marked out by which both of you could walk." *WGW,* vol. 32, 10-18-1792.
11 Hughes goes on to say of Jefferson's claim that Washington was a Deist, "This would seem to be the truth. In his time the 'deist' was a term of fierce reproach, almost worse than atheist, though a deist believed in an all-wise deity who cared for the world and provided a future reward for the good. This deity was not, however, the Israelite Jehovah and was not the father of Christ, who was considered a wise and virtuous man, but not of divine origin. Such was probably Washington's opinion on the subject, though there is little evidence either way.

In spite of his incessant allusions to providence, Washington was persistently silent as to his dogmatic beliefs." Rupert Hughes, *George Washington The Human Being*, p. 554.

12 For The Definition of Chalcedon written in 451, see Phillip Schaff, *The Creeds of Christendom* 6th edition (Grand Rapids: Baker Book House, 1983), vol. 2, pp. 62-63. The foundational language concerning Christ is "…consubstantial [coessential] with the Father according to the Godhead, and consubstantial with us according to the Manhood; in all things like unto us, without sin; begotten before all ages of the Father according to the Godhead, and in these latter days, for us and for our salvation, born of the Virgin Mary, the Mother of God, according to the Manhood; one and the same Christ, Son, Lord, Only-begotten, to be acknowledged in two natures; inconfusedly, unchangeably, indivisibly, inseparably; the distinction of natures being by no means taken away by the union, but rather the property of each nature being preserved, and concurring in one Person and one Subsistence, not parted or divided into two persons, but one and the same Son, and only begotten God the Word, the Lord Jesus Christ…."

13 See Schaff, *Creeds Of Christendom*, vol. 1, 651-52.

14 Thomas Jefferson was a critic of the theology of the Athanasian Creed: "The metaphysical insanities of Athanasius, of Loyola, and of Calvin, are, to my understanding, mere lapses into polytheism, differing from paganism only by being more unintelligible." — Thomas Jefferson to Jared Sparks, 1820. Andrew A. Lipscomb and Albert Ellery Bergh , ed. *The Writings of Thomas Jefferson*, 20 vols. (Washington, D.C., 1903-04), 15:288. And Thomas Jefferson to John Adams, 1813 "It is too late in the day for men of sincerity to pretend they believe in the Platonic mysticisms that three are one, and one is three; and yet that the one is not three, and the three are not one. But this constitutes the craft, the power and the profit of the priests." Ibid., 13:350.

15 Schaff, *The Creeds of Christendom*, vol. 2, p. 66-71, also JMD Kelly, *The Athenasian Creed* (New York: Harper & Row) 1963.

16 This principle well explains the alleged incident where Boller claims that Washington "avoids" speaking of Jesus Christ in an exchange of letters between Gouverneur Morris and Washington. Boller writes, "Washington frequently alluded to Providence in his private correspondence. But the name of Christ, in any connection whatsoever, does not appear anywhere in his many letters to friends and associates throughout his life. Gouverneur Morris once wrote him to say: "Had our Saviour addressed a Chapter to the Rulers of Mankind, I am persuaded his good Sense would have dictated this Text: Be not wise overmuch." In his reply, Washington avoided speaking of the "Saviour." "Had such a chapter as you speak of," he said, "been written to the rulers of Mankind, it would, I am persuaded, have been as unavailing as many others upon subjects of equal importance." Paul Boller, *George Washington And Religion*, p. 75. The problem with Boller's claim that Washington "avoids" referring to the "Saviour" and that it is thus an argument for Washington's Deism is that his remark in no way implies disbelief in the Saviour. What Washington avoids is the unnecessary and potentially profane use of the name of the "Saviour" in a discussion of the ponderous workings of government. Consider the actual letter of Washington to Morris on May 29, 1778: "Had such a chapter as you speak of been written to the rulers of mankind it would I am persuaded, have been as unavailing as many others upon subjects of equal importance. We may lament that things are not consonent with our wishes, but cannot change the nature of Men, and yet those who are distressed by the folly and perverseness of it, cannot help complaining, as I would do on the old score of regulation and arrangement, if I thought any good would come of it." Fitzpatrick, editor of the *WGW*, provides more of Morris' letter: "Gouverneur Morris wrote (May 21) to Washington: 'Had our Saviour addressed a Chapter to the Rulers of Mankind as he did many to the Subjects I am persuaded his Good Sense would have dictated this Text: Be not wise overmuch. Had the several Members which compose our multifarious Body been only wise enough Our Business would long since have been compleated. But our superior Abilities or the Desire of appearing to possess them lead us to such exquisite Tediousness of Debate, that the most precious Moments pass unheeded away like vulgar Things.'" See *WGW*, vol. 11, 5-29-1778. Given that the discussion between Morris and Washington is full of "complaining" and "vulgar Things," Washington's sense of honor prevented him from repeating the "Saviour's" name in what in itself could also be viewed as a profane act— proposing another chapter to the Gospels left untaught by Christ. But even beyond this, Boller's thesis does not stand the test of examination. If Washington operated under the principle advanced by Boller, he should never have mentioned the "Redeemer" either. Yet he does so as he writes to his military associates in his General Orders of November 27, 1779, speaking of "the merits of our gracious Redeemer." In the first instance he appropriately avoids repeating the profane use of the "Saviour's" name from Gouverneur Morris' letter dealing with complaints about government business. In the second instance he chooses to repeat the "Redeemer's" name from the call for prayer by the Continental Congress, since it is a worship context, and thus an appropriate use for Christ's sacred name.

17 Julian P. Boyd, ed., *The Papers of Thomas Jefferson*, vol. 13, March 7-October 1788 (Princeton, New Jersey: Princeton University Press, 1956): "I am truly sensible, Sir, of the honour you do me in proposing to me that of become one of the Sponsors of your child, and return you my sincere thanks for it. At the same time I am not a little mortified that scruples, perhaps not well founded, forbid my undertaking this honourable office. The person who becomes sponsor for a child, according to the ritual of the church in which I was educated, makes a solemn profession, before god and the world, of faith in articles, which I had never sense enough to comprehend, and it has always appeared to me that comprehension must precede assent. The difficulty of reconciling the ideas of Unity and Trinity, have, from a very early part of my life, excluded me from the office of sponsorship, often proposed to me by my friends, who would have trusted, for the faithful discharge of it, to morality alone instead of which the church requires faith. Accept therefore Sir this conscientious excuse which I make with regret, which must find it's apology in my heart, while perhaps it may do no great honour to my head."

18 Building on a study begun while president in 1804, and pursued in earnest in the summer of 1820, *The Life and Morals of Jesus of Nazareth Extracted Textually from the Gospels in Greek, Latin, French and English*, the so-called *Jefferson's Bible* was Thomas Jefferson's effort to summarize the teaching of Jesus, without being encumbered by the miraculous and the false additions to his teaching that he believed had been made to Jesus' historic word. Former President Jefferson wrote of his project to uncover the real words of Jesus from the faulty Gospel history in which they were contained. Jefferson explained that his project was a process of "abstracting what is really his [i.e., Christ's] from the rubbish in which it is buried [i.e., the Gospel history], easily distinguished by its lustre from the dross of his biographers, and as separate from that as the diamond from the dung hill." — Thomas Jefferson to W. Short, Oct. 31, 1819. Jefferson's work has no mention of

the beginning and the end of the Gospel story. There is no annunciation, virgin birth or appearance of angels to the shepherds. The resurrection of Jesus is entirely missing. Simply put, Jefferson's Jesus of Nazareth is not the Jesus Christ of Christianity. Nor is Jefferson's Jesus of Nazareth Washington's "Divine Author of our Blessed Religion." When Washington refers to "the religion of Jesus Christ" it is clearly not the Deistic and truncated religion of Thomas Jefferson. As a Deist, Jefferson had no scruple in frequently using Jesus' name:

"But the greatest of all reformers of the depraved religion of his own country, was *Jesus of Nazareth*. Abstracting what is really his from the rubbish in which it is buried, easily distinguished by its lustre from the dross of his biographers, and as separable from that as the diamond from the dunghill, we have the outlines of a system of the most sublime morality which has ever fallen from the lips of man. The establishment of the innocent and genuine character of this benevolent morality, and the rescuing it from the imputation of imposture, which has resulted fro artificial systems, invented by ultra-Christian sects (The immaculate conception of Jesus, his deification, the creation of the world by him, his miraculous powers, his resurrection and visible ascension, his corporeal presence in the Eucharist, the Trinity; original sin, atonement, regeneration, election, orders of the Hierarchy, etc.) is a most desirable object." Thomas Jefferson to W. Short, Oct. 31, 1819

"It is not to be understood that I am with him (*Jesus Christ*) in all his doctrines. I am a Materialist; he takes the side of Spiritualism; he preaches the efficacy of repentance toward forgiveness of sin; I require a counterpoise of good works to redeem it. Among the sayings and discourses imputed to him by his biographers, I find many passages of fine imagination, correct morality, and of the most lovely benevolence; and others, again, of so much ignorance, so much absurdity, so much untruth, charlatanism and imposture, as to pronounce it impossible that such contradictions should have proceeded from the same being. I separate, therefore, the gold from the dross; restore him to the former, and leave the latter to the stupidity of some, the roguery of others of his disciples. Of this band of dupes and imposters, Paul was the great Coryphaeus, and the first corruptor of the doctrines of *Jesus*." - Thomas Jefferson to W. Short, 1820

"The office of reformer of the superstitions of a nation, is ever more dangerous. *Jesus* had to work on the perilous confines of reason and religion; and a step to the right or left might place him within the grasp of the priests of the superstition, a bloodthirsty race, as cruel and remorseless as the being whom they represented as the family God of Abraham, of Isaac and of Jacob, and the local God of Israel. That *Jesus* did not mean to impose himself on mankind as the son of God, physically speaking, I have been convinced by the writings of men more learned than myself in that lore." — Thomas Jefferson to Story, Aug. 4, 1820

"The doctrines of *Jesus* are simple, and tend all to the happiness of man. But compare with these the demoralizing dogmas of Calvin.
1. That there are three Gods.
2. That good works, or the love of our neighbor, is nothing.
3. That faith is everything, and the more incomprehensible the proposition, the more merit the faith.
4. That reason in religion is of unlawful use.
5. That God, from the beginning, elected certain individuals to be saved, and certain others to be damned; and that no crimes of the former can damn them; no virtues of the latter save." — Thomas Jefferson to Benjamin Waterhouse, Jun. 26, 1822

"The truth is, that the greatest enemies of the doctrine of *Jesus* are those, calling themselves the expositors of them, who have perverted them to the structure of a system of fancy absolutely incomprehensible, and without any foundation in his genuine words. And the day will come, when the mystical generation of *Jesus*, by the Supreme Being as his father, in the womb of a virgin, will be classed with the fable of the generation of Minerva in the brain of Jupiter." — Thomas Jefferson to John Adams, April 11, 1823.

19   The radical unbelief in Jesus Christ expressed by Thomas Paine the Deist makes him very free to speak of Christ. The following passages of which there is not a shred of parallel with Washington are illustrative of Paine's deistic rejection of Christianity: "EVERY national church or religion has established itself by pretending some special mission from God, communicated to certain individuals. The Jews have their Moses; the Christians their *Jesus Christ*, their apostles and saints; and the Turks their Mahomet; as if the way to God was not open to every man alike.

"Each of those churches shows certain books, which they call revelation, or the Word of God. The Jews say that their Word of God was given by God to Moses face to face; the Christians say, that their Word of God came by divine inspiration; and the Turks say, that their Word of God (the Koran) was brought by an angel from heaven. Each of those churches accuses the other of unbelief; and, for my own part, I disbelieve them all....

"It is, however, not difficult to account for the credit that was given to the story of *Jesus Christ* being the Son of God. He was born when the heathen mythology had still some fashion and repute in the world, and that mythology had prepared the people for the belief of such a story. ...The Christian theory is little else than the idolatry of the ancient mythologists, accommodated to the purposes of power and revenue; and it yet remains to reason and philosophy to abolish the amphibious fraud...." Thomas Paine, *Age Of Reason*, Part One, Chapter two;

"It is certain that, in one point, all nations of the earth and all religions agree. All believe in a God, The things in which they disagree are the redundancies annexed to that belief; and therefore, if ever an universal religion should prevail, it will not be believing any thing new, but in getting rid of redundancies, and believing as man believed at first. Adam, if ever there was such a man, was created a *Deist*; but in the mean time, let every man follow, as he has a right to do, the religion and worship he prefers." Thomas Paine, *Age Of Reason*, Part One, Recapitulation.

20   The Nicene Creed was to be said in the morning prayer, the evening prayer, or the Communion service as a possible alternative to the Apostles Creed, according to the rubric of the 1789 *Book of Common Prayer*. This Trinitarian Creed declares: "I BELIEVE in one God the Father Almighty, Maker of heaven and earth, And of all things visible and invisible. And in one Lord Jesus Christ, the only-begotten Son of God; Begotten of his Father before all worlds, God of God, Light of Light, Very God of very God; Begotten, not made; Being of one substance with the Father; By whom all things were made: Who for us men and for our salvation came down from heaven, And was incarnate by the Holy Ghost of the Virgin Mary, And was made man: And was crucified also for us under Pontius Pilate; He suffered and was

buried: And the third day he rose again according to the Scriptures: And ascended into heaven, And sitteth on the right hand of the Father: And he shall come again, with glory, to judge both the quick and the dead: Whose kingdom shall have no end. And I believe in the Holy Ghost, The Lord, and Giver of Life, Who proceedeth from the Father and the Son; Who with the Father and the Son together is worshipped and glorified; Who spake by the Prophets: And I believe one Catholic and Apostolic Church: I acknowledge one Baptism for the remission of sins: And I look for the Resurrection of the dead: And the Life of the world to come. Amen."

21   *WGW* vol. 16, 7-29-1779.

22   Ibid., vol. 9, 9-19-1777 Note: "His Excellency General Washington was with the troops who passed us here to the Perkiomen. The procession lasted the whole night, and we had all kinds of visits from officers wet to the breast, who had to march in that condition the cold, damp night through, and to bear hunger and thirst at the same time. This robs them of courage and health, and instead of prayers we hear from most, the national evil, curses." —— *Muhlenberg's Diary* , Sept. 19, 1777.

23   Ibid., vol. 17, 11-27-1779.

24   Ibid., vol. 26, 6-8-1783.

25   Ibid., vol. 30, 10-3-1789.

26   Ibid., vol. 3, 9-14-1775.

27   Ibid., vol. 35, 3-3-1797.

28   Ibid., vol. 4, 3-6-1776.

29   Ibid., vol. 5, 5-15-1776.

30   Ibid., vol. 37, 9-22-1799.

31   Our founders were sometimes *explicit* in their use of the name of Jesus Christ in their public proclamations for prayer and fasting or thanksgiving, and at other times they were *implicit* in their Christian understanding. For examples of the *explict* use of Christ's name in a public yet holy context consider the following (which all can be found in *Journals of the Continental Congress*, on the dates specified):

In March 1776, the Congress said for a day of prayer and fasting, ". . . it becomes the indispensable duty of these hitherto free and happy colonies, with true penitence of heart, and the most reverent devotion, publickly to acknowledge the over ruling providence of God; to confess and deplore our offences against him; and to supplicate his interposition for averting the threatened danger, and prospering our strenuous efforts in the cause of freedom, virtue, and posterity. . . .Do earnestly recommend, that Friday, the Seventeenth day of May next, be observed by the said colonies as a day of humiliation, fasting, and prayer; that we may, with united hearts, confess and bewail our manifold sins and transgressions, *and, by a sincere repentance and amendment of life, appease his righteous displeasure, and through the merits and mediation of Jesus Christ, obtain his pardon and forgiveness*; . . .That he would be graciously please to bless all his people in these colonies with health and plenty, and grant that a spirit of incorruptible patriotism, and of pure undefiled religion, may universally prevail; and this continent be speedily restored to the blessings of peace and liberty, and enabled to transmit them inviolate the latest posterity. And it is recommended to Christians of all denominations, to assemble for public worship, and abstain from servile labour on the said day."
A Congressional Thanksgiving Proclamation on November 1, 1777 declared: "Forasmuch as it is the indispensable duty of all men to adore the superintending providence of Almighty God; . . .they may join the penitent confession of their manifold sins, whereby they had forfeited every favour, and their humble and earnest supplication that it may please God, through the merits of *Jesus Christ*, mercifully to forgive and blot them out of remembrance; that it may please him graciously to afford his blessing on the governments of these states respectively. . . and to prosper the means of religion for the promotion and enlargement of that kingdom which consisteth "in righteousness, peace and joy in the *Holy Ghost*."
Yet most often there is only an *implict* use of the name of Jesus Christ in such public proclamations. But they clearly do not imply an deistic intent since they either use honorific titles for Jesus Christ, or, they make clear that they are referring to Christianity.
The Congressional Proclamation in March 1782 is most remarkable because of the interest of the Congress in the expansion of the Christian religion. It says, ". . .that He would incline the hearts of all men to peace, and fill them with universal charity and benevolence, and that the religion of our *Divine Redeemer*, with all its benign influences, may cover the earth as the waters cover the seas."
In other Congressional Thanksgiving Proclamations, one can find a clear emphasis upon Christianity: In 1779, ". . .and above all, that he hath diffused the glorious light of the gospel, whereby, through the merits of our *gracious Redeemer*, we may become the heirs of his eternal glory. . . .prayer for the continuance of his favor and protection to these United States; to beseech him. . .that he would grant to his church the plentiful effusions of divine grace, and pour out his holy spirit on all ministers of the gospel; that he would bless and prosper the means of education, and spread the light of *Christian* knowledge through the remotest corners of the earth. . . ." In 1780, ". . .to cherish all schools and seminaries of education, and to cause the knowledge of *Christianity* to spread over all the earth." In 1783, ". . .and above all, that he hath been pleased to continue to us the light of the blessed *gospel*, and secured to us in the fullest extent the rights of conscience in faith and worship...to smile upon our seminaries and means of education, to cause pure religion and virtue to flourish." In 1784, "And above all, that he hath been pleased to continue to us the light of *gospel* truths, and secured to us, in the fullest manner, the rights of conscience in faith and worship."
Reverend Dr. John Witherspoon was a Presbyterian minister from New Jersey, President of the College of New Jersey in Princeton, and a member of Congress. He was the only clergyman to sign the Declaration of Independence. In 1782, he composed one of the Continental Congress' national calls for a day of thanksgiving: ". . . to testify their gratitude to God for his goodness, by a cheerful obedience to his laws, and by promoting, each in his station, and by his influence, the practice of *true and undefiled religion*, which is the great foundation of public prosperity and national happiness." Note that in his mind as an orthodox minister in the Presbyterian tradition, "true and undefiled religion" was a synonym for Christianity. Also, following the common custom of the day, Witherspoon did not directly mention the name of Jesus Christ in his proclamation, but this clearly had no anti-Christian or deistic intent.
A similar example of the *implicit* reference to Christianity is in the Reverend Dr. Jedidiah Morse's brief history of Washington. Morse

was an orthodox Christian New England clergyman who published America's first scholarly geography text. Not only did he correspond with Washington about this scholarly enterprise, but he also shared his sermons, which Washington read and approved, which we will consider in the chapter on Washington's sermons. He also published a brief history of Washington's life, which was actually the anonymous version of David Humphrey's notes on Washington. On p. 36 of Morse's "*Life of Washington*," we find the following "Federal Prayer" which reflects the "implicit" Christianity as just considered in Witherspoon's call for thanksgiving. It says, "FATHER of all! Thou who rulest the armies of Heaven above; look down upon us we beseech thee, and bless all orders of men in this lower world. In a particular manner we pray for our own country: Bless the Congress of these United States, and all our rulers; May they rule wisely, love mercy, and do justice at all times. Unite us more and more we beseech thee; lead us in the right way, and make us a great and a happy people. Bless all religious orders of men, O our heavenly Father! Enlighten their minds, subdue superstition,and grant that they may all unite to worship thee in truth, with one heart and one voice. Send discord far from us, we beseech thee, both from church and state, and give us hearts of unity and peace. Hasten the happy time when thy will shall be done here on earth, as it is done in Heaven: When sin and sorrow shall be no more: When all the inhabitants of the earth shall be blessed; and join in songs of praise to thee the only wise God, for ever and ever. Amen."

32 The dates on the title pages of the *Almanacks* that are extant are 1761, 1765, 1768, 1769, 1771, 1772, 1774. Each of them states "in the year of our Lord God." See these dates in Donald Jackson and Dorothy Twohig, ed. *The Diaries of George Washington* (Charlottesville: University Press of Virginia, 1976-79) [online] [http://memory.loc.gov/ammem/gwhtml/gwhome.html].

33 This was likely due to protest over the Stamp Act which was passed in 1765, and the additional cost this added to almanacs (See *A Tale of the Huguenots, or Memoirs of a French Refugee Family. Translated and compiled from the original manuscripts of James Fontaine, by one of his descendants, with an introduction by F. L. Hawks*. (New York: John S. Taylor, 1838), P. 257: "But what hath given a most general alarm to all the colonists upon this continent, and most of those in the islands, and struck us with the most universal consternation that ever seized a people so widely diffused, is a late Act of the British Parliament, subjecting us to a heavy tax by the imposition of stamp duties on all manner of papers requisite in trade, law or private dealings , on pamphlets, newspapers, almanacks, calendars ,and even advertisements, etc. etc.;"). It is also possible that the *Virginia Almanack* was only sold with the stamp, and Washington may have chosen not to buy it with a tax stamp affixed. It is clear that the Washington family was opposed to the Stamp Act. Four Washington family members signed a resolution in protest of the Stamp Act. Bishop Meade writes:

The following address and resolutions of the patriots of the Northern Neck of Virginia, in the year 1765, immediately after the passage of the Stamp Act, properly belongs to the article on Washington parish, Westmoreland. It was drawn up by Richard Henry Lee, whose name is first on the list. It is said to have been the first public association in the land for the resistance to the act.

Roused by danger, and alarmed at attempts, foreign and domestic, to reduce the people of this country to a state of abject and detestable slavery, by destroying that free and happy constitution of government under which they have hitherto lived,— We, who subscribe this paper, have associated, and do bind ourselves to each other, to God, and to our country, by the firmest ties that religion and virtue can frame, most sacredly and punctually to stand by , and with our lives and fortunes to support, maintain and defend each other in the observance and execution of these following articles.

First. – We declare all due allegiance and obedience to our lawful Sovereign, George the Third, King of Great Britain. And we determine to the utmost of our power to preserve the laws, the peace and good order of this colony, as far as is consistent with the preservation of our constitutional rights and liberty.

Secondly. – As we know it to be the birthright privilege of every British subject, (and of the people of Virginia as being such,) founded on reason, law, and compact, that he cannot be legally tried, but by his peers, and that he cannot be taxed, but by the consent of a Parliament, in which he is represented by persons chosen by the people, and who themselves pay a part of the tax they impose on others. If therefore any person or persons shall attempt, by any action or proceeding, to deprive this colony of those fundamental rights, we will immediately regard him or them as the most dangerous enemy of the community; and we will go to any extremity, not only to prevent the success of such attempts, but to stigmatize and punish the offender.

Thirdly. – As the Stamp Act does absolutely direct the property of the people to be taken from them without their consent expressed by their representatives, and as in many cases it deprives the British American subject of his right to trial by jury; we do determine, at every hazard, and paying no regard to danger or to death, we will exert every faculty to prevent the execution of the said Stamp Act in any instance whatsoever within this colony. And every abandoned wretch, who shall be so lost to virtue and public good, as wickedly to contribute to the introduction or fixture of the Stamp Act in this colony, by using stamp paper, or by any other means, we will, with the utmost expedition, convince all such profligates that immediate danger and disgrace shall attend their prostitute purposes.

Fourthly. – That the last article may surely and effectually be executed, we engage to each other, that whenever it shall be known to any of this association, that any person is so conducting himself as to favour the introduction of the Stamp Act, that immediately notice shall be given to as many of the association as possible; and that every individual so informed shall, with expedition, repair to a place of meeting to be appointed as near the scene of action as may be.

Fifthly. – Each associator shall do his true endeavour to obtain as many signers to this association as he possibly can.

Sixthly. – If any attempt shall be made on the liberty or property of any associator for any action or thing done in consequence of this agreement, we do most solemnly bind ourselves by the sacred engagements above entered into, at the utmost risk of our lives and fortunes, to restore such associate to his liberty, and to protect him in the enjoyment of his property.

In testimony of the good faith with which we resolve to execute this association, we have this 27th day of February, 1766, in Virginia, put our hands and seals hereto.

In Bishop Meade, *Old Churches And Families of Virginia*, vol. II, p. 434, appendix No. VI.

34 Boller, *George Washington and Religion* pp. 74-75 says, "Unlike Thomas Jefferson—and Thomas Paine, for that matter—Washington never even got around to recording his belief that Christ was a great ethical teacher. His reticence on the subject was truly remarkable."

35 Washington mentions Christmas 41 times. His special love for Christmas reflects his victory at the Christmas Day surprise attack on the Hessians in New Jersey (*WGW*, vol. 6, 12-28-1776, "I have the pleasure to inform you of the success of an enterprize, which took effect the 26th. Instant at Trenton; On the night of the preceding day, I cross'd the Delaware with a detachment of the Army under my Command, amounting to about 2400.) It also shows the impact of his final return from the war to Mount Vernon at the end of the war on Christmas Eve. (*WGW*, vol. 27, 2-1-1784, "I did, on the 23d. of December present them my commission, and made them my last bow, and on the Eve of Christmas entered these doors an older man by near nine years, than when I left them, is very uninteresting to any but myself.") But it also highlights an emphasis of his childhood education, which we will explore in the chapter on Washington's childhood education.

36 *WGW*, vol. 30, 4-1789. This text from Washington seems to refer to man's depravity seen in the abuse of a divinely given religious organization—the temple worship—which resulted in the crucifixion. See Matt. 26:57-68; 27:1-10, 41-44. Washington's childhood training, which we will consider in the chapters on Washington's childhood and Washington's childhood education, included an understanding of the redemptive sufferings of Christ.

37 In a later chapter, we will see that Easter and the Resurrection appear in his childhood training. We will also consider his Anglican tradition's teaching on theResurrection, and how that manifested itself in Washington's adult life.

38 *WGW* vol. 4, 12-8-1775; 24, 4-21-1782; 26, 6-8-1783; 35, 12-19-1796.

39 Ibid., vol. 30, 4-30-1789.

40 Ibid., vol. 28, 6-30-1786; 37, 4-25-1799.

41 Ibid., vol. 32, 1-27-1793; 3-6-1793.

42 Ibid., vol. 26, 6-8-1783.

43 Ibid., vol. 6, 12-6-1776; 37, 11-22-1799.

44 Ibid., vol. 30, 4-30-1789.

45 Ibid vol. 37, 8-28-1762.

46 Ibid., vol. 28, 6-30-1785; 29, 5-2-1788; 30, 7-6-1789, note; .

47 Ibid., vol. 29, 8-15-1787.

48 Ibid., vol. 35, 5-15-1797.

49 Ibid., vol. 36, 7-4-1798.

50 Ibid., vol. 21, 3-26-1781; 27, 2-1-1784.

51 Ibid., vol. 2, 7-1-1757; 15, 5-12-1779. In the second, "Ways of life" is paralleled with "the religion of Jesus Christ."

52 Ibid., vol. 29, 8-15-1787.

53 Ibid., vol. 17, 11-27-1779.

54 Ibid., vol. 17, 11-27-1779; 30, 10-23-1789.

55 Ibid., vol. 3, 1-31-1770-; 8, 7-28-1777; 12, 7-4-1778.

56 Ibid., vol. 4, 4-23-1776; 10-11-1777; 35, 5-15-1796.

57 Ibid., vol. 8, 6-17-1777; 15, 5-12-1779; 27, 7-10-1783; 37, 3-26-1762.

58 Ibid., vol. 1, 4-20-1756; 7, 1-21-1777; 21, 3-2-1781, note.

59 Ibid., vol. 35, 6-4-1797.

60 Ibid., vol. 10, 11-21-1777; 28, 7-25-1785.

61 Ibid., vol. 28, 7-25-1785.

62 Ibid., vol. 12, 9-6-1778; 17, 11-27-1779.

63 Ibid., vol. 29, 4-28-1788.

64 Ibid., vol. 30, 10-23-1789.

65 Ibid., vol. 25, 1-5-1785.

66 Nineteen times in all. Examples: *WGW*, vol. 3, 7-20-1770; 26, 1-15-1783; 26, 3-31-1783; 35, 11-15-1796.

67 *WGW* vol. 28, 7-26-1786.

68 Ibid., vol. 35, 11-28-1796.

69 Ibid., vol. 15, 7-4-1779; 37, 3-25-1799.

70 Ibid., vol. 1, "To the Speaker and Gentlemen of the House of Burgesses"; 31, 6-15-1791; 35, 3-5-1797.

71 Ibid., vol. 5, 5-31-1776; 27, 2-18-1784.

72 Ibid., vol. 28, 8-22-1785.

73 Ibid., vol. 28, 12-1-1785; 29, 2-5-1788; 31, 4-29-1790.

74 Ibid., vol. 16, 8-10-1779; 17, 11-25-1779; 1-23-1780; 24, 5-14-1782; 34, 2-7-1796.

75 Ibid., vol. 26, 6-8-1783.

76 Ibid., vol. 4, 3-31-1776.

77 Ibid., vol. 29, 4-25 to 5-1-1788.

78 Ibid., vol. 1, 5-28-1755.

79 Ibid., vol. 1, 9-6-1756.

80 Ibid., vol. 3, 8-10-1775; 4, 12-28-1775; 9, 9-4-1777; 23, 12-15-1782; 25, 11-13-1782.

81 Ibid., vol. 6, 9-30-1776.

82 Ibid., vol. 30, 2-5-1789.

83 Ibid., vol. 31, 6-4-1790.

84 Ibid., vol. 7, 2-22-1777.

85 Ibid., vol. 26, 4-18-1783.

86 Ibid., vol. 17, 11-27-1779.

87 Ibid., vol. 25, 11-16-1782; 36, 6-4-1798.

CHAPTER 4

1   *WGW,* vol. 35 5-15-1796.

2   See Peter A. Lillback, *Proclaim Liberty,* (Bryn Mawr: The Providence Forum, 2001), p. 11, n. 29. Mark A. Beliles and Stephen K. McDowell, *America's Providential History* (Charlottesville, Vir., Providence Press, 1989), p. 81.

3   Bishop Meade, *Old Churches,* vol. 1, p. 64

4   Mark A. Beliles & Stephen K. McDowell, *America's Providential History,* p. 81.

5   " ... When there was no service at the chapel or we were prevented from going, my father read the service and a sermon; and whenever a death occurred among the servants he performed the burial service himself, and read Blair's Sermon on Death the following Sunday. Of the character and conduct of the old clergy generally I have often heard them speak in terms of strong condemnation. My father, when a young man, was a vestryman in Price George county, Virginia, but resigned his place rather than consent to retain an unworthy clergyman in the parish." Meade, *Old Churches,* vol. I p. 22.

6   William W. Sweet, *Religion In Colonial America* (New York: Cooper Square Publishers, Inc., 1965), pp. 55-56.

7   "...Governors, Commissaries, and private individuals, in their communications with the Bishops of London and the Archbishops of Canterbury, all declare that such was the scanty and uncertain support of the clergy, the precarious tenure by which livings were held that but few of the clergy could support families and therefore respectable ladies would not marry them. Hence the immense number of unmarried, ever-shifting clergymen in the colony." Meade, *Old Churches,* vol. I. p. 92.

8   "The reigning vice among the clergy at that time was intemperance; as it probably has been ever since both among the clergy and laity of all denominations, having given great trouble to the Church of the every age. The difficulty of proof is stated in one of these schemes for reformation; and the following mortifying tests of intoxication are proposed to the Bishop of London, for the trial of the clergy in Virginia. They were these: "Sitting an hour or longer in company where they are drinking strong drink, and in the mean time drinking of healths, or otherwise taking the cups as they come round, like the rest of the company; striking, and challenging, or threatening to fight, or laying aside any of his garments for that purpose; staggering reeling, vomiting; incoherent, impertinent, or rude talking. Let the proof of these signs proceed so far, till the judges conclude that the minister's behaviour at such a time was scandalous, indecent, unbecoming the gravity of a minister." Bishop Meade, *Old Churches,* vol. I pp. 163-164.

9   Allan Nevins, *The American States: During and After the Revolution 1775-1789* (New York: Augustus M. Kelley Publishers, 1969) p. 429-230. "Every Anglican clergyman in Maryland had his house and glebe, or farm; he was guaranteed a tax, settled by law and collected by the sheriffs; and he had various fees, as those for performing marriages. Secure in his emoluments, and since he was appointed by the Proprietary of Governor, virtually free from fear of dismissal, the ordinary cleric was no model of virtue. The term "a Maryland parson" was a byword farther north. In 1753 Dr. Chandler, a frank American minister, wrote home that "the general character of the clergy is wretchedly bad," and that it would "make the ears of a sober heathen tingle to hear the stories" told of some of them. A contemporary tells us that a current couplet ran:

Who is a minister of the first renown?

A lettered sot, a drunkard in a gown.

There was no proper disciplinary authority, and favoritism entered into the appointments; so that the majority of the ministers had the brains, education, and moral elevation of Parson Trulliber. Yet the people were taxed heavily, as taxes went in America, for his clerical crew. The quarrel between the Legislature and Governor Eden which came to a head in 1770 involved, among other factors, the question whether every poll should pay thirty or forty pounds of tobacco to the Church, the Governor insisting on the latter amount. Since the price of tobacco was high, and they had other sources of income, the Maryland clergy were rated the best-paid in America. In 1767 one parish was worth about £500 a year. The people also had to pay special taxes for church-building, for fencing graveyards, and other purposes, and even in wartime beneficed clergymen were exempt from the general taxes. "I am as averse to having religion crammed down my throat," wrote Charles Carroll of Carrollton on July 1, 1773, "as to a proclamation"—Governor Eden having usurped certain legislative rights by proclamation. The burdens under which the Calvinists, Catholics, and Quakers lay were one of the real if minor causes of the Revolutionary spirit."

10 Peter Marshall & David Manuel, *The Light and the Glory* (Old Tappan, New Jersey, Fleming H. Revell 1977), pp. 80-105.

11 In 1733, for example, the Reverend Lawrence De Butts was called to preach three times a month in various churches, one of those times being "old Pohick Church," the church where Washington was baptized. His salary was to be "the sum of eight thousand pounds of tobacco clear of the Warehouse charges and abatements." Reverend Philip D. D. Slaughter, *The History of Truro Parish in Virginia* (Philadelphia: Geroge Jacobs & Co., 1907) p. 5. Washington was Church Warden in 1764. One of his duties was to auction tobacco at the Court House for the Vestry which is described in the Vestry minutes, "Ordered that 31,549 lb. Of tobo. In the hands of the Church Wardens for the year 1764, to wit, George Washington and George Wm. Fairfax Esqrs. be sold to the highest bidder, before the Court House door of this County on the first day of June Court next between the hours of 12 and 4, and that publick notice be given of the sale." Ibid., p. 51.

12 Sanford H. Cobb, *The Rise of Religious Liberty in America* (New York: Macmillan Company, 1902) p. 479, N. 3.

13 *The Diaries of George Washington.* vol. 1. Donald Jackson, ed.; Dorothy Twohig, assoc. ed. (Charlottesville: University Press of Virginia, 1976). "A Journal of my Journey over the Mountains began Fryday the 11th. of March 1747/8." Vol, 1, p. 7. 1748, "Wednesday March 23d. Rain'd till about two oClock & Clear'd when we were agreeably surpris'd at the sight of thirty odd Indians coming from War with only one

Scalp. We had some Liquor with us of which we gave them, Part it elevating there Spirits put them in the Humour of Dauncing of whom we had a War Daunce. There Manner of Dauncing is as follows Viz. They clear a Large Circle & make a great Fire in the Middle then seats themselves around it the Speaker makes a grand Speech telling them in what Manner they are to Daunce after he has finish'd the best Dauncer Jumps up as one awaked out of a Sleep & Runs & Jumps about the Ring in a most comicle Manner he is followd by the Rest then begins there Musicians to Play the Musick is a Pot half of Water with a Deerskin Streched over it as tight as it can & a goard with some Short in it to Rattle & a Piece of an horses Tail tied to it to make it look fine the one keeps Rattling and the other Drumming all the While the others is Dauncing."

14 *WGW*, vol., 37, Last Will And Testament.

15 "And to my Mulatto man William (calling himself William Lee) I give immediate freedom; or if he should prefer it (on account of the accidents which have befallen him, and which have rendered him incapable of walking or of any active employment) to remain in the situation he now is, it shall be optional in him to do so: In either case however, I allow him an annuity of thirty dollars during his natural life, which shall be independent of the victuals and cloaths he has been accustomed to receive, if he chuses the last alternative; but in full, with his freedom, if he prefers the first; and this I give him as a testimony of my sense of his attachment to me, and for his faithful services during the Revolutionary War." Ibid.,

16 Bishop Meade, *Old Churches*, vol. I. 14.

17 Ibid., p. 122.

18 Ibid., p. 66.

19 Ibid., p. 67.

20 Ibid., p. 63.

21 Ibid., p. 63

22 Ibid., p. 62.

23 *WGW*, vol. 29, 5-2-1788. Washington's letter began "Reverend Sir: I have received your obliging letter of the 28th of March, enclosing a copy of some remarks on the Customs, Languages &c. of the Indians, and a printed pamphlet containing the stated rules of a Society for propagating the Gospel among the Heathen for which tokens of polite attention and kind remembrance I must beg you to accept my best thanks."

24 Ibid., vol. 29, 5-2-1788.

25 One of the documents that accompanied Ettwein's letter to Washington read as follows:

Extract from the instruction or rules for the Society of the United Brethren as are used as missionaries or assistant in propagating the gospel among the Indians.

God our Saviour will have all men to be saved and to come unto the knowledge of the truth. 1st Timothy 2:4? He wills therefore in these our days as well as in the times of the apostles that the Gospel be preached to the heathen.

The United Brethren have undertaken to preach the Gospel to the heathen, firmly believing they thereby serve the will of God.

It is an undertaking of great importance to preach the gospel to the heathen that they be turned from darkness to light and from the power of Satan to God. Acts 26:18.

And it is likewise no light thing when heathen are converted and become sheep of Christ to exercise the faithfulness of a shepherd and servant of Christ.

It appeared in process of time and experience that the missionaries could not be of sufficient effectual service without the assistance of some sisters among the heathen women. To prevent some inevitable if not hurtful consequences, it was determined the sisters should accompany their husbands as helpers among the female heathen congregations of God, gathered among the heathen through the gospel.

When several brothers are engaged together in a mission among the heathen, they ought to be very careful to preserve and maintain in particular brotherly love among themselves, for nothing is more hurtful and shameful in a mission among the heathen then discord among those who are to preach peace and love and good will towards all men.

The more the lives of most people called after Christ, Christians, prove a scandal to the heathen, the more should our brethren be induced to God an unblameable life among them, for not withstanding all sins and abominations are generally practiced among the heathen. Yet they know they ought to do the very reverse, hence if they see people walking in love to God and their neighbors, they receive a good impression.

Our brethren are to take all possible pains to learn the language of those heathen with whom they have to do. They must be very careful what interpreter they use at public services, until they shall be able to express themselves intelligently to the heathen, they must rather be contented with preaching by their walk and conversation.

That custom to delay the baptism of the heathen until they have learned by heart so many questions and answers, which they are to repeat previous to their being admitted to baptism, is not to be recommended, but yet some instruction is required.

Those heathen who have the favor to be the first among their nation who become obedient to the gospel, should be to her care of with the utmost attention and faithfulness.

The baptized are to receive frequently further instructions; the more they are made acquainted with the doctrine of the Gospel, the more they lose those ideas which arose from the former heathenish ways. They are to be taught to observe all things, whatsoever Jesus has commanded his disciples and us.

As to morality, we are among other things, firmly to maintain 2 points: First, that everyone may arrive at such a personal connection with God our Saviour, that nothing in the whole world be dearer, yea not so dear and precious to him as he is. The second point is contained in the words of Christ: All things whatsoever you would that man should do unto you, do ye ever so to them.

Matthew 7:12. Stated Rules of a Society for Propagating the Gospel among the Heathen, lately incorporated by an Act of Assembly of this State. Reverend John Ettwein, Bethlehem, March 28, 1788

George Washington Papers at the Library of Congress, 1741-1799: Series 4. General Correspondence. 1697-1799. George Washington to John Ettwein, March 28, 1788, with Enclosures on Indian Languages and Cultures image 699ff.

26   The Preface to these Rules for the United Brethren's Missionary work was written by Bishop Ettwein himself. *Stated Rules of the Society of the United Brethren, For Propagating the Gospel among the Heathen*, Philadelphia: Printed by Charles Cist, in Race-Street Between Front and Second-streets, Nov. 1ft. 1787.

"Preface: Beloved Reader,

"The word of God, the bible, full of the most precious promises for the propagation and extension on the kingdom of God among the Heathen nations, (which we in a great measure for fulfilled in the different tongues and nations from which we come) with a feeling for the unhappy state of all such who live in heathenish darkness, has from the beginning of Christianity, caused in believers a heart desire, to help and to assist in that blessed work of preaching the gospel among all nations.

Such a pious desire, that Jesus Christ and his salvation might also be made known to the Indians in North America, moved the directions of the ancient Episcopal Church, called Unitas Frantrum or United Brethren near fifty years ago to begin a mission in this country, by which a number of Mahikans, Wampanos, Delawares, a few Shawanos, Nanitkoks and others, have been brought to the knowledge of the truth, and thereby collected into the Christian-church, in which they lived a civil, moral Christian life, under the care and tuition of the missionaries as a shining light to the wild Indians, until their towns on Mutkingum-river were unhappily destroyed in the last war.

"Above one thousand fouls have been received into the Christian-church by holy baptism from these Indian nations, more than fix hundred of them departed this life in faith, and about three hundred more live yet with the missionaries near Lake Erie, or are dispersed among their different tribes, on account of the sufferings and manifold troubles, which befel the Indian-congregation; the rest either died or live yet as aposlates in the wilderness.

"In the history of the Brethren's mission among the Indians, (which is preparing for the press) the reader will find a true account of the losses, persecutions, and great sufferings of the Indians converts to Christianity and a regular civil life, and what obstacles and difficulties the missionaries had to combat with in their calling; if faith, hope and love had not been their armour, they would have deserted the field long ago.

"The unavoidable expenses of the work were provided by charitable collections in the Brethren's congregations, made some but once, and in others twice a year, & the defect made up by our Brethren abroad.

"The change of government, the increase of the expenses by the local situation of the Indian-congregation, and great distance of the Indian nations, suggested a new arrangement, and the forming of a regular society for the support of the missions was proposed and resolved, upon the plan here subjoined.

"The holy scriptures teaches us to confider the whole race of me, as one great family. God created us all. We come all from one blood. We are all sinners. Jesus Christ died for us all, and commanded to preach the gospel to all nations, kindred and tongues, be they friend or foe.

"These are strong and solid reasons for true philanthropy, and for suppressing that inveterate, malicious hatred against the Indian nations. If you can think so, and you do moreover love our Lord Jesus Christ, the Saviour of the world, let your prayers and best wishes be for the success & prosperity of this society, and all gospel missionaries, that God may be praised among all the nations of this continent. John Ettwein, Epifc. Frrm. Bethlehem *George Washington Papers at the Library of Congress*, 1741-1799: Series 4. General Correspondence. 1697-1799 Society of United Brethren, November 1, 1787, Pamphlet on Propagating the Gospel among Indians Image 319ff.

27   Stated Rules of the Society of the United Brethren, For Propagating the Gospel among the Heathen (Philadelphia: Printed by Charles Cist, in Race-Street Between Front and Second-streets). *George Washington Papers at the Library of Congress*, 1741-1799: Series 4. General Correspondence. 1697-1799. Society of United Brethren, November 1, 1787, Pamphlet on Propagating the Gospel among Indians Image 319ff.

28   See under *WGW*, vol. 30, 7-6-1789. The letter is dated July 10, 1789. Washington also encountered the United Brethren of Wachovia in North Carolina during his tour of the south. See the letters between them and Washington dated 5-31-1791 as well as his diary for 6-1-1791. *George Washington Papers at the Library of Congress*, 1741-1799: Series 2 Letterbooks. George Washington to Wachovia, North Carolina, United Brethren, May 31, 1791 Letterbook 39 Image 97ff. Donald Jackson, and Dorothy Twohig, ed, *The Diaries of George Washington*. vol. 6., p. 153.

29   Meade, *Old Churches*, Vol I. p. 69.

30   Ibid.

31   The day of fasting was observed throughout the colony. "The people met generally with anxiety and alarm in their countenances, and the effect of the day, through the whole colony, was like a shock of electricity, arousing every man, and placing him erect and solidly on his center." (See Jefferson's *Works*, vol. I, p. 7.) "The fast was obeyed throughout Virginia with such rigor and scruples, as to interdict the tasting of food between the rising and setting sun. With the remembrance of the King [Ministry?], horror was associated; in churches, as well as in the circles of social conversation, he seemed to stalk like the arch-enemy of mankind." (See Moncure D. Conway's *Biography of Edmund Randolph.) WGW*, vol. 3, DIARY May 12, May 16

32   Meade, *Old Churches*, Vol I. p. 69.

33   Ibid.

34   Ibid.

35   Ibid., vol. I. p.73.

36   *WGW*, vol. 15, 5-12-1779.

37   It is under Whittaker's ministry that the remarkable events surrounding the Indian princess Pocahontas occurred. The evidence suggests that Pocahontas was the daughter of Powhatan, the dominant native king of the Indians inhabiting the Virginian forests. She first appears in history in the record of Captain Smith, who explains that as a twelve- or thirteen-year-old she rescued him from impending destruction. The captured Captain had not been released even though the young princess pleaded to her father for his life. As Smith's head was placed upon a rock and her father raised high a wooden club to crush his skull, she instantly interposed herself, placing her head upon Smith's head, while tightly embracing the doomed Captain with both arms, "hazarding' as Smith himself put it, "the beating out of her own brains instead of mine." (Meade, I.81.) Her father's heart melted, and the Captain's life was spared.

   The hostilities did not end immediately, and Pocahontas, on another occasion, brought a warning of an imminent attack to the English settlement. Smith wrote, "the dark night could not affright her, but, coming through the irksome woods, with watered eyes gave me intelligence." Meade, *Old Churches*, vol. I.81.

   Pocahontas' friendship with the English, however, did not keep her from being used as a pawn in negotiations to secure some captured settlers and confiscated goods from Powhatan's warriors. On one of her visits to the village, she was welcomed on board ship only to become a hostage, to begin the bargaining for the release of the other colonists. But unexpectedly to all, her stay aboard ship with the colonists produced an interest in Christianity and her engagement to John Rolph.

   While the order and the significance of the events in her life are still debated, the facts generally speaking are: having adopted Christianity, she was baptized in the Anglican Church; married an English settler named Mr. Rolph, had a child, and traveled with her family to England in 1616, where she died before the family returned to Virginia. Smith said, "She was the first Christian of that nation; the first who ever spake English, or had a child in marriage." She always spoke of Captain Smith as "father." When Pocahontas unexpectedly met him later in England, having been told before her voyage to England that he was dead, she joyfully greeted him again with her accustomed appellation of "father." But to her chagrin, the title of "daughter" that Smith had addressed her with in Virginia, he would not use in England.

The record of the story of Pocahontas' conversion was written in 1614 by Sir Thomas Dale, the High-Marshall of Jamestown:

   Powhatan's daughter I caused to be carefully instructed in the Christian religion, who, after she had made some good progress therein, renounced publicly her country's idolatry, openly confessed her Christian faith, was, as she desired, baptized, and is since married to an English gentleman of good understanding, (as by his letter unto me, containing the reasons of his marriage of her, you may perceive,) another knot to bind this peace the stronger. Her father and friends gave approbation to it, and her uncle gave her to him in the Church. She lives civilly and lovingly with him, and I trust will increase in goodness, as the knowledge of God increaseth in her. She will go into England with me; and, were it but the gaining of this one soul, I will think my time, toil, and present stay well spent. (Meade, *Old Churches*, vol., I:79.)

The spiritual rationale that motivated John Rolf is evident in his extended letter on the topic:
Meade, I:126-129 Rolph's Letter to Sir Thomas Dale

   "Honourable Sir, and Most worthy Governor:—When your leisure shall best serve you to peruse these lines, I trust in God the beginning will not strike you unto greater admiration than the end will give you good content. It is a matter of no small moment, concerning my own particular, which here I impart unto you, and which toucheth me so nearly as the tenderness of my salvation. Howbeit, I freely subject myself to your great and mature judgment, deliberation, approbation, and determination; assuring myself of your zealous admonition and godly comforts, either persuading me to desist, or encouraging me to persist therein, with a religious fear and godly care, for which (from the very instant that this began to root itself within the secret bosom of my breast) my daily and earnest prayers have been, still are, and ever shall bee poured forthwith, in a sincere a goodly zeal as I possibly may, to be directed, aided, and governed in all my thoughts, words and deeds, to the glory of God and for my eternal consolation; to persevere wherein I had never had more need, nor (till now) could ever imagine to have bin moved with the like occasion. But (my case standing as it doth) what better worldly refuge can I here seek, than to shelter myself under the safety of your favourable protection? And did not my care proceed from an unspotted conscience, I should not dare to offer to your view and approved judgment these passions of my troubled soul; so full of fear and trembling is hypocrisy and dissimulation. But, knowing my own innocency and godly fervour in the whole prosecution hereof, I doubt not of your benign acceptance and element construction. As for malicious depravers and turbulent spirits, to whom nothing is tasteful but what pleaseth their unsavory palate, I pass not for them, being well assured in my persuasion by the often trial and proving of myself in my holiest meditations and praises, that I am called hereunto by the Spirit of God; and it shall be sufficient for me to be protected by yourself in all virtuous and pious endeavors. And for me more happy proceedings herein my daily obligations shall ever be addressed to bring to pass to Good effects, that yourself and all the world may truly say, 'This is the work of God, an it is marvelous in our eyes.'

   "But to avoid tedious preambles, and to come nearer the matter: first, suffer with your patience to sweep and make clean the way wherein I walk from all suspicions and doubts, which may be covered therein, and faithfully to reveal unto you what should move me hereunto.

   "Let, therefore, this my well-advised protestations, which here I make before God and my own conscience, be a sufficient witness at the dreadful day of judgment, when the secret of all living harts shall be opened, to condemn me herein, if my deepest intent and purpose be not to strive with all my power of body and mind, in the undertaking of so mighty a matter, for the good of this plantation, for the honour of our country, for the glory of God, for my own salvation, and for the converting to the true knowledge of God and Jesus Christ an unbelieving creature, - viz. : Pokahontas. To whom my hearty and best thoughts are and have a long time bin so entangled and enthralled in so intricate a labyrinth, that I was even aweariied to unwind myself thereout. But Almighty God, who never faileth his that truly invocate his holy name, hath opened the gate and led me by the hand, that I might plainly see and discern the safe paths wherein to tread.

   "To you, therefore, (most noble sir,) the patron and father of us in this country, doe I utter the effects of this my settled and long-continued affection, (which hath made me mighty war in my meditations;) and here I do truly relate, to what issue this dangerous combat is come unto, wherein I have not only examined, but thoroughly tried and pared my thoughts, even to the quick, before I could find any fit, wholesome, and apt applications to cure so dangerous an ulcer. I never failed to offer my daily and faithful prayers to God for his sacred and holy assistance. I forgot not to set before mine eyes the frailty of mankind, his proneness to evil, his indulgence of wicked thoughts, with many other imperfections, wherein man is daily ensnared and oftentimes overthrown, and them compared to my present estate. Nor was I ignorant of the heavy displeasure which Almighty God conceived against the son of Levi and Israel for marrying strange wives, nor of the inconveniences which may thereby arise, with other the like good notions, which made me look about warily and with good circumspection into the grounds and principal agitations, which thus provoke me to be in love with one whose education hath been rude, her manners barbarous, her generation accursed, and so discrepant in all nurtreture from myself, that oftentimes with fear and trembling I have ended my private controversy with this : - 'Surely these are wicked instigations, hatched by him who seeketh and delighteth in man's destruction;' and so with fervent prayers to be ever preserved from such diabolical assaults (as I took those to be) I have taken some rest.

"Thus when I thought I had obtained some peace and quietness, behold, another but more gracious temptation hath made breaches into my holiest and strongest mediations, with which I have been put to a new trail, in a straighter manner than the former; for besides the many passions and sufferings which I have daily, hourly, yea, and in the my sleep endured, even awaking me to astonishment, taxing me with remissness and carelessness, refusing and neglecting to perform the duties of a good Christian, pulling me by the care, and crying, 'Why dost not thou endeavor to make her a Christian?' And these have happened to my greater wonder even when she hath bin furthest separated from me, which in common reason (were it not an undoubted work of God) might breed forgetfulness of a fare more worthy creature. Besides, I say, the Holy Spirit hath often demanded of me, why I was created, if not for transitory pleasures and worldly vanities, but to labour in the Lord's vineyard, there to sow and plant, to nourish and increase the fruits thereof, daily adding, with the good husband in the gospel, somewhat to the talent, that in the end the fruits may be reaped, to the comfort of the labourer in this life and his salvation in the world to come? And if this be, as undoubtedly this is, the service Jesus Christ requireth of his best servant, woe unto him that hath these instruments of piety put into his hands, and willfully despiseth to work with them! Likewise adding hereunto her great appearance of love to me, her desire to be taught and instructed in the knowledge of God, her capableness of understanding, her aptness and willingness to receive any good impression, and also the spirituall, beside her own incitements hereunto stirring me up. What should I doe? Shall I be of so untoward a disposition as to refuse to lead the blind into the right way? Shall I be so unnatural as not to give bread to the hungry, or uncharitable as not to cover the naked? Shall I despise to actuate these pious duties of a Christian? Shall the base fear of displeasing the world overpower and withhold me from revealing unto man these spiritual works of the Lord, which in my meditations and prayers I have daily made known unto him? God forbid! I assuredly trust he hath thus dealt with me for my eternal felicity and for his glory; and I hope so to be guarded by his heavenly grace, that in the end, by my faithful prayers and christianlike labour, I shall attain to that blessed promise pronounced by that holy prophet Daniel unto the righteous that bring many unto the knowledge of God, - namely: that 'They shall shine like the stars forever and ever.' A sweeter comfort cannot be to a true Christian, nor a greater encouragement to him to labour all the days of his life in performance thereof, to be desired at the hour of death and in the day of judgment. Again, by my reading and conference with honest and religious persons, have I received no small encouragement; besides *mea serena conscietia*, the cleanness of my conscience, clean from the filth of impurity, *quoe est instar muri ahenei*, which is to me a brazen wall. If I should set down at large the perturbations and godly motions which have striven within me, I should make but a tedious and unnecessary volume. But I doubt not these shall be sufficient, both to certify you of my true intent, in discharging of my duties to God and to yourself, to whose gracious Providence I humbly submit myself, for his glory, you honour, my country's good, the benefit of this Plantation, and for the converting of one unregenerate to regeneration, which I beseech God to grant for his dear Son Christ Jesus his sake. Nor am I in so desperate an estate that I regard not what becometh of me; nor am I out of hope but one day to see my country, nor so void of friends, nor mean in birth, but there to obtain a match to my great content; nor have I ignorantly passed over my hopes there, nor regardlessly seek to lose the love of my friends by taking this course: I know them all, and I have not rashly overslipped any.

"But shall it please God thus to dispose of me (which I earnestly desire to fulfill my end before set down) I will heartily accept of it, as a godly tax appointed me, and I will never cease (God assisting me) until I have accomplished and brought to perfection so holy a work, in which I will daily pray God to bless me, to mine and her eternal happiness. And thus desiring no longer to live, to enjoy the blessing of God, than this resolution doth tend to such godly ends, as are by me before declared, not doubting your favourable acceptance, I take my leave, beseeching Almighty God to rain down upon you such plenitude of his heavenly graces as your heart can wish and desire; and so I rest, 'At you command, most willingly to be disposed off, "John Rolph." (Bishop Meade, *Old Churches* Vol I, pp. 126-129.)

38   The legacy of Pocahontas has become a permanent part of the American story as can be seen in Washington, D.C., In the rotunda of our Capitol Building, one of the four majestic paintings commemorating America's colonial era is the scene of the baptism of Pocahontas in an Anglican Church. In "The Baptism of the Indian Princess Pocahontas in 1613," she kneels in the presence of family members, including her father Chief Powhatan. Her brother Nantequaus turns away from the ceremony. By this the artist may be implying the future hostility that will break out between the Native Americans and the Virginian colonists. The man behind here is her future husband, John Rolfe. Theirs became the first recorded marriage of a Native American and a European. Her story, while subject to all the interpolations and variations that often distort traditional stories especially those with potentially romantic themes, is nevertheless at the heart of the story of Virginia.

39   "On weekdays, early in the morning, the captain sent for tools, for which a receipt was given; the companies assembled, with the tools, in the place of arms, where "the serjeant-major, or captain of the watch, upon their knees, made public and faithful prayers to Almighty God for his blessing and protection to attend them in this their business the whole day after-succeeding. The men were divided into gangs, who worked on alternate days. The gang for the day was then delivered to the masters and overseers of the work appointed, who kept them at labour until nine or ten o'clock, according to the season of the year; then, at the beat of the drum, they were marched to the church to hear divine service. After dinner, and rest till two or three o'clock, at the beat of a drum, the captain drew them forth to the place of arms, to be thence taken to their work till five or six o'clock, when, at beat of drum, they were again marched to church to evening prayer: they were

then dismissed,—those that were to set the watch with charge to prepare their arms, the others unto their rest and lodgings. After order given out for the watch, the captain had to assemble his company, except his sentinels, upon his court of guard, and there "humbly present themselves on their knees, and, by faithful and zealous prayer to Almighty God, commend themselves and their endeavours to his merciful protections." Again, in the morning, an hour after the discharge of the watch, were they to repair to the court of guard, and there, "with public prayer, to give unto Almighty God humble thanks and praises for his merciful and safe protection through the night, and commend themselves to his no less merciful protection and safeguard for the day following. It was also the special duty of the captain to have religious and manly care over the poor sick soldiers or labourers under his command; to keep their lodgings sweet and their beds standing three feet from the ground, as provided in the public injunctions." (Meade, *Old Churches* vol. I. pp. 119-120.)

40 *The London Chronicle* in the September 21 to 23, 1779 edition (no. 3561, p. 288) carried an article that affirmed Washington's religious nature. It was entitled, "Character of General Washington, by an American Gentleman now in London, who is well acquainted with him." It states, "General Washington, altho' advanced in years is remarkably healthy, takes a great deal of exercise, and is very fond of riding on a favourite white horse; he is very reserved and loves retirement. . . . He regularly attends divine service in his tent every morning and evening, and seems very fervent in his prayers."

41 Meade, *Old Churches*, vol. I. pp. 74-75.

42 For the history and text of the Calvinistic "Lambeth Articles" see Schaff, *The Creeds of Christendom* vol. 3, p. 523.

43 Meade, *Old Churches* vol. I. pp. 77. We gain insight into the missions efforts of Whittaker from his "Tractate by Master Alexander Whittaker," written at Henrico in 1613.

"They (the Indians) acknowledge that there is a great good God, but know him not, having the eyes of their understanding as yet blinded; wherefore they serve the Devil for fear, after a most base manner, sacrificing sometime (as I have heard) their own children to him. I have sent one image of their god to the Council in England, which is painted on one side of a toadstool, much like unto a deformed monster. Their priests (whom they call Quickosoughs) are no other but such as our English witches are. They live naked in body, as if their shame of their sin deserved no covering. Their names are as naked as their body: they esteem it virtue to lye, deceive, and steal, as their master the Devil teacheth them.

"Their men are not so simple as some have supposed them, for they are of body lusty, strong, and very nimble; they are a very understanding generation, - quicke of apprehension, sudden in their dispatches, subtile in their dealings, exquisite in their intentions, and industrious in their labour. I suppose the world hath no better marksmen than they be: they will kill birds flying, fishes swimming, and beasts running. They shoot also with marvelous strength: they shot one of our men, being unarmed, quite through the body and nailed both his arms to his body with one arrow: one of their children also, about the age of twelve or thirteen years, killed a bird with his arrow, in my sight. The service of their god is answerable to their life, being performed with great fear and attention, and many strange dumb shews used in the same, stretching forth their limbs and straining their body, much like to the counterfeit women in England, who fancy themselves bewitched or possessed of some evil spirit. They stand in great awe of the Quickosoughs or priests, which are a generation of vipers, even Satan's own brood. The manner of their life is much like to the Popish hermits of our age; for they live along in the woods, in houses sequestered from the common course of men; neither may any man be suffered to come into their house, or speaks to them, but when the priest doth call him.

"He taketh no care for his victuals; for all such kind of things, both bread and water, &c., are brought into a place near his cottage and there left, which he fetcheth for his proper needs. If they would have raine, or have lost any thing, they have recourse to him, who conjureth for them and many times prevaileth. If they be sick, he is their physician; if they be wounded, he sucketh them. At his command they make war and peace, neither doe they any thing of moment without him. Finally, there is a civil government among them which they strictly observe, and show thereby that the law of nature dwelleth in them; for they have a rude kinde of commonwealth and rough government, wherein they both honour and obey their king, parents, and governors, both greater and lesser. They observe the limits of their own possessions. Murder is scarcely heard of; adultery and other offences severely punished." (Meade, *Old Churches* vol. I. pp. 134-135.)

44 The intermarriage of the Indian princess and the English settler brought on an era of peace in Virginia. But there were storm clouds brewing both in the mother country and secretly in the council fires of Powhatan's chiefs. The Reverend Peter Fontaine, corresponding with his brother in England while defending intermarriage with the Indians as a means of their civilization and Christianization, explains why the practice had ceased among the Virginians:

But this, our wise politicians at home put an effectual stop to at the beginning of our settlement here, for when they heard that Rolph had married Pocahontas, it was deliberated in Council whether he had not committed high treason by so doing, that is, marrying an Indian princess; and had not some troubles intervened, which put a stop to the enquiry, the poor man might have been hanged up for doing the most just, the most natural, the most generous and politic action, that ever was done on this side of the water. This put an effectual stop to all intermarriages afterwards. (Meade, *Old Churches* Vol I. p. 82.)

Pocahontas died while in England, although her family returned to America. Pocahontas' family legacy has included many illustrious American descendants, most notably, President Woodrow Wilson. But the frowns of the English leaders on the intermarriage of Virginians and Indians ended this form of "generous" diplomacy. Nevertheless, the good news of the gospel's advance in the wilds of the new world prompted responses of joy. Plans began to establish a University in Virginia. Gifts flowed in for the building up of the church across the ocean. In 1622, a clergyman was requested to bring a Thanksgiving message in London for all of God's mercies to the Virginian colony.

45 The struggle to Christianize the Indians was captured in a letter by Colonel Byrd: "The whole number of people belonging to the Nottoway Town, if you include women and children, amounts to about two hundred. These are the only Indians of any consequence now remaining within the limits of Virginia. The rest are either removed or dwindled to a very inconsiderable number, either by destroying one another, or else by smallpox or other diseases; though nothing has been so fatal to them as their ungovernable passion for rum, with which, I am

sorry to say it, they have been but too liberally supplied by the English that live near them. And here I must lament the bad success Mr. Boyle's charity has hitherto had toward converting any of these poor heathen to Christianity. Many children of our neighboring Indians have been brought up in the College of William and Mary. They have been taught to read and write, and have been carefully instructed in the Christian religion till they came to be men; yet after they returned home, instead of civilizing and converting the rest, they have immediately relapsed into infidelity and barbarism themselves. And some of them, too, have made the worst use of the knowledge they acquired among the English, by employing it against their benefactors. Besides, as they unhappily forget all the good they learn and remember the ill, they are apt to be more vicious and disorderly than the rest of their countrymen. I ought not to quit this subject without doing justice to the great prudence of Colonel Spottswood in this affair. This gentleman was Lieutenant-Governor of Virginia when Carolina was engaged in a bloody war with the Indians. At that critical time it was thought expedient to keep watchful eye upon our tributary savages, whom we knew had nothing to keep them to their duty but their fears. Then it was that he demanded of each nation a competent number of their great men's children to be sent to the College, where they served as so many hostages for the good behaviour of the rest, and, at the same time, were themselves principled in the Christian religion. He also placed a schoolmaster among the Saponi Indians, at a salary of fifty pounds annum, to instruct their children. ...I am sorry I cannot give a better account of the state of the poor Indians with respect to Christianity, although a great deal of pains has been taken and still continues to be take with them. For my part, I must be of the opinion, as I hinted before, that there is but one way of converting these poor infidels and reclaiming them from barbarity, and that is charitably to intermarry with them, according to the modern policy of the most Christian King in Canada and Louisiana. Had the English done this at the first settlement of the Colony, the infidelity of the Indians had been worn out at this day, with their dark complexions, and the country had swarmed with more people than insects. It was certainly and unreasonable nicety that prevented their entering into so good-natured an alliance. All nations of men have the same natural dignity, and we all know that very bright talents may be lodged under a very dark skin. The principal difference between one people and another proceeds only from the different opportunities of improvement. The Indians by no means want understanding, and are in figure tall and well proportioned. Even their copper-coloured complexions would admit of blanching, if not in the first, at the furthest in the second generation. I may safely venture to say, the Indian women would have made altogether as honest wives for the first planters as the damsels they used to purchase from aboard ships. It is strange, therefore, that any good Christian should have refused a wholesome straight bedfellow when he might have had so fair a portion with her as the merit of saving her soul." (Meade, *Old Churches*, vol. I. pp. 283ff.)

46   The marriage of the Princess to the Englishman created a sense of peace and well being between their formerly warring peoples. But things forever changed for the worse on March 22nd of that year. Unbeknown to the settlers that began to spread out without fear along the James River, a massacre had been secretly planned for a period of years. Bishop Meade describes this as "one of the most unexpected and direful calamities which had ever befallen the Colony":

On one and the same day the attack was made on every place. Jamestown, and some few points near to it, alone escaped, having received warning of the intended attack just in time to prepare for defenses. Besides the destruction of houses by fire, between three and four hundred persons were put to death in the most cruel manner. (Meade, *Old Churches*, vol. I. p. 85.)

The previous spiritual calls by the clergy and the crown for the evangelization of the Indians were instantly silenced by clamorous demands for merciless revenge to protect the devastated and vulnerable colonists. The East India Company that had strenuously worked to build the colony and good relationships with the Native Americans expressed the outrage that gripped the betrayed Anglicans:

We condemn their bodies, the saving of whose souls we have so zealously affected. Root them out from being any longer a people,— so cursed a nation, ungrateful for all benefits and incapable of all goodness,—or remove them so far as to be out of danger or fear. War perpetually, without peace or truce. Yet spare the young for servants. Starve them by destroying their corn, or reaping it for your own use. Pluck up their weirs (fishing-traps.) Obstruct their hunting. Employ foreign enemies against them at so much a head. Keep a band of your own men continually upon them, to be paid by the Colony, which is to have half of their captives and plunder. He that takes any of their chiefs to be doubly rewarded. He that takes Opochancono (the chief and brother of old Powhatan, who was now dead) shall have a great and singular reward.

Later an order was given, "The Indians being irreconcilable enemies, every commander, on the least molestation, to fall upon them." The tragic blueprint for dealing with the Indian tribes of North America was thus first written by the devastated colonists.

What then was to become of the colony's vision, said so well by the King's patent?:

So noble a work may, by the Providence of God, hereafter tend to the glorie of his divine majestie, in propagating of Christian religion to such people as sit in darkness and miserable ignorance of the true knowledge and worship of God, and may in time bring the infidels and savages (living in those parts) to human civility and quiet government. (Meade, *Old Churches* Vol I. p. 63.)

Bishop Meade describes the sense of the mother country at this nadir of despair,

The missionary effort was considered as a failure; the conversion, or even civilization, of the Indian, was regarded as hopeless. . . . The Indians were now objects of dread, of hate, of persecution. A sentiment and declaration is ascribed to one of the last of the ministers who came over, "that the only way to convert the Indians was to cut the throats of their chief men and priests." (Meade, *Old Churches*, vol. I. p. 87.)

47   Although the numbers of settlers continued to grow, there was a clear decline in the spiritual health of the clergy in the post-Pocahontas era. This historical reality was written in laws aimed at the clergy. "Laws now seem to be required to keep the ministers from cards, dice, drinking, and such like things; and even to constrain them to preach and administer the communion as often as was proper,— yea, even to visit the sick and dying." Meade, *Old Churches*, vol. I. p. 92.

48   See Alan Harding, *The Countess of Huntingdon's Connexion: A Sect in Action in Eighteenth-Century England* (Oxford University Press, 2003). This summary is dependent on the BBC's Making History: *The Countess of Huntingdon's Connexion* http://www.bbc.co.uk/education/beyond/factsheets/makhist/makhist7_prog5d.shtml. Lady Huntingdon appointed evangelist George

Whitefield (1714-70) to be her chaplain. Whitefield began preaching in the fields to miners at Kingswood near Bristol after being prevented from preaching in the churches. When Whitefield's ministry brought him to America, he became the first nationally famous preacher. James Hutson, the current Chief of the Manuscript Division of he Library of Congress, has compared the impact of Whitefield's coming to America in the mid-1700's to the British invasion of the Beatles in the1960's. After her husband's death, the Countess was called the "Elect Lady" of Methodism. She hoped to evangelize the upper class but when opposed by Anglicans she created her Connexion which Whitefield led from 1748. She developed chapels in connection with her residences, which she could accomplish because of her noble position. When she opened them for public evangelistic preaching, the Anglican Church resisted. So in 1781 her new movement left the Anglican fold.

The Countess proceeded to appoint evangelical ministers, but her determined efforts to win the souls of the nobility were not always welcomed. The Duchess of Buckingham declared that Lady Huntingdon's doctrines were "strongly tinctured with impertinence toward their superiors. It is monstrous to be told you have a heart as sinful as the common wretches who crawl the earth." Ultimately, Whitefield's Calvinist theology led to a division between Lady Huntingdon's Connexion and John Wesley, the Arminian (Anti-Calvinist) founder of the Methodist Church.

In all, Lady Huntingdon built sixty-four churches, targeting the aristocratic rich as well as a college for the education of her ministers. Most of the Countess of Huntingdon's Connexion chapels that remain are now part of the United Reform Church, though more than twenty chapels remain outside that Church, partly because they were owned by local trusts and could go the way trustees wanted. The Countess of Huntingdon's Connexion still exists as a small denomination with twenty-five chapels in this country and is affiliated with the Evangelical Alliance.

49 Jackson & Twohig, *The Diaries of George Washington. vol. 3*..[November] 1774, November 5.

50 *WGW*, vol. 27, 8-10-1783. For the full range of correspondence and strategic plan development of the mission, see the *Papers of George Washington*, Confederation Series vol. 2 (W. W. Abbot ed, Charlottesville: University Press of Virginia, 1992) pp. 200, 205-218; 330-332; 386, 392-396.

51 Ibid., 27, 8-10-1783, note.

52 Ibid., vol. 37, 1-20-1799. To Reverend Bryan, Lord Fairfax, Washington wrote on January 20, 1799, "Lady Huntington as you may have been told *was* a correspondent of mine, and did me the honor to claim me as a relation; but in what degree, or by what connexion it came to pass, she did not inform me, nor did I ever trouble her Ladyship with an enquiry. The favourable sentiments which others, you say, have been pleased to express respecting me, cannot but be pleasing to a mind [*sic*] who always walked on a straight line, and endeavoured as far as human frailties, and perhaps strong passions, would enable him, to discharge the relative duties to his Maker and fellow-men, without seeking any indirect or left handed attempts to acquire popularity."

53 *WGW*, vol. 27, 8-10-1783.

54 The letter continues: "I have been induced from this great object before me, to accept the obliging offers of Mr. James Jay (who was upon the point of embarking for America) to convey the outline of my design to each of the governors of those states, in which from nearest access to the Indian Nations and from soil and climate, a situation for many hundred families for the services of the Indians and the establishment of a people connected with me, should appear best. And whose object would be to support the Gospel, and render those missionaries sent by me for the Indians and their various ministrations among themselves, the more consistently useful for all.

"Should I be able to obtain a sufficient quantity of land suitable for such purposes, my intentions would be to transfer both my trust estate with all my own property in Georgia for this more extensive prospect, and which from the extreme heat of the climate renders the labours of missionaries there of little advantage. This with the poor and little, all I have to give on earth, has been long devoted to God, should so ever a happy a period arrive as in his tender mercy to us. We might be made the fortunate and honoured instruments in that great day approaching for calling the heathen nations as his inheritance, to the glorious light of the Gospel. Or should this offer any little prelude to so important an event, the hearts of all men for this purpose will be made subject. And as certainly no interested motives can appear, but on the contrary, a ready willingness to do and suffer his righteous will as his servants, so none can feel any effect from the accomplishment of the design but the increase of order, wealth, and the pure protestant faith, carrying the glad tidings of peace and Christian love over the earth.

"I indulge myself with the hope of your forgiveness for an openness so due to you on a subject that interesting in its views to me and also considering it as so great an honour done me by you admitting a representation for your attention, tho' but for an hour.

"My kind and most excellent friend Mr. Fairfax undertakes the care of this packet for me. His noble just and equitable mind renders him the friend of my highest regard and his ever willing and important services engage me as are under the greatest obligation to him and who on all occasions has my first confidence.

"You must yet bear with me by the liberty I take in sending the copy of the letter to the governor and outlines of the plan, as no reasons to you on the subject is compatible with the just honour and respect you must ever claim from me.

"Could my best compliments and best wishes to Mrs. Washington be rendered acceptable, she would help to plead my pardon with you to this unreasonable long letter but which does certainly contain in meaning the truest and most faithful regard, from Sir, Yours and Mrs. Most devoted obedient and most humble servant S. Huntingdon'

March 20, 1784. *George Washington Papers at the Library of Congress*, 1741-1799: Series 4. General Correspondence. 1697-1799 Selina S. Hastings to George Washington, March 20, 1784, Image 324ff.

55 *WGW* 28: 2-27-1785.

56 Ibid., vol. 28, 1-25-1785.

57 Ibid., vol. 28, 2-8-1785.

58 Ibid., vol. 28, 6-30-1785.

59   Ibid., vol. 31, 10-25-1791.   In Washington's Third Address To Congress on October 25, 1791, he wrote: "…the Executive of the United States should be enabled to employ the means to which the Indians have been long accustomed for uniting their immediate Interests with the preservation of Peace. And that efficacious provision should be made for inflicting adequate penalties upon all those who, by violating their rights, shall infringe the Treaties, and endanger the peace of the Union. A System corresponding with the mild principles of Religion and Philanthropy towards an unenlightened race of Men, whose happiness materially depends on the conduct of the United States, would be as honorable to the national character as conformable to the dictates of sound policy."

Compare President Washington's letter to Reverend John Carroll, the first Roman Catholic Bishop in the United States, on April 10, 1792. "Sir: I have received and duly considered your memorial of the 20th. ultimo, on the subject of the instructing the Indians within, and con-tiguous to the United States, in the principles and duties of Christianity.

The war now existing between the United States and some tribes of the western Indians prevents, for the present, any interference of this nature with them. The Indians of the five nations are, in their religious concerns, under the immediate superintendence of the Revd. Mr. Kirkland; and those who dwell in the eastern extremity of the United States are, according to the best information that I can obtain, so sit-uated as to be rather considered as a part of the inhabitants of the State of Massachusetts than otherwise, and that State has always con-sidered them as under its immediate care and protection. Any application therefore relative to these Indians, for the purposes mentioned in your memorial, would seem most proper to be made to the Government of Massachusetts. The original letters on this subject, which were submitted to my inspection, have been returned to Charles Carroll, Esq. of Carrollton.

Impressed as I am with an opinion, that the most effectual means of securing the permanent attachment of our savage neighbors, is to con-vince them that we are just, and to shew them that a proper and friendly intercourse with us would be for our mutual advantage: I cannot conclude without giving you my thanks for your pious and benevolent wishes to effect this desirable end, upon the mild principles of Religion and Philanthropy. And when a proper occasion shall offer, I have no doubt but such measures will be pursued as may seem best calculated to communicate liberal instruction, and the blessings of society, to their untutored minds. With very great esteem etc." *WGW*, vol. 32: 4-10-1792.

60   *WGW*, vol. 31, 1-11-1792. See also *The Papers of George Washington*, W. W. Abbot, Ed., Dorothy Twohig, Assoc. Ed., *Presidential Series* (Charlottesville: University Press of Virginia), vol. 9, pp. 394-395.

61   Ibid., vol. 35: 5-16-1796.

62   Ibid., vol. 35:11-14-1796.

63   Ibid., vol. 28, 12-8-1784.

64   Ibid., vol. 35: 5-16-1796.

CHAPTER 5

1   Rule 108 of the "Rules of Civility," copied by George Washington in his school paper 1746. The "Rules of Civility" are a part of the George Washington Papers and can be read on line at: http://memory.loc.gov/cgi-bin/query/P?mgw:1:./temp/~ammem_LB9I:: George Washington Papers at the Library of Congress, 1741-1799: Series 1a George Washington, Forms of Writing, and "The Rules of Civility and Decent Behavior in Company and Conversation," ante 1747. They have also been recently released in contemporary form. See: George Washington, *George-isms* (New York: Athenaeum Books for Young Readers, 2000). See also the appendix I.

2   Frank E. Grizzard Jr., *George Washington: A Biographical Companion* (Santa Barbara: ABC-CLIO, Inc. 2002) p. 331. Grizzard notes: "The Reverend Lawrence Washington, M.A., Fellow of Brasenose College, Oxford, and later a country rector allegedly ousted by the Puritans for drunkenness."

Historian Henry Cabot Lodge questions the moral charge, but explains that both poverty and politics made the move to the New World for this noble family a good decision: "The rector had been ejected on the grounds that he was "scandalous" and "malignant." That he was guilty of the former charge we may well doubt; but that he was, in the language of the time, "malignant," must be admitted, for all his fam-ily, including his brothers, Sir William Washington of Packington and Sir John Washington of Thrapston, his nephew, Sir Henry Washington, and his nephew-in-law, William Legge, ancestor of the Earl of Dartmouth were strongly on the side of the king. In a mar-riage which seems to have been regarded as beneath the dignity of the family, and in the poverty consequent upon the ejectment from his living, we can find the reason for the sons of the Reverend Lawrence Washington going forth into Virginia to find their fortune, and fly-ing from the world of victorious Puritanism which offered just then so little hope to royalists like themselves. Yet what was poverty in England was something much more agreeable in the New World of America. The emigrant brothers at all events seem to have had resources of a sufficient kind, and to have been men of substance, for they purchased lands and established themselves at Bridges Creek, in Westmoreland county. With this brief statement, Lawrence disappears, leaving us nothing further than the knowledge that he had numerous descendants." Henry Cabot Lodge, *George Washington*, (New Rochelle, NY, Arlington House, 1898), pp. 36-37.

3   *WGW*, vol. 32, 5-2-1792.

4   *Colonial Families of the United States of America* vol. II http://ftp.rootsweb.com/pub/usgenweb/va/rappahannock/wills/w2520001.txt Will of Lawrence Washington, Rappahannock co, 1677 Submitted by Sandra Ferguson <ferg@intelos.net> for use in the USGenWeb Archives In several sources it is noted that John, George Washington's great-grandfather, said in his will, "In the name of God, Amen. I, John Washington, of Washington parish, in the county of Westmoreland, in Virginia, gentleman, being of good and perfect memory, thanks be unto Almighty God for it, and calling to remembrance the uncertain state of this transitory life, that all flesh must yield unto death, do make, constitute, and ordain this my last will and testament and none other. And first, being heartily sorry, from the bottom of my heart, for my sins past, most humbly desiring forgiveness of the same from the Almighty God, my Saviour and Redeemer, in whom and by the merits of Jesus Christ I trust and believe assuredly to be saved, and to have full remission and forgiveness of all my sins, and that my soul with my body at the general resurrection shall rise again with joy. . . .through the merits of Jesus Christ's death and passion to possess and

inherit the kingdom of heaven prepared for his elect and chosen."

5   Historian James K. Paulding shuns the historical records of earlier Washingtons who were military leaders and heroes in British history.

6   Grizzard, *George Washington: A Biographical Companion*, p. 26.

7   Henry Cabot Lodge, *George Washington*, (New Rochelle: Arlington House, 1898), p. 37.

8   We will highlight John Washington's sense of justice in a story of his crossing the ocean to America in the Chapter on "George Washington and the Enlightenment."

9   Joseph D. Sawyer, *Washington* (New York: MacMillian, 1927), vol. I. p. 53.

10   Grizzard *George Washington: A Biographical Companion*, p. 53.

11   *WGW*, vol. 29, 10-1783, Biographical Memoranda. See Also David Humphreys, *Life of General Washington* (Athens and London: The University of Georgia Press) p.10.

12   Sawyer, *Washington*, vol. I. p. 53.

13   Ibid., p. 54.

14   Ibid., p. 53.

15   It is difficult to keep all of the Lawrence Washingtons distinct. Grizzard lists 11 Lawrence Washingtons from the years of George Washington's great-great-great-great-great-grandfather Lawrence Washington of Sulgrave Manor (c.1500-1584) to Lawrence Augustine Washington (1775-1824), George's nephew and son of his brother Samuel Washington. Grizzard *George Washington: A Biographical Companion*, p. 409.

16   Grizzard lists six other George Washingtons beside the first. These date from 1758—a nephew, son of half brother Augustine Washington and the last, a grandnephew born in 1790. George's adopted grandson (1781-1857) would unofficially be named Washington twice, George Washington Parke Custis Washington! Grizzard *George Washington: A Biographical Companion*, pp. 404, 408.

17   Ibid., p. 327.

18   Ibid., p. 326.

19   See, for example, the 39 *Articles* of the Church of England which can be found in Schaff, *Creeds of Christendom* vol. 3. p. 486. The *Catalogue of Homilies* are listed in Schaff, *The Creeds of Christendom*, vol. 3, pp. 509-511.

20   Slaughter, *The History of Truro Parish* p. 34ff.

21   Benson J. Lossing, *Mary and Martha: The Mother and Wife of George Washington* (New York: Harper & Brothers, 1886) p. 31.

22   Ibid.

23   Cited by Grizzard *George Washington: A Biographical Companion*, p. 327.

CHAPTER 6

1   *WGW*, vol. 35, 11-28-1796.

2   How much of Mason L. Weems' biography is grounded in fact? Consider the following example of how scholars have interacted with a traditional Washington story from Parson Weems. It comes from the time of Washington's early adult life as he was completing his service as a soldier and beginning to enter into politics. It well illustrates the difficulty in assessing the value for history of what Parson Weems preserved of Washington's life for posterity. John Corbin, *The Unknown Washington* (New York: Charles Scribner's Sons, 1930), pp. 44-45 gives the following summation: Washington Irving ignored the story. Bishop Meade offered local traditions that seemed to support Weems. Lodge utterly rejected it, declaring, "That Washington . . . allowed himself to be knocked down in the presence of his soldiers, and thereupon begged his assailant's pardon for having spoken roughly to him, [is a story] so silly and so foolish impossible that [it does not] deserve an instant's consideration." Yet Rupert Hughes accepted it as authentic. John Corbin believes the evidence is available to prove that it is an authentic event in the life of Washington. Thus some historians consider Weems' traditional stories to be historical, and others do not, and each judgment varies from case to case and author to author. It is here cited from Mason L. Weems, *The Life of Washington*, (The Belknap Press of Harvard University Press, 1962), p. 187-189.

    Brissot, another famous French traveller, assures us, that, "throughout the continent, every body spoke of Washington as of a father."

        That dearest and best of all appellations, "*the father of his country*," was the natural fruit of the *benevolence* which he so carefully cultivated through life. A singular instance of which we meet with in 1754, and the 22d year of his age.

        He was stationed at Alexandria with his regiment, the only one in the colony, and of which he was colonel. There happened at this time to be an election in Alexandria for members of assembly, and the contest ran high between colonel George Fairfax, and Mr. Elzey. Washington was the warm friend of Fairfax, and a Mr. Payne headed the friends of Elzey. A dispute happening to take place in the courthouse-yard, Washington, a thing very uncommon, said something that offended Payne; whereupon the little gentleman who, though but a cub in size, was the old lion in heart, raised his sturdy hickory, and, at a single blow, brought our hero to the ground. Several of Washington's officers being present, whipped out this cold irons in an instant, and it was believed that there would have been murder off-hand. To make bad worse, his regiment, hearing how he had been treated, bolted out from their barracks, with every man his weapon in his hand, threatening dreadful vengeance on those who had dared to knock down their beloved colonel. Happily for Mr. Payne and his party, Washington recovered, time enough to go out and meet his enraged soldiers; and, after thanking them for this expression of their love, and assuring them that he was not hurt in the least, he begged them, as they loved him or their duty, to return peaceably to their barracks. As for himself, he went to his room, generously chastising his imprudence, which had this struck up a spark that had like to have thrown the whole town into a flame. Finding on mature reflection, that he had been the aggressor, he resolved to make Mr. Payne honourable reparation, by asking his pardon on the morrow! No sooner had he made this noble resolution, than recovering that delicious gaiety which accompanies good purposes in a virtuous mind, he went to a ball that night, and behaved as pleasantly as though nothing had happened! Glorious proof that great souls, like great ships, are not affected by those little puffs which would overset feeble minds with passion, or sink them with spleen!

The next day he went to a tavern, and wrote a polite note to Mr. Payne, whom he requested to meet him. Mr. Payne took it for a challenge, and repaired to the tavern not without expecting to see a pair of pistols produced. But what was his surprise on entering the chamber, to see a decanter of wine and glasses on the table! Washington arose, and in a very friendly manner met him, and gave him his hand. "Mr. Payne," said he "to err is nature; to rectify error is glory; I find I was wrong yesterday, but wish to be right to-day. You have had some satisfaction; and if you think that sufficient, here's my hand, let us be friends.

3   The following story entitled, "The Poisoned Dish" allegedly comes from the time of Washington's military command of the revolutionary army. Yet it has all the signs of legend, even though it is in a book entitled, *True Stories of the Days of Washington*. It has no author, no source, and no other known record of the story occurring. It is, nevertheless, a valuable popular example of the fear of the possibility of Washington being assassinated.

The following story we also obtain from a communication to an old periodical. We have no reason to doubt its truth, although we do not find the circumstance mentioned elsewhere:

In the summer of 1776, when the American army was in New York, a young girl of the city went to her lover, one Francis, and communicated to him, as a secret she had overheard, a plan that was in operation among the government men to destroy the American commander-in-chief, by poison, which was to be plentifully mingled with his green peas, a favorite vegetable of his, on the following day, at Richmond Hill head-quarters, where he was to dine. Francis, who was a thorough Whig, although supposed to be friendly to the Royalists, went immediately to Washington and acquainted him with this diabolical plan for his destruction. Washington, having listened with attention said:

"My friend, I thank you; your fidelity has saved my life, to what reserve the Almighty knows! But, now, for your safety; I charge you to return to your house, and let not a word of what you have related to me, pass your lips; it would involve you in certain ruin; and heaven forbid that your life should be forfeited or endangered by your faith to me. I will take the necessary steps to prevent, and at the same time discover, the instrument of this wicked device."

The next day, about two hours before dinner, he sent for one of his guard, told him of the plot, and requested that he would disguise himself as a female, and go to the kitchen, there to keep a strict watch upon the peas, until they should be served up for the table. The young man carefully observed the directions he had received, and had not been long upon his post of duty, before a young man, another of the guard, came in anxiously to the door of the kitchen, looked in, and then passed away. In a few moments after, he returned and approached the hearth where the peas stood, and was about to mingle in the deadly substance, when suddenly he shrunk back as though from the sting of the fork-tongued adder, his color changing to the pale hue of death, and his limbs apparently palsied with fear, evidently horrorstruck with his own purpose; but soon, however, the operation of a more powerful incitement urged forward his reluctant hand, that trembling strewed the odious bane, and he left the kitchen, overwhelmed with conflicting passions, remorse and confusion.

"Harold sleeps no more; the cry has reached his heart ere the deed be accomplished," said the youth on duty, in a voice not devoid of pity, as he looked after the self-condemned wretch.

"What, Harold!" said the commander-in-chief, sorrowfully, upon receiving the information; "can it be possible – so young, so fair, and gentle! He would have been the last person upon whom a suspicion of that nature could have fallen, by right of countenance. You have done well," said he to the youth before him. "Go, join your comrades and be secret."

The young man went accordingly, and Washington returned to the piazza, where several officers were assembled, among whom was the hero of Saratoga, who was waiting for further instructions from Congress before he departed for Canada. In a few moments dinner was announced, and the party was ushered into a handsome apartment, where the sumptuous board was spread, covered with all the delicacies of the season.

The commander-in-chief took his seat, placing General Gates on his right hand, and General Wooster on the left. When the remainder of the officers and company were seated, and eager to commence the duties of the table, the chief said, impressively:

"Gentleman, I must request you to suspend your meal for a few moments. Let the guard attend me." All was silence and amazement. The guard entered and formed in a line toward the upper end of the apartment. Washington, having put upon his plate a spoonful of peas, fixed his eyes sternly upon the guilty man, and said: "Shall I eat of this vegetable?"

The youth turned pale and became dreadfully agitated, while his trembling lips faintly uttered, "I don't know."

"Shall I eat of these?" again demanded Washington, raising some upon his knife.

Here Harold elevated his hand, as if by an involuntary impulse, to prevent their being tasted.

A Chicken was then brought in, that a conclusive experiment might be made in the presence of all those witnesses. The animal ate of the peas and immediately died, and the wretched criminal, overcome with terror and remorse, fell fainting, and was borne from the apartment.

"The Poisoned Dish" in *True Stories of the Days of Washington* (New York: Phinney, Blakeman & Mason, 1861), p. 51-55.

4   A paradigm of authenticity might move in the direction from lesser reliability to greater reliability, beginning with myth, then moving consecutively to legend, to tradition, to verifiable historical event. Sometimes the only difference in actual history between tradition and historical event is verifiability. But the mere fact of the reality of historical occurrence is not the same as historical validity Thus, there is a strong wall of distinction between tradition and verifiable historical event. The recognition of this wall of separation between tradition and historical event, and the frustration and limitations it sometimes imposes on the historian, has encouraged the development of the study of oral history, as a legitimate attempt to utilize tradition without compromising the necessity of high standards for verifiable history. Oral history, then, is a preserver of tradition, a tradition that may in fact be a real event, yet an event not possessing the capability of independent verification by written record or other evidence. To overcome the inherent weakness of oral history's preserving of historical data with-

out external corroboration, various factors and standards have been conceived. Such factors to assess the strength and reliability of oral tradition include matters such as the reliability and credibility of the historical informants, the frequency of reports as well as the number of distinctive reporters, the extent of confusion in the story as to major or minor details, and as to whether the details are expressions of augmentation, or of contradiction. Thus, a largely uniform and frequently reported oral story expressed by several highly competent individuals is an expression of tradition that although falling short of the highest standards of verifiable historical fact, cannot be utterly dismissed as irrelevant. It is this intuitive understanding that causes the historian to frequently report an insightful anecdote that otherwise may not be able to stand on its own. In our study here, we will on occasion pursue the importance of certain potentially significant oral historical records, since there is no other data on which to build certain events, given the exigencies of the time and circumstances in which the event occurred.

So, as an example of a myth, consider "An Unknown Speaker Swayed Colonials to Sign the Declaration of Independence in 1776" in *The Justice Times* (Publishers Ajay Lowery & Anita Lowery, no date, no city.). The story here presented is historically situated, but it adds elements of the supernatural and of the impossible and historically unrecorded in any other setting.

Faced with the death penalty for high treason, courageous men debated long before they picked up the quill pen to si[g]n the parchment that declared the independence of the colonies from the mother country on July 4, 1776.

For many hours they had debated in the S[t]ate House at Philadelphia, with the lower chamber doors locked and a guard posted.

According to Jefferson, it was late in the afternoon before the delegates gathered their courage to the sticking point.

The talk was about axes, scaffolds, and the gibbet, when suddenly a strong, bold voice sounded:

"Gibbet! They may stretch our necks on all the gibbets in the land; they may turn every rock into a scaffold; every tree into a gallows; every home into a grave, and yet the words of that parchment can never die!

"They may pour our blood on a thousand scaffolds, and yet every drop that dyes the axe a new champion of freedom will spring into birth!

"The British King may blot out our stars of God from the sky, but he cannot blot out His words written on that parchment there.

"The works of God may perish: His words never! The words of this declaration will live in the world long after our bones are dust. To the mechanic in his workshop they will speak hope: to the slave in the mines, freedom: but to the coward kings, these words will speak in tones of warning they cannot choose but hear.

"Sign that parchment!

"Sign, if the next moment the gibbet's rope is about your neck! Sign, if the next minute this hall rings with the clash of falling axes!

"Sign, by all your hopes in life or death, as men, as husbands, as fathers, brothers, sign you names to the parchment, or be accursed forever! Sign, and not only for yourselves, but for all ages, for that parchment will be the textbook of freedom, the bible the rights of man forever.

"Nay, do not start and whisper with surprise! It is truth, your own hearts witness it: God proclaims it. Look at his strange band of exiles and outcasts, suddenly transformed into a people; a handful of men, weak in arms, but mighty in God-like faith; nay, look at your recent achievements, your Bunker Hill, your Lexington, and then tell me, if you can, that God has not given America to be free!

"It is not give to our poor human intellect to climb to the skies, and to pierce the Council of the Almighty One. But methinks I stand among the awful clouds which veil the brightness of Jehovah's throne.

"Methinks I see the recording Angel come trembling up to the throne and speak his dread message. 'Father the old world is baptized in blood. Father, look with one glance of Thine eternal eye, and behold evermore that terrible nations lost in blood, murder, and superstition, walking hand and hand over the graves of the victims, and not a single voice of hope to man!'

"He stands there, the Angel, trembling with the record of human guilt. But hark! The voice of God speaks from out the awful cloud: 'Let there be light again!

"Tell my people, the poor and oppressed, to go out from the old world, from oppression and blood, and build My alter in the new.'

"As I live, my friends, that to be His voice! Yes, were my soul trembling on the verge of eternity, were this hand freezing to death, were this voice, implore you to remember this truth— God has give America to be free!

"Yes, as I stare into the gloomy shadows of the grave, with my last faint whisper I would beg you to sign that parchment for the sake of those millions whose very breath is now hushed in intense expectation as they look up to you for the awful words: 'You are free.'"

The unknown speaker fell exhausted into his seat. The delegates, carried away by his enthusiasm, rushed forward. John Hancock scarcely had time to pen his bold signature before the quill was grasped by another… and another… and yet another.

It was done.

The delegates turned to express their gratitude to the unknown speaker for his eloquent words. He was not there.

Who was this strange man, who seemed to speak with a divine authority, whose solemn words gave courage to the doubters and sealed the destiny of the new nation?

His name is not recorded: none of those present knew him; or if they did, not one acknowledged the acquaintance. How he had entered into the locked and guarded room is not told, not is there any record of the manner of his departure.

5   R.T. Haines Halsey, *Pictures of Early New York on Dark Blue, Staffordshire Pottery* (New York: Dover Publications, 1974), pp. 302-306. See

photograph of the mug facing page 3.

6   Note that G.W.P.Custis, George's adopted grandson, accepts this story as true. See G. W. Parke Custis, *Recollections and Private Memoirs of Washington* (Bridgewater: American Foundation Publications, 1999), pp. 132-34.

7   *WGW*, vol. 30, 12-23-1788

8   Writing to the Learned Professions of Philadelphia, Washington spoke of "a higher and more efficient Cause" and "the greatest and best of Beings" (*WGW*, vol. 27, 12-13-1783); To mathematician Nicholas Pike, he spoke of how the tight logic of mathematics led one to even more sublime meditations: "the investigation of mathematical truths accustoms the mind to method and correctness in reasoning, and is an employment peculiarly worthy of rational beings. In a clouded state of existence, where so many things appear precarious to the bewildered research, it is here that the rational faculties find a firm foundation to rest upon. From the high ground of mathematical and philosophical demonstration, we are insensibly led to far nobler speculations and more sublime meditations. (*WGW*, vol. 30, 6-20-1788).

9   *WGW*, vol. 27. 12-13-1783.

10   Lodge claims that the cabbage seed story is untrue: "This tale is bodily taken from Dr. Beattie's biographical sketch of his son, published in England in 1799 and may be dismissed at once." Henry Cabot Lodge, *George Washington* (New Rochelle: Arlington House, 1898) p. 45.

11   Although Paulding does not give his source for the following alleged sayings of Washington, and therefore they cannot finally be historically established, the documented quotes we have just shared from Washington to the Philosophical Society ("the task of studying the works of the great Creator, inexpressibly delightful"), the Learned professions ("a higher and more efficient Cause" and "the greatest and best of Beings."), and the mathematician Nicholas Pike ("it is here that the rational faculties find a firm foundation to rest upon. From the high ground of mathematical and philosophical demonstration, we are insensibly led to far nobler speculations and sublimer meditations.") suggest that the following statements attributed to Washington by Paulding are within the realm of the possible: James K. Paulding, *A Life of Washington* (Port Washington: Kennikat Press, 1858), Vol II p. 208, 210. William J. Johnson, *George Washington The Christian*, (Arlington Heights: Christian Liberty Press, 1919 p. 263-64: "It is impossible to account for the creation of the universe without the agency of a Supreme Being." "It is impossible to govern the universe without the aid of a Supreme Being." "It is impossible to reason without arriving at a Supreme Being. Religion is as necessary to reason as reason is to religion. The one cannot exist without the other. A reasoning being would lose his reason in attempting to account for the great phenomena of nature, had he not a Supreme Being to refer to; and well has it been said, that if there had been no God, mankind would have been obliged to imagine one." The possibility of the authenticity of these statements is further buttressed by Washington's profound emphasis upon the activity and causation of providence in history as well of his use of "Supreme Being" as a title for deity. Also add to this the fact that Washington's view of religion maintains the compatibility of reason and faith as can be seen below in the Chapter entitled "George Washington's God: Religion, Reason, and Philosophy."

12   1731 by the Old (Julian) Calendar, 1732 by the New (Gregorian) Calendar. The New Calendar was adopted by Great Britain and the colonies in 1752. To bring the calendar in line with the solar year, it added 11 days and began the new year in January rather than March. Tobias Lear, secretary to Washington, to Clement Biddle, February 14, 1790, on the new calendar and Washington's birthday (http://memory.loc.gov/ammem/gwhtml/gwtime.html)

13   "Pa brought me two pretty books full of pictures. he got them in Alexandria. they have pictures of dogs and cats and tigers and elephants and ever so many pretty things. cousin bids me send you one of them. it has a picture of an elefant and a little Indian boy on his back like uncle jo's Sam. Pa says if I learn my tasks good he will let uncle jo bring me to see you. will you ask your ma to let you come to see me. Richard Henry Lee." Washington's reply: "Dear Dicky: I thank you very much for the pretty picture book you gave me. Sam asked me to show him the pictures and I showed him all the pictures in it; and I read to him how the tame Elephant took care of the master's little boy, and put him on his back and would not let any body touch his master's little son. I can read three or four pages sometimes without missing a word. Ma says I may go to see you and stay all day with you next week if it not be rainy. She says I may ride my pony Hero if Uncle Ben will go with me and lead Hero. I have a little piece of poetry about the picture book you gave me, but I mustn't tell you who wrote the poetry. 'G.W.'s compliments to R.H.L., And Likes his book full well, henceforth will count him his friend, And hopes many happy days he may spend' Your good friend, George Washington. I am going to get a whip top soon, and you may see it and whip it." Lossing, *Mary and Martha:* p. 37-38. Grizzard, *George Washington: A Biographical Companion*, p. 187, says that these letters are "undoubtedly apocryphal".

14   William Johnson writes about George during that period: "In that town [Fredericksburg] he went to school, and as Mrs. Washington was connected with the church there, her son no doubt shared, under her own eye, the benefits of divine worship, and such religion instruction as mothers in that day were eminently accustomed to give their children. It was the habit to teach the young the first principles of religion according to the formularies of the church, to inculcate the fear of God, and strict observance of the moral virtues, such as truth, justice, charity, humility, modesty, temperance, chastity, and industry." Johnson, *George Washington The Christian*, p.22.

15   See Custis, *Recollections* pp. 482-83. Also see Humphreys, *The Life of General Washington* p. 7.

16   The entries in the index of his *Diaries* include numerous instances of foxhunting, duck hunting, hunting, gunning, fishing, canoeing, and horseback riding.

17   See Custis, *Recollections*, pp. 483-84.

18   See *Diaries* under the entries of "balls." For Washington's dancing skills and remarkable horsemanship, see Custis, pp. 143-44, 386-87. As Jefferson said of Washington, "the best horseman of his age, and the most graceful figure that could be seen on horseback." (See Chapter 3 above)

19   See J. D. Sawyer, *George Washington*, (New York: MacMillian, 1927) vol. I. p. 104-05. Van Braam was also with Washington in the battle at Great Meadows in the French and Indian War, and was one of the interpreters whose knowledge of French was apparently not quite sufficient to prevent the infamous signing of the capitulation agreement that unwittingly affirmed the "assassination" of the French Ambassador.

20 Washington's relationship with Humphreys was very close, as can be seen in the following letter to David Humphreys *WGW*, vol. 27, 1-14-1784:

"My Dear Humphrys: I have been favored with your Letter of the 6th. Be assured that there are few things which would give me more pleasure than opportunities of evincing to you the sincerity of my friendship, and disposition to render you services at any time when it may be in my power.

Altho' all recommendations from me to Congress must now be considered as coming from a private character, yet I enter very chearfully into your views; and as far as my suggesting of them to that Honble body, accompanied by my testimonial of your competency to the execution of the duties of either of the offices in contemplation will go, you have them freely; and the enclosed Letter, which is a copy of the one I have written to Congress on the occasion, will be an evidence of my good wishes, whatever may be the success.

I cannot take my leave of you, without offering those acknowledgments of your long and zealous services to the public which your merits justly entitle you to, and which a grateful heart should not withhold: and I feel very sensibly the obligations I am personally under to you for the aid I have derived from your abilities, for the chearful assistance you have afforded me upon many interesting occasions, and for the attachment you have always manifested towards me. I shall hold in pleasing remembrance the friendship and intimacy which has subsisted between us, and shall neglect no opportunity on my part to cultivate and improve them; being, with unfeigned esteem and regard My Dear Humphrys Yrs. Etc".

21 See Humphreys, *The Life of General Washington* p. 6-8.

22 Grizzard, *George Washington: A Biographical Companion*, p. 109.

23 E.C.M'Guire, *Religious Opinions and Character of Washington* (New York: Harper & Brothers, 1836), p. 15.

24 Hughes, *George Washington The Human Being*, p. 33.

25 Ibid., p. 33.

26 Grizzard, *George Washington: A Biographical Companion* p. 331.

27 Benson J. Lossing, *Mary and Martha: The Mother and Wife of George Washington* (New York: Harper & Brothers, 1886) p. 39.

28 Benson J. Lossing, *The Home of Washington or Mount Vernon and Its Associations Historical, Biographical, and Pictorial* (New York: Virtue & Yorston, 1870) p. 45.

29 Lossing, *Mary and Martha*, p. 41.

30 See the chapter below on George Washington and Providence that deals extensively with his view of God's actions in history.

31 *WGW*, vol. 33, 5-25-1794.

32 A letter to Richard Henry Lee, *WGW*, vol. 22, 7-15-1781 note:, June 12, 1781. In this letter Lee enclosed a copy of one which he had written to James Lovell, Theodorick Bland, and Joseph Jones, in Congress, in which he proposed that Washington should "be immediately sent to Virginia, with 2 or 3000 good Troops. Let Congress, as the head of the federal union, in this crisis, direct that until the Legislature can convene and a Governor be appointed, the General be possessed of Dictatorial powers, and that it be strongly recommended to the Assembly when convened to continue those powers for 6.8 or 10 months: as the case may be. And the General may be desired instantly on his arrival in Virginia to summon the members of both houses to meet where he shall appoint, to organize and resettle their Government." These letters are in the *Washington Papers*.

33 See chapter Three.

34 *WGW*, vol. 27 2-14-1784.

35 Ibid., vol. 35, 11-28-1796.

36 Ibid., vol. 7, 4-15-1777. Washington's younger brother also had interest in the military and finally got Mary Washington's consent, as is seen in Washington's letter on his behalf to Robert Dinwiddie on April 16, 1756 (*WGW*, vol. 1, 4-16-1756): "I have a brother that has long discovered an Inclination to enter the Service; but has till this been dissuaded from it by my Mother, who now, I believe, will give consent. I must, therefore, beg that if your honour should issue any new Commissions before I come down, that you will think of him and reserve a Lieutenancy. I flatter myself that he will endeavour to deserve it as well as some that have, and others that may get [them]." *WGW*, however, notes: Dinwiddie answered this (April 23): "I have not the least objection to your broth's being a Lieut." The appointment, however, does not seem to have been made, as Washington's brother's name does not appear on any of the surviving returns of the Virginia Regiment

37 Johnson, *George Washington The Christian*, p. 21.

38 *The Papers of Thomas Jefferson*, vol. 13, March 7-October 1788 (Julian P. Boyd, Editor, Princeton, New Jersey: Princeton University Press, 1956): "I am truly sensible, Sir, of the honour you do me in proposing to me that of become one of the Sponsors of your child, and return you my sincere thanks for it. At the same time I am not a little mortified that scruples, perhaps not well founded, forbid my undertaking this honourable office. The person who become sponsor for a child, according to the ritual of the church in which I was educated, makes a solemn profession, before god and the world, of faith in articles, which I had never sense enough to comprehend, and it has always appeared to me that comprehension must precede assent. The difficulty of reconciling the ideas of Unity and Trinity, have, from a very early part of my life, excluded me from the office of sponsorship, often proposed to me by my friends, who would have trusted, for the faithful discharge of it, to morality alone instead of which the church requires faith. Accept therefore Sir this conscientious excuse which I make with regret, which must find its apology in my heart, while perhaps it may do no great honour to my head."

39 *George Washington Papers at the Library of Congress*, 11 - April 13, 1748, Image 2 of 70. http://memory.loc.gov/cgi-bin/ampage?collId=mgw1&fileName=mgw1b/gwpage481.db&recNum=1

CHAPTER 7

1 Grizzard, *George Washington: A Biographical Companion*, p. 93.

2 Washington's library has been fully catalogued by Appleton P.C. Griffin, *A Catalogue of the Washington Collection in The Boston Athenaeum*

(Cambridge: University Press, 1897).

3   *WGW,* vol. 28, 12-15-1784. To George Chapman, "Sir: Not until within a few days have I been honor'd with your favor of the 27th. of Septr. 1783, accompanying your treatise on Education. My sentiments are perfectly in unison with yours sir, that the best means of forming a manly, virtuous and happy people, will be found in the right education of youth. Without *this* foundation, every other means, in my opinion, must fail; and it gives me pleasure to find that Gentlemen of your abilities are devoting their time and attention in pointing out the way." *WGW,* vol. 27, 8-29-1784,

4   *WGW,* vol. 37, Last Will and Testament of George Washington, " give and bequeath in perpetuity the fifty shares which I hold in the Potomac Company (under the aforesaid Acts of the Legislature of Virginia) towards the endowment of a UNIVERSITY to be established within the limits of the District of Columbia, under the auspices of the General Government, if that government should incline to extend a fostering hand towards it; and until such Seminary is established, and the funds arising on these shares shall be required for its support, my further *Will* and desire is that the profit accruing therefrom shall, whenever the dividends are made, be laid out in purchasing Stock in the Bank of Columbia, or some other Bank, at the discretion of my Executors.."

5   *WGW* vol. 35, 12-7-1796 Eighth Annual Address to Congress. "I have heretofore proposed to the consideration of Congress, the expediency of establishing a National University; and also a Military Academy. The desirableness of both these Institutions, has so constantly increased with every new view I have taken of the subject, that I cannot omit the opportunity of once for all, recalling your attention to them."

6   *History of the George Washington Bicentennial Celebration,* p. 34, vol. 1 (United States George Washington Bicentennial Commission, 1932)

7   Johnson, *George Washington the Christian,* p. 269.

8   *History of the George Washington Bicentennial Celebration,* p. 34 vol. 1 (United States George Washington Bicentennial Commission, 1932

9   Grizzard, *George Washington: A Biographical Companion,* p. 93.

10 Sawyer, *Washington* vol. 1, p. 112.

11 For the story of one of the Huguenot families that made their way to Virginia and left a legacy of Christian faith, church leadership and patriotism, see *A Tale of the Huguenots, or Memoirs of a French Refugee Family.* Translated and compiled from the original manuscripts of James Fontaine, by one of his descendants, with an introduction by F. L. Hawks. (New York: John S. Taylor, 1838). The appendix is a letter written by Reverend James Maury on December 31, 1765, to Mr. John Fontaine, of South Wales, Great Britain. This is likely the son of the Reverend Marye, who opened the school that Washington attended. His letter shows how the descendents of this Huguenot family were among those who instinctively protested the Stamp Act: "But what hath given a most general alarm to all the colonists upon this continent, and most of those in the islands, and struck us with the most universal consternation that ever seized a people so widely diffused, is a late Act of the British Parliament, subjecting us to a heavy tax by the imposition of stamp duties on all manner of papers requisite in trade, law, or private dealings , on pamphlets, newspapers, almanacks, calendars ,and even advertisements, etc. etc.; and ordaining, that the causes of delinquents against the Act, wheresoever such delinquents may reside, shall be cognizable and finally determinable by any court of admiralty upon the continent, to which either plaintiff or defendant shall think proper to appeal from the sentence either of the inferior courts of justice or the supreme. The execution of this Act was to have commenced on the first of the last month all over British America; but hath been, with an unprecedented unanimity, opposed and prevented by every province on the continent, and by all the islands, whence we have had any advices since that date. For this 'tis probable some may brand us with the odious name of rebels; and others may applaud us for that generous love of liberty, which we inherit from our glorious forefathers; while some few may prudently suspend their judgment, till they shall have heard what may be said on either side of the questions. If the Parliament indeed have a right to impose taxes on the colonies, we are as absolute slaves as any in Asia, and consequently in a state of rebellion. If they have no such right, we are acting the noble and virtuous part, which every freeman and community of freemen hath a right, and is in duty bound to act. For my own part, I am not acquainted with all that may be said on the one part or the other, and therefore am in some sort obliged to suspend my judgment. But no arguments that have yet come in my way, have convinced me that the Parliament hath any such right." pp. 257-58.

12 Meade, *Old Churches,* vol. 2 p. 89. Bishop Meade notes in regard to Reverend James Marye, Jr.: "Mr. Marye was a worthy exception to a class of clergy that obtained in Virginia in olden time. So far as we can learn, he was a man of evangelical views and sincere piety. We have seen a manuscript sermon of his on the religious training of children, which would do honour to the head and heart of any clergyman, and whose evangelical tone and spirit might well commend it to every pious parent and every enlightened Christian…"

13 *WGW,* vol. 2, 5-30-1768.

14 See the later chapter on Washington and the clergy for the extensive correspondence that passed between these two.

15 Jonathan Boucher, *Reminiscences of an American Loyalist,* ed. J. Bouchier (Port Washington, NY: Kennikat, 1967) p. 113

16 Slaughter, *The History of Truro Parish* 25.

17 In our research for this book, we discovered an old note in the back of Washington's volume entitled *Dissertations on the Mosaical Creation, Deluge, Building of Babel, and Confusion of Tongues* by Simon Berington. It is clear that this was a book that Washington procured as a late teenager: the editors note "Autograph of Washington written at the age of 17 or thereabouts on the title-page." In Appleton P.C. Griffin, *A Catalogue of the Washington Collection in The Boston Athenaeum* (Cambridge: University Press 1897) p. 23. The faded and difficult to read note says: "I was running Hobby's dogs. .Says, as he has suffic. prov'd the swine begot of horses, a man of reason would soon distrust his own judgment, than question the truth of the mosaic law. Let it seemingly be efver so irrational and absurd." Whatever the precise meaning of this note might intend in regard to the origin of the species or the reliability of the Mosaic writings, should the note be authentic, it seems to substantiate the existence of someone named Hobby whom the apparently young Washington knew and accepted as an instructor.

18 M.D. Conway, *Washington and Mount Vernon* (Brooklyn, Long Island Historical Society, 1889) p. 500 n. 14.

19 Lossing, *Mary & Martha,* p. 29. Parson Weems says the following about Master Hobby: "The first place of education to which George

was ever sent, was a little "*old field school*" kept by one of his father's tenants, named Hobby; an honest, poor old man, who acted in the double character or sexton and schoolmaster. On his skill as a gravedigger, tradition is silent; but for a teacher of youth, his qualifications were certainly of the humbler sort; making what is generally called an A. B. C. schoolmaster. Such was the preceptor who first taught Washington the knowledge of letters! Hobby lived to see his young pupil in all his glory, and rejoiced exceedingly. In his cups – for, though a *sexton*, her would sometimes drink, particularly on the Gneral's birth-days – he used to boast, that "*'twas he, who, between his knees, had laid the foundation of George Washington's greatness.*" (Mason Weems, *The Life of Washington*, (Cambridge, Massachusetts: The Belknap Press of Harvard University, 1962) p. 8.

20   Johnson, *George Washington The Christian*, p. 18.

21   Ibid., p. 18, Hughes, *George Washington The Human Being*, p. 16.

22   Schaff, *Creeds of Christendom*, Vol 3 pp. 517-522.

23   Ibid., pp. 517-522.

24   See *WGW*, vol. 35, 12-19-1796 letter to George Washington Parke Custis.

25   See Griffin, *A Catalogue of the Washington Collection in The Boston Athenaeum*, p. 52 concerning Thomas Comber's work *Short Discourses upon the Whole Common-Prayer* published in London 1712. In the photo of the signatures, there are 3 different handwritings. The first is the original signature of Augustine and Mary Washington; the second is that of youthful George Washington and his own writing of his mother's signature. Under George's signatures a later family member has written 2 explanatory notes which read "the above is Genl. Washington's autograph when 13 years of age" . Under Washington's rendition of his mother's signature it reads: "The above name of his mother is in the handwriting of Genl. Washington at 13 years of age – which will be seen by comparing with his writing at that as in Sparks' work." Since he is called General Washington, it is presumed this was written before his presidency in 1787.

26   Griffin, *A Catalogue of the Washington Collection in The Boston Athenaeum*, p. 52.

27   Ofspring Blackall, D.D., *The Sufficiency of a Standing Revelation* (London: H. Hills, 1708) Sermon dated Feb. 15, 1700, p. 2.

28   Chevalier Ramsay, *The Travels of Cyrus* (London: James Bettenham, 1745) We know this book dates from his early days as it bears Washington's signature. *The Travels of Cyrus to which is annexed a Discourse upon the Theology and Mythology of the Pagans* by The Chevalier Ramsay printed in London in 1745, which was then in its seventh edition. Both of these were in Washington's library with dates that fall in the era of his early teen years, the time of study with his tutor and teachers. *The Travels of Cyrus* clearly bears the youthful form of his signature on the cover page. (Griffin/Lane, p. 170) What Ray was attempting to do in the scientific arena, so Ramsay was pursuing in the study of ancient cultures. *The Travels of Cyrus* is the story of the imaginary travels of the great monarch of the ancient world wherein he interacts with the worldviews and religions of the many different nations around him: Zoroaster, Hermes, Pythagoras, tradition, philosophy, Orientals, Egyptians, Greeks, and Romans. In the process of encountering these divergent views, he will finally encounter the Old Testament prophet Daniel and learn of the Judeo-Christian views that were in the scriptures. Simultaneously a travelogue, a philosophical debate and cultural experience of ancient civilization through the eyes of Cyrus, Ramsay's work had a distinct purpose. In answering the charge against his work, "far from doing homage to religion he degrades it."

He should think himself very unhappy to have produced a work so contrary to his intentions. All that he advances upon religion may be reduced to two principal points: the first is to prove against the Atheists the existence of a Supreme Deity, who produced the world by his power, and governs it by his wisdom. . . that the primitive system of the world was that of one supreme Deity.

The second point is to show, in opposition to the Deists, that the principal doctrines of revealed religion; concerning the state of innocence, corruption and renovation, are as ancient as the world; that they were foundation of Noah's religion; that he transmitted them to his children; that these traditions were thus spread thought all nations; that the Pagans' disfigured, degraded, and obscured them by their absurd fictions; and lastly, that these primitive truths have been no where preserved in their purity except in the true religion. (pp. 13-14.)

Reason in Ramsay's work is most important, but it is the divine reason that must be given final sway. The prophet Daniel explains to the young Cyrus,

All the systems that can be imagined are either dangerous or defective. The curiosity of seeing into every thing, explaining every thing, and adjusting it to our imperfect notions, is the most fatal disease of the human mind. The most sublime act of our feeble reason is to keep itself silent before the sovereign reason; let us leave to God the care of justifying one day the incomprehensible ways of his providence. Our pride and our impatience will not suffer us to wait for the unraveling; we would go before the light and by so doing we lose the use of it. (pp. 257-58.)

Ramsay's concluding discourse explains his views of ancient theology and mythology:

"In the first. . . the most celebrated Philosophers of all ages and all countries have had the notions of a supreme Deity, who produced the world by his Power and governs it by his Wisdom. From the second it will appear, that there are traces of the principal doctrines of revealed religion, with regard to the three states of the world, [the states of innocence, corruption and renovation] to be found in the Mythology of all nations. (p. 271.)....Thus much at least is plain, that the Chaldeans and Egyptians believed all the attributes of the Deity might be reduced to three, Power, Understanding and Love. In reality, whenever we disengage ourselves from matter, impose silence on the senses and imagination, and raise our thoughts to the contemplation of the infinitely infinite Being, we find that the eternal Essence presents itself to our mind under the three forms of Power, Wisdom and Goodness. These three attributes comprehend the totality of his nature, and whatever we can conceive of him." (p. 276.)

The Chevalier Ramsay summarizes the plan of the whole work,

. . . it is as follows: Each philosopher speaks to Cyrus the language of his own religion and country. The Orientals, Egyptians; Greeks and Tyrians all agree in the original purity, present corruption and future restoration of mankind, but they wrap up these truths in different fables, each according to these truths in different fables, each according to the genius of their nation. Eleazar clears their system from the Pagan fictions, but retains in his own opinions of his sect. The errors which prevail at this day resemble those of former times. The mind of man sees but a small number of ideas, reviews them continually, and thinks them new only because it expresses them differently in different ages The Magi in Cyrus's time were fallen into a kind of Atheism like that of Spinoza; Zoroaster, Hermes and Pythagoras adored one sole Deity, but yet were Deists; Elcazar resembled the Socinians, who are for subjecting religion to philosophy; Daniel represents a perfect Christian, and the Hero of this book a young Prince who began to be corrupted by the maxims of irrelgion. In order to set him right, the different philosophers with whom he converses successively unfold to him new truths mixt with errors. Zoroaster, confutes the mistakes of the Magi; Pythagoras those of Zoroaster; Eleazar those of Pythagoras ; Daniel rejects those of all others, and his doctrine is the only one which the author adopts. The order of conversations shews the progress of the mind, the matter being so disposed, that the Atheist becomes Deist, the Deist, Socinian, and the Socinian Christian, by a plain and natural chain of ideas. The great art in instructing is to lead the mind gradually on, and to take advantage even of its errors to make it relish truth. That Cyrus might thus be conducted step by step, it was necessary to introduce a person of the religion of the Hebrews, who should confute by reason, all the objections drawn from reason; Daniel could not act this part, it would not have become him to solve difficulties by uncertain conjectures; the philosopher might prepare the Prince by bare hypotheses, to submit to and to distrust his understanding: but is was necessary that the prophet should disengage Cyrus from all bold speculations, how refined and bright soever they might appear, and lead him to the belief of a supernatural religion, not by a philosophical demonstration of its doctrines, but by proving them to be divinely revealed." (pp. 15-16.)

29 *The Adventures of Peregrine Pickle* (London: Printed for J.F.Dove, Piccadilly).

30 Griffin, *A Catalogue of the Washington Collection in The Boston Athenaeum*, p. 23. "Washington's autograph, written when a youth, probably at the age of seventeen or eighteen."

31 Ibid., p. 555.

32 *WGW*, vol. 27, 12-13-1783, in an address to The American Philosophical Society. For examples of Washington's interest as a naturalist, see Washington Diaries, March 13, 1748; December 22, 1751; October 13, 1770; October 15, 1770; October 25, 770

33 These can be found at: http://memory.loc.gov/ammem/gwhtml/gwseries1.html.

34 *George Washington Papers* at the Library of Congress, 1741-1799: Series 1a., George Washington, Forms of Writing, and The Rules of Civility and Decent Behavior in Company and Conversation, ante 1747 http://memory.loc.gov/cgi-bin/ampage?collId=mgw1&fileName=mgw1a/gwpage001.db&recNum=25

TRUE HAPPINESS

These are the things when once possessed

Will make a life that's truly blessed

A good estate on healthy soil

Not got by vice nor yet by toil

Round a warm fire a pleasant joke

With chimney over free from smoke.

A strength within, a sparkling bowl.

A quiet wife, a quiet soul.

A mind as well as body whole

Prudent simplicity, constant friends.

A diet which no art commends,

A merry night without much drinking

A happy thought without much thinking

Each night by quiet sleep made short.

A will to be but what thou art

Possessed of these all else defy

And neither wish nor fear to die

These are things when once possessed

Will make a life that's truly blessed.

35 Grizzard, *George Washington: A Biographical Companion* p. 94.

36 *George Washington Papers* at the Library of Congress, 1741-1799: Series 1a.: http://memory.loc.gov/cgi-bin/ampage?collId=mgw1&fileName=mgw1a/gwpage001.db&recNum=24.

37 Hughes, *George Washington the Human Being*, p. 554. Also see Grizzard, *George Washington:* p. 94.

38 *George Washington Papers* at the Library of Congress, 1741-1799: Series 1a, George Washington, Forms of Writing, and The Rules of Civility and Decent Behavior in Company and Conversation, ante 1747, Image 25 of 36. (may be found online at www.loc.gov).The authors have not yet had the opportunity to examine the poem from the source from which Washington copied it, since his manuscript is illegible in the last 2 lines, the words used in its construction are based upon hints from the meter of the poem the logic of its conclusion and the few random stokes of Washington's pen that indicate certain letters.

39 To Robert Morris he wrote: Monday, December 24, [1781].

"Dear Sir: Knowing full well the multiplicity and importance of yr. business, it would give me more pain than pleasure if I thought your friendship, or respect for me did, in the smallest degree, interfere with it. At all times I shall be happy to see you, but wish it to be in your moments of leizure, if any such you have.

Mrs. Washington, myself and family, will have the honor of dining with you in the way proposed, to morrow, being Christmas day. I am etc."

To david Humphreys: "Peace and tranquillity prevail in this State. The Assembly by a very great majority, and in very emphatical terms, have rejected an application for paper money, and spurned the idea of fixing the value of military Certificates by a scale of depreciation. In some other respects too the proceedings of the present Session have been marked with justice and a strong desire of supporting the foederal system. Altho' I lament the effect, I am pleased at the cause which has deprived us of the pleasure of your aid in the attack of Christmas pies: we had one yesterday on which all the company, tho' pretty numerous, were hardly able to make an impression. Mrs. Washington and George and his wife (Mr. Lear I had occasion to send to the Western Country) join in affectione regards for you, and with sentiments, *WGW*, vol. 29 12-26-1786.

To John Bannister, April 21, 1778. vol. 11in general cases, any of the ties, the concerns or interests of Citizens or any other dependence, than what flowed from their Military employ; in short, from their being Mercenaries; hirelings. It is our policy to be prejudiced against them in time of *War*, and though they are Citizens having all the Ties, and interests of Citizens, and in most cases property totally unconnected with the Military Line. If we would pursue a right System of policy, in my Opinion, there should be none of these distinctions. We should all be considered, Congress, Army, &c. as one people, embarked in one Cause, in one interest; acting on the same principle and to the same End. The distinction, the Jealousies set up, or perhaps only incautiously let out, can answer not a single good purpose. They are impolitic in the extreme. Among Individuals, the most certain way to make a Man your Enemy, is to tell him, you esteem him such; so with public bodies; and the very jealousy, which the narrow politics of some may affect to entertain of the Army, in order to a due subordination to the supreme Civil Authority, is a likely mean to produce a contrary effect; to incline it to the pursuit of those measures which that may wish it to avoid. It is unjust, because no Order of Men in the thirteen States have paid a more sanctimonious regard to their proceedings than the Army; and, indeed, it may be questioned, whether there has been that scrupulus adherence had to them by any other, [for without arrogance, or the smallest deviation from truth it may be said, that no history, now extant, can furnish an instance of an Army's suffering such uncommon hardships as ours have done, and bearing them with the same patience and Fortitude. To see Men without Cloathes to cover their nakedness, without Blankets to lay on, without Shoes, by which their Marches might be traced by the Blood from their feet, and almost as often without Provisions as with; Marching through frost and Snow, and at Christmas taking up their Winter Quarters within a day's March of the enemy, without a House or Hurt to cover them till they could be built and submitting to it without a murmur, is a mark of patience and obedience which in my opinion can scarce be parallel'd.

40   See Grizzard, *George Washington: A Biographical Companion* p. 242, pp. 93-94 as an example. "Charles Moore, who traced these 110 Maxims back through various English and French versions to the sixteenth century in his 1931 book on the subject, rightly summed up the long-held view on the subject: 'These maxims were so fully exemplified in George Washington's life that biographers have regarded them as formative influences in the development of his character.'"

41   *George Washington Papers at the Library of Congress, 1741-1799: Series 1a.George Washington, Forms of Writing*, and "The Rules of Civility" and "Decent Behavior in Company and Conversation," ante 17: http://memory.loc.gov/cgibin/ampage?collId=mgw1&fileName=mgw1a/gwpage001.db&recNum=26: *George Washington Papers at the Library of Congress, 1741-1799: Series 1a. George Washington, Forms of Writing*, and "The Rules of Civility" and *Decent Behavior in Company and Conversation*, ante 1747; http://memory.loc.gov/cgi-bin/ampage (pages 24 and 36)

42   Grizzard, *George Washington: A Biographical Companion*, pp 361-365; For a contemporary take, see : George Washington, *Georgeisms* (New York: Atheneum Books for young Readers, 2000)

43   William H. Wilbur, *The Making of George Washington* (Caldwell: Caxton Printers, 1970 & 1973), p. 107.

44   Ibid., pp. 113-118.

45   *WGW*, vol. 28, 6-30-1786; 37, 4-25-1799.

46   Kitman, *The Making of the President*, p. 108

47   Grizzard, *George Washington: A Biographical Companion*, p. 94.

48   Sawyer, *Washington*, vol. I. p. 109.

49   Mather, *The Young Man's Companion*, p. 310

50   Ibid.

51   Ibid., p. 5b.

52   See images from: *George Washington Papers* at the Library of Congress, 1741-1799: Series 1a, George Washington, *Forms of Writing*, and "The Rules of Civility" and 'Decent Behavior in Company and Conversation," ante 1747.

53   Image 9 in *George Washington Papers* at the Library of Congress, 1741-1799: Series 1a, George Washington, *Forms of Writing*, and 'The Rules of Civility" and "Decent Behavior in Company and Conversation, ante *1747*

54   Appleton P.C. Griffin, *A Catalogue of the Washington Collection in The Boston Athenaeum* (Cambridge: University Press 1897), p. 554-555.

55   Ibid., p. 554-555.

56   Ibid., p. 554.

57   Francis Osborn, *Advice to a Son or Directions for Your Better Conduct through the various and most important Encounters of this Life*. (Oxford: H.H. for Tho: Robinson, 1658) p. 148.

58   Ibid., p. 157.

59   Ibid., p. 162.

60   James Hervey, *Meditations and Contemplations* (London: J. Walker & Co., 1816), A facsimile of the title page of Hervey's work which Mary Washington signed four times can be seen in Joseph Dillaway Sawyer, *Washington* (New York: MacMillian, 1927), vol. I p. 56 and the history of the book's sale listed in Appleton P.C. Griffin, *A Catalogue of the Washington Collection in The Boston Athenaeum* (Cambridge: University Press 1897), p. 503.

61   Joseph Dillaway Sawyer, *Washington* (New York: MacMillian, 1927), vol. I, p.57; Benson J. Lossing, *Mary and Martha: The Mother and Wife of George Washington* (New York: Harper & Brothers, 1886), p. 28.

62   James K. Paulding, *A Life of Washington* (Port Washington: Kennikat Press, 1858) vol. I. 24.

63   Ibid., vol. 24-25.

64   Ibid., vol. 25.; Verna M. and Dorothy Dimmick Hall Comp. and Ed. *George Washington: The Character and Influence of One Man* (San Francisco: Foundation for American Christian Education, 1999), pp. 125-143 prints "The Great Audit" in full, this can be found in Sir Matthew Hale, *Contemplations Moral and Divine* (London: William Shrowsbery at the Bible in Duke-Lane, and John Leigh at Stationers-Hall, 1685) vol. 1 pp. 271-276.

65   Paulding, *A Life of Washington*, vol. I p. 31. Sir Matthew Hale, *Contemplations Moral and Divine* (London: William Shrowsbery at the Bible in Duke-Lane, and John Leigh at Stationers-Hall, 1685), I. 315.

66   The listing of the articles written by Chief-Justice Hale reveal the biblical character of his thought:
Of the Consideration of our Latter End, and the Benefits of it.—Duet. 32:29.
Of Wisdom and the Fear of God, That that is true Wisdom—Job 27:28.
Of the Knowledge of Christ Crucified—1 Cor. 2:2.
The Victory of Faith over the Word—1 John 5:4
Of Humility—Prov. 3:34; James 4:6; 1 Peter 5:5
Jacob's Vow—Gen. 28:20-21
Of Contentation—Phil. 4:11
Of Afflictions—Job 5:6-7
A good Method to entertain unstable and troublesome times
Changes and Troubles: A Poem
Of the Redemption of time—
The Great Audit, with the Account of the Good Steward
Directions touching the Keeping of the Lord's Day, Letter to his Children
Poems upon Christmas Day
An Inquiry touch Happiness
Of the Chief End of Man
Upon Eccles. 12:1, Remember thy Creator
Upon Psalm 51:10
The Folly and Mischief of Sin
Of Self-Denial
Motives to Watchfulness, in reference to the Good and Evil Angels
Of Moderation of the Affections
Of Worldly Hope, and Expectation
Upon Hebrews 13:14; We have here no continuing City
Of Contentedness and Patience
Of Moderation of Anger
A Preparative against Afflictions
Of Submission, Prayer, and Thanksgiving
Of Prayer, and Thanksgiving, on Psalm 116:12
Meditations upon the Lord's Prayer
A Paraphrase upon the Lord's Prayer.
Sir Matthew Hale, *Contemplations Moral and Divine* (London: William Shrowsbery at the Bible in Duke-Lane, and John Leigh at Stationers-Hall, 1685)

67   Ibid., p. 94.

68   Stephen DeCatur, *Private Affairs of George Washington From the Records and Accounts of Tobias Leer, Esquire, His Secretary* (Boston: Houghton Mifflin, 1933), p. 90.

CHAPTER 8

1   *WGW*, vol. 28, 8-18-1786.

2   Paul M. Zall, *Washington on Washington* (Lexington: University Press of Kentucky, 2003), pp. 9-23.

3   Saul K. Padover, ed. *The Washington Papers*, (Harper Brothers, 1955)

4   Benson Lossing, *Mary and Martha*, p. 304

5   William Johnson, *George Washington the Christian* (Arlington Heights: Christian Liberty Press, 1919), p. 247.

6   Ibid., p. 247.

7   *WGW*, vol. 29, 3-26-1788.

8   Jackson and Twohig, ed, *The Diaries of George Washington*, vol. 5 [July 1788] The Diary entry for Tuesday July 29, 1788, says, "A Mr. Vender Kemp—a Dutch Gentn. who had suffered by the troubles in Holland and who was introduced to me by the Marquis de la Fayette came here to Dinner." The note provided therein says, "Francis Adrian Van der Kemp (1752-1829), Dutch soldier, scholar, and Mennonite minister, had been imprisoned in his homeland during a part of the previous year for revolutionary activities connected with the Patriot party, a group of Dutch liberals who wished to implement the republican ideals of the American Revolution in their country. Upon being freed in December, Van der Kemp found himself much reduced in fortune and faced with further political repression in the Netherlands. For

some time he had thought of going to America to become a farmer, and in Mar. 1788 he sailed with his wife and children for New York. To ease his way, Dutch friends obtained for him several letters of introduction to prominent Americans, including a letter from Lafayette to GW (6 Mar. 1788, PEL). Soon after his arrival in New York on 4 May, Van der Kemp dispatched the letters to their intended recipients (Van der Kemp to GW, 15 May 1788, DLC:GW). GW's reply of 28 May contained a cordial invitation to visit Mount Vernon when convenient, an invitation that Van der Kemp could not decline, having a great desire "to know that man, to whom America so much was indebted for her liberty." Van der Kemp became an American citizen in 1789 and lived the remainder of his life in upstate New York farming and pursuing his scholarly interests.

9   *WGW*, vol. 35, 7-15-1796 has the following quote from an extract of Benjamin H. Latrobe's diary, July 16, 1796, describing his visit to Mount Vernon: "The President came to me. He was dressed in a plain blue coat, his hair dressed and powdered. There was a reserve, but no hauteur, in his manner….Washington has something uncommonly commanding and majestic in his walk, his address his figure and his countenance, His face is characterised by more intense and powerful thought than by quick and fiery conception. There is a mildness about his expression and an air of reserve in his manner covers its tone still more. He is about 64 but appears some years younger, and has sufficient apparent signs to his many years. He was sometimes entirely silent for many minutes, during which time an awkwardness seemed to prevail in every one present. His answers were sometimes short and approached to moroseness. He did not, at anytime, speak with any remarkable fluency. Perhaps the extreme correctness of his language which almost seemed studied produced this effect. He appeared to enjoy a humorous observation and made several himself. He laughed heartily some times and in a very good humored manner. On the morning of my departure he treated me as if I had lived years in his house with ease and attention. But in general I thought there was a slight air of moroseness about him as if something had vexed him." The original of this extract by J. H. B. Latrobe was made for President Hayes in November, 1878, and is now in the Hayes Memorial Library, Fremont, Ohio.

10   *The Journal of William Maclay: United States Senator from Pennsylvania, 1789-1791* (New York: Albert & Charles Boni, 1927), p. 364. Maclay's unflattering comments from his 1791 journal states, "I have now, however, seen him for the last time, perhaps. Let me take a review of him as he really is. In stature about six feet, with an unexceptionable make, but lax appearance. His frame would seem to want filling up. His motions rather slow than lively, though he showed no signs of having suffered by gout or rheumatism. His complexion pale, nay, almost cadaverous. His voice hallow and indistinct, owing, as I believe, to artificial teeth before his upper jaw, which occasioned a flatness of—[The following leaf, on which the rest of this description was written, has been torn out and is lost.]"

11   Custis, *Recollections*, p. 175. This incident adds a fair amount of incredibility to Gouverneur Morris' claim that he knew Washington well, and so was able to declare that Washington was not a believer. Paul Boller, *George Washington and Religion*, p. 85, writes, "'I know,' Jefferson had written, in concluding his entry, 'that Gouverneur Morris, who pretended to be in his secrets & believed himself to be so, has often told me that Genl. Washington believed no more of that system than he himself did." Washington did write to the French later recommending the virtues of Morris to the French. See two letters written on the same date, one to Marquis de Chastellux and the other to Joseph Mandrillon, *WGW*, vol. 30, 11-27-1788.

12   Jackson and Twohig, ed, *The Diaries of George Washington*. vol. 4. The diary entry for Thursday May 26, 1785, says, "Upon my return Found Mr. Magowan, and a Doctr. Coke & a Mr. Asbury here—the two last Methodest Preachers recommended by Genl. Roberdeau—the same who were expected yesterday…After Dinner Mr. Coke & Mr. Asbury went away." The note provided therein says, "Thomas Coke (1747—1814) and Francis Asbury (1745—1816) were sent to America by John Wesley as missionaries to superintend the Methodist movement in this country. Asbury came shortly before the Revolution and Coke in 1784. They were at Mount Vernon to ask GW to sign an antislavery petition which was to be presented to the Virginia legislature. Coke later wrote that GW informed them that "he was of our sentiments, and had signified his thoughts on the subject to most of the great men of the State: that he did not see it proper to sign the petition, but if the Assembly took it into consideration, would signify his sentiments to the Assembly by a letter"

13   Elmer T. Clark, ed., *The Journal and Letters of Francis Asbury in 3 Volumes* (Nashville: Abingdon Press 1958) vol. 1, p. 489.

14.   *Journals of Dr. Thomas Coke* (London, G. Paramore 1793.)

15   Just about four years later on May 29, 1789, in New York, Bishops Thomas Coke and Francis Asbury wrote a letter on behalf of the Methodist-Episcopal church. Their letter of congratulations to the new president expressed "the warm feelings of [their] hearts" but also thanked Washington for his dependence upon God. *George Washington Papers at the Library of Congress, 1741-1799*: Series 2 Letterbooks, image 41, image 42. Coke and Asbury wrote as the Methodist Episcopal Bishops to George Washington on May 29, 1789, "We have received the most grateful satisfaction, from the humble and entire dependence on the Great Governor of the universe which you have repeatedly expressed, acknowledging him the source of every blessing, and particularly of the most excellent constitution of these states, which is at present the admiration of the world, and may in future become its great exemplar for imitation: and hence we enjoy a holy expectation that you will always prove a faithful and impartial patron of genuine, vital religion—the grand end of our creation and present probationary existence. And we promise you our fervent prayers to the throne of grace, that God Almighty may endue you with all the graces and gifts of his Holy Spirit, that may enable you to fill up your important station in his glory, the good of his church, the happiness and prosperity of the United States, and the welfare of mankind." This letter makes it clear that Coke had not ceased praying for Washington for the gift of the "witness of the Spirit." Washington responded on the same day with his written answer, and his words imply that he was not only pleased with their prayer but promised to reciprocate: "…I hope, by the assistance of the Divine Providence, not altogether to disappoint the confidence which you have been pleased to repose in me. It always affords me satisfaction when I find a concurrence of sentiment and practice between all conscientious men, in acknowledgments of homage to the great Governor of the universe, and in professions of support to a just civil government. After mentioning that I trust the people of every denomination who demean themselves as good citizens will have occasion to be convinced that I shall always strive to prove a faithful and impartial patron of genuine vital religion, I must assure you, in particular, that I take in the kindest part the promise you make of presenting your prayers to the throne of grace for me; and that I likewise implore the Divine benediction on yourselves and your religious community." It seems that Coke and

990

Washington had made a true spiritual connection after all. When Washington died in 1799, Francis Asbury wrote in his journal, "Washington, the calm, intrepid chief, the disinterested friend, first father, and temporal saviour of his country, under divine protection and direction.... the expressions of sorrow... the marks of respect paid by his fellow-citizens to this great man. I am disposed to lose sight of all but Washington. Matchless man! At all times he acknowledged the providence of God, and never was he ashamed of his Redeemer. We believe he died not fearing death. . . ."

16   Paul M. Zall, *Washington on Washington* (Lexington: University Press of Kentucky, 2003), p. 12.

17   *WGW*, vol. 3 6-16-1775.

18   Honor was so important to Washington that he chose not to receive any pay for his services to our country during the war. After the war, he reminded his fellow Virginian, Patrick Henry, of his continuing commitment to this practice in a letter in 1785: "When I was first called to the station, with which I was honored during the late conflict for our liberties . . . I thought it my duty to . . . shut my hand against every pecuniary recompense. To this resolution I have invariably adhered, and from it, if I had the inclination, I do not feel at liberty now to depart." *WGW*, vol. 28, 10-29-1785. Instead of pecuniary compensation, Washington sought the approval of his country through his humble service: "The approbation of my country is what I wish; and, as far as my abilities and opportunities will permit, I hope I shall endeavor to deserve it. It is the highest reward to a feeing mind; and happy are they, who so conduct themselves as to merit it." *WGW*, vol. 11, 3-28-1778.

19   *WGW*, vol. 2, 7-20-1758 states, "A granddaughter of Mrs. Washington is authority for the statement that Martha Washington, shortly before her death, destroyed the letters that passed between George Washington and herself." Washington refers to Providence in the only two known letters from Washington to his wife Martha that have survived. Emphasis is added to the relevant lines. The first letter is *WGW*, vol. 3, 6-18-1775. Washington wrote, "My Dearest: I am now set down to write to you on a subject, which fills me with inexpressible concern, and this concern is greatly aggravated and increased, when I reflect upon the uneasiness I know it will give you. It has been determined in Congress, that the whole army raised for the defence of the American cause shall be put under my care, and that it is necessary for me to proceed immediately to Boston to take upon me the command of it. You may believe me, my dear Patsy, when I assure you, in the most solemn manner that, so far from seeking this appointment, I have used every endeavor in my power to avoid it, not only from my unwillingness to part with you and the family, but from a consciousness of its being a trust too great for my capacity, and that I should enjoy more real happiness in one month with you at home, than I have the most distant prospect of finding abroad, if my stay were to be seven times seven years. But as it has been a kind of destiny, that has thrown me upon this service, I shall hope that my undertaking it is designed to answer some good purpose. You might, and I suppose did perceive, from the tenor of my letters, that I was apprehensive I could not avoid this appointment, as I did not pretend to intimate when I should return. That was the case. It was utterly out of my power to refuse this appointment, without exposing my character to such censures, as would have reflected dishonor upon myself, and given pain to my friends. This, I am sure, could not, and ought not, to be pleasing to you, and must have lessened me considerably in my own esteem. I shall rely, therefore, confidently on that Providence, which has heretofore preserved and been bountiful to me, not doubting but that I shall return safe to you in the fall. I shall feel no pain from the toil or the danger of the campaign; my unhappiness will flow from the uneasiness I know you will feel from being left alone. I therefore beg, that you will summon your whole fortitude, and pass your time as agreeably as possible. Nothing will give me so much sincere satisfaction as to hear this, and to hear it from your own pen. My earnest and ardent desire is, that you would pursue any plan that is most likely to produce content, and a tolerable degree of tranquility; as it must add greatly to my uneasy feelings to hear, that you are dissatisfied or complaining at what I really could not avoid. As life is always uncertain, and common prudence dictates to every man the necessity of settling his temporal concerns, while it is in his power, and while the mind is calm and undisturbed, I have, since I came to this place (for I had not time to do it before I left home) got Colonel Pendleton to draft a will for me, by the directions I gave him, which I will now enclose. The provision made for you in case of my death will, I hope, be agreeable. I shall add nothing more, as I have several letters to write, but to desire that you will remember me to your friends, and to assure you that I am, with the most unfeigned regard, my dear Patsy, your affectionate, &c." The second letter is *WGW*, vol. 2, 7-20-1758. Washington wrote to Martha, "We have begun our march for the Ohio. A courier is starting for Williamsburg, and I embrace the opportunity to send a few words to one whose life is now inseparable from mine. Since that happy hour when we made our pledges to each other, my thoughts have been continually going to you as another Self. *That an all-powerful Providence may keep us both in safety is the prayer of your ever faithful and affectionate friend.*"

20   *WGW*, vol. 6. 12-20-1776.

21   Ibid.,vol. 3, 6-20-1775.

22   Zall, *Washington on Washington*, p. 10.

23   Ibid., p. 10.

24   Ibid., p. 16, James Hutton, ed., *Letters and Correspondence of Sir James Bland Burges* (London: John Murray, 1855).

25   *WGW*, vol. 37 1-27-1799.

26   Ibid., vol. 26, 1-15-1783.

27   Ibid., vol. 2, 4-5-1758.

28   Sparks, *Writings of George Washington*, vol. 12, p. 405-408.

29   *WGW*, vol. 17, 12-15-1779.

30   Ibid., vol. 37, 1-15-1799.

31   Ibid., vol. 36, 12-21-97. In his "Speech to the Delaware Chiefs, Washington said, "Brothers: I am a Warrior. My words are few and plain; but I will make good what I say." *WGW*, vol. 15, 5-12-1779. Writing to Richard Henry Lee, however, Washington was forced to explain his words: "Dear Sir: By your favor of the 22d ultimo, I perceive my letter of the 17th has been expressed in too strong terms. I did not mean by the words, "to get rid of importunity," to cast the smallest reflection; indeed the hurry with which I am obliged to write the few

private letters I attempt, will not allow me to consider the force and tendency of my words; nor should I have been surprised, if the fact had really been so, if I am to judge of their, I mean foreigners' applications to Congress, by those to myself; for it is not one, nor twenty explanations, that will satisfy the cravings of these people's demands." *WGW*, vol. 8, 6-1-1777. But Washington's deeds were sometimes misunderstood as well: "Conscious that it is the aim of my actions to promote the public good, and that no part of my conduct is influenced by personal enmity to individuals, I cannot be insensible to the artifices employed by some men to prejudice me in the public esteem." *WGW*, vol. 1, 4-14-1779.

32 Grizzard, *George Washington: A Biographical Companion*, p. 51.

33 On the western frontier, somewhere in the wilderness of Pennsylvania, Colonel George Washington, barely in his twenties, led an expedition on behalf of the British Governor of Virginia to counter the claims of the French. The Indians were on both sides of this conflict between Britain and France, concerning the possession and control of North America. He and his men, including several Indians, came across a hidden French military encampment. They opened fire killing and captured several French soldiers. To Washington, they were intruders and spies. The French, however, claimed they were a diplomatic military escort simply protecting an unarmed French ambassador who was one of the killed. This was the incident that triggered the French and Indian War. Without this shot by Washington, "the shot heard round the world" at the "rude bridge" of Lexington and Concord may not have been fired. The French retaliated with a larger force and forced Washington and his men to surrender, after a battle at Washington's hastily built Fort Necessity. As part of the terms of surrender Washington, who did not read French at all with the assistance of his translator who did not read French well enough, signed a French document in which he unwittingly confessed to having "assassinated" the ambassador! This agreement of capitulation was later called "the most infamous a British Subject ever put his Hand to." The French never forgave the British for this "outrage." Willard Sterne Randall, *George Washington: A Life* (New York: Henry Holt and Co., 1997), p. 103ff.

34 Ibid., p. 107.

35 *WGW*, vol. 1, 5-31-1754 Washington wrote to John Augustine Washington, " Since my last arrived at this place, where three days ago we had an engagement with the French, that is, a party of our men with one of theirs. Most of our men were out upon other detachments, so that I had scarcely 40 men remaining under my command, and about 10 or 12 Indians; nevertheless we obtained a most signal victory. The battle lasted about 10 or 15 minutes, with sharp firing on both sides, till the French gave ground and ran, but to no great purpose. There were 12 killed of the French, among whom was Mons. de Jumonville, their commander, and 21 taken prisoners, among whom are Mess. La Force and Drouillon, together with two cadets. I have sent them to his honour the Governor, at Winchester, under a guard of 20 men, conducted by Lieutenant West. We had but one man killed, and two or three wounded. Among the wounded on our side was Lieutenant Waggener, but no danger, it is hoped, will ensue. We expect every hour to be attacked by superior force, but, if they forbear one day longer, we shall be prepared for them. We have already got entrenchments, are about a pallisado which I hope will be finished to-day. The Mingoes have struck the French and I hope will give a good blow before they have done. I expect 40 odd of them here tonight, which, with out fort and some reinforcements from Col. Fry, will enable us to exert our noble courage with spirit. P.S. I fortunately escaped without any wound, for the right wing, where I stood, was exposed to and received all the enemy's fire, and it was the part where the man was killed, and the rest wounded. I heard the bullets whistle, and, believe me, there is something charming in the sound. *WGW* Note: "From the *London Magazine* (August, 1754). Horace Walpole's *Memoirs of George the Second* relates that the King, on hearing that Washington described the sound of whistling bullets as 'charming,' said: 'He would not say so, if he had been used to hear many.'"

36 Zall, *Washington on Washington*, p. 11.

37 The spurious letters were in essence forged letters intended to weaken Washington by damaging his character. *WGW*, vol. 5, 6-12-1776. Note: "The first of the "Spurious Letters." They were published in London in 1776 by J. Bew in a small pamphlet under the title of "Letters from General Washington, to several of his Friends in the year 1776," etc. Handbills of one of the letters therefrom to Mrs. Washington were struck off by Rivington, in New York, as soon as the pamphlet reached America. A photostat copy of one of these bills is in the Library of Congress (Manuscripts Division). A complete reprint of the London pamphlet was also issued in America in 1778, and Hildeburn claims it as a Philadelphia imprint. The letters were plainly political propaganda put out by the London publisher, as much, it seems, for profit as for mischief-making, though the influences behind the move have not been traced. In America the reprint was made in the hope of creating discord between the New England and Southern Colonies. Washington attributed them to John Randolph, the last royalist attorney general of Virginia. The English magazines of 1776 expressed doubt of the authenticity of the letters and their hoped-for effect fell flat. In 1796 these letters were printed again, in New York, under the title "Epistles, Domestic, Confidential and Glacial from General Washington," to injure Washington's political standing, and he then took the trouble to refute their authenticity in a letter to Timothy Pickering, pointing out their discrepancies at some length. (See Mar. 3, 1797, *post*.)"

38 *WGW*, vol. 21, 3-26-1781.

39 Ibid., vol. 27, 3-25-1784.

40 Ibid., vol. 32, 5-20-1792. Madison's notes of these conversations, May 5 and 9, are in the *Madison Papers* in the Library of Congress. They are printed in Victor Hugo Paltsits's, *Washington's Farewell Address* (New York Public Library: 1935).

41 David Humphreys, *Life of General Washington with George Washington's "Remarks"* (London: The University of George Press, 1991).

42 *WGW*, vol. 28, 7-25-1785.

43 *WGW*, vol. 28, 8-18-1786.

44 Zall, *Washington on Washington*, p. 13.

45 Ibid., p. 13.

46 Jackson and Twohig, ed, *The Diaries of George Washington*, Volume 5, November, Sunday 8th, 1789. "It being contrary to Law & disagreeable to the People of this State (Connecticut) to travel on the Sabbath day and my horses after passing through such intolerable Roads wanting rest, I stayed at Perkins's Tavern (which by the bye is not a good one) all day——and a meeting House being with in a few rod of

the Door, I attended Morning & evening Service, and heard very lame discourses from a Mr. Pond.

1 GW correctly interpreted New England attitudes toward travel on the Sabbath. The *Pennsylvania Packet*, 3 Nov. 1789, noted with approval that Tristram Dalton and John Adams, on their way to Boston, broke their journey at Springfield in order not to travel on Sunday. "How pleasing the idea, that the most venerable and respectable characters of our Federal Legislature, pay such strict attention to the Sabbath." See also *Mass. Centinel*, 24 Oct. 1789.

47 Jackson and Twohig, ed, *The Diaries of George Washington*, Friday Feb. 15th, 1760. "Went to a Ball at Alexandria—where Musick and Dancing was the chief Entertainment. However in a convenient Room detachd for the purpose abounded great plenty of Bread and Butter, some Biscuets with Tea, & Coffee which the Drinkers of coud not Distinguish from Hot water sweetned. Be it remembered that pocket handkerchiefs servd the purposes of Table Cloths & Napkins and that no Apologies were made for either. I shall therefore distinguish this Ball by the Stile & title of the Bread & Butter Ball." Editors add additional note: "The Proprietors of this Ball were Messrs. Carlyle Laurie & Robt. Wilson, but the Doctr. not getting it conducted agreeable to his own taste woud claim no share of the merit of it.

A man named Robert Wilson voted for GW in the 1758 Frederick County election for the House of Burgesses.

GW apparently played cards at the ball, because on the following day he recorded the loss of 7s. 'By Cards'"

48 Zall, *Washington on Washington*, pp. 13-14.

49 *WGW*, vol. 1, 7-18-1755.

50 *Washington humorously criticizes a family member for missing church due to having a baby by using Christian language. WGW*, vol. 37, 8-28-1762. Writing to Burwell Bassett on August 28, 1762, Washington writes with tongue in cheek, " Dear Sir: I was favoured with your Epistle wrote on a certain 25th of July when you ought to have been at Church, praying as becomes every good Christian Man who has as much to answer for as you have; strange it is that you will be so blind to truth that the enlightning sounds of the Gospel cannot reach your Ear, nor no Examples awaken you to a sense of Goodness; could you but behold with what religious zeal I hye me to Church on every Lords day, it would do your heart good, and fill it I hope with equal fervency; but heark'ee; I am told you have lately introduced into your Family, a certain production which you are lost in admiration of, and spend so much time in contemplating the just proportion of its parts, the ease, and conveniences with which it abounds, that it is thought you will have little time to animadvert upon the prospect of your crops &c; pray how will this be reconciled to that anxious care and vigilance, which is so escencially necessary at a time when our growing Property, meaning the Tobacco, is assailed by every villainous worm that has had an existence since the days of Noah (how unkind it was of Noah now I have mentioned his name to suffer such a brood of vermin to get a birth in the Ark) but perhaps you may be as well of as we are; that is, have no Tobacco for them to eat and there I think we nicked the Dogs, as I think to do you if you expect any more; but not without a full assurance of being with a very sincere regard etc."

Washington humorously writes a thank you note for a poem written in his honor by taking on the role of a spiritual confessor. WGW, vol. 27, 9-2-1783. Washington laughingly writes to Mrs. Annis Boucinot Stockton, "You apply to me, My dear Madam, for absolution as tho' I was your father Confessor; and as tho' you had committed a crime, great in itself, yet of the venial class You have reason good, for I find myself strangely disposed to be a very indulgent ghostly Adviser on this occasion; and, notwithstanding "you are the most offending Soul alive" (that is, if it is a crime to write elegant Poetry) yet if you will come and dine with me on Thursday and go through the proper course of penitence, which shall be prescribed, I will strive hard to assist you in expiating these poetical trespasses on this side of purgatory. Nay more, if it rests with me to direct your future lucubrations, I shall certainly urge you to a repetition of the same conduct, on purpose to shew what an admirable knack you have at confession and reformation; and so, without more hesitation, I shall venture to command the Muse not to be restrained by ill-grounded timidity, but to go on and prosper.

"You see Madam, when once the Woman has tempted us and we have tasted the forbidden fruit, there is no such thing as checking our appetites, whatever the consequences may be. You will I dare say, recognize our being the genuine Descendents of those who are reputed to be our great Progenitors.

"Before I come to the more serious Conclusion of my Letter, I must beg leave to say a word or two about these Fine things you have been telling in such harmonious and beautiful Numbers. Fiction is to be sure the very life and Soul of Poetry. All Poets and Poetesses have been indulged in the free and indisputable use of it, time out of Mind. And to oblige you to make such an excellent Poem, on such a subject, without any Materials but those of simple reality, would be as cruel as the Edict of Pharaoh which compelled the Children of Israel to Manufacture Bricks without the necessary Ingredients. Thus are you sheltered under the authority of prescription, and I will not dare to charge you with an intentional breach of the Rules of the decalogue in giving so bright a colouring to the services I have been enabled to render my Country; though I am not conscious of deserving any thing more at your hands, than what the purest and most disinterested friendship has a right to claim; actuated by which, you will permit me, to thank you in the most affectionate manner for the kind wishes you have so happily expressed for me and the partner of all my Domestic enjoyments."

51 *Washington humorously describes the very different world of a retired president laboring as a farmer than that of a busy Secretary of War. WGW*, vol. 35, to the Secretary of War on May 29, 1797 "Dear Sir: I am indebted to you for several unacknowledged letters; but ne'er mind that; go on as if you had them. You are at the source of information, and can find many things to relate; while I have nothing to say, that could either inform or amuse a Secretary of War in Philadelphia.

"I might tell him that I begin my diurnal course with the Sun; that if my hirelings are not in their places at that time I send them messages expressive of my sorrow for their indisposition; then having put these wheels in motion, I examine the state of things further; and the more they are probed, the deeper I find the wounds are which my buildings have sustained by an absence and neglect of eight years; by the time I have accomplished these matters, breakfast (a little after seven Oclock, about the time I presume you are taking leave of Mrs. McHenry) is ready. This over, I mount my horse and ride round my farms, which employs me until it is time to dress for dinner; at which I rarely miss seeing strange faces; come, as they say, out of respect to me. Pray, would not the word curiosity answer as well? and how different this, from having a few social friends at a cheerful board? The usual time of sitting at Table; a walk, and Tea, brings me within the dawn of Candlelight; previous to which, if not prevented by company, I resolve, that, as soon as the glimmering taper, supplies the place of the great luminary, I will retire to my writing Table and acknowledge the letters I have received; but when the lights are brought, I feel tired, and disinclined to engage in this work, conceiving that the next night will do as well: the next comes and with it the same causes for postponement, and effect, and so on.

"This will account for *your* letter remaining so long unacknowledged; and having given you the history of a day, it will serve for a year; and I am persuaded you will not require a second edition of it: but it may strike you, that in this detail no mention is made of any portion of time allotted for reading; the remark would be just, for I have not looked into a book since I came home, nor shall I be able to do it until I have discharged my Workmen; probably not before the nights grow longer; when possibly, I may be looking in doomsday book. On the score of the plated ware in your possession I will say something in a future letter. At present I shall only add, that I am always and affectionately yours."

52   Zall, *Washington on Washington*, pp. 12.

53   Saul K. Padover, ed. *The Washington Papers* (Harper Brothers, 1955), p. 3.

54   *WGW*, vol. 26, 4-18-1783.

55   Ibid., Note in vol. 26, 4-18-1783, quoting Heath's *Memories*.

56   Ibid., vol. 11, 4-21-1788.

57   Washington's writings use the words passion and passions nearly ninety times. For the following, see above, note 35   In his Speech "To the Officers of the Army", he wrote, "In the moment of this Summons, another anonymous production was sent into circulation, addressed more to the feelings and passions, than to the reason and judgment of the Army." "…the secret mover of this Scheme (whoever he may be) intended to take advantage of the passions, while they were warmed by the recollection of past distresses…."

58   In a subsequent chapter, we will address objections to Washington's Christianity. This will deal with in part the question of his attitudes toward swearing and sexual ethics.

59   John E. Ferling: *The First of Men*, (The University of Tennessee Press, 1988) pp. 84-85.

60   Padover, The Washington Papers, p. 2 and beyond.

61   G.W.P. Custis writes of the events at Monmouth, "…by Lee's order, a general retreat commenced, without any apparent cause. The British pursued; a panic seized the Americans, and they fled in great confusion. These were the fugitives met by Washington. The chief was surprised and exasperated, and on this occasion, his feelings completely controlled his judgment for a moment. When he met Lee, he exclaimed in fierce tones, "what is the meaning of all this, sir?" Lee hesitated a moment, when, according to Lafayette, the aspect of Washington became terrible, and he again demanded—"I desire to know the meaning of this disorder and confusion!" The fiery Lee, stung by Washington's manner, made an angry reply, when the chief, unable to control himself, called him "a damned poltroon." "This," said Lafayette, when relating the circumstance to Governor Tompkins, in 1824, while on his visit to this country, "was the only time I ever heard General Washington swear." Lee attempted a hurried explanation, and after a few more angry words between them, Washington departed to form his line….After the battle, Lee wrote insulting letters to Washington. He was arraigned before a court-martial, because of his conduct on the twenty-eighth, and was suspended from all command, for one year." . Custis, *Recollections*, pp. 218-19. Washington's letter to Lee, *WGW*, vol. 12, 6-30-1778, says: "Sir: I received your Letter (dated thro' mistake the 1st. of July) expressed as I conceive, in terms highly improper. I am not conscious of having made use of any very singular expressions at the time of my meeting you, as you intimate. What I recollect to have said was dictated by duty and warranted by the occasion. As soon as circumstances will permit, you shall have an opportunity, either of justifying yourself to the army, to Congress, to America, and to the world in General; or of convincing them that you were guilty of a breach of orders and of misbehaviour before the enemy on the 28th. Inst in not attacking them as you had been directed and in making an unnecessary, disorderly, and shameful retreat." Note: The phrase, "justifying yourself to the army, to Congress, to America, and to the world in General," was an exact repetition from Lee's letter.

62   There is some evidence that Lee, who also had been "captured" by the British earlier in the war, may have been acting as a traitor to the cause. See Benson J. Lossings' note in Custis, pp. 292-93.

63   Padover, *The Washington Papers*, p. 2.

64   Zall, *Washington on Washington*, pp. 17-18.

65   Richard Rush, *Washington in Domestic Life, From Original Letters and Manuscripts 1857* (Kessinger Publishing, 2004) p. 65.

66   *WGW*, vol. 1, 1749-1759. We will address the question of Washington's alleged passionate interest in Mrs. Sally Fairfax in the Chapter dealing with "Objections to Washington's Christianity." See *WGW*, vol. 2, 9-12-1758. Washington allegedly wrote to Mrs. George William Fairfax, on September 12, 1758, expressing his emotions for her as he was facing another military mission. While Fitzpatrick was not sure it was authentic (see his note at this letter's date), recent scholars have concluded that it is. (See Willard Sterne Randall, *George Washington: A Life* (New York: Henry Holt and Co., 1997), p. 179. We will address George Washington's letter to Sally Fairfax in the chapter on objections to Washington's Christianity as well as the broader consideration of Washington's sexual ethics.

67   Ibid., vol. 35, 11-28-1796.

68   In his will, Washington writes, "To my compatriot in arms, and old and intimate friend Doctr. Craik, I give my Bureau (or as the Cabinet makers call it, Tambour Secretary) and the circular chair, an appendage of my Study."
      On July 3, 1789, Washington wrote to James McHenry, "The habits of intimacy and friendship, in which I have long lived with Dr. Craik, and the opinion I have of his professional knowledge, would most certainly point him out as the man of my choice in all cases of sickness. …in justice to Dr. Bard, who has attended me during my late indisposition, declare, that neither skill nor attention has been wanting on his part, and, as I could not have the assistance of my good friend Dr. Craik, I think myself fortunate in having fallen into such good hands."

69   Washington spoke of "our good friend Colo. Fairfax," to Robert Carter Nicholas on November 7, 1780, and to the Countess of Huntingdon on February 27, 1785. On October 1, 1777, he had demonstrated his friendship to Bryan Fairfax when he gave him a pass-

port to cross all military lines so he could get to New York and go to England because of his loyalist views. Washington never broke his friendship with Fairfax in spite of their different views. Gen. George Washington wrote out the following passport for his friend…"The bearer hereof Bryan Fairfax, Esqr. together with his son Mr. Thomas Fairfax and their baggage has permission to pass all guards on their way to New York and the Commanding Officer at any advanced post is requested to furnish a Flag and give any other assistance to effect this purpose. Given under my hand, etc."

70   See *WGW*, vol. 15, 7-4-1779; *WGW*, vol. 18, 5-8-1780; *WGW*, vol. 28, 12-8-1784.

71   Ibid., vol. 29, 5-28-1788: "I embrace you, my dear Count, with all my heart."

72   Ibid., vol. 24, 8-10-1782, "I look forward with pleasure, to the epocha which will place us as conveniently in one Camp, as we are congenial in our sentiments. I shall embrace you when it happens with the warmth of perfect friendship." vol. 30, 11-27-1788: "with sincere wishes for the felicity of you and yours, I embrace you, my dear Marqs. and am now, as ever With Sentiments of esteem and Friendship."

73   Ibid., vol. 27, 12-23-1783. Washington wrote to Baron Steuben from Annapolis finally on the way home to Mount Vernon on December 23, 1783, "I beg you will be convinced, My dear Sir, that I should rejoice if it could ever be in my power to serve you more essentially than by expressions of regard and affection; but in the meantime, I am perswaded you will not be displeased with this farewell token of my sincere friendship and esteem for you. This is the last Letter I shall ever write while I continue in the service of my Country; the hour of my resignation is fixed at twelve this day; after which I shall become a private Citizen on the Banks of the Potomack, where I shall be glad to embrace you, and to testify the great esteem and consideration…"

74   Ibid., vol. 23 9-20-1781. "I hope ere long to have the happiness to embrace you again with the like Cordiality and Sincere Affection, on the Reduction of Lord Cornwallis and his Army, an Event, which I am sure will convey the greatest Pleasure to each of us."

75   Ibid., vol. 27, 1-14-1784. Washington wrote to David Humphreys on January 14, 1784, "Be assured that there are few things which would give me more pleasure than opportunities of evincing to you the sincerity of my friendship,…I shall hold in pleasing remembrance the friendship and intimacy which has subsisted between us, and shall neglect no opportunity on my part to cultivate and improve them."

76   *WGW*, vol. 30, 10-3-1788.

77   *WGW*, vol. 29, 5-31-1787, Washington wrote to Henry Knox: "…assurances of the sincerest friendship…" Ibid., vol. 30, vol. 4-1-1789, "With best wishes for Mrs. Knox, and sincere friendship for yourself." Ibid., vol. 36, 7-14-1798, In a "Private and confidential" letter to Alexander Hamilton, he wrote: "my friend General Knox, whom I love and esteem." Ibid., vol. 36, 9-25-1798, to President John Adams, "With respect to General Knox, I can say with truth, there is no man in the United States with whom I have been in habits of greater intimacy; no one whom I have loved more sincerely, nor any for whom I have had a greater friendship."

78   Ibid., vol. 37, 12-25-1798.

79   Ibid., vol. 27, 12-1-1783.

CHAPTER 9

1   *WGW*, vol. 5, 7-9-1776.

2   Ibid., vol. 1, 11-15-1754.

3   Ibid., vol. 12-28-1776, Writing to Brig. Gen. William Maxwell, Washington said, "I have the pleasure to inform you of the success of an enterprize, which took effect the 26th. Instant at Trenton; On the night of the preceding day, I cross'd the Delaware with a detachment of the Army under my Command, amounting to about 2400; the difficulties arising in the passage of the River, prevented my arriving at the Town so soon as I expected, by which means the attack did not commence till eight O'Clock; when our Troops pressed forward with so much Ardor, and Spirit, as never to suffer them to form completely, about Seven hundred of the enemy ran away in the begining of the action; the rest amounting to 1000 including 31 Officers, after making a feeble opposition, laid down their Arms and Surrendered themselves prisoners of War. We have taken about one thousand stand of Arms, four Standards and Six pieces of brass Artillery, with some other Stores. I have issued some orders to day for the encouragement of the Troops, whose terms are near expiring, which I shall be glad you will immediately communicate to them, in your Orders."

4   Washington's record of this amazing journey was published by Gov. Dinwiddie, and, the story can be found in Fitzpatrick, *The Diaries of George Washington*, vol. I. pp. 43ff.

5   Writing to a friend named Robin, in 1754 or 1755, Washington speaks of spending his time very pleasantly in the company of a young lady who was living at the house of one of his friends. He goes on to explain, "as that only added fuel to the fire, it makes me the more uneasy where my often and unavoidably being in company with her revives my former passion for your lowland beauty, whereas was I to live more retired from young women, I might in some measure alleviate my sorrows by burying that chaste and former passion in the grave of oblivion and eternal forgetfulness." In *WGW*, vol. I., p. 16. George Washington's "Lowland Beauty" may have been Lucy Grymes, who later became Mrs. Henry Lee. See Clarence Macartney, "George Washington: A Bi-Centennial Sermon" (Pittsburgh: First Presbyterian Church, 1932), p. 5.

6   Macartney, *George Washington*, p. 7.

7   Jackson and Twohig, *The Diaries of George Washington*. vol. 1. Expedition to the Ohio 31 March—27 June 1754. pp. 169-170. "In 1756 a pamphlet, Reasons Humbly Offered, to Prove That the Letter Printed at the End of the French Memorial of Justification, Is a French Forgery, and Falsely Ascribed to His R—l H—s, was published in London, challenging the authenticity of the letter on the basis of its content. See also *Monthly Review*, (1756), 302—4.) GW expressed reservations concerning the accuracy of the MEMOIR in a letter used by Jared Sparks in his edition of GW's writings: In regard to the journal, I can only observe in general, that I kept no regular one during that expedition; rough minutes of occurrences I certainly took, and find them as certainly and strangely metamorphosed; some parts left out, which I remember were entered, and many things added that never were thought of; the names of men and things egregiously miscalled; and the whole of what I saw Englished is very incorrect and nonsensical; yet, I will not pretend to say that the little body, who

brought it to me, has not made a literal translation, and a good one. Short as my time is, I cannot help remarking on Villiers' account of the battle of, and transactions at, the Meadows, as it is very extraordinary, and not less erroneous than inconsistent. He says the French received the first fire. It is well known, that we received it at six hundred paces' distance. He also says, our fears obliged us to retreat in a most disorderly manner after the capitulation. How is this consistent with his other account? He acknowledges, that we sustained the attack warmly from ten in the morning until dark, and that he called first to parley, which strongly indicates that we were not totally absorbed in fear. If the gentleman in his account had adhered to the truth, he must have confessed, that we looked upon his offer to parley as an artifice to get into and examine our trenches, and refused on this account, until they desired an officer might be sent to them, and gave their parole for his safe return. He might also, if he had been as great a lover of the truth as he was of vainglory, have said, that we absolutely refused their first and second proposals, and would consent to capitulate on no other terms than such as we obtained. That we were wilfully, or ignorantly, deceived by our interpreter in regard to the word *assassination*, I do aver, and will to my dying moment; so will every officer that was present. The interpreter was a Dutchman, little acquainted with the English tongue, therefore might not advert to the tone and meaning of the word in English; but, whatever his motives were for so doing, certain it is, he called it the *death*, or the *loss*, of the Sieur Jumonville. So we received and so we understood it, until, to our great surprise and mortification, we found it otherwise in a literal translation." This is found in a letter to George Washington's brother, dated July 18, 1755, in Sparks, *The Writings of George Washington*, vol. II, p. 89.

8   *WGW*, vol. 2, 9-20-1765. Washington wrote to Mrs. Washington's uncle in England, "The Stamp Act Imposed on the Colonies by the Parliament of Great Britain engrosses the conversation of the Speculative part of the Colonists, who look upon this unconstitutional method of Taxation as a direful attack upon their Liberties, and loudly exclaim against the Violation; what may be the result of this and some other (I think I may add) ill judgd Measures, I will not undertake to determine; but this I may venture to affirm, that the advantage accrueing to the Mother Country will fall greatly short of the expectations of the Ministry; for certain it is, our whole Substance does already in a manner flow to Great Britain and that whatsoever contributes to lessen our Importation's must be hurtful to their Manufacturers. And the Eyes of our People, already beginning to open, will perceive, that many Luxuries which we lavish our substance to Great Britain for, can well be dispensd with whilst the necessaries of Life are (mostly) to be had within ourselves. This consequently will introduce frugality, and be a necessary stimulation to Industry. If Great Britain therefore Loads her Manufactures with heavy Taxes, will it not facilitate these Measures? they will not compel us I think to give our Money for their exports, whether we will or no, and certain I am none of their Traders will part from them without a valuable consideration. Where then is the Utility of these Restrictions? As to the Stamp Act, taken in a single view, one, and the first bad consequences attending it I take to be this. Our Courts of Judicature must inevitably be shut up; for it is impossible (or next of kin to it) under our present Circumstances that the Act of Parliam't can be complyd with were we ever so willing to enforce the execution; for not to say, which alone woud be sufficient, that we have not Money to pay the Stamps, there are many other Cogent Reasons to prevent it; and if a stop be put to our judicial proceedings I fancy the Merchants of G. Britain trading to the Colonies will not be among the last to wish for a Repeal of it." When it was repealed, Washington openly expressed his approval. *WGW*, vol. 2, 7-21-1766, "The Repeal of the Stamp Act, to whatsoever causes owing, ought much to be rejoiced at, for had the Parliament of Great Britain resolvd upon enforcing it the consequences I conceive woud have been more direful than is generally apprehended both to the Mother Country and her Colonies. All therefore who were Instrumental in procuring the Repeal are entitled to the Thanks of every British Subject and have mine cordially."

9   Washington seems to never have written the phrase, "taxation without representation." However, he does show his deep concern for American liberty in his involvement with the Virginia non importation plan. See for example, *WGW*, vol. 2, 4-5-1769. Writing to George Mason (author of the Virginia non-importation resolutions of 1769, the Fairfax resolutions of 1774, and the Virginia bill of rights, 1776), he says, "At a time when our lordly Masters in Great Britain will be satisfied with nothing less than the deprecation of American freedom, it seems highly necessary that some thing shou'd be done to avert the stroke and maintain the liberty which we have derived from our Ancestors; but the manner of doing it to answer the purpose effectually is the point in question. That no man shou'd scruple, or hesitate a moment to use a[r]ms in defence of so valuable a blessing, on which all the good and evil of life depends; is clearly my opinion; yet A[r]ms I wou'd beg leave to add, should be the last resource; the denier resort. Addresses to the Throne, and remonstrances to parliament, we have already, it is said, proved the inefficacy of; how far then their attention to our rights and priviledges is to be awakened or alarmed by starving their Trade and manufactures, remains to be tryed. The northern Colonies, it appears, are endeavouring to adopt this scheme. In my opinion it is a good one, and must be attended with salutary effects, provided it can be carried pretty generally into execution; but how far it is practicable to do so, I will not take upon me to determine. That there will be difficulties attending the execution of it every where, from clashing interests, and selfish designing men (ever attentive to their own gain, and watchful of every turn that can assist their lucrative views, in preference to any other consideration) cannot be denied; but in the Tobacco Colonies where the Trade is so diffused, and in a manner wholly conducted by Factors for their principals at home, these difficulties are certainly enhanced, but I think not insurmountably increased, if the Gentlemen in their several Counties wou'd be at some pains to explain matters to the people, and stimulate them to a cordial agreement to purchase none but certain innumerated Articles out of any of the Stores after such a period, not import nor purchase any themselves. …Upon the whole therefore, I think the Scheme a good one, and that it ought to be tryed here." *WGW*, note on this dates says, "The assembly in May was the first that met after the arrival of Lord Botetourt as governor. The burgesses agreed upon an address to the King, which Governor Botetourt disapproved and dissolved the assembly. The dismissed burgesses reassembled in the Apollo room of the Raleigh Tavern and drew up the Virginia Non-Importation Association. Washington was on the drafting committee and notes expenses, in his accounts, arising there from."

10   *WGW*, vol. 37, 8-20-1770. Washington was most serious about supporting the Non-Importation Agreement: "You will perceive in looking over the several Invoices that some of the Goods there required, are upon condition that the Act of Parliament Imposing a Duty upon Tea, Paper &ca. for the purpose of raising a Revenue in America is totally repeald; and I beg the favour of you to be governd

strictly thereby, as it will not be in my power to receive any Articles contrary to our Non-Importation Agreement, to which I have Subscribd, and shall religeously adhere to, if it was, as I coud wish it to be ten times as strict."

11   Macartney, *George Washington*, p. 10.

12   David Humphreys', *Life of George Washington*.

13   David Barton, *The Bulletproof George* (Texas: Wallbuilders Press, 2003) p. 35

14   In Humphreys, Washington explained, "The folly & consequence of opposing compact bodies to the sparse manner of Indian fighting in woods, which had in a manner been predicted, was now so clearly verified that from hence forward another mode obtained in all future operations."

15   *WGW*, vol. 1: 7-18-1755, Washington wrote to Robert Dinwiddie, "We continued our March from Fort Cumberland to Frazier's (which is within 7 Miles of Duquisne) with't meet'g with any extraordinary event, hav'g only a stragler or two picked up by the French Indians. When we came to this place, we were attack'd (very unexpectedly I must own) by abt. 300 French and Ind'ns; Our numbers consisted of abt. 1300 well arm'd Men, chiefly Regular's, who were immediately struck with such a deadly Panick, that nothing but confusion and dis-obedience of order's prevail'd amongst them: The Officer's in gen'l behav'd with incomparable bravery, for which they greatly suffer'd, there being near 60 kill'd and wound'd. A large proportion, out of the number we had! The Virginian Companies behav'd like Men and died like Soldiers; for I believe out of the 3 Companys that were there that day, scarce 30 were left alive: Captn. Peyrouny and all his Officer's, down to a Corporal, were kill'd; Captn. Polson shar'd almost as hard a Fate, for only one of his Escap'd: In short the dastardly behaviour of the English Soldier's expos'd all those who were inclin'd to do their duty to almost certain Death; and at length, in despight of every effort to the contrary, broke and run as Sheep before the Hounds, leav'g the Artillery, Ammunition, Provisions, and, every individual thing we had with us a prey to the Enemy; and when we endeavour'd to rally them in hopes of regaining our invaluable loss, it was with as much suc-cess as if we had attempted to have stop'd the wild Bears of the Mountains. The Genl. was wounded behind in the shoulder, and into the Breast, of w'ch he died three days after; his two Aids de Camp were both wounded, but are in a fair way of Recovery; Colo. Burton and Sir Jno. St. Clair are also wounded, and I hope will get over it; Sir Peter Halket, with many other brave Officers were kill'd in the Field. I luckily escap'd with't a wound tho' I had four Bullets through my Coat and two Horses shot under me. It is supposed that we left 300 or more dead in the Field; about that number we brought of wounded; and it is imagin'd (I believe with great justice too) that two thirds of both received their shott from our own cowardly English Soldier's who gather'd themselves into a body contrary to orders 10 or 12 deep, wou'd then level, Fire and shoot down the Men before them. I tremble at the consequences that this defeat may have upon our back set-tlers, who I suppose will all leave their habitations unless there are proper measures taken for their security."

16   *WGW*, vol. 1, 7-18-1755, writing to his brother, John Augustine Washington, he says, "Dear Jack: As I have heard since my arriv'l at this place, a circumstantial acct. of my death and dying speech, I take this early oppertunity of contradicting both, and of assuring you that I now exist and appear in the land of the living by the miraculous care of Providence, that protected me beyond all human expectation; I had 4 Bullets through my Coat, and two Horses shot under me, and yet escaped unhurt. We have been most scandalously beaten by a trifling body of men; but fatigue and want of time prevents me from giving any of the details till I have the happiness of seeing you at home; which I now most ardently wish for, since we are drove in thus far. A Weak and Feeble state of Health, obliges me to halt here for 2 or 3 days, to recover a little strength, that I may thereby be enabled to proceed homewards with more ease; You may expect to see me there on Saturday or Sunday Se'night, which is as soon as I can well be down as I shall take my Bulb skin Plantation's in my way. Pray give my Compl'ts to all my F'ds. I am Dr. Jack, y'r most Affect. Broth'r."

17   Barton, *Bulletproof George*, p.-37-38. David Barton points out that Washington was a specially marked target by the Indians: "The Indians had singled them out, and every mounted officer, except Washington, was slain before Braddock fell." Bulletproof-38. Historian George Bancroft observed: "Of the British and Americans, one half were killed or wounded. General Braddock braved every danger. His secretary was shot dead; both his English aids were disabled early in the engagement, leaving the American [George Washington] alone to distrib-ute his orders." Bancroft IV 1854-p. 190Bancroft continued: "Who is Mr. Washington?" asked Lord Halifax a few months later. "I know nothing of him," he added," but that they say he behaved in Braddock's action as bravely as if he really loved the whistling of bullets." See also Aaron Bancroft, *The Life of George Washington, Commander in Chief of the American Army*, (Boston: Waster Street Bookstore, 1833), IV 1854 p. 190.

18   Ibid., vol. 1, 7-15-1755. Writing to Col. James Innes, Washington explains, "Sir: Captn. Orme being confined to his Litter and not well able to write, has desir'd me to acknowledge the receipt of your's; He begs the favour of you to have the room that the Gen'l. lodg'd in prepar'd for Colo. Burton, himself, and Capt. Morris, who are all wounded; also, that some small place may be had where convenient for Cooking; and, that if any fresh Provn. and other suitable necessarys for persons in their infirm condition, may be had, that you will be kind enough to engage it. He also begs, that, you will order the present w'ch was sent by Governour Morris to the Genl. and his Family, into the care of Mr. A. le Roy, the Steward, who is sent on for that, and other purposes. The Horses, that carry the wounded Gent'n. in Litters are so much fatigued that we dread their performance, therefore, it is desir'd that you will be kind enough to send out 8 or 10 fresh horses for their relief, which will enable us to reach the Fort this Evening. I doubt not but you have had an acot. of the poor Genl.'s death by some of the affrighted Waggoners, who ran off without taking leave." In Humphreys, Washington explained, "Happy was it for him, and the remains of the first division that they left such a quantity of valuable and enticing baggage on the field as to occasion a scramble and con-tention in the seizure & distribution of it among the enemy for had a pursuit taken place——by passing the defile which we had avoided; and they had got into our Rear, the whole except a few woodsmen, would have fallen victims to the merciless savages. Of about 12 or 13 hundred which were in this action eight or 9 hundred were either killed or wounded, among whom a large proportion of brave and valu-able Officers were included."

19   Ibid., vol. 1, 7-18-1755. Washington several years later improved his copy of the letter by changing his first words to, "As I have heard, since my arrival at this place, a circumstantial account of my death and dying speech, I take this early opportunity of contradicting the first,

and of assuring you, that I have not as yet composed the latter. But by the All-Powerful Dispensations of Providence, I have been protected beyond all human probability or expectation; for I had four bullets through my coat, and two horses shot under me, yet escaped unhurt, although death was leveling my companions on every side of me!"

20 Macartney, *George Washington*, p.1

21 The Reverend Samuel Davies, as a Presbyterian, was a non-Anglican dissenting clergyman in Hanover County, Virginia. He later became the President of the College of New Jersey, or Princeton. He preached a series of sermons, which were printed in Philadelphia and London, entitled *Religion and Patriotism the Constituents of a Good Soldier*. He called for not only patriotic spirit and military courage in the difficulties of the struggle in the French and Indian War, but also a deep commitment to the Protestant faith over against the Roman Catholicism of the French. Reverend Davies' remarkable words regarding Washington were nearly prophetic: "As a remarkable instance of this, I may point out to the public that heroic youth, Colonel Washington, whom I cannot but hope Providence has hitherto preserved in so signal a manner for some important service to his country."
Religion and Patriotism the Constituents of a Good Soldier
A S E R M O N preached to Captain *Overton's* Independent Company of Volunteers,
raised in *Hanover* County, *Virginia, Au- gust* 17, 1755.
By Samuel Davis, *A. M. Minister of theGospel there.*
PHILADELPHIA
Printed by J A M E S   C H A T T I N. 1755.

RELIGION AND PATRIOTISM the CONSTITUENTS
of a good S O L D I E R.
A S E R M O N

2 Sam. 10. 12. *Be of good Courage, and let us play the Men, for our People, and for the Cities of our God: And the Lord do that which him good* An Hundred Years of Peace and Liberty in such a World as this, is a very unusual Thing; and yet our Country has been the happy Spot that has been distinguished with such a long Series of Blessings, with little or no Interruption. Our Situation in the Middle of the *British* Colonies, and our Separation from the *French*, those eternal Enemies of Liberty and *Britons*, on the one Side by the vast *Atlantic*, and on the other by a long Ridge of Mountains, and a wide, extended Wilderness, have for many Years been a Barrier to us; and while other Nations have been involved in War, we have not been alarmed with the Sound of the Trumpet, nor seen *Garments rolled in Blood.*

But now the Scene is changed: Now we begin to experience in our Turn the Fate of the Nations of the Earth. Our Territories are invaded by the Power and Perfidy of *France;* our Frontiers ravaged by merciless Savages, and our Fellow-Subjects there murdered with all the horrid Arts of *Indian* and Popish Torture. Our General *unfortunately brave*, is fallen, an Army of 1300 choice Men routed, our fine Train of Artillery taken, and all this (Oh mortifying Thought!) all this by 4 or 500 dastardly, insidious Barbarians.

These Calamities have not come upon us without Warnings. We were long ago apprized of the ambitious Schemes of our Enemies, and their Motions to carry them into Execution: And had we taken timely Measures, they might have been crushed, before they could arrive at such a formidable Height. But how have we generally behaved in such a critical Time; Alas! Our country has been funk in a deep Sleep: A stupid Security has unmanned the Inhabitants: They could not realize a Danger at the Distance of 2 or 300 Miles: They would not be persuaded, that even *French Papists* could seriously design us an Injury: And hence little or nothing has been done for the Defence of our Country in Time, except by the Compulsion of Authority. And now, when the Cloud thickens over our Heads, and alarms every thoughtful Mind with its near Approach, Multitudes, I am afraid, are still dissolved in careless Security, or enervated with an effeminate, cowardly Spirit. When the melancholy News first reached us concerning the Fate of our Army, then we saw how natural it is for the Presumptuous to fall into the opposite Extreme of unmanly Despondence and Consternation; and how little Men could do in such a Pannic for their own Defence. We have also *suffered our poor Fellow-Subjects in the Frontier Counties to fall a helpless Prey to Blood-thirsty Savages, without affording them proper Assistance*, which as Members of the same Body Politic, they had a Right to expect. They might as well have continued *in a State of Nature*, as be united *in Society*, if in such an Article of extreme Danger, they are left to shift for themselves. The bloody Barbarians have exercised on some of them the most unnatural and leisurely Tortures; and others they have butchered in their Beds, or in some unguarded Hour. Can human Nature bear the Horror of the Sight! See yonder! The hairy Scalps, clotted with Gore! The mangled Limbs! The ript-up Woman! The Heart and Bowels, still palpitating with Life, smoking on the Ground! See the Savages swilling their Blood, and imbibing a more outrageous Fury with the inhuman Draught! Sure these are not *Men*; they are not *Beasts of Prey;* they are something worse; they must be *internal Furies* in human Shape. And have we tamely looked on, and suffered them to exercise these hellish Barbarities upon our Fellow-Men, our Fellow-Subjects, our Brethren? Alas! With what Horror must we look upon ourselves, as being little better than Accessories to their Blood?

And shall these Ravages go on unchecked? Shall *Virginia* incur the Guilt and the everlasting Shame, of tamely exchanging her Liberty, her Religion, and her All, for arbitrary *Gallic* Power, and for Popish Slavery, Tyranny and Massacre? Alas! Are there none of her Children, that enjoyed all the Blessings of her Peace, that will espouse her Cause, and befriend her now in the Time of her Danger? Are *Britons* utterly degenerated by so short a Remove from their Mother-Country? Is the Spirit of Patriotism entirely extinguished among us? And must I give thee up for lost, O my Country, and all that is included in that important Word? Must I look upon these as a conquered, enslaved Province of *France*, and the Range of *Indian* Savages? My Heart breaks at the Thought and must ye, our unhappy Brethren in our Frontiers, must ye stand the single Barriers of a ravaged Country, unassisted,...? Alas! Must I draw these shocking Conclusions?

No; I am agreeably checked by the happy, encouraging Prospect now before me. Is it a pleasing Dream? Or do I really see a Number of brave Men, without the Compulsion of Authority, without the Prospect of Gain, voluntarily associated in a Company, to march over horrendous Rocks and Mountains, into an hideous Wilderness, to succour their helpless Fellow-Subjects, and guard their Country? Yes, Gentlemen, I see you here upon this Design; and were you all united to my Heart by the most endearing Ties of Nature, or Friendship, I could not wish to see you engaged in a nobler Cause; and whatever the Fondness of Passion might carry me to, I am sure my Judgment would never suffer me to persuade you to desert it. You all generously put your Lives in your Hands; and sundry of you have nobly disengaged yourselves from the strong and tender Ties that twine about the Heart of a *Father*, or a *Husband*, to confine you at home in glorious Ease, and sneaking Retirement from Danger, when your Country calls for your Assistance. While I have you before me, I have high Thoughts of a *Virginian;* and I entertain the pleasing Hope that my Country will yet emerge out of her Distress and flourish with her usual Blessings. I am gratefully sensible of the unmerited Honour you have done me, in making Choice of me to address you upon so singular and important an Occasion: And I am sure I bring with me a Heart ardent to serve you and my Country, though I am afraid my inability, and the Hurry of my Preparations, may give you Reason to repent your Choice. I cannot begin my Address to you with more proper Words than those of a great General, which I have read to you: *Be of good Courage, and play the Man, for your People, and for the Cities of your God; and the Lord do what seemeth him good.*

…Courage is an essential Character of a good Soldier:—Not a savage ferocious Violence:—Not a fool-hardy Insensibility of Danger, or headstrong Rashness to rush into it:—Not the Fury of enflamed Passions, broke loose from the Government of Reason: But calm, deliberate, rational Courage; a steady, judicious, thoughtful Fortitude; the Courage of a Man, and not of a Tiger.......*As a remarkable Instance of this, I may point out to the Public that heroic Youth Col. Washington, whom I cannot but hope Providence has hitherto preserved in so signal a Manner, for some important Service to his Country.*

22 Humphreys' *Life of George Washington* "During this interval in one of his tours along the frontier posts — he narrowly escaped, according to the account afterwards given by some of our People who were Prisoners with them, and eye witnesses at the time [illegible] falling by an Indian party who had waylaid (for another purpose) the communication along which with a small party of horse only he was passing — The road in this place formed a curve and the prey they were in weight for being expected at the reverse part, the Captain of the party had gone across to observe the number & manner of their improvements etc in order that he might make his disposition accordingly leaving orders for the party not to take notice of any passengers the other way till he returned to them —- in the meantime in the opposite direction I passed & escaped almost certain destruction for the weather was raining and the few carbines unfit for use if we had escaped the first fire — This happened near Fort Vass."

23 *The Diaries of George Washington 1748-1799* edited by John C. Fitzpatrick, vol. 1, 1748-1770, Published for The Mount Vernon Ladies' Association of the Union (Boston and New York: Houghton Mifflin Company). See under the following dates:
September 1770
20, 1770—Set out for the Big Kanhawa with Dr. Craik, Captn. Crawford and others. Incampd abt. 14 Miles off.
28, 1770—Meeting with Kiashuta and other Indian Hunters we proceeded only 10 Miles to day.
October 1770
5th—Began a journey to the Ohio in Company with Doctr. Craik..[Kiashuta, an Indian who had accompanied Washington part of the way from Logs Town to Fort Le Boeuf in 1753]
Sunday 14, 1770—At Captn. Crawford's all day. Went to see a Coal Mine not far from his house on the Banks of the River; the Coal seemed to be of the very best kind, burning freely and abundance of it.
Wednesday 17.—Doctr. Craik and myself with Captn. Crawford and others arrivd at Fort Pill,..The fort is built in the point between the River Alligany and Monongahela..
Thursday 18th—Dined in the Fort with Colo. Croghan…dined with Colo. Croghan the next day at his Seat abt. 4 miles up the Alligany.
Friday 19th—Recd. A Message from Colo. Croghan that the white Mingo and other Chiefs of the 6 Nations had something to say to me, and desiring that I would be at his House abt. 11(where they were to meet). I went up and receivd a Speech with a String of Wampum [Wampum, the Indian ceremonial emblem, was a comparatively rare shell of some beauty, which was pierced, longitudinally, and strung upon deerskin thongs. These strings were woven into bands of belts, and the size of the belt was generally proportioned to what the Indians considered the significance of the occasion where it was used. The Indian method of sealing and recording treaties or councils, was by presenting a wampum belt. Wampum was, sometimes, used for personal adornment. As used in the councils, or treaty-making, the belts were presented to the opposite party, and in all future discussions of the subject these belts were produced when, in some curious way the sight of each belt recalled to the Indian speech-chronicler the speech made at the time that belt was presented. It is stated that this chronicler, who was styled 'the Keeper of the Belts' could repeat the speech almost verbatim, even though some years had elapsed since it had first been delivered. The Keeper of the Belts was usually an old Indian and kept in training under him a younger man, who was to take his place, and him he drilled in remembering the speeches, that the record of them might not be lost.] from the White Mingo to the following effect:
That I was a Person who some of them remember to have seen when I was sent on an Embassy to the French, and most of them had heard of; they were come to bid me welcome to this Country, and to desire that the People of Virginia would consider them as friends and Brothers linked together in one chair; that I wd. Inform the Governor, that it was their wish to live in peace and harmy. With the white People, and that tho their had been some unhappy differences between them and the People upon our Frontiers, it was all made up, and they hopd forgotten; and concluded with saying, that, their Brothers of Virginia did not come among them and Trade as the Inhabitants of the other Provences did; from whence they were afraid that we did not look upon them with so friendly an Eye as they coud wish.. (410-11)
Monday 22…Upon our arrival at the Mingo Town we receivd the disagreeable news of two Traders being killd at a Town calld the Grape Vine Town.
Tuesday 23….only one Person was killd… At the Mingo Town we found, and left, 60 odd Warriors of the six Nations going to the

Cerhokee Country to proceed to war against the Cuttaba's..

Wednesday 24th....and enquire into the truth of the report concerning the Murder..

Thursday 25th.—About Seven Oclock Nicholson and the Indian returnd; they found nobody at the Town but tow old Indian Women (the Men being a Hunting) from these they learnt that the Trader was not killd, but drownd in attempting to Ford the Ohio…About half an hour after 7 we set out from our Incampment around which, and up the Creek is a body of fine Land. In our Passage down to this, we see innumerable quantities of Turkeys, and many Deer watering…

Friday 26th....At the end of this reach we found one, Martin, and Lindsay two Traders; and from them learnt, that the Person drownd was one Philips attempting in Compa. With Rogers, another Indn. Trader, the Swim the River with their Horses at an improper place; Rogers himself narrowly escaping…

Sunday 28th...we found Kiashuta and his Hunting Party Incampd. Here we were under a necessity of paying our Compliments, As this person was one of the Six Nation Chiefs and the head of them upon this River. In the Person of Kiashuta I found an old acquaintance, he being one of the Indians that went with me to the French in 1753. He expressed a satisfaction in seeing me, and treated us with great kindness; giving us a Quarter of very fine Buffalo. He insisted upon our spending that Night with him, and in order to retard us as little as possible movd his Camp down the River about 3 Miles just below the Mouth of a Creek, the name of which I coud not learn (it not being large); at this place we all Incampd. After much Councelling the overnight, they all came to my fire the next Morning, with great formality; when Kiashuta rehearsing what had passd between me and the Sachems at Colo. Croghan's, thankd me for saying that Peace and friendship was the wish of the People of Virginia (with them) and for recommending it to the Traders to deal with them upon a fair and equitable footing; and then again expressd their desire of having a Trade opend with Virginia, and that the Governor thereof might not only be made acquainted therewith, but of their friendly disposition towards the white People; this I promisd to do.

Monday 29th—The tedious ceremony which the Indians observe in their Councellings and speeches, detaind us till 9 Oclock…On this Creek many Buffaloes use [d to be] according to the Indians acct…

24   G.W. Parke Custis in his *Recollections of Washington*, p.300-305. Custis actually turned this story into a play entitled, "The Indian Prophecy" that was performed in several cities.

25   *WGW*, vol. 3, 6-18-1775. Bancroft IV 212

26   Bancroft, *The Life of George Washington*, IV 212.

27   Ibid., IV 212.

28   Ibid., IV 212.

29   *WGW*, vol. 1, April 22, 1756.

30   Ibid., vol. 21, 4-7-1781. Writing to Maj. Gen. William Heath, Washington confided: "Dear Sir: I have received and thank you for your information of this date. To guard against Assassination (which I neither expect, nor dread) is impossible; but I have not been without my apprehensions of the other attempt. Not from the enemy at New York, but the Tories and disaffected of this place; who might, in the Night, carry me off in my own Boat; and all be ignorant of it till the Morning. If the Water at Night is well guarded, I shall be under no appre- hension of attempts of this kind." *WGW*, vol. 21, 4-7-1781. Washington promptly wrote to Gov. William Livingston, "Dear Sir: Intelligence has been sent to me by a Gentleman living near the enemy's lines and who has an opportunity of knowing what passes among them, that four parties had been sent out with orders to take or Assainate Your Excellency, Governor Clinton, Me and a fourth person name not known. I cannot say that I am under apprehensions on account of the latter, but I have no doubt they would execute the former could they find an opportunity. I shall take such precautions on the occasion as appear to me necessary, and I have thought it proper to advise your Excellency of what has come to my knowledge that you may do the same. That they may fail of success if they have any such plan in contemplation is the earnest wish of, Dear Sir etc." As a popular example of the very real fear of the possibility of Washington being assassinated, consider the legend, "The Poisoned Dish" in *True Stories of the Days of Washington* (New York: Phinney, Blakeman & Mason, 1861), p. 51-55. This is found in the footnotes of the chapter, "The Childhood of George Washington."

31   Custis, *Recollections*, pp. 201-202.

32   *WGW*, vol. 6, 1-5-1777 note says: Sparks notes that in both the actions at Trenton and Princeton General Washington encouraged the troops by his presence in the most exposed situations. An officer who was in these engagements wrote from Morristown (January 7): "Our army love their General very much, but they have one thing against him, which is the little care he takes of himself in any action. His per- sonal bravery, and the desire he has of animating his troops by example, make him fearless of danger. This occasions us much uneasiness. But Heaven, which has hitherto been his shield, I hope will still continue to guard so valuable a life."

33   Bancroft mentions that the only reason Washington did not charge alone on his horse directly into the enemy lines at that moment was because someone reached out and grasped the reins of his horse. "Sept. 14, 1776— The American lines at this place were capable of defence, but the men posted in them, on the firing of the ships, without waiting for the attack of the enemy, abandoned them. As soon as the can- nonading began, two brigades were detached from the main body to support the troops in the breast works, the fugitives communicated to them their panics, and General Washington, in riding to the scene of action, met his troops retreating in the utmost confusion, disre- garding the efforts of their Generals to stop them. While the Commander in Chief was, with some effect, exerting himself to rally them, a very small body of the enemy appeared in sight, on which the men again broke, and a most dastardly route ensued. At this unfortunate moment, and only at this moment through his whole life, General Washington appears to have lost his fortitude. All the shameful and disastrous consequences of the defection of his army, rushed upon his mind, and bore down his spirits. In a paroxysm of despair, he turned his horse towards the enemy, seemingly with the intention to avoid the disgrace of the day by the sacrifice of his life: his aids seized the horse's bridle, and with friendly violence, rescued him from the destruction that awaited him." Aaron Bancroft, *Life Of Washington* (Boston: Water Street Bookstore, 1830, vol. I. p. 87. Ibid., vol.6, 9-16-1776 notes: Ford quotes a "Letter from New York," Sept. 27, 1776, printed in the *London Chronicle* (Nov. 19, 1776): "I forgot to mention that Mr. Washington shortly after the landing on New York island, narrow-

ly escaped being made prisoner. He left Mr. Apthorpe's house, at Bloomingdale, a few minutes only before the British light infantry entered it." Spark's quotes a letter from General Greene (September 17): "Fellows's and Parsons's brigades ran away from about fifty men and left his Excellency on the ground within eighty yards of the Enemy, so vexed at the infamous conduct of the troops, that he sought death rather than life." The Reverend William Gordon, whose history of the Revolution must always be read with recollection that the author's enthusiasm for America had cooled before he published his work, recounts the episode as he is supposed to have gleaned it from first hand in the camp shortly after the retreat. Col. William Smallwood states that Washington caned and whipped the fleeing men, though he does not state with what. Howe reported to Germain (September 21) merely that the landing at Kips Bay was unexpected to the Americans and that the British cannonade was so severe that the descent was made without the least opposition. He made no mention of Washington. After making due allowance for the excited recollections on the American side, colored by the chagrin for the panic, the bald fact seems to be that Washington continued his efforts to check the retreat until the British were so close as to put him in grave jeopardy of death or capture.

34 Writing to his brother John Augustine Washington on July 4, 1778, he explained how victory was snatched from defeat at Monmouth. "Dear Brother: Your Letter of the 20th. Ulto. came to my hands last Night; before this will have reached you, the Acct. of the Battle of Monmouth probably will get to Virginia; which, from an unfortunate, and bad beginning, turned out a glorious and happy day. The Enemy evacuated Philadelphia on the 18th. Instt.; at ten oclock that day I got intelligence of it, and by two oclock, or soon after, had Six Brigades on their March for the Jerseys, and followed with the whole Army next Morning. On the 21st. we compleated our passage over the Delaware at Coryells ferry (abt. 33 Miles above Philadelphia) distant from Valley forge near 40 Miles. From this Ferry we moved down towards the Enemy, and on the 27th. got within Six Miles of them. General Lee having the command of the Van of the Army, consisting of fully 5000 chosen Men, was ordered to begin the Attack next Morning so soon as the enemy began their March, to be supported by me. But, strange to tell! when he came up with the enemy, a retreat commenced; whether by his order, or from other causes, is now the subject of inquiry, and consequently improper to be descanted on, as he is in arrest, and a Court Martial sitting for tryal of him. A Retreat however was the fact, be the causes as they may; and the disorder arising from it would have proved fatal to the Army had not that bountiful Providence which has never failed us in the hour of distress, enabled me to form a Regiment or two (of those that were retreating) in the face of the Enemy, and under their fire, by which means a stand was made long enough (the place through which the enemy were pursuing being narrow) to form the Troops that were advancing, upon an advantageous piece of Ground in the rear; hence our affairs took a favourable turn, and from being pursued, we drove the Enemy back, over the ground they had followed us, recovered the field of Battle, and possessed ourselves of their dead. but, as they retreated behind a Morass very difficult to pass, and had both Flanks secured with thick Woods, it was found impracticable with our Men fainting with fatigue, heat, and want of Water, to do any thing more that Night. In the Morning we expected to renew the Action, when behold the enemy had stole off as Silent as the Grave in the Night after having sent away their wounded. Getting a Nights March of us, and having but ten Miles to a strong post, it was judged inexpedient to follow them any further, but move towards the North River least they should have any design upon our posts there. We buried 245 of their dead on the field of Action; they buried several themselves, and many have been since found in the Woods, where, during the action they had drawn them to, and hid them. We have taken five Officers and upwards of One hundred Prisoners, but the amount of their wounded we have not learnt with any certainty; according to the common proportion of four or five to one, there should be at least a thousand or 1200. Without exagerating, their trip through the Jerseys in killed, Wounded, Prisoners, and deserters, has cost them at least 2000 Men and of their best Troops. We had 60 Men killed, 132 Wounded, and abt. 130 Missing, some of whom I suppose may yet come in. Among our Slain Officers is Majr. Dickenson, and Captn. Fauntleroy, two very valuable ones."

35 Custis, *Recollections*, pp. 222-23

36 *WGW*, vol. 6, 12-10-1776. The context of the letter explains his dire circumstances as follows: "I wish to Heaven it was in my power to give you a more favorable account of our situation than it is. Our numbers, quite inadequate to the task of opposing that part of the army under the command of General Howe, being reduced by sickness desertion, and political deaths (on or before the first instant, and having no assistance from the militia), were obliged to retire before the enemy, who were perfectly well informed of our situation, till we came to this place, where I have no idea of being able to make a stand, as my numbers, till joined by the Philadelphia militia, did not exceed three thousand men fit for duty. Now we may be about five thousand to oppose Howe's whole army, that part of it excepted which sailed under the command of Gen. Clinton. I tremble for Philadelphia. Nothing, in my opinion, but Gen. Lee's speedy arrival, who has been long expected, though still at a distance (with about three thousand men), can save it. We have brought over and destroyed all the boats we could lay our hands upon the Jersey shore for many miles above and below this place; but it is next to impossible to guard a shore for sixty miles, with less than half the enemy's numbers; when by force or strategem they may suddenly attempt a passage in many different places. At present they are encamped or quartered along the other shore above and below us (rather this place, for we are obliged to keep a face towards them) for fifteen miles…When I say none but militia, I am to except the Virginia regiments and the shattered remains of Smallwood's, which, by fatigue, want of clothes, &c., are reduced to nothing — Weedon's, which was the strongest, not having more than between one hundred and thirty to one hundred and forty men fit for duty, the rest being in the hospitals. The unhappy policy of short enlistments and a dependence upon militia will, I fear, prove the downfall of our cause, though early pointed out with an almost prophetic spirit ! Our cause has also received a severe blow in the captivity of Gen. Lee. Unhappy man! Taken by his own imprudence, going three or four miles from his own camp, and within twenty of the enemy, notice of which by a rascally Tory was given a party of light horse seized him in the morning after travelling all night, and carried him off in high triumph and with every mark of indignity, not even suffering him to get his hat or surtout coat. The troops that were under his command are not yet come up with us, though they, I think, may be expected to-morrow. A large part of the Jerseys have given every proof of disaffection that they can do, and this part of Pennsylvania are equally inimical. In short, your imagination can scarce extend to a situation more distressing than mine. Our only dependence now is upon the speedy enlistment of a new army. If this fails, I think the game will be pretty well up, as, from disaffection and want of spirit and fortitude,

the inhabitants, instead of resistance, are offering submission…."

37 Ibid., vol. 6, 12-18-1776. Washington wrote, "Dear Brother: …between you and me, I think our Affairs are in a very bad situation; not so much from the apprehension of Genl. Howe's Army, as from the defection of New York, Jerseys, and Pennsylvania. In short, the Conduct of the Jerseys has been most Infamous. Instead of turning out to defend their Country and affording aid to our Army, they are making their submissions as fast as they can. If they the Jerseys had given us any support, we might have made a stand at Hackensack and after that at Brunswick, but the few Militia that were in Arms, disbanded themselves [or slunk off in such a manner upon the appearance of danger as to leave us quite unsupported and to make the best shifts we could without them] and left the poor remains of our Army to make the best we could of it. I have no doubt but that General Howe will still make an attempt upon Philadelphia this Winter. I see nothing to oppose him a fortnight hence, as the time of all the Troops, except those of Virginia (reduced almost to nothing,) and Smallwood's Regiment of Maryland, (equally as bad) will expire in less than that time. In a word my dear Sir, if every nerve is not strain'd to recruit the New Army with all possible expedition, I think the game is pretty near up, owing, in a great measure, to the insidious Arts of the Enemy, and disaffection of the Colonies before mentioned, but principally to the accursed policy of short Inlistments, and placing too great a dependence on the Militia the Evil consequences of which were foretold 15 Months ago with a spirit almost Prophetick. Before this reaches you, you will no doubt have heard of the Captivity of Genl. Lee; this is an additional misfortune, and the more vexatious, as it was by his own folly and Imprudence (and without a view to answer any good) he was taken, going three Miles out of his own Camp [for the sake of a little better lodging] and with 20 of the Enemy to lodge, a rascally Tory rid in the Night to give notice of it to the Enemy who sent a party of light Horse that seized and carried him with every mark of triumph and indignity. You can form no Idea of the perplexity of my Situation. No Man, I believe, ever had a greater choice of difficulties and less means to extricate himself from them. However under a full persuasion of the justice of our Cause I cannot [but think the prospect will brighten, although for a wise purpose it is, at present hid under a cloud] entertain an Idea that it will finally sink tho' it may remain for some time under a Cloud."

38 Larkin Spivey is an American military historian and author. He is a decorated veteran of the Vietnam War and a retired Marine Corps officer. He commanded infantry and reconnaissance units in combat and was trained in parachute, submarine, and special forces operations. He was with the blockade force during the Cuban Missile Crisis and served in the White House during the Johnson and Nixon administrations. As a faculty member at The Citadel he taught college courses in U.S. military history, a subject of lifelong personal and professional interest. He conducted much of his research at the Naval War College in Newport, Rhode Island. These remarks were made by Spivey to co-author Jerry Newcombe, who interviewed Spivey for Coral Ridge Ministries-TV.

39 WGW, vol. 61-5-1777. Washington wrote to Maj. Gen. William Heath, "Sir: We have made a successful attack upon Princeton. Genl. Howe advanced upon Trenton, we evacuated the Town, and lay on the other side of the Mill Creek, until dark, then Stole a march and attacked Princeton about nine O'Clock in the Morning; There was three Regiments Quartered there, the killed, wounded, and taken prisoners amounts to about 500. The Enemy are in great consternation, and as the Panick affords us a favourable Opportunity to drive them out of the Jerseys, It has been determined in Council, that you should move down towards New York with a considerable force, as if you had a design upon the City. That being an Object of great importance, the Enemy will be reduced to the Necessity of withdrawing a considerable part of their force from the Jerseys, if not the whole, to secure the City. I shall draw the force on this side the North River together at Morristown, where I shall watch the motions of the Enemy and avail Myself of every favourable Circumstance." Ibid., vol. 6, 1-5-1777. Washington wrote to Maj. Gen. Israel Putnam, "Dear General: Fortune has favoured us in an Attack on Princeton. Genl. Howe advanced upon Trenton which we Evacuated on the Evening of the Second of this instant, and drew up the Troops on the south side of the Mill Creek and continued in that position until dark, then Marched for Princeton which we reached next Morning by about nine O'Clock. There were three Regiments Quartered there, of British Troops, which we attack'd and routed. The number of the Killed Wounded and taken prisoners amounts to about 5 or 600. We lost Several Officers and about thirty privates. Genl. Mercer is badly Wounded, if not Mortally. After the Action we immediately marched for this place. I shall remove from hence to Morristown, there shall wait a few days and refresh the Troops, during which time, I shall keep a strict Watch upon the Enemy's motions; They appear to be panick struck, and I am in some hopes of driving them out of the Jerseys. It is thought advisable for you to march the Troops under your Command to Crosswix, and keep a Strict watch upon the Enemy upon that Quarter. If the Enemy continue at Brunswick, you must act with great Circumspection lest you meet with a Surprize. As we have made two successful attacks upon the Enemy by way of Surprize, they will be pointed with resentment, and if there is any possibility of retaliating, will attempt it. You will give out your Strength to be twice as great as it is. Forward on all the Baggage and Scattered Troops belonging to this division of the Army as soon as may be. You will keep as many Spies out as you will see proper, a Number of Horsemen, in the dress of the Country, must be constantly kept going backwards and forwards for this purpose, and if you discover any Motion of the Enemy, which you can depend upon, and which you think of Consequence, Let me be informed thereof as soon as possible by Express."

40 Ibid., vol. 11, 5-25-1778.

41 Ibid., vol. 24, 5-10-1782.

42 Ibid., vol. 4, 1-14-1776.

43 Ibid., vol. 13, 12-18-1778.

44 Ibid., vol. 18, 5-19-1780.

45 Ibid., W vol. 26. 2-6-1783.

46 Federer, America's God And Country, pp. 639-40.

47 WGW, vol. 23, 10-20-1781. The General Orders said at the victory at Yorktown, "Divine Service is to be performed tomorrow in the several Brigades or Divisions. The Commander in Chief earnestly recommends that the troops not on duty should universally attend with that seriousness of Deportment and gratitude of Heart which the recognition of such reiterated and astonishing interpositions of Providence demand of us."

48   *American Minute* with Bill Federer, January 17, 2006.

49   Ibid., vol. 7, 4-12-1777. See also, *WGW*, vol. 7, 4-15-1777.

50   Ibid., vol. 27, 11-2-1783.

51   Ibid., vol. 5, 7-2-1776.

52   Ibid., vol. 4, 3-6-1776.

53   Ibid., vol. 5, 5-15-1776.

54   Ibid., vol. 27, 6-11-1783.

55   Ibid., vol. 27, 8-25-1783.

56   Ibid., vol. 4, 3-1776, "Answer To An Address From The Massachusetts Legislature", "That the metropolis of your colony is now relieved from the cruel and oppressive invasions of those, who were sent to erect the standard of lawless domination, and to trample on the rights of humanity, and is again open and free for its rightful possessors, must give pleasure to every virtuous and sympathetic heart; and its being effected without the blood of our soldiers and fellow-citizens must be ascribed to the interposition of that Providence, which has manifestly appeared in our behalf through the whole of this important struggle, as well as to the measures pursued for bringing about the happy event. May that being, who is powerful to save, and in whose hands is the fate of nations, look down with an eye of tender pity and compassion upon the whole of the United Colonies; may He continue to smile upon their counsels and arms, and crown them with success, whilst employed in the cause of virtue and mankind. May this distressed colony and its capital, and every part of this wide extended continent, through His divine favor, be restored to more than their former lustre and once happy state, and have peace, liberty, and safety secured upon a solid, permanent, and lasting foundation."

57   Ibid., vol. 27, 11-27-1783: "Disposed, at every suitable opportunity to acknowledge publicly our infinite obligations to the Supreme Ruler of the Universe for rescuing our Country from the brink of destruction; I cannot fail at this time to ascribe all the honor of our late successes to the same glorious Being." Ibid., vol. 27, 8-4-1783: "Gentlemen: I accept with heart-felt satisfaction your affectionate congratulations on the restoration of Peace, and the formal recognition of the Independence of the United States. We may indeed ascribe these most happy and glorious Events to the Smiles of Providence, the Virtue of our Citizens, and the bravery of our Troops, aided by the powerful interposition of our Magnanimous and illustrious Ally." Ibid., vol. 28, 4-10-1785: "And that my conduct should have met the approbation, and obtained the affectionate regard of the State of New York (where difficulties were numerous and complicated) may be ascribed more to the effect of divine wisdom, which has disposed the minds of the people, harrassed on all sides, to make allowances for the embarrassments of my situation, whilst with fortitude and patience they sustained the loss of their Capitol, and a valuable part of their territory, and to the liberal sentiments, and great exertion of her virtuous Citizens, than to any merit of mine." Ibid., vol. 32, 1-27-1793: "Gentlemen: It has ever been my pride to merit the approbation of my fellow Citizens by a faithful and honest discharge of the duties annexed to those stations in which they have been pleased to place me; and the dearest rewards of my services have been those testimonies of esteem and confidence with which they have honored me. But to the manifest interposition of an over-ruling Providence, and to the patriotic exertions of united America, are to be ascribed those events, which have given us a respectable rank among the nations of the Earth."

58   Ibid., vol. 23, 10-20-1781. Washington uses the word "gratitude" over 250 times and the word "thankful" 85 times and the words "thank" or "thanks" nearly two thousand times.

59   Ibid., vol. 31, 7-28-1791

60   The Reverend Dr. Donald Binder a rector for one of Pohick Church, where Washington worshiped. Here's what Dr. Binder says about Washington and Providence when we asked him if our first president was a Deist:

      It's quite evident from Jefferson's writings that he was a deist, and that's sometimes laid at Washington's feet because he was fairly quiet and introverted about his faith, but he had this great belief in Divine Providence and really saw, especially, the coming together—he called it a "concatenation of events"—with the Revolutionary War. There was no way we should have won that war. The odds were so highly stacked against us that the very fact that they were able to sustain themselves for the longest war in American history, and then achieve a victory over the greatest force on the planet at that time, was for him a miracle. And he always attributed that to God's Divine Providence. Now that clashes with one of the tenets of Deism, which [is that] God is sort of behind [the scenes and] sort of sets the world off and spins it into motion and doesn't have any type of interactivity with it. But the whole notion of Divine Providence, which Washington espoused, clashes totally with that. He saw God's hand in bringing him the victories and in sustaining him and his troops throughout the war."

61   *WGW* vol. 27, 7-8-1783.

62   Ibid., vol. 30, 8-31-1788.

63   Ibid., vol. 30, 5-9-1789.

64   Ibid., vol. 4, 11-14-1775. General Orders: "The Commander in Chief is confident, the Army under his immediate direction, will shew their Gratitude to providence, for thus favouring the Cause of Freedom and America; and by their thankfulness to God, their zeal and perseverance in this righteous Cause, continue to deserve his future blessings." Ibid., vol. 4, 12-5-1775. To Maj. Gen. Philip Schuyler, "The Cause we are engaged in is so just and righteous, that we must try to rise superior to every Obstacle in it's Support; and, therefore, I beg that you will not think of resigning, unless you have carried your Application to Congress too far to recede." *WGW*, vol. 6, 12-18-1776. To the Massachusetts Legislature, "I wrote for Genl. Lee to reinforce me, with the Troops under his immediate Command. By some means or other, their Arrival has been retarded and unhappily on friday last, the Genl., having left his Division and proceeded three or four Miles nearer the Enemy, then 18.Miles from him; of which they were informed by some Tories, was surprised and carried off about 11 o'Clock, by a party of 70 Light Horse; I will not comment upon this unhappy accident; I feel much for his Misfortune and am sensible that in his Captivity, our Country has lost a Warm friend and an able officer. upon the whole our affairs are in a Much less promising condition than could be wished; Yet I trust, under the Smiles of Providence and by our own exertions, we shall be happy. Our cause is righteous, and must

be Supported."

Ibid., vol. 7, 4-23-1777. To Brig. Gen. Samuel Holden Parsons, "All agree our claims are righteous and must be supported; Yet all, or at least, too great a part among us, withhold the means, as if Providence, who has already done much for us, would continue his gracious interposition and work miracles for our deliverance, without troubling ourselves about the matter."

Ibid., vol. 9, 10-3-1777. General Orders , "This army, the main American Army, will certainly not suffer itself to be out done by their northern Brethren; they will never endure such disgrace; but with an ambition becoming freemen, contending in the most righteous cause, rival the heroic spirit which swelled their bosoms, and which, so nobly exerted, has procured them deathless renown."

Ibid., vol. 11, 4-12-1778. General Orders. "The Honorable Congress having thought proper to recommend to The United States of America to set apart Wednesday the 22nd. instant to be observed as a day of Fasting, Humiliation and Prayer, that at one time and with one voice the righteous dispensations of Providence may be acknowledged and His Goodness and Mercy toward us and our Arms supplicated and implored; The General directs that this day *also* shall be religiously observed in the Army, that no work be done thereon and that the Chaplains prepare discourses suitable to the Occasion."

Ibid., vol. 24, 6-30-1782. To the Magistrates and Military Officers of Schenectady. "Gentlemen: I request you to accept my warmest thanks for your affectionate address. In a cause so just and righteous as ours, we have every reason to hope the divine Providence will still continue to crown our Arms with success, and finally compel our Enemies to grant us that Peace upon equitable terms, which we so ardently desire."

Ibid., vol. 27, 8-10-1783. To George Martin, "Your Congratulations to our happy-fated Country, are very agreeable, and your Expressions of personal Regard for me, claim my sincerest Thanks, as do your Exertions in favor of our righteous Cause, now so happily terminated."

Ibid., vol. 27, 11-27-1783. To the Ministers, Elders, Deacons, and Members of the Reformed German Congregation of New York. "Disposed, at every suitable opportunity to acknowledge publicly our infinite obligations to the Supreme Ruler of the Universe for rescuing our Country from the brink of destruction; I cannot fail at this time to ascribe all the honor of our late successes to the same glorious Being. And if my humble exertions have been made in any degree subservient to the execution of the divine purposes, a contemplation of the benediction of Heaven on our righteous Cause, the approbation of my virtuous Countrymen, and the testimony of my own Conscience, will be a sufficient reward and augment my felicity beyond anything which the world can bestow."

65   Ibid., vol. 31, 2-1792. In a note entitled, "Errors of Government Towards The Indians" Washington wrote, "But, we are involved in actual War! Is it just? or, is it unjust?"

Ibid., vol. 1, in a an "Address To His Command", Washington said, "You see, gentlemen soldiers, that it hath pleased our most gracious sovereign to declare war in form against the French King, and (for divers good causes, but more particularly for their ambitious usurpations and encroachments on his American dominions) to pronounce all the said French King's subjects and vassals to be enemies to his crown and dignity; and hath willed and required all his subjects and people, and in a more especial manner commanded his captain-general of his forces, his governors, and all other his commanders and officers, to do and execute all acts of hostility in the prosecution of, this just and honorable war."

Ibid., vol. 10, 11-30-1777. General Orders: "Forasmuch as it is the indispensible duty of all men, to adore the superintending providence of Almighty God; to acknowledge with gratitude their obligations to him for benefits received, and to implore such further blessings as they stand in need of; and it having pleased him in his abundant mercy, not only to continue to us the innumerable bounties of his common providence, but also, to smile upon us in the prosecution of a just and necessary war, for the defence of our unalienable rights and liberties."

Ibid., vol. 23, 11-21-1781. To Mayor John Bullen, "That the State in general and this City in particular may long enjoy the benefits which they have a right to expect from their very spirited exertions in the prosecution of this just War is the sincere Wish of Sir Your etc."

Ibid., vol. 24, 5-6-1782. To Gov. William Livingston, "I must beg you to make it known to all persons acting in a military capacity in your State that I shall hold myself obliged to deliver up to the Enemy or otherwise to punish such of them as shall commit any Act which is in the least contrary to the Laws of War. I doubt not of your doing the same with those who come under the Civil power."

Ibid., vol. 3, 8-8-1775. To the New York Legislature, "You cannot but have heard that the Disstresses of the Ministerial Troops, for fresh Provisions and many other Necessaries, at Boston, were very great; It is a Policy, Justifiable by all the Laws of War, to endeavour to increase them; Desertions, Discouragement, and a Dissatisfaction with the Service, besides weakening their strength, are some of the Natural Consequences of such a Situation; and, if continued, might afford the fairest Hope of Success, without further Effusion of human Blood."

Ibid., vol. 16, 8-19-1779. To John Beatty, "You are absolutely to reject every overture for exchanging those persons whom we do not consider as military prisoners of war. We do not hold General Clinton bound by any act of ours respecting this matter; but we reject their exchange solely on the principle that by the Laws and practice of war, we do not think they were proper subjects of military capture. From this we shall never recede."

Ibid., vol. 24, 5-6-1782.

67   Ibid., vol. 29, 3-31-1787. Writing to James Madison, Washington says, "We seem to have forgotten, or never to have learnt, the policy of placing one's enemy in the wrong. Had we observed good faith on our part, we might have told our tale to the world with a good grace."

Ibid., vol. 28, 7-26-1786. Writing to William Grayson, Washington says, "It is good policy at all times, to place one's adversary in the wrong. Had we observed good faith, and the western Posts had then been withheld from us by G: Britain, we might have appealed to god and man for justice, and if there are any guarantees to the treaty, we might have called upon them to see it fulfilled." But this approach can be misapplied by individuals as

Ibid., vol. 24, 6-16-1782 shows, "Mr. Sands who yielding nothing himself requiring every thing of others and failing in the most essential parts of his Contract adopts, as is too commonly the Case with little minds the policy of endeavoring to place the adverse party in the wrong, that he may appear in a more favorable point of View himself."

1004

68   Compare, for instance, *WGW*, vol. 32, 1-27-1793. To the Members of the New Church in Baltimore, "Your prayers for my present and future felicity are received with gratitude; and I sincerely wish, Gentlemen, that you may in your social and individual capacities taste those blessings, which a gracious God bestows upon the Righteous."

69   *Appleton's Cyclopedia of American Biography*, 1889, vol. VI, p. 383; William Johnson, *George Washington The Christian* (Arlington Heights: Christian Liberty Press, 1919), p. 67. This letter nor either of the two listed sources are not cited nor referenced in *"Worthy Partner": The Papers of Martha Washington* (Westport: Greenwood Press, 1994).

70   *WGW*, vol. 11, 4-12-1778.

71   Ibid., vol. 5, 7-9-1776.

72   Ibid., vol. 30, 4-30-1789.

73   Ibid., vol. 27, 9-2-1783.

74   Ibid., vol. 35, 12-19-1796. To his grandson, George Washington Parke Custis, he said, "...a proper sense of your duties to God and man...." Ibid., vol. 4, 12-18-1775. "The Law of Retaliation, is not only justifiable, in the Eyes of God and Man, but absolutely a duty, which in our present circumstances we owe to our Relations, Friends and Fellow Citizens."
Ibid., vol. 24, 4-21-1782. "To do this will mark the Justice of your Excelly's Character. In Failure of it, I shall hold myself justifiable in the Eyes of God and Man, for the measure to which I shall resort."
Ibid., vol. 26, 6-8-1783. "Congress, who have in all their Transaction shewn a great degree of magnanimity and justice, will stand justified in the sight of God and Man...."
Ibid., vol. 28, 6-26-1786. "...we might have appealed to God and man for justice...."

75   Ibid., vol. 27, 9-27-1783.

76   Ibid., vol. 308-31-1788. To Annis Boudinot Stockton, "And now that I am speaking of your Sex, I will ask whether they are not capable of doing something towards introducing foederal fashions and national manners? A good general government, without good morals and good habits, will not make us a happy People; and we shall deceive ourselves if we think it will. A good government will, unquestionably, tend to foster and confirm those qualities, on which public happiness must be engrafted. Is it not shameful that we should be the sport of European whims and caprices? Should we not blush to discourage our own industry and ingenuity; by purchasing foreign superfluities and adopting fantastic fashions, which are, at best, ill suited to our stage of Society? But I will preach no longer on so unpleasant a subject; because I am persuaded that you and I are both of a Sentiment, and because I fear the promulgation of it would work no reformation."

77   Ibid., vol. 30, 4-30-1789, Here we find that Washington believed there was "... an indissoluble union between virtue and happiness." So also: Ibid., vol. 35, 3-30-1796. To Tobias Lear, "She is now no more! but she must be happy, because her virtue has a claim to it. Ibid., vol. 11, 5-15-1778. To Brig. Gen. Thomas Nelson, Jr. "Matters appear abroad to be in as favourable a train as we could wish, and If we are not free and happy, it will be owing to a want of virtue, prudence and management among ourselves. Ibid., vol. 28, 3-30-1785. To Lucretia Wilhemina Van Winter, "At best I have only been an instrument in the hands of Providence, to effect, with the aid of France and many virtuous fellow Citizens of America, a revolution which is interesting to the general liberties of mankind, and to the emancipation of a country which may afford an Asylum, if we are wise enough to pursue the paths wch. lead to virtue and happiness, to the oppressed and needy of the Earth. Our region is extensive, our plains are productive, and if they are cultivated with liberallity and good sense, we may be happy ourselves, and diffuse happiness to all who wish to participate."

78   Ibid., vol. 35, 11-28-1796. To George Washington Parke Custis, "The assurances you give me of applying diligently to your studies, and fulfilling those obligations which are enjoined by your Creator and due to his creatures, are highly pleasing and satisfactory to me. I rejoice in it on two accounts; first, as it is the sure means of laying the foundation of your own happiness, and rendering you, if it should please God to spare your life, a useful member of society hereafter; and secondly, that I may, if I live to enjoy the pleasure, reflect that I have been, in some degree, instrumental in effecting these purposes.

79   Ibid., vol. 30, 4-30-1789. The "experiment" entrusted to the American people that Washington refers to here in his first inaugural, he viewed as a "success" in his eighth address to Congress at the conclusion of his presidency, "The situation in which I now stand, for the last time, in the midst of the Representatives of the People of the United States, naturally recalls the period when the Administration of the present form of Government commenced; and I cannot omit the occasion, to congratulate you and my Country, on the success of the experiment; nor to repeat my fervent supplications to the Supreme Ruler of the Universe, and Sovereign Arbiter of Nations, that his Providential care may still be extended to the United States; that the virtue and happiness of the People, may be preserved; and that the Government, which they have instituted, for the protection of their liberties, maybe perpetual." *WGW* vol. 35, 12-7-1796.

80   Ibid., vol. 27, 8-10-1783. To George Martin, "I would felicitate the Kingdom of Ireland on their Emancipation from British Controul, and extend my pious Entreaties, that Heaven may establish them in a happy and perpetuated Tranquility, enjoying a freedom of Legislation, and an unconfined Extension of Trade, that connecting Link, which binds together the remotest Countries."
Ibid., vol. 9, 10-18-1777. to Brig. Gen. James Potter, "I congratulate you upon the glorious Success of our Arms in the North [i.e. the victory at Saratoga] an account of which is enclosed. This singular favor of Providence is to be received with thankfulness and the happy moment which Heaven has pointed out for the firm establishment of American Liberty ought to be embraced with becoming spirit; it is incumbent upon every man of influence in his country to prevail upon the militia to take the field with that energy which the present crisis evidently demands."
WGW, vol. 30, 4-30-1789. The First Inaugural Address, "Having thus imparted to you my sentiments, as they have been awakened by the occasion which brings us together, I shall take my present leave; but not without resorting once more to the benign parent of the human race, in humble supplication that since he has been pleased to favour the American people, with opportunities for deliberating in perfect tranquility, and dispositions for deciding with unparellelled unanimity on a form of Government, for the security of their Union, and the advancement of their happiness; so his divine blessing may be equally *conspicuous* in the enlarged views, the temperate consultations, and

the wise measures on which the success of this Government must depend."

81   Ibid., vol. 5, 7-21-1776. General Orders: "...the General most earnestly exhorts every officer, and soldier, to pay the utmost attention to his Arms, and Health; to have the former in the best order for Action, and by Cleanliness and Care, to preserve the latter; to be exact in their discipline, obedient to their Superiors and vigilant on duty: With such preparation, and a suitable Spirit there can be no doubt, but by the blessing of Heaven, we shall repel our cruel Invaders; preserve our Country, and gain the greatest Honor."

Ibid., vol. 5, 8-3-1776. General Orders: "The General is sorry to be informed that the foolish, and wicked practice, of profane cursing and swearing (a Vice heretofore little known in an American Army) is growing into fashion; he hopes the officers will, by example, as well as influence, endeavour to check it, and that both they, and the men will reflect, that we can have little hopes of the blessing of Heaven on our Arms, if we insult it by our impiety, and folly; added to this, it is a vice so mean and low, without any temptation, that every man of sense, and character, detests and despises it."

Ibid., vol. 5, 8-8-1776. General Orders: "The Honor and safety of our bleeding Country, and every other motive that can influence the brave and heroic Patriot, call loudly upon us, to acquit ourselves with Spirit. In short, we must now determine to be enslaved or free. If we make Freedom our choice, we must obtain it, by the Blessing of Heaven on our United and Vigorous Efforts."

Ibid., vol. 5, 8-9-1776. General Orders: "The General exhorts every man, both officer and soldier, to be prepared for action, to have his arms in the best order, not to wander from his encampment or quarters; to remember what their Country expects of them, what a few brave men have lately done in South Carolina, against a powerful Fleet and Army; to acquit themselves like men and with the blessing of heaven on so just a Cause we cannot doubt of success."

Ibid., vol. 5, 8-14-1776. General Orders: "We must resolve to conquer, or die; with this resolution and the blessing of Heaven, Victory and Success certainly will attend us. There will then be a glorious Issue to this Campaign, and the General will reward, his brave Fellow Soldiers! with every Indulgence in his power."

WGW, vol. 5, 8-17-1776. General Orders: "Whereas a bombardment and attack upon the city of New York, by our cruel and inveterate enemy, may be hourly expected; and as there are great numbers of women, children, and infirm persons, yet remaining in the city, whose continuance will rather be prejudicial than advantageous to the army, and their persons exposed to great danger and hazard; I Do, therefore recommend it to all such persons, as they value their own safety and preservation, to remove with all expedition out of the said town, at this critical period, — trusting that, with the blessing of Heaven upon the American arms, they may soon return to it in perfect security. And I do enjoin and require all the officers and soldiers in the army under my command to forward and assist such persons in their compliance with this recommendation. Given under my hand,"

Ibid., vol. 6, 9-3-1776. General Orders: "The General hopes the justice of the great cause in which they are engaged, the necessity and importance of defending this Country, preserving its Liberties, and warding off the destruction meditated against it, will inspire every man with Firmness and Resolution in time of action, which is now approaching — Ever remembring that upon the blessing of Heaven, and the bravery of the men, our Country only can be saved."

Ibid., vol. 9, 9-13-1777. General Orders: "The General, with peculiar satisfaction, thanks those gallant officers and soldiers, who, on the 11th. instant, bravely fought in their country and its cause.... Altho' the event of that day, from some unfortunate circumstances, was not so favorable as could be wished, the General has the satisfaction of assuring the troops, that from every account he has been able to obtain, the enemy's loss greatly exceeded ours; and he has full confidence that in another Appeal to Heaven (with the blessing of providence, which it becomes every officer and soldier humbly to supplicate), we shall prove successful."

Ibid vol. 21, 3-14-1781. "To the inhabitants of Providence, The determination you are pleased to express of making every effort for giving vigour to our military operations is consonant with the Spirit that has uniformly actuated this State. It is by this disposition alone we can hope, under the protection of Heaven, to secure the important blessings for which we contend."

Ibid., vol. 22, 5-7-1781. "To Chevalier De Chastellux. May you participate in those blessings you have invoked heaven for me, and may you live to see a happy termn. of a struggle which was begun and has been continued for the purpose of rescuing America from impending Slavery, and securing to its Inhabitants their indubitable rights in which you bear a conspicuous part..."

Ibid., vol. 23, 9-23-1781. To Maj. Gen. William Heath "By Information, Lord Cornwallis is incessantly at Work on his Fortifications, and is probably preparing to defend himself to the last Extremity; a little Time will probably decide his Fate; with the Blessing of Heaven, I trust it will prove favorable to the Interests of America."

WGW vol. 26, 6-8-1783. Circular to the States,... "Heaven has crowned all its other blessings, by giving a fairer oppertunity for political happiness, than any other Nation has ever been favored with."

Ibid., vol. 27, 8-25-1783. To the inhabitants of Princeton. "I now return you Gentlemen my thanks for your benevolent wishes, and make it my earnest prayer to Heaven, that every temporal and divine blessing may be bestowed on the Inhabitants of Princeton, on the neighbourhood, and on the President and Faculty of the College of New Jersey, and that the usefulness of this Institution in promoting the interests of Religion and Learning may be universally extended."

Ibid., vol. 27, 12-12-1783. To the militia Officers of the City and Liberties of Philadelphia "While the various Scenes of the War, in which I have experienced the timely aid of the Militia of Philadelphia, recur to my mind, my ardent prayer ascends to Heaven that they may long enjoy the blessings of that Peace which has been obtained by the divine benediction on our common exertions."

WGW, vol. 28, 4-10-1785. To the Mayor, Recorder, Aldermen and Commonalty of the City of New York "I pray that Heaven may bestow its choicest blessings on your City. That the devastations of War, in which you found it, may soon be without a trace. That a well regulated and benificial Commerce may enrichen your Citizens. And that, your State (at present the Seat of the Empire) may set such examples of wisdom and liberality, as shall have a tendency to strengthen and give permanency to the Union at home, and credit and respectability to it abroad. The accomplishment whereof is a remaining wish, and the primary object of all my desires."

Ibid., vol. 30, April, 1789. Proposed Address To Congress, "If the blessings of Heaven showered thick around us should be spilled on the ground or converted to curses, through the fault of those for whom they were intended, it would not be the first instance of folly [34] or perverseness in short-sighted mortals. The blessed Religion revealed in the word of God will remain an eternal and awful monument to prove that the best Institutions may be abused by human depravity; and that they may even, in some instances be made subservient to the vilest of purposes."

Ibid., vol. 32, 6-13-1793. To the Marquise de Lafayette, "I can only add my most ardent prayers, that you may be again united to M. de la Fayette, under circumstances that may be joyful to you both; and that the evening of that life, whose morning has been devoted to the cause of liberty and humanity, may be crowned with the best of heaven's blessings."

Ibid., vol. 33, 8-4-1793. To the Inhabitants of the City of Hartford "'Tis from dispositions like these that we may hope to avoid an interruption of the numerous blessings which demand our gratitude to Heaven; or that we may be encouraged to meet with firmness, confiding in the protection of a just Providence, any attempts to disturb them, which intemperance or injustice, from whatever quarter, may at any time make it our duty to encounter?"

Ibid., vol. 37, 3-3-1799. To the President of the United States: "I sincerely pray, that in the discharge of these arduous and important duties committed to you, your health may be unimpaired, and that you may long live to enjoy those blessings which must flow to our Country, if we should be so happy as to pass this critical period in an honourable and dignified manner, without being involved in the horrors and calamities of War."

Ibid., vol. 37, 12-13-1798. To James Mc Henry, Secretary of War. (Washington's last use of the phrase "blessing of providence" is in the context of preparing for war.) "Regarding the overthrow of Europe at large as a matter not entirely chimerical, it will be our prudence to cultivate a spirit of self-dependence, and to endeavour by unremitting vigilance and exertion under the blessing of providence, to hold the scales of our destiny in our own hands. Standing, as it were in the midst of falling empires, it should be our aim to assume a station and attitude, which will preserve us from being overwhelmed in their ruins."

82   Ibid., vol. 3, 7-4-1775.

83   Ibid., vol. 5, 7-9-1776.

84   Ibid., vol. 1, 9-23-1756.

85   Ibid., vol. 1, 11-9-1756.

86   Ibid., vol. 1, 11-24-1756.

87   *WGW*, vol. 2, 4-21-1758.

88   Ibid., vol. 4, 12-15-1775, To Gov. Jonathan Trumbull, "Having heard that It's doubtful, whether the Reverend Mr. Leonard from your Colony, will have it in his power to Continue here as a Chaplain, I cannot but express some Concern, as I think his departure will be a loss. His General Conduct has been exemplary and praiseworthy: In discharging the duties of his Office, active and industrious; he has discovered himself warm and steady friend to his Country, and taken great pains to animate the Soldiery and Impress them with a knowledge of the important rights we are contending for. Upon the late desertion of the Troops, he gave a Sensible and judicious discourse, holding forth the Necessity of courage and bravery and at the same time of Obedience and Subordination to those in Command. In justice to the merits of this Gentleman, I thought it only right to give you this Testimonial of my Opinion of him and to mention him to you, as a person worthy of your esteem and that of the Public. I am Sir, &c."

89   Ibid., vol.4, 2-7-1776. General Orders: "The Continental Congress having been pleased to order, and direct, that there shall be one Chaplain to two Regiments, and that the pay of each Chaplain shall be *Thirty-three* dollars and *one third*, pr Kalendar Month — The Revd. Abiel Leonard is appointed Chaplain to the Regiment of Artillery, under the command of Col Knox, and to the 20th. Regiment, at present commanded by Lt. Col Durkee."

90   Along with the discourse mentioned in Washington's letter to Gov. Jonathan Trumbull, there is written record of two other sermons by Abiel Leonard that Washington heard.

On Sunday, December 3, 1775, he attended service at the Reverend Dr. Appleton's Church; discourse by Abiel Leonard, chaplain of General Putnam's command. This was the "old congregational church," which Washington attended while in Cambridge, the minister being the venerable Nathaniel Appleton...." (Johnson, *George Washington the Christian*, pp. 74-75.)

On the same day, [the evacuation of Boston by the British, March 17, 1776] a few hours after the departure of the British, Washington and his officers attended thanksgiving service, and listened to the Reverend Dr. Abiel Leonard preach from Exodus 14:25: "And he took off their chariot wheels, that they drave them heavily; so that the Egyptians said, Let us flee from the face of Israel; for the Lord fighteth for them against the Egyptians." (Johnson, *George Washington the Christian*, pp 78-79.)

The following from George Littell, *George Washington: Christian*, 1913, adds additional information about Abiel Leonard, his illustrious family and Washington's contact with him: "...in Cambridge on Sunday, Dec. 3, 1775, he [Washington] went to the Reverend Dr. Appleton's church, and heard a discourse by Abiel Leonard, Chaplain to Gen. Putman's command. This building was taken down in 1833, and the land sold to Harvard College. Abiel Leonard is easily remembered in both State and Church. His son was Capt. Nathaniel Leonard, whose son was Abiel Leonard, a Supreme Court Justice of Missouri, whose son was the Right Reverend Abiel Leonard, the heroic Bishop of Salt Lake in Utah, and the 145th Bishop of the American Church to which Washington belonged...." Sadly, Chaplain Leonard's life ended early after a struggle with mental illness. Ibid., vol. 4, 12-15-1775, Note: "Abiel Leonard, chaplain of the Third Connecticut Regiment; chaplain of Knox's Continental artillery through the year 1776. He became insane in 1777 and died in 1778."

91   See Appleton, *A Catalogue of the Washington Collection at the Boston Athenaeum*, p. 557.

92   Abiel Leonard's Prayer in its entirety can be found in the appendix.

93   *WGW*, vol. 31, 3-4-1791, note says, "On this same day (March 4) Washington also sent to the Senate the nominations of Arthur St. Clair to be major general, Samuel Hodgdon to be quartermaster, and John Hurt to be chaplain, in consequence of the new regiment added to the United States Army." Chaplain John Hurt had served in the Revolutionary War and was from Virginia. See chapter 2, note 28.

94   See William C. Lane, *A Catalogue of the Washington Collection at the Boston Athenaeum*, see under Evans

95   The title page goes on to say, "At a Meeting of the General and Field Officers of the Western Army, it was Voted, That Brigadier General Maxwell, Colonel Courtlandt, Colonel Cilley, Lieutenant Colonel Forest, and Major Edwards, be a Committee to wait on the Reverend Mr. Evans, and return him the thanks of the Army for this Discourse, delivered before the Troops, on the seventeenth instant; and that they request of him a copy for the Press: That a number of copies be procured and distributed amongst the federal Corps of the Army gratis."

96   *WGW*, vol. 11, 4-21-1778.

97   Ibid., vol. 8, 7-19-1777.

98   Ibid., vol. 26, 4-4-1783.

99   Noel Porter, Arch Deacon of California, San Francisco, California "The Religious Life of George Washington, in *History of the George Washington Bicentennial Celebration*, volume II, Literature Series, (Washington, D.C.: United States George Washington Bicentennial Commission, 1932).

CHAPTER 10

1   *WGW*, vol. 3, 9-21-1775: *WGW* September 21, 1775 has the following note: Trumbull had written: "I am surprised that mine of the 5th instant was not received, or not judged worthy of Notice, as no mention is made of it. Stonington had been Attacked, and severely cannonaded, and by divine Providence marvelously protected. New London and Norwich are still menaced by the Ministerial Ships and Troops, that the militia cannot be thought sufficient for their security. That is necessary to cast up some Entrenchments. We are obliged actually to raise more Men for their Security, and for the Towns of New Haven and Lyme. I hoped some of the new Levies might have been left here, till these dangers were over, without injury to any of your Operations. I own that must be left to your Judgment. Yet it would have given me pleasure to have been acquainted that you did consider it. I thank Divine Providence and you for this early warning to great care and watchfulness, that so the Union of the Colonies may be settled on a permanent and happy Basis... "You may depend on our utmost Exertions for the defence and security of the Constitutional Rights and Liberty of the Colonies, and of our own in particular. None have shown greater forwardness, and thereby rendered themselves more the Object of Ministerial Vengeance. I am, with great Esteem and Regard for your *personal Character*," etc. Trumbull's letter, dated Sept. 15, 1775, is in the *Washington Papers*.

2   *WGW*, vol. 11, 5-2-1778.

3   Ibid., vol. 2, 5-30-1768.   Quoted by Fitzpatrick from Boucher's autobiography.

4   See examples *WGW*, vol. 1, 1-6-1756; 1, 11-24-1756; vol. 7, 4-9-1777; vol.7 4-17-1777; vol. 8 5-12-1777; vol.8 5-14-1777; vol.8, 5-23-1777; vol. 8, 6-3-1777; vol. 8 6-6-1777; vol.8, 6-20-1777; vol.8, 7-18-1777; vol.8, 7-24-1777; vol.9, 8-28-1777; vol.9, 9-1-1777; vol.9, 10-7-1777; vol.9, 10-10-1777; vol.9, 10-22-1777; vol.9, 10-25-1777; vol.9, 10-26-1777; vol.10, 11-10-1777; vol.10, 11-18-1777; vol.10, 12-3-1777; vol.10, 12-22-1777; vol.10, 12-25-1777; vol.10, 1-1-1778; vol.10, 1-3-1778; vol.10, 1-11-1778; vol.10, 1-14-1778; vol.10, 1-18-1778; vol.10, 1-28-1778, vol.10, 2-4-1778; vol.10, 2-8-1778; vol.36, 9-25-1798; vol. 36, 9-24-1776; vol.36, 7-16-1798; vol.36, 7-22-1798; vol.17, 11-20-1779; vol.36, 7-4-1798; vol. 37, 6-6-1799; vol.10, 1-29-1778; vol.31, 3-9-1792; vol.36, 10-15-1798; vol.37, 4-23-1799; vol.12, 8-24-1778;   etc...

5   Ibid., vol. 7, 4-21-1777; vol. 8, 5-9-1777; vol. 8, 5-10-1777; vol. 8, 6-6-1777; vol. 8, 7-19-1777; vol. 9, 8-27-1777; vol. 9, 9-1-1777; vol. 9, 9-6-1777; vol. 10, 11-21-1777; vol. 10, 11-23-1777; vol. 11, 3-1-1778; vol. 11, 3-26-1778; vol. 25, 8-23-1782.

6   Ibid., vol. 1, 10-10-1756; vol. 5, 6-28-1776; vol. 6, 10-8-1776; vol. 6, 10-22-1776; vol. 6, 12-1-1776; vol. 6, 12-10-1776; vol. 7, 1-13-1777; vol. 8, 5-31-1777; vol. 9, 8-4-1777; vol. 10, 1-30-1778; vol. 11, 4-11-1778; 3, vol. 7-10-1775; vol. 12, 8-21-1778; vol. 18, 5-28-1780.

7   Ibid., vol. 6, 9-11-1776; vol. 10, 11-14-1777; vol. 10, 1-10-1778.

8   Ibid., vol. 6, 10-11-1776; vol. 7, 1-13-1777; vol. 8, 5-12-1777; vol. 8, 6-10-1777; vol. 8, 6-19-1777; vol. 11, 3-12-1778; vol. 11, 3-24-1778; vol. 11, 3-25, 1778; vol. 11, 3-31-1778; vol. 11, 3-22-1778; vol. 24, 7-5-1782.

9   Ibid., vol. 7, 4-30-1777; vol. 8, 6-4-1777; vol. 8, 6-7-1777; vol. 9, 8-9-1777; vol. 1, 5-29-1754; vol. 3, 8-1-1775; 7, vol. 2-14-1777; vol. 7, 2-24-1777; vol. 26, 4-18-1783; vol. 27, 11-2-1783.

10   Ibid., vol. 1, 13-19-1756; vol. 2, 9-18-1757; vol. 3, 6-18-1775; vol. 3, 6-19-1775; vol. 3, 9-26-1775; vol. 4, 3-31-1776; vol. 5, 5-5-1776; vol. 5, 7-14-1776; vol. 6, 9-30-1776; vol. 6, 11-6-1776; vol. 7, 2-4-1777; vol. 7, 4-9-1777; vol. 2, 1-1757; vol. 2, 9-17-1757; vol. 3, 9-21-1775; vol. 5, 7-22-1776; vol. 16, 7-29-1779; vol. 27, 1-3-1784; vol. 28, 9-5-1785; vol. 34, 9-7-1795; vol. 35, 5-15-1796; vol. 10, 1-4-1778; vol. 20, 11-20-1780; vol. 27, 12-6-1783; vol. 27, 12-19-1783; vol. 30, 1-9-1790; vol. 33, 4-8-1794; vol. 36, 9-25-1798.

11   Ibid., vol. 2, 4-23-1758; vol. 3, 8-20-1775; vol. 5, 8-17-1776; vol. 5, 4-29-1777; vol. 7, 2-4-1777; vol. 7, 2-10-1777; vol. 7, 2-18-1777; vol. 10, 2-6-1778; vol. 10,, 2-18-1778; vol. 11, 3-5-1778; vol. 11, 3-10-1778; vol. 2, 1-1757; vol. 30, 3-23-1789; vol. 37, 1-15-1799; vol. 8, 5-6-1777; vol. 26, 4-25-1783; vol. 26, 5-15-1783; vol. 27, 12-15-1783; vol. 27, 5-15-1784; vol. 31, 12-5-1790; vol. 31, 5-20-1791; vol. 34, 4-20-1795; vol. 35, 8-8-1796.

12   Ibid., vol. 1, 3-7-1778; vol. 3, 8-20-1775; vol. 26, 3-18-1783; vol. 29, 3-31-1787; vol. 29, 3-26-1788; vol. 29, 4-25-1788; vol. 30, 4-30-1789; vol. 35, 5-15-1796; vol. 26, 4-4-1783; vol. 26, 4-5-1783; vol. 28, 6-22-1785; vol. 28, 8-22-1785; vol. 28, 11-30-1785; vol. 29, 11-5-1786; vol. 29, 11-15-1786; vol. 31, 2-13-1790; vol. 34, 10-16-1794; vol. 34, 12-22-1795; vol. 36, 7-14-1798; vol. 35, 9-19-1796; vol. 26, 6-8-1783; vol. 33, 5-6-1794.

13   Ibid., vol. 35, 7-7-1797; vol. 3, 6-10-1774; vol. 5, 6-13-1776; vol. 5, 6-27-1776; vol. 5, 7-6-1776; vol. 5, 8-11-1776; vol. 5, 8-12-1776; vol. 7, 2-14-1777; vol. 7, 2-19-1777; vol. 7, 4-7-1777; vol. 5, 8-7-1776; vol. 8, 6-28-1777; vol. 14, 4-5-1779; vol. 20, 10-25-1780; vol. 20, 11-16-1780; vol. 21, 2-22-1781.

14   Ibid., vol. 36 3-8-1798; vol. 3, 9-26-1775; vol. 37, 7-21-1799; vol. 3, 10-9-1774; vol. 29, 10-18-1787; vol. 31, 3-28-1790; vol. 33, 7-21-1793; vol. 36, 3-1798; vol. 33, 8-26-1794.

15 Ibid., vol. 11, 4-10-1778; vol. 11, 4-17-1778; vol. 35, 4-7-1797; vol. 36, 1-29-1798; vol. 36, 2-12-1798; vol. 36, 4-8-1798; vol. 36, 9-14-1798; vol. 37, 11-24-1799; vol. 28, 6-30-1785; vol. 33, 12-18-1793; vol. 36, 9-4-1797; vol. 27, 9-6-1783; vol. 28, 8-17-1785; vol. 28, 11-10-1785; vol. 28, 6-26-1786; vol. 27, 9-6-1783; vol. 31, 4-8-1790; vol. 32, 1-6-1793; vol. 33, 12-23-1793; vol. 33, 7-27-1794; vol. 33, 8-3-1794; vol. 34, 5-24-1795; vol. 35, 4-7-1797.

16 Ibid., vol. 29, 4-25-1788; vol. 31, 3-8-1792; vol. 33, 1-23-1794; vol. 35, 8-19-1796; vol. 30, 1-18-1788; vol. 31, 9-20-1790; vol. 31, 11-15-1791; vol. 32, 8-31-1792; vol. 32, 11-14-1792; vol. 32, 11-17-1792; vol. 32, 11-30-1792; vol. 33, 4-11-1794; vol. 33, 3-6-1795; vol. 35, 7-25-1796; vol. 35, 8-5-1796; vol. 36, 9-25-1798; vol. 35, 7-15-1796; vol. 35, 12-7-1796; vol. 30, 5-10-1789; vol. 30, 8-1789; vol. 26, 5-10-1786; vol. 31, 9-16-1791; vol. 33, 7-21-1793; vol. 35, 7-8-1796.

17 Ibid., vol. 4, 11-15-1775; 30, 11-30-1789; 30, 11-22-1789; 30, 11-30-1789; 34, 9-27-1795; 34, 9-28-1795; 34 10-29-1795;

18 Ibid., vol. 9, 8-4-1777; vol. 36, 7-30-1798; vol. 36, 8-10-1798; vol. 36, 8-20-1798; vol. 37, 1-20-1799.

19 Ibid., vol. 11, 3-21-1778; vol. 1, 9-8-1756; vol. 28, 2-27-1786.

20 Ibid., vol. 9, 9-28-1777; vol. 10, 2-21-1778; vol. 2, 2-25-1768; vol. 3, 6-24-1771; vol. 32, 12-18-1792; vol. 37, 4-7-1799; vol. 2, 10-9-1769; vol. 15, 6-1-1779; vol. 17, 11-11-1779; vol. 28, 4-12-1785; vol. 28, 5-25-1785; vol. 29, 12-3-1787; vol. 31, 11-7-1791; vol. 34, 1-12-1795.

21 Ibid., vol. 11, 3-13-1778; vol. 36, 10-18-1798; vol. 1, 4-23-1754; vol. 1, 10-17-1755; vol. 1, 11-9-1756; vol. 2, 12-2-1758; vol. 4, 10-13-1775; vol. 5, 5-15-1776; vol. 5, 6-16-1776; vol. 5, 6-24-1776; vol. 27, 8-3-1783; vol. 32, 1-23-1793; vol. 33, 3-31-1794; vol. 35, 2-28-1797; vol. 35, 7-7-1794.

22 Ibid., vol. 32, 4-18-1793; vol. 36, 9-25-1798.

23 Ibid., vol. 34, 11-23-1794; vol. 34, 3-15-1795.

24 Ibid., vol. 9, 8-21-1777; vol. 1, 4-23-1755; vol. 2, 10-4-1763; vol. 3, 8-4-1775; vol. 23, 10-27-1781; vol. 27, 7-14-1784; vol. 29, 2-11-1788; vol. 34, 11-23-1895; vol. 34, 2-1-1796.

25 Ibid., vol. 3, 4-25-1773; vol. 34, 1-16-1795.

26 Ibid., vol. 5, 7-9-1776; vol. 5, 8-3-1776; vol. 11, 5-2-1778; 30, also see 5-26-1789: On May 26 the General Assembly of Presbyterian churches in the United States, meeting in Philadelphia, sent an address to Washington. His answer, which is undated in the "Letter Book," follows immediately after the copy of the address. In it he wrote in part: "While I reiterate the professions of my dependence upon Heaven as the source of all public and private blessings; I will observe that the general prevalence of piety, philanthropy, honesty, industry, and economy seems, in the ordinary course of human affairs, particularly necessary for advancing and confirming the happiness of our country. While all men within our territories are protected in worshipping the Deity according to the dictates of their consciences; it is rationally to be expected from them in return, that they will be emulous of evincing the sanctity of their professions by the innocence of their lives and the beneficence of their actions; for no man, who is profligate in his morals, or a bad member of the civil community, can possibly be a true Christian, or a credit to his own religious society. I desire you to accept my acknowledgments for your laudable endeavours to render men sober, honest, and good Citizens, and the obedient subjects of a lawful government."

27 Ibid., vol. 10, 1-2-1778; vol. 11, 3-11-1778; vol. 11, 3-13-1778; vol. 11, 3-27-1778; vol. 11, 4-10-1778; vol. 35, 5-15-1796.

28 Ibid., vol. 3, 9-21-1775: WGW, September 21, 1775 has the following note: Trumbull had written: "I am surprised that mine of the 5th instant was not received, or not judged worthy of Notice, as no mention is made of it. Stonington had been Attacked, and severely cannonaded, and by divine Providence marvelously protected. New London and Norwich are still menaced by the Ministerial Ships and Troops, that the militia cannot be thought sufficient for their security. That tis necessary to cast up some Entrenchments. We are obliged actually to raise more Men for their Security, and for the Towns of New Haven and Lyme. I hoped some of the new Levies might have been left here, till these dangers were over, without injury to any of your Operations. I own that must be left to your Judgment. Yet it would have given me pleasure to have been acquainted that you did consider it. I thank Divine Providence and you for this early warning to great care and watchfulness, that so the Union of the Colonies may be settled on a permanent and happy Basis... "You may depend on our utmost Exertions for the defence and security of the Constitutional Rights and Liberty of the Colonies, and of our own in particular. None have shown greater forwardness, and thereby rendered themselves more the Object of Ministerial Vengeance. I am, with great Esteem and Regard for your personal Character," etc. Trumbull's letter, dated Sept. 15, 1775, is in the Washington Papers.

29 Ibid., vol. 3, 9-21-1775.   Governor Trumbull graciously replied on October 9, 1775: "I have no disposition to increase the weight of your burdens, which, in the multiplicity of your business, must be sufficiently heavy, nor inclination to disturb the harmony so necessary to the happy success of our public operations. I am persuaded no such difficulty will any more happen. It is unhappy, that jealousies should be excited, or disputes of any sort litigated, between any of the colonies, to disunite them at a time, when our liberty, our property, our all is at stake. If our enemies prevail, which our disunion may occasion, our jealousies will then appear frivolous, and all our disputed claims of no value to either side." See WGW, vol. 3, 9-21-1775.

30 Ibid., vol. 28, 10-1-1785.

31 Ibid., vol. 1, 13-19-1756.

32 Ibid., vol. 9, 9-19-1777 Washington wrote to the President of Congress, "I was honored, this Morning, with your favors of the 17th and 18th with their Inclosures. I am much obliged to Congress for the late instance of their Confidence, expressed in their Resolution of the 17th, and shall be happy, if my conduct in discharging the objects they had in view, should be such, as to meet their approbation." The significance of this is that Congress had in essence given Washington the power of a dictator. Fitzpatrick writes in a note to this letter: "The necessity of a speedy removal of Congress from Philadelphia, and the uncertainty as to the time of the next meeting, moved Congress to confer powers upon Washington which practically made him a dictator: 'Resolved, That General Washington be authorized and directed to suspend all officers who shall misbehave, and to fill up all vacancies in the American army, under the rank of brigadiers, until the pleasure of Congress shall be communicated: to take, wherever he may be, all such provisions and other articles as may be necessary for the comfortable subsistence of the army under his command, paying or giving certificates for the same; to remove and secure for the benefit of

the owners, all goods and effects, which may be serviceable to the enemy; provided, that the powers hereby vested shall be exercised only in such parts of these states as may be within the circumference of 70 miles of the head quarters of the American army, and shall continue in force for the space of 60 days, unless sooner revoked by Congress.' (See *Journals of the Continental Congress* , Sept. 17, 1777.)"

33   Ibid., vol. 26, 3-4-1783.

34   Ibid., vol. 26, 3-4-1783.

35   Ibid., vol. 26, 3-4-1783.

36   Ibid., vol. 26, 3-4-1783.

37   Ibid., vol. 26, 3, 15, 1783 quotes this letter from Col. David Cobb.

38   Ibid., vol. 26, 3-15-1783.

39   Ibid., vol. 26, 3-15-1783.

40   Ibid., vol. 26, 3-15-1783.

41   Ibid., vol. 2 1-1757.

42   Ibid., vol. 34, 7-31-1795.

43   Ibid., vol. 28, 11-30-1785.

44   Ibid., vol. 10, 1-8-1778. See also the note from *WGW*, vol. 32, 6-30-1792.

45   Ibid., vol. 12, 6-11-1778.

46   Ibid., See note, vol. 2, 12-9-1758

47   Ibid., vol. 12-9-1758.

48   Ibid., vol. 1, 11-15-1754.

49   Ibid., vol. 1, 4-20-1755.   The full text of the letter says, "Dr. Sir: I was sorry it was not in my power to wait upon you at Westover last Christmas. I had enjoy'd much satisfaction in the thought when an unexpected accident put it entirely out of my power to comply either with my promise, or Inclination; both of which equally urg'd me to make the Visit. I am now preparing for, and shall in a few days sett off, to serve in the ensuing Campaige; with different Views from what I had before; for here, if I can gain any credit, or if I am entitled to the least countenance and esteem, it must be from serving my Country with a free, Voluntary will; for I can very truly say, I have no expectation of reward but the hope of meriting the love of my Country and friendly regard of my acquaintances; and as to any prospect of obtaining a Comn. I have none, and am pretty well assur'd it is not in Genl. Braddock's to give such a one as I wou'd accept off as I am told a Compa. is the highest Comn. that is now vested in his gift. He disir'd my Company this Campaigne, has honoured me with particular marks of Esteem, and kindly invited me into his Family; which will ease me of that expence, which otherwise wou'd undoubtedly have accrued in furnishing a proper Camp Provision; whereas the expence will now be easy, (comparatively speaking) as baggage Horses, tents and some other necessarys will constitute the whole of the charge tho' I mean to say to leave a Family just settling, and in the utmost confusion and disorder (as mine is in at present) will be the means of my using my private Fortune very greatly, but however this may happen, it shall be no hindrance to my making this Campaigne. I am Sir with very g't esteem, etc."

50   Ibid., vol. 6, 10-12-1776.

51   Ibid., vol. 36, 7-4-1798.

52   Ibid., vol. 36, 8-29-1797. Washington wrote to Thomas MacDonald, (Of the British Board of Agriculture.): "Little doubt can be entertained of harmonious proceedings in any business, where men of character and honor, well disposed to do justice, are appointed to conduct it." (*WGW* note: Thomas MacDonald and Henry Pye Rich were the British Commissioners for carrying into effect the VIth Article of Jay's Treaty. They visited Mount Vernon Oct. 14-16, 1797.)

53   Ibid., vol. 23, 7-23-1775. Washington wrote to Brig. Gen. John Thomas, as Thomas was considering resigning.   "Sir: The Retirement of a general Officer possessing the Confidence of his Country and the Army at so critical a Period, appears to me to be big with fatal Consequences both to the Publick Cause and his own Reputation. ...I think it my Duty to use this last Effort to prevent it; he may very properly insist upon his claims of Rank...but in such a cause as this, where the Object is neither Glory nor extent of territory, but a defence of all that is dear and valuable in Life, surely every post ought to be deemed honorable in which a Man can serve his Country. ...if at such a time and in such a cause smaller and partial considerations cannot give way to the great and general Interest. These remarks can only affect you as a member of the great American body, but as an inhabitant of Massachusetts Bay, your own Province and the other Colonies have a peculiar and unquestionable claim to your Services, and in my opinion you cannot refuse them without relinquishing in some degree that Character For publick Virtue and Honor which you have hitherto supported. If our Cause is just, it ought to be supported, but where shall it find support, if Gentlemen of merit and experience, unable to conquer the prejudices of a competition, withdraw themselves in an hour of Danger."

54   Ibid., vol. 19 To Col. Goose Van Schaick on June 20, 1780:   "...the Troops must not tarnish by an unbecoming or unsoldierly conduct, the honor and character of perseverance which they have justly acquired. The want of pay and necessaries are not peculiar to the Regiment garrisoning Fort Schuyler: The rest of the Army have experienced the same."

55   Ibid., vol. 23, 10-31-1781. General Orders, October 31, 1781, "The General in order that this declaration may have its proper Effect and that Colonel White may be totally freed from the aspersions cast on his Character in consequence of the Charges alluded to Directs it to be Published to the Army. The General cannot forbear adding that Accusations of so serious a nature should be made with the most scrupulous caution; an Officer's Character being too sacred to be impeached with Levity without a sufficient foundation."

56   The phrase "conduct unbecoming" is found nine times.   "Unsoldierly conduct" is found twice. The phrase "court martial" is found over one thousand times in Washington's writings. "Guilty" is found 550 times; "innocent" 80 times.

57   *WGW*, vol. 6, 9-16-1776. General Orders: " ...the abandoned and profligate part of our own Army, countenanced by a few officers, who are lost to every Sense of Honor and Virtue, as well as their Country's Good, are by Rapine and Plunder, spreading Ruin and Terror wher-

ever they go; thereby making themselves infinitely more to be dreaded than the common Enemy they are come to oppose; at the same time that it exposes Men who are strolling about after plunder to be surpriz'd and taken. The General therefore hopes it will be unnecessary, on any future Occasion, for him to repeat the Orders of yesterday, with respect to this matter, as he is determined to shew no Favor to officer, or soldier, who shall offend herein, but punish without exception, every person who shall be found guilty of this most abominable practice, which if continued, must prove the destruction of any Army on earth."

58   Ibid., vol. 6, 11-3-1776. General Orders: "The General is sorry to find, that there are some Soldiers, so lost to all Sense of Honor, and Honesty, as to leave the Army, when there is the greatest necessity for their services: He calls upon the Officers of every Rank, to exert themselves, in putting a stop to it, and absolutely forbids any officer, under the Rank of a Brigadier General, discharging any officer, or soldier, or giving any permission to leave the Camp on any pretence whatever."

59   Ibid., vol. 25, 11-13-1782. Washington wrote to Brig. Gen. Peter Muhlenberg, "an Officer of the Virginia Line ... has received a sum of Money for the recruiting service, which he declares he will apply in the first instance to the payment of his own arrearage of Pay, and the Balance, if any, to the purposes for which he drew the sum. The Governor further informs me, that he has furnished you with proofs of the fact, and has desired you to call the Officer to a proper account. I can have no doubt of your not only immediately doing this, but taking steps to put a stop to a practice of the like kind by others. Tho' I hope no other will be found so lost to all sense of honor and honesty as to attempt it. It will be necessary for you, not only for information, but to prevent misapplication of public Money, to call upon the Recruiting Officers very often for returns, and if Men are not sent in agreeable to Returns, you may well suspect improper Conduct. You will as before directed, make me monthly returns at least."

60   Ibid., vol. 8, 5-3-1777. Washington wrote, "I am well informed, from various parts of the Country, that the pernicious practice of Gaming has been exceedingly injurious to the recruiting Service; not only in point of the Officer's time being taken up; but that they have been so lost to all sense of Honor, that the Money drawn and intended for Bounty has been Squander'd this way. it therefore becomes a matter of great concern, that every Commander of a Regiment should be particularly attentive, that this Evil may be prevented from creeping in amongst them, and punish it in a most exemplary manner, upon its first appearance."

61   Ibid., vol. 15, 7-8-1779.   General Orders: "At a Brigade General Court Martial in the 1st. Pennsylvania brigade July 5th., Colonel Humpton President, Neil Megonigle soldier in the 7th. Pennsylvania regiment was tried for, "Desertion from his guard at an advanced post proceeding towards the enemy and opposing the party who took him." The Court are of opinion the prisoner is guilty of the several charges exhibited against him and in consequence of his former bad character and his late conduct do unanimously sentence him to suffer *death* . The Commander in Chief confirms the sentence and orders said Megonigle to be hung next Saturday, 10 o'clock in the forenoon at such place as Genl. Putnam shall direct."

62   Ibid., vol.18, 3-1-1780. Washington wrote to Col. Thomas Craig, "Sir: I have received your favor on the subject of Lieutenant Armstrong. Previous to the receipt, the sentence had been issued in Genl. Orders. You will there observe that Lt. Armstrong was found guilty and sentenced to be discharged, but that the Genl. in consequence of the favorable character given him of the Gentn. has restored him to his rank and command. So far from thinking your commission a trouble, he assured me if it was not in the line of my duty, I should be happy to serve you."

63   Ibid., vol. 26,2-4-1783. General Orders, February 4, 1783, "The General is happy in having the following honorable testimony to the Character and memory of Major General Lord Sterling recorded in the Annals of the Army. By the United States in Congress assembled January 28, 1783. The Commander in Chief having in a letter of the 20th , informed Congress of the death of Major General Lord Stirling. On motion, Resolved, That the President signify to the Commandr. in Chief, in a manner the most respectful to the memory of the late Major General the Earl of Stirling, the sense Congress entertain of the early and meritorius, exertions of that general in the common cause; and of the bravery, perseverance and military talents he possessed; which having fixed their esteem for his character, while living, induce a proportionate regret for the loss of an officer who has rendered such constant and important services to his country."

64   Ibid., vol. 20, 9-26-1780. Writing to Lt. Col. John Laurens on October 13, 1780, Washington further discussed the treason of Benedict Arnold: "In no instance since the commencement of the War has the interposition of Providence appeared more conspicuous than in the rescue of the Post and Garrison of West point from Arnolds villainous perfidy. How far he meant to involve me in the catastrophe of this place does not appear by any indubitable evidence, and I am rather inclined to think he did not wish to hazard the more important object of his treachery by attempting to combine two events the lesser of which might have marred the greater. [Note: Laurens had congratulated Washington on *his* escape from the machinations of Arnold's plot.]
"A combination of extraordinary circumstances. An unaccountable deprivation of presence of Mind in a man of the first abilities, and the virtuous conduct of three Militia men, threw the Adjutant General of the British forces in America (with full proofs of Arnolds treachery) into our hands; and but for the egregious folly, or the bewildered conception of Lieut. Colo. Jameson who seemed lost in astonishment and not to have known what he was doing I should as certainly have got Arnold. André has met his fate, and with that fortitude which was to be expected from an accomplished man, and gallant Officer. But I am mistaken if at *this time* , Arnold is undergoing the torments of a mental Hell. [Note: Laurens had written: "Arnold must undergo a punishment incomparably more severe in the permanent increasing torment of a mental hell."] He wants feeling! From some traits of his character which have lately come to my knowledge, he seems to have been so hackneyed in villainy, and so lost to all sense of honor and shame that while his faculties will enable him to continue his sordid pursuits there will be no time for remorse." *WGW,* vol. 20, 10-13-1780.

65   Ibid., vol. 24, 8-7-1780. Washington wrote, "Honorary Badges of distinction are to be conferred on the veteran Non commissioned officers and soldiers of the army who have served more than three years with bravery, fidelity and good conduct; for this purpose a narrow piece of white cloth of an angular form is to be fixed to the left arm on the uniform Coat. Non commissioned officers and soldiers who have served with equal reputation more than six years are to be distinguished by two pieces of cloth set in parallel to each other in a similar form; should any who are not entitled to these honors have the insolence to assume the badges of them they shall be severely punished.

On the other hand it is expected those gallant men who are thus designated will on all occasions be treated with particular confidence and consideration. The General ever desirous to cherish virtuous ambition in his soldiers, as well as to foster and encourage every species of Military merit, directs that whenever any singularly meritorious action is performed, the author of it shall be permitted to wear on his facings over the left breast, the figure of a heart in purple cloth, or silk, edged with narrow lace or binding. Not only instances of unusual gallantry, but also of extraordinary fidelity and essential service in any way shall meet with a due reward. Before this favor can be conferred on any man, the particular fact, or facts, on which it is to be grounded must be set forth to the Commander in chief accompanied with certificates from the Commanding officers of the regiment and brigade to which the Candidate for reward belonged, or other incontestable proofs, and upon granting it, the name and regiment of the person with the action so certified are to be enrolled in the book of merit which will be kept at the orderly office. Men who have merited this last distinction to be suffered to pass all guards and sentinels which officers are permitted to do. The road to glory in a patriot army and a free country is thus open to all. This order is also to have retrospect to the earliest stages of the war, and to be considered as a permanent one."

Ibid., vol. 24, 8-7-1782, note: "This decoration, now known as 'The Purple Heart,' was revived by the President of the United States, Feb. 22, 1933, and thrown open to all who served in the Army of the United States. As established by Washington, "The Badge of Military Merit" was unique, in that it was obtainable only by privates and noncommissioned officers."

67   Ibid., vol. 11, 4-27-1783. General Orders said, "The Board appointed to take into consideration the claims of the Candidates for the Badge of merit [Known today as the "Purple Heart."]   Report. That Serjeant Churchill of the 2d regt. of Light Dragoons and Serjeant Brown of the late 5th Connecticut regt. are in their opinion severally entitled to the badge of Military merit and do therefore recommend them to His Excellency the Commander in chief, as suitable characters for that honorary distinction."

68   Ibid., vol. 11, 5-2-1778.

69   Ibid., vol. 11, 5-2-1778.

CHAPTER 11

1   *WGW*, vol. 30, 4-30-1789.

2   Ibid., vol. 30, 10-3-1789.

3   Ibid., vol. 30, 5-5-1789. To James Madison, "As the first of every thing, *in our situation* will serve to establish a Precedent, it is devoutly wished on my part, that these precedent may be fixed on true principles."

4   Jedidiah Morse (1761-1836), *The Life of Gen. Washington* (Philadelphia: Jones, Hoff & Derrick, 1794).

5   *WGW*, vol. 30, 4-30-1789. A similar quotation is often attributed to James Madison. See Federer, *America's God And Country*, pp. 411, 780, n. 16. This may be incorrect, since the attribution appears to be an exposition of Washington's Inaugural Address, perhaps made by another historical commentator and inadvertently attributed to Madison. If Madison did say it, no specific place in his writings has been found thus far where he uses these words.

6   Willard Sterne Randall, *George Washington A Life* (New York: Henry Holt and Company, 1997) p. 256. He writes: "Washington was not a deeply religious man."

7   Douglas Southall Freeman, *George Washington, A Biography Victory with the Help of France* (New York: Charles Scribner's Sons, 1952), vol. 5, p. 493.

8   James Thomas Flexner, *The Indispensable Man*, p. 216.

9   David Humphreys, *Life of George Washington* (University of Georgia Press, 1991).

10 The specific religious phrases of Washington's "Circular to the States" from Newburgh on June 8, 1783, are:
    — the glorious events which Heaven has been pleased to produce in our favor,
    — to give my final blessing to that Country, in whose service I have spent the prime of my life
    —...we shall find the greatest possible reason for gratitude and rejoicing;
    —...the lot which Providence has assigned us,
    —whether we view it in a natural, a political or moral point of light.
    —...sole Lords and Proprietors of a vast Tract of Continent, comprehending all the various soils and climates of the World, and abounding with all the necessaries and conveniencies of life, are now by the late satisfactory pacification, acknowledged to be possessed of absolute freedom and Independency; They are, from this period, to be considered as the Actors on a most conspicuous Theatre, which seems to be peculiarly designated by Providence for the display of human greatness and felicity;
    —...Heaven has crowned all its other blessings,
    —...The foundation of our Empire was not laid in the gloomy age of Ignorance and Superstition, but at an Epocha when the rights of mankind were better understood and more clearly defined,
    —...and above all, the pure and benign light of Revelation, have had ameliorating influence on mankind and increased the blessings of Society.

    —Such is our situation, and such are our prospects: but notwithstanding the cup of blessing is thus reached out to us, notwithstanding happiness is ours, if we have a disposition to seize the occasion and make it our own;
    —For, according to the system of Policy the States shall adopt at this moment, they will stand or fall, and by their confirmation or lapse,
    —it is yet to be decided, whether the Revolution must ultimately be considered as a blessing or a curse: a blessing or a curse, not to the present age alone, for with our fate will the destiny of unborn Millions be involved.
    —... compelled to beg their daily bread from door to door!

—...the Legacy of One, who has ardently wished, on all occasions, to be useful to his Country, and who, even in the shade of Retirement, will not fail to implore the divine benediction upon it.

—I now make it my earnest prayer, that God would have you, and the State over which you preside, in his holy protection, that he would incline the hearts of the Citizens to cultivate a spirit of subordination and obedience to Government, to entertain a brotherly affection and love for one another, for their fellow Citizens of the United States at large, and particularly for their brethren who have served in the Field, and finally, that he would most graciously be pleased to dispose us all, to do Justice, to love mercy, and to demean ourselves with that Charity, humility and pacific temper of mind, which were the Characteristicks of the Divine Author of our blessed Religion, and without an humble imitation of whose example in these things, we can never hope to be a happy Nation.

11 *WGW*, vol. 34, 12-24-1795. To Doctor James Anderson, "I have no inclination to touch, much less to dilate on politics. For in politics, as in religion my tenets are few and simple: the leading one of which, and indeed that which embraces most others, is to be honest and just ourselves, and to exact it from others; medling as little as possible in their affairs where our own are not involved. If this maxim was generally adopted Wars would cease, and our swords would soon be converted into reap-hooks, and our harvests be more abundant, peaceful, and happy. 'Tis wonderful it should be otherwise and the earth should be moistened with human gore, instead of the refreshing streams, wch. the shedders of it might become, instruments to lead over its plains, to delight and render profitable our labours. But alas! the millenium will not I fear appear in our days. The restless mind of man can not be at peace; and when there is disorder within, it will appear without, and soon or late will shew itself in acts. So it is with Nations, whose mind is only the aggregate of those of the individuals, where the Government is Representative, and the voice of a Despot, where it is not."

12 Ibid., vol. 4, 3-6-1776.

13 Ibid., vol. 30, 10-3-1789.

14 Ibid., vol. 12-17-1778.

15 Ibid., vol. 5, 5-31-1776.

16 Ibid., vol. 30, 4-1789.

17 Ibid., vol. 2-7-1788. To Marquis de Lafayette. "You appear to be, as might be expected from a real friend to this Country, anxiously concerned about its present political situation. So far as I am able I shall be happy in gratifying that friendly solicitude. As to my sentiments with respect to the merits of the new Constitution, I will disclose them without reserve, (although by passing through the Post offices they should become known to all the world) for, in truth, I have nothing to conceal on that subject. It appears to me, then, little short of a miracle, that the Delegates from so many different States (which States you know are also different from each other in their manners, circumstances and prejudices) should unite in forming a system of national Government, so little liable to well founded objections. Nor am I yet such an enthusiastic, partial or undiscriminating admirer of it, as not to perceive it is tinctured with some real (though not radical) defects. The limits of a letter would not suffer me to go fully into an examination of them; nor would the discussion be entertaining or profitable, I therefore forbear to touch upon it. With regard to the two great points (the pivots upon which the whole machine must move,) my Creed is simply,

1st. That the general Government is not invested with more Powers than are indispensably necessary to perform the functions of a good Government; and, consequently, that no objection ought to be made against the quantity of Power delegated to it.

2nd. That these Powers (as the appointment of all Rulers will for ever arise from, and, at short stated intervals, recur to the free suffrage of the People) are so distributed among the Legislative, Executive, and Judicial Branches, into which the general Government is arranged, that it can never be in danger of degenerating into a monarchy, an Oligarchy, an Aristocracy, or any other despotic or oppressive form, so long as there shall remain any virtue in the body of the People.

I would not be understood my dear Marquis to speak of consequences which may be produced, in the revolution of ages, by corruption of morals, profligacy of manners, and listlessness for the preservation of the natural and unalienable rights of mankind; nor of the successful usurpations that may be established at such an unpropitious juncture, upon the ruins of liberty, however providently guarded and secured, as these are contingencies against which no human prudence can effectually provide. It will at least be a recommendation to the proposed Constitution that it is provided with more checks and barriers against the introduction of Tyranny, and those of a nature less liable to be surmounted, than any Government hitherto instituted among mortals, hath possessed. We are not to expect perfection in this world; but mankind, in modern times, have apparently made some progress in the science of government. Should that which is now offered to the People of America, be found on experiment less perfect than it can be made, a Constitutional door is left open for its amelioration."

18 Ibid., vol. 29, 11-10-1787. To Bushrod Washington. "The warmest friends and the best supporters the Constitution has, do not contend that it is free from imperfections; but they found them unavoidable and are sensible, if evil is likely to arise there from, the remedy must come hereafter; for in the present moment, it is not to be obtained; and, as there is a Constitutional door open for it, I think the People (for it is with them to Judge) can as they will have the advantage of experience on their Side, decide with as much propriety on the alterations and amendments which are necessary [as] ourselves. I do not think we are more inspired, have more wisdom, or possess more virtue, than those who will come after us.

"The power under the Constitution will always be in the People. It is entrusted for certain defined purposes, and for a certain limited period, to representatives of their own chusing; and whenever it is executed contrary to their Interest, or not agreeable to their wishes, their Servants can, and undoubtedly will be, recalled. It is agreed on all hands that no government can be well administered without powers; . . . No man is a warmer advocate for proper restraints and wholesome checks in every department of government than I am; but I have never yet been able to discover the propriety of placing it absolutely out of the power of men to render essential Services, because a possibility remains of their doing ill."

19 *Records of the Federal Convention*, Saturday, June 30, Yates: Mr. Bedford: That all the states at present are equally sovereign and independent, has been asserted from every quarter of this house. Our deliberations here are a confirmation of the position; and I may add to it, that

each of them act from interested, and many from ambitious motives. Look at the votes which have been given on the floor of this house, and it will be found that their numbers, wealth and local views, have actuated their determination; and that the larger states proceed as if our eyes were already perfectly blinded. Impartiality, with them, is already out of the question — the reported plan is their political creed, and they support it, right or wrong….Pretenses to support ambition are never wanting. Their cry is, where is the danger? And they insist that altho' the powers of the general government will be increased, yet it will be for the good of the whole; and although the three great states form nearly a majority of the people of America, they never will hurt or injure the lesser states. I do not, gentleman trust you. If you possess the power, the abuse of it could not be checked; and what then would prevent you from exercising it to our destruction?…"

Elliot's The Debates in the Several State Conventions on the Adoption of the Federal Constitution vol. 1 image 500 or 606. http://memory.loc.gov/cgibin/ampage?collId=llfr&fileName=001/llfr001.db&recNum=529&itemLink=r?ammem/hlaw:@field(DOCID+@lit(fr001145))%230010510&linkText=1

Friday, June 17, Section 8, was again read, and

"The Hon. Mr. SMITH rose. Perhaps there never was a government which, in the course of ten years, did not do something to be repented of. As for Rhode Island, I do not mean to justify her; she deserves to be condemned. If there were in the world but one example of political depravity, it would be hers; and no nation ever merited, or suffered, a more genuine infamy than a wicked administration has attached to her character. Massachusetts also has been guilty of errors, and has lately been distracted by an internal convulsion. Great Britain, notwithstanding her boasted constitution, has been a perpetual scene of revolutions and civil war. Her Parliaments have been abolished; her kings have been banished and murdered. I assert that the majority of the governments in the Union have operated better than any body had reason to expect, and that nothing but experience and habit is wanting to give the state laws all the stability and wisdom necessary to make them respectable, if these things be true, I think we ought not to exchange our condition, with a hazard of losing our state constitutions. We all agree that a general government is necessary; but it ought not to go so far as to destroy the authority of the members. We shall be unwise to make a new experiment, in so important a matter, without some known and sure grounds to go upon. The state constitutions should be the guardians of our domestic rights and interests, and should be both the support and the check of the federal government. Ibid., vol. 2, image 335 of 556.

Records of the Federal Convention, Saturday, July 11.

"Mr. <Madison> was not a little surprised to hear this implicit confidence urged by a member who on all occasions, had inculcated So strongly, the political depravity of men, and the necessity of checking one vice and interest by opposing to them another vice & interest." Ibid., vol. 5, image 298 of 641.

20 *WGW*, vol. 29, 4-28-1788. To Lafayette, This I lay out to be a letter of Politics. …at present, or under our existing form of Confederations, it would be idle to think of making commercial regulations on our part. One State passes a prohibitory law respecting some article, another State opens wide the avenue for its admission. One Assembly makes a system, another Assembly unmakes it. Virginia, in the very last session of her Legislature, was about to have passed some of the most extravagant and preposterous Edicts on the subject of trade, that ever stained the leaves of a Legislative Code. It is in vain to hope for a remedy of these and innumerable other evils, untill a general Government shall be adopted.

"The Conventions of Six States only have as yet accepted the new Constitution. No one has rejected it. It is believed that the Convention of Maryland, which is now in session; and that of South Carolina, which is to assemble on the 12th of May, will certainly adopt it. It is, also, since the elections of Members for the Convention have taken place in this State, more generally believed that it will be adopted here than it was before those elections were made. There will, however, be powerful and eloquent speeches on both sides of the question in the Virginia Convention; but as Pendleton, Wythe, Blair, Madison, Jones, Nicholas, Innis and many other of our first characters will be advocates for its adoption, you may suppose the weight of abilities will rest on that side. Henry and Mason are its great adversaries. The Governor, if he opposes it at all will do it feebly.

"On the general merits of this proposed Constitution, I wrote to you, some time ago, my sentiments pretty freely. That letter had not been received by you, when you addressed to me the last of yours which has come to my hands. I had never supposed that perfection could be the result of accommodation and mutual concession. The opinion of Mr. Jefferson and yourself is certainly a wise one, that the Constitution ought by all means to be accepted by nine States before any attempt should be made to procure amendments. For, if that acceptance shall not previously take place, men's minds will be so much agitated and soured, that the danger will be greater than ever of our becoming a disunited People. Whereas, on the other hand, with prudence in temper and a spirit of moderation, every essential alteration, may in the process of time, be expected.

"You will doubtless, have seen, that it was owing to this conciliatory and patriotic principle that the Convention of Massachusetts adopted the Constitution in toto; but recommended a number of specific alterations and quieting explanations, as an early, serious and unremitting subject of attention. Now, although it is not to be expected that every individual, in Society, will or can ever be brought to agree upon what is, exactly, the best form of government; yet, there are many things in the Constitution which only need to be explained, in order to prove equally satisfactory to all parties. For example: there was not a member of the convention, I believe, who had the least objection to what is contended for by the Advocates for a *Bill of Rights* and *Tryal by Jury* . The first, where the people evidently retained every thing which they did not in express terms give up, was considered nugatory as you will find to have been more fully explained by Mr. Wilson and others: And as to the second, it was only the difficulty of establishing a mode which should not interfere with the fixed modes of any of the States, that induced the Convention to leave it, as a matter of future adjustment.

"There are other points on which opinions would be more likely to vary. As for instance, on the ineligibility of the same person for President, after he should have served a certain course of years. Guarded so effectually as the proposed Constitution is, in respect to the prevention of bribery and undue influence in the choice of President: I confess, I differ widely myself from Mr. Jefferson and you, as to the necessity or expediency of rotation in that appointment. The matter was fairly discussed in the Convention, and to my full convictions;

though I cannot have time or room to sum up the argument in this letter. There cannot, in my judgment, be the least danger that the President will by any practicable intrigue ever be able to continue himself one moment in office, much less perpetuate himself in it; but in the last stage of corrupted morals and political depravity: and even then there is as much danger that any other species of domination would prevail. Though, when a people shall have become incapable of governing themselves and fit for a master, it is of little consequence from what quarter he comes. Under an extended view of this part of the subject, I can see no propriety in precluding ourselves from the services of any man, who on some great emergency shall be deemed universally, most capable of serving the Public."

21   Ibid., vol. 30, 4-1789. Proposed Address to Congress: ". …set up my judgment as the standard of perfection? And shall I arrogantly pronounce that whosoever differs from me, must discern the subject through a distorting medium, or be influenced by some nefarious design? The mind is so formed in different persons as to contemplate the same object in different points of view. Hence originates the difference on questions of the greatest import, both human and divine. In all Institutions of the former kind, great allowances are doubtless to be made for the fallibility and imperfection of their authors. Although the agency I had informing this system, and the high opinion I entertained of my Colleagues for their ability and integrity may have tended to warp my judgment in its favour; yet I will not pretend to say that it appears absolutely perfect to me, or that there may not be many faults which have escaped my discernment. ….Whether the Constitutional door that is opened for amendments in ours, be not the wisest and apparently the happiest expedient that has ever been suggested by human prudence I leave to every unprejudiced mind to determine. Under these circumstances I conclude it has been the part of wisdom to ad[vise] it. I pretend to no unusual foresight into futurity, and therefore cannot undertake to decide, with certainty, what may be its ultimate fate. If a promised good should terminate in an unexpected evil, it would not be a solitary example of disappointment in this mutable state of existence. If the blessings of Heaven showered thick around us should be spilled on the ground or converted to curses, through the fault of those for whom they were intended, it would not be the first instance of folly or perverseness in short-sighted mortals. The blessed Religion revealed in the word of God will remain an eternal and awful monument to prove that the best Institutions may be abused by human depravity; and that they may even, in some instances be made subservient to the vilest of purposes. Should, hereafter, those who are intrusted with the management of this government, incited by the lust of power and prompted by the Supineness or venality of their Constituents, overleap the known barriers of this Constitution and violate the unalienable rights of humanity: it will only serve to shew, that no compact among men (however provident in its construction and sacred in its ratification) can be pronounced everlasting and inviolable, and if I may so express myself, that no Wall of words, that no mound of parchmt. can be so formed as to stand against the sweeping torrent of boundless ambition on the one side, aided by the sapping current of corrupted morals on the other."

22   In the New England mind of the day, civil and religious liberty were inseparable, and thus the happiness of life required a full liberty to pursue both. The Declaration of Independence spoke of "inalienable rights" with which Americans had been endowed by "our Creator" which included "life, liberty and the pursuit of happiness." The word "happiness" in the American context included implications for eternal salvation. (See, for example, Noah Webster's *magnum opus*, *An American Dictionary of the English Language*, published in 1834, wherein his definitions of "happy" and "happiness" encompassed the blessedness of the afterlife in Heaven.) America's spiritual happiness was intimately connected with her political happiness, as seen in the words of the political triumvirate of the New England Adams dynasty:

Samuel Adams, John Adam's cousin and co-patriot said as he signed the Declaration, "We have this day restored the Sovereign to Whom alone men ought to be obedient. He reigns in heaven and … from rising to the setting sun, may His kingdom come." Samuel Adam's emphasis upon Christ's Kingship reflected the spirit of Massachusetts and the other colonies of his day. Statements such as these became commonplace: "No King but King Jesus!" (a slogan emanating from the Committees of Correspondence). A crown appointed governor to the Board of Trade in England wrote, "If you ask an American who is his master? He will tell you he has none, nor any governor but Jesus Christ." This needs a bit of explanation. The English colonialists were not inherently opposed to monarchy per se. But King George had, in the minds of many colonialists, usurped the rule of Christ in his actions toward New England. The third charge of *The Declaration of Independence* against the King says, "He has refused to pass other laws for the accommodation of large districts of people unless those people would relinquish the right of representation in the legislature, a right inestimable to them and formidable to tyrants only." Charge XX says, "For abolishing the free system of English laws in a neighboring province, establishing therein an arbitrary government, and enlarging its boundaries, so as to render it at once an example and fit instrument for introducing the same absolute rule into these colonies." The issue involved in both of these charges is the loss of the British form of government in favor of a French variety and the establishment of the Roman Catholic religion in Quebec. The vast majority of the people in Quebec were Roman Catholic, but the government had been English. By the "Quebec Act" British law was set aside and the Roman Catholic religion established. There were those who believed these concessions to the Canadian Roman Catholics were made so that the British army would have a friendly staging area for an invasion of the colonies, if the struggle with the crown came to blows. The Continental Congress declared, "That the late act of Parliament for establishing the Roman Catholic religion and the French laws in that extensive country now called Quebec, is dangerous in an extreme degree to the Protestant religion and to the civil rights and liberties of all America; and therefore as men and protestant Christians, we are indispensably obliged to take all proper measures for our security." (*Journal of the Proceedings of Congress*, Sept. 17, 1774, p. 35.); and again, "establishing an absolute Government and the Roman Catholic Religion throughout those vast regions, that border on the westerly and northerly boundaries of the free, protestant English settlements." P. 138.

It should not be thought, however, that the American colonies had no room for Roman Catholics in their lands. This was made clear by General Washington's instructions to Benedict Arnold (not then viewed as a traitor) prior to the American invasion of Canada. Washington said to Arnold, "I also give it in Charge to you to avoid all Disrespect to or Contempt of the Religion of the Country and its Ceremonies. Prudence, Policy, and a true Christian Spirit, will lead us to look with Compassion upon their Errors without insulting them. . .God alone is the Judge of the Hearts of Men, and to him only in the Case, they are answerable." (*WGW*, vol. 3, 9-14-1775.) Consider also the Continental Congress' letter to the Roman Catholic citizens of Quebec. The Continental

Congress wrote, "We are too well acquainted with the liberality of sentiment distinguishing your nation, to imagine, that difference of religion will prejudice you against a hearty amity with us. You know, that the transcendent nature of freedom elevates those, who unite in her cause, above all such low minded infirmities. The Swiss Cantons furnish a memorable proof of this truth. Their union is composed of Roman Catholic and Protestant States, living in the utmost second concord and peace with one another, and thereby enabled, ever since they bravely vindicated their freedom, to defy and defeat every tyrant that has invaded them." (*Journal of the Proceedings of Congress*, p. 129). *The Articles of Confederation*, the first form of government for the United States before the *Constitution*, provided for the annexation of Canada! In some measure, the Revolutionary War possessed an element of religious war—the desire to prevent the establishment of a politically coercive religion. Thus the early Americans at first emphasized that they were "protestants," "ancient free protestant colonies", "free, protestant, English settlements" (*Journal of the Proceedings of Congress*, p. 138.) etc. Nevertheless, their hope to have a peaceful co-existence with Roman Catholics ultimately occurred with the arrival of the French forces.

John Adams, cousin of Samuel Adams, was an early patriot and later second President of the United States. On July 3, 1776, in a letter to his wife Abigail Adams, he wrote that the day of the signing the Declaration of Independence "ought to be commemorated, as the Day of Deliverance, by solemn acts of devotion to God Almighty. It ought to be solemnized with pomp and parade, shows, games, sports, guns, bells, bonfires and illuminations from one end of this continent to the other, from this time forward forevermore." (*Letters of John Adams—Addressed to His Wife*, Charles Francis Adams, ed., (Boston: Charles C. Little and James Brown, 1841), vol. I, p. 128.)

John Quincy Adams, son of John Adams, and also a president of the U. S. said in an "Oration Delivered Before the Inhabitants of the Town of Newburyport": Why is it that, next to the birthday of the Savior of the World, your most joyous and most venerated festival returns on this day [on the Fourth of July]? Is it not that, in the chain of human events, the birthday of the nation is indissolubly linked with the birthday of the Savior? That it forms a leading event in the progress of the gospel dispensation? Is it not that the Declaration of Independence first organized the social compact on the foundation of the Redeemer's mission upon earth? That it laid the cornerstone of human government upon the first precepts of Christianity?" J. Q. Adams presented this oration at their request on the 61st anniversary of the Declaration of Independence, July 4, 1837.

23 This powerful and illuminating letter in terms of the Christian perspective of Washington's religion is here quoted in full. *The Papers of George Washington*, W. W. Abbot, Ed., Dorothy Twohig, Assoc. Ed., *Presidential Series* (Charlottesville: University Press of Virginia), vol. 6, pp. 279-282. This will be abbreviated by *PGW*, volume number, page number *PGW* vol. 4:275-277:

And now we devoutly offer our humble tribute of praise and thanksgiving to the all-gracious *Father* of *lights* who has inspired our public Councils with a wisdom and firmness, which have effected that desirable purpose, in so great a measure by the National-Constitution, and who has fixed the eyes of all America on you as the worthiest of its Citizens to be entrusted with the execution of it.

Whatever any may have supposed wanting in the original plan, we are happy to find so wisely providing in it amendments; and it is with peculiar satisfaction we behold how easily the entire confidence of the People, in the Man who sits at the helm of Government, has eradicated every remaining objection to its form.

Among these we never considered the want of *a religious test*, that grand engine of persecution in every tyrant's hand: but we should not have been alone in rejoicing to have seen some Explicit acknowledgement of the *only true God and Jesus Christ, whom he hath sent* inserted some where in the *Magna Charta* of our country.

We are happy to find, however, that this defect has been amply remedied, in the face of all the world, by the piety and devotion, in which your first public act of office was performed—by the religious observance of the Sabbath, and of the public worship of *God*, of which you have set so eminent an example—and by the warm strains of Christian and devout affections, which run through your late proclamation, for a general thanksgiving.

The catholic spirit breathed in all your public acts supports us in the pleasing assurance that no religious establishments—no exclusive privileges tending to elevate one denomination of Christians to the depression of the rest shall ever be ratified by the signature of the *President* during your administration

On the contrary we bless God that your whole deportment bids all denominations confidently to expect to find in you the watchful guardian of their equal liberties—the steady patron of genuine Christianity—and the bright Exemplar of those peculiar virtues, in which its distinguishing doctrines have their proper effect.

Under the nurturing hand of a Ruler of such virtues, and one so deservedly revered by all ranks, we joyfully indulge the hope that virtue and religion will revive and flourish—that infidelity and the vices ever attendant in its train, will be banished [from] every polite circle; and that rational piety will soon become fashionable there; and from thence be diffused among all other ranks in the community.

Captivated with the delightful prospect of a national reformation rising out of the influence of your authority and example; we find the fullest encouragement to cherish the hope of it, from the signal deeds of pious and patriotic heroism, which marked the steps of the Father of his country, from the memorable hour of his appearance in Congress, to declare the disinterested views with which he accepted the command of her armies, to that hour, not less memorable, when, having gloriously acquitted himself in that important trust, and completely accomplished the design of it, he appeared in the same great Assembly again; and resigned his commission into the hands that gave it.

But glorious as your course has been as a Soldier in arms, defending your country, and the rights of mankind; we exult in the presage that it will be far outshone by the superior luster of a more glorious career now before you, as the Chief Magistrate of your nation—protecting, by just and merciful laws—and by a wise, firm, and temperate execution of them, enhancing the value of those inestimable rights and privileges, which you have so worthily asserted to it by your sword.

Permit us then, great Sir, to assure you that whilst it ever shall be our care, in our several places to inculcate those principles, drawn from the pure fountains of light and truth, in the sacred scriptures, which can best recommend your virtues to their imitation, and which, if generally obeyed, would contribute essentially to render your people happy, and your government prosperous; Our unceasing prayers to the *great Sovereign of all* nations, shall be that your important life, and all your singular talents may be the special care of an indulgent Providence for many years to come; that your administration may be continued to your country, under the peculiar smiles of Heaven, long be continued to your country, under the peculiar smiles of Heaven, long enough to advance the interests of learning to the zenith—to carry the arts and sciences to their destined perfection—to chase ignorance, bigotry, and immorality off the stage—to restore true virtue, and the religion of *Jesus* to their deserved throne in our land: and to found the liberties of America, both religious and civil, on a basis which no era of futurity shall ever see removed: and, finally, that, when you have thus done—free grace may confer on you, as the reward of all your great labours, the unfading laurels of an everlasting crown. Joseph Prince, moderator on behalf of the First Presbytery

24 *Westminster Confession of Faith*, chapter I, paragraph 7, "All things in Scripture are not alike plain in themselves, nor alike clear unto all; yet those things which are necessary to be known, believed, and observed, for salvation, are so clearly propounded and opened in some place of Scripture or other, that not only the learned, but the unlearned, in a due use of the ordinary means, may attain unto a sufficient understanding of them." In Schaff, *Creeds of Christendom*, vol. III, p. 604.

25 *WGW*, vol. 30, 10-23-1789, note.

26 Reverend Dr. John Witherspoon was a Presbyterian Minister from New Jersey, President of the College of New Jersey in Princeton, and a member of Congress. He was the only clergyman to sign the Declaration of Independence. In 1782, he composed one of the Continental Congress' national calls for a day of thanksgiving: ". . . to testify their gratitude to God for his goodness, by a cheerful obedience to his laws, and by promoting, each in his station, and by his influence, the practice of true and undefiled religion, which is the great foundation of public prosperity and national happiness." Note that in his mind as an orthodox minister in the Presbyterian tradition, "true and undefiled religion" was a synonym for Christianity. Witherspoon did not directly mention the name of Jesus Christ in his proclamation, but this obviously had no anti-Christian or deistic intent. See *Journals of the Continental Congress*, on the date specified.

27 *PGW*, 2:424. As Washington said at the conclusion of his letter to the Virginia Baptists, "In the meantime be assured, Gentlemen, that I entertain a proper sense of your fervent supplications to God for my temporal and eternal happiness."

28 We will consider Washington's belief in heaven and eternal life in a latter chapter. For now, notice that he understands happiness as both temporal and future in the hereafter. The import of the "completion" of happiness is eternity. *WGW*, vol. 25, 11-16-1782. To the Reformed Protestant Dutch Church in Kingston. "In return for your kind concern for my temporal and eternal happiness, permit me to assure you that my wishes are reciprocal...." Ibid., vol. 6, 11-4-1798.to Reverend William Lynn, who had been Chaplain to Congress under Washington's Presidency and was a Reformed minister from New York City. "Revd. Sir: I received with thankfulness your favour of the 30th. Ulto., enclosing the discourse delivered by you on the day recommended by the President of the United States to be observed as a general Fast. I have read them both with pleasure; and feel grateful for the favourable sentiments you have been pleased to express in my behalf; but more especially for those good wishes which you offer for my temporal and eternal happiness; which I reciprocate with great cordiality...."

29 Ibid., vol. 30, 4-30-1789. "....it would be peculiarly improper to omit, in this first official act, my fervent supplications to that Almighty Being who rules over the universe, who presides in the councils of nations and whose providential aids can supply every human defect; that His benediction may consecrate to the liberties and happiness of the people of the United States a Government instituted by themselves for these essential purposes; and may enable every instrument employed in its administration to execute with success, the functions allotted to his charge.
In tendering this homage to the Great Author of every public and private good, I assure myself that it expresses your sentiments not less than my own...."

30 Ibid., vol. 30, 4-30-1789, "No People can be bound to acknowledge and adore the invisible hand, which conducts the Affairs of men more than the People of the United States. Every step, by which they have advanced to the character of an independent nation, seems to have been distinguished by some token of providential agency. And in the important revolution just accomplished in the system of their United Government, the tranquil deliberations and voluntary consent of so many distinct communities, from which the event has resulted, cannot be compared with the means by which most Governments have been established, without some return of pious gratitude along with an humble anticipation of the future blessings which the past seem to presage. These reflections, arising out of the present crisis, have forced themselves too strongly on my mind to be suppressed. You will join with me I trust in thinking, that there are none under the influence of which, the proceedings of a new and free Government can more auspiciously commence."

31 Ibid., vol. 30, 4-30-1789, "And in the important revolution just accomplished, in the system of their United government, the tranquil deliberations and voluntary consent of so many distinct communities, from which the event has resulted, can not be compared with the means by which most governments have been established, without some return of pious gratitude, along with an humble anticipation of the future blessings which the past seem to presage."

32 Ibid., vol. 30, 4-30-1789, "We ought to be no less persuaded that the propitious smiles of Heaven can never be expected on a nation that disregards the eternal rules of order and right which Heaven itself has ordained; and since the preservation of the sacred fire of liberty and the destiny of the republican model of government are justly considered as deeply, perhaps finally, staked on the experiment."

33 James Thomas Flexner, *The Indispensable Man*, p. 216.

34 Lillback, *Proclaim Liberty*, p. 84-86; Sanford H. Cobb, *The Rise of Religious Liberty in America* (New York: Macmillan Co., 1902), p. 419.

35 This was, of course, in New York City. The U.S. Capitol wasn't moved to Washington, D.C., until several years later. After the World Trade Center was destroyed on September 11, 2001, by Muslim extremists, Mayor Guiliani marveled to the world how St. Paul's Cathedral, with-

in the shadow of these towering giants, miraculously survived their destruction.

36 *Soldier and Servant Series: Mrs. Alexander Hamilton Witness that George Washington Was A Communicant of the Church* (Hartford: Church Missions Publishing Company, 1932).

37 *PGW,* 6:279-282.

38 Ibid., 5:299-301.

39 Ibid., 3:496-499.

40 Ibid., 2:179-181; *PGW,* 8:181-82.

41 Ibid., 3:92-93.

42 Ibid., 4:263-265.

43 Ibid., 2:420-422; *PGW,* 4:274-277.

44 Ibid., 4:198-199; *PGW,* 8:177-178.

45 Ibid., 3:466-467; *PGW,* 8:226-227.

46 Ibid., 2:411-412.

47 Ibid., 2:423-425.

48 Ibid., 4:265-269; *PGW,* 5:296-299.

49 Ibid., 6:287-288; *PGW,* 4:182-183.

50 Ibid., 6:223-225.

51 Ibid., 5:448-450; *PGW,* 6:284-286; *PGW,* 7:61-64.

52 Ibid., 12:40-41.

53 Ibid., 2:179-181.

54 Ibid., 2:411-412.

55 Ibid., 3:92.

56 See notes 2, 3, 4 above.

57 *WGW,* vol. 27, 6-11-1783. Responding to Reverend Rodgers proposal for Congress to present each soldier with a Bible, Washington wrote, "Dear Sir: I accept, with much pleasure your kind Congratulations on the happy Event of Peace, with the Establishment of our Liberties and Independence. Glorious indeed has been our Contest: glorious, if we consider the Prize for which we have contended, and glorious in its Issue; but in the midst of our Joys, I hope we shall not forget that, to divine Providence is to be ascribed the Glory and the Praise. Your proposition respecting Mr Aikins Bible would have been particularly noticed by me, had it been suggested in Season; but the late Resolution of Congress for discharging Part of the Army, takg off near two thirds of our Numbers, it is now too late to make the Attempt. It would have pleased me, if Congress should have made such an important present, to the brave fellows, who have done so much for the Security of their Country's Rights and Establishment."

58 *PGW,* 2:420-422.

59 Ibid., 2:420-421.

60 Ibid., 2:420-422, "While all men within our territo5ries are protected in worshipping eh Deity according to the dictates of their consciences; it is rationally to be expected from them in return. . . ."

61 *WGW* vol. 35, 7-6-1796. "In short, that I was no party man myself, and the first wish of my heart was, if parties did exist, to reconcile them."

62 Ibid., vol. 35, 7-6-1796.

63 Ibid., vol. 2 8-2-1758.

64 Ibid., vol. 38, 4-23-1799.

65 Ibid., vol. 37, 12-25-1798.

66 Ibid., vol. 32, 8-26-1792, note. From Edmund Randolph to Washington, "Randolph's long letter of this date is in the *Washington Papers* . In it he discusses the political situation of the United States and urges Washington to serve a second term. Among many important statements in that letter are these: "… we must gain time, for the purpose of attracting confidence in the government by an experience of its benefits, and that man alone, whose patronage secured the adoption of the constitution, can check the assaults, which it will sustain at the two next sessions of congress....Should a civil war arise, you cannot stay at home. And how much easier will it be, to disperse the factions, which are rushing to this catastrophe, than to subdue them, after they shall appear in arms? It is the fixed opinion of the world, that you surrender nothing incomplete. I am not unapprized of the many disagreeable sensations, which have laboured in your breast, But let them spring from any cause whatsoever, of one thing I am sure, (and I speak this from a satisfactory inquiry lately made) that if a second opportunity shall be given the people of showing their gratitude, they will not be less unanimous than before."

67 Ibid., vol. 37, 7-21-1799. To Gov. Jonathan Trumbull, "My dear Sir: To you, and to your brother Colo. Jno Trumbull, I feel much indebted for the full, frank, and interesting communication of the political sentiments contained in both your letters.

The project of the latter is rash and under any circumstances would require very mature consideration; but in its extent, and an eye being had to the disorganizing Party in the United States, I am sure it would be impracticable in the present order of things.

Not being able to convey my ideas to you on this subject in more concise terms than I have already done to your brother in answer to the letter he informs you he has written to me I shall take the liberty of giving you an extract thereof, as follow.

For the Political information contained in it (that is his letter) I feel grateful, as I always shall for the free…and within the short period which you suppose may be allowed to accomplish it.

I come now, my dear Sir, to pay particular attention to that part of your Letter which respects myself.

I remember well the conversation which you allude to, and have not forgot the answer I gave you. In my judgment it applies with as much force *now*, as *then* ; nay more, because at that time the line between Parties was not so clearly drawn, and the views of the opposition, so clearly developed as they are at present; of course, allowing your observation (as it respects myself) to be founded, personal influence would be of no avail.

Let that party set up a broomstick and call it a true son of Liberty; a Democrat, or give it any other epithet that will suit their purpose, and it will command their votes in toto! as an analysis of this position, look to the pending Election of Governor in Pennsylvania. Will not the Federalists meet them or rather defend their cause, on the opposite ground? Surely they must, or they will discover a want of Policy, indicative of weakness, and pregnant of mischief which cannot be admitted. Wherein then would lye the difference between the present Gentleman in Office [John Adams], and myself?

It would be matter of sore regret to me if I could believe that a serious thot. was turned towards me as his successor; not only as it respects my ardent wishes to pass through the rest of life in retiremt., undisturbed in the remnant of the days I have to sojourn here, unless called upon to defend my Country (which every citizen is bound to do), but on Public ground also; for although I have abundant cause to be thankful for the good health with whh. I am blessed, yet I am not insensible to my declination in other respects. It would be criminal therefore in me, although it should be the wish of my Countrymen, and I could be elected, to accept an Office under this conviction, which another would discharge with more ability; and this too at a time when I am thoroughly convinced I should not draw a *single* vote from the Anti-federal side; and of course, should stand upon no stronger ground than any other Federal character well supported; and when I should become a mark for the shafts of envenomed malice, and the basest calumny to fire at; when I should be charged not only with irresolution, but with concealed ambition, which waits only an occasion to blaze out; and, in short, with dotage and imbecility.

All this I grant, ought to be dust in the balance, when put in competion [*sic*] with a *great* public good, when the accomplishment of it is apparent. But as no problem is better defined in my mind than that principle, not men, is now, and will be, the object of contention; and that I could not obtain a *solitary* vote from that Party; that any other respectable Federal character would receive the same suffrages that I should; that at my time of life, (verging towards three score and ten) I should expose myself without rendering any essential service to my Country, or answering the end contemplated: Prudence on my part must arrest any attempt at the well meant, but mistaken views of my friends, to introduce me again into the chair of Government.

Lengthy as this letter is, I cannot conclude it without expressing an *earnest* wish that, some intimate and confidential friend of the Presidents would give him to understand that, his long absence from the Seat of Government in the present critical conjuncture, affords matter for severe animadversion by the friends of government; who speak of it with much disapprobation; while the other party chuckle at and set it down as a favourable omen for themselves. It has been suggested to me to make this Communication; but I have declined it, conceiving that it would be better received from a private character, more in the habits of social intercouse and friendship. With the most sincere friendship, and Affectionate regard, etc.

68   Ibid., vol. 10, 1-29-1778.
69   Ibid., vol.10, 12-18-1778.
70   Ibid., vol. 15, 5-18-1779.
71   Ibid., vol. 26, 4-30-1783.
72   Ibid., vol. 34, 4-17-1795. The note at this date of *The Writings Of George Washington* says:
     "Addresses of disapprobation of Jay's Treaty, urging that it be not ratified, poured in upon the President from cities, towns, and counties in nearly every State. The earliest being that from the Selectmen of Boston, dated July 13, and the last coming from the citizens of Lexington, Ky., in their meeting of September 8 (forwarded September 10). To most of these addresses the same answer was returned as that to the Boston Selectman, July 28. The text of the addresses, with the President's answers, are entered in the "Letter Book" in the *Washington Paper*."
     On the "Letter Book" copy of the resolutions of the citizens of Petersburg, Va., August 1, Washington has noted: "Tenor indecent No answer returned."
     On the "Letter Book" copy of the resolutions of the inhabitants of Bordentown, Crosswicks, Black Horse, and Reckless Town, N. J., Washington has noted: "No answer given. The Address too rude to merit one." The copyist's note to resolutions of the citizens of Laurens County, S. C., is "The foregoing Resolutions &ca. were sent under a blank cover, by (it is supposed) Jno. Matthews Esqr. No notice has been taken of them."
     On the "Letter Book" copy of the remonstrance and petition of the citizens of Scott County, Ky., August 25, Washington has noted: "The Ignorance and indecency of these proceedings forbad an answr."
     On the "Letter Book" copy of the address from the citizens of Lexington, Ky., Washington has noted: "It would now [be] out of time to answr this address when reed Novr. Indecent besides."
73   Ibid., vol. 30, 4-17-1789.
74   Ibid., vol. 12, 8-20-1778 to Gen. Thomas Nelson; Ibid., vol. 28, 9-5-1785, to Chevelier de Luzerne.

CHAPTER 12
1   *WGW*, vol. 28, 5-23-1785.
2   Ibid., For example vol. 28, 5-8-1786. To Thomas Cresap, "…the heir of my brother Augustine, who lives at the distance of an hundred miles from me; and is one whom I scarcely ever saw." Cf. *WGW*, vol. 37, 12-30-1798. See Frank E. Grizzard, Jr., *George Washington: A Biographical Companion* Santa Barbara: ABC-CLIO, 2002), pp. 403-410.
3   Ibid., vol. 32, 5-2-1792. Ibid., vol. 36, 10-3-1798. To William Augustine Washington. "I thank you for the old documents you sent me, respecting the family of our Ancestors. but I am possessed of Papers which prove beyond a doubt, that of the two brothers who Emigrated to this Country in the year 1657, during the troubles of that day, that John Washington, from whom we are descended, was the eldest. The

Pedigree from him, I have, and I believe very correct; but the descendants of Lawrence, in a regular course, I have not been able to trace. All those of our name, in and about Chotanck, are from the latter. John, was the Grandfather of my father and Uncle, and Great grand-father to Warner and me. He left two Sons, Lawrence and John; the former, who was the eldest, was the father of my father, Uncle and Aunt Willis. Mrs. Hayward must have been a daughter of the *first* Lawrence, and thence became the Cousen of the second Lawrence, and John. We all unite in best wishes for you and family."

4 Ibid., vol. 17, 1-22-1780. To Maj. Gen. Nathanael Greene. "Dear Sir: Appears. and facts must speak for themselves; to these I appeal. I have been at my prest. quarters since the 1st. day of Decr. and have not a Kitchen to Cook a Dinner in, altho' the Logs have been put together some considerable time by my own Guard; nor is there a place at this moment in which a servant can lodge with the smallest degree of comfort. Eighteen belonging to my family and all Mrs. Fords are crouded together in her Kitchen and scarce one of them able to speak for the colds they have caught."

WGW, vol. 36, 8-9-1798. To Maj. Gen. Alexander Hamilton. "My Aids, as you well know, *must* be men of business; and *ought* to be Officers of experience. Many, very many *young* Gentlemen of the first families in the Country have offered their Services; and all have received one answer, to the above effect. Indeed in the choice of my Aids, a variety of considerations must combine, political, geographical &ca. as well as experience. .. No Foreigner will be admitted as a member of my family, while I retain my present ideas; nor do I think they ought to be in any situation where they can come at secrets, and betray a trust."

Ibid., vol. 37, 11-6-1781. To Jonathan Trumbull Jr. "My dear Sir: I came here in time to see Mr. Custis breathe his last. About Eight o'clock yesterday Evening he expired. The deep and solemn distress of the Mother, and affliction of the Wife of this amiable young Man, requires every comfort in my power to afford them; the last rights of the deceased I must also see performed; these will take me three or four days; when I shall proceed with Mrs. Washington and Mrs. Custis to Mount Vernon.

As the dirty tavern you are now at cannot be very comfortable; and in spite of Mr. Sterne's observation the House of Mourning not very agreeable; it is my wish, that all of the Gentn of my family, except yourself, who I beg may come here and remain with me; may proceed on at their leizure to Mount Vernon, and wait for me there. Colo. Cobb will join you on the road at the Tavern we breakfasted at (this side Ruffens). My best wishes attend the Gentn. and with much sincerity and affectn."

5 Ibid., vol. 30, 3-25-1789. To Elizabeth Washington Lewis. "My dear Sister: Since you were speaking to me concerning your Son Bob, I have thought it probable that I may have occasion for a young person in my family of a good disposition, who writes a good hand, and who can confine himself [to] a certain reasonable number of hours in the 24 to the recording of letters in books, which will be provided for their reception from the separate papers on which they now are and will be first draughted.

If Bob is of opinion that this employment will suit his inclination, and he will take his chance for the allowance that will be made (which cannot be great) as there are hundreds who would be glad to come in. I should be very glad to give him the preference. He will be at no expence (except in the article of clothing) as he will be one of the family and live as we do.

Should he incline to engage I could wish to know it by the first post after this letter gets to you, because I shall have many solicitations on this head at or before I get to New York, at which place direct for me, as I presume a letter cannot reach Mount Vernon before I shall have set out.

If he comes, it may be with his Aunt, (and at her expence, as she will want some body to accompany her) when I send my horses back after I am fixed in New York.

He will want no horses there himself, for which reason those or the one that he takes on, should be such as will sell."

Ibid., vol. 30, 7-27-1789. to Thomas Nelson. "Sir: The sincere regard I had for your very worthy, deceased father, induces me to offer you a place in my family. How convenient and agreeable it may be for you to accept the offer, is with you to determine; and that you may be the better enabled to judge, I shall inform you that the emoluments will be about six hundred dollars pr. ann., and the expences trifling as your board, lodging and washing (as also that of your Servant if you bring one) will be in the family. Horses if you keep any must be at your own expence because there will be no public occasion for them.

Note: Nelson's letter of August 13, accepting the offer, is in the *Washington Papers* .

The duties that will be required of you, are, generally, to assist in writing, receiving and entertaining company, and in the discharge of such other matters as is not convenient or practicable for the President to attend to in person. Whether you accept this offer or not I should be glad to hear from you as soon as it is conveniently possible because there are a number of Gentlemen who are anxiously desirous of this appointment but whose applications will remain undecided on until I receive an answer from you."

6 Ibid., vol. 27, 7-28-1784. To Clement Biddle. "Dear Sir: The mulatto fellow William, 8 who has been with me all the War is attached (married he says) to one of his own colour a free woman, who, during the War was also of my family. She has been in an infirm state of health for sometime, and I had conceived that the connection between them had ceased, but I am mistaken; they are both applying to me to get her here, and tho' I never wished to see her more yet I cannot refuse his request (if it can be complied with on reasonable terms) as he has lived with me so long and followed my fortunes through the War with fidility."

Ibid., vol. 28, 11-10-1785. To George Chapman. "I have a little boy something turned of four, and a girl of six years old living with me, for whom I want a Tutor. They are both promising children, the latter is a very fine one, and altho' they are of an age when close confine-ment may be improper; yet a man of letters, most of composition, and a good accomptant, would in other respects be essentially useful to *me* for a year or two to come. May I ask you therefore Sir, if it is in your power, conveniently, to engage a person of this description for me?

"Having already informed you what my wants are, it is needless to add what those of the children must be; your own judgement, when I inform you that I mean to fit the boy, in my own family, for a University, will point these out. The greater the knowledge of his precep-tor is, the better he would suit. To teach French grammatically is essential, as it is now becoming a part of the education of youth in this Country.

"I could not afford to give more than £50 Sterlg. pr. ann:but this sum, except in the article of cloathing, wou'd be clear, as the Gentleman would eat at my table; and have his lodging and washing found him; and his Linen and stockings mended by the Servants of my Family. It may happen that an Episcopal clergyman with a small living, and unencumbered by a family may be had to answer this description, such an one would be preferred; but I except none who is competent to my purposes, if his character is unimpeached."

Ibid., vol. 30, 8-4-1788. To Dr. James Craik, "I also send you Thirty pounds Cash for one years allowance for the Schooling of your Son G.W. I wish it was in my power to send the like sum for the other year, which is now about, or near due; and that could discharge your account for attendance and ministries to the Sick of my family; but it really is not; for with much truth I can say, I never felt the want of money so sensibly since I was a boy of 15 years old as I have done for the last 12 months and probably shall do for 12 Months more to come."

7   Ibid., vol. 2, 3-10-1768. To Robert Cary & Co. "Gentn: This Letter will, I expect, be delivered to you by Mr. Walter Magowan, who for many years has livd in my Family a Tutor to Master and Miss Custis, and now comes to England to get admittance into Holy Orders. Any little Civilities therefore which you may occasionally shew him during his short stay there, or assistance give, woud be very obliging as he is perfectly a Stranger, and may need a little Introduction, altho' he comes provided with proper Certificates &ca. to the Bishop.

Ibid., vol. 2, 5-30-1768.   To Reverend Jonathan Boucher.

Reverend Sir: Mr. Magowan who lived several years in my Family, a Tutor to Master Custis (my Son-in-law and Ward) having taken his departure for England leaves the young Gentleman without any master at this time. I shoud be glad therefore to know if it woud be convenient for you to add him to the number of your Pupils. He is a boy of good genius, about 14 yrs. of age, untainted in his morals, and of innocent manners. Two yrs and upwards he has been reading of Virgil, and was (at the time Mr. Magowan left him) entered upon the Greek Testament, tho I presume he has grown not a little rusty in both; having had no benefit of his Tutor since Christmas, notwithstanding he left the Country in March only. If he comes, he will have a boy (well acquainted with House business, which may be made as useful as possible in your Family to keep him out of Idleness) and two Horses, to furnish him with the means of getting to Church and elsewhere as you may permit; for he will be put entirely and absolutely under your tuition, and direction to manage as you think proper in all respects."

8   Ibid., vol. 28, 2-6-1786. To Benjamin Lincoln. "Mr. Lear, or any other who may come into my family in the blended characters of preceptor to the Children, and as a Clerk or private Secretary to me, will sit at my Table, will live as I live, will mix with the Company which resort to the Ho., and will be treated in every respect with civility, and proper attention. He will have his washing done in the family, and may have his linnen and Stockings mended by the maids of it. The duties which will be required of him are, generally, such as appertain to the offices before mentioned. The first will be very trifling 'till the Children are a little more advanced; and the latter will be equally so as my corrispondencies decline (which I am endeavouring to effect); and after my accts; and other old matters are brought up. To descend more minutely into his avocations I am unable, because occasional matters may require particular Services; nothing however derogatory will be asked, or expected. After this explanation of my wants, I request Mr. Lear would mention the annual sum he will expect for these Services, and I will give him a decided answer by the return of the Stages, which now carry the Mail and travel quick. A good hand, as well as proper diction would be a recommendation; on acct. of fair entries; and for the benefit of the Children, who will have to copy after it."

Ibid., vol. 35, 1-12-1797. "Dear Walker: Permit me once more to give you the trouble of forwarding the enclosed letters to their respective addresses. If you read the *Aurora* of this City, or those Gazettes which are under the same influence, you cannot but have perceived with what malignant industry, and persevering falsehoods I am assailed, in order to weaken, if not destroy, the confidence of the Public.

"Amongst other attempts to effect this purpose, spurious letters, known at the time of their first publication (I believe in the year 1777) to be forgeries, to answer a similar purpose in the Revolution, are, or extracts from them, brought forward with the highest emblazoning of which they are susceptible, with a view to attach principles to me which every action of my life have given the lie to. But *that* is no stumbling block with the Editors of these Papers and their supporters. And now, *perceiving* a disinclination on my part, perhaps *knowing*, that I had determined not to take notice of such attacks, they are pressing this matter upon the public mind with more avidity than usual; urging, that my silence, is a proof of their genuineness.

"Although I never wrote, or ever saw one of these letters until they issued from New York, in Print; yet the Author of them must have been tolerably well acquainted in, or with some person of my family, to have given the names, and some circumstances which are grouped in the mass, of erroneous details. But of all the mistakes which have been committed in this business, none is more palpable, or susceptible of detection than the manner in which it is said they were obtained, by the capture of my Mulatto Billy, with a Portmanteau. *All the Army*, under my immediate command, could contradict this; and I believe most of them know, that no Attendant of mine, or a particle of my baggage ever fell into the hands of the enemy during the whole course of the War."

9   Ibid., vol.33, 20-1794. To the Artillery Co. of Newport, RI. "Gentlemen: For your kind congratulations on the anniversary of my birthday, and the other obliging expressions of your Address I pray you to accept my grateful thanks. To cherish those principles which effected the revolution, and laid the foundation of our free and happy Government, does honor to your patriotism; as do the sentiments of commiseration for the sufferings of the unfortunate, and the good wishes for the happiness of the great family of mankind, to your philanthropy. Your prayer for me, is reciprocated by the best vows I can offer for your welfare."

10 Ibid., vol. 29, 4-6-1787. To John Rumney, "Sir: However desirous I may be of accomodating the wishes of so deserving a Lady as you represent Mrs. Wilson to be, yet Mrs. Washington concurs in sentiment with me that my family already is, and soon will be too large to admit of an increase."

11 Ibid., vol.3, 6-19-1775. To Burwell Bassett. "Dear Sir: I am now Imbarked on a tempestuous Ocean, from whence perhaps, no friendly harbour is to be found. I have been called upon by the unanimous Voice of the Colonies to the Command of the Continental Army. It is an honour I by no means aspired to. It is an honour I wished to avoid, as well from an unwillingness to quit the peaceful enjoyment of my Family..."

12 *WGW*, vol. 4, 10-13-1775. To John Augustine Washington. "Dear Brother: ...I am obliged to you for your advice to My Wife, and for

your Intention of visiting of her; seeing no great prospect of returning to my Family and Friends this Winter I have sent an Invitation to Mrs. Washington to come to me, altho' I fear the Season is too far advanced (especially if she should, when my Letters get home, be in New Kent, as I believe the case will be) to admit this with any tolerable degree of convenience. I have laid a state of the difficulties, however which must attend the journey before her and left it to her own choice. My Love to my Sister and the little ones are sincerely tenderd and I am with true regard Yr. Most Affecte. Brother."

Ibid., vol. 33, 5-4-1794. To William Pearce. "In the Gardeners report is a query, if Apricots will be wanting to preserve. I answer No. for the situation of public business now is, and likely to remain such, that my family will not be able to spend any time at Mount Vernon this Summer, that is, I cannot do it, and Mrs. Washington would not chuse to be there without me. My present intention is, if public business will permit, to make a flying trip there soon after the rising of Congress; but when that will be is more than I [am] able to decide, at present."

Ibid., vol. 34, 7-12-1795. To William Pearce. "If nothing more than I foresee at present, happens to prevent it, I shall leave this place (with my family) for Mount Vernon on Wednesday next, the 15th. instt., but when I shall arrive at it, is more difficult to decide, as the weather is extremely hot, and my horses very fat. These circumstances must, at any rate, cause my movements to be slow; or I shall hazard too much in my horses."

13 Ibid., vol. 37, 5-13-1799. To the Secretary of War. "Under any circumstances, I consider this preparatory measure of the President's, to be eligable; but I am led to believe from his having adopted it, at *this* time, without any previous intimation thereof (that has come to my knowledge) before he left the Seat of Government, that stronger indications of hostility have been received, than appeared when he went away to have occasioned it; if so, I think it ought to be communicated to me in confidence; for it must not be expected that like a Mercenary, I can quit my family and private concerns at a moments warning. There are many matters necessary for me to settle before I could leave home with any tolerable convenience, and many things, the providing of which would run me to an unnecessary expence, if I am not called to the Field."

14 Ibid., vol. 7, 2-20-1777. To Col. William Crawford. "I regret exceedingly the loss of your two Brother's, and thank you for your kind offer of serving me in any business I may have West of the Alleganies; but my time is so constantly taken up and ingrossed by public matters, that I scarce bestow a thought on my private Affairs, beyond my Family at Mount Vernon."

15 Ibid., vol. 28, 6-30-1786. To George William Fairfax. "'Till my Country called my services to the field, in which I spent almost nine years, I acted in every respect for you as I should have done for myself. But after bidding adieu to my family and home, to which I never expected to return if the smiles of Heaven should prove unpropitious, a general wreck of my affairs as well as yours, took place."

16 Ibid., vol. 2, 7-20-1758. To Martha Parke Custis. "We have begun our march for the Ohio. A courier is starting for Williamsburg, and I embrace the opportunity to send a few words to one whose life is now inseparable from mine. Since that happy hour when we made our pledges to each other, my thoughts have been continually going to you as another Self. That an all-powerful Providence may keep us both in safety is the prayer of your ever faithful and affectionate friend."

Ibid., vol. 3, 6-18-1775.to Martha Washington. "My Dearest: I am now set down to write to you on a subject, which fills me with inexpressible concern, and this concern is greatly aggravated and increased, when I reflect upon the uneasiness I know it will give you. It has been determined in Congress, that the whole army raised for the defence of the American cause shall be put under my care, and that it is necessary for me to proceed immediately to Boston to take upon me the command of it.

"You may believe me, my dear Patsy, when I assure you, in the most solemn manner that, so far from seeking this appointment, I have used every endeavor in my power to avoid it, not only from my unwillingness to part with you and the family, but from a consciousness of its being a trust too great for my capacity, and that I should enjoy more real happiness in one month with you at home, than I have the most distant prospect of finding abroad, if my stay were to be seven times seven years. But as it has been a kind of destiny, that has thrown me upon this service, I shall hope that my undertaking it is designed to answer some good purpose. You might, and I suppose did perceive, from the tenor of my letters, that I was apprehensive I could not avoid this appointment, as I did not pretend to intimate when I should return. That was the case. It was utterly out of my power to refuse this appointment, without exposing my character to such censures, as would have reflected dishonor upon myself, and given pain to my friends. This, I am sure, could not, and ought not, to be pleasing to you, and must have lessened me considerably in my own esteem. I shall rely, therefore, confidently on that Providence, which has heretofore preserved and been bountiful to me, not doubting but that I shall return safe to you in the fall. I shall feel no pain from the toil or the danger of the campaign; my unhappiness will flow from the uneasiness I know you will feel from being left alone. I therefore beg, that you will summon your whole fortitude, and pass your time as agreeably as possible. Nothing will give me so much sincere satisfaction as to hear this, and to hear it from your own pen. My earnest and ardent desire is, that you would pursue any plan that is most likely to produce content, and a tolerable degree of tranquillity; as it must add greatly to my uneasy feelings to hear, that you are dissatisfied or complaining at what I really could not avoid.

"As life is always uncertain, and common prudence dictates to every man the necessity of settling his temporal concerns, while it is in his power, and while the mind is calm and undisturbed, I have, since I came to this place (for I had not time to do it before I left home) got Colonel Pendleton to draft a will for me, by the directions I gave him, which will I now enclose. The provision made for you in case of my death will, I hope, be agreeable.

"I shall add nothing more, as I have several letters to write, but to desire that you will remember me to your friends, and to assure you that I am, with the most unfeigned regard, my dear Patsy, your affectionate,…"

Ibid., vol. 3, 6-23-1775. "My Dearest: As I am within a few minutes of leaving this city, I would not think of departing from it with out dropping you a line, especially as I do not know whether it may be in my power to write again till I get to the camp at Boston. I go fully trusting in that providence, which has been more bountiful to me than I deserve and in full confidence of a happy meeting with you some time in the fall. I have no time to add more as I am surrounded with company to take leave of me. I return an unalterable affection for you which neither time or distance can change my best love to Jack and Nelly and regard for the rest of the family; conclude me with the utmost truth and Sincerety, Yr. entire."

17 Ibid., vol. 3, 6-20-1775, To John Augustine Washington, " Dear Brother: I am now to bid adieu to you, and to every kind of domestick ease, for a while. I am Imbarked on a wide Ocean, boundless in its prospect, and from whence, perhaps, no safe harbour is to be found. I have been called upon by the unanimous Voice of the Colonies to take Command of the Continental Army. ...I shall hope that my Friends will visit and endeavor to keep up the spirits of my Wife as much as they can, as my departure will, I know, be a cutting stroke upon her; and on this account alone, I have many very disagreeable sensations. I hope you and my sister (although the distance is great) will find as much leisure this Summer, as to spend a little time at Mount Vernon."

18 Ibid., vol. 7, 1-13-1777. To Robert Morris. " Dear Sir: If amidst a multiplicity of Important matters, you could suffer a trivial one to Intrude, I should thank you most heartily, for taking a Letter or two of mine, when you do your own, by the Southern Mail, and forwarding of them, as oppertunity offers, to the Camp. I have long since drop'd all private corrispondance with my friends in Virginia, finding it incompatable with my public business. A Letter or two from my Family are regularly sent by the Post, but very irregularly received, which is rather mortifying, as it deprives me of the consolation of hearing from home, on domestick matters."

19 Ibid., vol. 28, 11-20-1785. To Lund Washington. "However unlucky I may have been in Crops, &c. of late years, I shall always retain a grateful sense of your endeavors to serve me; for as I have repeatedly intimated to you in my Letters from Camp, nothing but that entire confidence which I reposed, could have made me easy under an absence of almost nine years from my family and Estate, or could have enabled me, consequently, to have given not only my time, but my whole attention to the public concerns of this Country for that space."

20 Washington's concern for his brothers was always evident. See Ibid., vol. 27, 1-22-1784. To James Nourse. WGW, vol. 27, 6-11-1783. To Lund Washington. WGW, vol. 8, 6-1-1777. To John Augustine Washington. WGW, vol. 37, 9-22-1799. To Burgess Ball. "Dear Sir: Your letter of the 16th. instt. has been received, informing me of the death of my brother. [Charles Washington.]The death of near relations always produces awful and affecting emotions, under whatsoever circumstances it may happen. That of my brother's has been so long expected, and his latter days so uncomfortable to himself, must have prepared all around him for the stroke; though painful in the effect. I was the *first*, and am now the *last*, of my fathers Children by the second marriage who remain. when I shall be called upon to follow them, is known only to the giver of life. When the summons comes I shall endeavour to obey it with a good grace. Mrs. Washington has been, and still is, very much indisposed, but unites with me in best wishes for you, Mrs. Ball and family." Ibid., vol. 37, 12-10-1776. To Lund Washington. "Matters to my view, but this I say in confidence to you, as a friend, wears so unfavourable an aspect (not that I apprehend half so much danger from Howes Army, as from the disaffection of the three States of New York, Jersey and Pennsylvania) that I would look forward to unfavorable Events, and prepare Accordingly in such a manner however as to give no alarm or suspicion to any one; as one step towards it, have my Papers in such a Situation as to remove at a short notice in case an Enemy's Fleet should come up the River. When they are removd let them go immediately to my Brothers in Berkeley." Ibid., vol. 28, 2-13-1784. To George Mason. "Dr. Sir: My brother John [John Augustine Washington] is much in want of four, five or six hundred pounds which he is desirous of borrowing on Interest. If it is in your power to supply him I will become security for the fulfilment of his agreement. He seems to have little expectation that money in these times, can be had at the common interest; and his own words will best express what he is willing to allow." He also sought to provide a quality education for other members of his extended family Ibid., vol. 35, 11-16-1796. To Tobias Lear. "Mr. Dandridge (as I presume he has informed you) applied, without encouragement, to the Reverend Mr. Medor of this City (one of the Moravian Clergy) for the Speedy admission of Maria [Anna Maria, daughter of George Augustine Washington] into the S[c]hool for young Ladies, at Bethlehem. Since then, I have written to the Principal of that School, The Revd. Mr. Venvleck, [Reverend Jacob Van Vleck] but have not received his answer. When it comes I will forward it to you. ...Washington Custis has got settled at Princeton College, and I think under favourable auspices, but the change from his former habits is so great and sudden; and his hours for study so much increased beyond what he has been accustomed to, that though he promises to be attentive, it is easy to be perceived he is not at all reconciled to it yet." Ibid., vol. 35, 4-7-1796. Ibid., vol. 33, 9-21-1794. Ibid., vol. 35, 4-15-1787.

21 Ibid., vol. 29, 5-7-1787. To Lund Washington. "I need not tell you, because a moment's recurrence to your own accounts will evince the fact, that there is no source from which I derive more than a sufficiency for the daily calls of my family, except what flows from the collection of old debts, and scanty and precarious enough, God knows this is. My estate for the last 11 years has not been able to make both ends meet. I am encumbered now with the deficiency. I mention this for no other purpose than to shew that however willing, I am not able to pay debts unless I could sell land, which I have publicly advertised without finding bidders."
Ibid., vol. 29, 10-29-1787. To Mathew Carey. "Sir: The last post brought me your letter of the 22d. your application to me for the loan of £100 is an evidence of your unacquaintedness with my inability to lend money. To be candid, my expenditures are never behind my income, and this year (occasioned by the severest drouth that ever was known in this neighborhood) instead of selling grain which heretofore has been my principal source of revenue it is not £500 that will purchase enough for the support of my family. after this disclosure of my situation you will be readily persuaded that inclination to serve without the means of accomplishing it, is of little avail. This however is the fact so far as it respects the point in question."
Ibid., vol. 36, 10-2-1797. To Thomas Law. "My expences are so great and my resources so small, that it is but little in my power to promote such plans as you advocate. To clear me out of Philadelphia, and to lay in a few necessaries for my family, I sold two valuable tracts of land in the State of Pennsylvania a short time before I left the City. for 22,000 dollars; and since my arrival have sold other lands in Virginia the proceeds of all which (so far at least as hath been received) are nearly expended. To encourage however a Hotel at the Capitol, I authorise you if the plan is likely to succeed, on the terms you have suggested to put my name down to five Shares."
Ibid., vol. 37, 1210-1799. To James Anderson. "And It is hoped, and will be expected, that more effectual measures will be pursued to make butter another year; for it is almost beyond belief, that from 101 Cows actually reported on a late enumeration of the Cattle, that I am obliged to *buy butter* for the use of my family."

1023

22 Ibid., vol. 29, 2-15-1787. To Mary Washington. "Hond. Madam: In consequence of your communication to George[Augustine] Washington, of your want of money, I take the (first safe) conveyance by Mr. John Dandridge to send you 15 Guineas, which believe me is all I have, and which indeed ought to have been paid many days ago to another, agreeable to my own assurances. I have now demands upon me for more than 500 £, three hundred and forty odd off of which is due for the tax of 1786; and I know not where or when, I shall receive one shilling with which to pay it. In the last two years I made no crops. In the first I was obliged to buy corn and this year have none to sell, and my wheat is so bad, I cannot either eat it myself nor sell it to others, and Tobacco I make none. Those who owe me money cannot or will not pay it without suits, and to sue is to do nothing; whilst my expences, not from any extravagance, or an inclination on my part to live splendidly, but for the absolute support of my family and the visitors who are constantly here, are exceedingly high; higher indeed than I can support without selling part of my estate, which I am disposed to do, rather than run in debt, or continue to be so; but this I cannot do, without taking much less than the lands I have offered for sale are worth. This is really and truely my situation. I do not however offer it as any excuse for not paying you what may really be due; for let this be little or much, I am willing, however unable, to pay to the utmost farthing; but it is really hard upon me when you have taken every thing you wanted from the Plantation by which money could be raised, when I have not received one farthing, directly nor indirectly from the place for more than twelve years, if ever, and when, in that time I have paid, as appears by Mr. Lund Washington's accounts against me (during my absence) Two hundred and sixty odd pounds, and by my own account Fifty odd pounds out of my own Pocket to you, besides (if I am rightly informed) every thing that has been raised by the Crops on the Plantation. Who to blame, or whether any body is to blame for these things I know not, but these are facts; and as the purposes for which I took the Estate are not answered, nor likely to be so, but dissatisfaction on all sides have taken place, I do not mean to have any thing more to say to your Plantation or negros since the first of January, except the fellow who is here, and who will not, as he has formed connections in this neighborhood, leave it. As experience has proved him, I will hire. Of this my intention, I informed my brother John sometime ago, whose death I sincerely lament on many accounts, and on this painful event condole with you most sincerely. I do not mean by this declaration to withhold any aid or support I can give from you; for whilst I have a shilling left, you shall have part, if it is wanted, whatever my own distresses may be. What I shall then give, I shall have credit for; now I have not, for tho' I have received nothing from your Quarter, and am told that every farthing goes to you, and have moreover paid between 3 and 4 hundred pounds besides out of my own pocket, I am viewed as a delinquent, and considered perhaps by the world as [an] unjust and undutiful son. My advice to you, therefore, is to do one of two things with the Plantation. Either let your grandson Bushrod Washington, to whom the land is given by his Father, have the whole interest there, that is, lands and negros, at a reasonable rent; or, next year (for I presume it is too late this, as the overseer may be engaged) to let him have the land at a certain yearly rent during your life; and hire out the negros. This would ease you of all care and trouble, make your income certain, and your support ample. Further, my sincere and pressing advice to you is, to break up housekeeping, hire out all the rest of your servants except a man and a maid, and live with one of your children. This would relieve you entirely from the cares of this world, and leave your mind at ease to reflect undisturbedly on that which ought to come. On this subject I have been full with my Brother John, and it was determined he should endeavor to get you to live with him. He alas is no more, and three, only of us remain. My house is at your service, and [I] would press you most sincerely and most devoutly to accept it, but I am sure, and candor requires me to say, it will never answer your purposes in any shape whatsoever. For in truth it may be compared to a well resorted tavern, as scarcely any strangers who are going from north to south, or from south to north, do not spend a day or two at it. This would, were you to be an inhabitant of it, oblige you to do one of 3 things: 1st, to be always dressing to appear in company; 2d, to come into [the room] in a dishabille, or 3d, to be as it were a prisoner in your own chamber. The first you'ld not like; indeed, for a person at your time of life it would be too fatiguing. The 2d, I should not like, because those who resort here are, as I observed before, strangers and people of the first distinction. And the 3d, more than probably, would not be pleasing to either of us. Nor indeed could you be retired in any room in my house; for what with the sitting up of company, the noise and bustle of servants, and many other things, you would not be able to enjoy that calmness and serenity of mind, which in my opinion you ought now to prefer to every other consideration in life. If you incline to follow this advice, the House and lots on which you now live you may rent, and enjoy the benefit of the money arising therefrom as long as you live. This with the rent of the land at the little falls [of the Rappahannock] and the hire of your negros, would bring you in an income which would be much more than sufficient to answer all your wants and make ample amends to the child you live with; for myself I should desire nothing; if it did not, I would most cheerfully contribute more. A man, a maid, the phaeton and two horses, are all you would want. To lay in a sufficiency for the support of these would not require ? of your income, the rest would purchase every necessary you could possibly want, and place it in your power to be serviceable to those with whom you may live, which no doubt would be agreeable to all parties.

"There are such powerful reasons in my mind for giving this advice that I cannot help urging it with a degree of earnestness which is uncommon for me to do. It is, I am convinced, the only means by which you can be happy. The cares of a family, without any body to assist you; the charge of an estate the profits of which depend upon wind, weather, a good overseer, and honest man, and a thousand other circumstances, cannot be right or proper at your advanced age, and for me, who am absolutely prevented from attending to my own plantations, which are almost within call of me, to attempt the care of yours, would be folly in the extreme; but [by] the mode I have pointed out, you may reduce your income to a certainty, be eased of all trouble, and if you are so disposed, may be perfectly happy; for happiness depends more upon the internal frame of a person's own mind, than on the externals in the world. Of the last, if you will pursue the plan here recommended, I am sure you can want nothing that is essential. The other depends wholly upon yourself, for the riches of the Indies cannot purchase it.

Mrs. Washington, George and Fanny join me in every good wish for you, and I am, honored madame, your most dutiful and aff. son."

23 Ibid., vol. 37. AND NOW

"First To my Nephew Bushrod Washington and his heirs (partly in consideration of an intimation to his deceased father while we were Bachelors, and he had kindly undertaken to superintend my Estate during my Military Services in the former War between Great Britain and France, that if I should fall therein, Mount Vernon (then less extensive in domain than at present) should become his property) ...

Third And whereas it has always been my intention, since my expectation of having Issue has ceased, to consider the Grand children of my wife in the same light as I do my own relations, and to act a friendly part by them; more especially by the two whom we have reared from their earliest infancy, namely: Eleanor Parke Custis, and George Washington Parke Custis. ...

"Fourth Actuated by the principal already mentioned, I give and bequeath to George Washington Parke Custis, the Grandson of my wife, and my Ward, and to his heirs, the tract I hold on four mile run in the vicinity of Alexandria, containing one thousd. two hundred acres, more or less, and my entire Square, number twenty one, in the City of Washington.

Lastly I constitute and appoint my dearly beloved wife Martha Washington, My Nephews William Augustine Washington, Bushrod Washington, George Steptoe Washington, Samuel Washington, and Lawrence Lewis, and my ward George Washington Parke Custis (when he shall have arrived at the age of twenty years) Executrix and Executors of this Will and testament, In the construction of which it will readily be perceived that no professional character has been consulted, or has had any Agency in the draught; and that, although it has occupied many of my leisure hours to digest, and to through it into its present form, it may, notwithstanding, appear crude and incorrect. But having endeavoured to be plain, and explicit in all the Devises, even at the expence of prolixity, perhaps of tautology, I hope, and trust, that no disputes will arise concerning them; but if, contrary to expectation, the case should be otherwise from the want of legal expression, or the usual technical terms, or because too much or too little has been said on any of the Devises to be consonant with law, My Will and direction expressly is, that all disputes (if unhappily any should arise) shall be decided by three impartial and intelligent men, known for their probity and good understanding; two to be chosen by the disputants, each having the choice of one, and the third by those two. Which three men thus chosen, shall, unfettered by Law, or legal constructions, declare their Sense of the Testators intention; and such decision is, to all intents and purposes to be as binding on the Parties as if it had been given in the Supreme Court of the United States."

24   Joseph Fields, *Worthy Partner: The Papers of Martha Washington* (Westport: Greenwood Press, 1994). p.224 footnote, "About the middle of June, 1789, the President developed a fever, followed by tenderness over the left thigh. Swelling and inflammation soon followed. Dr. Bard and two other consultants were unable to make a diagnosis. Consideration was given to the fact that the President might have contracted anthrax. As the swelling progressed, so did the discomfort until as last he was in excruciating pain. Cherry Street, in front of his home, was roped off to prevent the noisy wagons and carts from disturbing his rest. By the 20th the swelling "pointed" into an abscess or carbuncle. It was lanced and drained, whereupon the fever began to subside. For about three weeks it was difficult for him to move about or sit without discomfort. His condition gradually improved, but still continued to drain during September."

To Mercy Otis Warren New York, June the 12th 1790

...During the President sickness, the kindness which everybody manifested, and the interest which was universally taken in his fate, were really very affecting to me. He seemed less concerned himself as to the event, than peraps almost any other almost any other person in ye united states.

...But for the ties of affection which attract me so strongly to my near connections and worthy friends, I should feel myself indeed much weaned from all enjoyments of this transitory life. ...

In passing down the vale of time, and in journeying through such a mutable world as that in which we are placed, we must expect to meet with a great and continual mixture of afflictions and blessings. This a mingled cup which an overruling providence undoubtedly dispenses to us for the wises and best purposes. – and as you justly observe, shall we shortsighted mortals dare to arraign the decrees of eternal wisdom – that you and your may always be under the kind of protection and guardianship of the providence is the sincere wish of Footnote

On May 10, 1790, The President complained of "a bad cold." The cold increased in severity within the next two days. He then developed symptoms of pneumonia and for the next several days his physical condition rapidly deteriorated. Four physicians were called into attendance. They despaired of his life, and it became widely known throughout the city that he was dangerously ill, that he might not survive. On the morning of May 15th his breathing became labored. Those nearest him felt the end was near. Suddenly about 4:00 P.M. his fever suddenly dropped and he developed profuse perspiration. His condition improved rapidly and by the 20th of May he was considered out of danger. His convalescence continued for a period of six weeks.

To Janet Livingston Montgomery

Phila. January the 29th

...I am thank god now recovering.

The decision to be inoculated for the smallpox was often hard to make. *WGW*, vol. 3, 4-20-1771. *WGW*, vol. 4, 4-3291776. The yellow fever epidemic in Philadelphia was also a great concern since it was the seat of the government. *WGW*, vol. 33, 10-14-1793. To the Postmaster General. Sir: The numerous and various reports which I have lately received from people who were not possessed of any *accurate* information with respect to the State of the malignant fever with which Philadelphia is so unfortunately afflicted, and my intention being to return thither, or to its neighbourhood, about the first of next month, have induced me to ask this information from you, and I beg you will advise me as well of the State of the fever in Phil⸤delphia, as whether it has extended itself in its vicinity, German town &c., to which last I have heard it has reached.

Taking it for granted, that the fever will not have entirely disappeared in the City of Philadelphia, and the Place become quite purified, so as to admit the members of Congress to meet there, with safety by the first of December, what accomodations could be had for them in Germantown, if it should be free from infection? If however, this place should be thought unsafe or improper, what other has been in contemplation, for the next Session of Congress? Full information of these matters, and of the prevailing sense of those who have had an opportunity of Judging and are best acquainted with the true Situation of things, in and about Philadelphia, is what I very much want, as the accounts we receive here are so opposite and unsatisfactory that we know not on which to rely.

By report, we learn, that Mr. Willing (president of the Bank) Mr. John Ross, Mr. Jonathan Sergeant, Mr. Howell, Colo. Franks and many others of our acquaintance have fallen victims to the fatal fever. that near 4,000 have died and that the disorder is more violent than ever. Is this a faithful representation? I hope your family are out of the way of this dreadful contagion, and that you and Mrs. Pickering are well. with esteem and regard I am etc.

P.S. What sort of a place is Reading, and how would it answer for the accommodation of Congress the ensuing Session.

WGW, vol. 3, 2-15, 1773. To Burwell Bassett. "Mrs. Washington, Patsy Custis and Jack, who is now here, are much as usual, and the family not sicklier than common. Hoping this will find you perfectly restored, and the rest of the good folks of Eltham in better health than when you wrote last, I am with best wishes to Mrs. Bassett, yourself and the children, in which all here join." p.168 .

From John Parke Custis

Mount Airy June 9th . 1776

"My dear Mamma,

The receipt of your kind letter… gave Me the sincerest pleasure to hear You are in so fair a Way of getting favorably through the Smalpox: - the small Danger attending that Disorder by Inoculation when the patients follow the Directions of their Phycian,… I do with the truest affection congratulate you on and thank God for your recovery" p.180.

To Bartholomew Dandridge, November the 2d 1778, "…I am very sorry to head that my Mamma has been so unwell and thank god that she has recovered again –from MW"

25   *WGW*, vol. 29, 5-5-1787. To Robert Morris, "Dear Sir; When your favor of the 23d. Ulto. was sent here from the Post Office, I was at Fredericksburg (to which place I had been called, suddenly, by Express) to bid, as I was prepared to expect, the last adieu to an honoured parent, and an affectionate Sister whose watchful attention to my Mother during her illness had brought to death's door. The latter I hope is now out of danger, but the former cannot long Survive the disorder which has reduced her to a Skeleton, tho' she is somewhat amended." Martha Washington wrote of her grandson (George Washington Parke Custis) to Fanny Bassett Washington from Mount Vernon on February 25th 1788, "I cannot say but it makes me miserable if ever he complains let the cause be ever so trifeling- I hope the almighty will spare him to me." In Joseph E. Fields, *"Worthy Partner": The Papers of Martha Washington* (Westport, Connecticut: Greenwood Press, 1994), p. 205. *WGW*, vol. 28, 4-25-1785. To William Grayson. "…into that part of the country I am hurried by an express which is just arrived with the accot. of the deaths of the mother and Brother of Mrs. Washington, in the last of whose hands (Mr. B. Dandridge) the embarrassed affairs of Mr. Custis had been placed, and call for immediate attention."

26   Ibid., vol. 1, 5-29-1754. To Robert Dinwiddie. "I have a Constitution hardy enough to encounter and undergo the most severe tryals, and, I flatter myself, resolution to Face what any Man durst, as shall be prov'd when it comes to the Test, which I believe we are upon the Borders off."

27   Ibid., vol. 2, 3-4, 1758. To Col. John Stanwix. "I have never been able to return to my command, since I wrote to you last, my disorder at times returning obstinately upon me, in spite of the efforts of all the sons of Æsculapius, whom I have hitherto consulted. At certain periods I have been reduced to great extremity, and have now too much reason to apprehend an approaching decay, being visited with several symptoms of such a disease. I am now under a strict regimen, and shall set out to-morrow for Williamsburg to receive the advice of the best physicians there. My constitution is certainly greatly impaired, and as nothing can retrieve it, but the greatest care and the most circumspect conduct…."

28   Ibid., vol. 31, 6-15-1790. To David Stuart. "These public meetings and a dinner once a week to as many as my table will hold, with the references *to* and *from* the different Departments of State, and *other* Communications with *all* parts of the Union is as much, if not more, than I am able to undergo; for I have already had within less than a year, two *severe* attacks; the last worse than the first; a third more than probable, will put me to sleep with my fathers; at what distance this may be I know not. Within the last twelve months I have undergone more, and severer sickness than thirty preceding years afflicted me with, put it all together. I have abundant reason however to be thankful that I am so well recovered; though I still feel the remains of the violent affection of my lungs. The cough, pain in my breast, and shortness in breathing not having entirely left me. I propose in the recess of Congress to visit Mount Vernon; but when this recess will happen is beyond my ken, or the ken I believe of any of its members."

29   Ibid., vol. 5, 5-31-1776. To John Augustine Washington. Mrs. Washington is now under Innoculation in this City; and will, I expect, have the Small pox favourably, this is the 13th day, and she has very few Pustules; she would have wrote to my Sister but thought it prudent not to do so, notwithstanding there could be but little danger in conveying the Infection in this manner. She joins me in love to you, her, and all the little ones. I am, with every Sentiment of regard."

Ibid., vol. 11, 3-11-1778 "Lord Fairfax (as I have been told) after having bowed down to the grave, and in a manner shaken hands with death, is perfectly restored, and enjoys his usual good health, and as much vigour as falls to the lot of Ninety."

Ibid., vol. 37, 5-3-1781. To Dr. William Shippen. " Dear Sir: As Mrs. Washington never receiv'd the Jallop and Calomel you promised her. As the Small Pox, by my last advices from home, has got into my Family, and I suppose not less than three hundred Persons to take the disorder, I must beg you to furnish the bearer with so much of the above Articles for my use as you shall judge necessary;"

Ibid., vol. 27, 7-10-1783. To George William Fairfax, "Mrs. Washington enjoys an incompetent share of health; Billious Fevers and Cholic's attack her very often, and reduce her low; at this moment she is but barely recovering from one of them; at the same time that she thanks Mrs. Fairfax and you for your kind suggestion of Doctr. James's Annaliptic Pills, she begs you both to accept her most Affectionate regards; she would have conveyed these in a letter of her own, with grateful acknowledgments of Mrs. Fairfax's kind remembrance by Mr. Lee, if her health would have allowed it."

Ibid., vol. 27, 11-3-1784. To Reverend William Gordon, "In my absence I had a very sickly family, but no deaths. Mrs. Washington has been very unwell, Miss Custis very ill, and your friend *Tub* [George Washington Parke Custis] a good deal reduced by a diarrhea, he has got perfectly well, and is as fat and saucy as ever. Mrs. Washington is pretty well recovered, but Miss Custis remains in a puny state. the family unite in best wishes for you,"

Ibid., vol. 28, 12-8-1784. To Marquis de Lafayette. "Nothing of importance has occurred since I parted with you; I found my family well, and am now immersed in company...."

Ibid., vol. 28, 2-7-1785. To David Humphreys, "Mrs. Washington enjoys but indifferent health. My nephew Geo. A. Washington has been buffetting the seas from clime to clime, in pursuit of health, but, poor fellow! I believe in vain. At present, if alive, I expect he is at Charleston. All the rest of my family are perfectly well, and join me in best wishes for you...."

Ibid., vol. 28, 7-25-1785. To Marquis de Lafayette. "Mrs. Washington has but indifferent health; and the late loss of her mother, and only brother Mr. Barthw. Dandridge (one of the Judges of our Supreme Court) has rather added to her indisposition. My mother and friends enjoy good health. George has returned after his peregrination thro' the West Indies, to Bermuda, the Bahama Islands, and Charlestown; at the last place he spent the winter. He is in better health than when he set out, but not quite recovered: He is now on a journey to the Sweet Springs, to procure a stock sufficient to fit him for a matrimonial voyage in the Frigate F. Bassett, on board which he means to embark at his return in October: how far his case is desperate, I leave you to judge, if it is so, the remedy however pleasing at first, will certainly be violent."

Ibid., vol. 28, 10-1-1785. To Jonathan Trumbull. "My principal pursuits are of a rural nature, in which I have great delight, especially as I am blessed with the enjoyment of good health. Mrs. Washington on the contrary is hardly ever well, but thankful for your kind remembrance of her, and joins me in every good wish for you, Mrs. Trumbull and your family."

30   Ibid., vol. 3, 3-26-1762. To Gov. Horatio Sharpe. "Sir: Be so good as to pardon the liberty I presume to take in recommending to your Excellency's notice the Revd. Mr. West; a young Gentn. lately entered into Holy Orders, of a good Family, and unexceptionable Morals; this with truth I can venture to certifie as he is a neighbour of mine, and one of those few of whom every body speaks well. At present he is engagd to officiate as Curate to the Revd. Doctr. Swift of Port Tobo.; who it seems is in the last Stage of a Consumption, and attempting by a Voyage to England, the recovery of his health, but, should he fail in this (as most probably he will) and the Parish become vacant by his death. Mr. West woud think himself very happy in the honour of your presentment of him to the Cure, and I am fully persuaded that his endeavours woud merit the favour."

Ibid., vol. 3, 8-28, 1774. To Mrs. Sarah Bomford. "Mrs. Washington also thanks you for your polite notice of her and begs your acceptance of her Compliments and that you will take the trouble of presenting them to Mrs. Savage at the same time to whom please also to make a tender of my best respects and inform her (as I have also done in a former Letter wch. I suppose to be miscarried) that the black Wax on my Letter was occasion'd by the death of Miss Custis whom we were unhappily deprivd of in June...."

Ibid., vol. 3, 6-18-1775. To Mrs. Martha Washington. "My Dearest: I am now set down to write to you on a subject, which fills me with inexpressible concern, and this concern is greatly aggravated and increased, when I reflect upon the uneasiness I know it will give you. ...As life is always uncertain, and common prudence dictates to every man the necessity of settling his temporal concerns, while it is in his power, and while the mind is calm and undisturbed, I have, since I came to this place (for I had not time to do it before I left home) got Colonel Pendleton to draft a will for me, by the directions I gave him, which will I now enclose. The provision made for you in case of my death will, I hope, be agreeable." WGW, vol. 37, 9-22-1799.   To Burges Ball. "Dear Sir: Your letter of the 16th. instt. has been received, informing me of the death of my brother [Charles Washington]. The death of near relations always produces awful and affecting emotions, under whatsoever circumstances it may happen. That of my brother's has been so long expected, and his latter days so uncomfortable to himself, must have prepared all around him for the stroke; though painful in the effect. I was the *first*, and am now the *last*, of my fathers Children by the second marriage who remain. when I shall be called upon to follow them, is known only to the giver of life. When the summons comes I shall endeavour to obey it with a good grace."

Ibid., vol. 37, 11-6-1781 To Jonathan Trumbull Jr. "My dear Sir: I came here in time to see Mr. Custis breathe his last. About Eight o'clock yesterday Evening he expired. The deep and solemn distress of the Mother, and affliction of the Wife of this amiable young Man, requires every comfort in my power to afford them; the last rights of the deceased I must also see performed; these will take me three or four days; when I shall proceed with Mrs. Washington and Mrs. Custis to Mount Vernon. As the dirty tavern you are now at cannot be very comfortable; and in spite of Mr. Sterne's observation the House of Mourning not very agreeable; it is my wish, that all of the Gentn of my family, except yourself, who I beg may come here and remain with me; may proceed on at their leizure to Mount Vernon, and wait for me there. Colo. Cobb will join you on the road at the Tavern we breakfasted at (this side Ruffens). My best wishes attend the Gentn. and with much sincerity and affectn. I remain,"

Ibid., vol. 23, 11-18-1781. To Robert Hanson Harrison. "I thank you for your kind Congratulations on the Capitulation of Cornwallis....Mr. Custis' death has given much distress in this family."

Ibid., vol. 29, 1-10-1787.   To Bushrod Washington. "My Dear Bushrod: I condole most sincerely with you, my Sister and family, on the death of my Brother [John Augustine Washington]. I feel most sensibly for this event; but resignation being our duty, to attempt an expression of my sorrow on this occasion would be as feebly described, as it would be unavailing when related."

Ibid., vol. 29, 2-15-1787. To Mary Washington. "I informed my brother John sometime ago, whose death I sincerely lament on many accounts, and on this painful event condole with you most sincerely."

Ibid., vol. 29, 3-25-1787.   "My Dear Marquis: I have lately lost a Brother (Colo. John Augt. Washington which I mention to account for the black Seal of this letter) the rest of my friends, and every individual in the Family are tolerably well and join most cordially in every *vow* that can contribute to the health and happiness of Madam La Fayette yourself and family. Esqr Tub will soon be able to offer you his own homage as he begins to write very prettily. I have no expression that can convey to you the warmth of my friendship and affectionate attachment. Adieu."

Ibid., vol. 33, 10-27-1793. To William Pearce. "The season has been remarkably sickly, generally, but my family, except a few slight touches of the intermittant fever, chiefly among the blacks, have shared less of it, than I find from report, has been felt in most other places."

Ibid., vol. 34, 5-10-1795. To William Pearce. "I am sorry to find by your last reports that there has been two deaths in the family since I left Mount Vernon; and one of them a young fellow. I hope every necessary care and attention was afforded him. I expect little of this from McKoy, or indeed from most of his class; for they seem to consider a Negro much in the same light as they do the brute beasts, on the farms; and often times treat them as inhumanly."

Ibid., vol. 37, 9-22-1799. To Samuel Washington. "Dear Sir: Your letter, announcing the death of my Brother, came to hand last night. One from Colo. Ball, informing me of that event, arrived the evening before. I very sincerely condole with your mother and the family on this occasion. But as death, in this case, regular in its approaches; and evident, long before it happened; she, and all of you, must have been prepared for the stroke. Of course, though painful, it must have fallen much lighter on that account."

31   Ibid., vol. 3, 8-28, 1774. To Mrs. Sarah Bomford. "…it would be a wrong to suffer the small pittance she reservd to herself the time of her unhappy Marriage to fall into the hands of a v — n [villain]who has not only endeavourd to wrong of it but would I suppose deprive her of the very means of Existance if he could do it."

Ibid., vol. 29, 11-15-1786. To Mrs. Anne Ennis. Ibid., vol. 33, 9-6-1794. To Peter Trenor. Ibid., vol. 29, 4-28-1788. To Comte de Rochambeau. "My dear Count: I have just received the letter which you did me the honor to write to me on the 18th of January; and am sorry to learn that the Count de Grasse, our gallant coadjutor in the capture of Cornwallis, is no more. Yet his death is not, perhaps, so much to be deplored as his latter days were to be pitied. It seemed as if an unfortunate and unrelenting destiny pursued him, to destroy the enjoyment of all earthly comfort. For the disastrous battle of the 12th of April, the loss of the favor of his king, and the subsequent connection in marriage with an unworthy woman, were sufficient to have made him weary of the burden of life."

32   Ibid., vol. 33, 9-14, 1794. To Elizabeth Parke Custis. "My dear Betcy: Shall I, in answer to your letter of the 7th. instant say, when you are as near the *Pinnacle* of happiness as your sister Patcy conceives herself to be; or when your candour shines more conspicuously than it does in *that* letter, that I will *then*, comply with the request you have made, for my Picture?

No: I will grant it without either: for if the latter was to be a preliminary, it would be sometime I apprehend before *that* Picture would be found pendant *at* your breast; it not being within the bounds of probability that the contemplation of an inanimate thing, whatever might be the reflections arising from the possession of it, can be the *only* wish of your heart.

Respect may place it among the desirable objects of it, but there are emotions of a softer kind, to wch. the heart of a girl turned of eighteen, is susceptible, that must have generated much warmer ideas, although the fruition of them may, apparently, be more distant than those of your Sister's.

Having (by way of a hint) delivered a sentiment to Patty, [Martha Parke Custis, who became Mrs. Thomas Peter] which may be useful to her (if it be remembered after the change that is contemplated, is consummated) I will suggest another, more applicable to yourself.

Do not then in your contemplation of the marriage state, look for perfect felicity before you consent to wed. Nor conceive, from the fine tales the Poets and lovers of old have told us, of the transports of mutual love, that heaven has taken its abode on earth: Nor do not deceive yourself in supposing, that the only mean by which these are to be obtained, is to drink deep of the cup, and revel in an ocean of love. Love is a mighty pretty thing; but like all other delicious things, it is cloying; and when the first transports of the passion begins to subside, which it assuredly will do, and yield, oftentimes too late, to more sober reflections, it serves to evince, that love is too dainty a food to live upon *alone*, and ought not to be considered farther than as a necessary ingredient for that matrimonial happiness which results from a combination of causes; none of which are of greater importance, than that the object on whom it is placed, should possess good sense, good dispositions, and the means of supporting you in the way you have been brought up. Such qualifications cannot fail to attract (after marriage) your esteem and regard, into wch. or into disgust, sooner or later, love naturally resolves itself; and who at the sametime, has a claim to the respect, and esteem of the circle he moves in. Without these, whatever may be your first impressions of the man, they will end in disappointment; for be assured, and experience will convince you, that there is no truth more certain, than that all our enjoyments fall short of our expectations; and to none does it apply with more force, than to the gratification of the passions. You may believe me to be always, and sincerely Your Affectionate."

33   Ibid., vol. 3, 4-3-1773. "Dear Sir: I am now set down to write to you on a Subject of Importance, and of no small embarrassment to me. My Son in Law and Ward, Mr. Custis, has, as I have been informed, paid his Addresses to your Second Daughter, and having made some progress in her Affections has required her in Marriage. How far a union of this Sort may be agreeable to you, you best can tell, but I should think myself wanting in Candor was I not to acknowledge, that, Miss Nellie's amiable qualifications stands confess'd at all hands; and that, an alliance with your Family, will be pleasing to his. [Note: Eleanor Calvert. She married John Parke Custis Feb. 3, 1774, and, after his death, Dr. David Stuart. By her first husband she had Eleanor Parke (Nellie) Custis, two other daughters, and George Washington Parke Custis.]

"This acknowledgment being made you must permit me to add Sir, that at this, or in any short time, his youth, inexperience, and unripened Education, is, and will be insuperable obstacles in my eye, to the completion of the Marriage. As his Guardian, I conceive it to be my indispensable duty (to endeavor) to carry him through a regular course of Education, many branches of which, sorry I am to add, he is totally deficient of; and to guard his youth to a more advanced age before an Event, on which his own Peace and the happiness of another is to depend, takes place; not that I have any doubt of the warmth of his Affections, nor, I hope I may add, any fears of a change in them; but at present, I do not conceive that he is capable of bestowing that due attention to the Important consequences of a marriage State, which is necessary to be done by those, who are Inclin'd to enter into it; and of course, am unwilling he should do it till he is. If the Affection which they have avowd for each other is fixd upon a Solid Basis, it will receive no diminution in the course of two or three years, in which time he may prosecute his Studies, and thereby render himself more deserving of the Lady, and useful to Society; If unfortunately, (as they are both young) there should be an abatement of Affection on either side, or both, it had better precede, than follow after, Marriage.

"Delivering my Sentiments thus, will not, I hope, lead you into a belief that I am desirous of breaking off the Match; to postpone it, is all I have in view; for I shall recommend it to the young Gentleman with the warmth that becomes a man of honour, (notwithstanding he did not vouchsafe to consult either his Mother or me, on the occasion) to consider himself as much engaged to your Daughter as if the indissoluble Knot was tied; and, as the surest means of effecting this, to stick close to his Studies, (in which I flatter myself you will join me) by which he will, in a great measure, avoid those little Flirtations with other Girls which may, by dividing the Attention, contribute not a little to divide the Affection.

"It may be expected of me perhaps to say something of Fortune, But, to discend to particulars, at this time, may seem rather premature. In general therefore I shall inform you that Mr. Custis's Estate consists of about 15,000 Acres of Land, good part of it adjoining to the City of Williamsburg, and none 40 Miles from it; several Lotts in the said City; between two and three hundred Negroes; and about Eight or ten thousand Pounds upon Bond, and in the hands of his Merchants. This Estate he now holds Independent of his Mother's Dower, which will be an acquisition to it at her Death, and upon the whole such an one as you will readily acknowledge ought to entitle him to a handsome Portion in a Wife; But, as I should never require a Child of my own to make a Sacrifice of himself to Interest, so, neither do I think it incumbent on me to recommend it as a Guardian; but as I know you are full able, I should hope, and expect, if we were now upon the point of Settling these Preliminaries, that you would also be willing to do something genteel by your Daughter.

"At all times when you, Mrs. Calvert, or the young Ladies can make it convenient to favor us with a visit we should be happy in seeing you at this place. Mrs. Washington and Miss Custis join me in respectful Compliments and I am, dear Sir, etc."

Ibid., vol. 3, 4-25, 1773. To Burwell Bassett, "Mrs. Washington, in her letter to Mrs. Bassett, informs her of Jack Custis's engagement with Nelly Calvert, second daughter of Benedict Calvert, Esq., of Maryland. I shall say nothing further therefore on the subject than that I could have wished b e had postponed entering into that engagement till his studies were finished. Not that I have any objection to the match, as she is a girl of exceeding good character; but because I fear, as he has discovered much fickleness already, that he may either change, and therefore injure the young lady; or that it may precipitate him into a marriage before, I am certain, he has ever bestowed a serious thought of the consequences; by which means his education is interrupted and he perhaps wishing to be at liberty again before he is fairly embarked on those important duties."

34   Ibid., vol. 3, 2-15, 1773. To Burwell Bassett. "Our celebrated fortune, Miss French, whom half the world was in pursuit of, bestowed her hand on Wednesday last, being her birthday (you perceive I think myself under a necessity of accounting for the choice) upon Mr. Ben Dulany, who is to take her to Maryland in a month from this time. Mentioning of one wedding puts me in mind of another, tho' of less dignity; this is the marriage of Mr. Henderson (of Colchester) to a Miss More (of the same place) remarkable for a very frizzled head, and good singing, the latter of which I shall presume it was that captivated our merchant."

35   Ibid., vol. 11, 3-11-1778. *WGW*, vol. 9, 8-18-1777. To Capt. Thomas Nelson, Jr. Ibid., vol. 23, 2-8-1782. To William Fitzhugh. Ibid., vol. 27, 10-2-1783. To Lt. Col. Tench Tilghman. Ibid., vol. 28, 9-1-1785. To Marquis de Lafayette. Ibid., vol. 28, 8-10-1786. To Charles Armand-Tuffin. Ibid., vol. 37, 12-27-1780. To Lt. Col. Alexander Hamilton. Ibid., vol. 3, 2-15-1773. To Burwell Bassett. Ibid., vol. 3, 12-15-1773. To Reverend Myles Cooper. Ibid., vol. 2, 9-30-1757.

36   Ibid., vol. 5-23-1785. To Burwell Bassett. *Cf.* Ibid., vol. 27, 9-20-1783.

37   Fitzpatrick, *Diaries of George Washington*, Nov. 17, 1751. vol. 1, p. 25.

38   Fields, *Worthy Partner*, p. 152-153.

39   Fields, *Worthy Partner*, p. 153-154 footnote. "Mrs. Washington is alleged to have written a sentimental letter to Eleanor Calvert Custis. The text of the letter first appeared in Lossing, *Mary and Martha, the Mother and the Wife of George Washington*, p. 126, New York 1886. The text as given by Lossing is as follows: "My dear Nelly: God took from my Daughter when June Roses were blooming. He has now given me another daughter about her age when winter winds are blowing, to warm my heart again. I am as happy as one so afflicted and blest can be. Pray receive my benediction and a wish that you may long live the loving, wife of my happy son and a loving daughter of your affectionate mother, M Washington." Martha Washington did not attend the marriage ceremony, since she was in mourning and did not wish to detract from the gaiety of the occasion. Lossing states George Washington was instructed to present the letter to the bride immediately after the ceremony...."

40   *Cf.* Willard Sterne Randall, *George Washington A Life* (New York: Henry Holt and Company, 1997) p. 256.

41   See John Corbin, *The Unknown Washington: Biographic Origins of the Republic* (New York: Charles Scribner's Sons, 1930), pp. 51-75. Corbin writes, "In 1877, two love letters written by Washington to Mrs. George William Fairfax were published for the first time and caused a sensation which, though masked for decades by biographers, has steadily increased. They had been found among Mrs. Fairfax's papers upon her death in England in 1811, and her kinsfolk in America had treasured them through two generations in the awed silence of Victorian propriety. The Fairfaxes were Washington's nearest friends until shortly before the Revolution, their house, Belvoir, being five miles down the Potomac from Mount Vernon and in full view of it. Though George Fairfax was eight years older, the two men had been intimate, surveying electioneering and fox-hunting together, from the time Washington, aged sixteen, came to live with his brother Lawrence. There is abundant evidence, notably in Washington's diaries, that Mrs. Fairfax and Mrs. Washington were neighborly always, dining and visiting with each other, and were the first to offer sympathy in illness and bereavement. The letters were written in 1758, when Washington, aged twenty-six, was engaged to Martha Custis. Though they are reticently worded and indeed seem intentionally vague and obscure, they are now generally accepted as showing that he was passionately in love with Mrs. Fairfax. One of them speaks of the 'the recollection of a thousand tender passages that I could wish to obliterate, till I am bid to revive them'—and what follows, as we shall see, is proof enough that these passages were not with Martha. In two later letters, one of them written only nineteen months before he died, he declared that the moments he had spent in her company were 'the happiest in my life.' We have here, obviously, something very different from the legend of idyllic love which the Victorians wove about the lives of George and Martha Washington. Whether it is in the way of scandal depends upon the nature of the 'thousand tender passages.' That question has obsessed recent biographers." Pp. 51-52. Corbin then adds, "Every record of Washington's married life bespeaks affection and happiness, a loyal and unflagging co-operation in the high art of living—but also bespeaks, though in the highest sense of the word, a marriage of convenience. Knowing what we do of his instinctive wisdom and integrity, we may well believe that, so far as he as in honor bound, he did not conceal or embellish the state of his heart. It was literal truth

that their lives were 'inseparable'; nor can we doubt that he cherished her always as 'another self.' In a very different view are his two letters of the following September to Sally, letters which she treasured to her death. Paul Leicester Ford's objection that the evidence of their authenticity 'has not been produced' is scarcely worthy of consideration. In writing the first daft of his little biography, Captain Cary, a devoted antiquary and genealogist, had access to Sally's papers and copied them. The final draft was prepared as an answer to Ford, but was still in manuscript when Captain Cary died…In such matters family tradition is of great weight, and in this case it is of the clearest and most substantial. It is sustained, moreover, by evidence both external and internal, which is beyond the power of the cleverest impostor to invent. The letters as also that written in 1757 on Washington's return from the front to Mount Vernon fall in perfectly with all the evidence as to his mood and movements, most of which is now for the first time assembled; and they bear the stamp of his character and habit down to the unrevised sentence-structure and elaborate punctuation. The autograph originals could scarcely be more convincing." P. 64.

42   Howard F. Bremer, *George Washington 1732-1799: Chronology—Documents—Bibliographical Aids* (Dobbs Ferry, N. Y.: Oceana Publications, 1967), p. 1. Bremer writes, "December 17, 1748, "George William Fairfax married Sarah ("Sally") Cary. George Washington, two years her junior, fell in love with her and probably remained so all his life."

43   Hughes, *George Washington: The Human Being* vol. 1.
       "The Reverend Doctor Moncure D. Conway makes a statement that is impressive in view of the emphasis unjustifiably laid on the imaginary doctrine that Washington was brought up in an atmosphere of intense religion: "In his many letters to his adopted nephew and young relatives, he admonishes them about their morals, but in no case have I been able to discover any suggestion that they should read the Bible, keep the Sabbath, go to church, or any warning against Infidelity."

44   An important consideration that we must consider is why Washington did not do what his mother and various others of his progenitors had done, namely, placed a testimony of trust in Christ in their last will and testament. Washington did not do this. From this, some would infer that he was not a Christian, and that it thus stands as a proof of a belief in Deism. And as to his death without the presence of a clergyman, and thus the reception of the Eucharist, we find that this question was raised by Washington's grandson, George Washington Parke Custis. GWP Custis in *Recollections* asks the question, "It may be asked, Why was the ministry of religion wanting to shed its peaceful and benign luster upon the last hours of Washington? Why was he, to whom the observances of sacred things were ever primary duties throughout life, without their consolations in his last moments? We answer, circumstances did not permit. It was but for a little while that the disease assumed so threatening a character as to forbid the encouragement of hope; yet, to stay that summons which none may refuse, to give still farther length of days to him whose 'time-honored life' was so dear to mankind, prayer was not wanting to the throne of Grace. Close to the couch of the sufferer, resting her head upon that ancient book, with which she had been wont to hold pious communion a portion of every day, for more than a half a century, was the venerable consort, absorbed in silent prayer, and from which she only arose when the mourning group prepared to lead her from the chamber of the dead. Such were the last hours of Washington." p. 477.

45   Humphreys, *Life of George Washington*, p.6-8
       "By a domestic tutor (which was then generally & is now frequently the mode of education practiced in that part of the Continent) he was betimes instructed in the principles of grammar, the theory of reasoning, on speaking, the science of numbers, the elements of geometry, & the highest branches of mathematics, the art of mensuration, composing together with the rudiments of geography, history & the studies which are not improperly termed "the humanities." In the graceful accomplishments of dancing, fencing, riding & performing the military exercises he likewise made an early & conspicuous proficiency. In short, he was carefully initiated into whatever might be most useful to him, in making his way to preferment in the British army or navy, for which he was designed.
       "Though he was rather unsure & reserved in his appearance; he was frequently animated & fluent in conversation & always descreed in conduct. & In the performance of any business committed to him, he was active, indefatigable, persevering. [He was noted for] His tall stature, for he was clear six feet high without his shoes; his gentiel deportment, for he had something uncommonly noble in his manners; his modest behaviour, which, without being the result of ill-becoming diffidence.
       "[He was] remarkably robust & athletic. I several times heard him say, he never met any man who could throw a stone to so great a distance as himself; and, that when standing in the valley beneath the natural bridge in Virginia, he was thrown one up to that stupendous arch.
       "[H]unting & Surveying – the first gave him activity & boldness – the second the means of improving the *Coup d'oeil* in judging of military positions & measuring by the eye the distance between different places. – Patience & perseverance in reconnoitering – how often he spent whole days on horseback, braving the ravages of the most violent heat & cold that ever was experienced in our climate.
       "As it was the design of his Father that he should be bred for an Officer in the British navy, his mental acquisitions & exterior accomplishments were calculated to give him distinction in that profession. <GW note: it was rather the wish of my eldest brother (on whom the several concerns of the family devolved) that this should take place & the matter was contemplated by him – My father died with I was only 10 years old.> At 15 years old, he was entered a midshipman on board of the [blank] & his baggage prepared for embarkation: but the plan was abandoned in consequence of the earnest solicitations of his Mother.

46   Custis, *Recollections* p. 131.

47   Willard Sterne Randall, *George Washington A Life* (New York: Henry Holt and Company, 1997) p. 256. Sterne writes: "Washington was not a deeply religious man. Once he left his Bible-thumping mother's household he may never have taken Anglican communion again." We believe Sterne is wrong on all counts in this unsubstantiated, but characteristically dogmatic remark.

48   Sawyer, *Washington*, pp. 166-168.

49   *WGW*, vol. 1, 5-6-1755. To Mary Washington.

50   http://memory.loc.gov/mss/mgw/mgw2/014/0190013.jpg

51   Ibid., vol. 29, 8-15-1787.

52   Sawyer, *Washington*, Vol 2 p. 157.

53   *WGW,* vol. 2, 9-30-1757.

54   Ibid., vol. 29, 2-15-1787.

55   Washington was much concerned for the financial welfare of his mother, and made it clear in this letter to Benjamin Harrison that her children would ensure that she was taken care of, even to their own personal detriment: " …confident I am that she has not a child that would not divide the last sixpence to relive her from *real* distress. This she has been repeatedly assured of by me; and all of us I am certain would feel much hurt, at having our mother a pensioner, while we had the means of supporting her; but in fact she has an ample income of her own. I lament accordingly that your letter, which conveyed the first hint of this matter, did not come to my hands sooner; but I request, in pointed terms, if the matter is now in agitation in your Assembly, that all proceedings on it may be stopped, or in case of a decision in her favor, that it may be done away and repealed at my request." (to Benjamin Harrison, New Windsor, March 21, 1781) Ibid., vol. 21, 3-21-1781. One of the traditions of Mary Washington's impact on George's adult life from childhood training is the anecdote entitled, "Let The Pen-Knife take the place of the Hatchet." This is again unable to be substantiated, but it has been preserved as part of the legends of Washington's childhood. Reverend Littell writes,

    Unquestionably, a truth-loving disposition was imparted this child "virtuously brought to lead a godly and a Christian life," though we discard the story of the hatchet and the cherry tree. But there is a story of a pen-knife which illustrates at one and the same time his filial affection, his military spirit, and his good Christian hope in the final success of his country's just cause.

    "When Washington was about fifteen year old, his brother obtained for him a midshipman's warrant in the British navy. The boy's kit had been carried aboard, and he himself was on the point of following it, when a messenger from his mother overtook him and brought her final word that he was not to go. He went back home- back to school and mathematics which he did not like. In reward for his obedience, his mother presented him with a good pen-knife says, 'always obey your superiors,' All his life he carried that gift and from time to time he was accustomed to tell the story to some of his friends. One day at Valley Forge, when the half-naked men had eaten no meat for many days, and when once more Congress had failed to provide or even suggest a way for getting food and clothes, Washington wrote out his resignation as Commander-in-Chief of the Army. Among the generals present was Henry Knox, who spoke out reminding him of the pen-knife. 'What has that to do with it?' asked Washington. 'You were always to obey your superiors,' answered Knox; 'You were commanded to lead this army. No one has commanded you to cease leading it.' Washington paused and then answered: 'There is something in that. I will think it over.' Half an hour later, he tore his resignation to pieces." Reverend John Stockton Littell, D.D. *George Washington: Christian Stories of Cross and Flag* No 1 (Keene, N. H.: The Hampshire Art Press, 1913).

56   *WGW,* vol. 21, 3-21-1781. To Benjamin Harrison, "My Dr. Sir: Upon my return to this place last night, I met your private and friendly letter of the 25th. of February. I do not delay a moment to thank you for the interesting matter contained in it, and to express my surprize at that part which respects a pension for my mother. True it is, I am but little acquainted with her *present* situation, or distresses, if she is under any. As true it is, a year or two before I left Virginia (to make her latter days comfortable, and free from care) I did, at her request but at my own expence, purchase a commodious house, garden and Lotts (of her own choosing) in Fredericksburg, that she might be near my Sister Lewis, her only daughter; and did moreover agree to take her Land and negroes at a certain yearly rent, to be fixed by Colo. Lewis and others (of her own nomination) which has been an annual expence to me ever since, as the Estate never raised one half of the rent I was to pay. Before I left Virginia, I answered all her calls for money; and since that period, have directed my Steward to do the same. Whence her distresses can arise therefore, I know not, never having received any complaint of his inattention or neglect on that head; tho' his inability to pay my own taxes, is such I know, as to oblige me to sell negroes for this purpose; the taxes being the most unequal (I am told) in the world, some persons paying for things of equal value, four times, nay ten times, the rate that others do. But putting these things aside, which I could not avoid mentioning, in exculpation of a presumptive want of duty on my part; confident I am that she has not a child that would not divide the last sixpence to relieve her from *real* distress. This she has been repeatedly assured of by me: and all of us, I am certain, would feel much hurt, at having our mother a pensioner, while we had the means of supporting her; but in fact she has an ample income of her own. I lament accordingly that your letter, which conveyed the first hint of this matter, did not come to my hands sooner; but I request, in pointed terms if the matter is now in agitation in your assembly, that all proceedings on it may be stopped, or in case of a decision in her favor, that it may be done away, and repealed at my request."

57   Ibid., vol. 29, February 15, 1787.

58   Lossing, *Mary and Martha*, pp. 64 - 65. When Lafayette praised the illustrious character of her son affirming the plaudits that he would receive from future generations, she characteristically responded with "I am not surprised at what George has done, for he was always a good boy."; Sawyer, *Washington* vol. 2 p. 155. Ibid., vol. 28, 5-10-1786. To Marchionesse de Lafayette. "My Mother will receive the compliments you honor her with, as a flattering mark of your attention; and I shall have great pleasure in delivering them myself."

59   Ibid., vol. 29, 6-17-1788. My dear Sir: I received your letter of the 25th. of May, just when I was on the eve of a departure for Fredericksburgh to pay a visit to my mother from whence I returned only last evening." Ibid., vol. 29, 6-19-1788. To Richard Henderson. "Sir: Your favour of the 5th. instant was lodged at my house, while I was absent on a visit to my Mother."

60   Fitzpatrick, *Diaries of George Washington* vol. 1, January 1760, "Abt. Noon it began snowing, the Wind at So. West, but not Cold; was disappointed of seeing my Sister Lewis and getting a few things which I wanted our of the Stores. Returnd in the Evening to Mother's - all alone with herp. 115. Ibid., vol. 27, 2-18-1784. To Annis Boudinot Stockton. "Dr. Madam: The intemperate weather, and the very great care which the post riders take of themselves, prevented your Letter of the 4th. of last month from reaching my hands 'till the 10th. of this: I was then in the very act of setting off on a visit to my aged mother, from whence I am just returned. These reasons I beg leave to offer, as an apology for my silence 'till now." Ibid., vol. 27, 1-22-1784. To Charles Thomson. "We have been so fast locked in Snow and Ice since Christmas, that all kinds of intercourse have been suspended; and a duty which I owed my Mother, and intended 'ere this to have performed, has been forced to yield to the intemperance of the Weather: but, as this again must submit to the approaching Sun, I shall

soon be enabled, I expect, to discharge that duty on which Nature and inclination have a call; and shall be ready afterwards to welcome my friends to the shadow of this Vine and Fig tree."

61 Returning from Williamsburg, he stopped at his mother's home. See also vol. 2, April 11, 1773.

62 See Lossing, *Mary and Martha*, p. 67. *WGW*, vol. 29, 5-5-1787. To Robert Morris, "Dear Sir; When your favor of the 23d. Ulto. was sent here from the Post Office, I was at Fredericksburg (to which place I had been called, suddenly, by Express) to bid, as I was prepared to expect, the last adieu to an honoured parent, and an affectionate Sister whose watchful attention to my Mother during her illness had brought to death's door. The latter I hope is now out of danger, but the former cannot long Survive the disorder which has reduced her to a Skeleton, tho' she is somewhat amended." *WGW*, vol. 30, 3-6-1789. To Richard Conway. "I would have done it this day but being to set off tomorrow for Fredericksburg in order probably to discharge the last Act of *personal* duty, I may, (from her age) ever have it in my power to pay my Mother, it would be very inconvenient for me."

63 Ibid., vol. 30, 9-13-1789.

64 Ibid., vol. 29, 2-15-1787. "Further, my sincere and pressing advice to you is, to break up housekeeping, hire out all the rest of your servants except a man and a maid, and live with one of your children. This would relieve you entirely from the cares of this world, and leave your mind at ease to reflect undisturbedly on that which ought to come. On this subject I have been full with my Brother John, and it was determined he should endeavor to get you to live with him. He alas is no more, and three, only of us remain. ...Mrs. Washington, George and Fanny join me in every good wish for you, and I am, honored madame, your most dutiful and aff. son."

65 Ibid. vol. 29, 2-15-1787.

66 Fitzpatrick, *Diaries of George Washington*, under June 10, 1788, vol. III, p. 366.

67 Humphreys, *Life of George Washington* p. 24-25.

    The success of this campaign having restored tranquility on the frontiers of the Middle States and the health of Washington having become extremely debilitated by an inveterate pulmonary complaint, in 1759 he resigned his military appointment. The tender regret of the Virginia Line & the affectionate regard of their Commander might be illustrated by authentic documents.

    His health was gradually restored; he married Mrs. Custis, a handsome & amiable young widow, possessed of an ample jointure; and settled himself as a planter & farmer on the estate where he now resides in Fairfax County. After some years, he gave up planting tobacco & went altogether into the farming business. Before the war he raised [*blank*] bushels of wheat, in one year. <GW note: I believe about 7,000 Bushels of Wheat and 10,000 bushels of Indian corn which was more the staple on the farm> Although he has confined his own cultivation to this domestic tract of about 10,000 acres, yet he possesses excellent lands, in large quantities, in several other Counties. His judgment in the quality of soils, his command of money to avail himself of purchases, and his occasional employment in early life as a Surveyor, gave him opportunities of making advantageous locations, many of which are much improved.

    In the interval that took place, from the War between Great Britain & the House of Bourbon which ended in 1763, to the civil war between Great Britain & her Colonies which commenced in 1775, he cultivated the arts of peace. He was constantly a Member of the Assembly, a Magistrate of his County, & a Judge of the Court. He was elected Delegate to the first Continental Congress in 1774, as well as to that assembled in the year following.

68 Littell, *Washington: Christian* "Washington was married by the Reverend David Mossom, who, though born in London, is called on his epitaph the first American ever ordained to the priesthood. Bishop Meade and Washington Irving say that the marriage took place at "White House" the residence of the bride's family, but Bishop Tucker in 1896 said that the evidence points to St. Peter's Church, New Kent. In 1903 were published the views of Mrs. Pryor and Woodrow Wilson, both favorable to the Church at New Kent. Dr. Wilson said: "He was married to Martha Custis on the 6th of January, 1759. The sun shone very bright that day, and there was the fine glitter of gold, the brave show of resplendent uniforms, in the little church where the marriage was solemnized. Officers of his Majesty's service crowded there, in their gold lace and scarlet coats to see their comrade wedded; the new Governor, Francis Fauquier, himself came, clad as befitted his rank; and the bridegroom took the sun not less gallantly than the rest, as he rode, in blue and silver and scarlet beside the coach and six that bore his bride homeward amidst the thronging friends of the country side. The young soldier's love of a gallant array and a becoming ceremony were satisfied to the full, and he must have rejoiced to be so brave a horseman on such a day."

69 *WGW*, vol. 2, 5-1-1759. "Gentln. The Inclos'd is the Ministers Certificate of my Marriage with Mrs. Martha Custis, properly as I am told, Authenticated, You will therefore for the future please to address all your Letters which relate to the Affairs of the late Danl. Parke Custis Esqr. to me, as by Marriage I am entitled to a third part of that Estate, and Invested likewise with the care of the other two thirds by a Decree of our Genl. Court which I obtain'd in order to strengthen the Power I before had in consequence of my Wiles Administration."

70 Ibid., vol. 2, 9-20-1765.

71 See John Corbin, *The Unknown Washington: Biographic Origins of the Republic* (New York: Charles Scribner's Sons, 1930), pp. 51-75. Corbin says, "Every record of Washington's married life bespeaks affection and happiness, a loyal and unflagging co-operation in the high art of living—but also bespeaks, though in the highest sense of the word, a marriage of convenience."

72 Ibid., A few examples: vol. 2, 8-18-1769. Ibid., vol. 3, 2-20-1771. Ibid.,, vol. 32, 10-7-1792. Ibid,., vol. 35, 11-28-1796.

73 Ibid., vol. 29, 10-25-1786. p. 170

From John Parke Custis, Mount Airy August 21st 1776

"My dearest Mamma

... She is now thank God as well as can be expected and the pleasure of her Daughter give Her compensates for the Pain She suffered. ... that the General may obtain a compleat Victory over his Enemys, which I sincerely pray God may be the Case.

... I wrote to the General the last two Posts. I shall write you again next Post, and ask Him to stand with yourself for my little Lady. ...

In the summer of 1775 a belief persisted that he (Governor Dunmore) intended to sail up the Potomac and capture Mrs. Washington, but nothing came of it."

21. p.183

To Burwell Bassett, Mount Vernon July the 18th 1780

"...we were sorry thar we did not see you at the Camp – there was not much pleasure thar the distress of the army and other difficultys th'o I did not know the cause, the pore General was so unhappy that it distressed me exceedingly. MW"

32. p.223-224

To Mercy Otis Warren, New York December the 26th 1789

"...for you know me well enough to do me the justice to beleive that I am only fond of what comes from the heart....

.... it is owing to this kindness of our numerous friends in all quarters that my new and unwished for situation is not indeed a burden to me. When I was much younger I should, probably, have enjoyed the inoscent gayeties of life as much as most my age; - but I had long since placed all the prospects of my future worldly happyness in the still enjoyments of the fireside at Mount Vernon-

I little thought when the war was finished, that any circumstances could possible have happened which would call the General into public life again. I had anticipated, that from this moment we should have been left to grow old in solitude and tranquility togather: that was, my Dear madam, the first and dearest wish of my heart; - but in that I have been disapointed; I will not, however, contemplate with too much regret disapointments that were enevitable, though the generals feelings and my own were perfectly in unison with respect to our predilections for privet life, yet I cannot blame him for having acted according to his ideas of duty in obaying the voice of his country. The consciousness of having attempted to do all the good in his power, and the pleasure of finding his fellow citizens so well satisfied with the disinterestedness of his conduct, will, doubtless, be some compensation for the great sacrifices which I know he has made; indeed in his journeys from Mount Vernon – to this place; in his late Tour through the eastern states, by every public and by every privet information which has come to him, I am persuaded that he has experienced nothing to make him repent his having acted from what he concieved to be alone a sense of indespensable duty: on the contrary, all his sensibility has been awakened in receiving such repeated and unequivocal proofs of sincear regards from all his country men. With respect to myself, I sometimes think the arrangement is not quite as it ought to have been, that I, who had much rather be at home should occupy a place with which a great many younger and gayer women would be prodigiously pleased. – As my grand children and domestic connections made a great portion of felicity which I looked indemnify me for the Loss of a part of such endearing society. I do not say this because I feel dissatisfied with my present station – no, God forbid: - for everybody and everything conspire to make me as contented as possable in it; yet I have too much of the vanity of human affairs to expect felicity from the splendid scenes of public life. – I am still determined to be cheerful and to be happy in whatever situation I may be, for I have also learnt from experianence that the greater part of our happiness or misary depends upon our dispositions, and not upon our circumstances; we carry the seeds of the one, or the other about with us, in our minds, wherever we go.

I have two of my grand children with me who enjoy advantages in point of education, and who, I trust by the goodness of providence, will continue to be a great blessing to me, my other two grand children are with thair mother in Virginia. –

...I wish you the best of Heavens blessings...MW"

45. p.371

To Janet Livingston Montgomery, Mount Vernon, April 5th

"... your affliction I have often marked and as often have keenly felt for you but my own experience has taught me that griefs like these can not be removed by the condolence of friends however sincere—If the mingling tears of numerus friends – if the sympathy of a Nation and every testimoney of respect of veneration paid to the memory of the partners of our hearts could afford consolation you and myself would experience it in the highest degree but we know that there is but one source from whence comfort can be derived under afflictions life ours To this we must look with pious resignation and with that pure confidence which our holy releigion inspires.

...but as you justly observe it is certainly a consolation and flattering to poor mortality to believe that we shall meet here after in a better place."

87. *WGW*, vol. 33, 9-25-1793. "My dear Sir: I have not written to you since we parted, but had just set down to do it when your letter of the 13th. instt. was brought to me from the Post Office in Alexandria.

"It gave Mrs. Washington, myself and all who knew him, sincere pleasure to hear that our little favourite had arrived safe, and was in good health at Portsmouth. We sincerely wish him a long continuance of the latter, that he may always be as charming and promising as he now is, and that he may live to be a comfort and blessing to you and an ornament to his Country; as a testimony of my affection for him, I send him a Ticket in the lottery which is now drawing in the Federal City; and if it should be his fortune to draw the Hotel it will add to the pleasure I have in giving it.

Note: Lincoln Lear.

"We remained in Philadelphia until the 10th. instr. It was my wish to have continued there longer; but as Mrs. Washington was unwilling to leave me surrounded by the malignant fever wch. prevailed, I could not think of hazarding her and the Children any longer by *my* continuance in the City the house in which we lived being, in a manner blocaded, by the disorder and was becoming every day more and more fatal; I therefore came off with them on the above day and arrived at this place the 14th. without encountering the least accident on the Road.

"You will learn from Mr. Greenleaf, that he has dipped deeply, in the concerns of the Federal City. I think he has done so on very advantageous terms for himself, and I am pleased with it notwithstanding on public ground; as it may give facility to the operations at that place, at the same time that it is embarking him and his friends in a measure which although it could not well fail under any circumstances that are likely to happen; may be considerably promoted by men of Spirit with large Capitols. He can, so much better than I, detail his engagements and the situation of things in and about the city that I shall not attempt to do it at this time.

"Mrs. Washington having decided to let Nelly Custis have her watch and chain, is disposed to receive substitutes in lieu thereof at about 25 guineas price; and leaves the choice of them to you. The plainness of the watch &ca. she will not object to. 120 dollars in Bank notes are inclose[d] for the purchase of them."

88. *WGW*, vol. 15, 5-28-1779. To Lt. Col. Nicholas Rogers. Dear Sir: A few days ago I was hond. with your polite and obliging favor of the 6th. Instt. accompanied by a Miniature picture of Mrs. Washington. I wish it was in my power to express as forcably as I feel, the lively sense I have of the repeated instances of your polite attention to her and myself. Such tribute as unfeigned thanks afford, is presented to you with much sincerity; and, if I knew how to make a more acceptable offering it should not be wanting.

Note: The miniature was of a size to fit a ring and, according to Roger's letter of Apr. 6, 1779, in the *Washington Papers* , showed Mrs. Washington in an Elizabethan ruff and hood.

"Difficult as it is to strike a likeness on so small a scale, it is the opinion of many that you have not failed in the present attempt. The dress is not less pleasing for being a copy of antiquity, it would be happy for us, if in these days of depravity the imitation of our ancestors were extensively adopted; their virtues wd. not hurt us.

Mrs. Washington joins me in a tender of best wishes for you and with much esteem etc.

91. *WGW*, vol. 3, 2-3-1771. To Reverend Jonathan Boucher. Rev'd. Sir: Colo. Robert Fairfax, with whom I have often talk'd, and who much approves, of Jacks intended Tour for Improvement, purposes to leave this on his return to England sometime in March; before his doing of which he is desirous of seeing Jacky and has instructed me to say, that he shou'd be very glad of seeing you with him. The warmth with which he has made a tender of his Services, and the pressing Invitation to make use of Leeds Castle as a home, in vacation time, are too obliging to be neglected; I shou'd be glad therefore if it cou'd suit you both to be over sometime before the last of this Month, or as soon, after the 10th. of March as may be, as I expect to be in Frederick, indeed am obli'g to be so, from the first of the Month to that time and, I do not know but Mrs. Washington may accompany me to my Brothers. His Horses shall attend you at any appointed time.

"Company, and the suddeness of the oppertunity, prevents my enlarging, or taking notice of the contents of your last Letter further than to say, that it never was my Intention that Jacky shou'd be restrained from proper Company; to prevent as much as possible his connecting with Store boys, and that kind of low loose Company who wou'd not be displeas'd at the debauchery of his Manners, but perhaps endeavour to avail themselves of some advantages from it, is all I had in view.

"Mrs. Washington requests the favour of you to get her 2 oz. of the Spirit of Ether, if such a thing is to be had in Annapolis, for Miss Custis, and send it by Price Posey. Our Love and best Wishes attend yourself and Jacky and I am Dr. Sir, etc."

74   See *WGW*, vol. 12, 9-23-1778. To John Augustine Washington. *WGW*, vol. 3, 7-27-1775; vol. 6, 9-22-1776. ; vol. 7, 7-4-1778. vol. 37, 4-2-1799. To Samuel Washington. *WGW*, vol. 36, 8-12-1798. To Thomas Peter.

75   Fields, *Worthy Partner*. p. 163 To Mr. Devenport Eltham, November 5th 1775

"I desire you will lett Mrs Bayly, that lives at west point have corn or wheat as she may want it, while her husband is ill and unable to provide for her, you may let her have a barrel of corn and half a barrel of wheat as sends for it and give her a fat hog."

p. 165 Washington paid ?39 –9d to Dr. John Witherspoon, president of The College of New Jersey, for the school of young Ramsay. See supra January 14, 1774, n. 4; Ledger B folio 47, *The Papers of George Washington*, DLC:GW

p.236 From Anonymous

I hope Madam that pity will direct your heart to grant the Boon I have ask'd & I shall, in deity bound ever pray.

Washington also cared for extended family members who were orphaned such as Sally Haney. *WGW*, vol. 31, 12-27-1790. To Elizabeth Haynie. *WGW*, vol. 34, 2-22-1795. To Robert Lewis. *WGW*, vol. 35, 6-26-1796. To Robert Lewis. A young neighboring student, Lawrence Posey. *WGW*, vol. 28, 6-16-1785. But if the family connection could not be established, the challenge for long term charity was decisively rejected. *WGW*, vol. 27, 9-25-1783. To Mrs. Ruthy Jones.

76   Custis, *Recollections*, p. 528, "He wore around his neck the miniature-portrait of his wife. This he had worn through all the vicissitudes of his eventful career, from the period of his marriage to the last days at Mount Vernon. Lossing's note adds, "This miniature could not have been painted earlier than the visit of C. W. Peale to Mount Vernon, in 1772, by whom it was probably executed. We have no account of any painter in miniature in the colonies previous to that time, except Taylor who painted small heads in water-colors, in Philadelphia, in 1760."

77   *WGW*, vol. 2, Diary 1760. January. Tuesday. 1. Visited my Plantations …And found Mrs. Washington upon my arrival broke out with the Meazles. Wednesday, 2d. Mrs. Barnes who came to visit Mrs. Washington yesterday returnd home in my Chariot, the weather being too bad to travil in an open Carriage, which, together with Mrs. Washington's Indisposition, confind me to the House and gave me an opportunity of Posting my Books and putting them in good order. Thursday, 3d. The Weather continuing Bad & ye same causes subsisting I confind myself to the House. Morris who went to work yesterday caught cold, and was laid up bad again, and several of the Family were taken with the Measles, but no bad Symptoms seemd to attend any of them. Hauled the Sein and got some fish, but was near being disappointd. of my Boat by means of an Oyster Man who had lain at my Landing and plagud me a good deal by his disorderly behaviour. Sunday, 6th. The Chariot not returng. time enough from Colo. Fairfax's we were prevented from Church. Mrs. Washington was a good deal better to day but the Oyster Man still continuing his Disorderly behavior at my Landing, I was oblig'd in the most preemptory manner to order him and his compy. away which he did not incline to obey till next morning.

78   Fields, *Worthy Partner*. Daniel McCarty and his wife, Sarah Ball McCarty. The residence, "Mount Air," was in the Pohick Creek area of Prince William County. They were close friends of the Washingtons and frequently visited and dined together. Both men were vestrymen of Truro Parish. They were also fox-hunting comrades. Washington was distantly related to both Daniel McCarty and his wife through the Ball family.

Ibid. p. 184

Anne Randolph Fitzhugh, wife of William Fitzhugh of "Chatham." Their daughter, Mary Lee Fitzhugh, was to marry Mrs. Washington's only grandson, George Washington Park Custis.

Ibid., p.228

To Colonel Clement Biddle

...the list of the things when he has collected them altogether she beggs to know if he has remembered the gin and liquers the General desires to have them sent and they may be the best kind-

Ibid., p.229

To Abigail Adams

... to Let Miss Smith come to dance with Nelly & Washington

WGW, vol. 28, 6-26-1785. To Reverend Stephen bloomer Balch. "Sir: My nephews are desirous of going to the Dancing School in Georgetown kept by Mr. Tarterson (I think his name is), and as it is my wish that they should be introduced into life with those qualifications which are deemed necessary, I consent to it. Sometime ago I expressed my approbation of their learning French, and a wish that when you had got your House in order to receive them, they might again board with you: Altho' I have no occasion [sic] the care, attention and kindness of Mr. Bailey to them, I conceive they can board at no place so eligably as at their Preceptors; for it is my wish that their morals as well as education may be attended to; and tho' I do not desire they should be deprived of necessary and proper amusements, yet it is my earnest request that they may be kept close to their studies."

79   January 16, 1768. At home all day at Cards—it snowing. "The entries for gains and losses at cards and other play are as carefully entered in Washington's accounts as all other income and expenditure. (1765, Jan. 'By Cash set aside for Card money L5.') Grouped through the years from 1772 to January 1, 1775, for cash won and lost at home, Fredericksburg, Williamsburg, Annapolis, and other places, the entries show a total loss of L78.5.9 and a corresponding gain of L72.2.6; a loss at play of L6.3.3 in four years." Diaries, I.246.) Washington had to worry of being addicted to gambling. Yet Washington was deeply concerned about Gambling in the military because of the many abuses it lead to.

80   Washington memorized the entire play of Cato—See Zall, Washington on Washington, p.8.

81   WGW, vol. 22, 7-19-1781. To Chevalier de Chastellux. "Dear Sir: You have taken a most effectual method of obliging me to accept your Cask of Claret, as I find, by your ingenious manner of stating the case, that I shall, by a refusal, bring my patriotism into question, and incur a suspicion of want of attachment to the French Nation, and of regard to you, [which. of all things I wish to avoid] I will not enter into a discussion of the point of divinity, as I [perceive] you are a Master at that Weapon. In short, my dear sir, my only scruple arises from a fear of depriving you of an Article that you cannot conveniently replace in this Country. You can only relieve me by promising to partake very often of that hilarity which a Glass of good Claret seldom fails to produce." He owned and operated his own Distillery. He knew the Indian love of Rum (to Queen Alquippa). His military strategy included arguing for Rum rather than Wine for his soldiers due to the matter of issues of weight and transportation. He exchanged Slaves for Rum in his early years. History by Reverend Morse, written by Humphreys—mentions that he drank beer, wine at dinner. A story in GWP Custis about toast and American Officer's misunderstanding. Whiskey Rebellion (Pres. W's trip—it is whiskey country—no need to bring wine). Standard practice to give rations of rum to soldiers. Story of Franklin and men for prayers to chaplain—more would come if when chapel was immediately before rum was given. Celebration with extra gil of rum for army. Yet GW's letters against drunkenness. Articles of war on drunkenness. There were examples of losses in battle at Brandywine due to sleeping drunken guard.

82   Between Jan 26th and Feb. 2nd the mutilated diary record says, "A Great Main of . . . . cks [Cock-fight] fought in Yorktown . . bween Glouster and York for 5 Pistoles each battle and 100 ye odd I left it with Colo. Lewis before it was decided and had part of his chariot to his house. . . .Fitzpatrick, Diaries, I. 36. There appears to be no other record of Washington indulging in this bloody sport after this one entry in his Diary from his earliest years.

83   Fields, "Worthy Partner, p. 177

84   Ibid., p.201

85   WGW, vol. 16, 10-17-1779. "As I do not at this time know where my Winter Quarters will be, or when I shall get into them. As I have little prospect of seeing my own home this Winter and Mrs. Washington desirous of coming to me before the Roads get bad and weather severe, I shall be obliged to you for enquiring and informing me, if she can hire lodgings in some genteel (but not a common boarding) house in Phila. till I know where I shall be fixed for the Winter."

86   See Mount Vernon website under Martha Washington.

87   WGW, vol. 2, 9-20-1759.

88   Ibid., vol. 3, 6-18-1775 To Martha Washington.

89   Ibid., vol. 28, 5-23-1785.

90   Ibid., vol. 29, 10-25-1786. To George Augustine Washington. "...if Mrs. Washington should survive me there is a moral certainty of my dying without issue, and should I be the longest liver, the matter in my opinion is almost as certain; for whilst I retain the reasoning faculties I shall never marry a girl; and it is not probable that I should have children by a woman of an age suitable to my own, should I be disposed to enter into a second marriage."

91   Fields, Worthy Partner, To John Dandridge from Mount Vernon April the 20th 1789. "My Dear John: I am truly sorry to tell that the General is gone to New York, — Mr Charles Thompson came express to him, on the 14th — when, or wheather he will ever come hom again god only knows, — I think it was much too late for him to go into publick life again, but it was not to be avoided, our family will be deranged as I must follow him."

92   Ibid., p. 219. To Fanny Bassett Washington from New York October the 23d 1789. "...I beg you will give me the worked muslin apron you have like my gown that I made just before I left home or worked muslin as I wish to make a petticoat of the two aprons — for my gown — Mrs Sims will give you a better account of the fashions that I can— I live a very dull life hear and know nothing that passes in the town — I never goe to the publick place — indeed I think I am more like a state prisoner than anything else, there is certain bounds set for me which I must not depart from — and as I can not doe as I like I am obstinate and stay at home a great deal -... my dear chil-

dren has had very bad colds but thank god they are getting better...."

93 Ibid., pp.223-224. To Mercy Otis Warren from New York December the 26th 1789. "...for you know me well enough to do me the justice to beleive that I am only fond of what comes from the heart.... it is owing to this kindness of our numerous friends in all quarters that my new and unwished for situation is not indeed a burden to me. When I was much younger I should, probably, have enjoyed the inoscent gayeties of life as much as most my age; - but I had long since placed all the prospects of my future worldly happyness in the still enjoyments of the fireside at Mount Vernon-

I little thought when the war was finished, that any circumstances could possible have happened which would call the General into public life again. I had anticipated, that from this moment we should have been left to grow old in solitude and tranquility togather: that was, my Dear madam, the first and dearest wish of my heart; - but in that I have been disapointed; I will not, however, contemplate with too much regret disapointments that were enevitable, though the generals feelings and my own were perfectly in unison with respect to our predilections for privet life, yet I cannot blame him for having acted according to his ideas of duty in obaying the voice of his country. The consciousness of having attempted to do all the good in his power, and the pleasure of finding his fellow citizens so well satisfied with the disinterestedness of his conduct, will, doubtless, be some compensation for the great sacrifices which I know he has made; indeed in his journeys from Mount Vernon – to this place; in his late Tour through the eastern states, by every public and by every privet information which has come to him, I am persuaded that he has experienced nothing to make him repent his having acted from what he concieved to be alone a sense of indespensable duty: on the contrary, all his sensibility has been awakened in receiving such repeated and unequivocal proofs of sincear regards from all his country men. With respect to myself, I sometimes think the arrangement is not quite as it ought to have been, that I, who had much rather be at home should occupy a place with which a great many younger and gayer women would be prodigiously pleased. – As my grand children and domestic connections made a great portion of felicity which I looked indemnify me for the Loss of a part of such endearing society. I do not say this because I feel dissatisfied with my present station – no, God forbid: - for everybody and everything conspire to make me as contented as possable in it; yet I have too much of the vanity of human affairs to expect felicity from the splendid scenes of public life. – I am still determined to be cheerful and to be happy in whatever situation I may be, for I have also learnt from experiance that the greater part of our happiness or misary depends upon our dispositions, and not upon our circumstances; we carry the seeds of the one, or the other about with us, in our minds, wherever we go.

"I have two of my grand children with me who enjoy advantages in point of education, and who, I trust by the goodness of providence, will continue to be a great blessing to me, my other two grand children are with thair mother in Virginia. –...I wish the best of Heavens blessings....".

94 *WGW*, vol. 36, 2-11-1798. To Sally Ball Hayne. "Miss Salley: I have received your letter of the 28th. of last month, and without enquiry at this time why you left Mr. Lewis's family or how you employ your time, I have requested him to furnish you with ten pounds to supply you with such necessaries as you may be in immediate want.

"But as you have no fortune to support you, Industry, oeconomy, and a virtuous conduct are your surest resort, and best dependance. In every station of life, these are commendable. In the one in which it has pleased Providence to place you, it is indispensably necessary that they should mark all your footsteps. It is no disparagement to the first lady in the Land to be constantly employed, at some work or another; to you, it would prove, in addition to a chaste and unsullied reputation the surest means of attracting the notice of some man with whom your future fortune will be united in a Matrimonial bond and without which it would be in vain to expect a person of worth. I wish you well and am Your friend."

95 Fields, *Worthy Partner*, p. 3. From Robert Carter Nicholas to Martha Custis, 7th August, 1757, "...how great Christian patience and resignation you submitted to your late misfortune;...",

96 Ibid., To Burwell Bassett Mount Vernon December 22d 1777, "... she has I hope a happy exchange – and only gone a little before us the time draws near when I hope we shall meet never more to part- if to meet our departed Friends and know them was certain we could have very little reason to desire to stay in this world where if we are at ease one hour we are in affliction days...."

"... my dear sister in her life time often mentioned my taking my dear Fanny if should be taken away before she grew up- If you will lett her come to live with me, I will with the greatest pleasure take her and be a parent and mother to her as long as I live – and will come down for her as soon as I come from the northward, ..."

97 Ibid., p. 152. to Martha Washington from John Parke Custis from Kings-College July 5, 1773, p. 152. "I generally get up about Six or a little after, dress myself & go to chappel, by the time that Prayers are over Joe has me a little Breakfast to which I sit down very contended after eating heartyly. I thank God, and go to my Studys, with which I am employed till twelve then I take a walk and return about one dine with the professors, & after dinner study till Six at which time the Bell always rings for Prayers they being over college is broak up, and then we take what Amusement we please. Things My dear Mother were going on in this agreeable Manner, till last Thursday, the day I receiv'd Pappa's melancholy Letter, giveing an account of my dear & only Sister's Death. I myself met the Post, & brought the sad Epistle to Doctor Cooper who I beg'd to open his Letter immediately, the Direction I did not know, but the Seal I knew too well to be deceived. My confusion & uneasiness on this occasion is better conceiv'd that exprest. Her case is more to be envied than pitied, for if we mortals can distinguish between those who are deserveing of grace & who are not, I am confident she enjoys that Bliss prepar'd only for the good & virtuous, let these consideration, My dear Mother have their due weight with you and comfort yourself with reflecting that she now enjoys in substance what we in this world enjoy in imagination & that there is no real Happiness on this side of the grave. I must allow that to sustain a shock of this kind requires more Philosophy than we in general are (possest) off, my Nature could not bear the shock. (illegible) sunk under the load of oppression, and hindered me from administering any consolation to my dear and nearest relation, this Letter is the first thing I've done since I received the melancholy News, & could I think my Presence wou'd be condusive to the Restoration of your Tranquility neither the distance nor the Fatigue of traveling could detain me a moment here. I put myself & Joe into deep Mourning & shall do (all) Honour in my power to the Memory of a deceas'd & well belov'd Sister, I will no longer detain you on a subject which is

painful to us both but conclude with beging you to remember you are a Christian and that we ought to submit with Patience to the divine Will and that to render you happy shall be the constant care of your effectionate and dutiful son. John Parke Custis"

98 *WGW*, vol. 2, 6-18-1769.

99 Custis, *Recollections*, p. 21.

100 *WGW*, vol. 3, 6-20-1773. "Dear Sir: It is an easier matter to conceive, than to describe the distress of this Family; especially that of the unhappy Parent of our Dear Patsy Custis, when I inform you that yesterday removed [*sic*] the Sweet Innocent Girl Entered into a more happy and peaceful abode than any she has met with in the afflicted Path she hitherto has trod. She rose from Dinner about four o'clock in better health and spirits than she appeared to have been in for some time; soon after which she was seized with one of her usual Fits, and expired in it, in less than two minutes without uttering a word, a groan, or scarce a sigh. This sudden, and unexpected blow, I scarce need add has almost reduced my poor Wife to the lowest ebb of Misery; which is encreas'd by the absence of her son, (whom I have just fixed at the College in New York from whence I returned the 8th Inst) and want of the balmy consolation of her Relations; which leads me more than ever to wish she could see them, and that I was Master of Arguments powerful enough to prevail upon Mrs. Dandridge to make this place her entire and absolute home. I should think as she lives a lonesome life (Betsey being married) it might suit her well, and be agreeable, both to herself and my Wife, to me most assuredly it would. It do not purpose to add more at present, the end of my writing being only to inform you of this unhappy change."

101 Fields, *Worthy Partner*, p. 170. John Parke Custis wrote to Martha on August 21 1776, "My dearest Mamma, … that the General may obtain a compleat Victory over his Enemys, which I sincerely pray God may be the Case.… I wrote to the General the last two Posts. I shall write you again next Post, and ask Him to stand with yourself for my little Lady.

102 Custis, *Recollections*, p. 255.

103 Fields, *Worthy Partner*,p. 221. To Abigail Smith Adams, November 4, 1789 "…I intended yesterday after the sermon to bring the children out with me on a visit to you, but the weather prevented me ."

104 Ibid., p. 217 n. 1. *Worthy Partner*, "Mrs. Washington was a strict disciplinarian with regard to "practice time," and insisted on four or five hours of practice each day. Nelly rebelled and cried bitterly, but to no avail."

105 *WGW*, vol. 28, 11-20-1785. To Lund Washington. "Before their marriage he and Fanny were both told that it would be very agreeable to Mrs. W. and myself, that they should make this House their home 'till the squalling and trouble of children might become disagreeable."

106 Moncure D. Conway, quoted in Rupert Hughes, *George Washington: The Human Being* vol. 1, p. 555.

107 The *Prayer Book* and Bible were important tools of education. Fields, *Worthy Partner*, p.217. To Fanny Bassett Washington July 1789 "…I wish you to take a prayer book yourself and give one to Hariot the other two to be given to Betty & Patty Custis- …" *WGW*, vol. 2, 10-12-1761. An order for the needs of the Washington family included the following: "A Small Bible neatly bound in Turkey, and John Parke Custis wrote in gilt Letters on the Inside of the cover. A Neat small Prayer Book bd. as above, with &ca. A Neat Small Bible b'd in Turkey and Martha Parke Custis wrote on the Inside in gilt Letters. A Small Prayer Book neat and in the same manner."

108 *WGW*, vol. 37, 12-30-1798. To David Stuart. "When the applications for Military appointments came to be examined at Philadelphia, it was pleasing to find among them, so many Gentlemen of family, fortune and high expectations, soliciting commissions; and not in the high grades.

"This, and a thorough conviction that it was a vain attempt to keep Washington Custis to any literary pursuits, either in a public Siminary, or at home under the direction of any one, gave me the first idea of bringing him forward as a Cornet of Horse. To this measure too I was induced by a conviction paramount in my breast, that if real danger threatened the Country, no young man ought to be an idle Spectator of its defence; and that, if a state of preparation would avert the evil of an Invasion, he would be entitled to the merit of proffered service, without encountering the dangers of War: and besides, that it might divert his attention from a matrimonial pursuit (for a while at least) to which his constitution seems to be too prone.

"But, though actuated by these ideas, I intended to proceed no farther in the business than to provide a vacancy in one of the Troops of light Dragoons, and to consult Mrs. Stuart and his Grandmother, as to their inclinations respecting his filling it, before any intimation of it should be given to him: But, Mr. Lear hearing the matter talked of, and not knowing that this was the ground on which I meant to place the appointment (if the arrangement met the President's approbation) wrote to Washington on the subject, in order to know if it would be agreeable to him, or not, to receive it.

"Under these circumstances (and his appearing highly delighted) concealment, I mean an attempt at it, would have proved nugatory. He stands arranged therefore a Cornet in the Troop to be Commanded by Lawrence Lewis (who I intended as his Mentor), Lawrence Washington junr. (of Chotanck) is the Lieutenant of the Troop. But all this it will be remembered is to be approved, first by the President, and consented to by the Senate to make it a valid act; and therefore, the less it is *publicly* talked of the better.

"Mrs. Washington does not seem to have the least objection to his acceptance of the Commission; but it rests with Mrs. Stuart to express her Sentiments thereon, and soon; as I requested the Secretary of War to forward the Commissions for *this* Troop of Light Dragoons, under cover to me.

"The only hesitation I had, to induce the caution before mentioned, arose from his being an only Son; indeed the only male of his Great great Grandfathers family; but the same Providence that wd watch over and protect him in domestic walks, can extend the same protection to him in a Camp, or the field of battle, if he should ever be in one."

109 *WGW*, vol. 28, 11-10-1785. To George William Fairfax. "As I am in the habit of giving you trouble, I will add a little more to what my last, I fear, may have occasioned. The two youngest children of Mr. Custis: the oldest a girl of six years, the other a boy a little turned of four live with me. They are both promising children; but the latter is a remarkable fine one and my intention is to give him a liberal education; the rudiments of which shall, if I live, be in my own family. Having premised this, let me next, my good Sir, ask if it is in your power conveniently, to engage a proper preceptor for him? at present, and for a year or two to come, much confinement would be improper for

him; but this being the period in which I should derive more aid from a man of Letters and an accomptant than at any other, to assist me in my numerous correspondences, and to extricate the latter from the disordered state into which they have been thrown by the war, I could usefully employ him in this manner until his attention should be more immediately required for his pupil.

"Fifty or Sixty pounds Sterling pr. ann. with board, lodging, washing and mending, *in the family* , is the most my numerous expenditures will allow me to give; but how far it may command the services of a person well qualified to answer the purposes I have mentioned, is not for me to decide. To answer *my* purposes, the Gentleman must be a Master of composition, and a good Accomptant: to answer his pupil's, he must be a classical scholar, and capable of teaching the French language grammatically: the more universal his knowledge is, the better.

"It sometimes happens that very worthy men of the *Cloth* come under this description; men who are advanced in years, and not very comfortable in their circumstances: such an one, if unencumbered with a family, would be more agreeable to me than a young man just from college; but I except none of good moral character, answering my description, if he can be well recommended.

"To you my Dr. Sir, I have offered this my first address; but if you should think my purposes cannot be subserved in your circle, upon the terms here mentioned; I beg, in that case, that you will be so obliging as to forward the enclosed letter as it is directed. This gentleman has written to me upon another subject, and favored me with his lucubrations upon Education, wch mark him a man of abilities, at the same time that he is highly spoken of as a teacher, and a person of good character. In Scotland we all know that education is cheap, and wages not so high as in England: but I would prefer, on acct. of the dialect, an Englishman to a Scotchman, for all the purposes I want." *WGW*, vol. 29, 3-10-1787. To Pres. Joseph Willard. *WGW*, vol. 31, 10-3-1790.

"I request after you get to Philadelphia, and previous to our arrival there, that you wd. use your best endeavors to ascertain the characters, or reputation of such Schools as it may be proper to place [George Washington Parke] Washington at, as soon as we shall be fixed in our New habitation; particularly if there be any fit School in the College for him, under good and able Tutors, and well attended. His trip to Mount Vernon will be of no Service to him, but will render restraint more necessary than ever. If the College is under *good* regulations, and have proper Tutors there for boys of his standing to prepare them for the higher branches of education quere whether it would not be better to place him in it at once? the presumption being, that a system prevails, by which the gradations are better connected than they are in Schools which have no correspondence with each other. Mr. S[mith]is a man of acknowledged abilities, but it may not be well perhaps to say more in a letter, especially as his re-instatement may have given rise to a reform of that conduct wch. did not escape censure formerly."

110 *WGW*, vol. 3, 6-5-1771. To Reverend Jonathan Boucher.

111 Ibid., vol. 30, 3-23-1789. To George Steptoe Washington. *WGW*, vol. 31, 12-5-1790.

112 Ibid., vol. 30, 9-22-1788. To Henry Lee.

113 Ibid., vol. 36, 1-22-1798. To David Stuart Ibid., vol. 28, 11-10-1785. To George William Fairfax. *WGW*, vol. 34, 2-18-1795. To William Augustine Washington. Ibid., vol. 27, 8-29-1784. To Reverend David Griffith.

114 Bishop William Meade, vol. I, p. 175, "At the end of the century the College of William and Mary was regarded as the hotbed of the infidelity and the wild politics of France. Strong as the Virginia feeling was in favour of the Alma Mater of their parents, the Northern Colleges were filled with the sons of Virginia's best men. No wonder that God for so long a time withdrew the light of his countenance from it.... They complain, also, that those have been frequently sent to them 'who were extremely unfit for the employments assigned them; ' and on that account, the education of the youth has been very defective; ' a natural consequence of which have been riots, contentions, and a dissipation of manners as unbecoming their characters as vitally destructive of the ends of their appointments.'"
These concerns seem to be hinted at by Washington. *WGW*, vol. 37, 1-7-1773. To Reverend Jonathan Boucher, "Dear Sir: From the best enquiries I could make whilst I was in, and about Williamsburg I cannot think William and Mary College a desirable place to send Jack Custis to; the Inattention of the Masters, added to the number of Hollidays, is the Subject of general complaint; and affords no pleasing prospect to a youth who has a good deal to attain, and but a short while to do it in. These considerations, added to a desire of withdrawing the mind of my Ward as much as possible from the objects which seem at present to have engrossd too much of his Attention; and moreover, to give him every advantage which is to be derivd from the best Publick Schools we have here (as there no longer seems to be any thoughts of his crossing the Atlantic) I have I think, determind to send him to the Philadelphia College; which, from the best Information I have been able to get, from those who have been educated themselves there, or have Children at it, stands equally fair with any other, and being nearer, is more agreeable to his Mother. About the middle of March (so that I may return in time for the April Court) is the time I have thought of to carry him there; previous to which I should be very glad to consult Mr. Smith the President (with whom I have some small acquaintance) on the terms it is proper for him to enter College; and were you, my good Sir, to do him and me the favour of having this matter adjusted by communicating your opinion by Letter, either to Mr. Smith directly, or indirectly through me, of his proficiency in the Classics and other branches of knowledge, it would be an acceptable Service, at the sametime that it might be proper to know, whether it would be best for him to take Chambers in the College, or board in the City, for as I am extreamly anxious to have his Education advanced, I could wish to have him so placed as to promote it. Mrs. Washington and Miss Custis joins me in wishing you, Mrs. and Miss Boucher the Compliments of the Season, and the Return of many happy new Years."

115 *WGW*, vol. 36, 1-7-1798. To George Washington Parke Custis. (Emphasis added.) "*System* in all things should be aimed at; for in execution, it renders every thing more easy.

If now and then, of a morning before breakfast, you are inclined, by way of change, to go out with a Gun, I shall not object to it; provided you return by the hour we usually set down to that meal.

From breakfast, until about an hour before Dinner (allowed for dressing, and preparing for it, that you may appear decent) I shall expect you will confine yourself to *your studies; and diligently attend to them*; endeavouring to make yourself master of whatever is recommended to, or required of you.

While the afternoons are short, and but little interval between rising from dinner and assembling for Tea, you may employ that time in walking, or any other recreation. After Tea, if the studies you are engaged in require it, you will, no doubt perceive the propriety and advantage of returning to them, until the hour of rest.

Rise early, that by habit it may become familiar, agreeable, healthy, and profitable. It may for a while, be irksome to do this, but that will wear off; and the practise will produce a rich harvest forever thereafter; whether in public, or private walks of Life.

Make it an invariable rule to be in place (unless extraordinary circumstances prevent it) at the usual breakfasting, dining, and tea hours. It is not only disagreeable, but it is also very inconvenient, for servants to be running here, and there, and they know not where, to summon you to them, when their duties, and attendance, on the company who are seated, render it improper.

Saturday may be appropriated to riding; to your Gun, and other proper amusements.

Time disposed of in this manner, makes ample provision for exercise and every useful, or necessary recreation; at the same time that the hours allotted for study, *if really applied to it* instead of running up and down stairs, and wasted in conversation with any one who will talk with you, will enable you to make considerable progress in whatever line is marked out for you, and that you may do it, is my sincere wish."

116   Compare here Smith's sermon, "A Discourse on the Nature and Reasonableness of Fasting, And on The existing Causes that call us to that Duty. Delivered at *PRINCETON*, on Tuesday the 6th January 1795 Being the Day appointed By the Synod of New-York and New-Jersey, To be observed as a General Fast, By all the Churches of their Communion in those States; and now published in compliance with the request of the Students of Theology and Law in Princeton By SAMUEL STANHOPE SMITH, D.D. Vice-President and Professor of Moral Philosophy and Divinity, in the College of New-Jersey. Philadelphia: Printed by William Young, Bookseller, No. 52, Second Street, Corner of Chesnut-Street. Washington actually had in his library. Smith wrote, "Blessed Jesus! Thy gracious and heavenly mission has been rejected by blinded mortals who have no guide to certainty and truth but thee! Thy divine nature, and thy supreme dominion have been insulted by worms of the dust who have dared to rise in rebellion against thee!—Thy sole and meritorious atonement has been denied by miserable sinners who have no hope in eternity but thee!—My brethren! Shall not God punish by his righteous judgments, if he cannot bring to repentance, a *guilty age* which has impiously endeavored to drag the *Son of righteousness* from his sphere—which has insulted his glory, and blasphemed the astonishing stoops of his mercy? Every sincere believer in Jesus Christ must be deeply penetrated with these dishonors done to his Redeemer's name. And he will find, in these daring impieties, in the general voice that surrounds him, and in his own heart, the subjects of profound repentance and contrition before God. Arrest, Lord! The growing profanity of the age! When will the iniquities of men come to an end, and the reign of truth and righteousness be extended from the rising to the setting sun!

What, then my brethren is our duty on this day? Is it not to humble our souls before God under his corrections? Is it not to make confession of our sins, and to turn from them with all our heart to the living and true God? Let us fervently address our prayers to the throne of his grace, that he would protect and bless our country—that he would endue with that wisdom which is from above, our legislators, our magistrates, and our judges—that he would promote the means of general knowledge, and extend the influence of true religion as the surest basis of the public weal—that he would teach us with sobriety, temperance, and thankfulness of heart, to enjoy the blessings of his providence, assured that, if we do not glorify him in the use of his mercies, he will glorify himself in the execution of his judgments. Let us, finally, implore from his mercy that he would spare the blood of our brethren shed by cruel and ferocious hands—that he would allay the convulsions that agitate the Christian world—and that he, who has all events, and the hearts of all men in his hands, would bring from the bosom of that chaos, a new creation of liberty and peace, and true religion over the whole earth—AMEN."

117   *WGW*, vol. 35, 7-23-1797. To George Washington Parke Custis. "Dear Washington: Your letter of the 14th instant has been duly received, and gives us pleasure to hear that you enjoy good health, and are progressing well in your studies.

Far be it from me to discourage your correspondence with Dr. Stuart, Mr. Law, or Mr. Lewis, or indeed with any others, as well-disposed and capable as I believe they are to give you speciments of correct writing, proper subjects, and if it were necessary, good advice.

With respect to your *epistolary amusements* generally, I had nothing further in view than not to let them interfere with your studies, which were of more interesting concern; and with regard to *Mr. Z. Lewis*, I only meant that no suggestions of his, if he had proceeded to give them, were to be interposed to the course pointed out by *Dr. Smith*, or suffered to weaken your confidence therein. Mr. Lewis was educated at *Yale college*, and as is natural, may be prejudiced in favor of the mode pursued at that seminary; but no college has turned out better scholars, or more estimable characters, than *Nassau. Nor is there any one whose president is thought more capable to direct a proper system of education than Dr. Smith; for which reason, Mr. Lewis, or any other, was to prescribe a different course from the one you are engaged in by the direction of Dr. Smith, it would give me concern.* Upon the plan you propose to conduct your correspondence, none of the evils I was fearful of can happen, while advantages may result; for composition, like other things, is made more perfect by practice and attention, and just criticism thereon.

"I do not hear you mention anything of geography or mathematics as parts of your study; both these are necessary branches of useful knowledge. Nor ought you to let your knowledge of the *Latin* language and grammatical rules escape you. And the *French* language is now so universal, and so necessary with foreigners, or in a foreign country, that I think you would be injudicious not to make yourself master of it."

118   *WGW*, vol. 35, 11-28-1796. To George Washington Parke Custis. "The assurances you give me of applying diligently to your studies, and *fulfilling those obligations which are enjoined by your Creator and due to his creatures*, are highly pleasing and satisfactory to me. I rejoice in it on two accounts; first, as it is the sure means of laying the *foundation of your own happiness*, and rendering you, if it should *please God to spare your life*, a useful member of society hereafter; and secondly, that I may, if I live to enjoy the pleasure, reflect *that I have been, in some degree, instrumental in effecting these purposes.*

"You are now extending into that stage of life when good or bad habits are formed. When the mind will be turned to *things useful and praiseworthy, or to dissipation and vice*. Fix on whichever it may, it will stick by you; for you know it has been said, and truly, "*that as the twig is bent so it will grow.*"This, in a strong point of view, shows the propriety of letting your inexperience be directed by *maturer advice*, and in placing guard upon the avenues which lead to *idleness and vice*. The latter will *approach like a thief*, working upon your passions; encouraged, perhaps, by *bad examples*; the propensity to which will increase in proportion to the practice of it and your yielding. This admonition proceeds from the purest affection for you; *but I do not mean by it, that you are to become a stoic*, or to deprive yourself in the intervals of study of any recreations or manly exercise which reason approves.

'T is well to be on good terms with all your fellow-students, and I am pleased to hear you are so, but while a courteous behavior is due to all, select the most deserving only for your friendships, and before this becomes intimate, weigh their dispositions and character *well* . True friendship is a plant of slow growth; to be sincere, there must be a congeniality of temper and pursuits. *Virtue and vice can not be allied*; nor can idleness and industry; of course, if you resolve to adhere to the two former of these extremes, an intimacy with those who incline to the latter of them, would be extremely embarrassing to you; it would be *a stumbling block* in your way; and act like *a millstone hung to your neck*, for it is the nature of idleness and vice to obtain as many votaries as they can.

"I would guard you, too, against imbibing hasty and unfavorable impressions of any one. Let your judgment always balance well before you decide; and even then, where there is no occasion for expressing an opinion, *it is best to be silent, for there is nothing more certain than that it is at all times more easy to make enemies than friends*. And besides, *to speak evil of any one, unless there is unequivocal proofs of their deserving it, is an injury for which there is no adequate reparation*. For, as Shakespeare says "He that robs me of my good name enriches not himself, but renders me poor indeed," or words to that effect. Keep in mind that scarcely any change would be agreeable to you at *first* from the sudden transition, and from never having been accustomed to shift or rough it. And, moreover, that if you meet with collegiate fare, it will be unmanly to complain. My paper reminds me it is time to conclude. Affectionately, &c. "

119 *WGW*, vol. 36, 6-13-1798.

120 Custis, *Recollections*, pp. 173-174.

121 Ibid., p. 508.

122 *WGW*, vol. 34, 1-16-1795. To Eleanor Parke Custis. [Dear Nelly:] Your letter, the receipt of which I am now acknowledging, is written correctly and in fair characters, which is an evidence that you command, when you please, a fair hand. Possessed of these advantages, it will be your own fault if you do not avail yourself of them, and attention being paid to the choice of your subjects, you can have nothing to fear from the malignancy of criticism, as your ideas are lively, and your descriptions agreeable. Let me touch a little now on your Georgetown ball, and happy, thrice happy, for the fair who were assembled on the occasion, that there was a man to spare; for had there been 79 ladies and only 78 gentlemen, there might, in the course of the evening, have been some disorder among.the caps; notwithstanding the apathy which *one* of the company entertains for the " *youth* " of the present day, and her determination "never to give herself a moment's uneasiness on account of any of them." A hint here; men and women feel the same inclinations to each other *now* that they always have done, and which they will continue to do until there is a new order of things, and *you* , as others have done, may find, perhaps, that the passions of your sex arc easier raised than allayed. Do not therefore boast too soon or too strongly of your insensibility to, or resistance of, its powers. In the composition of the human frame there is a good deal of inflammable matter, however dormant it may lie for a time, and like an intimate acquaintance of yours, when the torch is put to it, *that* which is *within you* may burst into a blaze; for which reason and especially too, as I have entered upon the chapter of advices, I will read you a lecture drawn from this text.

"Love is said to be an involuntary passion, and it is, therefore, contended that it cannot be resisted. This is true in part only, for like all things else, when nourishes and supplied plentifully with ailment, it is rapid in its progress; but let these be withdrawn and it may be stifled in its birth or much stinted in its growth. For example, a woman (the same may be said of the other sex) all beautiful and accomplished, will, while her hand and heart are undisposed of, turn the heads and set the circle in which she moves on fire. Let her marry, and what is the consequence? The madness *ceases* and all is quiet again. Why? not because there is any diminution in the charms of the lady, but because there is an end of hope. Hence it follows, that love may and therefore ought to be under the guidance of reason, for although we cannot avoid first impressions, we may assuredly place them under guard; and my motives for treating on this subject are to show you, while you remain Eleanor Parke Custis, spinster, and retain the resolution to love with moderation, the propriety of adhering to the latter resolution, at least until you have secured your game, and the way by which it may be accomplished.

"When the fire is beginning to kindle, and your heart growing warm, propound these questions to it. Who is this invader? Have I a competent knowledge of him? Is he a man of good character; a man of sense? For, be assured, a sensible woman can never be happy with a fool? What has been his walk in life? Is he a gambler, a spendthrift, or drunkard? Is his fortune sufficient to maintain me in the manner I have been accustomed to live, and my sisters do live, and is he one to whom my friends can have no reasonable objection? If these interrogatories can be satisfactorily answered, there will remain but one more to be asked, that, however, is an important one. Have I sufficient ground to conclude that his affections are engaged by me? Without this the heart of sensibility will struggle against a passion that is not reciprocated; delicacy, custom, or call it by what epithet you will, having precluded all advances on your part. The declaration, without the *most indirect* invitation of yours, must proceed from the man, to render it permanent and valuable, and nothing short of good sense and an easy unaffected conduct can draw the line between prudery and coquetry. It would be no great departure from truth to say, that it rarely happens otherwise than that a thorough-paced coquette dies in celibacy, as a punishment for her attempts to mislead others, by encouraging looks, words, or actions, given for no other purpose than to draw men on to make overtures that they may be rejected.

"This day, according to our information, gives a husband to your elder sister, and consummates, it is to be presumed, her fondest desires. The dawn with us is bright, and propitious, I hope, of her future happiness, for a full measure of which she and Mr. Law have my earnest wishes. Compliments and congratulations on this occasion, and best regards are presented to your mamma, Dr. Stuart and family; and every blessing, among which a good husband when you want and deserve one, is bestowed on you by yours, affectionately."

123 *WGW*, vol. 34, 2-10-1796. To Elizabeth Parke Custis. "My dear Betsey: I have obeyed your injunction in not acknowledging the receipt of your letter of the first instant until I should hear from Mr. Law. This happened yesterday; I therefore proceed to assure you, if Mr. Law is the man of your choice, of wch. there can be no doubt, as he has merits to engage your affections, and you have declared that he has not

only done so, but that you find, after a careful examination of your heart, you cannot be happy without him; that your alliance with him meets my approbation. Yes, Betsey, and this approbation is accompanied with my fervent wishes that you may be as happy in this important event as your most Sanguine imagination has ever presented to your view. Along with these wishes, I bestow on you my choicest blessings.

"Nothing contained in your letter, in Mr. Laws, or in any other from our friends intimate *when* you are to taste the sweets of Matrimony; I therefore call upon *you* , who have more honesty than disguise, to give me the details. Nay more, that you will relate all your feelings to *me* on this occasion: or as a Quaker would say "all the workings of the spirit within."

"This, I have a right to expect in return for my blessing, so promptly bestowed, after you had concealed the matter from me so long. Being entitled therefore to this confidence, and to a compliance with my requests, I shall look forward to the fulfilment of it.

"If after marriage Mr. Laws business should call him to this the same room which Mr. Peter and your sister occupied will accomodate you two; and it will be equally at your service.

"You know how much I love you, how much I have been gratified by your attentions to those things which you had reason to believe were grateful to my feelings. And having *no* doubt of your continuing the *same* conduct, as the effect will be pleasing to *me* , and unattended with any disadvantage to *yourself* , I shall remain with the sincerest friendship, and the most Affectionate regard, etc."

124 *WGW*, vol. 34, 2-10-1796. To Thomas Law.   Sir: Yesterday's Mail brought me your letter of the 4th Instant; and that of Saturday announced from Miss Custis herself, the Union which is pending between you. No intimation of this event, from any quarter, having been communicated to us before, it may well be supposed that it was a matter of Surprize.

"This being premised, I have only to add, that as the parties most interested are agreed, my approbation, in which Mrs. Washington unites, is cordially given; accompanied with best wishes that both of you may be supremely happy in the alliance. I must however, tho' it is *no immediate* concern of mine, be permitted to hope, as the young lady is in her non-age, that preliminary measures has been, or will be arranged with her Mother and Guardian, before the Nuptials are Solemnized.

"We shall hope that your fortunes (if not before) will, by this event, be fixed in America; for it would be a heart rending circumstance, if you should seperate Eliza from her friends in this country. Whether the Marriage is to take place soon, or late, we have no data to judge from but be it as it will, if you should bring her to Philadelphia, we invite you both to this house. With very great esteem and regard I am etc.

WGW, vol. 37, 12-25-1798. To George Washington Motier de Lafayette.

"Your acquaintance Lawrence Lewis is appointed Captain of a Troop of Light Dragoons; but intends, before he enters the Camp of Mars to engage in that of Venus; Eleanor Custis and he having entered into a contract of marriage; which, I understand, is to be fulfilled on my birthday (the 22d. of Feby). Washington Custis prefering a Military career to literary pursuits, is appointed Cornet in Lewis's Troop, and Washington Craik a Lieutenancy. Young Carroll of Carrolton, will be a Volunteer Aid of mine, and Mr. Lear is my Secretary."

Washington's "Diary" for February 22 records: "Morning raining. Mer at 30. Wind a little more to the Northward. Afterwards very strong from the No. Wt. and turning clear and cold. The Revd. Mr. Davis and Mr. Geo. Calvert came to dinner and Mass Custis was married abt. Candle light to Mr. Lawe. Lewis."

On February 23 Washington wrote: "General and Mrs. Washington present their Compliments to Mr. Andw. Ramsay, Mrs. Ramsay and Mr. Willm. Ramsay and request the favour of their Company to dine on Tuesday next, with the couple Newly Married" A photograph of this letter is in the *Washington Papers* .

WGW, vol. 37, 2-19-1799. To George Deneale. Sir: You will please to grant a license for the Marriage of Eleanor Parke Custis with Lawrence Lewis, and this shall be your Authority for so doing from Sir Yr. etc."

125 *WGW*, vol. 37, 9-20-1799.

126 Sparks, *The Writings of George Washington*, vol. XII, pp. 405-407. See John Eidsmoe, *Christianity and the Constitution*, (Grand Rapids: Baker Book House, 1987), p. 140-141. "Did Washington embrace Christianity? His adopted daughter thought so. Nelly Custis was Martha Washington's granddaughter, and when Nelly's father died, George and Martha Washington adopted her and she lived in their home for twenty years. In 1833 she wrote to the historian Jared Sparks, expressing indignation that anyone would question Washington's Christianity.".

CHAPTER 13

1 *WGW*, vol. 35, 3-2-1797.

2 Grizzard, *George Washington A Biographical Companion*, p. 100.

3 Johnson, *George Washington The Christian*, p. 249; Littel, *Washington: Christian*. p. 14.

4 The breadth of words that reflect a knowledge of the life of the Church are extensive in Washington's writings. They include words of:
·Government: episcopate, bishop, ecclesiastical, vestry, holy orders, cure, commissary, benefice, glebe (parish farm), Parish;
·Ministry: Parson, Reverend, Curate, Pastor, Chaplain, Missionary, vestryman, deacon, clergyman, priest;
·Parishioner Worship: Sunday, Sabbath, first day, seventh day, sermon, votaries, benediction, blessing, curse, obsequies, vows, pew;
·Calendar: Lady's Day, Michaelmas, Dominical Number, Easter, Easter Monday, Christmas;
·Anglican History: [Oliver] Cromwell, the usurper; Gunpowder;
·*Book of Common Prayer:* Divine Service, Prayers;
·Sacramental terms: Sponsor, Christen, Little Christian, God-son, Cup of blessing;
·Theology: True Religion, errors, superstition, expiate, conversion, repentance, forgiveness, holy;
·Military Terms that reflect Christian vocabulary: Pardon, Redemption, Atonement, Grace, Mercy, forgiveness, salvation, justification;
·Religious Figures: St. Patrick, Cross, Knights of Divine Providence;

·Other Religious traditions: Jew, Muslim, Atheist, infidel, Father confessor, purgatory, penance.

5   Slaughter, *The History of Truro Parish*, p. 3.

6   Ibid., p. 82.

7   Boller, *George Washington And Religion*, p. 28-29.

8   Ford, *The True George Washington*, p. 78.

9   Boller, *George Washington & Religion*, p.28.

10 Jackson, Twohig, *Diaries of George Washington*, vol. 3, p. 366, 6-10-1778.

11 See Chapter 19 on Religious Liberty, where the gunpowder plot is more fully discussed in relation to Washington's efforts to end the anti-Catholic discrimination within his army.

12 Stephen DeCatur Jr., *Private Affairs of George Washington* (Boston: Houghton Mifflin Col, 1933) p. 90.

13 Jackson, Twohig, *Diaries of George Washington* vol. 2, p. 80, 9-27-1772.

14 Johnson, *George Washington The Christian*, p. 176-177; Donald Jackson, ed.; Jackson, Twohig, *Diaries of George Washington* vol. 1, p. 50, 11-8-1789.

15 Ibid., entry for 1-24-1768.

16 See the chapter on "Washington and the Clergy."

17 Custis, *Recollections*, p. 173-174.

18 *WGW*, vol. 28, 8-23-1786.

19 Ibid., vol. 37, 9-22-1799.

20 Ibid., vol. 30, 12-23-1788.

21 Slaughter, *The History of Truro Parish*, p. 123.

22 Jackson, Twohig, *Diaries of George Washington*, vol. 2, p. 419, 10-2-1785.

23 Slaughter, *The History of Truro Parish*, p. 97f.

24 Sparks, *The Writings of George Washington*, vol. 12, p. 405-408.

25 Johnson, *George Washington The Christian*, p. 199. Also cited in Ashabel Green, *The Life of Ashabel Green*, 1849, p. 267.

26 John N.Norton, *Life of General Washington*, 1870. p. 117; also Johnson, *George Washington The Christian*, p. 58.

27 M'Guire, *Religious Opinions and Character of Washington* (New York: Harper & Brothers, 1836), p. 154.

28 Ibid., p. 154.

29 Boller, *George Washington & Religion*, p.32.

30 M'Guire, *Religious Opinions*, p. 146.

CHAPTER 14

1   Slaughter, *The History of Truro Parish*, p. 89.

2   Ibid., p. 2-3.

3   Notes on the State of Virginia, Query XIV: Justice, *Thomas Jefferson* 1781, see http://teachingamericanhistory.org/library/index.asp?document=514

4   Slaughter, *The History of Truro Parish in Virginia*, pp. 3-4.

5   Can we claim Jefferson for the Christian fold? This is attempted by Catherine Millard in *Rewriting of America's History*, pp. 91-109.

    1. The problem is that Jefferson explicitly affirmed that he believed the following things:

    The Bible is not revealed of God.

    It is good to doubt religion and God to assert the oracle of reason.

    He opposed Calvinism and Trinitarianism.

    That he was a unitarian.

    That he was a member of a sect all his own.

    That clergy in general were the source of intolerance.

    That he was a "true Christian" in the sense of viewing Jesus' theology and morals as the same as his own.

    Paul was one of the worst corrupters of Jesus' teachings.

        A. The Jefferson Bible's purpose and history: To distill Jesus' ethics from corruptions to his system found in the Bible by his followers.

        B. Jefferson's religious doubts were carried out in secret, not the public eye, for fear of its impact upon his career.

        C. The irony of Jefferson's fears of the Supreme Court's unchecked power under the Constitution!

        D. But were Jefferson's ethics and politics contrary to Christianity?

            1. His view of the ethics of Jesus—the best the world has ever known.

            2. His view of the Bible in schools—to be used in schools for education.

            3. His view of Christianizing the Indians—approved of money given from government.

            4. His view of religion in the states—federalism permitted religious actions by state government, but not by federal government as he saw the First Amendment.

    The Point of his 1802 letter to Danbury Baptists, which uses the famous phrase, "separation of Church and State," was to reassure the Baptists that there would be no established federal denomination. He was not afraid of religious activity, and even worshiped on Sundays in a church that met in the Capitol Building in Washington, D.C.

    Boyd Stanley Schlenther, *Charles Thomson: A Patriot's Pursuit* (Newark: University of Delaware Press 1990), p. 216-217.

Not surprisingly, Thomson's translation of the Bible had left him as a target for several eccentric correspondents. Perhaps the most curious was the Master of the Masonic Order in Baltimore who was "determined… to unbosom my heart." This man urged Thomson to become a Mason to help him bring the order (which had "deviated from the truth) back to the "first principles" of Christianity. "I am in, you are out," wrote the Masonic Master. "Will you – can you- deem yourself called upon to lend your aid to do much good?" Thomson stayed out. In fact, thoughtout his life he appears never to have joined any organization that he did not feel was involved in some useful purpose. He never was a member of the Tammany Society; he never joined Philadelphia's Hibernian Club, organized in 1759 by bother Protestant and Roman Catholic Irish immigrants. It appears that any group that smacked of frivolity or that was mainly given to socializing was never to Thomson's taste, and even those organizations with which he had associated himself –such as the Philosophical Society and the Agricultural Society – soon lost their charm and interest, especially if they had appeared to have served their purpose for him.

To occupy his time after Hannah's death, Thomson turned once again to biblical studies. Even while the Bible was in the process of printing, Thomson had begun "to draw up a harmony of the four evangelists from my translation following the Order of Dr. Doddridge." Thomson believed that by arranging the facts presented in the Gospels, producing them in parallel columns, he had "removed the seeming inconsistencies with which they are charged & shewn that instead of contradicting, they strengthen & confirm one another's narrative."

In it, he justified publication on the grounds that though there had been many such harmonies, "infidels still continue to charge the Evangelist with inconsistency, and contradiction." As for himself, Thomson publicly admitted that the real reason he first undertook the task was for his own "solace."

One result of the publication of the synopsis was brief renewal of his correspondence with Jefferson, which had not been maintained, following their exchanges at the appearance of the full Bible in 1808. Early in 1816 Jefferson wrote that he had received a copy of the synopsis, and after perfunctory compliments, he proceeded to inform Thomson that he had made a "wee little book" of his own; by cutting the texts from the Gospels which include the words of Jesus, Jefferson had compiled what he called the "Philosophy of Jesus." This information led Thomson to an innocent but extremely awkward indiscretion. Delighted that Jefferson saw this project as proof of his own religious nature)"I am a real Christian – that is to say, a disciple of the doctrines of Jesus"), Thomson brought several Philadelphians to the conclusion that there was reason for "the Religious world. …[to be] daily congratulating each other," on Jefferson's "happy change of Religious belief." The miraculous had happened: Jefferson had made "a profession of faith." The matter had gone so far that Thomson nearly provided Jefferson's letter for publication, only to receive this rebuke: "I apprehend that [you] were not sufficiently aware of its private & personal nature, or of the impropriety of putting it in the power of an editor to publish, without the consent of the writer." Crestfallen, Thomson wrote immediately to apologize. Jefferson – who had been caused no little anxiety and trouble by the who affair – replied, saying that he had received a communication from a person in Philadelphia who had seen his letter to Thomson, asking Jefferson "questions which I answer only to one Being. To himself, therefore. I replied: 'Say nothing of my Religion; it is known to my God and myself alone.'" Under the circumstances, it was a kindly response to Thomson, but this really was the last letter ever to pass between the two men.

6   Meade, *Old Churches,* vol. II p. 48.

7   Ibid., vol. II p. 49.

8   Boller, George *Washington & Religion*, p.26.

9   Ibid., p.27.

10   Slaughter, *The History of Truro Parish,* p. 89.

11   Note. See oaths George had to take to assume role of public surveyor

12   Slaughter, *The History of Truro Parish* p. 34.

13   Ibid., p. 34.

14   Ibid., p. 21. The oaths of office of the vestryman are given to us in Meade, *Old Church Ministers,* Volume II, 41-42. Again, note how concerned they were that the participants not return to the control of the Roman Church. This is from Bishop Meade's book, *Old Church Ministers and Families of Virginia,*

"Oath of Allegiance: "I, A.B., do sincerely promise and swear that I will be faithful and bear true allegiance to his Majesty King George the Second, so help me God."

Oath of Abjuration: "I, A.B., do swear that I do from my heart abhor, detest and abjure, as impious and heretical, that damnable doctrine and position that Princes excommunicate or deprived by the Pope, or any authority of the See of Rome, may be deposed or murdered by their subjects or any other whatsoever. And I do declare that no foreign Prince, Prelate, Person, State, or Potentate, hath, or ought to have, any jurisdiction, power superiority, pre-eminence, or authority, ecclesiastical or spiritual, within this realm. So help me God."

II. Oath of Allegiance: "I, A.B., do truly and sincerely acknowledge and promise, testify and declare, in my conscience, before God and the world, that our sovereign Lord, King George the Second, is lawful and rightful King of this realm and all other his Majesty's dominions and countries hereunto belonging; and I do solemnly and sincerely declare that I do believe in my conscience that the person pretended to be Prince of Wales during the life of the late King James,1 and since his decease pretending to be, and taking upon himself the style and title of, the King of England, or by the name of James the Third, or of Scotland by the name of James the Eighth, or the style and title of King of Great Britain, hath not any right whatsoever to the crown of this realm, or any other dominions hereto belonging. And I do renounce, refuse, and abjure any allegiance or obedience to him and I do swear that I will bear faithful and true allegiance to his Majesty King George the Second, and him will defend to the utmost of my power against all traitorous conspiracies and attempts whatsoever which shall be made against his person, crown, or dignity; and I will do my utmost to endeavor to disclose and make known to his Majesty and his successors all treasonable and traitorous conspiracies which I shall know to be against him, or any of them; and I do faithfully promise to the utmost of my power to support, maintain, and defend the successor of the crown against him, the said James, and all other persons whatsoever, which succession, by an Act entitled 'An Act for the further limitation of the crown and better securing the rights and liberties of the subjects,' is, and stands limited to, the Princess Sophia, late Electress and Duchess-Dowager of Hanover, and the heirs of her body, being Protestants; and all other theses things I do plainly and sincerely acknowledge and swear, according to these express words by me spoken, and according to the plain and common sense understanding of the same words, without any equivocation, mental evasion, or secret reservation whatsoever; and I do make this recognition, acknowledgement, abjuration, renunciation, and promise, heartily, willingly, and truly, upon the true faith of a Christian, so help me God....

Test Oath: "I do declare that I do believe that there is not any transubstantiation in the Sacrament of the Lord's Supper, or in the Elements of bread and wine at or after the consecration thereof by any person whatsoever."

Thus, here we see a strong affirmation of the historic Protestant faith.

15 Ibid., p. 5.
16 Ibid., p. 7.
17 Ibid., p. 9.
18 Ibid., p. 8.
19 Ibid., p. 9.
20 Ibid., p. 16.
21 Ibid., p. 18.
22 Ibid., p. 10 n.
23 Ibid., p. 17.
24 Ibid., p. 30.
25 Ibid., p. 78.
26 Ibid., p. 51.
27 Ibid., p. 41.
28 Ibid., p. 43.
29 *WGW*, vol. 2, 11-13-1757.
30 Ibid., vol. 2, 8-26-1761.
31 Ibid., vol. 1, 1755.
32 Slaughter, *The History of Truro Parish*, p. 51.
33 Ibid., p. 54-55.
34 Ibid., p. 63.
35 Ibid., p. 63-64.
36 Interview with Peter Lillback and Jerry Newcombe with Reverend Donald S. Binder, Ph.D , 2005.
37 Washington wrote to Bryan Fairfax on July 4, 1774: "Dear Sir: John has just delivered to me your favor of yesterday, which I shall be obliged to answer in a more concise manner, than I could wish, as I am very much engaged in raising one of the additions to my house, which I think (perhaps it is fancy) goes on better whilst I am present, than in my absence from the workmen. I own to you, Sir, I wished much to hear of your making an open declaration of taking a poll for this county, upon Colonel West's publicly declining last Sunday; and I should have writ ten to you on the subject, but for information then received from several gentlemen in the churchyard, of your having re fused to do so, for the reasons assigned in your letter;[editors note:(Note: The poll here mentioned was for the election of delegates to the House of Burgesses.) Mr. Fairfax declined, as he said, chiefly because he thought he could not give satisfaction at that time; for he should think himself bound to oppose strong measures, and was in favor of petitioning, and giving Parliament a fair opportunity of repealing their obnoxious acts. ...]" upon which, as I think the country never stood more in need of men of abilities and liberal sentiments than now, I entreated several gentlemen at our church yesterday to press Colonel Mason to take a poll, as I really think Major Broadwater, though a good man, might do as well in the discharge of his domestic concerns, as in the capacity of a legislator. And therefore I again express my wish, that either you or Colonel Mason would offer. I can be of little assistance to either, because I early laid it down as a maxim not to propose myself, and solicit for a second...." *WGW*, vol. 3, 7-4-1774.
38 Fitzpatrick, *Diaries of George Washington*, vol. I, p. 315.
39 Slaughter, *The History of Truro Parish*, p. 88.
40 Ibid., p. 89.
41 *WGW*, vol. 27, 7-10-1783.
42 Slaughter, *The History of Truro Parish*, p. 95.
43 Ibid., p. 90.
44 Washington had mentioned his paying for the Fairfax pew when he wrote his draft of a letter to George William. He wrote from Williamsburg on June 10, 1774, "Inclosd you have a Copy of the Acct. I settled before I left home with Mr. Craven Peyton; as also of my Acct. with you in which you will perceive a charge for your Pew in the New Church at Pohick which is now conveyed to you by the Vestry and upon Record. The Balce. Of this Acct. to with £ is now Exchangd for Bills and remit viz." But he crossed it out before he sent it, thus not asking for repayment. *WGW*, vol. 3, 6-10-1774.
45 Philip Slaughter writes, "That pew has become historical. It was afterwards occupied by Gen. Robert E. Lee, and there are tablets on the walls of the Church in memory of these two heroic characters and devout Christians. This historic pew attracts every week streams of pilgrims to Christ Church." Slaughter, *The History of TruroParish*, p. 96.
46 *WGW*, vol. 3, 2-15-1773.

CHAPTER 15

1   *WGW*, vol. 3, 5-4-1772. To Reverend Jonathan Boucher.

2   Reverend Mason Gallagher, *A Chapter of Unwritten History. The Protestant Episcopacy of the Revolutionary Patriots Lost and Restored. A Centennial Offering* (Philadelphia: Reformed Episcopal Rooms, 1883), p. 3. The quote continues: "In an able article on "The Causes which drove the Puritans from England," the *New Englander* for November, 1882, says: 'It was the bishops who drove the Puritans into Holland; it was the bishops who hung the sword of Damocles over them as they sailed to Plymouth; it was the bishops who compelled the founding of New England, and the great Puritan exodus.'"

    When fifty years afterwards Archbishop Tillotson and other bishops of England expressed with such energy to increase Mather, their just resentment to the injury which had been done to the first planters of New England, the old Puritan exclaimed: 'If such had been the bishops there had never been a New England.'

3   John S. Littel puts it this way:

> Before our Independence, there was in the colonies no Confirmation for anyone, and of course both individual members and the welfare of the Church as a whole were hindered. It is certain that the Church cannot expect to attain her very best development when her children are not "sealed" with the spiritual grace which our Lord at Pentecost placed in His Church to be ministered by the Apostles in "the laying on of hands." Washington was never confirmed, but so far as he was able he was in close touch with the Church. We have it on the testimony of his political and military associates and members of his family that for many years he was accustomed to make his Communions. Littell, *George Washington: Christian.*

4   *WGW*, vol. 37 3-26-1762. to Gov. Horatio Sharpe. "Sir: Be so good as to pardon the liberty I presume to take in recommending to your Excellency's notice the Revd. Mr. West; a young Gentn. lately entered into Holy Orders, of a good Family, and unexceptionable Morals; this with truth I can venture to certifie as he is a neighbour of mine, and one of those few of whom every body speaks well. At present he is engagd to officiate as Curate to the Revd. Doctr. Swift of Port Tobo.; who it seems is in the last Stage of a Consumption, and attempting by a Voyage to England, the recovery of his health, but, should he fail in this (as most probably he will) and the Parish become vacant by his death. Mr. West woud think himself very happy in the honour of your presentment of him to the Cure, and I am fully persuaded that his endeavours woud merit the favour."

5   Griffith, *Virginia House of Burgesses 1750-1774.*, pp. 118-123, 127, 130, 147, 164, 194.

6   *WGW*, vol. 1, 5-28-1755.

7   Griffith, *Virginia House of Burgesses*, pp. 118-19. Lucille Griffith writes, "George Washington was more than a mere surveyor for Lord Fairfax, he was an intimate of the family; George William was one of his best friends and Sally Cary Fairfax his confidant. Anne Fairfax, sister to George William, was married to Lawrence Washington, George's elder half-brother. It is a truism that Fairfax interest and support launched the youthful George on a political career."

8   *WGW* Note: Washington was married on Jan. 6, 1759, to Martha Custis, widow of Daniel Parke Custis, and daughter of John Dandridge. Ford states that the ceremony was performed by the Reverend David Mossum in St. Peters Church, a few miles from the Custis White House, which was on the Pamunkey River, in New Kent County, Va., but documentary evidence that the ceremony was performed in St. Peters is not available.

9   Sawyer, *Washington*, I.214.

10   William Stith, A.M. President of William and Mary College. Published at the Request of the House of Burgesses Williamsburgh, Printed and Sold by William Hunter, MDCCLIII. Meade, *Old Churches*, vol. I. p.137-138 writes, "William Stith was the only son of Captain John Stith, of the county of Charles City, and of Mary, a daughter of "William Randolph, gentleman," of Turkey Island, in the adjoining county, Henrico, in the Colony of Virginia : their son William was born in the year 1689. On the death of her husband, Mrs. Stith, at the instance of her brother, Sir John Randolph, removed to Williamsburg and placed her son in the grammar-school attached to the College of William and Mary, where he pursued his academic studies and graduated. His theological studies were completed in England, where he was ordained a minister of the Episcopal Church. On his return to Virginia, in the year 1731, he was elected master of the grammar-school in the College and chaplain to the Hose of Burgesses. In June, 1738, he was called rector to Henrico parish, in the county of Henrico. He married his cousin Judith, a daughter of Thomas Randolph of Tuckahoe, the second son of William Randolph, of Turkey Island, and resided in the parsonage on the glebe near Varina, the seat of justice for the county of Henrico. There he wrote his *History of Virginia*, which was printed and bound in the city of Williamsburg, at the only printing-press then in the Colony. In August, 1752, he was elected President of William and Mary College, to which he removed and over which he presided until his death, in 1755."

11   William Stith, A.M. President of William and Mary College. Published at the Request of the House of Burgesses Williamsburgh, Printed and Sold by William Hunter, MDCCLIII: "AND lastly to shew the Universality of CHRIST's Redemption, that he is *the Propitiation for out Sins, and not for our Sins only, but also for the Sins of the whole World.* 1 John 2:2. And for the clearer and more distinct Explication of this Subject, I shall observe.

> 1 That there is no Remission of Sin, or Salvation, but by the Merits and Sufferings of our Lord JESUS CHRIST. He is the *Lamb of God, which taketh away the Sin of the World;* (John 1:29) who *not by the Blood of the Goats and Calves, but by his own Blood, entered in once into the holy Place having obtained eternal Redemption for us.* Heb. 9:3. It is by his propitiatory Sacrifice, *offered once for all,* and by the Satisfaction thereby made to GOD's Justice (in a Manner and upon Reasons, incomprehensible to our weak Sense and Understanding) that we can have Access *to the Throne of Grace, or Inheritance among the Saint's in Light.* He is therefore emphatically stiled by the Prophet, *The Lord, our Righteousness.* Jer. 23:6. *For with his Stripes we are Healed,* and by his imputed Righteousness we are justified and accepted in the Sight of GOD. *Neither is there Salvation in any other: For there is none other Name under Heaven, given among Men, whereby we must be saved.* Acts 4:12.

> 2 As we are thus, by CHRIST's Merits and Satisfaction, put into a Capacity of Salvation, so is Faith required on our Part, as an indis-

pensable Condition for entering into the Kingdom of Heaven: an indispensable Condition, I mean, to those who have the Christian Faith offered unto them, or who have the Opportunity to know and embrace the Gospel. *For by Grace are we saved, through Faith.* Eph. 2:8. *So must the Son of Man be lifted up, that whosoever believeth in him, should not perish, but have eternal Life.* John 3:14, 15. *He that believeth on the Son, hath everlasting Life: And he, that believeth not the Son, shall not see Life; but the Wrath of GOD abideth on him.* Ibid., 536.

12 See Lane, *Washington Collection*, Boston Athenaeum, pp. 76-77, 195.

13 Meade, *Old Churches, vol. 1,* p. 216, Two Penny Act., "…in the year 1758. The act of Assembly which produced the contest, and convulsed both Church and State, was called the Option Law or Two-Penny Act, because the people were allowed the option of paying as usual so much tobacco, or about two pence per pound instead of it." p. 223 Providence and Tobacco and 2 Penny Act, "They thought it hard, therefore, that when, in the course of Providence, an increase of funds occurred for one year, by which they might be set free from debt or be enabled to buy a few books, this should be prevented by such an act. …They said the history of Virginia proved that a small crop of tobacco was best for the Colony, that the Legislature was often endeavouring to stint the crop of tobacco by preventing the culture of so much, and in former days had even destroyed some which was already made, and the now, when Providence had stinted the crop, it was hard that the clergy should be the chief, indeed only sufferers."

Lane, Boston Athenaeum, *Catalogue of the Washington Collection,* p. 41, "…bought by Washington, as appears from an entry under date of April 16, 1764, in his Ledger preserved in the State Department." *The Rector Detected: Being A Just Defence of the Twopenny Act,* against the artful Misrepresentations of the Reverend John Camm, Rector of York-Hampton, in his Single and Distinct View. Containing also a plain Confutation of his several Hints, as a specimen of the Justice and Charity of Colonel Landon Carter by Land Carter of Sabine-Hall Williamsburg: Printed by Joseph Royle. 1764.

"…the Twopenny Act will appear to be calculated for a very general and good Purpose to the whole Community." (p. 5.)

"The Clergy should benefit with the poor. "No 2. The poor, who have an annual Allowance of Tobacco from the Parish to maintain themselves, other poor Persons (those that are boarded out, I suppose) the Clerk of the Church, and the Sexton, not only have no Part of the Charity, but lose two Thirds of their stated allowance, with the Parson by Means of the Act." (p. 6.)

"The charge that Carter is challenging is "One would think (says he) the poorer any Man was, he ought to receive the greater Share, in a Project for the Benefit of the Poor; but, in this Project, the poorer a Man is, the less he has." (p. 7)

"Need I appeal to the serious in Christianity to discover the Consistency in Behaviour in a Minister of the Gospel of Christ, thus endeavouring to ridicule and depreciate a Work of such a real Benefit to the Poor? With how much Contempt will it then be read that this witty Ridicule is the Sanctified Performance of the Reverend John Camm, Rector of York-Hampton? Does he not in so doing deny the Power of Godliness, whilst he wears the Form of it? . . .Yet methinks the Scripture should have cautioned him first to pull out his own Beams before he attempted to peck at the Motes of others, for there may be an Hypocrisy in Things of this Kind…." (p. 37.)

14 Meade, *Old Churches,* p. 220, "Patrick Henry and Davies …though they must find for the plaintiffs, yet one penny damages would suffice, in five minutes the jury brought in that verdict. …It is probable, also, that this time Mr. Henry may have been a little alienated from the Church of his father and relatives. The Revs. Mr. Davies and Mr. Waddell (the old blind preacher of whom Mr. Wirt speaks) were then in their height of zeal and eminence, and Mr. Henry often attended their services and admired them much. Disaffection to the Church was also getting quite strong in that region. Mr. Henry may for a time have sympathized in their religious views, though I have no testimony to this effect. The following extract of a letter of Mr. Roger Atkinson, of Mannsfield, near Petersburg, an old vestryman and staunch friend of the Church in that place, to his brother-in-law, Mr. Samuel Pleasants, may throw some light on this point. He is drawing the portraits of the members sent to the first Congress of Virginia. Of Mr. Henry he says, "He is a real half-Quaker, - your brother's man, - moderate and mild, and in religious matters a saint; but the very d——l in politics, - a son of thunder. He will shake the Senate. Some years ago he had liked to have talked treason into the House. Whatever may have been the feelings of Mr. Henry as to the Episcopal Church at that time, it is very certain that in after-life he gave full proof that he was no enemy to it, and had no desire to deprive it of any just rights. … Mr. Henry stood up in opposition to every attempt at their alienation."

"Patrick Henry also had a significant impact on religious liberty in Virginia as well. In what became known as "The Parson's Cause," he helped defeat the required payment of tithes to the state church by the citizens of Virginia, a law that forced many to support a church in which they did not believe. Eidsmoe writes, "Several Anglican clergymen were suing some tobacco planters under a Virginia colony law that required a certain portion of tobacco revenues be paid for the support of the clergy. Henry agreed to defend the planters when their previous attorney declared the case hopeless and withdrew. He assailed the Anglican clergy without mercy, amid a packed courtroom filled with Anglican clergymen confident of victory, and 'Dissenters' (Methodists, Baptists and Presbyterians) looking to Henry as their champion: 'We have heard a great deal about the benevolence and holy zeal of our reverend clergy, but how is this manifested? Do they manifest their zeal in the cause of religion and humanity by practicing the mild and benevolent precepts of the Gospel of Jesus? Do they feed the hungry and clothe the naked? Oh, no, gentlemen! Instead of feeding the hungry and clothing the naked, these rapacious harpies would, were their powers equal to their will, snatch from the hearth of their honest parishioner his last hoe-cake, from the widow and her orphan children their last milch cow! The last bed, nay, the last blanket from the lying-in woman!' Henry could not demand a verdict for the planters since the law was clearly on the side of the clergy. Instead, he asked the jury to bring forth a verdict for the clergy in the amount of one penny—which the jury did." John Eidsmoe, *Christianity and the Constitution* (Grand Rapids: Baker Book House, 1987), p. 301.

15 Lane, Boston Athenaeum, *Catalogue of the Washington Collection,* p. 99, "Bought by Washington as appears from the following:—1774. June 15. By Henley's defence agt ye cha: of Heresy…." *A Candid refutation of the Heresy Imputed By Ro. C. Nicholas Esquire to The Reverend S. Henley.* Williamsburg, Printed for B. White in London, D. Prince in Oxford, and J. Woodyer in Cambridge, 1774. The book explains, "Colonel Bland's imputation of Socinianism rests solely upon my interpretation of the first chapter to the Hebrews. By this I explained away the divinity of our Saviour. That gentleman affirms it, and therefore, it must be true. Now I would ask, whether upon so inconclusive

an evidence any criminal, hitherto, was ever condemned? …Further: Supposing my interpretation of that chapter to have been the Socinian interpretation, it will, by no means, follow that I am a Socinian. What are the notions you entertain of Socinus? For the only information you may find leisure to receive consult in some dictionary a catalogue of his tenets. You will then find that the Papist, the Protestant, the Arian, and the MONSTROUS Socinian, do, and must, agree in their interpretation of the greatest part of Scripture. What wonder then, if I were to explain one chapter according to Socinus? But, suppose I departed from the orthodox interpretation; yet this concession will profit you nothing. Here methinks, I see you prick up your attention. But be patient. I am, as a minister o the Church of England, obliged to believe in (what I have never denied) the divinity of our Saviour. But the Church does not confine me to prove it by this, or that text." (pp. 4-6.)

16 Ibid., p. 39, "Bought by Washington, as shown by an entry in the Invoice of Cary & Co. of London, March, 1766, preserved in the State Department at Washington." Burnet's work was a classic defense of orthodox Anglicanism, but with a more "broad church" perspective, sometimes called "Latitudinarianism," suggesting a more tolerant view of theological differences, and less interest in using state power to persecute non-conformists. Gilbert Bishop of Sarum, *An Exposition of the XXXIX Articles of the Church of England* (Oxford: University Press, 1845). Article I. Of Faith In The Holy Trinity. The last branch of this article is, the assertion of that great doctrine of the Christian religion concerning the Trinity, or three Persons in one divine essence. It is a vain attempt to go about to prove this by reason: for it must be confessed, that we should have had no cause to have thought of any such thing, if the scriptures had not revealed it to us. p. 40.

Article II. Of The Word Or Son Of God, Which Was Made Very Man.

The first of these leads me to prosecute what was begun in the former article: and to prove, that the *Son*, or *Word*, was from all eternity begotten of the same substance with the Father. It is here to be noted, that Christ is in two respects the *Son*, and the *only-begotten Son of God*. The one is, as he was man; the miraculous overshadowing of the blessed Virgin by the Holy Ghost, having, without the ordinary course of nature, formed the first beginnings of Christ's human body in the womb of the Virgin. Thus that miracle being instead of a natural begetting, he may in that respect be called *the begotten*, and the *only-begotten Son of God*. The other sense is, that the *Word*, or the divine Person, was in and of the substance of the Father, and so was truly God. (p. 47.)

Article IV. Of The Resurrection Of Christ.

Among all Christians the article of the resurrection and ascension of Christ was always looked on as the capital one upon which all the rest depended. (p. 65.)

Article VI. Of The Sufficiency Of Holy Scriptures For Salvation.

In this article there are two important heads, and to each of them a proper consequence does belong. The first is, that the holy scriptures do contain all things necessary to salvation: the negative consequence that ariseth out of that is, that no article that is not either read in it, or that may not be proved by it, is to be required to be believed as an article of faith, or to be thought necessary to salvation. …After the main foundations of religion in general, in the belief of a God, or more specially of the Christian religion in the doctrine of the Trinity, and of the death, resurrection, and ascension of Christ, are laid down; the next point to be settled is, what is *the rule of this faith*, where is it to be found, and with whom is it lodged?. . . We on the contrary affirm, that the scriptures are a complete *rule of faith*, and that the whole Christian religion is contained in them, and no where else…. (p. 79.)

17 *WGW*, vol. 37, 1-7-1773. To Reverend Jonathan Boucher. "From the best enquiries I could make whilst I was in, and about Williamsburg I cannot think William and Mary College a desirable place to send Jack Custis to; the Inattention of the Masters, added to the number of Hollidays, is the Subject of general complaint; and affords no pleasing prospect to a youth who has a good deal to attain, and but a short while to do it in." *WGW*, vol. 36, 1-22-1798. To David Stuart.

Washington leaves this today, on a visit to Hope Park, which will afford you an opportunity to examine the progress he has made in the studies he was directed to pursue.

I can, and I believe do, keep him in his room a certain portion of the 24 hours, but it will be impossible for me to make him attend to his Books, if inclination, on his part, is wanting; nor while I am out, if he chuses to be so too, is it in my power to prevent it. I will not say this is the case, nor will I run the hazard of doing him injustice by saying he does not apply, as he ought, to what has been prescribed; but no risk will be run, and candour requires I declare it as my opinion, that he will not derive much benefit in any course which can be marked out for him at this place, without an *able* Preceptor always with him, nor then, for reasons, which do not require to be detailed.

What is best to be done with him, I know not. My opinion always has been that the University in Massachusetts would have been the most eligable Seminary to have sent him to, 1st, because it is on a larger Scale than any other; and 2nd, because I believe that the habits of the youth there, whether from the discipline of the School. or from the greater attention of the People, generally, to morals and a more regular course of life, are less prone to dissipation and debauchery than they are at the Colleges South of it. It may be asked, if this was my opinion, why did I not send him there? the answer is as short, as to me it was weighty; being the only male of his family and knowing (although it would have been submitted to) that it would have proved a heart rending stroke to have him at that distance. I was disposed to try a nearer Seminary, of good repute; which from some cause, or combinations of causes, has not, after the experiment of a year, been found to answer the end that was contemplated. Whether to send him there *now*, or indeed to any other public School, is at least problematical, and to suffer him to mispend his time at this place, will be disgraceful to himself and me.

The more I think of his entering at William and Mary, (unless he could be placed in the Bishop's family) the more doubtful I am of its utility, on many accounts; which had better be the subject of oral communications than by letter. I shall wish to hear from you on the subject of this letter. On occasion of severe reprimand, I found it necessary to give Washington sometime ago, I received the enclosed from him. I have little doubt of his meaning well, but he has not resolution, or exertion enough to act well. (See also, *WGW*, vol. 36, 1-22-1798. To David Stuart.)

18 See Edwin S. Gaustad, *A Documentary History of Religion In America to the Civil War*, (Grand Rapids: Eerdmans, 1993), p. 202-03.

19 Ibid, p. 203.

20 *WGW*, vol. 29, 2-20-1788. To Samuel Griffin.

21 To see how Washington's life reflected the three primary missions of William and Mary's founding charter, see the chapters: "Washington Vs. Deistic Ethics" for moral issues, "George Washington's Family Life" for the importance of proper college education for young people, and "Washington's Virginia and the Anglican Mission to the Indians" for missionary outreach. As to teaching the catechism and assenting to the Articles of the Christian faith, Washington had Anglican and Episcopal tutors for his children and he himself had signed the oath of subscription to the *Thirty-Nine Articles* when he became a Vestryman.

22 "Washington was assigned to his old Committee, that of Propositions and Grievances ... Privileges and Elections, and later to the new Committee of Religion.....He served on the same three regular committees as in the previous House—Propositions and Grievances, Privileges and Elections, and Religion." Douglas Southall Freeman, *George Washington: A Biography* (New York: Charles Scribner's Sons, 1951) III.218, 237.

23 Inasmuch as Virginia had been most forward in support of Massachusetts, Adams was especially eager to meet the Virginia delegates, four of whom, Peyton Randolph, Benjamin Harrison, Richard Henry Lee, and Richard Bland, arrived in the afternoon of September 2. A little converse with them, and Adams declared, "These gentlemen from Virginia appear to be the most spirited and consistent of any. Harrison said he would have come on foot rather than not come. Bland said he would have gone, upon this occasion, if it had been to Jericho." After a breakfast-table talk with Lee next morning, Adams set Lee down as "a masterly man." Physically, Randolph was "a large, well looking man," Lee "a tall, spare man," Bland "a learned, bookish man." Silas Deane drew a better portrait of Randolph: "Of an affable, open, and majestic deportment, large in size, though not out of proportion, he commands respect and esteem by his very aspect." It was Deane who described Harrison as "an uncommonly large man... rather rough in his dress and speech"; but it was Adams who later characterized him as "an indolent, luxurious, heavy gentleman, of no use in Congress or committee, but a great embarrassment to both." This, however, was when enthusiasms had cooled and the wires of purposes had become crossed. As the other Virginia delegates, Edmund Pendleton, Patrick Henry, and George Washington, did not arrive until Sunday, they failed to get their portraits hung in the Adams gallery at this time. It was Deane again, who a few days later supplied sketches of them. Pendleton was "of easy and cheerful countenance, polite in address, and elegant if not eloquent in style and elocution." Henry was "the compleatest speaker" he had ever heard. (Congress had then had some "samples" of the celebrated Virginian's oratory.) Colonel Washington was a tall man, of a "hard" countenance, "yet with a very young look, and an easy, soldier like air and gesture... speaks very modestly and in determined style and accent". What particularly placed him high in the estimation of the New Englanders was the speech he was said to have made in the House of Burgesses, when he offered to raise and arm and lead one thousand men himself at his own expense for the defense of the country. "Edmund Cody Burnett, *The Continental Congress*, (New York: The MacMillian Company, 1941), p. 29-30.

24 Meade, *Old Churches*, I. p. 174. See also, Meade, II. p. 292-293.

25 Meade, *Old Churches*, II. P. 140.

26 For Richard Henry Lee, see Meade, *Old Churches*, I. p. 171, II. 140-142. For Edmund Pendleton, see Meade I. pp. 414-416. For the Randolphs see Meade I. p. 181-183, II. p. 292-293, For R. C. Nicholas, see Meade I. 184-185. For Colonel Bland, see Meade, I. 183. For Patrick Henry, see Meade II. p. 12.

27 Federer, *America's God and Country*, p. 289.

28 Meade, *Old Churches*, I. p. 175, II. P. 293.

29 *WGW*, vol. 36, 1-22-1798. To David Stuart. "The more I think of his [George Washington Parke Custis] entering at William and Mary, (unless he could be placed in the Bishop's family) the more doubtful I am of its utility, on many accounts; which had better be the subject of oral communications than by letter."

30 Meade, *Old Churches*, I. 182-183.

31 Ibid, II. p. 292.

32 Ibid, I. 182.

33 Ellis, *His Excellency: George Washington*, p. 45.

34 Paul K. Longmore, *The Invention of George Washington* (Berkeley: University of California Press, 1988), pp. 92-93. "When the Assembly convened on 8 May 1769, Washington as usual received appointment to the powerful committees of Propositions and Grievances and of Privileges and Elections. A week later, he was put on the newly created standing Committee for Religion. This marked another significant step in his rise in the House. For the remainder of his membership, he would serve on these three standing committees. He was becoming an increasingly influential and prominent Burgess. Washington now stood in the second circle of power, just outside the central core of leadership.

"Signs of corruption alarmed Virginia's leaders: Robinson scandal, the sensational Chiswell murder care, pervasive materialism among the gentry, a consequent massive increase in private debt, reputedly widespread immorality among the Anglican clergy, declining influence of the established church, and the rise of disruptive religious sects. The Committee for Religion was established to combat these ominous trends. It included leading members of the House: Colony Treasurer Robert Carter Nicholas (Chair), Attorney General John Randolph, Richard Bland, Benjamin Harrison, Patrick Henry, Richard Henry Lee, Edmund Pendleton, and George Washington.

"The committee worked to police the established church by regulating parish vestries. It drafted plans to block a proposed Anglican episcopate and keep the church under indigenous control. It sought to defuse the divisive question of religious dissent by preparing legislation that would extend toleration to Baptists. In short, its actions were part of the effort to restore communal unity and public virtue at a time when both seemed jeopardy. This task was essential as the province confronted the Crown. Virginia's unified front from 1769 to 1775 suggests that the effort succeeded. It was not coincidence that the colony's leaders created the Committee for Religion at the same time they fashioned means to resist the Townshend duties and other recent arbitrary measures.

The remonstrances of the Virginia Assembly in 1768 against the Townshend duties had angered Crown officials. They have sent a new governor, Lord Botetcourt, to enforce imperial policy vigorously. Unbeknownst to Virginians, he carried instructions either to persuade provincial leaders to stop their protests against parliamentary authority, or failing that, to dissolve the Assembly and call for new elections. Meanwhile, the House of Lords, probably at the instigation of Lord Hillsborough, invoked a statute from the reign of Henry VIII to threaten the leading militants in Massachusetts with transportation to England to face charges of treason."

35   Ellis, *His Excellency: George Washington*, p. 151.

36   Ibid., p. 9.

37   Allan Nevins, *The American States: During and After the Revolution 1775-1789*, (New York: Augustus M. Kelley Publishers, 1969), p. 435, n. 16.

38   *WGW*, vol. 28, 1-17-1785. To Samuel Chase. "As you expressed a desire to know what the Assembly of this State had done, or were about to do respecting an establishment for the teachers of religion, I do myself the honor to enclose you a copy of their proceedings in that matter."

39   Allan Nevins, *The American States*, p. 434-435.

40   See Peter A. Lillback, *Proclaim Liberty: A Broken Bell Proclaims Liberty To The World* (Bryn Mawr: The Providence Forum, 2001), p. 88, n. 72. "It is sometimes inferred that Madison's rejection of established religion was tantamount to a rejection of the Christian faith. While Madison was deeply opposed to Christianity's use of force and persecution to advance its message, it is not true that he opposed Christianity *per se*. This is evident in his most famous treatise in the defense of non-governmental support of religion, 'Memorial and Remonstrance Against Religious Assessments, 1785.' One of his arguments for not using public funds to support the teachers of religion in Virginia is that it would actually advance the growth of Christianity, a fact that history has thoroughly substantiated. Madison writes, '6. Because the establishment proposed by the Bill is not requisite for the support of the Christian Religion. To say that it is, is a contradiction to the Christina Religion itself. . . .12. Because the policy to the bill is adverse to the diffusion of the light of Christianity. The first wish of those who enjoy this precious gift, ought to be that it may be imparted to the whole race of mankind."

41   *WGW*, vol. 10-3-1785, To George Mason.

42   Ibid., vol. 30, 10-23-1789. To First Presbytery of the Eastward. ". . . you will permit me to observe that the path of true piety is so plain as to require but little political direction. To this consideration we ought to ascribe the absence of any regulation, respecting religion, from the Magna-Charta of our country. To the guidance of the ministers of the gospel this important object is, perhaps, more properly committed. It will be your care to instruct the ignorant, and to reclaim the devious, and, in the progress of morality and science, to which our government will give every furtherance, we may confidently expect the advancement of true religion, and the completion of our happiness."

43   Ibid., vol. 30, 10-23-1789.

44   Ibid., vol. 30, 10-23-1789. To First Presbytery of the Eastward.

45   Note in Ibid, on May 4, 1772.

46   Ibid., vol. 3, 5-4-1772. To Reverend Jonathan Boucher.

47   Ibid., vol. 3, 5-4-1772. To Reverend Jonathan Boucher.

48   Longmore, *The Invention of George Washington*, p. 93.

49   See Sawyer, *Washington*, I. 215.

50   Letter of Nelly Custis, Sparks, *The Writings of George Washington*, vol. XII, p.405-408.

51   "Samuel Seabury (1729—1796) was the first bishop of the Episcopal church in America. He had been an outspoken and active Tory before and during the Revolution, and his choice by the Episcopal clergy of Connecticut as their candidate for consecration caused much controversy among the American churchmen and laity. The fact that he was consecrated in Scotland rather than in England made some question the validity of his office, and he was a controversial figure until his death." [a quote from where?]

52   Samuel Provoost (1742—1815) a native New Yorker, was the first Protestant Episcopal bishop of New York. Educated at Cambridge, he was ordained by the bishop of London in 1766. Upon his return to America, he served as assistant minister at Trinity Church in New York City, but his Whig sympathies so incensed the Loyalist members of the parish that he was forced to resign in 1771. After the evacuation of New York by the British, the vestry invited him to return as rector. In 1786 he was elected bishop of New York and was consecrated in England in the chapel of Lambeth Palace in Feb. 1787. In addition he still acted as rector of Trinity Church and was chaplain of the Senate.

53   William White (1748—1836), a native of Philadelphia, was the assistant minister and then, during the Revolution, the successor to Jacob Duché as minister for Christ and St. Peter's Anglican churches in Philadelphia. White had recently returned from England, where earlier this year he had been consecrated an Anglican bishop, thus becoming empowered to consecrate deacons for the newly formed Protestant Episcopal Church of the United States of America, which he was instrumental in organizing following the Revolution. White's sister Mary was the wife of George Washington's Philadelphia host, Robert Morris.

54   See Schaff's *Creeds of Christendom*, vol. 1, paragraph 82.

55   See justus.anglican.org/resources/bcp/1786/BCP; David Griffiths', *Bibliography of the Book of Common Prayer*; Paul Marshall, *Prayer Book Parallels*; William McGarvey *Liturgiæ Americanæ* (1907).

56   "A FORM OF PRAYER AND THANKSGIVING TO ALMIGHTY GOD, For the inestimable Blessings of Religious and Civil Liberty; to be used yearly Fourth Day of July, unless it happen to be on Sunday, and then on following. *The Service shall be as usual, except where it is hereby otherwise appointed. Among the Sentences at Morning Prayer shall be the following:*

THe Eternal God is thy refuge, and underneath are the everlasting Arms. *Deut.* 33. 27.Israel then shall dwell in safety alone: The fountain of Jacob shall be upon a land of corn and wine: also his heavens shall drop down dew. *Verse 28.*Happy art thou, O Israel: who is like unto thee, O people favoured by the Lord, the shield of thy help, and who is the sword of thy Excellency. *Verse 29.*

The Lord hath been mindful of us, and he shall bless us; he shall bless them that fear him, both small and great. *Psalm* 115. 12, 13. O that men would therefore praise the Lord for his goodness, and declare the wonders that he doeth for the children of men. *Psalm* 107.21. *Instead of "*O come let us sing, &c.," *the following Hymn shall be said or sung.*

MY Song shall be alway of the loving kindness of the Lord : with my Mouth ever be shewing his Truth from one generation to another. *Psal.* 89. 1.The merciful and gracious Lord hath so done his marvellous Works : that they ought to be had in remembrance. *Psal.* 111. 4. Who can express the noble Acts of the Lord : or shew forth all his praise? *Psal.* 106. 2. The works of the Lord are great : sought out of all them that have pleasure therein. *Psal.* 111.2. For he will not alway be chiding : neither keepeth he his anger forever. *Psal.* 103.9. He hath not dealt with us after our sins : nor rewarded us according to our wickedness. *Verse* 10. For look how high the heaven is in comparison of the earth : so great is his mercy toward them that fear him. *Verse* 11. Yea, like as a father pitieth his own children : even so is the Lord merciful unto them that fear him. *Verse* 11. Thou, O God, hast proved us; thou also hast tried us, like as silver is tried. *Psal.* 66.9. Thou didst remember us in our low estate, and redeem us from our enemies for thy mercy endureth forever. *Psal.* 136. 23, 24. *Then shall be said or sung the Psalm; which shall be the same as is appointed Day, Part 2.*

The first Lesson shall be, Deut. 8; *and the second Lesson shall be,* [1] Thess. 5.12 to 24.

A thanksgiving for the day, to be said after the general thanksgiving.

O God, whose Name is excellent in all the earth, and thy glory above the heavens, who as on this day didst inspire the direct the hearts of our delegates in Congress, to lay the perpetual foundations of peace, liberty, and safety; we bless and adore thy glorious Majesty, for this thy loving kindness and providence. And we humbly pray that the devout sense of this signal mercy may renew and increase in us a spirit of love and thankfulness to thee its only author, a spirit of peaceable submission to the laws and government of our country, and a spirit of fervent zeal for our holy religion, which thou hast preserved and secured to us and our posterity. May we improve these inestimable blessing for the advancement of religion, liberty, and science throughout this land, till the wilderness and solitary place be glad through us, and the desert rejoice and blossom as the rose. This we beg through the merits of Jesus Christ our Saviour. *Amen.*

The Collect: to be used instead of that for the Day.

ALmighty God, who hast in all ages shewed forth thy power and mercy in the wonderful preservation of thy church, and in the protection of every nation and people professing thy holy and eternal Truth, and putting their sure trust in thee; We yield thee our unfeigned thanks and praise for all thy public mercies, and more especially for that signal and wonderful manifestation of thy providence which we commemorate this day; Wherefore not unto us, O Lord, not unto us, but unto thy Name be ascribed all honor and glory, in all churches of the Saints, from generation to generation, through Jesus Christ our Lord. *Amen.*

The Epistle. Philip. 4. 4.

REjoice in the Lord alway: and again I say, Rejoice. Let your moderation be known unto all men. The Lord is at hand. Be careful for nothing; but in every thing by prayer and supplication with thanksgiving let your requests be made known unto God. And the peace of God, which passeth all understanding, shall keep your hearts and minds through Christ Jesus. Finally, brethren, whatsoever things are true, whatsoever things are honest, whatsoever things are just, whatsoever things are pure, whatsoever things are lovely, whatsoever things are of good report; if there be any virtue, and if there be any praise, think on these things.

The Gospel. St. John 8.31.

Then said Jesus to those Jews which believed on him, If ye continue in my word, then are ye my disciples indeed; And ye shall know the truth, and the truth shall make you free. They answered him, We be Abraham's seed, and were never in bondage to any man: how sayest thou, Ye shall be made free? Jesus answered them, Verily, verily, I say unto you, Whosoever committeth sin is the servant of sin. And the servant abideth not in the house for ever: but the Son abideth ever. If the Son therefore shall make you free, ye shall be free indeed.

57   The comment continues, "and on which our communion, the true, legitimate, Protestant Episcopal Church is based; while Bishop Seabury, a non-juror in principle and orders, and a pensioner of the British Government till his death, has impressed his principles of Episcopal and Sacerdotal exclusiveness, and of Sacramental, mechanical grace, upon the liturgy and Rites of the Church we have been forced to abandon." *A Chapter of Unwritten History. The Protestant Episcopacy of the Revolutionary Patriots Lost and Restored. A Centennial Offering,* by Reverend Mason Gallagher (Philadelphia: Reformed Episcopal Rooms, 1833), p. 4.

58   See chapter on religious liberty.

59   *A Chapter of Unwritten History. The Protestant Episcopacy of the Revolutionary Patriots Lost and Restored.* A Centennial Offering, by Reverend Mason Gallagher (Philadelphia: Reformed Episcopal Rooms, 1833), pp.; 4-5, 12.

60   *A Revolution that Led To A Church, Prepared for the 200th Anniversary of the establishment of the Episcopal Church in the United States. Journal of the Proceedings of the Bishops, Clergy, and Laity of the Protestant Episcopal Church, 1789* (Cincinnati: Forward Movement Publications,: 1990). Seven years of war knocked the wind out of the Anglican churches in America. Without an episcopate and a common bond of union, the Church in America was in danger of disintegrating. As the war drew to a close, however, churches in some states took independent action to protect their rights and liberties and to establish their own identity without regard to the larger issue of union of the church as a whole. Maryland took the lead in 1780 when it was agreed that "the Church formally known as the Church of England should now be called the Protestant Episcopal Church." But there had to be more!

In the Summer of 1782, thirty-four-year-old William White, Rector of the United Churches of Christ Church and St. Peter's, Philadelphia, published a pamphlet titled, *The Case of the Protestant Episcopal Church... Considered.* As the most important writing on the subject of union and reorganization at the time, it made White the central figure in the reorganization of the church.

White argued that because the ties with England had been broken, the churches were free to decide to unite or to remain separate. If they decided for union, they should build their organization from the parish up and not for the diocese down, this allowing laity a voice in the formation and operation of the church. To provide a forum where problems and solutions could be aired, White advocated a state convention of clergy and elected lay representatives.

On the matter of the episcopacy, White proposed that until that "higher office" could be obtained (and only until then), there be a Presbyterian type of ordination, and clergymen elevated to the "superior order" would serve in a parish. Since he believed (then) that the episcopate would be long in coming, he was convinced that his plan was in the best interest of the churches. As was expected, his proposal met with mixed reviews.

But more important than the immediate reactions to "The Case" was that by the time the Treaty of Paris had been signed, the former colonial churches had the outline of a plan for reorganization. Though all churchmen would not agree with White's proposals, his pamphlet opened up communications among various church leaders and attention began to be paid to the needs of the churches. Moreover, by 1785 the reorganization of the Episcopal Churches from New York to South Carolina was accomplished in open conventions of clergy and laity.

In contrast, the clergy of Connecticut, who apparently had received an early copy of White's pamphlet, met secretly in 1783 to discuss what they called the "Philadelphia Plan." Horrified, they went their own way: the episcopate first, union second. They elected Tory Samuel Seabury as bishop. Armed with a letter from the clergy to the archbishops, Seabury sailed for England to seek consecration. Though cordially received, his request was refused; and he turned to the non-juror bishops of Scotland and was consecrated in 1784, returning to the States the following spring (wearing a mitre, an ornament not used by the English bishops in the eighteenth century).

61   Reverend Mason Gallagher, *A Chapter of Unwritten History*, p. 12.

CHAPTER 16

1   *WGW*, vol. 30, 4-1779.

2   Boller, *George Washington & Religion*, p. 40.

3   From an interview done by Jerry Newcombe for Coral Ridge Ministries, 2005.

4   Johnson, *Washington the Christian*, p. 18.

5   *WGW*, vol. 2, 10-12-1761.

6   Ibid., vol. 3, 7-15-1772.

7   Ibid., vol. 2, 5-30-1768.

8   See Lane, *Washington Collection*, Boston Athenaeum, p. 23.

9   See *WGW*, vol. 2, Catalogue of Books for Master Custis Referred to on the Other side.

10   See the chapter on the Godly Leader.

11   *WGW*, vol. 27, 6-11-1783. To Reverend John Rodgers, "Dear Sir: I accept, with much pleasure your kind Congratulations on the happy Event of Peace, with the Establishment of our Liberties and Independence.
Glorious indeed has been our Contest: glorious, if we consider the Prize for which we have contended, and glorious in its Issue; but in the midst of our Joys, I hope we shall not forget that, to divine Providence is to be ascribed the Glory and the Praise.1
"Your proposition respecting Mr Aikins Bibles [Note: Rodgers's letter (May 30) suggested that Congress present each soldier with a Bible. This letter is in the *Washington Papers*.] would have been particularly noticed by me, had it been suggested in Season; but the late Resolution of Congress for discharging Part of the Army, takg off near two thirds of our Numbers, it is now too late to make the Attempt. It would have pleased me, if Congress should have made such an important present, to the brave fellows, who have done so much for the Security of their Country's Rights and Establishment.
"I hope it will not be long before you will be able to go peaceably to N York; some patience however will yet be necessary; but Patience is a noble Virtue, and when rightly exercised, does not fail of its Reward."

12   *WGW*, vol. 3-5-1794. To Charles Thompson. "Dear Sir: Weeks have passed since I finished reading the first part of your translation of the Septuagent; but having neglected (when I had the pleasure to see you last) to ascertain the medium through which I was to return it, and being unwilling to hazard the production to an uncertain conveyance, I give this letter to the Post Office in hopes of its reaching you, and of my receiving the information above."

13   See Boller, *George Washington & Religion*, p. 40.

14   *WGW*, vol. 37, Last Will and Testament,

15   Reverend Bryan Fairfax, Minister of Christ Church, Alexandria, *Sermon*; from Christ Church, Rare BV 4500 P14.

16   "While President, Washington followed an invariable routine on Sundays, The day was passed very quietly, no company being invited to the house. After breakfast, the President read aloud a chapter from the Bible, then the whole family attended church together. Washington spent the afternoon writing personal letters, never neglecting his weekly instructions to his manager at Mount Vernon, while Mrs. Washington frequently went to church again, often taking the children with her. In the evening, Lear read aloud to the family some sermon or extracts from a book of a religious nature and everyone went to bed at an early hour. The President was an Episcopalian and in New York at first went to Saint Paul's Chapel, as Trinity Church, which had been burned in the great fire of September, 1776, was then being rebuilt. The new church, when completed in March following, contained the 'President's Pew,' which was offered to Washington and accepted and after the new edifice was consecrated on the twenty-fifth of March, 1790, he attended services there until his departure from the city the following autumn." (Stephen Decatur, *Private Affairs of George Washington: From the Records and Accounts of Tobias Lear, Esquire, his Secretary*, pp. 90-91.)

17   M'Guire, *Religious Opinions*, p. 134 and following; Johnson, *George Washington The Christian*, p. 229-230; Meade, *Old Churches*, vol. 2, p. 246.

18   Custis, *Recollections*, p. 477.

19   Boller, *George Washington & Religion*, p. 40. See also P. Marion Simms, *The Bible in America* (New York, 1936), p. 132.

20   Consider here Uzal Ogden's 1795 work, *Antidote to Deism*, against Thomas Paine's *Age of Reason* that Washington declined to endorse.

Boller, p. 80, following Eliot Morison (*The Young Man Washington* (Cambridge, 1932), p. 37), implies that this was because of his sympathies for Deism. Washington received the two volumes on March 22, 1796. Ogden had written, "Dear Sir—I beg your acceptance of a Publication (which I have taken the Liberty to inscribe to you) designed to check the Progress of Infidelity and Vice, and to promote the Interests of Truth and Virtue—I shall be happy if the work shall be honored with your approbation, and am with sincere and great Esteem, Dear Sir, Your most obedient and very humble Servant Uzal Ogden." (William Lane, *A Catalogue of the Washington Collection*, (The Boston Athenaeum, 1897) pp. 154-55; *The George Washington Papers at the Library of Congress*, Series 4. General Correspondence. 1697-1799, Uzal Ogden to George Washington, March 22, 1796, Image 20 of 1122.) The truth is Washington by this time had determined to deal with Paine in total silence. To have endorsed a book that critiqued Paine would have opened him up for further wrangling with his erstwhile friend. See chapter two above. This view is corroborated by the fact that Washington in this instance did not even acknowledge Ogden's letter, although earlier he had clearly enjoyed an evangelical and biblically based sermon by Ogden, as is evident from Washington's letter to Ogden (*WGW*, vol. 16, 8-5-1779), and in another instance, although declining to endorse a publication by him, he graciously explained that he could not (*WGW*, vol. 30, 7-6-1789.) Interestingly, Washington not only retained Ogden's anti-Deistic work in his library, but Washington's autograph is on the title page of both volumes. Lane, *Washington Collection*, Boston Athenaeum p. 154.

21 *WGW,* vol. 30, April 1789.

22 Ibid., vol. 29, 4-25-1788.

23 Ibid., vol. 26, 6-8-1783.

24 Ibid., vol. 28, 7-25-1785.

25 Ibid.

26 Ibid., vol. 29, 4-5-1788. To Marquis de Chastellux. "…but for the sake of humanity it is devoutly to be wished, that the manly employment of agriculture and the humanizing benefits of commerce, would supersede the waste of war and the rage of conquest; that the swords might be turned into plough-shares, the spears into pruning hooks, and, as the Scripture expresses it, "the nations learn war no more."

27 Ibid., vol. 3, 5-21-1772. To Reverend Jonathan Boucher.

28 Ibid., vol. 16, 9-30-1779. To Marquis de Lafayette.

29 Ibid., vol. 32, 6-21-1792. To Gouverneur Morris.

30 Ibid., vol. 33, 5-26-1794. To the Earl of Buchan. "But providence, for purposes beyond the reach of mortal scan, has suffered the restless and malignant passions of man, the ambitious and sordid views of those who direct them, to keep the affairs of this world in a continual state of disquietude; and will, it is to be feared, place the prospects of peace too far off, and the promised millenium at an awful distance from our day." The millennium refers to the biblical text of Revelation 20:6 where a period of one thousand years is mentioned.

31 Ibid., vol. 30, 10-23-1789. To the First Presbytery of the Eastward. "I am persuaded, you will permit me to observe that the path of true piety is so plain as to require but little political direction."

32 Ibid., vol. 30, 10-9-1789, note. "On October 9 the Synod of the Dutch Reformed Church in North America sent an address to Washington, the answer to which is undated, but recorded immediately…In the answer he stated: 'I readily join with you that 'while just government protects all in their religious rights, true religion affords to government its surest support.'" *WGW*, vol. 30, 10-3-1789. Washington's first Thanksgiving Proclamation declared in part, "And also that we may then unite in most humbly offering our prayers and supplications to the great Lord and Ruler of Nations and beseech him to pardon our national and other transgressions, to enable us all, whether in public or private stations, to perform our several and relative duties properly and punctually, to render our national government a blessing to all the People, by constantly being a government of wise, just and constitutional laws, discreetly and faithfully executed and obeyed, to protect and guide all Sovereigns and Nations (especially such as have shown kindness unto us) and to bless them with good government, peace, and concord. To promote the knowledge and practice of true religion and virtue,…" *WGW*, vol. 24, 6-28-1782. To the Ministers, Elders, and Deacons of the Reformed Dutch Church at Albany. "Your benevolent wishes and fervent prayers for my personal wellfare and felicity, demand all my gratitude. May the preservation of your civil and religious Liberties still be the care of an indulgent Providence; and may the rapid increase and universal extension of knowledge virtue and true Religion be the consequence of a speedy and honorable Peace."

33 Ibid., vol. 13, 12-17-1778.

34 Ibid., vol. 10, 1-29-1778.

35 Ibid., vol. 25, 12-18-1782.

36 Ibid., vol. 30, April 1789.

37 Ibid., vol. 7, 1-22-1777

38 Ibid., vol. 12, 8-20-1778.

39 Ibid., vol. 27, 12-13-1783.

40 Ibid., vol. 35, 11-18-1796.

41 Ibid., vol. 36, July 25, 1798

42 Ibid., vol. 35, 5-15-1796.

43 Ibid., vol. 35, May 15, 1796

44 Interview with Mary Thompson, with Jerry Newcombe and Peter Lillback, 2005.

45 Ibid., vol. 29, 6-19-1788.

46 Ibid., vol. 31, 8-17-1790.

47 Ibid., vol. 35, 2-21-1796.

48 Ibid., vol. 35, 10-17-1796.

49 Ibid., vol. 35, 2-28-1797.

50   Ibid., vol. 35, 4-7-1797.
51   Ibid., vol. 35, 5-15-1797.
52   Ibid., vol. 35, 5-28-1797.
53   Ibid., vol. 35, 6-24-1797.
54   Ibid., vol. 35, 6-24-1797.
55   Ibid., vol. 35, 6-25-1797.
56   Ibid., vol. 35, 6-25-1797.
57   Ibid., vol. 35, 6-26-1797.
58   Ibid., vol. 35, 7-4-1797.
59   Ibid., vol. 35, 7-8-1797.
60   Ibid., vol. 30, 8-29-1788 to Sir Edward Newenham; vol. 33 5-26-1794 to the Earl of Buchan; vol. 34, 12-24-1795 to Dr. James Anderson.
61   Boller, *George Washington And Religion*, p. 43, writes, "If Washington 'diligently searched the Holy volume,' as has been asserted, he seems to have utilized his findings largely for purposes of whimsy."
62   *WGW*, vol. 37, 8-28, 1762.
63   Ibid., vol. 27, 9-2-1783. Her poem and letter, dated Aug. 28, 1783, and signed "Emilia," are in the Jackson, Twohig, *Diaries of George Washington.*
64   WGW, vol. 31, 8-14-1790 to Gouveneur Morris, see note.
65   Transcript of a TV interview with Rabbi Daniel Lapin, Coral Ridge Ministries 17 May 2001.
66   *WGW,* vol. 28, 7-25-1785.
67   Ibid., vol. 27, 9-2-1783.
68   Ibid., vol. 36, 6-13-1798.
69   Ibid., vol. 30, April 1789.
70   Ibid., vol. 28, 1-5-1785.
71   Ibid., vol. 37, 8-30-1799.
72   *PGW*, 2:179-181.
73   Ibid., vol. 5, 7-20-1776.
74   Ibid., vol. 22 7-8-1781.
75   Ibid., vol. 13, 12-12-1778.
76   Ibid., vol. 36, 4-16-1798.
77   Ibid., vol. 4, 1-14-1776.
78   Ibid., vol. 26, 6-8-1783.
79   Ibid., vol. 26, 5-26-1794.
80   Ibid., vol. 9, 10-19-1777.
81   Ibid., vol. 6, 9-24-1776.
82   Ibid., vol. 9, 10-19-1777.
83   Ibid., vol. 27, 9-2-1783.
84   Ibid., vol. 23, 1-31-1782.
85   Ibid., vol. 13, 12-17-1778.
86   Ibid., vol. 36, 12-3-1797.
87   Ibid., vol. 36, 11-4-1797.
88   Ibid., vol. 22, 6-7-1781.
89   Ibid., vol. 29, 4-25-1788.
90   Ibid., vol. 29, 4-25-1788.
91   Ibid., vol. 26, 7-8-1783.
92   Ibid., vol. 20, 11-20-1780.
93   Ibid., vol. 30, 6-28-1788.
94   Ibid., vol. 14,3-31-1779.
95   Ibid., vol. 27, 6-11-1783.
96   Ibid., vol. 30, 8-28-1788.
97   Ibid., vol. 26, 3-15-1783.
98   Ibid., vol. 11, 4-30-1778.
99   Ibid., vol. 24, 5-24-1793
100 Ibid., vol. 27, 10-12-1783.
101 Ibid., vol.3, 2-23-1773.
102 Ibid., vol. 4, 3-6-1776.
103 Ibid., vol. 27, 11-2-1783.
104 M'Guire, *Religious Opinions*, p.158

CHAPTER 17
1   *WGW*, vol. 7, 4-15-1777.

2   Believing that these phrases are not critical to be found in any specific context, but rather that it be understood that Washington used them, we here simply refer our reader to the *WGW* search feature, and ask them to type in the phrase and consider any number of examples for the phrases selected here.

3   See *WGW* search feature online.

4   See search feature of *WGW*.

5   *WGW*, vol. 4, 11-26-1775.

6   Ibid., vol. 4, 11-26-1775.

7   Ibid., vol. 8, 7-16-1777.

8   Ibid., vol. 10, 2-21-1778.

9   Ibid., vol. 6, 12-10-1776.

10 Ibid., vol. 28, 8-1-1786.

11 Ibid., vol. 6, 12-18-1776.

12 Ibid., vol. 9, 1-27-1777.

13 Ibid., vol. 19, 8-26-1780.

14 Ibid., vol. 17, 1-28-1780.

15 Ibid., vol. 17, 1-31-1780.

16 Ibid., vol. 27, 8-21-1783.

17 Ibid., vol. 26, 4-9-1783.

18 Ibid., vol. 36, 5-27-1798.

19 Ibid., vol. 34, 7-29-1795.

20 Ibid., vol. 37, 6-24-1799.

21 Ibid., vol. 29, 5-28-1788.

22 Ibid., vol. 13, 10-12-1778.

23 Ibid., vol. 27, 11-10-1783.

24 Ibid., vol. 31, 3-15-1790.

25 Ibid., vol. 30, 8-29-1788.

26 Ibid., vol. 29, 10-1783.

27 Ibid., vol. 30, 1-12-1790.

28 Ibid., vol. 13, 10-4-1778.

29 Ibid., vol. 31, 6-4-1790.

30 Ibid., vol. 27, 6-24, 1783.

31 Ibid., vol. 30, 5-10-1789.

32 Ibid., vol. 17, 11-27-1779.

33 Ibid., vol. 3, 9-14-1775.

34 Ibid., vol. 31, 3-15-1790.

35 Ibid., vol. 30, 8-18-1789.

36 Ibid., vol. 34, 2-10-1796.

37 Ibid., vol. 27, 8-10-1783.

38 Ibid., vol. 29, 5-5-1787.

39 Ibid., vol. 35, 8-29-1796.

40 Ibid., vol. 4, 1-27-1776.

41 We will consider Washington's view of God in a subsequent chapter.

42 We will consider Washington's view of providence in a subsequent chapter..

43 We will consider these in the subsequent chapter on Washington's view of God.

44 A subsequent chapter will consider Washington's view of heaven and eternal life.

45 *WGW*, vol. 7, 4-12-1777.

46 Ibid., vol. 10, 11-30-1777.

47 Ibid., vol. 30, 4-30-1789.

48 Ibid., vol. 9, 10-18-1777.

49 Ibid., vol.2, 10-12-1761; *WGW*, vol. 3, 7-15-1772; *WGW*, vol. 3, 7-18-1771.

50 Ibid., vol. 3, Diary.

51 Ibid., vol. 27, 7-10-1783.

52 8 times, e.g. *WGW*, vol. 4, 3-29-1776.

53 5 times, e.g. *WGW*, vol. 2-14-1784.

54 10 times, e.g. *WGW*, vol. 26, 6-8-1783.

55 5 times, e.g. *WGW*, vol. 27, 12-12-1783.

56 Ibid., vol. 29, 6-8-1788.

57 8 times, e.g. *WGW*, vol. 4, 12-5-1775.

58 5 times, e.g. *WGW*, vol. 30, 4-30-1789.

59 21 times, e.g. *WGW*, vol. 35, 5-15-1796.

60   This word is used over 1,500 times. The phrase "devoutly wishes" is used once in *WGW*, vol.35, 6-24-1797 and "devout wishes" is used twice, *WGW*, vol. 27, 7-14-1783; *WGW*, vol. 24, 1-7-1796. The words "devout" and "wish" occur together in various arrangements 22 times.

61   Ibid., vol. 27, 8-10-1783.

62   Ibid., vol. 17, 11-27-1779.

63   Human intercession resulting in pardon. *WGW*, vol. 25, 10-11-1782.

64   3 times, e.g. *WGW*, vol. 26, 6-8-1783. Benediction of heaven is used twice, e.g., *WGW*, vol. 27, 11-27-1783.

65   11 times, e.g. *WGW*, vol. 3, 7-4-1775.

66   Ibid., vol. 35, 9-16-1796.

67   Ibid., vol. 30, 7-20-1788.

68   161 times, e.g., *WGW*, vol. 26, 6-8-1783.

69   7 times, e.g. *WGW*, vol. 4, 11-18-1775.

70   Ibid., vol. 10, 11-30-1777.

71   Ibid., vol. 3, 7-29-1775.

72   Ibid., vol. 34, 12-30-1794.

73   9 times, e.g. *WGW*, vol. 5, 15, 1776.

74   Ibid., vol. 30, 10-3-1789.

75   Ibid., vol. 4, 11-18-1775.

76   Ibid., vol. 35, 8-29-1796.

77   3 times e.g. *WGW*, vol. 2, 8-2-1758.

78   We will consider the specific written prayers of Washington in the next chapter/APPENDIX, so we will not specifically footnote these phrases, since any number of the several examples can easily be found with the *WGW* search feature.

79   Ibid., vol. 36, 6-18-1798.

80   Ibid., vol. 27, 5-28-1784.

81   Ibid., vol. 27, 11-2-1783

82   Ibid., vol. 30, 7-21-1788.

83   Ibid., vol. 26, 6-8-1783.

84   Ibid., vol. 26, 3-23-1783.

85   Ibid., vol. 27, 11-15-1783.

86   Ibid., vol. 30, 9-23-1789.

87   Ibid., vol. 14, 3-4-1779.

88   Ibid., vol. 23, 9-8-1781.

89   Ibid., vol. 27, 2-14-84.

90   Ibid., vol. 27, 5-28-1784.

91   Ibid., vol. 24, 6-28-1782.

92   Ibid., vol. 27, 11-10-1783.

93   Ibid., vol. 37, 1-20-1799.

94   Ibid., vol. 27, 8-10-1783.

95   Ibid., vol. 31, 4-6-1790.

96   Ibid., vol. 31, 2-21-1791.

97   Ibid., vol. 37, 5-13-1776.

98   Ibid., vol. 2, 7-20-1758.

99   Ibid., vol. 33, 1-1-1794.

100 See appendix on Washington's written prayers.

101 *WGW*, vol. 28, 8-18-1786.

102 Ibid., vol. 3, 6-23-1775.

103 Ibid., vol. 37, 1-20-1799.

104 Ibid., vol. 5. 5-31-1776.

105 Ibid, vol. 4, 1-14-1776.

106 Ibid., vol. 37, 10-27-1799.

107 Ibid., vol. 37, 11-22-1799.

108 Ibid., vol. 5, 8-13-1776.

109 Ibid., vol. 31, 7-28-1791.

110 Ibid., vol. 37, 5-13-1776.

111 Ibid., vol. 13, 12-18-1778.

112 Ibid., vol. 33, 8-4-1793.

113 Ibid., vol. 36, 7-13-1798.

114 Ibid., vol. 3, 8-20-1775.

115 Ibid., vol. 3, 7-18-1775.

116 Ibid., vol. 30, 8-28-1788.

117 Ibid., vol. 30, 9-22-1788.

118 Ibid., vol. 1, 12-1756.

119 Ibid., vol. 36, 8-9-1798.

120 Ibid., vol. 4, 4-20-1776.

121 Ibid., vol. 37, 1-20-1799.

122 Ibid., vol. 35, 12-19-1796.

123 Ibid., vol. 26, 6-8-1783.

124 Ibid., vol. 3, 8-20-1785.

125 Ibid., vol. 28, 7-26-1786.

126 Ibid., vol. 26, 3-121-1783.

127 Ibid., vol.

128 Ibid., vol. 3, 8-11-1775.

129 Ibid., vol. 3, 9-14-1775.

130 Ibid., vol. 7, 4-15-1777.

131 Steiner, *The Religious Beliefs Of Our Presidents*, 1936.

132 *WGW*, vol. 30, 8-28-1785. To Reverend Jonathan Edwards.

133 Ibid., vol. 15, 6-2-1779. To the Minister, Elders, and Deacons of the Dutch Reformed Church at Raritan.

134 Ibid., vol. 30, 5-26-1789. To the General Assembly of Presbyterian churches in the United States.

135 Ibid., vol. 30, 10-23-1789. To the First Presbytery of the Eastward, Newburyport.

136 Ibid., vol. 28, 1-25-1785. To Sir James Jay.

137 Ibid., vol. 28, 2-8-1785. To the President of the Congress, *WGW*, vol. 28, 1-25-1785. To Sir James Jay.

138 Ibid., vol. 28, 1-25-1785. To Sir James Jay.

139 Ibid., vol. 32, 4-10-1792. To Reverend John Carroll.

140 Ibid., vol. 27, 8-10-1783. To George Martin.

141 Ibid., vol.13, 12-18-1778. To Benjamin Harrison

142 Ibid., vol. 11, 5-2-1778. General Orders.

143 Ibid., vol. 5, 5-15-1776. General Orders.

144 Ibid., vol. 30, 7-20-1785. To Jonathan Trumbull.

145 Ibid., vol. 30, 4-30-1789. The First Inaugural Address.

146 Ibid., vol. 35, 9-19-1796. Farewell Address.

147 *A Discourse*, Delivered, On the 18th day of December 1777, the Day of Public Thanksgiving Appointed by the Honourable Continental Congress, By the Reverend Israel Evans, Available on the Evans Collection Early American Imprints, 1st series, no. 15791 (filmed), "A.M. Chaplain to General Poor's Brigade And now published at the Request of the General and Officers of the said Brigade, To be distributed among the Soldiers, Gratis. Lancaster: Printed by Francis Bailey 1778. Evans wrote, "Methinks I see the illustrious Washington, with but two or three thousand men, retreating indeed before 10 or 12,000 of the enemy; but yet checking their progress thro' the country, and when reinforced by the brave militia, turning upon the enemy, killing some, captivating many, and obliging so large an army to retire, and confine themselves, during the whole winter, within narrow bounds. Oh America, give glory to God, for such a faithful hero! Then you saw him greatest when most without your aid. Collected in himself, he greatly resolved, with his few faithful followers, to be the barrier of liberty, or fall in its defense. Oh sons of America, let it not again be said, that you seemed to desert liberty and Washington: But God supported and preserved him and us all; so that instead of being conquered, we gained strength and knowledge, in the art and means of defense, during the two last campaigns: And having now nearly concluded the third campaign, although victory has not fully attended us in every enterprise, the prospect is glorious, and far exceeds our former expectations or hopes, and calls us to praise God, and say, blessed be the Lord, who hath not given us to be a prey to our enemies.... I now enter upon a less joyful subject than the triumphs of victory; but it is to some the sure attendant of conquest. Suffer me, my dear fellow soldiers, to check, for a moment, the current of joy and gladness, and blame me not for doing honour to the memory of the brave heroes, who fell in battle, honourably defending their country. They well deserve the tribute of a tear, and are justly entitled to the honour of being recorded in our breasts, among the saviors of our country. For us and posterity they bravely fought, and bled, and died, and fell in the field of glory, and the arms of victory. With us they were acquainted, and to us they were dear. Neither officers nor soldiers shall be ungratefully forgotten by us; for they have done honour to their country, and made a generous sacrifice of their lives, to the rights and liberties of mankind. Such bravery is worthy of imitation, and gives a dignity to human nature. Follow therefore, ye men of war, their noble example, and to all your innate bravery, join love to all the friends of liberty, and true love to God, who covered your heads in the day of battle, and shielded you from death, when you saw his arrows fly so thick around you, and so many were slain. I beseech you, let not your near escape from death, harden us against God, and dispose you to forget and neglect him. He is continually doing you good; why will you offend him, and disregard the innumerable obligations, you are under, to be obedient to his laws and submissive to his will. Behold, how tenderly the Psalmist represents the care and kindness of the Lord, unto all those who put their trust in him. He shall cover thee with his feathers, and under his wings shalt thou trust. Thou shalt not be afraid for the terror by night; nor the arrow that flyeth by day. In the strength of God, therefore, go on ye heroes, who, in two battles with the enemy, bravely fought, and have survived those conflicts, and are happily before me this day, employed in the most reasonable and dignified service, of praising and adoring the Lord of hosts, the God of battle, who with infinite ease disposes all the events of war, and guides the seemingly casual revolutions of kingdoms and states, to his own appointed purposes. Walk in the road of glory, and the pleasant path of true virtue, and gather fresh laurels in every enterprise. Regret not your removal from the late successful command of the honourable General Gates, for here is His Excellency General Washington. Look on him, and catch the genuine patriot fire of liberty and independence. Look on

him, and learn to forget your own ease and comfort; like him resign the charms of domestic life, when the genius of America bids you grow great in her service, and liberty calls you to protect her. Look on your worthy general, and claim the happiness and honour of saying, he is ours. Like him love virtue, and like him, reverence the name of the great Jehovah. Be mindful of that public declaration which he has made. "That we cannot reasonably expect the blessing of God upon our arms, if we continue to prophane his holy name. Learn of him to endure watchings, cold and hardships, for you have just heard that he assures you, he is ready and willing, to endure whatever inconveniences and hardships may attend this winter. Are any of you startled at the prospect of hard winter quarters? Think of liberty and Washington, and your hardships will be forgotten and banished. Let Europe, nay let the world hear, that the American army, in the defense of their country, cheerfully submitted to the inconvenience of having no other houses of accommodation, than such as their own hands reared in the depth of winter. Be encouraged, therefore, to undertake all that has been proposed to you, in the generals orders. And let me assure you, from some little experience obtained, in three campaigns, that what has appeared hard and impractible, at a distance, has been found tolerable and easy, when the worst that could be imagined has arrived."

148   *WGW*, vol.11, 3-13-1778. To Israel Evans.

149   *WGW*, vol. 30, 8-28-1788.

150   *WGW*, vol. 11, 3-13-1778. To Israel Evans. Valley Forge, March 13, 1778, "Your favor of the 17th. Ulto., inclosing the discourse which you delivered on the 18th. of December; the day set a part for a general thanksgiving; to Genl. Poors Brigade, never came to my hands till yesterday.

   "I have read this performance with equal attention and pleasure, and at the same time that I admire, and feel the force of the reasoning which you have displayed through the whole, it is more especially incumbent upon me to thank you for the honorable, but partial mention you have made of my character; and to assure you, that it will ever be the first wish of my heart to aid your pious endeavours to inculcate a due sense of the dependance we ought to place in that all wise and powerful Being on whom alone our success depends."

151   See, for example, *The American Heritage Dictionary*, (Boston: Houghton Mifflin, 1982), p. 390 under "devout".

152   *WGW*, vol. 7, 4-12-1777

153   *WGW*, vol. 7, 4-15-1777.

154   *WGW*, vol. 36 7-13-1798, To THE PRESIDENT OF THE UNITED STATES
   "Satisfied therefore, that you have sincerely wished and endeavoured to avert war, and exhausted to the last drop, the cup of reconciliation, we can with pure hearts appeal to Heaven for the justice of our cause, and may confidently trust the final result to that kind Providence who has heretofore, and so often, signally favoured the People of these United States."

155   *WGW*, vol. 30, 9-22-1788., To HENRY LEE
   "Should the contingency you suggest take place, and (for argument sake alone let me say it) should my unfeigned reluctance to accept the office be overcome by a deference for the reasons and opinions of my friends; might I not, after the Declarations I have made (and Heaven knows they were made in the sincerity of my heart) in the judgment of the impartial World and of Posterity, be chargeable with levity and inconsistency; if not with rashness and ambition?
   "While doing what my conscience informed me was right, as it respected my God, my Country and myself, I could despise all the party clamor and unjust censure, which must be expected from some."

156   *WGW*, vol.1, 5-29-1754. To ROBERT DINWIDDIE.

157   *WGW*, vol. 30, 12-4-1788. To Arthur Young.

158   *WGW*, vol. 24, 4-20-1782. To BARTHOLOMEW DANDRIDGE
   "In a word, I see so many perplexing and intricate matters before me, which must be the work of time to arrange and bring to a conclusion, that It would be injurious to the Children, and madness in me, to undertake as a *principle* a trust which I could not discharge. Such aid however, as it ever may be with me to give to the Children, especially the boy, I will afford with all my heart, and with all my Soul, and on the assurances of it you may rely."

159   *WGW*, vol. 25, 12-14-1782. To COMTE DE ROCHAMBEAU
   "To this testimony of your Public character I should be wanting to the feelings of my heart, was I not to add expressions of the happiness I have enjoyed in your private friendship. The remembrance of which, will be one of the most pleasing Circumstances of my life."

160   *WGW*, vol. 34, 12-16-1795. To THE CITIZENS OF FREDERICK COUNTY, VIRGINIA
   "Next to the approbation of my own mind, arising from a consciousness of having uniformly, diligently and sincerely aimed, by doing my duty, to promote the true interests of my country, the approbation of my fellow citizens is dear to my heart. In a free country, such approbation *should* be a citizen's best reward; and so it *would* be, if Truth and Candour were always to estimate the conduct of public men. But the reverse is so often the case, that he who, wishing to serve his country, is not influenced by higher motives, runs the risk of being miserably disappointed. Under such discouragements, the good citizen will look beyond the applauses and reproaches of men, and persevering in his duty, stand firm in conscious rectitude, and in the hope of [an] approving Heaven."

161   Ibid., vol. 16, 7-29-1779. To PRESIDENT JOSEPH REED
   "..the first wish of my Soul is to return to that peaceful retirement, and domestick ease and happiness from whence I came."
   Ibid., vol. 30, 1-10-1789. To SAMUEL HANSON
   "The first wish of my Soul is to spend the evening of my days in the lot of a private citizen on my farm...."
   Ibid., vol. 24, 6-15-1782. To ARCHIBALD CARY
   "I can truly say that the first wish of my Soul is to return speedily into the bosom of that Country which gave me birth and in the sweet enjoyment of domestic pleasures and the Company of a few friends to end my days in quiet when I shall be called from this Stage."

162   Ibid., vol. 19, 10-17-1777. TO RICHARD HENRY LEE "You may believe me, my good Sir, that I have no Earthly views, but the public good, in what I have said. I have no prejudice against General Conway, nor desire to serve any other Brigadier, further than I think the

cause will be benefitted by it; to bring which to a speedy and happy conclusion, is the most fervent wish of my Soul"

Ibid., vol. 26, 4-4-1783. To THEODORICK BLAND

"As it is the first wish of my Soul to see the war happily and speedily terminated, and those who are now in Arms return to Citizenship with good dispositions, I think it a duty which I owe to candor and to friendship to point you to such things, as will have a tendency to harmony and to bring them to pass."

Ibid., vol. 13, 12-12-1778. To PRESIDENT JOSEPH REED

"Were I to give into private conveniency and amusement, I should not be able to resist the invitation of my friends to make Phila. (instead of a squeezed up room or two) my quarters for the Winter; but the affairs of the army require my constant attention and presence, and circumstanced as matters are at this time, calls for some degree of care and address to keep it from crumbling. As Peace and retirement are my ultimate aim, and the most pleasing and flattering hope of my Soul, every thing advansive of this end, contributes to my satisfaction, however difficult and inconvenient in the attainment; and will reconcile any place and all circumstances to my feelings whilst I continue in Service."

163 Ibid., vol. 29, 2-25-1787. To HENRY KNOX,

"...to see this Country happy whilst I am gliding down the stream of life in tranquil retirement is so much the wish of my Soul, that nothing on this side Elysium can be placed in competition with it."

164 Ibid., vol. 36, 8-4-1797. To LAWRENCE LEWIS

"I am sorry to hear of the loss of your servant; but it is my opinion these elopements will be MUCH MORE, before they are LESS frequent: and that the persons making them should never be retained, if they are recovered, as they are sure to contaminate and discontent others. I wish from my soul that the Legislature of this State could see the policy of a gradual Abolition of Slavery; It would prevt. much future mischief."

165 Ibid., vol. 27, 12-1-1783. To THE FREEHOLDERS AND INHABITANTS OF KINGS COUNTY.

166 Washington's deep emotions are very evident in his words to his Army at the time of the cease fire with Britain.

Friday, April 18, 1783.

"Although the proclamation before alluded to, extends only to the prohibition of hostilities and not to the annunciation of a general peace, yet it must afford the most rational and sincere satisfaction to every benevolent mind, as it puts a period to a long and doubtful contest, stops the effusion of human blood, opens the prospect to a more splendid scene, and like another morning star, promises the approach of a brighter day than hath hitherto illuminated the Western Hemisphere; on such a happy day, a day which is the harbinger of Peace, a day which completes the eighth year of the war, it would be ingratitude not to rejoice! It would be insensibility not to participate in the general felicity.

"The commander in chief far from endeavouring to stifle the feelings of Joy in his own bosom, offers his most cordial Congratulations on the occasion to all the Officers of every denomination, to all the Troops of the United States in General, and in particular to those gallant and persevering men who had resolved to defend the rights of their invaded country so long as the war should continue. For these are the men who ought to be considered as the pride and boast of the American Army; And, who crowned with well earned laurels, may soon withdraw from the field of Glory, to the more tranquil walks of civil life.

While the General recollects the almost infinite variety of Scenes thro which we have passed, with a mixture of pleasure, astonishment, and gratitude; While he contemplates the prospects before us with rapture; he can not help wishing that all the brave men (of whatever condition they may be) who have shared in the toils and dangers of effecting this glorious revolution, of rescuing Millions from the hand of oppression, and of laying the foundation of a great Empire, might be impressed with a proper idea of the dignified part they have been called to act (under the Smiles of providence) on the stage of human affairs: for, happy, thrice happy shall they be pronounced hereafter, who have contributed any thing, who have performed the meanest office in erecting this stupendous *fabrick* of *Freedom* and *Empire* on the broad basis of Independency; who have assisted in protecting the rights of humane nature and establishing an Asylum for the poor and oppressed of all nations and religions. The glorious task for which we first flew to Arms being thus accomplished, the liberties of our Country being fully acknowledged, and firmly secured by the smiles of heaven, on the purity of our cause, and the honest exertions of a feeble people (determined to be free) against a powerful Nation (disposed to oppress them) and the Character of those who have persevered, through every extremity of hardship; suffering and danger being immortalized by the illustrious appellation of the *patriot Army* Ibid., vol. 26, 4-18-1783..

167 Ibid., vol. 16, 7-29-1779. General Orders.

CHAPTER 18

1   *WGW,* vol. 7, 4-15-1777.

2   M'Guire, *Religious Opinions,* p. 162-167, This story was "taken from a respectable literary journal published in New York," p. 162.

3   Ibid., p.-156.

4   Meade, *Old Churches,* vol. II, p.490ff. No. XXIII. "Further Statements Concerning the Religious Character of Washington and the Question Whether he was a Communicant or Not."

5   *WGW,* vol. 3, 7-18-1771.

6   1662 *Book of Common Prayer,* see http://www.eskimo.com/~lhowell/bcp1662/index.html

7   Ibid.

8   Ibid.

9   *WGW,* vol. 10, General Orders Head Quarters, White Marsh, November 30, 1777.

"On the 25th of November instant, the Honorable Continental Congress passed the following resolve:

Resolved. ... Forasmuch as it is the indispensible duty of all men, to adore the superintending providence of Almighty God; to acknowledge with gratitude their obligations to him for benefits received, and to implore such further blessings as they stand in need of; and it having pleased him in his abundant mercy, not only to continue to us the innumerable bounties of his common providence, but also, to smile upon us in the prosecution of a just and necessary war, for the defence of our unalienable rights and liberties.

"It is therefore recommended by Congress, that Thursday the 18th. day of December next be set apart for Solemn Thanksgiving and Praise; that at one time, and with one voice, the good people may express the grateful feelings of their hearts, and consecrate themselves to the service of their divine benefactor; and that, together with their sincere acknowledgements and offerings they may join the penitent confession of their sins; and supplications for such further blessings as they stand in need of. The Chaplains will properly notice this recommendation, that the day of thanksgiving may be duly observed in the army, agreeably to the intentions of Congress."

10   Ibid., vol. 17, General Orders Head Quarters, Moore's House, Saturday, November 27, 1779.

"The Honorable the Congress has been pleased to pass the following proclamation.

Whereas it becomes us humbly to approach the throne of Almighty God, with gratitude and praise for the wonders which his goodness has wrought in conducting our fore-fathers to this western world; for his protection to them and to their posterity amid difficulties and dangers; for raising us, their children, from deep distress to be numbered among the nations of the earth; and for arming the hands of just and mighty princes in our deliverance; and especially for that he hath been pleased to grant us the enjoyment of health, and so to order the revolving seasons, that the earth hath produced her increase in abundance, blessing the labors of the husbandmen, and spreading plenty through the land; that he hath prospered our arms and those of our ally; been a shield to our troops in the hour of danger, pointed their swords to victory and led them in triumph over the bulwarks of the foe; that he hath gone with those who went out into the wilderness against the savage tribes; that he hath stayed the hand of the spoiler, and turned back his meditated destruction; that he hath prospered our commerce, and given success to those who sought the enemy on the face of the deep; and above all, that he hath diffused the glorious light of the gospel, whereby, through the merits of our gracious Redeemer, we may become the heirs of his eternal glory: therefore,

"RESOLVED, That it be recommended to the several states, to appoint Thursday, the 9th of December next, to be a day of public and solemn thanksgiving to Almighty God for his mercies, and of prayer for the continuance of his favor and protection to these United States; to beseech him that he would be graciously pleased to influence our public councils, and bless them with wisdom from on high, with unanimity, firmness, and success; that he would go forth with our hosts and crown our arms with victory; that he would grant to his church the plentiful effusions of divine grace, and pour out his holy spirit on all ministers of the gospel; that he would bless and prosper the means of education, and spread the light of christian knowledge through the remotest corners of the earth; that he would smile upon the labours of his people and cause the earth to bring forth her fruits in abundance; that we may with gratitude and gladness enjoy them; that he would take into his holy protection our illustrious ally, give him victory over his enemies, and render him signally great, as the father of his people and the protector of the rights of mankind; that he would graciously be pleased to turn the hearts of our enemies, and to dispense the blessings of peace to contending nations; that he would in mercy look down upon us, pardon our sins and receive us into his favor, and finally, that he would establish the independence of these United States upon the basis of religion and virtue, and support and protect them in the enjoyment of peace, liberty and safety. A strict observance to be paid by the Army to this proclamation and the Chaplains are to prepare and deliver discourses suitable to it."

11   Ibid., vol. 26, 4-18-1783.

12   *Cf.*, M'Guire, *Religious Opinions*, 151. During the Constitutional Convention (May to September 1787), over which George Washington presided, progress was slow-going for the first several weeks. Tempers flared. It was hot and muggy and unpleasant. Delegates were coming and going. Some left and never returned. We know there were 55 delegates, yet only 39 signed the document in September, the first being Washington. Progress was so slow that on June 28, the elder statesman amongst them, the well-respected Benjamin Franklin, stood up and gave a monumental speech. He called for them to pray. He told them that they would succeed no greater than the builders of the Tower of Babel if they neglected God. Franklin was not an orthodox Christian. He was one of the 5% amongst them who was not. Yet he gave an impassioned speech—one of the greatest in American history—calling for prayer. Here is one of his statements in that speech: "I have lived, Sir, a long time, and the longer I live, the more convincing proofs I see of this truth—that God Governs in the affairs of men. And if a sparrow cannot fall to the ground without His notice, is it probable that an empire can rise without His aid?" ...Immediately after Franklin spoke, New Jersey delegate Jonathan Dayton described the scene. Note what he says about Washington's reaction. "The Doctor sat down; and never did I behold a countenance at once so dignified and delighted as was that of Washington at the close of the address; nor were the members of the convention generally less affected. The words of the venerable Franklin fell upon our ears with a weight and authority, even greater that we may suppose an oracle to have had in a Roman senate!" See David C. Gibbs, Jr., Jerry Newcombe, *One Nation Under God: Ten things Every Christian Should Know About the Founding of America.* (Seminole, FL: Christian Law Association), pp. 159-160.

13   Boller, p. 169. *George Washington Papers at the Library of Congress*, 1741-1799: Series 2 Letterbooks, George Washington to Philadelphia German Lutherans, April 27, 1789 Letterbook 38, Image 40 of 166.

14   Boller, *George Washington & Religion*, p. 173. *PGW*: Series 2 Letterbooks, George Washington to Methodist Episcopal Bishops, May 29, 1789, Letterbook 38, Image 42 of 166.

15   *WGW*, vol. 30, 10-3-1789.

16   Ibid., vol. 34, 11-19-1794

17   Ibid., vol. 35, 12-7-1796.

18   This argument has been used to diminish the importance of Washington's commitment to providence. *Cf.* Douglas Southall Freeman *George Washington, A Biography*, 7 vols. *Victory with the Help of France* Volume Five (New York: Charles Scribner's Sons, 1952), pp. 493-94. "To this same uncertain frontier of Washington's mind his personal religion had been brought back after the years of peace had led him,

the vestryman and then the warden, to conform without heart searching to the practices of the church. He had believed that a God directed his path, but he had not been particularly ardent in his faith. The war had convinced him that a Providence had intervened to save America from ruin. So often had he remarked it that a French skeptic would have said of him, no doubt, that a fatalist had become superstitious. On the other hand, had a Chaplain at headquarters been privileged to look through Washington's files he would have been disappointed to find there no evidence of expressed personal belief in any creedal religion. It was almost as if the God of Battles had subordinated the God of the humble heart. The tone of Washington's addresses and circulars was distinctly more fervent, to be sure, than in 1775, if the theme touched religion, but this change had not become marked until Jonathan Trumbull, Jr., had joined the staff and had begun to write Washington's public papers of this type. Trumbull's alternate and successor in this capacity was David Humphreys, who, like the Connecticut Governor's son, was of theologically minded New England believers. The part these two men played in accentuating and enlarging with their pens the place that Providence had in the mind of Washington probably was among the most extraordinary and least considered influences of puritanism on the thoughts of the young nation. The people who heard the replies of Washington to their addresses doubtless thought they were listening to the General, as indeed they were, to the extent that Washington did not cancel what had been written; but the warmth of the faith was more definitely that of the aide than that of the Commander-in-Chief. Now that the war had ended and the Providence that Washington would observe was that of rain and sunshine and season and storm, not that of marches and battles, it remained for the returning soldier to see whether God again became personal to him."

19   WGW, vol. 32, 5-24-1793 (WGW note: The draft, in the writing of Jefferson, is in the *Jefferson Papers* in the Library of Congress.).

20   Ibid., vol. 14, 3-4-1779.

21   Ibid., vol. 21, 2-26-1781.

22   The address of the artillery company is dated Feb. 22, 1794, and it and this answer are entered in the "Letter Book" in the *Washington Papers*.

23   *WGW*, vol. 33 2-1794.

24   The original address of the ministers, etc., is in *PGW*, It is signed "George J: L: Doll. V. D. M

25   *WGW*, vol. 25 11-16-1782.

26   *PGW*, Series 4. General Correspondence. 1697-1799, William Linn to George Washington, May 30, 1798, image 243-244.

27   *WGW*, vol. 36, 6-4-1798.

28   *A Discourse on National Sins*: Delivered May 9, 1798 Being the day recommended by the President of the United States to be observed as a day of General Fast By William Linn, D.D. One of the ministers of the Reformed Dutch Church in the City of New York. New York: Printed by T. & J. Swords, No. 99 Pearl-Street, 1798. Linn wrote,

"In the fourth place, that the prevalence of infidelity is a cause of divine judgments. Not many years ago, a professed deist, in this country, was rare. If any doubted, they were ashamed to avow it, and they had so much decency as not to ridicule what the generality of mankind held sacred. But infidelity is now no longer concealed. Its advocates are numerous, and propagate their sentiments with a brazen front. Formerly, some of the most celebrated infidels attacked the Christian religion indirectly; but we have seen it represented as a fable not even cunningly devised, as destructive of morality, and the source of innumerable miseries. We have seen it loaded with all manner of reproach, and a bold attempt made to eradicate it from the earth. From an American press have issued the most horrid blasphemies which have ever been uttered. From an American press issued the first part of the "Age of Reason;" and the second part was re-printed here; a multitude of copies were imported, and circulated with uncommon industry. Surely, if our ports be shut, it should be against such principles as these. Were it possible to lay an embargo on them in the country from which they come, it ought to be done; for they are infinitely more to be dreaded than all the fleets and armies of Europe...."

"Perhaps we may date the growth of infidelity among us, from the entrance of the French army. While they brought us the assistance we desired, and accelerated our independence, they leavened us with ungodliness, and it may yet be said of us, "The strength of Pharaoh shall be your shame, and the trust in the shadow of Egypt your confusion." Deism and atheism have long been propagated among their people, and at their revolution appeared in full maturity. Their very Clergy, the professed Ministers of the religion of Christ, headed by the Archbishop of Paris, came before the National Convention, and abjured the Christian religion, declaring that they considered it as an imposture. What else but horrid deeds were to be expected from those who gloried in the confession of their hypocrisy? What confidence can be placed in those who defy the Majesty of heaven and earth? ... As to the leading object of Thomas Paine, I have expressed an opinion. It is certain that his principles directly tend to confusion, and every evil work.... To the necessity of religion, President Washington has borne ample testimony, in his most excellent address on his resignation; an address fraught with political wisdom, and which, in matter and manner, is worthy the pen of the greatest philosopher and statesman in the world. "Of all the dispositions and habits," says he, "which lead to political prosperity, religion and morality are indispensable supports. In vain would that man claim the tribute of patriotism, who should labor to subvert these great pillars of human happiness, these firmest props of the duties of men and citizens. The mere politician, equally with the pious man, ought to respect and to cherish them. A volume could not trace all their connections with private and public felicity. Let it simply be asked, where is the security for property, for reputation, for life, if the sense of religious obligation desert the oaths, which are the instruments of investigation in courts of justice? And let us with caution indulge the supposition, that morality can be maintained "without religion."—If the heathen found their religious institutions and worship absolutely necessary, and highly beneficial, what advantages are to be expected from the profession and influence of the true religion? "There was never found," says the great Lord Bacon, who may be set against an host of infidels, "in any age of the world, either philosophy, or sect, or religion, which did so highly exalt the public good, as the Christian Faith."—The French legislators have not satisfied themselves with renouncing revealed religion, but have endeavored to destroy natural religion itself. They have denied the being of God and his providence; that there is any future state of existence; declared death to be an eternal sleep; and set up, no objects of worship, Reason and Liberty."

29   *WGW*, vol. 2, 7-20-1758

30   Ibid., vol. 4, 4-29-1776.
31   Ibid., vol. 7, 4-15-1777.
32   Ibid., vol. 11-18-1775.
33   Ibid., vol. 27, 12-12-1783.
34   Ibid., vol. 27, 11-2-1783.
35   Ibid., vol.27, 8-10-1783.
36   Ibid., vol. 26, 6-8-1783.
37   Ibid., vol.27, 8-25-1783.
38   Ibid., vol. 28, 4-10-1785.
39   Ibid., vol. 30, 9-28-1789.
40   Ibid., vol. 30, 10-3-1789.
41   Ibid., vol. 35, 9-19-1796.
42   Ibid., vol. 36, 10-24-1798.
43   Ibid., vol. 37, 1799.

CHAPTER 19

1   *WGW,* vol. 10, 12-17-1777.
2   This Psalm is indeed remarkable in this historical context. The following selection is taken from *The New International Version* of the Bible.
    1. Contend, O LORD, with those who contend with me;
    2. fight against those who fight against me.
    3. Take up shield and buckler; arise and come to my aid.
    4. Brandish spear and javelin against those who pursue me. Say to my soul, "I am your salvation."
    5. May those who seek my life be disgraced and put to shame; may those who plot my ruin be turned back in dismay.
    6. May they be like chaff before the wind, with the angel of the LORD driving them away;
    7. may their path be dark and slippery, with the angel of the LORD pursuing them.
    8. Since they hid their net for me without cause and without cause dug a pit for me,
    9. may ruin overtake them by surprise—may the net they hid entangle them, may they fall into the pit, to their ruin.
    10. Then my soul will rejoice in the LORD and delight in his salvation.
    11. My whole being will exclaim, "Who is like you, O LORD? You rescue the poor from those too strong for them, the poor and needy
    from those who rob them."
3   Cited in Robert Gordon Smith, ed., *One Nation Under God: An Anthology for Americans* (New York: Funk & Wagnalls, 1961), pp. 39-40.
    "Sadly for the American cause, Reverend Duché became a loyalist as the City of Philadelphia fell to the British. He wrote a letter calling
    on Washington to resign and end the war. Duché left for England. But when the War was over, he returned, and ever the gracious gentle-
    man, Washington answered Duché letter indicating that he held no ill will. Duché 's brother-in-law, Francis Hopkinson, signer of the
    Declaration and designer of the American flag, wrote a letter to Washington when he learned of the letter from Reverend Duché that had
    called on him to resign and to end the war." This was Washington's response. *WGW,* vol.10, 11-21, 1777. To Francis Hopkinson.
       "Sir: I am favoured with yours of the 14th. inclosing a letter for the Reverend Mr. Duché. I will endeavour to forward it to him, but I
    imagine it will never be permitted to reach his hands.
       [*WGW,* Note: Hopkinson's letter to Duché, who was his brother-in-law, is dated November 14 and is printed, in part, in *Life and Works
    of Hopkinson* , by George E. Hastings (Chicago, 1926): "Words cannot express the Grief and Consternation that wounded my Soul at the
    sight of this fatal Performance.... I could go thro' this extraordinary Letter and point out to you the Truth distorted in every leading Part;
    But the World will doubtless do this with a Severity that must be Daggers to the Sensibilities of your Heart. Read that Letter over again:
    and, if possible, divest yourself of the Fears and Influences, whatever they were, that induced you to pen it ... you have by a vain and weak
    Effort attempted the Integrity of one whose Virtue is impregnable to the Assaults of Fear or Flattery; whose Judgment needed not your
    Information and who, I am sure, would have resigned his Charge the Moment he found it likely to lead him out of the Paths of Virtue
    and Honour.... And with whom would you have him negotiate. Are they not those who, without the Sanction of any civil, moral or reli-
    gious Right, have come 3000 Miles to destroy our Peace and Property: to lay waste to *your* native Country with Fire and Sword and cru-
    elly muther its Inhabitants. Look for their Justice and Honour, in the Gaols of New York and Philada. and in your own Potter's Field. ..."]
       I confess to you, that I was not more surprised than concerned at receiving so extraordinary a Letter from Mr. Duché, of whom I had
    entertained the most favourable opinion, and I am still willing to suppose, that it was rather dictated by his fears than by his real senti-
    ments; but I very much doubt whether the great numbers of respectable Characters, in the State and Army, on whom he has bestowed the
    most unprovoked and unmerited abuse will ever attribute it to the same Cause, or forgive the Man who has artfully endeavoured to engage
    me to Sacrifice them to purchase my own safety.
       I never intended to have made the letter more public than by laying it before Congress. I thought this a duty which I owed to myself, for
    had any accident have happened to the Army intrusted to my command, and it had ever afterwards have appeared that such a letter had
    been wrote to and received by me, might it not have been said that I had betrayed my Country? and would not such a correspondence, if
    kept a secret, have given good Grounds for the suspicion?
       I thank you for the favourable sentiments which you are pleased to express of me, and I hope no act of mine will ever induce you to alter
    them."
4   *First Prayer in Congress—Beautiful Reminiscence* (Washington, D. C.: Library of Congress); John S. C. Abbot, *George Washington* (NY:

Dodd, Mead & Co., 1875, 1917), p. 187.

5   Consider the following from the pen of a revolutionary soldier: "Our enemy does not knock them on the head, or burn them to death with torches, or flay them alive, or gradually dismember them till they die, which is customary among Savages &Barbarians. No, they are worse by far. They suffer them to starve, to linger out their lives in extreme hunger. One of these poor unhappy men, driven to the last extreme by the rage of hunger, ate his own fingers up to the first joint of his hand, before he died...." John Joseph Stoudt, *Ordeal At Valley Forge: A Chronicle Compiled from the Sources* (Philadelphia: University of Pennsylvania Press, 1963.) p. 24-25

6   *WGW*, vol. 3, 8-20-1775. To Lt. Gen. Thomas Gage. "Sir: I addressed you on the 11th. Instant in Terms, which gave the fairest Scope for the Exercise of that Humanity, and Politeness, which were supposed to form a Part of your Character. I remonstrated with you on the unworthy Treatment, shewn to the officers and Citizens of America, whom the Fortune of War, Chance, or a mistaken Confidence, had thrown into your Hands."

"Whether British or American Mercy, Fortitude, and Patience are most preeminent, whether our virtuous Citizens, whom the Hand of Tyranny has forced into Arms to defend their Wives, their Children, and their Property, or the mercenary Instruments of lawless Domination, avarice and Revenge, best deserve the Appellation of Rebels, and the Punishment of that Cord, which your affected Clemency has forborne to inflict: whether the Authority, under which Fact, is usurped, or founded upon the genuine Principles of Liberty, were altogether foreign to the Subject. I purposely avoided all political Disquisition; nor shall I now avail myself of those Advantages, which the sacred Cause of my Country of Liberty, and human Nature, give me over you."

7   *WGW*, vol. 5, 7-7-1776. To Gov. Jonathan Trumbull The Interest of America is now in the Ballance, and it behoves all Attached to her Sacred Cause and the rights of Humanity, to hold forth their Utmost and most speedy Aid. I are Convinced nothing will be wanting in your power to Effect." *WGW*, vol. 8, 7-31-1777. To Gov. Jonathan Trumbull . "I sent Genls. Lincoln and Arnold to assist in that Command. These two Gentlemen are esteemed good Officers and, I think very deservedly. I am persuaded, nothing, that their judgements shall direct, will be omitted to stop the Progress of General Burgoyne's Arms, as far as in them lies — and, I am equally Sure, their personal exertions and Bravery will not be wanting in any instance. Their presence, I trust, will remove every Ground of diffidence and backwardness in the Militia, and that they will go on when and where their Services are demanded, with a Spirit and Resolution becoming Freemen and the Sacred Cause in which they are engaged."

8   Ibid., vol. 6, 9-4-1776. To Col. Fisher Gay. "Let me therefore not only Command, but exhort you and your Officers, as you regard your Reputation, your Country, and the sacred Cause of Freedom in which you are engaged, to Manly and Vigorous exertions at this time, each striving to excell the other in the respective duties of his department. I trust it is unnecessary for me to add further, and that these and all other Articles of your duty you will execute with a Spirit and punctuallity becoming your Station."

9   Ibid., vol. 5, 7-10-1776. To The President of Congress.

10   Ibid., vol.11, 4-21-1778, to John Banister.

11   The Congressional thanksgiving Proclamation states: Ibid., vol. 10, 11-30-1777. General Orders. "Forasmuch as it is the indispensible duty of all men, to adore the superintending providence of Almighty God; to acknowledge with gratitude their obligations to him for benefits received, and to implore such further blessings as they stand in need of; and it having pleased him in his abundant mercy, not only to continue to us the innumerable bounties of his common providence, but also, to smile upon us in the prosecution of a just and necessary war, for the defence of our unalienable rights and liberties.

It is therefore recommended by Congress, that Thursday the 18th. day of December next be set apart for Solemn Thanksgiving and Praise; that at one time, and with one voice, the good people may express the grateful feelings of their hearts, and consecrate themselves to the service of their divine benefactor; and that, together with their sincere acknowledgements and offerings they may join the penitent confession of their sins; and supplications for such further blessings as they stand in need of. The Chaplains will properly notice this recommendation, that the day of thanksgiving may be duly observed in the army, agreeably to the intentions of Congress.

12   Ibid., vol. 10, 12-17-1777. General Orders. Head Quarters, at the Gulph. "The Commander in Chief with the highest satisfaction expresses his thanks to the officers and soldiers for the fortitude and patience with which they have sustained the fatigues of the Campaign. Altho' in some instances we unfortunately failed, yet upon the whole Heaven hath smiled on our Arms and crowned them with signal success; and we may upon the best grounds conclude, that by a spirited continuance of the measures necessary for our defence we shall finally obtain the end of our Warfare, Independence, Liberty and Peace. These are blessings worth contending for at every hazard. But we hazard nothing. The power of America alone, duly exerted, would have nothing to dread from the force of Britain. Yet we stand not wholly upon our ground. France yields us every aid we ask, and there are reasons to believe the period is not very distant, when she will take a more active part, by declaring war against the British Crown. Every motive therefore, irresistably urges us, nay commands us, to a firm and manly perseverance in our opposition to our cruel oppressors, to slight difficulties, endure hardships, and contemn every danger. The General ardently wishes it were now in his power, to conduct the troops into the best winter quarters. But where are these to be found ? Should we retire to the interior parts of the State, we should find them crowded with virtuous citizens, who, sacrificing their all, have left Philadelphia, and fled thither for protection. To their distresses humanity forbids us to add. This is not all, we should leave a vast extent of fertile country to be despoiled and ravaged by the enemy, from which they would draw vast supplies, and where many of our firm friends would be exposed to all the miseries of the most insulting and wanton depredation. A train of evils might be enumerated, but these will suffice. These considerations make it indispensibly necessary for the army to take such a position, as will enable it most effectually to prevent distress and to give the most extensive security; and in that position we must make ourselves the best shelter in our power. With activity and diligence Huts may be erected that will be warm and dry. In these the troops will be compact, more secure against surprises than if in a divided state and at hand to protect the country. These cogent reasons have determined the General to take post in the neighbourhood of this camp; and influenced by them, he persuades himself, that the officers and soldiers, with one heart, and one mind, will resolve to surmount every difficulty, with a fortitude and patience, becoming their profession, and the sacred cause in which they are engaged. He himself will share

in the hardship, and partake of every inconvenience. To morrow being the day set apart by the Honorable Congress for public Thanksgiving and Praise; and duty calling us devoutely to express our grateful acknowledgements to God for the manifold blessings he has granted us. The General directs that the army remain in it's present quarters, and that the Chaplains perform divine service with their several Corps and brigades. And earnestly exhorts, all officers and soldiers, whose absence is not indispensibly necessary, to attend with reverence the solemnities of the day."

13 We considered a portion of that sermon in the earlier chapter on Washington's spirituality.

14 Israel Evans, *A Discourse, Delivered, on the 18th Day of December, 1777, the Day of Public Thanksgiving, Appointed by the Honourable Continental Congress*, by the Reverend Israel Evans, A. M. Chaplain to General Poor's Brigade. And now published at the Request of the General and Officers of the said Brigade, To be distributed among the Soldiers, Gratis. Lancaster: Printed by Francis Bailey, 1778.

15 *WGW*, vol. 5, 7-9-1776.

16 *Cf. WGW*, vol. 26, 3-18-1783. To the President of Congress. "Sir: The result of the proceedings of the grand Convention of the Officers, which I have the honor of enclosing to your Excellency for the inspection of Congress, will, I flatter myself, be considered as the last glorious proof of Patriotism which could have been given by Men who aspired to the distinction of a patriot Army; and will not only confirm their claim to the justice, but will increase their title to the gratitude of their Country. [*WGW* Note: Ford prints from a letter from Maj. J. A. Wright to Maj. John Webb, from West Point, Mar. 16, 1783, the following: "Yesterday there was a meeting of the officers. The Commander in Chief came among us, and made a most excellent address; he appeared sensibly agitated; as the writer advises to 'suspect the man who should advise to more moderation and longer forbearance,' this expression, together with a second anonymous letter, which I have not seen, gave reason to suppose that it was a plan laid against his Excellency, as every one who knows him must be sensible that he would recommend moderation. The general having finished his address, retired. Gen'l Gates took the chair; the business of the day was conducted with order, moderation, and decency."]

"Having seen the proceedings on the part of the Army terminate with perfect unanimity, and in a manner entirely consonant to my wishes; being impressed with the liveliest sentiments of affection for those who have so long, so patiently and so chearfully suffered and fought under my immediate direction; having from motives of justice, duty and gratitude, spontaneously offered myself as an advocate for their rights; and having been requested to write to your Excellency earnestly entreating the most speedy decision of Congress upon the subjects of the late Address from the Army to that Honble. Body, it now only remains for me to perform the task I have assumed, and to intercede in their behalf, as I now do, that the Sovereign Power will be pleased to verify the predictions I have pronounced of, and the confidence the Army have reposed in the justice of their Country.

"And here, I humbly conceive it is altogether unnecessary, (while I am pleading the cause of an Army which have done and suffered more than any other Army ever did in the defence of the rights and liberties of human nature,) to expatiate on their *Claims* to the most ample compensation for their meritorious Services, because they are perfectly known to the whole World, and because, (altho' the topics are inexhaustible) enough has already been said on the subject."

17 Ibid., vol.11, 5-2-1778.

18 In Federer, *America's God and Country*, pp. 459-60.

19 Ibid., p. 460: "John Peter Gabriel Muhlenberg (1746-1807), a member of the Virginia House of Burgesses in 1774, was a 30 year-old pastor who preached on the Christian's responsibility to be involved in securing freedom for America. He was the son of Henry Melchior Muhlenberg, one of the founders of the Lutheran Church in America. In 1775, after preaching a message on Ecclesiastes 3:1, 'For everything there is a season, and a time for every matter under heaven,' John Peter Muhlenberg closed his message by saying: 'In the language of the Holy Writ, there is a time for all things. There is a time to preach and a time to fight. And now is the time to fight.' He then threw off his clerical robes to reveal the uniform of an officer in the Revolutionary Army. That afternoon, at the head of 300 men, John Peter Muhlenberg marched off to join General Washington's troops and became Colonel of the 8th Virginia Regiment. He served until the end of the war, during which he was promoted to the rank of Major General. In 1785 he became the Vice-President of Pennsylvania, and in 1790 was a member of the Pennsylvania constitutional Convention. He then served as a U.S. Congressman from Pennsylvania, and in 1801 he was elected to the United States Senate. In 1889, the State of Pennsylvania placed his statue in the Statuary Hall at Washington."

His younger brother, Frederick Augustus Conrad Muhlenberg (1750-1801), was also a Lutheran clergyman. He at first criticized his brother's support for the Revolution. But when the British invaded New York where he was pastoring, he was forced to leave and returned to his father's house in Trappe. Eventually Frederick Augustus entered politics as well. He served as the first Speaker of the United States House of Representatives in 1789. In that capacity, along with Vice-President John Adams, who was thus also President of the Senate, signed the Bill of Rights when it was sent to the states for ratification.

20 *WGW*, vol. 33 7-24-1793, to the overseers at Mt. Vernon, "You will recollect that your time is paid for by me, and if I am deprived of it, it is worse even than robbing my purse, because it is also a breach of trust, which every honest man ought to hold most sacred. You have found me, and you will continue to find me faithful to my part of the agreement which was made with you, whilst you are attentive to your part; but it is to be remembered, that a breach on one side releases the obligation on the other; if, therefore it shall be proved to me that you are absenting yourself from either the Farm or the people without just cause, I shall hold myself no more bound to pay the wages, than you do to attend strictly to the charge which is entrusted to you, by one who has every disposition to be, Your friend"

21 Ibid., vol. 12, 8-3-1778, "To JOHN PARKE CUSTIS, "I presume you are not unacquainted with the fact of £ 12,000 at compound Interest amounting to upwards of £ 48,000 in twenty four Years. Reason therefore must convince you that unless you avert the evil by a deposit of the like Sum in the loan Office, and there hold it sacred to the purpose of accumulating Interest in the proportion you pay, that you will have abundant cause to repent it. No Virginia Estate (except a very few under the best of management) can stand simple Interest how then can they bear compound Interest. You may be led away with Ideal profits; you may figure great matters to yourself to arise from this, that, or t'other Scheme, but depend upon it they will only exist in the imagination, and that year after year will produce nothing but disappoint-

ment and new hopes; these will waste time, whilst your Interest is accumg. and the period approaching when you will be called upon to be prepared perhaps to advance 4 times the original purchase money. Remember therefore, that as a friend, I call upon you with my advice to shun this rock by depositing the Sum you are to pay Alexander, in the loan Office; let it be considered as Alexanders money, and Sacred to that use and that only, for if you shd. be of opinion that pay day being a great way off will give you time enough to provide for it and consequently to apply your present Cash to other uses it does not require the gift of prophecy to predict the Sale of the purchased Estate or some other to pay for it."

22 Ibid., vol. 15, 5-10-1779. To COLONEL DANIEL BRODHEAD, "[I cannot conclude without recommending the strictest oeconomy in all your conduct and operations; you may be assured it is become indispensably necessary, and that you cannot pursue more effectual means of recommending yourself to public favor and thanks than by an attention to its interests,] at this period of its affairs. [I earnestly recommend that the Batteaux and other vessels, which are built for public use be held in a manner sacred otherwise they will get squandered and when the period arrives that they will be wanted none will be found.]"

23 Ibid., vol. 8, 6-10-1777., GENERAL ORDERS "It is with inexpressible regret the Commander in Chief has been driven to the necessity of doing a severe, but necessary act of Justice, as an example of what is to be expected by those daring offenders, who, lost to all sense of duty, and the obligations they owe to their Country, and to mankind, wantonly violate the most sacred engagements, and fly to the assistance of an enemy, they are bound by every tie to oppose. A spirit of desertion is alone the most fatal disease that can attend an army, and the basest principle that can actuate a soldier; Wherever it shews itself, it deserves detestation, and calls for the most exemplary punishment. What confidence can a General have in any Soldier, who he has reason to apprehend may desert in the most interesting moments? What, but the want of every moral and manly sentiment, can induce him to desert the cause, to which he has pledged his faith, even with the solemnity of an oath, and which he is bound to support, by every motive of justice and good will to himself, and his fellow creatures? When such a character appears, it may almost be said in reference to it, that forbearance is folly; and mercy degenerates into cruelty."

24 Ibid., vol. 7, 2-28-1777, To MAJOR GENERAL ISRAEL PUTNAM Head Quarters, Morris Town, February 28, 1777, "Dear Sir: Your several favours of the 25th and 26th. Instt. came safe to hand. The pass granted by Lord and Genl. Howe to William Taylor, dated the 18th, is of such a nature, as not to afford any protection to the Vessel and Crew, even on the most scrupulous construction of the Law of Nations, and She came in so suspicious a manner, without a flag flying, as would have justified severer treatment than mere detention. But 'tis possible, that Taylor and the master of the Vessel, not sufficiently informed of the practice necessarily observable in bearing Flags, or Strangers to the instances, in which Protection can with propriety be granted by an Enemy, came with no ill design; I would therefore have the Vessel and hands released, being desirous to remove from our Army every, the smallest, Imputation of an Infringement on the sacred dignity of a Flag. Indeed I would pass over unnoticed, any small deviation from the usual Line in these cases, if not attended with danger to us. They are to consider this early discharge as an Indulgence, which they, or any other person, must not expect a Repetition of. It may not be improper to send Colo. Foreman a Copy of this part of my answer, that Taylor may know my sentiments, and the Reasons that induce me to discharge his Vessel. When the English Letters, that were found on board, come to you, please to send them to me, if of any Consequence."

Ibid., vol. 11, 3-22-1778, To SIR WILLIAM HOWE, "The conduct of Lieutenant Col. Brooks in detaining John Miller, requires neither palliation nor excuse. I justify and approve it. There is nothing so sacred in the Character of the King's Trumpeter, even when sanctified by a flag, as to alter the nature of things, or consecrate infidelity and Guilt. He was a Deserter from the Army under my Command; and, whatever you have been pleased to assert to the Contrary, it is the Practice of War and Nations, to seize and punish Deserters Wherever they may be found. His appearing in the character he did, was an aggravation of his Offence, in as much as it added insolence to perfidy. My scrupulous regard to the priviledges of flags, and a desire to avoid every thing, that partiality itself might affect to consider as a violation of them, induced me to send orders for the release of the Trumpeter, before the receipt of your Letter; the improper and peremptory Terms of which, had it not been too late, would have strongly operated to produce a less compromising conduct; I intended at the time to assure you, and I wish it to be remembered, that my indulgence in this instance, is not to be drawn into precedent, and that, should any deserters from the American Army, hereafter have the daring folly to approach our Lines in a similar manner, they will fall victims to their rashness and presumption."

25 Ibid., vol. 10, 1-29-1778, To THE COMMITTEE OF CONGRESS, "In speaking of rank, as a spur to enterprise, I am led, by the way to hint an idea, which may be improved and turned to no small advantage. This is the institution of honorary rewards, differing in degree, to be conferred on those, who signalize themselves, by any meritorious actions, in proportion to the magnitude and brilliancy of the achievement. These should be sacred to the purpose of their institution, and unattainable by loose recommendations, or vague, though arrogating pretension; given only upon authentic vouchers of real desert, from some proper board. Congress have already adopted the idea, in particular instances; but it were to be wished, it could be extended to something more general and systematic. I have not sufficiently employed my thoughts upon the subject, to digest them into a proposition, as to the nature variety and extent of these rewards; but I would in general observe, that they may consist in things of very little cost, or real value, and that the more diversified they are, the better. If judiciously and impartially administered, they would be well calculated to kindle that emulous love of glory and distinction, to which may be imputed far the greater part of the most illustrious exploits performed among mankind, and which is peculiarly necessary to be cherished and cultivated in a military life."

26 Ibid., vol. 34 10-20-1794, To GOVERNOR HENRY LEE , "There is but one point on which I think it proper to add a special recommendation. It is this, that every officer and soldier will constantly bear in mind that he comes to support the laws and that it would be peculiarly unbecoming in him to be in any way the infractor of them; that the essential principles of a free government confine the provinces of the Military to these two objects: 1st: to combat and subdue all who may be found in arms in opposition to the National will and authority; 2dly to aid and support the civil Magistrate in bringing offenders to justice. The dispensation of this justice belongs to the civil Magistrate and let it ever be our pride and our glory to leave the sacred deposit there unviolated. Convey to my fellow citizens in arms my

warm acknowledgments for the readiness with which they have seconded me in the most delicate and momentous duty the chief Magistrate of a free people can have to perform and add my affectionate wishes for their health comfort and success. Could my further presence with them have been necessary or compatible with my civil duties at a period when the approaching commencement of a session of Congress particularly urges me to return to the seat of Government, it would not have been withheld. In leaving them I have the less regret, as I know I commit them to an able and faithful director; and that this director will be ably and faithfully seconded by all."

27   Ibid., vol. 22, 5-5-1781, To BRIGADIER GENERAL JAMES CLINTON, "Alarmed at the critical situation of the Garrison of Fort Schuyler, I ordered out of the small pittance in our Magazines, 50 Barrels of Meat and the same quantity of flour, to be transported from this Army, and instantly thrown into that Garrison, but the Commissary reports there are but 34 Bbs of Meat in store. I have directed this number to be sent, and the residue of the 50 Barrels to be made up, from the Fish lately barreled on the River. This supply (the Fish included, or not, as you think proper) you will be pleased to consider as solely designed for the relief of the Garrison of Fort Schuyler, and sacredly to be appropriated to that and no other purpose whatever: For in our present embarrassed circumstances, when we know not from whence the supplies of tomorrow are to be derived, no inferior object could have justified the Measure of stripping this Army of its last Mouthful."

Ibid., vol. 22, 7-11-1781, To COLONEL CHARLES STEWART, "Sir: It is his Excellency's request that you will take immediate and effectual Measures, to have such a number of the Beef Cattle from the Eastern part of Connecticut and that part of Massachusetts contiguous to Rhode Island, furnished for the Militia Stationed at R Island, that they may not be under the necessity of consuming a single Barrel of salted Provision, if it can possibly be avoided. The Salted Provision to be repacked (if necessary) and kept sacredly as a reserve in the Magazine where it now is."

28   Ibid., vol. 25, 9-25-1782. To COLONEL ELISHA SHELDON, "Sir: On friday next you will move from your Quarters (wherever they may be) with your whole Corps, at such time and manner, as to be at the White Plains positively between sunset and dark; your Men will require provisions for saturday and may be perfectly light. I send you the Paroles and Cr Signs untill the 29th inclusive, you will keep them sacredly to yourself, except when they are to be delivered to the Officers entitled to them, on the several days they are designed for."

29   Ibid., vol. 26, 3-3-1783. To LIEUTENANT COLONEL WILLIAM STEPHENS SMITH, "It is much to be regretted, that while I am using every means in my power to comply with the orders of Congress, founded, in my judgment, on our true interest and policy, that there should be such a counteraction as we daily experience by individuals. But lamentable indeed is our situation when States, or the Administration of them, are leaping over those bounds which should ever be deemed the sacred barrier betwn. us and the Enemy, without which all opposition to their measures must soon cease. or dwindle into something, ridiculous enough."

30   Ibid., vol. 26, 4-18-1783. To THE PRESIDENT OF CONGRESS "This Act, at a comparative small Expence, would be deemed an honorable Testimonial from Congress of the Regard they bear to those distinguished Worthies, and the Sense they have of their suffering Virtues and Services, which have been so happily instrumental towards the security and Establishment of the Rights Liberties and Independence of this rising Empire. These constant companions of their Toils and Dangers, preserved with sacred Care, would be handed down from the present possessors, to their Children, as honorable Badges of Bravery and military Merit; and would probably be bro't forth, on some future Occasion, with Pride and Exultation, to be improved, with the same military Ardor and Emulation, in the Hands of posterity, as they have been used by their forefathers in the present Establishment and foundation of our National Independence and Glory."

31   Ibid., vol. 25 10-23-1782. To REVEREND WILLIAM GORDON "It appears to me impracticable for the best Historiographer living, to write a full and correct history of the present revolution who has not free access to the Archives of Congress, those of Individual States, the Papers of the Commander in Chief, and Commanding Officers of seperate departments. Mine, while the War continues, I consider as a species of Public property, sacred in my hands; and of little Service to any Historian who has not that general information which is only to be derived with exactitude from the sources I have mentioned. When Congress then shall open their registers, and say it is proper for the Servants of the public to do so, it will give me much pleasure to afford all the Aid to your labors and laudable undertaking which my Papers can give; 'till one of those periods arrive I do not think myself justified in suffering an inspection of, and any extracts to be taken from my Records."

32   Ibid., vol. 26, 3-18-1783, To THE PRESIDENT OF CONGRESS, "To prove these assertions, to evince that my sentiments have ever been uniform, and to shew what my ideas of the rewards in question have always been, I appeal to the Archives of Congress, and call on those sacred deposits to witness for me."

33   Ibid, vol. 1, 5-27-1754, JOURNAL May 27, 1754. "Besides, an Embassador has princely attendants, whereas this was only a simple petty *French* officer; an Embassador has no need of spies, his person being always sacred: and since their intention was so good, why did they tarry two days, five miles distance from us, without acquainting me with the summons, or at least, with something that related to the Embassy? That alone would be sufficient to excite the strongest suspicions, and we must to do them the justice to say, that as they wanted to hide themselves, they could not have picked out better places than they had done."

34   Ibid., vol. 1, Address To His Command. "And though our utmost endeavors can contribute but little to the advancement of his Majesty's honor and the interest of his governments, yet let us show our willing obedience to the best of kings, and, by a strict attachment to his royal commands, demonstrate the love and loyalty we bear to his sacred person; let us, by rules of unerring bravery, strive to merit his royal favor, and a better establishment as reward for our services."

35   Ibid., vol. 19, 8-11-1780, To BRIGADIER GENERALS ANTHONY WAYNE AND WILLIAM IRVINE, "Citizens and good men to realize the consequences and to assure themselves they act upon substantial grounds before they venture to execute what they have intimated. They ought to recollect that they cannot hereafter be happy, if they find their conduct condemned by the country and by the army, especially if it has been the cause of any misfortune. They should remember that we have actually entered upon the operations of the campaign; that we are now in the vicinity of the enemy and in a position that makes an action not very improbable perhaps not very remote

[if my intelligence true.] When they duly weigh these things they cannot but be sensible that the love of their country; the obligations of their respective stations; what they owe to their own characters and to that discipline which ought to be sacred among military men; all these motives call upon them to relinquish the intention they have suggested. It is true, we have not many considerations of interest to attach us to the service; but we have those of honor and public good [in a high degree] and I flatter myself these ties will not prove too feeble."

Ibid., vol. 23, 10-31-1781, GENERAL ORDERS, "The General cannot forbear adding that Accusations of so serious a nature should be made with the most scrupulous caution; an Officer's Character being too sacred to be impeached with Levity without a sufficient foundation."

36   Ibid., vol. 26, 3-5-1783, To THE OFFICERS OF THE ARMY "And let me conjure you, in the name of our common Country, as you value your own sacred honor, as you respect the rights of humanity, and as you regard the Military and National character of America, to express your utmost horror and detestation of the Man who wishes, under any specious pretences, to overturn the liberties of our Country, and who wickedly attempts to open the flood Gates of Civil discord, and deluge our rising Empire in Blood. By thus determining, and thus acting, you will pursue the plain and direct road to the attainment of your wishes. You will defeat the insidious designs of our Enemies, who are compelled to resort from open force to secret Artifice. You will give one more distinguished proof of unexampled patriotism and patient virtue, rising superior to the pressure of the most complicated sufferings; And you will, by the dignity of your Conduct, afford occasion for Posterity to say, when speaking of the glorious example you have exhibited to Mankind, "had this day been wanting, the World had never seen the last stage of perfection to which human nature is capable of attaining."

37   Ibid., vol. 5, 7-15-1776, To THE PRESIDENT OF CONGRESS New York, July 15, 1776. "The Inhuman Treatment to the whole, and Murder of part of our People after their Surrender and Capitulation, was certainly a flagrant violation of that Faith which ought to be held sacred by all civilized nations, and founded in the most Savage barbarity. It highly deserved the severest reprobation, and I trust the Spirited Measures Congress have adopted upon the Occasion, will prevent the like in future: But if they should not, and the claims of humanity are disregarded, Justice and Policy will require recourse to be had to the Law of retaliation, however abhorrent and disagreeable to our natures in cases of Torture and Capital Punishments".

38   Ibid., vol. 3, 4-5-1775, To GEORGE MERCER "I enclose you a copy of my last letter of the 4th. of December, and an account of the proceedings of the Convention held at Richmond the 20th. ulto. A great number of very good companies were raised in many Counties in this Colony, before it was recommended to them by the Convention, and are now in excellent training; the people being resolved, altho' they wish for nothing, more ardently, than a happy and lasting reconciliation with the parent State, not to purchase it at the expence of their liberty, and the sacred compacts of Government."

Ibid, vol. 34, 1-22-1795, To EDMUND PENDLETON "My communications to Congress at the last and present Session, have proceeded upon similar ideas with those expressed in your letter, namely, to make *fair* treaties with the Savage tribes, (by this I mean, that they shall *perfectly* understand every article and clause of them, from correct and repeated interpretations); that these treaties shall be held sacred, and the infractors on either side punished exemplarily; and to furnish them plentifully with goods under wholesome regulations, without aiming at higher prices than is adequate to cover the cost, and charges. If measures like these were adopted, we might hope to live in peace and amity with these borderers; but not whilst our citizens, in violation of law and justice, are guilty of the offences I have mentioned, and are carrying on unauthorised expeditions against them; and when, for the most attrocious murders, even of those of whom we have the least cause of complaint, a Jury on the frontiers, can hardly be got to listen to a charge, much less to convict a culprit."

39   Ibid., vol. 4, ANSWER TO AN ADDRESS FROM THE MASSACHUSETTS LEGISLATURE. "When the councils of the British nation had formed a plan for enslaving America, and depriving her sons of their most sacred and invaluable privileges, against the clearest remonstrances of the constitution, of justice, and of truth, and, to execute their schemes, had appealed to the sword, I esteemed it my duty to take a part in the contest, and more especially on account of my being called thereto by the unsolicited suffrages of the representatives of a free people; wishing for no other reward, than that arising from a conscientious discharge of the important trust, and that my services might contribute to the establishment of freedom and peace, upon a permanent foundation, and merit the applause of my countrymen, and every virtuous citizen."

40   Ibid., vol. 34, 12-8-1795, SEVENTH ANNUAL ADDRESS , "It is a valuable ingredient in the general estimate of our welfare, that the part of our country, which was lately the scene of disorder and insurrections, now enjoys the blessings of quiet and order. The misled have abandoned their errors, and pay the respect to our Constitution and laws which is due from good citizens, to the public authorities of the society. These circumstances, have induced me to pardon, generally, the offenders here referred to; and to extend forgiveness to those who had been adjudged to capital punishment. For though I shall always think it a sacred duty, to exercise with firmness and energy, the Constitutional powers with which I am vested, yet it appears to me no less consistent with the public good, than it is with my personal feelings, to mingle in the operations of government, every degree of moderation and tenderness, which the national justice, dignity and safety may permit."

Ibid. vol. 35, 5-5-1769 To JOSEPH LEECH, "A sacred regard to the constitution, and to the best interests of the United States as involved in its preservation, having governed my conduct on that occasion, the consciousness thereof would at all times have furnished me with strong ground of satisfaction."

41   Ibid., vol. 35, FAREWELL ADDRESS, 9-19-1796, "The Unity of Government which constitutes you one people is also now dear to you. It is justly so; for it is a main Pillar in the Edifice of your real independence, the support of your tranquility at home; your peace abroad; of your safety; of your prosperity; of that very Liberty which you so highly prize. But as it is easy to foresee, that from different causes and from different quarters, much pains will be taken, many artifices employed, to weaken in your minds the conviction of this truth; as this is the point in your political fortress against which the batteries of internal and external enemies will be most constantly and actively (though often covertly and insidiously) directed, it is of infinite moment, that you should properly estimate the immense value of your national

Union to your collective and individual happiness; that you should cherish a cordial, habitual and immoveable attachment to it; accustoming yourselves to think and speak of it as of the Palladium of your political safety and prosperity; watching for its preservation with jealous anxiety; discountenancing whatever may suggest even a suspicion that it can in any event be abandoned, and indignantly frowning upon the first dawning of every attempt to alienate any portion of our Country from the rest, or to enfeeble the sacred ties which now link together the various parts."

42   This seems to fit both categories of Washington's use of the word "sacred" so it is included here as well.
Ibid., vol. 8, 6-10-1777, GENERAL ORDERS , "It is with inexpressible regret the Commander in Chief has been driven to the necessity of doing a severe, but necessary act of Justice, as an example of what is to be expected by those daring offenders, who, lost to all sense of duty, and the obligations they owe to their Country, and to mankind, wantonly violate the most sacred engagements, and fly to the assistance of an enemy, they are bound by every tie to oppose."

43   Ibid., vol. 2, 6-8-1768., To MRS. WILLIAM SAVAGE June 28, 1768. , "Madam: If the most solemn asseverations of a man are sufficient to give credit to his report. If the honor and veracity of a Gentleman are things sacred enough to extort the truth, we have all the reasons imaginable to conclude that Doctr. Savage is entirely ignorant of the part you act in respect to the bond given in Trust to Mr. Fairfax and myself for your use;"

44   Ibid., vol. 26, 6-8-1783, CIRCULAR TO THE STATES "There are four things, which I humbly conceive, are essential to the well being, I may even venture to say, to the existence of the United States as an Independent Power: 1st. An indissoluble Union of the States under one Federal Head. 2dly. A Sacred regard to Public Justice."

45   Ibid., vol. 15, 5-29-1779. To COLONEL CLEMENT BIDDLE,"It is my wish that every possible respect should be paid in all cases to the Laws of this and every other State and a sacred regard to the property of each Individual Member as far as it can be done; but if necessity will not admit of their strict observance it must justify a deviation and such infringements as she compells. However, to prevent as much as possible any just ground of complaint and the charge of a wanton exercise of power, you should use every practicable exertion to obtain forage in the Ordinary way and where this cannot be effected, wherever circumstances will permit, you should make written requisitions to the Magistrates for pasturage and Meadows and obtain them by their allotment. If they will not permit or the Mgistrates refuse to designate them, or to make a competent provision, the exigency of the Public service must decide the conduct you are to pursue. I have mentioned the precautions because (tho' all regulations must yield to necessity) the principle should be introduced with caution, and practised upon with still more delicacy."
Ibid., vol. 24, 7-11-1782, To GOVERNOR GEORGE CLINTON "To remedy these evils, I have taken the liberty to trouble you with this, and to entreat that your Excellency will have the goodness to use your assistance and influence in devising some efficacious mode for furnishing Forage, without imposing upon the Public, or injury to the owners; taking care at the same time, that the value of the property taken may be justly ascertained in such manner, as that the debt shall be equitably paid by the Public, without breaking in upon the present arrangements of the Financier, which ought to be supported and maintained inviolably sacred, as we regard the safety and preservation of our Country."

46   Ibid., vol. 36, 7-13-1798, To THE PRESIDENT OF THE UNITED STATES, "Satisfied therefore, that you have sincerely wished and endeavoured to avert war, and exhausted to the last drop, the cup of reconciliation, we can with pure hearts appeal to Heaven for the justice of our cause, and may confidently trust the final result to that kind Providence who has heretofore, and so often, signally favoured the People of these United States.
"Thinking in this manner, and feeling how incumbent it is upon every person, of every description, to contribute at all times to his Country's welfare, and especially in a moment like the present, when every thing we hold clear and Sacred it so seriously threatned, I have finally determined to accept the Commission of Commander in Chief of the Armies of the United States, with the reserve only, that I shall not be called into the field until the Army is in a situation to require my presence, or it becomes indispensable by the urgency of circumstances."
Ibid., vol. 36, 7-16-1798, To HENRY KNOX, "Viewing things in this light, I would fain hope, as we are forming an Army *A New*, which Army, if needful *at all*, is to fight for every thing that ought to be dear and sacred to freemen that former rank will be forgot; and among the fit and chosen characters, the only contention will be, who shall be foremost in zeal at this crisis, to serve his Country, in whatever situation circumstances may place him. Most of those, who are best qualified to oppose the enemy, will have sacrifices of ease, Interest, or Inclination to make; but what are these, when put in competition with the loss of our Independence or the Subjugation of our Government? both of which are evidently struck at, by an intoxicated, ambitious, and domineering Foe."
Ibid., vol. 36, 7-25-1798, To DOCTOR JAMES ANDERSON, "When every thing Sacred, and dear to Freemen is thus threatned, I could not consistent with the principles which have actuated me through life, remain an idle spectator, and refuse to obey the call of my Country to lead its Armies for *defence* and therefore have pledged myself to come forward whensoever the exigency shall require it."

47   Ibid., vol. 2, CATALOGUE OF BOOKS FOR MASTER CUSTIS REFERRED TO ON THE OTHERSIDE, VIZ. Blackwells Sacred Classics, 2 vols.

48   Ibid., vol. 26, 2-15-1783, GENERAL ORDERS, "The Commander in Chief also desires and expects the Chaplains in addition to their public functions will in turn constantly attend the Hospitals and visit the sick, and while they are thus publickly and privately engaged in performing the sacred duties of their office they may depend upon his utmost encouragement and support on all occasions, and that they will be considered in a very respectable point of light by the whole Army."

49   Ibid., vol. 4, 3-6-1776, GENERAL ORDERS Head Quarters, Cambridge, March 6, 1776. , "Thursday the seventh Instant, being set apart by the Honourable the Legislature of this province, as a day of fasting, prayer, and humiliation, "to implore the Lord, and Giver of all victory, to pardon our manifold sins and wickedness's, and that it would please him to bless the Continental Arms, with his divine favour and protection" — All Officers, and Soldiers, are strictly enjoined to pay all due reverance, and attention on that day, to the sacred duties

due to the Lord of hosts, for his mercies already received, and for those blessings, which our Holiness and Uprightness of life can alone encourage us to hope through his mercy to obtain."

50 *WGW*, vol. 27, 8-20-1783. To John Gabriel Tegelaar.

51 *WGW*, vol. 30, 6-15-1789. Note. Answer to the Address of the Governor and Council of North Carolina. "A difference of opinion on political points is not to be imputed to Freemen as a fault since it is to be presumed that they are all actuated by an equally laudable and sacred regard for the liberties of their Country. If the mind is so formed in different persons as to consider the same object to be somewhat different in its nature and consequences as it happens to be placed in different points of view; and if the oldest, the ablest, and the most virtuous Statesmen have often differed in judgment, as to the best forms of Government, we ought, indeed rather to rejoice that so much has been effected, than to regret that more could not all at once be accomplished."

52 *WGW*, vol.11, 4-21-1778, to John Banister.

53 *WGW*, vol. 10, 12-17-1777.

54 Throughout this section, all of the references unless otherwise noted are to John Joseph Stoudt, *Ordeal At Valley Forge* (Philadelphia: University of Pennsylvania Press,1963.) Page numbers will simply be included in the text without footnote.

55 *WGW*, vol. 10, 12-20-1777

56 Stoudt, *Ordeal*, 3-10-1778, p. 176, 123, 176, 299, 250

57 Ibid., p. 250, 4-26-1778.

58 Ibid., p. 46.

59 Ibid., p. 66.

60 Ibid., p. 68.

61 Ibid., p. 133.

62 Ibid., p. 158.

63 Ibid., p. 225.

64 Ibid., p. 53.

65 Ibid., p. 49.

66 Ibid., p. 89.

67 Ibid., p. 101.

68 Ibid., p. 110.

69 Ibid., p.104, 156.

70 Ibid., p.121.

71 Ibid., p. 121.

72 Ibid., p. 30.

73 Ibid., p. 147.

74 Ibid., p. 45.

75 Ibid., p. 123, 134, 137, 190.

76 Ibid., p. 62.

77 Ibid., p. 137.

78 Ibid., p. 143.

79 Ibid., p. 216.

80 Ibid., p. 178, 181, 232.

81 Ibid., p. 188.

82 Ibid., p. 97, 67, 151, 39, 206, 235.

83 Ibid., p. 142.

84 Ibid., p.111, 268.

85 Ibid., p. 87.

86 Ibid., p. 115.

87 Ibid., p. 35.

88 Ibid., p. 136.

89 Ibid., p. 115.

90 Ibid., p. 31.

91 Ibid., p. 39.

92 Ibid., p. 40.

93 Ibid., p. 249.

94 Ibid., p. 45, 46, 241.

95 Ibid., p. 45.

96 Ibid., p. 124.

97 Ibid., p. 223.

98 Ibid., p. 140.

99 Ibid., p. 101.

100 Ibid., p. 116, 237.

101 Ibid., p. 70-71.

102 Ibid., p. 116.

103 Ibid., p.70.

104 Ibid., p. 107, 115.

105 Ibid., p.88.

106 Ibid., p. 61-62.

107 Ibid., p. 243.

108 *WGW*, vol. 10, 1-23-1778. To Reverend William Gordon. "I have attended to your information and remark, on the supposed intention of placing General L—, [Lee] at the head of the army: whether a serious design of that kind had ever entered into the head of a member of C —[Congress] or not, I never was at the trouble of enquiring. I am told a scheme of that kind is now on foot by some, in behalf of another gentleman, but whether true or false, whether serious, or merely to try the pulse, I neither know nor care; neither interested nor ambitious views led me into the service, I did not solicit the command, but accepted it after much entreaty, with all that diffidence which a conscious want of ability and experience equal to the discharge of so important a trust, must naturally create in a mind not quite devoid of thought; and after I did engage, pursued the great line of my duty, and the object in view (as far as my judgement could direct) as pointedly as the needle to the pole. So soon then as the public gets dissatisfied with my services, or a person is found better qualified to answer her expectation, I shall quit the helm with as much satisfaction, and retire to a private station with as much content, as ever the wearied pilgrim felt upon his safe arrival in the Holy-land, or haven of hope; and shall wish most devoutly, that those who come after may meet with more prosperous gales than I have done, and less difficulty. If the expectation of the public has not been answered by my endeavours, I have more reasons than one to regret it; but at present shall only add, that a day may come when the public cause is no longer to be benefited by a concealment of our circumstances; and till that period arrives, I shall not be among the first to disclose such truths as may injure it."

109 Stoudt, *Ordeal*, p. 128.

110 Ibid., p. 87.

111 Ibid., p.242.

112 Ibid., p. 243-44.

113 Ibid., p. 198, 260.

114 Ibid., p. 205, 212.

115 Ibid., p. 61, 97, 125, 139, 141, 155, 199.

116 Ibid., p. 145, 161-62, 188, 196.

117 Ibid., p. 209, 259.

118 Ibid., p. 249.

119 Ibid., p. 330.

120 Ibid., p. 171.

121 Ibid., p. 157-58.

122 Ibid., p. 187.

123 Ibid., p. 192.

124 Ibid., p. 260.

125 Ibid., p. 100.

126 Ibid., p. 110.

127 Ibid., p. 112, 129, 154.

128 Ibid., p. 106, 201.

129 Ibid., p. 117.

130 Ibid., p. 160.

131 *WGW*, vol. 11, 5-30-1778. To Landon Carter.

132 Boller, *George Washington & Religion*, p. 10-11.

133 Ibid., pp. 9-10.

134 Ibid., pp. 9-10.

135 See Peter A. Lillback, *Freedom's Holy Light*, (Bryn Mawr: The Providence Forum, 2000), p. 35.

136 Johnson, Weems, *Life of Washington*, p. 181. "In the winter of 1777-78, Washington, with the American army, was encamped at Valley Forge, amidst all the perplexities and troubles and sufferings, the Commander-in-chief sought for direction and comfort from God. He was frequently observed to visit a secluded grove. One day a Tory Quaker by the name of Isaac Potts "had occasion to pass through the woods near headquarters. Treading in his way along the venerable grove, suddenly he heard the sound of a human voice, which, as he advanced, increased in his ear; and at length became like the voice of one speaking much in earnest. As he approached the spot with a cautious step, whom should be behold, in a dark natural bower of ancient oaks, but the Commander-in-chief of the American armies on his knees at prayer! Motionless with surprise, Friend Potts continued on the place till the genera, having ended his devotions, arose, and with a countenance of angelic serenity, retired to headquarters.

Friend Potts then went home, and on entering his parlor called out to his wife, "Sarah! My dear Sarah! All's well! All's well! George Washington will yet prevail."

"What's the matter, Isaac?" replied she; "thee seems moved."

"Well, if I seem moved, tis' no more than what I really am. I have this day seen what I never expected. Thee knows that I always thought that the sword and the gospel were utterly inconsistent; and that no man could be a soldier and a Christian at the same time. But George

Washington has this day convinced me of my mistake." He then related what he had seen, and concluded with this prophetical remark! "If George Washington be not a man of God, I am greatly deceived – and still more shall I be deceived, if God do not, though him, work out a great salvation for America."

137 Benson J. Lossing, *Pictorial Field-Book of the Revolution* (1860), vol. II. P. 130. "Isaac Potts, at whose house Washington was quartered. Related that one day, while the Americans were encamped at Valley Forge, he strolled up the creek, when, not far from his den, he heard a solemn voice. He walked quietly in the direction of it, and saw Washington's horse tied to a sapling. In a thicket near by was the beloved chief upon his knees in prayer, his cheeks suffused with tears. Like Moses at the bush, Isaac felt that he was upon holy ground, and withdrew unobserved. He was much agitated, and one entering the room where his wife was, he burst into tears. On her inquiring the cause, he informed her of what he had seen, and added, "It there is anyone on this earth whom the Lord will listen to, it is George Washington; and I feel a presentiment that under such a commander there can be no doubt of our eventually establishing our independence, and that God in his providence has willed it so."

138 M'Guire, *Religious Opinions* , p. 158. Extract of a letter from a Baptist minister to the editor of the (Boston) Christian Watchman, dated Baltimore, January 13, 1832:
"The meetinghouse (which is built of stone) belonging to the church just alluded to is in sight of the spot on which the American army, under the command of General Washington, was encamped during a most severe winter. This, you know, was then called 'Valley Forge.' It is affecting to hear the old people narrate the sufferings of the army, when the soldiers were frequently tracked by the blood from the sore and bare feet, lacerated by the rough and frozen roads over which there were obliged to pass.
"You will recollect that a most interesting incident, in relation to the life of the great America commander-in-chief, has been related as follows: That while stationed here with the army he was frequently observed to visit a secluded grove. This excited the curiosity of a Mr. Potts, of the denomination of 'Friends,' who watched his movements at one of these seasons of retirement, till he perceived that he was one his knees and engaged in prayer. Mr. Potts when returned, and said to his family, 'Our cause is lost' (he was with the Tories), assigning his reasons for this opinion. There is a man by the name of Devault Beaver, now living on this spot (and is eighty years of age), who says he has this statement from Mr. Potts and his family.
"I have before heard this interesting anecdote in the life of our venerated Washington, but had some misgivings about it, all of which are now fully removed."

139 Theodore Wm. John Wylie, *Washington, A Christian*, (1862), pp. 28, 29. The following note was written to the Reverend T.E.J. Wylie, D.D., pastor of the First Reformed Presbyterian Church, of Philadelphia, February 28, 1862:
"My Dear Sir,
Referring to your request, I have to say that I cannot lay my hands at present upon my father's papers. I recollect that among his manuscript "Reminiscences," was a statement of his interview with Mr. Potts, A Friend, near Valley Forge, who pointed out to him the spot where he saw General Washington at prayer in the winter of 1777. This event induced Friend Potts to become a Whig; and he told his wife Betty, that the cause of America was a good cause, and would prevail, and that they must now support it. Mr. Weems, in his "Life of Washington," mentions this incident a little differently; but my father had it from Mr. Potts personally, and the statement herein made may therefore be relied on as accurate.
I am, with great regard,
Yours truly,
James Ross Snowden
Dr. Wylie says, "We have heard the incident just related from the lops of the late Dr. N.R. Snowden, who was informed it by the person himself."

140 M'Guire, *Religious Opinions* , p. 159. "It may be added that besides the individual named above as having witnessed the private devotions of General Washington at Valley Forge, it is known that General Knox also was an accidental witness of the same, and was fully apprised that *prayer* was the object of the Commander's frequent visits to the grove. This officer was especially devoted to the person of the Commander-in-Chief, and had very free and familiar access to him, which may in some measure account for his particular knowledge of his habits. That an adjacent wood should have been selected as his private oratory, while regularly encamped for the winter, may excite the inquiry of some. The cause may possibly be found in the fact that, in common with the officers and soldiers of the army, he lodged during that winter in a log hut, which, from the presence of Mrs. Washington, and perhaps other inmates, and the fewness of the apartments, did not admit of that privacy proper for such a duty."

141 *WGW,* vol. 7, 4-15-1777.

142 Ibid., vol. 7, 4-12-1777. To Edmund Pendleton.

143 Henry C. Watson, "Story of General Washington" in *Old Bell of Independence, or, Philadelphia in 1776* (Philadelphia: Lindsay & Blakiston, 1851), pp. 19-23.
"Grandfather," said Thomas Jefferson Harmar, "won't you tell us something about General Washington?" "I could tell you many a thing about that man, my child," replied old Harmar, "But I suppose people know everything concerning him by this time. You see, these history writers go about hunting up every incident relating to the war, now , and after a while they'll know more about it – or say they do- than the men who were actors in it."
"That's not improbable," said young Harmar. "These historians may not know as much of the real spirit of the people at that period, but that they should be better acquainted with the mass of facts relating to battles and to political affairs is perfectly natural." The old man demurred, however, and mumbled over, that nobody could know the real state of things who was not living among them at the time.
"But the little boy wants to hear a story about Washington," said Wilson. "Can't you tell him something about the man? I think I could. Any one who wants to appreciate the character of Washington, and the extent of his services during the Revolution, should know the his-

tory of the campaign of 1776, when every body was desponding, and thinking of giving up the good cause. I tell you, if Washington had not been superior to all other men, that cause must have sunk into darkness."

"You say well," said Smith. "We, who were at Valley Forge, know something of his character."

"I remember an incident," said Wilson, "that will give you some idea, Mrs. Harmar, of the heart of George Washington had in his bosom. I suppose Mr. Harmar has told you something of the sufferings of our men during the winter we lay at Valley Forge. It was a terrible season. It's hard to give a faint idea of it in words; but you may imagine a party of men, with ragged clothes and no shoes, huddled around a fire in a log hut – the snow about two feet deep on the ground, and the wind driving fierce and bitter through the chinks of the rude hovel. Many of the men had their feet frost-bitten, and there were no remedies to be had, like there is now-a-days. The sentinels suffered terribly, and looked more like ghosts than men, as they paced up and down before the lines of huts."

"I wonder the men didn't all desert," remarked Mrs. Harmar. "They must have been uncommon men."

"They were uncommon men, or at least, they suffered in an uncommon cause," replied Wilson. "But about General Washington. He saw how the men were situated, and I really believe, his heart bled for them. He would write to Congress of the state of affairs, and entreat that body to procure supplies; but, you see, Congress hadn't the power to comply. All it could do was to call on the States, and await the action of their Assemblies.

"Washington's head-quarters was near the camp, and he often came over to see the poor fellows, and to try to soothe and comfort them; and, I tell you, the men loved that man as if he had been their father, and would rather have died with him than have lived in luxury with the red-coat general.

"I recollect a scene I beheld in the next hut to the one in which I messed. An old friend, named Josiah Jones, was dying. He was lying on a scant straw bed, with nothing but rags to cover him. He had been sick for several days, but wouldn't go under the doctor's hands, as he always said it was like going into battle, certain of being killed. One day, when we had no notion of anything of the kind, Josiah called out to us, as we sat talking near his bed, that he was dying, and wanted us to pray for him. We were all anxious to do anything for the man, for we loved him as a brother; but as for praying, we didn't exactly know how to go about it. To get clear of the service, I ran to obtain the poor fellow a drink of water to moisten his parched lips.

"While the rest were standing about, not knowing what to do, some one heard the voice of General Washington in the next hut, where he was comforting some poor wretches who had their feet almost frozen off. Directly, he came to our door, and one of the men went and told him the state of things. Now, you see, a commander-in-chief might have been justified in being angry that the regulations for the sick had been disobeyed, and have turned away; but he was a nobler sort of man than could do that. He entered the hut, and went up to poor Josiah, and asked him how he was. Josiah told him the he felt as if he was dying, and wanted some one to pray for him. Washington saw that a doctor could do the man no good, and he knelt on the ground by him and prayed. We all knelt down too; we couldn't help it. An old comrade was dying, away from his home and friends, and there was our general kneeling by him, with his face turned towards heaven, looking, I thought, like an angel's. Well, he prayed for Heaven to have mercy on the dying man's soul; to pardon his sins; and to take him to Himself; and then he prayed for us all. Before the prayer was concluded, Josiah's spirit had fled, and his body was cold and stiff. Washington felt the brow of the poor fellow, and, seeing that his life was out, gave the men directions how to dispose of the corpse, and then left us to visit the other parts of the camp."

"That was, indeed, noble conduct," said young Harmar. "Did he ever speak to you afterwards about violating the regulations of the army?"

"No," replied Wilson. "He knew that strict discipline could not be, and should not have been maintained in that camp. He was satisfied if we were true to the cause amid all our sufferings."

"Praying at the death-bed of a private," mused Smith aloud. "Well, I might have conjectured what he would do in such a case, from what I saw of him. I wonder if history ever spoke of a greater and better man?"

Young Mr. Harmar here felt inclined to launch out into an elaborate panegyric on the character of Washington, but reflected that it might be out of place, and therefore contented himself with remarking, "We shall ne'er look upon his like again."

"He was a dear, good man," remarked Mrs. Harmar.

"Yes," said old Harmar, "General Washington was the main pillar of the Revolution. As a general, he was vigilant and skilful; but if he had not been anything more, we might have been defeated and crushed by the enemy. He had the love and confidence of the men, on account of his character as a man, and that enabled him to remain firm and full of hope when his countrymen saw nothing but a gloomy prospect."

144 Sparks, *The Writings of George Washington*, vol. II, p. 54.

145 *The London Chronicle* for 1779, Sept. 21-23.

146 Custis, *Recollections* , p. 493.

147 Sparks, *The Writings of George Washington*, vol. III.491.

148 Meade, *Old Churches*, vol. II, p. 492.

149 *Solder and ◉rvant Series: Mrs. Alexander Hamilton Witness that George Washington was A Communicant of the Church* (Church Missions Publishing Company Feb. 1932), pp. 3-4. General Burgoyne's soldiers had burned her father's house at Albany in October, 1777. John Fiske says that "As the poor soldiers marched on the 17th of December [1777] to their winter quarters [at Valley Forge], their route could be traced on the snow by the blood that oozed form bare, frost-bitten feet." And, "On the morning of the 18th of June, 1778, the rear-guard of the British marched out of Philadelphia, and before sunset the American advance marched in, and took possession of the city." Apparently the homeless daughter of the colonial general found domicile with her father in what an English writer, the Rt. Hon. Sir George Otto Trevelyan, has said, "bids fair to be the most celebrated encampment in the world's history." General Burgoyne afterward expressed to General Schuyler his regret for the burning of his home."

150 *WGW*, vol. 17, 1-29-1780.

151 Ibid., vol. 11, 4-12-1778.

152 Israel Evans, *A Discourse, Delivered, on the 18th Day of December, 1777.*

CHAPTER 20

1   *WGW,* vol. 26, 6-8-1783, Circular to the States.

2   Bishop William Meade, *Old Churches and Families of Virginia,* 1857, II, pp. 254-55.

3   Boller, *George Washington & Religion,* p 15.

4   Ibid., p 18.

5   Ibid., p 17.

6   Moncure D. Conway, *The Religion of George Washington in the Open Court,* October 24, 1889.

7   Letter to Jared Sparks from Nelly Custis.

8   Meade, *Old Churches,* vol. II, p.491-492. No. XXIII.

9   E. C. M'Guire, *Religious Opinions,* p. 411.

10 M'Guire, *Religious Opinions,* p. 414.

11 Meade, *Old Churches,* vol. II, p.490ff. No. XXIII.
    Further Statements Concerning the Religious Character of Washington and the Question Whether He Was a Communicant or Not. Extract from a letter of the Reverend Dr. Berrian, of New York, to Mrs. Jane Washington, of Mount Vernon, in answer to some inquiries about General Washington during his residence in New York as President of the United States: –
    "About a fortnight since I was administering the Communion to a sick daughter of Major Popham, and, after the service was over, happening to speak on this subject, I was greatly rejoiced to obtain the information which you so earnestly desired.
    "Major Popham served under General Washington during the Revolutionary War, and I believe he was brought as near to him as their difference of rank would admit, being himself a man of great respectability, and connected by marriage with the Morrises, one of the first families in the country. He has still an erect and military air, and a body but little broken at his advanced age. His memory does not seem to be impaired nor his mind to be enfeebled."
    To the above I can add my own testimony, having in different ways become acquainted with the character of Major Popham, and having visited him about the same time mentioned by Dr. Berrian.
    Extract from Major Popham's Letter to Mrs. Jane Washington, New York, March 14, 1839
    My Dear Madam: —You will doubtless be not a little surprised at receiving a letter from an individual whose name may possibly never have reached you; but an accidental circumstance has given me the extreme pleasure of introducing myself to your notice. In a conversation with the Reverend Dr. Berrian a few day since, he informed me that he had lately paid a visit to Mount Vernon, and that Mrs. Washington had expressed a wish to have a doubt removed from her mind, which had long oppressed her, as to the certainty of the General's having attended the Communion while residing in the city of New York subsequent to the Revolution. As nearly all the remnants of those days are now sleeping with their fathers, it is not very probable that at this late day an individual can be found who could satisfy this pious wish of your virtuous heart, except the writer. It was my great good fortune to have attended St. Paul's Church in this city with the General during the whole period of his residence in New York as President of the United States. The pew of Chief-Justice Morris was situated next to that of the President, close to whom I constantly sat in Judge Morris's pew, and I am as confident as a memory now labouring under the pressure of fourscore years and seven can make me, that the President had more than once – I believe I say often-attended at the sacramental table, at which I had the privilege and happiness to kneel with him. And I am aided in my associations by my elder daughter, who distinctly recollects her grandmamma – Mrs. Morris– often mention that fact with great pleasure. Indeed, I am further confirmed in my assurance by the perfect recollection of the President's uniform deportment during divine service in church. The steady seriousness of his manner, the solemn, audible, but subdued tone of voice in which he read and repeated the responses, the Christian humility which overspread and adorned the native dignity of the saviour of his country, at once exhibited him a pattern to all who had the honour of access to him. It was my good fortune, my dear madam, to have had frequent intercourse with him. It is my pride and boast to have seen him various situations,—in the flush of victory, in the field and in the tent, - in the church and at the altar, always himself, ever the same.

12 Ibid., p 490-491.

13 Alfred Nevin, D.D., LL.D. Editor. *Encyclopedia of the Presbyterian Church in the United States of America: Including the Northern and Southern Assemblies* (Philadelphia: Presbyterian Publishing Co., 1884.) p. 259-263.

14 Johnson, *George Washington The Christian,* p. 96, "In commemoration of this event the spot has been marked by a sundial, placed there by the Daughters of the American Revolution."

15 J. I. Good, *History of the German Reformed Church in the United States, 1725-1792* (Reading, Pennsylvania, 1899), pp. 616-617.

16 David Hosack, M.D., *Memoir of DeWitt Clinton,* 1859, p. 183. Johnson, *Washington the Christian,* p. 86.

17 *Harper's Magazine,* 1859, vol. XVIII, p. 293.

18 *The Presbyterian Magazine,* ed. C. Van Rensselaer, Philadelphia, Pa. February, 1851, vol. 1, p. 71.

19 Andrew M. Sherman, *Historic Morristown, New Jersey,* 1905, p. 237.

20 M'Guire, *Religious Opinions,* p. 412.

21 Ibid., pp. 413-14.

22 *Presbyterian Magazine,* vol. I, p. 569.

23 Ibid., vol. I, p. 569.

24 Boller, *George Washington & Religion,* p. 14.

25 See www.answers.com/topic/oral-history. Columbia University Press

Oral history, compilation of historical data through interviews, usually tape-recorded and sometimes videotaped, with participants in, or observers of, significant events or times. Primitive societies have long relied on oral tradition to preserve a record of the past in the absence of written histories. In Western society, the use of oral material goes back to the early Greek historians Herodotus (in his history of the Persian Wars) and Thucydides (in his *History of the Peloponnesian War*), both of whom made extensive use of oral reports from witnesses. The modern concept of oral history was developed in the 1940s by Allan Nevins and his associates at Columbia Univ. In creating oral histories, interviews are conducted to obtain information from different perspectives, many of which are often unavailable from written sources. Such materials provide data on individuals, families, important events, or day-to-day life.

The discipline came into its own in the 1960s and early 70s when inexpensive tape recorders were available to document such rising social movements as civil rights, feminism, and anti–Vietnam War protest. …By the end of the 20th cent. oral history had become a respected discipline in many colleges and universities. At that time the Italian historian Alessandro Portelli and his associates began to study the role that memory itself, whether accurate or faulty, plays in the themes and structures of oral history. Their published work has since become standard material in the field, and many oral historians now include in their research the study of the subjective memory of the persons they interview.

Bibliography. See S. Caunce, *Oral History* (1994); V. R. Yow, *Recording Oral History* (1994), R. Perks and A. Thomson, *The Oral History Reader* (repr. 1998).

Wikipedia oral history

Oral history is an account of something passed down by word of mouth from one generation to another. Oral history is considered by some historians to be an unreliable source for the study of history. However, oral history is a valid means for preserving and transmitting history. Experience within literate cultures indicates that each time anyone reconstructs a memory, there are changes in the memory, but the core of the story is usually retained. Over time, however, minor changes can accumulate until the story becomes unrecognizable.

A person within a literate culture thus has presuppositions that may falsely affect her judgement of the validity of oral history within pre-literate cultures. In these cultures children are usually selected and specially trained for the role of historian, and develop extraordinary memory skills known as eidetic or photographic memory.

Before the development of written language in a given society, oral history is the primary means of conveying information from one generation to the next. The most common form of this transmission is through storytelling and the recitation of epic poetry, with the stories and poems collectively known as the *oral tradition* of a people. The combination of this oral tradition with morals and rituals passed down by word of mouth is known as the folklore of a society. Although not as prevalent now as in the past, oral history is still very much alive among many North American native groups….

The most popular examples of oral history are the works of several authors that have, over the span of many hundred years BC, collected folklore which ultimately resulted in these works being included in a collective book known as the Old Testament, The New Testament was created by four different original authors whose slightly differing versions of many biblical events were combined. The Bible was therefore 'nearly' entirely created using oral history.

Contemporary oral history is much different. It involves recording or transcribing eyewitness accounts of historical events. …

One of the most important rules for those collecting oral history is to avoid asking leading questions, for many people will tend to say what they think the historian wants them to say.

Oral historians attempt to record the memories of many different people when researching a given event. Since any given individual may misremember events or distort their account for personal reasons, the historical documentation is considered to reside in the points of agreement of many different sources, rather than the account of any one person.

26 Interestingly, these words at the taking of an oath were required and written for those taking oaths in Virginia during the colonial era as can be seen in Bishop William Meade, *Old Churches and Families of Virginia*, (Philadelphia: J.B.Lippincott & Co. 1857), vol. II, pp. 41-2. Washington took these vows for the first time when he became a public surveyor:

Oath of Allegiance

"I, A.B., do sincerely promise and swear that I will be faithful and bear true allegiance to his Majesty King George the Second, so help me God.

"Oath of Abjuration.

"I, A.B., do swear that I do from my heart abhor, detest and abjure, as impious and heretical, that damnable doctrine and position that Princes excommunicate or deprived by the Pope, or any authority of the See of Rome, may be deposed or murdered by their subjects or any other whatsoever. And I do declared that no foreign Prince, Prelate, Person, State, or Potentate, hath, or ought to have, any jurisdiction, power superiority, pre-eminence, or authority, ecclesiastical or spiritual, within this realm. So help me God.

The test oath, however, did not conclude with "So help me God." Apparently the very act of denying transubstantiation was a matter of witness before God:

"Test Oath

"I do declare that I do believe that there is not any transubstantiation in the Sacrament of the Lord's Supper, or in the Elements of bread and wine at or after the consecration thereof by any person whatsoever."

27 *Encyclopedia_* oral history, compilation of historical data through interviews, usually tape-recorded and sometimes videotaped, with participants in, or observers of, significant events or times. Primitive societies have long relied on oral tradition to preserve a record of the past in the absence of written histories. In Western society, the use of oral material goes back to the early Greek historians Herodotus (in his history of the Persian Wars) and Thucydides (in his *History of the Peloponnesian War*), both of whom made extensive use of oral reports from witnesses. The modern concept of oral history was developed in the 1940s by Allan Nevins and his associates at Columbia Univ. In creating oral histories, interviews are conducted to obtain information from different perspectives, many of which are often unavailable from

written sources. Such materials provide data on individuals, families, important events, or day-to-day life.

The discipline came into its own in the 1960s and early 70s when inexpensive tape recorders were available to document such rising social movements as civil rights, feminism, and anti–Vietnam War protest. Authors such as Studs Terkel, Alex Haley, and Oscar Lewis have employed oral history in their books, many of which are largely based on interviews. In another important example of the genre, a massive archive covering the oral history of American music has been compiled at the Yale School of Music. By the end of the 20th cent. oral history had become a respected discipline in many colleges and universities. At that time the Italian historian Alessandro Portelli and his associates began to study the role that memory itself, whether accurate or faulty, plays in the themes and structures of oral history. Their published work has since become standard material in the field, and many oral historians now include in their research the study of the subjective memory of the persons they interview.

Bibliography

See S. Caunce, *Oral History* (1994); V. R. Yow, *Recording Oral History* (1994), R. Perks and A. Thomson, *The Oral History Reader* (repr. 1998).

Oral history is an account of something passed down by word of mouth from one generation to another. Oral history is considered by some historians to be an unreliable source for the study of history. However, oral history is a valid means for preserving and transmitting history. Experience within literate cultures indicates that each time anyone reconstructs a memory, there are changes in the memory, but the core of the story is usually retained. Over time, however, minor changes can accumulate until the story becomes unrecognizable.

The information passed on has occasionally shown a surprising accuracy over long periods of time. For example, the *Iliad*, an epic poem of Homer describing the conquest of Troy, was passed down as oral history from perhaps the 8th century BC, until being recorded in writing by Pisistratos. Nonetheless, factual elements of the *Iliad* were at least partially validated by the discovery of ruins discovered by Heinrich Schliemann in 1870, thought to be those of the city described in the poem.

The most popular examples of oral history are the works of several authors that have, over the span of many hundred years BC, collected folklore which ultimately resulted in these works being included in a collective book known as the Old Testament. The New Testament was created by four different original authors whose slightly differing versions of many biblical events were combined. The Bible was therefore 'nearly' entirely created using oral history.

Oral historians attempt to record the memories of many different people when researching a given event. Since any given individual may misremember events or distort their account for personal reasons, the historical documentation is considered to reside in the points of agreement of many different sources, rather than the account of any one person.

28 *Soldier and Servant Series*: "Mrs. Alexander Hamilton Witness that George Washington Was A Communicant of the Church" (Hartford: Church Missions Publishing Company, February, 1932), p. 2.

29 This whole account is preserved in "Mrs. Alexander Hamilton, Witness That Washington Was A Communicant Of The Church."

30 Meade, *Old Churches*, II, p. 244.

31 Ibid.

32 Johnson, *Washington the Christian*, p. 58.

33 Meade, *Old Churches*, II. 495.

34 Sparks, *The Writings of George Washington*, XII, pp. 405ff.

35 Ibid., p. 409.

36 *WGW*, vol. 37, 9-14-1799.

37 Ibid., 12-10-1799.

38 Interview with Mary Thompson for Coral Ridge Ministries.

39 Ibid.

40 "Almighty God, whose kingdom is everlasting, and power infinite; Have mercy upon the whole Church, and so rule the heart of thy chosen servant GEORGE our King and Governor, that he (knowing whose Minister he is) may above all things seek thy honour and glory; and that we and all his subjects (duly considering whose authority he hath) may faithfully serve honour and humbly obey him, in thee, and for thee, according to thy blessed word and ordinance, through Jesus Christ our Lord, who with thee, and the Holy Ghost, liveth and reigneth ever one God, world without end. *Amen*." [online] http://justus.anglican.org/resources/bcp/1662/HC.pdf p. 3.

41 "We beseech thee also to save and defend all Christian Kings, Princes, and Governors; and especially thy servant GEORGE our King, that under him we may be godly and quietly governed: and grant unto his whole council, and to all that are put in authority under him, that they may truly and indifferently minister justice, to the punishment of wickedness and vice, and to the maintenance of thy true Religion and Virtue. Give grace, O heavenly Father, to all Bishops and Curates, that they may both by their life and doctrine set forth thy true and lively word, and rightly and duly administer thy holy Sacraments: And to all thy people give thy heavenly grace; and especially to this Congregation here present...." [online] http://justus.anglican.org/resources/bcp/1662/HC.pdf p. 6.

42 "O Lord our heavenly Father, high and mighty, King of kings, Lord of Lords, the only ruler of princes, who dost from thy throne behold all the dwellers upon earth; Most heartily we beseech thee with thy favour to behold our most gracious Sovereign Lord King GEORGE, and so replenish him with the grace of thy Holy Spirit, that he may always incline to thy will, and walk in thy way: Endue him plenteously with heavenly gifts, grant him in health and wealth long to live, strengthen him that he may vanquish and overcome all his enemies; and finally after this life, he may attain everlasting joy and felicity, through Jesus Christ our Lord. *Amen*." [online] http://justus.anglican.org/resources/bcp/1662/mp.pdf p. 8.

43 In Johnson, *Washington the Christian*, p. 75.

44 *WGW*, vol. 11, 3-1-1778.

45 Lane, *Washington Collection*, Boston Athenaeum, pp. 30-31.

46 Ibid, p. 31.

47 "The Duty of Standing Fast in Our Spiritual and Temporal Liberties," A Sermon Preached in Christ Church July 7th 1775 To his
    Excellency George Washington, Esquire, General and Commander In Chief of all the forces of the Untied English Colonies in North
    America, this sermon, as a small tribute of respect for many amiable virtues as well in private as in public life, is most humbly and affec-
    tionately inscribed by the author.

48 Duché reasoned, Perhaps it may be said, that it is 'better to die than be Slaves.' This indeed is a splendid maxim in theory: And perhaps
    in some instances may be found experimentally true. But where there is the least Probability of an happy Accommodation, surely Wisdom
    and Humanity call for some Sacrifices to be made, to prevent inevitable Destruction. You, well know, that there is but one invincible Bar
    to such an Accommodation. Could this be removed, other obstacles might readily be overcome. 'Tis to you, and you alone your bleeding
    Country looks, and calls aloud for this Sacrifice. Your Arm alone has Strength sufficient to remove this Bar. May Heaven inspire you with
    the glorious Resolution of exerting this Strength at so interesting a Crisis, and thus immortalizing Yourself as Friend and Guardian of Your
    Country! Your penetrating Eye needs no more explicit Language to discern my meaning.
        Speaking of his sermon, "The Duty of Standing Fast", Duche writes: I was pressed to publish this sermon, and reluctantly consented.
    – From a personal attachment of near twenty years standing, and a high respect for your character, in private, as well as in public life, I took
    the liberty of dedicating this sermon to you. I had your affectionate thanks for my performance, in a letter, wherein was expressed in the
    most delicate and obliging terms, your regard for me, and your wishes for a continuance of my friendship and approbation of your con-
    duct. Farther than this I intended not to proceed. My sermon speaks for itself, and wholly disclaims the idea of independency….A very
    few days after the fatal declaration of independency, I received a letter from Mr. Hancock, sent by express to Germantown, where my fam-
    ily were for the summer season, acquainting me I was appointed Chaplain of the Congress, and desired my attendance next morning at 9
    o'clock. Surprised and distressed, as I was, by an event I was not prepared to expect; obliged to give an immediate attendance, without the
    opportunity of consulting my friends, I easily accepted the appointment. I could have but one motive for accepting this step. I thought the
    churches in danger ….I then looked upon independency as an expedient and hazardous, or, indeed, thrown out *in terrorem*, in order to pro-
    cure some favorable terms….My sudden change of conduct will clearly evince this to have been my idea of the matter. …independency
    was the idol they had long wished to set up, and that, rather than sacrifice this, they would deluge their country with blood. From this
    moment I determined upon my resignation, and, in the beginning of October 1776, sent it in form to Mr. Hancock, after having officiat-
    ed only two months and three weeks; and from that time, as far as safety would permit, I have been opposed to all their measures. This cir-
    cumstantial account of my conduct, I think due to the friendship you were obliging as to express for me, and I hope will be sufficient to
    justify my seeming inconsistencies in the part I have acted….If the arguments made use of in this letter should have so much influence as
    to engage you in the glorious work, which I have warmly recommended, I shall ever deem my success the highest temporal favour that
    Providence could grant me. Your interposition and advice, I am confident, would meet with a favourable reception from the authority under
    which you act. If it should not, you have an infallible recourse still left, negotiate for your country at the head of your army. After all it may
    appear presumption as an individual to address himself to you on a subject of such magnitude, or to say what measures would best secure
    the interest and welfare of a whole continent. The friendly and favourable opinion you have always expressed for me, emboldens me to
    undertake it, and which has greatly added to the weight of this motive; I have been strongly impressed with a sense of duty upon the occa-
    sion, which left my conscience uneasy, and my heart afflicted till I fully discharged it. I am no enthusiast; the cause is new and singular to
    me, but I could not enjoy one moment's peace till this letter was written, with the most ardent prayers for your spiritual, as well as tempo-
    ral welfare.
        I am your most obedient, And humble Friend and Servant, Jacob Duché

49 Weems, *Life of Washington*, pp. 187-189, relates the story of a fight that the youthful Washington had with a Mr. Payne, that resulted in
    his own apology, and need to be forgiven.
        "… the *benevolence* which he so carefully cultivated through life. A singular instance of which we meet with in 1754, and the 22d year
    of his age.
        "He was stationed at Alexandria with his regiment, the only one in the colony, and of which he was colonel. There happened at this
    time to be an election in Alexandria for members of assembly, and the contest ran high between colonel George Fairfax, and Mr. Elzey.
    Washington was the warm friend of Fairfax, and a Mr. Payne headed the friends of Elzey. A dispute happening to take place in the court-
    house-yard, Washington, a thing very uncommon, said something that offended Payne; whereupon the little gentleman who, though but
    a cub in size, was the old lion in heart, raised his sturdy hickory, and, at a single blow, brought our hero to the ground. Several of
    Washington's officers being present, whipped out this cold irons in an instant, and it was believed that there would have been murder off-
    hand. To make bad worse, his regiment, hearing how he had been treated, bolted out from their barracks, with every man his weapon in
    his hand, threatening dreadful vengeance on those who had dared to knock down their beloved colonel. Happily for Mr. Payne and his
    party, Washington recovered, time enough to go out and meet his enraged soldiers; and, after thanking them for this expression of their
    love, and assuring them that he was not hurt in the least, he begged them, as they loved him or their duty, to return peaceably to their bar-
    racks. As for himself, he went to his room, generously chastising his imprudence, which had this struck up a spark, that had like to have
    thrown the whole town into a flame. Finding on mature reflection, that he had been the aggressor, he resolved to make Mr. Payne hon-
    ourable reparation, by asking his pardon on the morrow! No sooner had he made this noble resolution, than recovering that delicious gai-
    ety which accompanies good purposes in a virtuous mind, he went to a ball that night, and behaved as pleasantly as though nothing had
    happened! Glorious proof that great souls, like great ships, are not affected by those little puffs which would overset feeble minds with pas-
    sion, or sink them with spleen!
        The next day he went to a tavern, and wrote a polite note to Mr. Payne, whom he requested to meet him. Mr. Payne took it for a chal-
    lenge, and repaired to the tavern not without expecting to see a pair of pistols produced. But what was his surprise on entering the cham-

ber, to see a decanter of wine and glasses on the table! Washington arose, and in a very friendly manner met him, and gave him his hand. "Mr. Payne," said he "to err is nature; to rectify error is glory; I find I was wrong yesterday, but wish to be right to-day. You have had some satisfaction; and if you think that sufficient here's my hand, let us be friends."

Lest we think that this was an easy matter for Washington, we need to understand that his soul struggled with the intense emotions that this civil war inevitably produced. Consider his poignant letter to Major Gen. Robert Howe written from West Point on November 20, 1779,

> I do not know which rises highest, my indignation or contempt for the Sentiments which pervade the Ministerial writings of this day; these hireling scribblers labour to describe and prove the ingratitude of America in not breaking faith with France, and returning to her Allegiance to the Crown of Great Britain after its having offered such advantageous terms of accommodation. Such Sentiments as these are insulting to common sense and affrontive to every principle of sound policy and common honesty. Why has She offered these terms? because after a bloody contest, carried on with unrelenting and savage fury on her part the issue (which was somewhat doubtful while we stood alone) is now become certain by the aid we derive from our Alliance; notwithstanding the manifest advantages of which, and the blood and treasure which has been spent to resist a tyranny which was unremitted as long as there remained a hope of subjugation we are told with an effrontery altogether unparalleled that every cause of complaint is now done away by the generous offers of a tender parent; that it is ungrateful in us not to accept the proffered terms; and impolitic not to abandon a power (dangerous I confess to her but) which held out a Saving hand to us in the hour of our distress. What epithet does such Sentiments merit? How much should a people possessed of them be despised? From my Soul I abhor them! A Manly struggle, had it been conducted upon liberal ground; an honest confession that they were unequal to conquest, and wished for our friendship, would have had its proper weight; but their cruelties, exercised upon those who have fallen within their power; the wanton depredations committed by themselves and their faithful Allies the Indians; their low and dirty practices of Counterfeiting our money, forging letters, and condescending to adopt such arts as the meanest villain in private life would blush at being charged with has made me their fixed enemy. *(WGW,* vol. 17, 11-20-1779.)

50 *WGW,* vol. 26, 6-8-1783.

51 Ibid., vol. 36, Circular to the States.

52 *WGW,* vol. 34, 12-24-1795.

CHAPTER 21

1 *WGW,* vol. 29, 2-16-1787. To Thomas Stone.

2 Boller, *George Washington & Religion,* pp. 22-23. "What, then, are we to say about Washington's actual religious faith and practices? It is clear that the popular legends about Washington—the valley Forge and the Morristown stories and the innumerable tales of Washington at prayer—must be dismissed as totally lacking in any kind of evidence that would hold up in a court of law."

3 See the previous chapter, "Did Washington Take Communion?"

4 Littell, *George Washington: Christian.* Boller writes in *George Washington & Religion,* pp. 33-34 "In 1835, Bishop White, in answer to Colonel Hugh Mercer's question as to "whether General Washington was a *regular communicant* in the Episcopal Church in Philadelphia," replied: "In regard to the subject of your inquiry, truth requires me to say, that General Washington never received the communion, in the churches of which I am parochial minister. Mrs. Washington was an habitual communicant."

5 Ibid., p.16.

6 Ibid., pp. 17-18.

7 Ibid., p. 33-34. Dr. James Abercrombie to Origen Bacheler, November 29, 1831, *Magazine of American History,* XIII (June, 1885), p. 597.

8 Ibid., pp. 33-34, writes "On communion Sundays," according to Mrs. Custis, "he left the church with me, after the blessing, and returned home, and we sent the carriage back for my grandmother." This comes from the letter of Nelly Custis to Jared Sparks. Nelly Custis to Jared Sparks in *The Writings of George Washington* (New York: Harper & Brothers, 1847), vol. XII, pp. 405-408. This can also be found in Johnson, *George Washington the Christian,* pp. 242-245 and Eidsmoe, *Christianity and the Constitution,* p. 141.

9 Ibid., p. 33.

10 *The Book Of Common Prayer* that I have in front of me for this page count is the 1662 edition printed in Oxford by Thomas Baskett, Printer to the University in 1751.

11 This can also be found in Johnson, *George Washington the Christian,* pp. 242-245 and Eidsmoe, *Christianity and the Constitution,* p. 141.

12 Nelly Custis to Jared Sparks in *The Writings of George Washington,* vol. XII, pp. 405-408.

13 Boller, *George Washington & Religion,* pp. 34-35.

14 Mrs. *Alexander Hamilton Witnesses?? that George Washington Was A Communicant of the Church,* p. 3. This testimony, however, was not limited to Mrs. Hamilton's clergyman great-grandson. She also communicated the same facts to General Schuyler Hamilton, who said, "I have it on the absolute authority of my great-grand-mother (Mrs. Alexander Hamilton, 1st.) that George Washington communed in the Episcopal Church; that is sufficient for me, as my great-grand-mother would not have said so unless it was a fact known to her by personal observation." Ibid., p. 6. The editor of the text adds, "Practically every fact mentioned by Mrs. Hamilton, other than the Service of Holy Communion at St. Paul's Chapel, is recorded by contemporaneous writers. Mrs. Washington was not at the Inaugural, Washington rode away from Mount Vernon with only two attendants, the Inauguration was at Federal Hall, the procession did walk instead of riding from Wall Street to Fulton; the Service was at St. Paul's instead of Trinity because Trinity Church had been burned and not yet rebuilt; and Bishop Provoost was Rector of Trinity Parish, of which St. Paul's was a chapel , as well as Bishop of New York, and so was rightly called 'the rector' by Mrs. Hamilton. In the perfect pattern recorded in historical works only one item is missing, the Holy Communion with Washington and his friends as communicants , and that was supplied by Mrs. Alexander Hamilton in the vivid and distinctive conversa-

tion reported by her great-grandson.", pp. 5-6.

15   Littell, *George Washington*.

16   "For example: *WGW*, vol. 2, 4-27-1763. To Robert Stewart. "On my honor and the faith of a Christian." *WGW*, vol. 29, 2-11-1788. To Benjamin Lincoln. "…our Religion holds out to us such hopes as will, upon proper reflection, enable us to bear with fortitude the most calamitous incidents of life…." *WGW* , vol. 26, 6-8-1783. "… the Divine Author of our blessed Religion…." *WGW*, vol. 11, 5-2-1778. "While we are zealously performing the duties of good Citizens and soldiers we certainly ought not to be inattentive to the higher duties of Religion. To the distinguished Character of Patriot, it should be our highest Glory to add the more distinguished Character of Christian."

17   Ibid., vol. 30, 9-28-1789. To Reverend Samuel Langdon, "The man must be bad indeed who can look upon the events of the American Revolution without feeling the warmest gratitude towards the great Author of the Universe whose divine interposition was so frequently manifested in our behalf. And it is my earnest prayer that we may so conduct ourselves as to merit a continuance of those blessings …." Ibid., vol. 12, 8-20-1778. To Brig. Gen. Thomas Nelson. "The hand of Providence has been so conspicuous in all this, that he must be worse than an infidel that lacks faith, and more than wicked, that has not gratitude enough to acknowledge his obligations, but, it will be time enough for me to turn preacher, when my present appointment ceases; and therefore, I shall add no more on the Doctrine of Providence."

18   Ibid., vol. 35, 9-19-1796. Farewell Address.

19   See the chapter on "George Washington and the Bible."

20   See the chapter entitled, "George Washington's God: Religion, Reason and Philosophy".

21   See the chapter entitled, "Did Washington Avoid the Name of Jesus Christ?"

22   See his first Thanksgiving Proclamation in 1789.

23   See the chapters entitled, "George Washington's Christian Worldview", "The Gospel According to George Washington."

24   See the chapters entitled, "Washington's Virginia and the Anglican Mission to the Indians."

25   See the chapter entitled, "George Washington on Heaven and Eternal Life."

26   See the chapter on "The Sacred Fire of Liberty."

27   See the chapter on "George Washington's Clergy and Their Sermons."

28   See the chapter on "George Washington's Sermons."

29   *WGW*, vol.35, 9-19-1796. Farewell Address; *WGW*, vol.30, 10-29-1789. To the First Presbytery of the Eastward. See the chapter on "The Spirituality of George Washington."
     Nelly Custis to Jared Sparks in *The Writings of George Washington*, vol. XII, pp. 405-408.

CHAPTER 22

1   Jackson, Twohig, *Diaries of George Washington*.(Monday October, 10, 1785).

2   J. I. Good, *History of the German Reformed Church in the United States, 1725-1792* (Reading, Pennsylvania, 1899), pp. 616-617. *WGW*, vol. 33, 9-30-1793, note: "The house occupied by Washington in Germantown is stated by W. S. Baker to have been owned by Col. Isaac Franks. It was on Germantown Avenue, about 6 miles northwest of Independence Hall, in Philadelphia. Reverend J. B. Stoudt states that the President occupied the first floor of Reverend Lebrecht Herman's parsonage as an office."

3   *WGW*, vol. 32, 7-3-1792. To Governor Henry Lee. "Dear Sir: Your letter of the 20th. Ulto.?? was presented to me yesterday by Mr. Williams, [William J. Williams] who, as a professional man, may, or may not be, a luminary of the first magnitude for aught I know to the contrary. But to be frank, and I hope you will not be displeased with me for being so, I am so heartily tired of the attendance which, from one cause or another, I have bestowed on these kind of people, that it is now more than two years since I have resolved to sit no more for any of them; and have adhered to it; except in instances where it has been requested by public bodies, or for a particular purpose (not of the Painters) and could not, without offence, be refused. [*WGW* note: The portrait was not executed until September, 1794, in Philadelphia. Having been refused a sitting at the above time, Williams offered the Masonic Lodge No. 22 of Alexandria the finished work, if the lodge would request him to make a portrait. The lodge approved this idea Aug. 29, 1793. The resultant portrait was executed in pastel, and is now in the possession of the lodge.] I have been led to make this resolution for another reason besides the irksomeness of sitting, and the time I loose by it, which is, that these productions have, in my estimation, been made use of as a sort of tax upon individuals, by being engraved, and that badly, and hawked, or advertised for Sale. With very great Esteem and regard I am &c."

4   Jackson, Twohig, *Diaries of George Washington* (Monday October, 10, 1785)

5   Washington had in his library another anonymous work by Reverend Samuel Seabury: *Free Thoughts, on the Proceedings of the Continental Congress*, held at Philadelphia, Sept. 5, 1774; wherein their Errors are exhibited, their Reasonings confuted, and the fatal Tendency of their Non-Importation, Non-Exportation, and Non-Consumption Measures, are laid open to the plainest Understandings; and the only Means pointed out for preserving and securing our present happy Constitution: in a Letter to the Farmers, and other Inhabitants of North America in general, and to those of the Province of New-York in particular. By a Farmer. Lane in *A Catalogue of the Washington Collection*, pp. 177-78 writes, "Prior to this, the colonial interests had been discussed in two pamphlets printed without the name of author or publisher, and one of them, entitled, 'Free thoughts on the Proceedings of the Continental Congress' was signed 'A. W. Farmer,' and attributed at the time and since to Isaac Wilkins, then an influential member of the loyal Provincial Assembly of New York, and an intimate friend of the rector of the church in Westchester. . . . A bitter feeling was excited towards the unknown author of these pamphlets, which were extensively and gratuitously circulated among the people of New York and other provinces. Vengeance was denounced upon him, and failing to find him, copies of the pamphlets were gathered and burnt, and in some instances they were tarred, feathered, and nailed to the whipping-post, as an indication of the treatment which their author would receive if he were detected. . . . But who was the spirited writer

that signed himself 'A. W. Farmer'? Seabury at an earlier day, had entered into a compact with his clerical friends, Dr. Chandler of New Jersey, and Dr. Inglis, rector of Trinity Church, New York, to watch and confute all publications in pamphlets or newspapers that threatened mischief to the Church of England and the British government in America. Out of this compact undoubtedly sprung 'Free Thoughts on the Proceedings of the Congress at Philadelphia,' which was from his pen, as were the other publications that immediately followed on the same side of the question." Beardsley. *Life and Correspondence of Samuel Seabury, D.D.* the task of defending the cause of the colonies against the attacks of "A.W. Farmer" was confided to Alexander Hamilton, then a youth of eighteen, about to close his studies at King's College."

6   Notes from *A Revolution That Led To A Church* by F. Lee Richards (Cincinnati: Forward Movement Publications, 1990). "The break with England seriously impacted the Anglican Church. The revolution caused the loss of half the clergy, meaning many rural churches had to close.

With peace in 1783, a process to rebuild the Church began, which reached its climax in 1789. Journal of the Proceedings of the Bishops, Clergy and Laity, of the Protestant Episcopal Church in the United States of America in a Convention held in the City of Philadelphia, from Tuesday, September 29th to Friday, October 16th, 1789 Printed in Philadelphia: by Hall and Sellers in 1790.

7   From note in *Diaries of Washington*. "John Lowe (1750—1798), a minor Scottish poet, was born in the Galloway district of Scotland and educated at the University of Edinburgh. He came to Virginia in 1772 and became a tutor in the family of John Augustine Washington. He later ran an academy in Fredericksburg attended by Fielding Lewis's children. After his ordination at St. George's Church, Hempstead, Long Island, he became minister at Hanover Parish in King George County, Va."

8   *WGW*, vol. 32, 10-20-1792. To Dr. William Davies Shipley.

9   Ibid., vol. 37, last Will and testament.

10   This occurred in Scotland by "non-juror" bishops. To be a "non-juror," as we have already noted, meant that such a bishop was one who had not taken an oath of loyalty to William and Mary, the Protestant monarchs of the House of Orange. who ascended to the English throne in 1688. concluding the "Glorious Revolution." What were the principles of the non-jurors? Thomas Lathbury, *A History of the Nonjurors: Their Controversies and Writings; With Remarks on Some of the Rubrics in the Book of Common Prayer* (London: William Pickering, 1845), pp. 419-20, says, "As William supported Presbytery in Scotland, because the Episcopalians refused to recognize him as their Sovereign, the Presbyterians have no room for boasting that their system was adopted in preference to Episcopacy. It certainly was not chosen on account of its purity, as they choose to imagine or to assert, but because King William found them more ready to render him their support, than the Bishops and Clergy. Whether the refusal of the latter was a blot upon their memory, posterity will decide. At all events, they were honest in their course, for it led to the loss of all their worldly goods. The bishop of Edinburgh's reply was frank and open. He had not expected any such Revolution, and he had the courage to say so. Perceiving that the Bishops and Clergy would not support him, the King threw himself into the arms of the Presbyterians." He adds on pp. 423-24, "All the Clergy, who refused to take the Oath of Allegiance to the new Sovereigns, were removed from their Parishes; and "from their refusal, they soon acquired the appellation of Nonjurors."... Such Episcopal Clergymen as took the Oath of Allegiance, and acknowledged Presbytery as the only legal establishment, were allowed by the State to retain their churches, and also to be admitted, with the Presbyterian clergy, to a share in the Ecclesiastical government. To assent to Presbytery, as established by law, did not involve any opinion respecting its Scriptural or primitive character, which no Episcopalian could possibly admit. Besides, as no form of Prayer was imposed by the Presbyterians, the Clergy could proceed in the management of public worship, nearly in the same manner as previous to the Revolution. Accordingly a considerable number of the Episcopal Clergy complied, and continued in their respective Parishes."

11   Search P.G.W. on line under John C. Ogden. None of his letters were personally answered by Washington and several were not answered.

12   See chapter 2 "Deism Defined: Shades of Meaning, Shading the Truth"

13   See chapter 11 "The Sacred Fire of Liberty"

14   Reverend Ogden wrote to Washington 7 times. George Washington's Secretary Tobias Lear responded to one on behalf of Washington. The rest were left unaddressed. http://memory.loc.gov/cgi-in/query/P?mgw:14:./temp/~ammem_3u3s::

15   First, there was the Protestant-Catholic sensitivities. Seabury had been ordained by the Protestant Bishops who had been most sympathetic to the Roman Catholic heir to the British throne. Second, Seabury's ordination amounted to a new connection with post-wWar England, establishing the American Episcopate, which Virginia and Washington and the Committee on Religion had resisted. Third, Bishop Seabury's ordination by the non-jurors appeared to sever a direct connection with Anglican ordination, which was not consistent with the methodical approach of George Washington. If there was eventually going to be a Bishop in America, Anglicans, including Washington, knew that the genius of the Anglican Church's authenticity required that they take the necessary steps to assure the appropriate connection with the British bishops. Fourth, it put an Anglican bishop in New England, which meant that episcopacy would soon be moving south to Virginia. And there were even more disquieting issues at work for Washington and fellow low churchmen caused by the ordination of Bishop Seabury.

16   The early mid 1800's saw a renewed emphasis upon the Episcopalian doctrine of apostolic succession. Some representative works include: John Henry Hopkins, *The Primitive Church, Compared with The Protestant Episcopal Church of the Present Day: Being an Examination of the Ordinary Objections against the Church, in doctrine, worship, and government, designed for popular use; with a dissertation on sundry points of theology and practice, connected with the subject of episcopacy, etc.* (Burlington: Vernon Harrington:, 1836); Reverend Wm. Ingraham Kip, *The Double Witness of the Church,* (New York: D. Appleton & Co, 1843); Reverend A. P. Perceval, *An Apology For the Doctrine Of Apostolic Succession: With An Appendix On The English Orders* (New York: Protestant Episcopal Tract Society, 1839); W. D. Snodgrass, *Discourses on the Apostolical Succession* (Troy, N.Y.: Stedman & Redfield, 1844).

17   In an anonymously published treatise by Bishop Seabury that Washington had in his library, we find his theological application of apostolic succession to the Presbyterian and Independent Churches that surrounded him in New England:

An Address to the Ministers and Congregations of the Presbyterian and Independent Persuasions in the United States of America. By a Member of the Episcopal Church [by Samuel Seabury], pp. 40-41, 49, 51.

> The Presbyterians and Independents departed from the church, making a schism in it. It is therefore reasonable they should make the first advances towards a reunion. I know not how this reason can be evaded but on two grounds: one is justifying the schism ; the other is, the at the local situation of both parties in this country takes away the imputation of schism. .... I conclude again, that those presbyters who separated from the church of England did not, and could not bring off with them the apostolical power of ordination, because they never had received it. Their separation made them schismatics, but gave them no new ecclesiastical powers. ... "Do you then," you will ask, "unchurch us all? Have our congregations no authorized ministers? No valid sacraments?" I answer, I unchurch nobody. If you were true churches before I wrote, you are so still. If you were not, all the bustle you can make will do you no good. Quietness and patience will be the best palliation for your disease—a radical cure can only be effected by your return to the church from which you departed. You ask, "have we no authorized ministers? No valid sacraments?" To these questions, I fear, I shall return disagreeable answers. You have ministers of the people, I confess; and if I may be allowed to make a supposition (and I have made a good many without any leave at all) I must suppose that such as your ministry is, such are your sacraments. These, in short, are matters that neither concern me, nor my argument, any farther than as they influence my benevolence in your behalf. To be a member of the true church of Christ is a matter of important concern to every body. I have pointed out this true church to you; into it you can enter; and in it you will have, in your own judgment, an authorized ministry, and valid sacraments. I hope you will avail yourselves of this information and then, and not till then, all your doubts and misgiving will be at an end.

18   As the American Episcopalian Church took hold, several defenses of its doctrine of apostolic succession appeared. Here is a representative list from the 1830-40's: John Henry Hopkins, *The Primitive Church, Compared with The Protestant Episcopal Church of the Present Day: Being an Examination of the Ordinary Objections against the Church, in doctrine, worship, and government, designed for popular use; with a dissertation on sundry points of theology and practice, connected with the subject of episcopacy, etc.* (Burlington: Vernon Harrington:, 1836); Reverend Wm. Ingraham Kip, *The Double Witness of the Church*, (New York: D. Appleton & Co, 1843); Reverend A. P. Perceval, *An Apology For the Doctrine Of Apostolic Succession: With An Appendix On The English Orders* (New York: Protestant Episcopal Tract Society, 1839); W. D. Snodgrass, *Discourses on the Apostolical Succession* (Troy, N.Y.: Stedman & Redfield, 1844).

19   Reverend Mason Gallagher,. A Chapter of Unwritten History. The Protestant Episcopacy of the Revolutionary Patriots Lost and Restored. A Centennial Offering. Philadelphia: Reformed Episcopal Rooms, 1883.

20   Ibid., Preface. But compare here, Lathworthy's description of the latitudinarianism of Tillotson and Burnet, p. 156: "That many of the clergy of the Revolution [i.e., the British Glorious Revolution] were latitudinarian in their opinions, is, as we have seen, admitted by Mr. Hallam, than whom a more unexceptionable witness could not be adduced. This charge is strongly urged by Hickes against Burnet. In his sermon, Burnet had said, that Tillotson left men to use their own discretion in small matters. Hickes, commenting on this assertion, states, that the Archbishop was accustomed to administer the Lord's Supper to some persons sitting, and that especially a certain lady of Dr. Owen's congregation was so accustomed to receive it in the chapel of Lincoln's Inn: that he walked around the chapel, administering the elements first to those who were seated in their pews, and then to those who were kneeling at the rails, not, however, going within himself, but standing without. This was a direct breach of the order of the Church, and may be regarded as an evidence of the extent of latitudinarian practices." It seems that Tillotson did not stand alone in this particular: For Hickes asserts, that the Bishop of St. Asaph adopted the same practice, at Kidder's church, in administering the Lord's Supper to Dr. Bates, and other nonconformists. When we contemplate such proceedings of the part of men high in station in the Church, we cannot close our eyes to the fact that the latitudinarian principles which prevailed to a considerable extent after the Revolution, did really place the Church in some danger. By the good providence of God, however, the Clergy in general were actuated by purer notions: and within a few years the danger was averted.

21   *WGW*, vol. 29, 8-15-1787. To Marquis de Lafayette.

22   Reverend Mason Gallagher, *A Chapter of Unwritten History. The Protestant Episcopacy of the Revolutionary Patriots Lost and Restored. A Centennial Offering*, (Philadelphia: Reformed Episcopal Rooms, 1883), Preface.

23   Ibid.

24   *WGW*, vol. 35, 3-2-1797.

25   We discussed this incident in the Chapter "Shadow or Substance?"

26   The theological system behind the Low Church was developed especially by English Bishop Gilbert Burnet. To see how Washington's theology comports with the Latitudinarian system, please see the appendix entitled "George Washington and Latitudinarianism."

27   In 1793, he solicited, under the most respectable patronage, the office of Treasurer of the Mint; but General Washington, in consequence of a resolution, which he had formed not to appoint two persons from the same State as officers in any one department, felt obliged to deny the application. He subsequently took an office in the Bank of the United States, but found it so totally uncongenial with his taste, that he resigned it, after the labour of a single day... When he [Abercrombie] communicated his wish to the Bishop and some Clergy, they warmly seconded it; and he was according examined, and ordained Deacon in St. Peter's Church, Philadelphia, December 29, 1793. His preference was for a country parish; but his many friends in the city chose to detain him there, and in compliance with their wishes, he became Assistance Minister of Christ Church and St. Peter's in June, 1794. On the 28th of December following, he received Priest's Orders from Bishop White. In 1797, he was elected a member of the American Philosophical Society.
William B. Sprague, D.D. *Annals of the American Pulpit* (New York: Robert Carter and Brothers, 1861) p. 50

28   Boller, *George Washington & Religion*, pp. 17-18.

29   See appendix entitled "George Washington and the Anglican Theology Latitudinarianism."

30   But compare here, Lathworthy's description of the latitudinarianism of Tillotson and Burnet, p. 156: "That many of the clergy of the Revolution [i.e., the British Glorious Revolution] were latitudinarian in their opinions, is, as we have seen, admitted by Mr. Hallam, than

whom a more unexceptionable witness could not be adduced. This charge is strongly urged by Hickes against Burnet. In his sermon, Burnet had said, that Tillotson left men to use their own discretion in small matters. Hickes, commenting on this assertion, states, that the Archbishop was accustomed to administer the Lord's Supper to some persons sitting, and that especially a certain lady of Dr. Owen's congregation was so accustomed to receive it in the chapel of Lincoln's Inn: that he walked around the chapel, administering the elements first to those who were seated in their pews, and then to those who were kneeling at the rails, not, however, going within himself, but standing without. This was a direct breach of the order of the Church, and may be regarded as an evidence of the extent of latitudinarian practices. It seems that Tillotson did not stand alone in this particular: For Hickes asserts, that the Bishop of St. Asaph adopted the same practice, at Kidder's church, in administering the Lord's Supper to Dr. Bates, and other nonconformists. When we contemplate such proceedings of the part of men high in station in the Church, we cannot close our eyes to the fact that the latitudinarian principles which prevailed to a considerable extent after the Revolution, did really place the Church in some danger. By the good providence of God, however, the Clergy in general were actuated by purer notions: and within a few years the danger was averted."

31   See footnote 10 of this chapter.

32   This summary is based on, "A Revolution That Created A Church."

33   Normally, except for the consecration of Samuel Seabury by the Scottish non-juror bishops.

34   Jackson, Twohig, *Diaries of George Washington*, June 17, 1787. p. 224.

35   April 1790 Sunday 11th. Went to Trinity Church in the forenoon and [wrote] several private letters in the afternoon Jackson, Twohig, *Diaries of George Washington*, 4-11-1790, p. 114

"Thursday 15th. Returned the above Act (presented to me on Tuesday) to the House of Representatives in Congress in which it originated with my approbation & signature. The following Company dined here to day—viz— The Vice President & Lady, the Chief Justice of the United States & Lady, Mr. Izard & Lady, Mr. Dalton and Lady, Bishop Provost & Lady, Judge Griffin & Lady Christina, Colo. Griffin & Lady, Colo. Smith & Lady, The Secretary of State, Mr. Langdon Mr. King, & Major Butler. Mrs. King was invited but was indisposed." *Diaries*, 4-15-1790, p.115..

36   Washington's words concerning Christian charity to clergy was not only given to the Episcopalians. He also wrote to the Presbyterians about the conduct that demonstrates that men are "true Christians."

WGW, vol. 30, 5-26-1786. Note to the General Assembly of Presbyterian Churches in the U.S.

New York, May 26, 1789.

"On May 26 the general assembly of Presbyterian churches in the United States, meeting in Philadelphia, sent an address to Washington. His answer, which is undated in the "Letter Book," follows immediately after the copy of the address. In it he wrote in part:

"While I reiterate the professions of my dependence upon Heaven as the source of all public and private blessings; I will observe that the general prevalence of piety, philanthropy, honesty, industry, and oeconomy seems, in the ordinary course of human affairs, particularly necessary for advancing and confirming the happiness of our country. While all men within our territories are protected in worshipping the Deity according to the dictates of their consciences; it is rationally to be expected from them in return, that they will be emulous of evincing the sanctity of their professions by the innocence of their lives and the beneficence of their actions; for no man, who is profligate in his morals, or a bad member of the civil community, can possibly be a true Christian, or a credit to his own religious society.

"I desire you to accept my acknowledgments for your laudable endeavours to render men sober, honest, and good Citizens, and the obedient subjects of a lawful government."

WGW, vol. 3, 9-14-1775, To COLONEL BENEDICT ARNOLD, "I also give it in Charge to you to avoid all Disrespect to or Contempt of the Religion of the Country and its Ceremonies. Prudence, Policy, and a true Christian Spirit, will lead us to look with Compassion upon their Errors without insulting them. While we are contending for our own Liberty, we should be very cautious of violating the Rights of Conscience in others, ever considering that God alone is the Judge of the Hearts of Men, and to him only in this Case, they are answerable. Upon the whole, Sir, I beg you to inculcate upon the Officers and Soldiers, the Necessity of preserving the strictest Order during their March through Canada; to represent to them the Shame, Disgrace and Ruin to themselves and Country, if they should by their Conduct, turn the Hearts of our Brethren in Canada against us. And on the other Hand, the Honours and Rewards which await them, if by their Prudence and good Behaviour, they conciliate the Affections of the Canadians and Indians, to the great Interests of America, and convert those favorable Dispositions they have shewn into a lasting Union and Affection. Thus wishing you and the Officers and Soldiers under your Command, all Honour, Safety and Success."

Ibid., vol., 35, 3-3-1797. To THE CLERGY OF DIFFERENT DENOMINATIONS RESIDING IN AND NEAR THE CITY OF PHILADELPHIA, "Believing, as I do, that *Religion* and *Morality* are the essential pillars of Civil society, I view, with unspeakable pleasure, that harmony and brotherly love which characterizes the Clergy of different denominations, as well in this, as in other parts of the United States; exhibiting to the world a new and interesting spectacle, at once the pride of our Country and the surest basis of universal Harmony.

"That your labours for the good of Mankind may be crowned with success; that your temporal enjoyments may be commensurate with your merits; and that the future reward of good and faithful Servants may be your's, I shall not cease to supplicate the Divine Author of life and felicity."

His words concerning Roman Catholics

United States, March 15, 1790.

Note: From the "Letter Book" copy in the *Washington Papers* .

"...may be the members of your Society in America, animated alone by the pure spirit of christianity, and still conducting themselves as the faithful subjects of our free government, enjoy every temporal and spiritual felicity."

37   See letters to Reformed Churches on these dates: November 3, 1780. November 16, 1782. June 2, 1779. November 27, 1783. June 28,

1782. June 30, 1782. November 10, 1783. June 11, 1789. October 9, 1789. December 24, 1789.

38 Boller, p. 35.

39 See the warmth and intimacy of their "reciprocal prayers" in the chapter on "George Washington's and Prayer."

40 Washington's diary references to William White occur only after his presidency, when he returned to Philadelphia to visit:
"November 5, 1798. Mr. White went away before breakfast. I set out on a journey to Phila. about 9 Oclock with Mr. Lear my Secretary—
was met at the Turnpike by a party of horse & escorted to the Ferry at George Town where I was recd. with Military honors. Lodged at
Mr. T. Peters. [GW was going to Philadelphia to make plans for the provisional army then being raised in case of an invasion by the French.
…] 9. Breakfasted in Wilmington & dined & lodged at Chester—waitg. at the latter the return of an Exps. At this place was met by sevl.
Troops of Phila. horse.
10. With this Escort I arrived in the City about 9 oclock & was recd. by Genl. McPhersons Blues & was escorted to my lodgings in 8th.
Street (Mrs. Whites) by them & the Horse….
11, 12, & 13. Dined at my Lodgings receiving many Visits. Weather clear & pleasant.
19. Do. at Doctr. Whites—Bishop. Raining."

41 Washington would not discuss politics with a foreign visitor. From the note on May 19, 1798, we learn: Julian Ursyn Niemcewicz (1758—
1841) visited Mount Vernon on 2 June. Niemcewicz was a Polish literary and political figure who came to America in 1797 …President
and Mrs. Washington came to the Law home on 23 May for a two-day stay while Niemcewicz was still there. Niemcewicz described this
event: "The whole time he [George Washington] was courteous, polite, even attentive; he talked very little, now and then on agriculture,
on natural history, on all that one would wish, except politics, on which he maintains an absolute silence and reserve." *The Diaries of George
Washington*, vol. 6. Donald Jackson, and Dorothy Twohig, ed. *The Papers of George Washington*. Charlottesville: University Press of
Virginia, 1979.

42 Reverend Mason Gallagher, *A Chapter of Unwritten History. The Protestant Episcopacy of the Revolutionary Patriots Lost and Restored. A
Centennial Offering*, (Philadelphia: Reformed Episcopal Rooms, 1883).
Low Churchman and Reformed Episcopalian, Reverend Gallagher put is this way: "The Seabury leaven of Sacerdotalism, exclusive Divine
right and sacramental grace, was allowed admittance. The Prayer Book of 1785 was essentially changed. The Romish alterations of
Elizabeth and Charles were reintroduced. The leaven has spread through the lump, and most significantly though White survived Seabury
a generation, the latter has thoroughly supplanted the patriotic Low Churchman, as the acknowledged Father of the Church, among those
who control and direct its affairs, and wield predominating influence therein. While the power of the laity was in the ascendant, the Church
was Protestant and Scriptural in its services. As the priestly influence became more general the Communion became naturally more sacerdotal, sacramental and exclusive. But these wise patriots were over powered by the insane passion for uniformity, and a hollow, unscrip-
tural unity, which has been the bane of the Protestant Episcopal Church."

43 *PGW*, vol. 2: 423-425. To the Baptist of Virginia.

44 See for example, *WGW*, vol. 3, 9-14-1775 to Col. Benedict Arnold.

45 Boller, *George Washington and Religion*, p. 90-91. "Bird Wilson, in reconsidering his views on Washington's religion, finally decided that
these were sufficient to characterize Washington as such. Washington's "aid given for the support of the Church, in his own parish—the
correct sentiments on religion contained in several of his public addresses—the unimpeached sincerity of his character, manifested through
life, and forbidding a suspicion that those sentiments were not really entertained—and his attendance on the public services of the house
of God, furnish satisfactory proof of his respect for religion and of his belief in Christianity. . . ." On the other hand, if to believe in the
divinity and resurrection of Christ and his atonement for the sins of man and to participate in the sacrament of the Lord's supper are req-
uisites for the Christian faith, then Washington, on the evidence which we have examined, can hardly be considered a Christian, except in
the most nominal sense. "That Washington was a professing Christian," declared Dr. James Abercrombie, "is evident from his regular attendance in our church; but , Sir, I cannot consider any man as a real Christian who uniformly disregards an ordinance so solemnly enjoined
by the divine Author of our holy religion, and considered as a channel of divine grace."
        One may indeed define Christianity broadly enough (as it is increasingly defined In the United States today) to include Washington
within the fold; but this is to place him at a considerable distance from the kind of Christianity which the pietists are talking about when
they claim Washington as one of their own. If Washington was a Christian, he was surely a Protestant of the most liberal persuasion. He
was, as Bird Wilson lamented in his Albany sermon, more of a "Unitarian" than anything else in his apparent lack of doctrinal convictions.
p. 92. There is every reason to believe, from a careful analysis of religious references in his private correspondence, that Washington's reliance
upon a Grand Designer along Deist lines was as deep-seated and meaningful for his life as, say, Ralph Waldo Emerson's serene confidence
in a Universal Spirit permeating the ever-shifting appearances of the everyday world.
p. 93. Twentieth-century scholars customarily lump Washington with Jefferson, Franklin, and Paine as a Deist and let it go at that. But
Washington was not a Jefferson or a Franklin or a Paine, and his religious views were by no means identical with theirs. Broadly speaking,
of course, Washington can be classified as a Deist. But this is to tell us little of a specific nature about his religious opinions, which were,
as a matter of fact, somewhat at variance with those of Jefferson, Franklin, and Paine.
p. 100. No matter what the odds, the human struggle was always worthwhile for Washington. Like the old-fashioned predestinarian
Calvinist (and like many modern secular determinists), Washington was stimulated and energized psychologically by the conviction that
the course of events followed an orderly pattern and was not the product of mere blind, senseless chance.
        The misinterpretation of Washington's guarded silence was not a unique phenomenon, as can be seen by a consideration of the debate
caused by his careful response to the Philadelphia clergy's letter.
P. 81. So frequently has this passage been cited by freethinkers as evidence of Washington's anticlerical bent, as well as his lack of Christian
orthodoxy, that the entire episode to which Jefferson referred somewhat vaguely is worth examining with some care.

The reason this is not true is the address itself, and second, Green's own refutation of the story. The address says, p. 81, "in our special character as ministers of the gospel of Christ, we are more immediately bound to acknowledge the countenance which you have uniformly given to his holy religion." Moreover, Green wrote, p. 83-84,

In all of the "consultations of the clergy," Green insisted, not a "single syllable" was uttered regarding Washington's failure to state publicly his commitment to the Christian faith. Any such "allegation," declared Green, would have been "palpably false," since, in his opinion, there was never any doubt as to Washington's orthodoxy. Bishop White,

Moreover, Green went on to say, "has assured us, that he has no trace of recollection that anything was said in the two meetings of the clergy, relative to the neglect of the President to declare his belief on the subject of divine revelation . . . ." The contents of the address itself, finally Green emphasized, reveal that there was no intention of forcing Washington to declare whether he was a Christian or not.

p. 84 Green also wrote, that in penning the address, it was in the mind of the writer (he knows not that it was in any other mind) that a full and fair opportunity should be given him to speak, on leaving the chair of state, as he had spoken of quitting his military command, and that the address was framed with some reference to this subject.

Pp. 85-86. Washington was in no sense an infidel retorted Green.

The writer of the address most assuredly never did think, or say, that General Washington was an infidel; but he has said, and he says now, that it would have given him gratification, if that great man had thought proper, during his presidency or at its close, to speak out again, as he had once spoken before—spoken in such a manner as not to permit the enemies of revealed truth to use even his silence, for the vile purposes for which they now endeavour to employ it. What were the considerations which..."

46 p. 66. Bishop William White. "I knew no man who seemed so carefully to guard against the discoursing of himself or of his acts, or of any thing pertaining to him; and it has occasionally occurred to me, when in his company, that if a stranger to his person were present, he would never have known, from anything said by the President, that he was conscious of having distinguished himself in the eyes of the world. His ordinary behaviour, although unexceptionably courteous, was not such as to encourage intrusion nor what might be in his mind."

47 this is a repeat of the above. Is that intentional? p. 66. Bishop William White. "I knew no man who seemed so carefully to guard against the discoursing of himself or of his acts, or of any thing pertaining to him; and it has occasionally occurred to me, when in his company, that if a stranger to his person were present, he would never have known, from anything said by the President, that he was conscious of having distinguished himself in the eyes of the world. His ordinary behaviour, although unexceptionably courteous, was not such as to encourage intrusion non what might be in his mind."

CHAPTER 23

1 *WGW*, vol. 32, 1-27-1793, to the members of the New Church in Baltimore.

2 "How the Founders built a nation on religion, philosophy," Review by Will Morrisey of Michael Novak's *On Two Wings: Humble Faith and Common Sense at the American Founding* (January 28-February 3, 2002 National Weekly Edition, *The Washington Times*, 28.

3 Sawyer, *Washington*, vol. I p. 49-50.

4 James Hutson, *Religion and the Founding of the American Republic*, p. 4. (Library of Congress distributed by University Press of New England, 1998) p. 4.

5 Washington Irving, *The Life of George Washington*, vol. I—cited by Character & Influence, p. 31.

6 Lillback, *Proclaim Liberty*, pp.16-24.

7 *WGW*, vol. 26, 6-8-1783, Circular to the States.

8 We explore this more fully in the chapter "Minds of Peculiar Structure."

9 George Washington wrote, "I now make it my earnest prayer that God would have you, and the State over which you preside, in His holy protection . . . that He would most graciously be pleased to dispose us all to do justice, to love mercy, and to demean ourselves with that charity, humility, and pacific temper of mind, which were the characteristics of the Divine Author of our blessed religion, and without an humble imitation of whose example in these things, we can never hope to be a happy nation." George Washington, "Circular to State Governments," June 8, 1783, *Writings* (New York: The Library of America, 1997), 526.

10 *Funk & Wagnalls New Encyclopedia* 1979, vol. 18, p. 249. Also, for more on this see Chapter 2, "Deism Defined: Shades of Meaning, Shading the Truth."

11 Benjamin Franklin, Reasons Against Satirizing Religion, December 13, 1757. See
http://teachingamericanhistory.org/library/index.asp?document=473

12 If one reads Paine's 1776 classic, *Common Sense*, he may note biblical references and allusions (in a positive way). Paine grew up in England and was a Quaker. His anti-Christian bias did not fully emerge until decades later. For example, here are a few sentences from *Common Sense*: "But where, say some, is the king of America? I'll tell you, friend, he reigns above, and doth not make havoc of mankind like the royal brute of Great Britain. Yet that we may not appear to be defective even in earthly honors, let a day be solemnly set apart for proclaiming the charter; let it be brought forth placed on the divine law, the Word of God; let a crown be placed thereon, by which the world may know, that so far as we approve of monarchy, that in America the law is king." (Bruce Frohnen, ed., *The American Republic: Primary Sources* (Indianapolis: Liberty Fund, 2002), 188.).

13 *WGW*, vol. 25, 9-18-1792.

14 Ibid., see note.

15 Ibid.

16 Ibid.

17 *WGW*, vol. 28, 8-18-1786.

18 Edwards, Tryon, *The New Dictionary of Thoughts – A Cyclopedia of Quotations*, (Garden City, NY, Hanover House, 1852; revised and

enlarged by C.H. Catrevas, et al. 1891, The Standard Book Company 1963), p.46

19 Blackstone, *Commentaries*, vol. 1, 38.

20 Ibid., 41.

21 Ibid., vol. 1, 42.

22 Ibid.

23 Rupert Hughes, *George Washington The Savior of the States 1777-1781* (New York: William Morrow & Company) 1930. pp. 398-399. The footnote to this text reads:

> "Lee Papers, IV., p. 31. In a letter to Dr. Rush, Sept. 26, 1779 he says: "You and many others accuse me of want of religion, there never was a greater mistake – to convince you I send you my proem, from Cicero de legibus – I am perswaded that no Society can exist without religion, and I think the Christian; unincumbered of its sophistications, is the most excellent and [of course] of a divine nature as comprehending the most divine system of which but at the same time, I own, I quarrel with the tediousness and impertinence of the liturgies of the various sects, which so far from being the support are the ruin of all religion – as to the dogmas they are many of 'em not only absurd but impious as they are dishonorable to the Godhead or visible rule and moderator of the infinity of worlds which surround us I therefore cannot help esteeming myself the [champion] vindicator rather than the Denyer and Blasphemer of the Almighty." (Lee Papers, III, pp. 373-4.

24 Although Lee could be classified as a skeptic, he seems to long for genuine Christianity lived out without all the interdenominational infighting.

> In his project for an ideal state, a military colony, General Lee says: "I speak to men and soldiers, who wish and are able to assert and defend the rights of humanity; and, let me add, to vindicate the character of God Almighty, and real Christianity, which have been so long dishonored by sectarists of every kind and complexion; catholics, church of England men, Presbyterians, and Methodists. I could wish, therefore, that the community of soldiers (who are to be all Christians) should establish one common form of worship, with which every member must acquiesce, at least in attendance of divine worship, and the observation of the prescribed ceremonies; but this so contrived as not to shock any an who ahs been bred up in any of the different sects. for which reason, let all expositions of the scripture, and all dogmas, be fore ever banished. Let it be sufficient that he acknowledges the existence, providence, and goodness of God Almighty; the he reverences Jesus Christ: but let the question never be asked, whether he considers Jesus Christ as only a divine person, commissioned by God for divine purposes, as the son of God, or as God himself. These sophistical subtleties only lead to a doubt of the whole; let it be sufficient therefore that whether a real God or only a divinely inspired mortal; for which reason to prevent the impertinence and ill consequences of dogmatizing, no professional priests of any sort whatever shall be admitted in the community. but still I am of opinion, that a sacred order, or hierarchy, should be established, and in the following manner: that this hierarchy are not to be expositors of the divine law, which ought to be understood by every member of common capacity; but as the servitors, or administrators of the solemn ceremonies to be observed in the worship of the Supreme Being, of his Son, or missionary." Lee Papers, III, p. 325.

25 *WGW*, vol. 35, 12-7-1796, 8th Annual Address to Congress.

26 Ibid., vol. 35, Farewell Address.

27 Ibid., vol. 30, 6-22-1788.

28 Ibid., vol. 30, 6-25-1788.

29 Ibid., 1-8-1790

30 Northwest Ordinance, Article III in *The Annals of America*, vol. 3, 194-195.

31 *WGW* vol. 32, 6-22-1792.

32 Ibid., 10-20-1792.

33 *WGW*, vol. 32, 1-27-1793.

34 Ibid., vol. 3, 9-14-1775.

35 Ibid., vol. 5, 7-9-1776.

36 Lillback, *Proclaim Liberty*, pp.15-24.

37 *PGW*, George Washington Papers at the Library of Congress, 1741-1799: Series 2 Letterbooks, George Washington to Savannah, Georgis, Hebrew Congregation, May, 1790 image 147 of 166.

38 *WGW*, vol. 30, Proposed Address to Congress.

39 Works of Jonathan Edwards, vol. 2 p 253

CHAPTER 24

1 Sparks, ed., *The Writings of George Washington*, vol. XII, 152.

2 Charles Francis Adams, ed., *Letters of John Adams—Addressed to His Wife* (Boston: Charles C. Little and James Brown, 1841), vol. I, 23-24.

3 *Journal of the Proceedings of Congress*, 1774 (Philadelphia: Printed for the Library Company of Philadelphia, 1974), September 10, 1774, see 30-33.

4 Ibid.

5 Ibid.

6 *WGW*, vol. 3, 6-15-1772

7 Their instructions will be found spread on the *Journals of the Continental Congress* of March 10, 1774.

8 John Rhodehame, ed., *George Washington: Writings* (New York: The Library of America, 1997), 187-189.

9 *WGW*, vol. 3, 9- 4-1775.

10 *WGW*, vol. 4, 11- 5-1775.

11 Benjamin Hart, "The Wall That Protestantism Built: The Religious Reasons for the Separation of Church and State," *Policy Review* (Washington, D.C.: Heritage Foundation, Fall 1988), 44.

12 *WGW*, vol. 31 , 3-15-1790, and Eidsmoe, *Christianity and the Constitution* p. 121.

13 William Barclay Allen, ed., *George Washington - A Collection* (Indianapolis: Liberty Classics, Liberty Fund, Inc., 1988), 547-548.

14 Sparks, *The Writings of George Washington,* vol. IX, p. 262.

15 For a discussion of Christianity's role in the establishment of religious liberty in America see, Peter A. Lillback, *Proclaim Liberty*.

16 WGW, vol. 31, 3-1-1790. and. Boller, , *George Washington & Religion* p. 182.

17 Sparks, *The Writings of George Washington,* vol. XII, p. 154.

18 *WGW*, vol. 30, 4-30-1789.

19 Ibid., vol.24, 6-28-1782.

20 Ibid., vol. 26, 4-18-1783. General Orders.

Ibid., vol. 28, 3-30-1785. To Lucretia Wilhemina Van Winter, "At best I have only been an instrument in the hands of Providence, to effect, with the aid of France and many virtuous fellow Citizens of America, a revolution which is interesting to the general liberties of mankind, and to the emancipation of a country which may afford an Asylum, if we are wise enough to pursue the paths wch. lead to virtue and happiness, to the oppressed and needy of the Earth. Our region is extensive, our plains are productive, and if they are cultivated with liberality and good sense, we may be happy ourselves, and diffuse happiness to all who wish to participate."

Ibid., vol. 29, 4-25-1788. To Marquis De Chastellux, "Hitherto there has been much greater unanimity in favour of the proposed government than could have reasonably been expected. Should it be adopted (and I think it will be) America will lift up her head again and in a few years become respectable among the nations. It is a flattering and consolatory reflection, that our rising Republics have the good wishes of all the Philosophers, Patriots, and virtuous men in all nations: and that they look upon them as a kind of Asylum for mankind. God grant that we may not disappoint their honest expectations, by our folly or perverseness."

Ibid., vol. 29, 5-28-1788. To Reverend Francis Adrian Vanderkemp. "...I take the speediest occasion to well-come your arrival on the American shore. I had always hoped that this land might become a safe and agreeable Asylum to the virtuous and persecuted part of mankind, to whatever nation they might belong; but I shall be the more particularly happy, if this Country can be, by any means, useful to the Patriots of Holland, with whose situation I am peculiarly touched, and of whose public virtue I entertain a great opinion."

Ibid., vol. 30, 8-29-1788. To Joseph Mandrillon. "We flatter ourselves your patriotic wishes and sanguine hopes respecting the political felicity of this Country, will not prove abortive. We hope, from the general acquiescence of the States so far, with small exceptions, in the proposed Constitution, that the foundation is laid for the enjoyment of much purer civil liberty and greater public happiness than have hitherto been the portion of Mankind. And we trust the western World will yet verify the predictions of its friends and prove an Asylum for the persecuted of all Nations."

Ibid., vol. 30, 8-31-1788. To Thomas Jefferson. "...this will become the great avenue into the Western Country; a country which is now settling in an extraordinarily rapid manner, under uncommonly favorable circumstances, and which promises to afford a capacious asylum for the poor and persecuted of the Earth."

Ibid., vol. 30, 9-27-1788. To Reverend Francis Adrian Vanderkepm. "Sir. The letter with which you was pleased to favor me dated the 29th. of Augt. came duly to hand, and afforded me the pleasure of hearing that you had made a purchase agreeable to your wishes in the vicinity of Esopus. I sincerely hope that it may prove an agreeable retreat, and a happy Asylum from your late troubles in Holland."

Ibid., vol. 32, 6-7-1793. To the Mechanical Society of Baltimore. "If the Citizens of the United States have obtained the character of an enlightened and liberal people, they will prove that they deserve it, by shewing themselves the true friends of mankind and making their Country not only an Asylum for the oppressed of every Nation, but a desirable residence for the virtuous and industrious of every Country."

21 *Liberty* is defined as follows by Noah Webster in his *First American Dictionary of the English Language* published in 1828: "Freedom from restraint, in a general sense, and applicable to the body, or to the will or mind. The body is at liberty, when not confined; the will or mind is at liberty, when not checked or controlled. A man enjoys liberty, when no physical force operates to restrain his actions or volitions." *Natural liberty* "consists in the power of acting as one thinks fit, without any restraint or control, except from the laws of nature. It is a state of exemption from the control of others, and from positive laws and the institutions of social life. This liberty is abridged by the establishment of government." *Civil liberty* is " the liberty of men in a state of society, or natural liberty, so far only abridged and restrained, as is necessary and expedient for the safety and interest of the society, state or nation. A restraint of natural liberty, not necessary or expedient for the public, is tyranny or oppression. Civil liberty is an exemption from the arbitrary will of others, which exemption is secured by established laws, which restrain every man from injuring or controlling another. Hence the restraints of law are essential to civil liberty." He further defines political liberty, "*Political liberty*, is sometimes used as synonymous with civil liberty. But it more properly designates the liberty of a nation, the freedom of a nation or state from all unjust abridgment of its rights and independence by another nation. Hence we often speak of the political liberties of Europe, or the nations of Europe." *Religious liberty*, "is the free right of adopting and enjoying opinions on religious subjects, and worshiping the Supreme Being according to the dictates of conscience, without external control." Clearly liberty was a critical concept in early America.

22 The full name for the Statue of Liberty is *Liberty Enlightening the World. WGW*, vol. 26, 6-8-1783. Washington's sense of enlightenment is closely related to religious liberty: "The Citizens of America, placed in the most enviable condition, as the sole Lords and Proprietors of a vast Tract of Continent, comprehending all the various soils and climates of the World, and abounding with all the necessaries and conveniencies of life, are now by the late satisfactory pacification, acknowledged to be possessed of absolute freedom and Independency; They are, from this period, to be considered as the Actors on a most conspicuous Theatre, which seems to be peculiarly designated by Providence for the display of human greatness and felicity; Here, they are not only surrounded with every thing which can contribute to the comple-

tion of private and domestic enjoyment, but Heaven has crowned all its other blessings, by giving a fairer oppertunity for political happiness, than any other Nation has ever been favored with. Nothing can illustrate these observations more forcibly, than a recollection of the happy conjuncture of times and circumstances, under which our Republic assumed its rank among the Nations; The foundation of our Empire was not laid in the gloomy age of Ignorance and Superstition, but at an Epocha when the rights of mankind were better understood and more clearly defined, than at any former period, the researches of the human mind, after social happiness, have been carried to a great extent, the Treasures of knowledge, acquired by the labours of Philosophers, Sages and Legislatures, through a long succession of years, are laid open for our use, and their collected wisdom may be happily applied in the Establishment of our forms of Government; the free cultivation of Letters, the unbounded extension of Commerce, the progressive refinement of Manners, the growing liberality of sentiment, and above all, the pure and benign light of Revelation, have had ameliorating influence on mankind and increased the blessings of Society. At this auspicious period, the United States came into existence as a Nation, and if their Citizens should not be completely free and happy, the fault will be intirely their own."

23 The names for our country reflect our discoverers and our history. "America" is an anglicized version of "Amerigo," which in turn is the first name of the explorer, Amerigo Vespuci, who first recognized that North America was not the Indies, but a hitherto unknown continent. Amerigo is a version of the German name "Emerick" which is a corruption of the German word, *Himmelreich,* meaning "Kingdom of Heaven." It has been suggested by some that this is an excellent name for America—"a corrupted version of the Kingdom of Heaven!" 2007 is the five hundredth anniversary of America being named America. The title was given by German monk named Martin Waldsemuller to honor Vespuchi as the first to understand that Columbus' discovery was not the Indies, but an entirely new continent—a New World. Thus, the monk put America on his map of the "new world." A second name for America is Columbia. This is a feminine version of Columbus, the great first discoverer of the Western Hemisphere. We have Columbus' name present in our nation's capitol, Washington D. C.—or the District of Columbia. Columbia—the feminine version of Christopher Columbus' last name, is a personification of our nation. Columbia stands at the top of our Capitol building in the District of Columbia, where our Congress meets on Capitol Hill. It is interesting that Columbus is the word for dove—the symbol for hope in a new world in the story of Noah's flood from Genesis 6-9. Further, his first name is Christopher, meaning, "the bearer of Christ." In a medieval legend, a man carried Christ over a raging stream, and thus was named "The Christ-Bearer" or "Christopher." One can see why for many years in the Roman Catholic tradition, St. Christopher was the patron saint of travelers. It is most fascinating that the discoverer of America's name implies one who carries Christ over the waters coming as a dove of hope for a new world after a flood! This may all be coincidence, or then again, it may be a gift of divine Providence. The third, and official name of our country is The United States of America. This reflects the "miracle of Philadelphia" where thirteen sovereign states or nations chose to become one nation of United States. This had never happened before nor has it happened since. Only in America did such a remarkable union of political entities ever occur. This unparalleled event is captured in our Latin mottoes seen on our Dollar Bill: *E Pluribus Unum* and *Novus Ordo Seculorum.* The first means, "one out of many" and the second means, "a new order of the ages." Perhaps it would also be appropriate to note another Latin motto on the dDollar bill—"Annuit Coeptis." This means "God has smiled at our undertakings." A providential perspective on history would suggest that such is indeed the case.

24 This phrase comes from one of the earliest publications on the life of Washington, by the Reverend Dr. Jedidiah Morse, a clergyman-scholar and correspondent of Washington. At the end of his thirty-three long page summary of General Washington's life, based upon the anonymously written and approved life of Washington by David Humphreys, we find the following poem, which probably came from the pen of Humphreys as well.

GENERAL WASHINGTON

GREAT without pomp, without ambition brave—
Proud, not to conquer fellow men, but save—
Friend to the weak—a foe to none but those,
Who plan their greatness on their brethren's woes—
Aw'd by no titles—undefil'd by lust—
Free without faction, obstinately just—
Too wise to learn, form Machiavel's school,
That truth and perfidy by turns should rule.
Warm'd by Religion's sacred, genuine ray,
Which points to future bliss, th' unerring way;
Yet ne'er controul'd by Superstition's laws,
The worst of tyrants in the noblest cause..

Jedidiah Morse (1761-1836), *The Life of Gen. Washington* (Philadelphia: Jones, Hoff & Derrick, 1794).

25 America, the custodian of Washington's "sacred fire of liberty," has learned to sing of the "sacred fire" in terms of "freedom's holy light." These words come from the patriotic hymn, "My Country 'Tis of Thee" written by Samuel Francis Smith (1808-1895). A graduate of Harvard and a Baptist pastor, with interest in the American Baptist Missionary Union, Smith wrote the words in less than a half hour at the age of twenty-three, while in seminary. The occasion was a children's celebration held in a Boston church on July 4t, 1832, the hundredth anniversary year of the birth of Washington. The melody is identical to the British national anthem, "God Save the King" making the last line "Great God our King" a rekindling of the spirit of '76 that blazed in Washington's Patriot Army. The first and *last* stanzas are:

My country 'tis of thee,
Sweet land of liberty,
Of thee I sing:
Land where my fathers died,

Land of the pilgrim's pride,
From ev'ry mountain side
Let freedom ring!
Our fathers' God, to Thee,
Author of liberty,
To Thee we sing:
Long may our land be bright
With Freedom's holy light;
Protect us by Thy might,
Great God, our King!

26   William J. Federer, remarks in D. James Kennedy's, *One Nation Under God* (Ft. Lauderdale: Coral Ridge Ministries, 2005), a video.
27   WGW, vol. 29, 4-25-1788.
28   Ibid., vol. 30, 8-31-1788.

CHAPTER 25

1   *WGW*, vol. 31, 8-17-1790. To the master, wardens, and brethren of King David's Lodge of Masons in Newport.
2   John Warwick Montgomery, *The Shaping of America* (Minneapolis: Bethany Fellowship, Inc., 1976), p. 54 and p. 56.
3   *WGW*, vol. 35, 4-24-1797. To THE GRAND LODGE OF ANCIENT, FREE AND ACCEPTED MASONS OF THE COM-MONWEALTH OF MASSACHUSETTS, "Brothers: In that retirement which declining years induced me to seek, and which repose, to a mind long employed in public concerns, rendered necessary, my wishes that bounteous Providence will continue to bless and preserve our country in Peace, and in the prosperity it has enjoyed, will be warm and sincere; And my attachment to the Society of which we are members will dispose me, always, to contribute my best endeavours to promote the honor and interest of the *Craft* . For the Prayer you offer in my behalf I entreat you to accept the thanks of a grateful heart; with the assurance of fraternal regard and best wishes for the honor, happiness and prosperity of all the Members of the Grand-lodge of Massachusetts."
Ibid., vol. 35, 4-1-1797. To THE BROTHERS OF ANCIENT YORK MASONS OF LODGE NO. 22 (Alexandria, Va.) "While my heart acknowledges with Brotherly Love, your affectionate congratulations on my retirement from the arduous toils of past years, my gratitude is no less excited by your kind wishes for my future happiness.
If it has pleased the Supreme Architect of the Universe to make me an humble instrument to promote the welfare and happiness of my fellow men, my exertions have been abundantly recompensed by the kind partiality with which they have been received; and the assurance you give me of your belief that I have acted upon the Square in my public Capacity, will be among my principle enjoyments in this Terrestial Lodge."
Ibid., vol. 35, 11-8-1798, To THE MARYLAND GRAND LODGE OF FREE MASONS
"Gentlemen and Brothers: Your obliging and affectionate letter, together with a Copy of the constitutions of Masonry, has been put into my hands by your Grand Master; for which I pray you to accept my best thanks.
So far as I am acquainted with the principles and doctrines of Free Masonry, I conceive it to be founded in benevolence, and to be exercised only for the good of Mankind; I cannot, therefore, upon this ground, withhold my approbation of it."
Ibid., vol. 24, 8-10-1782 To WATSON & CASSOUL, "Gentn: The Masonick Ornaments which accompanied your Brotherly Address of the 23d. of the first Month, tho' elegant in themselves, were rendered more valuable by the flattering sentiments, and affectionate manner, in which they were offered. If my endeavours to avert the evil, with which this Country was threatened, by a deliberate plan of Tyranny, should be crowned with the success that is wished; the praise is due to the *Grand Architect* of the Universe; who did not see fit to Suffer his Superstructures, and justice, to be subjected to the ambition of the princes of this World, or to the rod of oppression, in the hands of any power upon Earth. For your affectionate Vows, permit me to be grateful; and offer mine for true Brothers in all parts of the World; and to assure you of the sincerity with which I am etc."
4   Paul Johnson, *George Washington: The Founding Father* (HarperCollins Publishers, 2005), p. 11.
5   Randall, *George Washington: A Life*, p. 67.
6   Boller, *George Washington & Religion*, pp. 111-112.
7   Albert G. Mackey, M. D., *The Encyclopedia of Free Masonry* (Philadelphia: McClure Publishing Co., 1917), pp. 9-10 says, "The acacia, which, in Scripture, is always called *Shittah*, and in the plural *Shittim*, was esteemed a sacred wood among the Hebrews. Of it Moses was ordered to make a tabernacle, the ark of the covenant, the table for the shewbread, and the rest of the sacred furniture....the acacia, in the mythic system of Freemasonry, is preeminently the symbol of the IMMORTALITY OF THE SOUL—that important doctrine which it is the great design of the Institution to teach."
8   For Washington's Masonic Sermon Collection see Lane, *Washington Collection of the Boston Athenaeum*, p. 132.
9   In Washington's Masonic Sermon collection were sermons preached by some of the great clergymen of the day, such as Reverend Samuel Miller, one of the leading Presbyterian preachers.

A
DISCOURSE
Delivered in the
NEW PRESBYTERIAN CHURCH.
NEW-YORK:
Before the

GRAND LODGE
Of the STATE OF NEW-YORK,
AND THE BRETHREN OF THAT FRATERNITY,
ASSEMBLED IN GENERAL COMMUNICATION,
OF THE FESTIVAL OF
ST. JOHN THE BAPTIST,
June 24th, 1795
By SAMUEL MILLER, A.M.
One of the Ministers of the United Presbyterian
Churches, in the City of New-York
New-York: - Printed by F. Childs.
1795

10 Uzal Ogden, "Sermon Delivered at Morristown, On Monday December 27, 1784, it being the Festival of St. John the Evangelist, Before the Fraternity of Free and Accepted Masons, of Lodge No. 10 in the State of New Jersey." The page after the title page declares, "In Lodge No. 10, State of New-Jersey, Morris-Town, December 27, 5784. Resolved, That the thanks of this Lodge, be presented to the Reverend Mr. Uzal Ogden, for his sermon delivered this day before them, convened for the celebration of the Festival of St. John the Evangelist. And that Brothers, ... be desired to request the Reverend Mr. Ogden, to commit said discourse to writing, and to beg the favour of the manuscript for publication." Reverend Ogden's sermon was Gospel focused, "But, to deliver us from the curse of the law, even the Son of God himself, in condescension and goodness infinite, assumed our nature; 'bore our iniquities;' expiated our guilt; became 'accursed for us' the just having suffered for the unjust.'...We perceive, therefore, that the Gospel is a dispensation of divine Mercy;—that our redemption is of free 'Grace;' by us altogether unmerited; that Christianity was most graciously designed to counteract the effects of sin.;...As salvation is attainable only through Christ, of necessity, therefore, those who reject his dispensation of grace, must be consigned over to eternal woe...." p. 21ff. "And remember Sirs, you are Christian-Masons!—That you are under obligations numerous and most sacred, to make conscience of all your deeds, and so to live, that, in truth, you may—-fear God;—-honour the Government;—-honour all men, and love your Christian and Masonic Brotherhoods! How many have there been who have done honour to Christianity and Masonry;—who have been Christian Masons indeed?" pp. 39-40.

11 See chapter two.

12 *WGW*, vol. 1, 6-12-1754. To Robert Dinwiddie. "I am much grieved to find our Stores so slow advancing. *God* knows when we shall [be] able to do any thing for to deserve better of our Country." An example of one of Washington's earliest written prayers to God is in *WGW*, vol. 2, 6-10-1757. To John Robinson, "*God* send them success and a safe return, I pray."

13 The Masonic Constitution was printed at the beginning of Uzal Ogden's Masonic sermon preached in 1795, which was also in Washington's Masonic sermon collection. Reverend Uzal Ogden was an evangelical Episcopalian, whose Gospel sermons had been read and enjoyed by Washington. (See *WGW*, vol. 16, 8-5-1779. To Uzal Ogden.) Thus Gospel sermons were preached in the Masonic Order of Washington's day. Washington also autographed his copy of Uzal Ogden's *Antidote to Deism. The Deist unmasked; or an ample Refutation of all the Objections of Thomas Paine, against the Christian Religion,* 2 vol. (Newark: John Woods, 1795). Apparently Washington did not respond to Reverend Ogden's request for Washington's approbation of the work in his March 22 1796 letter to the president.

14 See Uzal Ogden's sermon quoted in note 13 above.

15 See Samuel Miller's sermon cited in note 12 above.

16 Reverend Dr. William Smith, A Sermon preached in Christ-Church Philadelphia, [For the Benefit of the Poor] by appointment of and before the General Communication of Free and Accepted Masons of the State of Pennsylvania, On Monday December 28, 1779.

17 THE
PHILANTHROPIST
OR
A GOOD TWELVE CENTS WORTH OF POLITICAL LOVE POWDER,
FOR THE FAIR DAUGHTERS AND PATRIOTIC SONS OF AMERICA

By the Reverend M.L. Weems, (of Lodge No. 50)
Dumfries

———————————

ALEXANDRIA
Printed by John & James D. Westcott
MDCCXCIX

To his Excellency George Washington, Esquire,
Lieutenant General of the Armies of the United States.

Most Honor'd General,
...
On the Square of Justice,

And on the Scale of Love,
I remain, Most Honored General,
Your very sincere friend,
And Masonic Brother,
M.L. Weems

18   Mackey, *The Encyclopedia of Free Masonry*, p. 182 has an article entitled, "the Christianization of Freemasonry." It states that wherever Christianity is strong, it often brings its faith directly into the Masonic Order.

The interpretation of the symbols of Freemasonry from a Christian point of view is a theory adopted by some of the most distinguished Masonic writers of England and this country, but one of which I think does not belong to the ancient system. Hutchinson, and after him Oliver, - profoundly philosophical as are the Masonic speculations of both, -have, I am constrained to believe, fallen into a great error in calling the Master Mason's degree a Christian institution. It is true that it embraces within its scheme the great truths of Christianity upon the subject of the immortality of the soul and the resurrection of the body; but this was to be presumed, because Freemasonry is truth, and all truth must be identical. But the origin of each is different; their histories are dissimilar. The principles of Freemasonry preceded the advent of Christianity. Its symbols and its legends are derived from the Solomonic Temple and the people even anterior to that. Its religion comes from the ancient priesthood; its faith was that primitive one of Noah and his immediate descendents. If Masonry were simply a Christian institution, the Jew and the Moslem, the Brahman and the Buddhist, could not conscientiously partake of its illumination. But its universality is its boast. In its language citizens of every nation may converse; at its altar men of all religions man kneel; to its creed disciples of every faith may subscribe.

Yet it cannot be denied that since the advent of Christianity a Christian element had been almost imperceptibly infused into the Masonic system, at least among Christian Masons. This has been a necessity; for it is the tendency of every predominant religion to pervade with its influence all that surrounds it or is about it, whether religious, political, or social. This arises from a need of the human heart. To the man deeply imbued with the spirit of his religion, there is an almost unconscious desire to accommodate and adapt all the business and the amusements of life, - the labors and the employments of his every-day existence,—to the I-dwelling faith of his soul.

The Christian Mason, therefore, while acknowledging and appreciating the great doctrines taught in Masonry, and also while grateful that these doctrines were preserved in the bosom of his ancient Order at a time when they were unknown to the multitudes of the surrounding nations, is still anxious to give them a Christian character; to invest them, in some measure, with the peculiarities of his own creed, and to bring the interpretation of their symbolism more nearly home to his own religious sentiments.

The feeling is an instinctive one, belonging to the noblest aspiration of our human nature; and hence we find Christian Masonic writers indulging in it to an almost unwarrantable excess, and, by the extent of their sectarian interpretations, materially affecting the cosmopolitan character of the Institution.

This tendency to Christianization has, in some instances, been so universal, and has prevailed for so long a period, and has prevailed for so long a period, that certain symbols and myths have been in this way, so deeply and thoroughly imbued with the Christian element as to leave those who have not penetrated into the cause of the peculiarity, in doubt whether they should attribute to the symbol an ancient or a modern and Christian origin.

19   See, for example, the articles on "Freemasonry" in *Documents of Synod: Study Papers and Actions of the Reformed Presbyterian Church, Evangelical synod—1965-1982*, ed. Paul R. Gilchrist (New Castle, Delaware: Reformed Presbyterian Church, Evangelical Synod, 1982), pp. 252-264.

20   Alexander D.D., Reverend Archibald. *Evidences of the Authenticity, Inspiration, and Canonical Authority of the Holy Scriptures.*(Philadelphia: Presbyterian Board of Publication)., p.27-30

Again, if deism be the true religion, why has piety never flourished among its professors? Why have they not been the most zealous and consistent worshippers of God? Does not truth promote piety? And will it not ever be the case that they who hold the truth will love God most ardently, and serve him most faithfully? But what is the fact in regard to this class of men? Have they ever been distinguished for the spirit of devotion; have they produced numerous instances of exemplary piety? It is so much the reverse, that even the asking such reasonable questions has the appearance of ridicule. And when people heat the word "pious deist," they have the same sort of feeling as when mention is made of an honest thief, or a sober drunkard.

There is no slander in making this statement, for deists do not affect to be pious. They have no love for devotion. If the truth were known, this is the very thing they wish to get rid of; and if they believed that professing themselves to be deist laid them under greater obligations to be devout, they would not be so zealous for the system. Believe me, the contest is not between one religion and another, it is between religion and irreligion. It is impossible that a man of truly pious temper should reject the Bible, even if he were unacquainted with its historical evidences. He would find it to be so congenial to his taste, and so salutary in its effects on his own spirit, that he would conclude that it must have derived its origin from heaven. But we find no such spirit in the writings of deists. There is not in them a tincture of piety; but they have more than a sprinkling of profane ridicule. When you turn to them from the Bible, you are sensible of as great a transition, as if you passed suddenly from a warm and genial climate to a frigid zone. If deists expect ever to conciliate regard for their religion they must appear to be truly pious men, sincerely engaged in the service of God; and this will have more effect than all their arguments. But whenever this event shall occur, they will be found no longer opposing the Bible, but will esteem it as the best of books, and will come to it for fuel to feed the flame of pure devotion. An African prince, who was brought to England and resided there some time, being asked what he thought of the Bible, answered, that he believed it to be from God, for he found all the good people in favour of it, and all the bad people against it!

The want of a spirit of piety and devotion, must be reckoned the principal reason why the deists have never been able to establish and keep up any religious worship among themselves. The thing has been attempted at several different times and in different countries, but never with success.

It is said, that the first enterprise of this kind was that of David Williams, an Englishman, who had been a dissenting minister in Liverpool, but passing over first to Socinianism, and then to deism, when to London, where, being patronized by some persons of influence, he opened a house for deistical worship, and formed a liturgy, consisting principally of praise to the Creator. Here he preached for a short time, and collected some followers; but he complained that most of his congregation went on to atheism. After four years' trial, the scheme came to nothing. There were neither funds nor congregation remaining, and the Priest of Nature,' (as Williams styled himself) through discouragement and ill health, abandoned the project.

Some feeble attempts of the same kind have been made in the United States; but they are unworthy of being particularly noticed.

Federick II., the deistical king of Prussia, had once formed the plan of a Pantheon in Berlin for the worshippers of all sects and all religions, the chief object of which was the subversion of Christianity; but the scheme was never carried into execution.

The most interesting experiment of this kind was that made by the Theophilanthropists in France, during the period of the revolution. After some trial had been made of atheism and irreligion, and when the want of public worship was felt by many reflecting persons, a society was formed for the worship of God, upon the pure principles of Natural Religion. Among the patrons of this society, were men beloved for their philanthropy, and distinguished for their learning, and some high in power.

La Revellière Lepaux, one of the directory of France, was a zealous patron of the new religion. By his influence, permission was obtained to make use of the churches for their worship. In the city of Paris alone, eighteen or twenty were assigned to them, among which was the cathedral church of Notre Dame.

Their creed was simple, consisting of the great articles, *The Existence of God, and the Immortality of the Soul*. Their moral system also embraced two great principles, *The Love of God, And The Love of Man*; - which were indicated by the name Theophilanthropists. Their worship consisted of prayers and hymns of praise, which were comprehended in a manual prepared for a directory in worship. Lectures were delivered by the members, which, however, underwent the inspection of the society, before they were pronounced in public. To these were added some simple ceremonies, such as placing a basket of fruit and flowers on the altar. Music, vocal and instrumental, was used; for the latter, they availed themselves of the organs in the churches. Great efforts were made to have this worship generally introduced in all the principal towns in France; and the views of the society were even extended to foreign countries. Their manual was sent into all parts of the republic by the Minister of the interior, free of expense.

Never did a society enjoy greater advantages at its commencement. Christianity had been rejected with scorn; atheism had for a short time been tried, but was found to be intolerable; the government was favourable to the project; men of learning and influence patronized it, and churches ready built were at the service of the new denomination. The system of Natural Religion which was adopted was the best that could have been selected, and considerable wisdom was discovered in the construction of their liturgy. But with all these circumstances in their favour, the society could not subsist. At first, indeed, while the scene was novel, large audiences attended, most of whom however were merely spectators; but in a short time, they dwindled away to such a degree, that instead of occupying twenty churches in Paris, they needed only four; and in some of the provincial towns, where they began under the most favourable auspices, they soon came to nothing. Thus they went on declining until, under the consular government, they were prohibited the use of the churches any longer; upon which they immediately expired without a struggle, and it is believed that not a vestige of the society now remains.

It will be instructive and interesting to inquire into the reasons of this want of success, in a society enjoying so many advantages. Undoubtedly, the chief reason was, the want of a truly devotional spirit. This was observed from the beginning of their meetings. There was nothing to interest the feelings of the heart. Their orators might be men of learning, and might produce good moral discourses, but they were not men of piety, and not always men of pure morals. Their hymns were said to be well composed, and the music good; but the musicians were hired from the stage. There was also a strange defect of liberality in contributing to the funds of the society. They found it impossible to raise, in some their societies, a sum which every Christian congregation, even in the poorest of any sect, would have collected in one day. It is a fact, that one of the societies petitioned government to grant them relief from a debt which they had contracted in providing the apparatus of their worship, not amounting to more than fifty dollars, stating, that their annual income did not exceed twenty dollars. In the other towns their musicians deserted them, because they were not paid, and frequently no person could be found to deliver lectures.

21 *WGW*, vol. 32, 7-3-1792. *WGW* note: "The portrait was not executed until September, 1794, in Philadelphia. Having been refused a sitting at the above time, Williams offered the Masonic Lodge No. 22 of Alexandria the finished work, if the lodge would request him to make a portrait. The lodge approved this idea Aug. 29, 1793. The resultant portrait was executed in pastel, and is now in the possession of the lodge." Mrs. Washington said it was her favorite portrait of the President, because the stylization and embellishment of portrait painters was not followed, and Williams painted Washington as he saw him, even with imperfections like small pox marks.

22 Eidsmoe, *Christianity and the Constitution*, 125.

23 *WGW*, vol. 36, 9-25-1798. To Reverend G. W. Snyder. *WGW* note says, "In a letter from Snyder (Aug. 22, 1798, which is in the *Washington Papers*), it is stated that this book 'gives a full Account of a Society of Free-Masons, that distinguishes itself by the Name of 'Illuminati,' whose Plan is to overturn all Government and all Religion, even natural.'" Washington followed up the letter a few weeks later. *WGW*, 10-24-1798. To Reverend G. W. Snyder. "Revd Sir: I have your favor of the 17th. instant before me; and my only motive to trouble you with the receipt of this letter, is to explain, and correct a mistake which I perceive the hurry in which I am obliged, often, to write letters, have led you into. It was not my intention to doubt that, the Doctrines of the Illuminati, and principles of Jacobinism had not spread in the United States. On the contrary, no one is more truly satisfied of this fact than I am. The idea that I meant to convey, was, that I did not believe that the *Lodges* of Free Masons in *this* Country had, as *Societies*, endeavoured to propagate the diabolical tenets of the first, or per-

nicious principles of the latter (if they are susceptible of seperation). That Individuals of them may have done it, or that the *founder*, or *instrument* employed to found, the Democratic Societies in the United States, may have had these objects; and actually had a seperation of the *People* from their *Government* in view, is too evident to be questioned. My occupations are such, that but little leisure is allowed me to read News Papers, or Books of any kind; the reading of letters, and preparing answers, absorb much of my time. With respect, etc."

24   Timothy Dwight, "The Duty of Americans at the Present Crisis" (1798) in *Annals of America*, (Chicago, 1976), vol. 4.

25   Thomson compiled and published a harmony of the Gospels, and served as an elder in the Presbyterian Church. As a classics scholar, he was the source of the Latin motto, *Annuit Coeptis*, meaning "He [God] has smiled on our undertakings" that is back of the Great Seal of the United States and on the reverse of the American dollar bill. See Peter A. Lillback, *Freedom's Holy Light*, (Bryn Mawr: The Providence Forum, 2000), pp. 4-7.

26   *WGW*, vol. 33, 3-5-1794. to Charles Thomson.

27   Boyd Stanley Schlenther, *Charles Thomson: A Patriot's Pursuit* (Newark: University of Delaware Press, 1990), pp. 216-217. "…the Master of the Masonic Order in Baltimore who was "determined… to unbosom my heart." This man urged Thomson to become a Mason to help him bring the order (which had "deviated from the truth") back to the "first principles" of Christianity. "I am in, you are out," wrote the Masonic Master. "Will you–can you–deem yourself called upon to lend your aid to do much good?" Thomson stayed out. In fact, through-out his life he appears never to have joined any organization that he did not feel was involved in some useful purpose. He never was a mem-ber of the Tammany Society; he never joined Philadelphia's Hibernian Club, organized in 1759 by bother Protestant and Roman Catholic Irish immigrants. It appears that any group that smacked of frivolity or that was mainly given to socializing was never to Thomson's taste, and even those organizations with which he had associated himself –such as the Philosophical Society and the Agricultural Society—soon lost their charm, and interest, especially if they had appeared to have served their purpose for him.

         To occupy his time after Hannah's death, Thomson turned once again to biblical studies. Even while the Bible was in the process of printing, Thomson had begun "to draw up a harmony of the four evangelists from my translation following the Order of Dr. Doddridge." Thomson believed that by arranging the facts presented in the Gospels, producing them in parallel columns, he had "removed the seeming inconsistencies with which they are charged & shewn that instead of contradicting, they strengthen & confirm one another's narrative."

         In it, he justified publication on the grounds that though there had been many such harmonies, "infidels still continue to charge the Evangelist with inconsistency, and contradiction." As for himself, Thomson publicly admitted that the real reason he first undertook the task was for his own "solace."

         One result of the publication of the *Synopsis* was brief renewal of his correspondence with Jefferson, which had not been maintained following their exchanges at the appearance of the full Bible in 1808. Early in 1816 Jefferson wrote that he had received a copy of the *Synopsis*, and after perfunctory compliments he proceeded to inform Thomson that he had made a "wee little book" of his own; by cutting the texts from the Gospels which include the words of Jesus, Jefferson had compiled what he called the "Philosophy of Jesus." This infor-mation led Thomson to an innocent but extremely awkward indiscretion. Delighted that Jefferson saw this project as proof of his own reli-gious nature)"I am a real Christian—that is to say, a disciple of the doctrines of Jesus"), Thomson brought several Philadelphians to the conclusion that there was reason for "the Religious world. …[to be] daily congratulating each other," on Jefferson's "happy change of Religious belief." The miraculous had happened: Jefferson had made "a profession of faith." The matter had gone so far that Thomson near-ly provided Jefferson's letter for publication, only to receive this rebuke: "I apprehend that [you] were no sufficiently aware of its private & personal nature, or of the impropriety of putting it in the power of an editor to publish, without the consent of the writer." Crestfallen, Thomson wrote immediately to apologize. Jefferson – who had been caused no little anxiety and trouble by the who affair—replied, say-ing that he had received a communication from a person in Philadelphia who had seen his letter to Thomson, asking Jefferson "questions which I answer only to one Being. To himself, therefore. I replied: 'Say nothing of my Religion; it is known to my God and myself alone.'" Under the circumstances, it was a kindly response to Thomson, but this really was the last letter ever to pass between the two men."

28   Michael Novak and Jana Novak, *Washington's God: Religion, Liberty, and the Father of Our Country*, (New York: Basic Books, 2006), p. 97, "Some object that he was a member of the Freemasons for many years (although his attendance at lodge meetings was extremely rare), and that that is incompatible with Christian belief. (Roman Catholics, even today, are forbidden to belong to the Masons; in Europe, unlike in the United States, Freemasonry has been rabidly, sometimes violently, anti-Catholic.) But many American Christian then and now have found nothing incompatible between Freemasonry and Christianity and have looked at the former as a kind of service arm of the latter. Indeed, in Washington's day many bishops and clergymen were active members of their local Masonic lodges."

29   John Warwick Montgomery, *The Shaping of America* (Minneapolis: Bethany Fellowship, Inc., 1976), pp. 54 and p. 56.

30   Randall, *George Washington: A Life*, (New York: Henry Holt and Company, 1997), p. 67.

31   Johnson, *George Washington: The Founding Father* (HarperCollins Publishers, 2005), pp. 10-11, "But neither did Washington look back to the seventeenth century and its religious zeal. . . He was never indifferent to Christianity—quite the contrary: he saw it as an essential ele-ment of social control and good government—but his intellect and emotions inclined him more to the substitute for formal dogma, freema-sonry, whose spread among males of the Anglo-Saxon world was such a feature of the eighteenth century. It was introduced into the colonies only three years before his birth. The first true Masonic Lodge in America was founded in 1734 in Philadelphia…."

CHAPTER 26

1   *WGW*, vol. 36, 8-4-1797. To Lawrence Lewis.

2   Rupert Hughes, *George Washington: The Human Being & The Hero 1732-1762*, (New York: William Morrow & Company, 1926), vol. 1, p. 552-559.

3   Bancroft, *History of the United States of America*, vol. IV, 34.

4   *WGW*, vol. 2, 7-2-1766. To Captain John Thompson. "With this letter comes a negro (Tom), which I beg the favor of you to sell in any of the Islands you may go to, for whatever he will fetch, and bring me in return from him."

        One hhd (Hogshead—a cask containing from 63 to 140 gallons)

        One ditto of best rum

        One barrel of lymes, if good and cheap

        One pot of tamarinds, containing about 10 lbs.

        Two small ditto of mixed sweetmeats, about 5 lbs each.

5   Ibid., vol. 28, 4-12-1786. To Robert Morris. "There is not a man living, who wishes more sincerely than I do, to see a plan adopted, for the abolition of slavery. But there is only one proper way and effectual mode by which it can be accomplished, and this by legislative authority." *WGW*, vol. 28, 5-10-1786. To Lafayette. "To set the slaves afloat, at once would I believe be productive of much inconvenience and mischief; but, by degrees, it certainly might and assuredly ought to be effected, and that, too, by legislative authority." *WGW*, vol. 34, 11-23-1794. To Alexander Spotswood. "With respect to the other species of property, concerning which you ask my opinion, I shall frankly declare to you that I do not like even to think, much less to talk of it. However, as you have put the question, I shall, in a few words, give you *my ideas* of it. Were it not then, that I am principled against selling negroes, as you would do cattle at a market, I would not in twelve months from this date, be possessed of one, as a slave. I shall be happily mistaken, if they are not found to be very troublesome species of property ere many years pass over our heads."

6   Ibid., vol., 29, 9-9-1786. To John Francis Mercer. "I never mean, unless some particular circumstance should compel me to it, to possess another slave by purchase, it being among my first wishes to see some plan adopted by which Slavery, in this country may be abolished by law." "I had resolved never to become the Master of another slave by purchase." Ibid., vol. 36, 11-13-1797. To George Lewis.

7   Ibid., vol. 36, 11-13-1797 To George Lewis. "The running off of my Cook, has been a most inconvenient thing to this family; and what renders it more disagreeable, is, that I had resolved never to become the Master of another Slave by *purchase* ; but this resolution I fear I must break. I have endeavoured to hire, black or white, but am not yet supplied." Ibid., vol. 37, 4-12-1791. To Tobias Lear. "…whilst my residence is incidental as an Officer of Government only, but whether among people who are in the practice of *enticing* slaves *even* where there is *no* colour of law for it, this distinction will avail, I know not, and therefore beg you will take the best advise you can on the subject, and in case it shall be found that any of my Slaves may, or any for them shall attempt their freedom at the expiration of six months, it is my wish and desire that you would send the whole, or such part of them as Mrs. Washington may not chuse to keep, home, for although I do not think they would be benefitted by the change, yet the idea of freedom might be too great a temptation for them to resist. At any rate it might, if they conceived they had a right to it, make them insolent in a State of Slavery. As all except Hercules and Paris are dower negroes, it behoves me to prevent the emancipation of them, otherwise I *shall* not only loose the use of them, but may have them to pay for. If upon taking good advise it is found expedient to send them back to Virginia, I wish to have it accomplished under pretext that may deceive both them and the Public; and none I think would so effectually do this, as Mrs. Washington coming to Virginia next month (towards the middle or latter end of it, as she seemed to have a wish to do) if she can accomplish it by any convenient and agreeable means, with the assistance of the Stage Horses &c. This would naturally bring her maid and Austin, and Hercules under the idea of coming home to *Cook* whilst we remained there might be sent on in the Stage. Whether there is occasion for this or not according to the result of your enquiries, or issue the thing as it may, I request that these Sentiments and this advise may be known to none but *yourself* and *Mrs. Washington* . From the following expression in your letter "that those who were of age might follow the example of his (the Attorney's people) after a residence of six months", it would seem that *none* could apply before the end of May, and that the non age of Christopher, Richmond and Oney is a bar to them."

    Worthy Partner, footnote, p. 213, says, "Austin, a dower negro slave who had been with the Washingtons in New York and Philadelphia, was returned to Mount Vernon to visit his wife and friends. It is likely the reason for returning him to Virginia was to prevent his possible emancipation. According to Pennsylvania law, when a slave owner took up citizenship in that state, his slaves, providing they were of age, would become emancipated at the end of six months. … all but three of the servants were dower slaves, and [Washington] did not wish to lose them, and thus be required to reimburse Mrs. Washington's estates for them."

8   John C. Fitzpatrick, "The George Washington Slanders" in *Washington Bicentennial Committee* (Washington, D. C.: 1932), vol. III. pp. 314-319.

9   Howard F. Bremer, *George Washington 1732-1799: Chronology—Documents—Bibliographical Aids* (Dobbs Ferry, N. Y.: Oceana Publications, 1967), p. 1. Bremer writes, "December 17, 1748, "George William Fairfax married Sarah ("Sally") Cary. George Washington, two years her junior, fell in love with her and probably remained so all his life."

10   *WGW*, vol. 2, 9-12-1758. To Mrs. George William Fairfax. "Dear Madam: Yesterday I was honored with your short but very agreeable favor of the first inst. How joyfully I catch at the happy occasion of renewing a correspondence which I feared was disrelished on your part, I leave to time, that never failing expositor of all things, and to a monitor equally faithful in my own breast, to testify. In silence I now express my joy; silence, which in some cases, I wish the present, speaks more intelligently than the sweetest eloquence.

    "If you allow that any honor can be derived from my opposition to our present system of management, you destroy the merit of it entirely in me by attributing my anxiety to the animating prospect of possessing Mrs. Custis, when—I need not tell you, guess yourself. Should not my own Honor and country's welfare be the excitement? 'Tis true, I profess myself a votary of love. I acknowledge that a lady is in the case, and further I confess that this lady is known to you. Yes, Madame, as well as she is to one who is too sensible of her charms to deny the Power whose influence he feels and must ever submit to. I feel the force of her amiable beauties in the recollection of a thousand tender passages that I could wish to obliterate, till I am bid to revive them. But experience, alas! sadly reminds me how impossible this is, and evinces an opinion which I have long entertained, that there is a Destiny which has the control of our actions, not to be resisted by the strongest efforts of Human Nature.

"You have drawn me, dear Madame, or rather I have drawn myself, into an honest confession of a simple Fact. Misconstrue not my meaning; doubt it not, nor expose it. The world has no business to know the object of my Love, declared in this manner to you, when I want to conceal it. One thing above all things in this world I wish to know, and only one person of your acquaintance can solve me that, or guess my meaning. But adieu to this till happier times, if I ever shall see them. The hours at present are melancholy dull. Neither the rugged toils of war, no the gentler conflict of A — B — s, [Assembly Balls?] is in my choice. I dare believe you are as happy as you say, I wish I was happy also. Mirth, good humor, ease of mind, and — what else — cannot fail to render you so and consummate your wishes.

"If one agreeable lady could almost wish herself a fine gentleman for the sake of another, I apprehend that many fine gentlemen will wish themselves finer e'er Mrs. Spotswood is possest. She has already become a reigning toast in this camp, and many there are in it who intend (fortune favoring) to make honorable scars speak the fullness of their merit, and be a messenger of their Love to Her.

"I cannot easily forgive the unseasonable haste of my last express, if he deprived me thereby of a single word you intended to add. The time of the present messenger is, as the last might have been, entirely at your disposal. I can't expect to hear from my friends more than this once before the fate of the expedition will some how or other be determined. I therefore beg to know when you set out for Hampton, and when you expect to return to Belvoir again. And I should be glad also to hear of your speedy departure, as I shall thereby hope for your return before I get down. The disappointment of seeing your family would give me much concern. From any thing I can yet see 'tis hardly possible to say when we shall finish. I don't think there is a probability of it till the middle of November. Your letter to Captain Gist I forwarded by a safe hand the moment it came to me. His answer shall be carefully transmitted.

"Col. Mercer, to whom I delivered your message and compliments, joins me very heartily in wishing you and the Ladies of Belvoir the perfect enjoyment of every happiness this world affords. Be assured that I am, dear Madame, with the most unfeigned regard, your most obedient and most obliged humble servant.

"N. B. Many accidents happening (to use a vulgar saying) between the cup and the lip, I choose to make the exchange of carpets myself, since I find you will not do me the honor to accept mine."

11 *WGW*, vol. 2, 9-12-1758. To Sally Cary Fairfax.

12 Ibid., vol. 2, 9-12-1758. *WGW* note explains: "The only authority for this letter that has so far appeared is the text printed in the *New York Herald* (Mar. 30, 1877), and in Welles's *Pedigree and History of the Washington Family* (New York: 1879). The letter was sold by Bangs & Co., auctioneers in New York, and the Herald, after printing this letter the day before, merely reported the sale as disposing of two Washington letters, one at $13 and one at $11.50, leaving it a matter of guess as to which one of these prices belonged to this much discussed epistle." The letter drops from sight after this sale, and its present whereabouts is unknown. Constance Cary Harrison, in *Scribner's Monthly* (July, 1876), wrote: "Mrs. George William Fairfax, the object of George Washington's early and passionate love, lived to an advanced age, in Bath, England, widowed, childless, and utterly infirm. Upon her death, at the age of eighty-one, letters (still in possession of the Fairfax family) were found among her effects, showing that Washington had never forgotton the influence of his youthful disappointment. But these conclusions are by no means unquestionable. The editor debated for some time the inclusion of this letter and finally concluded to use it after thus noting its unsettled status."

See John Corbin, *The Unknown Washington: Biographic Origins of the Republic* (New York: Charles Scribner's Sons, 1930), pp. 51-75. Corbin says, "In a very different view are his two letters of the following September to Sally, letters which she treasured to her death. Paul Leicester Ford's objection that the evidence of their authenticity 'has not been produced' is scarcely worthy of consideration. In writing the first daft of his little biography, Captain Cary, a devoted antiquary and genealogist, had access to Sally's papers and copied them. The final draft was prepared as an answer to Ford, but was still in manuscript when Captain Cary died…In such matters family tradition is of great weight, and in this case it is of the clearest and most substantial. It is sustained, moreover, by evidence both external and internal which is beyond the power of the cleverest impostor to invent. The letters as also that written in 1757 on Washington's return from the front to Mount Vernon fall in perfectly with all the evidence as to his mood and movements, most of which is now for the first time assembled; and they bear the stamp of his character and habit down to the unrevised sentence-structure and elaborate punctuation. The autograph originals could scarcely be more convincing." P. 64. See Willard Sterne Randall, *George Washington: A Life* (New York: Henry Holt and Co., 1997), p. 179.

13 John Corbin, *The Unknown Washington: Biographic Origins of the Republic* (New York: Charles Scribner's Sons, 1930), pp. 51-75. Corbin writes, "In 1877, two love letters written by Washington to Mrs. George William Fairfax were published for the first time and caused a sensation which, though masked for decades by biographers, has steadily increased. They had been found among Mrs. Fairfax's papers upon her death in England in 1811, and her kinsfolk in America had treasured them through two generations in the awed silence of Victorian propriety. The Fairfaxes were Washington's nearest friends until shortly before the Revolution, their house, Belvoir, being five miles down the Potomac from Mount Vernon and in full view of it. Though George Fairfax was eight years older, the two men had been intimate, surveying electioneering and fox-hunting together, from the time Washington, aged sixteen, came to live with his brother Lawrence. There is abundant evidence, notably in Washington's diaries, that Mrs. Fairfax and Mrs. Washington were neighborly always, dining and visiting with each other, and were the first to offer sympathy in illness and bereavement. The letters were written in 1758, when Washington, aged twenty-six, was engaged to Martha Custis. Though they are reticently worded and indeed seem intentionally vague and obscure, they are now generally accepted as showing that he was passionately in love with Mrs. Fairfax. One of them speaks of the 'the recollection of a thousand tender passages that I could wish to obliterate, till I am bid to revive them'—and what follows, as we shall see, is proof enough that these passages were not with Martha. In two later letters, one of them written only nineteen months before he died, he declared that the moments he had spent in her company were 'the happiest in my life.' We have here, obviously, something very different from the legend of idyllic love which the Victorians wove about the lives of George and Martha Washington. Whether it is in the way of scandal depends upon the nature of the 'thousand tender passages.' That question has obsessed recent biographers." Pp. 51-52. Kitman, *The Making of the President*, p. 267-268, 269.

14 *WGW*, vol. 27, 7-10-1783. To George William Fairfax. "My dear Sir: With very sincere pleasure I receiv'd your favor of the 26th. Of March. It came to hand a few days ago only; and gave me the satisfaction of learning that you enjoyed good health, and that Mrs. Fairfax had improved in hers. there was nothing wanting in this Letter to give compleat satisfaction to Mrs. Washington and myself, but some expression to induce us to believe you would once more become our Neighbours. Your House at Belvoir I am sorry to add is no more, but mine (which is enlarged since you saw it) is most sincerely and heartily at your Service till you could rebuild it. As the path, after being closed by a long, arduous, and painful contest, is to use an Indian Methaphor, now opened and made smooth, I shall please myself with the hope of hearing from you frequently; and till you forbid me to endulge the wish I shall not *despair* of seeing you and Mrs. Fairfax once more the Inhabitants of Belvoir, and greeting you both there, the intimate companions of our old Age, as you have been of our younger years."

15 Zall, *Washington on Washington*, p. 37. Zall writes, "Washington's ill health was reason enough to retire from military life. His malaria and dysentery had turned so severe in March of 1758 that he left his command at Winchester for treatment in Williamsburg. Six months later he was composing a celebrated letter confessing love to his neighbor's fun-loving wife, Sally Fairfax (12 Septermber 1758). At eighteen, a slender, tall brunet with sparkling dark eyes, she and her sisters exchanged teasing letters with Washington, apparently tutoring him in the art of courtly correspondence. The love letter could have been another exercise in courtly composition rather than the overflow of powerful feelings, since he carefully revised the expression."

16 *WGW*, vol. 11, 4-21-1778.

17 Ibid., vol. 28, 8-1-1786.

18 Ibid., vol. 27, 9-2-1783.

19 Kitman, *The Making of the President* p. 267-268, 269.

20 Ibid., 267.

21 Flexner, *Washington: The Indispensable Man*, pp. 17-18.

22 *WGW*, vol. 1, [1749-50]. To —— —. "Dear Friend Robin: As its the greatest mark of friendship and esteem Absent Friends can shew each other in Writing and often communicating their thoughts to his fellow Companions makes me endeavor to signalize myself in acquainting you from time to time and at all times my situation and employments of Life and could wish you would take half the Pains of contriving me a letter by any oppertunity as you may be well assured of its meeting with a very welcome reception my Place of Residence is at present at His Lordships where I might was my heart disengag'd pass my time very pleasantly [agreeably] as theres a very agreeable Young Lady Lives in the same House (Colo. George Fairfax's Wife's Sister) but as that's only adding Fuel to fire it makes me the more uneasy for by often and unavoidably being in Company with her revives my former Passion for your Low Land Beauty whereas was I to live more retired from young Women I might in some measure eliviate my sorrows by burying that chast and troublesome Passion in the grave of oblivion or etarnall forgetfulness for as I am very well assured that's the only antidote or remedy that I ever shall be releiv'd by or only recess than can administer any cure or help to me as I am well convinced were I ever to attempt any thing I should only get a denial which would be only adding grief to uneasiness."

23 Ibid., vol. 1, [1749-50]. To —— —. "Dear Friend Robin…."

24 Ibid., vol. 34, 1-16-1795. To Eleanor Parke Custis. [Dear Nelly:] Your letter, the receipt of which I am now acknowledging, is written correctly and in fair characters, which is an evidence that you command, when you please, a fair hand. Possessed of these advantages, it will be your own fault if you do not avail yourself of them, and attention being paid to the choice of your subjects, you can have nothing to fear from the malignancy of criticism, as your ideas are lively, and your descriptions agreeable. Let me touch a little now on your Georgetown ball, and happy, thrice happy, for the fair who were assembled on the occasion, that there was a man to spare; for had there been 79 ladies and only 78 gentlemen, there might, in the course of the evening, have been some disorder among the caps; notwithstanding the apathy which *one* of the company entertains for the " *youth* " of the present day, and her determination "never to give herself a moment's uneasiness on account of any of them." A hint here; men and women feel the same inclinations to each other *now* that they always have done, and which they will continue to do until there is a new order of things, and *you*, as others have done, may find, perhaps, that the passions of your sex are easier raised than allayed. Do not therefore boast too soon or too strongly of your insensibility to, or resistance of, its powers. In the composition of the human frame there is a good deal of inflammable matter, however dormant it may lie for a time, and like an intimate acquaintance of yours, when the torch is put to it, *that* which is *within you* may burst into a blaze; for which reason and especially too, as I have entered upon the chapter of advices, I will read you a lecture drawn from this text.

Love is said to be an involuntary passion, and it is, therefore, contended that it cannot be resisted. This is true in part only, for like all things else, when nourishes and supplied plentifully with ailment, it is rapid in its progress; but let these be withdrawn and it may be stifled in its birth or much stinted in its growth. For example, a woman (the same may be said of the other sex) all beautiful and accomplished, will, while her hand and heart are undisposed of, turn the heads and set the circle in which she moves on fire. Let her marry, and what is the consequence? The madness *ceases* and all is quiet again. Why? not because there is any diminution in the charms of the lady, but because there is an end of hope. Hence it follows, that love may and therefore ought to be under the guidance of reason, for although we cannot avoid first impressions, we may assuredly place them under guard; and my motives for treating on this subject are to show you, while you remain Eleanor Parke Custis, spinster, and retain the resolution to love with moderation, the propriety of adhering to the latter resolution, at least until you have secured your game, and the way by which it may be accomplished.

"When the fire is beginning to kindle, and your heart growing warm, propound these questions to it. Who is this invader? Have I a competent knowledge of him? Is he a man of good character; a man of sense? For, be assured, a sensible woman can never be happy with a fool? What has been his walk in life? Is he a gambler, a spendthrift, or drunkard? Is his fortune sufficient to maintain me in the manner I have been accustomed to live, and my sisters do live, and is he one to whom my friends can have no reasonable objection? If these interrogatories can be satisfactorily answered, there will remain but one more to be asked, that, however, is an important one. Have I sufficient ground to conclude that his affections are engaged by me? Without this the heart of sensibility will struggle against a passion that is not reciprocated; delicacy, custom, or call it by what epithet you will, having precluded all advances on your part. The declaration, without the *most indirect* invitation of yours, must proceed from the man, to render it permanent and valuable, and nothing short of good sense and an easy unaffected conduct can draw the line between prudery and coquetry. It would be no great departure from truth to say, that it rarely happens otherwise than that a thorough-paced coquette dies in celibacy, as a punishment for her attempts to mislead others, by encouraging looks, words, or actions, given for no other purpose than to draw men on to make overtures that they may be rejected.

"This day, according to our information, gives a husband to your elder sister, and consummates, it is to be presumed, her fondest desires. The dawn with us is bright, and propitious, I hope, of her future happiness, for a full measure of which she and Mr. Law have my earnest wishes. Compliments and congratulations on this occasion, and best regards are presented to your mamma, Dr. Stuart and family; and every blessing, among which a good husband when you want and deserve one, is bestowed on you by yours, affectionately."

25   *WGW*, vol. 2, 9-12-1758. To Sally Cary Fairfax.

26   Francis Rufus Bellamy, *The Private Life of George Washington*, (New York: Thomas Y. Crowell Co., 1951), p.53.

27   Flexner, *Washington: The Indispensable Man*, pp. 17-18.

28   *WGW*, vol. 11, 5-29-1778.

29   Ibid., vol. 12, 9-1-1778.

30   Ibid., vol. 10, 1-28-1778.

31   Ibid., vol. 11, 4-21-1778.

32   Ibid., vol. 24, 7-10-1782.

33   Ibid., vol. 28, 8-1-1786.

34   Ibid., vol., 36, 12-4-1797.

35   Ibid., vol. 28, 5-18-1786.

36   Francis Rufus Bellamy, *The Private Life of George Washington* (New York: Thomas Y. Crowell Co., 1951), pp.53-54.

37   See *WGW*, vol. 3, 1-29-1774. *Cf.* John Corbin, *The Unknown Washington*, (New York: Charles Scribner's Sons, 1930), pp. 43-44.

38   There is ambiguity surrounding the authenticity of this phrase in the Treaty. In *Treaties and Other International Agreements of the United Sates of America 1776-1949*, ed. Charles I. Bevans (Washington: Dept. Of State), vol. 11:1070, n. 3, one reads, "This translation from the Arabic by Joel Barlow, Consul General at Algiers, has been printed in all official and unofficial treaty collections since it first appeared in 1797 in the Session Laws of the Fifth Congress, first session. In a 'Note Regarding the Barlow Translation' Hunter miller stated: '. . .Most extraordinary (and wholly unexplained) is the fact that Article 11 of the Barlow translation, with its famous phrase, "the government of the United States of America is not in any sense founded on the Christian Religion." Does not exist at all. There is no Article 11. The Arabic text which is between Articles 10 and 12 is in form a letter, crude and flamboyant and withal quite unimportant, from the Dey of Algiers to the Pasha of Tripoli. How that script came to be written and to be regarded as in the Barlow translation, as Article 11 of the treaty as there written, is a mystery and seemingly must remain so. Nothing in the diplomatic correspondence of the time throws any light whatever on the point.'"

39   *Cf.* Boller: *Washington & Religion*, p. 87-88; John Eidsmoe's *Christianity and the Constitution* (Grand Rapids: Baker Book House, 1987), p. 413-15; Gary DeMar, *America's Christian History: The Untold Story* (Atlanta: American Vision Inc., 1995), p. 131-42. It is a myth because Washington did not sign this treaty, since he was not president when it was ratified. John Adams was the president that signed it into law on June 10, 1797. It was superseded on April 17, 1806. Leo Pfeffer, *Church, State and Freedom* (Boston: Beacon Press, 1953), p. 211 points out that following the war with Tripoli in 1801, the subsequent Treaty of 1806 during the Jefferson administration does not use this phrase again. This appears ironic given Jefferson's penchant for deistic thought.

40   See the following all written after Boller's 1963 study who continue to attribute this remark to Washington: Ernest Campbell Mossner, "Deism," *The Encyclopedia of Philosophy*, ed. Paul Edwards, 8 vols. (New York: Macmillan, 1967), 2:334; Norman L. Geisler, *Is Man the Measure: An Evaluation of Contemporary Humanism* (Grand Rapids: Baker Book House, 1983), p. 124-25; Mike Horton, *The Horses's Mouth* (April, 1994), p. 1-2.

41   *Treaties and Other International Agreements of the United Sates of America 1776-1949*, ed. Charles I. Bevans (Washington: Dept. Of State), vol. 11:1070, n. 3.

42   Joel Barlow's extended notes on atheism are found in his papers that are preserved in the Harvard University archives. We provide here a few examples of Barlow's investigation of atheism in his private reflections based on various French encyclopedia articles. Based upon such musings, one can understand why he interpolated the text that denies any connection between Christianity and the United States. The language of the Treaty was discussed in note 28 above. Barlow wrote:

...Critius, a famous atheist, agreed that the stars etc. were the first objects of worship.—but accounts for it in a singular manner. He says men were first disorderly and unjust, and lived by open violence. They soon found it was best to have laws to repress these evils. These served very well for a while. But their authority soon grew feeble, and men found the means to allude them by committing their crimes in secret. To repress these, some wise politician invented the fable of gods. He said every planet was a god, and he placed gods everywhere to watch men's secret actions and made them believe they would be punished hereafter. Such is his idea of the origin of religion. ...

...The monotheist, such as the Jews, the Christians, and the Mehomitans, whose history is best known to us, are remarkable for religious wars. The Jews founded their empire upon them.—the Mehomitans did the same; and the Christians, if we reckon their sectarians wars, their Mehomitan wars, their South American wars and their pagan wars, have probably destroyed more men than both the other classes of monotheists.

...In this examination of monotheism I do not bring into view the ancient philosophers, who believed in one God only, nor the modern Deists. The hands of those classes of men never formed a national religion and consequently have had very little affect on the moral or political character of any people. These teach in speculation are certainly repectable, but if they were reduced to dogmas, and formed into a system of worship, it is probable that such a system would degenerate into something like the Jewish or Mehometan. They might avoid the absurdities of the Christian system, but who could guarantee them against other absurdities as great?

Questions.

If man in all ages and countries had understood astronomy and physics as well as they do now generally in Europe would the ideas of God and religion have ever come into their minds?

Have not these ideas been greater sources of human calamity than all other moral causes?

Is it not necessary in the nature of things that they should be so, as long as they exist in the minds of men in such a strong degree as to form the basis of education?

If we admit that these ideas are wholly chimerical having arisen altogether from ignorance of natural causes is it not the duty of every person who sees this evil tendency to use his influence to banish them as much as possible from society?

Is it not possible wholly to destroy their influence and reduce them to the rank of other ancient fables to be found only in the history of human errors?

If the existence of philosophy would have prevented their existence why shall it not destroy them?

Had it been known that the earth moved round the sun, the latter would not have been considered a god. The knowledge of this movement would have been the key to all the science of astronomy and prevented mankind from being deceived for so many ages by false appearances in the movements of the heavenly bodies. Those false appearances gave the idea of life and intelligence in those bodies. Their influence on the earth was apparent, and if we suppose those influences to be directed by their intelligence the consequence is that they control us and either make or destroy our happiness. They are therefore gods, good or bad according as we are affected by their influence.

Darkness, storms, whirlwinds, thunders, inundations, were deified on the same principles, being unexplained they were supposed to act from their own will or that of their masters, they were therefore feared and adored as beings whom we could not control but might hope to soften by our prayers as we might a passionate master who had us in his power.

Joel Barlow was one of the few atheists among the early American governmental leaders. It seems that he kept his thoughts on this topic mainly to himself in his notes. Could it be that the anomalous and disputed text distancing America from the Christian religion in his version of the Treaty of Tripoli may reflect his own philosophical approach addressed above—"If the existence of philosophy would have prevented their existence [i.e. the errors of religion] why shall it not destroy them?"

CHAPTER 27

1   *WGW*, vol. 35, Farewell Address, 1796.

2   *Cf.* W. T. Jones, *Kant to Wittgenstein and Sartre* (New York: Harcourt, Brace & World, Inc., 1969), p. 8.

3   Alexander Pope again found the words to describe this new deistic creed of Enlightenment religion: "Father of all! In every age, In every clime adored, By saint, by savage, and by sage." "The Universal Prayer", 1738.

4   Noah Webster, *American Dictionary of the English Language*, 1828.

5   Norman Cousins, 'In God We Trust' The Religious Beliefs and Ideas of The American Founding Fathers, (Harper & Brothers, New York, p. 6).

6   *Adams Family Correspondence*, L.H. Butterfield, Editor volume 1 – December 1761-May 1776, pp. 626-27.

7   *The Works of Benjamin Franklin*, ed. Jared Sparks (Chicago: Townsend MacCoun., 1882), x. 281-82.

8   Bishop Meade, *Old Church Ministers and Families of Virginia* p. 223-224.

The strength as well as tenderness of Judge Marshall's attachment to Mrs. Marshall will appear from the following affecting tribute to her memory, written by himself, December 25, 1832:

"This day of joy and festivity to the whole Christian world is, to my sad heart, the anniversary of the keenest affliction which humanity can sustain. While all around is gladness, my mind dwells on the silent tomb, and cherishes the remembrance of the beloved object which it contains.

"On the 25th of December, 1831, it was the will of Heaven to take to itself the companion who had sweetened the choicest part of my life, had rendered toil a pleasure, had partaken of all my feelings and was enthroned in the inmost recess of my heart. Never can I cease to feel the loss and to deplore it. Grief for her is too sacred ever to be profaned on the day, which shall be, during my existence, marked by a recollection of her virtue.

"On the 3rd of January 1783, I was united by the holiest bonds to the woman I adored. From the moment of our union to that of our separation, I never ceased to thank Heaven for this its best gift. Not a moment passed in which I did not consider her as a blessing from which the chief happiness of my life was derived. This never-dying sentiment, originating in love, was cherished by a long and close observation of as amiable and estimable qualities as ever adorned the female bosom. To a person which in youth was very attractive, to manners uncommonly pleasing, she added a fine understanding, and the sweetest temper which can accompany a just and modest sense of what was due to herself. She was educated with a profound reverence for religion, which she preserved to her last moments. This sentiment, among her earliest and deepest impressions, gave a colouring to her whole life. Hers was the religion taught by the Savior of man. She was a firm believer in the faith inculcated by the Church (Episcopal) in which she was bred.

"I have lost her, and with her have lost the solace of my life! Yet she remains still the companion of my retired hours, still occupies my inmost bosom. When alone and unemployed, my mind still recurs to her. More that a thousand times since the 25th of December 1831, have I repeated to myself the beautiful lines written by General Burgoyne, under a similar affliction, substitution 'Mary' for 'Anna':

"'Encompass'd in an angle's frame,

An angel's virtues lay;

Too soon did Heaven assert its claim

And take its own away!

My Mary's worth, my Mary's charms,

Can never more return!

What now shall fill these widow'd arms?

Ah me! My Mary's urn!

Ah me! Ah me! My Mary's urn'"

As to the religious opinions of Judge Marshall, the following extract from a letter of the Reverend Mr. Norwood may be entirely relied on: "I have read some remarks of yours in regard to Chief-Justice Marshall, which have suggested to me to communicate to you the following facts, which may be useful should you again publish any thing in relation to his religious opinions. I often visited Mrs. General Harvey during her last illness. From her I received this statement. She was much with her father during the last months of his life, and told me that the reason why he never communed, was, that he was a Unitarian in opinion, thought he never joined their society. He told her that he believed in the truth of the Christian revelation, but not in the divinity of Christ; therefore he could not commune in the Episcopal Church. But during the last months of his life, he read Keith on Prophecy, where our Saviour's divinity is incidentally treated, and was convinced by his work, and the fuller investigation to which it led, of the supreme divinity of the Saviour. He determined to apply for admission to the Communion of our Church, objected to commune in private, because he thought it his duty to make a public confession of the Saviour, and which waiting of improved health to enable him to go the church for the purpose, he grew worse and died, without ever communing. Mrs. Harvey was a lady of the strictest probity, the most humble piety, and of a clear discriminating mind, and her statement, the substance of which I give you accurately (having reduced it to writing) maybe entirely relied on.

"I remember to have heard Bishop Moore repeatedly express his surprise (when speaking of Judge Marshall) that, though he was so punctual in his attendance at church, and reproved Mr. – and Mr. – and Mr. – when they were absent, and knelt during the prayers and responded fervently, yet he never communed. The reason was that which he gave to his daughter, Mrs. Harvey. She said he died an humble, penitent believer in Christ, according to the orthodox creed of the church.

Very truly, your friend and brother in Christ, Wm. Norwood.

"P.S. – Another fact, illustrating the lasting influence of maternal instruction, was mentioned by Mrs. Harvey. Her father told here that he never went to bed without concluding his prayer with those which he mother taught him when a child – viz.: the Lord's Prayer and the prayer beginning, 'Now I lay me down to sleep.'"

9   Ibid., p. 33 – Randolph's Repentance

"It being known that there was a family connection and some intimacy and correspondence between Mr. Randolph and myself, I have been often asked my opinion as to his religious character. It is as difficult to answer this as to explain some other things about this most talented, eccentric, and unhappy man. My acquaintance and correspondence with him commenced in 1813 and terminated in 1818, although at his death he confided a most difficult and important trust to myself, in conjunction with our common and most valued friend, Mr. Francis S. Key. I publish the following letter written in 1815, when his mind seemed to be in a state of anxiety on the subject of religion and an extract from another paper in my possession showing a supposed relief in the year 1818. Other letters I have, during the period of our intimacy, of the same character. The reader must judge for himself, taking into consideration the great inconsistencies of his subsequent life, and making all allowances for his most peculiar and unhappy temperament, his most diseased body, and the trying circumstances of his life and death."

Richmond, May 19 1815

"It is with very great regret that I leave town about the time that you are confidently expected to arrive. Nothing short of necessity should carry me away at this time. I have a very great desire to see you, to converse with you on the subject before which all others sink into insignificance. It continues daily to occupy more and more of my attention, which it ahs nearly engrossed to the exclusion of every other, and it is a source of pain as well as of occasional comfort to me. May He who alone can do it shed light upon my mind, and conduct me, through faith, to salvation. Give me your prayers. I have the most earnest desire for a more perfect faith than I fear I possess. What shall I do to be saved? I know the answer, but it is not free from difficulty. Lord, be merciful to me, a sinner. I do submit myself most implicitly to his holy will, and great is my reliance on his mercy. But when I reflect on the corruptions of my nature I tremble whilst I adore. The merits of an all-atoning Saviour I hardly dare to plead when I think of my weak faith. Help, Lord, or I perish, but thy will be done on earth as it is in heaven. I know that I deserve to suffer for my sins; for time misspent, faculties misemployed; but, above all, that I have not loved God and my neighbour as we are commanded to do. But I will try to confide in the promises we have received, or rather to comply with their conditions. Whatever be my fate, I will not harbour a murmur in my breast against the justice of my Creator. Your afflicted friend, John Randolph, of Roanoke"

"Reverend William Meade, August 1818,

"It is now just nineteen years since sin first began to sit heavy upon my soul. For a very great part of that time I have been as a conscious thief; hiding or trying to hide from my fellow-sinners, from myself, from my God. After much true repentance, followed by relapses into deadly sin, it hath pleased Almighty God to draw me to him; reconciling me to him, and, by the love which drives out fear, to show me the mighty scheme of his salvation, which hath been to me, as also to the Jews, a stumbling block and, as to the Greeks, foolishness. I am now, for the first time, grateful and happy; nor would I exchange my present feeling and assurances, although in rage, for any throne in Christendom."

p. 95- Bishop Madison- infidelity?

"In the year 1785, the Reverend James Madison, afterward Bishop of Virginia, became its minister, and continued so until his death in 1812, long before which the congregation had dwindled into almost nothing,- ... A young friend of mine, who was in Williamsburg about the year 1810, informed me that, being desirous of hearing the oratory of Bishop Madison, he had once or twice gone out on a Sabbath morning to this church, but that the required number for a sermon was not there, though it was a very small one, and so he was disappointed. ... In the year 1774 he became Professor in the College of William and Mary, in the year 1777, President of the College, and in the year 1799 was consecrated Bishop of Virginia. His addresses to the Convention breathe a spirit of zealous piety, and his recommendations are sensible and practical. ... I again repeat my conviction that the reports as to his abandonment of the Christian faith in his latter years are groundless; although it is to be feared that the failure of the Church in his hands, and which at that time might have failed in any hands, his secular and philosophical pursuits, had much abated the spirit with which he entered upon the ministry. The old church at Jamestown is no longer to be seen, except the base of its ruined tower."

10   The reformation envisaged by the Deists was an education founded on reason, coupled with an opposition to revelation and the clergy. As deist Charles Blount wrote in his *Oracles of Reason*:

"By education most have been misled,

So they believe, because they were so bred;

The priest continues what the nurse began,

And thus the child imposes on the man. Cited in J. A. Leo Lemay, "The Amerindian in the Early American Enlilghtenment" in *Deism, Masonry, and the Enlightenment* ed. by J. A. Leo Lemay (Newark: University of Delaware Press, 1987), p. 86-87.

Similarly, Deist John Toland in his *Letters to Serena* showed the danger of the clergy with their religious mysteries:

"Natural religion was easy first and plain,

Tales made it mystery, offerings made it gain;

Sacrifices and shows were at length prepared,

The priests ate roast meat and the people starved." Cited in Byrne, *Natural Relgion*, p. 80.

11   *The Virginia Almanack For the Year of our Lord God 1761* by Theophilus Weeg (Williamsburg: Printed and Sold by William Hunter, 1761). The book summary in the *Almanack* said:

"An Impartial Enquiry into the True Nature of the Faith, which is required in the Gospel as necessary to salvation, In which is briefly shown, upon how righteous terms of Unbelievers may become true Christians: And the Case of Deists is reduced to a short Issue. Containing Section I. Nature of Faith, or Belief, in the general. 2. Showing how much, and how readily, all Men act in the most important Affairs of this World, upon Faith, or upon Grounds less certain. 3. True Nature of the Christian Faith. 4. In which the Nature of Christian Faith is more fully explained, by examining the Properties of Abraham's Faith, which Christians are bound to imitate. The first Property attributed to Abraham's Faith is considered; viz. That it was grounded on Reason. 5. In which the second Property of Abraham's Faith is considered; viz. The Righteousness of his Faith. 6. In which the third Property of Abraham's Faith is considered; viz; That it was grounded on Reason. 6. In which the third Property of Abraham's Faith is considered; viz. That it was a Full Persuasion of his Mind. 7. In which the fourth Property of Abraham's Faith is considered; viz. That he gave Glory to God. 8. Shows in what Sense the Practice of Virtue is necessary to the producing of Faith in Christ Jesus. 9. Showing that no Man can attain to true Christian Faith, without the Assistance of the Divine Spirit influencing his Soul. 10. Concerning the due Submission of Reason, with regard to the Mysteries of Religion: In which the Nature of a Christian Mystery is explained. 11. In which the Influence and Efficacy of Divine Faith is considered. 12. Containing a summary Account of the Evidences which prove that Jesus was the Messiah, sent from God to instruct and redeem Mankind. In which is shown, that there was in the Jewish Scriptures a Prophesy made to Mankind, and from thence an Expectation of an extraordinary Person sent from God, at a particular Time. 13. Showing that, as Jesus declared himself to be this extraordinary Person, so he gave the fullest and strongest Proofs that could be desired, that he was the promised Messiah. In which the Evidence is examined, which ariseth from his fulfilling the other Prophecies, which foretold the Messiah. 14. In which the Evidence is examined, that ariseth from the Miracles which Jesus wrought: showing that the first condition, that should attend all Miracles, took Place in those wrought by Jesus, viz. That they should be so repeated, so publick, and so evident to Numbers, as to leave no Doubt. 15. Showing that the moral Doctrines, which Jesus taught, all manifestly tend to promote the Happiness of Mankind and the Glory of God. In which they are compared with those taught by the Heathens. 16. In which it is examined whether the peculiar Doctrines of Christianity be worthy of God and whether they tend to promote the Glory of God, and the Good of Mankind. 17. In which is examined the Evidence that ariseth from the Fulfilling of Prophecies foretold by Jesus. 18. The fifth Proof, that Jesus was a Teacher sent from God, viz. his rising from the Dead. 19. In which the Nature of the Evidence which we have for the Resurrection is examined, and the Objections to it, as witnessed by the Apostles, are answered. 20. In which the case of the Unbelievers of these Days is compared with that of the Jews, who saw the Miracles of Jesus; showing that we have several Proofs and Advantages which the Jews wanted; and that (upon the Whole) they who now reject the Christian religion, would reject it, thought the same Evidence which the Jews had, were offered to them. 21. Containing a short state of the Deist's Case, being the Result of the former Sections. 22. That no man can have true Christian Faith, without Freedom in Thought and Action; and that true Free-thinking and true Christian Faith, as it is the Act of the Mind, are evidently one and the same Thing. 23. Showing that Infidelity took its Rise from *Rome*, and hath been propagated from thence to us; and that our Deists, however contrary to their Intentions, carry on and greatly forward the Interests and Designs of popery."

12   *Cf.* Herbert Morais, *Deism in Eighteenth Century America* (New York: Russell & Russell, 1960), p. 31.

13   See Peter Byrne, *Natural Religion and the Nature of Religion: The Legacy of Deism* (New York: Routledge, 1989), p. 25. "How could I believe that a just God could take pleasure in the eternal reprobation of those to whom he never afforded any means of salvation . . . and whom he foresaw must be damned of absolute necessity, without the least hopes of escaping it?"

14 *Age of Reason* in *The Writings of Thomas Paine* (Wiltshire: Routledge/Thoemmes Press, 1996,) IV. 25.

15 See the chapter: "The Struggle for the Episcopal Church: Washington's Non-Communication and Non-Communion in Philadelphia"

16 See Kerry S. Walters, *The American Deists: Voices of Reason and Dissent in the Early Republic* (University Press of Kansas, 1992), p. 1. Kerry shows that Deism's impact on American colleges was wide spread by the end of the eighteenth century, including Dartmouth, William and Mary, Princeton and Harvard, p. 1-2. George Washington had corresponded with Stiles and had in his library a copy of Stile's sermon entitled, "America Elevated To Glory And Honor." See Appleton Griffin, *A Catalogue of the Washington Collection in the Boston Athenaeum*, (1897), p. 194.

17 Timothy Dwight, *The Nature and Danger of Infidel Philosophy, Exhibited in Two Discourses, Addressed to the Candidates for the Baccalaureate, in Yale College* (New Haven: George Bunce, 1798).

18 Dwight, *Infidel Philosophy*, p. 11.

19 The supremacy of reason was brought to English Christianity through Locke. The English and Continental civil wars of religion resulted in a focus on reason and toleration. *Treatises on Civil Government* & *Letter on Toleration*. Locke developed a philosophy that emphasized knowledge through experience or empiricism that was written on the blank slate or *tabula rasa* of the human mind.

    Yet we must not overlook his religious perspectives. He wrote a book entitled, *The Reasonableness of Christianity* as well as commentaries on Scripture. While Locke affirmed the importance of reason yet he still insisted on revelation. ; For example, Locke affirmed the inspiration of the Scriptures:

    "You ask me, "what is the shortest and surest way for a young gentleman, to attain a true knowledge of the Christian religion, in the full and just extent of it?" For so I understand your question; if I have mistaken in it, you must set me right. And to this I have a short and plain answer: "let him study the Holy Scripture, especially the New Testament." Therein are contained the words of eternal life. It has God for its author; salvation for its end; and truth, without any mixture of error, for its matter. So that it is a wonder to me, how any one professing Christianity, that would seriously set himself to know his religion, should be in doubt where to employ his search, and lay out his pains for his information; when he knows a book, where it is all contained pure and entire; and whither, at last, every one must have recourse, to verify that of it, which he finds any where else.

    Locke actually composed the constitution of the Colony of Carolina. In it, he continueD the English common law tradition of taking an oath before God in a legal setting by kissing the Bible. This is what Washington did at his inauguration as president. Locke's views led to the idea of a "Christian Enlightenment."

20 Ibid., p. 58.

21 Herbert: "That all Revealed Religion (viz Christianity) is absolutely uncertain, and of little of no use." Reverend Timothy Dwight, *The Nature and Danger of Infidel Philosophy Exhibited in Two Discourses, Addressed to the Candidates for the Baccalaureate, in Yale College, September 9th, 1797* (New Haven: George Bunce, 1798), *WGW*, vol. 11, 5-2-1778. General Orders.

22 Thomas Hobbes: "That Man is a mere machine: and That the Soul is material and mortal"; Timothy Dwight, *The Nature and Danger of Infidel Philosophy*. *WGW*, vol. 27, 8-21-1783. To the Magistrates and Inhabitants of the Borough of Elizabeth. *WGW*, vol. 13, 10-12-1778. To Reverend Alexander McWhorter. "Besides the humanity of affording them the benefit of your profession, …it serves to prepare them for the other world…." *WGW*, vol. 25, 11-16, 1782. To the Reformed Protestant Dutch Church. "In return for your kind concern for my temporal and eternal happiness, permit me to assure you that my wishes are reciprocal." *WGW*, vol. 36, 6-4-1798. To Reverend William Linn. "…grateful for the favourable sentiments you have been pleased to express in my behalf; but more especially for those good wishes which you offer for my temporal and eternal happiness; which I reciprocate with great cordiality…."

23 Charles Blount: "That Christianity is safer than Deism: and yet that Revelation is not sufficiently supported because men differ about it." Timothy Dwight, *The Nature and Danger of Infidel Philosophy*. *WGW*, vol. 26, 6-8-1783. Circular to the States.

24 *WGW*, vol. 30, April 1789. The Proposed Address to Congress.

25 Ibid., vol. 32, 6-21-1792. To Gouverneur Morris. *WGW*, vol. 16, 9-23-1779. To Marquis de Lafayette. "all the wonders recorded in holy writ" Ibid, vol. 16, 9-30-1779. To Marquis de Lafayette. "the Wonders of former ages may be revived in this." Ibid., vol. 30, 7-20-1788. To Jonathan Trumbull. "he shall begin to suspect that miracles have not ceased

26 Robert Collins: "That the Prophets were mere fortune-tellers and discoverers of lost goods; That Christianity stands wholly on a false foundation." Timothy Dwight, *The Nature and Danger of Infidel Philosophy*. Ibid., vol. 24, 6-28-1782. To Minister of the Reformed Dutch Church. Ibid., vol. 28, 2-8-1785. To the President of Congress. "If the union continues, and this is not the case, I will agree to be classed among the false prophets, and suffer for evil prediction." Ibid., vol. 26, 6-8-1783. Circular to the States, "…the Characteristicks of the Divine Author of our blessed Religion, and without an humble imitation of whose example in these things, we can never hope to be a happy Nation." Ibid, vol. 35, 3-3-1797. To the Clergy in Philadelphia. "That your labours for the good of Mankind may be crowned with success; that your temporal enjoyments may be commensurate with your merits; and that the future reward of good and faithful Servants may be your's, I shall not cease to supplicate the Divine Author of life and felicity."

27 Ibid, vol. 30, 4-30-1789. The First Inaugural Address. "Since we ought to be no less persuaded that the propitious smiles of Heaven, can never be expected on a nation that disregards the eternal rules of order and right, which Heaven itself has ordained."

28 William Tindal: "That the Scriptures are obscure, and fit only to perplex men, and that the two great parts of them are contradictory; That the Precepts of Christianity are loose, undetermined, incapable of being understood by mankind at large, give wrong and unworthy apprehensions of God, and are generally false and pernicious;" Timothy Dwight, *The Nature and Danger of Infidel Philosophy*. *WGW*, vol. 30, 10-23, 1789. To First Presbytery of the Eastward. "I am persuaded, you will permit me to observe that the path of true piety is so plain as to require but little political direction. To this consideration we ought to ascribe the absence of any regulation, respecting religion, from the Magna- Charta of our country. To the guidance of the ministers of the gospel this important object is, perhaps, more properly committed. It will be your care to instruct the ignorant, and to reclaim the devious, and, in the progress of morality and science, to which our govern-

ment will give every furtherance, we may confidently expect the advancement of true religion, and the completion of our happiness."

29   Ibid., vol. 30, 7-20-1788. To Jonathan Trumbull. "Or at least we may, with a kind of grateful and pious exultation, trace the finger of Providence through those dark and mysterious events, which first induced the States to appoint a general Convention and then led them one after another (by such steps as were best calculated to effect the object) into an adoption of the system recommended by that general Convention; thereby, in all human probability, laying a lasting foundation for tranquillity and happiness; when we had but too much reason to fear that confusion and misery were coming rapidly upon us. That the same good Providence may still continue to protect us and prevent us from dashing the cup of national felicity just as it has been lifted to our lips, is the earnest prayer of My Dear Sir, your faithful friend."

30   Thomas Chubb: "That God does not interpose in the affairs of this world, at all, and has nothing to do with the good, or evil, done by men here, That Prayer may be useful, as a positive Institution, by introducing proper thoughts, affections, and actions; and yet he intimates, That it must be displeasing to God, and directly improper; That Christ's birth and resurrection were ridiculous, and incredible; and that his institutions and precepts were less excellent, than those of other teachers and lawgivers; That the Apostles were impostors; and that the Gospels and Acts of the Apostles resemble Jewish fables, and Popish legends, rather than accounts of facts;" Timothy Dwight, *The Nature and Danger of Infidel Philosophy. WGW*, vol. 3, 7-4-1775. Answer to an Address of the Massachusetts Legislature. "In return for your affectionate wishes to myself, permit me to say, that I earnestly implore the divine Being, in whose hands are all human events, to make you and your constituents as distinguished in private and public happiness, as you have been by ministerial oppression, and private and public distress." *WGW*, vol. 30, 4-1789. Proposed Address to Congress. "The blessed Religion revealed in the word of God will remain an eternal and awful monument to prove that the best Institutions may be abused by human depravity; and that they may even, in some instances be made subservient to the vilest of purposes."

31   *WGW*, vol. 26, Circular to the States.

32   David Hume: "That what we believe to be a perfection in God may be a defect. (i.e. Holiness, Justice, Wisdom, Goodness, Mercy, and Truth, may be defects in God;) Of consequence, Injustice, Folly, Malice, and Falsehood, may be excellencies in his character;" Timothy Dwight, *The Nature and Danger of Infidel Philosophy. WGW*, vol. 3, 7-16-1775; *WGW*, vol., 5-26-1789. To the Presbyterian General Assembly. "While I reiterate the professions of my dependence upon Heaven as the source of all public and private blessings; I will observe that the general prevalence of piety, philanthropy, honesty, industry, and oeconomy seems, in the ordinary course of human affairs, particularly necessary for advancing and confirming the happiness of our country. While all men within our territories are protected in worshipping the Deity according to the dictates of their consciences; it is rationally to be expected from them in return, that they will be emulous of evincing the sanctity of their professions by the innocence of their lives and the beneficence of their actions; for no man, who is profligate in his morals, or a bad member of the civil community, can possibly be a true Christian, or a credit to his own religious society."

33   Lord Bolingbroke: "That he will not presume to deny, that there have been particular providences; and yet, That there is no foundation for the belief of any such providences; and that it is absurd and profane to assert, or believe, them; That God doth not so measure out rewards, or punishments; and that, if he did, he would subvert human affairs; that he concerns not himself with the affairs of men at all; or, if he does, that he regards only collective bodies of men, not individuals; that he punishes none except through the Magistrate; and that there will be no state of future rewards, or punishments Timothy Dwight, *The Nature and Danger of Infidel Philosophy.*

34   *WGW*, vol. 29, 4-28-1788. to Pierre Charles L'Enfant. "...of your good father; you will permit me to remind you, as an inexhaustible subject of consolation, that there is a good Providence which will never fail to take care of his Children." *WGW*, vol. 26, 6-8-1783. Circular to the States. "...and were it possible that such a flagrant instance of Injustice could ever happen, would it not excite the general indignation, and tend to bring down, upon the Authors of such measures, the aggravated vengeance of Heaven? If after all, a spirit of dis-union or a temper of obstinacy and perverseness, should manifest itself in any of the States, if such an ungracious disposition should attempt to frustrate all the happy effects that might be expected to flow from the Union, if there should be a refusal to comply with the requisitions for Funds to discharge the annual interest of the public debts, and if that refusal should revive again all those jealousies and produce all those evils, which are now happily removed, Congress, who have in all their Transaction shewn a great degree of magnanimity and justice, will stand justified in the sight of God and Man, and the State alone which puts itself in opposition to the aggregate Wisdom of the Continent, and follows such mistaken and pernicious Councils, will be responsible for all the consequences." *WGW*, vol. 28, 8-18-1786. To Marquis de Chastellux. "Perhaps nothing can excite more perfect harmony in the soul than to have this string vibrate in unison with the internal consciousness of rectitude in our intentions and an humble hope of approbation from the supreme disposer of all things." *WGW*, vol. 26, 6-8-1783. Circular to the States. "I now make it my earnest prayer, that God ...would most graciously be pleased to dispose us all, to do Justice, to love mercy, and to demean ourselves with that Charity, humility and pacific temper of mind, which were the Characteristicks of the Divine Author of our blessed Religion, and without an humble imitation of whose example in these things, we can never hope to be a happy Nation."

35   Ibid., vol. 4, 2-26-1776. General Orders. "All Officers, non-commissioned Officers and Soldiers are positively forbid playing at Cards, and other Games of Chance. At this time of public distress, men may find enough to do in the service of their God, and their Country, without abandoning themselves to vice and immorality."

    Ibid., vol. 8, 5-26-1777. To Brig. Gen. William Smallwood. "Let Vice, and Immorality of every kind, be discouraged, as much as possible, in your Brigade; and as a Chaplain is allowed to each Regiment, see that the Men regularly attend divine Worship. Gaming of every kind is expressly forbid, as the foundation of evil, and the cause of many Gallant and Brave Officer's Ruin. Games of exercise, for amusement, may not only be permitted but encouraged."

    Ibid., vol. 8, 5-31-1777. General Orders. "It is much to be lamented, that the foolish and scandalous practice of *profane Swearing* is exceedingly prevalent in the American Army — Officers of every rank are bound to discourage it, first by their example, and then by punishing offenders — As a mean to abolish this, and every other species of immorality — Brigadiers are enjoined, to take effectual care, to have divine service duly performed in their respective brigades." GENERAL INSTRUCTIONS FOR THE COLONELS AND COM-MANDING OFFICERS OF REGIMENTS IN THE CONTINENTAL SERVICE 1777.] "Let Vice and immorality of every kind be discouraged as much as possible in your Regiment; and see, as a Chaplain is allowed to it, that the Men regularly attend divine Worship. Gaming of every kind is expressly forbid as the foundation of evil, and the ruin of many a brave, and good Officer. Games of exercise, for amusement, may be not only allowed of, but Incouraged."

Ibid., vol. 1, 4-18-1756. To Robert Dinwiddie."It gave me infinite concern to find in yours by Governor Innes, that any representations should inflame the Assembly against the Virginia regiment, or give cause to suspect the morality and good behaviour of the officers. How far any of the individuals may have deserved such invidious reflections, I will not take upon me to determine, but *this* I am certain of, and can call my conscience, and what, I suppose, will still be a more demonstrable proof in the eyes of the world, my orders, to witness how much I have, both by threats and persuasive means, endeavoured to discountenance gaming, drinking, swearing, and irregularities of every other kind; while I have, on the other hand, practised every artifice to inspire a laudable emulation in the officers for the service of their country, and to encourage the soldiers in the unerring exercise of their duty. How far I have failed in this desirable end, I cannot pretend to say. But it is nevertheless a point, which does in my opinion merit some scrutiny, before it meets with a final condemnation. Yet I will not undertake to vouch for the conduct of many of the officers, as I know there are some, who have the seeds of idleness very strongly ingrafted in their natures; and I also know, that the unhappy difference about the command, which has kept me from Fort Cumberland, has consequently prevented me from *enforcing* the orders, which I never fail to *send.*"

Note: Dinwiddie had reported that "the Assembly were greatly inflamed, being told that the greatest immoralities and drunkenness have been much countenanced and proper discipline neglected." — *Ford.*

36 Lord Herbert: "that men are not hastily, or on small ground to be condemned, who are led to sin by bodily constitution: that the indulgence of lust, and of anger, is no more to be blamed, than the thirst, occasioned by the Dropsy; or the sleepiness , produced by the Lethargy," Timothy Dwight, *The Nature and Danger of Infidel Philosophy. WGW,* vol. 3, 7-16-1775, general orders

37 Hobbes: "That the Scriptures are the foundation of all obligation; and yet That they are of no obligatory force, except as enjoined by the Civil Magistrate: That, where there is no civil law, every man's judgment is the only standard of right and wrong." Timothy Dwight, *The Nature and Danger of Infidel Philosophy. WGW,* vol. 30, 4-30-1789. The First Inaugural Address. "I dwell on this prospect with every satisfaction which an ardent love for my Country can inspire: since there is no truth more thoroughly established, than that there exists in the oeconomy and course of nature, an indissoluble union between virtue and happiness, between duty and advantage, between the genuine maxims of an honest and magnanimous policy, and the solid rewards of public prosperity and felicity: Since we ought to be no less persuaded that the propitious smiles of Heaven, can never be expected on a nation that disregards the eternal rules of order and right, which Heaven itself has ordained: And since the preservation of the sacred fire of liberty, and the destiny of the Republican model of Government, are justly considered as *deeply*, perhaps as *finally* staked, on the experiment entrusted to the hands of the American people."

38 Shaftsbury, "That the hope of rewards, and the fear of punishments, makes virtue mercenary; That Atheists often conduct so well, as to seem to force us to confess them virtuous;" Ibid.

39 *WGW*, vol. 27, 11-27-1783. To the Ministers of the Reformed German Congregation.
"Disposed, at every suitable opportunity to acknowledge publicly our infinite obligations to the Supreme Ruler of the Universe for rescuing our Country from the brink of destruction; I cannot fail at this time to ascribe all the honor of our late successes to the same glorious Being. And if my humble exertions have been made in any degree subservient to the execution of the divine purposes, a contemplation of the benediction of Heaven on our righteous Cause, the approbation of my virtuous Countrymen, and the testimony of my own Conscience, will be a sufficient reward and augment my felicity ."

40 Ibid., vol. 35, 3-3-1797. To the Clergy of Philadelphia. "That your labours for the good of Mankind may be crowned with success; that your temporal enjoyments may be commensurate with your merits; and that the future reward of good and faithful Servants may be your's, I shall not cease to supplicate the Divine Author of life and felicity."

41 Ibid., vol. 12, 8-20-1778. To Brig. Gen. Thomas Nelson. "It is not a little pleasing, nor less wonderful to contemplate, that after two years Manoeuvring and undergoing the strangest vicissitudes that perhaps ever attended any one contest since the creation both Armies are brought back to the very point they set out from and, that that, which was the offending party in the beginning is now reduced to the use of the spade and pick axe for defence. The hand of Providence has been so conspicuous in all this, that he must be worse than an infidel that lacks faith, and more than wicked, that has not gratitude enough to acknowledge his obligations, but, it will be time enough for me to turn preacher, when my present appointment ceases; and therefore, I shall add no more on the Doctrine of Providence."

42 Ibid., vol. 30, 9-28-1789. To Reverend Samuel Langdon. "The man must be bad indeed who can look upon the events of the American Revolution without feeling the warmest gratitude towards the great Author of the Universe whose divine interposition was so frequently manifested in our behalf. And it is my earnest prayer that we may so conduct ourselves as to merit a continuance of those blessings with which we have hitherto been favored."

43 Tindal: "That the goodness or wickedness, of all actions is wholly measured by their tendency; that this tendency is wholly to be judged of by every man, according to his circumstances; and that these circumstances are continually changing;" Timothy Dwight, *The Nature and Danger of Infidel Philosophy. WGW,* vol. 4, 3-6-1776. General Orders. "Thursday the seventh Instant, being set apart by the Honourable the Legislature of this province, as a day of fasting, prayer, and humiliation, "to implore the Lord, and Giver of all victory, to pardon our manifold sins and wickedness's, and that it would please him to bless the Continental Arms, with his divine favour and protection." *WGW,* vol. 8, 6-10-1777. General Orders. "It is with inexpressible regret the Commander in Chief has been driven to the necessity of doing a severe, but necessary act of Justice, as an example of what is to be expected by those daring offenders, who, lost to all sense of duty, and the obligations they owe to their Country, and to mankind, wantonly violate the most sacred engagements, and fly to the assistance of an enemy, they are bound by every tie to oppose. A spirit of desertion is alone the most fatal disease that can attend an army, and the basest princi-

ple that can actuate a soldier; Wherever it shews itself, it deserves detestation, and calls for the most exemplary punishment. What confidence can a General have in any Soldier, who he has reason to apprehend may desert in the most interesting moments? What, but the want of every moral and manly sentiment, can induce him to desert the cause, to which he has pledged his faith, even with the solemnity of an oath, and which he is bound to support, by every motive of justice and good will to himself, and his fellow creatures ? When such a character appears, it may almost be said in reference to it, that forbearance is folly; and mercy degenerates into cruelty.

Notwithstanding this, and tho' the General is determined to convince every man, that crimes of so atrocious a nature shall not be committed with impunity; yet as He is earnestly desirous to shew that he prefers clemency to severity — pardoning to punishing — He is happy to proclaim, the remission of their offences, to all the other prisoners now under sentence, and a releasement to all those now under confinement for trial — He hopes that they, and all others will have a proper sense of this Act of lenity, and will not be ungrateful or foolish enough to abuse it. They will do well to remember that Justice may speedily overtake them, as it has done the unhappy man, whom they have seen fall a Victim to his own folly and wickedness. Those who are pardoned can expect no favor on a second offence. But, Why will Soldiers force down punishment upon their own heads ? Why will they not be satisfied to do their duty, and reap the benefits of it ? WGW, vol. 10, 12-26-1777. General Orders.

"It is with inexpressible grief and indignation that the General has received information of the cruel outrages and robberies lately committed by soldiers, on the other side of the Schuylkill: Were we in an enemy's country such practices would be unwarrantable; but committed against our friends are in the highest degree base, cruel, and injurious to the cause in which we are engaged. They demand therefore, and shall receive the severest punishment. Such crimes have brought reproach upon the army; and every officer and soldier suffers by the practices of such villains; and 'tis the interest, as well as duty, of every honest man to detect them, and prevent a repetition of such crimes. The General earnestly desires the General Officers, and those commanding Corps, to represent to their men, the cruelty, baseness and wickedness, of such practices, and the injury they do the army, and the common cause. And still further, to prevent the commission of those crimes, the General positively orders. WGW, vol. 19, 8-28-1780. Proclamation of Pardon to Deserters. "Whereas many Soldiers belonging to the Battalions raised by the Commonwealth of Virginia to serve in the Continental Army have deserted from them, and the Honourable the General Assembly of the said Commonwealth apprehending that many of them sensible of their folly and wickedness in violating their faith and Oaths, in dishonourably abandoning the cause of their Country by desertion, would gladly be restored to the favour of their fellow Citizens, by a speedy return to their duty during the war, or for a certain time over and above their several engagements, were it not for the fear of an ignominious punishment, were pleased by an Act passed at their last session, entitled "An Act the more effectually to prevent and punish desertion" which was published "to proclaim pardon to all Deserters from the Virginia line of the Continental Army, who should within Two Months after the publication of the said Act return to their several Companies, if on land, and if at sea, within Two Months after their return, and serve during the War, if so engaged, and if otherwise should serve Two Years over and above the time for which he or they engaged."

44 WGW, vol. 5, 8-3-1776. General Orders. "The General is sorry to be informed that the foolish, and wicked practice, of profane cursing and swearing (a Vice heretofore little known in an American Army) is growing into fashion; he hopes the officers will, by example, as well as influence, endeavour to check it, and that both they, and the men will reflect, that we can have little hopes of the blessing of Heaven on our Arms, if we insult it by our impiety, and folly; added to this, it is a vice so mean and low, without any temptation, that every man of sense, and character, detests and despises it."

45 Chubb: "That men will not be judged for their impiety or ingratitude to God, nor for their injustice and unkindness to each other; but only for voluntary injuries to the public; and that even this is unnecessary and useless;" Timothy Dwight, *The Nature and Danger of Infidel Philosophy*. WGW, vol. 1, 5-29-1754. To Robert Dinwiddie. "I am much concern'd, that your Honour should seem to charge me with ingratitude for your generous, and my undeserved favours; for I assure you, Hon'ble Sir, nothing is a greater stranger to my Breast, or a Sin that my Soul abhors, than that black and detestable one Ingratitude."

WGW, vol. 2, 10-5-1757. "I do not know, that I ever gave your Honor cause to suspect me of ingratitude, a crime I detest, and would most carefully avoid. If an open, disinterested behavior carries offence, I may have offended; because I have all along laid it down as a maxim, to represent facts freely and impartially, but no more to others, than I have to you, Sir. If instances of my ungrateful behavior had been particularized, I would have answered to them. But I have long been convinced, that my actions and their motives have been maliciously aggravated."

46 WGW, vol. 19, 8-20-1780. To the President of Congress. "On the whole, if something satisfactory be not done, the Army (already so much reduced in Officers by daily resignations as not to have a sufficiency to do the common duties of it) must either cease to exist at the end of the Campaign, or it will exhibit an example of more virtue, fortitude, self denial, and perseverance than has perhaps ever yet been paralleled in the history of human enthusiasm." WGW, vol. 19, 9-5-1780. General Orders. "That patience and self-denial, fortitude and perseverance, and the cheerful sacrifice of time, health, and fortune, are necessary virtues which both the citizen and soldier are called to exercise while struggling for the libertys of their country; and that moderation, frugality and temperance, must be among the chief supports, as well as the brightest ornaments, of that kind of civil government which is wisely instituted by the several states in this union."

47 Hume: "That self-denial, self-mortification, and humility, are not virtues, but are useless and mischievous; that they stupify the understanding, sour the temper, and harden the heart (and of course are gross crimes); That suicide, or self-murder, is lawful and commendable (and of course virtuous);That Adultery must be practised, if we would obtain all the advantages of life: That Female Infidelity (or Adultery) when known, is a small thing; when unknown, nothing;" WGW, vol. 26, 6-8-1783. Circular to the States. "I now make it my earnest prayer, that God would have you, and the State over which you preside, in his holy protection, that he would incline the hearts of the Citizens to cultivate a spirit of subordination and obedience to Government, to entertain a brotherly affection and love for one another, for their fellow Citizens of the United States at large, and particularly for their brethren who have served in the Field, and finally, that he would most graciously be pleased to dispose us all, to do Justice, to love mercy, and to demean ourselves with that Charity, humility and pacific temper

of mind, which were the Characteristicks of the Divine Author of our blessed Religion, and without an humble imitation of whose example in these things, we can never hope to be a happy Nation." *WGW*, vol. 27, 12-13-1783. To the Learned Professions of Philadelphia "I am sensible at the same time, it becomes me to receive with humility the warm commendations you are pleased to bestow on my conduct: … For the re-establishment of our once violated rights; for the confirmation of our Independence; for the protection of Virtue, Philosophy and Literature: for the present flourishing state of the Sciences, and for the enlarged prospect of human happiness, it is our common duty to pay the tribute of gratitude to the greatest and best of Beings."

48 "That Man's chief End is to gratify the appetites and inclinations of the flesh: That Modesty is inspired by mere prejudice: That Polygamy is a part of the Law, or Religion, of Nature; That Adultery is no violation of the Law or Religion of Nature; That there is no wrong in Lewdness, except in the highest Incest: That the Law or Religion of Nature forbids no incest, except between the nearest Relations: and plainly supposes, That all Men and Women are unchaste, and that there is no such thing, as Conjugal Fidelity." Timothy Dwight, *The Nature and Danger of Infidel Philosophy*, pp. 21-35.

49 *WGW*, vol. 5, 6-28-1776. General Orders. "The unhappy Fate of Thomas Hickey, executed this day for Mutiny, Sedition and Treachery, the General hopes will be a warning to every Soldier, in the Army, to avoid those crimes, and all others, so disgraceful to the character of a Soldier, and pernicious to his country, whose pay he receives and Bread he eats — And in order to avoid those Crimes the most certain method is to keep out of the temptation of them, and particularly to avoid lewd Women, who, by the dying Confession of this poor Criminal, first led him into practices which ended in an untimely and ignominious Death." *WGW*, vol. 10, 2-4-1778. General Orders. "The most pernicious consequences having arisen from suffering persons, women in particular to pass and repass from Philadelphia to camp under Pretence of coming out to visit their Friends in the Army and returning with necessaries to their families, but really with an intent to intice the soldiers to desert; All officers are desired to exert their utmost endeavors to prevent such interviews in future by forbiding the soldiers under the severest penalties from having any communication with such persons and by ordering them when found in camp to be immediately turned out of it. If any of them appear under peculiar circumstances of suspicion they are to be brought to immediate trial and punishment, if found guilty." "The Camp whores, who have now become more numerous are being used also as nurses." In John Joseph Stoudt, *Ordeal at Valley Forge*, (Philadelphia: University of Pennsylvania), p. 237.

50 *WGW*, vol. 11, 3-14-1778. General Orders. "At a General Court Martial …Lieutt. Enslin of Colo. Malcom's Regiment tried for attempting to commit *sodomy*, with John Monhort a soldier; Secondly, For Perjury in swearing to false Accounts, found guilty of the charges exhibited against him, being breaches of 5th. Article 18th. Section of the Articles of War and do sentence him to be dismiss'd the service with Infamy. His Excellency the Commander in Chief approves the sentence and with Abhorrence and Detestation of such Infamous Crimes orders Lieutt. Enslin to be drummed out of Camp tomorrow morning by all the Drummers and Fifers …."

51 *WGW*, vol. 13, 10-21-1778. General Orders. Cf. John Joseph Stoudt, *Ordeal at Valley Forge*, (Philadelphia: University of Pennsylvania, 1963), pp.70-71, "The Congress has resolved that ten dollars be paid by every Officer and four dollars by every soldier who shall enter or be sent to any Hospital to be cured of venereal disease. These sums are to be deducted from the pay and shall be used for blankets, shirts & other items for sick soldiers."

52 Isaac Lewis, "The divine mission of Jesus Christ evident from his life, and from the nature and tendency of his doctrines." A sermon preached at Stamford, October 11, 1796. before the Consociation of the Western District in Fairfield County. By Isaac Lewis, D.D. Pastor of a consociated church in Greenwich.

53 Boller, *George Washington & Religion*, p. 78.

54 By Isaac Lewis, D. D. Pastor of a Church in Greenwich. Hartford: Printed by Hudson & Goodwin. 1797. ELECTION SERMON "The Political Advantages of Godliness." By Isaac Lewis, D. D. Pastor of a Church in Greenwich. Hartford: Printed by Hudson & Goodwin. 1797. At a General Assembly of the State of Connecticut, holden at Hartford on the second Thursday of May, Anno Domini 1797.

55 *WGW*, vol. 36, 8-14-1797.

56 January 1, 1776. GENERAL ORDERS.

57 Philadelphia, November 28, 1796. To GEORGE WASHINGTON PARKE CUSTIS
"You are now extending into that stage of life when good or bad habits are formed. When the mind will be turned to things useful and praiseworthy, or to dissipation and vice. Fix on whichever it may, it will stick by you; for you know it has been said, and truly, "that as the twig is bent so it will grow." This, in a strong point of view, shows the propriety of letting your inexperience be directed by maturer advice, and in placing guard upon the avenues which lead to idleness and vice. The latter will approach like a thief, working upon your passions; encouraged, perhaps, by bad examples;…Virtue and vice can not be allied; nor can idleness and industry; of course, if you resolve to adhere to the two former of these extremes, an intimacy with those who incline to the latter of them, would be extremely embarrassing to you; it would be a stumbling block in your way; and act like a millstone hung to your neck, for it is the nature of idleness and vice to obtain as many votaries as they can."
February 18, 1778. GENERAL ORDERS
"The Commander in Chief approves the sentence, but is concern'd he cannot reinstate Lt. Rust in compliance with the recommendation of the Court founded upon his former good Character as an Officer. His behavior in the several instances alledged was so flagrant and scandalous that the General thinks his continuance in the service would be a disgrace to it and as one part of the charge against him was *gaming*, that alone would exclude him from all Indulgence; a Vice of so pernicious a nature that it never will escape the Severest punishment with His approbation."
December, 1756. To JOHN ROBINSON
"Dear Sir: It gave me infinite concern to hear by several letters, that the Assembly are incensed against the Virginia Regiment; and think they have cause to accuse the officers of all inordinate vices; but more especially of drunkenness and profanity! How far any *one* individual may have subjected himself to such reflections, I will not pretend to determine, but this I am certain of; and can with the highest safety

call my conscience, my God! and (what I suppose will still be a more demonstrable proof, at least in the eye of the World) the Orders and Instructions which I have given, to evince the purity of my own intentions and to shew on the one hand, that my incessant endeavours have been directed to discountenance Gaming, drinking, swearing, and other vices, with which all camps too much abound: while on the other, I have used every expedient to inspire a laudable emulation in the officers, and an unerring exercise of Duty in the Soldiers."

58   Farewell Address.

59   June 10, 1754. To ROBERT DINWIDDIE, "I hope Capt. McKay will have more sense than to insist upon any unreasonable distinction, tho' he and His have Com'ns from his Majest; let him consider tho' we are greatly inferior in respect to profitable advantages, yet we have the same Spirit to serve our Gracious King as they have, and are as ready and willing to sacrifice our lives for our Country's as them; and here once more and for the last time, I must say this Will be a cancer that will grate some Officers of this Regiment beyond all measure, to serve upon such different terms, when their Lives, their Fortunes, and their Characters are equally, and I dare say as effectually expos'd as those who are happy enough to have King's Commissions."

April 22, 1756. To ROBERT DINWIDDIE, "The supplicating tears of the women, and moving petitions from the men, melt me into such deadly sorrow, that I solemnly declare, if I know my own mind, I could offer myself a willing sacrifice to the butchering enemy, provided that would contribute to the people's ease."

60   WGW, vol. 5, 7-25-1776.

61   February 6, 1781. To BARON STEUBEN, "The oaths of the Men respecting the terms of their inlistments were precipitately admitted before the documents could be produced; by which it afterwards appeared, the greater part had perjured themselves, to get rid of the service." To MAJOR GENERAL ARTHUR ST. CLAIR, February 3, 1781, "It seems a great part of the soldiers of your line have fraudulently procured a discharge by the precipitate admission of their oaths, before the papers relative to their inlistments could be produced." January 30, 1781. GENERAL ORDERS, "He considers the patience with which they endured the fatigues of the march through rough and mountainous roads rendered almost impassable by the depth of the Snow and the cheerfulness with which they performed every other part of their duty as the strongest proof of their Fidelity, attachment to the service, sense of subordination and abhorrence of the principles which actuated the Mutineers in so daring and atrocious a departure from what they owed to their Country, to their Officers to their Oaths and to themselves."

August 29, 1780. PROCLAMATION OF PARDON TO DESERTERS. "Whereas many Soldiers belonging to the Battalions raised by the Commonwealth of Virginia to serve in the Continental Army have deserted from them, and the Honourable the General Assembly of the said Commonwealth apprehending that many of them sensible of their folly and wickedness in violating their faith and Oaths, in dishonourably abandoning the cause of their Country by desertion, would gladly be restored to the favour of their fellow Citizens, by a speedy return to their duty during the war, or for a certain time over and above their several engagements, were it not for the fear of an ignominious punishment, were pleased by an Act passed at their last session, entitled "An Act the more effectually to prevent and punish desertion" which was published "to proclaim pardon to all Deserters from the Virginia line of the Continental Army, who should within Two Months after the publication of the said Act return to their several Companies, if on land, and if at sea, within Two Months after their return, and serve during the War, if so engaged, and if otherwise should serve Two Years over and above the time for which he or they engaged."

May 7, 1778. GENERAL ORDERS. "The Honorable Congress have been pleased by their resolution of the 3rd. of February last to require all Officers as well civil as military, holding Commissions under them to take and subscribe the following Oath or Affirmation according to the Circumstances of the Parties. I do acknowledge The United States of America to be Free, Independent and Sovereign States and declare that the People thereof owe no Allegiance or Obedience to George the Third, King of Great Britain and I renounce refuse and abjure any Allegiance or Obedience to him, and I do swear (or affirm) that I will to the utmost of my Power support, maintain and defend the said United States against the said King George the third, his heirs and Successors and his and their Abettors, Assistants and Adherents and will serve the said United States in the office of which I now hold with Fidelity according to the best of my skill and understanding."

Valley Forge, March 1, 1778. To BRYAN FAIRFAX, "The determinations of Providence are all ways wise; often inscrutable, and though its decrees appear to bear hard upon us at times is nevertheless meant for gracious purposes; in this light I cannot help viewing your late disappointment; for if you had been permitted to have gone to england, unrestrained even by the rigid oaths which are administred on those occns. your feelings as a husband, Parent, &ca. must have been considerably wounded in the prospect of a long, perhaps lasting seperation from your nearest relatives. What then must they have been if the obligation of an oath had left you without a Will? Your hope of being instrumental in restoring Peace would prove as unsubstantial as mist before the Noon days Sun and would as soon dispel: for believe me Sir great Britain understood herself perfectly well in this dispute but did not comprehend America."

April 16, 1777. To GOVERNOR WILLIAM LIVINGSTON, "He said, that he could not in Conscience take the Oaths to the State, as he had taken the Oath of Allegiance to the King; that the People in the Country threatened his life, and that he thought he had better return. General Greene asked him, if he had not considered the Matter of taking the Oaths to the State before he came out, as he owned he had seen the Proclamation; but he gave such evasive Answers, that it convinced us, that he only came out to get intelligence and I therefore had him apprehended and sent to Philadelphia, where he has since been Confined."

"By his Excellency GEORGE WASHINGTON, Esq; General and Commander in Chief of all the forces of the United States of America, PROCLAMATION. *Whereas* Several Persons, Inhabitants Of The United States Of America, Influenced By Inimical Motives, Intimidated By The Threats Of The Enemy, Or Deluded By A Proclamation Issued The 30th Of November Last, By Lord And General Howe, stiled the King's Commissioners for granting pardons, &c. (now at open war and invading these states) have been so lost to the interest and welfare of their country, as to repair to the enemy, sign a declaration of fidelity, and, in some instances, have been compelled to take oaths of allegiance, and to engage not to take up arms, or encourage others so to do, against the King of Great-Britain. And whereas it has become necessary to distinguish between the friends of America and those of Great-Britain, inhabitants of these States and that every man who receives a protection from and is a subject of any State (not being conscientiously scrupulous against bearing arms) should stand ready to defend the fame against every hostile invasion, I do therefore. in behalf of the United States, by virtue of the powers committed to me by Congress, hereby strictly command and require every person having subscribed such declaration, taken loch oaths, and accepted protection and certificates from Lord or General Howe, or any person acting under their authority, forthwith to repair to Head-Quarters, or to the quarters of the nearest general officer of the Continental Army or Militia (until farther provision can be made by the civil authority) and there deliver up such protections, certificates, and passports, and take the oath of allegiance to the United States of America. Nevertheless, hereby granting full liberty to all such as prefer the interest and protection of Great-Britain to the freedom and happiness of their country, forthwith to withdraw themselves and families within the enemy's lines. And I do hereby declare that all and every person, who may neglect or refuse to comply with this order, within thirty days from the date hereof, will be deemed adherents to the King of Great- Britain, and treated as common enemies of the American States."

62 Farewell Address. "Of all the dispositions and habits, says he, which lead to political prosperity, religion and morality are indispensable supports. In vain would that man claim the tribute of patriotism who should labor to subvert these great pillars of human happiness, these firmest props of the duties of men and citizens. The mere politician equally with the pious man ought to respect and to cherish them. A volume could not trace all their connections with private and public felicity. Let it simply be asked, where is the security for property, for reputation, for life, if the sense of religious obligation desert the oaths, which are the instruments of investigation in the courts of justice? And let us with caution indulge the supposition, that morality can be maintained without religion. Whatever may be conceded to the influence of refined education on minds of a peculiar structure; reason and experience both forbid us to expect, that national morality can prevail in exclusion of religious principle.

"It is substantially true, that virtue or morality is a necessary spring of popular government. The rule indeed extends with more or less force to every species of free government. Who that is a sincere friend to it, can look with indifference on attempts to shake the foundation of the fabric?"

63 *WGW*, vol. 11, 5-7-1778.

64 July 12, 1757. To CAPTAIN JOHN DAGWORTHY, "Sir: I recd. your's of the 10th. Inst. Covering the Drummer's Deposition about the Enemys Motions and Designs which I hope will prove as favourable to us as the last Intelligence from that Quarter. I have Transmitted Governor Dinwiddie a Copy of it and would have sent another to Colo. Stanwix did not the Bearer assure me that there cou'd be no doubt of your Expresses reaching him in due time. If you shou'd at anytime hereafter have occasion to send an Express here you need not be at the Trouble of sendg. it further than Pearsalls from whence Captn. McKenzie will immediately forward it here, the Bearer seems unfit for the Service he is now on being a Drunken delatory Fellow. I am Sir, etc."

WGW, vol. 30, 3-31, 1789. To Thomas Green. "Thomas Green: I am about to leave my home whether for a length of time, is more than I can tell at present. But be this as it may I expect the agreement to which we have subscribed, will be as strictly complied with on your part as it shall be punctually fulfilled on mine. To enable you to do this, you would do well to keep two things always in remembrance. First that all Bargains are intended, for the Mutual benefit of and are equally binding on both the Parties, and are either binding in all their parts or are of no use at all. If then a man receives [pay] for his labour and he withholds that labour or if he trifles away that time for which he is paid, it is a robbery; and a robbery of the worst kind, because it is not only a fraud but a dishonorable, unmanly and a deceitful fraud; but it is unnecessary to dwell on this because there is no Man so ignorant of the common obligations of Justice, as not to know it; altho' there are hundreds who do not scruple to practice it at the same time that they would think hard, on the other hand if they were to be deprived of their money. The other matter which I advise you to keep always in remembrance is the good name which common policy as well as common honesty, makes it necessary for every workman who wishes to pass thro' life With reputation and to secure employment. Having said thus much by way of exhortation I shall inform you in the most serious and positive terms that I have left strict orders with the Major my Nephew, who is vested with full powers to transact all my business, that if he should find you unfaithful to your engagements, either from the love of liquor from a disposition to be running about, or from proneness to idle when at your work to discard you immediately and to remove your family from their present abode. The sure means to avoid this evil is, first to refrain from drink which is the source of all evil, and the ruin of half the workmen in this Country; and next to avoid bad Company which is the bane of good morals, economy and industry. You have every inducement to do this. Reputation the care and support of a growing family and society which this family affords within your own doors which may not be the case with some of the idle (to say nothing worse of them) characters who may lead you into temptation. Were you to look back, and had the means, either from recollection, or accounts, to ascertain the cost of the liquor you have expended it would astonish you. In the manner this expence is generally incurred that is by getting a little now, a little then, the impropriety of it is not seen, in as much as it passes away without much thought. But view it in the aggregate you will be convinced at once, whether any man who depends upon the labour of his hands not only for his own support, but that of an encreasing family can afford such a proportion of his wages to that article. But the expence is not the worst consequence that attends it for it naturally leads a man into the company of those who encourage dissipation and idleness by which he is led by degrees to the perpetration of acts which may terminate in his Ruin; but supposing this not to happen a disordered frame, and a body debilitated, renders him unfit (even if his mind was disposed to discharge the duties of his station with honor to himself or fidelity to his employer) from the execution of it. An aching head and trembling limbs which are the inevitable effects of drinking disincline the hands from work; hence begins sloth and that Listlessness which end in idleness; but which are no reasons for withholding that labour for which money is paid."

July 25, 1776. GENERAL ORDERS

"Henry Davis tried for "Desertion" is sentenced to receive Twenty Lashes; Patrick Lyons for "Drunkenness and sleeping on his post," Thirty Lashes."

March 30, 1777. To MAJOR GENERAL WILLIAM HEATH

"Major Austin is a Gentleman and a Man of Sense, and, before the unfortunate Step at the plains, was esteemed an excellent Officer. His excuse for his conduct is certainly, strictly considered, rather an aggravation of his crime, for there cannot be a greater failing in a Soldier than drunkenness. This, however, might have been the effect of an unguarded hour; if so, Major Austin has undergone a punishment equal to the offence; But I think I have heard that he is apt to drink, that is a matter that should be fully cleared up, before I could consent to his coming into the Army again. If upon inquiry, you find that his general Character, before and since, is that of a Man of Sobriety, I should think he might be intrusted with a Commission again. I am etc."

February 25, 1781. To MARQUIS DE LAFAYETTE

"As your March will be rapid to the head of Elk, leave good Officers to bring up the tired, lazy, and drunken Soldiers. With every wish for your success and glory. I am etc."

May 16, 1782. GENERAL ORDERS

"The General is extremely concerned to learn that an Article so salutary as that of distilled Liquors was expected to be when properly used, and which was designed for the comfort and refreshment of the troops has been in many instances productive of very ill consequences. He calls the attention of officers of every grade to remedy these abuses and to watch over the health of their men, for which purpose he suggests the expedient of keeping liquor Rolls in every Corps, from which the Name of every soldier shall be struck off who addicts himself to drunkenness or injures his Constitution by intemperence; such soldiers as are Struck off are not to draw liquor on any occasion, but are to receive other articles in lieu thereof."

Rocky Hill, October 16, 1783. To ROBERT LEWIS & SONS

"There is no Miller in America I would exchange Roberts for, if he could be broke of his abominable drunken and quarrelsome frolicks; the opinion I entertain of his skill, and an unwillingness to part with him, have been the inducements to my keeping him fourteen years, when I ought not to have borne with him for the last seven of them."

November 3, 1784. To JACOB READ

"Supposing this to be the case, their will be an interregnum, during which the works will be left without guards, and being obnoxious to British policy, and Indian prejudices, will, by *accidental* fires, or Indian Drunkeness end in conflagration."

Mount Vernon, August 1, 1792. To THE SECRETARY OF WAR

"So long as the vice of drunkenness exists in the Army so long I hope, Ejections of those Officers who are found guilty of it will continue; for that and gaming will debilitate and render unfit for active service any Army whatsoever."

December 23, 1793. To JOHN CHRISTIAN EHLER

"I shall not close this letter with out exhorting you to refrain from Spirituous liquors, they will prove your ruin if you do not. Consider how little a drunken Man differs from a beast; the latter is not endowed with reason, the former deprives himself of it; and when that is the case acts like a brute; annoying, and disturbing everyone around him. But this is not all, nor as it respects himself the worst of it; By degrees it renders a person feeble and not only unable to serve others but to help himself, and being an act of his own he fall[s] from a state of usefulness into contempt and at length suffers, if not perishes in penury and want.

"Don't let this be your case. Shew yourself more of a man, and a Christian, than to yield to so intolerable a vice; which cannot, I am certain (to the greatest lover of liquor) give more pleasure to sip in the poison (for it is no better) than the consequences of it in bad behaviour, at the moment, and the more serious evils produced by it afterward, must give pain. I am Your friend."

65   George Washington,. February 2, 1756, in a letter to Governor Dinwiddie written from Alexandria, Virginia. Sparks, *Writings of George Washington*, vol. II, p. 132.

66   Washington, George. October 2, 1775, orders issued. Elizabeth Bryant Johnston, George Washington, Day by Day (1894), p. 146. Johnson, *George Washington - The Christian*, p. 72.

67   *WGW,* vol. 26. 1-15-1783.

68   "Let vice and immorality of every kind be discouraged as much as possible in your brigade; and, as a chaplain is allowed to each regiment, see that the men regularly attend divine worship. Gaming of every kind is expressly forbidden, as being the foundation of evil, and the cause on many a brave and gallant officer's ruin. Games of exercise for amusement may not only be permitted but encouraged. Washington, George. May 26, 1777, in a circular to the brigadier-generals." Sparks, *Writings of George Washington*, vol. IV, p. 436.

Winchester, April 18, 1756. To ROBERT DINWIDDIE.

"this I am certain of, and can call my conscience, and what, I suppose, will still be a more demonstrable proof in the eyes of the world, my orders, to witness how much I have, both by threats and persuasive means, endeavoured to discountenance gaming, drinking, swearing, and irregularities of every other kind; while I have, on the other hand, practised every artifice to inspire a laudable emulation in the officers for the service of their country, and to encourage the soldiers in the unerring exercise of their duty."

May 21, 1778. GENERAL ORDERS

"At a Brigade Court Martial May 18th, 1778, Lieutt. Colo. Cropper, President, Captain Edward Hull of the 15th. Virginia Regiment tried for gaming when he ought to have been on the Parade the 12th. instant unanimously found guilty of that part of the Charge relative to gaming but acquitted of nonattendance on the Parade and sentenced to be reprimanded by the Commanding Officer of the Brigade in presence of all the Officers thereof.

"The Commander in Chief however unwilling to dissent from the judgment of a Court Martial is obliged utterly to disapprove the sentences, the punishment being in his opinion totally inadequate to the offence. A practice so pernicious in itself as that of gaming, so prejudicial to good order and military discipline; So contrary to positive and repeated General Orders, carried to so Enormous a height as it appears, and aggravated certainly in Case of Lieutt. Lewis by an additional offence of no trifling military consequence, Absence from Parade, demanded a much severer Penalty than simply a reprimand. Captn. Hull and Lieutt. Lewis are to be released from their Arrest."

Head-Quarters, Morristown, May 8, 1777. GENERAL ORDERS

"As few vices are attended with more pernicious consequences, in civil life; so there are none more fatal in a military one, than that of *Gaming* ; which often brings disgrace and ruin upon officers, and injury and punishment upon the Soldiery: and reports prevailing, which, it is to be feared are too well founded, that this destructive vice has spread its baneful influence in the army, and, in a peculiar manner, to the prejudice of the recruiting Service, The Commander in chief, in the most pointed and explicit terms, forbids *All* officers and soldiers, playing at cards, dice or at any games, except those of *Exercise,* for diversion; it being impossible, if the practice be allowed, at all, to dis-criminate between innocent play, for amusement, and criminal gaming, for pecuniary and sordid purposes."

January 8, 1778. GENERAL ORDERS

"The commander in chief is informed that gaming is again creeping into the Army; in a more especial manner among the lower staff in the environs of the camp. He therefore in the most solemn terms declares, that this Vice in either Officer or soldier, shall not when detected, escape exemplary punishment; and to avoid discrimination between play and gaming forbids Cards and Dice under any pretence whatsoever. Being also informed that many men are render'd unfit for duty by the Itch, He orders and directs the Regimental Surgeons to look attentively into this matter and as Soon as the men (who are infected with this disorder) are properly disposed in huts to have them annointed for it."

Head Quarters, Middle Brook, Friday, April 2, 1779. GENERAL ORDERS

"All General Orders are in force 'till they are set aside or altered by subsequent ones issuing from proper authority or 'till the occasion ceases which produced them. Colo. Ogdon knows this and he must have known also that the particular order which was the subject of the Court Martial's consideration of the 4th. charge against him, remained unalter'd and the infraction of it is more censurable, if possible, than that of any other, inasmuch as the order was intended to prevent the most pernicious Vice that can obtain in an Army, the vice of gam-ing!"

Mount Vernon, August 1, 1792. To THE SECRETARY OF WAR

"So long as the vice of drunkenness exists in the Army so long I hope, Ejections of those Officers who are found guilty of it will con-tinue; for that and gaming will debilitate and render unfit for active service any Army whatsoever."

Newburgh, January 15, 1783. To BUSHROD WASHINGTON

"The last thing I shall mention, is first of importance. and that is, to avoid Gaming. This is a vice which is productive of every pos-sible evil. equally injurious to the morals and health of its rotaries. It is the child of Avarice, the brother of inequity, and father of Mischief. It has been the ruin of many worthy familys; the loss of many a man's honor; and the cause of Suicide. To all those who enter the list, it is equally fascinating; the Successful gamester pushes his good fortune till it is over taken by a reverse; the loosing gamester, in hopes of retrieving past misfortunes, goes on from bad to worse; till grown desperate, he pushes at every thing; and loos-es his all. In a word, few gain by this abominable practice (the profit, if any, being diffused) while thousands are injured."

69   Sparks, *Writings of George Washington*, vol. III, 491.

70   May 10, 1776. GENERAL ORDERS

"Joseph Child of the New York Train of Artillery tried at a late General Court Martial whereof Col. Huntington was President for "defrauding Christopher Stetson of a dollar, also for drinking Damnation to all Whigs, and Sons of Liberty, and for profane cursing and swearing." The Court finding the prisoner guilty of profane cursing and swearing and speaking contemptuously of the American Army, do sentence him to be drum'd out of the army.

The Court are of opinion, that the Prisoner, Watkins, is guilty of being out of his quarters at unseasonable hours, and of profane curs-ing and swearing, and do sentence him to be confin'd six days; upon bread and water and be fined one sixth of a dollar for profane swearing, as by the 3rd Article is prescribed."

September 19, 1755. ORDERS

"Any Soldier who is guilty of any breach of the Articles of War, by Swearing, getting Drunk, or using an Obscene Language; shall be severely Punished, without the Benefit of a Court Martial."

May 18, 1756. To LIEUTENANT COLONEL ADAM STEPHEN

"Do take great pains to prevent all irregularities in the Garrison; but especially those of Drinking, Swearing and Gaming!"

July 29, 1757. GENERAL INSTRUCTIONS TO ALL THE CAPTAINS OF COMPANIES

"You are to use every imaginable precaution to prevent irregular suttling, licentious swearing, and all other unbecoming irregularities and to neglect no pains or diligence in training your men (when off duty) to the true use and exercise of their arms; and teaching them in all other respects, the duties of their profession."

July 4, 1775. GENERAL ORDERS

"The General most earnestly requires, and expects, a due observance of those articles of war, established for the Government of the army, which forbid profane cursing, swearing and drunkeness; And in like manner requires and expects, of all Officers, and Soldiers, not engaged on actual duty, a punctual attendance on divine Service, to implore the blessings of heaven upon the means used for our safety and defence."

August 3, 1776. GENERAL ORDERS

"The General is sorry to be informed that the foolish, and wicked practice, of profane cursing and swearing (a Vice heretofore little known in an American Army) is growing into fashion; he hopes the officers will, by example, as well as influence, endeavour to check it, and that both they, and the men will reflect, that we can have little hopes of the blessing of Heaven on our Arms, if we insult it by our impiety, and folly; added to this, it is a vice so mean and low, without any temptation, that every man of sense, and charac-ter, detests and despises it."

May 31, 1777. GENERAL ORDERS

"It is much to be lamented, that the foolish and scandalous practice of *profane Swearing* is exceedingly prevalent in the American

Army Officers of every rank are bound to discourage it, first by their example, and then by punishing offenders As a mean to abolish this, and every other species of immorality Brigadiers are enjoined, to take effectual care, to have divine service duly performed in their respective brigades."

Head Quarters, Moores House, Thursday, July 29, 1779. GENERAL ORDERS

"Many and pointed orders have been issued against that unmeaning and abominable custom of *Swearing* , not withstanding which, with much regret the General observes that it prevails, *if possible* , more than ever; His feelings are continually wounded by the Oaths and Imprecations of the soldiers whenever he is in hearing of them."

June 4, 1797. To GEORGE WASHINGTON PARKE CUSTIS

"an idle habit of hankering after unprofitable amusements at your time of life, before you have acquired that knowledge which would be found beneficial in every situation; I say *before*, because it is not my wish that, having gone through the essentials, you should be deprived of any rational amusements at your time of life, before you have acquired that knowledge which would be found beneficial in every situation; I say before, because it is not my wish that, having gone through the essentials, you should be deprived of any rational amusement afterward ; or, lastly, from dissipation in such company as you would most likely meet under such circumstances, who but too often, mistake ribaldry for wit, and rioting, swearing, intoxication, and gambling for manliness."

71   *WGW*, Farewell Address.

CHAPTER 28

1   *WGW*, vol. 30, 4-1789, First proposed address to Congress.

2   Flexner, *The Indispensable Man*, p. 216.

3   See chapter 2.

4   As noted earlier, these writings are available at John Clement Fitzpatrick, ed., *The Writings of George Washington, from the Original Manuscript Sources 1749-1799*, 39 vols. (Washington, D.C.: United States Government Printing Office, 1931-1944). Visit http://etext.lib.virginia.edu/washington/.

5   *Book of Common Prayer* Communion service

6   Washington also employed the explitives: God forbid, Wish to God, For God's sake – hurry!, My God!, Good God! That these were not profanity in his mind is seen in context where he uses to condemn swearing.

7   These phrases seem to suggest an acquaintance with the traditional philosophical arguments for God's existence: The "Greatest Efficient" referencing the Cosmological argument and the "Greatest and Best," referencing the Ontological argument.

8   We address George Washington's Masonic relationship in the chapter 25.

9   See chapter 2.

10   *WGW*, vol. 2 4-27-1763.

11   Over 197 references.

12   See for example *WGW*, vol. 2, 9-28-1760; vol. 4, 3-6-1776.

13   Ibid., vol. 30, 5-10-1789; vol. 30, 5-26-1789.

14   Ibid., vol. 30 4-1789.

15   Ibid., vol. 31, 12-29-1790; vol. 35 8-29-1796.

16   Over 133 matches.

17   *PGW*, Letterbook 38, image 148; letter to the Savannah Hebrew Congregation, May 1790.

18   Ibid.

19   See for example *WGW*, vol. 5, 7-2-1776; vol. 24, 6-30-1782; vol. 26, 2-15-1783. etc.

20   Ibid., vol. 27, 8-10-1783; vol. 30, 8-3-1788.

21   WGW vol. 27, August 10, 1783

22   See for example Ibid vol. 3, 1-13-1775; vol. 4, 11-28-1775; vol. 4, 12-5-1775; vol. 11, 5-5-1778; vol. 27, 12-22-1783, etc.

23   Ibid., vol. 18, 6-11-1780.

24   Ibid., vol. 30, Thanksgiving Proclamation.

25   See above references.

26   *WGW* vol. 30, 7-31-1788.

27   See for example Ibid vol. 3, 7-16-1775; vol. 3, 9-8-1775; vol. 4, 2-1-1776, etc.

28   Ibid., vol. 28, August 18, 1786

29   Ibid., vol. 34, 9-20-1795.

30   Ibid., vol. 37, 5-13-1776.

31   Ibid., vol. 29, 4-28-1788

32   Ibid., vol. 30, 5-29-1789.

33   Ibid., vol. 27, 12-13-1783.

34   Ibid., vol. 27, 12-13-1783.

35   Ibid., vol. 27, 12-13-1783.

36   Ibid., vol. 5, 7-2-1776, for example.

37   Ibid., vol. 35, 4-1-1797.

38   Ibid., vol. 34, Seventh Annual Address to Congress.

39   Ibid., vol. 7, 4-23-1777.

40 Ibid., vol. 35, 4-1-1797.

41 Ibid., vol. 4, 11-18-1775.

42 Ibid., vol. 34 December 8, 1795.

43 Ibid., vol. 35, 3-3-1797.

44 Ibid., vol. 35, 3-3-1797.

45 Ibid., vol. 5, 5-15-1776.

46 Ibid., vol. 4, 3-6-1776.

47 Ibid., vol. 7, 4-12-1777; vol. 7, 4-15-1777; vol. 27, 11-2-1783.

48 Ibid., vol. 23, 11- 19-1781.

49 Ibid., vol. 3, 7-16-1775; vol. 3, 9-8-1775; vol. 4, 2-1-1776; vol. 27, 5-15-1784.

50 See for example Ibid., vol. 30, 4-30-1789; vol. 35, 5-15-1796; vol. 3, 7-4-1775.

51 Ibid., Vol 11, 5-5-1778.

52 Ibid., vol. 17, 11-27-1779.

53 Ibid., vol. 6, 12-6-1776.

54 Ibid., vol. 27, 2-10-1784.

55 Ibid., vol. 28, 2-7-1785; vol. 30, 6-29-1788.

56 See for example Ibid., vol. 35, 12-7-1796; vol. 5, 8-12-1776; vol. 11, 5-5-1778.

57 Ibid., vol. 5, 7-10-1776.

58 Ibid., vol. 1, 7-18-1755; vol. 2, 7-20-1758; vol. 27, 1-18-1784.

59 Ibid., vol. 20, 10-18-1780.

60 Ibid., vol. 5, 8-13-1776; vol. 9, 10-27-1777; vol. 10, 11-30-1777; vol. 28, 8-18-1786.

61 Ibid., vol. 24, Answer to the Address of Congress. There are many other examples.

62 Ibid., vol. 4, 3-6-1776.

63 Ibid., vol. 34, 11-19-1794.

64 Ibid., vol. 35, 12-7-1796.

65 Ibid., vol. 35, 12-7-1796.

66 Ibid., vol. 5, 8-12-1776.

67 Ibid., vol. 4, 1-27-1776.

68 Ibid., vol. 30, 4-10-1789.

69 Ibid., vol. 30, Proposed Address to Congress.

70 Ibid., vol. 26, Circular to the States

71 Ibid., vol. 30, 4-1789.

72 Ibid., vol. 15, 5-12-1779.

73 Ibid., vol. 30, 4-30-1789.

74 Ibid., vol. 4, ANSWER TO AN ADDRESS FROM THE MASSACHUSETTS LEGISLATURE.

75 Ibid., vol. 28, 7-25-1785.

76 Ibid., vol. 15, 5-12-1779.

77 Ibid., vol., 2-14-1784.

78 Ibid., vol. 26, 6-8-1783.

79 See chapter 2.

80 Ibid., vol. 3, 4-25-1773; vol. 29, 4-25-1788; vol. 30, 6-22-1788.

81 Ibid., vol. 29, 10-10-1787; vol. 31, 1-6-1792; vol. 35, 3-2-1797; vol. 35, 3-30-1796 (To Elizabeth Parke Custis law); vol. 35, 3-30-1796 (To Tobias Lear).

82 Ibid., vol. 27, 2-1-1784; vol. 35, 6-24-1797; vol. 35, 6-25-1797; vol. 35, 6-26-1797; vol. 35, 7-4-1797.

83 Ibid., vol. 27, 12-13-1783; vol. 28, 8-18-1786; vol. 30, 8-18-1789; vol. 30, 1-9-1790; vol. 35, 9-19-1796.

84 Ibid., vol. 23, 11-23-1781 – CHECK that this is the right nuance

85 Ibid., – over 55 references

86 Ibid., vol. 3, 4- 25-1773.

87 Ibid., vol. 29, 10-10-1787.

88 Ibid., vol. 35, 3-2-1789.

89 Ibid., vol. 29, 4-25-1788.

90 Ibid., vol. 30, April 1789. Note Boller had no comment on this passage

91 *WGW*, vol. 13, 11-11-1778.

92 Ibid., vol. 23, 11-23-1781.

93 *The London Chronicle* in the September 21 to 23, 1779 edition no. 3561, p. 288.

94 James McGoldrick tells more details of Reverend Boucher's break with the colonists: "Fearing an open breach with Britain, Boucher tried unsuccessfully to organize the Anglican clergy in America into a solid block of support for the crown. As a minister of the Church of England, Boucher had taken a solemn oath of allegiance to the crown, and no amount of pressure could persuade him to violate it. ...When Britain closed Boston harbor after the Tea party, American resisters appeared for supplies to be sent to Boston so that the Patriots would suffer no loss of physical necessities. When asked to appeal from his pulpit for aid to the Boston rebels, Boucher refused. After this he was

a marked man, and several threats were made against his life." (James McGoldrick, "1776: A Christian Loyalist View" in *Fides Et Historia*, fall 1977, p. 32.) The stress of the final days of his ministry in the colonies became so great, that he literally preached with armed force close at hand. Boucher himself wrote, "I never after went into a pulpit without something very disagreeable happening. I received sundry messages and letters threatening me with the most fatal consequences if I did not . . . preach what should be agreeable to the friends of America. All the answer I gave to these threats was in my sermons, in which I uniformly and resolutely declared that I never would suffer any merely human authority to intimidate me from performing what . . . I . . . knew to be my duty to God and His Church." Jonathan Boucher, *Reminiscences of a American Loyalist*, ed. J. Bouchier (Port Washington, NY: Kennikat, 1967), p. 113.

Thereafter, Boucher's pulpit ministry was adorned with pistols on the pulpit itself and his own public declaration of "repelling violence with violence." (Ibid.)

95 Boucher, *Reminiscences*, p. 49
96 McGoldrick, "1776: A Christian Loyalist View" p. 33.
97 Flexner, Johnson, His Excellency, etc
98 *WGW*, vol. 7, 2-22-1777.
99 Ibid., vol. 37, Last Will and Testament, 1799.
100 Ibid., vol. 25, 11-14-1782.
101 To Lt. Col. John Laurens, he wrote,

"Believe me sincere when I assure you, that my warmest wishes accompany Captn. Wallops endeavours and your expectations of exchange; and that nothing but the principle of Justice and policy wch. I have *religiously* adhered to of exchanging Officers in the order of their Captivity (where rank would apply) has prevented my every exertion to obtain your release and restoration to a family where you will be receiv'd with open arms by every individual of it; but from none with more cordiality and true affection than Your Sincere friend etc."
In General Orders he writes,

"The Honorable The Congress having been pleased by their Proclamation of the 21st. of November last to appoint Wednesday the 30th. instant as a day of Thanksgiving and Praise for the great and numerous Providential Mercies experienced by the People of These States in the course of the present War, the same is to be *religiously* observed throughout the Army in the manner therein directed, and the different Chaplains will prepare discourses suited to the Occasion."
In General Orders, he writes,

The Honorable Congress having thought proper to recommend to The United States of America to set apart Wednesday the 22nd. instant to be observed as a day of Fasting, Humiliation and Prayer, that at one time and with one voice the righteous dispensations of Providence may be acknowledged and His Goodness and Mercy toward us and our Arms supplicated and implored; The General directs that this day *also* shall be *religiously* observed in the Army, that no work be clone thereon and that the Chaplains prepare discourses suitable to the Occasion."
He wrote to Robert Cary & Co. from Mount Vernon on July 25, 1769:

"Gentn: Inclosd you will receive Invoices of Goods wanted for myself and Master Custis for this place and our Plantations on York River, as also for Miss Custis which I beg may be sent by Captn. Johnstoun if the Orders gets to hand in time, if not by any other Vessel bound to this River. But if there are any Articles containd in either of the respective Invoices (Paper only excepted) which are Tax'd by Act of Parliament for the purpose of Raising a Revenue in America, it is my express desire and request, that they may not be sent, as I have very heartily enterd into an Association (Copies of which, I make no doubt you have seen otherwise I shoud have Inclosed one) not to Import any Article which now is or hereafter shall be Taxed for this purpose untill the said Act or Acts are repeal'd. I am therefore particular in mentioning this matter as I am fully determined to adhere *religiously* to it, and may perhaps have wrote for some things unwittingly which may be under these Circumstances."
He wrote in his General Orders from Head Quarters in Cambridge on July 16, 1775,

"The Continental Congress having earnestly recommended, that "Thursday next the 20th. Instant, be observed by the Inhabitants of all the english Colonies upon this Continent, as a Day of public Humiliation, Fasting and Prayer; that they may with united Hearts and Voice unfeignedly confess their Sins before God, and supplicate the all wise and merciful disposer of events, to avert the Desolation and Calamities of an unnatural war." The General orders, that Day to be *religiously* observed by the Forces under his Command, exactly in manner directed by the proclamation of the Continental Congress: It is therefore strictly enjoin'd on all Officers and Soldiers, (not upon duty) to attend Divine Service, at the accustomed places of worship, as well in the Lines, as the Encampments and Quarters; and it is expected, that all those who go to worship, do take their Arms, Ammunitions and Accoutrements and are prepared for immediate Action if called upon. If in the judgment of the Officers, the Works should appear to be in such forwardness as the utmost security of the Camp requires, they will command their men to abstain from all Labour upon that solemn day".
He wrote to Brig. Gen. Wm. Maxwell from Head Quarters in Morris Town on February 12, 1777,

"Sir: In answer to your Letter of the 9th. Instt., respecting the case of the young Men of Eliza. Town, who refuse to take the Oath of Allegiance to the States, or to withdraw within the Enemy's lines, and discourage all the Militia round about them; I would observe, that tho' it is my desire to have the terms and Conditions of my Proclamation *religiously* complied with, yet I do not intend that it shall be made a Shelter for our Enemies to injure us under, with impunity."
102 *WGW*, vol. 35, 10-9-1795.
103 Ibid., vol. 34, 1-22-1795.
104 Ibid., vol. 20, 10-18-1780.
105 Ibid., vol. 2, 4-17-1758.
106 Ibid., vol. 34, 12-24-1795.

107 Ibid., vol. 30, 5-29-1789.

108 Ibid., vol. 30, 9-28-1789.

109 Ibid., vol. 8, 6-8-1777.

110 Ibid., vol. 32, 6-22-1792.

111 Ibid., vol. 35, 3-3-1797.

112 Ibid., vol. 31, 12-1790.

113 Ibid., vol. 30, 10-9-1789.

CHAPTER 29

1   *WGW,* vol. 29 4-28-1788.

2   Flexner, *The Indispensable Man,* p. 216.

3   There are many examples. For one example, see *WGW,* vol. 9, 10-18-1777. See also the sermon by Ezra Stiles in Washington's library entitled: *The United States elevated to Glory and Honor....May 8, 1783.* Lane, *Washington Collection,* Boston Athenaeum, p. 194.

4   The Reverend Dr. Donald Binder, in an interview with Peter Lillback and Jerry Newcombe, 2005.

5   *WGW,* vol. 6, 12-18-1776.

6   Ibid., vol. 21, 3-9-1781. To Reverend William Gordon.

7   *WGW* vol. 29 4-28-1788.

8   See Ibid., vol. 9, 10-27-1777; vol.11, 3-1-1778; vol. 11, 5-30-1778;vol. 21, 3-89-1781; vol. 24, 6-5-1782; vol. 28, 8-1-1786; vol. 33, 9-25-1794; vol. 35, 3-30-1796; vol. 35, 6-8-1769; vol. 35, 10-12-1796; vol. 35, 3-2-1797; vol. 35, 3-3-1797; vol. 37, 11-22-1799.

9   See Ibid., vol. 17, 11-1-1779; vol. 21, 1-31-1781; vol. 30, 8-28-1788.

10 See Ibid., vol. 15, 5-29-1779; vol. 27, 10-15-1783.

11 See Ibid., vol. 30, 1-18-1790.

12 There are many examples. For a sampling, see Ibid., vol. 26, 4-18-1783; vol. 5, 6-16-1776; vol. 5, 7-10-1776; vol. 5, 8-12-1776; vol. 5, 8-13-1776; vol. 6, 12-14-1776; vol. 9, 9-10-1777; vol. 31, 8-14-1790; vol. 27, 12-9-1783.

13 See Ibid., vol. 12, 8-20-1778; vol. 21, 3-26-1781.

14 See Ibid., vol. 4, 1-14-1776; vol. 29, 5-28-1788; vol. 30, 7-20-1788.

15 See Ibid., vol. 27, 12-6-1783.

16 See Ibid., vol. 10. 11-8-1777.

17 See Ibid., vol. 27, 10-12-1783.

18 See Ibid,. vol. 10, 11-30-1777; vol. 3, 8-20-1775; vol. 5, 8-20-1776; vol. 9, 10-19-1777; vol. 11, 4-2-1778; vol. 29, 4-28-1788; vol. 32, 6-10-1792.

19 See Ibid., vol. 31, 7-28-1791; vol. 12, 9-6-1778; vol. 36, 7-13-1798; vol. 36, 7-25-1798; vol. 36, 8-15-1798.

20 See Ibid., vol. 30, 4-16-1789.

21 See Ibid., vol. 21, 3-26-1781.

22 See Ibid., vol. 27, 7-10-1783.

23 See Ibid., vol. 27, 6-11-1783; vol. 27, 8-21-1783; vol. 11, 5-2-1778; vol. 21, 4-15-1781.

24 See George Washington Papers at the Library of Congress, 1741-1799: Series 2 Letterbooks, Letter book 38, Images 147-148.

25 Mary Thompson interview with Peter Lillback and Jerry Newcombe, 2005.

26 According to the Noah Webster's 1828 Dictionary, a Deist was "One who believes in the existence of a God, but denies revealed religion, but follows the light of nature and reason, as his only guides in doctrine and practice; a freethinker." *Noah Webster's 1828 American Dictionary.*

27 *WGW,* vol. 12, 8-20-1778.

28 Ibid., vol. 11, 8-20-1778.

29 Ibid., 31, 8-17-1790; 3, 9-15-1755; 24, 3-21-1782; 3, 7-18-1775; 5, 7-11-1776; 27, 8-21-1783; 27, 11-7-1783; 27, 11-10 1783; 31, 6-4-1790; 30, 5-9-1789; 32, 11-6-1792; 33, 9-23-1793; 35, 2-17-1797.

30 Ibid., 1, 7-18-1755; 2, 7-20-1758; 36, 8-15-1798; 5, 5-13-1776; [see also 21, 4-15-1781; 11, 5-2-1778]

31 Ibid., 37, 1-20-1799; 30, 7-20-1788; 30, 8-31-1788; 2, 9-1-1758; 3, 4-25-1773; 30, 8-18-1788.

32 Ibid., 2, 9-1-1758; 3, 4-25-1773; 7,2-24-1777; 11, 3-1-1778; 17, 11-18-1779; 7, 2-24-1777; 33, 5-26-1794; 35, 3-30-1796; 35, 3-2-1797; 36, 8-31-1797; 36, 7-4-1798; 37, 12-28-1798; 37, 1-20-1799; 37, 6-24-1799; 5, 5-13-1776.

33 Ibid., 9, 8-10-1777; 35, 3-30-1796.

34 Ibid., 27, 7-10-1783; 27, 12-6-1783; 4, 3-25-1776; 11, 3-1-1778; 12, 9-6-1778; 28, 9-5-1785; 28, 5-10-1786; 35, 3-30-1796 (3); 35, 5-15-1796; 35, 3-2-1797; 36, 2-27-1798; 36, 7-25-1798; 36, 8-15-1798; 33, 5-25-1794.

35 Ibid., 9, 10-27-1777; 10, 11-30-1777; 27, 7-10-1783; 5, 8-13-1776; 28, 8-18-1786.

36 Ibid., 23, 1-27-1793.

37 Ibid., 27, 7-8-1783; 29, 5-28-1788; 21, 4-15-1781.

38 Ibid., 4, 3-28-1776; 5, 5-13-1776; 2, 4-23-1758; 2, 6-20-1762; 4, 3-24-1776; 4, 3-25-1776; 4, 3-31-1776; 27, 12-6-1783; 30, 10-3-1789; 11, 5-30-1778; 14, 4-2-1779; 20, 10-13-1780; 21, 3-9-1781; 17, 11-18-1779; 21, 3-26-1781; 23, 10-20-1781; 27, 11-2-1783; 27, 11-10-1782; 27, 12-13-1783; 27, 12-23-1783; 29, 12-4-1786; 30, 5-9-1789; 32, 6-10-1792; 32, 1-27-1793; 5, 5-13-1776; 20, 9-26-1780; 34, 2-22-1795.

39 Ibid., 11, 3-1-1778; 12, 9-6-1778; 15, 5-29-1779; 28, 5-10-1786; 29, 6-19-1788; 33, 5-26-1794; 36, 7-4-1798; 33, 9-14-1794.

40 Ibid., 9, 10-27-1777; 28, 9-5-1785; 32, 6-10-1792; 33, 3-2-1794; 35, 5-15-1796.

41   Ibid., 26, 6-8-1783; 27, 12-6-1783; 9, 10-18-1777; 13, 10-15-1778; 37, 1-20-1799.

42   Ibid., 14, 5-4-1779; 30, 8-29-1788.

43   Ibid., 11, 3-1-1778.

44   Ibid., 21, 4-15-1781(2).

45   Ibid., 31, 7-28-1791; 36, 8-15-1798.

46   Ibid., 27, 7-10-1783; 12, 9-6-1778; 21, 3-26-1781; 36, 7-25-1798; 36, 8-15-1798.

47   Ibid., 3, 4-25-1773.

48   Ibid., 10, 2-28-1778; 27, 7-10-1783; 28, 5-10-1786; 33, -26-1794; 36, 8-15-1798.

49   Ibid., 26, 6-2-1783; 28, 8-1-1786; 36, 7-13-1798; 36, 7-25-1798.

50   Ibid., 3, 4-25-1773; 11, 3-1-1778; 17, 11-18-1779; 24, 6-30-1782; 33, 8-4-1793; 35, 3-30-1796; 35, 6-8-1796; 35, 3-2-1797; 36, 3-27-1798; 36, 8-15-1798; 37, 6-24-1799; 33, 9-14-1794; 35, 3-30-1796.

51   Ibid., 31, 8-17-1790; 27, 8-2-1783; 5, 6-16-1776; 5, 7-10-1776; 5, 8-8-1776, 5, 8-12-1776; 5, 8-13-1776; 5, 8-14-1776; 5, 8-18-1776; 5, 8-22-1776; 6, 12-14-1776; 6, 12-18-1776; 9, 10-3-1777; 9, 9-10,1777;9, 10-10-1777;10, 11-20-1777; 26, 4-18-1783; 27, 8-4-1783; 27, 12-13-1783.

52   Ibid.,., 37, 11-22-1799.

53   Ibid., 11, 8-20-1778; 2, 9-28-1758; 21, 3-26-1781; 21, 5-15-1781; 35, 10-12-1796; 9, 10-15-1777.

54   Ibid., 30, 7-20-1788; 4, 1-14-1776; 29, 5-28-1788.

55   Ibid., 9, 10-18-1777; 2, 9-10-1757; 5, 5-13-176; 11, 5-2-1778.

56   Ibid., 9, 10-27-1777; 9, 10-18-1777.

57   Ibid., 30, 10-3-1789; 4, 11-28-1775; 4, 11-13-1775; 4, 2-17-1776; 5, 7-11-1776; 23, 11-23-1781.

58   Ibid., 27, 12-6-1783; 5, 6-13-1776; 5, 6-24-1776; 11, 3-1-1778; 14, 4-2-1779; 27, 7-10-1783; 27, 8-21-1783; 27, 11-10-1783; 30, 4-16-1789; 30, 1-8-17990; 33, 9-25-1794.

59   Ibid.,30, 7-20-1788; 30, 8-31-1788; 27, 10-12-1783; 17, 11-1-1779; 17, 11-18-1779; 29, 4-28-1788; 31, 7-28-1791; 33, 9-25-1794; 11, 5-2-1778.

60   Ibid., 35, 12-13-1796.

61   Ibid.,1, 8-2-1755; 27, 10-15-1783.

62   Ibid.,30, 10-3-1789; 5, 8-20-1776; 13, 12-22-1778.

63   Ibid.,27, 10-12-1783; 12, 7-4-1778; 21, 1-31-1781; 22, 7-21-1781; 35, 4-24-1797; 36, 2-11-1798; 31, 10-25-1791.

64   Ibid.,27, 10-15-1783; 27, 2-14-1784; 35, 10-12-1796.

65   Ibid.,30, 5-9-1789; 33, 9-2-1793; 33, 9-23-1793; 33, 10-4-1794; 33, 3-2-1794; 36, 7-13-1798.

66   Ibid.,24, 6-28-1782; 30, 4-16-1789.

67   Ibid.,4, 3-28-1776; 31, 7-28-1791; 37, 12-13-1798; 9, 9-13-1777; 27, 8-1-1783; 24, 5-4-1782; 24, 6-5-1782; 30, 1-8-1790; 31, 6-4-1790; 32, 5-20-1792; 33, 8-19-1792; 33, 9-2-1793; 35, 12-15-1796; 35, 4-24-1797.

68   Ibid.,30, 6-28-1788.

69   Ibid.,1, 7-18-1775.

70   Ibid.,2, 9-10-1757; 3, 5-10-1774; 31, 10-15-1791; 33, 5-25-1794.

71   Ibid.,3, 4-25-1773; 9, 8-10-1777; 31 3-8-1792; 33,12-28-1793; 35, 3-30-1796; 35, 3-30-1796; 35, 6-8-1796; 35,3-2-1797; 36, 8-31-1797; 36, 2-27-1798; 36, 8-15-1798; 37, 6-24-1799; 33, 9-14-1794.

72   Ibid.,4, 3-7-1776.

73   Ibid.,15, 5-29-1779.

74   Ibid.,4, 3-7-1776; 34, 3-27-1796; 35, 3-30-1796; 35. 3-30-1796; 36, 2-27-1798; 37, 6-24-1799; 33, 5-25-1794.

75   Ibid.,9, 10-27-1777; 12, 9-6-1778; 30, 8-18-1788; 33, 10-4-1794; 37, 10-27-1799; 37, 11-22-1799; 33, 5-25-1794.

76   Ibid.,28, 5-10-1786.

77   Ibid.,30, 7-20-1788; 31, 7-28-1791; 21, 3-26-1781; 35, 3-3-1797.

78   Ibid.,13, 10-15-1778; 32, 8-19-1792; 33, 5-26-1794.

79   Ibid.,13, 10-15-1778.

80   Ibid.,4, 3-7-1776; 11, 4-12-1778.

81   Ibid.,3, 8-20-1775; 3, 12-10-1775; 4, 1-1-1776; 4, 2-26-1776; 5, 8-14-1776; 5, 8-22-1776; 6, 10-9-1776; 6, 12-14-1776; 6, 12-18-1776; 7, 2-14-1777; 9, 9-10-1777; 9, 10-3-1777; 9, 10-10-1777; 9, 10-15-1777; 26, 4-18-1783; 27, 11-7-1783; 28, 8-22-1785; 32, 11-6-1792; 33, 9-23-1793; 34, 12-16-1795; 35, 11-28-1796; 35, 12-13-1796; 35, 2-17-1797.

82   Ibid.,30, 10-3-1789; 11, 4-12-1778; 14, 4-2-1779; 21, 4-15-1781; 31, 10-25-1791.

83   Ibid.,4, 11-14-1775; 11, 5-30-1778; 27, 8-21-1783; 27, 11-10-1783; 27, 12-23-1783; 30, 1-18-1790; 33, 8-4-1793; 36, 10-15-1797; 11, 5-2-1778; 31, 10-25-1791.

84   Ibid.,9, 10-18-1777; 11, 5-30-1778; 21, 3-9-1781; 27, 12-23-1783; 13, 12-22-1778.

85   Ibid.,11, 5-30-1778; 27, 11-10-1783; 33, 3-2-1794.

86   Ibid.,27, 8-21-1783; 21, 4-15-1781.

87   Ibid.,27, 6-11-1783; 31, 7-28-1791.

88   Ibid.,27, 6-11-1783; 13;12-22-1778.

89   Ibid.,30,5-9-1789; 33, 9-23-1793.

90   Ibid.,11, 5-2-1778.

1111

91   Ibid.,23, 10-20-1781.
92   Ibid.,37, 1-20-1799, 5, 5-31-1776; 4, 1-14-1776; 23, 11-23-1781; 29, 6-19-1788; 36, 3-27-1798; 37, 11-22-1799.
93   Ibid.,5, 8-13-1776; 7, 3-2-1777; 30, 6-28-1788; 37, 11-22-1799.
94   Ibid.,31, 7-28-1791; 5, 5-13-1776; 37, 12-13-1798; 13, 12-18-1778; 33, 8-4-1793; 33, 9-23-1793; 35, 6-26-1797; 36, 7-13-1798; 5, 5-13-1776.
95   Ibid.,37, 1-20-1799; 3, 7-18-1775; 6, 12-18-1776; 5, 8-8-1776; 3, 6-23-1775; 9, 9-10-1777; 9, 10-3-1777; 9, 10-19-1777; 15, 7-29-1779; 30, 8-28-1788; 28, 8-18-1786; 35, 8-5-1796; 35, 10-12-1796; 36, 7-13-1798; 37, 10-27-1799; 37, 11-3-1799.
96   Ibid.,4, 4-15-1776; 21, 3-9-1781.
97   Ibid.,5, 5-13-1776; 3, 6-18-1775; 7, 1-22-1777; 33, 9-25-1794; 33, 10-4-1794; 5, 5-13-1776.
98   Ibid.,33, 5-25-1794.
99   Ibid.,2, 7-20-1758; 33, 9-2-1793; 21, 4-15-1781.
100 Ibid.,9, 9-13-1777; 32, 5-20-1792.
101 Ibid.,2, 7-20-1758; 17, 11-1-1779; 30, 4-16-1789; 32, 6-10-1792.
102 Ibid.,29, 4-28-1788.
103 Ibid.,37, 11-22-1799.
104 Ibid.,24, 7-18-1782; 27, 12-9-1783; 35, 10-12-1796.
105 Ibid.,10, 1-29-1778; 13, 11-11-1778; 14, 5-4-1779; 16, 10-20-1779; 19, 8-20-1780; 36, 2-11-1798.
106 Ibid.,30, 1-8-1790; 27, 10-25-1784.
107 Ibid.,5, 8-7-1776; 7, 1-24-1777.
108 Ibid.,12, 9-6-1778; 21, 1-31-1781.
109 Ibid.,10, 11-8-1777; 14, 5-4-1779.
110 Ibid.,10, 11-20-1777.
111 Ibid.,35, 9-19-1796.
112 Ibid.,29, 4-28-1788.
113 Ibid.,5, 5-31-1776.
114 Ibid.,7, 3-2-1777; 21, 4-15-1781.
115 Ibid., 9, 10-18-1777.
116 Ibid., 26, 6-8-1783, 36, 2-11-1798.
117 Ibid., 4, 3-28-1776; 10, 11-30-1777.
118 Ibid., 1, 8-17-1755; 3, 6-18-1775; 27, 8-21-1783; 35, 4-24-1797.
119 Ibid., 24,3-21-1782; 1, 11-9-1756; 30, 7-20-1788; 4, 4-15-1776; 5, 8-20-1776; 6, 12-18-1776; 4, 3-31-1776; 7, 1-22-1777; 1, 7-18-1755; 11, 5-30-1778; 27, 11-10-1783; 32, 6-10-1792; 33, 8-4-1793; 33, 9-23-1793; 35, 10-12-1796; 35, 3-3-1797; 35, 6-26-1797; 36, 10-15-1797; 36, 8-15-1798; 37, 12-30-1798; 37, 11-3-1799; 20, 9-26-1780.
120 Ibid., 27, 7-10-1783; 5, 5-20-1776; 5, 6-13-1776; 27, 12-6-1783; 11, 5-30-1778; 12, 9-6-1778; 30, 6-29, 1788; 35, 3-3-1797; 36, 10-15-1797; 37, 11-3-1799.
121 Ibid., 31, 7-28-1791; 5, 5-31-1776; 17, 11-1-1779.
122 Ibid., 3, 6-18-1775; 3, 6-23-1775; 35, 10-12-1796.
123 Ibid., 4, 3-28-1776; 27, 8-2-1783; 5, 7-10-1776; 12, 9-6-1778.
124 Ibid., 1, 6-12-1754.
125 Ibid., 37, 1-20-1799; 19, 8-14-1780; 7, 3-2-1777; 13, 12-18-1778; 15, 7-29-1779; 32, 6-10-1792.
126 Ibid., 27, 10-15-1783; 27, 10-15-1783; 28, 3-30-1785.
127 Ibid., 30, 4-17-1789; 21, 4-15-1781.
128 Ibid., 2, 9-10-1757; 3, 5-10-1774; 31, 10-25-1791.
129 Ibid., 30, 8-31-1788; 27, 9-23-1784; 29, 12-4-1786; 30, 3-22-1789; 37, 8-19-1799; 31, 10-15-1791; 34, 2-22-1795.
130 Ibid., 28, 5-10-1786.
131 Ibid., 33, 5-26-1794.
132 Ibid., 2, 7-20-1758; 4, 3-28-1776.
133 Ibid., 31, 8-17-1790; 4, 11-13-1775; 5, 6-24-1776; 9, 10-19-1777; 9, 9-13-1777; 24, 6-30-1782; 27, 12-13-1783; 11, 5-2-1778.
134 Ibid., 5, 6-13-1776; 12, 9-6-1778; 9, 10-15-1777.
135 Ibid., 9, 10-27-1777; 2, 11-28-1758.
136 Ibid., 9, 10-18-1777.
137 Ibid., 4, 1-14-1776.
138 Ibid., 5, 5-13-1776, 5, 5-13-1776; 21, 4-15-1781.
139 Ibid., 11, 8-20-1778.
140 Ibid., 6, 10-6-1776.
141 Ibid., 8, 7-4-1777.
142 Ibid., 10, 11-20-1777.
143 Ibid., 12, 7-4-1778.
144 Ibid., 17, 11-18-1779; 17, 11-18-1779.
145 Ibid., 20, 10-13-1780; 28, 8-18-1786; 20, 10-1-1780.

146 Ibid., 11, 8-20-1778; 7, 1-24-1777.

147 Ibid., 9, 10-15-1777.

148 Ibid., 30, 11-18-1789.

149 Ibid., 33, 9-23-1793; 36, 7-25-1798; 35, 3-3-1797.

150 Ibid., 7, 1-22-1777; 27, 8-21-1783; 30, 8-28-1788.

151 Ibid., 28,8-22-1785; 27, 11-7-1783.

152 Ibid., 5, 5-13-1776; 4, 10-5-1775; 9, 10-15-1777; 20, 9-26-1780; 20, 9-26-1780; 20, 10-10-1780.

153 Ibid., 24, 6-30-1782; 33, 5-26-1794; 35, 10-12-1796.

154 Ibid., 27, 1-21-1784; 27, 1-22-1784.

155 Ibid., 21, 4-15-1781; 35, 12-7-1796; 37, 11-3-1799.

156 Ibid., 27, 8-2-1783; 4, 11-14-1775; 5, 8-20-1776; 5, 8-8-1776; 36, 7-13-1798; 37, 11-22-1799; 21, 4-15-1781.

157 Ibid., 30, 7-20-1788.

158 Ibid., 30, 7-20-1788; 30, 1-18-1790.

159 Ibid., 32, 6-10-1792; 33, 3-2-1794.

160 Ibid., 35, 5-15-1796.

161 Ibid., 35, 8-5-1796.

162 Ibid., 35, 10-12-1796; 35, 4-24-1797.

163 Ibid., 35, 10-12-1796; 35, 4-24-1797; 37, 11-3-1799; 31, 10-25-1791; 35, 12-7-1796.

164 Ibid., 35, 12-15-1796; 36, 3-27-1798; 32, 8-26-1792.

165 Ibid., 1st inaugural address, final remarks to Congress. In light of this extensive, expansive and heartfelt belief in Providence, Flexner's claim that Washington owed the Providential language to his speech writers is simply ludicrous. Washington used his "Doctrine of Providence" throughout his life. His dramatic experiences of Providential care were expressed in his many private letters, as well as in his public speeches that were prepared for him.

166 Ibid., vol. 3, 6-18-1775.

167 Ibid., vol. 3, 6-23-1775.

168 Ibid., vol. 30, 7-20-1788.

169 Sparks, *The Writings of George Washington*, vol. III, p. 341.

170 *WGW* vol. 4, 3-31-1776 to John Augustine.

171 Ibid., vol. 8, 7-4-1777.

172 Ibid., vol. 9, 10-19-1777.

173 Ibid., vol. 9, 10-27-1777.

174 Ibid., vol. 35, 1796.

175 Ibid., vol. 26, 6-8-1783.

176 Ibid., vol. 27, 6-11-1783.

177 Ibid., vol. 29, 6-19-1788.

CHAPTER 30

1 *WGW*, vol. 10, 1-29-1778. To the Committee of Congress.

2 Jackson, Twohig, *Diaries of George Washington*, search April 3, 1768.

3 Ibid., May 29, 1768.

4 1662 *Book of Common Prayer*

5 *WGW*, vol. 29, 4-28-1788.

6 Ibid., vol. 11, 3-1-1778.

7 Ibid., vol. 35, 3-30-1796.

8 Ibid., vol. 36, 2-27-1798.

9 Ibid., vol. 36, 8-15-1798.

10 Varnum Lansing Collins, *President Witherspoon* (New York: Arno Press and The New York Times, 1969), I:197-98.

11 *WGW*, vol. 26, Circular to the States.

12 Schaff, *Creeds of Christendom*, vol. 3 p. 488.

13 *WGW*, vol. 30, Thanksgiving Proclamation.

14 Ibid., vol. 34, Sixth Annual Address to Congress.

15 Ibid., vol. 35, 3-3-1797.

16 Ibid., vol. 30, Proposed Address to Congress. Paul Boller co-wrote a book in 1989 entitled *They Never Said It* and there he included this quote. The facts are this: It is true that Washington did not use this lengthy speech that he had written. He may have used various sources along with his own text to compose it. But it is undeniable that he wrote it in his own hand, and the text is in the *Washington Papers*. Thus it is truly his writing. For him to have anticipated using it for his speech shows that it was well within his personal understanding of what he believed. So he may never "said it," but he in fact "wrote it," which is all that matters for our purposes. Thus the fact that Joseph J. Ellis refers to this proposed speech, but he does not include the text, does not minimize or negate the force of these words that Washington wrote and contemplated sending to Congress.

17 *WGW*, vol. 29, 4-25-1788.

18 Ibid., vol. 26, Circular to the States.

19 Ibid., vol. 7, 1-22-1777.

20 Ibid., vol. 12, 8-20-1778..

21 Ibid., vol. 35,11-28-1796.

22 Ibid., vol. 36, 7-25-1798.

23 Rhodehamel, *George Washington: Writings*, p. 944.

24 *WGW*, vol. 10, 1-29-1778. To the Committee of Congress.

25 See Chapter 30. For instance, Christmas in 1769 fell on Monday. Washington's diary entry for Christmas Sunday, December 24, says, "Went to Prayers, and dined afterwards at Colo. Lewis.

26 Here are the scripture passages George Washington and the other worshipers heard during the Christmas service. These passages come from the Anglican Church's *Book of Common Prayer* (1662):
    "The Nativity of our Lord, or the Birth-day of Christ, Commonly called Christmas-Day.
    The Epistle. Heb. 1. 1.
    God, who at sundry times and in divers manners spake in time past unto the fathers by the prophets, Hath in these last days spoken unto us by his Son, whom he hath appointed heir of all things, by whom also he made the worlds; Who being the brightness of his glory, and the express image of his person, and upholding all things by the word of his power, when he had by himself purged our sins, sat down on the right hand of the Majesty on high: Being made so much better than the angels, as he hath by inheritance obtained a more excellent name than they. For unto which of the angels said he at any time, Thou art my Son, this day have I begotten thee? And again, I will be to him a Father, and he shall be to me a Son? And again, when he bringeth in the first begotten into the world, he saith, And let all the angels of God worship him. And of the angels he saith, Who maketh his angels spirits, and his ministers a flame of fire. But unto the Son he saith, Thy throne, O God, is for ever and ever: a sceptre of righteousness is the sceptre of thy kingdom. Thou hast loved righteousness, and hated iniquity; therefore God, even thy God, hath anointed thee with the oil of gladness above thy fellows. And, Thou, Lord, in the beginning hast laid the foundation of the earth; and the heavens are the works of thine hands: They shall perish; but thou remainest; and they all shall wax old as doth a garment; And as a vesture shalt thou fold them up, and they shall be changed: but thou art the same, and thy years shall not fail.
    The Gospel. St. John. 1. 1.
    "In the beginning was the Word, and the Word was with God, and the Word was God. The same was in the beginning with God. All things were made by him; and without him was not any thing made that was made. In him was life; and the life was the light of men. And the light shineth in darkness; and the darkness comprehended it not. There was a man sent from God, whose name was John. The same came for a witness, to bear witness of the Light, that all men through him might believe. He was not that Light, but was sent to bear witness of that Light. That was the true Light, which lighteth every man that cometh into the world. He was in the world, and the world was made by him, and the world knew him not. He came unto his own, and his own received him not. But as many as received him, to them gave he power to become the sons of God, even to them that believe on his name: Which were born, not of blood, nor of the will of the flesh, nor of the will of man, but of God. And the Word was made flesh, and dwelt among us, (and we beheld his glory, the glory as of the only begotten of the Father,) full of grace and truth."

27 Jackson, Twohig, *Diaries of George Washington*, December 25, 1770

28 One of Washington's important victories, i.e., important for morale, was the Battle of Trenton, fought on Christmas day 1776.

29 Rhodehamel, *George Washington: Writings* ,p. 526.

30 *WGW,* vol. 35, December 19, 1796.

31 Ibid., vol. 37, January 20, 1799.

32 Ibid., vol. 37, April 25, 1799.

33 See the chapters on "Did Washington Avoid the Name of Jesus Christ?," "Washington and the Bible," and the appendix of Washington's Biblical Allusions.

34 The *Book of Common Prayer*

35 Jackson, Twohig, *Diaries of George Washington* 1768, Easter fell on April 3.

36 *GWP:* Series 1a. George Washington, School Copy Book: Volume 1, 1745 Images 50-54.

37 *WGW,* vol. 17, general Orders, November 27, 1779.

38 Jackson, Twohig, *Diaries of George Washington,* June 2, 1754.

39 *Book of Common Prayer.*

40 Norman Cousins, *In God We Trust—The Religious Beliefs and Ideas of the American Founding Fathers* (NY: Harper & Brothers, 1958), p. 60.

41 Sparks, *The Writings of George Washington*, vol. VI, p. 36.

42 We considered these in the previous chapter.

43 Schaff, *Creeds of Christendom*, vol. 3 p. 486.

44 Rhodehamel, *George Washington: Writings*, p. 582.

45 *WGW,* vol. 17, 11-27-1779.

46 Jackson, Twohig, *Diaries of George Washington,* 11-11-1751.

47 Ibid., 11-17.

48 Descriptions of Washington would not overlook the fact that he was a smallpox survivor. "I would not mention to you the person of this excellent man, were I not convinced that it bears great analogy to the qualifications of his mind. General Washington is now in the forty-

seventh year of his age; he is a tall well-made man, rather large boned, and has a tolerably genteel address: his features are manly and bold, his eyes of a bluish cast and very lively; his hair a deep brown, his face rather long and marked with the small pox; his complexion sun burnt and without much colour, and his countenance sensible, composed and thoughtful; there is a remarkable air of dignity about him, with a striking degree of gracefulness: he has an excellent understanding without much quickness; is strictly just, vigilant, and generous; an affectionate husband, a faithful friend, a father to the deserving soldier; gentle in his manners, in temper rather reserved; a total stranger to religious prejudices, which have so often excited Christians of one denomination to cut the throats of those of another; in his morals irreproachable; he was never known to exceed the bounds of the most rigid temperance: in a word, all his friends and acquaintance universally allow, that no man ever united in his own person a more perfect alliance of the virtues of a philosopher with the talents of a general." W. S. Baker, *Character Portraits of George Washington* (Philadelphia: Robert M. Lindsay, 1887), p. 12 John Bell.

49   *WGW*, vol. 6, December 20, 1776.
50   Ibid., vol. 5 June 13, 1776.
51   1660 *Book of Common Prayer*.
52   Boller, *George Washington & Religion*, p. 181.
53   Rhodehamel, *George Washington: Writings*, p. 351.
54   *WGW*, vol. 35, June 4, 1797.
55   See the chapter "George Washington and Communion."
56   Johnson, *George Washington The Christian*, p. 59.
57   Rhodehamel, *George Washington: Writings*, p. 733.
58   *WGW*, vol. 29, February 11, 1788.
59   "But providence, for purposes beyond the reach of mortal scan, has suffered the restless and malignant passions of man, the ambitious and sordid views of those who direct them, to keep the affairs of this world in a continual state of disquietude; and will, it is to be feared, place the prospects of peace too far off, and the promised millenium at an awful distance from our day."
60   "If this maxim [meddling as little as possible in their affairs where our own are not involved] was generally adopted Wars would cease, and our swords would soon be converted into reap-hooks, and our harvests be more abundant, peaceful, and happy. 'Tis wonderful it should be otherwise and the earth should be moistened with human gore, instead of the refreshing streams, wch. the shedders of it might become, instruments to lead over its plains, to delight and render profitable our labours. But alas! the millenium will not I fear appear in our days."
61   Rhodehamel, *George Washington: Writings*, p. 693.
62   See the appendix of Washington's Biblical allusions.
63   *WGW*, vol. 3, 6-20-1773. To Burwell Bassett.

CHAPTER 31

1   *WGW*, vol. 17, 11-27-1779. General Orders.
2   Joseph J. Ellis, *His Excellency: George Washington* (New York: Alfred A. Knopf, 2004), 7. In general, he talks about "Parson Weems' fabrications." Ellis, *His Excellency*, p. 11.
3   We have provided the *Daily Sacrifice* prayers in full as an appendix.
4   Washington wrote to John Sullivan, December 15, 1779, "A slender acquaintance with the world must convince every man that actions, not words are the true criterion of the attachment of his friends...." He noted to Captain John Posey, September 24, 1767: "...it is Works and not Words that People will judge from, and where one Man deceives another from time to time his word being disregarded all confidence is lost." He penned to Henry Lee a similar observation (February 13, 1789): "For I hold it necessary that one should not only be conscious of the purest *intentions*; but that one should also have it in his power to demonstrate the disinterestedness of his *words* and actions at all times, and upon all occasions." He noted to William Heath (May 20, 1797): "there will always be found a wide difference between the words and actions of any of them [the European powers]." And one final example should cement the point that deeds were more important to Washington than mere words. He noted to John Trumbull (June 25, 1799): "the words and actions of the governing powers of that Nation [France] can not be reconciled."
5   George Washington, 1763, George Washington letter to Robert Stewart, April 27, 1763, John Rhodehamel, ed., *George Washington: Writings* (New York: The Library of America, 1997), 108.
6   George Washington, speech to the Delaware Indian Chiefs, May 12, 1779, John Rhodehamel, ed., *George Washington: Writings* (New York: The Library of America, 1997), 351.
7   *WGW*, vol. 29, 5-2-1788.
8   Slaughter, *The History of Truro Parish*, p. 34.
9   Schaff's *Creeds of Christendom*, vol. III, p. 494.
10   *Book of Common Prayer* (Oxford: Thomas Baskett, 1751).
11   Online Book of Common Prayer 1662
12   See Chapter 14, note 5.
13   John Rhodehamel, ed., *George Washington: Writings* (New York: The Library of America, 1997), 279.
14   *WGW*, vol. 33, 12-23-1793.
15   Ibid., vol. 3, 9-14-1775.
16   Fitzpatrick, *The Writings of George Washington*, vol. V, pp. 244-245.
17   *WGW*, vol. 14, 4-12-1779.
18   Benson J. Lossing, *The Pictorial Field-Book of the Revolution* (1886), vol. II, p. 140.

19   *WGW*, vol. 12, 9-6-1778.

20   Rhodehamel, *George Washington: Writings*, p. 526.

21   *WGW*, vol. 30, 10-23-1789.

22   Ibid., vol. 34, 12-24-1795. To Dr. James Anderson.

23   Ibid., vol. 34, 12-24-1795. To Dr. James Anderson.

24   Ibid., vol. 17, 11-27-1779. General Orders. "Whereas it becomes us humbly to approach the throne of Almighty God, with gratitude and praise for the wonders which his goodness has wrought in conducting our fore-fathers to this western world; for his protection to them and to their posterity amid difficulties and dangers; for raising us, their children, from deep distress to be numbered among the nations of the earth; and for arming the hands of just and mighty princes in our deliverance; and especially for that he hath been pleased to grant us the enjoyment of health, and so to order the revolving seasons, that the earth hath produced her increase in abundance, blessing the labors of the husbandmen, and spreading plenty through the land; that he hath prospered our arms and those of our ally; been a shield to our troops in the hour of danger, pointed their swords to victory and led them in triumph over the bulwarks of the foe; that he hath gone with those who went out into the wilderness against the savage tribes; that he hath stayed the hand of the spoiler, and turned back his meditated destruction; that he hath prospered our commerce, and given success to those who sought the enemy on the face of the deep; and above all, that he hath diffused the glorious light of the gospel, whereby, through the merits of our gracious Redeemer, we may become the heirs of his eternal glory: therefore,

RESOLVED, That it be recommended to the several states, to appoint Thursday, the 9th of December next, to be a day of public and solemn thanksgiving to Almighty God for his mercies, and of prayer for the continuance of his favor and protection to these United States; to beseech him that he would be graciously pleased to influence our public councils, and bless them with wisdom from on high, with unanimity, firmness, and success; that he would go forth with our hosts and crown our arms with victory; that he would grant to his church the plentiful effusions of divine grace, and pour out his holy spirit on all ministers of the gospel; that he would bless and prosper the means of education, and spread the light of Christian knowledge through the remotest corners of the earth; that he would smile upon the labours of his people and cause the earth to bring forth her fruits in abundance; that we may with gratitude and gladness enjoy them; that he would take into his holy protection our illustrious ally, give him victory over his enemies, and render him signally great, as the father of his people and the protector of the rights of mankind; that he would graciously be pleased to turn the hearts of our enemies, and to dispense the blessings of peace to contending nations; that he would in mercy look down upon us, pardon our sins and receive us into his favor, and finally, that he would establish the independence of these United States upon the basis of religion and virtue, and support and protect them in the enjoyment of peace, liberty and safety."

Ibid., vol. 28, 6-30-1785. To the Countess of Huntingdon. "My Lady: In the last letter which I had the honor to write to you, I informed your Ladyship of the communication I had made to the President of Congress of your wishes to obtain Lands in the Western Territory for a number of Emigrants as a means of civilizing the Savages, and propagating the Gospel among them."

Ibid., vol. 29, 5-2-1788. To Reverend John Ettwein. "Reverend Sir: I have received your obliging letter of the 28th of March, enclosing a copy of some remarks on the Customs, Languages &c. of the Indians, and a printed pamphlet containing the stated rules of a Society for propagating the Gospel among the Heathen for which tokens of polite attention and kind remembrance I must beg you to accept my best thanks."

So far as I am capable of judging, the principles upon which the society is founded and the rules laid down for its government, appear to be well calculated to promote so laudable and arduous an undertaking, and you will permit me to add that if an event so long and so earnestly desired as that of converting the Indians to Christianity and consequently to civilization, can be effected, the Society of Bethlehem bids fair to bear a very considerable part in it."

Ibid., vol. 30, 7-6-1789. To the Society of United Brethren for Propagating the Gospel. *WGW*, note, "On July 10 an address from the directors of the Society of United Brethren for Propagating the Gospel Among the Heathen was sent to the President from Bethlehem, Pa. …One paragraph of the reply stated: "In proportion as the general Government of the United States shall acquire strength by duration, it is probable they may have it in their power to extend a salutary influence to the Aborigines in the extremities of their Territory. In the meantime, it will be a desirable thing for the protection of the Union to co-operate, as far as circumstances may conveniently admit, with the disinterested endeavours of your Society to civilize and Christianize the Savages of the Wilderness."

Ibid., vol. 30, 10-23-1789. To the First Presbytery of the Eastward. "I am persuaded, you will permit me to observe that the path of true piety is so plain as to require but little political direction. To this consideration we ought to ascribe the absence of any regulation, respecting religion, from the Magna- Charta of our country. To the guidance of the ministers of the gospel this important object is, perhaps, more properly committed. It will be your care to instruct the ignorant, and to reclaim the devious, and, in the progress of morality and science, to which our government will give every furtherance, we may confidently expect the advancement of true religion, and the completion of our happiness."

Ibid., vol. 37, 8-28-1762. To Burwell Bassett. "Dear Sir: I was favoured with your Epistle wrote on a certain 25th of July when you ought to have been at Church, praying as becomes every good Christian Man who has as much to answer for as you have; strange it is that you will be so blind to truth that the enlightning sounds of the Gospel cannot reach your Ear, nor no Examples awaken you to a sense of Goodness; could you but behold with what religious zeal I hye me to Church on every Lords day, it would do your heart good, and fill it I hope with equal fervency."

25   Ibid., vol. 26, 6-8-1783. Circular to the States.

26   Ibid., vol. 5, 5-12-1779. Speech to the Delaware Chiefs.

27   Ibid., vol. 30, 4-1789. Proposed Speech to Congress.

28   Ibid., vol. 24, 6-28-1782. To Ministers of the Reformed Dutch Church.

29 Ibid., vol. 3, 9-14-1775. To Benedict Arnold.

30 Ibid., vol. 29, 4-25-1788. To Marquis de Chastellux.

31 Ibid., vol. 26, 6-8-1783. Circular to the States.

32 Ibid., vol. 32, 6-21-1792. To Gouverneur Morris.

33 Some 25 times, Washington will refer in his writings to "my soul" and thereby gives us a look into his inner life. For example, Ibid., vol. 1, 5-29-1754. To Robert Dinwiddie. "…for I assure you, Hon'ble Sir, nothing is a greater stranger to my Breast, or a Sin that *my Soul* abhors, than that black and detestable one Ingratitude." Ibid., vol. 2, 4-27-1763. To Robert Stewart. "…but alas! to shew my inability in this respect, I inclose you a copy of Mr. Cary's last Acct. currt. against me, which upon my honr and the faith of a Christian is a true one, and transmitted to me with the additional aggravation of a hint at the largeness of it. Messrs. Hanbury's have also a Ball'e against me, and I have no other corrispondants in England with whom I deal, unless it be with a namesake for trifles such as Cloaths; and for these I do not know whether the Balle. is for or against me. This upon *my Soul* is a genuine Acct. of my Affairs in England, here." Ibid., vol. 7, 4-15-1777. To Landon Carter. "Your friendly and affectionate wishes for my health and success has a claim to my most grateful acknowledgements. That the God of Armies may Incline the Hearts of my American Brethren to support, and bestow sufficient abilities on me to bring the present contest to a speedy and happy conclusion, thereby enabling me to sink into sweet retirement, and the full enjoyment of that Peace and happiness which will accompany a domestick Life, is the first wish, and most fervent prayer of *my Soul.*"

34 *WGW*, vol. 26, 6-8-1783. Circular to the States.

35 Ibid., vol. 29, 2-11-1788. To Benjamin Lincoln.

36 Ibid., vol. 30, 11-3-1789. Thanksgiving Proclamation.

37 Ibid., vol. 35, 3-3-1797. To the Clergy of Philadelphia.

38 Ibid., vol. 26, 1-10-1783. To Maj. Gen. John Armstrong.

39 GWP Series 1a, George Washington, Forms of Writing, and The Rules of Civility and Decent Behavior in Company and Conversation, ante 1747, Image 25 of 36. (may be found online at www.loc.gov).

40 *WGW*, vol. 6, 12-25-1776. To Robert Morris.

41 Ibid., vol.23, 12-24-1781. To Major General William Heath.

42 Ibid., vol. 37, 8-28-1762. To Burwell Bassett.

43 Ibid., vol. 17, 11-27-1779. General Orders.

44 Image 9 in *George Washington Papers* at the Library of Congress, 1741-1799: Series 1a, George Washington, Forms of Writing, and The Rules of Civility and Decent Behavior in Company and Conversation, ante 1747

45 *WGW*, vol. 30, 11-23-1789.

46 Ibid., vol. 13, 11-12-1778. To Reverend Alexander McWhorter.

47 Ibid., vol. 30, 11-23-1789.

48 Ibid., vol. 28, 6-30-1785. To the Countess of Huntingdon.

49 Ibid., vol. 28, 1-25-1785. To James Jay.

50 Ibid., vol. 3, 7-16-1775. vol. 3, General Orders. "The Continental Congress having earnestly recommended, that 'Thursday next the 20th. Instant, be observed by the Inhabitants of all the english Colonies upon this Continent, as a Day of public Humiliation, Fasting and Prayer; that they may with united Hearts and Voice unfeignedly confess their *Sins* before God, and supplicate the all wise and merciful disposer of events, to avert the Desolation and Calamities of an unnatural war'." Ibid., vol. 4, 3-6-1776. General Orders. "Thursday the seventh Instant, being set apart by the Honourable the Legislature of this province, as a day of fasting, prayer, and humiliation, 'to implore the Lord, and Giver of all victory, to pardon our manifold *sins* and wickedness's, and that it would please him to bless the Continental Arms, with his divine favour and protection."Ibid., vol. 5, 5-15-1776. General Orders. "The Continental Congress having ordered, Friday the 17th. Instant to be observed as a day of 'fasting, humiliation and prayer, humbly to supplicate the mercy of Almighty God, that it would please him to pardon all our manifold *sins* and transgressions, and to prosper the Arms of the United Colonies, and, finally, establish the peace and freedom of America, upon a solid and lasting foundation.'" Ibid., vol. 10, 11-30-1777. General Orders. "It is therefore recommended by Congress, that Thursday the 18th. day of December next be set apart for Solemn Thanksgiving and Praise; that at one time, and with one voice, the good people may express the grateful feelings of their hearts, and consecrate themselves to the service of their divine benefactor; and that, together with their sincere acknowledgements and offerings they may join the penitent confession of their *sins*; and supplications for such further blessings as they stand in need of. The Chaplains will properly notice this recommendation, that the day of thanksgiving may be duly observed in the army, agreeably to the intentions of Congress." Ibid., vol. 14, 4-12-1779. General Orders The Honorable the Congress having recommended it to the United States to set apart Thursday the 6th. day of May next to be observed as a day of fasting, humiliation and prayer, to acknowledge the gracious interpositions of *Providence* ; to deprecate deserved punishment for our *Sins* and Ingratitude, to unitedly implore the Protection of Heaven; Success to our Arms and the Arms of our Ally: The Commander in Chief enjoins a religious observance of said day and directs the Chaplains to prepare discourses proper for the occasion; strictly forbidding all recreations and unnecessary labor. Ibid., vol. 17, 11-27-1779. General Orders. "RESOLVED, That it be recommended to the several states, to appoint Thursday, the 9th of December next, to be a day of public and solemn thanksgiving to Almighty God for his mercies, and of prayer for the continuance of his favor and protection to these United States… and to dispense the blessings of peace to contending nations; that he would in mercy look down upon us, pardon our *sins* and receive us into his favor, and finally, that he would establish the independence of these United States upon the basis of religion and virtue, and support and protect them in the enjoyment of peace, liberty and safety." Ibid., vol. 25, 12-18-1782. To Bartholomew Dandridge. "…for be assured Sir that a Man so devoid of principle as he is to be guilty, not only of the barefaced frauds with which he is accused; but the *abominable Sin of ingratitude*, will neglect no oppertunity of converting to his own use when he can do it with impunity every species of property that is committed to his care; and will do it the

more readily after his reputation will have Suffered, than before. The most hardened villain, altho' he *Sins* without remorse, wishes to cloak his iniquity, if possible, under specious appearances; but when character is no more, he bids defiance to the opinions of Mankind, and is under no other restraint than that of the Law, and the punishments it inflicts. Posey, I am perswaded, will be no exception to this rule; and that the sooner the Estate can be taken out of his hands the less it will suffer; as it cannot be in worse." Ibid., vol. 1, 5-29-1754. To Robert Dinwiddie. "I am much concern'd, that your Honour should seem to charge me with ingratitude for your generous, and my undeserved favours; for I assure you, Hon'ble Sir, nothing is a greater stranger to my Breast, or a *Sin* that my Soul abhors, than that black and detestable one Ingratitude." Ibid., vol. 31, 6-19-1791. To Tobias Lear. I shall communicate the same sentiments to those who are with me, that, if they do *sin*, it shall be with their eyes open, and under a knowledge of the consequences. Ibid., vol. 25, 1782. To Bartholomew Dandridge. "...the abominable *Sin* of ingratitude, will neglect no oppertunity of converting to his own use when he can do it with impunity every species of property that is committed to his care; and will do it the more readily after his reputation will have Suffered, than before. The most hardened villain, altho' he *Sins* without remorse, wishes to cloak his iniquity, if possible, under specious appearances; but when character is no more, he bids defiance to the opinions of Mankind, and is under no other restraint than that of the Law, and the punishments it inflicts."

51   Ibid., vol. 24, 6-13-1782. To Brig. Gen. Jacob Bayley. "I can only advise you to attend very critically to the Movements of the Enemy on your Borders, and to the internal Machinations of evil Men and Emissaries who may be sent among you, or be contained in your own Bosoms. And to counteract them by every Means in your power; And at the same time to keep the Exertions of the people active and alert, and always prepared for speedy Action, in Case of an Appearance of the Enemy on your frontiers."

52   Ibid., vol. 5, 7-19-1776. "Lord Howe is arrived. He and the Genl. his Brother are appointed Commissioners to dispense pardons to Repenting *Sinners*." Ibid., vol. 28, 12-17-1785. "I never should have thought of this mode of punishment, had I not viewed the Defendants as wilful and obstinate *sinners*; presevering after timely and repeated admonition, in a design to injure me, ..."

53   Ibid., vol. 10, 1-29-1778. To the Committee of Congress. "It is vain to exclaim against the depravity of human nature ... the experience of every age and nation has proved it .... No institution, not built on the presumptive truth of these maxims can succeed."

54   Ibid., vol. 14, 3-31-1779. To James Warren. "Our conflict is not likely to cease so soon as every good Man would wish. The measure of *iniquity* is not yet filled; and unless we can return a little more to first principles, and act a little more upon patriotic ground, I do not know when it will, or, what may be the Issue of the contest." Ibid., vol. 30, 6-28-1788. To Charles Cotesworth Pinckney. "After New York shall have acted, then only one little State will remain; suffice it to say, *it is universally believed, that the scales are ready to drop from the eyes and the infatuation to be removed from the heart, of Rhode Island* . May this be the case, before that inconsiderate People shall have filled up the measure of *iniquity* before it shall be too late!"

55   Ibid., vol. 10, 1-29-1778. "It is vain to exclaim against the depravity of human nature on this account; the fact is so, the experience of every age and nation has proved it and we must in a great measure...." Ibid., vol. 3, 5-5-1772. To Thomas Johnson. "I cannot help adding, that, his Principles have been loose; whether from a natural depravity, or distress'd circumstances, I shall not undertake to determine; change the constitution of man, before we can make it otherwise. No institution, not built on the presumptive truth of these maxims can succeed." Ibid., vol. 10, 1-29-1778. To the Committee of Congress. "A small knowledge of human nature will convince us, that, with far the greatest part of mankind, interest is the governing principle; and that almost every man is more or less, under its influence. Motives of public virtue may for a time, or in particular instances, actuate men to the observance of a conduct purely disinterested; but they are not of themselves sufficient to produce a persevering conformity to the refined dictates and obligations of social duty. Few men are capable of making a continual sacrifice of all views of private interest, or advantage, to the common good. It is vain to exclaim against the depravity of human nature on this account; the fact is so, the experience of every age and nation has proved it and we must in a great measure, change the constitution of man, before we can make it otherwise. No institution, not built on the presumptive truth of these maxims can succeed." Ibid., vol. 15, 5-28-1779. To Lt. col. Nicholas Rogers. "Difficult as it is to strike a likeness on so small a scale, it is the opinion of many that you have not failed in the present attempt. The dress is not less pleasing for being a copy of antiquity, it would be happy for us, if in these days of depravity the imitation of our ancestors were extensively adopted; their virtues wd. not hurt us." *Ibid.,*vol. 26, 3-19-1783. To the Secretary for Foreign Affairs. "By Hook or by Crook, they are certain of acquittal. In truth I am quite discouraged, and have scarce any thing left but lamentation for the want of Virtue and depravity of my Countrymen." Ibid., vol. 29, 11-15-1786. To Bushrod Washington. "It was to these things that we owe the present depravity of the minds of so many people of this Country, and filled it with so many knaves and designing characters." Ibid., vol. 30, 4-1789. Proposed Address to Congress. "The blessed Religion revealed in the word of God will remain an eternal and awful monument to prove that the best Institutions may be abused by human depravity; and that they may even, in some instances be made subservient to the vilest of purposes. Should, hereafter, those who are intrusted with the management of this government, incited by the lust of power and prompted by the Supineness or venality of their Constituents, overleap the known barriers of this Constitution and violate the unalienable rights of humanity: it will only serve to shew, that no compact among men (however provident in its construction and sacred in its ratification) can be pronounced everlasting and inviolable, and if I may so express myself, that no Wall of words, that no mound of parchmt. can be so formed as to stand against the sweeping torrent of boundless ambition on the one side, aided by the sapping current of corrupted morals on the other." Ibid., vol. 29, 4-28-1788. To Marquis de Lafayette. "As for instance, on the ineligibility of the same person for President, after he should have served a certain course of years. Guarded so effectually as the proposed Constitution is, in respect to the prevention of bribery and undue influence in the choice of President: I confess, I differ widely myself from Mr. Jefferson and you, as to the necessity or expediency of rotation in that appointment. The matter was fairly discussed in the Convention, and to my full convictions; though I cannot have time or room to sum up the argument in this letter. There cannot, in my judgment, be the least danger that the President will by any practicable intrigue ever be able to continue himself one moment in office, much less perpetuate himself in it; but in the last stage of corrupted morals and political depravity: and even then there is as much danger that any other species of domination would prevail. Though, when a people shall have become incapable of governing themselves and fit for a master, it is of little con-

sequence from what quarter he comes. Under an extended view of this part of the subject, I can see no propriety in precluding ourselves from the services of any man, who on some great emergency shall be deemed universally, most capable of serving the Public. Ibid., vol. 29, 12-16-1786. To James Madison. "These, and such like things, in my humble opinion, are extremely hurtful, and are among the principal causes that present depravity and corruption without accomplishing the object in view for it is not the shadow, but the substance with which Taxes must be paid, if we mean to be honest. With sentiments of sincere esteem etc." Ibid., vol. 29, 12-26-1786. To Henry Knox. "I feel, my dear Genl. Knox, infinitely more than I can express to you, for the disorders which have arisen in these States. Good God! who besides a tory could have foreseen, or a Briton predicted them! were these people wiser than others, or did they judge of us from the corruption, and depravity of their own hearts? The latter I am persuaded was the case, and that notwithstanding the boasted virtue of America, we are far gone in every thing ignoble and bad."

56 Ibid., vol. 13, 12-17-1778. "I see so many instances of the rascallity of Mankind, that I am almost out of conceit of my own species; and am convinced that the only way to make men honest, is to prevent their being otherwise, by tying them firmly to the accomplishmt. of their contracts."

57 Ibid., vol. 24, 8-7-1782. To John Price Posey. "If what I have heard, or the half of it be true, you must not only be lost to the feelings of virtue, honor and common honesty; but you must have suffered an unwarrantable thirst of gain to lead you into errors which are so pregnant with folly and indiscretion, as to render you a mark for every mans arrow to level at. Can you suppose Sir, that a Manager, can dissipate his Employers Estate with impunity? That there are not Laws in every free Country by which justice is to be obtained? or, that the Heirs of Mr. Custis will not find friends who will pursue you to the end of the Earth in order to come at it? If you do, you are proceeding upon exceedingly mistaken principles. but, for a moment only let us suppose that you have taken the advantage of an unsuspecting friend; for such I am sure Mr. Custis was *to you* . and, that you have acted so covertly, as to elude the Law; do you believe that in the hours of cool reflection, in the moment perhaps, when you shall find that ill-gotten pelf can no longer avail you; that your *conscience* will not smite you severely for such complicated inequity as arises not only from acts of injustice, but the horrors of ingratitude; in abusing the confidence of a man who supposed you incapable of deceiving him, and who was willing, and I believe did, in a great degree, commit his whole property to your care? But this by the by, I do not mean to put this matter upon the footing of *Conscience. Conscience*, must have been kicked out of doors before you could have proceeded to the length of selling another Mans Negros for your own emolument and this too after having applyed the greatest part, or the whole of the profits of his Estate to your own benefit. *Conscience* again seldom comes to a Mans aid while he is in the zenith of health, and revelling in pomp and luxury upon ill gotten spoils; it is generally the *last* act of his life and comes too late to be of much service to others here, or to himself hereafter."

58 Ibid., vol. 35, 12-19-1796. To George Washington Parke Custis.

59 Ibid., vol. 4, Answer to an Address from the Massachusetts Legislature. "May that being, who is *powerful to save*, and in whose hands is the fate of nations, look down with an eye of tender pity and compassion upon the whole of the United Colonies; may He continue to smile upon their counsels and arms, and crown them with success, whilst employed in the cause of virtue and mankind. May this distressed colony and its capital, and every part of this wide extended continent, through His divine favor, be restored to more than their former lustre and once happy state, and have peace, liberty, and safety secured upon a solid, permanent, and lasting foundation."

60 Ibid., vol. 31, 7-28-1791. to Marquis de Lafayette.

61 Ibid., vol. 33, 11-6-1793. To the Trustees of the Public School of Germantown.

62 Ibid., vol. 35, 12-7-1796. Eighth Annual Address to Congress.

63 *PGW*, 2:179-181. To the Lutheran Church; *PGW*, 2:411-412, To the Methodist Bishops.

64 *WGW*, vol. 17, 11-27-1779. General Orders. "and above all, that he hath diffused the glorious light of the gospel, whereby, through the merits of our *gracious* Redeemer, we may become the heirs of his eternal glory: therefore,
RESOLVED, That it be recommended to the several states, to appoint Thursday, the 9th of December next, to be a day of public and solemn thanksgiving to Almighty God for his mercies, and of prayer for the continuance of his favor and protection to these United States; to beseech him that he would be *graciously* pleased to influence our public councils, and bless them with wisdom from on high, with unanimity, firmness, and success; ... that he would *graciously* be pleased to turn the hearts of our enemies, and to dispense the blessings of peace to contending nations; that he would in mercy look down upon us, pardon our sins and receive us into his favor, and finally, that he would establish the independence of these United States upon the basis of religion and virtue, and support and protect them in the enjoyment of peace, liberty and safety.
Ibid., vol. 4, 11-18-1775. General Orders. "a day of public thanksgiving "to offer up our praises, and prayers to Almighty God, the Source and Benevolent Bestower of all good; That he would be pleased *graciously* to continue, to smile upon our Endeavours, to restore peace, preserve our Rights, and Privileges, to the latest posterity."
Ibid., vol. 5, 6-13-1776. To Brig. Gen. John Sullivan. "...and wishing you and your Brothers, under the Direction of a *gracious* Providence, to lead your Army to Conquest and Victory."
Ibid., vol. 5, 7-10-1776. "... it behoves us to adopt such, as under the smiles of a *Gracious* and all kind Providence will be most likely to promote our happiness."
Ibid., vol. 7, 4-23-1777. "All agree our claims are righteous and must be supported; Yet all, or at least, too great a part among us, withhold the means, as if Providence, who has already done much for us, would continue his *gracious* interposition and work miracles for our deliverance, without troubling ourselves about the matter."
Ibid., vol. 11, 3-1-1778. To Bryan Fairfax. "The determinations of Providence are all ways wise; often inscrutable, and though its decrees appear to bear hard upon us at times is nevertheless meant for *gracious* purposes; in this light I cannot help viewing your late disappointment...."
Ibid., vol. 4-12-1779. General Orders. "...a day of fasting, humiliation and prayer, to acknowledge the *gracious* interpositions of *Providence*

; to deprecate deserved punishment for our Sins and Ingratitude...."

Ibid., vol. 26, 1-10-1783. To Maj. Gen. John Armstrong. "I offer you the compliments of the Season and wish you may possess health and spirits to enjoy, after we shall have seated ourselves under our own Vines and Figtrees, if it is the *gracious* will of Providence to permit it, the return of many happy years."

Ibid., vol. 26, 6-8-1783. Circular to the States. "I now make it my earnest prayer, that God would have you, and the State over which you preside, in his holy protection, ...that he would most *graciously* be pleased to dispose us all, to do Justice, to love mercy, and to demean ourselves with that Charity, humility and pacific temper of mind, which were the Characteristicks of the Divine Author of our blessed Religion...."

Ibid., vol. 27, 11-10-1783. To Ministers of the Dutch Reformed Churches. "Having shared in common, the hardships and dangers of the War with my virtuous fellow Citizens in the field, as well as with those who on the Lines have been immediately exposed to the Arts and Arms of the Enemy, I feel the most lively sentiments of gratitude to that divine Providence which has *graciously* interposed for the protection of our Civil and Religious Liberties."

Ibid., vol. 27, 12-6-1783. To the Legislature of New Jersey. "I am heartily disposed to join with you, Gentlemen, in adoration to that all-wise and most *gracious* Providence which hath so conspicuously interposed in the direction of our public affairs and the establishment of our national Independence."

Ibid., vol. 30, 4-16-1789. To the Mayor of Alexandria. "All that now remains for me is to commit myself and you to the protection of that beneficent Being, who, on a former occasion has happly brought us together, after a long and distressing separation. Perhaps the same *gracious* Providence will again indulge us with the same heartfelt felicity. But words, my fellow- citizens, fail me: *Unutterable sensations must then be left to more expressive silence: while, from an aching heart, I bid you all, my affectionate friends and kind neighbours, farewell!*"

Ibid., vol. 30, 1-8-1790. "... to secure the blessings which a *Gracious* Providence has placed within our reach, will in the course of the present important Session, call for the cool and deliberate exertion of your patriotism, firmness and wisdom."

Ibid.,vol. 32, 1-27-1793. To the New Church in Baltimore. "Your prayers for my present and future felicity are received with gratitude; and I sincerely wish, Gentlemen, that you may in your social and individual capacities taste those blessings, which a *gracious* God bestows upon the Righteous."

Ibid., vol. 33, 9-25-1794. Proclamation. "Now, therefore, I, *George Washington*, President of the United States, in obedience to that high and irresistible duty, consigned to me by the Constitution, "to take care that the laws be faithfully executed;" deploring that the American name should be sullied by the outrages of citizens on their: own Government; commiserating such as remain obstinate from delusion; but resolved, in perfect reliance on that *gracious* Providence which so signally displays its goodness towards this country, to reduce the refractory to a due subordination to the laws...."

Ibid., vol. 34, 11-199-1794. Sixth Annual Address to Congress. "Fellow Citizens of the Senate and of the House of Representatives: When we call to mind the *gracious* indulgence of Heaven, by which the American People became a nation; when we survey the general prosperity of our country, and look forward to the riches, power, and happiness, to which it seems destined; with the deepest regret do I announce to you, that during your recess, some of the citizens of the United States have been found capable of an insurrection."

65   Ibid., vol. 3, 7-26-1775. General Orders. "The Court Martial upon the prisoners pleading Guilty and promising to behave obediently for the future, recommended him to the General's *mercy*, who is pleased to pardon the prisoner."

Ibid., vol. 4, 3-6-1776. General Orders. "Thursday the seventh Instant, being set apart by the Honourable the Legislature of this province, as a day of fasting, prayer, and humiliation, "to implore the Lord, and Giver of all victory, to pardon our manifold sins and wickedness's, and that it would please him to bless the Continental Arms, with his divine favour and protection" — All Officers, and Soldiers, are strictly enjoined to pay all due reverance, and attention on that day, to the sacred duties due to the Lord of hosts, for his mercies already received, and for those blessings, which our Holiness and Uprightness of life can alone encourage us to hope through his *mercy* to obtain."

Ibid., vol. 5, 5-15-1776. "The Continental Congress having ordered, Friday the 17th. Instant to be observed as a day of "fasting, humiliation and prayer, humbly to supplicate the *mercy* of Almighty God, that it would please him to pardon all our manifold sins and transgressions, and to prosper the Arms of the United Colonies, and finally, establish the peace and freedom of America, upon a solid and lasting foundation" — The General commands all officers, and soldiers, to pay strict obedience to the Orders of the Continental Congress, and by their unfeigned, and pious observance of their religious duties, incline the Lord, and Giver of Victory, to prosper our arms."

Ibid., vol. 9, 8-10-1777. "From the Representation made to me respecting Brown and Murphy, I then thought that it became necessary to execute one of them by way of Example, but as you are of Opinion that the necessity is in some degree removed, and from late discoveries, that there is a possibility of their not being guilty, you have my free consent to pardon them both, as it is my most sincere wish, that whenever we are guilty of an Error in matters of this Nature, it may be on the Side of *Mercy* and forgiveness."

Ibid., vol. 9, 8-17-1777. General Orders. "William Rickett of the 12th. Pennsylv. Battalion, charged with "being a sleep on his post when over prisoners," pleaded guilty, and begged for *mercy*; sentenced to receive thirty nine lashes on his bare back."

Ibid., vol. 9, 9-3-1777. General Orders. "James Martin of the 2nd. Pennsylv. regt. charged with"Being drunk and asleep on his post while sentinel over prisoners," found guilty, and sentenced to receive one hundred lashes on his bare back; and to have the hair from the front part of his head shaved off without soap, and tar and feathers substituted in the room of the hair. Henry Hargood charged with "Desertion from the German regiment"; found guilty, and sentenced to suffer death: But for the reasons mentioned by the court, they recommend him to the Commander in Chief's clemency and *mercy*. The Commander in Chief pardons the offender."

Ibid., vol. 10, 11-3-1777. General Orders. "Forasmuch as it is the indispensible duty of all men, to adore the superintending providence of Almighty God; to acknowledge with gratitude their obligations to him for benefits received, and to implore such further blessings as they stand in need of; and it having pleased him in his abundant *mercy*, not only to continue to us the innumerable bounties of his common providence, but also, to smile upon us in the prosecution of a just and necessary war, for the defence of our unalienable rights and liberties."

Ibid., vol. 11, 4-12-1778. General Orders. "The Honorable Congress having thought proper to recommend to The United States of America to set apart Wednesday the 22nd. instant to be observed as a day of Fasting, Humiliation and Prayer, that at one time and with one voice the righteous dispensations of Providence may be acknowledged and His Goodness and *Mercy* toward us and our Arms supplicated and implored; The General directs that this day *also* shall be religiously observed in the Army, that no work be done thereon and that the Chaplains prepare discourses suitable to the Occasion."

Ibid., vol. 17, 11-27-1779. General Orders. "Whereas it becomes us humbly to approach the throne of Almighty God, with gratitude and praise for the wonders which his goodness has wrought in conducting our fore-fathers to this western world; for his protection to them and to their posterity amid difficulties and dangers; for raising us, their children, from deep distress to be numbered among the nations of the earth; and for arming the hands of just and mighty princes in our deliverance; and especially for that he hath been pleased to grant us the enjoyment of health, and so to order the revolving seasons, that the earth hath produced her increase in abundance, blessing the labors of the husbandmen, and spreading plenty through the land; that he hath prospered our arms and those of our ally; been a shield to our troops in the hour of danger, pointed their swords to victory and led them in triumph over the bulwarks of the foe; that he hath gone with those who went out into the wilderness against the savage tribes; that he hath stayed the hand of the spoiler, and turned back his meditated destruction; that he hath prospered our commerce, and given success to those who sought the enemy on the face of the deep; and above all, that he hath diffused the glorious light of the gospel, whereby, through the merits of our gracious Redeemer, we may become the heirs of his eternal glory: therefore,

RESOLVED, That it be recommended to the several states, to appoint Thursday, the 9th of December next, to be a day of public and solemn thanksgiving to Almighty God for his mercies, and of prayer for the continuance of his favor and protection to these United States; to beseech him that he would be graciously pleased to influence our public councils, and bless them with wisdom from on high, with unanimity, firmness, and success; that he would go forth with our hosts and crown our arms with victory; that he would grant to his church the plentiful effusions of divine grace, and pour out his holy spirit on all ministers of the gospel; that he would bless and prosper the means of education, and spread the light of christian knowledge through the remotest corners of the earth; that he would smile upon the labours of his people and cause the earth to bring forth her fruits in abundance; that we may with gratitude and gladness enjoy them; that he would take into his holy protection our illustrious ally, give him victory over his enemies, and render him signally great, as the father of his people and the protector of the rights of mankind; that he would graciously be pleased to turn the hearts of our enemies, and to dispense the blessings of peace to contending nations; that he would in mercy look down upon us, pardon our sins and receive us into his favor, and finally, that he would establish the independence of these United States upon the basis of religion and virtue, and support and protect them in the enjoyment of peace, liberty and safety

Ibid., vol. 26, 6-8-1783. "I now make it my earnest prayer, that God would have you, and the State over which you preside, in his holy protection, that he would incline the hearts of the Citizens to cultivate a spirit of subordination and obedience to Government, to entertain a brotherly affection and love for one another, for their fellow Citizens of the United States at large, and particularly for their brethren who have served in the Field, and finally, that he would most graciously be pleased to dispose us all, to do Justice, to love mercy, and to demean ourselves with that Charity, humility and pacific temper of mind, which were the Characteristicks of the Divine Author of our blessed Religion, and without an humble imitation of whose example in these things, we can never hope to be a happy Nation."

66   Propitious means kind or gracious.

Ibid., vol. 11, 5-5-1778. General Orders. "It having pleased the Almighty ruler of the Universe propitiously to defend the Cause of the United American-States and finally by raising us up a powerful Friend among the Princes of the Earth to establish our liberty and Independence up lasting foundations, it becomes us to set apart a day for gratefully acknowledging the divine Goodness and celebrating the important Event which we owe to his benign Interposition."

Ibid., vol. 27, 8-2-1783. To John Gabriel Tegelaar. "May Heaven, whose propitious smiles have hitherto watched over the freedom of your republic still Guard her Liberties with the most sacred protection. And while I thus regard the welfare of your Country at large, permit me to assure you, that I shall feel a very particular desire that Providence may ever smile on your private happiness and domestic pleasures."

Ibid., vol. 30, 4-30-1789. The First Inaugural Address. "Since we ought to be no less persuaded that the propitious smiles of Heaven, can never be expected on a nation that disregards the eternal rules of order and right, which Heaven itself has ordained: And since the preservation of the sacred fire of liberty, and the destiny of the Republican model of Government, are justly considered as *deeply*, perhaps as *finally* staked, on the experiment entrusted to the hands of the American people."

67   Ibid., vol. 29, 8-15-1787. To Marquis de Lafayette. "Being no bigot myself to any mode of worship, I am disposed to indulge the professors of Christianity in the church, that road to Heaven, which to them shall seem the most direct plainest easiest and least liable to exception."

68   *George Washington Papers* at the Library of Congress, 1741-1799: Series 1a, George Washington, Forms of Writing, and The Rules of Civility and Decent Behavior in Company and Conversation, ante 1747, Image 25 of 36. (may be found online at www.loc.gov).

69   Ibid., vol. 30, 4-1789. Proposed Address to Congress.

70   Ibid., vol. 37, 4-23-1799. To the Secretary of War.

71   See *George Washington Papers at the Library of Congress, 1741-1799: Series 1a.* George Washington, School Copy Book: Volume 1, 1745 Images 50-54.

72   The Collect for Easter-Day in the 1662 *Book of Common Prayer.*

73   *WGW*, vol. 26, 3-12-1783. To Alexander Hamilton.

74   Ibid., vol. 37, 8-28-1762. To Burwell Bassett.

75   Ibid., vol. 4, 12-18-1775. To Sir William Howe; *Ibid.,*vol. 24, 4-21-1782. To Sir Henry Clinton.

76   Ibid., vol. 3, 9-14-1775. Instructions to Benedict Arnold.
77   Ibid., vol. 30, note, 12-21-1789. To the General Assembly of Georgia.
78   *WGW*, vol. 26, 6-8-1783. Circular to the States. "In what part of the Continent shall we find any Man, or body of Men, who would not blush to stand up and propose measures, purposely calculated to rob the Soldier of his Stipend, and the Public Creditor of his due? and were it possible that such a flagrant instance of Injustice could ever happen, would it not excite the general indignation, and tend to bring down, upon the Authors of such measures, the aggravated vengeance of Heaven?"
79   In deep earnestness, however, he describes the depth of Benedict Arnold's treacherous soul as even being beyond the qualms of a "mental Hell." Ibid., vol. 10-13-1780. To Lt. col. John Laurens. "In no instance since the commencement of the War has the interposition of Providence appeared more conspicuous than in the rescue of the Post and Garrison of West point from Arnolds villainous perfidy. How far he meant to involve me in the catastrophe of this place does not appear by any indubitable evidence, and I am rather inclined to think he did not wish to hazard the more important object of his treachery by attempting to combine two events the lesser of which might have marred the greater. A combination of extraordinary circumstances. An unaccountable deprivation of presence of Mind in a man of the first abilities, and the virtuous conduct of three Militia men, threw the Adjutant General of the British forces in America (with full proofs of Arnolds treachery) into our hands; and but for the egregious folly, or the bewildered conception of Lieutt. Colo. Jameson who seemed lost in astonishment and not to have known what he was doing I should as certainly have got Arnold. André has met his fate, and with that fortitude which was to be expected from an accomplished man, and gallant Officer. But I am mistaken if at *this time*, Arnold is undergoing the torments of a mental Hell. He wants feeling! From some traits of his character which have lately come to my knowledge, he seems to have been so hackneyed in villainy, and so lost to all sense of honor and shame that while his faculties will enable him to continue his sordid pursuits there will be no time for remorse."
80   Ibid., vol. 30, 2-5-1789. To Francis Hopkinson. "Dear Sir: We are told of the amazing powers of musick in ancient times; but the stories of its effects are so surprizing that we are not obliged to believe them unless they had been founded upon better authority than Poetic assertion; for the Poets of old (whatever they may do in these days) were strangely addicted to the Marvellous; and If I before *doubted* the truth of their relations with respect to the power of musick, I am now fully convinced of their falsity, because I would not, for the honor of my Country, allow that we are left by Ancients at an immeasurable distance in everything; and if they could sooth the ferocity of wild beasts, could draw the trees and the Stones after them, and could even charm the powers of Hell by their musick, I am sure that your productions would have had at least virtue enough in them (without the aid of voice or instrument) to melt the Ice of the Delaware and Potomack, and in that case you should have had an earlier acknowledgment of your favor of the 1st. of December which came to hand but last Saturday."
81   Ibid., vol. 26, 6-8-1783. Circular to States
82   In this next letter, Washington's despair is palpable. He believes he is as low as one can go, yet his circumstances are only "the bitterest curse…on this side of the grave." *Ibid.*, vol. 9-30-1776. To Lund Washington. "In short, such is my situation that if I were to wish the bitterest curse to an enemy on this side of the grave, I should put him in my stead with my feelings; and yet I do not know what plan of conduct to pursue. I see the impossibility of serving with reputation, or doing any essential service to the cause by continuing in command, and yet I am told that if I quit the command inevitable ruin will follow from the distraction that will ensue. In confidence I tell you that I never was in such an unhappy, divided state since I was born. To lose all comfort and happiness on the one hand, whilst I am fully persuaded that under such a system of management as has been adopted, I cannot have the least chance for reputation, nor those allowances made which the nature of the case requires; and to be told, on the other, that if I leave the service all will be lost, is, at the same time that I am bereft of every peaceful moment, distressing to a degree. But I will be done with the subject, with the precaution to you that it is not a fit one to be publicly known or discussed. If I fall, it may not be amiss that these circumstances be known, and declaration made in credit to the justice of my character. And if the men will stand by me (which by the by I despair of), I am resolved not to be forced from this ground while I have life; and a few days will determine the point, if the enemy should not change their plan of operations; for they certainly will not — I am sure they ought not — to waste the season that is now fast advancing, and must be precious to them. I thought to have given you a more explicit account of my situation, expectation, and feelings, but I have not time. I am wearied to death all day with a variety of perplexing circumstances — disturbed at the conduct of the militia, whose behavior and want of discipline has done great injury to the other troops, who never had officers, except in a few instances, worth the bread they eat. My time, in short, is so much engrossed that I have not leisure for corresponding, unless it is on mere matters of public business.
83   *WGW*, vol. 24, 8-7-1782. To John Price Posey.
84   Ibid., vol. 3, 7-16-1775. General Orders.
85   Ibid., vol. 4, 3-6-1776. General Orders.
86   Ibid., vol. 17, 11-27-1779. General Orders.
87   Ibid., vol. 12, 8-20-1778. To Brig. Gen. Thomas Nelson.
88   Ibid., vol. 28, 7-25-1785. To Marquis de Lafayette.
89   For example, *WGW*, vol. 13, 11-5-1778. To Lt. Col. Samuel Smith.
90   For example, *WGW*, vol. 21, 1-30-1781. To Lt. Col. John Laurens.
91   For example, *WGW*, vol. 9, 8-7-1777. General Orders.
92   *WGW*, vol. 5, 7-9-1776. General Orders.
93   Ibid., vol. 33, 12-23-1793. To John Christian Ehler.
94   Ibid., vol. 11, 5-2-1778. General Orders.
95   Man's spiritual nature and need of the Holy Spirit is especially seen in Washington's General Orders for November 27, 1779 that declare Congress' day of thanksgiving. *WGW*, vol. 17, 11-27-1779. General Orders. "The Honorable the Congress has been pleased to pass the following proclamation. Whereas it becomes us humbly to approach the throne of Almighty God, with gratitude and praise for the won-

ders which his goodness has wrought in conducting our fore-fathers to this western world; for his protection to them and to their posterity amid difficulties and dangers; for raising us, their children, from deep distress to be numbered among the nations of the earth; and for arming the hands of just and mighty princes in our deliverance; and especially for that he hath been pleased to grant us the enjoyment of health, and so to order the revolving seasons, that the earth hath produced her increase in abundance, blessing the labors of the husbandmen, and spreading plenty through the land; that he hath prospered our arms and those of our ally; been a shield to our troops in the hour of danger, pointed their swords to victory and led them in triumph over the bulwarks of the foe; that he hath gone with those who went out into the wilderness against the savage tribes; that he hath stayed the hand of the spoiler, and turned back his meditated destruction; that he hath prospered our commerce, and given success to those who sought the enemy on the face of the deep; and above all, that he hath diffused the glorious light of the gospel, whereby, through the merits of our gracious Redeemer, we may become the heirs of his eternal glory: therefore, RESOLVED, That it be recommended to the several states, to appoint Thursday, the 9th of December next, to be a day of public and solemn thanksgiving to Almighty God for his mercies, and of prayer for the continuance of his favor and protection to these United States; to beseech him that he would be graciously pleased to influence our public councils, and bless them with wisdom from on high, with unanimity, firmness, and success; that he would go forth with our hosts and crown our arms with victory; that he would grant to his church the plentiful effusions of divine grace, and pour out his *Holy Spirit* on all ministers of the gospel; that he would bless and prosper the means of education, and spread the light of christian knowledge through the remotest corners of the earth...."

96 *WGW*, vol. 34, 2-10-1796.
97 Ibid., vol. 30, 8-18-1789.
98 Ibid., vol. 3, 9-14-1775.
99 Ibid., vol. 31, 3-15-1790. To a Committee of Roman Catholics.
100 Ibid., vol. 4, 1-27-1776.
101 Ibid., vol. 30, 5-26-1789.
102 Ibid., vol. 30, 5-26-1789.
103 Ibid., vol. 30, 10-29-1789.
104 Ibid., vol. 30, 10-9-1789. To the Synod of the Dutch Reformed Church in North America.
105 Ibid., vol. 30, 10-9-1789. To the Synod of the Dutch Reformed Church in North America.
106 Ibid., vol. 35, 9-19-1796.
107 Ibid., Vol 30, 10-23-1789.
108 Ibid., Vol 30, 10-23-1789.
109 Ibid.,vol.4, 12-18-1775.
110 Ibid., vol. 27, 8-21-1783. To the Magistrate and Inhabitants of Elizabeth.
111 Ibid., vol. 35, 3-2-1797. To the Rector, Church Wardens, and Vestrymen of the United Episcopal Churches. "Gentlemen: To this public testimony of your approbation of my conduct and affection for my person I am not insensible, and your prayers for my present and future happiness merit my warmest acknowledgments....Believing that that Government alone can be approved by Heaven, which promotes peace and secures protection to its Citizens in every thing that is dear and interesting to them, it has been the great object of my administration to insure those invaluable ends; and when, to a consciousness of the purity of intentions, is added the approbation of my fellow Citizens, I shall experience in my retirement that heartfelt satisfaction which can only be exceeded by the hope of future happiness." We know that this "hope of future happiness" to which Washington refers is eternal life because the letter that Washington is responding to says, "May you have the additional enjoyment of health; and of whatever else can tend to the happiness of the remainder of your life. And above all, it is our prayer, that you may at last enjoy a better Rest, in which no labor for the happiness of your fellow men will have been in vain." *George Washington Papers at the Library of Congress*, 1741-1799: Series 2 Letterbooks Philadelphia United Episcopal Church to George Washington, March 2, 1797 Letterbook 40, Image 290 of 307.
112 Ibid., vol. 28, 10-1-1785.
113 Ibid., vol. 29, 5-5-1787.
114 Ibid., vol. 13, 10-12-1778.
115 Ibid., Vol 33, 5-26-1794.
116 Ibid., vol.4, 3-31-1776.
117 Ibid., vol. 1, 9- 6-1756.
118 Ibid., vol. 5, 7-2-1776.

CHAPTER 32
1 *WGW*, vol. 35, 6-4-1797.
2 Ibid.
3 Ibid., vol. 30, 7-20-1788. To Jonathan Trumbull. "My dear Trumbull: I have received your favor of the 20th of June and thank you heartily for the confidential information contained in it. The character given of a certain great Personage, who is remarkable for neither forgetting nor forgiving, [Note: King George III.].
4 See the chapters on Washington and Communion.
5 John Corbin, *The Unknown Washington of the Republic* (New York: Charles Scribner Sons, 1930), p. 43-47.
6 Weems, *Life of Washington.* p. 187-189.
7 *WGW*, vol. 8, 6-10-1777. General Orders. "It is with inexpressible regret the Commander in Chief has been driven to the necessity of doing a severe, but necessary act of Justice, as an example of what is to be expected by those daring offenders, who, lost to all sense of duty, and

the obligations they owe to their Country, and to mankind, wantonly violate the most sacred engagements, and fly to the assistance of an enemy, they are bound by every tie to oppose. A spirit of desertion is alone the most fatal disease that can attend an army, and the basest principle that can actuate a soldier; Wherever it shews itself, it deserves detestation, and calls for the most exemplary punishment. What confidence can a General have in any Soldier, who he has reason to apprehend may desert in the most interesting moments ? What, but the want of every moral and manly sentiment, can induce him to desert the cause, to which he has pledged his faith, even with the solemnity of an oath, and which he is bound to support, by every motive of justice and good will to himself, and his fellow creatures ? When such a character appears, it may almost be said in reference to it, that forbearance is folly; and mercy degenerates into cruelty. Notwithstanding this, and tho' the General is determined to convince every man, that crimes of so atrocious a nature shall not be committed with impunity; yet as He is earnestly desirous to shew that he prefers clemency to severity — pardoning to punishing — He is happy to proclaim, the remission of their offences, to all the other prisoners now under sentence, and a releasement to all those now under confinement for trial — He hopes that they, and all others will have a proper sense of this Act of lenity, and will not be ungrateful or foolish enough to abuse it. They will do well to remember that Justice may speedily overtake them, as it has done the unhappy man, whom they have seen fall a Victim to his own folly and wickedness. Those who are pardoned can expect no favor on a second offence. But, Why will Soldiers force down punishment upon their own heads ? Why will they not be satisfied to do their duty, and reap the benefits of it ? The General addresses himself to the feelings of every man in the army; exhorting one and all to consult their own honor and wellfare — to refrain from a conduct that can only serve to bring disgrace and destruction upon themselves, and ruin to their country. He intreats them not to sully the Arms of America, by their Infidelity, Cowardice or Baseness, and save him the anguish of giving Guilt the chastisement it demands. They are engaged in the justest cause men can defend; they have every prospect of success, if they do their part. Why will they abandon, or betray so great a trust? Why will they madly turn their backs upon glory, freedom and happiness?"

8   Fields, *Worthy Partner*, p.189. February 7, 1783. "Yesterday there was an interesting scene at Headquarters. Over fifty soldiers, thinly clad, and with pale but happy faces, whom the General had pardoned in the morning for various crimes, came to express their gratitude for his mercy and kindness to them. They had come in a body. One of them was spokesman for the rest. My heart was touched and my eyes were filled with tears. I gave the speaker some money to divide among them all, and bad them 'go, and sin no more.' The poor fellow kissed my hand and said 'God bless Lady Washington.' Poor fellows." Location unknown. From Lossing , *Mary and Martha*, p220. "Lossing does not give his source, although he states it was written to Mrs. Washington's sister, Anna Maria Bassett. This is obviously incorrect, since Mrs. Bassett died in 1777. If based on an authentic letter, it has been substantially edited. In the General Orders of February 6, 1783, General Washington granted 'a full and free pardon to all military prisoners now in confinement.' *Writings* 25:102-03."

9   James Baldwin, *An American Book of Golden Deeds*, (1907), p. 102-107.

10   E. Gordon Alderfer, *The Ephrata Commune: An Early American Counterculture*, (University of Pittsburgh Press, 1985), pp. 166-167. Note at end of paragraph — The story of Widman has no known contemporary documentation, but see Sachse, *Sectarians*, II, 426-432; Zerfass, *Souvenir Book*, 11, 22-23; and Randolph, *German Seventh Day Baptists*, 1163-67, who claims he got the story "from the original manuscript," otherwise unidentified.

11   Douglas Harper, "The Widman Incident: Revolutionary Revisions To An Ephrata Tale," in *Journal of the Lancaster Country Historical Society*, vol. 97, Num. 3, 1995, pp. 94, 96.

12   The following discussion of the details of the Widman-Miller-Washington story is the result of a synthesis of the following relevant historical documents:

Joseph Townsend, *Some Account of the British Army, Under the Command of General Howe, and of The Battle of Brandywine on the Memorable September 11th, 1777, and the Adventures of that day, which came to the Knowledge and Observation of Joseph Townsend*, (Philadelphia: Townsend Ward, 1846).

Charles William Heathcote, *Washington in Chester County* (Washington Bi-Centennial bulletin, 1732-1932).

A History of Chester Country Pennsylvania, eds. C.W. Heathcote, Lucile Shenk (Harrisburg: National Historical Association, Inc., 1932).

James I. Good, (Reading: Danile Miller, Publisher, 1899) *History of the Reformed Church in the United States 1725-1792*

Joseph Henry Dubbs, *The Reformed Church in Pennsylvania* (Lancaster: Pennsylvania-German Society, 1902).

Life and Letters of the Reverend John Philip Boehm: Founder of the Reformed Church in Pennsylvania, 1683-1749, Ed. William J. Hinke, (Philadelphia: Publication and Sunday School Board of the Reformed Church in the United States, 1916).

Minutes and Letters of the Coetus of the German Reformed Congregations in Pennsylvania 1747-1792 together with Three Preliminary Reports of Reverend John Philip Boehm, 1734-1744 (Philadelphia: Reformed Church Publication Board, 1903).

Joseph Mortimer Levering, *A History of Bethlehem, Pennsylvania 1741-1892 with Some Account of Its Founders and Their Early Activity in America* (Bethlehem: Times Publishing Co., 1903).

John Hill Martin, *Historical Sketch of Bethlehem in Pennsylvania, With Some Account of the Moravian Church* (New York: AMS Press,1971).

Julius Friedrich Sachse, *The German Sectarians of Pennsylvania 1742-1800. A Critical and Legendary History of the Ephrata Cloister and the Dunkers* (Philadelphia: Printed for the Author, 1900).

Douglas Harper, "The Witman Incident: Revolutionary Revisions To An Ephrata Tale" in *Journal of the Lancaster Country Historical Society* vol. 97, Num. 3, 1995, pp. 90-97.

A. Monroe Aurand, Jr., *Historical Account of the Ephrata Cloister and the Seventh Day Baptist Society*, (Harrisburg: The Aurand Press, 1940)

Martin Grove Brumbaugh, *A History of The German Baptist Brethren in Europe and America* (Mount Morris, Ill.: Brethren Publishing House, 1899).

William M. Fahnestock, M.D., "An Historical Sketch of Ephrata" in *Hazard's Register of Pennsylvania. Devoted to the Preservation of Every Kind of Useful Information Respecting the State*, (Philadelphia, March 14, 1835, No. 375), vol. XV, No. 11, pp. 161-167.

The Ephrata Cloisters: An Annotated Bibliography, Compiled by Eugene E. Doll and Anneliese M. Funke (Philadelphia: Carl Schurz

Memorial Foundation, Inc, 1944).

Franklin Ellis and Samuel Evans, *History of Lancaster County, Pennsylvania, with Biographical Sketches of Many of Its Pioneers and Prominent Men*, (Philadelphia: Everts & Peck, 1833).

The Pennsylvania Gazette, (Philadelphia, May 7, 1761, March 16, 1769, March 19, 1772).

"Michael Witman, Loyalist," in *Lancaster County Historical Society*, vol. 14, pp. 181-185.

"Peter Miller—Michael Witman," in *Lancaster County Historical Society*, vol. 6, pp. 46-49.

Joseph Henry Dubbs, "The Founding of the German Churches of Pennsylvania" in *The Pennsylvania Magazine of History and Biography*, vol. XVII, 1893, No. 3, pp. 241-262.

"John Penn's Journal of a Visit to Reading, Harrisburg, Carlisle, and Lancaster, in 1788," in The *Pennsylvania Magazine of History and Biography*, (1877-1906), 1879, pp. 284-95.

"A Protestant Convent," in *Hours at Home: A Popular Monthly of Instruction and Recreation* (1865-1870); Mar. 1867, pp. 458-464.

Christian Endress, "An Account of the Settlement of the Dunkers, at Ephrata," in *The Register of Pennsylvania* (1828-1831); May 22, 1830, pp. 331-334.

"Religious Denominations in Pennsylvania," in *Christian Disciple* (1812-1818); April 1818, pp. 100-103.

E. Gordon Alderfer, *The Ephrata Commune: An Early American Counterculture*, (University of Pittsburgh Press, 1985).

S. G. Zerfass, *Souvenir Book of the Ephrata Cloister, Complete History from Its Settlement in 1728 to the Present Time. Included is the Organization of Ephrata Borough and Other Information of Ephrata Connected With the Cloister* (New York: AMS Press, Inc, 1975).

Samuel W. Pennypacker, *Valley Forge. An Address*, (Philadelphia, June 18, 1898).

John B. B. Trussell, Jr. *Birthplace of an Army: A Study of the Valley Forge Encampment*, (Harrisburg: Pennsylvania Historical And Museum Commission, 1990).

Stephen R. Taaffe, The Philadelphia Campaign, 1777-1778 (Lawrence: University Press of Kansas, 2003).

13   *WGW*, vol. 11, 3-28-1778 and vol. 29, 5-2-1788.

14   Stoudt, *Ordeal at Valley Forge*, p. 61.

15   Stoudt, *Ordeal at Valley Forge*, p. 97.

16   Stoudt, *Ordeal at Valley Forge*, p. 125.

17   Stoudt, *Ordeal at Valley Forge*, p. 139.

18   Stoudt, *Ordeal at Valley Forge*, p. 123.

19   Stoudt, *Ordeal at Valley Forge*, p. 190.

20   Stoudt, *Ordeal at Valley Forge*, p. 62.

21   Stoudt, *Ordeal at Valley Forge*, p. 137.

22   Stoudt, *Ordeal at Valley Forge*, p. 134.

23   Stoudt, *Ordeal at Valley Forge*, p. 97.

24   *WGW*, vol. 28, 3-8-1785; *WGW*, vol. 1, 3-31-1754, Journal of March toward the Ohio.

25   Ibid., vol. 23, 10-17-1781. To Philip Schuyler. "Dear Sir: I do myself the pleasure to acknowledge your favr. of the 26th. of Septemr. which I received a few Days since Had Colo Hamilton given me Time, before his Departure, I should have answered it by him. Mrs Fisher may be consoled respecting the Fate of her Son; the sentence of Death against him will not be confirmed, and he will be released from Confinement. [Note: Myndert Fisher, of Detroit, accused of corresponding with the British. John Dodge had interceded for his pardon or a stay of execution in July, 1781. (See Washington's letter to Brig. Gen. William Irvine, Nov. 1, 1781, *post* .)]*WGW*, vol. 25, 12-3-1782. To Brig. Gen. David Forman. "You must have the Resolve of Congress by which Capt. Asgill was released. All things considered, I question whether the determination of Congress upon the proceedings of Lippencots Court Martial would have been different from what it has been, had not the Court of France interceded warmly in Captain Asgill's favor: but after a request made by the prime Ministers, in which he expresses the wishes of their Majesties, that Capt. Asgill's life might be spared, there was scarcely a possibility of refusing,..."

CHAPTER 33

1   *WGW,* vol. 26, 3-22-1783.

2   Steiner "The Religious Beliefs Of Our Presidents" (1936).

3   Hughes, *George Washington: The Human Being & The Hero*, vol. 1, p. 555.

4   Reverend Charles Green, 5-28-1755 (to John Augustine Washington); 11-13-1757; (to Sally Cary Fairfax) 11-15-1757; 3-26-1761; 8-26-1761; Reverend Lee Massey, 7-10-1784; Reverend Thomas Davis, 4-7-1793 (to Samuel Hanson); 11-19-1794 (to Lund Washington); 1-17-1796 (to William Pearce); *Diaries*, 2-22-1799.

5   There are some 30 letters in the *WGW* from Washington to Reverend Jonathan Boucher, tutor of Jack Custis, Washington's stepson, 5-30-1768; 9-4-1768; 2-3-1771; 2-20-1771; 4-20-1771; 6-5-1771; 9-4-1768; 1-26-1769; 10-14-1769; 2-3-1770; 5-13-1770; 6-2-1770; 7-30-1770; 12-16-1770; 1-2-1771; 2-3-1771; 2-20-1771; 4-20-1771; 6-5-1771; 7-9-1771; 2-21-1772; 5-4-1772; 5-21-1772; 8-18-1772; 12-18-1772; 1-7-1773; 8-2-1773; 8-5-1773; 10-6-1773 (to Robert Cary & Co.); 2-15-1774; 8-15-1798. Other Washington family Tutors who were ordained clergyman at the time were Reverend Samuel Stanhope Smith, 5-24-1797; 10-9-1797; Reverend Myles Cooper, 5-31-1773 (to Robert Cary & Co.); 12-15-1773; 4-15-1774; 9-24-1782; Reverend Stephen Bloomer Balch, 10-30-1784; 6-26-1785; 11-22-1785; Reverend David Griffith, 8-29-1784; Reverend William McWhir, 12-25-1787; 10-12-1789; 2-17-1793; Reverend Jacob Van Vleck, 12-7-1796; 6-14-1797; Rev Dr. Smith Provost, 12-5-1790 (to George Steptoe Washington). Two other Washington family tutors, Walter McGowan, 10-12-1761 (to Robert Cary & Co.), 5-30-1768 (to Reverend Jonathan Boucher); 7-20-1784 and Zechariah Lewis (7-17-1797; 8-14-1797; 9-28-1798) would later become clergyman as well.

6   There are more than 20 letters either to or that mention Reverend Bryan Fairfax. These letters touch deaths in the family (3-6-1793; 4-9-1793); the conveyance of letters (5-18-1798); news from America while Fairfax was abroad (1-20-1799); surveying questions (5-17-1795; 11-26-1799; 11-30-1799); legal matters of an estate (2-19-1789; 4-6-1789); introduction of Fairfax to friends of Washington's in England (5-15-1798). Several of them are in regard to an estate problem of Mrs. Charles Green, the widow of Washington's childhood pastor, Reverend Chares Green. (See note below.)

7   Reverend Dr. William Smith provided his home for a meeting of Washington's officers, 8-6-1777, General Orders. Reverend Lebrecht Herman provided President Washington a study in Germantown, during the yellow fever epidemic for several weeks in 1793. Reverend Joseph Eckley was asked to assist in canceling a newspaper (5-10-1786). Reverend Mr. Bracken was given a case of pictures to care for that were to be shipped to Washington (2-27-1785.) Washington declined the offer for help in Europe on any matters before Reverend John Gabriel Gebhard came to America, who was also interested in a possible job in the new government, 5-26-1789.

8   Washington introduced young Bryan Fairfax, traveling to New York to catch a ship, to the Reverend Richard Peters of Philadelphia in1757. Twenty-five year old Washington had clearly become acquainted with the Philadelphia clergyman at some earlier point, perhaps when he had been traveling through Philadelphia to address his issue of the relative authority of rank of an officer with a colonial commission versus a royal commission. Washington wrote, "Permit me to recommend Colo. Fairfax, the bearer of this to your Friendly notice, while he stays in Philadelphia. He is Son of our late President [Col. George William Fairfax] ... and being a stranger in your City wanted Introduction; to whom then can I better introduce him than the agreeable Mr. Peters. I hope in doing this I make use of no unwelcome liberty; if I do, your genteel treatment of myself made me assume it and must plead my excuse." *WGW*, vol. 2, 9-30-1757 to Reverend Richard Peters.

9   Reverend H. Addison was assisted in traveling through military controlled areas, 11-29-1780. Reverend William Smith was assisted in securing a reimbursement, 2-18-1784 (to James Milligan). Reverend David Griffith was assisted in securing a loan for a building, 4-5-1786; Reverend Francis Adrian Vanderkemp, a Mennonite minister from Holland who had Unitarian inclinations, was welcomed to visit Mount Vernon as a religious refugee, having been referred to Washington's good graces by Marquis de Lafayette, 5-28-1788 (also see Washington's *Diaries*.) Reverend Belknap was assisted with securing information for his American Biography, 6-17-1798; Reverend Walter Magowan was given a pastoral recommendation in an application for a parish ministry, 7-20-1784; Reverend William West and family were served as Washington acted as an executor of a family estate on their behalf, 2-28-1789. Reverend John Witherspoon had been attempting to assist Reverend James Wilson, a Scotch Presbyterian minister, to find a pulpit and had written to Washington. He responded on 8-23-1786, "You have been misinformed respecting the congregation of Pohick. It is of the Episcopal Church and at this time has an incumbent; of which I give you the earliest notice for the information of Mr. Wilson. A Church above this, formerly under the same Ministry, is, I believe, unprovided; but of what Religion the people thereabout now are, I am unable to say. Most probably a medley as they have had Methodist, and Baptist preachers of all kinds among them."

10   *WGW*, vol. 21, 2-13-1781, To Mrs. Susan Blair (wife of Reverend Samuel Blair) et al,.

11   Ibid., vol. 28, 2-17-1785 to George William Fairfax, Mrs. Morton, wife of Reverend Andrew Morton.

12   Mrs. Charles Green, the widow of Washington's childhood pastor, Reverend Chares Green, married Dr. William Savage, which turned out to be a troubled marriage and left a troubled estate. Washington described the problems of the estate as "an affair which originated in an evil hour, by an injudicious and unhappy marriage, and will end, it is to be feared, in vexation and loss to all those who have had any concern in the affairs of the unfortunate Mrs. Savage." (to Peter Trenor, 9-6-1794.) To follow Washington's role in this affair, see 4-25-1767 (to Dr. William Savage); 5-27-1767 (to Dr. William Savage); 8-28-1774 (to Mrs. Sarah Bomford); 10-11-1783 (to Francis Moore); 11-15-1786 (to Mrs. Anne Ennis); 1-6-1790 (to Reverend Bryan Fairfax); 3-18-1792 (to Reverend Bryan Fairfax); 3-19-1792 (to Reverend Bryan Fairfax); 12-25-1792 (to Thomas Newton, Jr.); 3-6-1793 (to Reverend Bryan Fairfax); 9-6-1794 (to Peter Trenor); 9-8-1794 (to Reverend Bryan, Lord Fairfax); 1-3-1796 (to Reverend Bryan, Lord Fairfax); 8-20-1797 (to Reverend Newburgh Burroughs); 4-22-1798 (to George Deneale). The wrangling over the estate of Mrs. Savage prompted Washington to write to Reverend Bryan Fairfax on 3-6-1793, who was also responsible for helping the widow's estate. "Before I conclude, permit me to ask if anything is done, or likely to be done in the case of Savage. I am extremely anxious to see all matters in which I have had any agency, brought to a close, altho' the issue therof should be unfavorable, before I quit the stage of life." Washington's final word on the matter on 4-22-1798 to George Deneale declared, "...Doctr. Savage while living, and his followers since, have had recourse to all the chicane and subterfuge which could be practiced, to wrong the above Lady and defraud her creditors; of whom I am one for money *lent her*." It is perhaps this experience that prompted Washington to say. as he wrote to Burgess Ball. who was helping Washington with the estate of his deceased mother: "I hope you have got through your difficulties on account of your surety-ship for Major Willis, and without loss. When you engaged in this business you neglected the advice of the Wise man, than which no better I believe is to be found in his whole book, or among all his sayings, 'Beware of surety-ship'" *WGW*, vol. 30, 1-18-1790.

13   General Washington was favorable to Reverend John Rodgers' proposal to give to the American Army copies of the newly published and congressionally sanctioned American Bible, 6-11-1783. See the following for examples of Washington's various charitable gifts: Reverend William Smith, 8-18-1782; 8-25-1784; Reverend John Henry Livingston, 12-24-1789; Reverend Mr. Muir, 2-24-1794; 1-22-1798; 2-24-1794; Reverend Hezekiah Balch, see *WGW* note on 12-16-1795; Reverend John Rodgers, 11-28-1789; 8-39-1790; Reverend Auley Macauley, 11-14-1791; Reverend William White, 12-31-1793; 1-1-1794;1-2-1794.

14   See note on the Washington family's tutors above.

15   The word "chaplain" occurs in Washington's writings well over 100 times. Reverend Mr. Doyles, 8-5-1775 (General Orders). In the chapter on "Washington and Prayer," we discussed Washington's appreciation for Chaplain Abiel Leonard, 12-15-1775 (to Gov. Jonathan Trumbull.) Reverend Timothy Dwight, Jr. was a chaplain of Parson's brigade, 3-18-1778 (to Brig. Gen. Samuel Holden Parsons). Dwight would later become President of Yale College. Revd. Doctr. Israel Evans, chaplain of the New York Brigade proposed erecting of a public

building, which the General approved. Some chaplains required more attention than others: 2-7-1781 (to Maj. Gen. William Heath, "Inclosed is a letter which is one of many I have received upon the same subject from the Revd. Mr. Allen. I refer the matter to you, and if you find that he has the least shadow of right to his claim, pray pay him his demand, or he will write me, and travel himself to death." Reverend David Jones was involved in a Court Martial wherein he complained that Maj. Murnam took "possession of his quarters", a complaint which the clergyman lost (to Maj. Gen. John Sullivan, 5-15-1779; 9-21-1780). The General Orders of 2-18-1781 record a Court Martial against a Maj. Reid that included "unofficer and ungentlemanlike conduct" because of the content of a letter he had written about his superior officer to the Reverend Mr. Powers. Reverend William Rogers, 12-13-1778.was written to by Washington about his request for service as a Chaplain, which was referred to Congress. Washington wrote to Congress concerning the Reverend Mr. Tetard, who had "suffered in the extreme," to present his claim "to a generous notice", 9-4-1778 (to the President of Congress). Washington addressed questions of the status of chaplains as prisoners of war, the lack of pay of soldiers, the need for horses and land grants for men who served in the military to Reverend John Hurt, Chaplain to the Virginia Brigade, 9-25-1782; 8-28-1789. He wrote on 3-23-1781 to Reverend Jacob Johnson of his inability to appoint him as a chaplain to the Garrison at Wyoming. since he lacked congressional provision, even though he was "disposed to give every species of countenance and encouragement to the cultivation of Virtue, Morality and Religion." The note of *WGW* on April 18, 1783 says, "At noon the proclamation of Congress for a cessation of hostilities was proclaimed at the door of the New building, followed by three huzzas; after which a prayer was made by the Reverend Mr. Ganno, and an anthem (*Independence*, from Billings,) was performed by vocal and instrumental music."—Heath's *Memories.*"

16   Reverend Bishop Samuel Provoost was chaplain in the U.S. Senate; Reverend William Linn was chaplain in the House of Representatives; Reverend. Bishop William White served as Chaplain to the Continental Congress and then again as chaplain to Congress, when the new government convened in Philadelphia. Washington knew each of these men. See Fitzpatrick, *Diaries.*

17   The best known revolutionary clergyman, who also served as an active military officer, was General Peter Muhlenberg, who we discussed in the chapter on "Washington the Soldier." An unsung hero in this category was Reverend James Caldwell, chaplain of the Third New Jersey Regiment, but who was also an active military officer serving as Assistant Quartermaster. Reverend Caldwell was killed by a sentinel in November 1781. Caldwell first appears in Washington's letters on 12-6-1776 with his humorous quote of Reverend Caldwell, written to the President of Congress: "By a letter of the 4th Inst. from a Mr. Caldwell, a Clergyman and a staunch friend to the Cause, and who has fled from Elizabeth Town and taken refuge in the Mountains about Ten Miles from thence, I am informed, that Genl. or Lord Howe was expected in that Town, to publish pardon and peace. His words are, 'I have not seen his proclamation, but only can say, he gives 60 days of Grace and Pardons from the Congress down to the Committee. No one man in the Continent is to be denied his Mercy.' In the language of this Good Man, the Lord deliver us from his Mercy." Writing to Maj. Gen. Israel Putnam on 2-3-1777, Washington said about the need to secure forage, "On the success of this business, very much depends; let me therefore, call your utmost attention to it. Doctr. Caldwell will be the best person you can apply to, he will give you every possible Assistance." Other references to Reverend Caldwell are: 5-13-1778 (to Maj. Benjamin Tallmadge); 8-8-1778 (to Brig. Gen. William Maxwell); 8-22-1778 (to Maj. Gen. John Sullivan); 10-29-1778 (to Maj. Gen. Nathanael Greene); 10-31-1779 (to Maj. Gen. John Sullivan); 6-13-1778; 8-8-1778; 1-10-1780; 1-21-1780; 2-1-1780; 2-7-1781.

18   Reverend Samuel Kirkland, 9-28-1775 (to the Massachusetts Legislature); 2-26-1779 (to Maj. Gen. Philip Schuyler); 1-29-1778 (to the Committee of Congress with the Army); Reverend John Carroll, 5-15-1776 (to Maj. Gen. Philip Schuyler); 4-10-1792; Reverend John Ettwein, 3-28-1778; 5-2-1788; Reverend Mr. De La Motte, 12-17-1779 (to the President of Congress); Reverend John C. Kunze, 1-12-1790.

19   Reverend Alexander McWhorter, Chaplain of the Artillery brigade, 10-12-1778.

20   Reverend Charles Green, 11-13-1757.

21   Reverend Dr. John Wheelock, President of Dartmouth College, 12-18-1775 (to Maj. Gen. Philip Schuyler); 6-9-1781; Reverend Mr. Madison, 8-8-1776 (to the President of Congress); Reverend Dirck Romeyn, 11-3-1780.

22   Reverend Thornton Fleming, 1-30-1793; Reverend James Madison, 9-23-1793.

23   Reverend William Smith, 11-15-1780, was thanked as secretary of the American Philosophical Society for Washington's election to membership in the society. Reverend David Zeisberger, Moravian missionary, provided Washington with a list of Indian words for Marquis de Lafayette, 1-10-1788 (to Marquis de Lafayette). Reverend Jedidiah Morse's *American Geography* was discussed, 6-19-1788 (to Richard Henderson). Reverend Morse was also thanked for gifts of his works, 7-17-1793; 6-20-1797. Reverend George Skene Keith's work on weights, measures, and coins was received with thanks and with the declaration that his "Book is of high importance to society in general, and particularly to the Commercial World", 6-22-1792. Reverend John Lathrop's publications of the Humane Society were read with "singular satisfaction", 6-22-1788; 2-22-1788. He thanked Reverend Joseph Willard for his election as a member of the American Academy of Arts and Sciences, 3-22-1781. He acknowledged the good work in educating the Indians done by Reverend John Wheelock, President of Dartmouth College. He thanked Reverend Jeremy Belknap for his history of New Hampshire, 1-5-1785. He also thanked Reverend Belknap for his American Biography and promised him that he would assist in the effort to secure additional subscribers, 5-9-1794; 7-12-1798. He thanked and commended Reverend Jonathan Edwards for providing scholarly information on Indian languages, 8-28-1788. Reverend William Maunsell was congratulated for a publication that detailed a new method of cultivating potatoes, 2-20-1795. Reverend Samuel Knox was congratulated on his study on a "Uniform System of Education, adapted to the United States," 10-14-1798.

24   Reverend Clement Cruttwell was thanked for sending Bishop Wilson's *Bible* (published in 1785) and his *Works* (published in 1781), 7-10-1795. *WGW* note on this date says, "Reverend Thomas Wilson's (Bishop of Sodor and Man) *Works* were published in 1781, the Bishop having died in 1755. Reverend Thomas Wilson, son of Bishop, died in 1784....Washington's copy of the Bishop of Sodor and Man's *Bible*, which accompanied the Bishop's *Works*, is now in the Library of Congress." Washington bequeathed this *Bible* to his lifelong clergy friend, Bryan Fairfax. Washington's will says, "To the Reverend, now Bryan, Lord Fairfax, I give a Bible in three large folio volumes, with notes,

presented to me by the Right Reverend Thomas Wilson, Bishop of Sodor and Man." *WGW*, vol. 37, Last Will and Testament. *WGW* note says, "Washington's mistaken recollection that it had been presented to him by Reverend Thomas Wilson, Bishop of Sodor and Man, was due to the fact that it had been bequeathed to him by the son of the bishop, the Reverend Thomas Wilson, Prebendary of Westminster." We will consider Washington's endorsement of Reverend Mason Weem's *The Immortal Mentor* in a subsequent chapter. See also, *WGW*, vol. 32, 10-20-1792. To Dr. William Davies Shipley.

25   Reverend Dr. John Witherspoon, President of Princeton, Member of Congress, only Clergyman to sign the Declaration of Independence, Presbyterian minister, was written to concerning "partial exchanges" and a written memorial, 10-8-1782; 9-8-1783.

26   Clergymen were interested in writing histories of the American Revolution, such as Reverend William Smith, 5-8-1792. But it was especially Reverend William Gordon who pursued the matter, corresponding extensively with Washington throughout the War and after: the note on 9-16-1776 (to the President of Congress); 1-23-1778; note on 4-22-1779 (to Burwell Bassett); 5-2-1780 (to Lt. Col. Alexander Hamilton); 1-20-1786 (to James Mercer); 5-13-1776; 6-29-1777; 1-23-1778; 2-15-1778; 8-2-1779; 5-3-1780; 3-9-1781; 10-23-1782; 7-8-1783; 5-8-1784; 11-3-1784; 12-20-1784; 3-8-1785; 8-31-1785; 12-5-1785; 4-20-1786; 4-10-1787; 1-1-1788; 12-23-1788; 2-23-1789; 2-25-1791; 10-15-1797. Reverend Dr. John Witherspoon had a student named John Bowie who was willing to write the memoirs of Washington's life, but Washington, at first willing, subsequently declined because, when checking his papers for this project, he "found a mere mass of confusion (occasioned by frequently shifting them into trunks and suddenly removing them from the reach of the enemy)" 3-8-1775, (to John Witherspoon).

27   Reverend Charles Inglis, 12-16-1776 (to Maj. Gen. William Heath); Reverend Jonathan Boucher see note on 5-30-1768.

28   Reverend Jacob Duché, 8-10-1783; Reverend Jonathan Boucher, 8-15-1798.

29   See Lane, *Washington Collection*, Boston Athenaeum, for a listing of these.

30   *WGW*, vol. 26, 3-22-1783.

31   Meade, *Old Churches, Ministers, and Families of Virginia*, vol. I, p.22
       " ... When there was no service at the chapel or we were prevented from going, my father read the service and a sermon; and whenever a death occurred among the servants he performed the burial service himself, and read Blair's Sermon on Death the following Sunday. Of the character and conduct of the old clergy generally I have often heard them speak in terms of strong condemnation. My father, when a young man, was a vestryman in Price George county, Virginia, but resigned his place rather than consent to retain an unworthy clergyman in the parish. Of two clergymen, however, in King George county, – the Stewarts, – I have heard my mother, who lived for some time under the ministry of one of them, speak in terms of high condemnation, as exceptions to the general rule....(Ibid., p.25)
       ..." I think this a proper time for some notice of the character of the sermons which were preached and the books which were read among the Episcopalians of Virginia. This was the period when the poet Cowper upbraided the clergy of the English Church with substituting morality for religion saying '*How oft, when Paul has served us with a text, Has Plato, Tully, Epictetus preached!*' In the Church of Virginia, with the exception of Mr. Jarrett and perhaps a few others, I fear the preaching had for a long time been almost entirely of the moral kind."
       The books most in use were *Blair's Sermons*, *Sterne's Works*, *The Spectator*, *The Whole Duty of Man*, sometimes Tillotson's Sermons, which last were of the highest grade of worth then in use. But *Blair's Sermons*, on account of their elegant style and great moderation in all things, were most popular."
       The Washington family possessed Blair's sermons and bought them from Parson Mason L. Weems. See Lane, *The Boston Athenaeum Washington Collection*, p. 503.

32   See Stephen DeCatur Jr., *Private Affairs of George Washington* (Boston: Houghton Mifflin Col, 1933) p. 90. See Custis, *Recollections*, p. 508.

33   See Lane, *Washington Collection*, Boston Athenaeum, pp. 498, 502, 503.

34   A careful review of *the Boston Athenaeum's Catalogue of the Washington Collection* will show the vast number of printed sermons that were part of Washington's library.

35   See the chapter on Washington's education.

36   Thus Parson Mason L. Weems as a book seller, or colporteur, sold sermons to the Washington family, the specific example able to be documented is *Blair's Sermons*. See Lane, *Washington Collection, Boston Athenaeum, and the Washington Papers of the Library of Congress* under Weems.

37   Examples of printed funeral sermons in Washington's library include Mrs. Samuel Magaw, Benjamin Franklin, Governor James Bowdoin, Lord Pepperell. See Lane, *Washington Collection*, Boston Athenaeum.

38   *WGW*, vol. 32, 10-20-1792. To Dr. William Davies Shipley. "Sir: I have been honored with your polite Letter of the 23d. of May, together with the works of your late Right Reverend father Lord bishop of St. Asaph, which accompanied it. For the character and sentiments of that venerable Divine while living, I entertained the most perfect esteem, and have a sincere respect for his memory now he is no more. My best thanks are due to you for his works, and the mark of your attention in sending them to me; and especially for the flattering expressions respecting myself, which are contained in your letter." Reverend Jacob Duché dedicated "Stand Fast Therefore In The Liberty With Which Christ Has Made You Free" to Washington in 1775. Bishop William White dedicated *Sermon on The Reciprocal Influence of Civil Policy and Religious Duty* Delivered in the City of Philadelphia, the 19th day of February, 1795, Day of General Thanksgiving by William White, D.D. Bishop of the Episcopal Church, in the Commonwealth of Pennsylvania. Philadelphia: Ormrod & Conrad.
       Dedication to the President of the United States
       Sir,
              The liberty which I take, of sending the following Sermon from the press, with a dedication to the first Magistrate, is not from the thought, that I can, in any way, add to a reputation, so high as his, in our own country and throughout the world; but for a use, which arises out of my argument.
              The relation which I have asserted of religion to civil policy, is well known to be considered as chimerical by some; while it is

contemplated by others, as involved in whatever relates to the prosperity of the commonwealth. If a question should be raised, concerning the sense of the governments under which we live, it cannot be denied, that persons of the latter description may appeal to many particulars, in law and in practice, which can be defended on no other ground, than that of the propriety of the states availing itself of the religious principle in the minds of its citizens, in order to answer the purposes of its institution. When, therefore, in addition to constantly operating sanctions, we hear the voice of our country calling on us to assemble, for the express design of offering our acknowledgments to the Almighty Ruler of the Universe, for his prospering of its counsels, and of involving the continuance of his mercies; it is another sanction of the latter opinion, which the advocates of it cannot fail to notice, as being to their purpose; especially if it be aided by the reputation of those, from whose authority it proceeds.

It cannot have escaped the notice of any, that, since your elevation to the seat of supreme Executive authority, you have, in your official capacity, on all fit occasions, directed the public attention to the Being and Providence of God: And this implies a sense, as well of the relation, which nations, in their collective capacities, bear to him, their Supreme Ruler; as of the responsibility to him of earthly Governors, for the execution of the truths committed to them. Even had such acknowledgements come from any one, whose conversation or whose conduct were in opposition to the principle implied; still they might have been pleaded, as an homage to the truth, extorted by existing circumstances, or by some selfish views; at the expence of the violation of theory, or else of the crimination of the person. In the present instance, it is to my purpose to remark; and, but for this circumstance I should not now remark it; that an unimpeached sincerity of character, accompanied by the public acknowledgment of a Divine Being, not attached to station but evidenced throughout life, warrants, on every rule of evidence, a much stronger construction. We have a right, to apply the testimony of such a character, as the result of an enlightened conscience; and to think it an advantage to our cause, to pronounce, that a mind, which has embraced all the civil interests of the American people, has not overlooked the relation which they all bear, to the great truths of religion and of morals.

On this ground, Sir, I presumed, in the following discourse, delivered in your presence, to apply the summons under which we were assembled, to the doctrine which it was my object to establish: In doing which, it could not escape my recollection, that the sanction would come, with especial weight, before a Congregation, who have been witnesses of a correspondent conduct of the person, in his attendance on divine worship among them, during the frequent occasions of his temporary residence in this city, within the twenty years last past. For the truth of the construction of the act of government, the preacher only is responsible: The right of making the construction, if it be done with decency, seemed to come within his privileges as a citizen: And for any censure he might hazard, as to the propriety of the reasoning, he was willing to commit himself in that respect; considering, as he did, that the point intended to be established, was not mere matter of speculation, but involved important duties of civil rulers and equally important rights of Christian ministers: The former, as a conformity to professions brought forward to the public eye; and the latter, as giving us an opportunity to remind our civil superiors, when occasion and prospect of usefulness occur, of practicing duties, which with a view to the happiness of the civil state, they, officially and with great propriety, recommend to us and to our congregations.

From this statement of circumstances, the design, and I hope, the propriety of the Dedication, must be evident. It is, Sir, that in proof of a point, which I believe to be essential to the duties and to the felicities of public and of private life, I may, in the most explicit and pointed manner that occurs to me, avail myself of the aids which I think I discover, in the measures of your administration and in the weight of your character: A use of human authority, which cannot be objected to, as inapplicable to the subject; because it is of the essence of my argument, that, in every permanent government, civil rulers will be drawn to confess the principle asserted; either, as in the present instance, by a declaration of truths believed and felt; or, as may happen, by a compliance with what they suppose to be popular prejudices and weakness. And this is a circumstance, which I apply in proof, that my doctrine is involved in, and inseparable from social order.

The time, Sir, may come, and I believe it must come, when the doctrine here maintained will be held a much more important subject, than it has yet been, of political investigation; and when the acknowledging of it will be demonstrated by facts, to be a trait in the character of the enlightened statesman and in that of the virtuous citizen. In the event, it will be no small part of the praise of the chief magistrate of the present day, that, as the result of his own judgment and consistently with his own practice, he made acknowledgements, which are in contrariety to a theory, that sets open the flood-gates of immorality....

That you may enjoy that best reward of your present labors; and that the remainder of your life may be crowned with a measure of felicity, proportioned to the glory of the past period of it; is, Sir, the sincere wish and the devout prayer, of your respectful, affectionate and obliged humble servant,

WILLIAM WHITE

Feb. 28th, 1795.

See Lane, *Washington Collection*, Boston Athenaeum.

39 Reverend Samuel Davies, "Religion and patriotism the constituents of a good soldier." A sermon preached to Captain Overton's Independent Company of Volunteers, raised in Hanover County, Virginia, August 17, 1755. By Samuel Davies, A.M. Minister of the Gospel there. (Philadelphia: Printed by James Chattin, 1755.).

40 We saw this in the case of Uzal Ogden's request for Washington to endorse his critique of Thomas Paine's *Age of Reason*. Also, Reverend Knox mentioned above, who had written on a uniform system of education, had requested Washington's endorsement. Washington declined in both instances. But that is what makes his endorsement of Parson Weem's *Immortal Mentor* so remarkable, because it was not the practice of Washington to issue an endorsement. We will consider the Weem's publication in a subsequent chapter.

41 For the history of the Stith family, see Meade, *Old Churches*, p.137-138:
William Stith was the only son of Captain John Stith, of the county of Charles City, and of Mary, a daughter of "William Randolph, gentleman," of Turkey Island, in the adjoining county, Henrico, in the Colony of Virginia : their son William was born in the year 1689. On

the death of her husband, Mrs. Stith, at the instance of her brother, Sir John Randolph, removed to Williamsburg and placed her son in the grammar-school attached to the College of William and Mary, where he pursued his academic studies and graduated. His theological studies were completed in England, where he was ordained a minister of the Episcopal Church. On his return to Virginia, in the year 1731, he was elected master of the grammar-school in the College and chaplain to the House of Burgesses. In June, 1738, he was called rector to Henrico parish, in the county of Henrico. He marred his cousin Judith, a daughter of Thomas Randolph of Tuckahoe, the second son of William Randolph, of Turkey Island, and resided in the parsonage on the glebe near Varina, the seat of justice for the county of Henrico. There he wrote his *History of Virginia*, which was printed and bound in the city of Williamsburg, at the only printing-press then in the Colony. In August, 1752, he was elected President of William and Mary College, to which he removed and over which he presided until his death, in 1755....A third married William Stith, and was the mother of Reverend Mr. Stith, the historian of Virginia, minister of Henrico, and afterward President of William and Mary College. His sister married Commissary Dawson, and he himself married Miss Judith Randolph of Tuckahoe. Another of the family married the Reverend Mr. Keith, who settled in Fauquier, and was the ancestor of Judge Marshall. ... Bishop Randolph, of the latter part of the last century, was first Archdeacon of Jersey, then Bishop of Oxford, and then of London, in all which stations he was most highly esteemed. His collection of tracts for the benefit of young students for the ministry show him to have been a Bishop of sound doctrines and of a truly catholic spirit."

42 See the chapter entitled, "Washington the Low Churchman."

43 *WGW,* vol. 36, 9-25-1798. To Reverend G. W. Snyder.

44 Twohig, *The Diaries of George Washington*, vol. 5, November, Sunday 8th, 1789. "It being contrary to Law & disagreeable to the People of this State (Connecticut) to travel on the Sabbath day and my horses after passing through such intolerable Roads wanting rest, I stayed at Perkins's Tavern (which by the bye is not a good one) all day—and a meeting House being with in a few rod of the Door, I attended Morning & evening Service, and heard very lame discourses from a Mr. Pond."

45 Twohig, *Diaries,* Monday October 10, 1785.

46 Twohig, *Diaries,* Sunday July 3, 1791. "Received, and answered an address from the Inhabitants of York town—& there being no Episcopal Minister *present* in the place, I went to hear morning Service performed in the Dutch reformed Church—which, being in that language not a word of which I understood I was in no danger of becoming a proselyte to its religion by the eloquence of the Preacher." *PGW* vol. 6.

47 *WGW,* vol. 31, 3-28-1791. To Tobias Lear.

48 Ibid., vol. 3, 7-9-1771. To Jonathan Boucher.

49 Ibid., vol. 28, 7-25-1785. To David Humphreys.

50 See for example, *GWP*, Series 8 Miscellaneous Papers, where Washington's extensive personal notes on various topics, such as farming, history and constitutional forms of government are copied by him from various books he had read.

51 *WGW,* vol. 36, 12-21-1797. To James Anderson. "If a person only sees, or directs from day to day what is to be done, business can never go on methodically or well, for in case of sickness, or the absence of the Director, delays must follow. System to all things is the soul of business. To deliberate maturely, and execute promptly is the way to conduct it to advantage. With me, it has always been a maxim, rather to let my designs appear from my works than by my expressions. To talk long before hand, of things to be done, is unpleasant, if those things can as well be done at one time or another; but I do not mean by this to discourage you from proposing any plans to me which you may conceive to be beneficial, after having weighed them well in your own mind; on the contrary, I request you to do it with the utmost freedom, for the more combined, and distant things are seen, the more likely they are to be turned to advantage."

52 Custis writes in *Recollections*, pp. 162-163, "General Washington, during the whole of both his public and private life, was a very early riser; indeed, in the maternal mansion, at which his first habits were formed, the character of a sluggard was abhorred. Whether as chief magistrate, or the retired citizen, we find this man of method and labor seated in his library from one to two hours before day, in winter and at daybreak in summer. We wonder at the amazing amount of work which he performed. Nothing but a method the most remarkable and exemplary, could have enabled him to accomplish such a world of labor, an amount which might have given pretty full employment to half a dozen ordinary, and not idle men, all their lies. When we consider the volume of his official papers—his vast foreign, public, and private correspondence—we are scarcely able to believe that the space of one man's life should have comprehended the doing of so many things and doing them so well."

53 *WGW*, vol. 30, 4-1789. "I will only say, that, during and since the Session of the Convention, I have attentively heard and read every oral and printed information of both sides of the question that could readily be procured. This long and laborious investigation, in which I endeavoured as far as the frailty of nature would permit to act with candour has resulted in a fixed belief that this Constitution, is really in its formation a government of the people." Washington's concern for the constitutional crisis looming in America is well seen in *WGW*, vol. 29, 11-15-1786, To Bushrod Washington. "Among the great objects which you took into consideration at your meeting at Richmond, how comes it to pass, that you never turned your eyes to the inefficacy of the Federal Government, so as to instruct your Delegates to accede to the propositions of the Commrs. at Annapolis; or to devise some other mode to give it that energy, which is necessary to support a national character? Every man who considers the present constitution of it, and sees to what it is verging, trembles. The fabrick which took nine years, at the expense of much blood and treasure, to rear, now totters to the foundation, and without support must soon fall." Washington's written study notes on constitutional forms are found in *The George Washington Papers of the Library of Congress*, Series 8, "Miscellaneous Papers," images 344-366.

54 As for example, the sermons by Stith, "The Nature and Extent of Christ's Redemption" and Clark, "An Answer to the Question of Why I Am a Christian," and the study by Berrington that have been included as illustrations in this study.

55 See, for example, Lane, *Washington Collection*, Boston Athenaeum, pp. 76-77, 132, 145, 162-163, 195.

56 Lane, *Washington Collection*, Boston Athenaeum, p. 502.

57 Ibid., p. 503.
58 Ibid., p. 510.
59 Ibid., p. 500.
60 Ibid., p. 39.
61 Ibid., p. 221.
62 *WGW,* vol. 33, 8-29-1793.
63 Ibid., vol. , 9-9-1797
64 "The divine mission of Jesus Christ evident from his life, and from the nature and tendency of his doctrines." A sermon preached at Stamford, October 11, 1796, before the Consocation of the Western District in Fairfield County. By Isaac Lewis, D.D., Pastor of a consociated church in Greenwich. New Haven] Printed by T. and S. Green—New-Haven., [1796]
"The political advantages of godliness." A sermon preached before His Excellency the governor, and the honorable legislature of the state of Connecticut, convened at Hartford on the anniversary election. May 11, 1797. By Isaac Lewis, D.D., Pastor of a church in Greenwich. Hartford: Printed by Hudson & Goodwin., 1797.
65 *WGW,* vol. 7, 3-31-1777 to BRIGADIER GENERAL GEORGE CLINTON "I congratulate you most cordially on your late appointment to a command in the Continental Army. I assure you it gave me great pleasure when I read the Resolve, and wishing that your exertions may be crown'd with a suitable success. I am etc." Ibid., vol. 16, 8-5-1779 to Reverend Uzal Odgen, " Reverend. Sir: I have received, and with pleasure read, the Sermon you were so obliging as to send me. I thank you for this proof of your attention. I thank you also for the favourable sentiments you have been pleased to express of me. But in a more especial mannr. I thank you for the good wishes and prayers you offer in my behalf." Ibid., vol. 24, 5-29-1782 to Governor Jonathan Trumbull, "Your Excellency's reply to Deans Letter I read with great Satisfaction, and this pleasure was hightened by findg. that it contained not only your own Sentiments, but also conveys the Sense of the Legislative Body of your State. From a variety of circumstances I view the present, as the most critical moment, that we have almost ever experienced throughout the present contest."; Ibid., vol. 26, 3-10-1783 to Jame Mitchell Varnum, "Dear Sir: I have had the honor to receive your favor of the 21st. Ulto. and beg your acceptance of my particular acknowledgments for the honorauble and flattering manner in which you have spoken of me, in the dedication to your Oration, delivered before our Brethren at Providence. The Sentiments which you have expressed in your Oration I have read with pleasure, and am with great esteem etc. [*WGW* Note: "An Oration: delivered in The Episcopal Church in Providence (Rhode-Island) Before the Most Ancient and Honorable Fraternity of Free and Accepted Masons, On the American Festival of St. John the Evangelist, December 27, 1782, Providence: Printed by John Carter.]"; Ibid., vol. 26, 3-30-1783 to President Boudinot of Congress, "Dear Sir: I was upon the point of closing the Packet which affords a cover to this Letter when the Baron de Steuben arrived and put your obliging favor of the 17th. Instt. into my hands. I read it with great pleasure and gratitude, and beg you to accept my sincere thanks for the trouble you have taken to communicate the several matters therein contained many parts of which 'till then were altogether New to me."; Ibid., vol. 28, 2-5-1785 to Benjamin Vaughn, " Sir: I pray you to accept my acknowledgment of your polite letter of the 31st. of October, and thanks for the flattering expressions of it. These are also due in a very particular manner to Doctr. Price [by Reverend Richard Price, an English nonconformist minister], for the honble mention he has made of the American General in his excellent observations on the importance of the American revolution addressed, "To the free and United States of America," which I have seen and read with much pleasure."; Ibid., vol. 28, 10-30-1785 to Daivd Humphreys "My dear Humphreys: … I am very much obliged to you for the poem you sent me, I have read it with pleasure, and it is much admired by all those to whom I have showed it."; Ibid., vol. 33, 7-20-1794 to Sir John Sinclair, "I have read with peculiar pleasure and approbation, the work you patronise, so much to your own honor and the utility of the public. Such a general view of the Agriculture in the several Counties of Great Britain is extremely interesting; and cannot fail of being very beneficial to the Agricultural concerns of your Country and to those of every other wherein they are read, and must entitle you to their warmest thanks for having set such a plan on foot, and for prosecuting it with the zeal and intelligence you do. I am so much pleased with the plan and execution myself, as to pray you to have the goodness to direct your Book-seller to continue to forward them to me, accompanied with the cost which shall be paid to his order or remitted so soon as the amount is made known to me. When the whole are received I will promote, as far as in me lays, the reprinting of them here." There are many others as well.
66 Washington rarely gave this glowing phrase, "read with pleasure." On the 19 instances when he did, it was always with an implied or expressed approval. This included sermons, books on history, and books on agriculture. See Lane, *Catalogue of the Washington Collection*, pp. 90-91,: "Account of the Origin of the Board of Agriculture, and its Progress for three Years after its Establishment. By the President. (London, 1796), and "Agricultural survey of the Counties of Great Britain; William Heath, *Memoirs of Major-General Heath.* (Boston, 1798), Lane, *Washington Collection*, Boston Athenaeum, p. 99. For other examples, see Ibid., pp. 105, 126, 137, 146, 169.
67 See the chapter on "George Washington and Prayer." See *WGW,* vol. 36, To REVEREND WILLIAM LYNN, June 4, 1798. "Revd. Sir: I received with thankfulness your favour of the 30th. Ulto., enclosing the discourse delivered by you on the day recommended by the President of the United States to be observed as a general Fast. I have read them both with pleasure; and feel grateful for the favourable sentiments you have been pleased to express in my behalf; but more especially for those good wishes which you offer for my temporal and eternal happiness; which I reciprocate with great cordiality, being with esteem and respect…."
68 Boller, *George Washington & Religion*, p. 78.
69 Boller, *George Washington & Religion*, p. 78.
70 *WGW* Note: "Of Newton, Sussex County, N. J. He was elected Protestant Episcopal Bishop of New Jersey in 1798, but consecration was refused him in 1799; later he became a Presbyterian. The sermon was "A sermon on practical religion. Inscribed to Christians of every denomination. No. I. (Chatham: Printed by Shepard Kollock)." Copies of nos. II and III are in the Washington Collection in the Boston Athenaeum."

71 This sermon was delivered in the evening, and spoken extemporaneously. A few weeks after its delivery it was committed to writing and as nearly verbatim as the author's memory would serve. The sermon in its fuller form:

In all the compass of language, there is not, perhaps, a word that speaks greater terror, more dread to the impious sons of jollity and mirth, than death. How doth it damp every evil joy, embitter the impure draught of sensual pleasure, and fill the wicked with dreadful forebodings of what shall be hereafter!

As disagreeable as the subject of death is to the ungodly, it is the duty of the sincerest, best friends, the faithful ministers of the gospel, frequently to dwell upon it; to remind of it's certainty; it's necessary preparation, it consequences; and to use such arguments as shall have a tendency to cause sinners to escape all the exquisite, the inconceivable pains of death-eternal.

Be this our attempt this night, and be our text the following words of sacred writ:

Psalm 89:48

What man is he that liveth and shall not see death?

Suppose a person blessed with a most healthy constitution; breathing the air of some friendly and in the practice of exercise and temperance, the great promoters and preservers of health; imagine him not smitten with the sword of war, wasted by famine, nor consumed by pestilence, but year after year to roll, and he still be possessed of the enjoyment of life, yet the fatal line is drawn over which he cannot pass; the awful, the important moment must arrive, when he, in his own *person*, shall have verified the truth contained in the text, "that there is no man that *liveth* who shall not see *death*."

The historic as well as sacred page, fully evinces the truth of this assertion. Where are all those illustrious heroes, famed orators, sage philosophers, celebrated poets, whose names grace the volumes of antiquity? Where, indeed all the posterity of Adam, the noble and ignoble? All, all have paid their last great debt of nature, have, in the language of the Psalmist, seen death two only excepted, and those also whose existence hath been only as of a day.

"Dust thou art, and to dust shalt thou return" said God to Adam on his transgression.

"Man that is born of a woman," saith Job, "is of few days and full of trouble. He cometh up like a flower and is cut down; he fleeth also as a shadow and continueth not."

"It is appointed, "saith St. Paul, unto men once to die." Unto all men that shall ever live, except those who shall be found alive at the second advent of the Redeemer, such, faith the same apostle, "shall not sleep, but shall be changed in a moment, in the twinkling of an eye, at the last trump."

But why cite we authorities to prove that which none pretend to deny? Since we all confess the mortality of man, it must be of the utmost moment to be informed of the preparation that death requires.

It was the observation of a certain Pagan, that when the Supreme called into being the heavens and the earth, he transformed himself into Love. True it is, "That God is Love," and that all nature exhibits a rich display of the divine munificence. But in nothing did the goodness of the Almighty Creator shine forth more conspicuous, than in the formation and state of Man. How majestic, how beauteous his person! How noble, now divine his soul! Placed in the fairest part of all the fair creation, possessing the heavenly image, and enjoying communion with the most bounteous Author of his Being, nothing was wanting to consummate his felicity; nothing necessary for ever to perpetuate it, but a due observance of that easy and good law which God had given him. Had Adam paid proper respect to the divine command, it is the opinion of the best writers, both Jewish and Christian, that after his obedience had been sufficiently tried, he would have been translated from an earthly to a heavenly paradise.

By his apostasy, what did he not lose?

He lost the immortality of his person; or his body became mortal.

He lost the favour and friendship of heaven.

He lost the divine image, or the moral restitute of his nature, and consequently his happiness: And he became subject to miseries here, to endless and intolerable torments hereafter.

Unhappy Adam, thou sole father of mankind! Happy was it for thee, and for thy progeny, that thy Creator's goodness was not exhausted in thy formation, but that mercy infinite yet remained for thy redemption!

The divine Jesus was appointed by the Father of Mercies to interpose in our favor. He most graciously undertook to restore to man all that he had left, and to deliver him from all the evils to which he is exposed. The Son of God is, therefore, emphatically stiled our Redeemer, our Deliverer, our Saviour.

The human body became mortal; but shall it not be restored to immortality by the omnipotence of the Redeemer? Although it shall be laid, it shall not be lost in the grave. For "the hour is coming when the Dead shall hear the voice of the Son of God, and shall live." "The trumpet shall sound," we are told, "and the dead shall be raised incorruptible, and we shall be changed, for this corruptible must put on incorruption, and this mortal must put on immortality."

Man lost the divine favour and friendship. No sooner had he violated the sacred precept, but war, as it were, was declared between heaven and earth. Our first great friend, most justly became our enemy. We were exposed to vanquishment, ruin, death. This we fully merited; this we should have fatally experienced had not the Almighty ceased to contend. Unsolicited, the sword of vengeance, is sheathed, and O astonishing! The Omnipotent himself, He before whom all the Angels of heaven bow with the profoundest reverence, and at whose mighty name all the devils of hell tremble, deigns to sue for peace; most mercifully condescends to lay aside the robes of celestial glory; to take upon him the humble garb of humanity, and to labour, and toil, and bleed, to effect the Reconciliation.

"The Word was made flesh and dwelt among us, and we beheld his glory, the glory as of the only begotten of the Father, full of grace and truth." This divine Logos "bore our griefs, carried our sorrows, was wounded for our transgressions, bruised for our iniquities. The chastisement of our peace was upon him; and with his stripes we are healed."

It being most reasonable that the offending party should manifest some signs of contrition, previous to future favor and friendship, to this they were excited by the Prince of Peace, upon his entrance on his mediatorial office. "Repent," saith he, "for the kingdom of heaven is at hand."

"Recollect, O ye sons of men! Your ungrateful, repeated, unjustifiable offences against your Almighty Father; let a due sense of them fill you with remorse, cover you with shame, and cause you to be willing to accept the divine clemency; for now it is proclaimed; the gospel dispensation hath taken place; the doors of heaven are open to every repenting, returning offender."

Thus did the merciful Saviour endeavour to dispose men to be reconciled with their offended Maker. Thus, "was God in Christ reconciling the world unto himself, restoring us to his favour and friendship.

The medium of reconciliation, is the blood of Jesus, apprehended by faith, with a disposition of penitence and sincere obedience.

With what fervor of affection are we entreated by the apostle to accept of this favour? "We are ambassadors for Christ," says he "as though God did beseech you by us: We pray you, in Christ's stead, be ye reconciled to God; for he hath made him to be sin for us, who knew no sin, that we might be made the righteousness of God in him."

And how highly are those honoured who are obedient to the voice of the Redeemer, who suffer themselves to be redeemed by him. No longer are they stiled enemies, but friends of God. "Ye are my Friends, if ye do whatsoever I command you."

By the fall we lost also the divine image, and, of course, our happiness; for when we ceased to resemble God, we became incapable of the enjoyment of him. Without a similarity of temper and disposition between two beings, there cannot be any affection, agreement, or felicity. Man was at first created holy, that he might be happy; that he might possess, in some sort, the happiness which God himself enjoys. So absolutely necessary is purity of soul, to render us capable of celestial enjoyments, that we are assured in the most peremptory manner, that "without holiness no man shall see the Lord," or can be qualified for the enjoyment of him.

The great Mediator affords the means to regain the heavenly temper we lost. His holy ordinances are ordained for this very end. They are rendered efficacious through the assistance of the divine Spirit; and it's powerful aid, it's sanctifying saving graces, together with every other favor, we are assured of upon our due application to the throne of grace. "If men," says he, "being evil, know how to give good gifts unto their children, how much more will their heavenly father give his Holy Spirit to those that ask it." If mankind, who possess the principles of affection for their children in an imperfect degree, are yet most readily inclined to confer favours on them, How much more readily will the Father of Heaven bestow blessings on his offspring; even with as much greater freedom as he is better, more perfect than the sons of men?" "Ask" every spiritual and necessary blessing, "and it shall be given you; seek and ye shall find; knock and it shall be opened to you. For every one that asketh," in a proper manner "receiveth; and he that seeketh findeth; and to him that knocketh, it shall be opened." This gracious permission to supplicate divine benefits, with a most kind promise of having our petitions heard, our saviour was pleased thus to repeat to his disciples. "If ye shall ask anything in my name," for the sake of my merits and mediation, "I will do it," it shall be granted you.

72 *A Sermon Preached at Charlestown November 29, 1798 On the Anniversary Thanksgiving In Massachusetts*—With An Appendix Designed to illustrate some parts of the discourse; exhibiting proof of the early existence, progress, and deleterious effects of French intrigue and influence in the United States. By Jedidah Morse, D.D. Pastor of the Church in Charlestown Published by Request, Second Edition. Printed by Samuel Hall, No. 53, Cornhill, Boston, 1799.

73 Boller, *George Washington & Religion*, p. 78. says, "He expressed similar satisfaction with a thanksgiving sermon delivered by Jedidiah Morse, Congregational minister, staunch Federalist, and 'father of American geography,' to celebrate the passing of the French crisis in 1798. But what Washington particularly liked was the appendix, which Morse had added to the sermon, 'exhibiting proofs of the early existence, progress and deleterious effects of French intrigue and influence in the United States.' Washington told Morse that he had read the appendix 'with pleasure' and wished that it 'could meet a more general circulation' because it contained 'important information.' What he thought of the sermon itself he did not say." It is true that Washington seemingly approved the sermon. But note that the argument misses the point, since the appendix is thoroughly Christian as well as the sermon. Either Boller suppresses this fact, or has not read the sermon and the appendix. Either way, this is substandard research.

74 The text continues, "Foreign intrigue, the bane of our independence, peace, and prosperity, has been operating, in this country, in various ways, for more than twenty years past, in insidious efforts to diminish our national limits, importance, and resources, &c." (Preceding Discourse, p. 15)

"It is the object of this appendix to substantiate, from facts, the truth of that article in the preceding Discourse, of which the above is a part. In doing this, I consider myself as discharging an important duty of my profession. The interests of religion and good government, in the present state of the world, if we may judge from the condition of France, and her conquered countries, Holland, Geneva, and Switzerland, are inseparably interwoven, and must prosper or decay together. Anarchy is fatal to the religion and morals, as well as to the political health and prosperity of a nation; and so, I believe, for the same reason, is French influence. To develop and oppose it, therefore, is to espouse the cause of the *Church* as well as of the *State*.

"The intrigues, and consequent influence of France, in this country, I conceive, have corrupted, to an incalculable extent, all the sources of our true happiness. Our political divisions and embarrassments, and much of that Atheistical infidelity and irreligion, which, during the last twenty years, have made such alarming progress among us, are probably but the poisonous fruits of our alliance and intimate intercourse with the French nation. Her schemes and views concerning us, through all our vicissitudes, have been uniformly hostile to our dearest rights and interests. In proof of this, I appeal to the facts hereafter related.

"At a time when our holy religion and our government are formidably assailed, by the secret and subtle artifices of foreign enemies, it is incumbent on every friend to Christianity, and to his country, to unite in opposing their insidious and wicked designs. He is unworthy the name of a Christian or a patriot, who, in such a crisis as the present, is silent or inactive. Surely the ministers of religion ought not to be considered as deviating from the duties of their profession, while they unveil those political intrigues, which, in their progress and opera-tion, are undermining the foundations, and blasting the fair fruits of that holy religion, which they preach, and which they are under the oath of God to vindicate against every species of attack....

"I confess that I have been one of the many thousands of my countrymen, who have felt an honest esteem for, and a sincere gratitude to France, for the aid she afforded us during our war with Great Britain, and who unfeignedly rejoiced with her at the commencement of her revolution, in the prospect of her enjoying the sweets of freedom, and the blessings of an equal government. But I am not ashamed now to acknowledge, (and thousands have done the same) that this esteem, gratitude, and joy, were the offspring of *ignorance*. A develop-ment of the motives and designs of France, in respect to her alliance and intercourse with us, and of the real nature and object of her rev-olution, has produced an entire change in my own feelings and opinions. I can no longer consider her government, at any period, either under the monarchy or the republic, as having been truly friendly to the interests of the United Stateş; . . .

"....infidelity and licentiousness are too numerous, they are yet the minority of the nation, as we will hope and are now on the decline, both in numbers and influence. The lamentable issue of the great experiment, made in France, of governing a civilized people without the aids of religion, has procured for Christianity many able advocates, and furnished many strong motives to the Christian to cherish his faith. While France, both in a political and religious view, exhibits an awful example for us to shun, we cannot but feel for her present deplorable wretchedness, and the tremendous calamities, which, in all probability, still await this profligate nation. Although the "prejudices of philoso-phers (philosophists) and systemists", have been pronounced "incorrigible," we will indulge the hope, that the uncommon afflictions and miseries which the atheistical conspirators against religion and government have brought upon France, and those under her control, will operate conviction and regret in the blindest understanding and the hardest heart; and thus all this "wrath of man" be made ultimately to "praise God." How much soever we detest the principles and the conduct of the French, we shall most sincerely wish them well; that they may speedily enjoy the fruits of true repentance and reformation; the blessings of good government, peace, and pure Christianity. Then we will embrace them as FRIENDS; till then, we ought to hold them as ENEMIES."

75 Boller, *George Washington & Religion*, p. 78. says, "In the second instance, however, we can speak with some precision. In 1789, a few months after Washington's inauguration, Reverend Joseph Buckminster of New Hampshire sent the new President a sermon which presumably might be of particular interest to Washington as he assumed the highest office in the new federal government. It was an old sermon. It had been preached by Benjamin Stevens, pastor of the first church in Kittery, Maine, on the occasion of the death of Sir William Pepperell in 1759.... Washington voiced his hearty 'approbation of the doctrine therein inculcated.' Whether it was the humility or the conscientious-ness enjoined upon men in high office that appealed to Washington we have no way of knowing. Probably it was both. In any case, the doctrine which he approved was primarily of political significance and does not enlighten us as to his attitude toward the tenets of the Christian faith."

Paul Boller here follows the cut and paste presentation of this sermon given initially by Moncure Conway. Reverend Conway was the edi-tor of *The Works of Thomas Paine*, the leading Deist of Washington's day. Conway was quoted by Lane in *The Catalogue to the Washington Library at the Boston Athenaeum*, p. 194, "This letter to Dr. Buckminster is especially notable, because, though the larger part was dictated, Washington has added in his own hand his approbation of the doctrine of the discourse. It is doubtful if in all his writings similar approval of any statement of doctrine can be found. . . . The text selected for [this sermon] was from the 82nd Psalm, 'But ye shall die like men.' Referring to the previous part of the verse (7), 'I have said ye are Gods,' the preacher said that rulers might in a sense be properly so styled, because governments being appointed of God, magistrates were his representatives, He defined God as a moral governor, engaged in a great plan of wisdom and benevolence. As this world is not a state of retribution, it is requisite that these earthly Gods should be removed by Death as well as other men, in order to compleat the Plan of the Divine government. Indeed the great ends of the moral administra-tion of God seem to require this, to suppress the progress of vice and promote virtue and goodness in the present state, but especially for the final adjustment of all things with equity.' This, probably, is the doctrine of which Washington intimates his approval."

Steven's sermon, edited and summarized by Conway, is presented in such a way that one would have thought it was a sermon preached by a Deist. Nevertheless, if one is permitted actually to see the words of the sermon, it is clear that Steven's sermon is an orthodox Christian sermon. One would never know that fact from Conway's careful cutting and pasting of the message. Further, this method of parsing out the sections that Washington would have agreed with is not only entirely prejudicial and unscientific, it is inconsistent with the glowing affirmation that Washington wrote in his own hand. The sermon was addressed as a whole. The sermon as a whole was Christian. How could there not be Christian doctrine in view? This was a Christian funeral sermon, which as a whole was filled with Christian doctrine. The method employed here by Reverend Conway and Professor Boller is an overt act of deflection to keep the reader from knowing what Washington actually had read and approved. Astonishingly, the generally skeptical Professor Boller apparently can set aside all doubt and tell us what parts of the sermon Washington liked, although Washington's letter did not limited his approval to any specific doctrinal teach-ing. We believe this approach by Conway and Boller is an expression of a method of desperation to cover over the obvious Christian views that Washington had to possess to approve this sermon.

76 "A Sermon occasioned by the death of the Honorable Sir William Pepperell, Bart. Lieutenant-General in his Majesty's Service." Who died at his seat in Kittery, July 6th, 1759, aged 63. Preached the next Lord's-Day after his funeral by Benjamin Stevens, A.M. Pastor of the First Church in Kittery.

77 A Funeral Sermon. Psalm 82:7. But ye shall die like men.

As the benevolent Author of our Being, who knows our weakness, and wishes our welfare, is represented by the great Prophet of the Jews, saying to his people, *O that they were wise, that they understood this, that they would consider their latter end!* We have hereby plain-ly intimated, that serious reflections on our mortality, and the issue of things at death, would ... excite us faithfully to act the parts assigned us here, and daily solicitous to focus on the happiness of the world to come. ...

...The words are, *I have said ye are Gods, and all of you are children of the most High*. It follows, *But ye shall die like men*. ... Civil rulers are here, and in several other places in the sacred oracles, stiled Gods, not only on account of their authority and dominion, or the dignity of their character and office: but to point out the end and design for which they are exalted to power, viz. That they might in their limited sphere, imitate Him, who is the Supreme Ruler of the Universe, who governs the whole in infinite wisdom, perfect righteousness and goodness. ....Christ also says, John 10, 35 – *He called them Gods to whom the Word of the Lord came*, i.e. God, in his Word, has called those Gods, to whom he had delegated Power, and who were commissioned by Him, to the Office of Magistrates and Rulers....Now since in this sense civil Rulers *are of God*, and *his Establishment* and *Appointment*, ...they may without Impropriety be stilled *Gods*. But such, however dignified by Titles of Honor and Respect—And by *that* which is given to the sovereign Majesty of Heaven and Earth—Such, I say, however elevated their Station or extensive their Power and Usefulness, must die like other Men...

This is a Truth taught in our Text, and a Truth too evident to admit of any laboured Proof....In a Word, "The Lord Jehovah, only hath Immorality"—"He is the living God" "and an everlasting King" "His Throne remaineth from Generation to Generation while *the* Gods that have not made the Heavens and the Earth, even they shall perish from the Earth, and from under the Heavens."
...

Now as the most exalted in Dignity, whatever may be their boasted Pedigree, tho' they may lay Claim to noble, royal or divine Extraction, are Descendents of *Adam*: by whom "Sin entered into the World, and Death by Sin;" Death passes upon them as well as others. And however they may be distinguished in other Respects, they equally share with others in the Consequences of the first Transgression: and are involved in the same general Sentence of Death, with the whole Posterity of *Adam*....Infinite Wisdom cannot *err*, nor perfect *Rectitude* do *wrong*. Farther let it be observed that *Immortality* here was not the *Right* of Mankind, not even of *Adam* in Innocency:... however some of them may be distinguished and exalted above the Rest of his Posterity, yet they too, in Respect of their Mortality, must be equal Sharers with the common Parent of all. ...

... this Part of the divine Government may be, to prevent an undue *Trust* and *Dependence* in *Men*, and to lead us to place it in *Him*, to whom it belongs, and on *whom alone*, it can be placed with Safety. As this Appointment tends to suppress the Pride of those who may arrogate *Divinity* to themselves, so also to check the *Impiety* of those who *idolize* such false *Gods*.

... It is equally apparent that his moral Administration is not perfect here, but that it extends to a future State, in which all are to be dealt with according to their respective Characters.—Here there is often *one Event to the Righteous and to the Wicked*. But as all are to be removed hence by Death, and as Death stands in Connection with the Judgment of the great Day: Since the Great as well as the Small are to stand before the Tribunal of the universal Judge; they shall be judged in like Manner without Respect of Persons, and receive according to the deeds done in the Body. And *the Kings of the Earth, and the great Men, and the rich men, and the chief Captains and mighty Men*, were told, shall be struck with Terror and Amazement at the Appearance of Him *that sitteth on the Throne, and the Wrath of the Lamb*.

... If such Persons behave well in Life, and view Death in the Light the Gospel represents it to the Righteous; not as the End of our Being, but the Commencement of a happy Immorality: such being conformed to *Him who is the Resurrection and the Life*, have Reason with Thankfulness to adore that gracious Plan of Things which removes them from this World to a better; although the dark Valley of Death be the Passage thereto.— For then, instead of being abased, they shall be exalted to true Dignity. Then they shall be crowned with everlasting honors. Tho' their Bodies lie down in the Dust and see Corruption; tho' they mingle with the common Earth, and with the Dust of the lowest of Men; yet shall they be raised again in the Resurrection of the Just. And at the Judgment of the great Day, those who in this Life faithfully acted the Parts assigned them, shall meet with the Approbation of the universal Judge;—The unerring Discerner of true Worth—and whose Approbation is an Honor infinitely superior to the united Applause and Homage of all Mankind.—And those, *who have been faithful over a few Things, shall be made Ruler over many, and enter into the Joy of their Lord.*

...But before I finish, it deserves Notice, that in these degenerate Days in which too many are asham'd of Christ and his Cross, especially among those who are in high Life, he [Pepperell] consider'd the Christian Character as truly honourable.—And as he was favor'd with a Christian Education; so he made a public and open Profession of the Religion of Christ: and his regular Attendance on his holy Institutions, both in his Family, and in the House of God;—his becoming Seriousness and Gravity when engaged in solemn Acts of Worship;—and his Disposition to maintain peace and Order, and to support the Gospel, shew, that he was not insensible of the sacred Obligations of Christianity. And tho' he ever openly avowed, and steadily adhered to his religious Sentiments, he was far from being Ostentatious in his Religion—And, I believe, abhorred the Practice of cloaking wicked and sinister Intentions under the specious Disguise of Piety. Being also firmly attached to our Ecclesiastical Constitution, and a Friend to Learning, he always treated the Ministers of the Gospel with peculiar Marks of Distinction.

... *My Little Children*, Be concerned to remember your Creator in the Days of your Youth; let it be your first Concern to be good: In order to which acquaint yourselves with God, with his Son Christ Jesus, and with his Gospel; and live as the Word of God directs you....and you will be Blessings in this World, and happy to all Eternity.... find Consolation in him who so tenderly sympathized with his afflicted Friends in the Days of his Flesh! – In him who is the Resurrection and the Life! – And believing in him may they have Life eternal!

...May we be taught hereby to cease from Man, and to put our Trust in and expect our Happiness from him who is the ever-living God! – the Voice of this Providence speaks aloud to all to prepare for Death; – to prepare to follow him who is gone before us.— Every instance of Mortality enforces with peculiar Energy that important Admonition of our great Instructor Jesus Christ, *Be ye also ready for in such on Hour as you think not, the Son of Man cometh*. None we see are exempted from Death; – its Approach is intirely uncertain, it can be but at a little Distance at farthest, and is besides such an important and interesting Event, that it demands our most serious Consideration and our greatest Solicitude to prepare for it, that so it may be joyful and happy.

The life of Sir William Pepperell, as highlighted by Reverend Stevens, must have impressed Washington as well. The many striking parallels between Washington's and Pepperell's lives must have been the impetus for Lady Pepperell to send this sermon to Washington just before she died. Washington had made his presidential tour of the area only a short time before and had then met Reverend Buckminster, the clergyman who sent the sermon to the President. See *Washington's Diaries*. We add a few other quotes from the sermon that fill out the fascinating life of Sir Pepperell.

> … a just Character of Sir WILLIAM PEPPERELL; yet I shall attempt some Sketches thereof, and a brief Detail of those Services which render'd him so conspicuous both at Home and Abroad. In which Nothing, I trust, will be said, but what those who truly knew him, and are unprejudic'd, would readily subscribe to.
>
> … So high was he in the Esteem of his Country at that *important Crisis*, when the Scheme was laid by the *New-England* Governments for the Reduction of *Louis-bourg*, that He was wisely made Choice of by his Excellency our Governor, and commissioned by Him, …Every Circumstance consider'd, it was a Conquest heard of by all with Surprise, and will be transmitted to future Ages with Wonder.
>
> It is true, there was a most remarkable Series of Providences concurring in this whole Affair, and tho' Praise is ever to be ascrib'd to God *who did marvelous Things for us*, yet a *grateful Memorial* is due to him who was the principal Agent in obtaining this glorious Acquisition; … he ought ever to be accounted *honourable, because by him the Lord hath given Deliverance to us.*
>
> As there was so remarkable an Interposition of Heaven conspiring to bring this Enterprize to its happy Issue, so our General not only, as became an heroic spirit, was modest in Victory, but as became a Christian ever ascrib'd, even to his dying Breath, the Honor and Praise *to the Lord of Hosts and the God of Armies:* And as in the Undertaking and Prosecution of this important Affair, he was concern'd by Prayer and Supplication to engage the divine Blessing, and like the pious Heroes of old went forth *in the Name of the Lord;* so likewise did he acknowledge with Gratitude to the honor of the great Governour of the Universe, that *His right Hand and his holy Arm had gotten him the Victory.* He had a due Sense likewise of "the heroic Resolution, and exemplary Bravery of the Officers and Soldiers who were with him, and always estem'd it his great Honor to have commanded them.
>
> This illustrious Undertaking being thus happily accomplished, and such important Consequences having been the Result of that Conquest of *Lewisbourg;* as it has already caus'd the Name of Sir William Peppernell to spread far and wide, so will it occasion it to be remembered with Gratitude and Respect by all succeeding Generations.…It was upon this great Action's being so bravely attempted, and so happily accomplish'd, that our gracious Sovereign conferr'd the *Title* and *Dignity* of a BARONET of *Great-Britain* upon *our deceased Friend;* —An Honor never before or since confer'd on a Native of *New-England…*

78   Robert Davidson, D.D., A Sermon, on the Freedom and Happiness of the United Sates of America, preached in Carlisle, on the 5th Oct. 1794. Published at the request of the Officers of the Philadelphia and Lancaster Troops of Light Horse. By Robert Davidson, D.D. Pastor of the Presbyterian Church in Carlisle, and One of the Professors in Dickinson College. (Philadelphia: printed by Samuel H. Smith for Robert Campbell. 1794), 29 pp. See Lane, *The Washington Collection*, pp. 64-65.

79   Twohig, *Diaries*, October 5, 1794.

80   Davidson, *Sermon on the Freedom and Happiness.*

81   Davidson, *Sermon on the Freedom and Happiness:* As a Divine Providence, then, must be acknowledged over the affairs of men; and something may be learned on this subject even from *the light of nature*, and the general voice of nations;—how thankful should we be for *the light of revelation*, by which our views are so greatly enlarged, and our thoughts are carried back to the creation and forward to the consummation of all things! For the representations which are every where given of God, in the Jewish writings, lead us to conceive of him as the creator, Preserver, and Lord of heaven and earth; as having all nations under his direction; and employing all the shining armies of heaven as his ministers, in the government of this lower world.… They had also the moral law, written by the finger of God himself, which gives a full view of all those duties which we owe to God and to one another. For the sum of the commandments is, *To love the Lord our God with all our hearts, and our neighbour as ourselves.*" "…in the second pace, consider the great goodness of the Divine Being to our state and nation in particular;–our high privileges; the gratitude which we owe to God for them; and the wise improvement which we ought to make of them."

82   Ibid., …He then added, "And as to Religion, the choicest blessing of heaven to men, and without which no nation can be truly happy;–is she not left at liberty, to display to every advantage her celestial charms, and to exert her renovating powers on the minds of men, free both from the aids and the restraints of the civil arm? What would the people of these States have or wish for more? Are not these the very objects for which our patriots bled? And to obtain which the greatest sacrifices have been made by all ranks of citizens?" .…This then brought Dr. Davidson to address the reality of the officers of the federal army worshiping in his presence along with the Commander in Chief and President, George Washington. Dr. Davidson said, "But when I look around me, and see multitudes of men in the garb of soldiers, and handling the instruments of war,—I cannot but feel the most painful emotions, and ask,—What these things mean?...These preparations are …to teach those who will not otherwise be taught,—that we ought all to be obedient to lawful authority; that we ought to respect the government which ourselves have made, and whose protection we have enjoyed; that in a pure republic the will of the majority must be submitted to, and no lawless attempts made to weaken the energy of good government.…what heart, that is not hardened into an entire insensibility, does not bleed at the thought of an unprovoked insurrection, by some of our deluded fellow-citizens, against the mildest and freest government under heaven!"

83   Ibid.

84   Cited in Lane, *The Washington Collection*, p. 3.

85   *The Albany Centinal*, 1798-06-05; vol. I; Iss. 97; p. 3.

86   Reverend Alexander Addison, An Oration on the Rise and progress of the United States of America, to the Present Crisis; and on the Duties of the Citizens. (Philadelphia: Printed by John Ormrod, no. 41, Chesnut-Street,, 1798.)

87   Reverend M. L. Weems, *The Philanthropist;* or *A Good Twelve Cents Worth of Political Love Power, for the Fair Daughters and Patriotic Sons of America.* Dedicated to that great *Lover* and *Love* of his Country, George Washington, Esq (Alexandria: John & James D. Westcott, 1799).

88   *WGW,* vol. 37, 8-29-1799. To Reverend Mason L. Weems.

89   Weems, *The Philanthropist.* ....*it is not good for man* to be alone; that *alone*, he is a feeble helpless wretch…that *alone*, he is but as a poor ship-wrecked sailor cast on a desolate island, … our *associated state*, we are like a great family of brothers whom God has placed together as mutual aids, …Is it not as much a law of nature that we should love one another, as it is that the members of the body should love one another? As that the eyes should love the feet for carrying them to gaze on the dear objects of their affections? Or, that the feet should love the eyes for directing them to flowery walks to ramble in? Do the members of the body ever repine at each others perfections? Does the foot repine because the eye is quick sighted to see a thousand charming objects; because the ear with admirable nicety can distinguish enchanting sounds; or because the arms are strong and able to get an abundance of good things? No: they rejoice in each *other's perfections*, as in the instruments of their own glory and happiness. In like manner ought not every member of the great body of society to rejoice in the perfections of his brother member?

…how then must it affect, how *torture* the soul of humanity to see us men, whom God placed here to live in love, thus dreadfully abusing our powers to curse each others existence, and to crush one another into an untimely grave! …Thus, as in the natural body no member could be amputated without great detriment to the whole, so in the social body no class of the citizens could be taken away without great detriment to the rest. Thus has God, the common Parent, removed far from us all ground of pride on the part of the rich, and of dejection on the part of the poor, "the rich and the poor, says Solomon, meet together, the Lord is the maker of them all."….

Thus, secure in each others protection, thus abundant and happy in the sweet rewards of their mutual labours, they can eat, drink, and rejoice together like brothers, under the shade of their own vine and fig-tree, none daring to make them afraid. O how goodly a thing it is to see a whole nation living thus together in unity! …

O blessed land of well *secured liberty*, of *equal laws, of moderate taxes*, and *of universal toleration!*…O that we did but know in this our day the many felicities we enjoy under this our government, and did but love the government as we ought!

But how shall we *manifest* our love? By splitting into parties and mortally hating one another? No, God forbid, for a furious party spirit is the greatest *judgment*, the *heaviest curse* that can befall our country. It extinguishes loves.…

"Honor *all men* – Love *the brotherhood* – Fear *God* – Honor *the king.*"

Let us, *honor all men*; yes, even those who differ from us in political sentiments.

To make this more easy and pleasant; *Love the brotherhood*…. one *great political body*. Let us *fear God*. That is the only firm base on which the happiness of individuals, the prosperity of nations can rest securely. It is the only root from which every branch of duty can spring in *full vigor*, be *fed* and *enlivened*.

Wise and blessed above all nations should we be if we would but adopt such a conduct, a conduct honorable to human nature, and worthy of *Christianity*, which represents men to each other as children of one parent, as members of one family, journeying together through the chequer'd scenes of this transitory world, towards a region where all the distinctions of *rich* and *poor*, *high* and *low* are unknown, and where virtue alone shall be exalted and vice degraded for ever.

90   *WGW,* vol. 32, 10-20-1792. To Dr. William Davies Shipley.

91   Jonathan Shipley Bishop of St. Asaph, 1714-1788. *Shipley's Works*, 2 vols., Reverend Jonathan Shipley. Works. 2 vols., London. 1792. Presentation copy "From the Reverend Wm. Davies Shipley Dean of St. Asaph," the son of the author. Washington acknowledged the gift in a letter dated Philadelphia, 20 Oct., 1792. Lane, *Catalogue of the Washington Collection*, p. 500.

92   *WGW,* vol. 16, 9-8-1779. Note: The eulogium was "An Eulogium of the brave men who have fallen in the contest with Great Britain," delivered July 5, 1779, in the German Calvinist Church in Philadelphia. A copy is in the Library of Congress.

93   *WGW,* vol. 37,11-6-1781. To Jonathan Trumbull, Jr. See *The Works & Life of Laurence Sterne*, 2 volumes (New York: J. F. Taylor and Co., 1904). Sterne's collection of sermons was also in Washington's library. See Lane, *Catalogue of the Washington Collection*, p. 192.

CHAPTER 34

1   *WGW,* vol. 30, 6-20-1773.

2   G.W.P. Custis, *Recollections*, p. 477

3   Ellis, *His Excellency*, p. 151.

4   Boller, *George Washington & Religion.* In fact, it is the only work that is cited in the article on Religion in the *Washington Biographical Companion* written by the University of Virginia Professor, Frank E. Grizzard, Jr., the editor of the Washington Papers.

5   Ibid., p. 114.

6   Ibid., p. 111. Frank E. Grizzard, Jr. writes on pp. 270-71, "Although Washington often wrote about the intervention of Providence in human affairs, he only rarely mentioned his beliefs about an afterlife. When a friend named a son after him, Washington wrote to express the hope that 'he will live long to enjoy it, long after I have taken my departure for the world of Spirits." On the eve of his leaving Mount Vernon for Philadelphia for the Constitutional Convention, he confided in Robert Morris of his internal conflict about whether to become involved again in a public life: 'My first remaining wish being, to glide gently down the stream of life in tranquil retirement till I shall arrive at the world of sperits.' When his mother died in August 1789, at the age of 83, he wrote to console his sister, Betty, expressing the 'hope that she is translated to a happier place.' To another he referred to being 'translated to a happier clime.' How literally Washington meant these references to a 'happier clime' and a 'land of Spirts' is unclear. Certainly there is a detached and almost fatalistic tone about them. In short, he did believe in immortality, but it is unclear whether he held the classical version of one's life and deeds living on in the effects and memory of subsequent generations or the more literal land of spirits, so totally 'other worldly' as to be unknowable and hence not worth

troubling oneself over. The mention of a happier clime and meeting in the future indicates that he leaned more in favor of some sort of literal afterlife."

7 Thomas Paine, *Age of Reason*, Part II. Paine explains the rational basis for belief in immortality as follows:

> That the consciousness of existence is not dependent on the same form or the same matter is demonstrated to our senses in the works of the creation, as far as our senses are capable of receiving that demonstration. A very numerous part of the animal creation preaches to us, far better that Paul, the belief of a life hereafter. Their little life resembles an earth and a heaven—a present and a future state, and comprises, if it may be so expressed, immortality in miniature.
>
> The most beautiful parts of the creation to our eye are the winged insects, and they are not so originally. They acquire that form and that inimitable brilliancy by progressive changes. The slow and creeping caterpillar-worm of today passes in a few days to a torpid figure and a state resembling death; and in the next change comes forth in all the miniature magnificence of life, a splendid butterfly. No resemblance of the former creature remains; everything is changed; all his powers are new, and life is to him another thing. We cannot conceive that the consciousness of existence is not the same in this state of the animal as before; why then must I believe that the resurrection of the same body is necessary to continue to me the consciousness of existence hereafter?
>
> In the former part of the *Age of Reason* I have called the creation the only true and real word of God; and this instance, or this text, in the book of creation, not only shows to us that this thing may be so, but that it is so; and that the belief of a future state is a rational belief, founded upon facts visible in the creation; for it is not more difficult to believe that we shall exist hereafter in a better state and form than at present, than that a worm should become a butterfly, and quit the dunghill for the atmosphere, if we did not know it as a fact.

8 "True religion is a system of moral theism, which Herbert elaborates in five propositions: (1) there is a supreme God; (2) this supreme God ought to be worshipped; (3) virtue joined with piety is the best method of divine worship; (4) vices and crimes and all sorts of wickedness must be expiated by repentance; and (5) there is reward or punishment after this life. The practice of true religion is supposed to result in eternal life, and all our cognitive faculties have been designed to this end. This explains the two main parts of Herbert's philosophy: a theory of knowledge and a philosophy of comparative religion." From www.thoemmes.com/encyclopedia/herbert.htm. See also, www.luminarium.org/sevenlit/chirbury/chirbio.htm.

9 As to Thomas Jefferson's belief in immortality, consider, theamericanrevolution.org/ipeople/tjeff.asp. "In another strictly private communication to Dr. Rush, made in his first term as president, Jefferson revealed his own religious opinions. He believed in God and immortality ..." For Benjamin Franklin's belief in immortality and the resurrection of the body, consider the following: The epitaph that Franklin wrote for himself, but which was not used reads, "The body of Benjamin Franklin, printer, like the cover of an old book, its contents torn out and stripped of its lettering and gilding, lies here, food for worms. But the work shall not be lost; for it will, as he believed, appear once more in a new and more elegant edition, revised and corrected by the Author." See www.fi.edu/franklin/timeline/epitaph.html.

10 Washington wrote in his Diary on February 12, 1785, "Received an Invitation to the Funeral of Willm. Ramsy, Esqr. Of Alexandria, the oldest Inhabitt. Of the Town; and went up. Walked in a procession as a free mason, Mr. Ramsay in his life being one, and now buried with the ceremonies and honors due to one." Jackson, Twohig, *Diaries of George Washington*.

11 *GWP* Series 4. General Correspondence. 1697-1799 Pennsylvania Grand Lodge Masons to George Washington, December 27, 1796, image 438.

12 Ibid., Series 2 Letterbooks George Washington to Pennsylvania Grand Lodge Masons, January, 1797 Letterbook 40 Image 257.

13 Schaff, *Creeds of Christendom*, III, p. 499.

14 On this text, Chief Justice Hale wrote: "Most certainly the wise consideration of our Latter End, and the employing of our selves, upon that Account ... renders [*this*] *life the most contenting and comfortable life in the World*. For as a Man... [He] takes his opportunity to gain a stock of Grace and Favour with God, [he] has made his peace with his Maker through Christ Jesus, [he] has done a great part of the chief business of his life, and [he] is ready upon all occasions, for all conditions whereunto the Divine Providence shall assign him, whether of life or death, or health or sickness, or poverty or riches... If God lend him longer life in this World, he carries on his great business to greater degrees of perfection, with ease, and without difficulty, trouble, or perturbation: But if Almighty God cut him shorter, and call him to give an account of his Stewardship, he is ready... *Blessed is that Servant whom his Master when he comes shall find so doing*. As thus this Consideration makes Life better, so it makes Death easie. 1. By frequent consideration of Death and Dissolution, he is taught not to fear it; he is, as it were, acquainted with it afore-hand, by often preparation for it....2. By frequent consideration of our Latter end, Death becomes to be no surprise unto us." Sir Matthew Hale, *Contemplations Moral and Divine* (London: Printed for William Shrowsbery at the Bible in Duke-Lane, and John Leigh at Stationers-Hall, MDCLXXXV), pp. 5-6.

15 *WGW* vol. 2, 10-20-1761. To Richard Washington.

16 We discussed this text in the chapter on Washington's childhood education. See Lane, *The Washington Collection*, p. 52.

17 Custis, *Recollections*, p. 21.

18 *WGW*, vol. 27, 7-10-1783, To George William Fairfax.

19 For example, *WGW*, vol. 32, 3-6-1793. To Reverend Bryan Fairfax, "I thank you for your kind condolence on the Death of my Nephew. It is a loss I sincerely regret, but as it is the will of Heaven, whose decrees are always just and wise, I submit to it without a murmur." See *WGW* vol. 35, 3-30-1796. To Tobias Lear. Washington recognized how difficult it was to bring consolation to a grieving family. He actually expresses this sentiment by quoting from a Christian sermon by Reverend Laurene Sterne: *WGW*, vol. 16, 9-8-1779. To Reverend Hugh Henry Brackenridge. "Sir: I have to thank you for your favor of the 10th of August, and your Eulogium. [*WGW* Note: The eulogium was "An Eulogium of the brave men who have fallen in the contest with Great Britain," delivered July 5, 1779, in the German Calvinist Church in Philadelphia.] You add motives to patriotism, and have made the army your debtor in the handsome tribute which is paid to the memory of those who have fallen in fighting for their country. I am sensible that none of these observations can have escaped you, and

that I can offer nothing which your own reason has not already suggested on this occasion; and being of Sterne's opinion, that "Before an affliction is digested, consolation comes too soon; and after it is digested, it comes too late: there is but a mark between these two, as fine almost as a hair, for a comforter to take aim at." I rarely attempt it, nor shall I add more on this subject to you, as it would only be a renewal of sorrow, by recalling a fresh to your remembrance things which had better be forgotten." (Emphasis added.)

20 *WGW*, vol. 32, 4-9-1793. To Reverend Bryan Fairfax. "Dear Sir: At One o'clock in the afternoon on Thursday next, I mean to pay the last respect to my deceased Nephew, by having the funeral obsequies performed. If you will do me the favor to officiate on the occasion, it will be grateful to myself, and pleasing to other friends of the deceased. No sermon is intended, and but few friends will be present: for these dinner will be ready at half after two Oclk, at which I should be happy and shall expect to see you."

21 Ibid., vol. 30, 9-13-1789 to Elizabeth Washington Lewis. "My dear Sister: Colonel Ball's letter gave me the first account of my Mother's death. Since that I have received Mrs. Carter's letter, written at your request, and previous to both I was prepared for the event by some advices of her illness communicated to your Son Robert.

Awful, and affecting as the death of a Parent is, there is consolation in knowing, that Heaven has spared ours to an age, beyond which few attain, and favored her with the full enjoyment of her mental faculties, and as much bodily strength as usually falls to the lot of fourscore. Under these considerations and a hope that she is translated to a happier place, it is the duty of her relatives to yield due submission to the decrees of the Creator. When I was last at Fredericksburg, I took a final leave of my Mother, never expecting to see her more."

22 Ibid., vol. 37, 9-22-1799. To Burgess Ball.

23 Ibid., vol. 32 4-9-1793. To Reverend Bryan Fairfax.

24 From the 1662 *Book of Common Prayer*:

When they come to the Grave, while the Corps is made ready to be laid into the earth, the Priest shall say, or the Priest and Clerks shall sing:
Man that is born of a woman hath but a short time to live, and is full of misery. He cometh up, and is cut down, like a flower; he fleeth as it were a shadow, and never continueth in one stay.

In the midst of life we are in death: of whom may we seek for succour, but of thee, O Lord, who for our sins art justly displeased?

Yet, O Lord God most holy, O Lord most mighty, O holy and most merciful Saviour, deliver us not into the bitter pains of eternal death.

Thou knowest, Lord, the secrets of our hearts: shut not thy merciful ears to our prayer; but spare us, Lord most holy, O God most mighty, O holy and merciful Saviour, thou most worthy Judge eternal , suffer us not, at our last hour for any pains of death, to fall from thee.

Then, while the earth shall be cast upon the body by some standing by, the Priest shall say,
Forasmuch as it hath pleased Almighty God of his great mercy to take unto himself the soul of our dear *brother* here departed, we therefore commit *his* body to the ground; earth to earth, ashes to ashes, dust to dust; in sure and certain hope of the resurrection to eternal life, through our Lord Jesus Christ; who shall change our vile body, that it may be like unto his glorious body, according to the mighty working, whereby he is able to subdue all things to himself.

Then shall be said or sung,
I heard a voice from heaven, saying unto me, Write, From henceforth blessed are the dead which die in the Lord: Even so, saith the Spirit, for they rest from their labours. *Reverend* 14.13.

Then the Priest shall say,
Lord, have mercy upon us.
Christ, have mercy upon us.
Lord have mercy upon us

Another book found in Washington's library when he died was the 1744 edition of *The Sick Man Visited: And Furnished with Instructions, Meditations, and Prayers, for putting him in mind of his Change; for supporting him under his Distemper; and for preparing him for, and carrying him through, his last conflict with Death* by Nathanael Spinckes, Late Prebendary of Sarum. Printed in London. We cannot be sure to what extent Washington ever used this particular book. But its message certainly was relevant because of the many serious illnesses that Washington had that nearly took his life at various times: Small pox in Barbados, a serious illness just before Braddock's defeat; the illness connected with his "grim King" reference. One illness was so severe that he wrote to his Pastor/Physician Reverend Charles Green, "Reverend Sir: Necessity (and that I hope will Apologize for the trouble I must give you), obliges me to ask the favour of a visit; that I may have an opportunity of consulting you on a disorder which I have linger'd under for three Months past. It is painful to me to write, Mr. Carlyle will say the rest, I shall only add, that I am with very great esteem, ..."(*WGW*, vol. 2, 11-13-1757. To Reverend Charles Green. See also *WGW*, vol. 2, 8-26-1761. Washington also survived two very severe illnesses while President (a case of near fatal pneumonia, a near fatal abscess on his thigh). Having lost her first husband, and her two children, death was never far from the mind of Martha Washington either, as she experienced many illnesses as well. (*WGW*, vol. 27, 7-10-1783. To George William Fairfax. Washington wrote, "Mrs. Washington enjoys an incompetent share of health; Billious Fevers and Cholic's attack her very often, and reduce her low; at this moment she is but barely recovering from one of them; at the same time that she thanks Mrs. Fairfax and you for your kind suggestion of Doctr. James's Annaliptic Pills, she begs you both to accept her most Affectionate regards; she would have conveyed these in a letter of her own, with grateful acknowledgements of Mrs. Fairfax's kind remembrance by Mr. Lee, if her health would have allowed it." The prayers from Spinkes include: "A Prayer for Patience and Resignation to the Divine Will", "A Prayer for a Sanctifies Use of Sickness," "A Prayer for Victory over Death." pp. 187-188, 289.

Washington's words describing Lord Fairfax were nearly as true of himself: "Lord Fairfax (as I have been told) after having bowed down to the grave, and in a manner shaken hands with death, is perfectly restored, and enjoys his usual good health, and as much vigour as falls to the lot of Ninety."(*WGW*, vol. 11, 3-11-1778. To George William Fairfax. Thus an intrepid recognition of his own mortality is evident throughout Washington's writings. The letters of the twenty-three year old soldier spoke of "almost certain death", (*WGW*, vol. 1, 7-18-1755. To Mrs. Mary Washington; to Robert Dinwiddie.) and humorously noted the report of "a circumstantial account of my death and dying speech." (*WGW*, vol. 1, 7-18-1755. To John Augustine Washington) We find the older Washington using the imagery of "wearied traveler" (*WGW*, vol. 27, 2-20-1784. To Maj. Gen. Henry Knox; 3-2-1797.) and "pilgrim"(*WGW*, vol. 10, 1-23-1778. To Reverend William Gordon) en route to a "haven of hope" (*WGW*, vol. 10, 1-23-1778. To Reverend William Gordon.) or a "haven of security and rest."(*WGW* vol. 21, 3-26-1781. To Maj. Gen. John Armstrong.

vol. 36, 3-2-1797. To John Luzac.) Washington, mindful that his pilgrimage would one day end, wrote to John Francis Mercer on September 26, 1792:

> If nothing impeaching my honor, or honesty, is said, I care little for the rest. I have pursued one uniform course for three score years, and am happy in *believing* that the world have thought it a right one: of it's being so, I am so well satisfied myself, that I shall not depart from it by turning either to the right or to the left, until I arrive at the end of my pilgrimage.(*WGW* vol. 32, 9-26-1792. To John Francis Mercer)

25   *WGW*, vol. 26, 4-5-1783. To Marquis de Lafayette.

26   Ibid., vol. 30, 9-8-1789. To Dr. James Craik. vol. 32, 9-21-1792. To Tobias Lear.

27   See Lane note re: Lathrop, Lane, *Washington Collection*, Boston Athenaeum p. 119.

28   *WGW*, vol. 30, 6-22-1788.

29   John Lathrop, "Discourse Before the Humane Society in Boston" (1787), p. 33.

30   *WGW* vol. 35, 1-12-1797. To Benjamin Walker. "It would be a singular satisfaction to me to learn, who was the Author of these letters; and from what source they originated. [Note: So far as is known the "singular satisfaction" of discovering who wrote the spurious letters was denied Washington.]"; *WGW*, vol. 2, February, 1757. To the right Honorable John, Earl of Loudoun: *General and Commander in Chief of All His Majesty's Forces in North America; and Governor and Commander in Chief of His Majesty's Most Antient Colony and Dominion of Virginia* February, 1757, "*We*, the Officers of the Virginia Regiment, beg leave to congratulate your Lordship on your safe arrival in America; and to express the deep sense We have of His Majesty's great *Wisdom* and paternal care for His Colonies, in sending your Lordship to their protection at this critical Juncture. We likewise beg leave to declare our singular satisfaction and sanguine hopes, on your Lordships immediate appointment over our Colony; as it in a more especial manner Entitles Us to your Lordships patronage." *WGW* vol. 23, 1-29-1782. To Philip Schuyler. "Every information tending to prove that the affairs respecting the Grants may be speedily and happily accommodated, gives me singular Satisfaction. I will flatter myself, both the Articles of intelligence you have recd. are well grounded, ..."; *WGW*, vol. 27, 12-13-1783. To the Trustees and Faculty of the University of the state of Pennsylvania. "I experience a singular satisfaction in receiving your congratulations on the establishment of Peace and the security of those important interests which were involved in the fate of the War." *WGW*, vol. 30, 8-28-1788. To George Richards Minot. "I will only add that I always feel a singular satisfaction in discovering proofs of talents and patriotism, in those who are soon to take the parts of the generation, [Minot was then 30 years of age] which is now hastening to leave the stage,..."

31   *WGW*, vol. 29, 2-22-1788. To Reverend John Lathrop.

32   Ellis, *His Excellency*, p. 269.

33   Craik's account of Washington's death was published as an appendix to a sermon entitled, "A Sermon Occasioned by the Death of Gen. George Washington, Commander in Chief of the Armies of the United Sates of America. Who departed this life, on Saturday the 14th December, 1799, after an illness of about 24 hours. Preached December 29, 1799. by the Reverend Hezekiah N. Woodruff A.M. Pastor of the First Church of Christ in Stamington. To which is Added, An Appendix Giving a particular account of the behaviour of Gen. Washington, during his distressing illness, also of the nature of the complaint of which he died, By Doctors James Craik and Elisha C. Dick, attending Physicians. Printed by Samuel Trumbull, For Messsrs. Edward & Nathan Smith, Stonington Prot, January, 1800. p. 16.

34   Meade, *Old Churches and Families of Virginia*, 1857, II, pp. 254-55.

35   *WGW*, vol. 37 Last Will and Testament. In his will he wrote: "The family Vault at Mount Vernon requiring repairs, and being improperly situated besides, I desire that a new one of Brick, and upon a larger Scale, may be built at the foot of what is commonly called the Vineyard Inclosure, on the ground which is marked out. In which my remains, with those of my deceased relatives (now in the old Vault) and such others of my family as may chuse to be entombed there, may be deposited. And it is my express desire that my Corpse may be Interred in a private manner, without parade, or funeral Oration. [Note: The new vault (the present one) was built in 1830-31 by Lawrence Lewis and George Washington Parke Custis.]

36   *WGW*, vol. 32, 2-24-1793. To Frances Bassett Washington. There are several other examples of Washington's strong calls for a religious and philosophical Christian-stoicism. Consider the following: *WGW*, vol. 36 To WILLIAM AUGUSTINE WASHINGTON, February 27, 1798.

My dear Sir: Mr. Rice called here in his way to Alexandria, and delivered me your letter of the 15th. instant. Of the recent afflicting event, which was related therein, we had received previous accounts; and on that as on former occasions of a similar nature, sympathised sincerely in your sorrows. But these are the decrees of an Allwise Providence, against whose dictates the skill, or foresight of man can be of no avail; it is incumbent upon him therefore, to submit with as little repining as the sensibility of his nature will admit. This will have its course, but may be greatly ameliorated by philosophical reflection and resignation. As you have three children left, I trust they will be spared to you, and sincerely hope that in them you will find consolation and comfort.

vol. 33, 5-25-1794 To WILLIAM PEARCE

"Mr. Pearce: I learn with concern from your letter of the 18th. instant, that your crops were still labouring under a drought, and most of them very much injured. At disappointments and losses which are the effects of Providential acts, I never repine; because I am sure the alwise disposer of events knows better than we do, what is best for us, or what we deserve."

vol. 3, 4-25-1773 To BURWELL BASSETT

"Dear Sir: The interruption of the post for several weeks, prevented our receiving the melancholy account of your loss until within these few days. That we sympathize in the misfortune, and lament the decree which has deprived you of so dutiful a child, and the world of so promising a young lady, stands in no need, I hope, of argument to prove; but the ways of Providence being inscrutable, and the justice of it not to be scanned by the shallow eye of humanity, nor to be counteracted by the utmost efforts of human power or wisdom, resignation, and as far as the strength of our reason and religion can carry us, a cheerful acquiescence to the Divine Will, is what we are to aim; and I am persuaded that your own good sense will arm you with fortitude to withstand the stroke, great as k is, and enable you to console Mrs. Bassett, whose loss and feelings are much to be pitied."

vol. 9, 8-11777 To SAMUEL WASHINGTON

"Dear Brothr: Your letter by Capt. Rice, without date came to my hand last night. Where my last was dated, or from whence, I cannot at this time recollect; but with truth can assure, that it is not owing to a want of Inclination that you do not hear from me oftener, nor is it altogether to be ascribed to the hurry of business in which I am immerc'd: but to your living out of the Post Road, and my want of knowledge of accidental or Casual Conveyance.I most sincerely condole with you on your late loss; and doubt not your feeling it in the most sensible manner; nor do I expect that human Fortitude, and reason, can so far overcome natural affection, as to enable us to look with calmness upon losses wh. distress us altho they are acts of Providence, and in themselves unavoidable, yet acquiescence to the divine will is not only a duty, but is to be aided by every manly exertion to forget the causes of such uneasiness."

vol. 35, 6-8-1796 To HENRY KNOX

"My dear Sir: I wou'd not let Mr. Bingham (who says he is about to Visit you) depart without acknowledging the receipt of several letters from you; and offering Mrs. Knox and yourself, my sincere condolence on your late heavy loss. Great and trying, as it must be to your sensibility, I am persuaded after the first severe pangs are over you both possess fortitude enough to view the event, as the dispensation of providence, and will submit to its decrees, with philosophical resignation."

vol. 35, 3-2-1797 To HENRY KNOX

"From the friendship I have always borne you, and from the interest I have ever taken in whatever relates to your prosperity and happiness, I participated in the sorrows which I know you must have felt for your late heavy losses. [The death of three children.] But is not for man to scan the wisdom of Providence. The best he can do, is to submit to its decrees. Reason, religion and Philosophy, teaches us to do this, but 'tis time alone that can ameliorate the pangs of humanity, and soften its woes."

37 Fields, *Worthy Partner*, p. 371. For Martha Washington's commitment to faith in divine providence and its connection to Christian and spiritual strength in the context of the lives of her family and friends, consider the following. All of these are from Fields, *Worthy Partner*, as noted.

p. 3 From Robert Carter Nicholas, Williamsburg, 7th August, 1757

"...how great Christian patience and resignation you submitted to your late misfortune;..."

p. 152, From John Parke Custis Kings-College July 5th (1773).

"I generally get up about Six or a little after, dress myself & go to chappel, by the time that Prayers are over Joe has me a little Breakfast to which I sit down very contended after eating heartyly. I thank God, and go to my Studys, with which I am employed till twelve then I take a walk and return about one dine with the professors, & after dinner study till Six at which time the Bell always rings for Prayers they being over college is broak up, and then we take what Amusement we please.

"Things My dear Mother were going on in this agreeable Manner, till last Thursday, the day I receiv'd Pappa's melancholy Letter, giveing an account of my dear & only Sister's Death. I myself met the Post, & brought the sad Epistle to Doctor Cooper who I beg'd to open his Letter immediately, the Direction I did not know, but the Seal I knew too well to be deceived. My confusion & uneasiness on this occasion is better conceiv'd that exprest. Her case is more to be envied than pitied, for if we mortals can distinguish between those who are deserveing of grace & who are not, I am confident she enjoys that Bliss prepar'd only for the good & virtuous, let these consideration, My dear Mother have their due weight with you and comfort yourself with reflecting that she now enjoys in substance what we in this world enjoy in imagination & that there is no real Happiness on this side of the grave. I must allow that to sustain a shock of this kind requires more Philosophy than we in general are (possest) off, my Nature could not bear the shock. (illegible) sunk under the load of oppression, and hindered me from administering any consolation to my dear and nearest relation, this Letter is the first thing I've done since I received the melanchoy News, & could I think my Presence wou'd be condusive to the Restoration of your Tranquility neither the distance nor the Fatigue of traveling could detain me a moment here. I put myself & Joe into deep Mourning & shall do (all) Honour in my power to the Memory of a deceas'd & well belov'd Sister, I will no longer detain you on a subject which is painful to us both but conclude with beging you to remember you are a Christian and that we ought to submit with Patience to the divine Will and that to render you happy shall be the constant care of your effectionate and dutiful son.

John Parke Custis"

p.159 From George Washington, Philadelphia June 18, 1775.

"I shall rely therefore, confidently, on that Providence which has heretofore preservd, & been bountiful to me, not doubting but that I shall return safe to you in the fall..."

p. 161 From George Washington, Phila. June 23rd. 1775.

"... I go fully trusting in that Providence, which has been more bountiful to me than I deserve, & in full confidence of happy Meeting with you sometime in the Fall-"

p. 175 To Burwell Bassett, My Dear Sir , Mount Vernon December 22d 1777.

"... she has I hope a happy exchange – and only gone a little before us the time draws near when I hope we shall meet never more to part-if to meet our departed Friends and know them was scertain we could have very little reason to desire to stay in this world where if we are at ease one hour we are in affliction days…

"… my dear sister in her life time often mentioned my taking my dear Fanny if should be taken away before she grew up- If you will lett her come to live with me, I will with the greatest pleasure take her and be a parent and mother to her as long as I live—and will come down for her as soon as I come from the northward, …"

p.223-224 To Mercy Otis Warren, New York December the 26th 1789

"…for you know me well enough to do me the justice to believe that I am only fond of what comes from the heart….

…. it is owing to this kindness of our numerous friends in all quarters that my new and unwished for situation is not indeed a burden to me. …With respect to myself, I sometimes think the arrangement is not quite as it ought to have been, that I, who had much rather be at home should occupy a place with which a great many younger and gayer women would be prodigiously pleased.—As my grand children and domestic connections made a great portion of felicity which I looked indemnify me for the Loss of a part of such endearing society. I do not say this because I feel dissatisfied with my present station—no, God forbid:—for everybody and everything conspire to make me as contented as possable in it; yet I have too much of the vanity of human affairs to expect felicity from the splendid scenes of public life. – I am still determined to be cheerful and to be happy in whatever situation I may be, for I have also learnt from experiance that the greater part of our happiness or misary depends upon our dispositions, and not upon our circumstances; we carry the seeds of the one, or the other about with us, in our minds, wherever we go."

p.339 To Jonathan Trumball Mount Vernon January 15, 1800

"…the good Christian will submit without repining to the Dispensations on Divine Providence and look for consolation to that Being who alone can pour balm into the bleeding Heart and who has promised to be the widows god -… your kind letter of condolence of the 30th of December was greatfull to my feeling….

…the loss is ours the gain is his….

"For myself I have only to bow with humble submission to the will of that God who giveth and who taketh away looking forward with faith and hope to the moment when I shall be again united with the Partner of my life But while I continue on Earth my prayers will be offered up for the welfare and Happiness of my Friends among who you will always be numbered being."

p.364 To Catherine Livingston Garretson Mount Vernon, March 15t, 1800

"The kind sympathy which you expressed for my affictive loss – and your fervent prayers for my present comfort and future happiness, impress my mind with gratitude. The precepts of our holy Religion have long since taught me, that in the severe and trying scenes of life, our only sure Rock of comfort and consolation is the Divine Being who orders and directs all things for our good.

"Bowing with humble submission, to the dispensations of his Providence, and relying upon that support which he has promised to those who put their trust in him, I hope I have borne my late irreparable loss with Christian fortitude. – To a feeling heart, the sympathy of friends, and the evidences of universal respect paid to the memory of the deceased, - are truly grateful. – But while these alleviate our grief, we find that the only sense of comfort is from above.

"It give me great pleasure to hear that your good Mother yet retains her health and faculties unimpaired, - and that you experience those comforts which the Scriptures promise to those who obey the Laws of God. – That you may continue to enjoy the blessings of this life – and receive hereafter the portion of the Just is the prayer of your sincere friend & obt Serv."

p.368 To Theodore Foster Mount Vernon, March 28, 1800

"While these evidences of respect and veneration paid to the memory of our illustrious Chief, make the most grateful impression on the heart of Mrs. Washington, she finds that the only source of Consolation is from that Divine Being who sends Comfort to the Afflicted, and has promised to be the Widow's God. Your prayers for her health and happiness are received with gratitude, and reciprocates with sincerity."

p. 371 To Janet Livingston Montgomery Mount Vernon, April 5th

"… your affliction I have often marked and as often have keenly felt for you but my own experience has taught me that griefs like these can not be removed by the condolence of friends however sincere – If the mingling tears of numerous friends – if the sympathy of a Nation and every testimony of respect of veneration paid to the memory of the partners of our hearts could afford consolation you and myself would experience it in the highest degree but we know that there is but one source from whence comfort can be derived under afflictions life ours To this we must look with pious resignation and with that pure confidence which our holy religion inspires.

…but as you justly observe it is certainly a consolation and flattering to poor mortality to believe that we shall meet here after in a better place."

38 Sparks, *The Writings of George Washington*, vol. XII, pp. 405-407. See John Eidsmoe, *Christianity and the Constitution*, (Grand Rapids: Baker Book House, 1987), p. 140-141.

39 Lathrop, *Discourse Before the Humane Society in Boston*, p. 5. A summary of the sermon is provided here:

Lathrop begins by asserting that "Publick institutions, founded on the general principles of benevolence, and calculated either to promote the happiness or to alleviate the sufferings of human life, are honoured and encouraged among all the civilized nations of the world." The establishment of the Humane Societies was based on the insight "That the total suspension of the vital functions of the animal body, is by no means incompatible with life….the success which has attended the exertions of societies formed for the recovery of persons visibly dead, particularly such as were drowned, has far exceeded expectation." But the Humane Society, although medical in focus, decided to "be introduced with a Religious Exercise, and that the first Discourse be rather on the general object of the society, than confined to the *Medical Science*." In other words, these were Christian physicians and Christian leaders coming together to do this good work in the very spirit of Christ Himself: "the words of our LORD, placed at the head of the Discourse, naturally lead us to consider the value of human life, and the duty of preserving it by every method in our power. The holy Evangelists who have faithfully recorded the life of JESUS

1142

CHRIST, abundantly testify that his actions perfectly corresponded with he declaration it the text: He constantly went about doing good." [Emphasis is in the original.] Lathrop's continuing explanation points out Jesus' resurrections of the widow's daughter, Jairus' daughter and Lazarus. He points to the man as the highest creature of God who bears the image of God and so is to rule over all creation, including in areas of science and medicine. Useful knowledge and knowledge of the heavenly regions are all to be part of man's scientific enterprise. In so doing, man is only being "the head of the creatures which dwell on the face of the earth…he longs to converse with superious beings, and feels the highest pleasure in contemplating the perfections of his Creator, in the boundless Universe."

Thus Lathrop concludes, "From all that has been said, human life appears highly valuable: It is our duty to preserve our own life, and the life of others. 'The Son of Man came not to destroy men's lives, but to save them.'" And thus the existence of the Humane Societies. Next Reverend Lathrop details stories of rescued drowning victims who had been under water for up to two hours; of the rescuing of a convict who had been hung, after the performance by a physician of what we would call today a tracheotomy—apparently the man rapidly revived and was able to successfully elude the law. The Humane Society in Great-Britain in the first ten years had 796 lives that had been "restored from apparent death." Lathrop adds examples of those spared after being hit by lightning, and in one case, of someone even being rescued on the third day laying in their coffin when he had died in France, but was then living in Philadelphia nearly six years after the event. The organizations that had performed these great works had actually had assemblies of those rescued and made sure that they were being instructed "at stated periods for religious worship, and devotional books, suited to their circumstances are distributed among them."

The conclusion of this most remarkable medical sermon that Washington read with "singular satisfaction" declares "let us present our grateful acknowledgments to the FATHER of LIFE, that he hath, in this age of rapid improvement, led to those important discoveries, by which many of the human race may be saved from an untimely end. The tender feelings of our heart, and the Spirit of our holy Religion, happily unite in the cause of Humanity. The Son of God came into the world to save the life, and promote the happiness of the children of men. Let it be our determination to follow his most amiable example. Let us be constant and unwearied in works of humanity, and we shall receive the full reward of our labours, when those who found relief from our hand, when ready to perish, shall rise up and call us BLESSED."

Did this medical sermon impact Washington? Clearly it did. He did not want to be placed in his tomb until he had been dead for three days. But was Washington's hesitancy for burial a potential rejection of Christianity as implied by Ellis? Not at all, it was an affirmation of the compassionate Christian Medical spirit that Washington had read with "singular satisfaction" twelve years earlier. Had the tracheotomy been done on Washington, instead of only on the convict mentioned in Lathrop's discourse, he might have lived too. Apparently, Washington's "singular satisfaction" was not diminished by the Reverend Dr. Lathrop's Gospel hope expressed in the words, "…they had tasted death, and sunk into a state of insensibility, from which, if left without assistance, they could not have awoke, 'till the morning of the resurrection.'" Given the serious science coupled with the sincere Christian faith combined in Lathrop's Discourse, there was no need for a man of faith and reason like Washington to abandon Christianity for Deism.

40   WGW, vol. 29, 8-15-1787.
41   Ibid., vol. 28, 7-25-1785.
42   Ibid., vol. 34, 12-16-1795.
43   Ibid., vol. 15-28-1755.
44   Ibid., vol. 1, 9-6-1756.
45   PGW, Letterbook 38, Image 147
46   WGW, vol. 35, 3-3-1797.
47   Ibid., vol. 5, 5-31-1776.
48   Ibid., vol. 32, 1-27-1793.
49   Ibid., 28, 1-5-1785.
50   Ibid., vol. 30, 8-29-1788.
51   Ibid., 4, 3-31-1776.
52   Ibid., 28, 9-5-1785.
53   Ibid., vol. 24, 8-7-1782. To John Price Posey.
54   Ibid., vol. 30, 8-31-1788. To Annis Boudinot Stockton.
55   Ibid., vol. 27, 8-21-1783. To the Magistrates and Inhabitants of the Borough of Elizabeth.
56   Ibid., vol. 13, 10-12-1778. To Reverend Alexander McWhorter. "Besides the humanity of affording them the benefit of your profession, …it serves to prepare them for the other world…."
57   Ibid., vol. 25, 11-16, 1782. To the Reformed Protestant Dutch Church. "In return for your kind concern for my temporal and eternal happiness, permit me to assure you that my wishes are reciprocal." WGW, vol. 36, 6-4-1798. To Reverend William Linn. "…grateful for the favourable sentiments you have been pleased to express in my behalf; but more especially for those good wishes which you offer for my temporal and eternal happiness; which I reciprocate with great cordiality…."
58   Washington here refers to his step-daughter Patsy Custis. WGW, vol. 3, 6-20-1773. To Burwell Basett.
59   Ibid., vol. 27, 1-5-11784. To Jonathan Trumbull, Jr. This passage implies continuing fellowship with a friend who was a Christian clergyman in the "happier clime."
60   Ibid., vol. 30, 9-13-1789 To Elizabeth Washington Lewis.
61   Ibid., vol. 28, 3-30-1785. To Lucretia Wilhemina Van Winter. vol. 28, 10-1-1785. To Jonathan Trumbull; vol. 30, 12-23-1788. To Reverend William Gordon. vol. 36, 8-29-1797. To George Washington Parke Custis.
62   Ibid., vol. 27, 11-2-1783. Farewell Orders to the Armies of the United States. At the death of Gov. Jonathan Trumbull, Washington wrote

to his son Jonathan Trumbull Jr. on October 1, 1785: "My dear Sir:... You know, too well, the sincere respect and regard I entertained for your venerable fathers public and private character, to require assurances of the concern I felt for his death; or of that sympathy in your feelings for the loss of him, which is prompted by friendship. Under this loss however, great as your pangs may have been at the first shock, you have every thing to console you. A long and well spent life in the Service of his Country, placed Govt. Trumbull amongst the first of Patriots. In the social duties he yielded to none. and his Lamp, from the common course of Nature, being nearly extinguished, worn down with age and cares, but retaining his mental faculties in perfection, are blessings which rarely attend advanced life. All these combining, have secured to his memory universal respect and love here, and no doubt immeasurable happiness hereafter." *WGW* vol. 28, 10-1-1785. Washington had "no doubt" that the "immeasurable happiness" of the "hereafter" was secured for his respected and loved fellow friend and patriot.

63   Ibid., vol. 35, 3-30-1796. To Tobias Lear.

64   *PGW* Series 2 Letterbooks Philadelphia United Episcopal Church to George Washington, March 2, 1797 Letterbook 40, Image 290-291 of 307

65   See letters between Washington and the Reformed Church of Kingston. In chapter on "Washington and Prayer."

66   *WGW* vol. 29, 2-11-1788 to Benjamin Lincoln.

67   Ibid., vol. 34, 12-16-1795 to Citizens of Frederick County, VA.

68   Ibid., vol. 35, 3-3-1797.

69   *PGW* 2:179-181

70   *WGW*, vol. 30, 6-22-1788. To Reverend John Lathrop.

71   Ibid., vol. 1, 9-6-1756 to Lt. Col. Adam Stephen; vol. 25, 11-16-1782; to ministers of the Reformed Church in Kingston.

72   Ibid., vol. 37, 3-25-1799.

73   Ibid., vol. 29, May 5, 1787.

74   Ibid., vol. 29, 2-25-1787. To Marquis de Lafayette.

75   Rhodehamel, *George Washington: Writings*, 1050.

76   Hale, *Contemplations Moral and Divine*, p. 10.

77   Reverend Nathanael Spinkes, *The Sick Man Visit ed.* (London, 1745), p. 395-96.

78   1662 *Book of Common Prayer.*

79   George Washington's will was signed on July 9, 1799. A contemporary copy, made by Albin Rawlins, one of his secretaries, also bears the same date. See, Prussing, *The Estate of George Washington, Deceased,* (Boston, 1927) pp. 36, 40.

80   Martha Washington was ill during this period. Her illness necessitated visits by Dr. James Craik on September 1st and the 6th. Diaries, 6: 363,366. The text is taken from Lossing, *Mary and Martha*, p 324-326. Lossing states the letter was sent to a "kinswoman in New Kent," and that he obtained the text from the letter at Arlington House. The letter seems consistent with the facts." Joseph E. Fields, *A Worthy Partner*, pp. 321-22. Lossing's account of this says:

> The long and eventful period of the sweet earthly companionship enjoyed by Martha Washington with her husband was now drawing to a close. At near the end of the year in which the happy wedding occurred at Mount Vernon, the spirit of Washington departed from the earth. The story of that departure is familiar to all my readers, and I will not repeat it here in detail.
>
> For several months before that event Washington appears to have had at times a presentiment of near approaching death. In July he executed his last will and testament. He also prepared, in minute details, a system for the management of his estate, for the guidance of whomsoever might have charge of it. That paper was complete four days before he died, and was accompanied by a letter to his manager, Mr. Lear, giving him special direction, as if the writer was about to depart on a long journey. He seems to have communicated his forebodings to Mrs. Washington, who, early in the autumn, when she was recovering from a severe illness, wrote a kinswoman in Kent:
>
> "At midsummer the General had a dream so deeply impressed on his mind that he could not shake it off for several days. He dreamed that he and I were sitting in the summer-house, conversing upon the happy life we had spent, and looking forward to many more years on the earth, when suddenly there was a great light all around us, and then an almost invisible figure of a sweet angel stood by my side and whispered in my ear. I suddenly turned pale and then began to vanish from his sight and he was left alone. I had just risen from the bed when he awoke and told me his dream saying, 'You know a contrary result indicated by dreams may be expected. I may soon leave *you.*' I tried to drive from his mind the sadness that had taken possession of it, by laughing at the absurdity of being disturbed by an idle dream, which, at the worst, indicated that I would not be taken from him; but I could not, and it was *not* until after dinner that he recovered any cheerfulness. I found in the library, a few days afterwards, some scraps of paper which showed that he had been writing a Will, and had copied it. When I was so very sick, lately, I thought of this dream, and concluded my time had come, and that I should be taken first." (Autograph letter at Arlington House, dates "September 18, 1799)

81   *WGW*, vol. 37, 11-12-1799.

82   An important consideration that we must consider is why Washington did not do what his mother and various others of his progenitors had done, namely, placed a testimony of trust in Christ in their last will and testament. Washington did not do this. From this some would infer that he was not a Christian, and that it thus stands as a proof of a belief in Deism. And as to his death without the presence of a clergyman, and thus the reception of the Eucharist, we find that this question was raised by Washington's grandson, George Washington Parke Custis. GWP Custis in *Recollections* asks the question, "It may be asked, Why was the ministry of religion wanting to shed its peaceful and benign luster upon the last hours of Washington? Why was he, to whom the observances of sacred things were ever primary duties throughout life, without their consolations in his last moments? We answer, circumstances did not permit. It was but for a little while that the disease assumed so threatening a character as to forbid the encouragement of hope; yet, to stay that summons which none may refuse,

to give still farther length of days to him whose 'time-honored life' was so dear to mankind, prayer was not wanting to the throne of Grace. Close to the couch of the sufferer, resting her head upon that ancient book, with which she had been wont to hold pious communion a portion of every day, for more than a half a century, was the venerable consort, absorbed in silent prayer, and from which she only arose when the mourning group prepared to lead her from the chamber of the dead. Such were the last hours of Washington." p. 477.

83   Consider here Washington's approval of Benjamin Stephens' sermon that was preached at Lord Pepperell's funeral, that taught that even though great men are called "gods" in the Bible, they are reminded by the Scriptures that will also die like men. Stephens sermon has already been mentioned in chapter two, note 14 and was considered in the chapter on Washington's Clergy and Sermons.

84   Various examples of Washington's severe illnesses can be offered: *WGW*, vol. 2, note 11-5-1757, "Colonel Washington was now laboring under an indisposition, which shortly increased to an alarming illness. He left the army at the pressing request of Doctor Craik, his physician and intimate friend through life, and retired to Mount Vernon, where he was reduced so low by dysentery and fever that it was more than four months before he was able to resume his command. Dinwiddie wrote to Captain Stewart (November 15): "The violent complaint Col. Washington labors under gives me great concern, it was unknown to me or he shou'd have had leave of absence sooner, and I am very glad he did not delay following the Doctrs. advice, to try a change of air. I sincerely wish him a speedy recovery."

Fields, *Worthy Partner* p. 224, Footnote 1 offers another example: "About the middle of June, 1789, the President developed a fever, followed by tenderness over the left thigh. Swelling and inflammation soon followed. Dr. Bard and two other consultants were unable to make a diagnosis. Consideration was given to the fact that the President might have contracted anthrax. As the swelling progressed, so did the discomfort until as last he was in excruciating pain. Cherry Street, in front of his home, was roped off to prevent the noisy wagons and carts from disturbing his rest. By the 20th the swelling "pointed" into an abscess or carbuncle. It was lanced and drained, whereupon the fever began to subside. For about three weeks it was difficult for him to move about or sit without discomfort. His condition gradually improved, but still continued to drain during September."

Washington wrote to Dr. James Craik concerning this malady on September 8, 1789: "Dear Sir: The letter with which you favored me on the 24th ultimo came duly to hand, and for the friendly sentiments contained in it, you have my sincere and hearty thanks. My disorder was of long and painful continuance, and though now freed from the latter, the wound given by the incision is not yet closed. Persuaded as I am that the case has been treated with skill, and with as much tenderness as the nature of the complaint would admit, yet I confess I often wished for your inspection of it. During the paroxysm, the distance rendered this impracticable, and after the paroxysm had passed I had no conception of being confined to a lying posture on one side six weeks, and that I should feel the remains of it more than twelve. The part affected is now reduced to the size of a barley corn, and by Saturday next (which will complete the thirteenth week) I expect it will be skinned over. Upon the whole, I have more reason to be thankful that it is no worse than to repine at the confinement. The want of regular exercise, with the cares of office, will, I have no doubt hasten my departure for that country from whence no Traveller returns; but a faithful discharge of whatsoever trust I accept, as it ever has, so it always will be the primary consideration in every transaction of my life be the consequences what they may. Mrs. Washington has, I think, better health than usual, and the children are well and in the way of improvement." *WGW*, vol. 30, 9-8-1789.

Similarly, on May 10, 1790, The President complained of "a bad cold." The cold increased in severity within the next two days. He then developed symptoms of pneumonia and for the next several days his physical condition rapidly deteriorated. Four physicians were called into attendance. They despaired of his life, and it became widely known throughout the city that he was dangerously ill, that he might not survive. On the morning of May 15th his breathing became labored. Those nearest him felt the end was near. Suddenly about 4:00 P.M. his fever suddenly dropped and he developed profuse perspiration. His condition improved rapidly and by the 20th of May he was considered out of danger. His convalescence continued for a period of six weeks." Fields, *Worthy Partner*, pp. 226-27 note 1.

85   We considered several instances of Washington's exposure to danger and death as a military officer in the chapter on Washington the soldier.

86   *Letters & Recollections of George Washington*, Being letters to Tobais Lear and others…With a diary of Washington's last days, kept by Mr. Lear. (Garden City, New York: Doubleday, Doran & Company, Inc., 1932), pp. 129-141.

87   See G.W.P. Custis, *Recollections and Private Memoirs of Washington*, p. 477.

88   *Letters & Recollections of George Washington*, Being letters to Tobais Lear and others…With a diary of Washington's last days, kept by Mr. Lear. (Garden City, New York: Doubleday, Doran & Company, Inc., 1932), p. 135.

89   *Letters & Recollections of George Washington*, p. 141.

90   This account of Washington's death helps to explain why he did not call for a clergyman and did not receive the Sacrament. It is true that there were no clergy present. But one of Washington's closest lifelong friends was present, namely, Dr. James Craik. Dr. Craik was a devout Scotch-Irish Presbyterian who was later buried in the Presbyterian Church yard in Alexandria. Dr. Craik's assessment of Washington's last day of life is significant. Dr. Craik's simple description of Washington's death says, "During the short period of his illness, he oeconomised his time, in the arrangement of such few concerns as required his attention, with the utmost serenity; and anticipated his approaching dissolution with every demonstration of that equanimity for which his whole life has been so uniformly and singularly conspicuous." Dr. Craik who had known Washington throughout his adult life saw no change in his dying moments from his whole life. What was the secret of Washington's "equanimity" or calmness? Craik knew, as we saw in the chapter on "Washington the Soldier," that Washington possessed an unwavering trust in divine providence. As Washington was dying, Martha Washington was praying with her Bible open at the foot of the bed. It is true that there were no Christian rituals offering the solace of everlasting life…. There are two reasons for this. It should be remembered that Washington's illness only lasted a short 24 hours. Washington's illness was a swollen throat that was so severe that he could not swallow, and eventually could not even breathe. The point here is that even if Washington could have swallowed, as a Low Churchman in the Virginian tradition, he would not have sought the Eucharist on his sickbed. But perhaps most importantly, he was not afraid to die, and was ready to die. Ibid.

91   Fields, *Worthy Partner*, p.265

92   Ibid., p.368

93   Ibid., *Worthy Partner* p.364

94   *WGW*, vol. 34, 12-16-1795 To THE CITIZENS OF FREDERICK COUNTY, VIRGINIA "Next to the approbation of my own mind, arising from a consciousness of having uniformly, diligently and sincerely aimed, by doing my duty, to promote the true interests of my country, the approbation of my fellow citizens is dear to my heart. In a free country, such approbation *should* be a citizen's best reward; and so it *would* be, if Truth and Candour were always to estimate the conduct of public men. But the reverse is so often the case, that he who, wishing to serve his country, is not influenced by higher motives, runs the risk of being miserably disappointed. Under such discouragements, the good citizen will look beyond the applauses and reproaches of men, and persevering in his duty, stand firm in conscious rectitude, and in the hope of [an] approving Heaven."

95   Consider here the exchange between Washington, the Earl of Buchan and Martha Washington. To EARL OF BUCHAN Philadelphia, May 26, 1794.

"My Lord: It is no uncommon thing to attempt, by excuses, to atone for acts of omission; and frequently too at the expense of as much time as (seasonable employed) would have superceded the occasion of their presentment. Sensible as I am of this, and ashamed as I am of resorting to an apology so common; yet I feel so forcibly the necessity of making one for suffering your Lordship's very polite and obliging favor of the 30 of last June, to remain so long unacknowledged, that I cannot avoid falling into the error I am reprobating.

"The truth is, the malignant fever which raged in this City during the months of August, September and October of last year (of which at least 5,000 of its inhabitants were swept off) occasioned my retreat therefrom on the 10th of September, and prevented my returning until sometime in November; between which and the meeting of Congress (the first Monday in December) I had hardly time to prepare for the session. The session has been long and interesting, and is not yet closed. Little leisure therefore have I had, during the period of its continuance, for the indulgence of private correspondences.

"I did however, from Germantown in the early part of November, give your lordship the trouble of receiving a few lines from me introductory of my friend Mr. Lear; and am exceedingly flattered by the polite attention with which he was honored, on my account, by your Lordship and the Countess of Buchan. He speaks of it (in a letter I have lately received from him in London) in the highest terms of respect and gratitude.

"The sentiments which are expressed in your lordship's letter of the 30th of June, do honor to the goodness of your heart, and ought to be engraved on every man's heart. And if, instead of the provocations to war, bloodshed and desolation, (oftentimes unjustly given) the strife of nations, and of individuals, was to excel each other in acts of philanthropy, industry and oeconomy; in encouraging *useful* arts and manufactures, promoting thereby the comfort and happiness of our fellow men, and in exchanging on liberal terms the products of one Country and clime, for those of another, how much happier would mankind be.

"But providence, for purposes beyond the reach of mortal scan, has suffered the restless and malignant passions of man, the ambitious and sordid views of those who direct them, to keep the affairs of this world in a continual state of disquietude; and will, it is to be feared, place the prospects of peace too far off, and the promised millenium at an awful distance from our day.

Whether you have, upon any occasion, expressed yourself in disrespectful terms of me, I know not: it has never been the subject of my enquiry. If nothing impeaching my honor, or honesty, is said, I care little for the rest. I have pursued one uniform course for three score years, and am happy in *believing* that the world have thought it a right one: of it's being so, I am so well satisfied myself, that I shall not depart from it by turning either to the right or to the left, until I arrive at the end of my pilgrimage. I am etc. " *WGW*, vol. 33, 5-26-1794. After Washington's death, the Earl of Buchan wrote the following to Martha Washington,

The Earl of Buchan to Mrs. Washington Dryburgh Abbey, Jan, 28, 1800.

Madam:

"I have this day received from my brother, at London, the afflicting tidings of the death of your admirable husband, my revered kinsman and friend. I am not afraid, even under this sudden and unexpected stroke of Divine Providence, to give vent to the immediate reflections excited by it, because my attachment to your illustrious consort was the pure result of reason, reflection, and congeniality of sentiment. He was one of those whom the Almighty, in successive ages, has chosen and raised up to promote the ultimate designs of his goodness and mercy, in the gradual melioration of his creatures and the coming of his kingdom, which is in heaven.

"It may be said of this great and good man who has been taken from among us, what was written by the wise and discerning Tacitus concerning his father-in-law Agricola, that, 'though he was snatched away while his age was not broken by infirmity or dimmed by bodily decay of reason, yet that, if his life be measured by his glory, he attained to a mighty length of days; for every true felicity, namely, all such as arise from virtue, he had already enjoyed to the full. As he has likewise held the supreme authority of the state with the confidence and applause of all wise and good men in every part of the world, as well as among those he governed, and had enjoyed triumphal honors in a way undertaken for the defense of the inalienable rights of mankind, what more humanly speaking, could fortune add to his luster and renown?

"After enormous wealth he sought not; a honorable share he possessed. His course he finished in the peaceful retreat of his own election, in the arms of a dutiful and affectionate wife, and bedewed with the tears of surrounding relatives and friends, with the unspeakably superior advantage to that of a Roman general, in the hopes afforded by the Gospel of pardon and peace! He therefore, Madam, to continue my parallel, may be accounted singularly happy, since by dying according to his own Christian and humble wish expressed on many occasions, while his credit was nowise impaired, his fame in all it splendor, his relations and friends not only in a state of comfort and security, but of honor, he was probably to escape many evils incident to declining years. Moreover, he saw the government of his country in hands conformable to our joint wishes and to the safety of the nation, and a contingent succession opening, not less favorable to the liberties and happiness of the people.

"Considering my uniform regard for the American States, manifested long before their forming a separate nation, I may be classed as it were among their citizens, especially as I am come of a worthy ancestor, Lord Cardross, who found refuge there in the last century, and had large property in Carolina, where Port Royal is now situated. I hope it will not be thought impertinent or officious, if I recommend to that country and nation of America at large the constant remembrance of the moral and political maxims conveyed to its citizens by the Father and Founder of the United States, in his farewell address, in that speech which he made to the Senate and House of Representatives, where the last hand was put to the formation of the Federal Constitution; *and may it be perpetual.*

"It seems to me that such maxims and such advice ought to be engraved on every forum or place of common assembly among the people, and read by parents, teachers, and guardians to their children and pupils, so that true religion, and virtue, its inseparable attendant, may be imbibed by the rising generation to remote ages; and the foundations of national policy be laid and continued in the superstructure, in the pure and immutable principles of private morality, since there is not truth more thoroughly established than that there exists in the economy and course of nature an indissoluble union between virtue and happiness, between duty and happiness, between duty and advantage, between the genuine maxims of an honest and magnanimous people, and the solid rewards of public prosperity and felicity; since we ought to be no less persuaded that the propitious smiles of heaven can never be expected on a nation that disregards the eternal rules of order and right which Heaven itself has ordained; and since the preservation of the sacred fire of liberty and the destiny of the Republican model of government are justly considered as deeply, perhaps finally, staked on the experiment entrusted to the hands of the American people....I am, Madam, with sincere esteem, Your obedient and faithful servant Buchan."

In Margaret Conkling, *Memoirs of the Mother and Wife of George Washington* (Auburn: Derby, Miller and Company, 1851), pp. 241-245

96 Ibid.

97 Fields, *Worthy Partner*, p. 355.

98 Ibid., p. 389.

99 Ibid., *Worthy Partner* pg. 331 From Jonathon Trumbull Lebanon, Dec. 30, 1799.

100 *WGW,* vol. 28, 10-1-1785.

101 Fields, *Worthy Partner*, p. 339.

102 Washington's commitment to immortality is absolutely necessary to make sense of his dialogue in the following exchange. The Hebrew Congregation of Newport Rhode Island believed in immortality, and expected that Washington did as well, as their blessing sent to him indicates,

> For all the blessings of civil and religious liberty which we enjoy under an equal and benign administration, we desire to send up our thanks to the antient of days, the great preserver of men beseeching him that the angel who conducted our forefathers through the wilderness into the promised land may graciously conduct you through all the dangers and difficulties of this mortal life and when like Joshua full of days, and full of honor, you are gathered to your fathers, may you be admitted into the heavenly paradise to partake of the water of life and the tree of immortality.

> Done and signed by order of the Hebrew Congregation in Newport Rhode Island, August 8, 1789. (*PGW*: Series 2 Letterbooks, Newport, Rhode Island, Hebrew Congregation to George Washington, August 17, 1790 Letterbook 39, images 19-20 of 222.)

In light of the remarkable letter and blessing, Washington responded:

> May the children of the stock of Abraham who dwell in this land continue to merit and enjoy the goodwill of the other inhabitants while every one shall sit in safety under his own vine and fig tree and there shall be none to make him afraid.

> May the father of all mercies scatter light and not darkness in our paths, and make us all in our several vocations useful here and in his own due time and way everlastingly happy. (PGW: Series 2 Letterbooks George Washington to Newport, Rhode Island, Hebrew Congregation, August 17, 1790 Letterbook 39, Image 22 of 222.)

> Washington clearly expressed a belief in everlasting life by the mercies of God's grace.

CHAPTER 35

1 *PGW, Retirement Series*, July 3, 1799, to Mason Locke Weems, Last Volume, pp. 173-74.

2 Weems. *The Life of Washington.* Ed. Marcus Cunliffe. Cambridge, Mass.: Belknap Press of Harvard University Press, 1962.

3 The account of the cherry tree was not included in *Life and Memorable Actions of George Washington* until the ninth edition in 1809.

4 Weems, *The Life of Washington* p. 22.n.1.

5 Ibid., pp. 7, 21

6 Ibid., p. 21.

7 Fitzpatrick, *The Diaries of George Washington*, vol. II., pp. 80, 81, 88, 89.

8 Ibid., I. 150, 352.

9 Weems, *The Life of Washington* , p. 9.

10 On the title page in the Cunliffe reprint.

11 Henry Cabot Lodge, *George Washington* (New Rochelle: Arlington House, 1898) p. 41, 48. Lodge continues his excoriation of Weems: "There has been in reality a good deal of needless confusion about Weems and his book, for he was not a complex character, and neither he nor his writings are difficult to value or understand. By profession a clergyman or preacher, by nature an adventurer, Weems loved notoriety, money, and a wandering life. So he wrote books which he correctly believed would be popular, and sold them not only through the regular channels, but by peddling them himself as he traveled about the country. In this way he gratified all his propensities, and no doubt derived from life a good deal of simple pleasure. Chance brought him near Washington in the closing days, and his commercial instinct told him that here was the subject of all others for his pen and his market. He accordingly produced the biography which had so much success. Judged solely as literature, the book is beneath contempt. The style is turgid, overloaded, and at times silly. The statements are

loose, the mode of narration confused and incoherent, and the moralizing is flat and commonplace to the last degree. Yet there was a certain sincerity of feeling underneath all the bombast and platitudes, and this saved the book. The biography did not go, and was not intended to go, into the hands of the polite society of the great eastern towns. It was meant for the farmers, the pioneers, and the backwoodsmen of the country. It went into their homes, and passed with them beyond the Alleghenies and out to the plains and valleys of the great West. The very defects of the book helped it to success among the simple, hard-working, hard-fighting race engaged in the conquest of the American continent. To them its heavy and tawdry style, its staring morals, and its real patriotism all seemed eminently befitting the national hero and thus Weems created the Washington of the popular fancy. The idea grew up with the country, and became so ingrained in the popular thought that finally everybody was affected by it and even the most stately and solemn of the Washington biographers adopted the unsupported tales of the itinerant parson and book-peddler.

In regard to the public life of Washington, Weems took the facts known to every one, and drawn for the most part from the gazettes. He then dressed them up in his own peculiar fashion and gave them to the world. All this, forming of course nine tenths of his book, has passed despite its success, into oblivion. The remaining tenth described Washington's boyhood until his fourteenth or fifteenth year, and this, which is the work of the author's imagination, has lived. Weems, having set himself up as absolutely the only authority as to this period, has been implicitly followed, and has thus come to demand serious consideration. Until Weems is weighed and disposed of, we cannot even begin an attempt to get at the real Washington.

Weems was not a cold-blooded liar, a mere forger of anecdotes, He was simply a man destitute of historical sense, training, or morals, ready to take the slenderest fact and work it up for the purpose of the market until it became almost as impossible to reduce it to its original dimensions as it was for the fisherman to get the Afrit back into his jar. In a word, Weems was an approved myth-maker. No better example can be given than the way in which he described himself. It is believed that he preached once, and possibly oftener, to a congregation which numbered Washington among its members. Thereupon he published himself in his book as the rector of Mount Vernon parish. There was, to begin with, no such parish. There was Truro parish, in which was a church called indifferently Pohick or Mount Vernon Church. Of this church Washington was a vestryman until 1785, when he joined the church as Alexandria. The Reverend Lee Massey was the clergyman of the Mount Vernon church, and the church at Alexandria had nothing to do with Mount Vernon. There never was, moreover, such a person as the rector of Mount Vernon parish, but it was the Weems way of treating his appearance before the great man, and of deceiving the world with the notion of an intimacy which the title implied.

Weems, of course, had no difficulty with the public life, but in describing the boyhood he was thrown on his own resources, and out of them he evolved the cherry-tree, the refusal to fight or permit fighting among the boys at school, and the initials in the garden. This last story is to the effect that Augustine Washington planted seeds in such a manner that when they sprouted they formed on the earth the initials of his son's name, and the boy being much delighted thereby, the father explained to him that it was the work of the Creator, and thus inculcated a profound belief in God. This tale is taken bodily from Dr. Beattie's biographical sketch of his son, published in England in 1799, and may be dismissed at once. As to the other two more familiar anecdotes there is not a scintilla of evidence that they had any foundation and with them may be included the colt story, told by Mr. Custis, a simple variation of the cherry-tree theme, which is Washington's early love of truth. Weems says that his stories were told him by a lady, and "a good old gentleman," who remembered the incidents, while Mr. Custis gives no authority for his minute account of a trivial event over a century old when he wrote. To a writer who invented the rector of Mount Vernon, the further invention of a couple of Boswells would be a trifle. I say Boswells advisedly, for these stories are told with the utmost minuteness, and the conversations between Washington and his father are given as if from a stenographic report. How Mr. Custis, usually so accurate, came to be so far infected with the Weems myth as to tell the colt story after the Weems manner, cannot now be determined. There can be no doubt that Washington, like most healthy boys, got into a good deal of mischief, and it is not at all impossible that he injured fruit-trees and confessed that he had done so. It may be accepted as certain that he rode and mastered many unbroken thoroughbred colts, and it is possible that one of them burst a blood-vessel in the process and died, and that the boy promptly told his mother of the accident. But this is the utmost credit which these two anecdotes can claim. Even so much as this cannot be said of certain other improving tales of like nature. That Washington lectured his playmates on the wickedness of fighting, and in the year 1754 allowed himself to be knocked down in the presence of his soldiers, and thereupon begged his assailant's pardon for having spoken roughly to him, are stories so silly and so foolishly impossible that they do not deserve an instant's consideration.

There is nothing intrinsically impossible in either the cherry-tree or the colt incident, nor would there be in a hundred others which might be readily invented. The real point is that these stories, as told by Weems and Mr. Custis, are on their face hopelessly and ridiculously false. They are so, not merely because they have no vestige of evidence to support them, but because they are in every word and line the offspring of a period more than fifty years later. No English-speaking people, certainly no Virginians, ever thought or behaved or talked in 1740 like the personages in Weems's stories, whatever they may have done in 1790, or at the beginning of the next century. These precise anecdotes belong to the age of Miss Edgeworth and Hannah More and Jane Taylor. They are engaging specimens of the "Harry and Lucy" and "Purple Jar" morality, and accurately reflect the pale didacticism which became fashionable in England at the close of the last century. They are as untrue to nature and to fact at the period to which they are assigned as would be efforts to depict Augustine Washington and his wife in the dress of the French revolution discussing the propriety of worshiping the Goddess of Reason." Pp. 41-48.

12   *PGW Diaries*, vol. 5, p. 112.
13   Slaughter, *The History of Truro Parish*, pp. 101-02.
14   Ibid.
15   See www.loper.org/~george/archives/2000/Feb/39.html "George Washington's Birthday: Mason Locke Weems and the Cherry Tree Legend," Mason Weems (1760 - 1825). Clergyman, author, bookseller (*Excerpts taken from "Footnote People in U.S. History", People's Almanac, David Wallechinsky, N.Y: Doubleday & Co, pp. 113-114*).
16   *GWP Diaries*, 5:112. The note there directs to: 6 July 1792, PHi: Gratz Collection.

17   Fitzpatrick, *The Diaries of George Washington*, vol. III. p. 174.

18   Ibid. p. 112.

19   This volume was written by Hugh Blair, D.D., a minister of the "High Church" and a professor at the University of Edinburgh. It was originally published in London, but "Re-printed for the Reverend M. L. Weems" in Baltimore in 1792 by "Samuel and John Adams, Book-Printers, in Market-Street, between South and Gay-Streets."

20   *George Washington Papers at the Library of Congress*, 1741-1799: Series 4. General Correspondence. 1697-1799 Mason L. Weems to George Washington, 1795, Image 745.

21   Washington had been included in the estate of Dr. Wilson, Prebendary of Westminster & Rector of S. Stephens Walbrook in London. He was Bishop Thomas Wilson's son. The son of the Bishop also bequeathed his father's study Bible as well as his father's works to Washington. These were sent to Washington by Clement Cruttwell, the famous compiler of the Biblical Concordance that bears his name. (See Lane, *Catalogue of the Washington Collection*, pp. 63, 498, 501-02.) Washington in turn, in his own will, passed the Bible on to his dear friend, the Reverend Bryan Fairfax: "To the Reverend, now Bryan, Lord Fairfax, I give a Bible in three large folio volumes, with notes, presented to me by the Right reverend Thomas Wilson, Bishop of Sodor and Man." [Actually it was the Bishop's son who bequeathed them to Washington.]

22   Washington was interested in the subject of the evidences of Christianity. In Washington's cash accounts, dated Sept. 12, 1787, we discover that he purchased *Evidences of the Christian Religion Briefly and Plainly Stated* (London, 1786) by James Beattie. See Lane, *A Catalogue of the Washington Collection in the Boston Athenaeum*, Boston: 1897, p. 502. The book was a great success: An 1804 publisher wrote, "Of the Evidences of Christianity, an Edition is generally sold every 12 to 18 months." from the "Introduction" to the 1996 Routledge/Thoemmes Press reprint, p. xiv. The simple structure of Beattie's work is, "Revelation is useful and necessary," "The Gospel History is true," and "Objections answered."

23   The letter states: His Excellency Genl. Washington, Very Honored Sir: I was the other day in Norfolk where a very particular friend of mine Capt. James Tucker, a man of merit and money, begged me to ask a favor of you which we both concluded your goodness would readily grant. Capt. Tucker is a wealthy merchant of Norfolk, largely in the importing line. He has lately been applied to for a quantity of merchandise on credit by a gentleman who calls himself Major James Welch and who says moreover that he is the man who purchased your Excellency's western lands of which a post says you sold so much some time ago. Capt. Tucker wishes to know whether a Major Welch did purchase your Excellency's lands or a part of them, and whether he met your Excellency's expectations in the way of payment. If your Excellency will condescend to honor me with a line on this subject it will be very gratefully acknowledged both by Capt. Tucker and your Excellency's most obliged M. L. Weems." See under March 26, 1799 in *George Washington Papers at the Library of* Congress.

24   Washington answered from Mount Vernon, "Sir: Your letter of the 26th instt came duly to hand. In answer thereto, I inform you that, my sale to Mr. James Welch, of the Lands I hold upon the Great Kanhawa, is conditional only. He has a Lease of them at a certain annual Rent, which if punctually paid, for Six years, and at the end thereof shall pay one fourth of the sum fixed on as the value of them; and the like sum by Instalments the three following years, and this without any let or hindrance that then, and in that case only, I am to convey them in Fee simple, not else. This is the nature of the agreemt. between Mr. Welch and Sir Your etc. PS. It may not be amiss to add that the first years Rent (due in Jan. last) is not yet paid." See under on March 31, 1799, in *George Washington Papers at the Library of* Congress.

25   *WGW*, vol. 37, 8-29-1799.

26   Weems, *The Immortal Mentor; or Man's Unerring Guide to a Healthy, Wealthy and Happy Life*. In Three Parts. By Lewis Cornaro, Dr. Franklin, and Dr. Scott. Philadelphia: Printed for the Reverend Mason L. Weems, by Francis and Robert Bailey, no. 116 High-Street, 1796.

27   This letter is not found in the *Writings of George Washington*, but it is in *The Papers of George Washington, Retirement Series*, July 3, 1799, to Mason Locke Weems, Last Volume, pp. 173-74.

28   Washington was careful to thank people when they dedicated their works to him. See for example *WGW* vol. 35, 1-21-1797 to Richard Peters; Ibid., vol. 36, 2-6-1798, to the Secretary of state; Ibid., vol. 36, 8-15-1798, to Reverend Jonathan Boucher. But he usually did not give permission to those who requested his permission to dedicate their works to him. See Ibid., vol. 28, 6-20-1786, to Nicholas Pike; Ibid., vol. 36, 7-4-1798, to Ferdinand Fairfax; Ibid., vol. 36, 10-14-1798, to Reverend Samuel Knox; and Ibid., vol. 29, 1-9-1787, to Dr. John Leigh. An example of an exception to this was for Reverend Timtothy Dwight, Jr., see Ibid., vol. 11, 3-18-1778.

      Similarly, compare here his general unwillingness to give endorsements. See, for example, his silence with respect to Uzal Odgen's request for an endorsement (Lane, *Washington Collection*, Boston Athenaeum, p. 154-155); His approbation (or approval of a work) was a high honor and rarely given. Examples include Reverend Jedidiah Morse, *WGW*, vol. 37, 2-18-1799; Nicholas Pike, Ibid., vol. 30, 6-20-1788; and Reverend Benjamin Stevens, Ibid., vol. 30, 12-23-1789. This makes Washington's support for Weems' work most exceptional.

29   For Washington's consistent use of the word "peruse" or "perusal" in its sense of "examining with great care" or "to read intensively", see *WGW*, vol. 1, 11-26-1753, Speech to Indians at Logstown; *WGW*, vol. 14, 4-14-1779, to John Jay; *WGW*, vol. 29, 9-30-1786, to Bushrod Washington; *WGW*, vol. 32, 6-20-1792, to Dr. James Anderson; *WGW*, vol.. 37, 4-23-1799, to the Secretary of War. For a clear example of this, consider Washington's letter to Mercy Warren, *WGW*, 31, 11-4-1790, "Madam: My engagements, since the receipt of your letter of the 12th of September, with which I was honored two days ago, have prevented an attentive perusal of the book that accompanied it, but from the reputation of its author, from the parts I have read, and a general idea of the pieces, I am persuaded of its gracious and distinguished reception by the friends of virtue and science."

30   Dr. Thomas Scott (1747-1821) was an Anglican clergyman and well-known biblical scholar from England. His conversion from Unitarianism to Calvinism was recorded in *The Force of Truth* (1779). His most notable work was a many times reissued commentary on the Bible in 4 volumes (1788-1792). He was also author of a work against Thomas Paine entitled *A vindication of the Divine inspiration of the Holy Scriptures, and of the doctrines contained in them: being an answer to the two parts of Mr. T. Paine's Age of Reason. By Thomas Scott,*

Chaplain to the Lock Hospital.]([New York] London, printed: New-York, reprinted by G. Forman, for C. Davis, book-seller, no. 94, Water-Street., —1797.—)

31   Weems, *The Immortal Mentor*, pp. 57-60.
32   Ibid., p. 116.
33   Ibid., p. 123-24.
34   Ibid.
35   Ibid., p. 130.
36   Ibid., pp. 133-34.
37   Ibid., pp. 150-51.
38   Ibid., p. 151.
39   Ibid., pp. 172-175.
40   Ibid., pp. 177-79.
41   Ibid., pp. 232-233.
42   Ibid., pp. 312-13.
43   *WGW,* vol. 30, 6-22-1788. To Reverend John Lathrop.

CHAPTER 36: CONCLUSION
1   *WGW,* vol. 30, First Inaugural Address.
2   *Journals of the Continental Congress,* 1774.
3   Weems, *Life of Washington,* first edition, 1880.
4   Paul Johnson, *A History of the American People* (Great Britain: Weidenfield & Nicolson, 1997).
5   Author Peter Marshall notes: "But the sad truth, today, is that this lie about the founding fathers all being a bunch of Deists is taught by the secularist professors in our universities and colleges, who don't do much original research. I think a lot of them don't want to be disturbed by the reality of this situation to find out they've been teaching wrong. They simply repeat each other's lies, and this has become, sort of, a common sense, "Well, of course," idea in modern America and it's flatly untrue." Peter Marshall in D. James Kennedy, *One Nation Under God* (Ft. Lauderdale: Coral Ridge Ministries, 2005), a video.
6   John Rhodehamel, ed., *George Washington: Writings* (New York: The Library of America, 1997), 279.
7   *WGW,* vol. 5, 7-9-1776, General Orders.
8   Benson J. Lossing, *The Pictorial Field-Book of the Revolution* (1886), vol. II, p. 140
9   Rhodehamel, *George Washington: Writings,* p. 526
10   Ibid., p. 34.
11   Ibid., p. 33.
12   Johnson, *George Washington The Christian,* pp. 251-252.
13   *WGW* vol. 27, 12-1-1783.
14   Johnson, *Geroge Washington The Christian,* p.255.
15   Sparks, *The Writings of George Washington,* vol. XII, pp. 405-407. See Eidsmoe, *Christianity and the Constitution,* p. 140-141. "Did Washington embrace Christianity? His adopted daughter thought so. Nelly Custis was Martha Washington's granddaughter, and when Nelly's father died, George and Martha Washington adopted her and she lived in their home for twenty years. In 1833 she wrote to the historian Jared Sparks, expressing indignation that anyone would question Washington's Christianity."
16   *WGW,* vol. 1, 4-2-1747/48. (there is some question as to whether this was written in 1747 or 1748.)
17   Ibid., vol. 26, 6-8-1783. Circular to the States.
18   Ibid., vol. 27, 6-15-1783. To John Augustine Washington.
19   Ibid., vol. 30, 1-8-1790. First Annual Address to Congress.
20   Ibid., vol. 27, 1-22-1784. To Charles Thompson.
21   Ibid., vol. 3, 7-18-1775, To Governor Jonathan Trumbull.

APPENDIX 1
1   Frank E. Grizzard, *George Washington: A Biographical Companion* (Santa Barbara: ABC-CLIO, Inc. 2002) pp 361-365; For a contemporary take, see :George Washington, *Georgeisms* (New York: Atheneum Books for young Readers, 2000)

APPENDIX 4
1   Hughes, *George Washington The Human Being & The Hero* pp. 552-559.
2   As found in:
    W. Herbert Burk, B.D., *Washington's Prayers.* Norristown: Washington Memorial Chapel, 1907.
    John Eidsmoe, Christianity and the Constitution;.William J. Federer, *America's God and Country Encyclopedia of Quotations.* Coppell: FAME Publishing, Inc., 1994, pp. 656-659.
3   Hughes, *George Washington The Human Being & The Hero,* pp. 555ff.
4   Ibid.
5   Ibid.
6   Ibid

7   Ibid.

APPENDIX 5

1   Dr. Donald S. Lutzin D. James Kennedy, *One Nation Under God*(Ft. Lauderdale: Coral Ridge Ministries-TV, 2005), a video.

2   *WGW*, vol. 33, 8-29-1793. See Lane, *Washington Collection*, Boston Athenaeum, p. 142.

3   *WGW*, vol. 29, 2-23-1787. Lane, *Washington Collection*, Boston Athenaeum, p. 194.

4   See *WGW*, vol. 30, 7-6-1789. It is unclear which of Ogden's Sermons this may have been from the evidence available here. See Lane, *Washington Collection*, Boston Athenaeum, p. 153-54.

5   See *WGW*, vol. 34, 4-14-1795. See Lane, *Washington Collection*, Boston Athenaeum, p. 195-196.

6   See *WGW*, vol. 36, 6-15-1798. See Lane, *Washington Collection*, Boston Athenaeum, p. 20-21.

7   See Lane, *Washington Collection*, Boston Athenaeum, p. 500.

8   *WGW*, vol. 32, 10-20-1792. To Dr. William Davies Shipley.

9   See Lane, *Washington Collection*, Boston Athenaeum, p. 70.

10   See Lane, *Washington Collection*, Boston Athenaeum, p. 226.

11   *WGW*, vol. 31, 3-28-1791.

12   Lane, *Washington Collection*, Boston Athenaeum, p. 118-119. See *WGW* vol. 30, 9-28-1789.

13   Ibid., p. 146-147. See *WGW*, vol. 37, 5-26-1799.

14   Ibid., p. 226. See *WGW*, vol. 37, 5-30-1799.

15   Ibid., p. 25.

16   Ibid., p. 195.

17   Ibid., p. 86-87.

18   Ibid., p. 184. See also *WGW*, vol. 35, 7-23-1797. To George Washington Parke Custis. "Dear Washington: Your letter of the 14th instant has been duly received, and gives us pleasure to hear that you enjoy good health, and are progressing well in your studies. Far be it from me to discourage your correspondence with Dr. Stuart, Mr. Law, or Mr. Lewis [Zechariah Lewis], or indeed with any others, as well-disposed and capable as I believe they are to give you speciments of correct writing, proper subjects, and if it were necessary, good advice. With respect to your epistolary amusements generally, I had nothing further in view than not to let them interfere with your studies, which were of more interesting concern; and with regard to Mr. Z. Lewis, I only meant that no suggestions of his, if he had proceeded to give them, were to be interposed to the course pointed out by Dr. Smith, or suffered to weaken your confidence therein. Mr. Lewis was educated at Yale college, and as is natural, may be prejudiced in favor of the mode pursued at that seminary; but no college has turned out better scholars, or more estimable characters, than Nassau. Nor is there any one whose president is thought more capable to direct a proper system of education than Dr. Smith; for which reason, Mr. Lewis, or any other, was to prescribe a different course from the one you are engaged in by the direction of Dr. Smith, it would give me concern. Upon the plan you propose to conduct your correspondence, none of the evils I was fearful of can happen, while advantages may result; for composition, like other things, is made more perfect by practice and attention, and just criticism thereon."

19   Lane, *Washington Collection*, Boston Athenaeum, p. 142.

20   Ibid., p. 154.

21   Ibid., p. 16.

22   Philadelphia: Printed by James Chattin., 1755.

23   Israel Evans. A discourse, delivered, on the 18th day of December, 1777, the day of public thanksgiving, appointed by the Honourable Continental Congress, by the Reverend Israel Evans, A.M. Chaplain to General Poor's brigade. And now published at the request of the general and officers of the said brigade, to be distributed among the soldiers, gratis (Lancaster [Pa.]: Printed by Francis Bailey., M,DCC,LXXVIII. [1778]).

24   *WGW*, vol. 11, 3-13-1778.

25   Printed by Shepard Kollock, at his office in Chatham., [1779]

26   *WGW*, vol. 16, 8-5-1779.

27   printed by JJohn Colerick, 1798.

28   Lane, *Washington Collection*, Boston Athenaeum, p. 3; *WGW*, vol. 36, 6-3-1798.

29   Ibid., p. 126.

30   Ibid., p. 146.

31   *WGW*, vol. 37, 2-28-1799

32   Lane, *Washington Collection*, Boston Athenaeum, p. 226-227.

33   *WGW*, vol. 10, 12-20-1777.

34   *WGW*, vol. 37, 8-29-1799.

35   This letter is not found in the *Writings of George Washington*, but it is in *The Papers of George Washington*, ed. Dorothy Twohig (University of Virginia), *Retirement Series*, July 3, 1799, to Mason Locke Weems, Last Volume, pp. 173-74.

36   Lane, *Washington Collection*, Boston Athenaeum, p. 193; *WGW*, vol. 30, 12-23-1789.

37   By Isaac Lewis, D. D. Pastor of a Church in Greenwich. Hartford: Printed by Hudson & Goodwin. 1797. ELECTION SERMON "The Political Advantages of Godliness." By Isaac Lewis, D. D. Pastor of a Church in Greenwich. Hartford: Printed by Hudson & Goodwin. 1797. At a General Assembly of the State of Connecticut, holden at Hartford on the second Thursday of May, Anno Domini 1797.

38 See *WGW*, vol. 36, 8-14-1797. These sermons are not in Lane, *Washington Collection*, Boston Athenaeum.

39 Lane, *Washington Collection*, Boston Athenaeum, p. 119.

40 *WGW*, vol. 29, 2-22-1788;

41 Ibid., vol. 30, 6-22-1788.

42 *WGW*, vol. 16 , 9-8-1779. Note: The eulogium was "An Eulogium of the brave men who have fallen in the contest with Great Britain," delivered July 5, 1779, in the German Calvinist Church in Philadelphia. A copy is in the Library of Congress. See Lane, *Washington Collection*, Boston Athenaeum, p. 192.

43 *WGW*, vol. 37,11-6-1781. To Jonathan Trumbull, Jr. See *The Works & Life of Laurence Sterne*, 2 Volumes (New York: J. F. Taylor and Co., 1904). Sterne's collection of sermons was also in Washington's library. See Lane, *Catalogue of the Washington Collection*, p. 192.

44 Boston: Printed by Samuel Hall, in School-Street., 177., Lane, *Washington Collection*, Boston Athenaeum p. 118.

45 By Isaac Lewis, D. D. Pastor of a Church in Greenwich. Hartford: Printed by Hudson & Goodwin. 1797. ELECTION SERMON "The Political Advantages of Godliness." By Isaac Lewis, D. D. Pastor of a Church in Greenwich. Hartford: Printed by Hudson & Goodwin. 1797. At a General Assembly of the State of Connecticut, holden at Hartford on the second Thursday of May, Anno Domini 1797.

46 See *WGW*, vol. 36, 8-14-1797. These sermons are not in Lane, *Washington Collection*, Boston Athenaeum

47 Lane, *Washington Collection*, Boston Athenaeum, p. 71.

48 Abiel Leonard, A prayer, composed for the benefit of the soldiery, in the American army, to assist them in their private devotions; and recommended to their particular use. By Abiel Leonard, A.M. Chaplain to General Putnam's regiment, in said army.,(Cambridge [Mass.]: Printed and sold by S. & E. Hall., 1775).

49 Lane, *Washington Collection*, Boston Athenaeum, p. 75.

50 Philadelphia: Printed by James Chattin., 1755

51 Philadelphia. Printed and sold by James Humphreys, Junior, the corner of Black-Horse Alley, Front-Street., M,DCC,LXXV. [1775], Lane, *Washington Collection*, Boston Athenaeum, p. 70

52 Philadelphia: Printed by Ormrod & Conrad, at the Old Franklin's Head, no. 41, Chesnut-Street., March, 2d. 1795. Lane, *Washington Collection*, Boston Athenaeum, p. 226.

53 Philadelphia: Printed by John Ormrod, no. 41, Chesnut-Street,, 1799., Lane, *Washington Collection*, Boston Athenaeum, p. 226.

54 Chatham, N.J. Printed by Shepard Kollock, at his office in Chatham., [1779]

55 Boston: Printed by Edes and Gill, in Queen-Street,, M,DCC,LIX. [1759], Lane, *Washington Collection*, Boston Athenaeum p. 193.

56 Philadelphia: Printed by William Young, bookseller, no. 52, Second-Street, corner of Chesnut-Street., M,DCC,XCV. [1795]

57 New-York— Printed by Thomas Greenleaf., [1793]

58 See Lane, *Washington Collection*, Boston Athenaeum, p. 154.

59 Robert Davidson, D.D., A Sermon, on the Freedom and Happiness of the United Sates of America, preached in Carlisle, on the 5th Oct. 1794. And published at the request of the Officers of the Philadelphia and Lancaster Troops of Light Horse. By Robert Davidson, D.D. Pastor of the Presbyterian Church in Carlisle, and One of the Professors in Dickinson College. (Philadelphia: printed by Samuel H. Smith for Robert Campbell. 1794), 29 pp. See Lane, *The Washington Collection*, pp. 64-65.

60 Twohig, *Diaries*, October 5, 1794.

61 Twohig, *The Diaries of George Washington*, volume 5, November, Sunday 8th, 1789. "It being contrary to Law & disagreeable to the People of this State (Connecticut) to travel on the Sabbath day and my horses after passing through such intolerable Roads wanting rest, I stayed at Perkins's Tavern (which by the bye is not a good one) all day—and a meeting House being with in a few rod of the Door, I attended Morning & evening Service, and heard very lame discourses from a Mr. Pond."

62 Twohig, *Diaries*, Sunday July 3, 1791. "Received, and answered an address from the Inhabitants of York town—& there being no Episcopal Minister *present* in the place, I went to hear morning Service performed in the Dutch reformed Church—which, being in that language not a word of which I understood I was in no danger of becoming a proselyte to its religion by the eloquence of the Preacher." *PGW*, vol. 6.

63 *The Diaries of George Washington*, vol. 5. Donald Jackson and Dorothy Twohig, eds. The Papers of George Washington. Charlottesville: University Press of Virginia, 1979. [November 1789]

64 *The Diaries of George Washington*, vol. 6. Donald Jackson and Dorothy Twohig, eds. The Papers of George Washington. Charlottesville: University Press of Virginia, 1979. [January 1797]

65 Lane, *Washington Collection*, Boston Athenaeum, p. 502.

66 Ibid., p. 503.

67 Ibid., p. 39.

APPENDIX 6

1 Abiel Leonard, A prayer, composed for the benefit of the soldiery, in the American army, to assist them in their private devotions; and recommended to their particular use. By Abiel Leonard, A.M. Chaplain to General Putnam's regiment, in said army. (Cambridge [Mass.]: Printed and sold by S. & E. Hall., 1775.)

2 *WGW*, vol. 4, 12-15-1775. To Governor Jonathan Trumbull

APPENDIX 7

1 Reverend Bryan Fairfax, *Sermon by the Reverend Bryan Fairfax*. Virginia Historical Society Rare BV 4500 P14, pp. 261-276.

APPENDIX 8

1   Johnson, *George Washington The Christian*, p. 67.

2   Fields, *Worthy Partner*, p. 371.

3   Fields, *Worthy Partner*, p. 339.

APPENDIX 9

1   Martin I. J. Griffin, Jr., *Latitudinarianism in the Seventeenth- Century Church of England, Brill's Studies in Intellectual History* (Leiden: E.J.Brill, 1992) From Introduction by Lila Freedman.

This study by the late Martin Griffin, written between 1958 and 1962, was conceived as a definition of the seventeenth-century English Latitudinarians, from their origins in the thought of the Great Tew circle to the diffusion of their beliefs in the eighteenth-century Church of England.

Projected both as an historical survey and as an essay in definition and analysis, the study was done at a time when very little attention had as yet been given to the individuals comprising the group here called Latitudinarian. The essay single out the group of divines – John Tillotson (1630-94), Edward Stillingfleet (1635-99), Gilbert Burnet (1643-1715), Simon Patrick (1626-1707), Thomas Tenison (1636-1715), William Lloyd (1627-1717), Joseph Glanvill (1636-90), and John Wilkins (1614-72) – and from their writings isolates the characteristics of their thought that distinguish them from their contemporaries. These Griffin lists as: "(1) orthodoxy in the historical sense of acceptance of the contents of the traditional Christian creeds; (2) conformity to the Church of England as by law established, with its episcopal government, its Thirty-Nine Articles, and the Book of Common Prayer; (3) an advocacy of 'reason' in religion; (4) theological minimalism;

(5) an Arminian scheme of justification; (6) an emphasis on practical morality above credal speculation and precision; (7) a distinctive sermon style; (8) certain connections with seventeenth-century science and the Royal Society." Next, Griffin distinguishes the Latitudinarians from the Cambridge Platonists, with whom they had many personal connections, and locates them instead within the tradition of Falkland's circle at Great Tew, tracing their conception of "moral certainty," on which they based the assurance of the truth of Christianity, to the influence of William Chillingworth. With their speculative theology they attempted to meet specifically the challenges of Hobbism, Deism, and Roman Catholic apologetics, and in both their speculative and moral theology they aimed to combat "practical atheism," emphasizing in their sermons that they chief design of Christianity was "to make men good." They also rejected the Calvinist notion of predestination, which they thought led to antinomianism, and though they were charitable to those who differed from them in opinions, they opposed the principle of Nonconformity. "Their solution to the problem of tender consciences was comprehension, not toleration in the modern sense of the word; in the attempts of 1668,1675, and 1689 to achieve some scheme of comprehension, the Latitudinarians therefore played prominent roles."

2   *WGW*, vol. 30, 8-18-1789.

3   Martin I. J. Griffin, Jr., *Latitudinarianism in the Seventeenth- Century Church of England, Brill's Studies in Intellectual History* (Leiden: E.J.Brill, 1992), p. 5.

4   "The moderation of the Latitudinarians in matters of Church government suggested to Dryden that they might be crypto-Presbyterians." Martin I. J. Griffin, Jr., *Latitudinarianism in the Seventeenth- Century Church of England, Brill's Studies in Intellectual History* (Leiden: E.J.Brill, 1992), p. 7.

5   "A dictionary published in 1699 defined "Latitudinarian" in these uncategorical terms: "a Churchman at large, one that is no slave to rubrick, canons, liturgy, or oath of canonical obedience, and in fine looks toward Lambeth, and rows to Geneva." Martin I. J. Griffin, Jr., *Latitudinarianism in the Seventeenth- Century Church of England, Brill's Studies in Intellectual History* (Leiden: E.J.Brill, 1992), p. 7.

6   "The Papists," Burnet wrote, "set themselves against them to decry them as atheists, deists, or at best Socinians." Socinianism was, in fact, a favorite charge from all sides. Sometimes it referred literally to alleged Trinitarian herterodoxy, but more often, the Latiudinarians were "suspect of Socinianism, for [they] magnify reason, and are often telling how rational a thing Christian religion is." This charge, that the Latitudinarians made "Reason, Reason, Reason, their only holy Trinity," was a cherished weapon of their enemies' arsenal. Martin I. J. Griffin, Jr., *Latitudinarianism in the Seventeenth- Century Church of England, Brill's Studies in Intellectual History* (Leiden: E.J.Brill, 1992), p. 7.

7   Further, their doctrine of justification turned "the grace of God into a wanton notion of morality." Their rejection of the doctrine of predestination gained for them the epithets of "Arminians." Martin I. J. Griffin, Jr., *Latitudinarianism in the Seventeenth- Century Church of England, Brill's Studies in Intellectual History* (Leiden: E.J.Brill, 1992), p. 8.

8   "Their doctrine of grace and their scheme of salvation were Pelagian." Martin I. J. Griffin, Jr., *Latitudinarianism in the Seventeenth- Century Church of England, Brill's Studies in Intellectual History* (Leiden: E.J.Brill, 1992), p. 9.

9   "...the Nonjurors bitterly complained that the Latitudinarians were conscienceless Erastians who for the sake of preferment had betrayed the divinely-constituted spiritual and sacerdotal privileges of the Church of England. From all sides, for whatever reason, the quality of their Christianity was impugned by their enemies as being heretical or at best heterodox." Martin I. J. Griffin, Jr., *Latitudinarianism in the Seventeenth- Century Church of England, Brill's Studies in Intellectual History* (Leiden: E.J.Brill, 1992), p. 9.

10   Martin I. J. Griffin, Jr., *Latitudinarianism in the Seventeenth- Century Church of England, Brill's Studies in Intellectual History* (Leiden: E.J.Brill, 1992), p. 9.

11   "In the middle of the nineteenth century, 'Latitudinarian' fell out of style, its technical and religious meanings being expressed in common usage by the phrase "Broad Churchman." Since then, the pejorative connotations which the word had almost always carried with it have virtually disappeared." Martin I. J. Griffin, Jr., *Latitudinarianism in the Seventeenth- Century Church of England, Brill's Studies in Intellectual History* (Leiden: E.J.Brill, 1992), p. 10.

12 "In ecclesiology and liturgy, 'Low Church' and 'Latitudinarian' for our period were equivalent terms. . . .Though all Latitudinarians were Low Churchmen, not all Low Churchmen were full-fledged Latitudinarians." Martin I. J. Griffin, Jr., *Latitudinarianism in the Seventeenth-Century Church of England, Brill's Studies in Intellectual History* (Leiden: E.J.Brill, 1992), p. 44.

13 Martin I. J. Griffin, Jr., *Latitudinarianism in the Seventeenth- Century Church of England, Brill's Studies in Intellectual History* (Leiden: E.J.Brill, 1992), p. 15.

14 Martin I. J. Griffin, Jr., *Latitudinarianism in the Seventeenth- Century Church of England, Brill's Studies in Intellectual History* (Leiden: E.J.Brill, 1992), p. 40.

15 Martin I. J. Griffin, Jr., *Latitudinarianism in the Seventeenth- Century Church of England, Brill's Studies in Intellectual History* (Leiden: E.J.Brill, 1992), p. 40.

16 Martin I. J. Griffin, Jr., *Latitudinarianism in the Seventeenth-Century Church of England Brill's Studies in Intellectual History* (Leiden: E. J. Brill, 1992). p. 40-41.

17 *WGW,* vol. 3, 4-25-1773.

18 Ibid., vol. 29, 2-11-1788.

19 Ibid., vol. 34, 12-24-1795.

20 Ibid., vol. 35, 3-30-1796.

21 *Worthy Partner,* p. 152.

22 *WGW,* vol. 3, 6-20-1773.

23 *WGW,* vol. 3, 4-25-1773.

24 Ibid., vol. 2, 9-24-1767.

25 Ibid., vol. 17, 12-15-1779.

26 Ibid., vol. 26, 3-22-1783.

27 Ibid., vol. 27, 12-13-1783.

28 See the chapter, "George Washington And Communion."

29 *WGW,* vol. 24, 6-28-1782.

30 Ibid., vol. 30, 10-9-1789.

31 Ibid., vol. 30, 10-23-1789,

32 Ibid., vol. 3, 9-14-1775.

33 Ibid., vol. 30, 5-26-1789.

34 Ibid., vol. 35, 3-30-1796.

35 Ibid., vol. 30, 6-20-1788.

36 Ibid., vol. 29, 2-11-1788.

37 Ibid., vol. 29, 8-15-1787.

38 Ibid., vol. 31, 8-14-1790.

39 Ibid., vol. 4, March 1776.

40 Ibid., vol. 26, 6-8-1783.

41 Ibid., vol. 30, 10-3-1789.

42 Ibid., vol. 26, 6-8-1783.

43 Ibid., vol. 37, 5-13-1776.

44 Ibid., vol. 12, 8-20-1778.

45 Ibid., vol. 30, 9-28-1789.

46 Ibid., vol. 35, 9-19-1796.

APPENDIX 10

1 Johnson, *George Washington The Christian,* p.250.

2 Ibid., pp. 250-251.

3 Ibid., pp. 251-252.

4 Ibid., p. 253.

5 Ibid., p. 253.

6 Ibid., p. 253-254.

7 Ibid., p. 254.

8 Ibid., pp. 254-255.

9 Ibid., p. 255.

10 Ibid., p. 256.

11 Ibid., p. 256-257.

12 Ibid., p. 257.

13 Ibid., p. 258.

14 Ibid., p. 258.

15 Ibid., p. 258-259.

16 Ibid., p. 260.

17 Ibid., p. 260.

18   Ibid., p. 260.
19   Ibid., p. 260.
20   Ibid., p. 260.
21   Ibid., p. 261.
22   Ibid., p. 262.
23   Ibid., p. 263-265.
24   Ibid., p. 266-267.
25   Ibid., p. 267-268.
26   Weems, *Life of Washington*, p.172.
27   Johnson, *George Washington The Christian*, p.269.
28   Hart, Albert Bushnell. *Tributes to Washington, Pamphlet No. 3* (Washington, D.C.: George Washington Bicentennial Commission, 1931, pp.31-32.
29   Hart, *Tributes to Washington*, p. 32.
30   Ibid., p. 32.
31   Ibid., p. 31.
32   Ibid., p. 31.
33   Ibid., p. 31.
34   Ibid., p. 32.
35   Ibid., p. 31.
36   Ibid., p. 31.
37   Ibid., p. 32.
38   Ibid., p. 30.
39   Ibid., p. 31.
40   Ibid., p. 31.
41   Ibid., p. 32.
42   Ibid., p. 32.
43   Ibid., p. 32.
44   Ibid., p. 30.
45   Ibid., p. 31.
46   Ibid., p. 31.
47   Griffin, Appleton P.C. comps. *A Catalogue of the Washington Collection in the Boston Athenaeum.* Cambridge: University Press, 1897, p. 65.
48   Hart, Albert Bushnell. *Tributes to Washington, Pamphlet No. 3* (Washington, D.C.: George Washington Bicentennial Commission, 1931, p. 34.
49   Ibid., p. 33.
50   Ibid., p. 33.
51   Ibid., p. 32.
52   Ibid., p. 33.
53   Ibid., p. 35.
54   Ibid., p. 33.
55   Ibid., p. 35.
56   Ibid., p. 33.
57   Ibid., p. 35.
58   Ibid., p. 33.
59   Ibid., p. 33.
60   Ibid., p. 33.
61   Ibid., p. 35.
62   Ibid., p. 35.
63   Ibid., pp. 35-36.
64   Ibid., p. 33.
65   Ibid., p. 34.
66   Ibid., p. 34.
67   Ibid., p. 35.
68   Ibid., p. 35.
69   Ibid., p. 33.
70   Ibid., p. 34.
71   Ibid., pp. 34-35.
72   Ibid., p. 35.
73   Ibid., p.34.
74   Ibid., p. 37.
75   Ibid., p. 37.

76 Ibid., p. 36.
77 Ibid., p. 38.
78 Ibid., p. 37.
79 Ibid., p. 36.
80 Ibid., p. 37.
81 Ibid., p. 38.
82 Ibid., p. 38.
83 Ibid., pp. 36-37.
84 Ibid., p.38.
85 Ibid., p. 38.
86 Ibid., p. 38.
87 Ibid., p. 38-39.
88 Ibid., p. 36.
89 Ibid., p. 37.
90 Ibid., p. 39.
91 Ibid., p. 37.
92 Ibid., p. 38.
93 Ibid., p. 38.
94 Ibid., p. 37.

ILLUSTRATION CREDITS

Front Cover   George Washington portrait by Gilbert Stuart from Corbis Images

Page 57   Virginia Almanack with George Washington's signature–George Washington Papers at the Library of Congress, 1741-1799: Series 1b. George Washington, Diary, January 1–December 31, 1769, Image 5 of 134

Page 74   Selina Hastings, Countess of Huntingdon–Library of Congress, Reproduction Number: LC-USZ62-93956, c1830-80

Page 80   Plaque in George Washington's crypt–Photo by Jerry Newcombe

Page 96   Map of Washington's Extended Neighborhood by Judy Mitchell. Also see color insert page X.

Page 97   George Washington and the cherry tree mug–R.T. Haines Halsey, *Pictures of Early New York on Dark Blue Staffordshire Pottery* (Dover Publications, 1974) p. 2

Page 101   Reverend Mason Locke Weems–Benson J. Lossing, *The Pictorial Field-Book of the Revolution* (New York: Harper & Brothers, 1852

Page 103   George Washington's parents' signatures–Courtesy of The Boston Athenaeum

Page 108   George Washington's surveyor's notebook–George Washington Papers at the Library of Congress, 1741-1799: Series 1b.George Washington, Diary, March 11–April 13, 1748, Image 2 of 7

Page 113   Geometry notes–George Washington Papers at the Library of Congress, 1741-1799: Series 1a. George Washington, School Copy Book: Volume 1, 1745, Image 2 of 112

Page 115   Field School–Photo by Jerry Newcombe

Page 116   Record of George Washington's baptism–Benson J. Lossing, *Mary and Martha: The Mother and Wife of George Washington* (New York: Harper & Brothers, 1886)

Page 120   "True Happiness" poem–George Washington Papers at the Library of Congress, 1741-1799: Series 1a George Washington, Forms of Writing, and The Rules of Civility and Decent Behavior in Company and Conversation, ante 1747, Image 26 of 36

Page 123   "On Christmas Day" poem–George Washington Papers at the Library of Congress, 1741-1799: Series 1a George Washington, Forms of Writing, and The Rules of Civility and Decent Behavior in Company and Conversation, ante 1747, Image 25 of 36

Page 125   "Rules of Civility"–George Washington Papers at the Library of Congress, 1741-1799: Series 1a George Washington, Forms of Writing, and The Rules of Civility and Decent Behavior in Company and Conversation, ante 1747, Images 27 & 36 of 36

Page 131   "Contemplations Moral and Divine"–*Contemplations Moral and Divine. In Two Part*s (Printed for William Shrowsbury [etc.], London, 1675/6)

Page 129   George Washington's Childhood will - George Washington Papers at the Library of Congress, 1741-1799: Series 1a George Washington, Forms of Writing, and The Rules of Civility and Decent Behavior in Company and Conversation, ante 1747, Image 9 of 36

Page 133   Childhood doodles–Courtesy of The Boston Athenaeum

Page 143   Book plate–Benson J. Lossing, *The Home of Washington: or Mount Vernon and its Associations, Historical, Biographical, and Pictorial* (Hartford, Conn.: A. S. Hale 1870)1

Page 151   Signature through the years–Joseph Dillaway Sawyer, *Washington* (New York: The Macmillan Company, 1927), vol. I, p. 75

Page 152   Painting of Washington and Lafayette–Library of Congress, Reproduction Number: LC-USZC4-6877, c1907

Page 158   "Dissertations on the Mosaical Creation . . ."–Courtesy of The Boston Athenaeum

Page 167   George Washington in military uniform–Library of Congress, Reproduction Number: LC-USZ62-96753, c1918 (painting by Charles Willson Peale 1741-1827)

Page 181   Braddock's Defeat–engraving by Félix Emmanuel Henri Philippoteaux (1815-1884), Library of Congress

Page 205   Badge of Merit & Purple Heart–Courtesy of The Military Order of the Purple Heart, Springfield, VA

Bibliography

PRIMARY SOURCES

Abbot, W. W., and Dorothy Twohig, eds. *The Papers of George Washington.* The University Press of Virginia, 1992ff.

Adams, Charles Francis, ed. *Letters of John Adams—Addressed to His Wife.* Boston: Charles C. Little and James Brown, 1841.

Blair, D.D. Hugh. *Sermons.* Baltimore: 1792.

Blackall, D.D., Ofspring. *The Sufficiency of a Standing Revelation.* London: H. Hills, 1708.

Book of Common Prayer. London: Thomas Baskett, 1751.

Book of Common Prayer. 1662

Boyd, Julian P., ed. *The Papers of Thomas Jefferson vol.13 March 7 to October 1788.* Princeton: Princeton University Press, 1956.

Bremer, Howard F. *George Washington 1732-1799: Chronology—Documents—Bibliographical Aids.* Dobbs Ferry, N. Y.: Oceana Publications, 1967.

Butterfield, L.H., ed. *Adams Family Correspondence,* Volume 1 – December 1761-May 1776.

Custis, George Washington Parke, and Benson J. Lossing. *Recollections and Private Memoirs of Washington by His Adopted Son with a Memoir of the Author by His Daughter and Illustrative and Explanatory Notes by Benson J. Lossing.* Bridgewater: American Foundation Publications, 1999.

Edwards, Jonathan and Edward Hickman Revisions. *The Works of Jonathan Edwards vol. 1 & 2.* Edinburgh: The Banner of Truth Trust, 1979.

Ellis, Franklin, and Samuel Evans. *History of Lancaster County, Pennsylvania, with Biographical Sketches of Many of its Pioneers and Prominent Men.* Philadelphia: Everts & Peck, 1833.

Endress, Christian. "An Account of the Settlement of the Dunkers, at Ephrata," in *The Register of Pennsylvania* (1828-1831); May 22, 1830, pp. 331-334.

Fahnestock, M. D., William M. "An Historical Sketch of Ephrata" in *Hazard's Register of Pennsylvania. Devoted to the Preservation of Every Kind of Useful Information Respecting the State.* Philadelphia, March 14, 1835, No. 375, vol. 15, No. 11.

Fields, Joseph E. *Worthy Partner: The Papers of Martha Washington.* Westport: Greenwood Press, 1994.

Fitzpatrick, John C., ed. *The Writings of George Washington from the Original Manuscript Sources 1745-1799.* Washington: United States Government Printing Office, 1937.

Fitzpatrick, John C., ed. *The Diaries of George Washington 1748-1799 vol. 1-4.* Boston: Houghton Mifflin Company, 1925.

Fontaine, James, trans. *A Tale of the Huguenots, or Memoirs of a French Refugee Family.* New York: John S. Taylor, 1838.

Franklin, Benjamin. *Information to Those Who Would Remove To America.* London: M Gurney, 1794.

George Washington's Rules of Civility & Decent Behaviour. Bedford, MA: Applewood Books, Inc., 1988.

George-isms by George Washington. New York: Simon & Schuster Inc., 2000.

Halyburton, Thomas. *Natural Religion Insufficient, and Revealed Necessary, to Man's Happiness in his Present State: or A Rational Inquiry into the Principles of the Modern Deists.* Albany: H.C. Southwick, 1812.

Hale, Sir Matthew. *Contemplations Moral and Divine.* London: William Shrowsbery at the Bible in Duke-Lane, and John Leigh At Stationers-Hall, 1685.

Hervey, A.M. James. *Meditations and Contemplations.* London: J.Walker and Co.,1816.

Hopkins, D.D., John Henry. *The Primitive Church, Compared With the Protestant Episcopal Church, of the Present Day: Being an examination of he Ordinary Objections Against the Church, in Doctrine, Worship, and Government, Designed for Popular Use; with a Dissertation on Sundry Points of Theology and Practice, Connected with the Subject of Episcopacy, etc.* Burlington: Vernon Harrington, 1836.

Jefferson, Thomas, "A Bill for Establishing Religious Freedom," 1786, Bruce Frohnen, ed., *The American Republic: Primary Sources.* Indianapolis: Liberty Fund, 2002.

Journal of the Proceedings of the Bishops, Clergy and Laity, of the Protestant Episcopal Church in the United States of America in a Convention held in the City of Philadelphia from Tuesday, September 29th to Friday, October 16th, One Thousand and Seven Hundred and Eighty-Nine. Philadelphia: Hall and Sellers, 1790.

Kip, M.A., Reverend Wm. Ingraham. *The Double Witness of the Church.* New York: Appleton & Co., 1843.

Lathbury, M.A., Thomas. *A History of Nonjurors: This Controversies and Writings; with Remarks on Some of the Rubrics in the Book of Common Prayer.* London: William Pickering, 1845.

Letters & Recollections of George Washington. Garden City, New York: Doubleday, Doran & Company, Inc., 1932.

Lipscomb, Andrew A., and Albert Ellery Bergh, eds. *The Writings of Thomas Jefferson,* 20 Vols. Washington, D.C., 1903-04.

Mather, William. *The Young Man's Companion.* London: T Snowdon, 1681.

Meade, Bishop. *Old Churches, Minister and Families of Virginia. vol. 1 & 2.* Philadelphia: J.B. Lippincott & Co., 1857.

Minutes and Letters of the Coetus of the German Reformed Congregations in Pennsylvania 1734-1744. Philadelphia: Reformed Church Publication Board, 1903.

Minutes and Letters of the Coetus of the German Reformed Congregations in Pennsylvania 1747-1792 together with Three Preliminary Reports of Reverend John Philip Boehm, 1734-1744. Philadelphia: Reformed Church Publication Board, 1903.

Morse, Jedidiah. *The Life of Gen. Washington.* Philadelphia: Jones, Hoff & Derrick, 1794.

Osborn, Francis. *Advice to a Son or Directions for Your Better Conduct through the various and most important Encounters of this Life.* Oxford: H.H. for Tho: Robinson, 1658.

Padover, Saul K., ed. *The Washington Papers.* Harper Brothers, 1955.

Paine, Thomas. *Age of Reason.* Luxembourg, 8th Pluviose, Second Year of the French Republic, one and indivisible. January 27, O.S. 1794.

Paine, Thomas. *Age of Reason* in *The Writings of Thomas Paine.* Wiltshire: Routledge/Thoemmes Press, 1996, IV. 25.

Paulding, James K. *A Life of Washington.* Port Washington: Kennikat Press, 1858.

Perceval, B.C.L., Hon. and Reverend A.P. *An Apology for the Doctrine of Apostolical Succession with an Appendix on the English Orders.* New York: Protestant Episcopal Tract Society, 1839.

Ogden, Uzal. *Antidote to Deism.* 1795.

Ramsay, Chevalier. *The Travels of Cyrus.* London: James Bettenham, 1745.

Ray, John. *The Wisdom of God: Manifested in the Works of the Creation (1691).* Hildesheim: Georg Olms Verlag, 1974.

Rhodehamel, John, ed. *George Washington: Writings.* New York: The Library of America, 1997.

Rush, Richard. *Washington in Domestic Life, From Original Letters and Manuscripts 1857.* Kessinger Publishing, 2004.

Sachse, Julius F., comp. *Washington's Masonic Correspondence As Found Among the Washington Papers in the Library of Congress.* Lancaster, PA: Press of the New Era Printing Company, 1915.

Schaff, Philip. *Creeds of Christendom In Tree Volumes.* Grand Rapids: Baker Book House, 1977.

Smollett, Tobias. *The Adventures of Peregrine Pickle.* London: Printed for J. F. Dove, Piccadilly, 1751 or 1758.

Snodgrass, D.D., W.D. *Discourses on the Apostolical Succession.* Troy: Stedman & Redfield, 1844.

Sparks, Jared. *The Writings of George Washington; Being His Correspondence, Addresses, Messages, and Other Papers, Official and Private.* New York: Harper & Brothers, 1847.

Sparks, Jared ed., *The Works of Benjamin Franklin.* Chicago: Townsend MacCoun, 1882.

Spinckes A.M., Nathanael. *The Sick Man Visited and Furnished with Instructions, Meditations, and Prayers, for Putting him in mind of his Change for Supporting him under his Distemper; and for Preparing him for, and Carrying him through his Last Conflict with Death.* London: J. Rivington, 1744.

Stated Rules of the Society of the United Brethren for Propagating the Gospel Among the Heathen. Philadelphia: Charles Cist, 1787.

Stoudt, John Joseph. *Ordeal At Valley Forge: A Chronicle Complied from the Sources.* Philadelphia: University of Pennsylvania Press, 1963.

The Papers of George Washington. Virginia: The University Press of Virginia, 1996.

Townsend, Joseph. *Some Account of the British Army, Under the Command of General Howe, and of The Battle of Brandywine on the Memorable September 11th, 1777, and the Adventures of that day, which came to the Knowledge and Observation of Joseph Townsend.* Philadelphia: Townsend Ward, 1846.

Vickers, John A., ed. *Journals of Dr. Thomas Coke.* Abington Press, 2005.

Walsh, Reverend W. J., D.D., ed. *Reeve's History of the Bible.* Dublin: M. H. Gill and Son, Ltd., 1905.

Webster, Noah. *First Edition of an American Dictionary of the English Language (1828).* San Francisco: Foundation for American Christian Education, 1967.

Weeg, Theophilus. *The Virginia Almanack For the Year of our Lord God 1761.* Williamsburg: Printed and Sold by William Hunter, 1761.

Weems, Mason L. and Marcus Cunliffe, ed. *The Life of Washington.* Cambridge: The Belknap Press of Harvard University Press, 1962.

PRIMARY SOURCES OF INTERVIEWS, JOURNALS, MAGAZINES AND NEWSPAPERS

The Albany Centinal, 1798-06-05; vol. I; Iss. 97; p. 3.

The London Chronicle in the September 21 to 23, 1779 edition (no. 3561, p. 288)

The Pennsylvania Gazette, (Philadelphia, May 7, 1761, March 16, 1769, March 19, 1772).

Van Rensselaer, C., ed. *The Presbyterian Magazine.* Philadelphia, Pa. February, 1851, vol. 1, p. 71.

SERMONS

Addison, Alexander. "Observations on the Speech of Albert Gallatin, in the House of Representatives of the Untied States, on the Foreign Intercourse Bill."

Addison, Reverend Alexander. "An Oration on the Rise and progress of the United States of America, to the Present Crisis; and on the Duties of the Citizens." Philadelphia: Printed by John Ormrod, no. 41, Chesnut-Street,1798.

Barlow, Joel. "An Oration, delivered at the North Church in Hartford, at the Meeting of the Connecticut Society of the Cincinnati, July 4th, 1787."

Beattie, Reverend James. "Evidences of the Christian religion briefly and plainly stated." 2 Vols. London. 1786.

Belknap D.D., Jeremy. "A Sermon, delivered on the 9th of May, 1798, the Day of the national Fast, recommended by the President of the United States." Boston: Samuel Hall, 1798.

Blackhall, Ofspring. "The Sufficiency of a Standing Revelation in General, and of the Scripture Revelation in particular. Both as to the Matter of it, and as to the Proof of it; and that new Revelations cannot reasonably be desired, and would probably be unsuccessful." (In eight Sermons), 1717.

Blair, Reverend Hugh. "Sermons. To which is prefixed that admired tract, On the internal evidence of the Christian religion." 2 vols. Baltimore, reprinted for the Reverend M. L. Weems. 1792-1793. (Published by and purchased from Reverend Mason Weems).

Burnet, Reverend Gilbert, Bishop of Sarum. "An Exposition of the Thirty Nine Articles of the Church of England." The sixth Edition corrected. London: printed for J. Knapton, C. Hitch, 1759.

Davidson, Robert D.D., "A Sermon, on the Freedom and Happiness of the United Sates of America, preached in Carlisle, on the 5th Oct. 1794." Philadelphia: printed by Samuel H. Smith for Robert Campbell. 1794.

Davies, Reverend Samuel. "Religion and patriotism the constituents of a good soldier." A sermon preached to Captain Overton's Independent Company of Volunteers, raised in Hanover County, Virginia, August 17, 1755. By Samuel Davies, A.M. Minister of the Gospel there. Philadelphia: Printed by James Chattin., 1755.

Duché, Jacob. "The Duty of Standing fast in our spiritual and temporal Liberties." July 7, 1775.

Dwight, D.D., Reverend Timothy. "The A. Nature and B. Danger of Infidel Philosophy Exhibited in Two Discourses, Addressed to the Candidates for the Baccalaureate, in Yale College." New Haven: George Bunce, 1798.

Evans, Israel. "A discourse, delivered, on the 18th day of December, 1777, the day of public thanksgiving, appointed by the Honourable Continental Congress."

Fairfax, Reverend Bryan. "He that Believeth On Me Hath Everlasting Life." Virginia Historical Society Rare BV 4500 P14.

Gordon, William. "The Separation of the Jewish Tribes, after the Death of Solomon, accounted for, and applied to the present Day," July the 4th, 1777. Boston: Printed by J. Gill, Printer to the General Assembly.

Langdon D.D., Samuel. "The Republic of the Israelites an Example to the American States." June 5, 1788. Exeter: printed by Lamson and Ranlet.

Langdon D.D, Samuel. "The Co-incidence of natural with revealed religion." November 1, 1775.

Lathrop, John. "Discourse Before the Humane Society in Boston," 1787.

Leonard, Abiel. "A Prayer Composed for the Spiritual Benefit of the soldiery in the American army to assist them in their private devotions, and recommended to their particular use." Cambridge, 1775.

Lewis, Isaac. "The Political Advantages of Godliness." May 11, 1797.

Lewis, Isaac. "The divine mission of Jesus Christ evident from his life, and from the nature and tendency of his doctrines." October 11, 1796. New Haven: Printed by T. and S. Green—New Haven, 1796.

Linn, William. "A Discourse on national Sins." May 9, 1798.

Miller, Samuel. "A Sermon, preached in New-York." July 4th, 1793.

Morse, D.D., Jedidah. "A Sermon Preached at Charlestown November 29, 1798 On the Anniversary Thanksgiving In Massachusetts"—With An Appendix Designed to illustrate some parts of the discourse; exhibiting proof of the early existence, progress, and deleterious effects of French intrigue and influence in the United States. Printed by Samuel Hall, No. 53, Cornhill, Boston, 1799.

Ogden, Uzal. "A sermon on practical religion." [Four lines of Scripture texts] Number I. Chatham, N.J.

Ogden, Uzal. "A Sermon delivered at Morris-Town, on Monday December 27, 1784, it being the Festival of St. John the Evangelist, before the Fraternity of Free and Accepted masons, of Lodge No. 10, in the State of New-Jersey."

Sandoz, Ellis, ed. "Political Sermons of the American Founding Era, 1730-1805 vol. 2." Indianapolis: Liberty Fund, 1998.

Scott, Thomas. "A vindication of the Divine inspiration of the Holy Scriptures, and of the doctrines contained in them: being an answer to the two parts of Mr. T. Paine's Age of Reason. By Thomas Scott Chaplain to the Lock Hospital." [New York] London, printed: New York, reprinted by G. Forman, for C. Davis, book-seller, no. 94, Water-Street., 1797.

Shipley, Reverend Jonathan. "Shipley's Works," 2 vols. London. 1792.

Smith D.D., Samuel Stanhope. "A Discourse on the Nature and Reasonableness of Fasting, and on the existing Causes that call us to that Duty." January 6, 1795. Philadelphia: printed by William Young, 1795.

Sterne, Lawrence. "The Sermons of Mr. Yorick vol. 1 & 2." New York: J.F. Taylor, 1904.

Stevens, Benjamin. "A Sermon occasioned by the death of the Honorable Sir William Pepperell, Bart. Lieutenant-General in his Majesty's Service." Who died at his seat in Kittery, July 6th, 1759, aged 63. Preached the next Lord's-Day after his funeral.

Stiles, D.D., Ezra. "The United States elevated to Glory and Honor." May 8th, 1783. New-Haven: printed by Thomas & Samuel Green, 1783.

Stith, William. "The Nature and Extent of Christ's Redemption." November 11, 1753. Published at the request of the House of Burgesses, 1753.

Story, Isaac. "A Discourse." February 15, 1795, Salem: Thomas C. Cushing.

Weems, Reverend Mason L. "The Immortal Mentor; or Man's Unerring Guide to a Healthy, Wealthy and Happy Life." In Three Parts. By Lewis Cornaro, Dr. Franklin, and Dr. Scott. Philadelphia: Printed for the Reverend Mason L. Weems, by Francis and Robert Bailey, no. 116 High-Street, 1796.

Weems, Reverend Mason L. "The Philanthropist; or A Good Twelve Cents Worth of Political Love Power, for the Fair Daughters and Patriotic Sons of America. Dedicated to that great Lover and Love of his Country, George Washington, Esq." Alexandria: John & James D. Westcott, 1799.

Whitaker, Nathaniel. "An Antidote Against Toryism. Or the Curse of Meroz, in a Discourse on Judges 5th 23." 1777.

White, William. "A sermon on the reciprocal influence of civil policy and religious duty." February 19, 1795.

White, William, "A sermon on the duty of civil obedience, as required in Scripture." April 25, 1799.

Access to some of these sermons was via "Early American Imprints, Series I: Evans, 1639-1800," published by Readex, a division of Newsbank, Inc. http://www.readex.com and http://infoweb.newsbank.com

SECONDARY SOURCES

Alderfer, E. Gordon. *The Ephrata Commune: An Early American Counterculture*. University of Pittsburgh Press, 1985.

Alexander D.D., Reverend Archibald. *Evidences of the Authenticity, Inspiration, and Canonical Authority of the Holy Scriptures*. Philadelphia: Presbyterian Board of Publication, 1836.

Allen, William Barclay, ed. *George Washington - A Collection*. Indianapolis: Liberty Classics, Liberty Fund, Inc., 1988.

Alves, Reverend Joseph Hodge, and Harold Spelman. *Near the Falls: Two Hundred Years of The Falls Church*. Annandale: The Turnpike Press, Inc., 1969

The American Heritage Dictionary: 2nd College Edition. Boston: Houghton Mifflin Co. 1985.

Amos, Gary, and Richard Gardiner. *Never Before in History: America's Inspired Birth*. Dallas: Pandas Publications, 1998.

Annual Report of the American Historical Association for the Year 1892. Washington: Government printing Office, 1893.

Appleton's Cyclopedia of American Biography vol. 6. 1889.

Aurand, Jr., A. Monroe. *Historical Account of the Ephrata Cloister and the Seventh Day Baptist Society*. Harrisburg: The Aurand Press, 1940.

Baker, W.S. ed. *Character Portraits of Washington as Delineated by Historians, Orators and Divines*. Philadelphia: Press of Globe Printing House, 1887.

Baldwin, James. *An American Book of Golden Deeds*. 1907.

Bancroft, D.D., Aaron. *The Life of George Washington, Commander in Chief of the American Army, through the Revolutionary War; and the First President of the United States*. Boston: Water Street Bookstore, 1833.

Barton, Charles. *The Bulletproof George Washington*. Texas: WallBuilder Press, 2003.

Beattie, James. *Evidences of the Christian Religion; Briefly and Plainly Stated*. London: Routledge/Thoemmes Press, 1996.

Bellamy, Francis Rufus. *The Private Life of George Washington*. New York: Thomas Y. Crowell Co.,1951.

Beliles, Mark A and Stephen K. McDowell, *America's Providential History*. Charlottesville, VA, Providence Press, 1989.

Bernard, Winfred E.A. *Fisher Ames Federalist and Statesman 1758- 1808*. Chapel Hill: University of North Carolina, 1965.

Bobrick, Benson. *Angel in the Whirlwind: The Triumph of the American Revolution*. New York: Penguin Books, 1997.

Boller, Jr., Paul F., *George Washington & Religion*. Dallas: Southern Methodist University Press, 1963.

Boller Jr., Paul F. *No Bigotry No Sanction*. Burke, VA: The Trinity Forum, 1997.

Boucher, Jonathan, ed. *Reminiscences of an American Loyalist*. Port Washington, NY: Kennikat, 1967.

Boudreau, Dr. Allan. *George Washington and New York City*. Silver Spring, MD: The Masonic Service Association, 1989.

Brinton, Crane. *The Shaping of Modern Thought*. Englewood Cliffs, N.J.: Prentice-Hall, Inc, 1963.

Brookhiser, Richard. *Founding Father: Rediscovering George Washington*. New York: The Free Press, 1996.

Brumbaugh, Martin Grove. *A History of The German Baptist Brethren in Europe and America*. Mount Morris, Ill.: Brethren Publishing House, 1899.

Burk, B.D., W. Herbert. *Washington's Prayers*. Norristown: Washington Memorial Chapel, 1907.

Burnett, Edmund Cody. *The Continental Congress*. New York: MacMillan Co., 1941.

Byrne, Peter. *Natural Religion and the Nature of Religion: The Legacy of Deism*. New York: Routledge, 1989.

Canby, Henry Seidel. *The Brandywine*. Exton, PA: Schiffer Ltd., 1941.

Case, James R. *Freemasons at the First Inauguration of George Washington*. Silver Spring, MD: The Masonic Service Association, 1989.

Clark, Elmer T., ed. *The Journal and Letters of Francis Asbury in 3 Volumes*. Nashville: Abingdon Press, 1958.

Claudy, Carl H. *Washington's Home and Fraternal Life*. Silver Spring, MD: The Masonic Service Association, 1981.

Cobb, Sanford H. *The Rise of Religious Liberty in America*. New York: Macmillan Company, 1902.

Collins, Varnum Lansing. *President Witherspoon*. New York: Arno Press and The New York Times, 1969.

Conkling, Margaret. *Memoirs of the Mother and Wife of George Washington*. Auburn: Derby, Miller and Company, 1851.

Conway, M.D. *Washington and Mount Vernon*. Brooklyn: Long Island Historical Society, 1889.

Conway, Moncure D. *The Religion of George Washington* in *the Open Court*, October 24, 1889.

Corbin, John. *The Unknown Washington: Biographic Origins of the Republic*. New York: Charles Scribner's Sons, 1930.

Cousins, Norman. '*In God We Trust' The Religious Beliefs and Ideas of The American Founding Fathers*. New York, Harper & Brothers, 1958.

DeCatur, Jr., Stephen. *Private Affairs of George Washington*. Boston: Houghton Mifflin Co, 1933.

DeMar, Gary. *America's Christian History: The Untold Story*. Atlanta: American Vision Inc., 1995.

Dixon, David. *Bushy Run Battlefield*. Mechanicsburg, PA: Stackpole Books, 2003.

Doll, Eugene E. & Anneliese M. Funke, Comps. *The Ephrata Cloisters: An Annotated Bibliography*. Philadelphia: Carl Schurz Memorial Foundation, Inc, 1944.

Dubbs, Joseph Henry. "The Founding of the German Churches of Pennsylvania" in *The Pennsylvania Magazine of History and Biography*, vol. XVII, 1893, No. 3.

Dubbs, Joseph Henry. *The Reformed Church in Pennsylvania*. Lancaster: Pennsylvania-German Society, 1902.

Eidsmoe, John. *Christianity and the Constitution*. Grand Rapids: Baker Book House, 1987.

Ellis, Joseph J. *His Excellency*. New York: Alfred K. Knopf, 2004.

Elkins, Stanely, and Eric McKitrick. *The Age of Federalism*. Oxford: Oxford University Press, 1993.

Federer, William J. *America's God and Country Encyclopedia of Quotations*. Coppell: FAME Publishing, Inc., 1994.

Ferling, John E. *The First of Men*. The University of Tennessee Press, 1988.

Fischer, David Hackett. *Paul Revere's Ride*. New York, NY: Oxford University Press, Inc., 1994.

Flexner, James Thomas. *George Washington Anguish and Farewell (1793-1799)*. Boston: Little, Brown & Co. 1969.

Flexner, James Thomas. *Washington: The Indispensable Man*. New York: Signet, 1984.

Forbes, Esther. *Paul Revere and the World He Lived In*. New York, NY: First Mariner Books, 1999.

Ford, Paul Leicester. *The True George Washington*. Philadelphia: J.B. Lippincott Company, 1903.

Freeman, Douglas Southall. *George Washington, A Biography*. 7 Vols. New York, 1948-57.

Freeman, Douglas Southall. *George Washington, A Biography Victory with the Help of France vol. 5*. New York: Charles Scribner's Sons, 1952.

Gallagher, Reverend Mason. *A Chapter of Unwritten History. The Protestant Episcopacy of the Revolutionary Patriots Lost and Restored. A Centennial Offering*. Philadelphia: Reformed Episcopal Rooms, 1883.

Garraty, John A. *The American Nation To 1877*. New York: Harper & Row Publishers, 1966.

Gaustad, Edwin S. Ed. *A Documentary History of Religion in America to the Civil War*. Grand Rapids: William B. Eerdmans Publishing Company, 1993.

Gilcrest, Paul R., ed. *Documents of Synod: Study Papers and Actions of the Reformed Presbyterian Church, Evangelical Synod –1965-1982*. New Castle, DE: TriMark Publishing Co. 1982.

Good, James I. *History of the Reformed Church in the United States 1725-1792*. Reading: Danile Miller, Publisher, 1899.

Griffin, Appleton P.C. comps. *A Catalogue of the Washington Collection in the Boston Athenaeum*. Cambridge: University Press, 1897.

Griffin, Jr., Martin I.J. *Latitudinarianism in the Seventeenth-Century Church of England*. Leiden: E.J. Brill, 1992.

Griffith, Lucille. *Virginia House of Burgesses 1750-1774*. Northport: Colonial Press, 1963.

Grizzard, Frank E. *George Washington: A Biographical Companion*. Santa Barbara: ABC-CLIO, Inc. 2002.

Hall, David W., ed. *Election Day Sermons*. Oak Ridge, TN: The Covenant Foundation, 1996.

Halsey, R.T. Haines. *Pictures of Early New York on Dark Blue Staffordshire Pottery*. New York: Dover Publications, Inc., 1974.

Hall, Verna M. and Dorothy Dimmick, comps. and eds. *George Washington: The Character and Influence of One Man*. San Francisco: Foundation for American Christian Education, 1999.

Harding, Alan. *The Countess of Huntingdon's Connexion: A Sect in Action in Eighteenth-Century England*. Oxford University Press, 2003.

Harper, Douglas. "The Witman Incident: Revolutionary Revisions To An Ephrata Tale" in *Journal of the Lancaster Country Historical Society* vol. 97, Num. 3, 1995.

Hart, Albert Bushnell, ed. *Tributes to Washington, Pamphlet No. 3*. Washington, D.C.: George Washington Bicentennial Commission, 1931.

Hart, Benjamin, "The Wall That Protestantism Built: The Religious Reasons for the Separation of Church and State," *Policy Review*, Fall 1988.

Heathcote, Charles William. *Washington in Chester County*. Washington Bi-Centennial bulletin, 1732-1932.

Heathcote, C.W., and Lucile Shenk, eds. *A History of Chester Country Pennsylvania*. Harrisburg: National Historical Association, Inc., 1932.

Heaton, Brother Ronald E. *Masonic Membership of the Signers of the Constitution of the United States*. Silver Spring, MD: The Masonic Service Association, 1986.

Heaton, Brother Ronald E. *Masonic Membership of the General Officers of the Continental Army*. Silver Spring, MD: The Masonic Service Association, 1993.

Heaton, Brother Ronald E. *Masonic Membership of the Founding Fathers*. Silver Spring, MD: The Masonic Service Association, 1997.

Hinke, William J., ed. *Life and Letters of the Reverend John Philip Boehm: Founder of the Reformed Church in Pennsylvania, 1683-1749*. Philadelphia: Publication and Sunday School Board of the Reformed Church in the Untied States, 1916.

Hirschfeld, Fritz. *George Washington and Slavery: A Documentary Portrayal*. Columbia: University of Missouri Press, 1997.

Hirschfeld, Fritz. *George Washington and the Jews*. Rosemont Publishing & Printing Corp., 2005.

History of the George Washington Bicentennial Celebration vol. 1 Literature Series. United States George Washington Bicentennial Commission, Washington, D.C., 1932.

Hosack, M.D., David. *Memoir of DeWitt Clinton.* 1859

Hughes, Rupert. *George Washington The Human Being & The Hero 1732-1762.* New York: William Morrow & Co., 1926.

Humphreys, David. *The Life of General Washington with George Washington's Remarks.* Athens: University of Georgia Press, 1991.

Hutson, James H., ed. *The Founders on Religion.* Princeton, NJ: Princeton University Press, 2005.

Irving, Washington. *Life of George Washington.* 1855-59.

Johnson, Paul. *A History of the American People.* Great Britain: Weidenfield & Nicolson, 1997.

Johnson, Paul. *George Washington: The Founding Father.* Harper Collins Publishers: Eminent Lives, 2005.

Johnson, William J. *George Washington The Christian.* Arlington Heights: Christian Liberty Press, 1919.

Johnston, Elizabeth Bryant. *George Washington Day by Day.* New York: Cycle Publishing Co., 1895

Johnston, A.M., Henry P., ed. *The Correspondence and Public Papers of John Jay 1782-1793.* New York: Burt Franklin, 1970.

Jones, Gilbert S. *Valley Forge Park.* Philadelphia: Ketterlinus.

Jones, W. T. *Kant to Wittgenstein and Sartre.* New York: Harcourt, Brace & World, Inc., 1969.

Kitman, Marvin. *The Making of the President 1789: the Unauthorized Campaign Biography.* New York: Harper & Row, 1989.

Lane, William. *A Catalogue of the Washington Collection in the Boston Athenaeum.* The Boston Athenaeum, 1897.

Lemay, J. A. Leo., ed. "The Amerindian in the Early American Enlightenment" in *Deism, Masonry, and the Enlightenment.* Newark: University of Delaware Press, 1987.

Levering, Joseph Mortimer. *A History of Bethlehem, Pennsylvania 1741-1892 with Some Account of Its Founders and Their Early Activity in America.* Bethlehem: Times Publishing Co., 1903.

Lillback, Peter A. *Proclaim Liberty.* Bryn Mawr: The Providence Forum, 2001.

Littell, D.D., Reverend John Stockton. *Washington: Christian – Stories of Cross and Flag No. 1.* Keene: The Hampshire Art Press, 1913.

Lodge, Henry Cabot. *George Washington.* New Rochelle: Arlington House, 1898.

Longmore, Paul K. *The Invention of George Washington.* Berkeley: University of California Press, 1988.

Lossing, Benson J., *The Home of Washington or Mount Vernon and its Associations, Historical, Biographical, and Pictorial.* New York: Virtue & Yorston, 1870.

Lossing, Benson J., *Mary and Martha: The Mother and Wife of George Washington.* New York: Harper & Brothers, 1886.

Lowery, Ajay and Anita Lowery. Publishers "An Unknown Speaker Swayed Colonials to Sign the Declaration of Independence in 1776" in *The Justice Times.* (no date, no city).

Macartney, Clarence. *George Washington: A Bi-Centennial Sermon.* Pittsburgh: First Presbyterian Church, 1932.

Mackey M.D., Albert G. *Encyclopedia of Freemasonry and its Kindred Sciences Comprising the Whole Range of Arts, Sciences, and Literature as Connected with the Institution.* Philadelphia: McClure Publishing Co., 1917.

Maclay, William. *The Journal of William Maclay United State Senator from Pennsylvania, 1789-1791.* New York: Albert & Charles Boni, 1927.

Marshall, Peter and David Manuel. *The Light and the Glory.* Old Tappan, New Jersey, Fleming H. Revell, 1977.

Martin, John Hill. *Historical Sketch of Bethlehem in Pennsylvania, With Some Account of the Moravian Church.* New York: AMS Press, 1971.

McDougal, Walter A. *Freedom Just Around the Corner.* New York: Harper Collins, 2004.

M'Guire, E.C. *Religious Opinions and Character of Washington.* New York: Harper & Brothers, 1836.

McGuire, Thomas J. *The Battle of Paoli.* Mechanicsburg: Stackpole Books, 2000.

Montgomery, John Warwick. *The Shaping of America*. Minneapolis: Bethany Fellowship, Inc. 1976.

Morais, Herbert. *Deism in Eighteenth Century America*. New York: Russell & Russell, 1960.

Morrissey, Brendan. *Saratoga 1777*. Oxford, UK: Osprey Publishing Ltd., 2000.

Nevin, D.D., LL.D., Alfred. ed. *Encyclopedia of the Presbyterian Church in the United States of America: Including the Northern and Southern Assemblies*. Philadelphia: Presbyterian Publishing Co., 1884.

Nevins, Allan. *The American States: During and After the Revolution 1775-1789*. New York: Augustus M. Kelley, 1969.

The Official Records of Robert Dinwiddie, Lieutenant-Governor of the Colony of Virginia, 1751-1758, Now First Printed from the Manuscript in the Collections of the Virginia Historical Society, with an Introduction and Notes by R.A. Brock, Corresponding Secretary and Librarian of the Society. vol. 1. Richmond: Virginia Historical Society, 1883.

Pennypacker, Samuel W. *Valley Forge: An Address*. Philadelphia, June 18, 1898.

Porter, Noel. *The Religious Life of George Washington, in History of the George Washington Bicentennial Celebration Volume II Literature Series*. Washington, DC: United States George Washington Bicentennial Commission, 1932.

Randall, Willard Sterne. *George Washington: A Life*. New York: Henry Holt and Co., 1997.

Sachse, Julius Friedrich. *The German Sectarians of Pennsylvania 1742-1800. A Critical and Legendary History of the Ephrata Cloister and the Dunkers*. Philadelphia: Printed for the Author, 1900.

Sawyer, Joseph Dillaway. *Washington vol. 1 & 2*. New York: MacMillian, 1927.

Schaff, Phillip. *The Creeds of Christendom 6th edition. vol. 2* Grand Rapids: Baker Book House, 1983.

Schlenther, Boyd Stanley. *Charles Thomson: A Patriot's Pursuit*. Newark: University of Delaware Press, 1990.

Schroeder, John Frederick, D.D., comp. and arr. *Maxims of Washington*. Mount Vernon, VA: The Mount Vernon Ladies' Association of the Union, 1942.

Sherman, Andrew M. *Historic Morristown, New Jersey*, 1905.

Skirvin, Dennis D. *The George Washington Primer*. Wilmington, DE: Dennis D. Skirvin Writing Service, 2002.

Slaughter, D.D., Reverend Philip. *The History of Truro Parish in Virginia*. Philadelphia: George W. Jacobs & Co., 1907.

Smith, Robert Gordon, ed. *One Nation Under God: An Anthology for Americans*. New York: Funk & Wagnalls, 1961.

Soldier and Servant Series: "Mrs. Alexander Hamilton Witness that George Washington Was A Communicant of the Church." Hartford: Church Missions Publishing Company, February, 1932.

Sprague, Reverend Delos E. *Descriptive Guide of the Battlefield of Saratoga*. Ballston Spa, NY: Battlefield Publishing Co., Inc., 1930.

Sprague, D.D, William B. *Annals of the American Pulpit*. New York: Robert Carter and Brothers, 1861.

Steiner, Franklin. *The Religious Beliefs Of Our Presidents From Washington to FDR*. New York: Prometheus Books, 1995.

Stetson, Charles W., *Washington and His Neighbors*. Richmond: Garrett & Massie, Inc. 1956.

Stringer, Col. *Discovering Australia's Christian Heritage*. Australia: Col Stringer Ministries Inc., 2001.

Sweet, William Warren. *Religion in Colonial America*. New York: Cooper Square Publishers, Inc. 1965.

Taaffe, Stephen R. *The Philadelphia Campaign, 1777-1778*. Lawrence: University Press of Kansas, 2003.

Taylor, Frank H. *Valley Forge*. Valley Forge, PA: Daniel J. Voorhees, 1922.

Thompson, Ray. *Washington at Germantown*. Fort Washington, PA: The Bicentennial Press, 1971.

True Stories of the Days of Washington. New York: Phinney, Blakeman & Mason, 1861.

Trussell, Jr., John B. B. *Birthplace of an Army: A Study of the Valley Forge Encampment*. Harrisburg: Pennsylvania Historical And Museum Commission, 1990.

Upton, Dell. *Holy Things and Profane: Anglican Parish Churches in Colonial Virginia.* Cambridge: The MIT Press, 1986.

Virginia: A Guide to the Old Dominion. Compiled by workers of the Writers' Program of the Work Projects Administration in the State of Virginia, New York: Oxford, 1992.

Walters, Kerry S. *The American Deists: Voices of Reason and Dissent in the Early Republic.* University Press of Kansas, 1992.

Watson, Henry C. *The Young American's Library the Old Bell of Independence; or Philadelphia in 1776.* Philadelphia: Lindsay and Blackiston, 1851.

Weigley, Russell F., ed. *Philadelphia: A 300 – Year History.* New York: Norton & Company, 1982.

Weintraub, Stanley. *General Washington's Christmas Farewell.* New York, NY: Plume, 2004.

Westminster Confession of Faith. Lawrenceville: Committee for Christian Educational & Publications, 1990.

Wiencek, Henry. *An Imperfect God: George Washington, His Slaves and the Creation of America.* New York: Farrar, Straus and Giroux, 2003.

Wigmore, Francis Marion. *The Old Parish Churches of Virginia: A Pictorial-Historic Exhibition of Photographs in Colors Lent to the Library of Congress.* Washington: Government Printing Office, 1929.

Wills, Gary. *Cincinnatus: George Washington And The Enlightenment.* Garden City: Doubleday & Co. Inc., 1984.

Wilbur, William H. *The Making of George Washington.* Caldwell: Caxton Printers, 1970 & 1973.

Zall, Paul M. *Washington on Washington.* Lexington: University Press of Kentucky, 2003.

Zerfass, S. G. *Souvenir Book of the Ephrata Cloister, Complete History from Its Settlement in 1728 to the Present Time. Included is the Organization of Ephrata Borough and Other Information of Ephrata Connected With the Cloister.* New York: AMS Press, Inc, 1975.

SECONDARY SOURCES OF INTERVIEWS, JOURNALS, MAGAZINES AND NEWSPAPERS

American Minute with Bill Federer, January 17, 2006. (Email newsletter)

"A Protestant Convent" in *Hours at Home: A Popular Monthly of Instruction and Recreation* (1865-1870); Mar. 1867, pp. 458-464.

Harper's Magazine, 1859, vol. XVIII, p. 293.

Hume, Brit. "The Political Grapevine," February 22, 2005, Fox News.

Hart, Benjamin. "The Wall That Protestantism Built: The Religious Reasons for the Separation of Church and State," *Policy Review.* Washington, DC: Heritage Foundation, Fall 1988.

"John Penn's Journal of a Visit to Reading, Harrisburg, Carlisle, and Lancaster, in 1788" in The *Pennsylvania Magazine of History and Biography*, (1877-1906), 1879, pp. 284-95.

Journal of the Proceedings of Congress, 1774. Philadelphia: Printed for the Library Company of Philadelphia, 1974, September 10, 1774, see 30-33.

Marshall, Peter. Interview in D. James Kennedy's, *One Nation Under God.* Ft. Lauderdale: Coral Ridge Ministries, 2005, a video.

McGoldrick, James E. "1776: A Christian Loyalist View" *Fides et Historia*, X (Fall 1977), p. 26-42.

"Michael Witman, Loyalist" in *Lancaster County Historical Society*, Volume 14, pp. 181-185.

"Peter Miller—Michael Witman" in *Lancaster County Historical Society*, Volume 6, pp. 46-49.

"Religious Denominations in Pennsylvania" in *Christian Disciple* (1812-1818); April 1818, pp. 100-103.

Sorokin, Ellen. "No Founding Fathers? That's Our New History," *Washington Times*, January 28, 2002.

Thompson, Mary. Research historian at Mount Vernon Personal Interview for Coral Ridge Ministries.

Virginia Magazine of History and Biography vol. 17. Richmond: Virginia Historical Society, 1909.

WEBSITES

George Washington's writings, papers, letters, photos of original letters can be found at the following websites:

Jackson, Donald. & Dorothy Twohig, ed. *The Diaries of George Washington* (Charlottesville: University Press of Virginia, 1976-79) [http://memory.loc.gov/ammem/gwhtml/gwhome.html].

George Washington Papers at the Library of Congress, 1741-1799. http://memory.loc.gov/ammem/gwhtml/gwhome.html

Washington, George. Writings of George Washington http://etext.lib.virginia.edu/washington/

Series 1: Exercise Books, Diaries, and Surveys. 1741-99 http://memory.loc.gov/ammem/gwhtml/gwseries1.html

ADDITIONAL WEBSITES

Early American Imprints, Series I: Evans, 1639-1800 http://www.readex.com and http://infoweb.newsbank.com

BBC's Making History: *The Countess of Huntingdon's Connexion* http://www.bbc.co.uk/education/beyond/factsheets/makhist/makhist7_prog5d.shtml.

Book of Common Prayer. 1662 http://justus.anglican.org/resources/bcp/1662/HC.pdf

Butler, John. *Edward Lord of Chirbury* www.luminarium.org/sevenlit/chirbury/chirbio.htm.

"Edward, 1st Lord Herbert of Cherbury (or Chirbury) Herbert," Thoemmes Continuum: History of Ideas

www.thoemmes.com/encyclopedia/herbert.htm.

Elliot's The Debates in the Several State Conventions on the Adoption of the Federal Constitution vol. 1 image 500 or 606. http://memory.loc.gov/cgi-bin/ampage?collId=llfr&fileName=001/llfr001.db&recNum=529&itemLink=r?ammem/hlaw:@field(DOCID+@lit(fr001145))%230010510&linkText=1

Oral History www.answers.com/topic/oral-history. Columbia University Press

Paine, Thomas. *Age of Reason* http://libertyonline.hypermall.com/Paine/AOR-Frame.html

Index

THE PROVIDENCE FORUM
...proclaiming liberty throughout the land

The doctrine of Providence declares that the world and our lives are not ruled by chance or by fate, but by God. The Providence Forum demonstrably acknowledges that the Providence of God continues to be at work, and calls us to action. It is a non-profit corporation whose mission is to reinstill and promote a Judeo-Christian worldview within our culture and to advance the faith, ethics, and moral values consistent with the spirit of our nation's founding, emphasizing America's historical Judeo-Christian roots. The Providence Forum reaches a broad, national audience using various means, including multimedia, radio, television and film, publications, conferences, and lectures among its many channels of communication. The Providence Forum has been raised up to help call our nation back to its historic dependence on what both George Washington and Thomas Jefferson called "an overruling Providence." Our founding father, George Washington, spoke of, "That overruling Providence which has so often, and so remarkably interposed in our favor." He wrote, "you will permit me to remind you, as an inexhaustible subject of consolation, that there is a good Providence which will never fail to take care of his Children."

PROVIDENCE
FORUM PRESS

Providence Forum Press is the publishing arm of The Providence Forum. Its mission is to present the facts and opinions of scholarly and mainstream authors on topics relating to the Judeo-Christian heritage of the United States and divine Providence in America and around the world.

The "all-seeing eye of Providence" is a symbol that has needlessly been shrouded in mystery and controversy throughout US history, in spite of its clear message and meaning. It is found on the Great Seal of the United States, which was conceived by various committees of the US Congress beginning in 1776, but the final form we see today was proposed in the summer of 1782 by Secretary of Congress Charles Thomson, a Christian theologian. His design of the Great Seal of the United States displayed the "eye of Providence," encased in a triangle representing the Trinity, signifying the historic Christian icon of God the Father, the first person of the Trinity, the Sovereign Agent of Providence. According to the records of the Continental Congress, " . . . the eye . . . allude[s] to the many signal interpositions of providence in favour of the American cause." Other organizations subsequently adopted similar symbolism as early as 1797 for purposes other than this original intent. Even The Masonic Service Association of North America confirms, "The eye on the [Great] Seal represents an active intervention of God in the affairs of men," and, "When placed in a triangle, the eye went beyond a general representation of God to a strongly Trinitarian statement." It goes on to conclude, referring to the back of the Great Seal, "The combining of the eye of Providence overlooking an unfinished pyramid is a uniquely American—not Masonic—icon, and must be interpreted as its designers intended. It has no Masonic context." (Masonic Service Association of North America, "Eye in the Pyramid" at http://www.msana.com/stb_eyepyramid.htm)

This historic image is both an American and Christian symbol of our founding fathers, and, is thus most appropriate as the publisher's mark of Providence Forum Press.

About the Authors

Peter A. Lillback, Ph.D., is the president of The Providence Forum, senior pastor at Proclamation Presbyterian Church in Bryn Mawr, Pennsylvania, and president of Westminster Theological Seminary, where he is also Professor of Historical Theology. He is the voice of *Proclaiming The Word*, a daily syndicated radio program, as well as *The Proclamation Worship Hour*. Dr. Lillback received a Ph.D. from Westminster Theological Seminary, a Th.M. from Dallas Theological Seminary, and a B.A. from Cedarville University in Ohio. He is the author of *The Binding of God: Calvin's Role in the Development of Covenant Theology* (Baker), *Freedom's Holy Light—With a Firm Reliance on Divine Providence* (Providence Forum Press), and *Proclaim Liberty: A Broken Bell Rings Freedom to the World* (Providence Forum Press).

Dr. Lillback's collaborator, Jerry Newcombe, is the co-author of several bestselling books, including *What If Jesus Had Never Been Born?* (Nelson) and *What If the Bible Had Never Been Written?* (Nelson). He is senior producer of the nationally syndicated television program *The Coral Ridge Hour* and has produced or coproduced more than thirty documentaries, one of which won a silver medal at the International New York Film and Television Festival. Mr. Newcombe has a B.A. in history from Tulane University and an M.A. in communications from Wheaton Graduate School.

Other Literature by Peter A. Lillback

available at www.ProvidenceForum.org

PROCLAIM LIBERTY...
A BROKEN BELL RINGS FREEDOM TO THE WORLD

Dr. Lillback has written this 122-page book in commemoration of the 300th anniversary of religious liberty in America. It is the exciting story of America's beloved Liberty Bell—but more than that, it is the story of America's experience of religious and civil liberty—blessings which began over 300 years ago with William Penn's Charter of Privileges. Written in a narrative form, this book explains how the Liberty Bell has become the worldwide symbol of mankind's aspiration for freedom from the tyranny of repressive governments. As Americans once again fly the flag with pride and sing God Bless America with inspiration, *Proclaim Liberty* will help every patriot, from school children to scholars, understand why the United States was intended to be and is still the "land of the free and the home of the brave."

LESSONS ON LIBERTY: A PRIMER FOR YOUNG PATRIOTS

(to be released in the fall of 2006)

Designed for all ages and packed with colorful illustrations, this entertaining and educational hardcover book uses a simple alphabet poem to guide the reader through the fundamental principles of American liberty. Incorporating early nineteenth century dictionary definitions and enhanced graphics, Bible quotations and *Poor Richard's Almanack*, this engaging book adds powerful historic quotes, surprising facts, and truths about our nation's founding to excite young and old about our country—this beacon of liberty for the world. Included also are activity pages to further teach young scholars with a hands-on approach—perforated for easy tear-out, these pages may be reproduced on a copier for group use. James Madison once declared, "*The diffusion of knowledge is the only guardian of true liberty.*" Whether in your family, or in a public, Christian or home school setting, please join us in striving to preserve our unparalleled heritage of freedom for future generations by introducing them to these timeless truths.

DOES THE SEPARATION OF CHURCH AND STATE
REQUIRE THE SEPARATION OF GOD AND GOVERNMENT?

How often have you heard it stated that our Constitution mandates the separation of church and state? In truth, the Constitution never uses the word "separation." Dr. Lillback's meticulous research and highly informative writing addresses our nation's historic understanding of and the founding fathers' intention in the relationship of our Constitution to matters of faith, ethics and morals. This sixty-page whitepaper explores these questions, taking into account their historical context as well as their relation to today's culture. This is an excellent resource for anyone interested in wrestling with and defending the intriguing truths and issues of church and state.

FREEDOM'S HOLY LIGHT...
WITH A FIRM RELIANCE ON DIVINE PROVIDENCE

The flagship publication of The Providence Forum, this easy to read, thirty-five-page booklet recaps America's Judeo-Christian heritage in the foundations and ongoing development of our nation. It presents the stories of the very first covenants of the colonies, leading to and including the Declaration of Independence, The Constitution, The Great Seal of the United States, our flag, the Pledge of Allegiance, our national motto and more. *Freedom's Holy Light* has been distributed coast to coast by individuals, at political and community leadership conferences, religious and homeschool networks, radio stations, Christian schools, and bookstores. *Freedom's Holy Light* is endorsed by, among others, Dr. John DiIulio, former Director of the White House Office of Faith-based and Community Initiatives, US Congressman Joe Pitts, Anthony Cardinal Bevilacqua, and Rabbi Daniel Lapin. This book is as entertaining as it is educational, illuminating the intersection of our Judeo-Christian faith, national history and government. The success of America is still dependent upon what our founders described as a "firm reliance on Divine Providence."

A TOUR OF THE DOLLAR BILL

One of the most profound tools of influence in our society, indeed in the world, is the almighty American dollar. Remarkably, the one-dollar bill has a story to tell about the history and founding principles of our nation, the men that have steered her course since, and our historic symbols and institutions. It reveals the distinctive principles of America, as determined by our founders. The dollar bill explains the founding faith and values of our nation in various ways, including outlining seven essential moral virtues and recognizing the role of Providence in the formation of our nation. Based on Dr. Lillback's renowned presentation seen around the world, Providence Forum Press designed a careful, but non-exact, replica of the one dollar bill with a written "tour" of America's history as told by Dr. Lillback and the dollar itself. Sadly, people are largely ignorant of the history they handle on a daily basis. This entertaining and educational tool fits in any wallet, just as the authentic dollar does, and can be used in many ways to spread the much forgotten history of America's providential founding.

For these and other unique items and resources, please visit
www.ProvidenceForum.org

NOTES

NOTES

NOTES

NOTES

NOTES

NOTES